THE ENCYCLOPEDIA OF WORLD THEATER

Austria, the BURGTHEATER in the Ringstrasse, Vienna, designed by Gottfried Semper and Karl Hasenauer, opened 1888

Introduction by Martin Esslin

THE ENCYCLOPEDIA OF WORLD THEATER

With 420 illustrations and an index of play titles

CHARLES SCRIBNER'S SONS

NEW YORK

Based on *Friedrichs Theaterlexikon*
by Karl Gröning and Werner Kliess
Edited by Henning Rischbieter
This English-language edition has been translated
by Estella Schmid, and adapted and amplified under
the general editorship of Martin Esslin

(*Half-title*) **Greece**, Hellenistic comic mask,
Agora Museum, Athens

1 3 5 7 9 11 13 15 17 19 I/C 20 18 16 14 12 10 8 6 4 2

Printed in Great Britain
Library of Congress Catalog Card Number 76-19741
ISBN 0-684-14834-X

INTRODUCTION

Encyclopaedias and reference books of all kinds – dictionaries, *thesauri*, gazetteers, almanacs, guide-books, even railway and airline timetables – have always exercised a powerful attraction. There are those – and they are among the most sophisticated users of the printed word – who consider them their favourite and most fruitful reading matter. And yet, on the face of it and in the common received opinion of mankind, these are, or ought to be, among the driest, most pedantic kinds of books. What, then, gives them such fascination?

One of the chief reasons may well be that such books respond to the urge not only to accumulate as much knowledge as possible but also to have it always accessible in clear and ordered form. If knowledge is power, accumulated knowledge, within easy reach and readily available, is not only a tool for work but an instrument of power. Instinctively we feel that what we know we can also master and dominate. Hence the ancient fears and *mystiques* connected with names. In some civilizations the individual had a public name which was disclosed to others, and a *real* name he kept secret to prevent others from gaining domination over him. The lists of names and registers of possessions that are a feature of ancient archaeological sites are, dimly and indirectly, precursors of reference books. And they *were* instruments of power.

That may be one of the deep instinctive sources of the feeling of security the possession of reference books and encyclopaedias gives many of us today. We may be ignorant of a subject, but owning a reference book on it makes us feel that we can instantly gain access to any aspect of it. What we do not know we can always look up.

But this is merely one side of the charm of encyclopaedias. It is generally thought to be their main utility that where there are questions they will provide the answers. This is the service they are designed to perform. And that is as it should be. Yet, if that was all they were good for, they really would be no more than pedantic, dryasdust utilitarian tools. In fact they are much more.

A body of knowledge, neatly ordered and laid out for inspection is a powerful stimulus to exploration. It may be systematic, as in the case of those – and they still exist – who set out to read a whole reference book from A to Z. Or it may be casual and spontaneous, light-hearted browsing.

Browsing of this kind is one of the best ways of improving the range of one's interests and knowledge. In systematic learning the student follows a predetermined course. In browsing he may discover areas of interest which he might otherwise never have approached at all. Before anyone decides to study a given subject he must know that it exists. In browsing, whether in bookshops or encyclopaedias, one can discover the existence of hitherto unknown fields of inquiry. In an age where narrow specialization of interests and skills has become a real cultural danger, the casual exploration of other disciplines must surely be a healthy antidote.

For, make no mistake about it, browsing in reference books is a *creative* activity. The reader of a novel or an essay is taken into a ready-made world along a prescribed path. The browser in an encyclopaedia or dictionary is presented with the raw material of such a world, a do-it-yourself construction kit from which he must build his own. Far from being dry, pedantic books, reference works of this kind are stimulants to the imagination. That is why even street directories or timetables are, for those who have the inner resources, magic keys into new worlds. In fact browsing in reference books is akin to, and anticipates, those tendencies of the contemporary avant-garde which aim at an *aleatory* work of art: novels which consist of loose pages that can be read in any order, or Raymond Queneau's basic pattern of a sonnet's rhyme scheme which by accidental combination can yield several million different poems. Contemporary avant-garde theatre also makes use of such aleatory techniques in productions like those of Ariane Mnouchkine's *Théâtre du Soleil* or Luca Ronconi's *Orlando Furioso*, in which the performance is taking place simultaneously in different locations and the spectators, freed from imprisonment in a static seat, must choose for themselves which of several simultaneous actions they will watch. The material to be looked at is there, but the choice is left to the spectator, just as it is to the reader of a reference work.

How does all this apply to a one-volume illustrated encyclopaedia of theatre?

While such an encyclopaedia will, it is hoped, provide an answer to a good many, even most, of the questions it will be asked to answer by those who come to it with the desire to look up a given entry, it should also be ideal for browsing. The world of the theatre is a wide and varied one, but it is also much dominated by fashion and the constant imitation of established patterns of success. Anyone whose fate it is to have to listen to aspiring actors auditioning for parts is painfully aware of this fact. The same scenes and speeches seem to occur with monotonous regularity. They vary from year to year, but, within each period, they repeat themselves. And the same is true of the repertoires of professional as well as amateur theatres. Anything that would widen the field from which theatres select their productions, actors their audition pieces, would be of considerable value. How can one come across hitherto neglected authors? Perhaps by casually flicking through a one-volume encyclopaedia like the present one.

Here the very fact that its roots are in a slightly different cultural sphere from our own English-speaking world might be of value. In the process of adapting it to our own requirements, it became very clear indeed how widely disparate the basic store of knowledge of a German-speaking and an English-speaking theatre-lover has become. The German repertoire is far more catholic than that of the English-speaking countries. The German theatre has always been offering many more plays from the classical Spanish or Italian repertoire and is today far more open to plays from Eastern Europe. That articles about British and American playwrights, actors, directors, designers had to be introduced to make up the deficiencies in this respect was obvious and was indeed done. Many of the original entries, on the other hand, which would have been meaningless or superfluous because too parochial could be eliminated. Yet, on the whole, a far more comprehensive, international mixture resulted from having started from a different type of ground-plan.

Moreover, this is an illustrated encyclopaedia and illustrations can be the most powerful aid and incentive to browsing. They capture the attention and arouse the desire to find out more about their subject. In a theatre encyclopaedia, illustrations can convey more than pages of description ever could and recapture the flavour, the guiding spirit, of past performance.

Yet the question may be put: is there any value in such knowledge, such awareness of the past in a field so thoroughly wedded to the present, so ephemeral as the live theatre? Does one need any solid knowledge about what many people still consider no more than a branch of the entertainment industry?

The theatre *is* ephemeral and it *does* provide much – sorely needed – entertainment. But it is becoming ever more apparent that it is also an important, perhaps even a vital, cultural factor. We are living in the era of the mass media. A large proportion of the immense flood of material with which the mass media are inundating their public (which in the developed countries today in practice comprises the entire population), is in dramatic form and thus ultimately derives from the techniques of the theatre. The difference is merely that the mass media (television and the cinema) are mechanized, industrial processes involving vast capital equipment and expenditure, while the theatre is still, as it were, handicrafted. The live theatre, and above all the increasingly important avant-garde sector which operates with a minimum of production expenditure, is thus the natural experimental laboratory and training ground for the mass media. It is here that new techniques of writing and production, new styles of acting, new forms of humour can be tried out and tested without the need for heavy expenditure. The live theatre stands to the mass media in the relationship of a pure research establishment to the highly industrialized mass-production process of the modern manufacture of consumer goods.

Television and the cinema need the live theatre. Without the constant experimentation and innovation carried out by it, there would be a grave danger of stagnation, staleness and ultimate boredom of the audience. And, what is even more important, television has become in the developed countries (and *will* soon in the rapidly developing third world) the most powerful cultural influence in shaping the ideas and life-styles of the masses. The full extent and scale of this influence have not yet been fully realized. Nevertheless it is already clear that any country will at its own peril neglect the power of television for the good or ill of its development. Lively, intelligent, stimulating television will be of enormous benefit to a society. Stereotyped, uninventive, repetitive television might well, in the long run, result in a lowering of creativeness, intelligence and competitive strength in whole populations and, in an age where the economic strength of a community depends on its intellectual and cultural level, even affect its standard of living.

There is thus an indirect, but nevertheless extremely important, link between the state of theatre and the general quality of life in a contemporary society. Far from being merely a branch of the entertainment industry the theatre is increasingly becoming a vitally important cultural factor, and the state of any culture is closely linked with its awareness of its tradition. For tradition is the basis even of innovation, which is no more than a reaction to the prevailing tradition and usually, as history develops in cycles or ascending spirals, a return to earlier aspects of the same tradition.

Here again, then, knowledge – knowledge of the past and its manifestation in the present – is ultimately power. A society with a healthy awareness of its theatrical tradition and consequently a lively and intelligent theatrical present will be able to produce stimulating mass entertainment and mass education in the media and thus be able to raise its cultural and social life to higher levels.

If the mass media are one aspect of the shaping of the consciousness and quality of life of modern societies, the educational system by which they train their individual members is the other. It may be a matter for debate whether even small children today do not acquire more of their education from the mass media than they ever get from their schooling, but no one will deny that education in schools is vital. And here too dramatic forms of expression are playing an increasingly important part, precisely because children who have grown up in a mass media culture have been conditioned to perceive the world in terms of drama and theatrical techniques of communication. Drama is thus bound to be used more and more as a means by which pupils are taught both by being induced to act out their own problems and situations and by being made aware of how to respond to and evaluate the immense amount of dramatic material which they will be offered on their television screens as passive recipients. A society dominated by the mass media needs a critical public, able to form its own judgment on the products of the mass media, as a vital counterbalancing factor. Otherwise we should get very near to the totally manipulated society predicted by Aldous Huxley in *Brave New World.* It goes without saying that a wide knowledge of the traditions of the past and the techniques of the present is indispensable in creating such an informed critical overview.

And yet – what use are the names and biographies, the faded portraits of long dead actors of past centuries in the context of all these contemporary requirements?

It is true: to recapture the quality and flavour of the work of the greatest artists among the actors of the past, Burbage, Champmeslé, Garrick, Kean, Duse is impossible. And yet these and other great actors have made vital contributions to the development of techniques of playwriting and production; they have been powerful personalities whose biographies are graphic documents in the life of their times. Thus the names and life stories and reputations of great actors of the past are not only an essential ingredient of the history of drama, they are part of its basic structure, the skeleton around which the whole fabric coheres.

For, after all, the actor is the essential element of all drama. Plays without actors are literature. It is the actor who contributes that mysterious but indispensable element which transmutes a piece of writing into a living theatrical experience. One goes to the theatre to watch actors; otherwise one might as well stay at home and just read the text of the play. And even in periods when dramatic literature, the quality of the written word in the theatre, was at a low ebb, the theatre flourished because it could produce actors whom thousands of people wanted to see.

The actor, basically, represents one of the chief human archetypes of a society. It would be difficult to understand or to recapture the flavour of our own century without a knowledge of figures like Rudolph Valentino, Greta Garbo, James Dean, Marilyn Monroe or Humphrey Bogart. The same is true of previous epochs. The actors of past centuries are thus highly relevant for an understanding not only of their theatre but of their society.

If, as Hamlet says, the theatre holds a mirror up to nature and thus mirrors the society of its epoch, then it follows that the society concerned can be studied with advantage in that mirror, which, as an art form, compresses, orders and simplifies the chaotic picture of nature – reality itself – by reducing it to its essential features. All literature does that, of course, but the theatre captures the actual everyday reality of human intercourse, including the small talk, the forms of politeness and invective, the give-and-take of the trivia of domestic and public life. And by its peculiar and ever mysterious alchemy it enables us to bring all these details back to actual life. For the spectators of a performance of an Elizabethan tragedy, a Restoration Comedy or a nineteenth-century social drama by Ibsen, these past epochs actually do live again, distorted perhaps by historical hindsight or by a director's attempts to make the action relevant for today, but still true in their essentials.

By its very nature the theatre is the art form most closely related to society and to life. I am referring here to the theatre in its strictest sense, as the performance of the written word: this is also the range of the present encyclopaedia, which therefore excludes the larger related fields of opera and ballet, though it does take a passing glance at such areas as cabaret, circuses and mime. The theatre is a synthesis of many arts, making use of poetry, music, painting, architecture. This may impair its purity, but it contributes to its richness. Being so rich, it also has the most fluid frontiers with life itself. Much of politics and its ritual, much of the church's liturgy can be seen as theatre. Restaurants in which the waiters wear national costumes against an appropriate decor use elements of the art of the theatre, and so do costume balls. Great sporting occasions are immensely theatrical. Commercial organizations provide their salesmen with routines that are learned in exactly the same way that an actor studies his role. Executives are trained in the art of decision-making by being made to act out elaborate scenarios of a variety of situations they might encounter in the course of their professional life. Indeed, whichever way you look at it one is compelled to agree with Shakespeare's Jaques that all the world's a stage and all the men and women merely players.

It is of this world of the stage which mirrors the world at large that this book endeavours to give a brief and far from comprehensive or all-embracing, yet wide enough conspectus. If it answers at least a fair proportion of the queries it is required to deal with and if it invites fruitful browsing which will stimulate its users to seek further knowledge, it will fulfil the aims of its compilers.

MARTIN ESSLIN

GUIDE TO THE USE OF THE ENCYCLOPAEDIA

Abbreviations

Bibl	= Bibliography	fp	= first performed
des	= designed by	post	= posthumous
dir	= directed by	pub	= published
ed	= edited by	rev	= revised
est	= established	trans	= translated by
		vol	= volume

Language references = Gk (Greek), Fr (French), etc.

Cross-references

SMALL CAPS are used to indicate that there is a separate entry for any item thus printed.

▷ = see

Dates of Plays

Most plays have three dates: when written, when first produced and when published. In general one date only is given here, that considered the most significant, but on occasion more than one date may be given when there is special relevance.

Play Titles

If an English translation already exists (acting version or published book), this is also given, in *italics* in the author entry, and this English version alone is generally used in non-indigenous entries. A rough translation is given in the author entries as a guide to the reader if there is no accepted translation and the language is less familiar than French.

In the *Index of Plays* (on page 296), the accepted English translation is used, except where none has been traced, in which case the title is rendered in the original language in *italics*; in either case, the author's name follows in SMALL CAPS, indicating a cross reference. If the author does not have a separate entry, a cross reference is given to the entry in which a play title occurs. For example: *Aria da Capo* (Millay) PROVINCETOWN PLAYERS.

Bibliographical references to individual entries are given only where they are considered to be specifically useful for further details. Where no title is given, this means that it is identical with the entry heading.

Abbey Theatre. Playhouse opened in Dublin, 1904, by LADY GREGORY and YEATS, with the help of ANNIE HORNIMAN, which became the focal point of the Irish Dramatic Movement (▷FAY). In 1924 it became the first state-subsidized theatre in the English-speaking world. Badly damaged by fire in 1951, it was rebuilt in 1966. The plays, written for the Abbey Theatre by Yeats, Lady Gregory, A E, SYNGE, BOYLE, ROBINSON, O'CASEY, Edward Martyn, Padraic Colum and T. C. Murray, dealt with subjects from Gaelic myth and everyday life in the countryside and town; some were actually written in Gaelic. The emphasis was on modern subjects rendered in poetic yet realistic language, especially under the influence of Synge and Robinson, who was associated with the theatre as producer and manager from 1910 till his death in 1958. The ENSEMBLE, partly amateurs at the beginning, cultivated a realism pared to essentials. It gained an international reputation by touring, notably in the USA.
Bibl: L. Robinson, IRELAND'S ABBEY THEATRE, A HISTORY, 1899–1951, 1951

Abbott, George (1887–), US director, dramatist and actor. Studied under BAKER at Harvard in 1912, and from 1913 worked as an actor. Particularly known for high-speed FARCE, he had his first success as a playwright with *The Fall Guy*, 1925, written with James Gleason, and achieved a spectacular hit with the brilliantly funny *Three Men on a Horse*, 1935, written with John Cecil Holm. One of BROADWAY's outstanding theatrical personalities, he directed a great number of MUSICAL COMEDIES, especially those of the '30s and '40s with music and lyrics by RODGERS and L. HART, among them: *Babes in Arms*, 1937; *The Boys From Syracuse*, 1938, an uproarious adaptation of SHAKESPEARE's *The Comedy of Errors*; *Too Many Girls*, 1939; *Pal Joey*, 1940 (book by John O'Hara). Other musicals he has directed include: *Best Foot Forward*, 1941; *On the Town*, 1944, with music by L. BERNSTEIN; *Where's Charley?*, 1948, an adaptation of W. B. THOMAS's *Charley's Aunt*, with music by LOESSER and starring Ray Bolger; *The Pajama Game*, 1954, and *Damn Yankees*, 1955, both with music and lyrics by Adler and Ross. G.A. published his autobiography in 1963.

Abele spelen (Middle-Dutch; Dutch *abele* =able, skilful; *spelen*=to play). A particular form of the Netherlands folk theatre in the 14th century; the oldest known non-liturgical plays in Dutch. The four plays preserved (*Hulthem manuscript*) are romantic love stories written in the dialect of Brabant. They were performed on a multiple stage by a maximum of eight actors (*Ghesellen van den spelen*) with masks. They began with a PROLOGUE describing the action and were followed by an EPILOGUE explaining the moral of the play and introducing the *sotternie* (▷SOTIE), which always followed.
Bibl: H. H. Borchert, DAS EUROPÄISCHE DRAMA IM MITTELALTER, 1935

Abell, Kjeld (1901–61), Danish dramatist and artist. He began as a stage designer in Paris, and worked with the choreographer George Balanchine in Copenhagen and London, 1930–31. From 1935 onwards he was active both as playwright and designer. His dramatic work was influenced by Hans Christian Andersen, and in his use of poetic language he resembles FRY. Among his plays, mainly concerned with social criticism, are: *Melodien, der blev væk* (*The Melody that Got Lost*), fp Copenhagen 1935, London 1936; *Eva aftjener sin barnepligt* (Eve Serves out Her Childhood), 1936; *Anna Sophie Hedvig*, 1939; *Dronningen går igen* (*The Queen on Tour*), 1943; *Silkeborg*, 1946; *Dage på en sky* (Days on a Cloud), 1947; *Den blå Pekingeser* (The Blue Pekinese), 1954; *Andersen, eller Hans livs eventyr* (Andersen, or the Fairy Tale of His Life), 1955; *Skriget* (*The Scream*), 1961.
Bibl: F. Schyberg, 1947

Abington, Frances (1737–1815), English actress. The daughter of a soldier named Barton, she was a flower-girl and street-singer until her first appearance as Miranda in *The Busybody* at the Haymarket Theatre in 1755. She was taken on at DRURY LANE, where she found herself overshadowed by KITTY CLIVE and Mrs Pritchard. Despairing of finding success in London she went to Dublin, but after five years GARRICK called her back to London. During the next 18 years at Drury Lane, she was one of the leading actresses, most outstanding in SHAKESPEARE's comedies (as Beatrice, Olivia, and Portia) as well as in his tragedies (as Desdemona and Ophelia); she was also known as the ideal interpreter of CONGREVE, and of SHERIDAN for whom she created the part of Lady Teazle in *The School for Scandal* in 1777; she was at COVENT GARDEN THEATRE 1782–90 and retired in 1799.
Bibl: E. Robins, TWELVE GREAT ACTRESSES, 1900

Absurd, Theatre of the ▷ THEATRE OF THE ABSURD.

Academy (Gk *Akademeia*). Originally a grove on the outskirts of Athens named Academe after the hero Academus. In ARISTOPHANES' time it was a place for exercise; *c.*385 BC it became the site of Plato's philosophical school; since the end of the 15th century the Academia Platonica in Florence, modelled on Plato, spreading from there throughout Europe (Académie française in France, 1635). The academies of the Renaissance often had their own theatres where they performed classical drama in Latin, e.g. the Academici Olimpici in Vicenza who performed SOPHOCLES' *Oedipus Rex* in their TEATRO OLIMPICO. The large opera house in Paris was first called Académie royale de musique; the first independent theatre with its own building in the Netherlands called itself Academy; EKHOF founded an academy for actors (Akademie der Schönemannschen Gesellschaft) in Germany, 1753. Today the name is given to schools of fine art, music, theatre and film, and to research institutes.

Accesi, The. A company of COMMEDIA DELL'ARTE actors, founded about 1590. In 1600 the group toured France, under the leadership of T. MARTINELLI and CECCHINI, with the actors D. MARTINELLI and Flaminio Scala. They travelled there again in 1608, this time without their ARLECCHINO, T. Martinelli. Later Cecchini joined forces with the younger ANDREINI; Cecchini's most outstanding actor between 1621 and 1632 was FIORILLO, the first Captain Matamoras.

Accius, Lucius (170–*c.*90 BC). Roman writer and dramatist. It was as a tragedian that his fame grew through antiquity. Fragments of some 46 named plays are extant. Most of the recognizable plays were translated from Euripides, some from Sophocles and a few from Aeschylus but he was an original poet in his own right who stamped his Greek material with his own powerful style. His outstanding qualities were the forcefulness of his rhetoric and the ability to concentrate the gist of his meaning in memorable phrases such as 'Oderint dum metuant' (Let them hate me so long as they fear me). He also wrote on the history of drama and theatre technique.
Bibl. B. Bilinki: ACCIUS ED I GRACCHI, 1958

Achard, Marcel (1899–1974), French playwright. He was known for COMEDIES with serious undertones praising the simple joys of life. Studied as a prompter at the THÉÂTRE DU VIEUX-COLOMBIER; later he became a journalist. Two of his early plays were *La Messe est dite*, 1922, and *Celui qui vivait sa mort*, 1923, but his first success was in 1923 with the merry-melancholy slapstick comedy *Voulez-vous jouer avec moâ?*, dir DULLIN, followed by *Jean de la lune*, 1929, dir JOUVET. After that came *Domino*, 1931; *Pétrus*, 1934; the poetic romance *Le Corsaire*, 1938, dir Jouvet, des BÉRARD; *Adam*, 1939, with a homosexual theme, and *Auprès de ma blonde*, 1946, adapted by BEHRMAN as *I Know My Love*. In his later plays, e.g. *Patate*, 1957, he returned to his original comedy style.
Bibl: M.-L. Bataille, L'ACTE D'APRÈS M. PAGNOL, M. ACHARD, ETC., 1947

Ackermann. A family of actors, whose work was of great importance in the development of German theatrical art. (1) **Konrad Ernst A.** (1712–71) worked with SCHÖNEMANN's company 1740–41, then toured as a strolling player through Europe (Hamburg, Danzig, St Petersburg, Moscow). In 1753 in Prussia he was author-

ized to build his own theatre; while it was being constructed, the Ackermann troupe went on tour to Warsaw, Breslau and Frankfurt where they gave the première of LESSING's *Miss Sara Sampson* in 1755. In the same year A. opened his own 800-seat theatre in Königsberg, the first private playhouse in Germany. Soon afterwards he started touring again, 1757–61, in Swi.zerland, where he met WIELAND, and in Alsace. Later, 1764–67, he was mostly in Hamburg where he opened the Comödienhaus, on the site of the former opera house, with which Lessing was connected. The latter's famous HAMBURGISCHE DRAMATURGIE, a cornerstone of modern dramatic criticism, is based on reviews of some of A.'s performances there. However, the indifference of his audiences forced him once again to go on tour. He excelled in realistic comedy parts, playing for example Major von Tellheim in Lessing's *Minna von Barnhelm*. Many members of his ensemble became celebrated actors: DÖBBELIN, EKHOF, Brockmann, Boeck, Susanne Mecour and KAROLINE KUMMERFELD.
A. was married to the actress, (2) **Sophie Charlotte A.** (1714–93). F. L. SCHRÖDER, her son by her first husband, later became one of Germany's greatest actors. Sophie first worked with Schönemann's company, then joined A.'s company and managed it very successfully after his death. Sophie and Konrad A. had two daughters; the elder, (3) **Dorothea A.** (1752–1821), was greatly admired in the title role of *Minna von Barnhelm* and as Countess Orsina in *Emilia Galotti* by Lessing; she retired from the theatre at the age of 21. The younger daughter, (4) **Charlotte A.** (1757–75), was a fragile beauty who gave her best performance as Emilia Galotti. When she died at the age of 17, Germany lost one of its finest and most beloved actresses.
Bibl: C. L. Costenoble, TAGEBÜCHER, 1912, 2 vols

Acquart, André (1922–), French stage designer. One of the most creative modern artists, he works with such leading French directors as VILAR, PLANCHON, BLIN, G. WILSON and Jean-Marie Serreau. He studied in Algiers and in 1951 went to Paris. Since then he has worked both there and in Germany on such productions as: *Les Nègres* by GENET, 1959, dir Blin; *The Resistible Rise of Arturo Ui* by BRECHT, 1960, TNP, dir Vilar and Wilson; *Red Roses for Me* by O'CASEY, 1961, TNP; Bizet's opera *Carmen*, Cologne 1962, dir LIETZAU; *Troilus and Cressida* by SHAKESPEARE, Villeurbanne 1964, dir Planchon; *Les Paravents* by Genet, Paris 1965, dir Blin.

Acrobat (Gk *akrobatein*=to go on tiptoe). Serious or comic circus performer. There are aerial acrobats (rope, trapeze, aerial swing) and floor acrobats; among the most ancient kind of performing artists. ▷CLOWN

Acta est fabula (Lat=the play is over). Announcement at the end of a performance in ancient Rome.

George Abbott's production of *Pal Joey*, New York 1940, music and lyrics by RODGERS and L. HART

Abbey Theatre production of LADY GREGORY's *Hyacinth Halvey*, Dublin 1906. Far left W. G. FAY, on the right SARA ALLGOOD

Acrobat at a 19th-century English MUSIC HALL

Acting versions. Plays printed with production notes. They first appeared in England in the 18th century. Some of them are important source material for the study of production techniques, e.g. Bell's edition of SHAKESPEARE, 1773, which describes how 24 of these plays were produced in GARRICK's time.

Actor-manager. A leading player who rents a theatre and runs his own company, or someone who tours a REPERTOIRE of plays under his own management, playing the leading roles himself. The actor-manager has been gradually disappearing since the 19th century. In the traditional sense he no longer exists.
Bibl: H. Pearson, THE LAST ACTOR-MANAGERS, 1950

Actors' Equity Association ▷EQUITY

Actors' Studio. Founded in New York, 1947, by CHERYL CRAWFORD, KAZAN, STRASBERG and Robert Lewis, its aim is in part to give actors an opportunity to widen their experience through team criticism. While only professional actors can be members, playwrights and directors are permitted to join as guests. Strasberg, who became director in 1951, based his concept on STANISLAVSKY's work, particularly with regard to improvisation, but extends the latter's psychological approach to the part by employing quasi-psychoanalytical techniques, the actor being encouraged to bring memories of earlier times in his life, especially from childhood, to bear on the interpretation of existential situations. Numerous STARS, many in films, known for their ability to interpret complex characters, emerged from the Actors' Studio, e.g. James Dean, Karl Malden, Paul Newman, JULIE HARRIS, Eva Marie Saint, etc. It has often been criticized because its technique is said to tend towards a rigid system, 'the Method', which places an undue emphasis on psychological insights and neglects more external skills. But it cannot be denied that it has made an original and important contribution to the development of the training and teaching of actors in the USA.
Bibl: C. Marowitz, THE METHOD AS MEANS, 1961

Adalbert, Max (1874–1933), German actor. One of the most successful comedians of the BERLIN theatre of the 1920s; he proved his enormous potential as an actor when he took over from KRAUSS the title role in ZUCKMAYER's *Der Hauptmann von Köpenick*, 1931, Deutsches-Theater, dir HILPERT.

Adam de la Halle (*c.* 1240–88), also known as Le Bossu d'Arras (Hunchback). French poet and composer, first writer of secular drama in France. *Le Jeu de la feuillée* is a witty and mischievous account of his forced departure from Arras in 1262. *Le Jeu de Robin et de Marion*, written for the court of Robert II, Count of Artois, is considered the earliest example of French PASTORAL DRAMA.
Bibl: G. Meyer, LEXIQUE DES ŒUVRES D'ADAM DE LA HALLE, 1946

Adamberger, Antonie (1791–1867), Austrian actress. Daughter of **Valentine A.**, first tenor at the Vienna Opera, and **Marie Anna A.**, tragedienne at the BURGTHEATER. Antonie A. was the first Klärchen in GOETHE's *Egmont*, and the leading tragedienne at the Burgtheater until 1817.
Bibl: H. Zimmer, THEODOR KÖRNERS BRAUT, 1918

Adamov, Arthur (1908–70), Russian-born French playwright. Left Russia in 1912, and eventually settled in France. Started writing poetry in Paris in the 1920s and suffered a mental breakdown in the 1930s, which is described in his autobiography *L'Aveu*, 1938–43. The subject of his first play, *La Parodie*, written 1947, fp Paris 1950, Théâtre Lancry, and also of *L'Invasion*, fp 1950, Studio des Champs-Elysées, dir VILAR, is man's solitude and the impossibility of communication between people. His world is a parody of man's search for meaning, his helplessness in the face of the unknown and the inevitability of death. With *Le Ping-Pong*, fp Paris 1955, dir MAUCLAIR, he gave more importance to political themes. His most ambitious play, *Paolo Paoli*, fp Lyons 1957, Théâtre de la Comédie, examines the egoism and the narrow-mindedness of the pre-war generation which contributed to the outbreak of World War I. Among his other plays are: *La Grande et la Petite Manœuvre*, 1950; *Le Professeur Taranne*, fp Lyons 1953, dir PLANCHON; *Tous contre tous*, fp Paris 1953, dir Jean-Marie Serreau; *Le Sens de la marche*, 1955; *Le Printemps '71*, 1961; *La Politique des restes*, 1963; *Off Limits*, fp Paris 1968, Théâtre d'Aubervilliers, dir G. Garran.
Bibl: M. Esslin, THE THEATRE OF THE ABSURD, 2/1968

Adams, Maude (1872–1953), US actress. Started her stage career at the age of nine months and had a resounding success when only five years old in *Fritz, Our German Cousin*, by A. Halliday. At 16 she came to New York (her first featured role 1889 in *A Midnight Bell* starring SOTHERN) where she achieved fame playing the parts of unfortunate and maltreated girls in MELODRAMA. BARRIE saw her performance in *Rosemary* (starring with J. DREW; ETHEL BARRYMORE playing her first part), 1896, and recognized her as an ideal interpreter for his delicate fey women. He wrote for her the part which established her as one of America's leading actresses, Lady Babbie in *The Little Minister*, 1897. Other parts in plays by Barrie which she made her own were in *Quality Street*, 1901; *What Every Woman Knows*, 1908; and above all the title role in *Peter Pan*, 1905. Barrie's manuscript of the play is dedicated to her. Maude A. was an actress of great beauty, sensitivity and intelligence.

ADC. The Amateur Dramatic Club of Cambridge University undergraduates.

Addison, Joseph (1672–1719), English essayist and politician. Famous for his contributions to the *Tatler*, *Spectator* and *Guardian*, he was the author of *The Drummer*, 1715, a moral COMEDY, and of *Cato*, 1713, a TRAGEDY following the classical French model, which had great success at DRURY LANE, starring B. BOOTH and ANNE OLDFIELD.
Bibl: B. Dobree, ESSAYS IN BIOGRAPHY, 1925

Ade, George (1866–1944), US journalist, short-story writer and playwright. He became known for his *Fables in Slang*, 1900, and its sequel, modelled on *Aesop's Fables*. On BROADWAY he began with a musical, *The Sultan of Sulu*, 1902; this was followed by some 20 successful light FARCES, most popular of which were *The College Widow*, 1904 (in 1917 it became a musical by KERN, Guy Bolton, etc., entitled *Leave It to Jane*, which was later revived and had a long OFF-BROADWAY run); *The Country Chairman*, 1903; *Just Out of College*, 1905; *Father and the Boys*, 1908.

Adler, Stella (1904–), US actress and teacher of acting. Member of a family well known in the YIDDISH THEATRE (father Jacob, mother Sarah). She studied with STANISLAVSKY. She and her brother Luther joined the GROUP THEATRE in 1931. Among plays in which she appeared were their productions of GREEN's *The House of Connelly*, 1931, and ODETS' *Awake and Sing*, 1935.

Admiral's Men (also known as Lord Admiral's Men). A theatrical company that shared the honours of the Elizabethan stage with the CHAMBERLAIN'S MEN with whom SHAKESPEARE was associated. Their protector was Charles Howard, who became Lord Admiral in 1585; their most prominent author was MARLOWE; their star actor was ALLEYN. Their business manager, HENSLOWE, kept a combined diary and account book, 1594–1604, which is one of the most important sources for the history of the ELIZABETHAN THEATRE. The 8–12 actors shared the profits of the enterprise. They had a large REPERTOIRE of new and old plays, and besides those by Marlowe they performed some of CHAPMAN's early works as well as plays by DEKKER and Henry Chettle. They played, 1594–1600, at the ROSE THEATRE and 1600–21 in the newly opened FORTUNE THEATRE, where they subsequently called themselves Prince Henry's Men, and later Palsgrave's Men. In 1621 the Fortune Theatre was burnt down, and a new one was opened in 1623. None of the new plays, however, proved to be successful, and after two years the company was disbanded.

A E (George William Russell; 1867–1935), Irish poet. An important figure in the Irish literary revival, he was connected with the early years of the modern Irish theatre through his only play *Deirdre*, fp 1902.

Aediles (Lat *aedilis*, from *aedes*=temple). Roman functionaries; originally temple officials, they came to be assistants to the tribunes and were responsible for judging the various games, including scenic performances. The *aedilis plebei*, after 494 BC, judged the *ludi plebei*, while the *aedilis curulis*, after 367 BC, judged the *ludi Romani* and also other games.

Aeschylus (Gk Aischylos; *c.* 525–*c.* 456 BC), earliest of the three great Athenian writers of TRAGEDY. Only seven of his 79–90 plays are extant: *The Suppliant Women*, *c.* 490 BC; *The Persians*, 472; *The Seven Against Thebes*, 467; *Prometheus Bound*, *c.* 460; the ORESTEIA, consisting of *Agamemnon*, the *Choephori* and the *Eumenides*, 458; the fourth play of the TETRALOGY, a SATYR PLAY, *Proteus*, is not preserved. Before him, tragedy consisted of long choral sections interspersed with DIALOGUE between the leader of the CHORUS and one principal actor, the PROTAGONIST. A. introduced a second actor, the DEUTERAGONIST, who played less important parts so that a more lively interplay became possible. Later he started using a third actor who had been introduced by his younger rival SOPHOCLES. A., who appeared in his own plays and rehearsed the chorus, thus acting as his own director, to use a modern term, also brought in numerous reforms and rearranged existing practices to suit his purpose. With A. the COSTUME of the tragic actor became a long garment with sleeves, boots reaching to the knees (*cothurnus*) and a cloth mask with a hair-style piled up high in front (*onkos*). For scenery he used graves, rocks, altars and a tent in the background, later a temporary wooden building (*skene*) representing a palace or a temple (▷AGATHARCOS). The chorus acted mainly in the ORCHESTRA – a circular dancing area – with the actors often close to the buildings which were possibly set tangentially to the orchestra. The actual scenic structure was probably fixed on low platforms, but a general raised stage did not exist in the period of A. and the other classical writers. The lyric parts, usually laments, were sung by the chorus and in antiphony (*kommos*) by the actors and the chorus and were accompanied by flute (the music is not preserved).
Bibl: Thomson, AESCHYLUS AND ATHENS, 3/1966; G. Murray, AESCHYLUS, THE CREATOR OF TRAGEDY, 1940

Afinogenov, Alexander Nikolaevich (1904–41), Soviet dramatist. His early plays were strongly influenced by the Proletcult, a left-wing literary movement: *Po tu storonu shcheli*, based on Jack London's story *South of the Slot*, 1926, about a San Francisco strike; *Na perelome* (At Breaking Point), 1926, a lampoon against German Democratic Socialism; *Glyadi v oba* (Look with Both Eyes), 1927; *Volchya tropa* (The Track of the Wolf), 1927. In 1928 he turned to SOCIALIST REALISM, a movement which at that time was still permitted some measure of social criticism. Despite this he was accused of sympathizing with the unpolitical intelligentsia in his play *Chudak* (The Eccentric), 1929. His most important and most discussed work is *Strakh* (Fear), 1929, fp Leningrad 1931. The hero is a psychologist who propounds the theory that fear governs the USSR but in the end is converted to Socialism. *Dalyokoe*, performed at the Vakhtangov Theatre in 1934, was first seen in London at the Gate Theatre in 1937 as *Distant Point*, translated by Hubert Griffith.
Bibl: A. N. Afinogenov, SIX SOVIET PLAYS (translated by C. Malamuth), 1936

Afranius, Lucius (active *c.* 150 BC), writer of Roman COMEDY. He was the most important and productive representative of the *fabula togata* (▷FABULA) and was greatly influenced by MENANDER and TERENCE. His themes were taken from everyday life in Rome. Of his work 44 titles and 250 fragments (400 verses) are preserved; some of the better-known plays are *Thais*, *The Cousins*, *The Importer* and *The Fire*.
Bibl: E. Courbaud, DE COMEDIA TOGATA, 1899

Africa (▷EGYPT; SOUTH AFRICA). Almost every area of Black Africa has its own dances. With political independence African countries have established national ballets, which combine native traditions with modern techniques of spectacle for the purpose of representation abroad. In many parts of Africa there are signs of an independent theatre with varied European influence, e.g. in the Nigerian Yoruba opera. The Zulu *Macbeth*, performed in London during the WORLD THEATRE SEASON, 1972, was much acclaimed. In recent years, some notable plays have been written by Africans working in English. Outstanding among them is the Nigerian poet SOYINKA.
Bibl: M. Amosu, PRELIMINARY BIBLIOGRAPHY OF CREATIVE AFRICAN WRITING IN EUROPEAN LANGUAGES, 1964

Afterpiece. A brief, one-act kind of nonsense piece, which was put on after the main play, e.g. the SATYR PLAY in ancient times, the Klucht in Holland, following the ABELE-SPELEN, the JIG of the ENGLISH COMEDIANS. It came into fashion as a comic antidote to the main play in England at the beginning of the 18th century. In the fight for the audience's favour these pieces, usually comedies with songs and dances, were often done with more care and display than the full-length play. They were meant to provide diversion for late-comers, shopkeepers, business men and so forth for whom the 6 o'clock curtain was too early. J. Weaver, the ballet master, was one of the main creators of the afterpiece, which remained in use until GARRICK's time.
Bibl: E. D. Every, DANCING AND PANTOMIME ON THE ENGLISH STAGE, 1934

Agate, James (1877–1947), English drama critic. The most influential critic of his time, he was with *The Sunday Times* 1923–47. His reviews were scholarly, witty, showing his deep love of the theatre and enthusiasm for the great star personalities among actors. He published many volumes of his collected reviews, as well as a series of personal diaries under the title *Ego*.

Agatharchos of Samos (5th century BC),

Maude Adams

Actors' Studio production of BALDWIN's *Blues for Mister Charlie*, WORLD THEATRE SEASON (▷DAUBENY), London 1965

Africa, drama group from Umabatha, in a local performance later presented in London during the WORLD THEATRE SEASON (▷DAUBENY) 1971

painter of scenery for the Attic TRAGEDY, e.g. plays by AESCHYLUS. He is mentioned by VITRUVIUS in the introduction to *De Architectura*, VII. Started by painting the *skene* (tents, then huts, for costume-changing) in 468 BC, and later wrote an essay on stage painting.
Bibl: A. W. Pickard-Cambridge, THE THEATRE OF DIONYSOS IN ATHENS, 1946

Agathon (447–400 BC), Athenian tragic poet and younger contemporary of EURIPIDES. He won top prize at the Lenaean Festival in 416 BC; his first victory. He was the first Greek to devise his own plots, instead of taking them from mythology, and, according to ARISTOTLE, he used choric odes that were unconnected with the PLOT, and turned from genuinely tragic subjects to melodramatic ones. Only about 40 lines of his work remain, from *Aerope*, *Alcmaeon*, *The Mysians*, *Telephus* and *Thyestes*.

Agitprop theatre. Agitation and propaganda theatre, in the form of REVUES and sometimes large shows; started in the USSR about 1920 by the Communist Party, it was used later in Germany. Actors were usually amateurs while the directors were professional though the reverse was also true, e.g. the Blue Blouses, who were professional actors. It had a strong influence on professional theatre and on directors like MEYERHOLD, BRECHT and PISCATOR.

Agon (Gk=contest). The ancient Greeks held regular athletic, musical and theatrical contests at their religious festivals at Olympia, Delphi, Corinth and elsewhere. As far as drama and the dramatic festivals of Athens in particular are concerned, the *agones* were originally between *choregi* (chorus leaders): later, *c.* 510 BC, there was also an *agon* between dramatists; not until 450 BC, when the DIALOGUE had become dominant, was an *agon* introduced for individual actors, the PROTAGONISTS of TRAGEDY; after *c.* 420 BC the comic protagonists also competed. The word *agon* is also used to designate one of the constituent parts of Attic COMEDY – the debate between two opposing characters in a play.

Agora (Gk=market place, referred to by Homer as a place of dance and sacrifice). It was the centre of commercial, social and often political activity. Before the slopes of the Acropolis were used, the earliest dramatic performances in Athens were given in the *agora*. The Athenian *agora* contained the first ORCHESTRA in Greek theatre, which was later moved from there to the theatre of Dionysos. ▷DIONYSOS, THEATRE OF

Aiorema. A type of STAGE MACHINERY used in ancient Greek theatre for appearances of gods (▷DEUS EX MACHINA). Presumably a mobile crane, it came into use at the time of EURIPIDES.

Akimov, Nikolai Pavlovich (1901–68), Soviet theatre designer and director. He fought for the acceptance of new Soviet dramatists, and attracted some attention with his designs for the sets of *Armoured Train 14–69* (IVANOV) 1927 and *Fear* (AFINOGENOV) 1931 at the Leningrad Academic Theatre. Then he joined the Vakhtangov Theatre in Moscow where he worked as a designer and director. In his first spectacular 'formalist' production, *Hamlet*, 1932, he used design to express the decadence of the Court. He returned to Leningrad in 1934, and became Art Director of the Theatre of Comedy in 1936. Among his productions were *Twelfth Night*, 1938, *Tartuffe* (design and costumes), and *As You Like It*, 1938. From 1955 he was head of the Faculty of Design and Production at the Leningrad Theatrical Institute.
Bibl: A. A. Bartosevich, 1933

Alarcón y Mendoza, Juan Ruiz de (*c.* 1580–1639), Mexican-born Spanish dramatist. Originally a lawyer, he wrote about 20 plays which, unlike those of his contemporary and bitter enemy LOPE DE VEGA, did not, primarily, aim at theatrical effectiveness but rather at economical plot construction, clever contrast of well defined characters and correct language. Though his plays were not popular during his lifetime, they had great influence on dramatists like CORNEILLE and GOLDONI. He published his works in two volumes in 1628 and 1634. His play *La verdad sospechosa* (The Suspect Truth), was the source for Corneille's *Le Menteur*. Other works include: *Los favores del mundo* (The Favours of the World); *El antichristo* (The Anti-Christ), his only religious work; *El tejedor de Segovia* (The Weaver of Seville).
Bibl: V. Valbuena Prat, HISTORIA DEL TEATRO ESPAÑOL, 1956

Albania. The 450 years of occupation by the Turks prevented the growth of a national theatre in Albania. After the end of Turkish rule in 1912, second-rate European companies toured the country; during the occupation by Italy, 1939–44, it was visited by somewhat better Italian companies. Today it has a state theatre in the capital, Tirana, with its own ENSEMBLE and the beginning of a national tradition of drama.

Albee, Edward (1928–), US dramatist. In his works he attacks the complacent optimism of US society, and writes of the isolation and despair of contemporary civilization. His early play *The Zoo Story* illustrates, in a park-bench dialogue between a conformist, bourgeois family man and an outcast and lonely bohemian rebel, that violence is the only means of communication, even if it involves murder. First performed in Berlin 1959, it opened OFF-BROADWAY, New York 1960. *The Death of Bessie Smith*, fp Berlin 1961, was performed in the Provincetown Playhouse, New York 1961. It concerns the death of the Black American blues singer, following her rejection by White hospitals in the South, after a motor accident. *Exorcism* and *The Sandbox*, fp Off-Broadway, 1960, were sketches in the style of the THEATRE OF THE ABSURD. *The American Dream*, 1961, a longer version of *The Sandbox*, is a devastating caricature of American values and types, using the means of the Theatre of the Absurd (IONESCO, *The Bald Soprano*). *Who's Afraid of Virginia Woolf?*, fp New York 1962, Billy Rose Theatre, dir SCHNEIDER, his first full-length play, won the NYDCC and Antoinette Perry awards and became an international success. It shows how, in the course of a night of drinking, two couples – the men professors at a small-town New England college – destroy their hopes and illusions. *Tiny Alice*, fp 1963, Billy Rose Theatre, dir Schneider, leads played by IRENE WORTH and GIELGUD, is a forceful and controversial play, mixing games with sensual and religious themes. *A Delicate Balance*, fp New York 1966, which won a PULITZER PRIZE, shows nervous, subtle and mysterious relationships between the members of a US middle-class family. *Box/Quotations from Chairman Mao Tse-tung/Box* or *Box/Mao/Box*, fp 1968 Buffalo, N.Y., Arts Festival, consists of a series of independent MONOLOGUES on themes of birth, death and civilization interspersed with revolutionary aphorisms delivered by Mao Tse-tung. Adaptations: *The Ballad of the Sad Café*, after a novella by CARSON MCCULLERS, 1963; *Malcolm*, after a novel by James Purdy, 1966; *Everything in the Garden*, after a play by COOPER, fp New York 1967. Most recent plays are *All Over*, fp New York, 1971, dir Gielgud; *Seascape*, 1975.
Bibl: M. E. Rutenberg, EDWARD ALBEE, PLAYWRIGHT IN PROTEST, 1969; M. Esslin, THE THEATRE OF THE ABSURD, 2/1968

Albers, Hans (1892–1960), German actor. After World War I he appeared mainly in BERLIN, first in various operettas, and later at the Deutsches-Theater, 1926. His greatness lay in the portrayal of swaggering daredevils and adventurous social outcasts; he was also noted for his musical talent. His most brilliant parts included title roles in *Liliom* by MOLNÁR, 1931, and IBSEN's *Peer Gynt*. Also a successful film actor in the 1930s and 1940s.

Albertazzi, Giorgio (1923–), outstanding Italian actor of the post-World War II generation. In 1952 he helped found a theatrical company, from 1956 known as the Compagnia Proclemer-Albertazzi which, for the next ten years, was the leading group in Italy. An intelligent modern actor, he has adapted plays and written theoretical articles for newspapers. His most important parts include: Lysander in *A Midsummer Night's Dream*, 1951–52, the Fool in *King Lear*, 1955, and the title role in ZEFFIRELLI's famous production of *Hamlet* in 1963. He has worked as a director since 1959, his first production being *Les Séquestrés d'Altona* by SARTRE, in which he also played the lead.

Alberti, Rafael (1902–), Spanish poet and playwright. He was a friend of LORCA. His plays are lyrical; among them are *El adefesio* (The Ridiculous One), 1944, and *El trébol florido* (The Elegant Shamrock), 1950.
Bibl: C. Bo, 1940

Alcestis. Character in Greek mythology. Wife of King Admetos who offered herself to Death when he came to take away her husband. *Alcestis*, a play by EURIPIDES, 438 BC, formed the afterpiece of the TRILOGY *The Cretan Women*, *Alcmaeon in Psophis* and *Telephus*. Adaptations and works influenced by the Alcestis story – operas: Philippe Quinault, *Alceste*, 1674; Handel, *Admeto*, 1727, and Gluck, *Alceste*, 1767; plays: SACHS, *Alcestis*, 1551; Alexandre Hardy, *Alceste*, 1602; ALFIERI, *Alceste Seconda*, 1798; Herder, *Admetus Haus* (House of Admetos), 1803; BROWNING, *Balaustion's Adventure*, 1871; HOFMANNSTHAL, *Alkestis*, 1909; ELIOT, *The Cocktail Party*, fp 1949; WILDER, *A Life in the Sun*, 1955.

Aleichem ▷SHOLEM ALEICHEM

Aleotti, Giovan Battista (nicknamed L'Argenta: 1546–1636), Italian architect and stage designer. He introduced WINGS, consisting of flats mounted in wooden frames which replaced the former system of TELARI, which were three-sided prisms modelled on the PERIAKTOS of the ancients restricting each play to three sets of scenery. This new device used for the first time at the Teatro dell'Accademia degli Intrepidi, Ferrara, 1606, and then at the Teatro Farnese in Parma, which he designed 1618–19, laid the foundation for the numerous and magical scene-changes of BAROQUE THEATRE. His pupil Torelli (1608–78) further developed A's invention into the system of wings slotted into the stage floor which prevailed till the end of the 19th century.
Bibl: H. Leclerc, LES ORIGINES ITALIENNES DE L'ARCHITECTURE THÉÂTRALE MODERNE, 1946

Alexander, Sir George (1858–1918), English ACTOR-MANAGER. Knighted in 1911. Joined IRVING's Lyceum Theatre as an actor, then went into management on his own in 1889. He was manager of St James's, the leading London theatre of his time, from 1891 until his death. Altogether he produced over 80 plays, ranging from SHAKESPEARE to PINERO, whose *The Second Mrs Tanqueray* he produced in 1895 with MRS PATRICK CAMPBELL, who had made a spectacular hit as Paula in the first performance, 1893. He encouraged writers like WILDE whose *Lady Windermere's Fan* was first performed at the St James's Theatre in 1892 and *The Importance of Being Earnest* in 1895, which was produced by A. who also played John Worthing. A man of great charm and wit on the stage, he typified the ideal English gentleman of the pre-World War I era. His own greatest acting success was in the dual role in Anthony Hope's *The Prisoner of Zenda*, 1896.
Bibl: H. Pearson, THE LAST ACTOR-MANAGERS, 1950

Alexandrine. Dodecasyllabic, iambic verse, which emerged in the 11th century in France and later, usually in rhyming couplets, became the metre of the classical French TRAGEDY of CORNEILLE and RACINE.

Aleotti's Teatro Farnese in Parma

Edward Albee's *Who's Afraid of Virginia Woolf?*, New York 1962, with Uta Hagen, George Grizzard and Arthur Hall

George Alexander and Lily Hanbury in WILDE's *Lady Windermere's Fan*, London 1892

Alexis (born *c.* 372 BC in Italy, died in Athens 270 BC), Greek comic poet. Together with Antiphanes, the most outstanding writer of the Middle Comedy; 135 titles recorded and 346 fragments (1,200 verses) preserved. He introduced the character of the parasite into comic literature. His themes seem to have been love stories, adventures, and satires on philosophers; many of his titles suggest that he introduced the study of character types, which was to be a major feature of the New Comedy. ▷COMEDY, GREEK

Alfieri, Count Vittorio Amadeo (1749–1803), the most important dramatist of 18th-century ITALY. He wrote plays on classical, biblical and romantic subjects. For him TRAGEDY was the dramatic presentation of a great theme: praise of the heroic, the free individual, rebellion against tyranny. His style was influenced by the French classics, while in his verse he owes much to Cesaretti. His first play *Cleopatra* was successfully presented at Turin in 1775. Best known of his tragedies are *Saul*, 1782–84, and *Mirra*, 1784–86. Another is *Agamennone*. These plays expressed the Italians' striving for freedom and still retain their effectiveness. A.'s bicentenary started a renaissance of his work in Italy; *Oreste*, dir VISCONTI, Rome 1949; *Filippo*, seen at his birthplace, Asti, in 1949, presented by the ENSEMBLE of the PICCOLO TEATRO DI MILANO, dir COSTA, and *Oreste*, 1951, director and leading actor GASSMAN.
Bibl: M. Fubini, 2/1953; G. A. Levi, 1950

Alhambra. A famous MUSIC HALL in Leicester Square, London, built in Moorish style. It opened in 1854 as the Panopticon and in 1858 was first called the Alhambra (Palace). It burnt down in 1882, but was rebuilt the following year, and had its heyday as a music hall from 1890 to 1910, when it had a resident ballet. Diaghilev's Ballets Russes company made its first appearance there in 1911. The same year it went over to REVUES with great success, e.g. *The Bing Boys Are Here*, 1916, by GROSSMITH, with ROBEY. It then reverted to variety until it was demolished in 1936, and replaced by the Odeon Cinema.

Alienation effect. (*Verfremdungseffekt*, abbreviated to *V-Effekt*), a theatrical device, or series of such devices, designed by BRECHT to make the spectator see the world with fresh eyes, 'as though he were seeing it for the first time' so that 'the familiar should become strange'. Brecht's intention in using such means as non-naturalistic acting, stylized sets, film-projections, non-identification of the actors with their parts, etc., was to arouse the spectators' critical faculties so that they would learn from what they saw in the theatre.

Allegory. The representation of abstract concepts of ethics (moral allegory) or political, historical events (historical allegory) by means of the characters, setting and action of a play. The first type is historically identified with the MORALITY PLAY such as the medieval drama EVERYMAN. The technique employed is that of personification. *Everyman* features characters with names like Good Deeds, Fellowship and Worldly Goods. The second type, historical allegory, treats contemporary problems, with which it may not be possible to deal openly, by presenting historical events involving similar situations, for example, MIDDLETON's *A Game at Chess*, 1624, a satirical allegory, or A. MILLER's *The Crucible*, 1953, which drew a parallel between the McCarthy 'witch-hunts' and the witch trials of Salem, or *Armstrong's Last Goodnight*, 1965, by ARDEN, based on the Scottish *Ballad of Johnny Armstrong*.
Bibl: H. J. Newinger, METAPHOR AND ALLEGORY, 1957

Alleyn, Edward (1566–1626), one of the best-known actors of the ELIZABETHAN THEATRE. He was the son-in-law and business partner of HENSLOWE. The major actor of the ADMIRAL'S MEN, for whom MARLOWE was the chief dramatist, some of his successful appearances were in *Dr Faustus*, *The Jew of Malta*, *Tamburlaine the Great*, and GREENE's *Orlando Furioso*. He was considered a rival of the versatile actor R. BURBAGE, the leading Shakespearean player, but A. personified the more powerful expressive hero.
Bibl: G. L. Hocking, THE LIFE AND TIMES OF EDWARD ALLEYN, 1952

Allgood, Sara (1883–1950), Irish actress. One of the leading players at the ABBEY THEATRE, Dublin, during its great period, she appeared there in the first productions when it opened in 1904. She went to Liverpool and Manchester in 1914 to work with ANNIE HORNIMAN, later appeared in London and increasingly often in the USA. After 1940 she settled in Hollywood and concentrated on films. Among her most famous theatrical roles were Cathleen in *Riders to the Sea*, and Widow Quin in *The Playboy of the Western World*, both by SYNGE; Cathleen in *Cathleen ni Houlihan* (YEATS); Peg in *Peg o' My Heart* (J. H. Manners); Mrs Peachum in GAY's *The Beggar's Opera*; and Juno in *Juno and the Paycock* (O'CASEY).

Allio, René (1921–), French stage designer and director. Worked with PLANCHON at the Théâtre de la Cité de Villeurbanne, and contributed greatly to the development of the Brechtian style of production in France. Has also worked in England, at STRATFORD-UPON-AVON, and at the NATIONAL THEATRE, where he designed GASKILL's production of FARQUHAR's *The Recruiting Officer*, 1963; he drew plans for the conversion of the Roundhouse, London, under the auspices of CENTRE 42, and worked on the rebuilding of theatres in France (Aubervilliers; Théâtre de la Ville, Paris). He has also directed a number of films.

Altar (Lat *alta ara*=raised fireplace, place for worship and sacrifice). Origin of religious drama; one piece of evidence is a Greek cup by the Brygos Painter (*c.* 490 BC), on which satyrs dance round an altar. In the Greek theatre the altar (*thymele*), sacred to DIONYSOS, stood in the middle of the ORCHESTRA or dancing area, subsequently at the periphery. The Greek drama preceded a sacrifice, indicating the religious nature of the performance. The Romans maintained the outward aspects of the religious tradition by setting up two altars, though the Roman theatre had no national mythological TRAGEDY. In the religious theatre of the early Middle Ages, which took place at first in churches, the altar represented the grave of Christ, and marked the centre of dynamic action. The mobile altar, developed from the Corpus Christi processions, played an important part in the religious theatre of Spain.

Alvarez Quintero, Serafín (1871–1938) and **Joaquín** (1873–1944), Spanish dramatists. They were brothers and wrote all their plays in collaboration. The best known are: *Los galeotes* (The Galley Slaves), 1900, *Cabrita que tira al monte* (The Engine which cast Stones at the Mountain), 1912, *Los mosquitos* (The Mosquitoes), 1928.
Bibl: J. Losada de la Torre, 1945

Amanat (Saiyed Agha Hasan; 1816–59), Indian dramatist. He was the founder of Urdu drama with his musical play *Indar-Sabha* (Indar's Court).
Bibl: Ram Baku Saksena, A HISTORY OF URDU LITERATURE, 1940

American National Theatre and Academy (ANTA). Established by Congressional Charter in 1935, with the support of President Roosevelt, to develop drama in the USA and encourage serious theatrical activities; it is privately financed. It gives information about theatres, holds an annual congress, promotes new playwrights (Experimental Theatre 1948/49) and individual productions, sponsors US companies touring abroad and the visits of foreign companies to the USA.

Ames, Winthrop (1871–1937), US director and manager. Son of a railway magnate, he was educated at Harvard. He managed the Castle Square Theatre in Boston from 1904 to 1907. His ambition was to establish serious REPERTORY theatre in the USA and, with this purpose in mind, opened the New Theatre in New York in 1909, but without lasting success. After three seasons of productions of SHAKESPEARE, and contemporary playwrights such as GALSWORTHY and MAETERLINCK, the theatre had to close with a deficit of $400,000. In 1912 he founded the Little Theatre and later added the Booth Theatre to his enterprise, where he was more successful, and concentrated on a modern REPERTOIRE including plays by PINERO and GRANVILLE-BARKER. He retired in 1932.

Amiel, Denys (1884–), French playwright. Started as secretary to BATAILLE, about whom he published a critical biography. His early plays were influenced by the ideas of the 'theatre of silence', formulated by a group of dramatists, headed by OBEY and including J.-J. BERNARD, who were inspired by MAETERLINCK. Later his work tended towards the more popular effects of BOULEVARD THEATRE. His plays include: *La Souriante Madame Beudet*, written with OBEY, 1921; *Le Voyageur*, 1923; *Monsieur et Madame Un Tel*, 1925; *Carcasse*, with Obey, 1926; *L'Image*, 1927; *Décalage*, 1931; *Trois et une*, 1932; *L'Homme*, 1934; *La Femme en fleur*, 1935; *Ma liberté*, 1936; *La Maison Monestier*, 1939.

Amoroso (Ital=lover). In modern Italian theatre, descendant of the INNAMORATI (lovers) of the COMMEDIA DELL'ARTE.

Amphitheatre (Gk *amphi*=around+*theatron*, from *theaomai*=behold). Type of theatre building in classical antiquity. In ancient GREECE the usual form of the amphitheatre consisted of a circular space or dancing area (*orchestra*), largely enclosed by an auditorium of tiered seats (*theatron*) and the stage (*skene*). The *theatron*, originally built of wood, after 330 BC of stone, was often on a slope, using the natural incline for the tiered seats of the spectators, who entered the amphitheatre from the orchestra on sloping (*kerkides*) or horizontal (*diazomata*) passageways. In the centre of the orchestra was an ALTAR (*thymele*) which was later moved to the periphery. The *skene*, in its earliest form a hut used for costume changes, was separated from the *theatron* by entrances or runways (*parodoi*); built of stone, it had a high, narrow platform (*proskenion*) facing the audience, and side wings (*paraskenia*). Later the *skene* was raised and provided with STAGE MACHINERY (*eccyclema*=stage cart, CHARONIAN STEPS, etc.) and then with sets, movable (*periaktoi*) or painted (*pinakoi*). The Renaissance architects, PALLADIO and ALEOTTI, designed their auditoriums on the model of the amphitheatre, elements of which occur in the THEATRE-IN-THE-ROUND and other modern forms of theatre. The Greek amphitheatres originated at the same time as Greek TRAGEDY – in the second half of the 6th century BC – the orchestra being the most ancient part. Ruined remains of about 80 still survive, among them the theatres of: DIONYSOS in Athens; EPIDAUROS, 400 BC: Priene, 300 BC: Delos, 269 BC: Oropos, 200 BC. The Roman half-amphitheatre was greatly influenced by the Greek amphitheatre and by the Latin ATELLAN stage. Since the chorus had lost its importance in ROMAN THEATRE, the Greek circular orchestra was replaced by a free-standing, semicircular amphitheatre. The *skene* became a much broader, raised stage, richly decorated (*scaenae frons*). The *paraskenia* disappeared, stage and auditorium fused into a whole and so could be covered over with a *velum*. The Roman amphitheatre already had a front curtain (▷AULEUM). For gladiatorial fights, etc., a full amphitheatre was built round the arena, e.g. Balbus-Marcellus theatre, Colosseum. Notable amphitheatres are those at Orange, Aspendos, Pompeii and Taormina. The largest could accommodate 17,000 spectators.

Bibl: M. Bieber, HISTORY OF THE GREEK AND ROMAN THEATRE, 1961

Alhambra, London, interior of the 1883 building

Edward Alleyn, portrait at Dulwich College Gallery, London

Amphitheatre at EPIDAUROS, built 400 BC

Amphitryon. Greek mythological character. The king of Tiryns, whose shape was assumed by Zeus in order to gain access to the latter's wife, Alcmene, and thus father Hercules. Tragedies by AESCHYLUS, SOPHOCLES and EURIPIDES not preserved. PLAUTUS' comedy *Amphitruo*, variously dated from 215 to 186 BC, was the prototype of many later plays: ROTROU, *Les Sosies*, 1638; MOLIÈRE, *Amphitryon*, 1668; DRYDEN, *Amphitryon*, 1690; KLEIST, *Amphitryon*, 1807; GIRAUDOUX, *Amphitryon 38*, 1929, which, according to the author, was the 38th version of the play: KAISER, *Zweimal Amphitryon*, 1944.

Anagnorisis (Gk=recognition). As defined by ARISTOTLE in the *Poetics*, the discovery of the true identity of a character in drama, for example the recognition of Orestes by Electra in AESCHYLUS' *Choephori*. Modern critics interpret the term in a wider sense, to include the recognition by a character of his own or another's true condition, or of the real meaning of his actions, for example, Oedipus' self-recognition in SOPHOCLES' *Oedipus Rex*.

Anapiesmata (Gk=something pressed upward). A trapdoor used on the classical Greek stage for entrances from the world of the dead.

Ancey, Georges (1860–1917), French dramatist. Originally a diplomat, he became one of the spiritual leaders of the THÉÂTRE LIBRE. He was a frank, almost cruel observer of reality, and, along with BECQUE, the most important dramatist of French NATURALISM. His works include *Autres choses*, 1886; *Monsieur Lamblin*, 1888; *Les Inséparables*, 1889; *L'Ecole des veufs*, 1889; *Grand-mère*, 1890; *La Dupe*, 1891; *L'Avenir*, 1899; *Ces Messieurs*, 1903.
Bibl: R. Dournic, DE SCRIBE À IBSEN, 1896

Anderson, Judith (1898–), Australian-born US actress. She made her début in Sydney in 1915 and in 1918 went to the USA where she has remained ever since. A powerful actress excelling in strong roles, capable of expressing overpowering yet suppressed emotion, her most memorable appearances have been in *Behold the Bridegroom* by KELLY, 1927; *As You Desire Me* by PIRANDELLO, 1931; O'NEILL's *Mourning Becomes Electra*, 1931; *Come of Age* by Clemence Dane, 1934; *The Old Maid* by Zoë Akins (▷NYDCC AWARD), 1935; as the Queen in *Hamlet*, with GIELGUD, 1936; as Lady Macbeth, opposite EVANS, 1941; *Three Sisters* by CHEKHOV, 1942; the name part in EURIPIDES' *Medea* (adapted by Robinson Jeffers), 1947. She has also appeared in many films.

Anderson, Lindsay (1923–), British director, who began as a film critic. Worked as a stage producer mainly at the ROYAL COURT THEATRE; productions include W. HALL's *The Long and the Short and the Tall*, 1959; OWEN's *Progress to the Park*, 1959; ARDEN's *Serjeant Musgrave's Dance*, 1959; Keith Waterhouse and W. Hall's *Billy Liar*, 1960; Christopher Logue's *Trials by Logue*, 1960; TRAVERS, *The Bed Before Yesterday*, London 1975. Together with Karel Reisz he launched the 'free cinema', a British documentary movement. Main short films: *Wakefield Express*, 1952; *O Dreamland*; *Thursday's Children*, 1953; Main feature films: *This Sporting Life*, 1963; *Red White and Zero*, 1966; *Come the Revolution*, 1968, and *If*, 1969.

Anderson, Maxwell (1888–1959), US journalist who turned to playwriting. In this he was encouraged by Laurence Stallings, a colleague at the *New York World*, who helped to get his first play, *White Desert*, produced in 1923. A commercial failure, it nevertheless received good reviews and his next play, written in collaboration with Stallings, *What Price Glory?*, 1924, a provocative and realistic war play, was a hit. This was followed by *Saturday's Children* (with RUTH GORDON), 1927, a 'serious comedy', and *Gods of the Lightning*, 1928, a harrowing drama about the Sacco–Vanzetti case, which created a sensation. Favouring VERSE DRAMA, he experimented with a number of theatrical forms: probably his finest verse play is *Winterset*, 1935, an imaginative sequel to *Gods of the Lightning*. He had a great success with *Elizabeth the Queen*, 1930, a historical play starring the LUNTS. Other notable plays include: *Both Your Houses*, 1933, a satire on political corruption, which won the PULITZER PRIZE; *Mary of Scotland*, 1933, with HELEN HAYES; *Valley Forge*, 1934; *The Wingless Victory*, 1936, with KATHARINE CORNELL; *High Tor*, 1936, with PEGGY ASHCROFT making her New York début; *The Masque of Kings*, 1937, a costume drama; *Key Largo*, 1939, with MUNI; *Joan of Lorraine*, 1946, with Ingrid Bergman; *Anne of the Thousand Days*, 1948, with HARRISON as Henry VIII; *Barefoot in Athens*, 1951, and *The Golden Six*, 1958. Founder member of the PLAYWRIGHTS' COMPANY, 1937, his first play for them was *Knickerbocker Holiday*, 1938, music WEILL, with Walter Huston. He collaborated again with Weill on the musical drama, *Lost in the Stars*, 1949, based on the novel *Cry the Beloved Country*. Many of his plays have been filmed, and he collaborated on a number of film scripts, e.g. *All Quiet on the Western Front*, 1931. He published a collection of articles on drama: *The Essence of Tragedy and Other Footnotes*, 1929.
Bibl: M. D. Bailey, MAXWELL ANDERSON, THE PLAYWRIGHT AS PROPHET, 1957.

Anderson, Robert (1917–), US poet and dramatist. He taught drama and writing at Harvard, and served in the US Navy in World War II when he wrote the play *Come Marching Home*, New York 1945, which won the National Theatre Conference prize for the best play written by a serviceman on overseas duty. In 1946 he started playwriting courses at the American Theatre Wing and taught there for four years. From this group sprang the New Dramatists' Committee which he helped form and of which he became president. He achieved his biggest success with *Tea and Sympathy*, New York 1953, Ethel Barrymore Theatre, dir KAZAN, with Deborah Kerr, following which he was elected a member of the PLAYWRIGHTS' COMPANY. Other plays include: *Love Revisited*, 1951; *All Summer Long*, 1953; *Silent Night, Lonely Night*, 1959; *The Days Between*, 1965; *You Know I Can't Hear You When the Water's Running*, a programme of one-act plays, 1967; *I Never Sang for My Father*, 1968, and *Solitaire/Double Solitaire*, 1971. He has also written a number of screenplays, notably *The Nun's Story*, 1959, with Audrey Hepburn, which won an Oscar.

Andersson, Bibi (1935–), Swedish actress. One of the leading performers of the younger generation in her country, her main roles include: Karin Mansdotter in STRINDBERG's *Erik XIV*, 1956, Malmö Theatre, dir I. BERGMAN; Irina in CHEKHOV's *Three Sisters*, Stockholm 1959, Royal Dramatic Theatre; Prince Arthur in SHAKESPEARE's *King John*, 1959, Dramatic Theatre, dir SJÖBERG; Carmen in GENET's *Le Balcon*, Uppsala 1961. Subsequently she has been under contract to the Dramatic Theatre managed by Bergman. She played Juliet in Shakespeare's play, Maggie in A. MILLER's *After the Fall*, 1965; she has appeared in many of Bergman's films, e.g. *Smiles of a Summer Night*; *The Seventh Seal*; *Wild Strawberries*; *The Island*; *Persona*; *The Girls*.

Andreini. Italian family of actors of the COMMEDIA DELL'ARTE. (1) **Francesco A.** (1548–1624) was one of the leaders of the GELOSI, with whom he went to Paris in 1600. He was best known for his performance as CAPITANO in *Bravure del Capitano Spavente* (Exploits of Captain S.), 1607, which fully developed the character. His wife (2) **Isabella Canali** (1562–1604) was the leading lady of the Gelosi and many parts were named after her. They had seven sons; the most famous was (3) **Giovanni Battista A.** (*c.* 1578–1654), also known as Lelio. He was one of the outstanding actors of the c. dell'a. as well as a writer of COMEDIES.

Andreyev, Leonid Nikolayevich (1871–1919), Russian dramatist. He studied at Moscow and St Petersburg universities, then worked as a journalist. Although very attracted to the revolutionary movement in his youth, he emigrated to Finland after the October Revolution. His short stories, in the realistic tradition of the 19th century, were greatly influenced by CHEKHOV, DOSTOYEVSKY, TOLSTOY and MAETERLINCK. His plays during the period 1905–17, profoundly pessimistic and bitter, were mostly in Symbolist style; they include: *Zhizn cheloveka* (*The Life of Man*), 1907; *Tsar Golod* (King Hunger), 1908; *Chornye Maski* (The Black Maskers), 1909; *Anatema* (*Anathema*), 1909; *Prekrasnye Sabinyanki* (The Sabine Women), 1911; *Tot, kto poluchaet poshchochiny* (*He Who Gets Slapped*), 1914, the best known outside the USSR, produced in London (1927 and 1947) and in New York (1922, 1946 and

Maxwell Anderson's *Winterset*, New York 1935, stage set by MIELZINER, featuring MEREDITH

Jean Anouilh's *Ring Round the Moon* (trans FRY), London 1950, with MARGARET RUTHERFORD, Claire Bloom and SCOFIELD; costumes and set by MESSEL

Robert Anderson's *Tea and Sympathy*, New York 1953, with Deborah Kerr and Leif Erickson

1956). In 1912 he wrote two realistic plays, *Yekaterina Ivanovna* and *Professor Storitsyn*. In 1914 *Mysl* (*The Thought*) was performed at the MOSCOW ART THEATRE, dir STANISLAVSKY.
Bibl: D. S. Mirsky, CONTEMPORARY RUSSIAN LITERATURE, 1926

Andrieux, François (1759–1833), French dramatist. Politically active during the French Revolution, member of the Tribune of 1,000 and secretary to the Académie française. A classicist who resisted Romanticism, he wrote witty COMEDIES, the TRAGEDY *Junius Brutus*, 1830, and the LIBRETTO to the comic opera *L'Enfance de J.-J. Rousseau*, by Dalayrac, 1794. His other works include *Anaximandre*, 1782; *Les Etourdis ou la Mort Supposée*, 1788; *Helvétius ou la Vengeance du menteur*, 1803 (after CORNEILLE); *Le Trésor*, 1894; *La Soirée d'Auteuil ou Molière avec ses amis*, 1894; *Le Vieux Fat*, 1810; *La Comédienne*, 1816; *Louis IX en Egypte*, 1790, libretto written with Guillard, music Dalayrac.
Bibl: M. Carlson, THE THEATRE OF THE FRENCH REVOLUTION, 1966

Angely, Louis (1787–1835), German playwright, and from 1822 actor and director at the Königstädtisches Theater, BERLIN. He wrote more than 100 FARCES, mostly adapted from French VAUDEVILLE and very cleverly localized in Berlin: *Das Fest der Handwerker* (The Artisans' Festival); *Sieben Mädchen in Uniform* (Seven Girls in Uniform); *Die Reise auf gemeinschaftliche Kosten* (The Journey at Shared Expense); *Paris in Pommern* (Paris in Pomerania); *Wohnungen zu vermieten* (Apartments to Let).

Anouilh, Jean (1910–), French dramatist. Influenced by GIRAUDOUX whose play *Siegfried*, dir JOUVET, 1928, had an enduring effect on him. His plays are characterized by the portrayal of loneliness and the impossibility of making contact, disgust, the sadness of lost innocence and the melancholy of old age. Highly successful as a writer, he is a skilled dramatic craftsman, his virtuosity deriving on the one hand from MARIVAUX and MUSSET, on the other from VAUDEVILLE. The basic pattern of his work is the 'play within the play', a device which he frequently employs, from the heroine of *Antigone*, who sees herself as the one destined to fulfil a role, to plays like *La Foire d'empoigne* and *Pauvre Bitos*, which are based on the interplay and tension between fantasy and reality. He gained his first success in the theatre in 1937 with *Le Voyageur sans bagage*, followed in 1938 with *La Sauvage* (*The Restless Heart*) written 1934, both plays directed by PITOËFF. BARSACQ directed and produced *Le Bal des voleurs* in 1938 and, after taking over the Théâtre de l'Atelier from DULLIN in 1941, also produced *Le Rendezvous de Senlis* (*Dinner with the Family*); in 1942 *Eurydice* (*Point of Departure*, or *Legend of Lovers*), a modern version of this theme; in 1943 *Antigone*, which became a world-wide success; in 1946 *Roméo et Jeannette* (*Fading Mansions*); in 1947 *L'Invitation au château* (*Ring Round the Moon*); and in 1950

Colombe. Some of the later plays were directed by Roland Pietri, e.g. *Ardèle, ou la Marguerite*, 1948, and *La Valse des toréadors*, 1952, and others by the author, e.g. *L'Alouette*, 1953, on the theme of Joan of Arc.
The world première of *La Foire d'empoigne* took place in Germany 1960 at the Ruhrfestspiele at Recklinghausen. In 1962 A. produced with Pietri VITRAC's *Victor, ou les Enfants au pouvoir* at the Théâtre de l' Ambigue. A. directed his own play *Le Boulanger, la boulangère et le petit mitron* in Paris in 1968. His other works include: *L'Hermine*, 1931; *Jézabel*, 1932; *Léocadia* (*Time Remembered*), 1939; *Médée*, 1946; *La Répétition, ou l'Amour puni*, 1950; *Cécile, ou l'école des pères*, 1953; *Ornifle, ou le Courant d'air*, 1956; *Pauvre Bitos, ou le Dîner des têtes*, 1956; *La Petite Molière*, 1959; *L'Hurluberlu, ou le Réactionnaire amoureux*, 1959; *Becket, ou l'Honneur de Dieu*, 1959; *La Grotte*, 1961; *L'Orchestre*, 1961; *Cher Antoine*, 1970.
Bibl: R. Vandromme, 1966; L. C. Pronko, THE WORLD OF JEAN ANOUILH, 1961

Anschütz, Heinrich (1785–1865), German actor. For 40 years he was one of the leading members of the company of the Vienna BURGTHEATER. Tall and strongly built, he corresponded to the image of the 'heroic leading man' of his time and was a famous Lear, Othello and Falstaff.

Ansky, Scholom (Solomon Rappoport; 1863–1920, Jewish playwright, essayist and short-story writer, who wrote in Yiddish. Born in Russia, he was also an ethnologist, and studied Russian and Jewish folklore, making ethnographic expeditions to the Ukraine, later incorporating some of the material in his best-known play *Der Dibuk* (*The Dybbuk*), 1920, a study of demonic possession and the Hassidic doctrine of pre-ordained relationships. The play owes its fame to VAKHTANGOV's production for the Moscow HABIMAH company in 1922. It was seen in Hebrew in New York, 1925, and London, 1930. It has also been filmed and made into an opera.
Bibl: J. C. Landis, THE DYBBUK AND OTHER GREAT YIDDISH PLAYS, 1966

ANTA ▷AMERICAN NATIONAL THEATRE AND ACADEMY

Antagonist. Actor who played opposite principal actor, the PROTAGONIST, in the ancient Greek theatre.

Antigone. Greek mythological character. Daughter of Oedipus; killed by Creon for burying her brother who had led an invasion force against Thebes and whose burial had been forbidden by the king. TRAGEDY by SOPHOCLES, 441 BC. Adaptations and works based on the subject: ROTROU, *Antigone*, 1638; RACINE, *La Thébaïde*, 1664; ALFIERI, *Antigone*, 1783; HASENCLEVER, *Antigone*, trans Chamberlain, *The Death of Antigone*, 1917; COCTEAU, *Antigone*, 1922; ANOUILH, *Antigone*, 1943; BRECHT, *Antigone*, 1948.

Antoine, André (1858–1943), French actor, producer and manager. One of the pioneers of modern theatre. In 1887, while employed by a gas company, he founded the Théâtre Libre. With the help of writers such as ZOLA, he attacked the conventions of the COMÉDIE-FRANÇAISE and the shallowness of the BOULEVARD THEATRE. He produced BALZAC, BECQUE, MAUPASSANT, TOLSTOY, G. HAUPTMANN, STRINDBERG, BJØRNSON, TURGENEV, and notably IBSEN (*Ghosts*, 1890). He taught his company, former amateurs, a natural style of acting, and replaced painted flats with three-dimensional sets. In 1888 while on tour in Brussels, he saw the MEININGER company whose ENSEMBLE playing confirmed his own theories on theatre. The Théâtre Libre performed irregularly in rented halls and on tour; he founded the more permanent Théâtre Antoine in 1897. In 1906 he was appointed director of the Odéon, in recognition of his work; retiring in 1914, he worked subsequently as a theatre critic and film director. He helped to establish naturalistic drama in France and extended his influence towards a theatre based on the essence of the play and its relationship to real life, rather than on convention or theatrical effectiveness. Inspired by him, BRAHM founded the FREIE BÜHNE in Berlin, 1889, and GREIN the Independent Theatre Club in London, 1891. He also wrote two volumes of memoirs: *Mes Souvenirs sur le Théâtre Libre*, 1921, and *Mes Souvenirs sur le Théâtre Antoine et sur l'Odéon*, 1928.
Bibl: S. M. Waxman, ANTOINE AND THE THÉÂTRE LIBRE, 2/1964

Antrobus, John (1933–), English scriptwriter and comedian. His stage plays include *The Bedsitting Room*, 1963, written in collaboration with MILLIGAN, later filmed by Dick Lester; *You'll Come to Love your Sperm Test!*, *One Orange for the Baby* and *Trixie and Baba*, three ROYAL COURT THEATRE productions, 1967, dir Jane Howell; *Captain Oates's Left Sock*, 1968, for which he won the Writer's Guild Award; *Crete and Sergeant Pepper*, 1972, dir Peter Gill. He has also written a number of TV and film comedies.

Anzengruber, Ludwig (1839–89), Austrian playwright and essayist. He started as a strolling player, then became a clerk. After the performance of his peasant play *Der Pfarrer von Kirchfeld* (The Parson of Kirchfeld), 1870, he became a resident dramatist in Vienna, first at the Theater an der Wien, and later at the WIENER VOLKSTHEATER. He holds an important place in Austrian theatrical history as the last of the writers of classical Viennese dialect comedies, which deal with the problems of lowly people, particularly peasants. They are realistic, with anticlerical liberal tendencies. Examples are *Der Meineidbauer* (The Perjured Peasant), 1872; *Der Kreuzelschreiber* (He Who Signed with a Cross), 1872, and *Das Vierte Gebot* (The Fourth Commandment), 1877.
Bibl: L. Koessler, 1943

Apollinaire, Guillaume (Wilhelm Apollinaris de Kostrovitsky; 1880–1918), French poet of Polish descent. One of the most influential critics and theoreticians of the Cubist Movement, he invented the term SURREALISM, later applied to an entire literary and artistic movement. He aimed at a total theatre with equal emphasis on sound, colour, movement, action and the spoken word, anticipating the theories of ARTAUD. With his play *Les Mamelles de Tirésias*, written 1903, produced 1917, he criticized the conventional BOULEVARD THEATRE and the realism of ANTOINE. This *drame surréaliste*, as he called it, was a grotesque VAUDEVILLE, claiming a serious political message – a radical policy to increase the population of France. The main character changes sex twice. Thérèse becomes Tirésias and fathers 40,049 children. Two other plays, *Couleur du Temps* and *Casanova* were never finished.
Bibl: C. Mackworth, APOLLINAIRE AND THE CUBISTS, 1962

Apotheosis (Gk = deification). Solemn celebratory final scene or tableau which shows the exaltation or elevation of heroes to immortality. Frequent in Baroque opera, JESUIT DRAMA, plays written to celebrate special occasions or rulers, fairy-tales and PANTOMIMES.

Appen, Karl von (1900–), German stage designer. Started working in Frankfurt at the Frankfurter Künstlertheater, 1921–23. After World War II, he worked at the Dresden National Theatre and has been with the BERLINER ENSEMBLE since 1954, working with directors such as BRECHT (*Der kaukasische Kreidekreis*, 1954), BESSON, PALITZSCH, WEKWERTH and Tenschert. His work is in the same tradition as NEHER, aiming at precise detail, historical accuracy and realism, with special emphasis on theatrical effectiveness and the avoidance of illusionary theatre.

Appia, Adolphe (1862–1928), Swiss stage designer and theoretician. His revolutionary reforms of scenic design, above all demands for a stage-floor structured sculpturally on several levels and for three-dimensional sets, form the basis of contemporary stage design. In his architecturally conceived designs, he eschewed all realistically detailed ornamentation and description of milieu in favour of clean stylized lines. In his early designs he anticipated the functional use of light which was remarkable because the STAGE LIGHTING of that time was generally inadequate (electricity did not come into general use until the end of the 1880s). He was able to put his ideas into practice in relatively few productions: in 1913 *Orpheus* by Gluck in Hellerau. He was particularly concerned with the works of Wagner and was the first to recognize the inadequacy of the stage techniques of Wagner's own time for performance of his operas: in 1923 *Tristan und Isolde* at La Scala, Milan; 1924 *Das Rheingold* and *Die Walküre* in Basle; 1925 *Prometheus* in Basle. These performances did not have much impact, largely because his designs were badly and inaccurately carried out. Later stage designers successfully realized his ideas which he had

recorded in his books: *La Mise en scène du drame wagnérien*, 1895; *Die Musik und die Inszenierung*, 1889, and *Goethe's Faust I*, 1920.
Bibl: W. R. Volbach, APPIA, PROPHET OF THE MODERN THEATRE, 1968

Applause (Lat *applausus*). Approval, clapping, acclaim, the cheers of the spectators expressing their endorsement. Practised in the Greek theatre; by Roman times it had been formalized into waving with the pointed ends of the toga (after the time of Aurelian with strips of material which were distributed for that purpose), snapping of the fingers and eventually clapping with both hands. Since the 17th century it has been practised in the theatre throughout Europe; in some countries approval is also expressed by whistling or stamping the feet. ▷CLAQUE

Arbuzov, Alexey Nikolayevich (1908–), Soviet dramatist, actor and director. In 1941 he organized a youth theatre in Moscow. His best-known play in Europe is *Irkutskaya istoriya* (*It happened in Irkutsk*), 1960. Strongly influenced in form by WILDER's *Our Town*, it is a series of dramatic sequences about a construction collective in a small town in Siberia. It was performed by the Vakhtangov Theatre at the THÉÂTRE DES NATIONS in Paris, 1961; produced in Sheffield, England, 1967. It is one of the most popular plays of the contemporary Soviet theatre, and like many of his other plays has a permanent place in the Soviet REPERTORY. In 1963 five of them were running simultaneously in some 71 Russian theatres. Among his plays are: *Klass* (Class), 1930; *Tanya*, 1939; *Yevropeiskaya kronika* (European Chronicle), 1953; *Gody stranstvii* (The Years of Wandering), 1954; *Dvenadtsaty chas* (The Twelfth Hour), 1959, written in memory of MEYERHOLD; *Moi bedny Marat* (*The Promise*), 1965, prod Oxford 1967, later transferred to London; *Old World*, London 1976. His plays are in general characterized by sharp, vital conflicts and psychological complexity.

Archer, William (1856–1924), Scottish critic and dramatist. A close friend of SHAW, he was a journalist on the *Edinburgh Evening News* before settling in London in 1878, where he worked successively for the London *Figaro*, the *World*, the *Tribune*, the *Nation* and the *Star*. Notable for his serious treatment of the theatre as an art, he translated IBSEN (collected works published 1906–08) whose work he used to exemplify his ideals of realism and craftsmanship in the theatre. He supported the British dramatists of his day, arguing against the overestimation of plays with a classical reputation. Publications include: *English Dramatists of Today*, 1882; *Henry Irving*, 1883; *Masks or Faces*, 1888; *William Charles Macready*, 1890; *Study and Stage*, 1899; *America Today*, 1900; *The Old Drama and the New*, 1923, and *A National Theatre: Scheme and Estimates*, 1907, with GRANVILLE-BARKER. His play *The Green Goddess*, a

André Antoine's Théâtre Antoine, 1901, where Eugène Brieux is reading his banned play *Les Avariés* to a private audience

Adolphe Appia, stage set for Gluck's opera *Orpheus*, 1913

Karl von Appen, stage set for BRECHT's *Der kaukasische Kreidekreis*, at the BERLINER ENSEMBLE, 1954

MELODRAMA, seen in the USA, 1920, was produced at the St James's Theatre, London, in 1923 and ran for 416 performances.
Bibl: G. B. Shaw, PEN PORTRAITS AND REVIEWS, 1931

Archimime (Lat *archimimus, archimima*). Chief actor or actress in a mime play (▷ MIME). Often also the director of a troupe of actors of mime.

Arden, John (1930–), English dramatist. Won a prize in the BBC North Region drama competition with the radio play, *The Life of Man*, 1956. Then the ENGLISH STAGE COMPANY presented four of his works, *The Waters of Babylon*, 1957; *Live Like Pigs*, 1958; *Serjeant Musgrave's Dance*, 1959; *The Happy Haven*, 1960. Later plays include: *The Workhouse Donkey*, a satire on English provincial politics, 1963; *Armstrong's Last Goodnight*, 1965, with FINNEY, both performed at the CHICHESTER FESTIVAL, and *Left-Handed Liberty*, 1965. Since then he has been involved in EXPERIMENTAL THEATRE. Other works include: *Soldier, Soldier*, 1960, and *Wet Fish*, 1961, both televised; *Ironhand*, 1963, Bristol Old Vic, dir Val May; *The Hero Rises Up* (on the life of Nelson), 1969; *The Island of the Mighty*, written with Margaretta D'Arcy, and *The Ballygombeen Bequest*, 1972. His plays are about relationships between groups in which the characters usually represent a corporate interest, while he attempts to view the community as a whole. His sociological sensitivity is combined with a great historical sense. As with BRECHT, part of his reason for turning to historical subjects is to stand at some distance from the contemporary scene and to be able to comment on it with more impact, which he also achieves by the use of language that alternates between prose and verse.

Arena (Lat=*sand, sandy place*). Originally the area of action in the Roman AMPHITHEATRE.

Arena stage. A type of stage where the acting arena is surrounded on all four sides by the tiered seats of the spectators. In modern times first used in the USSR: common in American university theatres. The seating arrangements are often changeable. With a circular layout it is known as THEATRE-IN-THE-ROUND.

Aretino, Pietro (1492–1556), Italian pamphleteer, dramatist and poet. *Orazio*, 1546, his only TRAGEDY, written in verse, was judged by Benedetto Croce to be 'the most beautiful tragedy in the 16th century'. However, he is principally remembered for his COMEDIES: *La Cortigiana* (The Courtesan), 1526; *Il Marescalco* (The Farrier), 1527; *Il Filosofo* (The Philosopher), 1544. His work was free in form, reflecting contemporary life with great spontaneity and a lively satirical wit. Though his plays had little impact on the theatre of his day, his style had widespread influence on, e.g., MOLIÈRE, JONSON (*Epicœne*) and the COMMEDIA ERUDITA.
Bibl: G. Petrocci, 1948

Argentina ▷LATIN AMERICA

Argument. The summary of the theme, subject matter or plot of a play which precedes it, either in its printed edition, or on stage. In the Middle Ages and the Renaissance, vernacular plot summaries, which were recited before the performance of plays in Latin. Sometimes in European SCHOOL DRAMA an 'Argumentator' explained the text. Also, in BAROQUE THEATRE, the allegorical PANTOMIMES which prepared the ground for the play (i.e. in the performance which Hamlet presents to King Claudius).

Ariadne. Greek mythological character. Daughter of King Minos of Crete; helped Theseus to slay the Minotaur, fled with him but was abandoned on the island of Naxos, where DIONYSOS found her and made her his wife. Her story (often together with that of her sister Phaedra) is dealt with in plays by LOPE DE VEGA, 1621; CALDERÓN, 1636; KOTZEBUE, *Travestie*, 1803; many operas from Monteverdi, 1608, to Richard Strauss (*Ariadne auf Naxos*, 1912, LIBRETTO by HOFMANNSTHAL).

Ariosto, Ludovico (1474–1533), Italian poet and playwright. Author of the romantic epic *Orlando Furioso*, first published in 1516, completed in 1532, written in honour of the d'Este family of Ferrara, under whose patronage he remained throughout his life. One of the first important writers of early Italian comedy, he helped to establish the literary form of the COMMEDIA ERUDITA. He wrote several comedies which were produced in Ferrara: *La Cassaria* (The Strong Box), 1508; *I Suppositi*, 1509 (performed in Rome in 1519 before Pope Leo X, des RAPHAEL: English version by George Gascoigne, called *The Supposes*, performed at Gray's Inn, 1566); *Il Negromante* (The Necromancer), written 1520, prod 1530; *La Lena*, 1528. *Gli Studenti*, written 1519, was never finished. The characters and dialogue of his comedies were drawn from real life but he retained the structure and technique of the classical Roman COMEDY. From 1528 he managed the COURT THEATRE of the Dukes of Ferrara, a wooden building in classical style, built to his own specification, which enabled him to participate in all stages of the production, both as writer and actor. His style of production influenced the Renaissance theatre throughout Europe.
Bibl: C. Grabher, SUL TEATRO DELL' ARIOSTO, 1946

Aristophanes (*c.* 445–*c.* 385 BC), Greek playwright. Wrote some 40 comedies of which 11 are extant; they include the only surviving examples of the Attic Old Comedy. (▷COMEDY (GREEK)) The Old Comedy fused elements of the Doric farce (hero-travesty with types, favourite characters were Heracles, Odysseus, Parasite, Braggart, Cook) with elements of the SATYR PLAY (animal-masquerade, phallic rituals, dance, songs). The scenic structure of the *prologos, parados, stasima*, and *episodia* developed in analogy to the earlier literary form of the TRAGEDY. A. used a series of loosely connected scenes in various metres. The central situation from which he developed his comedy was one that had direct reference to the political situation of the moment or some urgent social question often involving a contest or struggle between the hero and the CHORUS. He attacked politicians in *The Knights*, 424 BC, specifically the warmonger Creon; poets in *The Frogs*, 405, which gives an account of a contest in Hades between AESCHYLUS and EURIPIDES; philosophers in *The Clouds*, 423, especially Socrates; his fellow countrymen's passion for litigation in *The Wasps*, 422. His main theme was the desire for freedom: *Peace*, 421, and *Lysistrata*, 411. Other complete plays are *The Acharnians*, 425; *The Birds*, 414; *Thesmophoriazousae* (The Festival of Women), 410; *Ecclesiazousae* (Women in Parliament), 392, and *Plutus*, 388. His plays, especially the early ones in which the chorus plays a prominent part, are a mixture of fantasy, satire, verbal wit, political propaganda and FARCE. His wit was rude, aggressive and obscene. His actors wore masks and under the short tunic a giant phallus of leather. The parts of the women were played by men. The chorus, consisting of 24 singers and dancers, often appeared in animal disguise, e.g. *The Wasps, The Frogs*.
Bibl: C. H. Whitman, ARISTOPHANES AND THE COMIC HERO, 1964; G. Murray, ARISTOPHANES, A STUDY, 1933

Aristotle (384–322 BC), Greek philosopher and scientist. Pupil of Plato in Athens and teacher of Alexander the Great. Founded the Lyceum (or Peripatetic) School of Philosophy. His *Poetics*, 330 BC, of which only Book One (on tragedy and epic) is extant, ranks as the most influential single work of literary criticism – on the theory of TRAGEDY in particular – ever written (▷ANAGNORISIS). Using SOPHOCLES as his chief model, he discusses the origins of tragedy and analyzes contemporary works. Historically his most influential ideas concerned his theory of catharsis, defined as the ritual purging of the emotions through pity and fear; he believed that tragedy should maintain unity of action; he also remarked that Sophocles' plays usually observed unity of place.
Bibl: G. F. Else, ARISTOTLE'S POETICS, 1967; G. M. A. Grube, THE GREEK AND ROMAN CRITICS, 1965

Arlecchino (Fr *Arlequin*; Ger *Harlekin*; Engl *Harlequin*). One of the ZANNI, the domestic servants, of the COMMEDIA DELL' ARTE. The role was played originally as a comic and naïve peasant boy from Bergamo, speaking the local dialect and dressed in rags. D. MARTINELLI was the first actor to adopt the name and develop the character. The well-known costume, made of multicoloured triangular and rhomboid patches, with a black leather half-mask, was created by G. D. BIANCOLELLI, the most famous Arlecchino. TRUFFALDINO, MEZZETTINO, Pasquino, Tabarino and Gradiella are all variations of the character.
Bibl: A. Nicoll, THE WORLD OF HARLEQUIN, 1963

Arlen, Harold (Hyman Arluck; 1905–), US composer. Best known for songs written for films (*The Wizard of Oz*, 1939; *A Star is Born*, 1954), he has also provided scores for several Broadway MUSICAL COMEDIES, including: *Bloomer Girl*, 1944; *St Louis Woman*, 1946; *House of Flowers*, 1954; *Jamaica*, 1957, with Lena Horne.

Arletty (Arlette-Léonie Bathia; 1898–), French actress. Her early career was in leading roles in REVUE, operetta and BOULEVARD THEATRE, acting the witty, intelligent and independent Parisienne. Her most famous role in the theatre was Blanche in *A Streetcar Named Desire*, 1949, by T. WILLIAMS, adapted by COCTEAU. She has also appeared in many films, e.g. *Hôtel du Nord*, 1939, and *Les Enfants du Paradis*, 1944, dir Marcel Carné.

Arliss, George (1868–1946), English actor. Best known in his later years as a film actor, he won an Oscar for the title role in *Disraeli*, 1930. His first major stage success was as Keane in *Mr and Mrs Daventry*, a scenario by WILDE, turned into a four-act play by Frank Harris, with MRS PATRICK CAMPBELL, 1900, London. In New York, 1902, he played Cayley Drummle in PINERO's *The Second Mrs Tanqueray* opposite MRS FISKE and Blanche Bates. Leading parts included the title role in *The Devil*, by MOLNÁR, New York 1908, and *Disraeli* by L. N. Parker, Montreal 1911. He spent one year in London in 1923 and then appeared on BROADWAY and in films. His last theatrical role was Shylock, 1928, but he appeared in films until 1937. He wrote several plays and his autobiography, *Up the Years from Bloomsbury*, 1927.

Arnoux, Alexandre (1884–1973), French dramatist. He aimed at a theatrical lyricism, employing legendary elements imitative of Italian COMEDY. *L'Amour des trois oranges*, 1947, deals with the life of GOZZI and the situation of the theatre in the 18th century. Among his other plays are *Huon de Bordeaux*, 1923, Théâtre de l'Atelier, dir DULLIN; *Petite lumière et l'ourse*, 1924; *Les Taureaux*, 1949. Adaptations for the Théâtre de l'Atelier included CALDERÓN's *Life's a Dream*.

Arrabal, Fernando (1932–), Spanish-born French dramatist. One of the exponents of the THEATRE OF THE ABSURD, he was influenced by BECKETT, IONESCO and particularly by ARTAUD. Other influences on his writings: CALDERÓN, LOPE DE VEGA, TIRSO DE MOLINA, DOSTOYEVSKY, KAFKA, CAMUS, FAULKNER and STEINBECK. He combines comedy and dream-like elements with youthful innocence and visions of sadistic cruelty. His traumatic experiences as a child during the Spanish Civil War are probably responsible for the ferocity and element of shock which dominate his early plays, such as the anti-military satire, *Pique-nique en campagne*, written 1952, fp Paris 1959, Théâtre de Lutèce, dir Jean-Marie Serreau. Other plays of his early period are *Le Tricycle*, written 1953, fp Paris 1967; *Oraison*, 1958; *Fando et Lis*, 1958; *La Communiante*, fp 1966 Théâtre de

Arlecchino, engraving, 1689

Pietro Aretino, detail of portrait by Titian, Frick Collection, New York

John Arden's *The Hero Rises Up*, Nottingham Playhouse, 1969

Poche, Montparnasse, a shock drama reminiscent of the film *The Cabinet of Dr Caligari*. From 1962 onwards he proclaimed his faith in a ceremonial or ritualistic theatre which he called 'Théâtre Panique', related to SURREALISM, Pop Art and HAPPENINGS. In *L'Architecte et L'Empereur d'Assyrie*, written 1966, fp 1967, Théâtre Montparnasse, dir J. Lavelli, he says that he hoped to fuse humour and poetry, panic and love, and thus to produce a text that would recall the fantasies of Don Quixote, the nightmares of Alice, the delirium of KAFKA and the dreams of an IBM machine. Other plays: *Le Jardin des délices*, 1967; *... et ils passèrent des menottes aux fleurs*, 1969 (prod London 1973, Open Space Theatre, dir author as *And They Handcuffed the Flowers*); *L'Aurore rouge et noire*, 1969; *Ars Amandi* (*Opéra Panique*), 1970; *Dieu par les mathématiques* (*Orchestration théâtrale*), 1970.
Bibl: B. Gille, 1970; M. Esslin, THE THEATRE OF THE ABSURD, 2/1968

Arronge, Adolf L' (A. Aaron; 1838–1908), German dramatist and theatre manager. He founded the Deutsches-Theater, BERLIN, which he managed 1883–94. Author of numerous sentimental folk comedies and FARCES which gained him great popularity. His family comedies remained for many years in the REPERTORY of German theatres, e.g. *Mein Leopold*, 1873, and *Hasemanns Töchter* (H.'s Daughters), 1877.
Bibl: K. Raeck, DAS DEUTSCHE THEATER IN BERLIN UNTER L'ARRONGE, 1928

Artaud, Antonin (1896–1948), French poet, actor, director and playwright. An outstanding member of the French theatrical avant-garde between the two world wars. He started his career as an actor in 1921 working with LUGNÉ-POË, DULLIN and PITOËFF. Between 1923 and 1927 he was actively connected with the Surrealist movement in literature. In 1927 he founded with VITRAC the Théâtre Alfred Jarry which gave four productions: his one-act play *Le Ventre brûle ou La Mère folle*, CLAUDEL's *Partage de Midi*, STRINDBERG's *A Dream Play*, and Vitrac's *Victor, ou les Enfants au pouvoir*, all in 1928. In 1931 a performance by a group of Balinese dancers stimulated him to attempt to redefine the meaning of the theatre. He wrote his first manifesto of 'Le Théâtre de la Cruauté' in 1932, the second in 1933, and gave practical expression to his theories in 1935 with a production of his own play *Les Cenci*, based on Stendhal and SHELLEY (▷THEATRE OF CRUELTY). However, his theoretical writings were more influential than his production which was hampered by lack of funds and rehearsal time. A series of essays appeared in 1938: *Le Théâtre et son double*. His conception of the theatre can be summed up as follows: the action should be similar to a religious incantation involving all the spectators. The cruelty should have the power to stir the spectator to the depth of his being and to liberate forces within his subconscious. Using a variety of techniques the production should hold the audience, bewitch and entrance them. To this end he invoked the oriental theatre's use of symbolic gesture, movement and sound and of light, colour texture and masks. He called for audience participation to be stimulated by simultaneous action in different parts of the theatre. The drama should subordinate DIALOGUE to action, the text of the play serving as only one constituent; the director is the author of the play. A. strongly influenced artists as divergent as BARRAULT, VILAR, BLIN, BROOK (Theatre of Cruelty season, London 1964), Julian Beck and Judith Malina (LIVING THEATRE, e.g. *Mysteries*, 1964) and writers such as ADAMOV, GENET, CAMUS and AUDIBERTI. As an actor he appeared in his own productions and, in Dullin's Théâtre de l'Atelier, as king in CALDERÓN's *Life's a Dream* and also in films, e.g. Dreyer's *La Passion de Jeanne d'Arc*, Abel Gance's *Mater Dolorosa*.
Bibl: E. Sellin, THE DRAMATIC CONCEPTS OF ANTONIN ARTAUD, 1968; M. Esslin, THE THEATRE OF THE ABSURD, 2/1968; L. C. Pronko, THE AVANT-GARDE, THE EXPERIMENTAL THEATRE IN FRANCE, 1962

Arts Council of Great Britain. A public body consisting of 16 members which distributes government subsidies to the arts in Britain. Money is allocated to music, including opera and ballet, the theatre, fine arts and literature. Founded in 1940 as the Council for the Encouragement of Music and the Arts (CEMA). As far as drama is concerned, the Arts Council subsidizes not only the NATIONAL THEATRE, the ROYAL SHAKESPEARE COMPANY and the ENGLISH STAGE COMPANY, but also some 40 repertory theatres throughout Britain. Subsidies are also given to playwrights, young directors, designers and theatre administrators as well as to experimental companies. For the year 1976/77 the total sum allocated by the Ministry of Arts to the Arts Council for England, Scotland and Wales was £37,150,000 of which £8,720,000 was for the Royal Opera House, Covent Garden Ltd, the Sadler's Wells Trust, the National Theatre Board and the Royal Shakespeare Theatre. A further £7,596,750 was allocated for drama generally.

Asch, Sholem (1880–1957), Jewish novelist and dramatist. Born and raised in Kutno, he went to Palestine in 1908, and then to the USA. In 1954 he moved to Israel. His earliest writings were in Hebrew but he later turned to German and Yiddish, influenced by PERETZ. His reputation rests largely on his novels, of which probably the best known is *Three Cities*, 1930, and he did much to raise the standard of Yiddish writing and give it a place in world literature. As a dramatist he first gained fame with *Got fun Nekome* (*God of Vengeance*), and REINHARDT's production in Berlin, 1907, brought the author international renown. Set in a brothel, it is a tragedy of self-deception and of delusions destroyed by a God of Vengeance, manifested in the retribution of worldly reality. Frequently banned because of its setting and the portrayal of lesbianism, it has nevertheless been translated into many languages, including English (1918), and was produced in Paris 1928 by DULLIN. He wrote some 20 other plays, and adapted his own novels and short stories, the most successful of which were *Motke Ganev* (Motke the Thief), 1917, and *Der T'hilim Yid* (Salvation), 1939.
Bibl: A. Madison, YIDDISH LITERATURE: ITS SCOPE AND MAJOR WRITERS, 1968

Asche, Oscar (John Stanger Heiss; 1871–1936), English actor, born in Australia. His first stage appearance was in 1893. He was with BENSON's company and later became an ACTOR-MANAGER, 1907. He produced plays together with his wife, the actress Lily Brayton, both taking the lead parts in SHAKESPEARE's *As You Like It*, *Othello*, and *The Taming of the Shrew*, in London and on tours throughout Australia. His own show *Chu-Chin-Chow*, first produced in 1916, ran for a record five years, a success which may have ruined him as a creative artist. When his plays *Mecca*, 1920, and *Cairo*, 1921, were not successful, he toured Australia again, where he was received with acclaim. His autobiography *Oscar Asche by Himself*, published in 1929, is remarkable for its frankness.
Bibl: H. Pearson, THE LAST ACTOR-MANAGERS, 1950

Ashcroft, Dame Peggy (1907–), English actress. She made her début at the BIRMINGHAM REPERTORY THEATRE, as Margaret in BARRIE's *Dear Brutus*, 1926. In London she first attracted attention as Naomi in DUKES's adaptation of FEUCHTWANGER's *Jew Süss*, 1929, which established her as a player of innocent young girls. She made her New York début in 1936 in M. ANDERSON's *High Tor*. Noted performances include Juliet with OLIVIER (alternating with GIELGUD) as Romeo, in Gielgud's production, London 1935, New Theatre; Nina in CHEKHOV's *The Seagull*, London 1936, dir KOMISARJEVSKY; and Irina in *Three Sisters*, London 1937, dir SAINT-DENIS; the Duchess of Malfi in Gielgud's 1944–45 season at the Haymarket Theatre, London; Cordelia with Gielgud as Lear at STRATFORD-UPON-AVON, 1950. Comedy parts include Cecily Cardew in *The Importance of Being Earnest*, 1939, dir Gielgud; Lady Teazle in *The School for Scandal*; Beatrice in *Much Ado About Nothing* and Mistress Page in *The Merry Wives of Windsor*. Later she appeared in modern dramas such as MORLEY's *Edward, My Son*; JAMES's *The Heiress*, dramatized by Ruth and Augustus Goetz; RATTIGAN's *The Deep Blue Sea* and notably in *The Chalk Garden* by ENID BAGNOLD, 1956, DRURY LANE, and as Shen-Te in BRECHT's *The Good Woman of Setzuan*, 1957, ROYAL COURT. Among her finest mature parts: the title role in *Hedda Gabler*, 1954, in which play she toured Norway where she received the King's Medal; and Queen Margaret in HALL's production of *The Wars of the Roses* (BARTON's cycle adapted from SHAKESPEARE's *Henry VI* and *Richard III*), at Stratford in 1963. Other recent appearances: *Ghosts* (IBSEN), 1967; *Days in the Trees* (DURAS), 1967; *John Gabriel Borkman* (IBSEN) and *Happy Days* (BECKETT), 1975; *Old World* (ARBUZOV), 1976. She was appointed DBE in 1956 and in 1962 a theatre, named after her, was opened in Croydon.

Aslan, Raoul (1890–1958), Austrian actor. Prominent at the BURGTHEATER in Vienna from 1920. He was artistic director 1945–48. He played the title roles in *Gyges und sein Ring* by HEBBEL, and in *Hamlet*, 1920; in *Torquato Tasso* by GOETHE, 1921. His greatest part was the main role in SOPHOCLES' *Oedipus Rex*, 1930. While these roles are all of the classical 'heavy hero' type, he was also successful playing witty, sophisticated gentlemen such as Bolingbroke in SCRIBE's *A Glass of Water*.
Bibl: E. Buschbeck, RAOUL ASLAN UND DAS BURGTHEATER, 1946

Asphaleian system (Gk *asphaleia*=security). One of the earliest modern stage systems, it involved the use mainly of steel in its construction and marked the beginning of a new era in stage technique, constituting a breakthrough in safety since it lessened the danger of fire. Named after the Austrian Asphaleia company, it was first employed in the Budapest Opera House, 1884. The whole stage area is divided into individual platforms, on hydraulic pistons, each of which can be separately raised, lowered or tipped.

Astaire, Fred (Frederick E. Austerlitz; 1899–), US dancer, singer and actor, of Austrian descent. Best known for his brilliant dancing, he epitomized the urbane, sophisticated American; his versatility and technical mastery suited him for MUSICAL COMEDY. After training as a dancer he appeared on stage with his sister, Adele A. (1898–) until 1931. His first success was in 1917 with the BROADWAY revue, *Over the Top*, then in numerous revues and musicals, e.g. *The Passing Show of 1918*; *Apple Blossoms*, 1919; *The Love Letter*, 1921; *For Goodness Sake*, 1922; *Lady, Be Good*, 1924 and *Funny Face*, 1927, both with GERSHWIN music; *The Band Wagon*, 1931, music by A. SCHWARTZ. After the marriage of his sister, he starred with Claire Luce in *The Gay Divorce*, 1932, music PORTER. From 1933 he appeared only in films (where he had a long collaboration with Ginger Rogers).

Atellan farce (after Atella in Campania, Italy). Known as *fabula atellana* (▷FABULA), also called *ludi Osci*, it originally consisted of a masked MIME dance, accompanied by the flute at religious festivities, later a crude, rural improvised play full of obscene allusions, containing sharp characterization and simple worldly wisdom; possibly influenced by the PHLYAKES farces, it reached Rome between 364 and 240 BC. Primarily played in Oscan dialect by citizens of Campania; four stock characters stand out: *Bucco* (a glutton and boaster), *Dossenus* (hunchbacked, cunning trickster), *Maccus* (a stupid clown, harlequin, buffoon), *Pappus* (a gullible old man, greedy and often cheated). The Latinized *atellan* was performed by professional actors (*Atellani histriones*) between 125 and 103 BC as an exodium or after-play to the *fabula togata*. It was played

Peggy Ashcroft in IBSEN's *Hedda Gabler*, with DEVINE, London 1954

Antonin Artaud, self-portrait

Oscar Asche as Angelo in *Measure for Measure*

Fred and **Adele Astaire** in *Stop Flirting*, London 1923

in front of the curtain (SIPARIUM). At that time the *atellan* was already played unmasked and sometimes without the phallus. Novius and Pomponius established the literary form of the *atellan* in *c.*90 BC; later the *atellan* was overshadowed by the PALLIATA and by the mime. Some characters anticipated the COMMEDIA DELL'ARTE, but a direct influence cannot be proved.
Bibl: W. Beare, THE ROMAN STAGE, 3/1965

Atkins, Sir Robert (1886–1972), English actor and director. After training at RADA, was engaged by TREE for His Majesty's Theatre in 1906, where he first appeared in *Henry IV*, Part I. He joined the OLD VIC company in 1915 and, after war service, returned 1920–25. Produced and appeared in a number of SHAKESPEARE's plays including *Titus Andronicus* and *Troilus and Cressida*, and IBSEN's *Peer Gynt* (first London production). Subsequently founded the Bankside Players, and produced *Henry V*, *Much Ado About Nothing*, *The Merry Wives of Windsor*. He was also a producer at the Shakespeare Memorial Theatre, STRATFORD-UPON-AVON and at the London Open Air Theatre in Regent's Park, his most successful parts included Sir Toby Belch, Touchstone, Caliban, Bottom, Sir Giles Overreach in *A New Way to Pay Old Debts* by MASSINGER, and James Telfer in PINERO's *Trelawny of the 'Wells'*. He was knighted in 1971.

Atkinson, Brooks (1894–), US theatre critic. Began reviewing plays as a reporter for the *Boston Evening Transcript* in 1919. For 30 years, from 1925, he was theatre critic for the *New York Times*, a position of great influence. After World War II, he also wrote for the London *Daily Telegraph*. In 1947 he received a PULITZER PRIZE for journalism, and is the only drama critic to have had a theatre named after him (the Mansfield, now the Brooks Atkinson Theatre, New York). He has written a number of books on American literature and also on the theatre, e.g. *Broadway*, 1970.

Aubignac, François Hédelin, Abbé d' (1604–76), French dramatist and important theoretical writer on drama. In his *La Pratique du Théâtre*, published 1657, translated into English 1684, he supported ARISTOTLE's theories of drama which later, indirectly, formed the basis of the French classical style, of which his first tragedy, *Zénovie*, 1640, was an early example.
Bibl: P. Mélèze, LE THÉÂTRE SOUS LOUIS XIV, 1934

Auclair, Michel (Wladimir Vujovíc; 1922–), French actor of Yugoslav origin. Between 1941 and 1946 he appeared at various theatres in Paris, in plays such as CLAUDEL's *L'Annonce faite à Marie*; SYNGE's *Deirdre of the Sorrows*; COPEAU's adaptation of DOSTOYEVSKY's *The Brothers Karamazov*. After 1945 he acted in many films, then went back to the theatre with the play *Le Bal du Lieutenant* by G. Arout, 1950. Later he successfully appeared at PLANCHON's Théâtre de la Cité de Villeurbanne, Lyons, in among others, MOLIÈRE's *Tartuffe*, 1960.

Auden, Wystan Hugh (1907–73), English poet. In 1938 he went to the USA and taught at various colleges and universities, eventually becoming an American citizen. He used poetic forms, from the ode to the popular ballad, in plays with an emphasis on topical themes including *The Dance of Death*, fp London 1935; *The Dog Beneath the Skin*, fp London 1936; *The Ascent of F6*, London 1936; *On the Frontier*, fp London 1939. The last three were written in collaboration with ISHERWOOD. He also wrote LIBRETTI for Stravinsky's opera *The Rake's Progress*, 1951, and Henze's *Elegy for Young Lovers*, 1961, and verse commentaries for documentary films, e.g. *Coalface*, 1935; *Night Mail*, 1936.

Audiberti, Jacques (1899–1965), French journalist, novelist, poet and dramatist. His plays belong to the poetic avant-garde of contemporary French theatre, embracing writers such as GHELDERODE, VAUTHIER, Georges Neveux and Henry Pichette, an important parallel trend to the THEATRE OF THE ABSURD. Unlike the Absurd theatre he uses poetic speech consciously; the plays are in effect poems sustained by complex imagery. He is basically concerned with the struggle between good and evil, between the spirit and the flesh. Though his plays can be seen as modern parables with a simple moral message, the action is often obscure and allusive, the language exotic and laden with symbolism. His world is fantastic and grotesque, often doom-ridden and malignant; half rational, half irrational, mixing mythological image and verbal coarseness. He made his début in the theatre with *Quoat-Quoat*, Paris 1946, Théâtre de la Gaîté-Montparnasse. Other works include: *Le Mal court*, 1947; *Les Femmes du bœuf*, 1949; *La Fête noire*, 1948; *L'Ampelour*, 1950; *Pucelle*, 1950; *Les Naturels du Bordelais* (Don Juan theme), 1953; *La Logeuse*, 1954; *La Hobereauté*, 1958; *L'Effet Glapion*, 1959; *La Fourmi dans le corps*, 1962; *Pomme, pomme, pomme*, 1962; *La Brigitta*, 1962; *La Guérite*, 1967.
Bibl: G. E. Wellwarth, THE THEATRE OF PROTEST AND PARADOX, 1964; L. C. Pronko, THE AVANT-GARDE, THE EXPERIMENTAL THEATRE IN FRANCE, 1962

Augier, (Guillaume Victor) Emile (1820–89), French dramatist. He reacted against French Romantic theatre, concentrating on middle-class subjects and social questions of his time. He was in favour of business and moral sobriety, but fought for the rights of unmarried mothers. In *Le Mariage d'Olympe*, 1855, he depicted realistically the life of a courtesan, as opposed to DUMAS *fils'* idealized *La Dame aux camélias*. He had begun as a neo-classicist writing VERSE DRAMAS, in which RACHEL had enormous success, and later followed SCRIBE's technique of the WELL-MADE PLAY. His plays, some written in collaboration with other dramatists, were: *La Cigüe*, 1844; *L'Aventurière*, 1848; *Gabrielle*, 1849; *La Chasse au roman*, 1851, with J. Sandeau; *Sappho*, 1851, opera LIBRETTO for Gounod; *Diane*, 1852; *La Pierre de touche*, 1853; *Philiberte*, 1853; *La Gendre de M. Poirier*, 1854, with J. Sandeau; *La Ceinture dorée*, 1855; *La Jeunesse*, 1858; *Les Lionnes pauvres*, 1858, with E. Foussier; *Un Beau mariage*, 1859, with E. Foussier; *Les Effrontés*, 1861; *Le Fils de Giboyer*, 1862; *Maître Guérin*, 1864; *Paul Forestier*, 1868; *Post-Scriptum*, 1868; *Lions et renards*, 1869; *Jean de Thomeray*, 1873, with J. Sandeau; *Le Prix Martin*, 1875, with LABICHE; *Madame Caverlet*, 1876; *Les Fourchambault*, 1878.
Bibl: H. A. Smith, MAIN CURRENTS OF MODERN FRENCH DRAMA, 1925; H. Gaillard de Chapris, 1910

Auleum. Woven and richly decorated front curtain of the Roman theatre; used during the 1st century BC. It perhaps originated in MIME. At the opening of the play it was lowered into a deep groove at the front of the stage (preserved at Pompeii and Herculaneum), and drawn up at the end of a performance or act. By the 2nd century AD the *auleum* was manipulated from above like the curtain in the modern theatre: it was raised at the play's beginning, held suspended, and lowered at the end. Occasionally a combination of *auleum* and SIPARIUM was used.

Austin, Charles (1878–1944), a famous and very popular English MUSIC HALL comedian, and a well-known figure in PANTOMIME. He created the amusing character of Parker P. C., and wrote sketches around him.

Australia. The first theatre production was in 1789, one year after the beginning of colonization. In 1800 the first permanent company was formed in Sydney; in 1833 Barnett Levey founded the Royal Theatre. The English actor and director George Selth Coppin established almost a dozen provincial theatres including Hobart, 1839; Adelaide, 1839; Melbourne, 1841. Between 1880 and 1890 the theatre flourished. There were guest appearances by European stars, productions of GILBERT AND SULLIVAN operas, and plays, including IBSEN. A decline in the early 20th century was followed by revitalization after 1945 by amateur REPERTORY and UNIVERSITY THEATRES, stimulated through the visits of the OLD VIC company in 1948 and the Stratford-upon-Avon Festival Company in 1949, which led to proposals for an Australian NATIONAL THEATRE.
Bibl: I. B. Fowlic, STARS IN MY BACKYARD: A SURVEY OF THE AUSTRALIAN STAGE, 1962; H. Hunt, THE MAKING OF THE AUSTRALIAN STAGE, 1960

Austria. The history of the Austrian theatre is closely linked with the development of the German-speaking theatre (▷ GERMANY). Vienna is the centre of theatre life. Among its most important theatres are the BURGTHEATER, founded in the late 18th century; the WIENER VOLKSTHEATER, founded in the 19th century. Also noteworthy are the Theater an der Wien and the Theater in der Josefstadt.

There are also a number of small EXPERIMENTAL THEATRES with literary pretensions. Today Austria has a subsidized theatre system, and permanent ENSEMBLE and REPERTORY companies in the other main cities such as Bregenz, Innsbruck, Salzburg, Linz, Klagenfurt and Graz.
Bibl: H. F. Garten, MODERN GERMAN DRAMA, 1959; O. Rommel, DIE ALT-WIENER VOLKSKOMÖDIE, 1952; J. Gregor, GESCHICHTE DES ÖSTERREICHISCHEN THEATERS, 1948, and DAS THEATER DES VOLKES IN DER OSTMARK, 1943

Auto sacramental (sacramental act), Spanish dramatic genre. A one-act play in verse which presents an allegorical dramatization of ideas related to the Eucharist, with personified abstractions, e.g. Holiness, Sin, the Devil, etc., as characters. The *auto*, like the secular drama, arose from simple LITURGICAL DRAMA, e.g. the Nativity play. In the 16th century they were performed in the open air to celebrate Corpus Christi. The most important early exponent was Diego Sánchez de Badajoz; TIRSO DE MOLINA, and LOPE DE VEGA also used the genre, drawing analogies between profane tales of adventure or love, and the divine mysteries. The master of this form was CALDERÓN DE LA BARCA, responsible for more than 70 *autos*, who often combined biblical stories with the abstract world of the sacraments, e.g. *El gran teatro del mundo* (The Great Theatre of the World) and *No hay más fortuna que Dios* (There is no Fortune other than God). In 1765 a royal decree prohibited the performance of *autos*. In the 20th century, apart from revivals of Calderón's *autos sacramentales*, there was renewed interest in the genre, e.g. ALBERTI and Miguel Hernández have written modern, secularized imitations of the old *autos*.
Bibl: R. B. Donovan, THE LITURGICAL DRAMA IN MEDIEVAL SPAIN, 1958

Avancini, Nikolaus (1611–86), Austrian dramatist of Italian origin. He wrote Latin SCHOOL DRAMAS and Baroque spectacles. In Austria he was the most prominent writer of JESUIT DRAMA and became court poet to Leopold I. For themes he drew on the classics, history and the Bible; he also wrote plays which were chiefly concerned with prophecy or praise for the House of Habsburg (*ludi Caesarii*). He raised the Viennese BAROQUE THEATRE to an apex of spectacle and splendour. Among his most important works are *Pietas Victrix*, 1659, and *Curae Caesarum*, 1654.
Bibl: N. Scheid, AVANCINI ALS DRAMATIKER, 1913

Avignon Festival. Annual drama festival, founded by VILAR, inaugurated in 1947 with a production by his own company of SHAKESPEARE's *Richard II*. The plays are staged in the forecourt of the Palais des Papes. When Vilar was appointed director of the THÉÂTRE NATIONAL POPULAIRE, this company supplied the festival with productions. The outstanding actors seen in Avignon have included MARIA CASARÈS,

Austria, the original BURGTHEATER in the Hofballhaus, founded 1741

Auto sacramental, 'La Piedra, el Rayo y el Fuego', by CALDERÓN, illustration from the original 17th-century MS

Nikolaus Avancini, *Pietas Victrix*, engraving from the original edition, 1659

SORANO and PHILIPE, e.g. in *Le Cid*. Among modern plays seen at Avignon are Supervielle's *Schéhérazade*, CLAUDEL's *La Ville*, PIRANDELLO's *Henry IV*, BRECHT's *Mother Courage* and BOLT's *A Man for All Seasons*. More recently companies such as M. BÉJART's Ballet du XXe siècle, the LIVING THEATRE and PLANCHON's Théâtre de la Comédie de Lyon have performed at Avignon. Originally the festival ran for a fortnight, sometimes playing to an audience of up to 50,000; since 1966 it has run for four weeks each year.
Bibl: AVIGNON, 20 ANS DE FÉSTIVAL, 1966

Axer, Erwin (1917–), Polish director. He was a pupil of L. SCHILLER. In 1940 he founded the Contemporary Theatre in Warsaw, which he made internationally famous with a REPERTOIRE of modern drama by such playwrights as GIRAUDOUX, SARTRE, WILDER, FRISCH, BRECHT (*Arturo Ui*, first seen in Warsaw in 1962), MROŻEK (*Tango*, first seen in Belgrade 1965). He has worked as a visiting director in New York, Leningrad and Düsseldorf.

Ayckbourn, Alan (1939–), English dramatist. He became known with *Standing Room Only*, 1961. *Mister Whatnot*, staged by the Studio Theatre at Stoke-on-Trent in 1963, was his first play to reach the West End. *Relatively Speaking*, 1967, had a long run at the Duke of York's Theatre, and became established as a major popular success; it was translated into many languages and produced all over the world. *How the Other Half Loves*, 1970, enjoyed almost the same success. He has also written works for the Theatre-in-the-Round at Scarborough, Yorks., e.g. *The Story So Far*, 1970, a number of shorter pieces, such as 'Countdown', one of the sketches in *Mixed Doubles*, 1969; a full-length play, *Absurd Person Singular*, London 1973, and a TRILOGY consisting of *Table Manners*, *Living Together* and *Round and Round the Garden*, each a full-length play, performed on consecutive evenings, under the general title *The Norman Conquests*, London 1974. In 1975 he provided the book and lyrics for the musical comedy *Jeeves*, based on WODEHOUSE.

Aylmer, Sir Felix (1889–), English actor. Made his début in 1911 with Sir Seymour Hicks at the London Coliseum, played small parts with Fred Terry's and TREE's companies. Joined the BIRMINGHAM REPERTORY THEATRE in 1913 where he appeared in a number of Shakespearean roles (Orsino, Malvolio, Prospero, Bassanio, Jaques) and in SHAW (Morell in *Candida*, Bohun in *You Never Can Tell*). On his return to the London and later the New York stage he became a leading actor of character parts and in his old age one of the finest and most subtle portrayers of noble and witty elderly gentlemen. Knighted in 1965. President of the British Actors' Equity Association, 1949–69 (▷EQUITY).

Aymé, Marcel (1902–67), French novelist, humorist and dramatist. He was a very original satirist, tending to SURREALISM and the GROTESQUE. He achieved his first success with the TRAGICOMEDY *Lucienne et le boucher* written in 1932 and first seen at the THÉÂTRE DU VIEUX-COLOMBIER in 1948. It was followed by *Clérambard*, 1950; *La Tête des autres*, 1952; *Les Quatre vérités*, 1954; *La Mouche bleue*, 1957; *Les Oiseaux de lune*, 1956; *Le Patron*, 1959; *Louisiana*, 1961; *Les Sorcières de Salem*, French version of A. MILLER's *The Crucible*.

Ayrer, Jakob (1543–1605), German dramatist. He was born in Nuremberg and was probably a MEISTERSINGER. He was the successor to SACHS and, like him, wrote long carnival plays and SINGSPIELE, e.g. *Phänicia* and *Sidea*. His work was mostly influenced by the English who travelled in GERMANY in the 1590s. His themes were taken from history and legend. Adapted SHAKESPEARE's plays, wrote numerous production notes demanding rich extravagant sets, but his own plays have no particular literary merit.

Azevedo, Artur (1855–1908), Brazilian journalist, poet, short-story writer, translator and dramatist. Started writing plays at the age of 9 and subsequently wrote a great number of COMEDIES, dramas, VAUDEVILLES, parodies, MUSICAL COMEDIES and operettas, some in collaboration with other playwrights. His works are vivid and humorous portrayals of the manners of his time. His own best-known plays are: the musical comedies, *A capital federal* (The Federal Capital) 1897, and *O Mambembe* (The second-rate travelling theatre) 1896; *O dote* (The Dowry) 1907; *A jóia* (The Jewel) 1879; *Casa de orates* (House of Madmen) 1882; *A fonte castália*, 1904; *Vida e morte* (Life and Death) 1908.

Bab, Julius (1880–1955), German drama critic. He wrote for the magazine *Die Schaubühne* and such newspapers as *Die Welt am Montag* and *Berliner Volkszeitung*. Emigrated to the USA in 1939. Best known for numerous theoretical studies of the drama, e.g. *Chronik des deutschen Dramas*, 1900–26, 5 vols; *Shaw*, 1910; *Der Wille zum Drama*, 1919; *Schauspielkunst und Schauspieler*, 1920; *Goethe*, 1921; *Gerhart Hauptmann*, 1922; *Hebbel*, 1923; *Shakespeare*, 1925; *Das Theater im Lichte der Soziologie*, 1930; *Kränze der Mimen*, 1954. His monographs on actors include KAINZ and BASSERMANN. He also worked as a DRAMATURG with JESSNER in Königsberg and at the VOLKSBÜHNE in Berlin. For his part in the conflict over PISCATOR's political conceptions he advocated a REPERTOIRE based rather on the German classics than the latter's topical propaganda spectacles.

Babel, Isaak (1894–c. 1941), Soviet writer and dramatist. His most famous work is the short-story cycle *Red Cavalry*, 1923–25, in which he portrays Jewish life in Odessa. 1937 marked the last publication of his work in the USSR. In 1939 he was denounced, arrested and sentenced on undisclosed charges; 17 March 1941 is the official date given for his death in a prison camp. But, despite 20 years' official suppression, 1937–57, his two plays are now considered to rank with GOGOL, CHEKHOV and GORKY. In 1957 Ilya Ehrenburg, his lifelong friend, edited a collection of B.'s work including these plays: *Sunset*, fp by STANISLAVSKY at the MOSCOW ART THEATRE, 1923; and *Marya*, first published in the USSR in 1935, but never performed there professionally. There have been performances of *Marya* in London, ROYAL COURT THEATRE, 1967, dir Robert Kidd, and in GERMANY, Stuttgart 1967, dir PALITZSCH; the play presents a picture of life in Russia during the St Petersburg insurrection in 1905.

Bacchae. In ancient Greece the female celebrants of the Dionysiac orgies. Bacchanalia, the orgiastic festivities of the Romans in honour of Bacchus, were prohibited in 186 BC by the Roman senate because of excesses. *The Bacchae* is also the title of a play by EURIPIDES. Modern adaptations include an opera by Hans Werner Henze, *Die Bassariden* (*The Bassarids*), 1966, with LIBRETTO by AUDEN and Chester Kallman.

Bagnold, Enid (1899–), English novelist and playwright. Her plays include: *Lottie Dundass*, 1943; *National Velvet*, 1946, a dramatization of her novel written 1935, which was later filmed with the young Elizabeth Taylor making her début; *The Chalk Garden*, New York 1955, with GLADYS COOPER and SIOBHAN MCKENNA; London 1956, with EDITH EVANS and PEGGY ASHCROFT; *The Chinese Prime Minister*, New York 1964, with MARGARET LEIGHTON and Edith Evans, London 1965. She published her autobiography in 1969.

Bahr, Hermann (1863–1934), Austrian dramatist and critic. As an author, DRAMATURG and critic he was closely involved with the Art Nouveau movement and was a pioneer in the theatre of NATURALISM, neo-Romanticism, Impressionism and EXPRESSIONISM. He collaborated 1884–87 with HOLZ and BRAHM in BERLIN on the paper *Die Freie Bühne*; after 1894 freelance writer, co-editor of the liberal weekly magazine *Die Zeit*; 1898 critic for the *Neues Wiener Tageblatt*. In 1907 he became director at the Deutsches-Theater, Berlin, under the artistic direction of REINHARDT. Dramaturg at the BURGTHEATER, Vienna, 1918. The best known of his numerous comedies are *Das Tschapperl*, 1898, and *Das Konzert*, 1909.

Baierl, Helmut (1926–), German dramatist. His plays are intended to present everyday life in East Germany. First known for his play *Die Feststellung* (The Arrangement), 1958; has worked since 1959 with the BERLINER ENSEMBLE where his play *Frau Flinz* (an attempt at portraying a modern character on the lines of BRECHT's *Mutter Courage*) was first staged in 1961 by PALITZSCH and WEKWERTH, with the lead played by HELENE WEIGEL; it was followed by *Johanna von Döbeln*, 1969.

Bajor, Gizi (1894–1951), Hungarian actress. One of the outstanding performers of her time at the National Theatre in Budapest, the Nemzeti Szinhàz. She was honoured as 'People's Artist' of the Republic in 1950. Her famous parts include Nora in IBSEN's *A Doll's House*, and the title roles in *La Dame aux camélias* by DUMAS *fils* and SHAW's *Saint Joan*, in addition to parts in contemporary Hungarian plays.

Baker, George Pierce (1866–1935), US drama teacher. The first Professor of Dramatic Literature at Harvard where, in 1905, he instituted a course of practical playwriting that led to the founding of the 47 Workshop in which he encouraged his students to criticize and discuss dramatic technique and theory, and to stage the plays they had written. It became the training ground for a whole generation of American dramatists, including O'NEILL, S. HOWARD, P. BARRY, BEHRMAN, ABBOTT and SHELDON. He was Director of the Graduate Department of Drama at Yale 1925–33, where he was provided with his own theatre, a library and studios, etc. His pioneer work in planning and teaching methods served to influence the development of drama departments in other American universities where lectures in theatre history were combined with exercises in playwriting and practical theatre. His main works include *Dramatic Technique*, 1919, a standard work for aspiring playwrights, and *The Development of Shakespeare as a Dramatist*, 1907.
Bibl: GEORGE PIERCE BAKER: A MEMORIAL, 1939

Bakst, Léon (Lev Samoylovich B. Rosenberg; 1866–1924), Russian designer. He became world famous with his designs for Diaghilev's Ballets Russes: *Cléopâtre*, 1909 (various composers); *Schéhérazade*, 1910 (Rimsky-Korsakov); *Firebird*, 1910 (Stravinsky); *Le Martyre de Saint Sébastien*, 1911 (Debussy), based on D'ANNUNZIO's MYSTERY PLAY; *Daphnis et Chloë*, 1912 (Ravel) and *The Legend of Joseph*, 1914 (Richard Strauss). He combined stylistic elements of archaic Greek art with oriental and 19th-century motives to produce an Art Nouveau style.
Bibl: R. Lister, THE MOSCOVITE PEACOCK, 1954

Baldwin, James (1924–), Black US novelist and playwright. Son of a Holy Roller lay preacher, he expressed his feelings in brilliant prose which gradually brought him fame. He received his theatrical apprenticeship with KAZAN. His play, *The Amen Corner*, staged by Howard University in 1955, in New York 1965, later toured

Alan Ayckbourn, scene from *Table Manners* in the trilogy *The Norman Conquests*, London 1974

Leon Bakst, costume design for the Blue Sultana in *Schéhérazade*

Europe. It concerns the everyday life of a small church community in New York; acted by a Black cast including Spiritual singers, the play gently probes the genuine and self-deluded elements in Black religious experience. *Blues for Mister Charlie*, fp New York 1964, ACTORS' STUDIO, dir MEREDITH, is inflammatory in the AGITPROP tradition. It portrays racialism as being due to White envy of supposed Black sexual superiority. With stereotype characters, it has a skeletal setting and there is a constant shift of time from past to present.

Bale, John (1495–1563), English dramatist. Bishop of Ossory in Ireland, he was the author of MIRACLE and MORALITY PLAYS (with anti-clerical tendencies). The most important is *Kynge Johan*, *c.* 1538, which is considered to be the first English historical play and marks the transition from medieval to Elizabethan drama.
Bibl: E. K. Chambers, THE MEDIEVAL STAGE, 1903, 2 vols.

Ballad opera. A play with songs based on well-known popular melodies. The first and most successful of the genre was GAY's *The Beggar's Opera*, 1728, with music arranged by Pepusch (1667–1752). It remained in vogue as a style of entertainment for more than a hundred years. BRECHT's *Dreigroschen Oper*, 1928, was based on it.
Bibl: G. Kitchin, A SURVEY OF BURLESQUE AND PARODY IN ENGLISH, 1931.

Ballet de Cour. Developed from the courtly entertainments and festivities in France, especially the masquerades. Reached its climax in the reign of Louis XIV, who established the first Académie Royale de Danse in 1661, and danced there himself. He encouraged artists like the poet Isaac de Benserade, the composer Lully and the choreographer Charles-Louis Beauchamps. The most famous name connected with this entertainment was that of MOLIÈRE, who developed the COMÉDIE-BALLET which he wrote in collaboration with Lully, e.g. *Les Fâcheux* and *Le Bourgeois gentilhomme*. This form gradually disappeared and merged into the opera-ballet (early form of French opera) in 1671, and the *ballet pur*, performed only by professional dancers.
Bibl: M.-F. Christout, LE BALLET DE COUR DE LOUIS XIV 1643–1672, 1967

Balucki, Michal (1837–1901), Polish poet and author. He wrote successful satires on society, also produced in other countries, e.g. *Radcy pana radcy*, depicting a kindly but incompetent municipal official, Cracow 1869; Vienna 1880. He suffered bitter attacks by the younger generation of critics, supporters of IBSEN and G. HAUPTMANN, which, combined with private difficulties, led to his suicide. Since World War II there has been renewed interest in his works.

Balzac, Honoré de (1799–1850), French writer. His influence on the theatre of the 19th century was enormous though his dramatic work is not extensive and cannot be compared in quality with his novels: he prepared rather careless adaptations of his own short stories, mostly in collaboration with friends such as the actor LEMAÎTRE; first *Le Père Goriot*, 1835, then *Vautrin*, 1840, a failure despite the fact that Lemaître played the main part; B. was accused of 'immorality' and the play was banned soon after the opening; then *Les Ressources de Quinola*, 1842; *Paméla Giraud*, 1843. He had his first success with *La Marâtre*, 1848; an even greater success with *Mercadet*, an original play, fp posthumously under the title *Le Faiseur* in 1851; as late as 1910 ANTOINE produced his *L'Ecole des ménages*, written in 1839. Numerous short stories and novels have subsequently been adapted for the theatre.
Bibl: D. Z. Milztchitch, LE THÉÂTRE D'HONORÉ DE BALZAC, 1930

Bancroft, Lady (Marie Effie Wilton; 1839–1921) and her husband **Sir Squire B.** (1841–1926), English ACTOR-MANAGERS. She appeared with great success in popular BURLESQUE (e.g. H. J. BYRON, Strand Theatre). They opened the Prince of Wales Theatre (formerly the Queen's Theatre) in 1865, which was to become one of London's leading playhouses. Most successful productions were the domestic comedies of ROBERTSON: *Society*, 1865; and *Caste*, 1867, in which S.B. gave one of his best performances; READE's *Masks and Faces*. Then they undertook a more demanding REPERTOIRE: e.g. SHERIDAN's *The School for Scandal* and *The Rivals*, SHAKESPEARE's *The Merchant of Venice* and PINERO's *Lords and Commons*. In 1880 they took over the management of the Haymarket Theatre which they ran successfully till their retirement from the stage in 1885. S.B. was knighted in 1897. They used their reputation as popular actors and their business talent to raise the economic and social standing of actors and introduced many reforms to the English stage such as practical scenery, real doors and windows in three-wall rooms with ceiling (box-set). Autobiographies *On and Off the Stage*, 1888, and *Recollections of Sixty Years*, 1909 (both written jointly), and (S.B.) *Empty Chairs*, 1923.
Bibl: A. Nicoll, A HISTORY OF ENGLISH DRAMA, Vol. V, 1959

Bankhead, Tallulah (1903–68), US actress. Made her stage début in 1918 in New York in Frederick Hatton's *The Squab Farm*. After a fairly successful BROADWAY career she went to London and made a sensation in Hubert Parson's *The Dancers*. An exceptionally striking woman with a husky voice whose reputation for extravagant and scandalous behaviour was as celebrated as her acting, she became the idol of fashionable young people in England. On her return to the USA after eight years she was not taken seriously as an actress and had an abortive film career. Among the plays in which she appeared in New York during that period were: *Forsaking All Others*, 1933; *Dark Victory*, 1934; *Reflected Glory* by KELLY, 1936; MAUGHAM's *The Circle*, 1938. Not till 1939 did she gain the recognition of American critics with her stage performance as Regina Giddens in LILLIAN HELLMAN's *The Little Foxes*. Other characteristic parts were Sabina in WILDER's *The Skin of Our Teeth*, 1942; the queen in COCTEAU's *The Eagle Has Two Heads*, 1947, and Blanche in T. WILLIAMS's *A Streetcar Named Desire*, a 1956 revival. Her memoirs were published as *Tallulah, My Autobiography*, 1952.

Bannister. (1) **Charles B.** (1741–1804), English actor. After some years in the provinces he went to London and appeared in 1762 at the Haymarket Theatre in FOOTE's *The Orators*. In 1767 he made his début at DRURY LANE under the direction of GARRICK in the latter's play *Cymon*. Famous as a comic actor and mimic, he could imitate both *castrati* and bass-singers. His fame was overshadowed by that of his son (2) **John B.** (1760–1836), who gained early success in tragic parts at Drury Lane, in which he was however soon superseded by HENDERSON and J. P. KEMBLE. J.B. was the first Don Ferolo Whiskerandos in SHERIDAN's *The Critic*, 1779, in which he later played Sir Fretful Plagiary; he then played Sir Anthony Absolute in Sheridan's *The Rivals*; Tony Lumpkin in GOLDSMITH's *She Stoops to Conquer*. Eventually he became one of the managers at Drury Lane and retired from the stage in 1815.
Bibl: J. L. Adolphus, MEMOIRS OF CHARLES BANNISTER, 1838

Banville, Théodore Faullin de (1823–91), French poet. He caused a sensation with his classicist poems *Les Cariatides*; also an influential critic who advocated the return of VERSE DRAMA. His plays *Le Feuilleton d'Aristophane*, 1852, and *Les Fourberies de Nérine*, pub 1864, are COMEDIES written in verse, the latter a variation on MOLIÈRE's *Les Fourberies de Scapin*. He was most successful with one of his few prose dramas, *Gringoire*, 1866, which contained a STAR part brilliantly performed by actors like COQUELIN *aîné* and ZACCONI.
Bibl: J. Charpentier, THÉÂTRE DE BANVILLE, 1925

Baraka, Imamu Amiri ▷JONES, LEROI.

Barker ▷GRANVILLE-BARKER.

Barlach, Ernst (1870–1938), German sculptor and poet. Leading exponent of German Expressionist drama, concerned with religious and mystical subjects; men searching for God: *Der tote Tag* (The Dead Day), fp 1919, most important production by FALCKENBERG for the Munich Kammerspiele, 1924; *Der arme Vetter* (The Poor Cousin), fp 1919; *Die echten Sedemunds* (The True Sedemunds), fp Berlin 1922, dir JESSNER; *Der blaue Boll* (The Blue Bulb), fp Berlin 1929, dir FEHLING. A cycle of Barlach plays was produced by LIETZAU for the Schillertheater, Berlin 1956–60.
Bibl: H. Maier, DER VERBORGENE GOTT, 1963

Barlog, Boleslaw (1906–), German director. From 1945 artistic director of the Schlossparktheater in BERLIN and since

1951 of the Schillertheater. As a director best known for contemporary plays of psychological realism; productions include: ZUCKMAYER's *Des Teufels General*, 1948; SAROYAN's *The Time of Your Life*, 1948; Zuckmayer's *Der Hauptmann von Köpenick*, 1954 and 1967; OSBORNE's *Look Back in Anger*, 1957; and ALBEE's *Who's Afraid of Virginia Woolf?*, 1964. He has also directed operas.

Barnay, Ludwig (1842–1924), German actor and theatre manager. Leading man and character actor of the MEININGER company, he founded the Genossenschaft Deutscher Bühnenangehörigen (the German equivalent of EQUITY) in 1871; also one of the founders of the Deutsches-Theater, and in 1906 artistic manager of the Royal Theatre, both in BERLIN, and 1908–11 of the Court Theatre in Hanover.

Barnay, Paul (1884–1960), Austrian actor, director and theatre manager in Breslau, Hamburg and Vienna (VOLKSTHEATER). Played leading parts in LESSING's *Nathan der Weise*, SHAKESPEARE's *Richard III* and GOETHE's *Faust* (Mephistopheles).

Barnes, Peter (1931–), English dramatist. First worked as a film critic and organized seasons for the National Film Theatre. Early attempts at drama were mainly TV plays, from 1956, among them *The Man with a Feather in His Hat*, 1960. His one-act play *Sclerosis* was produced at the Traverse Theatre, Edinburgh, 1965, and seen in London at the Aldwych. Established himself with his 'Baroque comedy' *The Ruling Class*, fp 1968, Nottingham Playhouse, transferred to the Piccadilly Theatre, 1969, filmed 1971, with O'TOOLE; it holds up a satirical mirror to the socio-sexual power structure, and won him the John Whiting Award in 1968. Subsequent work has included the one-act plays: *Leonardo's Last Supper*, and *Noonday Demons*, presented as a double bill at the Open Space Theatre, 1969. He adapted WEDEKIND's *Earth Spirit* and *Pandora's Box* produced jointly under the title *Lulu*, fp 1970, Nottingham Playhouse, transferred to the ROYAL COURT and later to the Apollo Theatre.

Barnowsky, Victor (1875–1952), German director and producer. One of the most successful theatre managers of the 1920s in BERLIN: 1905–13 at the Kleines-Theater, 1913–24 at the Lessingtheater and the Komödienhaus. Outstanding German actors like BASSERMANN, JANNINGS, PALLENBERG, KÄTHE DORSCH and ELISABETH BERGNER appeared under his management. His REPERTORY provided an alternative to REINHARDT's productions which tended towards classicism.
Bibl: J. Berstl, 25 JAHRE BERLINER THEATER UND VICTOR BARNOWSKY, 1930

Barnum, Phineas Taylor (1810–91), US theatre manager and showman. A pioneer of show business, he founded such theatres as the American Museum (also known as Barnum's), New York, 1842, made a star

Ballet de Cour, engraving from the *Ballet Comique de la Reine*, 1582, the first Court ballet produced in France

Tallulah Bankhead in MAUGHAM's *Rain*, New York 1935

Squire and **Lady Bancroft** in *Society* by ROBERTSON, London 1865

of Tom Thumb, 1842 (touring throughout Europe in 1844); organized the American tour of Jenny Lind, the singer, and in 1871 founded his first circus 'The Greatest Show on Earth'; from 1881, in partnership with J. A. Bailey.
Bibl: N. Harris, HUMBUG: THE ART OF P. T. BARNUM, 1973

Baron, French family of actors. (1) **André B.** (1600–55), whose real name was Boyron, but kept the name Baron after being wrongly addressed by Louis XIV as 'Le Sieur Baron'. Left the Théâtre du Marais for the HÔTEL DE BOURGOGNE, playing kings in TRAGEDY and peasants in COMEDY – a usual combination in the 17th century. Married to (2) **Jeanne Auzoult** (1625–62), an outstanding interpreter of boys' parts, much admired by CORNEILLE. The youngest of their six children was (3) **Michel B.** (1653–1729), who was discovered and trained by MOLIÈRE, and appeared in his troupe in small parts. He left Molière after a disagreement with the latter's wife, but returned in 1670 and played young lovers like Octave in *Les Fourberies de Scapin* and Ariste in *Les Femmes savantes.* Left Molière again for the Hôtel de Bourgogne where for the first time he played young tragic heroes in RACINE's plays, e.g. Achille in *Iphigénie*, Hippolyte in *Phèdre.* In 1680 he became the principal actor of the newly formed COMÉDIE-FRANÇAISE. In 1691 at the height of his career he retired suddenly, returning to the stage nearly 30 years later in 1720; he continued to act in his old roles but helped to establish a new style of acting aimed at revealing the inner truth of the character instead of relying on the existing declamatory style. He patronized and encouraged the young and talented actress ADRIENNE LECOUVREUR, and acted in the first plays of MARIVAUX. M.B. also wrote several comedies, the best of which are: *Les Rendez-vous des Tuileries ou le Coquet*, 1685, and *L'Homme à bonnes fortunes*, 1686.
Bibl: B. E. Young, MICHEL BARON, ACTEUR ET AUTEUR DRAMATIQUE, 1905

Baroque theatre. Reached its peak in the 17th and 18th centuries in the princely courts and sumptuous monasteries of Roman Catholic countries, particularly SPAIN, ITALY, AUSTRIA and Bavaria. Performances often took the form of great festivals with productions that transcended the confines of the stage. The performances, springing from Humanism and the Renaissance, enriched the existing theatrical tradition. The texts that have been preserved are frequently no more than blueprints for the use of machinery and stage effects on a vast and fantastic scale. Fireworks and water displays often formed part of the stage effects that aimed at a kind of total theatre representing the whole world. The emphasis was on the crowd scenes with people and animals rather than on DIALOGUE. Baroque theatre was the concrete, allegorical embodiment of a new inspiration in the arts centred on a tension between illusion and reality. The Baroque idea of the transience of all being was expressed theatrically in the use of changeable scenery. The backgrounds, painted in perspective, and the *trompe-l'œil* architectural painting had the function of blurring the borderline between appearance and actuality. Man was seen in the abstract rather than as a psychological individual and it was felt necessary also to show those forces which battled for him in the heavens and in the underworld; allegories and emblems of supernatural and infernal creatures were shown, in the shape of clouds, comets, sun, moon, fire, angels, eagles, peacocks and swans. The scene of action shifted from the horizontal, objective, interpersonal sphere of conflict of the Renaissance to the vertical plan which led to a movement away from the two-dimensional erections of RENAISSANCE THEATRE to a three-dimensional structural concept of space. All aspects of the theatre were encouraged through patronage; writers, musicians, architects and designers (e.g. the PARIGI, BURNACINI and GALLI-BIBIENA families) brought in available resources to build up illusion and create brilliant effects.
Outside the courts theatre flourished in the schools as a means of disseminating education. JESUIT DRAMA was produced in Latin with comic or balletic interludes to make it acceptable to a wider audience, from which elaborate visual spectacles developed. Amateur theatre flourished among the populace with endless productions of the Passion of Christ, perpetuated today in the decennial performances at OBERAMMERGAU. Literary works of the period include the plays of BIDERMANN in Germany (*Cenodoxus*, the Faust theme of the Scholar between God and the Underworld), GRYPHIUS; AVANCINI, the Austrian Jesuit writer; CALDERÓN in Spain; the later works of SHAKESPEARE, *The Winter's Tale* and *The Tempest*, with their elements of Baroque fantasy; the MASQUES of JONSON, and I. JONES. In France, Louis XIV, himself very fond of ballet, encouraged MOLIÈRE who collaborated with LULLY to produce COMÉDIE-BALLETS (*Le Bourgeois gentilhomme*) and was the model emulated by other courts. Gradually as the performances increased in splendour, the spoken word diminished in importance, while opera became more popular. In Vienna in 1667 the wedding of the Emperor Leopold I and the Spanish Infanta was signalized by the cosmic drama *La Contesa dell'aria e dell'acqua*, a glorification of the divine right of princes; in Dresden 1676 a gathering of the Royal House culminated in the *Musikalische Oper*, a ballet symbolizing the royal meeting by a dance of the seven planets. The changed cultural atmosphere of the 18th century was also reflected at court where the pastoral and idyll came into favour in place of allegories of power and dynasty. Baroque theatre declined as cultural nationalism arose, during the second half of the 18th century. French drama and Italian opera lost their position of preeminence, individual nations created their own drama and operas. National diversity, springing from the demands of the new middle-class public, replaced its glories.
Bibl: M. Baur-Heinhold, BAROQUE THEATRE, 1967; H. Tintelnot, BAROCKTHEATER UND BAROCKE KUNST, 1939

Barrault, Jean-Louis (1910–), French actor, director and producer. Pupil of DULLIN with whom he worked as an actor at the Théâtre de l'Atelier, 1931–35, during which period he was also a pupil of the great mime DECROUX; MIME later became an important part of his technique. In 1935 he produced the mime drama *Autour d'une mère* based on William Faulkner's novel *As I Lay Dying*. He left the Théâtre de l'Atelier with a group of actors and founded a studio, Le Grenier des Augustins, where he collaborated with painters and writers such as André Breton, Jacques Prévert and ARTAUD, who became his close friend. His group revived CERVANTES' only tragedy *El Cerco de Numancia* in 1937, repeated in 1965; *Hamlet* in the free adaptation by Jules Laforgue; and *Faim*, a dramatization of the novel by HAMSUN. In 1940 COPEAU engaged B. for the COMÉDIE-FRANÇAISE; he became a SOCIÉTAIRE in 1942. He made his début as Rodrigue in CORNEILLE's *Le Cid* and played the title role in SHAKESPEARE's *Hamlet.* Also responsible for noted productions of RACINE's *Phèdre* (with MARIE BELL in the lead), 1942; CLAUDEL's *Le Soulier de satin*, 1943; and Shakespeare's *Antony and Cleopatra*, 1945. In 1946 he left the CF to form with his wife, the actress MADELEINE RENAUD, his own company which played at the Théâtre Marigny from 1946 to 1956; productions included *Hamlet* (GIDE's translation, with B. playing the lead), 1946; MARIVAUX's *Les Fausses Confidences*, 1946; *Baptiste* (ballet-pantomime about DEBURAU by Prévert); SALACROU's *Les Nuits de la colère* in which B. gave a fine performance as Jean Cordet; *Le Procès* (based on KAFKA's novel *The Trial*, adapted by Gide and B.), 1947; MOLIÈRE's *Amphitryon* with EDWIGE FEUILLÈRE, 1947; CAMUS's *L'Etat de siège*, 1948; Claudel's *Partage de midi*, 1948; Molière's *Les Fourberies de Scapin* (B. played the title role), dir JOUVET, 1949; MONTHERLANT's *Malatesta*, 1950; ANOUILH's *La Répétition*, 1950; Gide's *Œdipe*, 1951; COCTEAU's *Bacchus*, 1951; OBEY's *Lazare*, 1951; Claudel's *Christophe Colomb*, 1953; AESCHYLUS' *Oresteia* trans Obey, 1955; SCHÉHADÉ's *Histoire de Vasco*, 1957. In 1959 he was appointed director of the Théâtre de l'Odéon (renamed THÉATRE DE FRANCE), the second national theatre after the CF, where he produced numerous revivals of earlier plays. Outstanding in this period: Schéhadé's *Le Voyage*, 1961; IONESCO's *Le Piéton de l'air*, fp in France, 1963; BILLETDOUX's *Il faut passer par les nuages*, fp 1964; MARGUERITE DURAS's *Des journées entières dans les arbres*, fp 1966; GENET's *Les Paravents*, fp in France 1966, dir BLIN; FLAUBERT's *La Tentation de St Antoine*, dir BÉJART, 1967. In 1968, dismissed from the Odéon for political reasons, B. then produced *Rabelais* (after *Gargantua*) in a hall formerly used as a wrestling ring in Montmartre. In his productions, heightened use of gesture produces a style particularly adapted to comedies, e.g. his famous Scapin, and serious plays which invite the use of mime, e.g. Claudel's *Christophe Colomb.* His skill as a mime is shown best in his performance as Baptiste Deburau in Marcel Carné's film *Les Enfants du Paradis*,

1944. His theoretical works include *Réflexions sur le théâtre*, 1949, and *Nouvelles réflexions sur le théâtre*, 1959; he also initiated the *Cahiers de la Compagnie Renaud-Barrault*. His autobiography was published in 1974.

Barrie, Sir James Matthew (1860–1937), Scottish playwright and novelist. Wrote *c.* 40 plays which combine the traditions of DRAWING-ROOM COMEDY with fantastic, fairy-tale elements and social satire. His most widely known and performed work is *Peter Pan*, 1904, a fairy-tale about a 'boy who did not want to grow up' and who takes the children of the Darling family with him into the Never-Never-Land inhabited by those denizens of children's books, Indians and Pirates. *Peter Pan* is performed in London every year as a Christmas show for children. Among his other well-known plays are: *Walker, London*, 1892; *The Little Minister*, 1897; *The Admirable Crichton*, 1902; *What Every Woman Knows*, 1908; *The Twelve-Pound Look*, 1910; *A Kiss for Cinderella*, 1916; *Dear Brutus*, 1917; *Mary Rose*, 1920; *The Boy David*, 1936, written especially for ELISABETH BERGNER.
Bibl: J. Dunbar, THE MAN BEHIND THE IMAGE, 1970

Barry, Elizabeth (1658–1713), English actress. Early career unsuccessful despite her training by DAVENANT and the protection of the Earl of Rochester, but later she became one of the leading tragediennes of her day, acting in many plays opposite BETTERTON; well known especially as the heroine in OTWAY's tragedies, e.g. Belvidera in *Venice Preserved*. Other parts included Cordelia in Nahum Tate's adaptation of *King Lear*, Lady Brute in VANBRUGH's *The Provok'd Wife* and Zara in CONGREVE's *The Mourning Bride*.

Barry, Philip (1896–1949), US playwright. Studied in BAKER's 47 Workshop at Harvard; member of the THEATRE GUILD. First made an impact with *You and I*, 1923. He followed this with *The Youngest* which reached BROADWAY in 1924, although it had been written before his previous success; *In a Garden*, 1925; *White Wings*, 1926; the biblical tragedy *John*, 1927; *Cock Robin*, in collaboration with RICE, 1928; *Paris Bound*, 1927; *Holiday*, 1928; *Hotel Universe*, 1930; *The Animal Kingdom*, 1931, starring L. HOWARD; *The Philadelphia Story*, 1939 – his most popular work, the epitome of the sophisticated American DRAWING-ROOM COMEDY of the 1930s – in which KATHARINE HEPBURN had a triumph; *Foolish Notion*, 1945, starring TALLULAH BANKHEAD; *Second Threshold*, finished by SHERWOOD and first performed 1951.
Bibl: J. P. Roppolo, 1965

Barry, Spranger (1719–77), Irish-born actor. One of the leading stage lovers of his time; said to have looked as 'handsome as a Greek God'. First performed on stage at the Smock Alley Theatre in Dublin 1744–46, then went to DRURY LANE where he appeared in great Shakespearean parts

Baroque theatre, design by Torelli for the opera *Les Noces de Pelée et de Thétis*, mid-17th century

Jean-Louis Barrault and Geneviève Page in RACINE's *Andromaque*

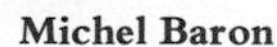

Michel Baron

Elizabeth Barry

(Othello, Henry V) and in many plays with GARRICK, e.g. Pierre in *Venice Preserved* with Garrick as Jaffier. In 1750 he moved to COVENT GARDEN, where he played the lead in John Home's *Douglas* opposite PEG WOFFINGTON in 1757 (▷SCOTLAND). By playing Romeo, Lear and Richard III he engaged in rivalry with Garrick, who nevertheless called him back to Drury Lane in 1767. B.'s second wife **Ann Dancer** (1734–1801) was a successful actress best known for her comic parts, e.g. Polly in GAY's *The Beggar's Opera* but her most famous role was Desdemona.

Barrymore, US family of actors. (1) **Maurice B.** (1847–1905) was an Englishman, real name Herbert Blythe, born in India. He studied law at Cambridge, and made his stage début in London in 1875 and in the same year in Boston, Mass., in DALY's *Under the Gaslight*. He was a handsome, witty and intelligent man and during his London seasons mixed with the circle around WILDE. He appeared with almost all the important actresses of his time: HELENA MODJESKA, LILLIE LANGTRY and MRS FISKE, mostly in plays which are forgotten today. His wife was GEORGIANA EMMA DREW, whom he married in 1876. The Barrymores had three children who all became actors. (2) **Lionel B.** (1878–1954) made his stage début at the age of 15 at the Arch Street Theatre, Philadelphia, managed by his grandmother, achieving an outstanding success in *The Copperhead*, 1918, by Augustus Thomas but soon left the stage to work in films. His sister (3) **Ethel B.** (1879–1959), was admired both for her beauty and for her acting, and had a long career. Her first hit was as Madame Trentoni in *Captain Jinks of the Horse Marines*, by FITCH, 1901; particularly noteworthy was her performance as Nora in IBSEN's *A Doll's House* with her brother, John B. (see below), as Dr Rank, and she appeared in classic roles such as Ophelia, Juliet, Portia and Camille and later Lady Teazle in SHERIDAN's *The School for Scandal*, the name part in G. HAUPTMANN's *Rose Bernd*, and in more contemporary plays, e.g. *Déclassée*, by Zoë Akins, 1919. Her most popular performance was probably as Miss Moffat in *The Corn is Green*, by E. WILLIAMS, 1940. In 1928 she opened her own theatre in New York which was named after her. The three children of her marriage with R. C. Colt are also actors. (4) **John B.** (1882–1942), younger brother of Lionel and Ethel, was one of the most talented actors of the English-speaking stage. In his early career he mainly appeared in popular farces and light comedies (he had great success in GALSWORTHY's *Justice*) but later proved his excellence in classic roles, notably Richard III, 1920, and Hamlet, 1922, at the Sam H. Harris Theatre, New York. He repeated his success in London at the Haymarket Theatre in 1925. In later years he appeared mainly in films and on radio. Two of his three children, **Diana B.** (1921–60) and **John B.** (1932–), became actors.
Bibl: G. Fowler, GOODNIGHT SWEET PRINCE, 1943

Barsacq, André (1909–73), French director and designer. Started his career at DULLIN's Théâtre de l'Atelier designing sets for JONSON's *Volpone* (adaptation by Stefan Zweig and ROMAINS), 1928; he then collaborated with COPEAU at the Vieux-Colombier; founded the Compagnie des Quatre Saisons in 1937 where he did his first work as a director and designer of GOZZI's *Il Re cervo*. 1937–38 he was in New York; after his return to France he took over the management of Dullin's Atelier in 1941. He tried to reproduce the atmosphere of the play in his stage designs, to give the actors a 'frame' within which to realize their emotions. He formulated his theories in 'Lois scéniques' in the magazine *Revue théâtrale*, April 1947, and in *Architecture et dramaturgie* (a collection of essays by JOUVET, BATY, etc.) Paris 1950. He produced many of ANOUILH's plays such as *Le Bal des voleurs*, 1938; *Le Rendez-vous de Senlis*, 1941; *Eurydice*, 1942; *Antigone*, 1943; *Roméo et Jeannette*, 1946; *L'Invitation au château*, 1947; other productions include ACHARD's *Jean de la lune*, 1937; MOLIÈRE's *Les Fourberies de Scapin*, 1940; CLAUDEL's *Le pain dur*, 1949; PIRANDELLO's *Enrico IV*, 1950; MARCEAU's *L'Oeuf*, 1956; Françoise Sagan's *Un Château en Suède*, 1960; and DÜRRENMATT's *Frank V*, 1963.

Bart, Lionel (1930–), English composer, lyricist and librettist. Emerged from JOAN LITTLEWOOD's company at the Theatre Royal, Stratford East, London: wrote the songs and lyrics for the musical *Fings Ain't Wot They Used T'Be*, 1959; also wrote lyrics for MILES's musical play *Lock Up Your Daughters*, 1959; book, lyrics and music for *Oliver!*, 1960; co-authored the book and wrote lyrics and music for *Blitz*, 1962, and *Maggie May*, 1964, and was sole author of *Twang!*, 1965.

Barton, John (1928–), director and adaptor of SHAKESPEARE. He was a Fellow of King's College, Cambridge, 1954–60. Directed *Macbeth*, his first production, at the ADC theatre, Cambridge, in 1949. While at the university directed numerous productions for the Marlowe Society. His first London production was *Henry V*, 1953, for the ELIZABETHAN STAGE SOCIETY. In 1960 he joined the RSC in Stratford-upon-Avon, and directed *The Taming of the Shrew*. He devised for the company two anthology performances: *The Hollow Crown*, 1961, and *The Art of Seduction*, 1962, which he also directed. In 1963 he adapted and edited Shakespeare's *Henry VI* and *Richard III* as the three-play cycle *The Wars of the Roses*, assisting HALL, who directed it. Appointed Associate Director of the RSC, 1964, in which year he co-directed at Stratford: *Richard II* and *Henry IV* (Parts I, II); *Henry V*, *The Wars of the Roses*; 1965, directed *Love's Labour's Lost* and co-directed *Henry V* at the Aldwych Theatre, London. In 1966 co-directed *Henry IV* (Parts I, II), *Henry V*; in 1967 *Coriolanus* and *All's Well That Ends Well* at Stratford; in 1968 *Troilus and Cressida* and *Julius Caesar* at Stratford and Aldwych. At Stratford, *Twelfth Night*, 1969; *Othello*, 1971, and *Richard II*, 1973.

Basoche. In pre-revolutionary France a guild of lawyers (*clercs*). The first group may have been founded by Philip the Fair in the early 14th century. The Clercs de la Basoche were among the original interpreters of early French FARCE. The most famous group was the Basoche du Palais in Paris which first performed in 1442.
Bibl: G. Harvey, THE THEATRE OF THE BASOCHE, 1941

Bassermann, Albert (1867–1952), German actor. One of the greatest actors of the naturalistic theatre, he started with the MEININGER company and appeared from 1900 at the Deutsches-Theater, BERLIN, under BRAHM and later REINHARDT. His range was immensely wide, extending from exuberant comedy to the great heroic roles, from IBSEN and G. HAUPTMANN to the classics, e.g. Philip II in SCHILLER's *Don Carlos*, Wallenstein in Schiller's trilogy, Shylock in *The Merchant of Venice*, Mephistopheles in GOETHE's *Faust*. Left GERMANY after Hitler came to power and later went to the USA where he appeared in Hollywood films. Returned to Europe in 1946.
Bibl: I. Richter-Haase, DIE SCHAUSPIELKUNST ALBERT BASSERMANNS, 1964

Bataille, Henry (1872–1922), French dramatist. With his play *Maman Colibri*, 1904, he became the most successful playwright of the pre-war period in France; influenced in his analytical dramatic technique by writers such as IBSEN and MAETERLINCK. Among his plays were: *La Marche nuptiale*, 1905; *La Femme nue*, 1908; *La Vierge folle*, 1910; *La Phalène*, 1913; *L'Amazone*, 1916; *L'Homme à la rose*, 1920.
Bibl: J. B. Besançon, 1928

Bates, Alan (1934–), English actor. Studied at RADA. First appeared in London at the ROYAL COURT THEATRE in *The Mulberry Bush*, 1956. Subsequent roles at the Royal Court included: in 1956, Hopkins in A. MILLER's *The Crucible*; Cliff Lewis in OSBORNE's *Look Back in Anger*, Stapleton in DENNIS's *Cards of Identity*; in 1957 Mr Hartcourt in WYCHERLEY's *The Country Wife*, and Monsieur le Cracheton in GIRAUDOUX's *L'Apollon de Bellac*. For his performances as Edmund Tyrone in O'NEILL's *Long Day's Journey Into Night*, EDINBURGH FESTIVAL, and London 1958, he received the Clarence Derwent Award. Created the part of Mick in PINTER's *The Caretaker*, fp London 1960, Arts Theatre, transferred to Duchess Theatre, and produced in New York 1961. Starred in STOREY's *In Celebration*, 1969, Royal Court; title role in GRAY's *Butley*, 1971, Criterion Theatre, dir Pinter, New York 1972; Storey's *Life Class*, 1974; Gray's *Otherwise Engaged*, 1975. Has also appeared in films.

Bathyllus, Roman pantomimist originally from Alexandria. Towards the end of the 1st century BC he established with his rival Pylades (from Cilicia in Asia Minor) a form of pantomime in which dance predominated.

Baty, Gaston (1885–1952), French director and designer. First studied law, then German

literature in Munich; influenced by the Munich Künstlertheater (especially by the designer Fritz Erler), he returned to Paris where he produced the work of new dramatists and founded his own company, La Chimère, 1922 (Baraque de la Chimère, 1923; Studio des Champs-Elysées, 1923–28; Théâtre de l'Avenue, 1928; Théâtre Pigalle, 1929), settling in the Théâtre Montparnasse in 1930 where his productions included: BRECHT's *The Threepenny Opera*, 1930; *Crime and Punishment*, 1932 (a dramatized version of DOSTOYEVSKY's novel); MUSSET's *Les Caprices de Marianne*, 1935; *Madame Bovary*, 1936 (based on FLAUBERT's novel); RACINE's *Phèdre*, 1939; SHAKESPEARE's *Macbeth* (an adaptation). In 1936 he was appointed a producer at the COMÉDIE-FRANÇAISE: LABICHE's *Le Chapeau de paille d'Italie*, 1937; Racine's *Bérénice*, 1946; SALACROU's *L'Inconnue d'Arras*, 1948. In his productions he combined an intellectual approach with practical expertise, mostly designing his own sets. He introduced a new aesthetic of the theatre in *Le Masque et l'encensoir*, Paris, 1929, and also wrote historical works like *Vie de l'art théâtral des origines à nos jours*, Paris 1932, in collaboration with R. Chavance. B. advocated a 'total theatre' in which language is of secondary importance. In practice this sometimes led to an over-emphasis on the visual and decorative elements. He wrote one play, *Dulcinée*, 1938, based on an episode in *Don Quixote*. He retired from the theatre in 1949 to concentrate on puppet plays. ▷PUPPET THEATRE.
Bibl: R. Cogniat, 1953

Baudissin, Wolf Graf von (1789–1878), German translator. Danish diplomat who lived from 1827 in Dresden. A friend of the German Romantic writer, TIECK, he translated 13 plays for the famous German SHAKESPEARE Schlegel-Tieck edition. Also translated MOLIÈRE, 1865–67, and Italian COMEDIES by GOZZI and GOLDONI, 1877.

Bauer, Wolfgang (1941–), Austrian avant-garde playwright. Uses his experiences of HAPPENINGS and improvisation exercises to create a form of highly theatrical and grotesquely realistic WELL-MADE PLAY, characterized by biting wit and the exact and concise use of Austrian dialect. His first major success was *Magic Afternoon*, fp 1968, followed by *Change*, fp 1969, which like most of his other work is set in the pop culture of Vienna; *Party For Six*, fp 1967, *Film und Frau* (Film and Woman), fp 1971, *Silvester oder Das Massaker im Hotel Sacher* (Silvester or The Massacre in the Hotel Sacher), fp 1971.

Bauernfeld, Eduard von (1802–90), Austrian dramatist. Friend of prominent Austrian writers and musicians, such as GRILLPARZER, RAIMUND, and Schubert. He was dismissed from the Civil Service in 1848 because of his liberal ideas. Author of numerous Viennese COMEDIES in the French tradition, e.g. *Der Graf von Gleichen*, 1825; *Leichtsinn aus Liebe* (Indiscretion through Love), 1826; *Das Liebesprotokoll* (The Protocol of Love), 1831; *Bürgerlich und Roman-*

Albert Bassermann as Mephistopheles in GOETHE's *Faust*

John Barrymore, 1918

Ethel and **John Barrymore** in BARRIE's *A Slice of Life*, New York 1912

John Barton's production of SHAKESPEARE's *The Taming of the Shrew*, Stratford-upon-Avon 1960, des Alix Stone

tisch (Simple and Romantic), 1835; *Das Tagebuch* (The Diary), 1836; *Grossjährig* (Of Age), 1846; *Der kategorische Imperativ* (The Categorical Imperative), 1851; *Der Landfrieden* (Public Peace), 1867.
Bibl: F. Horner, 1900

Baylis, Lilian (1874–1937), English theatre manager. Founder of the OLD VIC and Sadler's Wells companies. Trained as a musician, she appeared in concerts with her parents, both singers, and later settled in Johannesburg as a music teacher until she was recalled to England by her aunt, Emma Cons, to assist in running the Victoria Theatre (then called the Royal Victoria Hall and Coffee Tavern and managed by E. Cons since 1880). In 1912 L.B. took over the management and soon became the leading manageress in London for opera and ballet. Her aim was to provide opera and good drama for a wide public. She made the Old Vic a centre for SHAKESPEARE and between 1914 and 1923 produced all his plays; in 1932 she rebuilt and opened the Sadler's Wells where the productions of opera and ballet rapidly achieved fame and great popularity with the assistance of Charles Corri (as director of the opera) and Ninette de Valois (as head of the ballet company). She was appointed a Companion of Honour in 1929.
Bibl: A. Dent, A THEATRE FOR EVERYBODY: THE STORY OF THE OLD VIC AND SADLER'S WELLS, 1945; R. Findlater, L.B.: THE LADY OF THE OLD VIC, 1975

Bayreuth. City in Upper Bavaria, where Richard Wagner founded his Festival Theatre, which was built 1872–76, according to the ideas of Wagner himself and the architects G. Semper and O. Brückwald, with STAGE MACHINERY designed by K. Brandt. Most notable features of Wagner's revolutionary concept were the concealed orchestra and the tiered auditorium which did away with the traditional division between stalls and several balconies and galleries, creating 1,800 seats, all giving a clear view of the stage. This concept has become the norm for theatre construction in the 20th century. Bayreuth also has an old, historic opera house, built between 1744 and 1748. The simple façade (designed by Joseph Saint-Pierre) conceals a sumptuous interior by the Italian Baroque artists G. and C. GALLI-BIBIENA.

Beaton, Sir Cecil (1904–), English designer, photographer and writer. Since 1935 has designed COSTUMES and sets for theatre and ballet, e.g. Ballets Russes de Monte Carlo, COVENT GARDEN, London 1937, and since 1946 also in the USA, e.g. WILDE's *Lady Windermere's Fan*, San Francisco 1946. Other designs: LONSDALE's *Aren't We All?*, London 1953; COWARD's *Quadrille*, New York 1954; ENID BAGNOLD's *The Chalk Garden*, New York 1955; Coward's *Look After Lulu* (after FEYDEAU's *Occupe-toi d'Amélie*), fp New York 1959; the musical *Saratoga* (based on EDNA FERBER), New York 1960. He gained international fame for his costume designs for *My Fair Lady* (musical by LERNER and LOEWE, New York 1956, London 1958; film version in 1964). He is also a leading photographer with a world-wide reputation and has published books of photographs, his diaries, reminiscences and a play, *The Gainsborough Girls*, London 1951. Knighted in 1972.

Beaumarchais, Pierre Augustin Caron de (1732–99), French playwright and essayist. The son of a watchmaker, he led an eventful life: gave harp lessons to the daughter of Louis XV, married three times, was a secret agent, a financier, went bankrupt and was in prison several times during the Revolution and finally was forced to leave France until 1796. Inspired by DIDEROT's *Le Père de famille*, 1758, and by Michel Jean Sedaine's *Le Philosophe sans le savoir*, 1765, B. wrote his first play *Eugénie*, 1767, according to Diderot's theories of DRAME BOURGEOIS; it was followed in 1770 by *Les Deux amis, ou le Négociant de Lyon*. His two masterpieces which had worldwide success were *La Précaution inutile, ou le Barbier de Séville*, 1775, and *La Folle Journée, ou le Mariage de Figaro*, 1784, on both of which famous operas were based, by Rossini and Mozart respectively. The central character in each comedy is the comic barber Figaro, a character in whom elements of the COMMEDIA DELL'ARTE, which had already been used by MOLIÈRE, are perfectly integrated with French sensibility. Figaro is a mouthpiece for biting attacks on the aristocracy and their privileges, criticizing society as a whole, and B.'s plays consequently suffered from censorship. These two comedies remain valid through his masterly and relaxed use of the theatrical techniques of FARCE, COMEDY and polemical DIALOGUE. With his later sentimental play *L'Autre Tartuffe, ou La Mère coupable*, 1792, B. completed a Figaro TRILOGY.
Bibl: C. Fox, THE REAL FIGARO, 1962

Beaumont, Francis (*c.* 1584–1616), English playwright, with a special talent for dramatic craftsmanship. His name is generally associated with FLETCHER, who was the more imaginative and practically gifted of the two. They worked together from *c.* 1608, writing theatrically effective plays. Although there are 53 plays in the *Collected Works of Beaumont and Fletcher*, published 1647 and 1679, probably no more than 6–12 of these were actually written in collaboration. The rest are now attributed to Fletcher working with other writers, e.g. MASSINGER, JONSON, TOURNEUR, MIDDLETON, etc. Attributed to Beaumont alone are several plays, including *The Woman Hater*, 1606, and most of *The Knight of the Burning Pestle*, 1607, but his best works derive from his partnership with Fletcher, e.g. *Philaster*, *A King and No King*, 1611, *The Maid's Tragedy*, written *c.* 1608–11.
Bibl: E. Waith, THE PATTERN OF TRAGICOMEDY IN BEAUMONT AND FLETCHER, 1952; B. Maxwell, STUDIES IN BEAUMONT, FLETCHER AND MASSINGER, 1940

Beauval (Jean Pitel; *c.* 1635–1709), French actor. With his wife Jeanne Olivier de Bourguignon, known as **Mme Beauval** (*c.* 1648–1720), he joined MOLIÈRE's company in 1670, and appeared in small parts, e.g. Thomas Diafoirus in *Le Malade imaginaire*. Mme B. gained a reputation as an excellent comic actress (she was known for her laughing parts), e.g. as Nicole in Molière's *Le Bourgeois gentilhomme* and Zerbinette in *Les Fourberies de Scapin*. After Molière's death in 1673 they went to the HÔTEL DE BOURGOGNE, where Mme B. also appeared in tragic parts, e.g. in RACINE's *Phèdre* as the confidant, Œnone. Later they both became members of the COMÉDIE-FRANÇAISE, and retired in 1704.
Bibl: A. Copin, HISTOIRE DES COMÉDIENS DE LA TROUPE DE MOLIÈRE, 1886

Becher, Johannes R. (1891–1958), German dramatist and poet. In his early youth he was a leading German Expressionist writer. He emigrated to the USSR in 1933 and after his return to East Germany served there 1954–58 as Minister of Culture. His most important play *Winterschlacht* (Winter Battle), fp Prague 1952; Leipzig 1954; dir BRECHT for the BERLINER ENSEMBLE, 1955, deals with an episode during Hitler's invasion of the USSR.

Beck, Julian ▷LIVING THEATRE.

Becker, Maria (1920–), German actress. From 1938 mainly at the ZURICH SCHAUSPIELHAUS, then the BURGTHEATER, Vienna, Hamburg Schauspielhaus and Schlossparktheater, BERLIN. Since 1960, with her husband Robert Freytag and QUADFLIEG, she has managed a touring company, Die Schauspieltruppe. Among her famous parts: Lady Macbeth; title roles in SHAW's *Saint Joan* and SOPHOCLES' *Antigone*; Elizabeth in SCHILLER's *Maria Stuart*; Electra in SARTRE's *Les Mouches*; Martha in ALBEE's *Who's Afraid of Virginia Woolf?*, and Irma in GENET's *Le Balcon*.

Beckett, Samuel (1906–), Irish writer and playwright. He has written many of his most important works in French. After studying Romance languages at Trinity College, Dublin, he resigned his post as a lecturer there and, following a period of wanderings through Europe, settled in Paris in 1937, where he befriended JOYCE. During the war he remained, as a neutral Eire citizen, in Occupied France and belonged to a resistance group in Paris. In 1942, on receiving news that members of the group had been arrested, he fled to Unoccupied France where he lived in hiding as an agricultural labourer in the Vaucluse. After the liberation he briefly returned to Ireland, and went back to France in the autumn of 1945. In a period of intense creativity 1946–47 he wrote an unpublished play *Eleutheria* and *En attendant Godot* (*Waiting for Godot*), his most famous play, as well as a TRILOGY of prose narratives (*Molloy*, *Malone meurt*, *L'Innommable*). *En attendant Godot* was first performed in Paris in 1953, dir BLIN. After initial resistance it broke through and became a success. It was produced at the Arts Theatre, London

1955, by HALL and opened in the USA, Miami 1956, dir SCHNEIDER, before coming to BROADWAY. B.'s other dramatic works: *Fin de Partie* (*Endgame*), fp in the original French at the ROYAL COURT THEATRE, London 1957, dir Blin; *Krapp's Last Tape*, fp London 1958; *Embers*, radio play, fp BBC Third Programme, 1959; *Happy Days*, fp New York 1961, dir Schneider; *Play*, fp in German, Ulm 1963, in the original English, New York 1964, London, 1964 NATIONAL THEATRE; *Breath* (short sketch lasting less than a minute), fp as opening sketch of the revue *Oh! Calcutta!*, New York 1969; *Not I*, fp New York 1972, London 1973.

B.'s dramatic work is characterized by the extreme concreteness of the poetic metaphors he puts on the stage: each of his plays is, above all, an image: an empty road on which two men wait for an appointment with someone who may or may not come becomes an image of man's hoping to discover the purpose of his existence on earth. That is the intensely graphic image of *Waiting for Godot*; in *Endgame* blind Hamm sitting motionless, Clov restlessly moving about unable to sit and the parents stuffed into dustbins give an image of the interdependence of human beings on each other and at the same time may be an allegory of the split mind of a single individual about to die; Krapp listening to the tapes of his own voice without recognizing his former self. Both in English and in French (and he usually translates his own works from the language in which he wrote them into his second language) he is a supreme stylist with an incomparable mastery of form, e.g. the two parallel, symmetrical acts of *Waiting for Godot*; he is always striving for the utmost compression of content, by reducing the action and characters to the essentials and omitting all inessential features (thus his characters mostly lack a social status, a past history) and by restricting his style to the utmost economy of expression. Hence the increasing brevity of many of his dramatic works. He was awarded the Nobel Prize for Literature in 1969.

Bibl: H. Kenner, A READER'S GUIDE TO SAMUEL BECKETT, 1973; M. Esslin, THE THEATRE OF THE ABSURD, 2/1968, and SAMUEL BECKETT, A COLLECTION OF CRITICAL ESSAYS, 1965

Becque, Henry (1837–99), French dramatist. One of the most important exponents of naturalistic drama in France following in the tradition of ZOLA. B. portrays and parodies the immorality of bourgeois life in Paris. His technique was to present characters and events realistically and without comment. His main plays are: *Les Corbeaux*, 1882, and *La Parisienne*, 1885. Among his other dramatic works are: *Sardanapale*, 1867; LIBRETTO for *L'Enfant prodigue*, 1868, composer Victorin Joncières; *Michel Pauper*, 1870; *L'Enlèvement*, 1871; *La Navette*, 1878; *Les Honnêtes femmes*, 1880; *Les Polichinelles* (unfinished) and a one-act play *Le Départ*, pub. posthumously, 1924.

Bibl: S. M. Waxman, ANTOINE AND

Beaumarchais's *Le Mariage de Figaro*, lithograph by Fragonard, 1784

Lilian Baylis, crayon drawing by Sir William Rothenstein

Samuel Beckett's *Endgame*, London, with Patrick Magee and Jack MacGowran

THE THÉÂTRE LIBRE, 2/1964; A. Descotes, 1962

Beer-Hofmann, Richard (1866–1945), Austrian poet and playwright. He was a friend of HOFMANNSTHAL and SCHNITZLER. Among his sensitively poetic VERSE DRAMAS: *Der Graf von Charolais*; an adaptation of an English Elizabethan TRAGEDY, *The Fatal Dowry* by MASSINGER and FIELD, 1905; *Jaakobs Traum* (Jacob's Dream), 1919.

Beerbohm, Sir Max (1872–1956), English essayist and caricaturist. One of the finest writers of his generation, he was also famous as a drama critic. He was a half-brother of Sir Herbert Beerbohm-Tree (▷TREE). Succeeded SHAW as drama critic for the *Saturday Review*, 1898–1910; Shaw called him 'the incomparable Max'. He enjoyed both serious drama and MUSIC HALL entertainment; with his intuitive grasp he helped to establish dramatic criticism as a distinct journalistic form. He was also well known for his caricatures of famous artists and politicians. His criticism was collected in *Around Theatres*, 1924. His dramatic works were of minor importance: *The Happy Hypocrite*, fp 1900, Royalty Theatre, staged by MRS PATRICK CAMPBELL; *A Social Success*, fp 1913, Palace Theatre; ALEXANDER's first music hall appearance, *The Fly on the Wheel*, 1902, written with Murray Carson.

Behan, Brendan (1923–64), Irish dramatist. Member of a family of rebellious nationalists, he joined the Irish Republican Army at 16. He was sent to Borstal for three years for his part in attempting to blow up a British warship. Back in Dublin, he was sent to prison for 14 years for political activities, but released after six years in the 1946 general amnesty. He began his career as a journalist. His earliest play *The Quare Fellow*, Dublin 1954, portrays with humour the crudities of everyday life in prison, and was followed by *The Hostage*, described by TYNAN as 'a COMMEDIA DELL' ARTE of the 20th century', a bitter, ironic close-up of working-class life in Ireland. Both plays achieved success in productions by JOAN LITTLEWOOD at her Theatre Workshop, the first in 1956, the second in 1958, the production emphasizing in music-hall technique his use of song and dance, interspersed with DIALOGUE directed at the audience. His other works include the radio drama, *The Big House*, 1958, and *Borstal Boy*, an autobiography which was performed in a dramatized version at the ABBEY THEATRE, Dublin, 1967.
Bibl: D. Behan, MY BROTHER BRENDAN, 1965; J. R. Taylor, ANGER AND AFTER, 1963

Behn, Mrs Aphra (1640–89), English dramatist, poet and novelist. The first English woman to write professionally for the theatre; a friend of other prominent writers of her time, e.g. OTWAY, DRYDEN and SOUTHERNE. She wrote numerous witty, theatrically effective plays, especially comedies of intrigue, which were frivolous and salacious, in keeping with the fashion of her time. Her most successful play was *The Rover, or, the Banished Cavaliers*, 1677. Other works include: *The Forced Marriage, or, the Jealous Bridegroom*, 1670; *The Feign'd Curtizans, or, a Night's Intrigue*, 1679; *The Roundhead, or, the Good Old Cause*, 1681; *The City-Heiress, or, Sir Timothy Treat-All*, 1682; *The Emperor of the Moon*, 1687, one of the earliest examples of English PANTOMIME.
Bibl: G. Woodcock, 1948

Behrman, Samuel Nathaniel (1893–1973), US playwright. Pupil of BAKER and member of the PLAYWRIGHTS' COMPANY, he wrote a large number of successful BROADWAY plays. Much of his best original work appeared during the twelve years preceding World War II, including *The Second Man*, 1927, with the LUNTS; *Biography*, with INA CLAIRE, 1932; *Rain from Heaven*, with JANE COWL, 1934. A craftsman, he wrote witty DIALOGUE and provided splendid parts for star actors. He became increasingly concerned with the contemporary social problems, such as the rise of Fascism, and began injecting serious ideas into his highly entertaining DRAWING-ROOM COMEDIES, though they tended to remain subservient to the main comic theme. His most important and successful play, *No Time for Comedy*, 1939, starring KATHARINE CORNELL and OLIVIER, described the dilemma of a playwright who had to decide whether to continue writing slick comedies or compose more serious drama appropriate to the age, e.g. to concern himself with the fate of Loyalist Spain.
Behrman's development as a significant original playwright was not fully realized and he began increasingly to turn out adaptations and translations of other people's original work, brilliantly done nevertheless. In 1937 he wrote *Amphitryon 38*, based on GIRAUDOUX; in 1944 *Jacobowsky and the Colonel*, based on WERFEL; in 1946 *Jane*, based on MAUGHAM, and in 1954 *Fanny* a musical, with songs with Harold Rome, based on the PAGNOL trilogy.
Bibl: Joseph Wood Krutch, THE AMERICAN DRAMA SINCE 1918, 1957. Gerald Rabkin, DRAMA AND COMMITMENT, 1964

Béjart. French family of actors in the 17th century. Children of Joseph B. and Marie Hervé: (1) **Marie-Madeleine B.** (1618–72), who was MOLIÈRE's mistress, created the parts of many young girls in his plays, e.g. Lisette in *L'Ecole des femmes*, Mlle Béjart in *L'Impromptu de Versailles*, Frosine in *L'Avare*, Dorine in *Tartuffe*. Her brothers (2) **Joseph B.** (1616/17–59) and (3) **Louis B.** (nicknamed L'Eguisé; 1630–78), and her sister (4) **Geneviève B.** (called Mlle Hervé; 1624–75) also belonged to Molière's company. (5) **Armande B.** (1642–1700), whom Molière married, may also have been a sister of Marie-Madeleine B., or perhaps her daughter. When Molière married her in 1662 the actor Montfleury accused him of having relations with his mistress's daughter. The marriage was unhappy. After Molière's death Armande B. married the actor Guérin d'Estriche. Armande played the parts of the first ingénue in Molière's plays: Elise in *La Critique de l'Ecole des femmes*, Mlle Molière in *L'Impromptu de Versailles*, Célimène in *Le Misanthrope*, Elmire in *Tartuffe*, Alcmène in *Amphitryon*, Elise in *L'Avare*, Angélique in *George Dandin*, Lucile in *Le Bourgeois gentilhomme*, Hyacinthe in *Les Fourberies de Scapin*, Henriette in *Les Femmes savantes*, Angélique in *Le Malade imaginaire*. She was a brilliant, energetic, perhaps somewhat cold actress. After her husband's death she presided over the company with considerable ability. Joined the COMÉDIE-FRANÇAISE in 1680, retired from the stage in 1694.
Bibl: F. Hillemacher, GALERIE HISTORIQUE DES PORTRAITS DES COMÉDIENS DE LA TROUPE DE MOLIÈRE, 1869

Béjart, Maurice (1927–), French dancer and choreographer. Important advocate and representative of modern free dance compositions, he founded the Ballet de l'Etoile with Jean Laurent and created the first example of the new style with *La Symphonie pour un homme seul* with musique concrète by P. Schaefer and P. Henry; he also collaborated with Michèle Seigneuret. He became internationally successful with *Le Sacre du printemps*, music Stravinsky, for the THÉÂTRE DES NATIONS on the occasion of the World's Fair in Brussels, 1959. In 1960 he was appointed director of the Théâtre de la Monnaie in Brussels and went on tour with the Ballet du XXe siècle, a new company which emerged from there. He aimed at total theatre combining text, music, dance and spectacular crowd scenes: *La Douceur de tonnerre*, music Duke Ellington; *Divertimento*, 1961; *Les sept péchés capitaux de la petite-bourgeoisie*, 1961, libretto BRECHT, music WEILL; *Boléro*, 1961, music Ravel; *Neuvième symphonie de Beethoven*, 1964; *Roméo et Juliette*, Brussels 1967; *A la recherche de . . .*, Avignon 1968, which was strongly influenced by the music and movement of the East. He also produced Offenbach's *Tales of Hoffmann* and Lehár's *The Merry Widow* in Brussels.

Belasco, David (1853–1931), US producer, ACTOR-MANAGER and dramatist. Originating from a Portuguese-Jewish family of actors, he was a child actor with touring companies (appeared with KEAN in *Richard III*, 1864), later became a director and author. Adapted and dramatized foreign plays, novels, short stories (mostly in collaboration with other writers) according to the theatre practice of his time, aiming at a theatre of illusion and effect. He discovered and managed stars like WARFIELD, ARLISS, Blanche Bates, etc. However, he showed little understanding for the new movements which developed in the last ten years of his life. He is best known for the extreme realism of his productions and as a director of action-filled plays. He wrote his first play *Chums* (retitled *Hearts of Oak*, written in collaboration with James A. Herne) in 1879 while still in San Francisco where he had worked as an actor and stage manager. In 1882 he went to New York and in 1884 became manager of the Madison Square Theatre where his most popular play to be produced was *May Blossom*. In

1886 he became a partner of D. FROHMAN at the Lyceum Theatre and in 1890 left to become an independent producer. By 1900 he had become a major force in American theatre. Between 1887 and 1890 he collaborated with Henry C. De Mille (father of Cecil B. De M.) on four successful plays: *The Wife*, *Lord Chumley*, *Charity Ball* and *Men and Women*. He made his real breakthrough as a dramatist with *The Girl I Left Behind Me* in 1893, written with Franklyn Fyles for the opening of the Empire Theatre and with *Heart of Maryland* (with M. BARRYMORE), 1895, a melodrama about the American Civil War. Two of his plays, *Madame Butterfly*, 1900, written with John Luther Long, and *The Girl of the Golden West*, 1905, were used by Puccini as LIBRETTI for his operas. Other dramatic works include: *The Darling of the Gods*, 1902; *Adrea*, 1904, and *The Return of Peter Grimm*, 1911. In 1901 he bought the Republic Theatre and in 1906 built a new theatre, first known as the Stuyvesant and renamed the Belasco in 1910.
Bibl: W. Winter, THE LIFE OF DAVID BELASCO, 1916

Bel Geddes, Norman (1893–1958), US stage designer. A follower of CRAIG and APPIA, he reproduced the interior of a Gothic cathedral for REINHARDT's New York production of *The Miracle* in 1924. Best known for his abstract style of design; bold use of space and of staircases constructed in simple geometrical shapes, and use of lighting to achieve atmospheric effects; e.g. *Arabesque*, 1925; *Lysistrata*, 1930; *Hamlet*, 1931; *Dead End*, 1935. His tendency to use monumental scenery was seen in his film sets for De Mille, the costumes and designs for Sonja Henie's ice revues and his designs (unrealized) for a spectacular production of Dante's *Divine Comedy*, 1921, involving a specially constructed AMPHITHEATRE. His daughter **Barbara B. G.** is a well-known actress.
Bibl: M. Gorelik, NEW THEATRES FOR OLD, 1947

Belgium. The theatrical activity of the French-speaking part of the country was and still is modelled after the Paris theatre, while in the Flemish region it follows the example of the theatre in the NETHERLANDS. In Brussels there exist two theatres with a long tradition: the Théâtre Royal de la Monnaie, since 1700 used mainly for opera, and the Théâtre Royal du Parc, since 1782 used for drama. One of the greatest Belgian dramatists emerged around the turn of the century, MAETERLINCK (1862–1949), whose works became known in Paris and all over the world; at that time in Brussels a great number of small theatres with a literary orientation were formed. Since 1934, influenced by the ideas of COPEAU, the Comédiens Routiers have toured the country, presenting classical works and plays of the Middle Ages. During the German occupation, their production of *Les Quatre Fils Aymon* was perceived as an expression of resistance. The director of the company, Jacques Huisman, became director of the newly formed NATIONAL THEATRE in 1945, which performs in Brussels in French and tours the country with its own literary and versatile REPERTOIRE.
The Flemish region has been campaigning since the 19th century for its own language. After 1919 Het Vlaamsche Volkstooneel was founded by Oskar de Gruyter, under the direction of Johan de Meester; it was strongly influenced by Russian CONSTRUCTIVISM, notably in Pol de Mont's *Reineke Vos* and VONDEL's *Lucifer*. The most important Flemish dramatist since 1945 is CLAUS, who has made his career in the Netherlands.
Bibl: S. Lilar, THE BELGIAN THEATRE SINCE 1890, 1957

Belinskii, Vissarion Grigorevich (1811–48), leading Russian critic of the time. In 1841 he introduced his ideas of social criticism through literary criticism. In 1848 in a celebrated letter to GOGOL he announced his disillusionment with the writers whom he had admired.

Bell, Marie (Marie-Jeanne Belon; 1900–), French actress. Made her début in 1921 in AUGIER's *L'Aventurière* at the COMÉDIE-FRANÇAISE, which was, however, not as successful as her appearance as Angélique in MOLIÈRE's *Le Malade imaginaire* later the same year. She played Célimène in Molière's *Le Misanthrope* and appeared in the world première of COCTEAU's *Renaud et Armide*, CF, 1943; also in CLAUDEL's *Le Soulier de satin*; but her most impressive performances were in tragic parts, e.g. title roles in RACINE's *Esther* and *Phèdre* (1942 in a new production by BARRAULT). A SOCIÉTAIRE in 1928; she left to manage the Théâtre des Ambassadeurs in 1934, returning to the CF as an honorary member. She has also appeared in films, notably *Carnet de Bal*.

Bellerose (Pierre Le Messier; *c.* 1592–1670), French actor. Came to Paris in 1622 and joined the Comédiens du Roi who played at the HÔTEL DE BOURGOGNE until the COMÉDIE-FRANÇAISE was founded in 1673. Unlike his declamatory rival MONTDORY, B.'s style of acting was restrained and thoughtful. His most famous performance was the title part in CORNEILLE's *Le Menteur*, 1643, for which play RICHELIEU provided him with a valuable costume. Because of his elegance and good manners, he was considered the most accomplished actor of his time, though his enemies dismissed him as sentimental and boring. His wife **Nicole Gassot**, known as **Mlle B.** (d. 1680) was an excellent tragedienne; she probably created the title role in Corneille's *Rodogune*.
Bibl: G. Mongrédien, LES GRANDS COMÉDIENS DU XVIIe SIÈCLE, 1927

Bellotti-Bon, Luigi (1820–83), Italian actor and manager. Son of Luigi Bellotti and Luigia Ristori, trained by the actor F. A. Bon, from 1845 by MODENA. In 1854 he joined the Compagnia Reale Sarda which included ADELAIDE RISTORI and E. ROSSI. In 1859 he founded his own company of outstanding actors, encouraging many young dramatists; he was an influential luminary of the Italian theatre for about

Armande Béjart in *Psyche*, 1671, a *tragédie-ballet* by MOLIÈRE, CORNEILLE and Quinault, music by Lully

Marie Bell and Aimé Clarioud in CLAUDEL's *Le Soulier de satin*, COMÉDIE-FRANÇAISE, 1943

ten years. On the basis of this success the company was split into three groups in 1873; however he soon overreached himself financially, running into debt which led to his suicide.
Bibl: E. Montazio, 1965

Bema. In the Greek theatre name given to the speaker's platform, when the theatre was used for political assemblies. Later the term was identified with the stage itself, which was low and broad and often protected by a movable balustrade; sometimes also the PROSCENIUM.

Benavente, Jacinte (1866–1954), Spanish dramatist. Leading writer of the first quarter of the 20th century, he was the author of about 200 plays; in 1909, with the actor Porredón, he founded a children's theatre for which he also wrote plays, e.g. *El principe que todo lo apprendió en los libros* (The Prince who learned everything out of books), 1909. He managed the Spanish National Theatre for a short period from 1920. In 1922 he was awarded the Nobel Prize for Literature. His best-known play, which was also produced in other countries, *Los intereses creados* (*The Bonds of Interest*), 1908, was based on the convention of the COMMEDIA DELL'ARTE. It was the first play to be produced by the American THEATRE GUILD in 1919. Among his other important works: *Señora ama*, 1908; *El marido de la Téllez* (The Husband of Téllez), 1897; *La malquerida* (The Passion Flower), 1913; *Más fuerte que el amor* (More Force than Love), 1906. His plays were studies of contemporary society ironically exposing its follies and vices; he also translated several plays by SHAKESPEARE and MOLIÈRE.
Bibl: S. Cordoba, 1959

Bennett, (Enoch) Arnold (1867–1931), English novelist and dramatist. His reputation is based more on his novels, which are realistic accounts of life in industrial England, well constructed with vividly drawn characters, than on his dramatic writing though several of his plays were very successful on the stage, e.g. *Milestones*, written with KNOBLOCK, 1911, fp at the Royalty Theatre in 1912 where it ran for 607 performances, revived in 1920, and at the Yvonne Arnaud Theatre, Guildford, in 1965; *The Great Adventure*, 1913, based on his novel *Buried Alive*. His other plays include: *Cupid and Commonsense*, 1908; *The Honeymoon*, 1911; *London Life*, 1924, and *Mr Prohack*, 1927, also with Knoblock.
Bibl: J. G. Hepburn, THE ART OF ARNOLD BENNETT, 1963

Bennett, Richard (1873–1944), US actor and producer. Among plays that he acted in were RICE's *For the Defense*, 1919; O'NEILL's *Beyond the Horizon*, 1919, which he helped to produce; THEATRE GUILD productions such as *He Who Gets Slapped* by ANDREYEV; S. HOWARD's *They Knew What They Wanted*, 1924, and *Winterset*, 1935, by M. ANDERSON, with MEREDITH and Margo. His three daughters, Barbara, Constance and Joan became well known as film actresses.

Benois, Alexandre (1870–1960), Russian painter and critic, who also wrote LIBRETTI for ballets and was a stage designer of prime importance. From 1898 he worked with Diaghilev and BAKST on their magazine *The World of Art* which was the focal point for a group of painters and musicians. In 1901 he did his first design for the ballet *Sylvia* at the Maryinsky Theatre, Leningrad. For the first seasons of the Ballets Russes in Paris he designed many productions including *Pavillon d'Armide*, 1907; *Giselle*, 1910; *Petrushka*, 1911. His use of colour, derived from Russian folklore, avoided the contemporary preoccupation with Art Nouveau. He emigrated to Paris in 1924, and also worked at La Scala, Milan, and in London and New York. He was a great-uncle of USTINOV. His son **Nicola B.** (1901–) also works as a stage designer, much influenced by his father's style, mainly at La Scala.

Benson, Frank (Sir Francis Robert B.; 1858–1939), English ACTOR-MANAGER. Knighted in 1916. After his early success as a leading member of the OUDS, made his professional stage début in 1882 in IRVING's company at the Lyceum. He formed his own company in 1883 and went on tour through the provinces producing nearly all of SHAKESPEARE's plays, and also gave seasons in London, in 1889–90, at the Globe Theatre, and in 1916 on the occasion of the Shakespeare tercentenary celebrations at DRURY LANE. From 1886 to 1919 director of the Shakespeare Memorial Theatre in STRATFORD-UPON-AVON. Though not an outstanding actor himself, he was talented in discovering and training young actors and might be called the founder of ENSEMBLE playing in the English theatre.

Bentley, Eric (1916–), English-born US theatre critic and director. Educated at Oxford and Yale, a lecturer at various colleges, he first became known through his book *The Playwright as Thinker*, 1949, a series of essays on the trends of 20th-century drama. In 1948 he travelled through Europe: guest director at the ABBEY THEATRE, Dublin; Municipal Theatre in Zurich; Teatro Universitario, Padua; assisted BRECHT with his Munich production of *Mutter Courage* in 1950. Drama critic of *Harper's* magazine in the 1940s and of the *New Republic*, 1952–62; 1954–70 Professor of Drama and Literature at Columbia University, New York. In 1957 he directed Brecht's *The Good Woman of Setzuan* (Phoenix Theatre, New York). He has a high reputation for his translations of Brecht, whose principal spokesman and advocate he has been in the USA; he has also translated PIRANDELLO.

Beolco, Angelo ▷RUZANTE.

Bérain, Jean (1637–1711), French designer. Worked first at the Paris Opéra from 1674 as creator of court spectacles for the king; mainly designed for works by Lully. His style influenced the interior design and furniture of his period; he was specially important in developing the High Baroque style of stage COSTUME.
Bibl: P. Sonrel, TRAITÉ DE SCÉNOGRAPHIE, 1943

Bérard, Christian (1902–49), French stage designer. One of the most outstanding and influential designers of the modern theatre in France. His sets were light, graceful and airy; his designs for MOLIÈRE's plays recreated the Baroque stage forms with their use of light, shape and colour. He attracted attention through his work with BARRAULT and JOUVET, especially with his designs for the latter's productions of COCTEAU's *La Voix humaine*, 1930, and *La Machine infernale*, 1934; Molière's *L'Ecole des femmes*, 1936; GIRAUDOUX's *La Folle de Chaillot*, 1945, and Molière's *Dom Juan*, 1947. For the Compagnie Renaud-Barrault he designed: Giraudoux's *Amphitryon 38*, 1947; Molière's *Les Fourberies de Scapin*, 1949, dir Jouvet. He was associated with most of the famous choreographers of his time, e.g. Lifar, Massine, Lichine and Petit.

Bergman, Hjalmar (1883–1931), Swedish novelist and dramatist. Influenced by STRINDBERG, IBSEN and MAETERLINCK, his first play *Maria, Jesu moder* (Mary Mother of Jesus), pub 1905, was unsuccessful but he gained critical acclaim for his Maeterlinckian dramas *Det underbara leendet* (The Wonderful Smile), 1907, and the *Marionettspel* (Marionette plays): *Herr Sleeman kommer* (Mr Sleeman is coming), *Dödens Arlekin* (Death's Harlequin), pub 1917. His most important work is the comedy *Swedenhielms* (The Swedenhielms), 1925, fp England 1960 by the BIRMINGHAM REPERTORY THEATRE as *The Family First* (in the USA as *The Nobel Prize*). Other plays include the Expressionist works: *Ett experiment* (An Experiment), 1918, and three short plays *Vävaren i Bagdad* (The Weaver of Baghdad); *Spelhuset* (The Gaming House), and *Porten* (The Doorway); the comedy *Patrasket* (The Rabble), 1928; dramatizations of his novels; *Markurells i Wadköping*, 1910, as the play *God's Orchid*, 1929, and *Hans nåds testamente*, 1910, as the play *His Grace's Last Testament*, 1931.
Bibl: R. G. Berg, 1949

Bergman, Ingmar (1918–), Swedish director. In his tendency towards deep psychological interpretations and extreme dramatic intensification he follows STRINDBERG. The theatricality of his productions serves to demonstrate the inner motivation and conflict of the characters. He began working in amateur productions; 1940–42 assistant director at the Royal Opera in Stockholm; début as director in 1943 with the light comedy *Hotellrummet* (The Hotel Room) by J. Lochner. In 1944 started writing film scripts; 1946–49 director at the Göteborg Municipal Theatre, where he produced CAMUS's *Caligula*, and T. WILLIAMS's *A Streetcar Named Desire*; since 1950 at the Intimate Theatre, Stockholm: BRECHT's *The Threepenny Opera*, 1950; Malmö Municipal Theatre: PIRANDELLO's *Six Characters in Search of an Author* and STRINDBERG's *The Ghost Sonata*, 1953. 1963–66 director of the Royal Dramatic Theatre, Stockholm: CHEKHOV's *The Sea-*

Alexandre Benois, design for the ballet *Les Noces de Psyché*

Jean Bérain, design for Lully's opera *L'Armide*, 1686

Elisabeth Bergner in *Escape Me Never*, London 1935, by Margaret Kennedy, prod COCHRAN, dir KOMISARJEVSKY

gull, ALBEE's *Who's Afraid of Virginia Woolf?*, IBSEN's *Hedda Gabler* and BÜCHNER's *Woyzeck*, 1969. As a film director he is outstanding; his principal productions include *Wild Strawberries, The Seventh Seal* and *Silence*.

Bergner, Elisabeth (1897–), Austrian actress. She made her stage début in Zurich in 1916 as Rosalind in *As You Like It*, which remained one of her most celebrated parts. Later she worked at theatres in BERLIN, then Vienna and Munich, returning to Berlin in 1922 (Barnowsky-Bühnen, Deutsches-Theater, State Theatre) appearing in STRINDBERG's *Queen Christina*, 1922, and *Miss Julie*, 1923; in SHAKESPEARE as Viola, 1923, and Portia, 1927; Nora in IBSEN's *A Doll's House*; the title role in SHAW's *Saint Joan*, 1924; Nina in O'NEILL's *Strange Interlude*, 1929. She went on tour from 1928. In 1933 she emigrated to England and appeared in *Escape Me Never* by Margaret Kennedy, 1935, and in *The Boy David*, 1936, written for her by BARRIE; then travelled to the USA (successful in M. Vale's *The Two Mrs Carrolls*, which ran for two years). Graceful, slim and boyish-looking, with large dreamy eyes and a soft soulful voice, she epitomized the erotic ideal of Berlin in the 1920s. She appeared in many films, e.g. *Der Geiger von Florenz* (The Violinist of Florence), 1926; *Ariane*, 1931; *Der träumende Mund* (Dreaming Lips), 1932; and after emigrating *As You Like It*, 1936; *Stolen Life*, 1939. In 1973 she appeared in *Catsplay* by Istvan Orkeny, at the Greenwich Theatre.
Bibl: S. Melchinger, SCHAUSPIELER, 1965

Berlin. Essentially its theatre history resembles that of other German cities: in 1787 Friedrich Wilhelm III of Prussia founded a Royal National Theatre, which had its golden era under the direction of IFFLAND (1796–1814) and was characterized by the adoption and cultivation of the Weimar classical style. In the 1830s and 1840s the most popular plays were dialect 'Berlin farces'. With the rapid expansion of the city more and more private theatre buildings emerged. Light entertainment dominated in REPERTORY: French and German BOULEVARD plays, light COMEDY, MELODRAMA, SINGSPIELE, etc.

It was only with the founding of the FREIE BÜHNE in 1889 and subsequently the takeover of the Deutsches-Theater by BRAHM in 1894 that a modern literary theatre began to dominate the scene. Brahm produced IBSEN, G. HAUPTMANN and SCHNITZLER. He managed the Lessingtheater from 1905 to 1912. At the other extreme from his cool, naturalistic theatre was REINHARDT's theatre – Kleines-Theater, 1902; Deutsches-Theater, where he took over the management in 1905 – which, more colourful and theatrical in style, combined symbolic and neo-Romantic elements, reaching its high-point in a series of Shakespearean productions around 1910. Reinhardt at one time managed four theatres: the Deutsches-Theater and the Kammerspiele – his small theatre adjoining, which he opened in 1906 – the Grosses Schauspielhaus and the VOLKSBÜHNE. Other Berlin theatres of the time with a literary emphasis included: Berliner-Theater; Theater in der Königgrätzer Strasse; Komödienhaus, managed by Carl Meinhardt and Rudolf Bernauer; Kleines-Theater managed by BARNOWSKY, 1905–13.

From about 1900 Berlin was not only the political capital but also the theatrical capital of GERMANY. Only an engagement at a Berlin theatre could establish an actor, only a success in Berlin, the reputation of a playwright. A great variety of talent including foreign playwrights (Ibsen, STRINDBERG, GORKY, SHAW, PIRANDELLO) produced a high standard of theatre in Berlin. The last years of World War I saw the first signs of EXPRESSIONISM in Reinhardt's Das Junge Deutschland productions and MARTIN's Die Tribüne productions. The November Revolution in 1918 changed the situation; the Königliches Hoftheater was taken over as a Prussian State theatre by the director JESSNER. His Expressionist productions of classical works exemplified in theatrical terms the mood of the young Republic. Reinhardt divided his attention between Berlin and Vienna. The theatres showed a sudden burst of activity: STAR cult, rapid movement of actors from one theatre to another, founding of commercial combines (the Rotter brothers), crisis in private theatres. But the Berlin theatre of the 1920s reflected and even formulated the life-style of its contemporaries. The productions of PISCATOR incorporated journalistic forms, technical devices and communist polemics. The economic and political crisis, which began in 1929, paralyzed the theatre and eventually commercial theatre collapsed. The Piscator-Bühne was closed down in 1929, and Jessner's rule overthrown. BRECHT (first striking success: *Die Dreigroschenoper* in 1928 at the Theater am Schiffbauerdamm) fell back on work with amateur companies and workers' groups.

Under the Nazi dictatorship the commercial theatre system finally superseded a great number of state-subsidized theatres. The following were appointed as INTENDANT: GRÜNDGENS, State Theatre; HILPERT, Deutsches-Theater; GEORGE, Schillertheater and Eugen Klöpfer, Volksbühne. Classical plays dominated the REPERTOIRE; most important were FEHLING's productions at the State Theatre, and ENGEL's at the Deutsches-Theater which were considered artistic high-points of the time. The Nazi era produced no dramatist of any importance.

In 1944 all theatres were closed down to enable total concentration on the war effort; in 1945 almost all were destroyed or severely damaged. The Deutsches-Theater was preserved and reopened in 1945 with a production of LESSING's *Nathan der Weise* (title role: WEGENER). Under the management of LANGHOFF, 1946–62, and HEINZ, since 1962, it has developed into the National Theatre of East Berlin. Great artistic successes: the productions of BESSON. Worldwide fame was attained in East Berlin, capital of the German Democratic Republic, by Brecht's BERLINER ENSEMBLE, by the Volksbühne and the Maxim Gorky Theater. In West Berlin after 1945 smaller theatres emerged, including the Schlossparktheater in Steglitz and the Hebbel-Theater (manager Martin, stage directors Fehling and KORTNER). In 1951 came the opening of the newly built Schillertheater, the biggest state theatre in West Berlin, under the management of BARLOG. In 1962 the new theatre building of the FREIE VOLKSBÜHNE was opened under the Intendant Piscator, 1962–66.

Bibl: F. Kienzl, DIE BERLINER UND IHR THEATER, 1967; A. Muhr, RUND UM DEN GENDARMENMARKT, 1965; H. Jhering, VON REINHARDT BIS BRECHT, 1961

Berlin, Irving (originally Israel, 'Izzy', Baline; 1888–), Russian-born US composer. One of the most famous composers of American popular music: *Alexander's Ragtime Band* which he wrote in 1911 introduced a new style of 'rag-time' jazz. Like PORTER, he has always himself provided the lyrics to his songs. His stage musicals include *Yip Yip Yaphank*, 1918; *The Cocoanuts*, 1925, produced with the Marx Brothers; *Face the Music*, 1932, and the revue *As Thousands Cheer*, 1933, both with book by M. HART; *Louisiana Purchase*, 1940. International success with *This Is the Army*, 1942; *Annie Get Your Gun* (book: H. and DOROTHY FIELDS), 1946; *Miss Liberty*, with SHERWOOD, 1949, and *Call Me Madam* (book: LINDSAY and CROUSE), 1950

Berliner Ensemble. Founded in 1949 by BRECHT and his wife HELENE WEIGEL as a group within the Deutsches-Theater in East Berlin, it was not until 1954 that they obtained their own premises, the Theater am Schiffbauerdamm (Das Berliner Ensemble am Bertolt Brecht-Platz). It developed a style of production which was to become a model for the performance of Brecht's plays. His aesthetic finesse combined with his precise definition of social and political realities rapidly won him world-wide acclaim: first prize at the THÉÂTRE DES NATIONS in 1954 and 1955. He called on his close collaborators of the 1920s, the designer NEHER, the director ENGEL, the performers Helene Weigel, THERESE GIEHSE, BUSCH and STECKEL, to join the ensemble but he also trained young directors: MONK, BESSON, PALITZSCH and WEKWERTH. After Brecht's death in 1956, the Berliner Ensemble continued its work according to his conception. Their most successful productions were: Brecht's *Der Aufhaltsame Aufstieg des Arturo Ui*, dir Palitzsch/Wekwerth, 1959; Shakespeare/Brecht *Coriolan*, dir Wekwerth/Tenschert, 1964. They first visited London in 1956 with *Mutter Courage, Pauken und Trompeten*, and *Der kaukasische Kreidekreis* at the Palace Theatre. During their second visit in 1965 they appeared at the NATIONAL THEATRE with *Die Dreigroschenoper, Coriolan, Die Tage der Kommune* and *Arturo Ui*. The directorship was entrusted to Ruth Berghaus, wife of the composer DESSAU, after the death of Brecht's widow, but already during her lifetime the Berliner Ensemble was in danger of becoming a mere showcase of a fossilized style. Fewer plays were produced and rehearsal times lengthened, resulting in productions that seemed mainly concerned with structure and form for their own sake, e.g. *Mann ist Mann*, dir Birnbaum, 1967; *Die heilige Johanna der Schlachthöfe*, dir Wekwerth/Tenschert, 1968.

Bibl: M. Wekwerth, NOTATE, 1967; THEATERARBEIT, 1952; ▷BRECHT

Berman, Eugene (1899–), Soviet stage designer. Left the USSR in 1920 and worked in England, Germany and France (*The Threepenny Opera*, Paris, 1937); went to the USA in 1945 where he has worked mainly in ballet and opera, e.g. *Rigoletto*, 1952, and *The Barber of Seville*, 1954, at the Metropolitan Opera.

Bernanos, Georges (1888–1948), French religious novelist. He wrote his only dramatic work, *Dialogues des Carmélites*, in 1948. Originally a film script, it was adapted for the stage by Albert Béguin and performed in 1952, used for an opera by Poulenc and filmed in 1960.

Bernard. (1) **Tristan B.** (1866–1947), French dramatist, novelist and journalist. Writer of innumerable successful light FARCES, satires and COMEDIES in which he proved himself an excellent technical craftsman. In his plays such as *Le Prince charmant, Monsieur Colomat, Le Petit café, Sa Sœur* he depicts human weakness and unheroic failure. Several of his plays have been translated into English, e.g. *Triplepatte*, written with André Godfernaux, adapted by FITCH as *Toddles*, 1905, which was popular in London and New York.

His son (2) **Jean-Jacques B.** (1888–1972), belonged to a group of dramatists who developed the 'theatre of silence' based on the ideas of MAETERLINCK, who advocated a form of spiritual drama which illuminates the unspoken truths behind the spoken words. His main plays, often on the theme of unrequited love, were *Le Voyage à deux*, 1909; *La Joie du sacrifice*, 1912; *Martine*, 1922; *Notre-Dame d'En-Haut*, 1951; *La Route de France*, 1952. Several have been translated into English and seen in New York and London, e.g. *Le Feu qui reprend mal* (*The Sulky Fire*), 1921, and *L'Ame en peine* (*The Unquiet Love*), 1926.

Bibl: ▷H. BERNSTEIN

Bernhardt, Sarah (Henriette Rosine Bernard; 1844–1923), French actress. A legendary actress, one of the most successful of all time. An excellent speaker, she combined perfect elocution with artistic range, added to which she was naturally graceful and slim, seemingly translucent and incorporeal. Her talents were suited to clear expressive acting rather than to emotional parts. In 1862 she made her first appearance in a small part in RACINE's *Iphigénie* at the COMÉDIE-FRANÇAISE, but left there in 1880, because she lacked scope for her creative development. After an unsuccessful attempt to sing in BURLESQUE she attracted attention in Coppée's *Le Passant* in 1869 at the Théâtre de l'Odéon.

The Franco-Prussian War interrupted her career. She then returned to the CF and appeared there in DUMAS *père*'s *Mademoiselle de Belle Isle*, 1872; as Cherubino in BEAUMARCHAIS's *Le Mariage de Figaro*; in Racine's *Andromaque* and *Phèdre*; VOLTAIRE's *Zaïre*; Doña Sol in HUGO's *Hernani*; again left the CF and went on to travel all over the world, giving visiting performances. She first appeared in London in 1879 in *Phèdre*, and in 1881 she first played her greatest role, Marguerite in DUMAS *fils*'s *La Dame aux camélias*. In 1893 she took over the Théâtre de la Renaissance which she renamed the Théâtre Sarah Bernhardt. Her most famous appearances were in SARDOU's *Fédora*, and *La Tosca*; ROSTAND's *L'Aiglon*, MUSSET's *Lorenzaccio* and as Hamlet. Artistically gifted, she was also a painter and sculptress, and wrote poetry and plays.
Bibl: S. Bernhardt, MY DOUBLE LIFE, REMINISCENCES, 2/1968; C. Otis-Skinner, MADAME SARAH, 1968

Bernini, Giovanni Lorenzo (1598–1680), painter, sculptor and one of the most important Italian representatives of European Baroque architecture. Also worked as theatre architect and inventor of STAGE MACHINERY (described by Richard Lascelles in his *Italian voyage*, 1670). He wrote numerous comedies and adaptations.

Bernstein, Henry (1876–1953), French playwright. Successful author of light satirical COMEDIES (some seen on BROADWAY in translation) depicting unscrupulous businessmen and immoral officials. His plays include: *Le Marché*, 1900; *Le Détour*, 1902; *Frère Jacques* (with P. Weber), 1904; *La Rafale*, 1905; *Ses Yeux bleus*, 1906; *Mélo*, 1926; *L'Espoir*, 1934.
Bibl: E. See, LE THÉÂTRE FRANÇAIS CONTEMPORAIN, 1950; B. H. Clark, CONTEMPORARY FRENCH DRAMATISTS, 1916

Bernstein, Leonard (1918–), US conductor and composer. Educated at Harvard and the Curtis Institute of Music, Philadelphia. Has composed scores for ballets and musicals, including *On the Town*, 1944; *Wonderful Town* (based on the book *My Sister Eileen*), 1953; *Candide*, 1956 (successfully revived with alterations 1973); *West Side Story*, 1957, and is a leading symphonic and operatic conductor.

Bertinazzi, Carlo Antonio (known as Carlino or Carlin; 1710–83), Italian actor. The last of the great ARLECCHINI, famous in Italy, he reached his peak in the COMÉDIE-ITALIENNE in Paris, where he made his début in *Arlecchino muto per forza* (Arlecchino forced to be dumb), scenario by RICCOBONI. He was much admired by GOLDONI (as described in his *Mémoires*) and by GARRICK.
Bibl: M. Sand, MASQUES ET BOUFFONS, COMÉDIE-ITALIENNE, 1860

Bertolazzi, Carlo (1870–1916), Italian dramatist. Considered today as the foremost Italian representative of European NATURALISM, he wrote numerous realistic

Berlin, the new Schauspielhaus, designed by SCHINKEL, 1818–24

Berliner Ensemble, premises at the Theater am Schiffbauerdamm

Sarah Bernhardt in HUGO's *Ruy Blas*, 1879

folk dramas, some in the Milanese dialect, including *El Nost' Milan* (Our Milan), 1893 – Part I *La Povera gènte* (The Poor Ones); Part II *I Sciori* (The Rich Ones) – produced by STREHLER for the PICCOLO TEATRO DI MILANO in 1955; also *La Gibigianna* (The Reflection), 1898; *L'Egoista* (The Egoist), 1900; and *Lulu*, 1903.
Bibl: S. Pagani, IL TEATRO MILANESE, 1944

Besekow, Sam (1911–), Danish director. Studied in Germany under PISCATOR and REINHARDT. He worked at the private Riddersalen Theatre in Copenhagen 1938–40: O'NEILL's *The Emperor Jones*, and STEINBECK's *Of Mice and Men*. In 1943 he emigrated to SWEDEN; from 1945 he worked for various theatres in Copenhagen, in Sweden and other countries. He is one of the leading realistic directors in the Scandinavian theatre.

Besson, Benno (1922–), German director. Started in 1949 as assistant director and actor with the BERLINER ENSEMBLE. First production, MOLIÈRE's *Dom Juan*, Rostock 1952, which he produced again in 1954 at the Berliner Ensemble in their adaptation. Other productions there: BRECHT's *Pauken und Trompeten*, 1955, adapted from FARQUHAR's *The Recruiting Officer*, and *Der Gute Mensch von Setzuan*, 1957. In Rostock: Brecht's *Die Tage der Kommune*, fp 1956, dir WEKWERTH; *Mann ist Mann*, 1957. At the Scala, Vienna: JONSON's *Volpone*, 1953, and at the National Theatre, Stuttgart: Brecht's *Die heilige Johanna der Schlachthöfe*, 1961. In 1958 he left the Berliner Ensemble to work in theatres in Rostock, Vienna, Stuttgart, and from 1961 at the Deutsches-Theater in East Berlin, e.g. ARISTOPHANES' *Peace* (adapted by HACKS, 1962); his own adaptation of SHAKESPEARE's *The Two Gentlemen of Verona*, 1963; Molière's *Tartuffe*, 1963; Hacks' adaptation of Offenbach's *La Belle Hélène*, 1964; Hacks' *Moritz Tassow*, fp Berlin 1965, VOLKSBÜHNE; SOPHOCLES' *Oedipus Rex*, Deutsches-Theater, 1967; Molière's *Dom Juan*, Deutsches-Theater, 1968; Brecht's *Turandot oder der Kongress der Weisswäscher*, fp ZURICH SCHAUSPIELHAUS, 1969. Since autumn 1969 he has been artistic director at the Volksbühne in East Berlin. He is Brecht's most important pupil; in his productions he combines extreme precision with imagination and sensuous elegance.
Bibl: A. Müller, DER REGISSEUR, BENNO BESSON, 1967

Betterton, Thomas (1635–1710), leading English actor and director of Restoration theatre (▷RESTORATION DRAMA). Equally famous for tragic and comic parts, his performance as Hamlet was especially praised. He appeared in 1661 with the Duke of York's Servants under DAVENANT at the Lincoln's Inn Fields Theatre; in 1671, after the latter's death, he took over the management of the company, which joined with KILLIGREW's King's Players at the THEATRE ROYAL, DRURY LANE in 1682. In 1695 he left the company and reopened the Lincoln's Inn Fields Theatre. His best parts included Lear, Macbeth, Othello; he also acted in CONGREVE's *Love for Love*, 1695, and in DRYDEN's plays. He adapted Elizabethan and Jacobean plays to Restoration taste, e.g. FLETCHER's *The Prophetess*, which was set to music, in his version, as an opera (*Diocletian*) with music by Purcell. His wife **Mrs Mary B.** (*née* Sanderson; d. 1712) became famous playing Ianthe in Davenant's *The Siege of Rhodes* at Lincoln's Inn Fields, and was among the first actresses to appear in SHAKESPEARE's plays, e.g. as Juliet, Ophelia, Lady Macbeth. She is buried in Westminster Abbey.
Bibl: A. Nicoll, A HISTORY OF ENGLISH DRAMA, I/1952

Betti, Ugo (1892–1953), Italian poet and playwright. A lawyer by profession, he became a judge in 1930, and went to Rome in 1931 where he was attached to the court of appeals until his death. The structure of many of his plays resembles a law case with an investigation during which an attempt is made to determine the causes of an incident; eventually it is society as a whole and the conditions of human existence which are shown to be responsible. The best example is *Corruzione al Palazzo di giustizia* (Corruption at the Palace of Justice), 1949. Among his other important works: *Un Albergo sul porto* (A Hotel by the Harbour), 1930; *Frana allo Scalo Nord* (Landslide at North Station), 1932; *Ispezione* (The Inquiry), 1942; *Irene innocente* (Innocent Irene), 1946; *La Regina e gli insorti* (*The Queen and the Rebels*), 1949, *L'Aiuola bruciata* (*The Burnt Flower-bed*), produced posthumously in 1953.
Bibl: E. Barbetti, IL TEATRO DI UGO BETTI, 1943

Betty, William Henry West (1791–1874), English actor. At the age of 12 he was a child prodigy, known as the Young Roscius and a favourite with the public in London during the season 1804–05. Later he appeared in all the great Shakespearean roles including Hamlet at DRURY LANE. His success was short-lived and ended with his performance as Richard III, when he was hissed off the stage. His later attempts to return to the stage met with no success.
Bibl: G. Playfair, THE PRODIGY: THE STRANGE LIFE OF MASTER BETTY, 1957

Bhāna. Indian erotic monologue – a playlet, in which one character holds a conversation with an imaginary companion. This genre reached its peak in the 16th and 17th centuries.

Biancolelli. Family of actors of the COMMEDIA DELL'ARTE. (1) **Francesco B.** (d. *c.* 1640) married (2) **Isabella Franchini** (d. 1650), daughter of Francesco Franchini, the famous PANTALONE. She was much admired as COLOMBINA. Their son (3) **Giuseppe Domenico** (*c.* 1637–88), known as Dominique, belonged to the Italian troupe of Louis XIV, the Comédiens du Roi, gaining fame as Arlequin (▷ARLECCHINO), a part which he developed by introducing elements of acrobatics and dance. In 1663 Dominique married (4) **Orsola Cortesi** (*c.* 1632–1718) who played under the name of Eularia. Of their eight children three were actors: (5) **Francesca Marie Apolline B.** (1664–1747) known as Isabella, an intelligent player of amorous leading ladies, and (6) **Catarina B.** (d. 1716) known as Colombina, who overshadowed even the reputation of her grandmother in the part (she was often portrayed by Watteau); (7) **Pier Francesco B.** (1680–1734) known as Dominique *fils*, who played Arlequin and PIERROT in the COMÉDIE-ITALIENNE until 1697 and later in RICCOBONI's company.
Bibl: M. Sand, MASQUES ET BOUFFONS, COMÉDIE-ITALIENNE, 1860

Bibbiena (Bernardo Dovizi, known as Il Bibbiena; 1470–1520), Italian poet. Created a cardinal (1513) by Pope Leo X, he wrote only one play, *La Calandria*, freely adapted from PLAUTUS' *Menaechmi* with a sub-plot from Boccaccio. A frivolous comedy in the spirit of the Renaissance, it was first performed at Urbino in 1513, and in 1518 in Rome with décor by PERUZZI.
Bibl: G. L. Moncallero, 1953

Bidermann, Jakob (1578–1639), leading exponent of German JESUIT DRAMA written in Latin. His play *Cenodoxus*, written 1600, fp Munich 1609; new adaptation by H. Rommel, 1932, which shows a scholar who like Faust has to choose between Heaven and Hell, transcends the mere external spectacle of most of the German and Viennese Baroque theatres of his time by its realism and spiritual depth. His plays were collected in *Ludi teatrales sacri*, 1666; reprinted in 2 vols, 1967.
Bibl: D. G. Dyer, 1950; ▷JESUIT DRAMA

Biennale. International theatre festival in Venice, originally held every two years, now every September. Since 1941 the main performances have been held at the Teatro La Fenice.

Bill-Belotserkovsky, Vladimir Naumovich (1885–1970), Soviet dramatist. He came from a working-class background, and went to sea; in 1911 he went to the USA doing odd jobs and returned to Russia in 1917 to play an active part in the October Revolution. From 1921 he wrote heroic plays in praise of Socialism. *Shtorm* (Hurricane) fp 1926 at the Mossoviet Theatre, was a propaganda piece about the struggles of a revolutionary leader. His other works include *Zhiznzovyot* (Life is Calling), 1934, published in England 1938.
Bibl: P. Yershov, COMEDY IN THE SOVIET THEATRE, 1956

Billetdoux, François (1927–), French playwright, journalist, scenario writer, novelist and cabaret performer. Often dir his own plays which combine elements of BOULEVARD THEATRE and THEATRE OF THE ABSURD. His recurring theme is man's desperate search for an impossible love, in plays such as: *A la nuit la nuit*, 1955; *Tchin-Tchin*, 1959; *Va donc chez Törpe*, 1961, dir BOURSEILLER; *Pour Finalie* (one-act play), 1962; *Comment va le monde, môssieu? Il*

tourne, môssieu!, 1964; *Il faut passer par les nuages*, written especially for MADELEINE RENAUD, who played the lead in the world première at the Odéon in 1964, dir BARRAULT, des ALLIO.
Bibl: J. Guicharnaud, MODERN FRENCH THEATRE, 1967

Bio-mechanics. The basic concept behind MEYERHOLD's theory of directing in the theatre: rejecting STANISLAVSKY's concept of emotional authenticity reached through introspection, he demanded that primacy should be given to the efficiency and elegance of the actor's movement: 'A theatre built on psychological foundations is as certain to collapse as a house built on sand. On the other hand a theatre which relies on physical elements is at least assured of clarity. All psychological states are determined by specific physiological processes. By correctly resolving the nature of his state physically, the actor reaches the point where he experiences the excitement which communicates itself to the spectator and induces him to share the actor's performance . . .' Meyerhold, influenced by ideas of work efficiency and research into the economy of movement in sport, postulated a swift, elegant style approximating to ballet. 'A skilled worker at work invariably reminds one of a dancer; thus work borders on art. The spectacle of a man working efficiently affords positive pleasure. This applies equally to the work of the actor . . . The actor of the future will work without make-up and wear an overall, that is, a costume designed to serve as everyday clothing yet equally suited to the movements and concepts which the actor realizes on the stage.'
Bibl: E. Braun (ed), MEYERHOLD ON THEATRE, 1969

Birmingham Repertory Theatre. One of the fountainheads of the repertory movement in Britain. In 1907 JACKSON founded the Pilgrim Players with DRINKWATER, a semi-amateur company which performed plays of artistic worth at local halls. With funds provided by Jackson a permanent home was built for the professional company which emerged from the Pilgrim Players. The theatre was opened in February 1913. In the 1920s and 1930s the Birmingham Rep. was one of the focal points of drama in Britain. It pioneered SHAKESPEARE in modern dress and was the nursery of great acting talents, including AYLMER, HARDWICKE, OLIVIER, RICHARDSON, SCOFIELD, and Gwen Ffrangcon-Davies. The Birmingham company became the nucleus of the Malvern Festival which presented first performances of a number of SHAW's later plays. A new building was opened in 1972.
Bibl: T. C. Kemp, THE BIRMINGHAM REPERTORY THEATRE, 1948

Bjørnson, Bjørnstjerne (1832–1910), Norwegian novelist, poet, journalist and playwright. In his dramatic works he was, like IBSEN, concerned with exploring the moral shortcomings of contemporary society but his plays were more specific and localized, lacking the profundity and direct power of Ibsen. He was director of the theatre in Bergen 1857–63; of the theatre in Christiania (Oslo) 1865–67; and of the Møllergaten Theatre in Christiania 1870–72. He began his dramatic writings with historical and patriotic plays: *Mellem Slagene* (Between the Battles), 1857; *Kong Sverre* (King Sverre), 1861; *Sigurd Slembe* (*Sigurd the Bastard*), 1862; *Maria Stuart i Skotland*, 1864; followed by realistic social dramas, e.g. *Redaktøren* (The Editor), 1874; *En Fallit* (*A Bankruptcy*), 1875; *Det nye System* (*The New System*), 1879. His most interesting plays are psychological dramas, e.g. *Over Ævne I* (Beyond Our Power), 1883, (in London 1901, Royalty Theatre); *Over Ævne II*, 1895, and *Daglannet*, 1904; *Naar den ny Vin blomstrer* (*When the New Wine Blooms*), 1909, and the comedy *Geografi og Kjaerlighed* (Geography and Love). He was the first Scandinavian to be awarded the Nobel Prize for Literature, 1903. His son **Bjørn B.** (1859–1952) was an actor. He was one of the founders of the Norwegian National Theatre (1899–1909 and 1923–27).
Bibl: H. Beyer, A HISTORY OF NORWEGIAN LITERATURE, 1965; H. Larson, 1945

Blackfriars Theatre. One of London's principal theatres in Elizabethan and Jacobean times. From 1576 premises which had formed part of the Blackfriars monastery were used for performances by the CHILDREN OF THE CHAPEL, and later by other children's troupes. Another part of the old monastery was acquired in 1596 by J. BURBAGE who built a roofed theatre there for use in winter when it was impossible to appear in uncovered playhouses elsewhere; SHAKESPEARE, who belonged to Burbage's company, appeared at the Blackfriars Theatre, and from 1609 till the closure of theatres in 1642 it was used by the King's Players.

Blaga, Lucian (1896–1961), Rumanian philosopher, poet and playwright. In his dramatic writing he showed strong elements of EXPRESSIONISM, e.g. *Zamolxe*, a profane mystery play, 1921, and *Avram Iancu*, a historical drama, 1934.
Bib.: H. Stamatu, 1962

Blakemore, Michael (1928–), English director, born in Sydney, Australia. Started his career as an actor in REPERTORY with the Bristol Old Vic and in Birmingham and Coventry. In 1957 he toured Eastern Europe with OLIVIER in *Titus Andronicus* and played again with him in *Coriolanus* at STRATFORD-UPON-AVON in 1959. Co-director with Michael Meacham of the GLASGOW CITIZENS' THEATRE, 1966–68. Productions there included: WEISS's *The Investigation*, HALLIWELL's *Little Malcolm and His Struggle against the Eunuchs*, Hugh Leonard's *Stephen D.*, and BRECHT's *The Visions of Simone Machard* and *Arturo Ui* (which B. also directed at the EDINBURGH FESTIVAL in 1968; transferred 1969 to London); and NICHOLS' *A Day in the Death of Joe Egg*, 1967 (which he directed again in 1968 with FINNEY on BROADWAY). At the NATI-

Thomas Betterton

William Betty, aged 15, as Hamlet, 1804

Giuseppe Biancolelli in the costume of the Dottore of the COMMEDIA DELL'ARTE

ONAL THEATRE he has directed: Nichols' *The National Health*, 1969; O'NEILL's *Long Day's Journey Into Night*, 1972, and HECHT/MacARTHUR's *The Front Page*, 1972.

Blanchard, Pierre (1896–1963), French actor. Successful film career; a nervous and sensitive player recognized specially for his parts as a 'mysterious stranger'. He made his stage début at the Odéon (1919–23), then during the 1920s he distinguished himself in plays like BOURDET's *La Prisonnière*; PAGNOL's *Jazz*, 1925; SALACROU's *L'Inconnue d'Arras*, 1935; ACHARD's *Domino*, 1931. In 1939 he joined the COMÉDIE-FRANÇAISE, playing tragic parts like Oedipus and Julius Caesar. He left the CF in 1946 to appear both on the stage and in films. In the later stages of his career he mainly excelled in light comedy.

Blank verse. An unrhymed iambic pentameter (i.e. line with five beats) which is the metre most frequently used in English VERSE DRAMA. Reproducing the natural beat of English and extremely flexible in use, it is ideally suited for dramatic effect. Through the spread of SHAKESPEARE's influence, blank verse also became the prevailing metre in German and Russian verse drama, while French verse plays are dominated by the rhyming ALEXANDRINE (six iambic feet to the line), and Spanish classical drama by the trochaic tetrameter (four beats to the line).

Blin, Roger (1907–), French director. One of the leading directors of the modern theatre in France (especially of various works of the THEATRE OF THE ABSURD), he is best known for his definitive productions of BECKETT and GENET. Started as assistant director and actor in ARTAUD's *Les Cenci*, 1935. He worked with BARRAULT and as an actor under DULLIN. He managed the Théâtre de la Gaîté, Montparnasse, with Christine Tsingos, 1949–51. Among his most notable productions were: STRINDBERG's *The Ghost Sonata*, BÜCHNER's *Woyzeck*, ADAMOV's *La Parodie*, 1952; world première of Beckett's *En attendant Godot*, in which he played Pozzo, 1953; and *Fin de Partie*, 1957; *La Dernière Bande*, 1959; GENET's *Les Nègres*, 1959; and *Les Paravents*, 1966.
Bibl: J. Genet, LETTRES À ROGER BLIN, 1967

Blok, Alexander (1880–1921), Russian Symbolist poet. His VERSE DRAMAS include *Balaganchik* (The Puppet Show), 1906; and *Roza i krest* (The Rose and the Cross), 1916. The former created a stir in St Petersburg when first produced and B. was attacked as a blasphemer, but others praised the work and it established him as a leading Russian writer. B. served in World War I and supported the 1917 Revolution. In his most famous poem, *Dvenadtsat* (The Twelve), 1918, he depicts twelve workers as though they were the Apostles.
Bibl: F. D. Reeve, 1962

Blumenthal, Oskar (1852–1917), German critic and writer. Founder and manager of the Lessingtheater in BERLIN (1888–97). His light comedy, *Im weissen Rössl*, 1897, which he wrote in collaboration with KADELBURG, achieved international renown; in 1931 it served as the LIBRETTO for the operetta *The White Horse Inn* by Müller and Benatzky.

Bocage (Pierre-Martinien Tousez; 1797–1863), French actor. One of the most important actors of the Romantic period in France. Came to Paris in 1821 and tried twice but unsuccessfully to join the COMÉDIE-FRANÇAISE. He specialized in new drama and MELODRAMA and helped to increase the popularity of the dramatists of the Romantic movement, playing the title role in DUMAS *père*'s *Antony*, fp 1831, and Didier in HUGO's *Marion Delorme*, fp 1831, both at the Gaîté. After travelling in the provinces he became a director of the Odéon in 1845, where he produced George Sand's *Claudie*, 1851, and Dumas *père*'s *Marbier*, 1854. He was a very sensitive and hypnotic actor who was said to look like a Greek god. He became involved in abortive financial speculations and never benefited from his huge successes, dying in poverty at the height of his career.
Bibl: T. Gauthier, HISTOIRE DE L'ART DRAMATIQUE EN FRANCE DEPUIS 25 ANS, 1858–59, 8 vols

Bodel, Jean (or Jehan; second half of the 12th century–1210), French dramatist. With ADAM DE LA HALLE he was one of the pioneers of French secular drama. He wrote the MYSTERY PLAY *Jeu de Saint Nicolas*, performed on the vigil of the saint, 5 December, which included scenes from the Crusades and crude realistic inn sketches.
Bibl: G. Cohen, LE THÉÂTRE EN FRANCE DU MOYEN AGE, 1928

Boguslawski, Woyciech (1757–1829), Polish actor, playwright and theatre manager. A pioneer of the theatre in POLAND; from 1783 to 1814 he managed the National Theatre. He translated *Hamlet* and succeeded with playwrights like LESSING (*Emilia Galotti*) and MOLIÈRE.
Bibl: Z. Krawczykowski, 1954

Boileau-Despréaux, Nicolas (1636–1711), French writer and critic. A friend of MOLIÈRE, RACINE and La Fontaine, he exercised great influence on French literature and drama as a critic. In his theoretical work *Art poétique*, 1674, based on Horace's *Ars poetica*, he defined the rules for poetry which became binding for French classical literature. He regarded TRAGEDY, which should adhere to ARISTOTLE's rules, as the highest form of poetry.
Bibl: E. Magne, 1929

Bois, Curt (1901–), German actor. One of the leading comic performers on the contemporary German stage. He appeared at variety theatres in Germany, Austria, Hungary, Switzerland 1914–21, and in MUSICAL COMEDIES at the Kurfürstendamm Theater, Berlin 1923–25, then went on tour till 1932; emigrated to the USA in 1933, and appeared mainly in Hollywood films; returned to Berlin in 1950, where he joined the Deutsches-Theater as both actor and director, 1950–53. One of his best-known performances was in the title role of BRECHT's *Herr Puntila*, produced by the author at the BERLINER ENSEMBLE.

Boisrobert, François le Métel de, Abbé (1592–1662), French writer and priest. Friend and adviser of RICHELIEU and Mazarin. He played an important role in the creation of the Académie française of which he was one of the first members (1635). He wrote 18 plays of various genres for the stage, which were performed at the Théâtre du Marais and the HÔTEL DE BOURGOGNE. Though his plays are now forgotten, some of his comedies inspired MOLIÈRE to write *L'Avare* and *L'Ecole des maris*.
Bibl: E. Magne, LE PLAISANT ABBÉ BOISROBERT, 1909

Bolshoi Theatre (Russ *bolshoi* = big). USSR national theatre founded in 1774. In Moscow it is used for opera and ballet. The present building, erected in 1856 (rebuilt from a theatre of 1825), is one of the largest theatres in the world: it has five circles and a capacity of 2,000.

Bolt, Robert (1924–), English playwright. Originally a teacher, he started writing radio plays for the BBC in his spare time and in 1957 wrote the stage plays *The Last of the Wine* and *The Critic and the Heart*. His first play to have a successful London production was *The Flowering Cherry* in 1957. He achieved international fame with *A Man for All Seasons*, 1960, an historical play about Sir Thomas More, with SCOFIELD (who also starred in the film version). Subsequent plays: *The Tiger and the Horse*, 1960; *Gentle Jack*, 1963; *The Thwarting of Baron Bolligrew*, 1965, a children's play; *Brother and Sister*, 1967; *Vivat! Vivat Regina!*, fp CHICHESTER FESTIVAL, 1970. His plays, realistic in style and traditional in form, relate modern ideas to a historical context and offer exacting parts for principal actors. He has also written successful screenplays, e.g. *Lawrence of Arabia*, *Dr Zhivago*, *Ryan's Daughter*, and *Lady Caroline Lamb*.

Bond, Edward (1935–), English playwright. Deeply concerned with the violence of modern life, he started with two plays which show the life of people on the lowest social level who are practically inarticulate. With great skill he succeeds in making their emotions and thoughts apparent in *The Pope's Wedding*, 1962, and *Saved*, 1965, which caused an outrage through the scene in which a baby in its pram is killed by hooligans. When he was accused of gratuitous sadism, a number of prominent personalities, including OLIVIER, sprang to his defence, pointing out that the purpose of the scene was the exposure of the inhumanity of social conditions which lead to such brutality. *Early Morning*, 1968, satirizes the Court of Queen Victoria as a scene of preposterous crime. This play also caused a scandal and was banned, but ultimately gave the impetus to the abolition of stage CENSORSHIP in England. Other plays include: *Narrow Road to the Deep North*, 1968; *Black Mass*, 1970; *Passion*, 1971; *Lear*, 1971, a bold retelling of SHAKESPEARE's fable, designed to show the madness of power.

Booth. Anglo-American family of actors, important in US theatre history. (1) **Junius Brutus B.** (1796–1852). After touring the English provinces he made his stage début in London as Richard III, immediately becoming a rival to KEAN; he played Iago opposite Kean's Othello (DRURY LANE, 1817), Edgar to his Lear, etc. In 1821 he went to New York, where he rapidly became one of the leading actors, laying the foundations for the US tradition of tragic acting; his first appearance was in *Richard III* in 1821; later one of his best performances was as Oreste in RACINE's *Andromaque*. He was also manager of several theatres. An alcoholic, he tended to melancholy and religious fanaticism. Of his erratic genius Walt Whitman said: 'Terms like enthusiasm, energy and devotion achieved through him a new creative meaning.' His son (2) **Edwin Thomas B.** (1833–93) was one of the first great American actors who also gained a European reputation. He made his initial appearance when he was 16, then toured AUSTRALIA in 1854 with LAURA KEENE, arriving in London in 1861 where he appeared at the Haymarket Theatre (Shylock, Overreach, Richelieu) without great success. Returning to New York he took over the Winter Garden Theatre in 1863 and managed it until 1867 (a record 100 performances of *Hamlet*). After the theatre burned down he built his own, Booth's Theatre, in 1869, opening the same year with *Romeo and Juliet*. Went bankrupt in 1873, then toured the USA and came to England in 1880 and 1882 (at the Lyceum Theatre, London, where his acting was now highly appreciated), and to Germany in 1883. E.B. was an important interpreter of Shakespearean parts like Lear, Othello, Iago, Shylock, Romeo. His Hamlet ranks as one of the most accomplished interpretations of the role. He was a sensitive and natural actor, outstanding in his use of expressive gesture and movement. His elder brother (3) **Junius Brutus B.** (1821–83), though not an outstanding actor, was an excellent producer and manager, who organized the companies of his father and brother. E.B.'s youngest son (4) **Sydney Barton B.** (1873–1937) made his name on the American stage as a leading actor. E.B.'s younger brother, (5) **John Wilkes B.** (1839–65), assassinated President Lincoln on 14 April 1865 during a performance of Tom Taylor's *Our American Cousin* at Ford's Theatre, Washington, D.C.
Bibl: E. Ruggles, PRINCE OF PLAYERS, 1953; S. Kimmel, THE MAD BOOTHS OF MARYLAND, 1940

Booth, Barton (1681–1733), English ACTOR-MANAGER (no relation to JUNIUS BRUTUS B.). Born into a wealthy family, he first attracted attention as a schoolboy at Westminster. After working in Dublin and the provinces, he was called by BETTER-

Bolshoi Theatre, Moscow

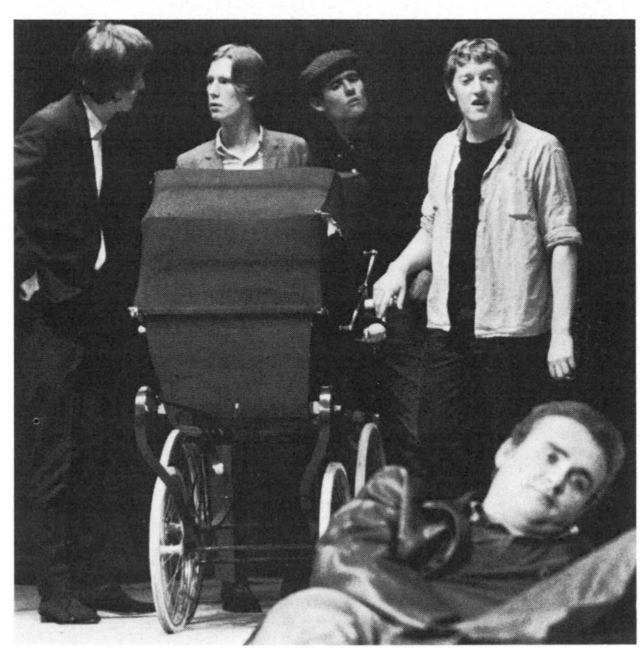

Edward Bond's *Saved*, ROYAL COURT THEATRE, 1965

Pierre Blanchard in *Le Trompeur de Séville*, Paris 1937

TON to the Lincoln's Inn Fields Theatre in 1700; later he moved with the company to the Haymarket Theatre, and in 1708 to DRURY LANE, where he became one of the managers 1713–25. In 1710 he took over the part of Othello from Betterton, but he gained greater success in 1712 as Pyrrhus in *The Distressed Mother* (an adaptation of RACINE's *Andromaque*) and in 1713 with the title role in ADDISON's *Cato*. His most striking qualities in a wide range of tragic roles were his way of moving and his use of the languages of gesture and MIME, particularly in his reactions to the speeches of his fellow actors.

Borboni, Paola (1900–), Italian actress. Made her stage début in 1916; she was the leading actress 1921–29 in Armando Falconi's company, appearing mainly in light comedies. Noted initially for her beauty and eccentricity, she developed a REPERTOIRE of more literary roles, making a breakthrough in 1935 in PIRANDELLO's *Come prima, meglio di prima* (*As Well as Before, Better than Before*) acting with her own company. Subsequently she worked with leading actors and directors in plays ranging from STRINDBERG's *Easter*, 1949, to SHAKESPEARE's *The Merry Wives of Windsor*, 1949. She has also appeared in films.

Borchert, Wolfgang (1921–47), German playwright, poet and novelist, who became known posthumously for his play *Draussen vor der Tür* (The Man Outside), 1947. Originally conceived as a radio play, it was the first outstanding example of post-war German drama; dealing with the topical theme of the homecoming soldier, written in stylized, highly colourful language, reminiscent of EXPRESSIONISM.
Bibl: S. Spender (ed), BORCHERT, THE MAN OUTSIDE, 1952

Borelli. Italian actresses. (1) **Alda B.** (1882–) had a major success in 1903 as Micol in *Saul*, a performance to celebrate the 100th anniversary of ALFIERI's death. In 1920 she appeared in MAETERLINCK's *Monna Vanna*, in 1921 in the title role of *La Dame aux camélias* by DUMAS *fils*, gaining a reputation as an intelligent, sensitive actress. She was with the Compagnia Nazionale 1921–23 together with TALLI and RUGGERI where she gave her best performance in D'ANNUNZIO's *Parisina*, 1921. She retired from the theatre in 1928. (2) **Lyda B.** (1887–), sister of Alda, was one of the leading Italian actresses before World War I. She was admired for her exquisite style and her temperament. Her main parts: WILDE's *Salomé*; S. Benelli's *Gorgana*, 1913; D'ANNUNZIO's *Il Ferro*, 1914. She retired in 1918.

Börne, Ludwig (1786–1837), German journalist. He maintained that the theatre is an indicator of national development and dramatic criticism a vehicle for criticism of both the state and society.

Boucher, François (1703–70), French painter. One of the most important exponents of rococo art. He illustrated the MOLIÈRE edition of 1734; designed sets and costumes for the Opéra in Paris: Lully's *Atys*, 1740; Rameau's *Les Indes galantes*, 1743; Noverre's *Les Fêtes des Chinoises*, 1744. After doing some work at the Opéra Comique, he returned to design for the Opéra 1761–66, e.g. Lully's *Armide*, 1761.

Boucicault, Dion (also Bourcicault or Boursiquot, Dionysius Lardner; 1822–90), Irish-born US dramatist and actor. He worked in England and the USA, where he eventually settled and was associated with the WALLACKS' company. A prolific writer, he is credited with about 150 plays, many of them adaptations from the French and dramatizations of novels. His plays were theatrically very effective, and he appeared in many of them. The best known and most successful were: *London Assurance*, fp COVENT GARDEN THEATRE, 1841, leads played by MATHEWS, MADAME VESTRIS, W. FARREN (a play that has frequently been revived, most recently by the RSC in 1970); *The Corsican Brothers*, London 1852, Princess Theatre; a MELODRAMA about slavery, *The Octoroon; or, Life in Louisiana*, 1859, the first serious play concerned with the American Negro; the Irish comedy *The Colleen Bawn*, 1860, and *Rip Van Winkle*, 1865, with J. JEFFERSON. His other works include: *Louis XI*, 1855; *Jessie Brown*; *Dot* (based on Dickens's *The Cricket on the Hearth*) 1859; *Belle Lamar* (based on the American Civil War), 1874. B. was married twice; his second wife, the English actress **Agnes Kelly Robertson**, became very popular in the USA.
Bibl: A. H. Quinn, A HISTORY OF THE AMERICAN DRAMA, 1945; A. Nicoll, HISTORY OF ENGLISH DRAMA, V/1959

Bouffes-Parisiens. Theatre opened by Jacques Offenbach in Paris in 1855 (Champs-Elysées, Salle Lacaze), mainly for light opera; his most successful production there was *Orphée aux Enfers*. After World War II it became a legitimate theatre.
Bibl: G. Verdot, 1962

Boulevard du Temple ▷NICOLET.

Boulevard theatre. The commercial theatre of Paris, centred in the medium and smaller theatres of the Paris boulevards which sprang up at the turn of the century. They presented, and still present, plays designed for light, pleasant entertainment, usually with a cast built round a STAR actor or actress. Hence the term boulevard theatre is also generally applied to the lighter, commercial, French WELL-MADE PLAY.
Bibl: G. Pillement, ANTHOLOGIE DU THÉÂTRE CONTEMPORAIN, 1946

Bourdet, Edouard (1887–1945), French dramatist and theatre manager. Director of the COMÉDIE-FRANÇAISE 1936–40, he supported modern drama. Using BECQUE as his model he wrote plays dealing with urgent social and moral questions, particularly controversial subjects such as homosexuality in *La Fleur des pois*, 1932, and lesbianism in *La Prisonnière*, 1926. His most important work is his satire *Vient de paraître*, 1927. Famous actors like FRESNAY and ARLETTY appeared in his plays.
Bibl: R. Lalou, LE THÉÂTRE EN FRANCE DEPUIS 1900, 1951; E. See, LE THÉÂTRE FRANÇAIS CONTEMPORAIN, 1950

Bourget, Paul (1852–1935), French writer. Best known for his novels, several of which he turned into thesis plays, some in collaboration with other writers, e.g. *Mensonges*, adaptation with L. Lacour, 1889; *Un Divorce*, adaptation with A. Gury, 1908; *L'Emigré*, adaptation, 1908; *La Barricade*, 1910; *Un Cas de conscience*, written with S. Basset, 1910; *Le Tribun*, 1911; *La Crise*, written with A. Beaunier, 1912. These topical plays dealt with divorce, politics and social themes.

Boursault, Edmé (1638–1701), French dramatist. In his one-act play *Le Portrait du peintre*, 1663, very successfully produced at the HÔTEL DE BOURGOGNE, he accused MOLIÈRE of using recognizable contemporary characters in *La Critique de l'Ecole des femmes*, feeling himself to be attacked therein. Molière answered him with another play, *L'Impromptu de Versailles*, 1663. B. also attacked BOILEAU, but later became friendly with both writers. Among his plays are *Le Médecin volant*, 1661, *La Comédie sans titre ou le Mercure galant*, 1683. Most interesting are his later plays, e.g. *Esope à la cour*, 1701, adapted into English by VANBRUGH.

Bourseiller, Antoine (1930–), French actor and director. He works mainly in small experimental theatres; plays he has directed include BILLETDOUX's *Va donc chez Törpe*, 1961; BRECHT's *In the Jungle of the Cities*, 1963; L. JONES's *The Dutchman*, 1964; an adaptation of KAFKA's *America*, 1965; Adrien's *La Baye* at the AVIGNON FESTIVAL, fp 1967, and works by IONESCO. His controversial productions at the COMÉDIE-FRANÇAISE, e.g. MOLIÈRE's *Dom Juan*, 1967, show elements of the ceremonial and unreal. Since 1968 he has been director of the CENTRE DRAMATIQUE at Aix-en-Provence.

Boyle, William (1853–1923), Irish dramatist, poet and short-story writer. One of the resident dramatists of the ABBEY THEATRE, Dublin, who advocated a new 'realistic' theatre; the best example of his work is *The Building Fund*, 1905, which was produced there. Later plays include, in 1906, *The Eloquent Dempsey*, and *The Mineral Workers*.
Bibl: L. Robinson, IRELAND'S ABBEY THEATRE, A HISTORY 1899–1951, 1951

Bracegirdle, Anne (*c.* 1674–1748), English actress. Much admired in her time, she first appeared as a child actress at the age of 6. A pupil of BETTERTON, she was probably the first woman to play Portia. She made her most successful appearances as the heroine in plays by VANBRUGH, ROWE and especially CONGREVE, who wrote a leading part for her in each of his plays, notably Angelica in *Love for Love* and Millamant in

The Way of the World. Congreve was obviously in love with her for years and left her £200 in his will. She retired in 1707 at the height of her career following the first big successes of ANNE OLDFIELD. She is buried in Westminster Abbey.
Bibl: E. Robins, TWELVE GREAT ACTRESSES, 1900

Bragaglia, Anton Giulio (1890–1960), Italian director and essayist. In his productions and theoretical works he advocated a form of theatre in which all those involved adopt a creative role: theatre of the director, the designer and the actor (as in the COMMEDIA DELL'ARTE) contrary to the existing tradition, based on STAR actors and the writer's text. Essay: *Del teatro teatrale*, 1927. Worked 1921–24 on the topical periodical *Cronache d'attualità.* Managed 1922–31 the EXPERIMENTAL THEATRE, Teatro degli Indipendenti; produced plays ranging from STRINDBERG's *A Dream Play* to GHELDERODE's *La Mort du Docteur Faust*, 1928; APOLLINAIRE's *Les Mamelles de Tirésias*, 1927; JARRY's *Ubu Roi*, 1926, and original theatrical spectacles like the *Cabaret epilettico* (which he wrote with MARINETTI) and PANTOMIMES. He was manager 1937–43 of the Teatro delle Arti in Rome, with a REPERTORY of modern world theatre: O'NEILL, O'CASEY, WILDER, SALACROU.

Brahm, Otto (1856–1912), German literary critic, theatre manager and director. Collaborated with HOLZ and BAHR on the paper *Die Freie Bühne*, 1884–87, and then, inspired by the work of ANTOINE's Théâtre Libre in Paris, he founded his own theatre, the FREIE BÜHNE in 1889, the main purpose of which was to further the work of the new naturalistic playwrights. He was manager 1894–1905 of the Deutsches-Theater, BERLIN, where he assembled a remarkably strong company including ELSE LEHMANN and BASSERMANN. His REPERTORY of plays was chosen mainly from IBSEN and G. HAUPTMANN and he was the first to perfect ENSEMBLE playing in Germany. One of the outstanding members of his company was REINHARDT, who later reacted against B.'s consistently nautralistic style with a more colourful neo-Romantic approach. B. was artistic director 1905–12 of the Lessingtheater. He did much to rid the German stage of outmoded traditions, and to bring it into the mainstream of European drama.

Braque, Georges (1882–1963), French painter. Worked as a stage designer for the Ballets Russes: *Les Fâcheux*, 1924, *Zéphire et Floré*, 1925, and for JOUVET in MOLIÈRE's *Tartuffe*, 1950, Théâtre de l' Athénée. He applied his delicate range of colours and the technique of cubist collage to stage scenery.
Bibl: H. Rischbieter (ed), BÜHNE UND BILDENDE KUNST IM 20. JAHRHUNDERT, 1968

Brasseur, Pierre (1905–72), French actor. Since 1925 a much admired STAR of light comedy; especially successful in L. Descaves's *Le Cœur ébloui*; BOURDET's *Le Sexe*

Dion Boucicault, slave market scene from *The Octoroon*, 1859

Edwin Booth, above, in a performance of *Richard III*, 1879, when an attempt was made to assassinate him, and below, as Richelieu in BULWER-LYTTON's play

faible, 1929, and *La Fleur des pois*, 1932. He mainly played the part of the gigolo. He gained artistic maturity with the COMPAGNIE RENAUD-BARRAULT playing in the world première of CAMUS's *L'Etat de siège*, 1948; CLAUDEL's *Partage de Midi*, 1948; and ANOUILH's *La Répétition*, fp 1950. He had great personal success in parts like Goetz in SARTRE's *Le Diable et le Bon Dieu*, fp 1951, dir JOUVET, and the title role in Sartre's *Kean* (after DUMAS), 1953; Sam in PINTER's *The Homecoming*, 1966. Also appeared in many films and wrote a number of COMEDIES.

Bread and Puppet Theatre. US OFF-OFF-BROADWAY theatre group, founded and managed by German-born Peter H. Schumann, who act with masks, and lifesize or giant puppets. Characterized by ritualistic, slow-motion, symbolic productions without words (e.g. *Fire*, 1966); they have also organized street shows or participated in demonstrations against, e.g. the war in Vietnam or racism. They appeared in London in 1969 at the ROYAL COURT THEATRE.

Brecht, Bertolt (1898–1956), German poet, playwright, director and theoretician of the theatre. One of the most influential personalities of 20th-century drama, he came from a middle-class family and began medical studies in Munich in 1918, but drifted into the theatre. His earliest plays, influenced by BÜCHNER and WEDEKIND, express an anarchic acceptance of life and a cynical, nihilistic attitude towards society: *Baal*, written 1918, fp Leipzig, 1923, depicts the life of a vagabond-poet who drifts through existence in a haze of sensuality; *Trommeln in der Nacht* (*Drums in the Night*), written 1919, fp Munich 1922, tells the story of a soldier who returns from the war and decides not to take part in revolution; *Im Dickicht der Städte* (*In the Jungle of the Cities*), fp Munich 1923, shows the 'motiveless' struggle between two men in Chicago and is a precursor of late Absurdist drama. In 1924 he moved to BERLIN where he worked for a time as a DRAMATURG for REINHARDT. There he became involved in left-wing politics and increasingly interested in Marxism. His first parable play *Mann ist Mann* (*Man is Man*), fp Darmstadt 1926, describes the transformation of a human being from a humble and meek individual into a ferocious soldier. He achieved his first big popular success with *Die Dreigroschenoper* (*The Threepenny Opera*), fp Berlin 1928, a modernization of GAY's *The Beggar's Opera* with catchy tunes by WEILL, who also wrote the score for the opera *Aufstieg und Fall der Stadt Mahagonny* (*The Rise and Fall of the City of Mahagonny*), fp Leipzig 1930, a picture of the anarchy and greed of capitalist society seen as a wide-open gold-diggers' settlement on the fringes of the Alaska gold-rush.
His didactic plays (*Lehrstücke*) are terse, simple, and highly schematized exercises in the demonstration of the basic truths about human behaviour: *Der Flug des Lindberghs* (The Lindbergh Flight) which shows man's ability to overcome nature, and *Das Badener Lehrstück vom Einverständnis* (The Didactic Play of Baden: on Consent), both fp Baden-Baden 1929, music Weill/Hindemith.
B. and his family left Germany in 1933 and settled in Denmark where he devoted himself mainly to work which was intended to be a direct contribution to the struggle against Hitler: *Furcht und Elend des Dritten Reiches* (*Fear and Misery of the Third Reich*, also known in the USA as *The Private Life of the Master Race*), fp Paris 1938, is a sequence of short scenes of life in Nazi Germany; *Die Rundköpfe und die Spitzköpfe* (Roundheads and Peakheads), written 1931–34, fp Copenhagen 1936, a parable on the race problem. In 1941 he travelled to the USA via the USSR and settled in California. During his period of exile he wrote his greatest and most mature plays: *Leben des Galilei* (*Life of Galileo*), written 1937–39, fp Zurich 1943, in Birmingham at the university, and New York 1947, London 1963, Mermaid Theatre, a profound study of the dilemma of a creative genius and the social responsibility of the scientist; *Mutter Courage und ihre Kinder* (*Mother Courage and Her Children*), written 1938–39, fp Zurich 1941, which shows how anyone who tries to make profit out of war is a destructive, evil force; *Der Gute Mensch von Setzuan* (*The Good Woman of Setzuan*), written 1938–42, fp Zurich 1943, a parable on the theme that one cannot be a good human being in an evil society; *Herr Puntila und sein Knecht Matti* (*Mr Puntila and His Servant Matti*), written 1940, fp Zurich 1948, a folk play set in Finland which shows that one cannot be a successful landowner and a good man at the same time. The last of his major plays was *Der kaukasische Kreidekreis* (*The Caucasian Chalk Circle*), written 1943–45, the story of a girl who rescues an abandoned aristocratic child and retains it when the mother claims it back, with the help of the roguish judge Azdak, who takes the side of the common people.
In 1947 he was involved in the 'witch-hunt' against Communists in the Hollywood film industry and although he emerged unscathed, he decided to return to Europe and accepted an invitation to become artistic director of the Theater am Schiffbauerdamm in East Berlin where, with his wife HELENE WEIGEL, he founded the BERLINER ENSEMBLE. Here he was able to put into practice his theories of epic, non-Aristotelian drama, a technique of playwriting and production which avoided the direct assault on the audience's emotions and substituted for it the lucid demonstration of human behaviour which would enable them to arrive at a cool, critical judgment. B.'s main aim is to prevent the spectator from identifying with the characters by a variety of *Verfremdungseffekte* (▷ ALIENATION EFFECT). While leading the Berliner Ensemble, B. devoted himself mainly to directing his own plays and making adaptations to enrich the REPERTOIRE. Among these are *Antigone* (after SOPHOCLES), fp under B.'s direction at Chur 1948; *Die Tage der Kommune* (*The Days of the Commune*), written 1948–49, fp 1956; *Der Hofmeister* (*The Tutor*, after the play by LENZ), 1950; *Don Juan* (after MOLIÈRE), 1952; *Pauken und Trompeten* (Trumpets and Drums, after FARQUHAR's *The Recruiting Officer*), 1955; *Coriolan* (after SHAKESPEARE), 1951–53, fp 1962.
Bibl: M. Esslin, A CHOICE OF EVILS, 2/1971; J. Willett, THE THEATRE OF BRECHT, 2/1967; J. Willett (ed), BRECHT ON THEATRE, 1964

Brécourt, Guillaume Marcoureau, Sieur de (1638–85), French actor. For a short period he was a member of MOLIÈRE's company, where he played Alain in *L'Ecole des femmes* in 1662 and Dorante in *La Critique de l'Ecole des femmes* in 1663. Later, because of a quarrel with Molière, he joined FLORIDOR at the HÔTEL DE BOURGOGNE, where he became the leading man in RACINE's plays: Chicaneau in *Les Plaideurs*, 1668; title roles in *Britannicus*, 1669, and *Bajazet*, 1672; Antiochus in *Bérénice*, 1670; Xipharès in *Mithridate*, 1673. Became a member of the COMÉDIE-FRANÇAISE in 1682.
Bibl: G. Mongrédien, LES GRANDS COMÉDIENS DU XVIIe SIÈCLE, 1927

Bremer, Claus (1924–), German DRAMATURG and theoretician. Trained as actor and director in Hamburg and Freiburg, he started his career as an actor at the Landestheater, Darmstadt, from 1952 to 1961 under SELLNER, where he later became resident director, and Dramaturg which he also was 1962–65 at the experimental theatre in Ulm. He supported the literary and theatrical avant-garde. In his repertory were: POUND, JARRY, AUDIBERTI, BECKETT, IONESCO; translations and adaptations, e.g. SOPHOCLES, BEAUMONT and FLETCHER, and GATTI. Edited 1957–61 the *Darmstädter Blätter für Theater und Kunst*; wrote essays ('Theater ohne Vorhang', 1962; 'Shakespeare und die Avant-garde von 1964', *Shakespeare Jahrbuch*, 1964) and with the playwright Paul Pörtner developed the experimental playlets (*Mitspiele*), *Drei* (Three), 1962; *Scherenschnitt* (Scissors Cut), 1963; *Entscheiden Sie sich!* (Decide!), 1965.

Brenton, Howard (1944–), English dramatist who read English at Cambridge. After some years as a stage manager he joined a theatre group called the Brighton Combination in 1967/68. He adapted *Gargantua* by Rabelais and wrote *Gum and Go*, 1968; first full-length play *Revenge* at the ROYAL COURT THEATRE Upstairs, 1969 (a play about the police). For the Portable Theatre he wrote: *Christie in Love*, 1969; and *Fruit*, 1970. Other plays: *Wesley* and *Scott of the Antarctic*, performed 1969 and 1970 respectively at the Bradford Festival; *Moby Dick*, 1970. His play *Hitler Dances*, 1972, was written for the Traverse Theatre, Edinburgh. In his work he is concerned with public and private violence, seeing every 'law and order' restraint as a threat to the individual.

Bressart, Felix (1893–1949), German comedian. Very popular in German films

Bertolt Brecht

and on the Berlin stage up to 1933 when he emigrated to the USA and became well known for his impersonations of gangling, fussy, grotesque gentlemen in films, above all in Lubitsch's comedies.

Brice, Fanny (1891–1951), US comedian and singer. Celebrated for her Yiddish dialect songs. Appeared in many BROADWAY revues, including various *Ziegfeld Follies* (1910, 1911, 1916).

Bridie, James (Dr Osborne Henry Mavor; 1888–1951), Scottish dramatist. Studied medicine at Glasgow University and became a medical practitioner and consultant. During World War I he served in the Army Medical Corps; remained in practice till 1938. Started his career as a playwright late in life. His plays were mostly written in the tradition of SHAW. He gained his first success through the Scottish National Theatre Society (▷SCOTLAND) who commissioned him to write plays for the Scottish National Theatre movement which was founded to develop Scottish drama. He also helped to found the GLASGOW CITIZENS' THEATRE. His dramatic works include: *The Sunlight Sonata*, 1928; *The Anatomist*, 1930; *Tobias and the Angel*, 1930; *Jonah and the Whale*, 1932; *A Sleeping Clergyman*, 1933; *The Black Eye*, 1935; *Storm in a Teacup* (based on FRANK's *Sturm im Wasserglas*), 1936; *Susannah and the Elders*, 1937; *The King of Nowhere*, 1938; *What Say They?*, 1939; *Mr Bolfry*, 1943; *It Depends What You Mean*, 1944; *The Forrigan Reel*, 1944; *Dr Angelus*, 1946; *Daphne Laureola*, 1949, London, with EDITH EVANS in the title role; *The Queen's Comedy*, 1951, written for the EDINBURGH FESTIVAL; *The Baikie Charivari*, 1952, and *Meeting at Night*, 1954, both produced posthumously. His other works include a witty autobiography *One Way of Living*, 1939, two books of essays, and a children's book.
Bibl: W. Bannister, 1955

Bread and Puppet Theatre in a pageant depicting the Last Supper, Washington, D.C., 1971

Brighella. Character of the COMMEDIA DELL'ARTE (first servant – one of the ZANNI) from about 1571; he was the wily youth from Bergamo. His costume was white with a linen blouse, long trousers, cloak and cap with green tassels, and he wore a dark mask with a beard.

Brignone, Lilla (1913–), Italian actress. Her father **Guido B.** was a well-known film actor and director, her grandfather **Giuseppe B.**, a well-known actor at the turn of the century and a STAR of silent films. Lilla B. made her début in 1934; by 1943 she had become the leading lady of the Stival company, and of Rascel's revue troupe in 1946; she reached her artistic maturity as the leading actress of the PICCOLO TEATRO DI MILANO, under STREHLER and GRASSI. Later she worked in other companies and has become a star actress who has appeared under directors like SALVINI, SIMONI, COSTA and VISCONTI; under Strehler's direction she played in SHAKESPEARE (Lady Macbeth, and Queen Margaret in *Richard III*); Mommina in PIRANDELLO's *Questa sera si recita a soggetto* (*Tonight We*

Pierre Brasseur in SARTRE's *Kean*, Paris 1953

Improvise); Célimène in MOLIÈRE's *The Misanthrope*; Nora in IBSEN's *A Doll's House*, etc.

British Actors' Equity Association ▷EQUITY.

British Drama League. Founded by WHITWORTH in 1919, the BDL is an association devoted to the fostering of drama of all kinds, professional as well as amateur, which has, however, become the representative organization of British amateur societies. The BDL maintains the most comprehensive library of plays in Britain, an excellent information service, and organizes training courses for directors, etc. In the premises in Fitzroy Square in London a number of other organizations are also housed, connected with the theatre, and collectively known as the British Theatre Centre. The BDL was renamed British Theatre Association in 1972 – an expression of its widening sphere of concern with all aspects of drama.

Broadway. The majority of New York's larger commercial theatres are concentrated in area from 42nd to 50th streets, bisected by Broadway. In contrast to OFF-BROADWAY and OFF-OFF-BROADWAY where plays, often of an experimental nature or foreign origin, are produced on shoestring budgets, made possible by cheaper running costs and waiving of union restrictions, Broadway theatre has to concentrate on plays of wide popular appeal and sustained commercial success. In recent decades this has increasingly meant musicals and light comedies, sure-fire hits with star casts, the success of which are dependent on a favourable critics' verdict. Thus the term 'Broadway theatre' has become synonymous with a high level of production and acting skill but tends to be unadventurous and orthodox, appealing to conventional taste. The range of theatre has become narrower than it was in the 1950s when the plays of T. WILLIAMS and A. MILLER were popular, and earlier when the THEATRE GUILD productions were still viable. It is significant that a revival of interest in the plays of O'NEILL was stimulated by an Off-Broadway production of *The Iceman Cometh* in the 1950s. *Long Day's Journey Into Night*, written 1940–41, received its first Broadway production in 1956.

Bronnen, Arnolt (1895–1959), Austrian dramatist. Started as a writer of Expressionist drama, became a friend of BRECHT, and wrote documentary plays. He supported the Nazi regime from 1933 but reverted to his left-wing views after 1945. In 1951 he was appointed assistant director and DRAMATURG of the Scala Theater in Vienna, and then moved to East Berlin. His dramatic works include: *Vatermord* (Patricide), fp Frankfurt 1922; Deutsches-Theater, BERLIN 1922, dir VIERTEL with sensational success; *Geburt der Jugend* (Birth of Adolescence), 1922; *Die Exzesse* (The Outrages), 1923; *Anarchie in Sillan* (Anarchy in Sillan), 1924; *Katalaunische Schlacht* (Catalan Battle), 1924. He wrote his autobiography *A.B. gibt zu Protokoll*, 1954, and *Tage mit B. Brecht*, 1960.

Brook, Peter (1925–), English director. Made his début with a production of MARLOWE's *Dr Faustus* in 1943; directed under JACKSON at the BIRMINGHAM REPERTORY THEATRE: SHAW's *Man and Superman*, SHAKESPEARE's *King John*; at STRATFORD *Love's Labour's Lost* and *Romeo and Juliet*, and in London three plays by SARTRE including *The Respectful Prostitute*; directed opera at COVENT GARDEN including Richard Strauss's *Salome*, 1949, des DALI. In 1962 he became a director of the ROYAL SHAKESPEARE COMPANY. Apart from his productions of controversial modern plays (DÜRRENMATT, ANOUILH, FRISCH, WEISS) and musicals, he is best known for his Shakespeare productions: *Measure for Measure*, 1950; *The Winter's Tale*, 1951, both with GIELGUD; *Hamlet*, 1955; *Titus Andronicus*, 1955, and particularly *King Lear*, 1962. (▷KOTT).
Experimental works under the influence of the ideas of ARTAUD: THEATRE OF CRUELTY, 1964: scenes from *The Tempest*, 1968; his collective improvisation *US*, 1966, combined techniques of the MUSIC HALL with a political attack on the Vietnam war. Ritualistic and orgiastic elements combined with great visual quality and extreme cleverness characterize his style of production: Weiss's *Marat/Sade*, 1963; SENECA's *Oedipus*, 1968, NATIONAL THEATRE, London; and his most recent and internationally successful *A Midsummer Night's Dream*, STRATFORD-UPON-AVON, later London 1971. Since then he has been concerned with the Centre for Theatre Research in Paris. In 1971 he visited the Shiraz-Persepolis Festival and produced *Orghast*, written by Ted Hughes. In 1975 he produced *Timon of Athens* and *Les Ikes* in Paris. The latter came to London in 1976.

Brown, Ivor (1891–1974), English critic: on the *Manchester Guardian* (1919–35), the *Observer* (1928–54) and the *Saturday Review* (1944–55). He also wrote for *Punch* and other newspapers and magazines. A collection of his journalistic work was published under the title *Two on the Aisle*, 1939. His other works on the theatre include *Masques and Phases*, 1926; *Amazing Movement, A Short History of the Shakespeare Industry*, 1939, with G. Fearon, and *Shakespeare*, 1949.

Browne, (Elliot) Martin (1900–), English director and actor. Supported the revival of poetic and religious drama. His first production in 1935 was ELIOT's *Murder in the Cathedral* at Canterbury Cathedral, later at the OLD VIC, then in New York. Became the leading director of other plays by Eliot: *The Family Reunion*, 1939; *The Cocktail Party*, 1949, EDINBURGH FESTIVAL; *The Confidential Clerk*, 1953, Edinburgh; *The Elder Statesman*, 1958. In 1945 he became director of the Mercury Theatre, London, where he tried to establish a poetic theatre by producing verse plays including N. S. Nicholson's *The Old Man of the Mountain*, DUNCAN's *This Way to the Tomb* and FRY's *A Phoenix Too Frequent*. He was director of the BRITISH DRAMA LEAGUE 1948–57.

Browne, Maurice (1881–1955), English writer, actor, director and manager. In 1912 he founded the first American Little Theatre in Chicago. From 1927 he worked in London where he had his greatest success with his production of SHERRIFF's *Journey's End* at the Savoy Theatre in 1929. In 1930 he produced *Othello* with ROBESON in the title role, playing Iago himself. Later he managed the Globe Theatre and the Queen's Theatre; among other productions he presented GIELGUD in *Hamlet* and seasons of MOISSI and the PITOËFF family. Later productions included: *The Improper Duchess*, 1931; *Viceroy Sarah*, 1935; *Quiet Wedding*, 1939. His most important dramatic works were: *The King of the Jews, What Men Call Honour*, and *Dr Job*.

Browning, Robert (1812–89), English poet. Author of nine dramatic works, mostly written in verse and mainly of literary interest. Only a few have been performed, e.g. *Strafford*, 1837, dedicated to and played by MACREADY; *A Blot in the 'Scutcheon*, 1843; *Colombe's Birthday*, 1844. *Pippa Passes*, written 1841, not originally intended to be performed, was staged in New York 1917; in Norwich, England, 1925; revived in Oxford, 1968.

Bruckner, Ferdinand (Theodor Tagger; 1891–1958), Austrian dramatist. In 1923 he founded the Renaissance Theater in BERLIN, where he remained as director till 1928. He emigrated in 1933, eventually settling in New York, and returned to Berlin in 1951 where he worked as a DRAMATURG. He started his career as an Expressionist writer turning to a drama of social and psychological conflict which rapidly earned him an international reputation, e.g. *Krankheit der Jugend* (Illness of Youth), 1926; *Die Verbrecher* (The Criminals), fp Berlin 1928, Deutsches-Theater, dir HILPERT. His later plays were historical dramas like *Elisabeth von England*, 1930, and VERSE DRAMAS like *Der Tod einer Puppe* (The Death of a Doll), 1956; and *Der Kampf mit dem Engel* (Fight with an Angel), 1956, attempting to create modern TRAGEDY. Other works: *Timon und das Gold*, 1931, based on SHAKESPEARE; *Die Marquise von O.*, 1933; *Simon Bolivar* (in two parts, 1943/45); and *Pyrrhus und Andromache*, 1952.

Brulin, Tone (1926–), Flemish dramatist. With Piet Sterckx and Jan Christiaens, one of the avant-garde dramatists of Flanders, increasingly involved with political themes. Among his plays are: *Neu het dorp niet meer bestaat* (Now that the village has disappeared), 1957; *Nonkel en de jukebox*, 1959; and *De honden* (The Dog), 1960. He also founded the Theatre in the Attic in Antwerp.

Buazzelli, Tino (1922–), Italian actor. One of the leading performers of the post-war Italian theatre, in range and versatility comparable with LAUGHTON. Made his stage début in 1947 playing the father in A. MILLER's *All My Sons*; worked at the Piccolo Teatro in Rome; Father in PIRANDELLO's *Sei personaggi in cerca d'autore*, Sganarelle in MOLIÈRE's *Dom Juan*, Egisto in ALFIERI's *Oreste*. At the PICCOLO TEATRO DI MILANO he played the lead in GOGOL's *The Government Inspector*, 1952; BRECHT's *Schweik in the Second World War*, 1960, and *Galileo*, 1962, dir STREHLER. He has also appeared in films.

Büchner, Georg (1813–37), German dramatist. Studied Medicine and Natural Sciences in Strasbourg (1831) and Giessen (1833). He died of typhoid fever at the age of 23. B.'s three plays and the unfinished novella *Lenz* were written between 1835 and 1837. *Dantons Tod* (*Danton's Death*) was published in 1835 and fp Hamburg in 1910. *Leonce und Lena*, written 1836 for a competition held by a publishing house, was not accepted as he had delivered it too late; it was first produced in Vienna in 1911. In 1836 he worked on *Woyzeck* (which remained unfinished), upon which Alban Berg later based his opera *Wozzeck*. The play was first produced in Munich in 1913. B.'s dramatic works anticipate the naturalistic tradition in German drama and greatly influenced BRECHT.
Bibl: A. H. J. Knight, 1951

Buckwitz, Harry (1904–), German director and producer. Was INTENDANT of the Frankfurt Municipal Theatre 1951–68. His productions of BRECHT during a period in which the latter's plays were ignored by other West German theatres rank as his most important work: *Der Gute Mensch von Setzuan*, 1952; *Der kaukasische Kreidekreis*, 1955; *Die Gesichte der Simone Machard*, fp 1957; *Mutter Courage und ihre Kinder*, 1958; *Schweyk im zweiten Weltkrieg*, 1959; *Leben des Galilei*, 1961; and several others in the following years, all designed by OTTO.

Buen Retiro. Castle near Madrid, where the theatre enthusiast Philip IV (1621–65) built a particularly splendid COURT THEATRE and open-air theatre on the French and Italian models. In 1635 CALDERÓN was appointed director of this theatre which quickly gained a reputation throughout Europe for its special use of effective STAGE MACHINERY and for the ingenuity of Italian scenic designers like Cosme Lotti and Cesare Fontana.

Bulgakov, Mikhail Afanasyevich (1891–1940), Soviet novelist, short-story writer and playwright. With KATAYEV, BABEL, OLESHA, Ilya Ilf and Yevgeny Petrov, he was one of the outstanding writers of modern Soviet literature. He came to Moscow in 1921, and wrote for the magazine *Gudok* (The Whistle). Although he had supported the Revolution from the beginning, he nevertheless suffered throughout his life from the repressive censorship of the Soviet regime. His most famous play *Dni Turbinykh* (The Days of the Turbins), 1926, produced in England in an adaptation

Peter Brook's production of *A Midsummer Night's Dream*, Stratford-upon-Avon 1970

Georg Büchner, *Danton's Death*, London 1971, produced by J. MILLER

by R. Ackland as *The White Guard*, 1938, was dramatized from his partly autobiographical novel, based on his experiences in Kiev, 1918–19, and deals with opponents of the Revolution who find their path to socialism. Despite the positive conclusion of the play it was attacked by official critics and banned after a few performances. Among his other important works: *Krasnyi ostrov* (The Red Island), 1928, a COMEDY; a dramatization of Gogol's *Dead Souls* for the MOSCOW ART THEATRE, 1932; *Kabala svyatosh* (The Cabal of Saintly Hypocrites), 1936, a play about MOLIÈRE; *Poslednye dni* (The Last Days), about PUSHKIN's death, produced posthumously, 1943; *Don Kikhot* (Don Quixote), 1940; *Blazhenstvo* (Bliss), written 1934, dramatizing the life of a time-machine inventor plagued by bureaucrats, which was banned and remained unpublished until 1966, and *Ivan Vasilyevich*, written 1936, a variation on this theme, which was banned from public performance and not produced till 1965.

Bulgaria. The 19th century saw attempts to create a National Theatre opposed to Turkish rule and the Greek influence of the upper class. It started in 1856 as the *Chitalishte* which used dance and theatre to encourage and promote a national culture. The first professional company was formed in 1883, followed in 1892 by a metropolitan company in Sofia, which became the basis of the NATIONAL THEATRE founded in 1904. Greatly influenced by Russian theatre, its best actors were trained by STANISLAVSKY. Since 1945 theatres have been under government control; at present the country has about 40 theatres.

Bullins, Ed (1935–), Black US poet, novelist and dramatist. Originally from Philadelphia, he has spent most of his life in California. First won acclaim with his powerful and haunting drama *Clara's Ole Man*, which was presented in New York with two companion pieces, *The Electronic Nigger* and *A Son Came Home*, fp 1967, American Place Theatre, later transferred to the Martinique. Won the NYVRDD award for outstanding achievement in OFF-BROADWAY 1967–68 season. His full-length play *In the Wine Time*, at the New Lafayette Theatre, New York, also had an enthusiastic reception. *The Gentleman Caller* formed part of *A Black Quartet* which comprised four short plays by B., L. JONES, Ronald Milner and Ben Caldwell; originally presented by the Chelsea Theatre Center, it transferred to Tombellini's Gate Theatre. B. was one of the founders of the Black Arts/West in San Francisco's Fillmore District, modelled on Jones's Black Arts Repertory Theatre School in Harlem. As a member of the Black Arts Alliance (an organization of Black theatre groups) he has assisted Jones in film-making and stage productions on the West Coast. In 1968 he edited the special issue of *The Drama Review* devoted to Black Theatre. A collection of the author's work, *Five Plays by Ed Bullins*, was published in 1969. Recipient of a Rockefeller Foundation grant.

Bulwer-Lytton, Edward George Earle, 1st Baron Lytton of Knebworth (1803–73), English novelist and playwright. He also played an important part in politics (M.P. in 1831, Colonial Secretary 1858–59, Viceroy of India 1876–80). Apart from many successful novels and historical romances, he wrote some highly successful melodramatic plays: *The Lady of Lyons*, 1838; *Richelieu, or The Conspiracy*, 1839; *Money*, 1840.
Bibl; M. Sadleir, 1946

Buontalenti, Bernardo (1536–1608), Italian theatre architect and engineer. Worked at the Court of the Medici and was an imaginative inventor, pioneering the use of movable scenery in the BAROQUE THEATRE. He built the Teatro degli Uffizi in Florence in honour of the marriage of Virginia de' Medici and Cesare d'Este in 1585, constructed the décor, STAGE MACHINERY and designed costumes for theatrical performances, court festivities and NAUMACHIAE (staged sea-battles).
Bibl: H. Tintelnot, BAROCKTHEATER UND BAROCKE KUNST, 1939

Burbage (Burbadge, Burbege, Burbige). English family of actors. (1) **James B.** (*c.*1530–97) built in 1576 the first English theatre entirely devoted to plays; it was known as THE THEATRE. In 1596 he took over and rebuilt the BLACKFRIARS THEATRE, which passed after his death to his eldest son, (2) **Cuthbert B.** (*c.*1566–1636), who dismantled The Theatre and used the timber to build the GLOBE, Southwark, in 1599; in this theatre SHAKESPEARE's plays were first performed. James's second son (3) **Richard B.** (*c.*1567–1619) was the first great English actor and creator of Shakespearean parts such as Richard III, Henry V, Brutus, Lear, Shylock, Romeo, Hamlet and Othello. He also appeared in plays by JONSON, KYD, WEBSTER, etc. R.B. was able to adapt to almost any part; unlike other contemporary actors who tended to have exaggerated declamatory styles his acting was natural, refined and sensitive, and it has been said, though not with any authority, that Shakespeare was greatly inspired by his performances.
Bibl: B. L. Joseph, ELIZABETHAN ACTING, 1952

Burgtheater. Austrian National Theatre in Vienna, founded by the Empress Maria Theresa in the Hofballhaus near the Hofburg in 1741 as a Court theatre. In 1776 by a decree of Emperor Franz Joseph II the Burgtheater was proclaimed Deutsches Nationaltheater under the administration of the Court, with an ENSEMBLE of German actors (known as K. K. National-Hofburg-Schauspieler). This marked the beginning of the great period of German acting in Vienna. Under the personal supervision of the emperor, the management of the theatre was committed to a board of directors (1776–89), succeeded 1789–92 by the first director of the Burgtheater, F. C. Brockmann. After 1789 the actors formed a permanent group and developed their own group spirit. The Burgtheater reached its peak in the 19th century under direction of SCHREYVOGEL, the critic, ('artistic secretary' 1814–32), who fostered the works of the Weimar classics and staged the first performances of plays by GRILLPARZER, and under LAUBE, 1849–67, in whose time French BOULEVARD comedies and contemporary German WELL-MADE PLAYS were predominant. Performances were presented at the old Ballhaus on the Michaelerplatz until 1888 when the new theatre on the Ringstrasse, designed by the architects Gottfried Semper and Karl Hasenauer, was opened. It was slightly damaged in 1945, and reopened in 1955. Franz Dingelstedt, director 1870–81, favoured lavish décor in contemporary style. After his retirement the directors changed frequently. The main strength of the theatre was the ensemble and the REPERTOIRE of world classics. As far as modern drama is concerned, the Burgtheater has on the whole been rather conservative in its policy; many years elapsed before the works of IBSEN, HOFMANNSTHAL, G. HAUPTMANN and SCHNITZLER were regularly performed. The company consisted of Austrian and German actors. Austria's greatest man of the theatre, REINHARDT, never became Burgtheater director; also the idea of a director's theatre was resisted for a long time. After World War II, the ensemble appeared in the Ronacher Saal, and in 1955 they moved back to their old house on the Ringstrasse. Today the Burgtheater has a second house, the Akademietheater. Recent directors of the Burgtheater include: E. Häussermann (1959–68), HOFFMANN (1968–71), and E. Klingenberg (1971–).
Bibl: E. Häussermann, VON SOPHOKLES BIS GRASS, 10 JAHRE BURGTHEATER, 1968; F. Hadamoswky, DIE WIENER HOFTHEATER, 1776–1966, 1966

Burian, Emil František (1904–59), Czech critic, actor, director playwright and musician. In 1934 he founded the 'D 34' theatre, which rapidly gained an international reputation as a centre for experimental plays and style of production. He tended towards radical simplification, definition of structure by light and music (which he composed himself) and free adaptations of classics (MOLIÈRE and SHAKESPEARE): e.g. he directed *Romeo and Juliet* as the dream of a concentration camp prisoner, 1946.

Burlesque (from Ital *burlesco* = mockery and raillery). A theatrical entertainment, mostly a full-length satirical play, aiming to caricature or parody contemporary literary and dramatic conventions. Reached its peak in the 18th century with SHERIDAN's *The Critic*, 1779. Other important examples are BEAUMONT's *The Knight of the Burning Pestle*, 1607; George Villiers' *The Rehearsal*, 1671; GAY's *The Beggar's Opera*, 1728; FIELDING's *Tom Thumb*, 1730; H. J. BYRON's *The Corsican Brothers*, 1869.
In the USA burlesque came to be kind of variety entertainment in which 'leg shows' and other erotic material (including striptease) alternated with bawdy comedy. American burlesque arose about the middle of the 19th century, reached its peak in the

period before 1914 and petered out after World War II.
Bibl: V. C. Clinton-Baddely, THE BURLESQUE TRADITION, 1952

Burletta. A verse play with music which originated in England in the 18th century as a device to avoid restrictions imposed upon the London theatre by the licensing laws which confined legitimate drama to DRURY LANE and COVENT GARDEN. Any three-act play with at least five songs escaped the restriction. The burletta thus enabled the minor London theatres to present COMEDIES and even plays by SHAKESPEARE through the interpolation of musical numbers.

Burnacini. Italian family of architects and stage designers. (1) **Giovanni B.** (b. early 17th century–1655) was an architect and stage designer *c.* 1640 at the COURT THEATRE in Vienna, where he introduced wing-settings. His son (2) **Ludovico Ottavio B.** (1636–1707) was one of the most important and influential stage designers of the early Baroque; he designed the costumes and settings for about 115 Court festivities and theatrical productions, mostly imaginative allegories, involving the use of ingenious STAGE MACHINERY crowned with fireworks.
Bibl: F. Hadamowsky, DAS HOFTHEATER LEOPOLD I. UND DAS KOSTÜMWERK DES LUDOVICO BURNACINI, 1948

Burton, Richard (1925–), British actor. He made his stage début in 1943 in Liverpool as Glan in *Druid's Rest*, by E. WILLIAMS. He then appeared in London in several of FRY's plays: as Richard in *The Lady's Not for Burning*, 1949, which he also played in 1950 for his New York stage début; and as Tegeus in *A Phoenix Too Frequent*, 1950. Subsequently he worked with leading companies in England and America, e.g. at the OLD VIC, where he appeared in 1953/54 as Hamlet and Caliban, and in 1956 alternating with John Neville as Othello and Iago. In the USA he made a successful appearance as Arthur in the musical *Camelot* (LERNER/LOEWE), New York 1960, and as Hamlet under GIELGUD's direction, New York 1964. Today mainly known as a film actor. Chief films: *Look Back in Anger*; *Becket*; *Who's Afraid of Virginia Woolf?*; *Dr Faustus* (also co-dir and prod).

Bury, John (1925–), English stage designer. Worked after World War II at JOAN LITTLEWOOD's Theatre Workshop and since 1963 as stage designer at the Shakespeare Memorial Theatre, STRATFORD-UPON-AVON. His principal objective in stage design was to escape from the technique of decorative and *anti*-illustrative stage sets and to achieve effects with a minimum of equipment and materials; for the prison play *The Quare Fellow* by BEHAN, 1956, he built a stage using blocks, iron chains and bars; *The Playboy of the Western World* by SYNGE, 1959, both Theatre Workshop. He designed 1962–64 SHAKESPEARE productions directed by HALL, of which the most important was the cycle *The Wars of the Roses*, adapted by BARTON from *Henry*

Bulwer-Lytton's play *Not So Bad as We Seem*, performed by Charles Dickens' group of amateur actors in the presence of the Royal family

Buontalenti, design for Florentine festivities, *Il combattimento pitici d'Apollo col Serpente*, 1589

Richard Burbage

Richard Burton as Iago at the OLD VIC, 1956

VI and *Richard III*, 1963. Among other productions he designed were: DÜRRENMATT's *The Physicists*, 1963, dir BROOK; and PINTER's *The Homecoming*, 1965, dir Hall.

Busch, Ernst (1900–), German actor and singer of proletarian political and protest songs. One of the leading actors of the BERLINER ENSEMBLE, he started his career at the VOLKSBÜHNE, Berlin, in PISCATOR's production of TOLLER's *Hoppla, wir leben!*. Emigrated in 1933; since 1945 he has appeared mainly at the Deutsches-Theater, BERLIN, and with the Berliner Ensemble, in parts like Semjon Lapkin in BRECHT's *Die Mutter*, adapted from GORKY, Berliner Ensemble, 1951; Iago in *Othello*, Deutsches-Theater, 1953. Parts in other Brecht plays: the cook in *Mutter Courage*, 1954; Azdak in *Der kaukasische Kreidekreis*, 1954; and the title role in *Leben des Galilei*, 1957.
Bibl: H. Weigl (ed) THEATERARBEIT, 1962

Buzzati, Dino (1906–72), Italian novelist and playwright. He was a journalist for the *Corriere della Sera*. His dramatic work combines Kafkaesque elements with bitter enigmatic topical SATIRE, e.g. his play *Un caso clinico* (A Clinical Case), fp 1953, PICCOLO TEATRO DI MILANO, Paris 1955, adapted by CAMUS, concerns a rich businessman, who is sent to hospital by his family, gradually loses contact with reality and inevitably dies. This was followed by a satire on a totalitarian revolution *Un verme al ministero* (A Worm at the Ministry); *Il mantello* (The Coat), 1960; and *L'uomo che andrà in America* (The Man Who Will Go To America), Naples 1962.
Bibl: M. Esslin, THE THEATRE OF THE ABSURD, 2/1968

Byron, George Gordon, Lord (1788–1824), English poet. His dramatic work consists of eight plays which have considerable impact as poetry but are hardly suitable for the stage. *Marino Faliero*, pub 1821, was the only play produced in his lifetime (DRURY LANE 1821). *Werner, or The Inheritance*, pub 1822, was acted by MACREADY in 1830 at Drury Lane; *The Two Foscari*, pub 1821, was staged at COVENT GARDEN in 1838. These historical plays are his most successful in theatrical terms. He gave dramatic form to his philosophical and theological ideas in his satirical VERSE DRAMAS which formed the basis of his reputation in his lifetime. In his dramatic poem, *Manfred*, pub 1817, fp Covent Garden, 1834; *Cain*, pub 1821 (apparently not produced in England but translated into German six times and latterly performed in Lucerne 1960); *Heaven and Earth*, pub 1823, and *The Deformed Transformed* (unfinished), pub 1824, the protagonists are damned Faustian souls. His tragedy, *Sardanapalus*, was staged by Macready in 1834.
Bibl: S. Chew, THE DRAMAS OF LORD BYRON, 1915

Byron, Henry James (1834–84), English actor and playwright. Best known for his BURLESQUES – dramatized parodies of themes from mythology, fairy-tale and legend in a heavily punning language, e.g. *The Corsican Brothers; or The Troublesome Twins*, 1869. He was manager of the Alexandra Theatre, Liverpool, 1867–74, then of the Criterion in London, where his most successful play *Our Boys*, 1875, ran for over four years.

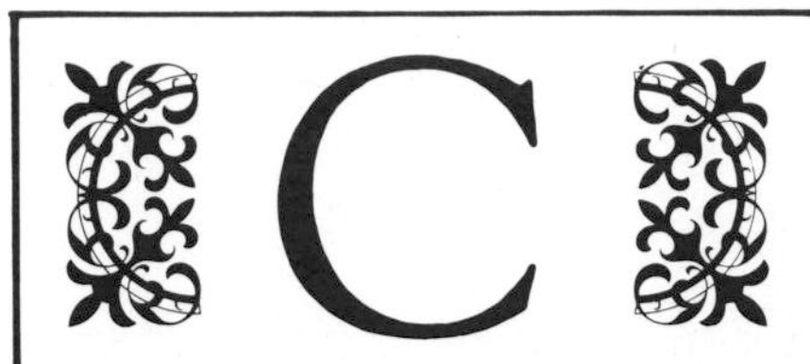

Cabaret (Fr = tavern, inn, probably derived from the Spanish *caba retta* = many-coloured bowl). Originally the small stage in a club or restaurant where solo artists, usually singers or comedians, performed CHANSONS and satirical sketches, commenting on the contemporary political and cultural climate, an intimate metropolitan entertainment. Cabaret was really launched in Paris, in 1881, in the Chat Noir Café of the painter R. Salis, which mostly staged improvised performances and chansons. A rival establishment was Le Mirliton, founded in 1885 by the anarchistic folk-singer Aristide Bruant, who used *argot* to mock the rich and sympathize with the poor; YVETTE GUILBERT was a follower of Bruant, first at the Divan Japonais, later at the Moulin Rouge. As a DISEUSE, in her sharply etched performances, she perfected the use of the chanson as a vehicle of social criticism. In 1901 O. J. Bierbaum and E. v. Wolzogen founded the Überbrettl in Berlin, which was criticized by KERR for its philistine tendencies. In Munich between 1901 and 1904 the cabaret 'Die elf Scharfrichter' flourished with contributions by painters and literary men like WEDEKIND. The programmes included parodies, grotesques, satirical chansons and folk-songs. In 1903 the Cabaret Simplizissimus opened in Munich, where the famous poet and *chansonnier* Joachim Ringelnatz appeared. During World War I the Cabaret Voltaire opened in Zurich; its members included Hugo Ball, Hans (Jean) Arp, Raoul Hausmann, and Richard Huelsenbeck, from among whom the DADA movement originated.
Cabaret flourished in Berlin in the 1920s, with writers like MEHRING, KÄSTNER and Kurt Tucholsky, and singers like Trude Hesterberg, Rosa Valetti, Kate Kühl, Blandine Ebinger, and Margo Lion. After 1929 Werner Finck appeared at the Katakombe, and continued to use cabaret even after 1933 for disguised political attacks against the Nazi regime. Anti-Fascist cabaret thrived in Vienna and Zurich in the 1930s (Pfeffermühle and Cornichon). After 1945 there was a revival of political and literary cabaret in West Germany: Die Schaubude (Munich), Das Kom(m)ödchen (Düsseldorf), Die Stachelschweine (Berlin), Die Lach- und Schiessgesellschaft (Munich). In the English-speaking world there is relatively little evidence of a continuous cabaret tradition. In pre-war England 'little revue' came closest to French or German cabaret, yet remained without the political bite of its Continental models. The term 'cabaret' is also used for the floor shows of restaurants and hotels. In the 1950s political cabaret arose from the sharper political conflicts of the period in Chicago (The Second City, The Premise), San Francisco (The Committee) and New York. It produced some of the best American comedians of the time: Mort Sahl, Shelley Berman, Lenny Bruce. In England satirical cabaret came to the fore in the wake of the great success of *Beyond the Fringe* by J. MILLER, Peter Cook, Alan Bennett and Dudley Moore and flourished briefly in clubs like The Establishment and in TV shows such as *That Was The Week That Was* (abbreviated to *TW3*) and the satirical late night shows that followed it in the mid-1960s.

Caecilius Statius (*c.* 220–168 BC), Roman comic playwright, one of the greatest writers of PALLIATAE. About 300 lines of his work from some 40 titles are extant. He took most of his themes from MENANDER, adding new ideas and jokes, and transforming the language.

Café La Mama ▷LA MAMA.

Caigniez, Louis-Charles (1762–1842), French dramatist. Wrote numerous MELODRAMAS for the BOULEVARD THEATRE with titles such as *La Forêt d'Hermanstadt ou La Fausse épouse* and *L'Enfant de l'amour*. Known by his contemporaries as the 'Racine of the boulevard theatre', he was described by GAUTIER as one of the 'unknown Shakespeares'.
Bibl: P. Ginisti, LE MÉLODRAME, 1911

Caillavet, Gaston de (1869–1915), French dramatist. He wrote, mostly in collaboration with FLERS, comedies and VAUDEVILLE plays which rely on the mechanism of intrigue and confusion. Though frivolous and superficial, they were never banal or in bad taste. Best known is his last play *Monsieur Brotonneau*, 1914.

Calderón de la Barca, Pedro (1600–81), Spanish dramatist. In 1628 became Court poet and head of the COURT THEATRE under Philip IV; *c.* 1650 ordained as a priest. Of his *c.* 300 plays, about 120 COMEDIAS, 80 AUTOS SACRAMENTALES and 20 ENTREMESES are extant; at an early stage in his career he was praised by LOPE DE VEGA. He started with COMEDIAS DE CAPA Y ESPADA (cloak-and-sword dramas), but also achieved considerable success and fame with comedies of intrigue, e.g. *La dama duende* (The Goblin Lady), *c.* 1629, which turns on the existence of a concealed door in a room enabling the heroine to make sudden appearances and to vanish equally abruptly. Later C.'s plays became more serious and philosophical. Among the best known of these, which have retained their place in the world REPERTOIRE, are: *El magico prodigioso* (The Miraculous Magician); *La devoción de la Cruz* (Devotion to the Cross); *La vida es sueño* (*Life's a Dream*); *El principe* *constante* (*The Constant Prince*); *El mayor monstruo los celos* (Jealousy, the Greatest Monster); *El médico de su honra* (The Physician of His Own Honour); *El pintor de su deshonra* (The Painter of His Own Shame); *La hija del aire* (The Daughter of the Air); *El Alcalde de Zalamea* (*The Mayor of Zalamea*), C.'s most famous play, is one of the first social dramas, in which a lowly but honourable peasant punishes the ravisher of his daughter, although he is a high-born soldier. For the open-air theatre at the royal palace of BUEN RETIRO, C. wrote, among other plays, *El mayor encanto amor* (Love the Greatest Charm). Among his religious plays the best known are *El gran teatro del mundo* (The Great Theatre of the World), an ALLEGORY which presents the world as a stage on which all men, beggars as well as kings, are assigned their roles by the supreme producer, God; and *La cena de Baltasar* (Belshazzar's Feast). Edward Fitzgerald published translations of six plays by him in 1853. C., a supreme poet and master of dramatic situation, is one of the great playwrights of the Western world.

Bibl: B. W. Wardropper (ed), CRITICAL ESSAYS ON THE THEATRE OF CALDERÓN, 1965; A. A. Parker, THE ALLEGORICAL DRAMA OF CALDERÓN, 1943

Callot, Jacques (1592–1622), French painter and graphic artist. Lived in Florence 1609–22 and was a pupil of the theatre architect PARIGI in 1614. In his series of illustrations *Trois Pantalons*, 1619, and the 24 prints of the *Balli di Sfessania* he depicts the typical characters of the COMMEDIA DELL'ARTE and conveys a vivid picture of the theatre of his time.

Calvert, Charles Alexander (1828–79), English actor and manager. Prominent in the theatrical life of Manchester where he became leading man and producer at the Theatre Royal in 1859, and manager of the Prince's Theatre 1864–75. He strove for historical accuracy in sets and costumes in performances of SHAKESPEARE. As an actor his good looks and sonorous voice attracted attention. His best parts were Henry IV and Shylock. His wife **Adelaide Helen Biddles** (1837–1921) created the part of Catherine Petkoff in SHAW's *Arms and the Man*, 1894. All his eight children took up acting, but only **Louis C.** (1859–1923) made his mark. He was a leading member of the Vedrenne-Barker company at the ROYAL COURT THEATRE and played Creon in REINHARDT's production of SOPHOCLES' *Oedipus Rex* at COVENT GARDEN in 1912. He wrote a book on *Problems of an Actor*, 1918.

Campbell, Mrs Patrick (*née* Beatrice Stella Tanner; 1865–1940), English actress. She made her first outstanding appearance in 1893 at the St James's Theatre as Paula in PINERO's *The Second Mrs Tanqueray*, a melodramatic play, which shows the influence of IBSEN in its criticism of social conventions. Her finest parts included the title role in SUDERMANN's *Magda*, London and New York; a number of leading Ibsen

Cabaret, poster by Toulouse-Lautrec advertising the Divan Japonais

Calderón, a setting, attributed to F. Ricci, for one of his plays

roles, such as Hedda Gabler, and Eliza Doolittle in SHAW's *Pygmalion* in the first production, 1914, and in subsequent revivals. Towards the end of her life, she was in Hollywood. Though notorious for being unmanageable and for throwing tantrums, she was a beautiful woman of great wit, with a melodious voice and dark shining eyes, and her admirers included Shaw, whose ardent correspondence with her was later dramatized by the US playwright Jerome Kilty under the title *Dear Liar*, 1960.

Campistron, Jean Gualbert de (1656–1723), French dramatist in the classical tradition. He was a friend and follower of RACINE. For some time, on the strength of his early plays (*Virginie*, 1683; *Arminius*, 1684; *Alcibiade*, 1685; and the most important, *Andronic*, 1685, lead played by M. BARON), he was considered a leading writer of TRAGEDIES, but his later plays failed. He also wrote LIBRETTI for Lully, e.g. his last opera, *Acis et Galatée*, 1686, and two COMEDIES.

Campton, David (1924–), English dramatist. His brief 'glimpses' or playlets use the technique of the THEATRE OF THE ABSURD, which he considers to be 'a weapon against complacency', to expose the dangers that threaten society, especially the atomic bomb. Most notable are the playlets *The Lunatic View*, 1957, and *A View from the Brink*, 1961, with the subtitle 'a comedy of menace'.

Camus, Albert (1913–60), Algerian-born French philosopher, novelist and playwright. He was the leader 1935–39 of avant-garde theatre groups in Algiers: the Théâtre du Travail, until 1937, and 1937–39 the Théâtre de l'Equipe. He also worked as a journalist in North Africa and later in Paris, where he became one of the leaders of the French resistance movement during World War II. As a philosopher he is regarded as one of the leading figures of the French existentialist school; he used drama to express his philosophical ideas in the most concrete possible form, through the fate of individual human beings. He saw the world as basically without purpose or meaning – 'absurd'. But as man is at liberty he can give his own life meaning by freely choosing the cause to which he commits himself. C.'s dramatic works include: *Le Malentendu*, written 1941, fp Paris 1944, with MARIA CASARÈS, dir HERRAND – the return of a long-lost son who wants to surprise his mother and sister and, unrecognized, is murdered and robbed by them; *Caligula*, written 1938, fp 1945 with PHILIPE in the title role – the Roman emperor whose supreme power gives him absolute freedom tries to reach the limits of free will by arbitrary murder and cruelty; *L'Etat de siège*, fp Paris 1948, dir BARRAULT – a parable play about totalitarianism and resistance against it, using the resources of total theatre, poetry, MIME, choruses, etc.; *Les Justes*, 1949 – a discussion play in a Russian anarchist setting on the subject of the rights and wrongs of political murder. C. also made adaptations of plays and novels, e.g. *La Dévotion à la Croix*, from CALDERÓN's play, 1953; *Un Cas intéressant* from BUZZATI's *Un caso clinico*, 1955; *Requiem pour une nonne*, from William Faulkner's novel, 1956; *Les Possédés*, after DOSTOYEVSKY's novel, 1959. He was awarded the Nobel Prize for Literature in 1957.
Bibl: E. Freeman, THE THEATRE OF ALBERT CAMUS, 1971; J. Cruikshank, ALBERT CAMUS AND THE LITERATURE OF REVOLT, 1959

Canada. Largely dominated by a highly developed amateur theatre, e.g. Hart House Theatre at the University of Toronto, founded 1919, with professional directors and technicians. 1930 saw the founding of the Toronto Children's Players and in 1933 the Dominion Drama Festival was established. In 1934 the Little Theatre in Ontario was formed; it now has 7,000 members. Amateur theatre in French-speaking areas is strongly influenced by the Church, e.g. Compagnons de Saint-Laurent under the direction of Père Emile Legault. Since the opening of the Shakespeare Festival at Stratford, Ontario, 1953, founded by GUTHRIE, a powerful movement for the creation of professional theatre has taken shape and REPERTORY theatres have been established in a number of cities.
Bibl: H. Whittaker, THE CULTURE OF CONTEMPORARY CANADA, 1967; M. S. Tait, LITERARY HISTORY OF CANADA, 1965

Canetti, Elias (1905–), Bulgarian-born novelist and dramatist who writes in German. Studied in Frankfurt, Zurich and Vienna, emigrating to London 1938. Apart from his novels, the best known of which is *Die Blendung* (Engl. ed.: *Auto da Fé*) and the sociological essay, *Masse und Macht* (Engl. ed.: *Crowds and Power*), his work includes dramas like *Hochzeit* (Marriage), written in Vienna 1932, fp Brunswick, Germany 1965, *Komödie der Eitelkeit* (Comedy of Conceit), 1934, fp Brunswick 1965; *Die Befristeten* (The Time Limit), 1952, fp Vienna 1967. His plays deal with extreme social situations, e.g. in *Hochzeit* he uses grotesquely exaggerated realism, reminiscent of BRECHT's *Die Kleinbürgerhochzeit* (The Petty-bourgeois Wedding), while the other two plays have a tendency to ALLEGORY.

Cannan, Dennis (1919–), English dramatist. Began his career as the author of *Captain Carvallo*, 1950, St James's Theatre, dir OLIVIER. Subsequently worked on many film scripts and, in close association with BROOK, on both *US* at the Aldwych and an adaptation of GREENE's *The Power and the Glory*. His play *One at Night* was produced at the ROYAL COURT THEATRE in 1971.

Canticum. In Roman COMEDY song (*solo*) in a six-beat iambic line with flute accompaniment as distinct from the DIALOGUE parts (*diverbium*). It continues the dramatic action, whereas the Greek CHORUS interrupts the action. Found in extant plays by PLAUTUS. Theories of its origins are speculative, but it is presumed to have derived from the mime play. ▷MIME

Čapek, Karel (1890–1938), Czech dramatist, novelist and essayist, who collaborated on several plays with his brother **Josef Č.** (1887–1945). He studied philosophy and, during a stay in Paris, became interested in French avant-garde literature, painting and the philosophy of Henry Bergson. At the end of World War I he worked temporarily for the liberal paper *Lidové noviny*. He was at the Prague Municipal Theatre 1921–23. His most famous play is the utopian 'collective drama', *R.U.R.* (Rossum's Universal Robots, from the Czech *robotit*=to drudge), 1920, which was the name of an international trust for the manufacture of robots. Robots are a symbol of the threat of modern technology. In the course of a struggle between the robots and the human race the secret of their manufacture is lost, but miraculously they turn into human beings; two fall in love and thus regenerate the human race. In this dramatic work he exercises a humanistic perspective rather than a substantive critique of the world and the conditions of modern life. The success of *R.U.R.* was followed by that of the allegorical revue written by both brothers, *Ze života hmyzu* (*The Insect Play*), 1922, inspired by the entomologist Jean-Henri Fabre, which draws on a variety of theatrical forms such as REVUE, film and PANTOMIME. His other major works include: *Loupežník* (The Brigand), 1920, which mingles realism and SYMBOLISM, has a strong dramatic construction and depicts the conflict between young love and the prudishness of the older generation. *Věc Makropulos* (The Makropulos Secret), 1922, on which Janáček based his opera, is a philosophical drama with a utopian theme, the dream of immortality. Both his last plays are anti-Fascist works, *Bílá nemoc* (The White Plague), 1937, and *Matka* (The Mother), 1938.
Bibl: W. E. Harkins, 1962

Capitano (Ital=captain). A braggart and brawler; a character of the COMMEDIA DELL'ARTE, already found in PLAUTUS (*Miles Gloriosus*) and TERENCE. Variations of the part were created by: F. ANDREINI, *Capitano Spavento* (Ital=fright); F. Fornari, *Capitan Coc(c)odrillo*, play on Ital cocco (=cock) and coccodrillo (=crocodile); G. Gavarini, *Capitan Rinoceronte* (Ital=rhinoceros); G. Bianchi, *Capitano Spezzaferro* (Ital=iron-breaker or strongman). His COSTUME was based on the uniform of officials of the Spanish occupation, with an extra long rapier, large moustache and spurs.

Capocomico (Ital=colloquial, 'chief actor'). Artistic and business manager of a theatrical company who is at the same time a leading actor; equivalent to the Anglo-American ACTOR-MANAGER and the *Prinzipal* of the 18th- and 19th-century companies in GERMANY.

Caragiale, Ion Luca (1852–1912), Rumanian novelist and playwright. Founder of the comic theatre in Rumania, he was the author of sharp satires on the bourgeoisie: *O noapte futurnoasa* (A Stormy Night), 1878; *Conu Leonida fata cu reactiunea* (Mister Leonida and the Reaction), 1879; *O scrisoare pierduta* (The Lost Love Letter), 1884.

Carraro, Tino (1910–), Italian actor. Made his stage début in 1939 and subsequently appeared with numerous leading companies, e.g. playing the title role in MOLIÈRE's *Le Malade imaginaire* in 1951. A leading actor of great versatility, he has been at the PICCOLO TEATRO DI MILANO since 1952 where he has appeared in SHAKESPEARE's *Julius Caesar*, played the title role in *Coriolanus*, and Lopakhin in CHEKHOV's *The Cherry Orchard*.

Carroll, Paul Vincent (1900–68), Irish playwright. Originally a teacher, he scored his first success with *Things That Are Caesar's*, 1932, winning a prize from the ABBEY THEATRE in Dublin. His best-known play is *Shadow and Substance*, written 1934, which was produced in New York 1938, winning the NYDCC award, and in London 1943. This was followed by *The White Steed*, which had been rejected by the Abbey Theatre, in New York 1939, London 1947. His experience as a schoolmaster in Glasgow 1921–37, where he helped BRIDIE found the Citizens' Theatre, provided material for a number of plays, e.g. *Green Cars Go East*, Glasgow 1940, and *The Strings, My Lord, Are False*, Dublin and New York 1942, but his main concern was with his native land, of which he proved himself a consistent though loyal critic in his satirical but sympathetic analysis of the Irish Catholic clergy, e.g. *The Old Foolishness*, 1940; *The Devil Came from Dublin*, 1950; *The Wayward Saint*, 1955.

Carros. Wagons used in the Spanish AUTOS SACRAMENTALES, decorated with great splendour in the Church's workshops.

Carros navalis (Gk). A cart, decorated like a boat, which was pulled out through the streets during the *Anthesteria*, the spring festival held in honour of DIONYSOS.

Cartel (Théâtres du). A union of French theatres directed by BATY, DULLIN, JOUVET and PITOËFF, formed in Paris in 1927. The cartel was opposed to the academic style of performance of the COMÉDIE-FRANÇAISE and even more opposed to the non-artistic commercial theatre. It is difficult to judge how successfully it achieved its ideals, but it certainly exercised a strong influence on French theatre at the time.
Bibl: F. Anders, JACQUES COPEAU ET LE CARTEL DES QUATRES, 1959

Casarès, Maria (1922–), Spanish-born French actress. She made her stage début in SYNGE's *Deirdre of the Sorrows*, Paris 1943, Théâtre des Mathurins, and subsequently became the principal actress in the early existentialist plays, three by CAMUS: as Marthe in *Le Malentendu*, fp 1944; as Victoria in *L'Etat de siège*, fp 1948, and as

Karel Čapek's *R.U.R.*, THEATRE GUILD, 1922

Mrs Patrick Campbell in PINERO's *The Notorious Mrs Ebbsmith*, 1895

Canada, scene from a performance of *Henry V* at the Stratford, Ontario, Shakespeare Festival, 1956

Dora in *Les Justes*, fp 1949; Hilda in SARTRE's *Le Diable et le Bon Dieu*, fp 1951; Julie in *La Dévotion à la Croix* (Camus/CALDERÓN), 1953; she also played Jeannette in ANOUILH's so-called *pièce noire, Roméo et Jeannette*, fp 1946. She was at the COMÉDIE-FRANÇAISE 1952–54 (noted performance as Phèdre), subsequently at the TNP: Lady Macbeth, AVIGNON FESTIVAL, 1954. In the 1960s at BARRAULT's Théâtre de France: the mother in GENET's *Les Paravents*, 1966, Margaret of Anjou in SHAKESPEARE's *Henry VI*. One of the leading actresses in France today, she has also appeared in films.
Bibl: B. Dussane, 1953

Casona, Alejandro (Alejandro Rodríguez Alvarez; 1903–65), Spanish dramatist. Originally a teacher, he founded a theatre troupe for children; from 1931 he managed a travelling company, Teatro del Pueblo, till he went into exile in 1937 in France, Central and Latin America, becoming DRAMATURG in Buenos Aires in 1939, and returned to Spain in 1962. He enjoyed world-wide success with *Los árboles mueren de pié* (*The Trees Die Standing*), 1949. Other works include: *La sirena varada* (The Stranded Siren), 1934; *Nuestra Natacha* (Our Natasha), 1936; *Otra vez el diablo* (Next Time the Devil), 1935; *Prohibido suicidarse en primavera* (*Suicide Prohibited in the Springtime*), 1938; *Romance en tre noches* (Romance in Three Nights), 1938; *La dama del alba retalbo* (The Lady of the White Dawn), 1944; *La barca sin pescador* (The Boat without a Fisherman), 1945; *La llave en el desván* (The Key to the Attic), 1951; *La tercera palabra* (The Third Word), 1953.

Cassandre (Adolphe Mouron; 1901–), Russian-born French painter and stage designer. He spent most of his childhood in Russia but was educated in Paris, where he did his first design in 1934 for GIRAUDOUX's *Amphitryon 38*, dir JOUVET; in 1936 designed Balanchine's *Aubade* for the Ballets Russes de Monte Carlo. After a short break in his career he was, from 1941, in demand as a designer for drama, opera and ballet.

Casson, Sir Lewis Thomas (1875–1969), English actor, husband of the actress SYBIL THORNDIKE. Began his career as an amateur actor, then was at the ROYAL COURT THEATRE under Vedrenne-Barker for one season. He was artistic manager 1911–14 of the Gaiety Theatre in Manchester. In 1912 he founded a company and toured the USA with a REPERTORY of 11 plays. His production of *Julius Caesar* in 1913 was staged simply, and was outstanding for its naturalistic approach to the text. After World War II he worked mainly as a director and continued organizing tours largely in South Africa and Australia. In 1940 he was with GRANVILLE-BARKER at the OLD VIC and appeared there as Kent in *King Lear*. He was knighted in 1945.

Castro y Bellvís, Guillén de (1569–1631), Spanish dramatist. Author of COMEDIAS EN CAPA Y ESPADA (cloak-and-sword dramas), a genre in which he followed his contemporary and friend, LOPE DE VEGA. His plays, *Las mocedades del Cid* (The Cid's Youth) and its sequel *Las bazañas del Cid* (The Cid's Exploits), which were dramatizations of ballads celebrating the great Spanish hero, became important in world literature as models for CORNEILLE's *Le Cid*, 1637. His other works include *Los malcasados de Valencia* (The Ill-wed of Valencia), *El Narciso en su opinión* (The Man Who Thought He was Narcissus) and *El conde de Alarcos* (The Count of Alarcos).
Bibl: H. Mérimée, L'ART DRAMATIQUE À VALENCIA, 1913

Cavea (Lat=hollow). The semicircular auditorium of the Roman theatre, rising more or less steeply, row by row. The categories of seating were: *prima c.* – first level; *c. media* – middle level; *c. ultima* or *c. summa* – highest level, the 'gallery'.

Cecchi, Giovanni Maria (1518–87), one of the most influential early Italian dramatists. His work marks an important stage in the transition from religious to secular drama (he intermingled mythological themes and scenes from contemporary life in biblical drama) and from popular FARCE to classical COMEDY, e.g. *Assiuolo*, 1550.

Cecchini, Pier Maria (known as FRITELLINO; 1575–1645). Important actor and author of the COMMEDIA DELL'ARTE from 1591, he appeared in the mask of the second ZANNI with his wife Orsola (known as Flaminia) (1580–?); toured Italy with the ACCESI company (with T. MARTINELLI) and made several successful visits to France; in 1600 to Lyons for the marriage of Henry IV and Maria de' Medici; and again in 1601, 1608; he was in Austria 1613–14 (Linz and Vienna).
Bibl: ▷COMMEDIA DELL'ARTE

Censorship ▷LORD CHAMBERLAIN.

Centlivre, Susanna (1667–1723), Irish-born English actress and playwright. A masculine-looking woman, she played mainly men's parts, though she was more successful as a writer, first with the sentimental drama *The Gamester*, 1705, Lincoln's Inn Fields. She made a breakthrough with her comedies of intrigue: *The Busybody*, 1709, THEATRE ROYAL, DRURY LANE, and *A Woman Keeps a Secret*, 1714, with ANNE OLDFIELD and Robert Wilks; GARRICK chose the play in 1776, with the part of Don Felix for his last stage performance. Her last play *A Bold Stroke for a Wife*, 1718, shows the influence of CONGREVE. All three were often revived.
Bibl: A. Nicoll, A HISTORY OF ENGLISH DRAMA 1600–1900, III/1952

Centre 42 ▷WESKER, ARNOLD.

Centres dramatiques. State and municipally subsidized theatres in FRANCE, designed to bring drama to the hitherto neglected areas outside Paris. Until World War II most provincial cities and towns in France had to rely on touring companies, which brought them mainly the current successes of the Paris boulevard. In 1937 DULLIN proposed the 'decentralization' of theatrical activity, an idea which had been first mooted by GÉMIER and later by COPEAU. After the war, in 1946, it was decided to create five Centres dramatiques. By 1967 there were nine such centres: Comédie de St Étienne; Grenier de Toulouse; Comédie de l'Ouest, at Rennes; Comédie de l'Est, at Strasbourg; Centre dramatique du Sud-Est, at Aix-en-Provence; Centre dramatique du Nord, at Tourcoing; Comédie de Bourges; Théâtre de la Cité de Villeurbanne, near Lyons, led by PLANCHON; and Théâtre de l'Est Parisien, which serves the industrial suburbs of Paris. The Centres dramatiques perform a wide-ranging modern and classical REPERTOIRE; three of them have their own drama school. MALRAUX, Minister of Culture in De Gaulle's administration, widened the programme of cultural decentralization by an ambitious plan for the creation of numerous *maisons de culture* – cultural centres, each with its own theatre, cinema, lecture rooms, exhibition halls, etc., in provincial towns. Many of these have, in fact, developed into local REPERTORY theatres of high quality so that the decentralization movement in France comprised at least 20 permanent companies in the early 1970s.

Cervantes Saavedra, Miguel de (1547–1616), Spanish novelist, playwright and poet. Famous mainly through his great work, *Don Quixote*; as a dramatist he stands apart from the mainstream of Spanish drama. He wrote about 30 plays, of which eight COMEDIAS – e.g. *Pedro de Urdemalas*, translated by Walter Starkie in 1964 as *Pedro, the Artful Dodger*; *El rufián dichoso* (The Blessed Pimp) – and eight ENTREMESES (interludes or sketches) – e.g. *El retablo de las maravillas* (The Wonder Show), *El juez de los divorcios* (The Divorce Court Judge), *El viejo celoso* (The Jealous Old Husband), *La cueva de Salamanca* (The Cave of Salamanca) – were published in 1615. These were his most effective works and his greatest contribution to the theatre. They gave a lively impression of contemporary life in Spain and contain satirical elements reflecting the social and political situation of his time. His only two extant full-length plays are the Senecan melodrama *El Cerco de Numancia* (The Blockade of Numancia) and the comedy *El Trato de Argel* (The Business at Algiers) where he deals with his personal adventures and the five years' imprisonment he experienced in Algiers. His influences were basically humanist; in his early youth he was an admirer of the actor-playwright LOPE DE RUEDA; though his prose writing shows dramatic talent and feeling for the theatre, he could not compete with the superior technique of LOPE DE VEGA.
Bibl: J. Casaduero, SENTITO Y FORMA DEL TEATRO DE CERVANTES, 2/1966

Cervi, Gino (1901–74), Italian actor. After early success with an amateur troupe, he appeared in 1924 with ALDA BORELLI's troupe and in 1925 at the Teatro d'Arte di Roma, under the direction of PIRANDELLO.

Later he worked with several companies, from 1935 as principal actor, and from 1938 at the Teatro Eliseo di Roma, which he managed after 1939. His noted performances include: Falstaff in *The Merry Wives of Windsor*, 1939, and the title role in *Othello*, 1940; from 1945 he appeared in a series of first productions of modern plays including: Georges in COCTEAU's *Intimate Relations*, dir VISCONTI, Hector in GIRAUDOUX's *Tiger at the Gates*, dir SALVINI. His most brilliant performance was the title role in ROSTAND's *Cyrano de Bergerac*, 1953. He was a vital actor, particularly successful in interpreting bourgeois characters, full of life, anti-romantic, never unsympathetic. He was also well known as a film actor, e.g. Peppone in the 'Don Camillo' films.

Césaire, Aimé (1913–), French poet and playwright born in Martinique. Also an important political personality, who tries in his work to link the African cultural tradition with European culture; his poems are very close to SURREALISM. In his dramatic work he is concerned with the fate of individual African political figures in a period of decolonization and their failure because of the inconsistency and political inexperience of the African people, showing the difficulties in recovering human dignity after centuries of slavery: *Et les chiens se taisaient*, pub 1956, a dramatic poem which deals with the fight for freedom in the Antilles; *La Tragédie du roi Christophe*, pub 1964, is based on the historical character of the king of Haiti (1811–20) and was first produced at the SALZBURG FESTIVAL in 1964 by Jean-Marie Serreau and performed at the Théâtre de France in 1965. *Une Saison au Congo*, pub 1966, is a semi-documentary commentary on the rise and death of Patrice Lumumba, hero of the Congolese struggle for freedom, fp Paris 1967, Théâtre de l'Est Parisien, dir Serreau.
Bibl: H. Hatzfeld, TRENDS AND STYLES IN 20TH-CENTURY FRENCH LITERATURE, 1966

Chagall, Marc (1887–), Russian painter, now living in France. Studied stage design under BAKST for a year in 1907, and between 1917 and 1921 designed several sets for the HABIMAH THEATRE and the Hebrew State Theatre in Moscow, which were only partly realized. In 1942 he designed Massine's ballet *Aleko* (Ballet Theatre, USA); in 1945 *L'Oiseau de feu*, ballet by A. Bolm, choreography by Balanchine; in 1967 Mozart's *The Magic Flute*, the opening production of the new Metropolitan Opera House at the LINCOLN CENTER in New York.
Bibl: M. Ayrton, 1950

Chaikin, Joseph ▷OPEN THEATRE.

Chamberlain's Men. Elizabethan theatre company with which SHAKESPEARE was mainly connected; he was one of the shareholders and wrote most of his plays for them. They appeared 1594–99 at J. BURBAGE's THEATRE, subsequently at the GLOBE. In 1603, under the patronage of James I, they became the King's Players. From 1608 Shakespeare gradually withdrew and BEAUMONT and FLETCHER became the resident playwrights of the company, with MASSINGER and SHIRLEY. In addition to the Globe, they also took over the BLACKFRIARS THEATRE and continued to appear as the leading company at Court, where they were consistently invited, even after the death of Shakespeare in 1616, and after the death in 1619 of the principal actor R. BURBAGE, the first interpreter of the great Shakespearean roles, until 1642 when the theatres were closed and the company ceased to exist.

Champmeslé. (1) **Charles Chevillet C.** (1642–1701), French actor. One of the earliest members of the COMÉDIE-FRANÇAISE after its foundation in 1680; also the author of several COMEDIES among the best of which were: *Les Grisettes ou Crispin chevalier*, fp Paris 1673, HÔTEL DE BOURGOGNE; *Le Florentin*, fp 1685, CF; *La Coupe enchantée*, 1688. He was a fine tragic actor, though overshadowed by his wife, the much celebrated actress (2) **Marie Desmares C.** (1642–98), known as La Champmeslé. With her husband she joined the Théâtre du Marais in 1669, and a year later went to the Hôtel de Bourgogne, where she created the part of Bérénice in RACINE's play; in 1679 she joined the Théâtre Guénégaud, which, after MOLIÈRE's death, was founded by a fusion of the Marais company and the Palais Royal; going on from there to be leading actress of the CF where she appeared as Phèdre in the opening production in 1680 and, until the end of her life, remained the most popular actress of the company. She was goodlooking and possessed a melodious, expressive voice with which she established the chanting, declamatory style for the classical French TRAGEDIES, which passed on to the actresses of the following generations. She was also admired for her charm and wit by many famous men of her time, including Racine and La Fontaine, who dedicated his *Belphégor* to her.
Bibl: E. Mas, LA CHAMPMESLÉ, 1927

Chancerel, Léon Louis (1886–1965), French dramatist. Pupil of COPEAU, collaborated with DULLIN at the Théâtre de l'Atelier; founder and director of several companies including the amateur ensemble, Les Comédiens-Routiers, and the children's Théâtre de l'Oncle Sébastien, 1935; one of the initiators and heads of the popular theatre movement of the CENTRES DRAMATIQUES. He succeeded JOUVET as president of the Société d'Histoire du Théâtre, and was the French representative on the Committee of the International Federation of Theatre Research. He also wrote critical, theoretical and historical essays.

Chanson. Originally any vocal epic or secular lyric poem, today generally a light popular song. The oldest are the *chansons de geste*, heroic legends, part-songs which were sung by minstrels in the Middle Ages. In the form of an interlude known as *canzone* or *canzonetta* in Italian, *canción* in

Maria Casarès as Lady Macbeth at the AVIGNON FESTIVAL, 1954

Marie Desmares Champmeslé

Chagall, costume design for SYNGE's *The Playboy of the Western World*, 1920

Spanish (they were sung by actors as distinct from trained singers who performed in opera and light comedy), they are found in the Italian INTERMEZZO, in the English BALLAD-OPERA, in the French OPÉRA-COMIQUE, in the German SINGSPIEL (a special form was the couplet of the local FARCES of Vienna and Berlin), in the Spanish ZARZUELA, in English and American MUSICAL COMEDY. The *chanson* is one of the most important elements of CABARET (mostly of political and erotic content), from which the form was adopted in BRECHT's plays (he preferred the harder sounding English word 'song'), and also in REVUES and musical comedies.

Chapman, George (1559–1634), English poet, dramatist and translator of Homer (the inspiration for a famous sonnet by Keats), Juvenal and other classics. He wrote *Eastward hoe!*, 1605, in collaboration with JONSON and MARSTON, fp by the CHILDREN OF ST PAUL'S; a satire on the investiture of knights held by James I, it gave offence and led to the imprisonment of Chapman and Jonson. *All Fools*, 1604, is strongly influenced by TERENCE and was described by Swinburne as one of the best COMEDIES in the English language. C.'s TRAGEDIES are generally MELODRAMAS of blood and horror with the exception of his most famous play *Bussy d'Ambois*, fp 1604, with FIELD playing the title role, and its sequel *The Revenge of Bussy d'Ambois*, *c.*1610, which are interspersed with philosophical reflections reminiscent of *Hamlet*.
Bibl: E. Rees, 1955; E. K. Chambers, THE ELIZABETHAN STAGE, 1923, 2 vols

Charon, Jacques (1920–75), French director. Started as assistant director to BATY, and became one of the leading directors of the COMÉDIE-FRANÇAISE, and from 1946 a SOCIÉTAIRE. He directed successful FARCES and VAUDEVILLE plays such as FLERS/CAILLAVET's *Le Roi*, 1959, and FEYDEAU's *La Puce à l'oreille*, 1966, which production later came to the OLD VIC in London. Other productions include Frank Martin's comic opera *Monsieur de Pourceaugnac*, fp Geneva 1964, and ROSTAND's *Cyrano de Bergerac*, 1964.

Charonian steps (Gk *Charoneia klimax*= staircase from the underworld). A feature of the Greek theatre leading from the *orchestra* on to the *proskenion*. An actor's entrance using these symbolized his appearance from the underworld.
▷AMPHITHEATRE.

Chase, Mary Coyle (1907–), US dramatist. She gained a world-wide reputation with her play *Harvey*, fp New York 1944, starring Frank Fay, a comedy about a man and his companion, an invisible six-foot white rabbit, for which she was awarded the PULITZER PRIZE in 1945. Among her other works: *Mrs McThing*, starring HELEN HAYES, and *Bernardine*, both 1952; *Midgie Purvis*, starring TALLULAH BANKHEAD, 1961.

Chayefsky, Paddy (1923–), US playwright, TV and screen writer. His plays include: *Middle of the Night*, with Edward G. Robinson, 1956; *The Tenth Man*, 1959; *Gideon*, with F. MARCH, 1961; *The Passion of Joseph D.*, 1964; *The Latent Heterosexual*, 1968. His best-known TV play is *Marty*, for the film version of which he received an Academy Award in 1955.

Cheeseman, Peter ▷VICTORIA THEATRE, STOKE-ON-TRENT.

Chekhov, Anton Pavlovich (1860–1904), Russian dramatist. A physician by profession, he wrote short stories for newspapers and periodicals while still a student. Later turned towards the theatre and wrote a number of short one-act farcical sketches as well as a number of major dramatic works which straddle the categories of COMEDY and TRAGEDY, and give a marvellous picture of Russian society at the end of the 19th century. One of the world's supreme playwrights, C. was an innovator of dramatic technique. In the wake of the NATURALIST movement he above all tried to create atmosphere; his plays rely on the subtle portrayal of complex moods among complex groups of people. This impressionistic, almost *pointilliste* technique goes hand in hand with major innovations in the art of DIALOGUE. One of the most acute observers of human nature and behaviour in the history of drama, C. realized that human communication often does not take place in the words that are actually said, but beneath the explicit meaning of what is spoken and left unsaid. The emphasis in his plays thus shifts from the text to the subtext and indeed into the silences between the characters. His first dramatic work was *Platonov* (written 1877–81), not performed in his lifetime, and published posthumously 1923; it was followed by the one-act plays *Na bolshoi doroge* (On the high road), 1885; *Lebedinnaya pesnaya* (The Swan Song), 1886; *O vrede tabaka* (*On the Hazards of Smoking Tobacco*), 1886–1902, in six different versions; *Noch pered sudom* (The Night before the Trial), 1890; *Tragik ponevole* (A Tragedian in Spite of Himself), 1890; *Yubilei* (The Anniversary), 1891. The most frequently performed one-act plays are: *Medved* (*The Bear*), 1888; *Predlozhenie* (*The Proposal*), 1889; and *Svadba* (*The Wedding*), 1889. Full length plays: *Ivanov*, St Petersburg 1887; *Chaika* (*The Seagull*), fp St Petersburg 1896, where it was a failure, revived by STANISLAVSKY at the MOSCOW ART THEATRE in 1898 with lasting success; *Dydya Vanya* (*Uncle Vanya*), 1899, MAT (revised version of an earlier play *Leshi* (*The Wood Demon*) which had been performed in Moscow in 1889 but withdrawn by C.); *Tri sestry* (*Three Sisters*), 1901, MAT; *Vishnyovy sad* (*The Cherry Orchard*), 1904, MAT. C.'s influence on the subsequent development of drama in the world has been immense.
Bibl: S. Lafitte, 1966; R. Hingley, 1950

Chénier, Marie-Joseph (1764–1811), French dramatist. Brother of the poet André de C., he was an important literary figure of the French Revolution (member of the Convention). Before 1789 his work was suppressed by censorship against which he protested in his essay 'De la Liberté du Théâtre', 1789. His tragedy *Charles IX ou l'Ecole des rois*, fp 1789, COMÉDIE-FRANÇAISE, became a revolutionary treatise; a revival in 1790 created a split in the CF. The play was enthusiastically received, partly because of the acting of TALMA, who later opened the Théâtre de la République with Chénier's *Henry VIII*, 1791, and produced his *Jean Calas*, 1791, and *Caïus Gracchus*, 1792. His work has an important place in the development of historical drama in FRANCE.
Bibl: A. J. Bingham, 1939

Chéri, Rose (Rose-Marie Cizos; 1824–61), French actress. One of a large family of actors, she made her stage début in 1842 at the Théâtre du Gymnase in Paris, where she remained throughout her career. She was a graceful and charming woman, one of the most admired and best loved actresses of her time. With her husband Montigny (Auguste Lemoine), whom she married in 1847 and who was the manager and director of the Théâtre du Gymnase, she achieved a notable simplicity of style in plays by AUGIER, DUMAS, VIGNY, SARDOU and George Sand. She also appeared several times in London.

Chevalier, Maurice (1888–1973), French actor, singer and dancer. From a humble background, he sang in cafés as a child and became the partner of MISTINGUETT at the FOLIES-BERGÈRE. Made his London début in 1919 in the revue *Hullo, America!*; in New York 1929, in a ZIEGFELD show; from that time on he was one of the greatest international STARS of his day in CABARET, REVUE, theatre and cinema. He was the embodiment of the elegant, Parisian charmer, whose working-class origins shone through his mischievous *gamin* smile. Among his most famous American films were *The Merry Widow*, *The Smiling Lieutenant*, *The Love Parade* and *Gigi*. Memoirs: *The Man in the Straw Hat*, 1949, and *I Remember It Well*, 1970.

Chiarelli, Luigi (1880–1947), Italian dramatist. Progenitor of the THEATRE OF THE GROTESQUE, launched by his major work, *La maschera e il volto*, an exploration of inadequacy and corruption, and the falseness of social man, which was successfully staged in 1916 by the avant-garde Compagnia Drammatica in Rome and, in the same year, in Milan by TALLI. Translated and adapted by C. B. Fernald, it was produced in London in 1924 as *The Mask and the Face*. His other works include: *Le lacrime e le stelle* (The Tears and the Stars), 1918; *Chimere* (Chimeras), 1920; *La morte degli amanti* (The Death of the Lovers), 1921; *Fuochi d'artificio*, 1923 (as *Money, Money* in England, 1927); *Les tripes à la mode de Caen*, 1925; *Jolly*, 1928; *K 41*, 1929; *La reginetta* (The Little Queen), 1931; *Un uomo da rifare* (A Man to Remake), 1932; *Una più due* (One plus Two), 1935; *Il cerchio magico* (The Magic Circle), 1937; *Il teatro in fiamme* (The Theatre in Flames), 1945; *Essere* (To Be), 1953.
Bibl: M. Lo Vecchio Musti, 1942

Chichester Festival. Founded by OLIVIER in 1961 in a large arena-type theatre building created by the initiative of local residents in the cathedral city of Chichester, West Sussex. The first season was in 1962. In 1966 CLEMENTS took over from Olivier as artistic director. The festival attracts large audiences in the summer months, with plays ranging from CHEKHOV and the Elizabethans to BRECHT, ARDEN, SHAFFER, ANOUILH, etc. In 1974 Keith Michell succeeded Clements.

Chiesa, Ivo (1920–), Italian journalist, writer and theatre manager. In 1946 he founded in Genoa with B. M. Guglielmino the theatre magazine *Sipario* (of which he remained a director till 1951), the main theatre magazine in Italy, now published in Milan. He is also author of plays, mainly adaptations, e.g. *Gente nel tempo* (People in Time), based on Bontempelli, a contemporary Italian playwright, journalist and novelist, himself influenced by PIRANDELLO and FUTURISM, fp 1949, PICCOLO TEATRO DI MILANO, dir STREHLER. C. worked as an associate manager there, then as director of the *Compagnia stabile* in the Teatro Via Manzoni; since 1955 director of the TEATRO STABILE in Genoa.

Chikamatsu, Monzaemon (1653–1725), Japanese playwright. One of the most important and popular dramatists after the period of the *Noh* plays (▷JAPAN). He wrote 160 plays for the *Kabuki* theatre and after 1706 exclusively for the *Joruri* (PUPPET THEATRE) which fall into two distinct groups: heroic or historical plays such as *Kokusenya–gassen* (The Battles of Coxinga), 1715, and *Shusse Kagekiyo* (Kagekiyo Victorious), 1685; and domestic plays such as *Sonezaki shinyu* (The Love Suicides at Sonezaki), 1703; *Yari no Gonza* (Gonza the Lancer), 1706; *Onnagoroshi Abura Jigoku* (The Woman Killer and the Hell of Oil), 1721. Best English translation by Donald Keene, *The Major Plays of Chikamatsu*, 1961.

Children of St Paul's and **Children of the Chapel.** The most important English boy troupes in the 16th century; the ENSEMBLE consisted of choir-boys, who acted in plays by leading dramatists of the time in competition with professional companies. ▷LYLY.

Children's theatre. (1) Children *as* performers. In the Elizabethan theatre female parts were always played by boys, and productions by companies of boys (CHILDREN OF ST PAUL'S) even competed with the professional theatre, several dramatists writing exclusively for them. (2) Theatre *for* children. Since the 19th century special productions for children have been presented, mostly on festive occasions, e.g. dramatized fairy stories at Christmas time, and the Christmas PANTOMIME in England. This form of entertainment for children continued into the 20th century and in addition several attempts were made to produce regular shows for children; among these were the Comédiens-Routiers founded by CHANCEREL in Paris, 1935; also the

Chekhov reading *The Seagull* to the company of the MOSCOW ART THEATRE, 1898. His wife, OLGA KNIPPER, sits to the right, NEMIROVICH-DANCHENKO stands at the far left

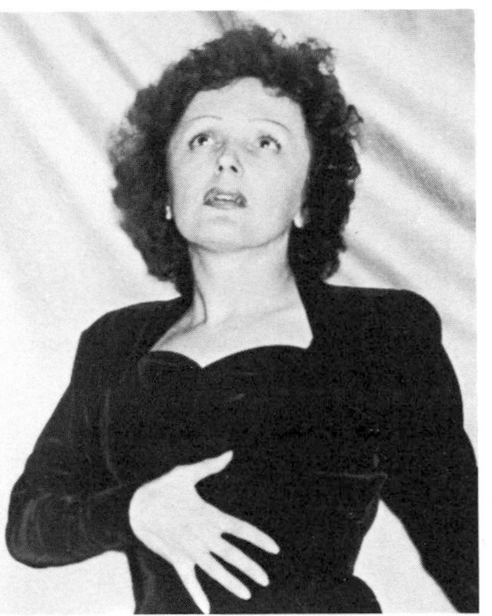

Chanson singer Edith Piaf

Maurice Chevalier

Chichester Festival, the large arena-type theatre building, interior

Young Vic in London which, as part of the OLD VIC, presents both children's and young people's drama and classics. There was systematic development of children's and youth theatre in the USSR after the October Revolution, where by 1935 there were 57 youth theatres. The modern Central Moscow Children's Theatre, dir Maria Knebel, produces many and varied forms of drama; the productions, in artistic and scenic quality, equal the theatre for adults. Similar developments can be seen in other Socialist countries. In the Western world there have been renewed attempts to develop theatrical forms which will have a special appeal and relevance for children and lay the foundations for an informed adult audience in the future: in England notably the work of Brian Way and Marjorie Sigley; in the US the work of the puppeteer Bil Baird and the New York Paper Bag Players.

China. Theatre is known to have existed in China since about the middle of the 8th century BC. It probably came from INDIA with Buddhism. The basic dramatic structures, characters and plots were written down in the 12th, 13th and 14th centuries. Peking was the cradle of Chinese theatre and has always remained its centre. Later theatre in China is characterized by a tradition of artistic presentation, which is a synthesis of song, dance, acrobatics, MIME and drama. The most austere form, the so-called Peking Opera, comprises a REPERTOIRE of almost 2,000 plays, but more importance is given to the actor than to the author. The PLOTS are well known to the audience, as are the traditional forms of presentation, so attention is focused mainly on the degree of artistic perfection of the individual performer. The actors are specialized and train from an early age. In Peking Opera female parts are played by men. Costumes are lavish and richly decorated, and their colours have great symbolic meaning. Animals are indicated by masks, gods and human beings by stylized make-up. Décor is scarcely used: to show a city wall, for instance, a piece of material is used, on which bricks are painted. Each movement has its own rhythm. The movement, conventionally stylized and characterized, expresses ideas, emotions and actions through highly refined and formalized technique. The musical accompaniment consists mainly of percussion instruments, which emphasize movement and rhythm. Vocal numbers, sung in falsetto, are generally accompanied by string instruments: Pipa-Pa, Chinese guitar, with great modular variation, allows all nuances of expression; Erhon, a Chinese violin with two strings of natural silk, with a snakeskin-covered body; Goutsing, Chinese lute with seven strings; and the flute, Ditza, already known 140 BC, made of bamboo, with six finger-holes and a stop. In Communist China a reinterpretation of the traditional theatre is taking place: the bad demons of the old plays become 'imperialists', the courageous young people are transformed into Communist fighters, while the traditional forms are preserved.
Bibl: Liu Wu-chi, AN INTRODUCTION TO CHINESE LITERATURE, 1966; A. C. Scott, THE CLASSICAL THEATRE OF CHINA, 1957

Chirico, Giorgio de (1888–1974), Greek-born Italian painter. In his stage designs he recreated the dream-like empty spaces of his early paintings and the exciting classicism of his later works: *La Jarre*, Ballet Suédois, Paris 1924; *Le Bal*, Ballets Russes de Monte Carlo, 1929; *Life of Orestes*, opera by Křenek, Berlin 1930; *The Legend of Joseph*, ballet with music by R. Strauss, 1951; *Apollon Musagète*, ballet with music by Stravinsky, 1956. The last two were produced at La Scala, Milan.

Chodowiecki, Daniel Nicolas (1726–1801), draughtsman and copperplate engraver. Worked in Germany from 1743; many of his engravings (mostly miniatures) are of great importance in theatre history. His first theatre portraits were 23 illustrations for MOLIÈRE's *L'Ecole des maris*; in 1770 he did 12 copper-engravings for LESSING's *Minna von Barnhelm*, based on DÖBBELIN's production in 1768 (during the performance he made sketches from which he developed the most important visual record of 18th-century theatre). His 15 Hamlet engravings of Johann Brockmann's Berlin performance in 1778/79 reveal much about the style of performance and décor. His other work includes: 12 copper-engravings for SCHILLER's *Kabale und Liebe*, 1785, with FLECK as Ferdinand, and 12 copper-engravings of BEAUMARCHAIS's *The Marriage of Figaro*, 1786, also with Fleck.

Choregos (Gk = chorus leader). In ancient Athens a citizen nominated by the State to pay the costs of a dramatic production. About 318 BC the State began to share in the expense thus incurred.

Chorodidaskalos (Gk = chorus teacher). Before 400 BC the playwright (poet), who later had the function of training or rehearsing the CHORUS as a professional teacher, paid by the State.

Chorus (Gk *choros* = place of dance; later the whole dance group). The foundation of Greek drama, which, according to ARISTOTLE, grew from the choral hymn (▷ DITHYRAMB) in honour of DIONYSOS. The dialogue between chorus and actor (PROTAGONIST) developed in the hands of THESPIS from the MONOLOGUE and DIALOGUE of the chorus; later AESCHYLUS introduced a second actor, the DEUTERAGONIST. The chorus dominated Greek drama (both TRAGEDY and COMEDY), commenting on and interrupting the action, even in some earlier plays functioning as the principal participant. Later, as less weight became attached to the elements of music and dancing, the chorus also diminished in importance. With EURIPIDES, it sometimes had only a poetical character which, in post-classical times, was its exclusive role. The structural function of the chorus was revived in the Middle Ages; in RENAISSANCE and BAROQUE THEATRE this was taken over by one character who acted as commentator and observer of the main action, e.g. the fool in Elizabethan tragedy, the confidante or maid-servant of French classical tragedy. In modern times several attempts have been made to revive the chorus in drama, mostly in providing a commentary to the action in plays by BRECHT, ELIOT and SARTRE.
Bibl: T. B. L. Webster, GREEK THEATRE PRODUCTION, 2/1970; A. W. Pickard Cambridge, THE DRAMATIC FESTIVALS OF ATHENS, 2/1968; M. Bieber, A HISTORY OF THE GREEK AND ROMAN THEATRE, 2/1961

Christie, Dame Agatha (1890–1976), English detective novelist and playwright. Most of her successes in the theatre are taken from her own works, notably *Alibi*, 1928, based on her novel *The Murder of Roger Ackroyd*; *Love from a Stranger*, 1936, based on a short story; *Ten Little Niggers* (US: *Ten Little Indians*), 1943; *Appointment with Death*, 1945; *Murder at the Vicarage*, 1950 (revived 1975); *The Mousetrap*, 1952 (still running in the West End of London in 1977, it has had the longest run in theatre history), based on her short story *Three Blind Mice*; *Witness for the Prosecution*, 1953; *Spider's Web*, 1954. Appointed a D.B.E. in 1971.

Cibber. English family of actors of the 18th century. (1) **Colley C.** (1671–1757), ACTOR-MANAGER and playwright. He was a brilliant comedian but his acting tended to rely on a rather shallow theatricality. Among the best of his plays are *Love's Last Shift or The Fool in Fashion*, 1696, in which he combines elements of the Restoration comedy of manners (▷ COMEDY) with the new vogue for sentiment and morality, and *The Careless Husband*, 1704. For a century his characters, especially in the late plays, were taken as representative of English upper-class society. In 1730 he was appointed Poet Laureate, probably for his Whig sympathies, but he was ridiculed by Pope in *The Dunciad*, a satire on hack-writers, and also by FIELDING and Dr Johnson. C. acted mainly at DRURY LANE, of which he later became co-director. His *Apology for the Life of Mr Colley Cibber, Comedian* (new edition, 1914) gives a detailed description of and insight into the nature of RESTORATION DRAMA. C.'s son (2) **Theophilus C.** (1703–58) was a talented actor, but his eccentric and extravagant behaviour destroyed his potential career. T.C.'s second wife (3) **Susanna Maria C.** (1714–66), sister of Thomas Arne the composer, known as Mrs Cibber, was originally a singer, much admired by Handel when she appeared in his *Acis and Galatea*. She was trained by C.C. after marrying his son and appeared in 1736 in VOLTAIRE's *Zaïre*. Later she became GARRICK's leading tragedienne. She was buried in Westminster Abbey. One of C.C.'s daughters, (4) **Charlotte C.** (1713–60), who married Richard Charke, a violinist, was an extravagant personality and a rather masculine woman who was at her best in men's parts, e.g. Roderigo in *Othello*. She also wrote comedies and was the author of the notable autobiography, *A Narrative of the Life of Mrs Charlotte Charke*, 1755.
Bibl: F. D. Senior, 1928

Circus. A space in the strictest sense circular, but sometimes oval or even oblong, intended for the exhibition of races and other contests. In Roman times it was an arena where the chariot-racing and gladiatorial combats took place, the oldest being the Circus Maximus, situated in the valley between the Palatine and the Aventine Hills. It was the only public spectacle where the men and women were not separated.

The circus of modern times is a form of popular entertainment which has little in common with the institution of classical Rome. It is frequently nomadic in character, the place of the permanent building known to the ancients being taken by a tent (the 'Big Top'). The traditional travelling circus consisted basically of feats of horsemanship and acrobatics, and by drolleries from the CLOWN. The popularity of the circus in England may be traced to that of Philip Astley (d. 1814) at the end of the 18th century. Ducrow who followed him had much to do with establishing the traditions of the circus which was perpetuated by shows such as Hengler's and Sanger's of a later generation.

In colonial days several English shows brought troupes to the US, among the first being Reckett's circus which exhibited in New York in 1797. The first American-born showman of note was Rufus Welch, who in 1818 managed a wagon show and later directed larger outfits. In 1826 the Mount Pitt Circus opened in New York, in a building seating 3,500, at that time the largest place of entertainment in America. In areas too large for DIALOGUE to be heard, stage feats such as aerobatics and other exhibitions of skill and daring using complex machinery, grew in importance. In 1869 Coup projected the largest circus known up to that time and originated performances in two rings. He persuaded the showman BARNUM to enter the field. Bailey introduced the third ring. Barnum and Bailey joined forces and in 1881 they had a positive claim to possess the 'greatest show on earth'. Barnum's influence on the development of entertainment was considerable.

After 1920 there was a considerable revival of interest in the circus. Largely a family enterprise the great names were still around; in England Mills and Sanger; in the US Ringling as well as Barnum and Bailey; there were others on the Continent. A state circus was founded in the USSR.

Today the circus can be divided basically into three types; in England the travelling caravan, on the Continent a music hall with arena and stables, in the US a mobile arsenal of amusements. Seasonal shows are given in huge permanent buildings such as Olympia in London and Madison Square Garden in New York; smaller ones in villages under a canvas bell tent. Circus acts are drawn from all over the world and performed internationally, but in its size and peculiar mobility the modern circus is American in character.

Bibl: H. R. Nutt, OUR RINGLING FAMILY STORY, 1960; E. C. May, CIRCUS FROM ROME TO RINGLING, 1932

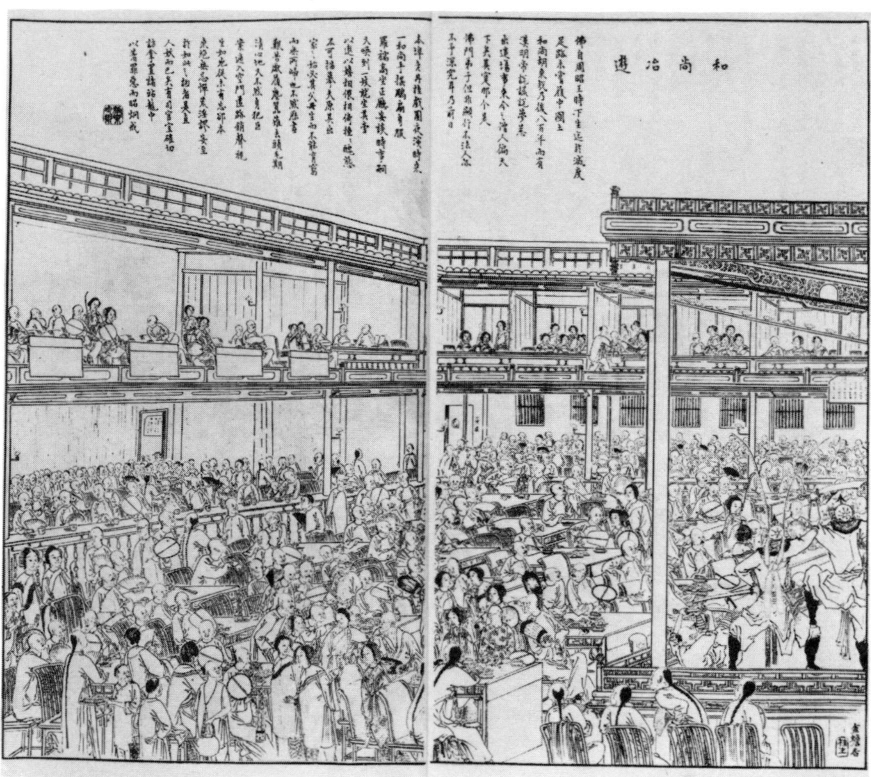

China, 19th-century theatre in Shanghai

Circus, Astley's Amphitheatre

Claire, Ina (1895–), US actress and singer, best known for stylish performances in light comedy. First appeared in VAUDEVILLE in 1907, making her New York début in 1909 in an impersonation of the Scottish comic singer, Harry Lauder. Trained by BELASCO, she appeared in the musical *Jumping Jupiter*, 1911, in New York and then as Prudence in *The Quaker Girl*, 1911, also a musical. Her London début was in *The Girl from Utah*, 1913. Among her later successes were *The Last of Mrs Cheyney* by LONSDALE, 1925; *Our Betters* by MAUGHAM, 1928; *Biography*, 1932, and *End of Summer*, 1936, both by BEHRMAN; *The Confidential Clerk* by T. S. ELIOT, 1954. She has also appeared in films.

Clairon, Mlle (Claire-Josèphe-Hippolyte de la Tude; 1723–1803), French actress. She joined the COMÉDIE-ITALIENNE at the age of 13. In 1743 she went to the Opéra as a singer but was transferred to the COMÉDIE-FRANÇAISE to understudy MLLE DANGEVILLE. For her début she asked to be allowed to tackle the difficult part of Phèdre in RACINE's play, which request was granted, the company thinking she would learn through failure, but her performance in September 1743 was a triumph, and from that time she was considered the leading tragedienne alongside her rival MLLE DUMESNIL. She appeared as Camille in CORNEILLE's *Horace*, Roxane in *Bajazet* and Aricie in *Phèdre*, both by Racine. Protégée and friend of VOLTAIRE, her main parts were in his plays: Electra in *Oreste*, Idame in *L'Orphelin de la Chine*, Amenaïde in *Tancrède* and the title role in *Olimpie*. Her style of acting avoided any hint of improvisation and spontaneity, emphasizing acting as 'art' in contrast to the 'realism' of Mlle Dumesnil; DIDEROT praises Mlle C. in his *Paradoxe sur le comédien*. She supported LEKAIN in his concern for historically accurate COSTUMES and stage sets. In about 1753, at the height of her career, she found her declamatory manner inadequate and superficial, and switched to a more subdued and simple style, encouraged by Jean François Marmontel, author and critic. After leaving the CF she appeared only in private performances, notably at Voltaire's own theatre at Ferney. In 1772 she went to Germany to appear at the Court of the Margrave of Ansbach where she remained for 17 years and worked on her *Mémoires et réflexions sur l'art dramatique*, published in 1799. On the death of the Margrave, *c.*1789, she returned to Paris.
Bibl: J. C. Lancaster, FRENCH TRAGEDY IN THE TIME OF LOUIS XIV AND VOLTAIRE 1715–74, 1950, 2 vols

Claque (Fr 'clap'). A group of people hired and paid to applaud (▷APPLAUSE). It had already existed in ancient times. Nero engaged more than 5,000 goodlooking and beautifully dressed young people (*plausores*) for his public appearances on stage. The claqueurs were usually highly paid for their rehearsed applause (*imbrex*=clapping with hollow hands; *testa*=clapping with flat hands). In the Roman folk theatre favourites were engaged and spread around the AUDITORIUM to encourage applause at pre-arranged times. The Spanish BAROQUE THEATRE also knew the claque (*mosqueteros*). In the 19th century there were claques in the metropolitan theatres in Europe; in Paris for example where the agency Assurance de Succès Dramatique, 1820, undertook orders for a fixed fee for approval or disapproval, and the Metropolitan Opera House in New York was famous for its claque. At the beginning of the 20th century this practice often led to excited demonstrations between rival claques at large theatres like the State Opera in Vienna. Nowadays there are hardly any such organized groups.

Claudel, Paul (1868–1955), French poet, diplomat and the outstanding Catholic dramatist of his age. He began his writing in 1883 with a short drama entitled *L'Endormie*, which was a predecessor of his *Protée, drame satirique*, written in 1913, a lyrical farce with a Greek classical setting. Son of a minor civil servant of peasant stock, C. showed great intellectual promise as a young man and worked hard. He went through a profound religious crisis as an adolescent, losing his faith and regaining it again in a dramatic way in 1886 as he experienced what he described as an 'ineffable revelation' during a Christmas mass in Notre Dame, though he continued to have spiritual conflicts. From that time on he was deeply involved with Catholicism in his elaborately poetic plays with long stylistic speeches and scant action, and he was concerned to predicate a Christian concept of Salvation, depicting the conflict between the worldly, physical life and the spiritual one. He believed that God used the mutual love of human beings as an instrument for inculcating His divine love, thereby enabling men ultimately to attain a state of grace. He had been impressed by Rimbaud's *Illuminations* and its ideas on the supernatural which he had read just prior to his religious conversion, and was briefly under the influence of Mallarmé, as well as WILDE, GIDE and MAETERLINCK. He had read SHAKESPEARE thoroughly from the age of 14, following on to the Greek classics and RACINE. In 1888 he wrote *Une Morte prématurée*, but destroyed it for family reasons. His dramatic technique is characterized by SYMBOLISM and pathos.
His distinguished career in the diplomatic service took him all over the world, first as consul in the USA, 1893, then in China, Japan, Germany, Denmark, later as ambassador to Japan, 1921, and the USA, 1926, and elsewhere. Most of his plays were written during his period of government service and some reflect the backgrounds of the countries he visited, i.e. *L'Echange*, written 1893 while in Boston, with an American setting and American French-born protagonists, and the verse MYSTERY PLAY, *Le Repos du septième jour*, written 1896 while in China, which is about a Chinese emperor who finally delivers a message of redemption through Christ. Although some of his plays were first presented in France, e.g. *L'Annonce faite à Marie*, Paris 1912, Théâtre de l'Œuvre, dir LUGNÉ-POË, he did not become well known there until 1941 when BARRAULT began producing his plays systematically. Their entertainment content, requiring magnificent settings, was ideal for Barrault's concept of *théâtre total*. C. first became known to the world at large through a production of *L'Annonce faite à Marie* in Hellerau, Germany, 1913.
Major works include: *Tête d'or*, written 1889, fp Paris 1949, Odéon, dir Barrault; *La Jeune fille violaine*, written 1892, then rewritten several times, eventually becoming *L'Annonce faite à Marie*; *L'Echange*, written 1893, fp Paris 1914, Théâtre du Vieux-Colombier, dir COPEAU; translation of AESCHYLUS' *Oresteia*, 1892–96; *Partage de Midi*, written 1905, fp Paris 1948, Théâtre Marigny, Compagnie Renaud-Barrault; *L'Otage*, written 1908–12, fp Paris 1914, Théâtre de l'Œuvre, dir Lugné-Poë, the first of a 'papal trilogy'; *Le Pain dur*, written 1914, fp Paris 1949, Théâtre de l'Atelier, dir BARSACQ, the second of the papal trilogy; *Le Père humilié*, written 1916, fp Paris 1945, Théâtre des Champs-Elysées, the third of the papal trilogy, written while in Rome (he was honoured by the Pope in 1950); *Le Soulier de satin, ou Le Pire n'est pas toujour sûr*, written 1919–24, considered by C. to be his masterpiece, shortened and revised in 1943 in collaboration with Barrault, who produced it at the COMÉDIE-FRANÇAISE, music Honegger; *Jeanne d'Arc au bûcher*, a scenic oratorio, music Honegger, fp Basle 1938, then Théâtre Municipal d'Orléans, 1939; *L'Histoire de Tobie et de Sara*, written 1942, fp Hamburg 1953.
Bibl: J. L. Barrault, 1967; L. Chaigne, VIE DE PAUL CLAUDEL ET GENÈSE DE SON ŒUVRE, 1961; W. Fowlie, 1957; J. Chiari, THE POETIC DRAMA OF PAUL CLAUDEL, 1954

Claus, Hugo (1929–), Flemish writer, essayist, poet and playwright. His numerous plays include: *Een bruid in de morgen* (A Bride in the Morning), 1955; *Het Lied van de Moordenar* (The Song of the Murderer) 1957; *Mama kijk, zoder Handen* (Look Mother, No Hands) 1958; *De dans van de Reiger* (The Dance of the Heron) 1961. He also wrote one-act plays and translated BÜCHNER and D. THOMAS.

Clements, Sir John (1910–), English ACTOR-MANAGER. A fine classical actor who also excels in high comedy and is an excellent director. After appearing in the West End of London, with the OLD VIC and in the USA for many years, he was director of the CHICHESTER FESTIVAL THEATRE 1965–73, which he managed with outstanding artistic and commercial success. Married to the actress Kay Hammond. Knighted 1968.

Clive, Kitty (Catherine Raftor; 1711–85), English actress. She won her great reputation playing high comedy and farce appearing mainly with GARRICK at DRURY LANE. She was a passionate woman, who had many prominent admirers including GOLDSMITH, Dr Johnson and Horace Walpole. She wrote a BURLESQUE and four FARCES.

Clown. A composite comic figure who was variously court jester, knave or fool. He was found in Elizabethan theatre in England. In this early form the clown existed in various guises and had complex origins: in the devils of medieval MYSTERY PLAYS, court jesters, ruffians and country yokels. SHAKESPEARE's clowns in *As You Like It*, for example, vary from the foolish country boy William to the professional jester Touchstone and the mephistophelian philosopher Jaques. Famous clowns of the Elizabethan theatre were TARLETON and KEMPE. 1607 marked the first appearance of HARLEQUIN (ARLECCHINO) on the English stage; thus the comic figure of the COMMEDIA DELL'ARTE became part of the English tradition. During the 18th century, and even more in the 19th, clowns were no longer acceptable in the serious theatre. PIERROT and Harlequin became the main characters of English PANTOMIME. The clown was made famous by GRIMALDI in the 18th century who gave the name Joey to this role, from a part he had in a Christmas pantomime written by Thomas Dibden. Joey is the name now commonly given to circus artists with comic numbers. The character of the clown has always been tragi-comic in his inability to adapt himself to the outside world, conveyed by his constant battle with inanimate objects and with mockingly superior figures. Great circus clowns of the 20th century include GROCK, the Fratellinis, the Rivels and POPOV.
Bibl: W. Willeford, THE FOOL AND HIS SCEPTRE, 1969

Clurman, Harold Edgar (1901–), US director, critic and author; a pupil of COPEAU who spent two years during World War I at the Garrick Theatre, New York. In 1925 he began working at the Greenwich Village Theatre as stage manager, actor and play-reader, and in 1931, in association with STRASBERG and CHERYL CRAWFORD, founded the GROUP THEATRE, which had an important influence on the development of the US theatre until 1941, with productions like P. GREEN's *The House of Connelly*, 1931, KINGSLEY's *Men in White*, 1933, and early plays by ODETS. After the Group Theatre closed, Clurman worked temporarily as a film director, returning to the theatre in 1946, and staging many important productions including A. MILLER's *All My Sons*, 1947; O'NEILL's *Desire under the Elms*, 1952 (revival); ANOUILH's *Colombe*, 1954; SHAW's *Saint Joan*, 1954; INGE's *Bus Stop*, 1955; GIRAUDOUX's *Tiger at the Gates* (trans FRY), London and New York 1955, with REDGRAVE in the lead. He has also written several books of essays and theatre criticism, as well as the history of the Group Theatre under the title *The Fervent Years*, New York 1945.

Coburn, Charles (1877–1961), US ACTOR-MANAGER, who with his wife, the actress **Ivah Wills** (1882–1937), founded the Coburn Shakespearean Players. Besides the main Shakespeare plays, in which they both appeared, their REPERTOIRE included EURIPIDES' *Electra* and SHERIDAN's *The Rivals*.

Ina Claire in *The Quaker Girl*, New York 1911

Mlle Clairon in VOLTAIRE's *L'Orphelin de la Chine*

Claque at the Odéon, Paris

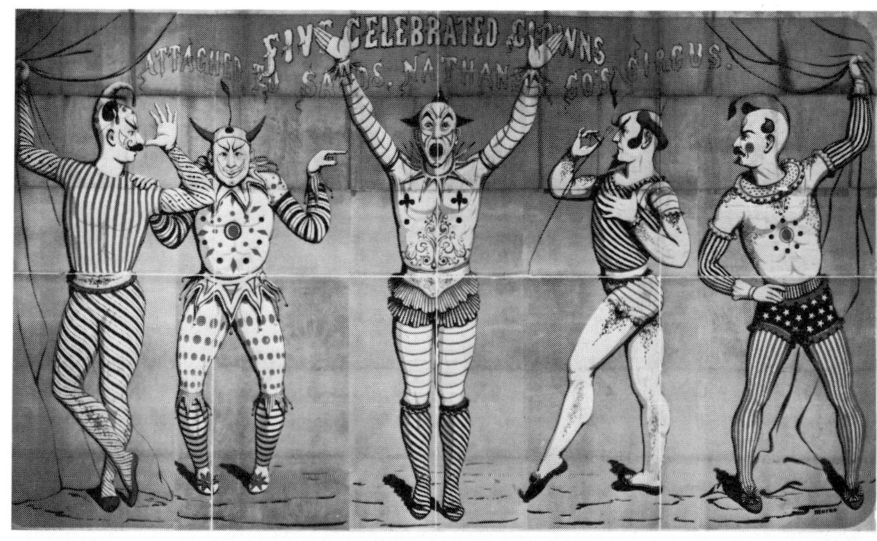

Clowns, in a circus poster

Coburn played Hamlet, Othello and Shylock, but had his greatest success as Old Bill in the contemporary light comedy *The Better 'Ole*, 1918, which ran for two years. His other well-known parts included James Telfer in *Trelawny of the 'Wells'* by PINERO and Wu Hoo Git in *The Yellow Jacket*, 1912, by George Hazelton and J. Harry Benrimo. He was one of the founders of the Mohawk Drama Festival in 1935, which later became an annual event. He left the stage after the death of his wife, but returned briefly in 1946 to act Falstaff for the THEATRE GUILD. Best known as a film actor.

Cochran, C. B. (Sir Charles Blake C.; 1872–1951), English theatrical producer, knighted in 1948. One of the most outstanding showmen of his time, he began his career as an actor in the USA, and served for five years as personal representative for MANSFIELD. He then went into management, his first production being IBSEN's *John Gabriel Borkman*, New York 1897. In 1911 he managed REINHARDT's production of Vollmöller's *The Miracle*, at Olympia, London, and in 1912 the German Hagenbeck CIRCUS, also at Olympia. From 1902 he made his reputation in London as an independent producer, mainly of MUSICAL COMEDIES and REVUES including *Sporting Simpson*, 1902, Royalty Theatre; *Odds and Ends*, 1914, and *Pell Mell*, 1916, both at the Ambassadors Theatre. His most famous productions at the London Pavilion: *As You Were*, 1918; *London, Paris and New York*, 1920. From 1925, he worked in association with COWARD, his greatest successes being *Bitter Sweet*, 1929, His Majesty's Theatre, and *Cavalcade*, 1931, DRURY LANE. His reminiscences were published as *Secrets of a Showman*, 1925; *I Had Almost Forgotten*, 1932; *Cock-a-Doodle-Do*, 1941, and *A Showman Looks On*, 1945.
Bibl: G. Graves, THE COCHRAN STORY, 1951

Cocteau, Jean (1889–1963), French poet, novelist, critic and playwright. At the age of 17 he published his first book of poetry and rapidly became a prominent figure in French intellectual circles, together with his friends ROSTAND, Daudet and Proust. His most popular novel was *Les Enfants terribles*, 1929, filmed in 1950. He also worked with the Russian ballet among artists who included PICASSO, Satie, Dufy, Diaghilev and Massine. Later he distinguished himself as a film director: *Le Sang d'un poète*, 1930, *Orphée*, 1950. In his dramatic work he was continually involved in EXPERIMENTAL THEATRE, writing in a variety of genres ranging from BOULEVARD THEATRE to classical TRAGEDY. He shows the poet struggling to transcend the preoccupations of everyday life. Of supreme importance in his theatre is his vision of death as a triumphant escape. His first produced work was the *ballet-réaliste*, *Parade*, 1917, in collaboration with Picasso and Satie, which created a scandal. His dramatic work includes: *Roméo et Juliette*, 1924, based on SHAKESPEARE; *Orphée*, fp 1926, Théâtre des Arts, dir PITOËFF; *Antigone*, fp 1922, Théâtre de l'Atelier, dir DULLIN, des Picasso, music Honegger; *La Voix humaine*, fp 1930, COMÉDIE-FRANÇAISE; *La Machine infernale*, fp 1934, Théâtre Jouvet, dir JOUVET; *Les Chevaliers de la Table ronde*, 1937; *Les Parents terribles* (*Intimate Relations*), 1938; *Les Monstres sacrés*, fp 1940, Théâtre Michel, dir A. Brulé, des BÉRARD; *La Machine à écrire*, 1941; *Renaud et Armide*, fp 1943, CF, dir Cocteau, des Bérard; *L'Aigle à deux têtes*, fp Brussels 1946; *Le Fantôme de Marseille*, fp 1952, Compiègne, a MONODRAMA written for Edith Piaf; *L'Epouse injustement soupçonnée*, 1950; *Bacchus*, fp 1951, Théâtre Marigny, prod Compagnie Renaud-Barrault.
Bibl: N. Oxenhandler, SCANDAL AND PARADE: THE THEATRE OF JEAN COCTEAU, 1957; M. Crosland, 1954; P. Dubourg, DRAMATURGIE OF JEAN COCTEAU, 1954

Cohan, George Michael (1878–1942), US actor, playwright, composer, lyricist and producer. As a small child he appeared with his parents and sister in a VAUDEVILLE act, *The Four Cohans*. At the age of 15 he started to write and compose popular songs and sketches for vaudeville. Among his more than 500 songs are all-time hits like 'I'm a Yankee Doodle Dandy', 1904; 'Give my regards to Broadway', 1904, and the wartime song 'Over There', 1917. His first MUSICAL COMEDY *The Governor's Son*, 1901, in which all four Cohans appeared, established the style of his subsequent successes by a mixture of popular music, FARCE, COMEDY and sentimental MELODRAMA. It was followed by *Running for Office*, 1903; *Forty-Five Minutes From Broadway*, 1906; *The Honeymooners*, 1907; *The Talk of New York*, 1908; *The Yankee Prince*, 1908; *Get-Rich-Quick Wallingford*, 1910; *Seven Keys to Baldpate*, 1913. In his later years he devoted himself to producing but also appeared as an actor in the work of other authors (e.g. Nat Miller in the THEATRE GUILD production of O'NEILL's *Ah, Wilderness!*, 1933). He wrote his autobiography *Twenty Years on Broadway; and the Years It Took to Get There*, 1925.

Coleridge, Samuel Taylor (1772–1834), English poet, critic and philosopher. Author of two VERSE DRAMAS of little theatrical merit: *The Fall of Robespierre*, pub 1794, and *Osorio*, 1797, later published as *Remorse*, fp 1813, DRURY LANE. His main importance for the theatre lies in his criticism and his work as an editor of SHAKESPEARE. He also translated several plays from the German, e.g. SCHILLER's *Wallenstein*.
Bibl: H. House, 1953

Colette (1873–1954), French writer. Many of her novels were dramatized by her and also by other writers; the most famous was *Chéri*, 1921, which she adapted with L. Marchand. Early in her career she also appeared as an actress and singer, e.g. in Van Lerberghe's *Pan*, 1906, Theatre de l'Œuvre, Compagnie LUGNÉ-POË.

Collé, Charles (1709–83), French dramatist and *chansonnier* (▷CHANSON). In 1729–39 a member of the Société du Caveau, a drinking club famous for its entertainment and good company. Subsequently he entered the service of the Duke of Orleans as his reader, adapted plays and wrote frivolous COMEDIES for the Duke's private performances: *La Vérité dans le vin*, 1747, a satire on the corruption of the clergy. The comedy *Dupuis et des Ronais*, fp 1759, was given at the COMÉDIE-FRANÇAISE in 1763; *La Partie de chasse d'Henri IV*, based on Robert Dodsley's *The King and the Miller of Mansfield*, 1739, was given a private performance in 1764, but not played in public till 1774, having been banned by Louis XV: it is an essay in democracy, in which a simple man teaches a king who is hunting incognito the principles of a state policy based on human worth.
Bibl: L. Breitholtz, LE THÉÂTRE HISTORIQUE EN FRANCE JUSQU'À LA RÉVOLUTION, 1952

Collier, Constance (1878–1955), English actress. Started her career at the age of three. She worked for TREE at His Majesty's Theatre, 1901–07; her roles included Pallas Athene in PHILLIPS's *Ulysses*, several Shakespearean parts such as Portia, Viola and Olivia, Cleopatra, and Mrs Ford in *The Merry Wives of Windsor*. In 1908 she made her stage début in New York, and from that time appeared alternately in England and the USA. Among her most famous parts were: the Duchesse de Surennes in MAUGHAM's *Our Betters*, 1923; the queen in *Hamlet*, with J. BARRYMORE in the title role, 1925; Judith Bliss in COWARD's *Hay Fever*, 1931. Under the pseudonym David L'Estrange she wrote two plays with NOVELLO, *The Rat*, 1924, and *Down Hill*, 1926. In 1929 she published her reminiscences under the title *Harlequinade*.

Colman. (1) **George C.** (the elder; 1732–94), English dramatist and theatre director. His play, *The Jealous Wife*, 1761, was one of the most popular COMEDIES of his time. He based his other main work, *The Clandestine Marriage*, 1766, on FIELDING's *Tom Jones*. Following a disagreement with GARRICK over the latter play he became an associate director of the COVENT GARDEN THEATRE 1764–74, and later of the Haymarket Theatre, 1777–85. He was succeeded in the management, 1794–1803, by his son (2) **George C.** (the younger; 1762–1836) who was an effective dramatist, and created many COMIC CHARACTERS which have survived as well-known comedy roles, e.g. Dr Pangloss and Dennis Brulgruddery. His plays include: *The Iron Chest*, 1796; *The Heir at Law*, 1797; *John Bull; or the Englishman's Fireside*, 1803; *The Actor of All Work; or, First and Second Floor*, 1817.
Bibl: A. Nicoll, HISTORY OF ENGLISH DRAMA, III/1952; E. R. Page, GEORGE COLMAN THE ELDER, 1935

Colomba, Giovanni Battista Innocenzo (1717–93), Swiss-Italian stage designer. Worked from 1737 in Germany and created the décor at the ducal court opera house in Stuttgart. He was a leading theatre architect of the classical late Baroque in Germany.

Bibl: M. Guidi, DIZIONARIO DEGLI ARTISTI TICINESI, 1932

Colombina (Ital = dove). Originally a mask of the COMMEDIA DELL'ARTE; the cunning maidservant and the confidante of her mistress. A counterpart to ARLECCHINO (HARLEQUIN), her stage lover, she was also known as Arlecchinetta and wore a corresponding costume, a multi-coloured dress originally with a black half-mask. In the French COMÉDIE-ITALIENNE she wears a very short white dress, the traditional 'tutu'. With the growing popularity of PANTOMIME she came to England in the 18th century as Columbine.

Comedia (Span), **comédie** (Fr), **commedia** (Ital). In the Romance languages originally a light-hearted or serious poem, e.g. Dante's *Divina Commedia*. Later the name given to all drama, both tragic and comic; today = COMEDY.

Comedia en capa y espada (Span = cloak-and-sword play). Comedy of Intrigue, named after the costume worn by aristocratic characters. It dealt mostly with affairs of honour, and incorporated a comic servant, e.g. GRACIOSO. The décor was simple, unlike the *comedia de ruido*, which was a lavishly spectacular production.

Comédie-ballet. A genre of theatre developed by MOLIÈRE in collaboration with the composer Lully; it lies midway between the Court ballet (▷BALLET DE COUR) and COMEDY. The PLOT gives occasion for elaborate balletic interludes. Most famous example: *Le Bourgeois gentilhomme*, 1670.

Comédie-Française. The national theatre of France, formerly the Théâtre Français. It was founded in 1680 by Louis XIV, with the merging of the company of the Théâtre du Marais and the HÔTEL DE BOURGOGNE with which MOLIÈRE's troupe was amalgamated in 1673. During the Revolution it split into the revolutionary Théâtre de la République, led by TALMA at the Palais Royal, and the conservative Théâtre de la Nation, but in 1803 the company of the CF was reformed. It is a co-operative society of actors, in which each holds a share; a new member is admitted first on probation, and called a *pensionnaire*, then after the resignation or death of one of the full members he may become a SOCIÉTAIRE. Until a reform in 1945 the earliest that an actor might leave the company was after ten years and, if a contract was broken, an actor risked being banned from the French stage for ten years. It is the oldest national theatre and has the longest continuous acting tradition, but its conservative REPERTOIRE, the casting of actors in recurring roles, and the inflexibility of its co-operative system has led to frequent criticism. Its golden age was determined by outstanding actors who included MLLE CLAIRON, MLLE CHAMPMESLÉ, BARON, LEKAIN, Talma, RACHEL (for a short time), SARAH BERNHARDT and MOUNET-SULLY. In this century several attempts have been made to rejuvenate it. Around 1940 directors of

Comédie-Française, a performance by MOLIÈRE's company

Constance Collier and TREE in *Antony and Cleopatra*

George M. Cohan in *Little Jonny Jones*, New York 1904

Colombina, a celebrated exponent of the part, CATARINA BIANCOLELLI

the CARTEL (COPEAU, DULLIN, JOUVET, BATY), who had been working in opposition to the CF occasionally produced there. BARRAULT directed CLAUDEL's *Le Soulier de satin* and MONTHERLANT's *La Reine morte*; the brilliant actor RAIMU appeared in the title role of Molière's *Le Malade imaginaire*. MADELEINE RENAUD and Barrault, who left the CF in 1946, managed the THÉÂTRE DE FRANCE (Odéon) in 1959–68 as the second national theatre. The REPERTORY of the CF includes the best of classical French literature, especially the COMEDIES of Molière and MARIVAUX, and the great French classical TRAGEDIES. It receives a state subsidy, which is part of an annual subsidy to all national theatres in France; in 1974 the subsidy was 109,508,320 francs.
Bibl: P. A. Touchard, HISTOIRE SENTIMENTALE DE LA COMÉDIE-FRANÇAISE, 1955

Comédie-Italienne. Italian companies of the COMMEDIA DELL'ARTE who often visited France at the end of the 16th century (first recorded visit, 1571, led by the GELOSI). From the middle of the 17th century they paid regular visits, from 1658 one company giving alternate performances with MOLIÈRE in the Petit-Bourbon, later in the Palais Royal. The name Comédie-Italienne was first used in 1680 to distinguish it from the COMÉDIE-FRANÇAISE which was founded in that year. About that time they began to intersperse the Italian text with French songs and DIALOGUE, which led to rivalry with the privileged actors of the CF. In 1697 they were expelled from France because they ridiculed Mme de Maintenon, the mistress of Louis XIV, by playing *La Fausse Prude*. In 1716 they returned, led by the elder RICCOBONI, and in 1723 were honoured with the title *Comédiens Ordinaires du Roi*, producing a great variety of shows, especially VAUDEVILLE. From the middle of the 18th century they gradually developed a musical theatre and when they amalgamated with the Opéra comique in 1801 the original CI, a vital part of French theatre history, ceased to exist.
Bibl: N. M. Bernardin, LA COMÉDIE-ITALIENNE EN FRANCE, 1902

Comédie larmoyante ▷LA CHAUSSÉE.

Comedy (Gk *komos* = a pageant or feast, and *oide* = a song). One of the two main genres of drama. If TRAGEDY deals with elevated subjects and usually has a sad ending, comedy in its widest sense (which comprises FARCE, BURLESQUE as well as subtler forms of humorous drama) deals with subjects of daily living and relatively trivial problems in a light-hearted manner with a happy solution. The main element of comedy in the narrower sense (as distinct from farce which deals with comical physical mishaps and external embarrassments arising from ludicrous situations) are the quirks and foibles of human character and the absurdities of the social scene. Another element of comedy is the wit and amusement derived from the DIALOGUE – the comic idiosyncrasies of language which, in their turn, arise out of the characters' peculiarities. A voluminous literature, concerned with the theory of dramatic genres and their definitions and subdivisions, has evolved various subdivisions of comedy: among these are the Elizabethan Comedy of Humours based on the four basic human temperaments or humours, as written by JONSON; the Restoration Comedy of Manners, as written by CONGREVE; the Renaissance Comedy of Intrigue from Spain (CALDERÓN) via France, in England as written by APHRA BEHN; the French *comédie larmoyante* of the 18th century as written by LA CHAUSSÉE, in which sentiment played an important part and which was influenced by the English sentimental comedies of STEELE. The writing and acting of comedy has also been divided into high comedy (with its emphasis on style and wit) and low comedy (based on characters from lower social orders and cruder, more physical effects). In recent years there has been talk of a Comedy of Menace (e.g. PINTER's plays). Drama which deals with comedy subjects (the trivia of life and the absurdities of society and human character) but contains elements of horror and sadness has been labelled Dark Comedy or TRAGICOMEDY.

Comedy (Greek). There are three categories:
(1) **Old Comedy** falls mainly into two divisions, Sicilian and Attic. Of the first little is known except that it was written in Doric, had no CHORUS, had a PLOT and was free from satire. Some of the stock characters foreshadow New Comedy. Sicilian comedy died out early giving place to the Attic comedy which began somewhere between 486 and 441 BC. The subject matter of Old Comedy is usually personal invective, mainly against political characters and individuals otherwise notorious, i.e. EURIPIDES and SOCRATES were attacked by Ameipsias in a comedy bearing his name. Another type of comedy is that of fantasy as typified by ARISTOPHANES in his *The Birds*, and yet another is mythological burlesque, more common in Middle Comedy but well established in Old Comedy as suggested by the titles of Aristophanes' plays. Old Comedy was written to a fixed plan (a) PROLOGUE, (b) entrance of chorus, (c) development of plot, with strict attention to metre.
(2) **Middle Comedy.** From Old Comedy there was continuous development through the Middle Period (*c.* 400–*c.* 320 BC), into the New. The downfall of Athens, 404 BC, vitally affected the comic stage; other themes replaced those which had evoked the wit and fancy of Aristophanes and his contemporaries. The structure was adapted to that of a play of intrigue in which the role of the chorus is greatly diminished. The transition is visible in Aristophanes' play *Plutus*, 388 BC. The realistic depiction of daily life became the chief aim in comedy and the most striking characteristic observation of contemporary types and manners. Diction and metre are much less elaborate than in the Old Comedy. About 50 names of poets are known, the main ones being ALEXIS and Antiphanes.
(3) **New Comedy** (320–250 BC). This continues the development begun by Middle Comedy away from the imaginative and fantastic. The chorus is almost altogether divorced from the action. The stock characters are shown by numerous masks. Personal ridicule is directed against parasites, gluttons, etc. and there are isolated attacks upon philosophers. The preponderant influence of Euripides, already marked in Middle Comedy, is seen in the dramatic treatment of modern problems. It is mainly serious in tone. Metre is even less elaborate than in Middle Comedy. About 70 names are known, the main ones being MENANDER, Philemon and Diphilus.

Comedy (Roman) ▷ROME.

Comic character. Theatrical character occurring in numerous national and historical variations; often improvised; universally recognized by a standard COSTUME and manner; in the Roman Comedy shrewd and clever slaves, in the PASSION PLAY of the Middle Ages, the cheated devil, in the COMMEDIA DELL'ARTE the ZANNI, DOTTORE, PANTALONE and CAPITANO, recognizable types with special features according to the country and social situations; from the Italian ARLECCHINO developed the French HARLEQUIN, the PICKELHERRING in GERMANY, the HANSWURST in Vienna in the 17th century; in more modern times the CLOWN in CIRCUS and variety shows.

Commedia dell'arte (meaning 'professional comedy'). Italian form of theatre which originated in Venice and Lombardy around the middle of the 16th century; often regarded as wholly improvised, because it has been mainly preserved through the scenarios and *canevas* – short outlines of the PLOT and the turning-points of the action – and because performances seemed so natural and spontaneous, as though the actors were inventing the DIALOGUE as they went along. In fact, the style and details of the performances were based on pre-arranged conventions and traditional formulae, e.g. the speeches, not written down in the outlines – even the carefully polished speeches of the young lovers – consisted largely of fixed rhetorical phrases, the learning of which formed part of the professional training of the actors. The themes usually were concerned with the love of a young couple (INNAMORATI), at first frustrated by the older generation but finally permitted, and the characters were stereotyped. Among the latter the two servants, ZANNI, were of central importance; it was from them that, among others, the ARLECCHINO developed – originally a peasant boy from Bergamo working in the big city, Venice. His COSTUME consisted of coloured diamond patchwork, broad-brimmed hat with a rabbit or fox tail, a black half-mask of leather, and a wooden sword. Variants of the zanni are the rustic TRUFFALDINO, the rascally and sly BRIGHELLA, the suggestive PULCINELLA (a forerunner of the German HANSWURST). Other stereotyped characters are: PANTALONE, the duped father and husband; the DOTTORE, a lawyer,

doctor or philosopher from Bologna, always represented as the garrulous, ridiculous scholar; the CAPITANO, a braggart and amorous soldier, always a Spaniard; Arlecchino's partner, the worldly-wise maidservant COLOMBINA, and the CORTIGIANA, the 'great lady'. In the sentimental plot FLORINDO and Isabella appear as lovers.
The c. dell'a. is an amalgam of artistic and literary traditions. Influences from ancient COMEDY (PLAUTUS) and the COMMEDIA ERUDITA combine with the acrobatics and pantomime of the jugglers (*saltimbanchi*) and create the peculiar dual character of the c. dell'a.: 'a scurrillous pairing of abstract geometry with animal exuberance' (Alewyn). The guiding principle was not originality of subject matter but formal variation of known elements. Everything had to meet the demand for the utmost perfection and agility of movement, both in the rhetorical and intellectual sphere in witty ideas (*concetti*: conceits) and repartee (*battute*) as in the mimed physical gags (LAZZI). The wider influence of the c. dell'a., which mainly came from the impact of the stereotyped characters, was carried abroad, notably to France, by touring companies, and extends to MOLIÈRE, English PANTOMIME (Harlequinades) and the WIENER VOLKSTHEATER of the late 18th and early 19th centuries. For a wholly theatrical, non-psychological theatre, the c. dell'a. remains a model to this day.
Bibl: V. Pandolfi, LA COMMEDIA DELL' ARTE STORIA E TESTI, 1957–61, 6 vols

Commedia dell'arte, ARLECCHINO in *The Seraglio*, 1690

Commedia erudita (Ital = educated comedy). Literary form of the comedy of intrigue of the Italian Renaissance as distinct from the COMMEDIA DELL'ARTE, which is based on the classic, especially the Roman, model. ARETINO, ARIOSTO and MACHIAVELLI are representative of this genre.

Compagnia dei Giovani. Italian theatrical company founded in 1954 by Giorgio de Lullo, director and actor, together with the actors BUAZZELLI, VALLI, ROSSELLA FALK and A. M. Guarnieri. It opened with MUSSET's *Lorenzaccio* and later produced COLETTE's *Gigi*, 1954, D. FABBRI's *Il Bugiardo*, 1955, seen in London 1965, WORLD THEATRE SEASON, and Frances Goodrich and Albert Hackett's *The Diary of Anne Frank*, 1957.

Compagnie des Quinze. Name given to COPEAU's original company 'Les Copiaux', after it had been taken over and reorganized by his nephew SAINT-DENIS in 1931. The plays produced were mainly those of OBEY (*Le Viol de Lucrèce* and *Noé*), and, though successful in Paris and London, it was dissolved in 1934.

Compagnie Renaud-Barrault ▷ BARRAULT.

Compton. English family of actors of the 19th and 20th centuries. (1) **Henry C.** (Charles Mackenzie; 1805–77), known as an excellent comic actor, e.g. as the gravedigger in *Hamlet*. He married the actress Emmeline Montague; they had nine children all of whom became connected with

Comédie-Italienne departing on banishment by Louis XIV, engraving after Watteau

the stage, and two of them became famous. (2) **Edward C.** (1854–1918) achieved a great reputation as an actor in COMEDIES, e.g. as Claudio in *Much Ado About Nothing* in 1879 at the Shakespeare Festival, STRATFORD-UPON-AVON, which he managed 1881–82. He also toured the provinces with comedies by FOOTE, SHERIDAN and GOLDSMITH. (3) **Katherine C.** (1858–1928) excelled in playing aristocratic ladies in the plays of her husband, R. C. Carton. E.C. married the actress Virginia Bateman (1853–1940) in 1882 and they had five children, one of whom was the novelist Compton Mackenzie (1883–1972). The other four became actors, outstanding among them (4) **Fay C.** (1894–) who has had a distinguished career in tragic and comic parts, as well as in PANTOMIME and VARIETY; her outstanding roles have included Ophelia, in 1925 with J. BARRYMORE and in 1939 with GIELGUD; Ruth in COWARD's *Blithe Spirit*, 1941; the title role in SHAW's *Candida*, 1947; the Virgin Mary in William Joyce Cowen and Lenore Coffee's *Family Portrait*, 1948; Lady Bracknell in WILDE's *The Importance of Being Earnest*, and Maman in CHEKHOV's *Uncle Vanya*, at the first CHICHESTER FESTIVAL, 1962. Her reminiscences were published under the title *Rosemary* in 1926.

Confidenti, Compagnia dei. Name of a COMMEDIA DELL'ARTE troupe which travelled throughout Europe, mainly in Italy and France from *c.* 1574 to 1640; most successful around 1587 when it included such actors as the brothers D. and T. MARTINELLI (as ARLECCHINO).

Congreve, William (1670–1729), English dramatist. One of the great exponents of the Restoration Comedy of Manners (▷ COMEDY). A critical observer of the morals and society of his time, he was also endowed with a mastery of dramatic technique, dazzling wit, and a prose style of great subtlety and beauty. His first play *The Old Bachelor* was produced in 1693 with BETTERTON and ANNE BRACEGIRDLE, for whom he wrote a leading part in each of his plays. It was followed by *The Double Dealer*, 1694, both at Drury Lane; *Love for Love*, 1695, Lincoln's Inn Fields; and his only TRAGEDY *The Mourning Bride*, 1697. His comedy *The Way of the World*, 1700, Lincoln's Inn Fields, is nowadays considered (with *Love for Love*) to be his finest work. The play was, however, coolly received at its first performance, almost certainly because of the change in public taste (away from the values expressed in most RESTORATION DRAMA towards a more bourgeois outlook) which had been given impetus by Jeremy Collins's *Short View of the Immorality and Profaneness of the English Stage*, 1699. It was probably this failure that decided C., though still at the height of his powers, to write no more plays. His later stage works were a MASQUE, *The Judgement of Paris*, an opera, *Semele*, and, in collaboration with VANBRUGH and William Walsh, a translation of MOLIÈRE's *Monsieur de Pourceaugnac*. In 1707 he briefly joined with Vanbrugh in managing the Haymarket Theatre.
Bibl: J. C. Hodges, WILLIAM CONGREVE, THE MAN, 1941

Connelly, Marc (1890–), US playwright. His greatest BROADWAY success was *The Green Pastures*, 1930, based on R. Bradford's *Ol' Man Adam an' His Chillun*, a dramatization of important events of the Old Testament as visualized by an aged Negro pastor in Louisiana; the play won the PULITZER PRIZE in 1930 and ran for two years. Several other plays, mostly satires, were written in collaboration with KAUFMAN, e.g. *Merton of the Movies*, 1922; *Beggar on Horseback*, 1924. He collaborated with J. F. Mankiewicz on *The Wild Man of Borneo*, 1927; with F. B. Elser on *The Farmer Takes a Wife*, 1934; with A. Sundgaard on *Everywhere I Roam*, 1938. He has also worked as an actor, director, producer and film scriptwriter (*I Married a Witch*, 1942, dir René Clair), and as a teacher of drama at Yale University, 1946–50.
Bibl: A. S. Downer, FIFTY YEARS OF AMERICAN DRAMA, 1941

Conservatoire d'Art Dramatique. State drama school in Paris, connected with the COMÉDIE-FRANÇAISE. Founded in 1795 as a school of music, the training of actors gradually became a feature, and talented young people are now trained there for the CF.

Constructivism. An artistic movement which originated *c.* 1912 mainly in Russia. The movement has been especially influential in architecture and also in typography. The theories combine rational and utopian elements, directed towards a man-made world. Theatrical manifestations: Malevich's production of the poem *Victory over the Sun*, St Petersburg 1913; phonetic poems and mask-dances in the Café Pittoresque in Moscow during World War I. After the Revolution the Constructivists held important positions in the world of art. In the critical situation in the civil war in the post-revolutionary period there was no possibility of Constructivists realizing their aims in architecture, so the Constructivist painters proceeded to produce 'architecture of stage' as Lissitzky formulated it. Constructivism found its purest expression in Tatlin's stage design for Chelbnikov's *Zanguesi*, Leningrad 1923, and Lissitzky's model of the structure of the stage for TRETYAKOV's play, *I Want a Child*, directed by MEYERHOLD, Moscow 1929. The stage designers V. and E. Stenburg, YAKULOV, L. Popova, and ALEXANDRA EXTER used Constructivist principles in their designs, especially for the productions of TAIROV and Meyerhold. The latter was influenced by Constructivism in the development of BIO-MECHANICS, the name he gave to his method of production.
Bibl: H. Rischbieter (ed), BÜHNE UND BILDENDE KUNST IM 20. JAHRUNDERT, 1968

Contat, Louise-Françoise (1760–1813), French actress. Her stage début in 1766 was unsuccessful, but after several good performances, she made her breakthrough as Suzanne in BEAUMARCHAIS's *Le Mariage de Figaro*, a part she undertook at the request of the author himself. This performance helped to establish her growing reputation as a comedienne of grace and intelligence. Until her retirement in 1809 she continued to appear in juvenile parts such as Elmire in *Tartuffe* and Célimène in *Le Misanthrope*. She much admired the plays of MARIVAUX, which suited her style of intellectual comic acting, and, as a SOCIÉTAIRE of the COMÉDIE-FRANÇAISE, advocated their inclusion in the REPERTOIRE.
Bibl: Dussane, LA CÉLIMÈNE DU THERMIDOR, LOUISE CONTAT, 1929

Conti, Italia (1874–1946), English actress. She founded a famous school for the training of children as dancers, singers and actors for the stage. The Italia Conti school started in 1911 and supplied generations of children's ballets to PANTOMIME as well as training such famous performers as GERTRUDE LAWRENCE, COWARD and the dancer Anton Dolin.

Cooper, Giles (1918–66), English dramatist. He became known as one of the finest radio dramatists of his time. His radio plays, which include *Mattury Beacon*, 1956; *The Disagreeable Oyster*, 1957; *Under the Loofah Tree*, and *Unman, Wittering and Zigo*, both 1958, are recognized as classics. He adapted Simenon's Maigret stories for TV. He wrote the stage plays *Never Get Out*, 1950; *Everything in the Garden*, 1962, adapted for the New York stage by ALBEE in 1967; *Out of the Crocodile*, 1963; and *Happy Family*, 1966.

Cooper, Gladys (1888–1971), English actress. She was appointed a DBE in 1967. Began her stage career at the age of 17, gaining her first experience in musicals as a chorus girl, and in PANTOMIME. Soon rose to STAR parts and appeared as Cecily Cardew in WILDE's *The Importance of Being Earnest* at the St James's Theatre, London 1911; she established herself as an outstanding actress in DRAWING-ROOM COMEDY as well as in the plays of SHAW, SHAKESPEARE, MAUGHAM and PINERO. A woman of dazzling beauty with classical features, impeccable bearing and brilliant wit, she was undoubtedly one of the outstanding actresses of her time, in London as well as in New York where she made her début in 1934. Among plays in which she performed later in life was ENID BAGNOLD's *The Chalk Garden*, New York 1955. She also acted in a number of films. Two volumes of autobiography: *Gladys Cooper*, 1931, and *Without Veils*, 1953.

Copeau, Jacques (1879–1949), French actor and director. His work has strongly influenced modern French theatre, and consequently American and European theatre in general. For more than a generation he was regarded as a model by theatre people as divergent as DULLIN, JOUVET, SAINT-DENIS, BARSACQ, DASTÉ, BARRAULT, and VILAR. He started as a drama critic, and, with GIDE and others, founded *La Nouvelle Revue Française* in 1911. After attracting attention with his adaptation of DOSTOYEVSKY's *The Brothers Karamazov* in 1911, he opened the Théâtre du Vieux-Colombier in 1913 with a production of *A Woman Killed with Kindness* by the Elizabethan playwright HEYWOOD. The war interrupted his work, and the ENSEMBLE split up. In 1917 he went with the remaining members of the company to New York, where until 1919 he produced classical and modern French plays at the Garrick Theatre. After his return to Paris he founded the drama school attached to the Vieux-Colombier. In 1924 he retired, partly due to bad health, partly because he had a religious crisis. Some of his pupils went with him to Pernand-Vergelesses in Burgundy, where he rehearsed classical FARCES and appeared at fairgrounds as the actors of the COMMEDIA DELL'ARTE had done. They were known as 'Les Copiaux', and some of them later joined the COMPAGNIE DES QUINZE, directed by SAINT-DENIS, C.'s nephew. C. pursued 'pure' theatre, despising superficiality and insincerity. At the Vieux-Colombier productions were of the utmost simplicity, relying mainly on a few simple stage properties. His theatre was one of language and of actors, whom he regarded as servants of the words. He and his followers criticized both the STAR system and the pedantic realism of ANTOINE. His admiration for classical dramatic literature and his own search for a precisely defined 'pure' theatre did not preclude a certain dignified conventionalism. Hence it is not surprising that he produced several plays at the COMÉDIE-FRANÇAISE, 1837–40, where for a short time he also acted as administrator.

Productions include: (Vieux-Colombier, Paris) ADAM DE LA HALLE's *Le Jeu de Robin et de Marion*, 1913; CLAUDEL's *L'Echange*, 1914; (Vieux-Colombier at the Garrick Theatre, New York) MUSSET's *Les Caprices de Marianne*, 1918; MAETERLINCK's *Pelléas et Mélisande*, 1919; MOLIÈRE's *Le Misanthrope*, 1919; (V.-C., Paris) CHEKHOV's *Uncle Vanya*, 1921; GIDE's *Saül*, fp 1922; Molière's *Sganarelle*, 1923; GOZZI's *Turandot*, 1923; GOLDONI's *Mirandolina*, 1923; (CF) RACINE's *Bajazet*, 1937; MAURIAC's *Asmodée*, 1937; OBEY's *Introduction pour le Cid* and CORNEILLE's *Le Cid*, both 1940.

Bibl: F. Anders, JACQUES COPEAU ET LE CARTEL DES QUATRES, 1959

Coquelin. French family of actors. (1) **Constant-Benoît C.** (1841–1909), known as Coquelin *aîné*. A pupil of Regnier at the CONSERVATOIRE D'ART DRAMATIQUE, he started his career at the COMÉDIE-FRANÇAISE and quickly won a reputation as an excellent leading actor in classical COMEDIES (Figaro in BEAUMARCHAIS's *Le Mariage de Figaro* and *Le Barbier de Séville*; Purgon in MOLIÈRE's *Le Malade imaginaire*) as well as in contemporary plays by BANVILLE, AUGIER, DUMAS *fils* and SARDOU. C. was an outstanding comedian and versatile mimic; he had a resonant voice, was inventive and possessed of a controlled alert intelligence. He left the CF several times after 1887 and in 1892 finally departed for a prolonged tour of Europe and the USA. Later he appeared at the Théâtre de la Porte Saint-Martin, where he created the part always associated with his name: the title role in ROSTAND's *Cyrano de Bergerac*, 1897. C. also wrote on the theory of theatre in *L'Art et le comédien*, 1880. He had political connections and founded a home for aging actors, in which he himself spent most of his late life. (2) **Ernest-Alexandre Honoré C.** (1848–1909), brother of Constant, known as Coquelin *cadet*; though he appeared at the CF in several leading parts (Figaro, Harpagon, Scapin), he was best in secondary comic parts. Coquelin *aîné*'s son (3) **Jean C.** (1865–1944) appeared for several years with his father at the CF after 1890, for example, as Ragueneau in *Cyrano* and later also in the title role. J.C.'s son (4) **Jean-Paul C.** (1924–) was in 1955 awarded a prize for his recording of *Cyrano*.

Corneille, Pierre (1606–84), French playwright and poet. Educated by the Jesuits, worked in law and administration at Rouen. The first great tragic French writer, he was one of the founders of French classical drama, which set out rules indirectly based on the theories formulated by ARISTOTLE in his *Poetics*. Among the French classic writers he was the least doctrinaire – he retained his independence within the classical rules and was therefore disapproved of and often strongly criticized, especially by his younger rivals. In his later work he departed from the clear refined style of speech of his earlier work, showing a preference for a more romantic approach. In 1652 he left the theatre for a while, because a play of his had failed, and translated *The Imitation of Christ* by Thomas à Kempis in a language full of emotion and vivid images. His first dramatic work was the COMEDY *Mélite*, written 1630, which the actor MONTDORY took on tour through the provinces before a Paris production in the same year. The TRAGICOMEDY *Clitandre*, 1631, was followed by four other comedies: *La Veuve*, 1631; *La Galérie du Palais*, 1632; *La Suivante*, 1633; *La Place Royale*, 1634. In the meantime he had moved to Paris and belonged for some time to a group of five dramatists, who wrote collectively for RICHELIEU. His first TRAGEDY *Médée*, 1635, was followed by the comedy *L'Illusion comique*, 1636, and finally *Le Cid*, 1637, which established his fame. This tragicomedy (in later publications 'tragedy') was presented, as all of his earlier plays, at the Théâtre du Marais, with which he had been connected, following his first dramatic achievement with Montdory. *Le Cid*, which was based on a play by the Spanish dramatist CASTRO, put forth a new concept of moral greatness, of pathos and power of diction, which is still considered an essential characteristic of tragedy. But C.'s contemporary and rival poets reproached the author for breaking theatrical rules, giving rise to a famous literary quarrel in 1637, finally settled at Richelieu's intervention. After Montdory's retirement from the stage in 1637, FLORIDOR succeeded him in leading roles, e.g. Dorante in *Le Menteur*, 1637, one of C.'s best comedies (▷ALARÇON Y MENDOZA). The following plays con-

Gladys Cooper as the Hon. Muriel Pym in *Milestones* by A. BENNETT and KNOBLOCK, London 1911

Jacques Copeau in MOLIÈRE's *Les Fourberies de Scapin*

Corneille's *Le Cid*, engraving by Gravelot, 1764

firmed C.'s position as the most prominent tragic dramatist in France: *Horace*, *Cinna*, both 1640; *Polyeucte*, 1641; *La Mort de Pompée*, 1643.
When Floridor left the Théâtre du Marais in 1646 to appear at the HÔTEL DE BOURGOGNE, C. transferred the premières of his plays to this theatre. *Rodogune*, 1644, and *Théodore, Vierge et martyre*, 1645, were still produced at the Marais; most of his subsequent work at the Bourgogne. C.'s poetic power declined and he produced failures, but it is not true – as is frequently maintained – that he died lonely and without recognition. His works were performed by leading companies and already during his lifetime he was recognized and respected as a classic writer (▷ALEXANDRINE). Other works: *Héraclius*, 1646; *Andromède*, 1650; *Don Sanche d'Aragon*, 1649; *Nicomède*, 1651; *Pertharite*, 1651; *Oedipe*, 1659; *La Conquête de la toison d'or*, 1660; *Sertorius*, 1662; *Sophonisbe*, 1663; *Othon*, 1664; *Agésilas*, 1666; *Attila*, 1667, and *Tite et Bérénice*, 1670, Palais Royal, Compagnie de Molière; *Psyché*, 1671, with MOLIÈRE; *Pulchérie*, 1672; *Suréna*, 1674.
Bibl: R. J. Nelson, CORNEILLE, HIS HEROES AND THEIR WORLDS, 1963; S. W. Deierkauf-Holsboer, LE THÉÂTRE DU MARAIS, 1954

Cornell, Katharine (1893–1974), US actress. Started with the WASHINGTON SQUARE PLAYERS in 1916, then in stock (▷ STOCK COMPANY) and on tour; first appearance in London as Jo in Louisa Alcott's *Little Women*, 1919; Broadway début in 1921 in CLEMENCE DANE'S *A Bill of Divorcement*; married the director McCLINTIC in the same year. Outstanding interpreter of SHAW (*Candida*, 1924; *Saint Joan*, 1936), also of SHAKESPEARE, CHEKHOV, and MAUGHAM (*The Constant Wife*), 1951. Starred with OLIVIER in BEHRMAN'S *No Time for Comedy*, New York 1939. Generally regarded as the leading US actress of her time. Published two volumes of reminiscences: *I Wanted to Be an Actress*, 1939, and *Curtain Going Up*, 1943.

Corral (Span=courtyard). The original Spanish term for a theatre, used because theatres for travelling companies were set up in courtyards. The stage (*tablada*), covered with a large canvas hood, was always erected at the rear of the courtyard with a simple platform; at the back was a changing-room shielded by a curtain. In the middle of the courtyard was the *patio*, often tiered in steps (*gradas*). Windows and balconies became the boxes. The first permanent theatres (Corral de la Cruz, 1579, and Corral del Príncipe, 1582, in Madrid) had rows of stalls (*bancos*); the seats opposite the stage were reserved for women.

Cortigiana (Ital=courtesan). The 'great lady' of the COMMEDIA DELL'ARTE, who appeared on stage without mask and wearing the typical costume of a rich courtesan of the time.

Coryphaeus (Gk *koryphaios*=at the head). The leading member of the CHORUS in Greek drama.

Costa, Orazio (1911–), Italian director. He was a pupil of COPEAU. In 1948 he founded the Piccolo Teatro della Città di Roma which he managed till 1954. One of the leading directors of the post-war generation of the anti-naturalistic, poetic theatre, producing among other plays TASSO'S *Aminta*, 1952; ALFIERI'S *Agamennone*, 1952; BETTI'S *L'Aiuola bruciata* (*The Burnt Flower-bed*), 1953, and a MYSTERY PLAY at the PICCOLO TEATRO DI MILANO in 1964.

Costantini (in France: Constantini), Italian family of actors. **Costantino C.** (*c.* 1634–*c.* 1696) played the leading ZANNI under the name of Gradellino, after 1687 also in Paris. His son **Angelo C.** (*c.* 1654–1729) acted with the troupe of Dominique (▷BIANCOLELLI) in Paris and created the character of MEZZETINO. After the death of G. BIANCOLELLI (1688) he succeeded him in the part of ARLECCHINO. After the dissolution of the Italian troupe in Paris, 1697, he went to Germany where he took service at the Court of Augustus the Strong at Dresden. Here he rose in the king's favour until discovered in a compromising situation with one of the king's numerous mistresses and thereafter spent 20 years in prison. He made a brief reappearance after his release, in Paris, 1729.

Costenoble, Karl Ludwig (1769–1837), German actor. In Hamburg, 1801–17, started as singer, became a comic and character actor; from 1818 with the ENSEMBLE of the BURGTHEATER in Vienna. His diaries (*Aus dem Burgtheater*, ed K. Glossy and J. Zeidler, 1889) are important documents in AUSTRIA'S theatrical history.

Costume. The clothes worn by actors on stage. One of the main elements of theatre, more basic and also more ancient than SCENERY. In the theatre of classical GREECE costume was simple in TRAGEDY, grotesquely fantastic in COMEDY. In the religious drama of the Middle Ages, in the theatre of the Renaissance and the Baroque, costume represented current fashion but tended to heighten it by being particularly sumptuous or colourful. Only in the 18th century were efforts made (e.g. by critics like VOLTAIRE and GOTTSCHED) to achieve a degree of historical accuracy in costume. In the popular theatre there were stereotype costumes (HARLEQUIN, PANTALOON, etc.). At the end of the 18th and throughout the 19th century standardized historical costume became prevalent. Companies of actors tended to have sets of classical, medieval or Renaissance costume. With the growing interest in history and historical painting at the end of the 19th century, there was a greater degree of individualization and accuracy. With the rise of the director in the 20th century different approaches and possibilities with regard to costume are open to each production: from a classic author like SHAKESPEARE played in modern costume, to adopting any one of a number of other historical epochs for the play, or clothing it in imaginative or stylized costume; BRECHT advocated 'realistic' costume in that he insisted that the actors' clothes appeared grubby and well worn rather than brand-new or freshly laundered. Contemporary trends involve actors appearing in rehearsal clothes and eclectic costumes borrowing from various trends and using all kinds of materials.
Bibl: J. Laver, A CONCISE HISTORY OF COSTUME, 1969

Côté cour, côté jardin. French terms: *côté jardin* (garden side) means right of the actor, *côté cour* (court side) left of the actor. Originally it was customary to have *côté du roi* (king's side for right) and *côté de la reine* (queen's side for left) based on the arrangements of the seats at court; after the Revolution the new terms were introduced in the Théâtre des Tuileries, situated between the garden and the palace.

Coup de théâtre. Unexpected, effective turning-point in a play.

Courteline, Georges (G. Moinaux; 1858–1929), French dramatist. He followed the tradition of early French FARCE in his satirical comedies. He portrays in precise detail, with bitter, often cruel wit, episodes of ordinary life, the squabbling between the petty bourgeoisie and the police, the tyranny of the law and the bureaucrats. His plays were first produced by ANTOINE at his Théâtre Libre (later at the Théâtre Antoine) whose leading comic playwright he became, and slowly found their way into the repertoire of the COMÉDIE-FRANÇAISE, where a few still remain popular. He also continued his work as a journalist for *L'Echo de Paris*. His best-known play is *Boubouroche*, 1893. Other works include: *Lidoire*, 1891; *Les Joyeuses Commères de Paris*, 1892; a musical fantasy, *Les Grimaces de Paris*, 1894; *Les Gaîtés de l'escadron*, 1895; *Un Client sérieux*, 1896; *Hortense, couche-toi!*, 1897; *Les Boulingrins*, 1898; *Le Gendarme est sans pitié*, 1899; *l'Article 330*, 1900; *La Paix chez soi*, 1903, etc. His work was praised by many contemporaries, including DUMAS *fils*, Mallarmé and Anatole France.
Bibl: A. Dubeux, LA CURIEUSE VIE DE GEORGES COURTELINE, 1958

Court theatre. Theatres of the European courts for amateur theatricals among the attendants or guest appearances of professional companies. It began in Italy during the Renaissance: there were theatres in classicist style in the Courts of Florence and Parma, where amateur productions were given by the aristocracy of classical comedies (PLAUTUS, TERENCE) and contemporary plays (Poliziano's *Orfeo*, Mantua, 1471; BIBBIENA'S *Calandria*, Urbino, 1507) as part of major Court festivities in collaboration with famous painters and architects; high points were the triumphal processions (*trionfi*), allegories, water-games and jousting games of the Baroque period (▷BAROQUE THEATRE); this contrasted with professional theatre outside the Courts which was mostly in the hands of public commercial companies. In the 17th century France showed its own specific development of the Court theatre (emergence of the BALLET DE COUR), and acting was only by Royal licence; in England the professional companies of the late 16th and 17th centuries were under the protection of the aristocracy; actors were first only nominally Court servants and after 1660 they were not connected at all; in the course of the 17th century, there was constant development of the professional theatre, so that Court theatre was increasingly arranged for the amusement of the courtiers by permanent companies; Court officials became responsible for the administration and censorship of these troupes. Court Theatre encouraged a supra-national European theatre and, at the same time, held back the development of national drama: Italian opera, French ballet and French comedy predominated in European Courts. The Court theatres (*Hoftheater*) in the many sovereign German-speaking countries of the 18th and 19th centuries were of social importance; professional theatre was largely in the hands of private Court companies. In 1776 in Vienna, the imperial capital, the theatre 'near the Burg' was raised to the rank of a German National Theatre, and national theatres were created in 1777 in Mannheim, 1786 in both Berlin and Weimar. In the 19th century the German Court theatres were bastions of the traditional, conservative style of acting; the last important new developments to be made were achieved by the Company of the Court theatre of Meiningen (MEININGER company). In 1918 the former Court theatres were renamed state theatres, municipal theatres, etc. when they were taken over by the state or local authorities. Notable surviving Court theatres are in BAYREUTH, Munich, Versailles, Leningrad and DROTTINGHOLM.

Court theatre in Vienna with a performance of *Il Pomo d'Oro*, 1666

Katharine Cornell and Brian Aherne in *The Barretts of Wimpole Street*, New York 1931

Covent Garden Theatre, London. The first building on this site was commissioned by John Rich and opened in 1732 with CONGREVE'S *The Way of the World*. The REPERTOIRE included plays, PANTOMIMES, spectacles. The golden age of the theatre was in the second half of the 18th century under the management of COLMAN. The theatre was burnt down twice (1808 and 1856); in 1858 the present theatre (with 2,800 seats) was built, designed by Sir Edward M. Barry. Outstanding English actors who appeared there include J. P. KEMBLE, his sister SARAH SIDDONS, KEAN and MACREADY. In 1847 it opened as the Royal Italian Opera House, and since then has been the main opera house in London; from 1948 Royal Opera House and home of the Royal Ballet; the opera and ballet jointly receive a considerable state subsidy through the ARTS COUNCIL OF GREAT BRITAIN. In 1975/76 it amounted to £3,350,000.

Covent Garden Theatre, the Royal family at a performance, 1804

Coviello (Jacoviello = Neapolitan dialect for the name Giacometto). Cunning and clever servant, a Neapolitan variation of the ZANNI of the COMMEDIA DELL'ARTE. He wore tight trousers, a black jacket with silver laces and a half-mask.

Coward, Sir Noël (1899–1973), English actor, playwright, composer and director. Knighted in 1970. Started as a child actor (first appearance: 1911 in a children's fairy play) and became one of the most versatile personalities of 20th-century theatre: an actor of great wit, elegance, suavity and perfect comic timing; a splendid performer in REVUE, frequently singing his own songs; composer and librettist of his own MUSICAL COMEDIES, often produced by COCHRAN with whom he worked closely from 1925. He proved himself a sharp but urbane social satirist in a series of brilliant DRAWING-ROOM COMEDIES, and also a serious playwright not averse to tackling daring and advanced subjects, such as drug-addiction in *The Vortex* (as early as 1924), though not ashamed of being a flag-waving patriot (in *Cavalcade*, 1931, and *This Happy Breed*, 1942). Other works include: *The Young Idea*, 1923; *Fallen Angels*, 1925; *Hay Fever*, 1925; *Easy Virtue*, 1926; *Sirocco*, 1927; *This Year of Grace*, a revue, 1928; *Bitter Sweet*, a musical, 1929; *Private Lives*, 1930; *Post-Mortem*, 1931; *Words and Music*, a revue, 1932; *Design for Living*, 1932; *Tonight at 7.30* (later *8.30*), a group of nine one-act plays (later ten) for three evenings, 1935; *Blithe Spirit*, 1941; *Present Laughter*, 1942; *Relative Values*, 1951; *Quadrille*, 1954; *Nude with Violin*, 1956; *Suite in Three Keys*, 1966. Wrote and directed the film *In Which We Serve* and played the lead in it, 1944. Also appeared in many other films. An anthology of his songs and sketches was presented in a successful revue, *Cowardy Custard*, at the MERMAID THEATRE, 1972, also presented in New York at the same time. Autobiographical works: *Present Indicative* and *Future Indicative* and *Future Indefinite*.
Bibl: S. Morley, A TALENT TO AMUSE, 1969; C. Lesley, *The Life of Noël Coward*, 1976

Cowl, Jane (1884–1950), US actress, known both for Shakespearean and DRAWING-ROOM COMEDY roles. Her first appearance was in *Sweet Kitty Bellairs*, 1903, produced by BELASCO. She wrote, with Jane Murfin, *Lilac Time*, 1917, in which she starred, and *Smilin' Through*, 1919, a sentimental play by A. L. Martin, was one of her early successes. Her finest performance was as Juliet to Rollo Peters' Romeo in 1923. Other plays in which she appeared include *The Road to Rome*, 1926, by SHERWOOD; *Jenny*, 1929, by SHELDON and Margaret Ayer Barnes; WILDER's *The Merchant of Yonkers*, 1938; and in M. EVANS's 'GI' *Hamlet*, 1945.

Cowley, Hannah (1743–1809), English playwright of the transition period from Restoration to 18th-century comedy. Her first play, *The Runaway*, a comedy of manners (▷COMEDY), was produced by GARRICK at DRURY LANE in 1776. *The Belle's Stratagem*, fp COVENT GARDEN 1780, based on DESTOUCHES's *Fausse Agnès* became her best-known work; through productions in the REPERTOIRE of L. HALLAM JR and John Hodgkinson in New York, 1794, it was one of the earliest comedies seen in America. The play was revived several times in London and New York up to the beginning of the 20th century.
Bibl: A. Nicoll, A HISTORY OF ENGLISH DRAMA, III/1952

Craig, Edward Gordon (1872–1966), English actor, director, stage designer and theoretician. Son of the actress ELLEN TERRY and the architect Edward William Godwin; he was a pioneer of the modern theatre, and like APPIA, his spiritual brother, he has had great influence on modern directing technique and stage design, and received the admiration of eminent men from YEATS (who called him to the ABBEY THEATRE) to BARRAULT. He started his career as an actor (e.g. he was with IRVING's company at the Lyceum 1889–98); produced two operas by Purcell, including *Dido and Aeneas*, and one by Handel, 1900–02; and 1902–03 designed plays for his mother's company, e.g. IBSEN's *The Vikings at Helgeland*, and Shakespeare's *Much Ado About Nothing*; in these designs he replaced the decorative pseudo-realism of his time with a simple structured stage defined by the expressive use of lighting. After he had left England in 1904 he was able to try out his theories in only five productions: HOFMANNSTHAL's adaptation of OTWAY's *Venice Preserved*, Berlin 1905, Lessingtheater; Ibsen's *Rosmersholm* for ELEONORA DUSE, Florence 1906; *Hamlet*, MOSCOW ART THEATRE, 1911; Ibsen's *The Pretenders*, Copenhagen 1926, Royal Theatre, designer co-director, and *Macbeth*, Knickerbocker Theatre, New York 1928, designer. His importance lies more in his theoretical writings than in his productions. In his *The Art of the Theatre*, 1905, C. wrote: 'STAGE DIRECTOR: No; the Art of the Theatre is neither acting nor the play, it is not scene nor dance, but it consists of all the elements of which these things are composed; action, which is the very spirit of acting; words, which are the body of the play; line and colour, which are the very heart of the stage; rhythm, which is the very essence of the dance.' He spent the latter part of his life in Italy and in Spain. He collected and published theatrical documents and edited the magazine *The Mask* 1908–29.
His works include: *On the Art of the Theatre*, 1911; *Towards a New Theatre*, 1913; *The Theatre Advancing*, 1919; *Puppets and Poets*, 1921; *The Scene*, 1923; *Books and Theatres*, 1925; *A Production*, 1926; *Henry Irving*, 1930; *Ellen Terry and Her Secret Life*, 1931; *Fourteen Notes*, 1931; *Index to the Story of My Days*, 1957.
Bibl: E. Craig, 1968

Crawford, Cheryl (1902–), US director and producer. One of the founders of the GROUP THEATRE (in 1931) and of the ACTORS' STUDIO (in 1947). Since 1939 she has been an independent producer, e.g. GERSHWIN's *Porgy and Bess* (new production); T. WILLIAMS's *The Rose Tattoo* and *Camino Real*. In 1952 she became vice-president of ANTA.

Crébillon, Prosper Jolyot de (1674–1762), French playwright. Very popular in his own day, he was considered as an important dramatist and successor to RACINE; honoured by Louis XV for *Catalina* in 1748, but vigorously attacked by VOLTAIRE who eventually eclipsed him. To achieve a terrifying COUP DE THÉÂTRE he concentrated on horror and brutality at the expense of psychological truth of motivation. The best known of his nine tragedies is *Rhadamiste et Zénobie*, 1711.
Bibl: H. C. Lancaster, SUNSET, 1945

Cregan, David (1931–), English dramatist. Studied at Cambridge University and from 1955 taught at several universities in England and the USA. By 1966 his two short plays *Transcending* and *Dancers*, and the full-length plays *Miniatures* and *Three Men for Colverton* had been produced at the ROYAL COURT THEATRE, and in 1968 *The Houses by the Green*, a kind of modern Restoration COMEDY, sharp and dry, with an ingenious plot. Other works: *Arthur*, 1969; *A Comedy of the Changing Years*, 1970; and *Tipper*, 1970.

Crispin (Fr *crisper*=to shrink). The quick-witted, unscrupulous, but clumsy valet (often interpreted as a stutterer) of French late 17th- and 18th-century COMEDY, originally derived from the COMMEDIA DELL'ARTE mask of SCARAMUCCIA (Scaramouche of the COMÉDIE-ITALIENNE). Crispin wore a black costume, a wide strip of yellow leather wound round the midriff, a black skull cap and a round hat, a short Spanish cloak and a short rapier. The first Crispin was R. Poisson (1630–90) in 1677. Hero of LESAGE's comedy *Crispin rival de son maître*, 1707.

Croft, Michael (1922–), English director. He started his career as an actor in 1939. After studying at Oxford, he was a teacher at Alleyn's School and Dulwich College, London, organizing school productions from which he developed his idea for a youth theatre, leading to a production of *Henry V* acted by students. The group became recognized as the National Youth Theatre. Subsequently he directed several plays by SHAKESPEARE (*Hamlet*, *Julius Caesar*, *Richard II*, *Coriolanus*, *A Midsummer Night's Dream*), toured the Netherlands, Belgium, Denmark, played at the Paris Festival, THÉÂTRE DES NATIONS, and the Berlin Festival (*Julius Caesar*, 1961). In 1965 the National Youth Theatre was invited to put on two plays at the OLD VIC: *Antony and Cleopatra* and *Troilus and Cressida*. Their greatest success was in 1967 with C.'s production at the Jeannetta Cochrane Theatre of TERSON's *Zigger-Zagger*, a play especially written for them. C. has also produced plays for other theatres. In 1971 the London Borough of Camden gave the NYT a home in London in its newly built Shaw Theatre.

Crommelynck, Fernand (1888–1970), Flemish dramatist who wrote in French. In his early days *Nous n'irons plus au bois*, 1906, and *Le Sculpteur de masques*, 1908, he was strongly influenced by the work of

MAETERLINCK. He established his reputation with the farcical TRAGEDY *Le Cocu magnifique*, fp 1920, dir LUGNÉ-POË; MEYERHOLD staged a famous production in Moscow in 1922. (London production 1932 with PEGGY ASHCROFT.) He was obsessed with sin; his major theme is jealousy which leads to destruction. His plays are rich in imagery and language, and show the influence of EXPRESSIONISM: *Les Amants puérils*, 1922; *Tripes d'or*, 1925; *Carine, ou la Jeune Fille folle de son âme*, 1929; *Une femme qu'a le cœur trop petit*, 1934; *Chaud et froid, ou l'Idée de Monsieur Dom*, 1934; *Léona*, 1944.
Bibl: S. Lilar, LE THÉÂTRE EN BELGIQUE, 1947

Crouse, Russel (1893–1966), US dramatist. His collaboration with LINDSAY resulted in some of BROADWAY's most successful plays: *Life with Father*, 1939, had a record run of over 3,000 performances; *The Sound of Music*, 1959, together with RODGERS and HAMMERSTEIN II, had a long stage run and also became a very successful musical film. Together with Lindsay he also directed, e.g. Joseph O. Kesselring's *Arsenic and Old Lace*, 1941, and KINGSLEY's *Detective Story*, 1949.

Cruelty, Theatre of ▷ THEATRE OF CRUELTY.

Csokor, Franz Theodor (1885–1969), Austrian dramatist. His early work was strongly influenced by EXPRESSIONISM; his later plays had Christian themes. He was DRAMATURG and director at the Raimund Theater and the VOLKSTHEATER, Vienna, 1923–27. His dramatic works include *Der grosse Kampf* (The Big Fight), 1914; *Die rote Strasse* (The Red Street), 1918; *Der dritte November, 1918* (3 November 1918), 1923; *Gottes General* (God's General), 1938; *Kalypso*, 1942; *Medea*, 1948; *Europäische Trilogie*, 1952; *Hebt den Stein ab* (Lift up the Stone), 1956; *Treibholz*, 1959; *Die Erwecking des Zosimir* (The Awakening of Zosimir), 1960.

Cumberland, Richard (1732–1811), English dramatist. He wrote several TRAGEDIES and sentimental COMEDIES, which portrayed the victory of virtue and the punishment of vice, e.g. *The Brothers*, 1769. Best known of his plays is *The West-Indian*, successfully produced by GARRICK in 1771. He was both extremely sensitive to criticism and an active plagiarist; SHERIDAN ridiculed him in *The Critic* as Sir Fretful Plagiary.
Bibl: A. Nicoll, A HISTORY OF ENGLISH DRAMA, IV/1955

Cuny, Alain (1908–), French actor. Studied architecture, worked as an assistant director in films and as film architect. After training under DULLIN, he has worked as an actor since the early 1940s, playing Orphée in ANOUILH's *Eurydice*, fp 1942; Orin in O'NEILL's *Mourning Becomes Electra*, 1947. In 1955 he joined the company of the THÉÂTRE NATIONAL POPULAIRE, playing Macbeth; he gave a brilliant performance as Romeo Daddi in PIRANDELLO's *Non si sa come*, 1962. He has also appeared in films, notably Fellini's *La Dolce Vita* and *Satyricon*.

Edward Gordon Craig, stage set for *The Vikings at Helgeland* by IBSEN, 1903

Noël Coward's *Private Lives*, London 1930, the author taking part in company with OLIVIER, GERTRUDE LAWRENCE and Adrienne Allen

Curel, François de (1854–1928), French dramatist, who belonged to the Naturalist movement. Originally a novelist and scientist who in his dramatic work analyzed the social life of his time, but his plays never gained wide popularity. His best-known play is *Le Repas du lion*, fp 1897 at ANTOINE's Théâtre Libre, and in 1920 at the COMÉDIE-FRANÇAISE; it is a study of the struggle between Socialism and traditional values. Among other plays: *L'Ame en folie*, 1919.

Curtain-raiser (Lever de rideau). A short one-act play in the French theatre in the second half of the 19th century; its prime function was to bridge the gap between the beginning of the performance and the late arrival of members of the audience. A relic of the beginnings of bourgeois theatre, where short plays by different authors were common before and after the main play or between the acts. Specialists in the genre included F. Carré, E. Dupré, E. Blum. Because these productions had nothing to do with the content of the main play, they were discontinued by the end of the 19th century.

Cuvilliés, François de (the elder; 1695–1768), French architect. He is important for his creation of the old Residenztheater in Munich, 1750–53, considered to be one of the world's most beautiful rococo theatres.

Cyclorama. The curved back wall of the stage which can suggest an open expanse of sky in the open air. When orthodox backdrops are used to suggest the blue sky behind an open landscape not only does it appear flat but also often shows the wrinkles of the canvas. The cyclorama was devised to overcome these weaknesses. It can form a permanent part of the stage, or may be movable, i.e. canvas stretched on a curved frame.

Cyrano de Bergerac (1619–55), French poet, soldier and philosopher. After being twice badly wounded in the siege of Arras, 1641, he came to Paris and started writing, first on scientific subjects, then the TRAGEDY *La Mort d'Agrippine*, 1653, and the COMEDY, *Le Pédant joué*, 1654; but he died soon after, having been struck on the head by a falling tile. Though his plays have little importance in themselves, they show talent and are remembered mainly as models for MOLIÈRE and SCARRON, who were both his friends. He became world-famous as the adventurous character depicted by ROSTAND in his *Cyrano de Bergerac*, 1897, written in lyric verse and since 1898 staged in many countries, though the portrait that Rostand draws is somewhat romanticized and idealized.

Czechoslovakia. Bohemia, Moravia (inhabited by Czech and German-speaking people) and Slovakia (Slovak and Hungarian-speaking people) were under varying political regimes until the formation of the Czechoslovakian Republic in 1918. In the Middle Ages ecclesiastical drama written in Latin and Czech; they were of considerable influence in the development of medieval European drama. Czech Renaissance drama dates from the middle of the 16th century, most of the themes being taken from the Old Testament; plays were performed mainly in schools. The Jesuits used this form in the Counter-Reformation. (▷SCHOOL DRAMA; JESUIT DRAMA) In the 17th and 18th centuries many foreign companies and professional actors appeared in Czechoslovakia at Courts performing Baroque operas. In 1737 the Kothentheater was founded in Prague, productions mainly given in German; in 1783 the theatre on St Caroline Square was opened with LESSING's *Emilia Galotti*; it became known as the National Theatre and between 1785 and 1805 productions in Czech were also given. From 1786 performances here were only in the Czech language, but soon after a bilingual REPERTOIRE developed which existed until the second half of the 19th century. In 1798 the city of Prague took over the National Theatre as the National Theatre of the Estates; managed from 1834 by August Stöger with mainly operas and operettas as well as German-speaking productions. Slow rise of the professional Czech theatre through the work of Josef Kajetán Tyl (1808–56), dramatist, director and actor and the leading Czech theatrical figure of his time. Though he belonged originally to the Romantic movement, he later became a fighter for the national and social rights of Czechs and turned to dramatic realism. He was director of the Kajetán Theatre and from 1846 also put on Czech productions in the Theatre of the Estates. The Czech Interims Theatre dates from 1862. In 1881 came the inauguration of the splendid new National Theatre, in which opera had priority; 1900–18 under the management of Jaroslav Kvapil, a director with great sensitivity for dialogue who became best known for his productions of SHAKESPEARE, IBSEN and symbolist drama.

The German Municipal Theatre under the management of Angelo Neumann, 1885–1910, produced a series of operas and dramas; in 1907 opening of the Czech Municipal Theatre (Municipal Theatre of Královské Vinohrady), managed 1914–21 by Karel Hugo Hilar, who greatly supported Czech actors and became best known for his grotesque and expressionistic style of production (*Peer Gynt*; *The Undivine Comedy*); in 1921 he took over the management of the National Theatre, where he encouraged the works of contemporary Czech dramatists including ČAPEK and LANGER. In the 1930s a number of small EXPERIMENTAL THEATRES emerged in Prague, the best known of which was the Collective D 34, founded by BURIAN.

After 1945 continuation of the experiments of the 1930s. From 1948 growing oppression by Stalinist dogmatism. Development of technically refined, playful forms of theatre and stage, mixing theatre, CABARET and films. The stage designer SVOBODA worked in collaboration with the director V. Kašlík in opera, also invented the LATERNA MAGICA and worked with KREJČA. From 1956 upsurge of new experimental theatres, e.g. Theatre on the Balustrade with GROSSMAN's drama group, and FIALKA's MIME company; Theatre Before the Gate with Krejča; the Semafor, a musical cabaret specializing in popular songs by J. Suchy and J. Slitre; the Rococo Theatre, and, in Brno, the Evening Theatre, devoted to political satire. In recent years several young playwrights have emerged, including TOPOL and HAVEL, the leading Czech writer of absurd comedies, best known for *The Garden Party*, 1963, and *The Memorandum*, 1965.

Bibl: S. M. Kimball, CZECH NATIONALISM: A STUDY OF THE NATIONAL THEATRE MOVEMENT, 1945–83, 1963

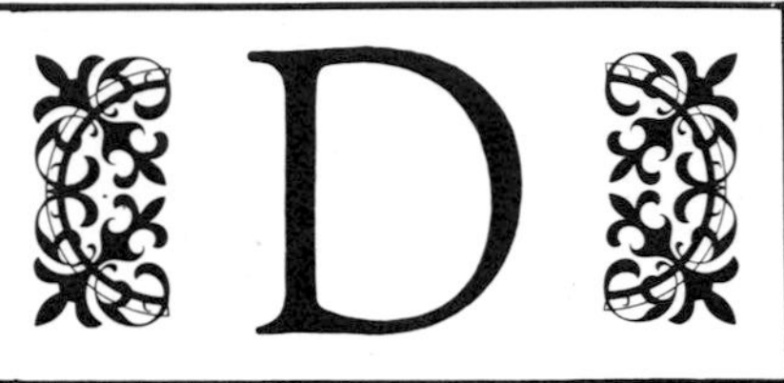

Dabrowski, Bronislaw (1903–), Polish director. Started his career as an actor in Warsaw, Lwów and Craców; director from 1932 (1932–36 Lwów and 1939–41; Poznań 1936–37; Lódz 1937–39). After World War II director of the theatres in Katowice and Craców; of the Teatr Polski in Warsaw, 1950–55; of the Slovacki Theatre in Craców, 1955. He has been strongly influenced by TAIROV and VAKHTANGOV (visit to the USSR in 1934). His most noted productions: SHAKESPEARE's *As You Like It*, 1936, 1946, 1947; LOPE DE VEGA's *Fuenta Ovejuna*, 1948. He was awarded a prize in 1949 for his direction of CHEKHOV's *Three Sisters*, which he also translated.

Dada (ism). An international art movement of provocative nihilism in opposition to, and dedicated to the destruction of, traditional art forms. It sprang up in 1915 in New York (Marcel Duchamp, Francis Picabia, Man Ray), 1916–18 in Zurich – Cabaret Voltaire of Hugo Ball, Richard Huelsenbeck, Raoul Hausmann, Hans (Jean) Arp, Marcel Janco, Tristan Tzara (▷ CABARET), then in BERLIN 1919–20 (the brothers Herzfelde ▷HEARTFIELD, GROSZ, MEHRING), and in Paris 1920–23 (Tzara, André Breton and VITRAC). Dada used a multiplicity of theatrical forms: masked dance, grotesque, often puppet-like costumes, recitation of phonetic poems and mechanical sounds. These performances lacked all logical PLOT and were completely abstract. Among Dada's more important manifestations was the Ballet Relâche, with designs by Picabia and music by Satie (Ballet Suédois, Paris 1924). Dada led to SURREALISM, CONSTRUCTIVISM and the THEATRE OF THE ABSURD, and foreshadowed the current avant-garde, especially the HAPPENINGS of the 1950s and 1960s.

Dagerman, Stig (1923–54), Swedish novelist and playwright. Member of a working-class family; active as a journalist

before turning to fiction and drama. His work was strongly influenced by EXISTENTIALISM; it is concerned with the absurdities of the human condition: *Den Dödsdömde* (*The Condemned*), 1947, *Skuggan av Mart* (The Shadow of Mart), 1947, *Streber* (The Upstart), 1949, *Ingen går fri* (No One Goes Free), 1949. He failed, however, to fulfil his early promise and committed suicide at the age of 31.
Bibl: O. Lagercrantz, STIG DAGERMAN, 1958; A. Gustafson, A HISTORY OF SWEDISH LITERATURE, 1961

Dagover, Lil (1894–), German actress. She became known chiefly as a film actress in Germany and the USA (after 1919). She also appeared on stage, generally as a guest star after 1945. Her main parts include: the title role in PATRICK's *The Curious Savage*, 1960, at the Berliner Theater (she later played the same part on tour); and Aurélie in GIRAUDOUX's *La Folle de Chaillot*, 1964.

Dalberg, Wolfgang Heribert, Baron von (1750–1806), German Minister of State, appointed director of the newly opened Mannheim National Theatre in 1779 (till 1803). He tried to establish a model theatre by engaging famous actors and staging first productions by new playwrights. He first engaged SEYLER, then called EKHOF's actors headed by IFFLAND from the Gotha Court Theatre to Mannheim, where Iffland directed his première productions of SCHILLER's first play *Die Räuber*, 1782, followed by *Fiesko* and *Kabale und Liebe*; he also appointed Schiller as resident playwright (1783–84). In 1785 he produced SHAKESPEARE's *Julius Caesar* for the first time in Germany in his own adaptation. He was the author of several COMEDIES and TRAGEDIES and in 1789 adapted Shakespeare's *Timon of Athens*.
Bibl: E. L. Stahl, DIE KLASSISCHE ZEIT DES MANNHEIMER THEATERS, 1940

Dalcroze, Émile Jacques (1865–1950), important innovator of the modern dance movement in Germany. Born in Vienna. In 1911 he founded with APPIA his school 'Bildungsanstalt [Institute] Jacques-Dalcroze' at Hellerau near Dresden. Here he developed and taught his system of eurythmics. In 1913 at the Festival Theatre at Hellerau he produced CLAUDEL's *L'Annonce faite à Marie*. According to his theories, gymnastics and rhythm are the basic principles of physical and moral balance. His method of developing rhythmical feeling consisted of interpreting music in body movement. He had considerable impact on large-scale productions and influenced Diaghilev in the creation of the ballet *Le Sacre du Printemps*. One of his famous pupils was the dancer and later teacher, Mary Wigman.

Dalí, Salvador (1904–), Spanish surrealist painter. His horror-stricken world of frozen and intense images contains many theatrical elements: he not only 'produces' his images but also himself as a personality, his attributes and appearances.

François de Cuvilliés' masterpiece, the old Residenztheater in Munich

Czechoslovakia, set for SOPHOCLES' *Oedipus Rex*, designed by SVOBODA, 1963

In 1927 he designed *Mariana Pineda*, a play by LORCA, his childhood friend. Later he became attracted to the world of Richard Wagner: he wrote the scenario and designed scenery and COSTUMES for Massine's *Bacchanale* (ballet after Wagner), given at the Metropolitan Opera House, New York 1939; scenery and costumes for the ballet *Mad Tristan*, New York 1944. He has worked with a variety of famous producers and artists: in 1948 with VISCONTI (*As You Like It*, at the Teatro Eliseo in Rome), in 1949 with BROOK (*Salome*, opera by R. Strauss, COVENT GARDEN, 1961), and with BÉJART (*Gala*, a ballet at the Teatro La Fenice, Venice).
Bibl: H. Rischbieter (ed), BÜHNE UND BILDENDE KUNST IM 20. JAHRHUNDERT, 1968

Daly, John Augustin (1838–99), US producer, playwright, critic and adapter of French and German works. First successful play, *Leah the Forsaken*, 1862, adapted from a German play, S. H. Mosenthal's *Deborah*. His best-known original plays are: *Under the Gaslight*, 1867, a MELODRAMA, and *Horizon*, 1871. His dramatic work contributed to the development of realistic drama about American life. In 1869 he founded his first acting company at the Fifth Avenue Theatre in New York City, which later became famous for its realistic productions. In 1873 he established the second Fifth Avenue Theatre and in 1879 Daly's Theatre with stars such as ADA REHAN and J. DREW. By 1882 he had become one of New York's leading producers; in 1893 with EDWARDES he opened Daly's Theatre in London. His Shakespearean productions, particularly of comedies (e.g. *The Merry Wives of Windsor*, 1885; *A Midsummer Night's Dream*, 1885; and *The Taming of the Shrew*, 1887), were noteworthy.
Bibl: M. Felheim, THE THEATRE OF AUGUSTIN DALY

Damiani, Luciano (1923–), Italian stage designer. Worked 1952–66 at the PICCOLO TEATRO DI MILANO. Together with STREHLER he developed a realistic style, concentrating on simplified basic elements, with subtle use of allusions to the style in which classical works were originally staged and refined lighting effects. He also worked for the Teatro La Fenice in Venice, for the Piccola Scala in Milan (BRECHT's *Mahagonny*, dir Strehler, 1965), and for the Bremen Municipal Theatre (Brecht's *Arturo Ui*, dir PALITZSCH, 1965). Among other designs by Damiani for the Piccolo Teatro are: LORCA's *The House of Bernarda Alba*, 1955; BERTOLAZZI's *El Nost' Milan*, 1955; PIRANDELLO's *Questa sera si recita a soggetto*, Edinburgh 1956; SHAKESPEARE's *Coriolanus*, 1957; DÜRRENMATT's *The Visit*, 1960; Brecht's *The Good Woman of Setzuan*, 1958; *Schweik in the Second World War*, 1961, and *Galileo*, 1963; GOLDONI's *Baruffe chiozzotte*, 1965.
Bibl: PICCOLO TEATRO 1947–58, 1968

D'Amico, Silvio (1887–1955), Italian theatre critic and historian. He edited the *Enciclopedia dello Spettacolo* (1954–62, 9 vols; supplementary volume 1966). Drama critic for Rome daily papers: from 1918, *Idea Nazionale* and *Tribuna*; 1941–43, *Giornale d'Italia*; from 1945, *Tempo*. In 1953 he founded the Accademia Nazionale dell' Arte Drammatica, in Rome, of which he remained president until his death. He also wrote many books on the theatre including: *Il teatro italiano*, 1932; edited *Storia del teatro italiano*, 1936; *Storia del teatro drammatico*, 1939–40; third edition in 4 vols, 1953; *Mettere in scena*, 1954.

Dancourt. French family of actors. (1) **Florent Carton** (1661–1725) known as Dancourt, was a dramatist and actor. While a law student in Paris he fell in love with the actress (2) **Marie-Thérèse Lenoir** (1663–1725), the daughter of La Thorillière, whom he married in 1680. They both joined the COMÉDIE-FRANÇAISE in 1685, he playing juvenile leads, she appearing opposite him; they remained there till 1718. He wrote more than 50 comedies, almost exclusively produced at the CF. Though his dramatic work tended to rely on superficial effects, his technical skill was of a high order; his description of the contemporary scene is particularly accomplished – the wealthy middle class with its love of money, its political weakness, its hedonism and narrow view of life. His best plays include: *Le Chevalier à la mode*, with Saint-Yon, 1687; *La Maison de campagne*, 1688; *La Foire de Bezons*, 1695; *Les Vendanges de Suresnes*, 1695; *Les Trois cousines*, 1700. His two daughters (3) **Marie-Anne-Armande D.** (1684–1745) known as Manon, and (4) **Marie-Anne-Michelle D.** (1685–1780) known as Mimi, both became members of the CF in 1701.
Bibl: P. Mélèse, LE THÉÂTRE ET LE PUBLIC À PARIS SOUS LOUIS XIV, 1659–1715, 1934

Dane, Clemence (pseud. of Winifred Ashton; *c.* 1890–1965), English novelist and playwright. Wrote a number of highly successful plays, among them *Bill of Divorcement*, 1921; *Will Shakespeare*, 1921; *Naboth's Vineyard*, 1925; *Granite*, 1926; *Mariners*, 1927; *Wild Decembers*, 1932; *Cousin Muriel*, 1940; *The Lion and the Unicorn*, 1943; *Call Home the Heart*, 1947; *Eighty in the Shade*, 1959. In the novel *Broome Stages*, 1931, she tells the story of a family of actors through several generations.

Dangeville, Marie-Anne Botot (1714–96), French actress. From a family of actors and dancers who were associated with the COMÉDIE-FRANÇAISE over three generations, she joined the CF in 1740 and excelled mainly in light comedy. After her retirement from the theatre in 1763 she staged private performances at her house in Vaugirard, e.g. COLLÉ's *La Partie de chasse d'Henri IV*, which Louis XV had banned from performance.

D'Annunzio, Gabriele (1863–1938), Italian novelist, poet and playwright. A flamboyant and controversial figure whose dramatic inspiration came from sources as diverse as MAETERLINCK's mystical plays, Nietzsche, with his concept of the superman, the madrigalists of the Baroque age, the Greek tragedians and Wagner's operas. His friendship with ELEONORA DUSE, 1894, provided the stimulus for his theatrical writing. His critical reception has been mixed. His works include: *Sogno di un mattino di primavera* (Dream of a Spring Morning), Paris 1897, at SARAH BERNHARDT's Théâtre de la Renaissance, lead played by Duse; *La città morta* (The Dead City), Paris 1898 with Bernhardt, in Milan 1901 with Duse and ZACCONI; *La Gioconda*, Palermo 1899, with Duse and SALVINI. His most important play is his pastoral tragedy in verse, *La Figlia di Jorio* (The Daughter of Jorio), Milan 1904, by the Compagnia Talli-Gramatica-Calabresi. Other works: *Francesca da Rimini*, 1902; *La Fiaccola sotto il moggio* (The Light Under the Bushel), 1905; *La Nave* (The Ship), 1908; *Le Martyre de Saint Sébastien*, MYSTERY PLAY, Paris 1911, music Debussy; *La Pisanella*, Paris 1913, music Pizzetti, dir MEYERHOLD, choreography Fokine, with IDA RUBINSTEIN; *Parisina*, music Mascagni, fp Milan 1913.
Bibl: G. Gatti, 1956

Darrieux, Danielle (1917–), French actress. Has worked mainly in films, but also a much admired star of the Paris BOULEVARD THEATRE. First appeared in 1937 in a play written for her by her husband, Henri Decoin, *Jeux d'argent*. Other parts: ANOUILH's *Léocadia*, 1949; BERNSTEIN's *Evangeline*, 1952; Françoise Sagan's *La Robe mauve de Valentine*, 1962.

Dasté, Jean (1904–), French actor and director. Joined COPEAU's drama school in 1922, and followed his teacher to the country in Burgundy; he was one of the founders of the COMPAGNIE DES QUINZE. With BARSACQ and M. Jacquemont he managed the Théâtre des Quatre Saisons which gave visiting performances in the USA 1937–39. In the 1940s he produced, e.g. at the Théâtre de l'Atelier, plays by ANOUILH: *Le Bal des voleurs*, *Le Rendezvous de Senlis*, and *Eurydice*. After the war he managed the first CENTRE DRAMATIQUE in the provinces (Grenoble) and since 1947 the Comédie at St-Etienne. As a pupil of Copeau, D. supports the 'théâtre pur' tending to theatricality for its own sake; as an actor, he prefers parts like BRIGHELLA in GOZZI's *Il Re cervo*, Scapin, Sganarelle, and comic roles in Anouilh's plays.
Bibl: P. Ackroyd, THE DRAMATIC ART OF LA COMPAGNIE DES QUINZE, 1935

Daubeny, Sir Peter (1921–75), English impresario. Started as an actor, but after losing an arm in World War II turned to management. After many successful West End productions, he became increasingly interested in bringing foreign dance, and later dramatic, companies to London, such as BARRAULT's company and the BERLINER ENSEMBLE on their first visit in 1956, the COMÉDIE-FRANÇAISE, the MOSCOW ART THEATRE, etc. From 1964 to 1973 he directed the annual World Theatre Season at the

Aldwych Theatre, London, which became one of the world's great showcases for international drama and exercised a considerable influence on the development of the English theatre. Knighted in 1973. He received many other decorations from countries he visited including Officier de Legion d'Honneur in 1971.
Autobiographies: *Stage by Stage*, 1952, and *My World of the Theatre*, 1971.

Davenant, Sir William (1606–68), English dramatist and theatre manager. Wrote and produced Court MASQUES in the style of JONSON, whom he succeeded as Poet Laureate in 1638. He also wrote a number of plays (e.g. *A Cruel Brother*). During the period when public theatres were closed by the Puritans (1642–60) he succeeded in staging private performances, e.g. in 1656 of his *The Siege of Rhodes*, a play with music, which marks the beginning of English opera. With the advent of the Restoration he and KILLIGREW were given patents by Charles II to re-open public theatres. D.'s company, the Duke of York's Servants, opened at the old theatre in Salisbury Court and then moved to the Duke's Theatre in Lincoln's Inn Fields, while Killigrew, after opening in a makeshift theatre in Vere Street, took the King's Players to his THEATRE ROYAL, DRURY LANE. D. was the first to introduce ballet, stage décor and mechanism into the English theatre in contrast to the simple staging of the ELIZABETHAN THEATRE.
Bibl: A. N. Nethercot, 1938

Daviot, Gordon (pseud. of Elizabeth Mackintosh; 1897–1952). English novelist and playwright. She wrote mystery stories under the name of Josephine Tey. Her most noteworthy play is *Richard of Bordeaux*, 1932, in which GIELGUD first made an impression on the London stage as a major actor.

Dawison, Bogumil (1818–72), German-speaking Polish actor. Made his début in Warsaw in 1837 and went to Germany in 1846, appearing at the Thalia Theater, Hamburg, in 1847. After guest performances in Vienna he joined the BURGTHEATER there in 1849. At the height of his career, 1854–64, he was engaged by the Dresden Theatre and toured Vienna, Berlin, Paris, and Leningrad with parts in plays by SCHILLER, SHAKESPEARE and GOETHE. He represented the travelling virtuoso: a brilliantly skilful actor with controlled movements, language and memory, who fascinated the audience with his eccentricity. Compared with his rival E. DEVRIENT (who appeared with him in Dresden), the 'idealist' of the Weimar School, he was the 'realist'. He was also known as the 'Polish fury'. After 1864 he gave guest performances at several theatres, and in 1866–67 he had a triumphant tour of the USA with the Theater an der Wien.
Bibl: E. Devrient, GESCHICHTE DER DEUTSCHEN SCHAUSPIELKUNST, 1848–74, new ed. 1957, 2 vols

Danielle Darrieux in *La Robe mauve de Valentine* by Françoise Sagan, Paris 1962

Gabriele d'Annunzio

Daly's Fifth Avenue Theatre

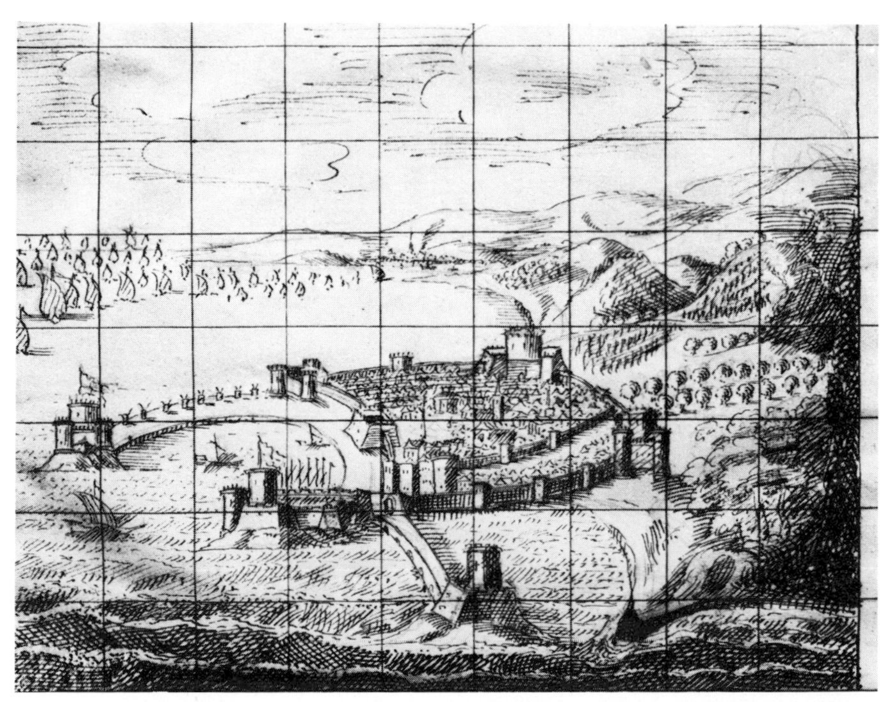

Sir William Davenant's *Siege of Rhodes*, backcloth design by John Webb, 1661

Dean, Basil (1888–), English director and manager. Started as an actor; joined the HORNIMAN company at the Gaiety Theatre, Manchester, in 1907. In 1911 became manager of the Liverpool Repertory Theatre. After World War I went into management in London and produced and directed numerous great successes, including FLECKER's *Hassan*, 1923; MARGARET KENNEDY's *The Constant Nymph*, 1926; and many plays by GALSWORTHY, BARRIE, CLEMENCE DANE and MAUGHAM. Also active as a producer on BROADWAY and as a film producer. Autobiography: *Seven Ages*, 1970, *The Theatre at War*, 1955.

De Bosio, Gianfranco (1924–), Italian director. Started working in 1949 with a company of students, Il Ruzzante, for whom he produced plays by writers ranging from AESCHYLUS to PIRANDELLO and BRECHT (first Italian production of *Man is Man* in 1953). In 1953 when Il Ruzzante amalgamated with the Tre Venezie company, he took over the management of the new group. In 1955 he became director of the TEATRO STABILE in Turin; later he worked as a freelance director. His main importance lies in his revival of RUZANTE, whose *La Moschetta* he produced in the open air at the Teatro di Venezia in Ferrara, 1956.

De Brie, Mlle (Catherine Le Clerc du Rozet; *c.* 1620–*c.* 1706), French actress. One of the first and most important members of MOLIÈRE's company, which she joined in 1650. She created many of his female parts, her greatest success being as Agnès in *L'Ecole des femmes*, 1662. Other roles: Cathos in *Les Précieuses ridicules*, 1659; Eliante in *Le Misanthrope*, 1666; Marianne in *Tartuffe*, 1668, and Alcmène in *Amphitryon*, 1668. Her husband **Edmé Villequin de B.** (1607–76) was a character actor in Molière's company.
Bibl: L. Lacour, LES MAÎTRESSES DE MOLIÈRE, 2/1932

Deburau, Jean-Baptiste Gaspard (1796–1846), French MIME. His family were acrobats. He arrived in Paris in 1812, moving in 1816 to the Théâtre des Funambules on the Boulevard du Temple, the home of acrobats and tightrope-walkers. At first he received little appreciation as a member of the company, but gained greater recognition as he developed his conception of PIERROT, the pale and unrequited lover, which he established as an eternal type. Eventually, he was as successful with the ordinary people of the Paris suburbs as he was with critics and sophisticated connoisseurs. He has since become a legendary figure of the French theatre, featuring in novels and as a character in plays: *Deburau* by J. Claetie, 1907, and S. GUITRY, 1918, and the film *Les Enfants du Paradis* by Marcel Carné in which BARRAULT played Deburau.
Bibl: T. Rémy, 1954

Decroux, Etienne (1898–), French actor and MIME. A pupil and collaborator of DULLIN, 1926–34, he was the first to develop a systematic language of physical expression, which led to the 20th-century revival of PANTOMIME. His pupils and followers include Elyane Guyon, Catherine Toth, BARRAULT, and MARCEAU. His first production at his school of pantomime in 1940 included a series of sketches (subsequent productions 1941, 1942); in 1943 he became a teacher of mime at the Théâtre Sarah Bernhardt; between 1947 and 1951 he toured Switzerland, Israel, Holland and England, then worked in Paris at the Cabaret Fontaine des Quatre Saisons, and subsequently at various other theatres. He taught mime at the New School of Social Research, New York. Also known as a film actor: mime in the film *Les Enfants du Paradis*, 1945. He is the author of *Paroles sur le Mime*, Paris 1963. His son **Maximilian D.** is also a mime and directs his father's school.

De Filippo. Family of Neapolitan actors and playwrights who revived the Neapolitan dialect in the theatre. (1) **Titina de F.** (1898–1963), (2) **Eduardo de F.** (1900–) and (3) **Peppino de F.** (1903–). T. de F. and E. de F. appeared together in 1916 in E. Scarpetta's company in juvenile parts, P. de F. worked first with the same company in 1919. In 1929 all three appeared in a revue company; in the following two years E. de F. wrote LIBRETTI for REVUES and his first one-act play; T. de F. and P. de F. also did some dramatic writing. In 1931 they formed their own company under the management of E. de F., the Teatro Umoristico I de Filippo, on which their reputation in the Italian theatre today is based. In 1945 the two brothers formed separate companies, T. de F. joined E. de F., with whom she remained until her death. E. de F. wrote major dramatic works including *Napoli milionaria* (Naples with its Millions), 1945; *Filumena Marturano*, 1946; *Sik Sik, l'artefice magico* (The Magician), 1930; *Le voci di dentro* (Voices from Within), 1948; *Pulcinella in cerca della sua fortuna per Napoli* (Pulcinella in search of his fortune in Naples), 1958; *Sindaco del rione Sanità* (The Mayor of the Sanità District), 1960. Some of his plays have been translated into English. In 1964 and again in 1973 P. de F. brought his own company to London for the WORLD THEATRE SEASON with his farce *The Metamorphosis of a Wandering Minstrel*, and E. de F.'s play *Saturday, Sunday, Monday*, written 1959, was produced at the NATIONAL THEATRE in 1973 with OLIVIER and his wife JOAN PLOWRIGHT in the leading roles.

Déjazet, Pauline-Virginie (1798–1875), French actress. At the age of five she was a potential ballerina but, after appearing with several children's companies and spending a few years in the provinces, she joined the Théâtre du Gymnase in 1821, where she excelled in VAUDEVILLE and MUSICAL COMEDIES, particularly in boys' parts – in which she was highly successful throughout her life. In 1831 she went to the Palais Royal where she won great fame and popularity. From 1859 she managed her own theatre for several years: the Théâtre des Folies-Nouvelles, which she renamed Théâtre Déjazet, and for which her son **Eugène D.** (1820/25–80) wrote LIBRETTI for musical comedies. In spite of some successes the theatre went bankrupt and was forced to become a touring company. She was a small, graceful woman with sharp expressive features; her mellow voice and her grace made her a natural star in REVUE, light comedy and VARIETY. She created on stage a type of woman, at once witty and malicious; such parts were named *Déjazets* after her. At the age of 62 she made a memorable appearance in a male part in SARDOU's *Monsieur Garat*.

Dejmek, Kazimierz (1924–), Polish director, who started his career as an actor in a small provincial theatre (1944). In 1945/46 he was in Craców, 1946–49 in Lódz under the management of L. SCHILLER, in 1949 he became director of the New Theatre in Lódz, and in 1960 of the National Theatre in Warsaw, but had to resign after disturbances caused by a performance of MICKIEWICZ's *Dziadý* in 1968. He is one of the outstanding figures in Polish theatre today; famous for his productions of classical plays (SHAKESPEARE's *Measure for Measure*, 1956; *Julius Caesar*, 1960); he gained a worldwide reputation with his rediscovery of Polish Renaissance plays: Rej's *Life of St Joseph*, in 1958, and *The Story of the Glorious Resurrection of Our Lord*, a 16th-century MYSTERY PLAY, first produced in 1961 by the National Theatre, Warsaw, for the Paris THÉÂTRE DES NATIONS festival.

Dekker, Thomas (*c.* 1572–*c.* 1632), English dramatist. Best known for his comic masterpiece *The Shoemaker's Holiday*, fp 1599, Rose Theatre. The most important of his other plays is *The Honest Whore*, in two parts, 1604, some passages of which may be the work of MIDDLETON. In *Satiromastix*, 1601, D. satirizes JONSON (▷ WAR OF THE THEATRES). Most of his plays were written in collaboration with other writers, e.g. *The Roaring Girl*, 1610, with Middleton; *The Virgin Martyr*, 1620, with MASSINGER. In his plays D., who mainly worked for HENSLOWE, reveals sunny good humour and deep human sympathy, especially for the poor and oppressed.
Bibl: G. E. Bentley, THE JACOBEAN AND CAROLINE STAGE, 1941–66, 7 vols

Delaney, Shelagh (1939–), English writer. At the age of 17 she wrote her first play, *A Taste of Honey*, initially produced by JOAN LITTLEWOOD at her Theatre Workshop in 1958, it was subsequently transferred to the West End and then had a BROADWAY run. She also scripted the film version in 1961 in collaboration with the director T. RICHARDSON. Her second play, *The Lion in Love*, 1960, was less successful.

Delaunay, Louis Arsène (1826–1903), French actor. He made his stage début at the Odéon in 1845 and three years later joined the COMÉDIE-FRANÇAISE where he had a brilliant career, excelling in plays by MUSSET; he was the original Fortunio in *Le Chandelier* and appeared as Valentin in *Il ne faut jurer de rien*, 1855, and Coelio in

Les Caprices de Marianne; he was so greatly admired in this part that the play was not performed again for a long time after his retirement from the theatre, 1886.
Bibl: H. Lyonnet, LES PREMIÈRES D'ALFRED DE MUSSET, 1927

Della Porta, Giovan Battista (1538–1613), Italian scientist, philosopher and playwright. Of some 30 plays 14 have survived. His subjects were taken from classical Rome and the Italian Renaissance, particularly PLAUTUS and Boccaccio (COMMEDIA ERUDITA). His *I due fratelli rivali* (The Two Rival Brothers), 1601, is taken from a story by Bandello on which SHAKESPEARE also based his *Much Ado About Nothing*. Other major works include: *La Fantesca* (The Maid), *L'Astrologo* (The Astrologer), *La Trappolaria* (The Trick).

De Lullo, Giorgio (1921–), Italian actor and director. Started working in the theatre in 1945. He was successful in the Compagnia Morelli-Stoppa (Orpheus in ANOUILH's *Eurydice*, 1946) and at the PICCOLO TEATRO DI MILANO (Mark Antony in *Julius Caesar*, 1953). With BUAZZELLI, ROSSELLA FALK, VALLI and A. M. Guarnieri he founded the COMPAGNIA DEI GIOVANI, in which he was active both as actor and director.

Denmark. In the late Middle Ages, Easter plays and plays on the lives of saints; after the Reformation, Humanist School theatre; in the 17th century, German, English and French itinerant companies. In 1722 the Frenchman René Magnon de Montaigu obtained a royal licence to open a Danish-language theatre; it began with MOLIÈRE, and was followed by HOLBERG's *Den politiske Kandestøber*. In 1748 the newly built Royal Theatre was opened, and in the 19th century it took over the function of a NATIONAL THEATRE. In 1917 the actress Betty Nansen, well known for her performances of IBSEN and STRINDBERG, established a playhouse with a literary programme, the Betty Nansen Theatre, Copenhagen; it was followed in 1938 by the Riddersalen Theatre under the important director BESEKOW. After 1945 gradual development of REPERTORY theatres outside the capital.

Dennis, Nigel (1912–), English dramatist; also well known as a novelist. A satirist in the tradition of VOLTAIRE and SHAW; in a Shavian-style preface to his first two plays he defines with great wit his favourite targets: the doctrine of Original Sin and the assumptions of psychoanalysis, which, he argues, both undermine natural self-reliance and may threaten personal individuality. His plays illustrate this thesis: *Cards of Identity*, 1956, adapted from his own novel, is about members of a club formed to give people a changed identity; *The Making of Moo*, 1957; *August for the People*, 1961.

Desiosi, The. COMMEDIA DELL'ARTE company; T. MARTINELLI, the famous Italian HARLEQUIN, made several appearances with them *c.* 1595. After it disbanded most of its actors later joined the ACCESI company.

Dessau, Paul (1894–), German composer. First conductor at the Municipal Opera in Berlin from 1925; he emigrated to Paris in 1933, then to the USA in 1939, where in 1942 he met BRECHT, for whom he wrote the music for several plays, among them: *Mutter Courage*, 1946; *Der gute Mensch von Setzuan*, 1947; *Die Ausnahme und die Regel*, 1948. He wrote two operas based on texts by Brecht: *Das Verurteilung des Lukullus* (on *Das Verhör des Lukullus*), East Berlin 1951, State Opera; *Puntila* (on *Herr Puntila und sein Knecht Matti*), East Berlin 1966, State Opera, dir Ruth Berghaus, D.'s wife, and he has also written stage music for other writers: BECHER's *Der Weg nach Füssen*, 1956, BERLINER ENSEMBLE; WEISS's *Diskurs über Vietnam*, 1968, Berliner Ensemble. He has composed film music in Germany and the USA.
Bibl: F. Hennelberg, DESSAU-BRECHT, 1963

Destouches, Philippe Néricault (1680–1754), French dramatist. One of the forerunners of the 18th-century DRAME BOURGEOIS and the COMÉDIE LARMOYANTE, he imitated the themes and intrigues of MOLIÈRE but emphasized the moral message. His best plays are: *Le Triple mariage*, 1716, at the COMÉDIE-FRANÇAISE; *Le Philosophe marié*, 1727; and *Le Glorieux*, 1732, at the CF (translated into English in 1791).

Deus ex machina (Lat = the god from the machine). In the Greek theatre a crane-like scaffold (Lat *machina*) designed to facilitate the sudden and surprise appearance of gods and heroes on top of the stage building as if they were coming from the clouds. A stage device often used by EURIPIDES to resolve plot complications which might otherwise have remained insoluble. The phrase is also used figuratively.

Deuteragonist (Gk *deuteragonistes*). The second actor in Greek classical TRAGEDY introduced by AESCHYLUS. He filled the lesser roles and women's parts. Inferior to the PROTAGONIST from whom he received payment.

Deval, Jacques (J. Boularan; 1890–1972), French dramatist. Writer of BOULEVARD plays in the French VAUDEVILLE tradition, successful with his first play *Une faible femme*, 1920. Other works include: *Dans sa candeur naïve*, 1926, adapted by Valerie Wingate and WODEHOUSE as *Her Cardboard Lover*; *Etienne*, 1930; *Prière pour les vivants*, 1933, in New York as *Another Love*; *Tovaritch*, 1933, worldwide success, English adaptation by SHERWOOD (*Tovarich*) fp New York 1936. He went to the US in the 1930s and served in the US Army during World War II. Further plays written first in English: *Lorelei*, 1938; *Behold the Bride*, 1939; *Oh Brother!*, 1945. After his return to France he wrote *Ce Soir à Samarcande*, 1950; *Charmante soirée*, 1955; *Un homme comblé*, 1964.

Devine, George Alexander Cassady (1910–66), English theatre director. Started as an actor in 1932; was director and

Jean-Baptiste Deburau, 1840

Eduardo de Filippo

Deus ex machina, eighteenth-century French print showing the descent of a 'cloud machine'

manager at SAINT-DENIS's London Theatre Studio, one of the first modern English drama schools, 1936–39. After the war he worked 1946–52 as part of a 'triumvirate' with Saint-Denis and GLEN BYAM SHAW, who succeeded in making the OLD VIC the unofficial English NATIONAL THEATRE. He was also director of the experimental group at the Old Vic – the Young Vic – and a teacher at the Old Vic Theatre School. After the break-up of the triumvirate, he endeavoured to create a theatre which would sponsor the work of new dramatists. In 1956 he succeeded in founding the ENGLISH STAGE COMPANY at the Royal Court Theatre, of which he was appointed director; it became a major influence in the London theatrical scene, supporting particularly such new-wave dramatists as OSBORNE (*Look Back in Anger*, 1956), PINTER, WESKER, ARDEN, and also staging plays by BRECHT, BECKETT, IONESCO (*Exit the King*, 1963), GENET and other writers of the European avant-garde.

Devrient. Family of German actors of Dutch origin. (1) **Ludwig D.** (1784–1832) began his career in 1804 with a travelling company, joined the COURT THEATRE in Dessau in 1805, where he appeared as Franz Moor (SCHILLER's *Die Räuber*), Wurm (Schiller's *Kabale und Liebe*) and Harpagon (MOLIÈRE's *Le Misanthrope*); in 1814 IFFLAND called him to the Royal Theatre in BERLIN, where he gave brilliant performances as a comedian (Falstaff was considered his finest part), but was at his best in tragic parts such as Shylock, Lear and Franz Moor. He later appeared in plays by Iffland and other contemporary dramatists. L.D. was a versatile temperamental talent of a restless nature; his style of acting could not be compared with any other – it was unique, he attempted to interpret his roles with intuition and imagination and was most convincing in parts which matched his sensibilities (Lear). He was one of the greatest actors in the history of the German theatre, his romantic genius being often compared with that of KEAN in England. L.D. had three nephews on the stage, the eldest (2) **Karl August D.** (1797–1872) made his stage début as Rudenz (Schiller's *Wilhelm Tell*) in Brunswick under KLINGEMANN, then joined the Court Theatre in Dresden, where he played Posa (Schiller's *Don Carlos*), title roles in *Hamlet*, *Egmont* (GOETHE), and *Wilhelm Tell* (Schiller). Later he appeared with the companies in Karlsruhe (1835) and Hanover (1839). He excelled in character roles – Faust, Lear, Shylock. His brother (3) **Eduard D.** (1801–77) began as a singer, wrote two LIBRETTI and was a member of the Royal Opera House; after his singing voice failed him in 1834 he turned to the theatre. He appeared successfully at the Royal Theatre (in such roles as Richard II) and also worked as a producer. In 1844 he went to the Court Theatre in Dresden, where rivalry with his brother Emil (see below) led him increasingly to producing. Besides this, he started writing on the theatre, his most important work being *Geschichte der Deutschen Schauspielkunst* (5 vols 1848–74; new ed in 2 vols 1967) – the first account of the development of the German theatre, and an important document for the theatrical history of the 19th century. In 1852 he was appointed director of the Court Theatre in Karlsruhe, where he remained until 1870; after he retired from the theatre he published German versions of SHAKESPEARE, the *Deutsche Bühnen- und Familien-Shakespeare*, 1873–76, with his son (4) **Otto D.** (1838–94) who was known mainly as a playwright and producer, actor and singer. His *Diaries* covering the period 1836–70 were published in 1964. L.D.'s youngest nephew (5) **Emil D.** (1803–72) made his début in 1821 at Brunswick, then appeared at Bremen, Leipzig, Magdeburg and Hamburg, until in 1831 he joined the Dresden Court Theatre, where he remained until 1868. He had a noble, sensitive voice, and heroic gestures; his academic acting was very much approved by his contemporaries; he was outstanding in juvenile heroic parts: Tasso, Orestes in *Iphigenia*, Egmont, and in Schiller's plays. Other notable members of the family were the actors: (6) **Friedrich Philipp D.** (1827–71), son of K.A.D. and his first wife, Wilhelmine Schröder (1804–60), a famous opera singer, and (7) **Max D.** (1857–1929), son of K.A.D. and his second wife Johanna Block. He was for many years at the Vienna BURGTHEATER, where he excelled in big tragic roles, particularly in Goethe, Schiller and Shakespeare.

Bibl: K. Reinholz, EDUARD DEVRIENTS GESCHICHTE DER DEUTSCHEN SCHAUSPIELKUNST, 1967, 2 vols; W. Drews, DIE GROSSEN DES DEUTSCHEN SCHAUSPIELS, 1941

Dexter, John (1925–), English director. He came to prominence with his first productions of WESKER's plays, all for the ENGLISH STAGE COMPANY: *Roots*, 1960; *Chicken Soup with Barley*, 1960; *I'm Talking about Jerusalem*, 1960; *The Kitchen*, 1961; *Chips with Everything*, 1962. With the founding of the NATIONAL THEATRE he became an associate director, staging SHAW's *Saint Joan*, OLD VIC, 1963; *Othello*, 1964, with OLIVIER (also at the CHICHESTER FESTIVAL and as a visiting director in BERLIN and Moscow); P. SHAFFER's *The Royal Hunt of the Sun*, Chichester and Old Vic, London, 1964, and New York, 1965. He co-directed with GASKILL ARDEN's *Armstrong's Last Goodnight*, 1965 and directed *The Devils*, opera by the Polish composer Krzysztof Penderečki, based on WHITING's play, London, 1973, and another successful P. Shaffer play, *Equus*, Old Vic, 1973, New York 197 .

Dialogue (Gk *dialogos* = exchange of speech, conversation). Verbal exchange between two or more characters on stage (as opposed to MONOLOGUE). It is the basis of all drama, and the art of dialogue the fundamental skill of the playwright. ▷ STICHOMYTHIA.

Didascalae (Gk *didaskalai* = instructions). In the Greek theatre records of productions, listing title, name of festival, festival officials, director, composer, playwright, PROTAGONIST, etc. Such lists appeared, for example, in the manuscripts of TERENCE's plays and of PLAUTUS' *Stichus* and *Pseudolus*. They are important sources of theatre history.

Didascalos (instructor). Greek name for the dramatic poet, who was responsible for training and instructing the CHORUS; the production was known as the *Didascalia*.

Diderot, Denis (1713–84), French philosopher, essayist, playwright and critic, whose work greatly influenced 19th-century drama. He edited (and largely wrote) at first with d'Alembert, later on his own, the famous *Encyclopédie*. In his dramatic work he transformed one of the most popular genres of his time, the COMÉDIE LARMOYANTE, into the DRAME BOURGEOIS which influenced BEAUMARCHAIS, DUMAS *fils* and AUGIER, and the German Romantics LESSING, GOETHE and SCHILLER. Though D. was not a good playwright himself, and over-sentimental, his plays were most important to the development of the new *drame bourgeois*; each play was accompanied by a long original essay expounding his ideas: *Le Fils naturel*, written 1757, fp 1771 at the COMÉDIE-FRANÇAISE; *Le Père de famille*, written 1758, fp 1760 in Marseilles, 1761 at the CF. In the essays 'Entretiens sur *Le Fils naturel*', 1757, and 'Discours sur la poésie dramatique', 1758, he demanded middle-class heroes and the depiction of their bourgeois lives with details of their occupation, origins, etc.; he emphasized the importance of action rather than the traditional declamatory style. In his *Le Paradoxe sur le comédien*, pub 1830, he calls coolness and conscious control the signs of great art in acting. His dialogue *Le Neveu de Rameau*, written between 1761 and 1774, which first became known through a translation into German by Goethe, 1821, was performed in Berlin and Paris in the 1960s; it is a character sketch in which the author gives a resumé of his ideas and theories on poetry and music, and also throws light on the corruption of contemporary society.

Dieterle, William (1899–1972), German director. Began his career as an actor in Heidelberg, Zurich, Munich and in BERLIN at the VOLKSBÜHNE and Deutsches-Theater (under the management of REINHARDT in 1918); from 1921 he also appeared in films. From 1930 to the end of the 1950s D. worked as film actor and director in the USA (e.g. *The Hunchback of Notre Dame*, 1939). Returning to Germany, he took over the management of the Festival in Bad Hersfeld (1961–65). From 1968 D. managed the touring company, Der Grüne Wagen.

Dietrich, Marlene (Maria Magdalena von Losch; 1902–), German actress and singer. Trained with REINHARDT in Berlin, then appeared on stage at his theatres in small parts, such as the Widow in SHAKESPEARE's *The Taming of the Shrew*, 1922. She made her first successful stage appearance in the REVUE by M. Schiffer and M. Spoliansky *Es liegt in der Luft*, 1923; she appeared at the National Theatre, Berlin 1926; she was also in KAISER's *Zwei Krawatten*, 1929. Since then she has appeared only in films. Under Joseph von Sternberg's direction in *The Blue Angel*, 1930, she achieved world fame and he continued to direct her in Hollywood in a series of exotic romances such as *Morocco*, *Shanghai Express*. Apart from *Destry Rides Again*, her screen work since leaving Von Sternberg has been unremarkable, and she has recently concentrated on concert appearances as DISEUSE.

Dingelstedt, Franz von (1814–81), German director and theatre manager. Began his career as a DRAMATURG at the COURT THEATRE in Stuttgart, 1845–51, subsequently became director in Munich, then in Weimar, and eventually director of the BURGTHEATER in Vienna, 1870–81. His productions, supported by the stage painter W. von Kaulbach, displayed a splendidly picturesque historic style, with emphasis on graphic effects, especially in crowd scenes. His Munich 'model productions' and his productions of SHAKESPEARE's plays in Weimar (1864) and Vienna (1875) were triumphant successes, making theatrical history. He is known as an author of satirical poems with political content, of novels and essays on the theatre and as a translator of Shakespeare's plays into German.

Dionysia. Greek festivals in honour of the god DIONYSOS (the earliest were held in Athens). At the Great, or City, Dionysia (after 535 BC in Athens), held during the spring festival in March/April, dramatic performances were given either in a three-day period, when a TETRALOGY followed by a COMEDY was presented each day, or in a four-day period with three days of tragic tetralogies and five comedies on the fourth day, performed by the ten dithyrambic choruses. The more ancient Rustic Dionysia – held in December to celebrate the wine harvest – originally consisted of eating and drinking, and games with processions.

Dionysos. Greek god, son of Zeus and Semele, who brought the cult of the vine to the ancient world. D. was many-named: Bromius, Lacchus, Nyctelius, Bacchus and Zagreus. The original meaning of his name is unknown; in evidence before Homer's time (although Homer himself virtually ignores him) D. occurs again in the 7th and 6th centuries BC in Asia Minor (Phrygia) and the north (Thrace). D.'s characteristic emblem was the thyrsus and he was commonly represented as the leader of a riotous group (Thiasos) made up of maenads and satyrs. Hence the rituals in his honour often took the form of processionals representing the revelry of the Thiasos. In Attica his festivals, the DIONYSIA and LENAEA, provided the source from which every kind of ancient drama grew.

Dionysos, Theatre of. Situated at the southern slope of the Acropolis of Athens in an area sacred to DIONYSOS near a temple

John Dexter's production of *Royal Hunt of the Sun* by P. SHAFFER at the NATIONAL THEATRE, 1964

Karl Devrient as Shylock

Dionysos with maenads, Greek red-figure cup

dating from the 6th century BC which is said to have contained a sacred image of the god from Eleuthera. The oldest acting area, created for the round dances of the chorus, was about 72 feet in diameter. Originally the spectators merely stood around its perimeter, later wooden benches and a tent for changing costumes at the edge of the dancing area (*orchestra*) were provided. The erection of a stone stage and auditorium started in the 5th century BC, the theatre in stone being completed under Lykurgos, 340–319 BC. The theatre at that time could hold 14,000 to 17,000 spectators. A stone *proskenion* was erected in the 2nd century BC and rebuilt under Nero (AD 54–68).

Diseur, Diseuse (Fr=reciter). CHANSON-singer of the genre which developed in Paris in 1880, involving singing with the main emphasis on the text. Famous interpreters: Aristide Bruant, YVETTE GUILBERT.

Dithyramb (Gk *dithyrambos*, origin unknown). Choral hymn in honour of DIONYSOS at the celebrations of the Dionysia. Performed in the dancing area (ORCHESTRA) around the god's statue by men and boys in choruses numbering about 50; it was accompanied by flute. The division of the verse into strophe (sung by the leader of the CHORUS) and anti-strophe (by the whole chorus) was attributed to the singer-poet Arion (*c*.600 BC); ARISTOTLE argued that drama developed from this point, although dithyrambs were not strictly dramatic and survived as an independent genre for a long time.

Döbbelin, Carl Theophilus (1727–93), German ACTOR-MANAGER. He began his career as a leading man in the companies of CAROLINE NEUBER and later of ACKERMANN and F. SCHUCH. GOTTSCHED, who had greatly admired D.'s performances in his play *Der sterbende Cato*, encouraged him to manage his own company, which D. founded in 1756 in Erfurt. After travelling (Weimar, Mainz, Koblenz, Cologne, Düsseldorf) he joined, temporarily, the company of Ackermann and later of Franz Schuch Jr, until, in 1765, he took over Schuch's company and went with them to BERLIN; here, in 1767, he obtained a licence to give performances. Besides visiting performances (with the company) in Leipzig, Halle, Brunswick and Dresden, Berlin remained his base. D. keenly supported the work of LESSING, producing very successfully the latter's *Minna von Barnhelm*, 1768; *Emilia Galotti* and *Nathan der Weise* (1783, with D. himself playing the lead). He built up a good REPERTORY of plays by Opitz, WEISE, F. L. SCHRÖDER and SHAKESPEARE; in 1786 he was given the Komödienhaus am Gendarmenplatz, Berlin, which he reopened a year later as the Royal National Theatre.

Documentary theatre. Topical name – arising out of the success of HOCHHUTH's *Der Stellvertreter*, 1962, and *Soldaten*, 1967; KIPPHARDT's *In der Sache J. Robert Oppenheimer*; WEISS's *Die Ermittlung*, 1965, and *Diskurs über . . . Viet Nam . . .* , 1969; BROOK's *US*, 1966; DORST's *Toller*, 1967, and D. Berrigan's *The Catonsville Nine*, 1970. It is used to describe plays and productions which employ or are based on material such as official documents, press reports and also films, records, photos and tapes. In general a theatre which presents fact instead of fiction. In the USA it is also called Theatre of Fact, and developed originally out of the FEDERAL THEATRE PROJECT's Living Newspaper which flourished in the 1930s and was among the most important American theatre forms. The themes have almost always an historical or political character. Often used forms are transcripts of lawsuits, trials or investigations. Usually, political and economic subject-matter is combined with educative, critical and didactic purposes. The combination of documentary and propagandist purpose was already to be found in the revolutionary Russian theatre (e.g. YEVREINOV's production of *The Storming of the Winter Palace*, 1920, and in PISCATOR's productions in the late 1920s (e.g. A. N. TOLSTOY's *Rasputin*).

Don Juan. One of the great characters in modern Western drama – a southern counterpart to FAUST. Don Juan derives from old Spanish legend, and first found expression in TIRSO DE MOLINA's *El burlador de Sevilla y Convidado de piedra* (before 1630) which consists of two parts: the first describes the hero's adventures, the second the visit of the marble statue and Don Juan's punishment for his crimes. The sensual and demonic figure of Don Juan coupled with his punishment by the statue (and the moral ending) inspired many variations on the theme; Don Juan is a constantly recurring figure right up to the 20th century. Among the best-known versions are: MOLIÈRE's *Dom Juan ou le Festin de Pierre*; Mozart's opera *Don Giovanni*; GOLDONI's *Il Dissoluto*; GRABBE's *Don Juan und Faust*; DUMAS *père*'s *Don Juan de Manara*; BYRON's poem 'Don Juan'; and ROSTAND's *La Dernière nuit de Don Juan*. He also appears in the third act of SHAW's *Man and Superman*.

Donat, Robert (1905–58), English actor. Was a member of BENSON's Shakespeare company 1923–28. Noted for his beautiful voice. Became an outstanding performer of plays by SHAKESPEARE and SHAW (Dick Dudgeon in *The Devil's Disciple*, 1940; Shotover in *Heartbreak House*, 1943). At the OLD VIC played Becket in ELIOT's *Murder in the Cathedral*, 1953. Also appeared in many films, among them René Clair's *The Ghost Goes West*, 1936; Hitchcock's *The Thirty-Nine Steps*, 1935; he received an Oscar for his performance in *Goodbye Mr Chips*, 1939.

Doronina, Tatyana (1933–), Soviet actress. Since 1959 with the Leningrad Gorky Theatre. Outstanding in TOVSTONOGOV's productions of CHEKHOV, e.g. Masha in *Three Sisters*, 1965.

Dorsch, Käthe (1890–1957), German actress. Started as a SOUBRETTE in MUSICAL COMEDY, later became one of the great tragic actresses of her generation in Germany. Excelled in many of the great classical roles of the German REPERTOIRE and in the plays of the Naturalists, notably G. HAUPTMANN.

Dorst, Tankred (1925–), German dramatist. Studied in Munich, then worked at a PUPPET THEATRE. His plays show changing influences: *Gesellschaft im Spätherbst* (Company in late Autumn), fp Mannheim 1960, National Theatre, suggests GIRAUDOUX and ANOUILH; the FARCES *Die Kurve* (The Bend in the Road), 1960, and *Freiheit für Clemens* (Freedom for Clemens), are reminiscent of IONESCO. In *Grosse Schmährede an der Stadtmauer* (Great Vituperation at the City Wall), 1961, he depicts a woman accusing a militarist male world. *Die Mohrin* (The Moorish Girl), fp Frankfurt 1964, tells the story of Aucassin and Nicolette in a very ironic and playful sequence of images. *Wittek geht um* (Wittek haunts the town), fp 1967, Düsseldorf Schauspielhaus, describes a petty-bourgeois mass-murderer. *Toller*, fp Stuttgart, 1968, dir PALITZSCH, tells the story of the failure of the Munich uprising in 1919, with the playwright TOLLER as the central character.

Dorval, Marie-Thomas Amélie (*née* Delaunay; 1798–1849), French actress. Prototype of the romantic actress: passionate in life and on stage, she was of almost vulgar originality. She appeared several times at the COMÉDIE-FRANÇAISE, but found its restrictions tiresome and never attained the rights and financial security of a SOCIÉTAIRE; she returned to the popular theatres, where she often appeared with success opposite LEMAÎTRE. She was also a friend of VIGNY, of whose plays she was, according to contemporaries (Jules Sandeau, George Sand, GAUTIER, among them) an ideal interpreter; as Kitty Bell in *Chatterton*, 1835, she gave an especially memorable performance. One of her last successes was the part of the unhappy mother in the sentimental drama *Marie-Jeanne ou La Femme du peuple* by Adolphe Dennery. Gautier wrote of her: 'She was nature itself, all womanhood united in one woman.'

Dossenus (Lat=the hunchback). Comic philosopher with grotesque mask (hunchback and big nose) of the Roman comedy (▷ATELLANA).

Dostoyevsky, Fyodor Mikhailovich (1821–81), Russian novelist. Though none of his original dramatic works (*Mary Stuart, Boris Godunov, The Jew Jankel*) has survived, his novels are probably the most often adapted and dramatized works of world literature; their scenic structure together with the intensity of his DIALOGUE almost demand dramatic representation. NEMIROVICH-DANCHENKO saw in adaptations of D.'s work a possible source for enlarging the small REPERTORY of original Russian TRAGEDIES and produced, between

1910 and 1917, at the MOSCOW ART THEATRE: *The Brothers Karamazov*; *Nikolai Stavrogin* (from *The Demons*); *The Village Stepanchikovo*; *The Insulted and the Humiliated*. Other notable adaptations include: *White Nights* and *The Village Stepanchikovo*, by the Czech director, BURIAN; *Crime and Punishment* by L. SCHILLER (Polish); *The Brothers Karamazov* by COPEAU/J. Croué, *Crime and Punishment* by BATY, and *The Possessed* by CAMUS (French); *The Brothers Karamazov* by C. Alvaro, and *The Demons* by D. FABBRI (both Italian); *Crime and Punishment*, adaptation by R. Ackland and L. Irving, London 1946, with GIELGUD, also in the USA; an opera by Prokofiev, *The Gambler*; *The Idiot*, adapted by GRAY, London 1970, OLD VIC, prod QUAYLE.
Bibl: Leonic Grossman, 1975

Dottore. Standard character and pedant of the COMMEDIA DELL'ARTE, usually depicted as a Bolognese lawyer; passed via MOLIÈRE into French comedy. COSTUME: long black cloak with white collar, black jacket with white cuffs, black short trousers, black stockings and shoes; leather belt, black cap and a hat with a broad upturned brim. Black half-mask with red cheeks.

Douking, Georges (G. Ladoubée; 1902–), French director and designer. Studied music and dance; was also a painter and appeared in CABARET. His engagement at the Théâtre Montparnasse under BATY was decisive: he adopted the latter's idea of the theatre as an homogeneous entity comprising actor, designer and all the other components of the production; like Baty he designed the sets himself. He became well known with his production of MUSSET's *Il ne faut jurer de rien*, the production notes of which he published in 1947. He managed the CENTRE DRAMATIQUE (C. D. du Sud-Est) at Aix-en-Provence 1953–56. Other major productions, for which he also designed sets and costumes: SYNGE's *Riders to the Sea*, 1937, Théâtre des Ambassadeurs; GIRAUDOUX's *Sodom et Gomorrhe*, 1943, Théâtre Hebertot, des BÉRARD.

Dramaturg (Gk *dramaturgein* = to compose a drama, in that sense still used in several languages; Fr *dramaturge* = dramatist). Title existing in Germany since the end of the 18th century, whose holder has the function of literary adviser to a permanent theatrical company, and whose responsibilities are to read submitted plays, to select the REPERTOIRE and sometimes undertake the translation, adaptation and revision of plays in collaboration with the director. He may also be responsible for public relations, e.g. programme notes, posters, organizing of lectures, press contacts, etc. for the company.

Drame bourgeois. Dramatic genre of the 18th and 19th centuries. Until the middle of the 18th century TRAGEDIES were largely concerned with people of higher social class, and were written in verse. With the emancipation of the bourgeoisie, middle-class people appeared on stage as tragic characters, at first in England (for example LILLO's *The London Merchant* in 1731). Their conditions were viewed seriously and the traditional declamatory poetic style gave way to prose. The central themes of the *drame bourgeois* deeply concerned the middle-class spectator. But the father of this genre was DIDEROT who adapted it from the COMÉDIE LARMOYANTE and describes the central ideas in his essays 'Entretiens sur *Le Fils naturel*': *Dorval et Moi* published in 1757 with his play *Le Fils naturel*. The first important German *drame bourgeois* (*Bürgerliches Trauerspiel*) after the French and English models was LESSING's *Miss Sara Sampson*.

Draper, Ruth (1884–1956), US actress and writer. She appeared in short MONODRAMAS written by herself, without make-up and hardly any props, conjuring up not only the personality of the character she portrayed but also that of the unseen people with whom she was talking. Best-known: *Three Women and Mr Clifford*, *In a Church in Italy*, *On a Maine Porch*. These sketches have been published in a volume, *The Art of Ruth Draper*, 1960.

Drawing-room comedy. Light sophisticated play, realistically staged, with contemporary PLOT, main characters drawn from the upper middle class, in which the chief action took place in the drawing-room or living-room. It had its heyday between the wars, in the US with P. BARRY, BEHRMAN and KELLY, in England with LONSDALE, MAUGHAM, and particularly COWARD as playwrights outstanding in this genre.

Drew. Family of US ACTOR-MANAGERS of Irish origin. (1) **John D.** (1827–62) excelled as an actor in portraying Irish character parts, e.g. Sir Lucius O'Trigger in *The Rivals*. His wife (2) **Louisa Lane D.** (Mrs John Drew; 1820–97), a woman of strong personality, was, after LAURA KEENE, the most important manageress in the American theatre; she ran the Arch Street Theatre, Philadelphia, 1860–92. The ENSEMBLE, under her firm rule, had a reputation for excellent diction and style. She went on tour, 1880–92, in *The Rivals*, as Mrs Malaprop (one of her best parts), with J. JEFFERSON as Bob Acres. She had three children, John, Louise and (3) **Georgiana Emma D.** (1856–92), the youngest, who became an actress, trained and managed by her mother. She married M. BARRYMORE in 1876. She appeared mainly under DALY at the Fifth Avenue Theatre and later in HELENA MODJESKA's company (*The Wages of Sin*, *The Senator*) and under the management of C. FROHMAN. She also appeared with Lawrence Barrett and E. BOOTH. (4) **John D.** (1853–1927) had the greatest acting talent in the family and was one of the outstanding performers of his time. He was under contract to Daly, 1875–92, for whom he appeared opposite ADA REHAN and Fanny Davenport, one of his mother's pupils. Although especially gifted in strong, heavy roles, he preferred character parts in comedies: Petruchio, Charles Surface, Orlando. He also visited London several

Dostoyevsky's *The Idiot*, costume designs by A. BENOIS

Ruth Draper in a Spanish character sketch

Louisa Lane Drew as Mrs Malaprop in SHERIDAN's *The Rivals*

times in the 1880s (in classics such as *As You Like It, The School for Scandal, The Taming of the Shrew*), and in 1893 in *Twelfth Night*. One of his best performances towards the end of his career was as Major Pendennis in a dramatization of Thackeray's novel. He wrote *My Years on the Stage*, 1922. (5) **Sidney D.** (S. White; 1864–1920) was the adopted son of Mrs John Drew. He began in VAUDEVILLE, but his later career was mainly as an actor and director in films.
Bibl: P. Wood, SPLENDID GIPSY: JOHN DREW, 1928; M. J. Moses, FAMOUS ACTOR FAMILIES IN AMERICA, 1906

Drinkwater, John (1882–1937), English poet and dramatist. He was one of the founders of JACKSON's Pilgrim Players (1907) from which later developed the BIRMINGHAM REPERTORY THEATRE, where he was for several years actor, director and general manager. After his early attempts to write VERSE DRAMA he turned to historical (prose) plays, with which he gained his reputation as a dramatist, the best among them probably *Abraham Lincoln*, London 1918, where it had a one-year run; frequently revived in London and New York. Other works include the historical plays: *Mary Stuart*, 1921; *Oliver Cromwell*, 1921, and *Robert E. Lee*, 1923; and the COMEDY *Bird in Hand*, 1927.
Bibl: B. Matthews, A HISTORY OF THE BIRMINGHAM REPERTORY THEATRE, 1924; T. C. Kemp, THE BIRMINGHAM REPERTORY THEATRE, 1948

Drottningholm Theatre. Royal Court Theatre situated near Stockholm. The original theatre built in 1754, probably after designs of the German architect George Greggenhofer for a French theatrical company, was burnt down in 1762 and rebuilt in 1766 by C. F. Adelcrantz as part of the palace of Queen Louisa Ulrika. Both the STAGE MACHINERY, by Donato Stopani, and the original décor have survived, and form one of the most important collections of the Drottningholm Museum. In the 19th century the theatre fell into disuse and was not restored and reopened till 1922; since 1934 it has been used for summer seasons, mainly of early opera.
Bibl: G. Hillestrom, THE DROTTNINGHOLM THEATRE – PAST, PRESENT, 1956

Drury Lane, Theatre Royal. One of the most famous English theatres, the oldest still in use today. It was founded and built by KILLIGREW, 1662, and opened in May 1663. Burnt down in 1672, it reopened in 1674 with DRYDEN as resident dramatist. BETTERTON was chief actor there from 1682 to 1695 and the theatre then came under the triumvirate of CIBBER, Dogget and Wilks, with ANNE OLDFIELD as leading actress. The theatre reached its apogee under GARRICK, who went there in 1742 as an actor, and managed the theatre 1746–76, introducing numerous reforms, e.g. he banished the privileged audience from the stage. He was succeeded by SHERIDAN under whose management SARAH SIDDONS and her brother, J. P. KEMBLE, had triumphant successes; in 1794 it was rebuilt, but burned down again in 1809. After being rebuilt in 1812 it found no long-term stable management for nearly a hundred years. Despite several successful years with KEAN and other outstanding actors, the house was used more and more for PANTOMIME, opera and CIRCUS, without bringing any special benefit to lessees. In the early 20th century it was IRVING (1903 and 1905) who resumed the old traditions; between World Wars I and II series of operas and pantomimes were produced there; today Drury Lane is used mainly for musicals.

Dryden, John (1631–1700), English poet, translator, dramatist and critic of the Restoration period (▷RESTORATION DRAMA). Of his COMEDIES the most successful were: *Marriage à la mode*, 1672, written in collaboration with the Duke of Newcastle, and *Sir Martin Mar-All, or the Feign'd Innocence*, 1667. His TRAGICOMEDIES include *The Rival Ladies*, 1664, *Secret Love, or the Maiden-Queen*, 1667, anticipating in many respects CONGREVE's *The Way of the World*, and based partly on Mme de Scudéry's novel *Le Grand Cyrus*. They were very successful at the time, although in comic wit he was soon excelled by WYCHERLEY and Congreve. In tragedy he wrote the best HEROIC DRAMAS, a new development in the English theatre, modelled after French classical TRAGEDY and composed in heroic couplets. Several of these were written in collaboration with other dramatists. The greatest of his heroic dramas is *Almanzor and Almahide, or The Conquest of Granada* – in two parts, 1670, 1671; it contains all the elements of the genre – rant, bombast, poetry, vigour, battle, murder and sudden death. His last important play in this style was *Aureng-Zebe*, 1675; he then turned to blank verse with *All for Love*, 1677, which is usually considered his finest play. Although in PLOT an imitation of SHAKESPEARE's *Antony and Cleopatra*, it observes more strictly the French conception of classical unities of time, place and action than any other play of the period; it was frequently revived in the 18th century. D.'s essays show him as an outstanding critic; they are major sources for the understanding of Restoration drama: *An Essay of Dramatic Poesy*, 1668, *Of Heroic Plays*, 1672, the preface to *All for Love* and the preface to *Troilus and Cressida*. In 1668 he was appointed Poet Laureate, and his greatest achievements, such as his verse satires *Absalom and Achitophel*, Part I, 1681, and *MacFlecknoe*, 1682, were non-dramatic.
Bibl: A. C. Kirsch, DRYDEN'S HEROIC DRAMA, 1965

Držić, Marin (*c.* 1508–67), Croatian dramatist. Creator of the Ragusan Renaissance Comedy, modelled on Plautus and Boccaccio. Of his several comedies, *Dundo Maroje* is the most frequently revived in the modern Croatian theatre; he is one of the main authors presented at the annual festival in Dubrovnik.
Bibl: J. Torbarina, ITALIAN INFLUENCE ON THE POETS OF THE RAGUSAN REPUBLIC, 1931

Dudek, Jaroslav (1932–), Czech director. One of the first post-war directors to be trained at the newly founded Academy of Arts (AMU) which had attached to it a faculty for training actors (DAMU). He began his career in 1954 at the S. K. Neumann Theatre, Prague, where he remained a director until 1962, then became first director at the Theatre of the Army (now Vinohradsky Divadlo) in Prague. For his production of POGODIN's *Aristokraty*, 1960, S. K. Neumann Theatre, he was awarded a national (State) prize.

Dugazon. French family of actors. (1) **Jean-Baptiste-Henry Gourgaud** (1746–1809) known as Dugazon, a comedian, who became a member of the COMÉDIE-FRANÇAISE in 1771, best in roles by SCARRON and LEGRAND. He was one of the first teachers at the newly founded School of Declamation, 1786, which in 1795 became the CONSERVATOIRE D'ART DRAMATIQUE; TALMA was among his pupils. Married (2) **Louise-Rose Lefèvre** (1755–1821) known as Mme D., daughter of a French dancer at the Berlin Opera House; she started her career as a singer and dancer and in 1774 became the leading actress of the COMÉDIE-ITALIENNE. She was much praised for her natural and sensitive playing, and gave her most brilliant performance as Nina in Marsollier's *Nina ou La Folle par amour*.

Dukes, Ashley (1885–1959), English playwright, adapter and theatre manager. His most successful original play is *The Man with a Load of Mischief*, 1925, with FAY COMPTON, an elegant period COMEDY. He translated and adapted many plays from German (TOLLER, KAISER, STERNHEIM, FEUCHTWANGER, etc.), French and Italian (MACHIAVELLI's *La Mandragola*), some of which he produced at his own theatre in London, the Mercury, which he ran from 1933 to 1952. It was under his inspiration that the movement towards the revival of VERSE DRAMA in England started with performances at the Mercury of, e.g. ELIOT's *Murder in the Cathedral*, 1935, and DUNCAN's *This Way to the Tomb*, 1945. Dukes was married to the choreographer Marie Rambert, whose own ballet company also performed at the Mercury Theatre.

Dullin, Charles (1885–1949), French actor, director and theatre manager. One of the pioneers of the concept of the modern director in France. Started by reciting poetry in the CABARET Lapin Agile and was befriended by members of the literary and artistic avant-garde: PICASSO, APOLLINAIRE, Max Jacob. Discovered as an actor by COPEAU whom he joined at the Théâtre du Vieux-Colombier in 1913 where he played, e.g. the title role in MOLIÈRE's *L'Avare* and Rosmer in IBSEN's *Rosmersholm*. Left Copeau in 1921 and founded a theatre school, Ecole nouvelle du comédien. In 1922 he acquired the Théâtre Montmartre which he renamed Théâtre de l'Atelier where he was joined by DECROUX, 1926–34. Many leading French actors were nurtured by him at the Atelier, among them BARRAULT,

MARAIS, VILAR, and the great mime MARCEAU. He produced the classics as well as modern authors, among them PIRANDELLO and SALACROU. Like Copeau, he was above all a developer of acting talent, a great teacher, and reacted against the French rhetorical tradition by insisting on 'truth' rather than 'beauty' of expression. Like Copeau he strove for simplicity in the visual side of production and avoided excessive richness of décor. Unlike Copeau, however, D. was an intuitive rather than a theoretical director; his productions, precise though they were, always had the lightness of touch of a great improviser. In 1941 he relinquished the Théâtre de l'Atelier to BARSACQ and directed in other theatres, with varying success: outstanding was his direction of the first performance of SARTRE's *Les Mouches* in 1943.
Bibl: P. Teillon-Dullin & C. Charras, 1955

Dumas. French writers. (1) **Alexandre D.** (Dumas *père*; 1803–70), novelist and dramatist, whose plays were an important part of the Romantic movement in France. His first breakthrough in Romantic tragedy was his historical play *Henri III et sa cour*, fp 1829, Théâtre Français (▷COMÉDIE-FRANÇAISE), gaining him the recognition of VIGNY and HUGO. He strengthened his position even more by his next play *Antony*, 1831, regarded as a prototype of the Romantic genre in France, and his most famous melodramatic piece *La Tour de Nesle*. Both were produced at the Théâtre de la Porte Saint-Martin and part of their great success was due to the excellent performances of MLLE DORVAL and BOCAGE, the best actors of the time. In the next 30 years he wrote plays in profusion (about 90 in all), many in collaboration with other authors; several were dramatizations of his own novels: *Le Comte de Monte Cristo*, 1848, *Les Trois Mousquetaires*, 1849. In a time when there existed only the conventional CF with its classical REPERTOIRE and the trivial entertainment of VAUDEVILLE, D. *père* created a popular drama which somehow linked the traditional with the contemporary scene. His plays describe adventurous actions, usually in foreign countries, showing splendid heroes and dark villains. He gives his audiences spectacle and his actors the opportunity for strong performances. Even in modern times he has been an influence on artists such as SARTRE (his adaptation of *Kean*, 1953) and PLANCHON, who dramatized and produced *Les Trois Mousquetaires*.
(2) **Alexandre D.** (Dumas *fils*; 1824–95), playwright, essayist and novelist, was the illegitimate son of the elder Dumas and Catherine Labay. His unhappy childhood made him rebel against what he considered a cruel and false society. This comes out in his works, where his desire to reform the morals and manners of his time can be seen in plays dealing with marriage, the evils of money, adultery, prostitution and illegitimacy. His plays were mostly 'problem' or 'thesis' plays – as opposed to Romantic drama and the WELL-MADE PLAY of SCRIBE – combining moral instruction with enter-

Drottningholm Theatre, view of the interior

Alexandre Dumas, *père*, a scene from his play *Antony*, woodcut by Tony Johannot

Drury Lane, the theatre built 1810–12, print by W. Hopwood

tainment. He introduced realistic social drama to the French stage with his first and most famous play *La Dame aux camélias* (a dramatization of his own novel), 1852, Théâtre du Vaudeville; this brought him the greatest triumph of the Paris theatre in the second half of the century. His other major works included: *Le Demi-monde*, 1855; *Le Fils naturel*, 1858; *Diane de Lys*, 1853; *La Question d'argent*, 1857; *Un Père prodigue*, 1859; *Les Idées de Mme Aubray*, 1867; *La Femme de Claude*, 1873; *Denise*, 1881.
Bibl: A. Maurois, THE TITANS, A THREE-GENERATION BIOGRAPHY OF THE DUMAS, 1957

Du Maurier, Sir Gerald (1873–1934), English ACTOR-MANAGER. Knighted in 1922. One of the leading actors of his time, notably in light drama and COMEDY; a master of understatement, he was discovered by FROHMAN. He created parts like *Raffles*, 1906, in the MELODRAMA with the same title by Presbrey and Hornung, also Arsène Lupin and the gentleman detective Bulldog Drummond. Other important parts: the title role in BARRIE's *The Admirable Crichton* and Captain Hook in *Peter Pan*. In 1910 he became one of the directors of Wyndham's Theatre, where he produced mainly light comedy. His father was the novelist and cartoonist **George Louis Palmella Busson du M.** (1834–96) in whose dramatized novel *Trilby* Gerald appeared in 1895. Gerald's brother **Guy du M.** (1865–1916) was the author of the patriotic drama *An Englishman's Home*, 1909, and Gerald's daughter is the novelist and dramatist **Daphne Du M.** (1907–) author of the well-known novel *Rebecca*.
Bibl: D. Du Maurier, GERALD: A PORTRAIT, 1934

Dumesnil, Marie-Françoise (1713–1803), French actress, contemporary of MLLE CLAIRON. She joined the COMÉDIE-FRANÇAISE in 1737, and was especially noted for her passionate roles; she became one of the most important interpreters of VOLTAIRE's plays, whose success owed much to her acting: *Zulime*, 1740; *Mérope*, 1743; *Sémiramis*, 1748, and Clytemnestre in *Oreste*, 1750. Unlike her rival Mlle Clairon, she had no interest in the reform of theatrical costume; she was always richly robed in contemporary style and laden with jewels. She retired in 1775.
Bibl: H. C. Lancaster, FRENCH TRAGEDY IN THE TIME OF LOUIS XV AND VOLTAIRE, 1715–74 1929–42, 2 vols

Dumont, Louise (1862–1932), German actress and manageress. Began her career as an actress in several permanent theatre companies: Deutsches-Theater, Berlin 1884 and 1898–1901; BURGTHEATER, Vienna 1887–88; Hoftheater, Stuttgart 1890–95; she toured Europe with productions of IBSEN's plays; in 1905 together with her husband Gustav Lindemann (1872–1960) she founded the Düsseldorf Schauspielhaus and remained director until her death. As the interpreter of female roles in Ibsen's plays (Mrs Alving in *Ghosts*, the name part in *Hedda Gabler*, Rebecca West in *Rosmersholm*, Irene in *When We Dead Awaken*, Ellida in *The Lady From the Sea*) she emphasized their emancipatory urge towards freedom and self-determination. Her acting style was regarded as the epitome of NATURALISM and *fin-de-siècle* Art Nouveau. She saw the theatre as a demanding and solemn institution, and employed literary advisers in the position of DRAMATURG at her theatre, founded an academy of theatrical arts (Hochschule für Bühnenkunst) and a programme-magazine *Masken*. Her REPERTOIRE also included: WILDE, *Salomé*; SHAKESPEARE, *A Midsummer Night's Dream*; G. HAUPTMANN, *Die Weber*; GOETHE, *Faust*; WEDEKIND, *Frühlings Erwachen*, and after World War I STRINDBERG and the Expressionists. Because of financial difficulties, the theatre was temporarily closed 1919/20 and 1922/24. Lindemann's production of Goethe's *Faust* (Part II), at the State Theatre, Berlin 1932, with Louise D.'s pupil GRÜNDGENS as Mephistopheles, gained a belated triumph for the couple's theatrical concept.
Bibl: M. Linke, GUSTAV LINDEMANN, 1969

Duncan, Ronald (1914–), English dramatist and poet who has also written short stories and LIBRETTI. *This Way to the Tomb* – a masque and anti-masque (▷ MASQUE) – was modelled on JONSON's masques, fp London 1945, dir E. MARTIN BROWNE, music Britten; libretto for Britten, *The Rape of Lucretia*, based on OBEY's *Le Viol de Lucrèce*, Glyndebourne, 1946; he is the author of TRAGEDIES in verse, e.g. *Stratton*, 1949, and the double-bill *Don Juan*, 1953, and *The Death of Satan*, 1954, in the REPERTORY of the ENGLISH STAGE COMPANY in 1956, which he helped found in 1955. He was one of the founders of the Devon Festival of the Arts, 1953, for which he adapted old English plays and translated a number of French plays, e.g. COCTEAU's *L'Aigle à deux têtes*.

Dunlap, William (1766–1839), pioneer of the theatre in America. He was the first American to attempt to make a profession of writing plays and the first to become a theatre historian. Son of a former officer in the British Army, he went to London in 1784 where he set up as a portrait painter. Inspired by SARAH SIDDONS and C. KEMBLE, he began to write plays. He returned to America in 1787 and made his début with *The Father, or American Shandyism*, fp American Company, 1789. In 1796, he combined with HALLAM and John Hodgkinson, and bought a quarter interest in the company, which he helped by bringing in J. JEFFERSON. In 1798 the company moved to the Park Theatre in New York when he became its sole manager. In 1805, however, following various difficulties, including an epidemic of yellow fever, he became bankrupt and the theatre closed. From 1807 to 1811 he served as assistant stage manager at the Park Theatre under its new lessee, Thomas Abthorne Cooper, an English actor, one of the first to become an American citizen. D. was author and co-author of altogether 29 plays and also worked as an adapter and translator; his works include sentimental COMEDY, romantic and historical TRAGEDY, patriotic drama and BALLAD OPERA. He wrote two biographies and several histories, including *History of the American Theatre*, 1832, and *History of the Rise and Progress of the Arts of Design in the United States*, 1834. A competent painter all his life, he was one of the founders of the National Academy of Design.
Bibl: O. Coad, WILLIAM DUNLAP, 1917; A. H. Quinn, A HISTORY OF THE AMERICAN DRAMA FROM THE BEGINNING TO THE CIVIL WAR, 1946

Dunsany, Lord (Edward Drax Plunkett, 18th Baron Dunsany; 1878–1957), Irish playwright and short-story writer. A prolific writer of fantastic short stories, he was persuaded by YEATS to write a play for the ABBEY THEATRE: *The Glittering Gate*, 1909, in which two burglars try to get into Heaven. Other plays in a similarly fantastic and ironical mythological vein are: *King Argimenes*, 1911; *The Gods of the Mountain*, 1911; *A Night at an Inn*, 1916; *The Tents of the Arabs*, 1920; *The Golden Doom*, 1912; *The Lost Silk Hat*, 1913.

Du Parc. French family of actors. (1) **René Berthelot**, who called himself at first Du Parc, then *Gros-René* after the character he created, *c.* 1630–64, a plump little comedian. MOLIÈRE, whose company he had joined very early in his career, wrote several parts for him in FARCES, most of which have not survived: *Gros-René écolier*; *Gros-René petit enfant*; *La Jalousie de Gros-René*. His wife (2) **Marquise Thérèse de Gorla**, was known as **La Du Parc** (1633–68). Her talent and beauty were much praised, and she was deeply admired and loved by Molière, both Thomas and PIERRE CORNEILLE, RACINE and La Fontaine. She appeared in Molière's company in such comic parts as Célimène in his *La Critique de l'Ecole des femmes* and Elvire in *Dom Juan*, but she was best in tragic parts like Axiane in Racine's *Alexandre et Porus*. She left Molière's company and was taken on by the HÔTEL DE BOURGOGNE in 1667 under the protection of Racine, and made her most successful appearance in the title role of his *Andromaque*. When she died suddenly at the height of her success, Racine, by whom she was believed to be pregnant, was alleged to have poisoned her, but it is probable that she died as the result of an abortion.
Bibl: L. Lacour, LES MAÎTRESSES DE MOLIÈRE, 2/1932

Duras, Marguerite (1914–), French novelist, journalist and playwright. Born in Indo-China, she studied in France; most of her plays are dramatizations of her novels, such as *Le Square*, 1956; longer version 1965; *Un Barrage contre le Pacifique*, adapted from her novel of the same title by Geneviève Serreau, fp 1960, dir J.-M. Serreau; her first full-length play *Des Journées entières dans les arbres* (*Days in the Trees*), 1966, based on an earlier story, in which MADELEINE RENAUD created the leading part at the Odéon, Paris, produced at the Aldwych, London 1966, with PEGGY ASHCROFT. Plays written directly for the stage include: *Les Viaducs de la Seine-et-Oise*, Marseilles 1960, Paris 1963; *Les Eaux et forêts*, 1965; *L'Amante anglaise* (*The Lover of Viorne*), 1969. She 'composes, out of apparently clear sentences, ambiguous states of suspense – she does not write drama, but leaves her novels to make music on the stage' (G. Hensel). She also became famous as a scriptwriter for films such as *Hiroshima, mon amour*, dir Alain Resnais, 1959.

Durieux, Tilla (1880–1971), Austrian actress. Trained in Vienna, she made her stage début in Olmütz 1902, and in 1903 became a member of the permanent company at the Deutsches-Theater, BERLIN, where she remained until 1911. Her most brilliant performance there was in the title role of WILDE's *Salomé*, 1903/04. She had a lively and passionate temperament but her acting was sensitive and discriminating. She worked at the Lessingtheater, Berlin, 1911–14; she was with the State Theatre, Berlin, 1915–20, where she gave a memorable performance as Countess Weidenfels in WEDEKIND's *Der Marquis von Keith*, 1920, dir JESSNER. In 1927 she part-financed PISCATOR's theatre and later appeared under his direction as the Tsarina in *Rasputin*. Emigrated in 1933 (her husband was a Jew) and played Lady Macbeth in Prague 1935. During World War II she worked in Yugoslavia with a PUPPET THEATRE. Returned to Germany in 1952, giving visiting performances in Berlin and several other German cities. She wrote also two autobiographical books: *Eine Tür fällt ins Schloss*, 1928; *Eine Tür steht offen*, 1954.

Dürrenmatt, Friedrich (1921–), Swiss playwright, novelist, short-story writer and dramatic theorist. His primary ambition was to be a painter, and it was not until 1943 he began to devote himself to writing. His first play to be published as *Es steht geschrieben* (*All As It is Written*), 1947, is clearly influenced by BRECHT. In his essay *Theaterprobleme*, 1955, he argues that a world like ours, which is so over-organized that the individual choice of the tragic hero has become impossible, can only be treated by COMEDY in the theatre. In comparison with Brecht, whom he follows in the parable-like form of his description of society, he tends to be basically pessimistic regarding the possibility of change. He sees man as an absurd and essentially pitiable creature, subject to the ultimate meaninglessness of death. Life in the last analysis is insignificant and man is usually corruptible; his two major themes are death and power that corrupts; this is true of all his work but is most apparent in his major plays: *Die Ehe des Herrn Mississippi* (*The Marriage of Mr Mississippi*), fp 1952 Munich Kammerspiele, dir SCHWEIKART, produced at the Arts Theatre, London 1959; *Der Besuch der alten Dame* (*The Visit*), fp Zurich 1956, in New York 1959, later London; dir WÄLTERLIN, des OTTO, with THERESE GIEHSE and Knuth; *Romulus der Grosse* (*Romulus the Great*), fp Basle 1949; *Ein Engel kommt*

Dürrenmatt's *Die Ehe des Herrn Mississippi*, 1952

Gerald du Maurier as Aramis (right) in DUMAS *père*'s *The Three Musketeers*, London 1899

nach Babylon (*An Angel Comes to Babylon*), 1953; *Frank der fünfte* (*Frank* V), 1959; *Die Physiker* (*The Physicists*), 1962, RSC production 1963; *Der Meteor* (*The Meteor*), 1966. He adapted SHAKESPEARE's *King John*, 1968, and STRINDBERG's *Dance of Death* as *Play Strindberg*, 1970; and wrote *Porträt eines Planeten* (Portrait of a Planet), 1971; *Der Mitmacher* (*The Collaborator*), 1973. D. is influenced by Greek tragedy, ARISTOPHANES, NESTROY and WEDEKIND. In his pessimistic comedies he uses satire, persiflage, FARCE, grotesque characters and situations. His 'theatre is that of meaningful exaggeration to the point of complete paradox'. Its effect lies not in nuances, but in the strongest possible contrasts. English translation: D., *Four Plays*, London 1964. Bibl: V. Jenny, DÜRRENMATT, A STUDY OF HIS PLAYS, 1971; G. Wellwarth, THE THEATRE OF PROTEST AND PARADOX, 1964; H. Mayer, DÜRRENMATT UND FRISCH, 1963

Duse, Eleonora (1858–1924), Italian actress. One of the great tragediennes of the international theatre. Her parents were strolling players and she was on stage at an early age, but had her first big success in 1878 in AUGIER's *Les Fourchambault*. In 1879 she was engaged as the leading lady in Rossi's company, where her most brilliant performances were in GOLDONI's *Mirandolina* and DUMAS *fils' La Princesse de Bagdad*. In 1881 she went with the Città di Roma company to Russia, where she was greatly admired by CHEKHOV; in 1885 on tour to Latin America; in London she and SARAH BERNHARDT both appeared in 1895 as Magda in *Heimat* by SUDERMANN, and SHAW proclaimed the supremacy of Duse. After her successful appearances in plays by contemporary authors, including Dumas *fils*, SARDOU, GIACOSA, and in the traditional classic parts, she looked out for new dramatists; she became friendly with D' ANNUNZIO, whose poetic drama she championed, and made him famous by playing in his *La Gioconda*, *Francesca da Rimini* and *La Città morta*. She was also outstanding in IBSEN, as Hedda Gabler, Nora in *A Doll's House*, Rebecca West in *Rosmersholm*, and Ellida in *The Lady From the Sea*. She retired from the theatre shortly before 1914, returned in 1923 to play in London and New York, and died in Pittsburgh the following year. She was noted for the beauty and expressiveness of her gestures, her lithe grace and the intensity of her emotional playing.

Dux, Pierre (1908–), French actor and director. Son of the actress Emilienne Dux (1874–1950), who was a member of the COMÉDIE-FRANÇAISE, 1915–32. After training at the CONSERVATOIRE D'ART DRAMATIQUE, he made his début in 1929 as Figaro in *Le Barbier de Séville* by BEAUMARCHAIS at the CF, and very quickly carved a career as an actor (Figaro in *Le Mariage de Figaro*, and Alceste in MOLIÈRE's *Le Misanthrope*) and also as a director; from 1935 he was a SOCIÉTAIRE, and 1944/45 'Administrateur' of the CF (the first actor to hold this post); 1948–52 co-director of the Théâtre de Paris (with K. Karsenty), where he produced Malaparte's *Le Capital*, VITRAC's *Le Sabre de mon père*, Arout's *Guillaume le Confident*, Roussin's *La Main de César*. As a director he has moved to a very cautious modernization of style, as in his productions of *Le Misanthrope* at the Théâtre de l'Œuvre 1962/63, played in modern costumes. Re-appointed Administrateur of the CF 1970.

Dyer, Charles (1928–), English actor and playwright. Started his acting career at the New Theatre, Crewe, in 1947. Wrote a number of plays before achieving his first major success with the two-character *Rattle of a Simple Man*, 1961. *Staircase*, 1965, achieved an equally great success with SCOFIELD and Patrick Magee at the Aldwych Theatre, London, and was subsequently filmed. *Mother Adam*, a third two-character play, 1970, was not quite so successful. He reaches considerable subtlety and psychological depths with techniques which derive from the popular theatre.

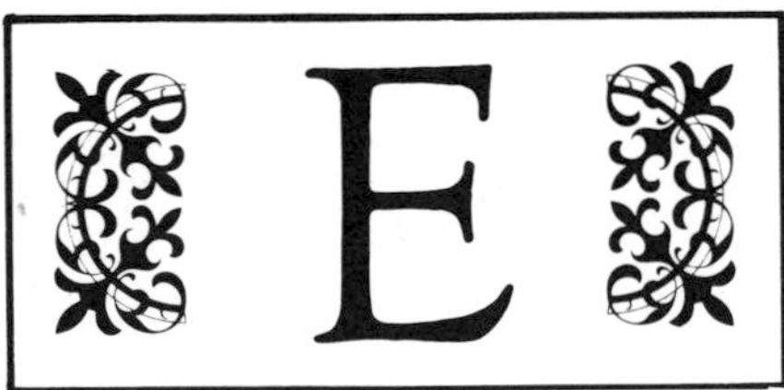

Ebert, Carl (1887–), German actor and director. Began his career acting under REINHARDT (1904–14) and after World War I joined the State Theatre, Berlin, where he appeared in parts including Faust, Petruchio and Karl Moor in SCHILLER's *Die Räuber*. He managed the Darmstadt theatre, 1927–31, and produced, besides classical pieces, plays by contemporary writers, such as BRECHT's *Im Dickicht der Städte*. In 1931 he became director of the State Opera in Berlin but emigrated in 1933; he worked in Buenos Aires, 1933–36; he was one of the founders of the Glyndebourne Festival in 1934; he was at the Turkish State Opera House in Ankara 1938–46; director at Glyndebourne and Edinburgh 1947–53; Professor of Drama at the University of Southern California (Los Angeles) 1948–54; director of the State (later Deutsche) Opera House, West Berlin 1954–62.

Ecclesiastical drama
▷ LITURGICAL DRAMA

Eccyclema (Gk *ekkyklema* = *something rolled out*). Stage cart in the Greek theatre. A low platform on rollers, it was pulled out through the stage door (*porta regia*) in the middle of the *skene* to reveal to the audience the results of events inside the house, e.g. the corpses of Clytemnestra and Aegisthus in AESCHYLUS' *Agamemnon*, 458 BC.

Echegaray, José (1832–1916), Spanish dramatist. Wrote romantic plays in verse, in which he dealt with urgent social questions. The most successful of his works, *El gran Galeoto*, 1881, is known in England as *Calumny*, in the USA as *The World and His Wife*. Other major works include: *O lucura o santidad* (Either Madness or Holiness), 1877; *El loco Dios* (The Mad God), 1900, and *El hijo de Don Juan* (The Son of Don Juan), 1892. Awarded the Nobel Prize for Literature in 1905.

Echeia (Gk, derived from *Echo*). Acoustic vases, used as resonators to improve audibility in the ancient Greek theatre. Referred to by the Roman architect VITRUVIUS (I, 1,9 and V, 5,1). No other documentary evidence extant.

Edinburgh Festival. Edinburgh has a theatre tradition going back to the Middle Ages. Its most famous theatre companies include the Edinburgh Gateway Theatre, and the Edinburgh Theatre Company (▷SCOTLAND). The Edinburgh International Festival of Music and Drama started in 1947. Although this is mainly a music festival the official programme always includes an element of drama from visiting companies, English REPERTORY theatres (e.g. the ENGLISH STAGE COMPANY, ROYAL SHAKESPEARE COMPANY) and first productions of new plays. Performances are mainly given at the Royal Lyceum Theatre and in the Assembly Hall, where GUTHRIE directed the most successful of all productions at the festival, the medieval Scottish play *The Three Estates*, in 1948. Famous visiting companies and artists have included JOUVET's company from the Athénée (MOLIÈRE's *L'Ecole des femmes* and GIRAUDOUX's *Ondine*), BARRAULT and MADELEINE RENAUD, the Düsseldorf company, the Théâtre de l' Atelier, the COMÉDIE-FRANÇAISE, the THÉÂTRE NATIONAL POPULAIRE, the PICCOLO TEATRO DI MILANO, the TEATRO STABILE, Genoa; and the mime MARCEAU. From the beginning the Edinburgh Festival has also attracted 'fringe' companies, numerous student, professional and semi-professional companies from Britain and other countries, who perform in church halls and improvised stages in other places. Many interesting experimental plays and productions have been discovered here. Edinburgh has a permanent EXPERIMENTAL THEATRE, the Traverse Theatre Club, one of the most influential centres of the avant-garde in Britain.

Edwardes, George (1852?–1915), theatre manager known as 'The Guv'nor'. An important figure in London at the turn of the century, he gave MUSICAL COMEDY its final form. Became business manager at the Savoy Theatre, when it was opened by D'Oyly Carte in 1881, then went into partnership with John Hollingshead at the old Gaiety and, after his partner's retirement, ran it on his own. In 1893 E. built Daly's Theatre in co-operation with the American manager DALY, which he managed together with the Gaiety; also controlled the Prince of Wales and the Apollo. He started with BURLESQUE: *Monte-Cristo Junior*, *Esmeralda* (for a tour to Australia in

1888), *Cinder Ellen* (first use of the Can-Can in England); he then supplanted burlesque with musical comedy which he made popular with *The Shop Girl*, 1893; *An Artist's Model*, 1895; *The Merry Widow*, 1907, and *The Quaker Girl*, 1910. He had enormous flair for giving the public what they wanted; the well-trained troupes known as 'Gaiety Girls' combined with splendid décor and costumes, guaranteed him lasting success and a great reputation in the world of entertainment.
Bibl: A. E. Wilson, EDWARDIAN THEATRE, 1951

Edwin, John (the elder; 1749–90), English actor. After a number of successful years in Bath, he made his London début at the Haymarket Theatre. A brilliant comedian with a fine voice, he was accounted the best BURLETTA singer of his time. His acting was praised for its subtlety and taste; at his best in SHAKESPEARE's comedies, he also excelled in 22 plays by John O'Keefe (1741–1833).
His son, (2) **John E.** (the younger; 1768–1803) had already made his reputation in his early youth, and, as a protégé of Richard Barry, Earl of Barrymore, appeared mainly in private performances for the aristocracy. He married (3) **Elizabeth Rebecca Richards** (*c.* 1771–1854), a graceful actress of great vivacity, who gave notable performances in COMEDY and FARCE.

Egypt. Records of dramatic scenes and productions at religious festivals exist dating from the Old Kingdom. Papyri have been discovered which prove the existence of classical MIME; there is also graphic evidence of jugglers (or CLOWNS). Following the conquest by Alexander the Great, 331 BC, Greek theatre became popular all over Egypt, especially in Alexandria, but with the Arab invasion of the early 7th century theatrical performances were stopped, apart from primitive FARCES. In the 18th century in Cairo there were theatrical companies consisting of Moslems, Christians and Jews. Modern Egyptian theatre started with European-influenced Syrian companies. Mahmud Taimur founded the NATIONAL THEATRE *c.* 1920; Taimur is also one of the most important dramatists in the Arab world.
Bibl: Jacob M. Landau, STUDIES IN THE ARAB THEATRE AND CINEMA, 1958

Eichendorff, Josef Freiherr von (1788–1857), writer of the German Romantic movement. A poet, who dealt with theatre in his essay *Zur Geschichte des Dramas*, 1854, he also wrote several dramatic works, e.g. *Ezzelin von Romano*, 1828, and *Der letzte Held von Marienburg* (The Last Hero of Marienburg), 1830; translated the AUTOS SACRAMENTALES by CALDERÓN into German (*Geistliche Schauspiele*, 1846–54), also ENTREMESES by CERVANTES, and wrote a parody on GRILLPARZER's *König Ottokars Glück und Ende* (King Ottokar's Luck and End), called *Meierbeths Glück und Ende*, 1828; his only successful work still performed on the stage is the romantic COMEDY *Die Freier* (The Suitors), 1883.

Eleonora Duse as Magda in SUDERMANN's *Heimat*, 1895

Edinburgh Festival, GUTHRIE's production (1948) of *The Three Estates* by D. LINDSAY

George Edwardes, a poster illustrating one of his 'Gaiety Girl' shows, 1895

Eisenstein, Sergei Mihailovich (1898–1948), Russian film director. Began his career in the theatre as a stage designer and director: *The Mexican* (a dramatization based on the novel by Jack London; 1921). He was a 'student director' under MEYERHOLD 1920–21; his productions included OSTROVSKY's *Even a Wise Man Stumbles*. He won international acclaim as the director of the film *Battleship Potemkin* and for many years was accepted as the cinema's leading theorist. His sense of design produced superb images which he juxtaposed by montage with immense dramatic effect.

Eisler, Hanns (1898–1962), German composer. Studied in Vienna under Schönberg. He wrote songs and choruses for Socialist groups in BERLIN 1924–33, and from 1930 composed music for films. He left Germany in 1933 and travelled all over Europe, meeting BRECHT in Denmark and subsequently collaborating with him on *Die Rundköpfe und die Spitzköpfe*, Copenhagen, 1936. He came to England in 1935 and while there wrote the music for TOLLER's play *No More Peace!* with lyrics adapted by AUDEN. In 1938 he went to the USA where he wrote theatre and film music and was awarded two Oscars. He returned to Europe after the war and became professor at the Academy of Music in East Berlin in 1950. He won a prize for composing the official East German national anthem (words by BECHER). His theoretical works include *Komposition für den Film*, 1948. E. also wrote music for other Brecht plays, including *Furcht und Elend des Drittes Reiches*, *Leben des Galilei*, and *Schweyk im zweiten Weltkrieg*, as well as for other productions by the BERLINER ENSEMBLE such as STRITTMATTER's *Katzgraben*; BECHER's *Winterschlacht*, and SYNGE's *The Playboy of the Western World*.

Ekhof, Konrad (1720–78), German ACTOR-MANAGER. A follower of CAROLINE NEUBER, he helped to raise the status of the professional theatre in Germany and laid the foundations of its acting tradition; he joined SCHÖNEMANN's company in 1740 for a small part in *Mithridate* and went on to become its leading actor, perfecting his art in the 17 years he was with them. Though short and not good-looking, he gained his power as an actor by the authority of his movements and his melodious voice. He was also the first German actor to attempt to pass on his experience to young actors; in 1753 he founded the first, short-lived Academy of Acting. After Schönemann's company was disbanded in 1757, he played for some time under KOCH and, at the height of his powers, joined the ACKERMANN company in 1764 appearing with them at the newly founded National Theatre in Hamburg, 1767–69. He acted in SCHLEGEL's *Canut*, played the uncle in LILLO's *The London Merchant*, gave an outstanding performance as Tellheim in LESSING's *Minna von Barnhelm* and – his finest role – portrayed Odoardo in the latter's *Emilia Galotti*. In 1771 he joined the company of SEYLER, who later founded the COURT THEATRE in Weimar; in 1775 he became director and chief actor of the first German Court Theatre in Gotha; in 1778 he made a guest appearance as the father in an amateur production of CUMBERLAND's *The West-Indian* with GOETHE as Belcour; his last appearance on stage in Gotha was as the Ghost in *Hamlet* in an adaptation by F. L. SCHRÖDER. Lessing, Goethe, IFFLAND and other contemporaries considered E. to be one of the greatest performers in the German language. He received much praise for the richness of his gestures, his subdued comic style and his discerning tragic manner; he prepared the way for the reforms and triumphs of Schröder, who in his youth severely attacked E.'s acting (they were for some time together in Ackermann's company), but later recognized him as his teacher. E. also translated plays and wrote several himself.

Ekman, Gösta (1890–1938), Swedish director. At the Svenska Teater in Stockholm, 1912–25, under the management of Albert Ranft. He excelled in classical parts (Lionel in SCHILLER's *The Maid of Orleans*, 1914; Romeo in 1919) and also in lighter roles (Karl Heinrich in Meyer-Förster's *Alt Heidelberg*). He worked with John and Pauline Brunius, 1926–30, at the Oscar Teater where he appeared several times as Petruchio in *The Taming of the Shrew*, Marchbanks in SHAW's *Candida*, and in MOLIÈRE's *Tartuffe*. He managed the Våsa Teater in Stockholm, 1931–35, playing Peer Gynt, and Fedya in TOLSTOY's *The Living Corpse*, subsequently touring with these productions. E. was an eccentric actor, his interpretations always individualistic, and he was often heavily attacked by the critics. He also became well known as a film actor.

Electra. A Greek mythological character. Daughter of Agamemnon and Clytemnestra, sister of Orestes, Iphigenia and Chrysothemis; her story was treated by the three great tragic writers: AESCHYLUS in the *Choephori* (second part of the ORESTEIA, 458 BC), EURIPIDES in *Electra*, 413 BC, and SOPHOCLES in *Electra*, *c.* 415 BC. Also appears in Euripides' *Orestes*. Adaptations and authors whose works were influenced by Elektra's story; VONDEL, *Elektra*, 1639; CRÉBILLON, *Electre*, 1709; VOLTAIRE, *Oreste*, 1750; ALFIERI, *Oreste*, 1786; HOFMANNSTHAL, *Elektra*, 1904, LIBRETTO for opera by Richard Strauss, 1909; O'NEILL, *Mourning Becomes Electra*, 1931; GIRAUDOUX, *Electre*, 1937; SARTRE, *Les Mouches*, 1943; G. HAUPTMANN, *Elektra*, 1947.

Eliot, Thomas Stearns (1888–1965), US-born English critic, poet and dramatist. Naturalized British in 1927; became an Anglo-Catholic. He initiated an important revival of VERSE DRAMA in order to create an appropriate form of expression and communication for the Christian 'order', which is central to his work. His early dramatic attempts were based on his critical essays on the ELIZABETHAN THEATRE and other subjects and resulted in a dramatic 'fragment', *Sweeney Agonistes: Fragments of an Aristophanic Melodrama*, followed by the didactic play *The Rock*, 1934. In 1935, having been commissioned by the Church, he wrote the religious drama *Murder in the Cathedral* which deals with the martyrdom of Thomas à Becket in 1170, fp Canterbury Festival, 1935. *The Family Reunion*, a VERSE DRAMA in a contemporary setting, is based on the ORESTEIA by AESCHYLUS. In his later plays E. moves closer to NATURALISM; on the surface they follow the conventional commercial DRAWING-ROOM COMEDY, with verse that is barely distinguishable from prose, except at moments of emotional climax. But they are full of SYMBOLISM and literary allusions and are all based on classical models: *The Cocktail Party* on EURIPIDES' *Alcestis*, fp EDINBURGH FESTIVAL 1949, and in New York and London, 1950; *The Confidential Clerk*, 1953, on Euripides' *Ion*; *The Elder Statesman*, 1958, on SOPHOCLES' *Oedipus at Colonus*. E. wrote many essays and critical studies, among them *Poetry and Drama*, 1951, in which he examined his own problems as a dramatist. He was also a director of the publishing house of Faber and Faber, London. In 1948 he was awarded the Nobel Prize for Literature.
Bibl: H. Smith, T. S. ELIOT'S DRAMATIC THEORY AND PRACTICE, 1963; D. E. Jones, THE PLAYS OF T. S. ELIOT, 1960

Elizabethan Stage Society ▷POEL.

Elizabethan theatre. English drama and theatre during the reign of Elizabeth I (1558–1603), though the theatrical conditions and creative impetus in question continued during the reign of James I (1603–25) and, with declining vigour, until just before the outbreak of the Civil War in 1642. A popular folk theatre in a time of economic prosperity and political power: flourishing trade and crafts, historiography (*Holinshed's Chronicle* served as collection of themes for the Elizabethan drama), knowledge of foreign languages and literature (Plutarch, SENECA, Italian and French Renaissance literature), the need and love of the English people of all classes for exciting entertainment, variety, information about the world, sensations and social life. A regular play-going audience was already in being and steadily increasing in number. The first regular London playhouse, THE THEATRE, had been built by the actor and carpenter J. BURBAGE in 1576 outside the City of London chiefly to escape the Puritan civic authorities. Up to this time players had been forced to perform mostly in inn yards, but the new building reproduced the main features of the inn yard with its platform stage, and seating arrangements in the yard and gallery. Features of the typical Elizabethan playhouse were: a ground plan, roughly round or octagonal in shape, in the middle an open space, or unroofed yard surrounded by galleries (one or two); the stage, an open platform, jutted out into the centre of the yard. Under the stage, hidden by drapery, was a cellar with machinery for projecting ghosts and devils through trapdoors. At the back of the stage was a tiring house, a permanent architectural feature with inset doors. Above this the first gallery provided an open balcony which could be used for appearances of actors (on city walls, etc.). Above the balcony was a hut to house machinery to raise or lower actors or property on to the stage. The audience could stand around the stage, on three sides, for the payment of a penny; in the galleries the best places cost as much as sixpence (according to the theatre, there were places for 2,000–3,000 spectators). The stage had no décor. There is little direct evidence but much has been deduced from various sources. It seems possible that the interior was brightly painted and that there were splendidly worked curtains. But the Restoration playhouses developed more from the private theatre (▷BLACKFRIARS) after the Puritan interregnum. Performances during the afternoon, beginning at 2 p.m. The Court and aristocracy supported the companies, ADMIRAL'S MEN, CHAMBERLAIN'S MEN, by patronage; the MASTER OF THE REVELS was in charge of the theatres and also responsible for CENSORSHIP. The companies, who engaged dramatists as resident playwrights formed the basis of this flourishing drama; a 'share' in a company could bring an actor or playwright great wealth. Among the most prominent dramatists were LYLY, KYD, PEELE, GREENE, MARLOWE, SHAKESPEARE, JONSON, BEAUMONT and FLETCHER, WEBSTER, TOURNEUR, MIDDLETON, FORD, MASSINGER, SHIRLEY.

Bibl: C. W. Hodges, SHAKESPEARE'S THEATRE, 1964; A. Nicoll, STUART MASQUES AND THE RENAISSANCE STAGECRAFT, 1937; E. K. Chambers, THE ELIZABETHAN STAGE, 1923, 4 vols

Elliott (US actresses). (1) **Maxine E.** (Jessie Dermot; 1868–1940) made her début with E. S. Willard's company in *The Middleman* and became a member of DALY's company in 1895, appearing in London and New York, mainly in Shakespearean roles. With her husband Nat Goodwin she toured Australia, and in 1908 founded the Maxine Elliott Theatre in New York. Shortly before World War I she retired to London where she was very popular, including Edward VII among her personal friends. In 1920 she returned to the USA and once again became a much admired actress. Her sister (2) **May Gertrude E.** (1874–1950) made her début in WILDE's *A Woman of No Importance*, 1894, with Rose Coghlan's company at Saratoga; she appeared in New York at the Star Theatre, and in 1899 gave her first performance in London at the Duke of York's Theatre; in 1900 she was engaged by FORBES-ROBERTSON (later her husband) with whom she toured the English provinces, Canada and the USA. After his retirement in 1913 she appeared under her own management and toured widely in South Africa and Australia. She returned to New York in 1936 when she played the Queen in L. HOWARD's production of *Hamlet* at the Imperial Theatre.

Elliston, Robert William (1774–1831), English ACTOR-MANAGER. A tall, good-looking man of great wit and taste, he led an eccentric and extravagant life. One of the most popular actors of his time, his

T. S. Eliot's *Murder in the Cathedral*, with Robert Speaight as Becket, prod E. MARTIN BROWNE, 1935

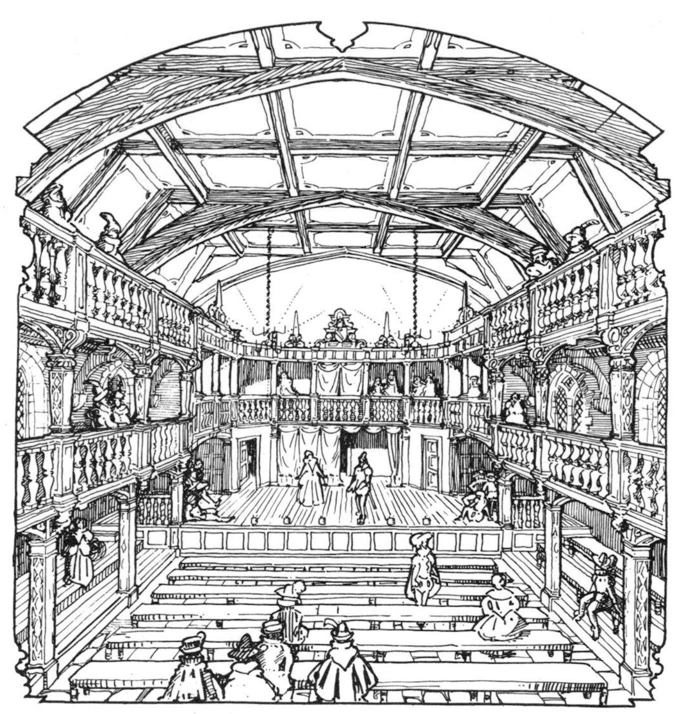

Elizabethan theatre, a reconstruction of the BLACKFRIARS THEATRE, 1597; and below, the GLOBE THEATRE, from Visscher's *View of London*, Amsterdam 1616

contemporaries placed him second only to GARRICK. He was noted for his Hamlet (1812), Richard III, Charles Surface, Romeo, Hotspur and in his later years Falstaff (1826). He was a fascinating personality of whom Lamb said: 'Wherever Elliston walked, sat or stood still, there was the theatre.' As a manager 1819–26 at DRURY LANE, where he had made his stage début in 1804, he surrounded himself with the best actors of his time: KEAN, MACREADY, C. M. Young. His expensive style of living and his drunkenness led him to bankruptcy in 1826. Shortly afterwards, however, he was able to reinstate himself with a production of Jerrold's *Black-Eyed Susan*, starring T. P. Cooke, at the Surrey Theatre.

Emery. English family of actors. (1) **John E.** (1777–1822) appeared mainly at the Haymarket Theatre and COVENT GARDEN, excelling in parts where he could use his Yorkshire dialect. Much praised were his appearances as Caliban and the First Gravedigger. His son (2) **Samuel Anderson E.** (1817–81) specialized in contemporary plays and was most successful as Anthony Latour in S. Brooks' *The Creole* and in dramatized versions of novels by Dickens (e.g. Jonas in *Martin Chuzzlewit*; Will Fern in *The Chimes*). Samuel's daughter (3) **Isabel Winifred E.** (1862–1924), a beautiful woman of great charm, appeared at the Vaudeville Theatre and later became the leading lady at the Haymarket Theatre under the management of her husband Cyril Maude; one of her best parts was as Lady Windermere in WILDE'S COMEDY. Her brother (4) **Edward E.** (?–1938) was not an outstanding actor and was outshone by his son (5) **John E.** (*c.* 1905–), who appeared first on stage as Edward Emery Jr. He was brilliant at playing young lovers and partnered many of the leading actresses of his time. In 1925 he joined the company of EVA LE GALLIENNE, appeared in 1932 opposite KATHARINE CORNELL in *The Barretts of Wimpole Street*, and in 1937 as Octavius in *Antony and Cleopatra* with TALLULAH BANKHEAD, whom he married. Other major performances include Laertes in GIELGUD'S *Hamlet* in 1936 and the title role in *King John* at Stratford, Conn., in 1956.

Encina, Juan del (*c.* 1469–1529?), Spanish dramatist. He was one of the originators of the secular Spanish drama. His *églogas*, dialogues between shepherds and shepherdesses, dealt with biblical subjects but also contained scenes from daily life, set in a rural environment, although written for performances at Court and private houses. Later adapted by travelling companies, his works were among the first plays performed by professional actors. His masterpiece was the *Egloga de Placida y Victoriano*, *c.* 1490.
Bibl: E. B. Rasmussen, 1937

Engagement. An actor's limited period of employment; for a single part in one show as in the US theatre, or in a company – sometimes for several months or even years – as in the German system. The COMÉDIE-FRANÇAISE offers contracts with shares (partnerships); the BURGTHEATER in Vienna has contracts with pension rights; a few European State Theatres offer one or other of these contracts instead of engagements limited to a specific number of performances. Also, an arrangement for a company to play in a theatre for a stipulated period of time.

Engel, Erich (1891–1966), German director. Trained as an actor at the drama school of JESSNER in Hamburg; director at the Hamburg Kammerspiele, 1918–21, at the State Theatre, Munich, 1922–24. Of great significance was his meeting with BRECHT, with whom he collaborated (with NEHER as designer) on the first production of *Im Dickicht der Städte*, 1923; revived Berlin 1924, Deutsches-Theater. This was followed in 1925 by the production of SHAKESPEARE'S *Coriolanus*, at the Lessingtheater, Berlin. To the theatre of Brecht he contributed an assured elegance and sober clarity: *Mann ist Mann*, Berlin 1928, Volksbühne; *Die Dreigroschenoper*, 1928; *Happy End*, 1929, a musical play by Brecht and Elisabeth Hauptmann, music WEILL; both at the Schiffbauerdamm Theater, BERLIN. E. reached the height of his career when directing Shakespeare's plays at the Deutsches-Theater, Berlin: *Measure for Measure*, 1935; *Coriolanus*, 1936; *Othello*, 1939. He was director of the Munich Kammerspiele, 1945–47; in 1949 he renewed his collaboration with Brecht with *Mutter Courage* and *Puntila* at the Deutsches-Theater, Berlin. In 1957, having finished the production of Brecht's *Leben des Galilei*, he joined the BERLINER ENSEMBLE, producing *Die Dreigroschenoper*, 1960, and *Schweyk im zweiten Weltkrieg*, 1963.
Bibl: K. H. Ruppel, GROSSES BERLINER THEATER 1935–43, 1962

Enghaus, Christine (1817–1910), German actress. In 1840 she joined the ensemble of the BURGTHEATER in Vienna where she married the dramatist HEBBEL in 1846; she gave her best performance in his plays, notably *Judith*.

England. From the 13th century there were performances of MYSTERY PLAYS (▷ LITURGICAL DRAMA), at intervals of several years because of the complexity of the productions. Actors were amateurs. Women took part only occasionally for specific parts. With the rise of vernacular theatre, professional actors emerged, in England under R. BURBAGE. In the second half of the 16th century and in the first half of the 17th century there was a flowering of popular theatre (▷ ELIZABETHAN THEATRE). The closure of the theatres by the Puritans in 1642 interrupted this, but with the Restoration and the return of Charles II to the throne in 1660 there was a great revival of drama, and many new playwrights came on to the scene. Women's parts could now be taken by actresses (▷ GWYNN, RESTORATION DRAMA). During the 16th and 17th centuries English actors (ENGLISH COMEDIANS) toured the Continent, particularly in Germany, giving impetus to the rise of professional theatre there.
The 18th century was a time of richness in the theatre, with great actors and ACTOR-MANAGERS (GARRICK, KEMBLE) and a SHAKESPEARE revival. At the beginning of the 19th century the dramatic star was KEAN. The second half of this century saw the dominance of the non-literary forms of drama, PANTOMIME, MELODRAMA, and MUSIC HALL but from 1891 there were attempts to revive drama as a serious art form. The Independent Theatre Club under GREIN, produced plays by SHAW and IBSEN. From 1904–07, during the VEDRENNE-BARKER seasons at the Royal Court, plays were produced with a repertory ranging from EURIPIDES to HAUPTMANN, MAETERLINCK and Shaw, and Barker himself. The repertory movement, begun by Grein, continued under ANNIE HORNIMAN (theatres refurbished in Manchester 1907, Liverpool 1911). LILIAN BAYLIS'S work at the OLD VIC started a tradition in 1912 culminating 74 years later with the opening of the new NATIONAL THEATRE on the South Bank in 1976 (first created in 1963 at the Old Vic under OLIVIER).
Following World War II there were subsidies to theatres from the ARTS COUNCIL. The Shakespeare Memorial Theatre at STRATFORD-UPON-AVON began to hold London seasons at the Aldwych Theatre from 1960, and DAUBENY organized World Theatre seasons there 1964–74. Theatre in the East End of London, experimental theatre, and drama festivals became part of the national scene (▷ DEVINE, JOAN LITTLEWOOD, CHICHESTER).
Bibl: A. Harbage, rev. S. Schoenbaum, ANNALS OF ENGLISH DRAMA, 975–1700, 1964; A. Nicoll, A HISTORY OF ENGLISH DRAMA, 1660–1900, 1952–59, 6 vols; E. K. Chambers, THE MEDIEVAL STAGE, 1903, 2 vols; E. K. Chambers, THE ELIZABETHAN STAGE, 1923, 4 vols; G. E. Bentley, THE JACOBEAN AND CAROLINE STAGE, 1641–66, 7 vols; B. Dobree, RESTORATION COMEDY, 1660–1720, 1924, and RESTORATION TRAGEDY, 1929; R. Genest, SOME ACCOUNT OF THE ENGLISH STAGE, 1660–1830, 2/1965.

England, Barry (1935–), English dramatist. Author of several TV dramas and the stage plays *End of a Conflict*, 1961, and *The Big Contract*, 1961, both performed at Coventry. *Conduct Unbecoming*, 1969, was a success in London and was also filmed.

English Comedians. Companies of English actors who went to Germany and Eastern Europe from *c.* 1585 and made their name especially in Germany as *Englische Komödianten* (▷ HEINRICH). They travelled with about 20 actors and a group of instrumentalists, led by the first comedian, the CLOWN, and played in English. The English Comedians initiated the development of the professional theatre in Germany; gradually they began to use the German vernacular, German actors were engaged, rival German companies formed, and after the 17th century only German travelling companies remained (the last authenticated record of an English company dates from 1659). The REPERTOIRE of the English

Comedians included plays by MARLOWE, SHAKESPEARE and their contemporaries; the Clown (from which originated the German PICKELHERRING, HANSWURST, Stockfisch, etc.) usually played an important role and also appeared in comic interludes during serious plays.

English Stage Company. An organization dedicated to the production of plays by living authors, set up in 1956, on the initiative of DUNCAN, DEVINE, Oscar Lewenstein and others. At the ROYAL COURT THEATRE, Sloane Square, London, under the artistic direction of Devine (until 1965) and, after his retirement, of a triumvirate of GASKILL, L. ANDERSON and Anthony Page until 1972, the company produced the work of some of the most important English playwrights, notably OSBORNE, whose play *Look Back in Anger* is generally considered to have inaugurated a new era in English drama (non-middle-class characters, etc.) at its first performance at the Royal Court on 8 May 1956. This was followed by works of WESKER, PINTER, ARDEN, SIMPSON, BOND as well as BECKETT, SARTRE, IONESCO, GENET and FRISCH from abroad. The Royal Court gave one-night Sunday performances of works by unknown writers. It also has the experimental Theatre Upstairs. Oscar Lewenstein was artistic director of the English Stage Company 1972–74.

Ensemble. A group of actors working together as a company, not by arbitrary association, but with emphasis on systematic development of their ability to harmonize their personalities by pursuing an agreed, common artistic objective, creating their own collective style. Most important examples in theatre history: the ensemble of the MOSCOW ART THEATRE under STANISLAVSKY and NEMIROVICH-DANCHENKO, and the BERLINER ENSEMBLE under BRECHT.

Entr'acte. An intermission or a brief entertainment provided during an intermission. Hence entr'acte music etc.

Entremes (pl. **entremeses**; Sp = insertion). In England INTERLUDE. Spanish term applied to brief dramatic or non-dramatic diversion, originally short comic pieces played in Corpus Christi processions, and at festivities, often ending in music or dance. Later in the 17th century played between acts of main drama but having no connection with it. Developed into the one-act play, epitomized by CERVANTES.

Epic theatre. A term which BRECHT made widely known; originally used by German Expressionists (Paquet, PISCATOR, FEUCHTWANGER), who wanted the theatre to contain a stronger 'narrative' element: e.g. in Feuchtwanger's 'dramatic novel' *Thomas Wendt*, 1919. Brecht used the term 'epic theatre' to contrast his conception of drama with the conventional 'Aristotelian' view of theatre, which demands that the audience should experience the play as something happening *here and now*, with which every member of the public can

England, a view of the OLD VIC showing the pit and galleries

England, the NATIONAL THEATRE, main foyer of the Lyttelton Theatre, opened 1976

instantly identify. As this, in Brecht's view, was achieved by the relentless progress of a unified action and the intense identification between the actors and the characters they portray, Brecht demanded that it should be made clear that the action lay in the past, *there and then*, a detached, 'cool' attitude on the part of the actors and a structure which interrupts the progress of the action towards an intense climax. Hence 'epic theatre' is not divided into long acts, but many short scenes, each of which is of roughly equivalent weight and can stand on its own; such an episodic structure is one of the elements of the technique aimed at producing the *Verfremdungseffekte* (abbreviated to V-Effekte) the *distancing* or ALIENATION EFFECTS which have been widely discussed since Brecht coined the term. All these are designed to inhibit emotional identification and to make the spectator think for himself, and think critically. They include: narrative elements in form of posters, placards, projected titles (as in the silent film); characters leaving their parts to comment on the action; filmed inserts; the use of songs to destroy the realism of the action; non-concealment of STAGE MACHINERY; unrealistic STAGE LIGHTING and an acting style which shows that the actor is not identifying himself with the character, but has his own critical attitude towards him.

Epidauros. City in Argolis on the southern coast of the Saronic Gulf in Greece. Epidauros was a centre for the cult of Asclepios. Its ancient theatre is one of the best preserved in Greece: a semi-AMPHITHEATRE built by the architect Polycleitus *c.* 340 BC, it has seats for 12,000 spectators. One of the most beautiful and harmonious theatres of antiquity, it still shows the full ring of the ORCHESTRA, and continues to be used for performances of Greek TRAGEDIES.

Epilogue (Gk *epilogos*). A scene or speech at the end of a dramatic performance. Introduced by PLAUTUS in Roman comedy. In the LITURGICAL DRAMA of the Middle Ages it consisted of a religious admonition, in the MORALITY PLAYS an instructive line of reasoning. In the latter, it was also used to name the author. Extensively used during the Restoration period, it survived well into the 18th century. Often witty, sometimes scurrilous comments on politics and social conditions, they were written by men like GARRICK and DRYDEN, and spoken by the leading characters. The form disappeared during the 19th century with the ever-increasingly crowded playbill but is found again in the 20th in the works of, among others, BRECHT, ELIOT, CLAUDEL.

Episode (Gk *epeisodion* = interspersion). Scene comprising action and dialogue between two choric odes in the Greek drama, especially in TRAGEDY. Today the episode is a side-action, interlinked with the main action. An episodic play is one which consists of linked incidents, rather than of fully integrated scenes and acts.

Equestrian drama, also known as **equestrian spectacle**. A spectacular type of entertainment in which horses (or, by extension, other animals) were used in the 19th century, which made popular the featuring of horses in plays; notable example *Mazeppa*, by the Polish dramatist SLOWACKI, 1847, one of the most successful MELODRAMAS of all time. Also known as hippodrama.

Equity. Actors' Equity Association, the professional guild for actors in the USA (est. 1913). The British equivalent is the British Actors' Equity Association (est. 1930).

Ernst, Paul (1866–1933), German novelist and dramatist. He wrote most of his plays for the Düsseldorf Schauspielhaus, where he worked as DRAMATURG, 1904–15. At first under the influence of NATURALISM, he wrote: *Lumpenbagasch* (Riffraff), *Im chambre séparé*, 1898–99; later tending to neo-classicism, in *Eine Nacht in Florenz* (A Night in Florence), 1906; *Paolo und Francesca*, 1907; *Canossa*, 1908; *Demetrius*, 1910; *Brunhild*, fp Munich 1911, Court Theatre; *Ninon de Lenclos*, Dresden 1911, Royal Theatre; *Ariadne auf Naxos*, Weimar 1914, Court Theatre; *Preussengeist* (Prussian Spirit), 1915; *Kassandra*, 1915; *Yorck*, 1917; *Chriemhild*, 1922.

Ervine, John St John Greer (1883–1971), Irish dramatist and critic. His early plays were performed at the ABBEY THEATRE, Dublin, of which he was manager for a while. They deal with the conflicts between Irish nationalists and the English, between Protestants and Catholics: *Mixed Marriage*, 1911; *John Ferguson*, 1915. His later plays concentrate on middle-class society: *Jane Clegg*, 1913; *The First Mrs Fraser*, 1929; *Robert's Wife*, 1937; *Friends and Relations*, 1941. He moved to England, where he became drama critic (*Observer*; *Morning Post*) and wrote essays on the theatre and dramatists: 'The Organized Theatre', 1924, 'Shaw', 1956. In 1937 he became president of the League of British Dramatists.
Bibl: L. Robinson, IRELAND'S ABBEY THEATRE, A HISTORY, 1899–1951, 1951

Espy, L'. ▷JODELET.

Etherege, Sir George (1634–*c.* 1691), English playwright. Early exponent of RESTORATION DRAMA who excelled in COMEDY. His first play *The Comical Revenge: or, Love in a Tub*, 1664, combines heroic action, written in verse, with comic and witty prose scenes. *She Would If She Could*, 1668, and *The Man of Mode: or, Sir Fopling Flutter*, 1676, his masterpiece and one of the finest plays of the Restoration School, are witty comedies dealing with love affairs in a light and cynical manner, with splendid character-drawing.

Euripides (*c.* 484–*c.* 406 BC), Greek tragic dramatist. Unlike the two other great Greek tragedians (AESCHYLUS and SOPHOCLES), he played little part in Athenian political life, which is probably why not much is known of his personal life. He is said to have written 92 plays of which 17 tragedies (16 authenticated) and one SATYR PLAY have been preserved; he was crowned victor at the DIONYSIA five times. When he started as a playwright he found a fixed form of TRAGEDY, which was predetermined in all details by the techniques of production and theatre building; he used this traditional form to express his views about the city state (*polis*), society and humanity, views which became increasingly sceptical as he grew older. In the DIALOGUE, he heightened the dialectical elements and hence was (wrongly) regarded as a sophist; he allowed the choric element to diminish in importance, frequently compensating for this by writing more lyrical dialogue, in which human beings are shown as autonomous personalities. He gives little importance to the exposition of what has occurred before the opening of the play; he invented the PROLOGUE, which briefly summarizes the previous events and so allowed him to throw all the interest into the inner life of his characters, especially the women. In order to satisfy the convention which demanded the correct moral solutions to the action, he often achieves these abruptly at the end through divine intervention (DEUS EX MACHINA). But as the solutions are more apparent than real, ARISTOTLE regarded him as the most 'tragic' of the antique dramatists.
Extant works: *Medea*, 431 BC; *The Heraclidae*, 430; *Andromache*, 429; *Hippolytus*, 428; *Hecuba*, 425; *The Suppliants*, 421; *Heracles*, 421; *The Trojan Women*, 415; *Iphigenia in Tauris*, 414; *Electra*, 413; *Ion*, 413; *Helena*, 412; *The Phoenician Women*, 410; *Orestes*, 408; *The Bacchae* and *Iphigenia in Aulis*, posthumously, 405; *Rhesus* (long considered spurious); one satyr play *The Cyclops*, and *Alcestis*, 438, which took the place of a satyr play in a TETRALOGY.
Bibl: D. J. Conacher, EURIPIDEAN DRAMA, 1967; H. D. F. Kitto, GREEK TRAGEDY, 4/1966

Evans, Dame Edith (1888–1976), English actress. Appointed DBE in 1946. First appearance in Cambridge under the direction of POEL in 1912 in *Śakuntalā* by KĀLIDĀSA, the Indian writer. First London appearance as Cressida, 1912. Joined the OLD VIC company in 1925 and appeared in the 1925/26 season as Portia, Queen Margaret in *Richard III*, Katharina in *The Taming of the Shrew*, Mariana in *Measure for Measure*, Cleopatra, Mistress Page in *The Merry Wives of Windsor*, Beatrice in *Much Ado about Nothing*, Rosalind in *As You Like It*, and the Nurse in *Romeo and Juliet*. Among her best parts were Millamant in CONGREVE's *The Way of the World* (1924, 1927); Lady Bracknell in WILDE's *The Importance of Being Earnest*, 1939, which she also played in a film. In 1954 she appeared in FRY's *The Dark is Light Enough*; in 1956 in ENID BAGNOLD's *The Chalk Garden*, and in 1958 as Queen Katharine in *Henry VIII* at the Old Vic. One of the finest actresses of her time, she was brilliant in COMEDY in which she excelled with her sense of style and timing.
Bibl: J. C. Trewin, 1954

Evans, Maurice (1901–), US actor of British origin. Joined the OLD VIC company in 1934, playing leading Shakespearean roles, and first went to the USA in 1935, when he had a great success as Romeo, playing opposite KATHARINE CORNELL in New York. Subsequently he appeared as Richard II, Hamlet, Malvolio and Macbeth. During World War II he entertained troops with a so-called 'G.I.' version of *Hamlet*. He has also appeared in some of SHAW's plays, in BROADWAY shows like *Dial 'M' for Murder* by Frederick Knott, and occasionally directed films and produced TV shows. He is a straight romantic actor, with some tendency towards mannerism.

Eveling, Stanley (1925–), English playwright, senior lecturer in philosophy at Edinburgh University. Writes plays in a style between absurdist farce and philosophical parable: *The Balchites*, 1963; *The Strange Case of the Lunatic, the Secret Sportsman and the Woman Next Door*, 1968; *Dear Janet Rosenberg, Dear Mr Kooning*, 1969; *Mister*, 1970.

Everding, August (1929–), German theatre manager and director. Beginning as an assistant artistic director at the Munich Kammerspiele, he became artistic director in 1959 and INTENDANT in 1963. His major productions include SHAW's *The Apple Cart*, 1957; SARTRE's *Huis Clos*, 1960; Reinhard Raffalt's *Der Nachfolger*, 1962; ALBEE's *A Delicate Balance*, 1966; SPERR's *Landshuter Erzählungen*, fp 1967. He also directed operas such as Wagner's *Tristan and Isolde*, Vienna 1967, State Opera.

Everyman. A medieval MORALITY PLAY, developed *c.* 1495; the earliest text was probably Dutch (translated from *Elckerlijc* by Petrus van Dienst). An allegorical play, *Everyman* is a warning that in the moment of death man must lose friends, family and worldly goods and that his worldly qualities – beauty, intelligence and strength – are also of no avail. Only Good Deeds can speak for his salvation. The characters are personifications of concepts such as Fellowship, Worldly Goods, etc. The action revolves around Death's summoning of Everyman to a general reckoning before God. Everyman asks in turn Fellowship, Kindred, Cousin, etc. to accompany him, but they all desert him except his Good Deeds. The famous German version, *Jedermann*, a free adaptation by HOFMANNSTHAL, is shown annually in front of the cathedral at the SALZBURG FESTIVAL.

Examiner of Plays. In British terminology, an official serving under the LORD CHAMBERLAIN, charged with the licensing (until 1968) of stage productions within the London area.

Existentialism. The philosophy known as Existentialism is concerned with existence (specifically human) in an active sense rather than with the abstract nature of existence or of the universe. It derives ultimately from concepts expressed by the Danish writer Sören Kierkegaard, which

Edith Evans in *The Dark is Light Enough* by FRY, 1954

Equestrian drama, cartoon illustrating *Timour the Tartar*

Everyman, title page, woodcut dated 1530

was elaborated by two German philosophers, Martin Heidegger and Karl Jaspers. The Existentialism of the contemporary French writer, philosopher and playwright, SARTRE, is the pessimistic form in which, since about 1945, Existentialist doctrines have penetrated far beyond the philosophic world to a wide public of novel-readers and play-goers. The postulate common to the various forms of Existentialism is that existence precedes essence, for man exists only in so far as he shapes his own existence and thus confers an essence upon it by his own conscious choice. In 1946 Sartre published his essay *L'Existentialisme est un humanisme*, according to which it seems that man can succeed in escaping from a miserable state of indetermination by a supreme act of will in committing himself to a positive part in social and political affairs, achieving an awareness of others as well as himself. Sartre's formal Existentialism was a powerful influence on thought, literature and dramatic writing in the post-war years, not only in France. The term itself is said to have been given currency by MARCEL.

Exodus (Gk *exodos*=the way out, exit). Song in ancient Greek theatre intoned by the chorus as it went out at the end of a play; as a more general term, the conclusion of a dramatic work with the catastrophe.

Experimental theatre. With the rise of the director in the 20th century and the consequent breakdown of the dominance of tradition in production, new theories of drama and methods of production developed which had to be tested, hence the introduction of the concept of experimentation derived from science, into the theatre. Among the first important producers to work experimentally with new theories and methods were STANISLAVSKY (1863–1938), and MEYERHOLD (1874–1942), followed TAIROV (1885–1950), ARTAUD (1896–1948) and BRECHT (1898–1956). Today among the most prominent experimenters are GROTOWSKI (1933–) and BROOK (1925–). New forms of theatre building, as suggested by SCHLEMMER and the Bauhaus in the 1920s, and the advocates of THEATRE-IN-THE-ROUND in the 1950s–60s, also gave new impetus to experimental theatre. Other forms of experimentation with new kinds of theatre which may transcend the old concept of drama range from JOAN LITTLEWOOD's Theatre Workshop (London) and the attempts at participatory theatre exemplified by ARIANE MNOUCHKINE's Théâtre du Soleil (Paris), the collective productions of Joseph Chaikin's OPEN THEATRE and beck's LIVING THEATRE (New York), the SAN FRANCISCO MIME TROUPE (San Francisco), and RONCONI's Teatro Libero di Roma (Rome) to the *Happening* movement.
Bibl: R. Kostelanetz, THE THEATRE OF MIXED MEANS, 1970; A. Veinstein, LE THÉÂTRE EXPÉRIMENTAL, 1968

Exposition (Lat *expositio*=explanation). In drama an introduction to the personal and factual circumstances of the situation and the complications to be expected; it also indicates events preceding the dramatic action. Sometimes takes the form of a PROLOGUE, e.g. in classical drama and in the Middle Ages: as the interest and suspense of a play depend on it, the technique of exposition is one of the essential elements of the playwright's art.

Expressionism. A literary and artistic movement which started in the decade before World War I, initially in the German-speaking world. It is anti-realistic and against subtle nuances, aiming at ecstasy, pathos, comprehensiveness and simplification. Expressionism was anti-authoritarian, directed against Victorian paternalism. Reality is to be transcended and thus Expressionism can also be seen as an attempt to renew an idealistic attitude. Language is foreshortened, heightened, over-simplified. The first Expressionist play was SORGE's *Der Bettler*, published in 1912. The main playwrights of German Expressionism were: KAISER, HASENCLEVER, JOHST, KORNFELD, WERFEL, UNRUH, TOLLER. Among its forerunners were WEDEKIND, with his exaggerated character drawing and theatrical dynamics, not only in his writing, but also as an actor; and STRINDBERG, whose later plays had their greatest impact in the years between 1910 and 1919. The Expressionist theatre came into being later than Expressionism in the fine arts and it is significant that in its German form it did not start in BERLIN, where a strong realistic tradition was entrenched, but in the provinces: it was initiated in Mannheim in 1916, under the director WEICHERT, and also in the same year at the Albert Theater in Dresden, where Hasenclever's *Der Sohn* was first performed. The avant-garde theatre, Das junge Deutschland, founded in Berlin by REINHARDT in December, 1917, showed 12 plays in three seasons, usually at special matinées: the first two were Sorge's *Der Bettler*, December 1917, and GOERING's *Die Seeschlacht*, March 1918. Reinhardt staged the plays on an almost empty stage and worked with strong lighting effects. The most important early Expressionist production in Berlin was Toller's *Die Wandlung*, first performed at the newly founded Tribüne on 30 September 1918, directed by MARTIN. The Expressionist style of production was characterized by the subordination of detail to a principal 'vision', with essential features dramatically picked out by spotlight, tremendous emphasis on tempo, symbolical decor and costume, exaggerated volume of sound, and rhythmic articulation by the actors. Such methods were applied to the productions of the classics by JESSNER at the Berlin State Theatre: SCHILLER's *Wilhelm Tell*, 1919, SHAKESPEARE's *Richard III*, 1920. It spread to the USA and elsewhere. Playwrights like O'NEILL (*The Hairy Ape*), KAUFMAN and CONNELLY (*Beggar on Horseback*) and RICE (*The Adding Machine*), were influenced by Expressionism which, however, lost its main impetus after 1920. Its second phase was no longer idealistic, but merely aggressive; the emotional and partly anti-intellectual 'black' Expressionism as found in the early plays of BRONNEN (*Vatermord*), BRECHT (*Baal, Im Dickicht der Städte*) and JAHNN (*Medea*).
Bibl: G. Rühle, THEATER FÜR DIE REPUBLIK, 1967; W. Sokel (ed), AN ANTHOLOGY OF GERMAN EXPRESSIONIST DRAMA, 1963, 3. C. Hill & Ralph Ley, THE DRAMA OF GERMAN EXPRESSIONISM, 1960

Extempore acting (Lat *ex tempore*=out of the time). Speaking without reference to a script or notes. Hence to 'extemporize' in popular light comedy it was, and still is sometimes today, an important source of comic spontaneity, which reached its height in the comic parts of the COMMEDIA DELL' ARTE.

Exter, Alexandra (1884–1949), Russian stage designer. Her work derived initially from Art Nouveau, but was later influenced by CONSTRUCTIVISM. From 1916 she was an important collaborator of TAIROV (designs for WILDE's *Salomé*, Paris, 1919). She eventually settled in France and held numerous exhibitions in Paris, showing many designs, which remained to a great extent unrealized.

Extravaganza. A popular form of entertainment very similar to BURLESQUE though without the satiric content which flourished in the 19th century but no longer exists today. The productions were lavish and spectacular, the improbable plots were based on well-known folk-tales or myths, with attendant music, the DIALOGUE often in outrageously rhyming couplets. A master of the genre was PLANCHÉ. The present-day PANTOMIME has derived from it.

Eyre, Ronald (1929–), English director. Originally a teacher, then a TV director. First stage production: *Titus Andronicus*, Birmingham, 1963. His successes include: *London Assurance*, RSC, 1970; *Mrs Warren's Profession*, NATIONAL THEATRE, 1970; *Veterans*, by WOOD, ROYAL COURT, 1972. Has written a number of TV features and plays, one of which, *A Crack in the Ice*, formed the basis of a stage play of the same title.

Eysoldt, Gertrud (1870–1950), German actress. Trained in Munich, she made her first appearance at the COURT THEATRE there, subsequently playing in companies in Riga and Berlin. In 1902 she joined REINHARDT's ENSEMBLE, remaining with them until 1933. She was at her best in realistic parts, particularly in plays by WEDEKIND (Lulu in *Erdgeist*, 1902, in which she played opposite Wedekind), then in plays by IBSEN, STRINDBERG, title role in *Miss Julie*, 1903. Other major parts included: the title role in WILDE's *Salomé*, 1903, and Puck in *A Midsummer Night's Dream* in Reinhardt's famous production which remained in the REPERTOIRE from 1905 to 1921. Later in life her most famous performance was as the mother in BRECHT's *Im Dickicht der Städte*, 1924. She also managed the Kleines Schauspielhaus in Berlin, 1920–21.

Alexandra Exter, design for *La dama duende* by CALDERÓN

Experimental theatre, scene from GROTOWSKI's *Apocalypsis cum figuris*

Jacques Fabbri's *La Famille Arlequin*, Paris 1955

Fabbri, Diego (1911–), Italian playwright. Strongly influenced by PIRANDELLO and BETTI. Originally a lawyer by profession. Much concerned with 'tragic Christianity', his plays mainly deal with religious themes: his importance lies therefore in the development of religious drama. His best-known work is *Processo a Gesù* (*Between Two Thieves*) fp PICCOLO TEATRO DI MILANO, 1955, dir COSTA. Other significant works include: *Inquisizione* (Inquisition), 1950; *Processo di famiglia* (Family Trial), 1953, and *Il Bugiardo* (The Liar), 1953, seen in London at the WORLD THEATRE SEASON in 1965, produced by the COMPAGNIA DEI GIOVANI.

Fabbri, Jacques (J. Fabbricotti; 1925–), French director and actor. Awarded several director's prizes for his high-comedy productions modelled on the COMMEDIA DELL' ARTE, whose acrobatic numbers (LAZZI) and improvisations he copied; amongst these were *La Famille Arlequin* by C. Santelli in 1955 at the Théâtre du Vieux-Colombier, for which he was awarded the Prix Molière.

Fabula, generic name for a play in ancient Rome. It included many different types of drama: *fabula atellana*, a folk comedy (▷ ATELLAN FARCE); *fabula praetexta*, based on themes from Roman history and legend, named after the *toga praetexta*, the purple-bordered robe worn by magistrates and by youths before they reached manhood; *fabula togata*, a COMEDY, so called after the *toga*, the Roman form of dress, and dealing with Roman life and customs, contrasted with the *fabula palliata* which was acted in Greek COSTUME, and consisted largely of plays by PLAUTUS and TERENCE (▷PALLIATA and ROME).

Falckenberg, Otto (1873–1947), German director and manager. Joined the Munich Kammerspiele in 1913, under the management of ZIEGEL, and had his first success there with the production of STRINDBERG's *The Ghost Sonata*, fp 1915; in 1917 he was appointed the theatre's artistic director and remained there until 1944. He did excellent work with actors and greatly advanced the careers of such important artists as KÄTHE GOLD, Heidemarie Hatheyer, ELISABETH FLICKENSCHILDT, RÜHMANN, HASSE, and Ewald Balser. At first a disciple of Strindberg, he used SYMBOLISM and tried 'to reveal the visionary through realism'. As he developed as a director, his tendency towards Impressionism became increasingly pronounced. He also encouraged playwrights, notably KAISER, JOHST, BRECHT and BARLACH.
Bibl: W. Petzet, 1939

Falk, Rossella (R. Falzacappa; 1926–), Italian actress. While still a pupil of the Accademia dell'Arte Drammatica, she won first prize at an international youth theatre competition in Prague; she made her stage début in 1948 in PIRANDELLO's *Sei personaggi in cerca d'autore*, Venice Festival, directed by COSTA; appeared subsequently at the Piccolo Teatro in Rome (under the management of Costa) in classical roles (Electra in ALFIERI's *Oreste*), later increasingly in modern plays, e.g. Stella in T. WILLIAMS's *A Streetcar Named Desire*, Natasha in CHEKHOV's *Three Sisters*, both between 1951 and 1953, in a company led by VISCONTI; in 1954 she played the lead in Moravia's *La Mascherata* (The Masquerade) at the PICCOLO TEATRO DI MILANO. In 1954 she founded, with actors of her own age (DE LULLO, BUAZZELLI, VALLI, A. M. Guarnieri) the COMPAGNIA DEI GIOVANI which opened with MUSSET's *Lorenzaccio* and later produced such contemporary successes as COLETTE's *Gigi*, 1954 and D. FABBRI's *Il Bugiardo*, 1955.

Fantesca (Ital = lady's maid, chambermaid). Stock character of the COMMEDIA DELL'ARTE, originally a peasant woman, later developed into the character of COLOMBINA.

Farce (Fr = stuffing). Although identifiable in early Greek drama, farce, as we know it, traces its development originally from the interlude in the French MYSTERY PLAYS of the Middle Ages, e.g. *Maistre Pierre Pathelin*. It was made popular in France, especially in the 17th century, by the farce players (e.g. Turlupin, Gros-Guillaume) who strongly influenced MOLIÈRE. Later it developed, as a distinct theatrical form, into short satirical one-act plays. Farce in its present form probably originated in France in the 19th century; as distinct from COMEDY, it is a humorous play which derives laughter from physical action and the mechanism of the PLOT (mistaken identities, lovers hiding in cupboards, etc.) rather than subtlety of characterization. LABICHE and FEYDEAU are the great masters of 19th-century French farce. In England the genre remains popular to this day – between the wars the Aldwych Theatre was the home of the famous Aldwych farces; in the 1960s and 1970s Brian Rix became one of the main exponents of farce in London.
Bibl: E. Bentley, LIFE OF THE DRAMA, 1965

Farquhar, George (1678–1707), Irish-born English dramatist. Began his career as an actor in Dublin; went in 1697 or 1698 to England, where his first play *Love and a Bottle* was produced at DRURY LANE in 1698. With *The Constant Couple; or, a Trip to the Jubilee*, 1699, Drury Lane, he established his popular reputation as a playwright. *The Recruiting Officer*, 1706, was based on personal experience; the play was adapted by BRECHT, in collaboration with Elisabeth Hauptmann and BESSON, in 1955 under the title *Pauken und Trompeten*. *The Beaux' Stratagem*, given at the King's Theatre in the Haymarket in 1707 with Robert Wilks and ANNE OLDFIELD, is considered his finest play; it shows his mastery of characterization and his handling of polished DIALOGUE. He was the last important writer of RESTORATION DRAMA. His plays are less sharp-tongued than those of his predecessors, but display more vitality, naturalness, depth of feeling and humour than most of them. His other plays are: *Sir Harry Wildair, Being The Sequel of the Trip to the Jubilee*, 1701; *The Inconstant; or, the Way to win him*, 1702; *The Twin Rivals*, 1702; and *The Stage Coach*, 1704.
Bibl: W. Connelly, YOUNG GEORGE FARQUHAR, 1949

Farren. English family of actors. (1) **William F.** (1725–95) was at DRURY LANE 1776–84, where he was the first Careless in *The School for Scandal* and Leicester in *The Critic*, both by SHERIDAN; among his other parts were: Lear, Buckingham in *Henry VIII* and the Ghost in *Hamlet*. His son (2) **Percival F.** (1784–1843), who started as an actor, later managed theatres in Plymouth and Dublin and, 1828–31, the Plymouth Theatre in London; he was a teacher of HELEN FAUCIT, and is credited with inspiring her career. His younger brother (3) **William F.** (1786–1861) made his début under Percival's management in Plymouth, but had his first major success as Sir Peter Teazle at COVENT GARDEN, London, in 1818. His other noted parts were: Malvolio, Polonius, and Lord Ogleby in GARRICK's *The Clandestine Marriage*. His son (4) **William F.** (1825–1908) appeared for 15 years at the Haymarket Theatre (1853–67), subsequently at the Vaudeville, and with H. B. Conway founded the Conway-Farren Company in 1887; he established a REPERTOIRE which included plays by COLMAN, FARQUHAR, GOLDSMITH, SHERIDAN and Thomas Holcroft. W.F. liked to play parts in which his father had appeared but never achieved the same stature. His own son (5) **Percival William F.** (1853–1937) was also an actor and playwright. W.F. (4)'s brother (6) **Henry F.** (1826–60) was an actor who never attracted particular attention, while H.F.'s daughter was the famous actress (7) **Ellen F.** (1848–1904), known as Nellie, one of the favourite actresses of the Gaiety Theatre, who appeared in BURLESQUE from 1868–91, excelling in boys' parts. A contemporary critic said of her: 'Miss Farren may be a wife and a mother, but she is certainly one of the best boys in existence.'
Bibl: W. Davenport Adams, A DICTIONARY OF DRAMA, 1904

Fastnachtspiel (Carnival play). Early form of German secular drama; farce-like plays, which originated in the pre-Lenten carnival Shrove Tuesday of the later Middle Ages in Germany and Switzerland. The most representative writers of the *Fastnachtspiel* in Nuremberg were Hans Rosenplüt and Hans Folz, but the form reached its peak in the work of SACHS in the 16th century.

Faucit, Helen (Helena Saville; *c.* 1817–98), English actress. Trained by P. FARREN, she made her stage début in 1836 at COVENT GARDEN, appearing in several of SHAKESPEARE's plays (as Juliet, Portia, Desdemona) and also in plays by contemporary authors such as BROWNING's *Strafford*, 1837, *A Blot in the 'Scutcheon*, 1843, and *Colombe's Birthday*, 1853, as well as *The Lady of Lyons*, 1838, by BULWER-LYTTON. When MACREADY took over the management of the Haymarket Theatre she appeared there; she made a successful French tour, 1844–45, as Lady Macbeth and Ophelia, which became her most celebrated performances. After her marriage in 1851 to the novelist Theodore Martin her appearances became rare. She also wrote the well-known book *On Some of Shakespeare's Female Characters*, 1885. She was a very beautiful woman of great charm, as successful in society as she was on stage. She became a personal friend of Queen Victoria.
Bibl: H. Simpson & C. Braun, A CENTURY OF FAMOUS ACTRESSES, 1913

Faust, The Legend of. One of the great themes of dramatic world literature, based on the historical figure of Georg Faust (later often called Dr Johann Faust), *c.* 1480–1536(?39), a magician and astrologer whose exploits soon became the subject of popular fiction and legend. Reports of earlier magicians and scientists merged to produce in 1587 the first version of the Faust legend, *Historia von Dr Johann Fausten*, printed by Johann Spiess in Frankfurt. According to this story Faustus studied theology in Wittenberg and then turned to medicine and magic (witchcraft) and concluded a pact with Mephistopheles for 24 years; Faust's love for a poor girl is an addition by Johann Nikolaus Pfizer (1674), whose short version was very popular in the 18th century (also as a puppet play); GOETHE made the acquaintance of the story in this version. MARLOWE dramatized an English translation of Spiess's Faust story in 1589. 18th-century versions included: LESSING, 1759, a fragment; Maler Müller, *Situationen aus Fausts Leben*, 1776, and *Fausts Leben dramatisiert*, 1778. Goethe made his first draft, *Urfaust*, in 1772–75, completing the first part in 1806, the second in 1831. Further adaptations by GRABBE, *Don Juan und Faust*, 1829; VALÉRY, *Mon Faust*, 1946; operatic versions by Gounod, 1859; Boito, 1868; Busoni, 1920; as a novel by T. MANN, 1948.
Bibl: R. Petsch, FAUSTSAGE UND FAUSTDICHTUNG, 1966

Fay, William George (1872–1947), Irish actor and director. With his brother **Frank F.** (1870–1931), the true creator of the realistic and precise acting style at the ABBEY THEATRE, which was founded in 1904 through the merging of their amateur company (Ormande Dramatic Society, founded in 1898) and the circle of dramatists around LADY GREGORY. One of his finest roles was Christy Mahon in the original production of SYNGE's *The Playboy of the Western World*, 1907. After some disagreement with YEATS and Lady Gregory the brothers left for the USA in 1908, where they produced a series of Irish plays for FROHMAN. Frank J. returned to the Abbey Theatre some years later to play in Yeats's *The Hour-Glass* and settled in Dublin.

W.G. returned to England in 1914 and played in repertory. Among his later parts in London were: Tramp in Synge's *In The Shadow of the Glen*, 1930; and Mr Cassidy in BRIDIE's *Storm in a Teacup*, 1935, which he also produced. He also wrote several books including *The Fays of the Abbey Theatre*, 1935; *Merely Players*; *A Short Glossary of Theatrical Terms*, 1932.
Bibl: ▷ABBEY THEATRE

Fechter, Charles Albert (1824–79), French actor, brought up in England. He appeared for a short time at the COMÉDIE-FRANÇAISE, making his début there in 1840, then toured Germany and England. After returning to France he played Armand in DUMAS *fils' La Dame aux camélias*, 1852, with great success; at this time he was also co-director of the Odéon. He then went back to England and made his London début in HUGO's *Ruy Blas*, 1861, and a year later gave a revolutionary interpretation of Hamlet, being praised for his sensitive and imaginative performance. He managed the Lyceum Theatre in London 1863–67; he went to the USA in 1869, where he re-opened the former Globe Theatre in New York as Fechter's, reviving his old successful roles and appearing in new plays with varying success. He retired in 1876 and died near Philadelphia.

Fedeli (Ital=faithful followers). Leading company of the COMMEDIA DELL'ARTE in the last quarter of the 17th century, led and probably founded by the younger ANDREINI (Giovanni Battista, who played Lelio); they were very successful from 1613 in Paris with T. MARTINELLI (Arlecchino), Barbieri (Beltrame), and GABRIELLI (Scapino), the leading actors of the company.

Federal Theatre Project. Founded in 1935 by the US Government within the framework of the Works Progress Administration (WPA) in order to give socially useful employment to needy professional theatre people. Directed by Hallie Flanagan (1890–1969), professor of Drama and Director of the Experimental Theatre at Vassar, later at Smith College, it encouraged writers to carry out experimental work with actors, designers and musicians, and did much to encourage theatrical activity all over the country. Apart from revivals of well-known classics, Sinclair Lewis's *It Can't Happen Here*, 1936 was produced simultaneously in 21 cities. Other productions included GREEN's *The Lost Colony*, 1937, in North Carolina, and *The Swing Mikado*, 1939, put on by a Black company. A. MILLER worked for the Project in 1938 after graduating. Another creation of the Project was the Living Newspaper which used cinema technique to present important living issues (*Triple-A Plowed Under*, 1936, and *One-Third of a Nation*, 1938, by A. Arent). The Federal Theatre Project was closed down on 30 June 1939, on political grounds, in some degree as a result of the Living Newspaper's unbiased and outspoken productions, but the technique of the latter was successfully used in England

Faust, engraving by Delacroix, 1828, illustrating Part I of GOETHE's play

William Fay, portrait by Jack Yeats

for adult education and propaganda in the armed forces during World War II. It has also influenced the development of DOCUMENTARY THEATRE.

Fehling, Jürgen (1885–1968), German director. First gained prominence in the 1920s as the realist among the EXPRESSIONIST directors; later developed his very personal style of violent, demonic theatre, sparse, with box-like sets and steeply raked floors. His productions of BARLACH, KLEIST, GOETHE and SHAKESPEARE were outstanding. He was one of the dominant personalities of the BERLIN theatre of the 1930s.

Feiffer, Jules (1929–), US dramatist. Best known for his cartoons, which first appeared in New York in *The Village Voice* in 1956. Today these appear in 75 newspapers throughout the USA and in other countries. Author of the one-act play *Crawling Arnold*, London 1965, Arts Theatre; the full-length plays: *Little Murders*, RSC, 1968, which gained the London Variety Critics Award for the best play by a foreign author; *God Bless*, fp Yale 1968, RSC, 1968, dir Reeves; *The Whitehouse Murder Case*, 1970. He wrote the screenplay for the film *Carnal Knowledge*, 1971.

Fellner, Ferdinand (1847–1916) and **Hermann Helmer** (1849–1919), theatre architects. Two of the most famous and successful architects at the end of the 19th century, their theatres can be found throughout the area of the former Austro-Hungarian Empire and Germany; they worked at first in the style of the High Renaissance, later incorporating Baroque and Rococo elements: municipal theatres in Vienna, 1872; Augsburg, 1876; Brno, 1881, etc. Altogether they built about 60 theatres.
Bibl: H. C. Hoffmann, DIE THEATERBAUTEN VON FELLNER UND HELMER, 1966

Felsenreitschule. Open-air theatre in Salzburg. Originally an arena for jousting and riding displays; it was built in 1694 into the vertical walls of an old quarry with three galleries and 93 boxes cut out of the rock. First used by REINHARDT for productions at the SALZBURG FESTIVAL in 1926. In 1933 Reinhardt asked the architect HOLZMEISTER to convert it, for his production of *Faust*, into a multiple stage 30 yards wide containing all the sets for the production. Now the theatre, which can be covered by a canvas roof in case of rain, is in regular use during the festival for the performance of operas and plays.

Felsenstein, Walter (1901–75), Austrian actor and director. He worked with major REPERTORY theatres in Germany, including the Frankfurt Städtische Bühnen, the Zurich Stadttheater, and the Schillertheater and Hebbeltheater, BERLIN. In 1947 he was appointed director of the Komische Oper in East Berlin and became a leading director of contemporary opera, adapting and translating numerous operas (Bizet's *Carmen*, 1949; Verdi's *La Traviata*, 1955). His best-known operatic productions include Mozart's *Die Zauberflöte*, 1954; Offenbach's *Hoffmanns Erzählungen*, 1958; Verdi's *Otello*, 1959. His conception of opera emphasized realistic acting in contrast to the conventional posturing of singers; at its best the borderline between theatre and opera vanished – the singing became an essential expression of a certain 'dramatic situation'. F.'s principal dramatic productions were at the BURGTHEATER in Vienna (SCHILLER's *Die Räuber*, 1946; IBSEN's *John Gabriel Borkman*, 1950).

Ferber, Edna (1887–1968), US novelist and playwright. Best known for her massive novels, in particular *Show Boat* which was turned into an operetta in 1927 by KERN and HAMMERSTEIN II, the London production of which established ROBESON as a singer. She collaborated with KAUFMAN on a number of successful plays, notably *The Royal Family*, a satire on the BARRYMORE dynasty of actors, 1927, produced in London 1934 as *Theatre Royal*; *Dinner at Eight*, 1932; and *Stage Door*, 1936.

Ferdinand, Roger (1898–1967), French dramatist. He enjoyed world-wide success with his BOULEVARD comedies about the life of young people, *Les J 3 ou la nouvelle école*, 1943, and *Trois garçons, une fille*, 1947.

Ferrati, Sarah (1906–), Italian actress. Made her stage début in 1928. Since 1938 she has played leading roles in light comedies including WILDE's *A Woman of No Importance*, 1939/40, and SHAW's *Mrs Warren's Profession*, 1943; she has also appeared in tragic parts, most famous of which was her Medea (EURIPIDES) in 1948.

Ferrer, José (1912–), US actor, producer and director. One of the most versatile performers in the US theatre (he has also appeared in opera and ballet), Ferrer is above all an outstanding character actor in classical parts, notably Iago, a part he played opposite ROBESON in a successful run of *Othello* in 1943, and *Cyrano de Bergerac*, in which he has appeared repeatedly, in the original play as well as in a musical and a film version. Another of his favourite parts is *Richard III*. But he has also more than once played Lord Fancourt Babberley in *Charley's Aunt*. He is a much sought-after film actor.

Fersen, Alessandro (1911–), Polish-born Italian director. He has lived since childhood in Italy. He made his début as a director in 1947 at the Teatro Ebraico with *Lea Lebowitz*, script by Fersen, based on a Hassidic legend, then became organizer of the Stagione Mediterranea in Nervi 1949 (*The Merry Wives of Windsor*); in 1951 he founded a short-lived studio called I nottambuli, and in 1957 he started a workshop for young actors. He has also written several articles on the theatre and acting, especially on the method of STANISLAVSKY. His productions included plays by MOLIÈRE, e.g. *Le Malade imaginaire*, 1953; PIRANDELLO, *Liolà*, 1956; Malipiero, *Il figlio prodigo* (The Prodigal Son) and *Venere prigioniera* (Venus Imprisoned), Florence 1957, Maggio Musicale. He is known also as a film actor.

Festivals. The earliest theatrical performances were organically linked to religious feasts, as the theatre emerged from ritual, e.g. the feast of DIONYSOS in Athens, at which plays were performed; the same is true of the religious drama of the Middle Ages, the Renaissance and the Baroque. With the rise of the professional theatre and urban bourgeois culture, the theatre becomes, in a negative as well as a positive sense, an everyday occurrence – hence from the mid-19th century onwards attempts to reinvest theatrical performances with the sense of occasion they had possessed in previous epochs. Special performances were mounted to mark exceptional artistic or social occasions, e.g. Verdi's *Aida*, commissioned to celebrate the opening of the Suez Canal in 1869 and first performed on 24 December 1871. Wagner instituted the Bayreuth Festival, 1876 (▷BAYREUTH), for the festive performance of his operas, and built a special theatre for it. REINHARDT and HOFMANNSTHAL started the SALZBURG FESTIVAL (opera and drama) with open-air performances of *Jedermann* (*Everyman*) in front of Salzburg Cathedral. Since then the festival idea has spread far and wide. AVIGNON FESTIVAL, 1947, initiated by VILAR; Venice Festival (BIENNALE) of Theatre, since 1934; Maggio Musicale in Florence, since 1933; STRATFORD-UPON-AVON, regular seasons at the Shakespeare Memorial Theatre since 1879; other Shakespeare festivals take place in Canada (Stratford, Ont.), since 1953, and the USA (Stratford, Conn.), since 1955; Opera Festival at Glyndebourne, Sussex, since 1934; EDINBURGH FESTIVAL since 1947; CHICHESTER FESTIVAL THEATRE, since 1962. Other important international festivals: the Paris THÉÂTRE DES NATIONS, since 1957, and the WORLD THEATRE SEASON at the Aldwych Theatre, London, 1964–73, which brought together leading companies from a number of countries.

Feuchtwanger, Lion (1884–1958), German writer. Best known as a historical novelist who started his career as a playwright with free versions of Greek classics, e.g. *The Persians* (after AESCHYLUS), 1915; *Peace* (after ARISTOPHANES), 1916. Collaborated with BRECHT on *Leben Eduards des Zweiten*, 1924, and *Die Gesichte der Simone Machard*, 1942. Also wrote *Jud Süss* (*Jew Süss*), 1917, which he adapted as a novel; *Kalkutta, 4 Mai*, 1927, written with Brecht and based on a novel by F. called *Warren Hastings, gouverneur von Indien*, 1916; *Die Petroleuminseln* (The Oil Islands), 1927; *Wird Hill amnestiert?* (Will Hill Be Pardoned?), 1930; *Wahn oder der Teufel in Boston* (Madness or the Devil in Boston), 1948; *Die Witwe Capet* (The Widow Capet), 1957.

Feuillère, Edwige (*née* Cunati; 1907–), French actress. First appeared in light comedies at the Palais-Royal and Bouffes-Parisiens under the name Cora Lynn; in 1931 she became a member of the COMÉDIE-

FRANÇAISE, where she appeared as Suzanne in BEAUMARCHAIS's *Le Mariage de Figaro.* Leaving the CF in 1933, because she did not get enough parts, she made her breakthrough as an actress in BECQUE's *La Parisienne*, 1937, and DUMAS *fils' La Dame aux camélias*, 1937, in which role she made several tours in foreign countries (London, 1955). After 1931 she appeared in films, and in only a few, carefully chosen stage roles: GIRAUDOUX's *Sodome et Gomorrhe*, 1943; COCTEAU's *L'Aigle à deux têtes*, 1946; MOLIÈRE's *Amphitryon* with BARRAULT, 1947; CLAUDEL's *Le Partage de Midi*, 1948, seen in London 1951 and 1968. In 1957 she appeared in London with her own company at the Palace Theatre, in RACINE's *Phèdre* and BECQUE's *La Parisienne.* Highly praised for her particularly lovely voice, her beauty, intelligence and vitality, she is one of the leading actresses in the Paris theatre. Main films: *Mam'zelle Nitouche, Topaze, L'Idiot, L'Aigle à deux têtes, Le Crime ne paie pas*, etc.
Bibl: R. Kemp, 1951

Feydeau, Georges (1862–1921), French playwright. Master of French FARCE in the tradition of SARDOU, LABICHE, BEAUMARCHAIS, and MOLIÈRE. He and his friend COURTELINE succeeded Sardou in the popular esteem of Paris audiences. His farces involved more complicated situations than had those of his predecessors, the action being based on an almost geometric pattern of intrigue, and the mockery was much sharper. Like Molière, he attacked people and institutions with equal vigour. Beginning his career in 1880 with *Par la fenêtre*, a one-act comedy translated as *Wooed and Viewed*, he went on to write numerous works including: *Monsieur chasse!* and *Champignol malgré lui*, both in 1892 at the Palais-Royal and the Théâtre des Nouveautés; each ran for more than 1,000 performances; *Un Fil à la patte*, 1894 (adapted by MORTIMER as *Cat among the Pigeons*, 1970); *L'Hôtel du libre échange*, 1894 (*Hotel Paradiso*, 1957); *Le Système ribadier*, 1892; *La Dame de chez Maxim*, 1899; *Occupe-toi d'Amélie*, 1908 (adapted by COWARD as *Look After Lulu*, 1959); and his masterpiece *La Puce à l'oreille*, 1907, which is the one most frequently revived (best-known modern production at the COMÉDIE-FRANÇAISE, dir CHARON; in an English version by Mortimer, *A Flea in Her Ear*, London 1965, OLD VIC). Many of his farces are regularly produced by the CF.
Bibl: E. Bentley, LIFE OF THE DRAMA, 1965; N. Shapiro, FOUR FARCES BY FEYDEAU, 1970

Fialka, Ladislav (1931–), Czech MIME. Trained as a ballet dancer; he was one of the founders of the Theatre on the Balustrade in Prague in 1958. Within this company he established a mime troupe in the genre of MARCEAU. Director and principal mime in his productions, he wears the traditional white mask of PIERROT. Unlike the other contemporary mimes (Marceau, Molcho) he has his own company. His mime dramas are based mostly on traditional PANTOMIME themes, e.g. *Les Amants de la Lune*, 1959,

Edna Ferber's *Show Boat* at DRURY LANE, 1928, with ROBESON

Edwige Feuillère and BARRAULT IN CLAUDEL's *Le Partage de Midi*, 1948

on a pantomime by DEBURAU; *The Castaways*, a grotesque in the manner of a silent film pantomime; *The Masks*, 1959. His other works include: *The Way*, history of the 'white mime'; *The Fools*, 1965, characters taken from the Bible, SHAKESPEARE and KAFKA. He also collaborated in productions of plays: *Hamlet*, National Theatre in Prague, 1959; JARRY's *Ubu Roi*, Theatre on the Balustrade, 1964; he produced mime plays on TV and has toured successfully with his company throughout Europe and the American continent.

Field, Nathan (1587–*c.* 1620), English actor and playwright. At the age of 13 he was the leading boy actor of the CHILDREN OF THE CHAPEL ROYAL. He appeared in the first productions of JONSON's plays at the BLACKFRIARS THEATRE: *Cynthia's Revels*, 1600 or 1601; *Poetaster*, 1601; and *The Silent Woman*, 1609. Unlike the majority of child actors he succeeded in gaining entry to professional companies. He mainly played the parts of young lovers; his most noted performance was the title role in CHAPMAN's *Bussy d'Ambois*. He worked successively for the Children of Her Majesty's Revels, Princess Elizabeth's Men, and the King's Players. Little is known about his acting, but he was considered one of the most important actors of the Elizabethan theatre. He also wrote plays: *A Woman is a Weathercock*, 1609 or 1610; *Amends for Ladies*, *c.* 1610–11; and collaborated on several plays with MASSINGER and FLETCHER.
Bibl: R. F. Brinkley, 1928

Fielding, Henry (1707–54), English novelist, journalist and comic playwright. Wrote very successfully for the theatre from 1727 to *c.* 1737, mainly BURLESQUE and satirical plays including parodies of contemporary plays: *The Tragedy of Tragedies; or, the Life and Death of Tom Thumb the Great*, 1731. He ridiculed Sir Robert Walpole and his Whig administration, King George II and Queen Caroline in his plays, resulting in a tightening of CENSORSHIP and the passing of the Stage Licensing Act of 1737. The Haymarket Theatre, where all his plays had been produced, was closed that year and he retired to write novels. His dramatic works include: *The Author's Farce*, 1730; *The Covent Garden Tragedy*, 1732; *The Distressed Mother*, 1712; *The Welsh Opera*, 1731; *Don Quixote in England*, 1734, *Pasquin*, 1736.
Bibl: F. H. Dudden, HENRY FIELDING: HIS LIFE, WORKS AND TIMES, 1952, 2 vols

Fields. US theatrical family. **Lew F.** (1867–1941) actor, producer. Performed in BURLESQUE with Joe Weber at the New York Music Hall till it closed in 1904. He then produced shows like *Hit the Deck*, *The Connecticut Yankee*, both 1927. His son **Joseph F.** (1895–1966) was a playwright, producer and director, best known for his collaboration with Jerome Chodorov, with whom he wrote *My Sister Eileen*, 1944, later to become the award-winning musical *Wonderful Town*, with music by BERNSTEIN. He also collaborated with Anita Loos on a musical version of her novel *Gentlemen Prefer Blondes*, 1949, and with RODGERS and HAMMERSTEIN on the musical *Flower Drum Song*, 1958. His sister **Dorothy F.** (1905–74) and brother **Herbert F.** (1898–1958) were successful librettists who wrote the books for a number of Broadway musicals, the most outstanding of which was *Annie Get Your Gun*, 1946, with ETHEL MERMAN and music by BERLIN. Dorothy was also a highly talented and successful writer of lyrics (particularly with KERN).

Finland. Visiting performances of Swedish, Russian and German companies in the 19th century; in 1827 first theatre in Helsinki, in 1866 foundation of the Swedish theatre. Finnish theatrical activities developed together with the fight for the Finnish language and with the struggle for independence. In 1870 the national poet Aleksis Kivi (or Stenvall) dramatized and produced *The Seven Brothers* in Finnish, following which the Finnish critic and dramatist Kaarlo Bergbom inspired the idea of a national theatre. In 1873 the first professional Finnish theatre was established. In 1902 the Finnish National Theatre obtained its own permanent house, and under the management of Eino Kalima, 1917–50, it showed the dominating influence of STANISLAVSKY's ideas: productions of CHEKHOV's *Three Sisters* toured the country and Europe. In 1950 Arvi Kivimaa was appointed director of the National Theatre and built up a world theatre REPERTOIRE.

Finney, Albert (1936–), English actor. Began his career in 1956 at the BIRMINGHAM REPERTORY THEATRE and in 1958 made his first West End appearance in a small part in Jane Arden's *The Party*, for which he won an award as best supporting actor. In 1959 he was at STRATFORD-UPON-AVON playing Cassio in *Othello* and Edgar in *King Lear* and then had his first real break when he took over as Coriolanus from OLIVIER during that season. His first major success was the title role in *Billy Liar* by W. HALL and Keith Waterhouse, 1960; he enhanced his reputation with his interpretation of OSBORNE's *Luther*, 1961, ROYAL COURT THEATRE; on BROADWAY 1963. His temperament and vitality enable him to excel in comic as well as tragic parts; his heroes are full of strength and the spirit of revolt, e.g. the Scottish rebel in JOHN ARDEN's *Armstrong's Last Goodnight*, 1965, National Theatre at the CHICHESTER FESTIVAL. He made a notable appearance in WHITEHEAD's *Alpha Beta*, 1972, at the Royal Court Theatre, with which he has had strong links. In 1975–76 he played an uncut *Hamlet* at the NATIONAL THEATRE, and in 1976 starred in MARLOWE's *Tamburlaine the Great* in the HALL production with which the new Olivier Theatre opened. F. has also appeared in many films of a wide gamut, ranging from *Tom Jones*, 1963, to *Murder on the Orient Express*, 1975.

Fiorilli, Tiberio (known as Scaramuccia or Scaramouche; 1608–94), Italian actor. His name is sometimes given as Fiorillo, the name of another actor, SILVIO FIORILLO, who may have been his father. He was one of the best itinerant comedians of the 17th century in ITALY and FRANCE, and also visited London. He was the first and greatest SCARAMUCCIA, a mixture of the ZANNI and the CAPITANO who, as Scaramouche, became a stock character in French COMEDY. He was specially praised by his contemporaries for his charm and spontaneity (he played unmasked) and his skill as a dancer and acrobat. In 1658 he played alternately with MOLIÈRE, who was much inspired by him, at the Petit-Bourbon in Paris. His biography was written by A. COSTANTINI, 1695.
Bibl: ▷COMMEDIA DELL'ARTE

Fiorillo, Silvio (second half of the 16th century–1630), Italian actor. The original Capitano Matamoros. Later in Naples *c.* 1609 he was probably the first PULCINELLA. He also wrote several scenarios in the COMMEDIA DELL'ARTE tradition. His son **Giovan Battista F.** (*c.* 1614–51) played the part of the second ZANNI under the name Trappolino, and also SCARAMUCCIA. He was married to **Beatrice F. Vitellini** (d. 1654) who played one of the INNAMORATI.
Bibl: ▷COMMEDIA DELL'ARTE

Fire. Stage effect already in use in the antique theatre, e.g. the burning city in EURIPIDES' *The Trojan Women*: in the BAROQUE THEATRE fire was used in combination with other stage resources of the time such as hangings, borders and wings, to depict hell. Later, in the open-air theatre, fireworks were also used. Naked lights (candles, chandeliers) which caused fires in the theatre, were still in use in the 19th century. They were prohibited from the beginning of the 20th century. Today all fire-effects (fireplaces, fires) are created by STAGE LIGHTING (projections, films) with sound-effects. Candles which burn unprotected on stage are only allowed with increased safety precautions. The fire curtain, flats and other objects are fire-proofed by chemical means.

Firework spectacles. The first use of fireworks goes back to the MYSTERY PLAYS of the 14th century; fireworks became part of the devil's wardrobe and were often used for stage effect, e.g. in the fiery mouth of hell, already known in early Florentine INTERLUDES, which became a firm property of the medieval and BAROQUE THEATRE. In Munich an open-air stage was built on the river Isar in 1662 on the occasion of a festival given by the Elector of Bavaria which concluded with a *Drama di fuoco* (Ital= firework spectacle). In Molière's comedy ballet *La Princesse d'Elide*, 1664, the final witches' spell was broken by a firework display. These spectacles were particularly popular at Court festivals in Vienna, Dresden and in Italy, France, the Netherlands and England from the 17th to the 19th centuries. Today firework displays are held to celebrate world-famous events or anniversaries though rarely used in connection with the theatre (e.g. 4 July in the USA; 14 July in France). In England, the annual Guy Fawkes Day, on the 5th of November, purportedly commemorates the foiling of the Gunpowder Plot to blow up the Houses of Parliament in 1605, but it is little more than an excuse for the children of England to have their own individual firework displays.

Fiske, Mrs (*née* Marie Augusta Davey, stage name: Minnie Maddern until she married Harrison Grey Fiske, 1890; 1865–1932), US director and actress. One of the greatest actresses of her period, she started as a child performer before she was five years old; returned to the stage at the age of 13 after a brief period of schooling, retired from the stage briefly after her marriage, but re-emerged again three years later, in 1893, in a series of plays in the then modern, serious, socially conscious vein, including IBSEN's *A Doll's House* and an adaptation of Thomas Hardy's *Tess of the d'Urbervilles*. She and her husband managed the Manhattan Theatre in New York and produced a series of outstanding plays, including several by Ibsen, which she herself directed with outstanding success. In her later years she excelled in COMEDY parts.

Fitch, William Clyde (1865–1909), US dramatist. One of the most prolific writers in the USA in the last decade of the 19th and the first of the 20th century. He achieved success in: historical dramas on American subjects – *Nathan Hale*, 1898, and *Barbara Frietchie*, 1899; social COMEDIES, making use of contemporary problems and conditions – *The Climbers*, 1901; *Lover's Lane*, 1901; *Captain Jinks of the Horse Marines*, 1901; and in MELODRAMAS – *The Moth and the Flame*, 1898; *The Cowboy and the Lady*, 1899. Among 50 other plays that he wrote are: *The Girl with Green Eyes*, 1902; *The Truth*, 1906; *The Woman in the Case*, 1909.

Flanagan, Hallie ▷FEDERAL THEATRE PROJECT.

Flaubert, Gustave (1821–80), French writer. Several of his novels were dramatized, e.g. *Madame Bovary* by BATY (Théâtre Montparnasse, 1936). His COMEDY *Le Candidat* was produced with little success in 1873; it served the German dramatist STERNHEIM as a model for his own comedy *Der Kandidat*, 1915.
Bibl: J. Canu, FLAUBERT, AUTEUR DRAMATIQUE, 1946

Flautino. Stock character of the COMMEDIA DELL'ARTE, derived from the character of BRIGHELLA.

Fleck, Johann Friedrich Ferdinand (1757–1801), German actor. Started his career in 1777 with the company of J. Brandes; 1779/80 he worked with F. L. SCHRÖDER in Hamburg, where among other parts he played in SCHILLER's *Fiesko*; in 1783 he went to work with DÖBBELIN in Berlin; after 1786 he was a member of the Berlin National Theatre (under the direction of J. J. Engel, and from 1796 under IFFLAND) acting (Macbeth, Lear) and

Firework spectacle, as performed before the Duke of Richmond at Whitehall, 1749

Albert Finney as Cassio in *Othello*, with Zoe Caldwell as Bianca, STRATFORD-UPON-AVON, 1959

Minnie Maddern Fiske with George Arliss in IBSEN's *Hedda Gabler*, 1904

directing plays. His best remembered parts are: Odoardo in LESSING's *Emilia Galotti*, Karl Moor in Schiller's *Die Räuber*, and especially Wallenstein in the first production of Schiller's play in Berlin, 1799. In 1798 he gave a visiting performance in his home town, Dresden, with his wife, the actress, **Sophie Louise F.** (1777–1846). He was the first important heroic actor in the German theatre, whose performances in Schiller's plays earned him much praise.
Bibl: S. Troizkij, DIE ANFÄNGE DER REALISTISCHEN SCHAUSPIELKUNST, 1949

Flecker, James Elroy (1884–1915), English poet. Studied Persian and Arabic and joined the Consular Service, spending two years in Beirut. His health broke down and he died of tuberculosis. His most notable dramatic work is the VERSE DRAMA *Hassan*, produced posthumously by DEAN, who adapted the shortened stage version in 1922. Another play in verse is *Don Juan*, pub 1925.
Bibl: J. Sherwood, 1973

Fleisser, Marieluise (1901–74), German dramatist. After 1923 she collaborated with BRECHT on a number of realistic plays which dealt with everyday life in Bavaria: *Fegefeuer* (Purgatory), 1926; *Pioniere in Ingolstadt* (Pioneers in Ingolstadt), fp Berlin 1929, Theater am Schiffbauerdamm. After World War II she wrote *Karl Stuart* and *Der starke Stamm* (The Strong Tribe), 1946. She was also the author of an autobiographical story *Avantgarde*, 1943.

Flers, Robert de (R. de Pellevé de la Motte Angro, Marquis de Flers; 1872–1927), French dramatist. He wrote his best plays in collaboration with CAILLAVET; very clever and well-made unpretentious COMEDIES with a slight hint of satire: *Les Travaux d'Hercule*, 1901; *Papa*, 1911; *L'Habit vert*, 1912; *Monsieur Brotonneau*, 1914. After the death of Caillavet, 1915, he worked mainly with F. de Croisset. In 1914 he became editor of *Le Figaro*.
Bibl: F. de Croisset, LE SOUVENIR DE ROBERT DE FLERS, 1929

Fletcher, John (1579–1625), English poet and dramatist. He wrote his best plays in collaboration with BEAUMONT, and they are among the most important examples of romantic English TRAGICOMEDY. From what can be deduced, F. was the finer poet and had the more inventive mind; Beaumont brought to the partnership a critical intelligence and a talent for revision. Their best work includes *The Maid's Tragedy*, *c.* 1608–11; the tragicomedies *Philaster; or, Love Lies a-Bleeding*, 1608–10, and *A King and No King*, 1611; and the COMEDY *The Scornful Lady*, 1613. At some time during 1612 F. succeeded SHAKESPEARE as chief dramatist of the King's Players. After Beaumont's death in 1616 F. wrote some plays together with other dramatists including MASSINGER, MIDDLETON, ROWLEY and FIELD, and is believed to have collaborated with Shakespeare (probably on *Henry VIII*, 1613, and *The Two Noble Kinsmen*, 1613–16, revived in 1973 at the York Festival). Plays written by F. alone include *The Faithful Shepherdess*, 1608–09, a PASTORAL PLAY for the Queen's Revels; the comedies *The Woman's Prize; or, The Tamer Tamed*, 1604–*c.* 1617, *Monsieur Thomas*, 1610–*c.* 1616, and *Wit without Money*, 1614–20; and the historical TRAGEDY *Bonduca*, 1611–14. F.'s comedy *The Chances*, 1613–25, adapted by Buckingham in 1666, was revived in 1962 at the first CHICHESTER FESTIVAL.
Bibl: ▷BEAUMONT

Flickenschildt, Elisabeth (1905–), German actress. Started in Hamburg and became one of the leading interpreters of women of forceful personality in Germany in the late 1930s. She was outstanding as a character actress: Mistress Quickly in *The Merry Wives of Windsor*, Berlin State Theatre, 1941; Clytemnestra in SARTRE's *The Flies*, 1947, and Arkadina in CHEKHOV's *The Seagull*, 1948; Queen Elizabeth in SCHILLER's *Maria Stuart*, Berlin 1952, Schillertheater; Dr von Zahnd in DÜRRENMATT's *Die Physiker*, Hamburg 1962. With her high-cheekboned, expressive face, she is a heroic actress in the grand manner. Often directed by GRÜNDGENS, she proved a capable partner of this great German actor in GOETHE's *Faust* and other plays.

Flon, Suzanne (1923–), French actress. Famous for her interpretations of ANOUILH: Ismène in *Antigone*, 1944, Jeannette in *Roméo et Jeannette*, 1946, both first performed at the Théâtre de l'Atelier; *L'Alouette*, 1953. She also created leading roles in Roussin's *La Petite Hutte*, 1947, AUDIBERTI's *Le Mal court*, 1947, 1957, and Katharina in the latter's adaptation of SHAKESPEARE's *The Taming of the Shrew*, 1957. She has also appeared in films.

Floridor (Josias de Soulas; 1608–71), a leading actor of the French classical period. He gave up a military career to join a company of travelling players in the provinces, with whom he appeared at DRURY LANE in London. In 1637 he settled in Paris and joined the company of the Théâtre du Marais, succeeding MONTDORY in the leading roles, one of his first parts being Dorante in CORNEILLE's *Le Menteur*. He took over the management in 1642. At this theatre, which later moved to the HÔTEL DE BOURGOGNE, were given the first performances of Corneille's plays, in most of which he appeared: *Horace*, 1640; *Cinna*, 1640; *Oedipe*, 1659; Massinissa in *Sophonisbe*, 1663; *Othon*, 1664. His notable parts in RACINE's plays included: *Alexandre et Porus*, 1665; Pyrrhus in *Andromaque*, 1667; Néron in *Britannicus*, 1669; Titus in *Bérénice*, 1670. He was a refined, authoritative and sensitive actor with a well-trained voice, the only one spared by MOLIÈRE in his critical pronouncement on actors in *L'Impromptu de Versailles*.
Bibl: S. W. Deierkauf-Holsboer, LE THÉÂTRE DU MARAIS, 1954

Florindo. One of the INNAMORATI of the COMMEDIA DELL'ARTE, who dressed after the fashion of the day and appeared without a mask.

Fo, Dario (1926–), Italian playwright, ACTOR-MANAGER and MIME. While studying architecture in Milan, he became known as a comedian in the theatre and on the radio. With his wife Franca Rame, an actress whose family had been associated with the theatre for generations, he founded a small company in 1952, which included Jacques Lecoq, a former pupil of MARCEAU. They staged mainly short plays written by Fo at the PICCOLO TEATRO DI MILANO. In 1957 he was able to establish a larger company, the Franca Rame-Dario Fo company with Fo as author, leading actor, producer, and designer of the sets and costumes. More recently he founded Nuova Scena, a company which toured Italy in a successful attempt to take theatre to small towns and to 'working' people, who were encouraged to use theatre as a forum. The English titles of his longer plays are *Archangels Don't Play Flipper*; *He Had Two Pistols With Black and White Eyes*; *Who Steals a Foot Is Lucky in Love*; *Isabella*; *Three Ships and a Knave*; *It's Always the Devil's Fault*; *This Woman Is Expendable*; *The Seventh Commandment*.

Folies-Bergère. A famous CABARET in Paris, which opened in 1869 with a mixed programme of songs and PANTOMIME (Paul Legrand as PIERROT) and gained worldwide fame under E. Marchand's management (1886–1901) who introduced the first company of dancing girls in France. After World War I the theatre reached a second high point under the management of Paul Derval. Many of the most famous names in REVUE appeared there at the peak of their careers: YVETTE GUILBERT, Josephine Baker, MISTINGUETT, CHEVALIER, etc. Today the programme consists largely of spectacular revues with acrobatic numbers, sketches and CHANSONS, but the main attraction is still the display of naked dancers.

Fontane, Theodor (1819–98), German novelist and critic. During the time he spent in London (1855–59) he studied the popular English theatre of his day in his book *Die Londoner Theater*. He was theatre critic of the *Vossische Zeitung*, 1870–89, in Berlin. He welcomed the realistic tendencies in the acting of the great virtuoso performers of his time and was an advocate of the plays of IBSEN and HAUPTMANN, the first production of whose *Vor Sonnenaufgang* he reviewed in 1889. Complete edition of his reviews: *Sämtliche Werke*, Munich 1959, volume XXII/1–3 (with bibliography).

Fontanne, Lynn (1887–), English-born US actress. She first appeared in London in 1905 before going to New York in 1910. She and her husband LUNT whom she married in 1922 gained a reputation as the best acting couple in the American theatre when they joined the company of the THEATRE GUILD in the '20s. Later some of their most brilliant performances were in plays by SHAW, SHERWOOD (*Reunion in Vienna*, 1931; *Idiot's Delight*,

1936), COWARD (*Design for Living*, 1933; *Quadrille*, 1954) and GIRAUDOUX (*Amphitryon 38*, 1937). In 1959 the Lunts appeared memorably in DÜRRENMATT's *The Visit* at the former Globe Theatre (renamed Lunt-Fontanne) in New York, and later in London.
Bibl: G. Freedley, THE LUNTS, 1957

Fool. Comic character. Originally took two forms: the licensed buffoon of the medieval Feast of Fools, and the Court Fool or King's Jester, often the classical dwarf-buffoon, a permanent member of the Royal Household, whose origins might be traced back to the Court of Haroun-al-Rashid. His traditional costume is a cap with horns and ass's ears, sometimes with bells, covering head and shoulders, particoloured jacket and trousers, tight-fitting, occasionally a tail. He carries a *marotte* or bauble or a bladder filled with dried peas. SHAKESPEARE's 'fools' (*Twelfth Night, King Lear*) derived from the Court jester, by this time already a traditional figure in England.
Bibl: W. Willeford, THE FOOL AND HIS SCEPTRE, 1969

Foote, Samuel (1720–77), English ACTOR-MANAGER and dramatist. He studied at Oxford till lack of money drove him into the theatre in 1744. He had his first success in Dublin. In 1747 he took over the Haymarket Theatre in London, managing to evade the Stage Licensing Act (▷LORD CHAMBERLAIN) by inviting his friends to a dish of tea or chocolate, their invitation cards providing admittance to an entertainment in which he displayed his gifts as a brilliant mimic and parodist of famous personalities (e.g. GARRICK). He was known to his contemporaries as the English ARISTOPHANES. He also used this talent in his plays which were intended to caricature one individual. They were FARCES containing brilliant sketches of contemporary manners: *The Englishman in Paris*, 1753; sequel *The Englishman Returned from Paris*, 1756; *The Minor*, considered his best play, which he staged himself in Dublin, 1760; *The Devil Upon Two Sticks*, 1768; *A Trip to Calais*, 1776. He was given a Royal patent for the Haymarket in 1766. He also wrote theoretical works on the theatre.
Bibl: M. M. Belden, THE DRAMATIC WORKS OF SAMUEL FOOTE, 1929

Forbes-Robertson, Sir Johnston (1853–1937), English ACTOR-MANAGER. Leading actor between the turn of the century and World War I. Son of an art critic and writer, he had successfully trained as a painter when the writer W. G. Wills saw him acting with an amateur company and offered him a contract. He made his professional début as Chasteland in Wills' *Mary Queen of Scots* at the Princess Theatre in 1874. He then took acting lessons with PHELPS, subsequently appearing at all the major London theatres playing juvenile leads, mainly in modern plays until he made his name as a Shakespearean actor, based mainly on two parts: Buckingham in *Henry VIII*, 1892, and the title role in *Hamlet*, 1897. His magnificent performance has classed him among the great Hamlets. He had a fine-featured sensitive face, a voice which, though lacking volume, was well modulated, and had great rhythmical virtuosity. He was also famous for his performances: as Romeo, 1895, with MRS PATRICK CAMPBELL as Juliet; as Macbeth, 1898; in PINERO's *The Second Mrs Tanqueray*; in SHAW's *The Devil's Disciple*, 1900, and *Caesar and Cleopatra*, 1906; as Othello and Shylock. He was knighted in 1913 on his retirement from the stage. He was married to the American actress GERTRUDE ELLIOTT. Other members of his family were also actors; the best known was his daughter **Jean F.-R.** (1905–62), the most famous interpreter of Peter Pan, who also played parts like Puck, Oberon and Jim Hawkins in *Treasure Island*, and excelled in IBSEN's plays.

Ford, John (1586–?1639), English dramatist. Little is known of his life. Early in his career he collaborated with other playwrights, including WEBSTER, DEKKER and ROWLEY, on *The Witch of Edmonton* (with Dekker and Rowley), 1621, and *The Sun's Darling* (with Dekker), 1624. The latter may also have worked with him on his historical play, *Perkin Warbeck*, *c.* 1629–34. F. collaborated as well on plays which were published under the names of other writers. The finest of the plays which he wrote alone are: *The Lover's Melancholy*, 1628, a TRAGICOMEDY; and three TRAGEDIES, *The Broken Heart*, *c.* 1625–33; *Love's Sacrifice*, ?1632; and his masterpiece *'Tis Pity She's a Whore*, 1629–33, which has frequently been revived, notably in VISCONTI's famous production in Paris, *Dommage qu'elle soit putain*, 1961. He exaggerates human weaknesses to the point where they become abnormal. His blank verse is poignant and clear, and his analytical exploration of the human mind owes much to Burton's *Anatomy of Melancholy*.
Bibl: C. Leech, JOHN FORD AND THE DRAMA OF HIS TIME, 1957; T. S. Eliot, ELIZABETHAN DRAMATISTS, 1963

Forrest, Edwin (1806–72), US actor. Perhaps the finest, certainly the most famous American tragic actor of his time. Made his début at the age of 14 as young Norval in the Reverend John Home's *Douglas* and obtained an instant success (Philadelphia 1820). To gain experience he joined a travelling company which took him as far west as Cincinnati, and south to New Orleans. He returned to New York in 1825 where he appeared in the Albany Theatre opposite KEAN. It is said that F. developed his 'gladiatorial', impassioned manner, known as 'the American style' under Kean's influence. In 1826 he achieved his first major success as Othello at the Park Theatre, New York. Among his greatest parts were Jaffier in OTWAY's *Venice Preserved*, the title role in Sheridan Knowles's *William Tell* and as Lear. To encourage American writing talent, but also to get parts written for him, F. sponsored playwriting competitions. These produced, among others, plays like John H. Stone's *Metamora, or The Last of the*

Fool, German engraving of 1635

Johnston Forbes-Robertson as Hamlet, 1897

Edwin Forrest as Spartacus, 1831

Wampanoags, 1829, in which F. appeared in the part of an Indian chief, and Robert M. Bird's *The Gladiators*, 1831, which gave him a fat part in the role of Spartacus. In 1836 he appeared in London at DRURY LANE as Spartacus and achieved a triumph. When in 1845 during a second British tour he failed to repeat this, he suspected MACREADY, his rival as the greatest tragic actor of the time, of having intrigued against him. The bitter enmity between the two actors led in 1849, during Macready's stay in New York, to the famous Astor Place riots. On 8 May 1849 Macready, appearing as Macbeth at the Astor Place Opera House, was compelled by supporters of F. to abandon the stage. On 10 May he appeared again; inside the theatre the audience seemed more friendly towards him, but a large crowd of F. supporters had gathered in the street outside. Stones were thrown against the theatre and, when the situation seemed to be getting out of hand, troops were called in and fired into the crowd with the result that there were 22 dead and 36 wounded. The suspicion that he may have had a part in causing this incident (although never proven) remained with F. to the end of his life. He continued to appear with great acclaim in his most popular parts until 1865 when a partial paralysis diminished his acting ability. He retired alone to the vast house he had built for himself in his native Philadelphia. The Edwin Forrest Actors Home was founded there.
Bibl: R. Moody, 1960

Fort, Paul (1872–1960), French writer, director and theatre manager. Leading symbolist who founded the Théâtre d'Art (formerly Théâtre Mixte), a theatre of painters and poets, when only 18 years old, as a reaction to ANTOINE's naturalistic theatre (▷SYMBOLISM). He set anti-naturalistic plays in a symbolic décor, but after two years of this enterprise his only success was MAETERLINCK's *Les Aveugles*, 1891, and he gave up the theatre. He was succeeded by LUGNÉ-POË.

Fortune Theatre. Elizabethan theatre in London. A second and more modern theatre for the ADMIRAL'S MEN, successor to the Rose Theatre, financed by HENSLOWE. A square open building, it was opened in 1600 north of the City of London. It was burnt down in 1621, rebuilt and in use until 1642. Above the entrance door there was a statue of the goddess Fortuna.

Foyer (Fr=fireplace). The area in the theatre between the outer lobby and the auditorium reserved for the use of the audience during the intervals; first found in the opera house at Versailles, the last major COURT THEATRE in France, built in 1753.

France. First secular drama in the late 13th century ADAM DE LA HALLE; in the 14th and 15th centuries SOTIES and FARCES, e.g. *Maistre Pierre Pathelin*, anonymous *c.* 1470, played by semi-professional companies. In the 16th century, emergence of professional theatre; TRAGEDIES by JODELLE, COMEDIES by Pierre Larivey, influenced by the COMMEDIA DELL' ARTE. The French theatre reached its first high point in the 17th century with the tragedies of CORNEILLE (*Le Cid*, 1637) and RACINE and the comedies of MOLIÈRE; founding of the French National Theatre, the COMÉDIE-FRANÇAISE, through the fusion of leading French companies in 1680. In the 18th century the CF established itself as the leading European theatre of its time, with the outstanding actors: MLLE LECOUVREUR, MLLE CLAIRON, MLLE DUMESNIL, LEKAIN and TALMA. In addition to the works of classical dramatists such as CRÉBILLON and VOLTAIRE and the comedy-writer MARIVAUX, there was the DRAME BOURGEOIS of DESTOUCHES and DIDEROT, and towards the end of the 18th century, as precursors of the Revolution, the comedies of BEAUMARCHAIS (*Le Mariage de Figaro*, 1784). During the Revolution the CF ceased to hold a monopoly, and numerous private theatres emerged, situated mainly on the boulevards, most famous among them the Odéon; they competed with the CF, which in 1812 was given the status of a state theatre by Napoleon.
The Revolution did not produce any specific form of drama and it was not until the Romantic movement and its most representative writers, DUMAS *père*, VIGNY and HUGO, that the theatre received fresh impetus; most outstanding writer of comedy at that time was MUSSET. The great number of theatres and the fame of certain actors assisted the development of what was called the WELL-MADE PLAY, a class of drama perfected by SCRIBE. About the middle of the 19th century criticism of social conditions found its voice in the works of AUGIER and DUMAS *fils*; the tradition of Scribe was continued by SARDOU. Decisive social commitment came from the Théâtre Libre of ANTOINE; one of his most important authors was the naturalistic writer BECQUE; as a counter movement to NATURALISM the symbolist dramas of the Belgian writer MAETERLINCK and the Théâtre de L'Œuvre directed by LUGNÉ-POË.
The beginning of the 20th century was largely dominated by the traditions of the previous century; it was not until COPEAU founded the Théâtre du Vieux-Colombier in 1913 that a new epoch began; here theatre was reduced to bare essentials, with emphasis on text and gesture. Besides Copeau's pupils DULLIN and JOUVET (who first staged plays by GIRAUDOUX), BATY and PITOËFF were the most influential figures in French theatre until World War II. Dullin's pupil BARRAULT left the CF in 1946 with the actress MADELEINE RENAUD to form his own company (the Compagnie Renaud-Barrault in the Marigny, later, 1959–68, at the THÉÂTRE DE FRANCE in the Odéon) as the second national theatre. Among the most outstanding dramatists of the 1940s were: ANOUILH, SARTRE, CAMUS; and the dramatists of the THEATRE OF THE ABSURD (IONESCO, BECKETT and GENET). Attempts to form a popular theatre (THÉÂTRE NATIONAL POPULAIRE) were made by VILAR and his successor G. WILSON; since *c.* 1954 there has been strong influence by the guest appearances by the BERLINER ENSEMBLE, especially in the regional Théâtre de la Cité de Villeurbanne at Lyons under PLANCHON; attempts towards cultural decentralization by founding of regional CENTRES DRAMATIQUES. In 1974 the total subsidy to all national theatres was 109,508,320 francs.
Bibl: W. Fowlie, A GUIDE TO CONTEMPORARY FRENCH LITERATURE FROM VALÉRY TO SARTRE, 1972; G. Wellwarth, THEATRE OF PROTEST AND PARADOX, 1964; L. C. Pronko, AVANT-GARDE, THE EXPERIMENTAL THEATER IN FRANCE, 1962; R. Lalou, LE THÉÂTRE EN FRANCE DEPUIS 1900, 1951; M. Turnell, THE CLASSICAL MONUMENT, 1947, 2 vols; H. C. Lancaster, A HISTORY OF FRENCH DRAMATIC LITERATURE IN THE 17TH CENTURY, 1929–42, 9 vols; G. Cohen, LE THÉÂTRE EN FRANCE AU MOYEN AGE, 1928–31, 2 vols

Frank, Bruno (1887–1945), German novelist, dramatist, poet and short-story writer. Originally an Expressionist, he later turned to the technique of the WELL-MADE PLAY: *Die treue Magd* (The Faithful Girl), Vienna 1916, BURGTHEATER; *Bibikopf* (based on DOSTOYEVSKY), 1921; *Zwölftausend* (Twelve Thousand), BERLIN 1926, New York 1928, London 1931, dir REINHARDT, with KRAUSS and STEINRÜCK, which concerned the sale of soldiers by German princes in the 18th century; *Sturm im Wasserglas* (adapted by BRIDIE as *Storm in a Teacup*), Dresden 1930; *Der General und das Gold* (The General and the Gold), Munich Kammerspiele 1932; dir FALCKENBERG, with BASSERMANN. He emigrated in 1933 and after 1939 lived in the USA, where he died.

Fraser, Claude Lovat (1890–1921), English graphic artist and stage designer. Achieved his greatest success with the sets and costumes for PLAYFAIR's production of GAY's *The Beggar's Opera* at the Lyric, Hammersmith, 1920. The panache of his style, characterized by bright colours, had considerable influence on the development of British stage design.

Freie Bühne. Founded in 1889 in Berlin as a society for private production of plays which would otherwise have been censored. Founder members were: BRAHM, HARDEN, REICHER, SCHLENTHER, etc. Since they had no theatre of their own, they rented one for matinées and opened with IBSEN's *Ghosts* in 1889. The first German play given there was HAUPTMANN's *Vor Sonnenaufgang*, 1889. The Freie Bühne advocated a theatre of dramatic realism with plays of the new naturalistic school of writers – modelled on ANTOINE's Théâtre Libre. In 1894 with the amalgamation of the Freie Bühne and the Deutsches-Theater – under Brahm – it fulfilled its aims. Brahm formed a permanent company with Reicher as chief actor. The magazine *Freie Bühne für modernes Leben*, founded in 1890 by Brahm, was from 1894 published under the title *Neue Deutsche Rundschau* and after 1904 *Neue Rundschau*. Some of the founders of the Freie Bühne were also founders of the VOLKSBÜHNE.

Bibl: G. Schley, DIE FREIE BÜHNE IN BERLIN, 1967

Freie Volksbühne ▷VOLKSBÜHNE.

Fresnay, Pierre (Pierre-Jules-Louis Laudenbach; 1897–1975), French actor. In 1915, at the age of 18, he appeared at the COMÉDIE-FRANÇAISE in RACINE's *Britannicus*; in 1923 he became a SOCIÉTAIRE, but left the CF in 1926 to work as a freelance actor in the theatre and in films. He appeared very successfully in PAGNOL's *Marius*, 1929, also in the film version, made in 1931, and in the film sequels *Fanny*, 1932, and *César*, 1933. For a short time he was with the COMPAGNIE DES QUINZE, appearing in OBEY's *Noé* and in plays by two new playwrights, C. A. Pouget and ANOUILH (*L'Hermine*, 1932). In 1932 he married the actress Yvonne Printemps, who took over the management of the Théâtre de la Michodière. He acted there and produced Anouilh's *Léocadia*, 1940; ACHARD's *Auprès de ma blonde*, 1946, and *Bille en tête*, by Fresnay's son R. Laudenbach, 1957. He was one of the leading French actors of his generation, whose controlled and sensitive acting lost nothing in intensity in his transition from the juvenile hero of the CF to the character actor of his later years. An important film actor, his main pictures were: *Le Roman d'un jeune homme pauvre, La Grande Illusion*, dir Jean Renoir; *Le Duel*; *Le Corbeau*, dir Clouzot; *Le Voyageur sans bagage* by Anouilh; *Monsieur Vincent*.

Freytag, Gustav (1816–95), German novelist and dramatist. Author of several COMEDIES, of which *Die Journalisten*, 1852, a portrayal of party politics, is still produced today in Germany. He was also an important dramatic theoretician of the 19th-century WELL-MADE PLAY. His *Die Technik des Dramas*, 1863, is an excellent analysis of the rules of craftsmanship of plot construction.
Bibl: J. Hofmann, 1922

Friedell, Egon (1878–1938), Austrian writer and actor. Artistic director, 1908–10, of the CABARET Die Fledermaus in Vienna; 1919–22 drama critic; 1922–27 character actor at REINHARDT's theatres in Vienna and Berlin, subsequently mainly successful as writer, essayist, witty aphorist, dramatist (*Die Judastragödie*, 1920) and cultural historian, who wrote an important and influential *Cultural History of Europe*. He committed suicide when the Germans occupied Vienna. His essays on the theatre and some of his cabaret pieces are collected in *Wozu das Theater?*, 1965.

Frigerio, Ezio (1930–), Italian stage and costume designer. Started as a painter. From 1955 with STREHLER's company at the PICCOLO TEATRO DI MILANO, first as costume designer (BRECHT's *The Threepenny Opera*, 1956; *The Good Woman of Setzuan*, 1950; PIRANDELLO's *I giganti della montagna*, first staged in Düsseldorf 1958, and in Milan 1966), and after 1958 also as stage designer (GOLDONI's *Il Servitore di due Padroni*, 1958). He worked with Strehler

France, *Le Malade imaginaire* by MOLIÈRE, 1674, performed at Versailles

France, uproar during the first night of HUGO's *Hernani*, at the COMÉDIE-FRANÇAISE, painting by Albert Bernard

C. Lovat Fraser, costume designs for *The Beggar's Opera* by GAY, prod PLAYFAIR, 1920

on all his productions, but also with other directors including DE FILIPPO, SQUARZINA, PUECHER, BOSIO, J. QUAGLIO and B. Menegatti. His designs incorporate his experience as a painter, and his work in collaboration with the designers M. Chiari and DAMIANI and with Strehler: they are extremely functional and influenced by the Venetian painters of the 16th century.

Friml, Rudolf (1879–1972), composer of MUSICAL COMEDIES. Born in Prague, he became naturalized in the USA in 1925. Among his immensely successful musicals were *Rose Marie*, 1924 with lyrics by HAMMERSTEIN II; *The Vagabond King*, 1925, and *The Three Musketeers*, 1928. The 'Indian Love Call' (from *Rose Marie*) and 'Only a Rose' (from *The Vagabond King*) are among his numerous hit tunes which swept the world.

Frisch, Max (1911–), Swiss playwright, novelist, journalist and architect. With DÜRRENMATT, considered one of the leading contemporary Swiss dramatists and one of the most influential writers in contemporary European theatre. His plays stress the inability of man to control his destiny in the face of external events. He questions the habits and convictions of the average human being, and decries the tendency to treat the image we build up of other people as definitive. He uses the widest variety of anti-illusionist theatrical forms, at one time borrowing the psychological sensitivity of STRINDBERG, at another the structures of BRECHT. He began with poetic dream plays: *Nun singen sie wieder* (Now They Sing Again), 1945, dir HORWITZ; *Santa Cruz*, 1946, dir HILPERT; *Die chinesische Mauer* (*The Chinese Wall*), 1946, dir STECKEL, a FARCE about man's inability to learn to avoid the danger of total annihilation; the naturalistic play *Als der Krieg zu Ende war* (*When the War was Over*), 1948, dir Horwitz, all at the ZURICH SCHAUSPIELHAUS; the MORALITY PLAY *Graf Öderland* (1st version: Zurich 1951; 2nd version: Frankfurt 1956, Städtische Bühnen; 3rd version: BERLIN 1961, Schillertheater); the brilliant conversational COMEDY *Don Juan oder die Liebe zur Geometrie* (Don Juan or the Love of Geometry), Zurich and Berlin, Schillertheater, 1953, shows the great lover as more interested in mathematics than amorous adventures; the parable *Biedermann und die Brandstifter* (*The Fire Raisers*), Zurich 1958; *Andorra*, Zurich 1961, dir HIRSCHFELD, des OTTO. *Andorra* is considered the most successful post-war German play; first performances in Germany took place simultaneously in Munich, Hamburg and Düsseldorf. In his most recent play *Biografie* (Biography), Zurich 1968, dir LINDTBERG, des Otto, F. deals with the unpredictability of life.
Bibl: U. Weisstein, 1968; H. Banziger, FRISCH UND DÜRRENMATT, 2/1962; H. F. Garten, MODERN GERMAN DRAMA, 1959

Fritellino. Stock character of the COMMEDIA DELL'ARTE, a variant of ARLECCHINO, created by CECCHINI. Costume: white jacket and trousers, brown half-mask, with a beard, a wooden sword and a belt with a pouch.

Frohman. (1) **Charles** (1860–1915), US theatre manager. The first to make consistent use of the advantages of transferring productions between New York and London, he achieved remarkable success in both cities. After his first visit to England in 1880, he became business manager of Haverley's Minstrels; started his own production company in New York and became a manager, a dramatic agent and an organizer of touring companies. He made his breakthrough with *Shenandoah*, 1888–89, by B. HOWARD; in 1890 he founded his own STOCK COMPANY, and with it opened the Empire Theatre in 1893. His first London success came in 1896 with *A Night Out* at the Vaudeville; he subsequently took EDWARDES'S MUSICAL COMEDIES and BARRIE'S plays to the USA. At one time he controlled five theatres in London, including the Duke of York's where his notable productions included *Peter Pan*, 1904. He had six theatres under his control in New York at the time of his death (he was drowned when the *Lusitania* was torpedoed in 1915). His brother (2) **Daniel F.** (1851–1940), a journalist in his early days, became business manager of the Madison Square Theatre in 1880 and went into management on his own in 1885 taking over the Lyceum Theatre in New York and producing plays by PINERO and H. A. JONES. He also managed DALY'S Theatre in New York, 1899–1903. He fostered the career of BELASCO and, in 1912, with Zukor and Loew Enterprises, founded the Players Film Company. Wrote autobiographical works including: *Memoirs of a Manager*, 1911; *Daniel Frohman Presents*, 1935; *Encore*, 1937.
Bibl: I. F. Marcosson & D. Frohman, CHARLES FROHMAN: MANAGER AND MAN, 1916

Fry, Christopher (1907–), English dramatist and poet. Shares responsibility with ELIOT for the revival of VERSE DRAMA in England in the 1950s. Began his career as a teacher, actor and director with amateur companies, wrote PAGEANTS and religious plays for performances in church (*Youth and the Peregrines, The Boy with a Cart, Thursday's Child, The Town, The Firstborn*), almost all written between 1924 and 1946 and originally produced by amateur companies; later some were produced by professional companies. His breakthrough as a playwright came with his one-act verse comedy *A Phoenix Too Frequent*, fp 1946, Mercury Theatre, for the E. MARTIN BROWNE season of verse plays, followed by the first in his TETRALOGY of the seasons, *The Lady's Not for Burning*, fp 1948, Arts Theatre Club, with GIELGUD and Pamela Brown, transferred to the West End in 1949. For the Canterbury Festival he wrote *Thor, With Angels*, 1948. His next play, written for OLIVIER, was *Venus Observed*, 1950, the second in the tetralogy, followed by a biblical play *A Sleep of Prisoners*, 1951, performed at St Thomas's Church, Regent Street, which has frequently been revived. In 1954 EDITH EVANS starred in *The Dark is Light Enough*, the third in the tetralogy. For a period he stopped writing plays, and translated and adapted ANOUILH'S *L'Invitation au château* as *Ring Round the Moon*, 1950, *L'Alouette* as *The Lark*, 1955, and GIRAUDOUX'S *La Guerre de Troie n'aura pas lieu* as *Tiger at the Gates*, 1955. He wrote the historical play *Curtmantle*, 1961, about Henry II and *Thomas à Becket*, fp Tilburg (in Dutch), then produced by the RSC, Aldwych. The last in his tetralogy of the seasons was *A Yard of Sun*, fp Nottingham 1970. He has also written many screen plays.
Bibl: D. Stanford, 1952

Fuchs, Georg (1868–1949), German dramatic theorist. In *Die Schaubühne der Zukunft*, 1904, he advocated the 'theatricalization' of the theatre and tried to realize his ideas in the Munich Künstlertheater, built by LITTMANN in collaboration with the director Zavrel and the painter Fritz Erler. He also translated CALDERÓN and SHAKESPEARE, and wrote a Passion play *Christus*, 1916.

Fuentes, Giorgio (1756–1821), Italian theatre painter. Worked in Frankfurt 1796–1805. GOETHE tried unsuccessfully in 1797 to persuade him to come to Weimar. He was the last major exponent of the painted stage, achieving a pure classical line and historical authenticity.

Fugard, Athol (1932–), South African dramatist. Born in Cape Province of an English-speaking South African father and an Afrikaans-speaking mother. He left Cape Town University before finishing his philosophy course to travel in Africa and the Far East, but returned to South Africa to work as a journalist; left journalism to work in the theatre. His sympathy with the non-white people in South Africa is the basis for nearly all his work and in 1967 the Government withdrew his passport. He now lives in Port Elizabeth, which is the setting of most of his plays. He first gained recognition with his play *No-Good Friday*, which was followed by *Nogogo*, 1960; *The Blood Knot*, 1961, London 1966, Hampstead Theatre Club; *People Are Living There*, 1968; *Hello and Goodbye*, 1969, and *Boesman and Lena*, London 1971, Royal Court Theatre Upstairs. He directed a season of South African plays at the ROYAL COURT THEATRE, London 1974, experiments in play-making, in which he collaborated with the actors who performed in these plays: *The Island, Sizwe Bansi is Dead* and *Statements after an Arrest under the Immorality Act*. In 1976, his play *Dimetos* with SCOFIELD was produced at the Comedy Theatre.

Fulda, Ludwig (1862–1939), German dramatist. Originally influenced by NATURALISM (one of the founders of the FREIE BÜHNE, Berlin): *Die Aufrichtigen* (The Honest Ones), 1883; *Das Recht der Frauen* (The Right of Women), 1888. Later plays: (in verse) *Der Talisman*, 1893; (a romantic COMEDY) *Der heimliche König* (The Secret King), 1906; attractive BOULEVARD plays, e.g. *Die verlorene Tochter* (The Lost

Daughter), 1916, etc. Also a well-known translator of works by IBSEN (*Peer Gynt*), BEAUMARCHAIS, MOLIÈRE, GOLDONI, and of several Spanish comedies.
Bibl: A. Klaar, 1922

Furttenbach, Josef (1591–1667), German theatre architect. Studied in Italy and edited several works on Italian theatre architecture: *Architectura civilis*, 1628; *Mannhaffter Kunstspiegel*, 1663. He built the first German municipal theatre, the Theater am Binderhof in Ulm (1641).

Futurism. Literary and artistic movement which originated in Italy *c.* 1909, expounded by F. T. Marinetti in manifestos which celebrate technology, speed and automation: 'with Futurism art has become action, as will, attack, possession, penetration, joy and brutal reality'. A symbiosis of art and life phrased in a dynamic, rhetorical gesture. The Futurists rejoiced in irrationality, adventure and war. Marinetti's 'poèmes' which tend towards onomatopoeia and the abstraction of logic and content were recited at Futurist soirées (the first in Turin, 1910). These concepts were used in painting, music (brutish noise concerts by L. Russolo) and the theatre (First Manifesto in 1913, Second Manifesto in 1915), with mechanical ballet, rapidly changing lighting and sudden noises, performances of spectacular variety. Most important Futurist theatre work: *Feu d'artifice*, music Stravinsky, Ballets Russes, Rome 1917, for which the painter Giacomo Balla designed sculptural forms lit from the inside to move in rhythm to the music on stage. Futurism declined during World War I. Futurist theatrical experiments in the development of the mechanical ballet were made by Fortunato Depero, *Balli plastici*, Rome 1918, and PRAMPOLINI, mainly in Paris, also a stage designer.
Bibl: F. T. Marinetti, IL TEATRO FUTURISTA, 1941; M. Kirby, FUTURIST PERFORMANCE, 1971

Fyffe, Will (1885–1947), Scottish music-hall comedian. Started as an actor and achieved immense popularity as a brilliant character comic and singer of comic songs. He also appeared with great success in PANTOMIME.

Gabrielli. Family of COMMEDIA DELL'ARTE actors. (1) **Giovanni G.** (?–between 1603 and 1611) known as Sivello, was a great mimic, who could impersonate the characters of a whole company. His son (2) **Francesco G.** (1588–1636) created the character of Scapino, toured Italy and

Christopher Fry's *A Yard of Sun*, in rehearsal at the Nottingham Playhouse, 1970, Fry second left

Athol Fugard's *The Island*, ROYAL COURT THEATRE, 1974

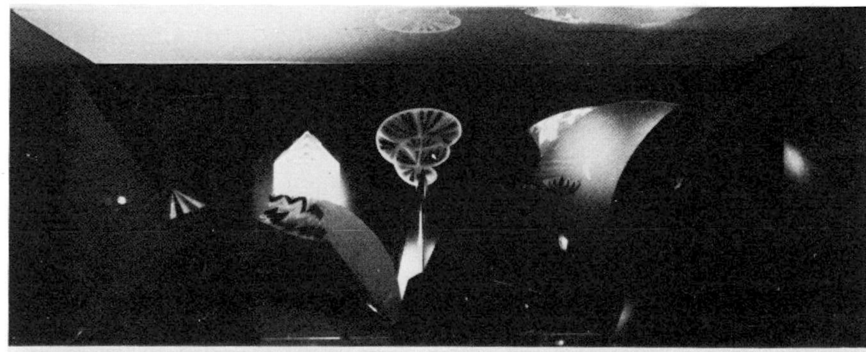

Futurism, a reconstruction of a stage setting for the ballet *Feu d'Artifice*, 1917, directed by Diaghilev in Rome

France (1624–25 in Paris with G. B. ANDREINI) appearing mainly with the ACCESI company; most famous were his musical numbers.
Bibl: N. Leonelli, ATTORI TRAGICI E ATTORI COMICI ITALIANI, 1940

Gade, Svend (1877–1952), Swedish stage designer and director. Worked in Oslo and Stockholm, 1898–1904, and 1904–23 in BERLIN, mainly at theatres under the management of Meinhard and Bernauer. In his stage designs he concentrated on tableaux based on simplified Realism: STRINDBERG's *A Dream Play*, fp 1915. At the Royal Theatre of Copenhagen, 1930–47. He also wrote a book of reminiscences *Mit Livs Drejescene* (My Life's Revolving Stage), 1941.

Gallery. (1) The cheapest seats in the theatre, usually upper balcony (sometimes one of two such balconies). (2) Any raised working platform at the side or rear of the stage. Also fly-gallery from which scenery is 'flown' until required when it is lowered into position.

Galliari. Italian family of stage designers. (1) **Bernardino G.** (1707–94), (2) **Fabrizio G.** (1709–90) and (3) **Giovanni Antonio G.** (1714–83). Their works, on most of which they collaborated, fall between the Baroque and Classical styles. In 1778 they designed the opening production of the new Teatro alla Scala in Milan.

Galli-Bibiena. Italian family of theatre architects and designers. (1) **Giovanni Maria Galli** (1619–65). (2) **Ferdinando** (1657–1743), son of Giovanni, was the first theatre architect at the Court of Vienna, 1712–26; designed the COURT THEATRE in Mantua; author of the famous book *L' Architettura civile*, Parma, 1711. (3) **Francesco** (1659–1739) Ferdinando's brother, also became theatre architect in Vienna and designed the theatres in Nancy and Verona. (4) **Alessandro** (1687–1769), eldest son of Ferdinando, worked from 1726 at the Mannheim Court Theatre. (5) **Giuseppe** (1696–1757), second son of Ferdinando, probably the most outstanding member of the family, first collaborated with his father in Vienna, then succeeded him in 1727; he was the creator of the Castle Garden Theatre in Prague, 1723, and of the Margrave's Opera House in Bayreuth, 1744–48, which is among the few BAROQUE THEATRES preserved; stage and auditorium are harmoniously constructed and form a perfect unity. After his activities at the Dresden Court Theatre, 1748–54, he worked for two years at the Royal theatres in BERLIN; some of his designs for stage theatre architecture can be found in his book of copper engravings *Architetture e Prospective*, 1740. (6) **Antonio** (1700–74), third son of Ferdinando, also worked in Vienna, where he designed the Redoutensaal in the Hofburg in 1743; from 1750 he worked in Italy. (7) **Giovanni Maria** (1704–69) youngest son of Ferdinando, worked in Austria, Italy, Spain and Portugal. (8) **Carlo** (1725–87), youngest son of Giuseppe, the last member of this important family, with whose work the late Baroque art of stage design reached its peak; mastery of perspective is the most outstanding characteristic of their art.
Bibl: A. Hyatt-Mayor, THE BIBIENA FAMILY, 1945; H. Tintelnot, BAROCK-THEATER UND BAROCKE KUNST, 1939

Gallmeyer, Josephine (1838–84), Austrian actress and singer. She made her début in the theatre at the age of 15 in Brno and first achieved major success in 1862 in a small part at the Theater an der Wien. She established her reputation as the most admired comic actress in light opera and COMEDY of her time in 1865 at the Carltheater in Vienna (Offenbach's *La Vie parisienne*); her finest, and last appearance was as Rosa in RAIMUND's *Der Verschwender* (The Spendthrift). She also wrote two plays: *Aus purem Hass* (Out of Pure Hate), 1883, and *Sarah Bernhardt*, 1884, a parody.

Galsworthy, John (1867–1933), English dramatist and novelist, author of the series of novels called *The Forsyte Saga*. Under the influence of SHAW he dealt with social topics of the time in precise realistic plays; in his first play *The Silver Box*, fp ROYAL COURT THEATRE under the management of VEDRENNE/BARKER, 1906, he showed the injustice of the law to the poor; it was followed by *Strife*, 1909, the story of a strike; *Justice*, 1910, which established his fame as a dramatist. Till about 1926 he continued to write plays, in which social concerns increasingly predominated: *The Skin Game*, 1920; *Loyalties*, 1922; *Windows*, 1922; *The Forest*, 1924; *Escape*, 1926. He was awarded the Order of Merit in 1929 and received the Nobel Prize for Literature in 1932.
Bibl: J. Russell Taylor, THE RISE AND FALL OF THE WELL-MADE PLAY, 1967; H. V. Marrot, THE LIFE AND LETTERS OF JOHN GALSWORTHY, 1935

Ganassa, Zan (Alberto Naseli; *c.*1540–*c.* 1584), actor of the COMMEDIA DELL'ARTE. He was among the first to take a company abroad; he was in Paris from 1572, then toured Spain on frequent occasions over a period of about ten years.
Bibl: J. V. Falcinieri, UNA HISTORIA DE LA COMMEDIA DELL'ARTE EN ESPAÑA, 1958

Garden Theatre. Special form of BAROQUE THEATRE, produced at summer festivities first with improvised buildings, then permanent sitings were constructed in the parks of palaces or country houses. Plants and trees in the garden were incorporated into the stage set. Later, proscenium arches of stone were erected partly formed as ruins. Best-known examples: BUEN RETIRO, near Madrid; Boboli Gardens, Florence; and in GERMANY, Herrenhausen near Hanover, 1690, Dresden, 1719 and Nymphenburg, 1720.
Bibl: R. Meyer, HECKEN UND GARTEN-THEATER IN DEUTSCHLAND, 1933

Garrick Club. Established by the Duke of Sussex, who also acted as patron when the club opened in London in 1831. Its present premises opened in 1864. It is restricted to about 800 members who include great names of the English stage (though originally it admitted no actors, who were regarded as socially inferior); it has a famous collection of theatre portraits.

Garrick, David (1717–79), English actor, dramatist and theatre manager of Huguenot descent. One of England's greatest actors of all time, he began his career with amateur companies, and created a sensation with his début as SHAKESPEARE's Richard III in Goodman's Fields, London 1741. Opposed to the declamatory and elaborate style fashionable at the time, he relied on simplicity and freshness, basing his acting on sharp observation. Described as being 'a small man of middle height, with good mobile features and flashing expressive eyes' his style was easy and familiar, yet forcible in speaking and acting with 'the concurring expression of the features from the genuine workings of nature' (Davies). He was unsurpassed in his playing of tragic heroes of the contemporary theatre and also Shakespearean leads such as Hamlet, Macbeth, Romeo, Henry IV and particularly Lear. He was also much admired in comedy, including Abel Drugger in *The Alchemist*, Benedick in *Much Ado About Nothing*, Bayes in *The Rehearsal*. He joined DRURY LANE theatre in 1742 and became associate manager in 1746. Some years later he took over the management which he retained until his retirement in 1776. He introduced many reforms in the English theatre, the most important of which were: banishing the audience from the stage, technical innovations like concealed STAGE LIGHTING, and naturalistically painted backdrops. He was a competent dramatist, and his plays include: *Miss in Her Teens*, 1747; and *Bon Ton; or High Life Above Stairs*, 1775. He also adapted plays, e.g. WYCHERLEY's *The Country Wife* (retitled *The Country Girl*) and SHAKESPEARE. His collaboration with other writers included the well-known play *The Clandestine Marriage*, 1766, with COLMAN the elder. He was buried in Westminster Abbey.
Bibl: K. A. Burnim, DAVID GARRICK, DIRECTOR, 1961; C. Oman, 1958

Gaskill, William (1930–), English director. Began as a TV director; produced for the ENGLISH STAGE COMPANY at the ROYAL COURT THEATRE, which he joined in 1957 and of which he later became associate director; *Epitaph for George Dillon* by OSBORNE and Anthony Creighton, 1958; and three plays by SIMPSON, *A Resounding Tinkle*, *The Hole*, and *One Way Pendulum*. Then followed SHAKESPEARE productions for the RSC at Stratford-upon-Avon including *Richard III*, *Cymbeline*, 1961; at the Aldwych Theatre BRECHT's *The Caucasian Chalk Circle*, 1962; subsequently he managed the Actors' Studio at the Royal Court; with DEXTER, at the NATIONAL THEATRE, 1963–65, where he directed FARQUHAR's *The Recruiting Officer*, 1963, and Brecht's *Mother Courage*, 1965. In 1965 he succeeded DEVINE as director of the English Stage Co.

Gaslight. Used for the first time in the theatre in 1817 at DRURY LANE. It was easier to regulate than the earlier oil-lighting and gave more light, but it was the cause of many fires; today its use is prohibited. ▷ STAGE LIGHTING.

Gassman, Vittorio (1922–), Italian ACTOR-MANAGER. His début in Milan in 1943 in Niccodemi's *Nemica* made him a star of the Italian theatre; his athletic figure, perfectly modulated voice, his romantic flair and enormous talent, also for comic roles, made him exceptional in contemporary Italian theatre. Immediately after his first success he played with leading companies directed by SQUARZINA (A. MILLER's *All My Sons*; *Antony* by DUMAS *père*, 1947–48) and by VISCONTI (Orlando in *As You Like It*, Stanley Kowalski in T. WILLIAMS's *A Streetcar Named Desire*, and in ALFIERI's *Oreste*, 1948–49). Among his productions, in most of which he starred himself, were IBSEN's *Peer Gynt* and BETTI's *Il Giocatore*, both at the Teatro Nazionale 1950–51; 1951–53 he managed the Teatro dell'Arti together with Squarzina in a REPERTORY of first productions of new plays and classical TRAGEDIES, most famous of which were *Hamlet* and *The Persians* (AESCHYLUS). Among his best parts are the title role in ALFIERI's *Oreste*, Kean in SARTRE's play based on DUMAS, Othello and Iago, 1956–57 alternating the roles with RANDONE; he toured Paris, London and Latin America. He made several attempts to popularize the theatre, founded the Teatro Popolare Italiano on the lines of VILAR's TNP and toured the provinces in 1960–61 (with MANZONI's *Adelchi*). He brought his company to London in 1963 with a production called *The Heroes*, consisting of excerpts from his REPERTOIRE. Also a well-known film actor, reciter and essayist.

Gassner, John Waldhorn (1903–69), Hungarian-born US drama critic. Lecturer at the THEATRE GUILD in 1930. Worked as a critic 1935–43; also professor at Columbia University and the Yale School of Drama; his students included T. WILLIAMS and A. MILLER. Editor of several anthologies: *A Treasury of the Theatre*, 1935; a series of *Twenty Best Plays of the Modern American Theatre*, 1939. His critical and theoretical works include: *Masters of the Drama*, 1940; *Producing a Play*, 1941; *The Theatre in Our Time*, 1954; *The Reader's Encyclopedia of World Drama*, 1969 (with Edward Quinn).

Gatti, Armand (1924–), French dramatist, journalist and film scriptwriter. His plays have open dramatic structures, discontinuous short scenes, and the cutting, in film-editing style, is reminiscent of a William Faulkner novel; PLOT is replaced by the simultaneous juxtaposition of objective and subjective reality, memories, external realities and visionary images. In all his plays G. expresses his humanitarian socialism in sympathy with the oppressed – the working class, prisoners, and the exploited peoples of the Third World. His dramatic works include: *La Vie imaginaire*

Galli-Bibiena, stage design

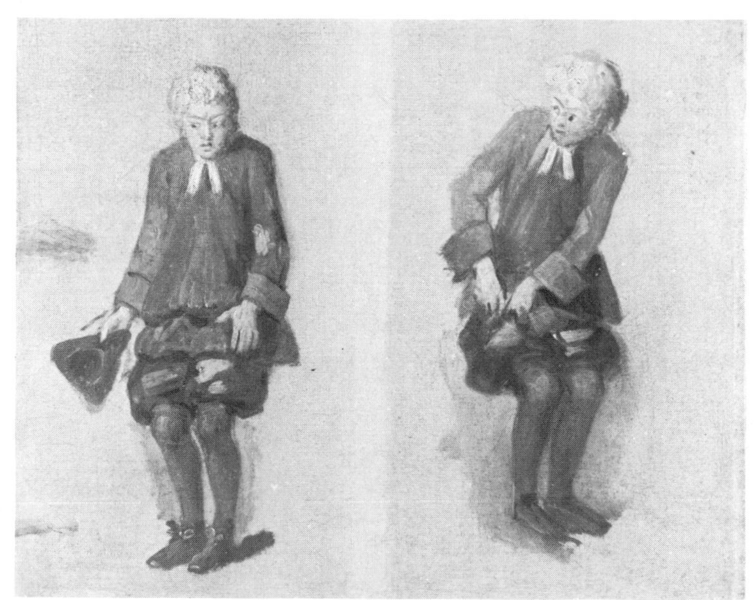

David Garrick as Abel Drugger in *The Alchemist* by JONSON, 1769, oil sketch by Zoffany.

de l'éboueur Auguste Geai, 1956, fp Lyons 1962; *Le Poisson noir*, 1957, fp Toulouse 1964; *Le Crapaud-buffle*, fp Paris 1959, TNP; *Le Voyage du Grand Tchou*, fp Marseilles 1962; *La Deuxième existence du camp de Tatenberg*, fp Lyons 1962; *Chronique d'une planète provisoire*, fp Toulouse 1963; *Chant publique devant deux chaises électriques*, fp Paris 1966, TNP; *Un homme seul*, fp Saint-Etienne 1966; *Les Passions du Général Franco*, fp Kassel 1967; *V comme Vietnam*, fp Toulouse 1967; *La Naissance*, 1968; *Les 13 soleils de la rue Saint-Blaise*, 1968. He has also directed films, e.g. the prize-winning *L'Enclos*.
Bibl: M. Corvin, LE THÉÂTRE NOUVEAU EN FRANCE, 1963

Gautier, Théophile (1811–72), French novelist, poet, dramatic critic and playwright. One of the supporters of the Romantic movement in the French theatre, he organized a CLAQUE to support HUGO at the famous first night of *Hernani* in 1830. He himself wrote only a few insignificant plays, mostly in collaboration, but his influence as a critic was immense. A collection of his notices appeared in six volumes in Paris, 1858–59, under the title *Histoire dramatique en France depuis vingt-cing ans*. Gautier was also a devotee of ballet, and one of the founders of serious ballet criticism; he was deeply in love with the ballerina Carlotta Grisi whom he met in 1841. Some of the ballet scenarios he wrote are still in the standard REPERTOIRE, notably *Giselle ou les Wilis*, music Adam, fp Paris 1841, and *La Péri*, music Burgmüller, fp 1843.
Bibl: J. Richardson, THÉOPHILE GAUTIER, HIS LIFE AND TIMES, 1958; S. Lifar, GISELLE, 1942

Gavella, Branko (1885–1962), Yugoslav director. He is noted for his craftsmanship and technical expertise, e.g. rotating cylindrical sets designed by Babic for his production of *As You Like It*, Zagreb 1924. Apart from directing plays of classical world literature, he revived the work of native playwrights and staged first productions of contemporary dramatists, e.g. KRLEŽA. He also worked as a producer in theatres in Prague, Sofia and Milan.

Gay, John (1685–1732), English poet and playwright. Came to London from his native Devon to make his fortune as a poet and journalist and became a member of the circle around Pope and Swift. His plays include: *The Mohocks, A Tragi-Comical Farce*, 1712; *The What d'ye Call It: A Tragi-Comic Pastoral Farce*, 1715; *Three Hours after Marriage* (in collaboration with Pope and Arbuthnot), 1717; but his main claim to fame is *The Beggar's Opera*, music mainly based on popular folk-tunes and arranged by Pepusch, fp Lincoln's Inn Fields, London 1728, which created the genre of the BALLAD OPERA and caused a political sensation by satirizing the government of Sir Robert Walpole in the shape of a thieves' kitchen. *Polly*, 1729, a sequel, was banned. *The Beggar's Opera* has been frequently revived; it inspired BRECHT's *The Threepenny Opera*, music WEILL, 1928.
Bibl: S. Armens, 1954; B. H. Bronson, THE BEGGAR'S OPERA, 1941

Gélin, Daniel (1921–), French actor. Best known as a film actor (since 1941), also a star of the Paris BOULEVARD THEATRE; his outstanding performances have been in M. ANDERSON's *Winterset*, 1964; PRIESTLEY's *Dangerous Corner*, 1948, and a dramatization of Simenon's novel *La Neige était sale*, 1950; less successful as a tragic actor, e.g. Antiochus in CORNEILLE's *Bérénice* in 1955 at the Festival in Algiers.

Gellner, Julius (1900–), Czech-born director, now living in London. Directed at the Munich Kammerspiele 1926–33; in 1933 became artistic director of the German theatre in Prague. His first production in London was in 1942 at the OLD VIC THEATRE: *Othello* with Frederick Valk and MILES. Later he directed at the MERMAID THEATRE. His most notable production is CAMUS's *Les Possédés*, Tel Aviv 1962, Habimah Theatre.

Gelosi, Compagnia dei. One of the earliest and most famous COMMEDIA DELL' ARTE companies, which later exerted great influence on the French theatre. They visited Paris several times: 1571; 1576–77; 1588; 1600; 1602; performing in the Petit-Bourbon and, for the first time in France, demonstrated the superiority of professional actors. Their REPERTOIRE consisted partly of scripted plays, partly of c. dell'a improvisations. Famous members of the company included FRANCESCO and ISABELLA ANDREINI.

Gémier, Firmin (1869–1933), French actor and producer. Pupil of ANTOINE, with whom he worked at the Théâtre de l'Œuvre, under the direction of LUGNÉ-POË. In 1901 he took over the management of the Théâtre de la Renaissance, where he also established his reputation as a director; in 1906 he succeeded Antoine at the Théâtre Antoine until 1921 when he was appointed director of the Odéon where he remained till 1930. A very powerful actor with a tendency to grand gesture and simplification, his best parts included: Père Ubu in *Ubu Roi* by JARRY and Petruchio in *The Taming of the Shrew*. He staged highly topical, lavish productions, and made several attempts to establish a popular theatre: in 1911 with the travelling company Théâtre National Ambulant, and in 1920 with productions at the Paris Cirque d'Hiver (Saint-Georges de Bouhélier's *Oedipe roi de Thebes*). This was the germ of the later CENTRES DRAMATIQUES; many of his ideas were also later realized by the THÉÂTRE NATIONAL POPULAIRE. His major importance was as a teacher, the first to emphasize the importance of improvisation and systematic training in the style of STANISLAVSKY. His most famous pupil was DULLIN.
Bibl: P. Gsell, 1921

Generalintendant ▷INTENDANT.

Genesius, St, Roman actor, who was ordered to enact a parody of baptism on stage, but instead professed his Christian faith and was consequently martyred in AD 297. He is the patron saint of actors and his feast day is annually celebrated in Paris on 25 August with a special Mass attended by actors. He occurs as a character in LOPE DE VEGA's play *Lo fingido verdadero*.

Genet, Jean (1910–), French novelist, playwright and poet. Born illegitimate, he spent part of his youth in an institution for juvenile delinquents and later became a thief and male prostitute. Started to write in prison. His works embody some of the fantasy life of a social outcast who sees the 'respectable' world as a vast sham. His plays have a haunting dreamlike quality and – as he sees the Mass as the most effective form of dream – the power of ritual, inverted religious ceremonial. *Haute Surveillance*, fp Paris 1949, set in a prison cell, deals with the lives of three criminals and their struggle for power. His second play *Les Bonnes*, fp Paris 1949, dir JOUVET, shows a ritualistic act of two maids playing out a servant-mistress relationship in a ceremonial which culminates in the killing of the one who enacts the mistress. *Le Balcon*, written 1956, fp London 1957, Arts Theatre, dir ZADEK, in English; fp in French, Paris 1960, Théâtre du Gymnase, dir BROOK, is set in a brothel designed for the fulfilment of any fantasy however bizarre or outrageous, peopled with characters relentlessly driven by their most private compulsions, played against a background of revolutionary violence. In *Les Nègres*, fp Paris 1959, dir BLIN, des ACQUART, a group of Blacks perform the ritual re-enactment of their resentments and desire for revenge before a White audience. *Les Paravents*, fp BERLIN 1961, dir LIETZAU, Paris 1966, Odéon, dir Blin, des Acquart, is Genet's comment on the Algerian revolution. He has also written film scripts including *Mademoiselle*, dir RICHARDSON, with Jeanne Moreau, 1966, and produced a silent picture *Un Chant d'amour*, c. 1949.
Bibl: P. Thody, JEAN GENET: A STUDY OF HIS WORK, 1968; J. P. Sartre, ST GENET, COMÉDIEN ET MARTYR, 1952

Georg II, Duke of Saxe-Meiningen (1826–1914), founder and inspirer of the MEININGER company in Germany.

George, Heinrich (1893–1946), German actor. Began his career as a champion of EXPRESSIONISM, acting in, and co-directing, the one-act plays of KOKOSCHKA, at the Albert Theater, Dresden, in 1917. He subsequently appeared in plays by other exponents of the Expressionist movement such as HASENCLEVER, UNRUH, BARLACH, REHFISCH; he worked with various directors – PISCATOR in GORKY's *The Lower Depths*, Berlin 1926, VOLKSBÜHNE, with ENGEL as Galy Gay in BRECHT's *Mann ist Mann*, 1928, Volksbühne; with FEHLING; and with JESSNER in *Othello* at the Berlin State Theatre, 1932. Later, 1933–44, he was director of the Schillertheater, Berlin, and specialized mainly in classical plays by GOETHE, KLEIST and CALDERÓN. A powerful actor, one of his best performances was as

Falstaff in SHAKESPEARE's *Henry IV*, 1940, dir Fehling. He also appeared in many films.
Bibl: B. Drews, 1962

George, Mlle (Marguerite-Joséphine Weymer; 1787–1867), French actress. One of the leading romantic actresses in France, she had her first major success at the COMÉDIE-FRANÇAISE in 1802 in the name part of RACINE's *Iphigénie*; the audience was split into rival groups: fans of Mlle G. and of her rival Duchênois. Because Mlle G. was a protegée of Napoleon, whose mistress she was 1802–08, she became a SOCIÉTAIRE of the CF; in 1808 she suddenly disappeared to St Petersburg with a dancer; from there she went to Sweden, where she appeared before the Court in Stockholm, 1813; returning to Paris she rejoined the CF; in 1817 she left and travelled to England and the provinces where she met Charles Jean Harel, who engaged her first at the Odéon and later at the Porte Saint-Martin in contemporary roles: DUMAS pere's *Christine*, 1829, and *La Tour de Nesle*, 1832; VIGNY's *La Maréchale d'Ancre*, 1831, HUGO's *Lucrèce Borgia*, 1833, and *Marie Tudor*, 1833.
Bibl: Fleischmann, UNE MAÎTRESSE DE NAPOLÉON: MLLE GEORGE, 1908

Germany. In the Middle Ages religious plays; in the Renaissance secular theatre: *Meistersang*, SCHOOL DRAMA. Beginning of the professional theatre in the 17th century with the appearances of the ENGLISH COMEDIANS. The Thirty Years War set back the development of the theatre. Leading theatre managers of travelling companies included VELTHEN (1640–93) and CAROLINE NEUBER (1697–1760). Classicist theatre reform attempted by GOTTSCHED. An attempt to create a NATIONAL THEATRE in Hamburg, 1767–68, was made with the support of the great critic and playwright LESSING. Outstanding managers and actors of the time were EKHOF (1720–78), F. L. SCHRÖDER (1744–1816). Founding of the Mannheim National Theatre under the direction of DALBERG (1750–1806). Development of the Weimar classicist style by GOETHE, after 1791, and SCHILLER. In the 19th century COURT THEATRE and emergence of municipal theatres; exceptional position of the Vienna BURGTHEATER; efforts at reform by German directors including KLINGEMANN in Brunswick, IMMERMANN in Düsseldorf, and TIECK in Dresden. By the middle of the 19th century the REPERTOIRE of German theatres was dominated by French light COMEDIES, German FARCES and sentimental dramas, conventional productions of classical works, and guest appearances of virtuoso actors.
Beginning of the director's theatre: LAUBE at the Vienna Burgtheater, the MEININGER company from 1874, VOLKSTHEATER in Vienna and in BERLIN. From *c.* 1890 Berlin became the chief centre of theatre and from then until 1944 there was interplay between the metropolitan and provincial theatres; after a rapid succession of many styles, the principle of the director's theatre finally succeeded. Breakdown of

John Gay, *The Beggar's Opera*, painting by Hogarth

Jean Genet

Germany, a troupe of actors preparing for a performance in Nuremberg, *c.* 1730

the private theatre system in the 1920s, since then the subsidized ensemble and REPERTORY theatre has dominated, with a literary repertoire of a high standard and regular audiences (subscription system). After World War II the division of Germany led to a special development of the theatre in East Germany, where the East Berlin theatres, including the BERLINER ENSEMBLE and the Deutsches-Theater, still dominate the theatre scene. With Berlin's loss of capital city status, theatrical life in West Germany has become decentralized with the consequence that there are a number of rival theatrical 'capitals' which present a repertoire of world literature. In the 1940s and 1950s productions were still strongly influenced by EXPRESSIONISM. Tendencies towards stylization can be seen in the works of leading directors in these other 'capitals': SELLNER in Darmstadt; SCHALLA in Bochum; STROUX in Düsseldorf; KOCH in Frankfurt; SCHUH in Berlin and Hamburg. Other important centres are Hanover, Bremen and Stuttgart. A dominant figure in modern German theatre was GRÜNDGENS who, as INTENDANT, director and actor, worked mainly in Düsseldorf and Hamburg. Realistic tendencies showed in the work of KORTNER and NOELTE, who gained great influence in the 1960s. There are now about 185 public theatres (including opera and ballet). The total subsidy in West Germany to all arts including music in 1975 was about 2,000,088,000 DM.
Bibl: K. Reinholz, EDUARD DEVRIENTS GESCHICHTE DER DEUTSCHEN SCHAUSPIELKUNST, 2/1967; W. P. Friedrich, AN OUTLINE HISTORY OF GERMAN LITERATURE, 1966; H. Rischbieter and E. Went, DEUTSCHE DRAMATIK IN WEST UND OST, 1965; R. R. Heitner, GERMAN TRAGEDY IN THE AGE OF ENLIGHTENMENT, 1963; H. F. Garten, MODERN GERMAN DRAMA, 2/1962

Gershwin, George (1898–1937), US composer. He trained as a pianist and became a writer of songs and scores for numerous successful musicals, often working in collaboration with his brother **Ira G.** who wrote the lyrics. His brilliant jazz-inspired compositions set the style for popular music in the 1920s. He first attracted attention with his song 'Swanee', sung by JOLSON, and went on to write the lilting tunes for shows like *Lady Be Good*, 1924, and *Funny Face*, 1927, with the ASTAIRES; *Oh Kay!*, 1926, with GERTRUDE LAWRENCE; *Girl Crazy*, 1930, with ETHEL MERMAN, and the Pulitzer Prize-winning musical by KAUFMAN and Morrie Ryskind, *Of Thee I Sing*, 1932, while also composing symphonic works, e.g. *Rhapsody in Blue*, 1924, and *Concerto in F*, 1928, in which he demonstrated his conviction that jazz could be treated seriously as legitimate music. His masterpiece, the opera *Porgy and Bess*, 1935, was based on the stage play *Porgy* by Dorothy and Du Bose Heyward with whom he collaborated, his brother writing many of the lyrics. His last work was for the film *Shall We Dance*, 1937, with Astaire and Ginger Rogers.
Bibl: G. Chase, AMERICA'S MUSIC, 1955; C. Smith, MUSICAL COMEDY IN AMERICA, 1950

Ghelderode, Michel de (1898–1962), Flemish dramatist who wrote in French. He belongs with AUDIBERTI and George Neveux to the 'poetic avant-garde' of contemporary theatre; preoccupied with the absurdity and the uncertainty of human existence. His plays are based on folklore and biblical themes, and he is much concerned with the fear of death. His ideas and techniques spring from the traditions of the Flemish theatre – the PUPPET THEATRE, VAUDEVILLE, and improvised fairground drama; he was influenced by the world of Flanders in the past as depicted in the paintings of Brueghel and Bosch. He wrote more than 50 plays, most of which remain unperformed. He was little known outside his own country till *Hop! Signor*, written 1936, was produced in Paris 1947, followed by *Escurial*, 1948 (written 1928). His best-known work is probably *Fastes d'enfer*, written 1929, which achieved a *succès de scandale* when produced in Paris, 1949. Other significant works include *La Mort du docteur Faust*, 1926; the biblical drama *Barabbas*, 1929; *La Ballade du Grand Macabre*, 1935; *Sire Halewyn*, 1936.
Bibl: J. Francis, 1949

Ghéon, Henri (Henri Vangeon; 1875–1944), French dramatist. A Catholic poet, whose dramatic works were modelled on the medieval MYSTERY PLAYS; they were used by COPEAU as texts for his *théâtre pur*, theatre reduced to its essentials. Copeau was also responsible for G.'s first success: he produced his *L'Eau de vie* at the Vieux-Colombier, 1914. Today G.'s plays are produced by professional companies as well as by religious amateur companies. They include: *Le Pauvre sous l'escalier*, 1920; *Saint Maurice ou l'Obéissance*, 1922; *Le Triomphe de Saint Thomas d'Aquin*, 1924; *La Parade du pont au diable*, 1925; *La Mort de Lazare*, 1933; *Violante*, 1933; *La Complainte de Pranzini et de Sainte Thérèse de Lisieux*, 1934; *Le Noël de Greccio*, 1936; *Judith*, 1948, and *Oedipe ou le Crépuscule des Dieux*, 1951, both posthumous.
Bibl: M. Deleglise, LE THÉÂTRE D'HENRI GHÉON, 1947

Gherardi. Italian family of actors. (1) **Giovanni G.** (middle of 17th century–1683), COMMEDIA DELL'ARTE actor who joined a company in Paris in 1674 or 1675. He was a much admired musical comedian, who imitated musical instruments (the guitar and flute – from which he derived his name 'Flautino'). His son (2) **Evaristo G.** (1663–1700) was a sophisticated ARLECCHINO, whose collection of plays produced at the HÔTEL DE BOURGOGNE is one of the most important sources for the history of the c. dell'a.
Bibl: O. Klinger, DIE COMÉDIE ITALIENNE IN PARIS NACH DER SAMMLUNG VON GHERARDI, 1902

Giacosa, Giuseppe (1847–1906), Italian playwright and librettist. Accomplished realistic chronicler of Italian middle-class life in the style of IBSEN's social plays. First success with *Tristi amori* (Unhappy Loves), a realistic portrayal of provincial life. His COMEDIES, very successful in his day, were *La zampa del gatto* (The Cat's Paw), 1883, and *Una partita a scacchi* (*The Wager*), 1871; for SARAH BERNHARDT he wrote *Signora di Challant* which she played in New York under the title *La Dame de Challant*; ELEONORA DUSE appeared in 1891 in Turin in the same part. He also wrote LIBRETTI (with Luigi Illica) for Puccini: *La Bohème*, *Tosca*, and *Madame Butterfly*.
Bibl: P. Nardi, 1949

Gibbs, Wolcott (1902–58), US drama critic. He wrote mainly for *The New Yorker*. A fine stylist whose humour and sardonic detachment made his work immensely readable, though he tended to write better about bad plays than good ones. The irony he injected into his reviews acted as a tonic to BROADWAY, providing a positive stimulus to theatrical production. His book *A Season in the Sun* contains a number of biting burlesques of contemporary novelists and playwrights; these he turned into a play in 1951.

Gibson, William (1914–), US poet, novelist and playwright. He is best known for his powerful drama *The Miracle Worker*, written for TV 1957, fp 1959, 'The story of the magnificent determination of Annie Sullivan to teach the blind and deaf Helen Keller the fundamentals of knowledge . . . altogether a superior television achievement' (*New York Times*). His first BROADWAY success came with *Two for the Seesaw*, 1958, which gained world-wide fame. Other plays include the OFF-BROADWAY fantasy, *Dinny and the Witches*, 1959, and *A Cry of Players*, first written 1948, refurbished 1968. He has also written a VERSE DRAMA, *I lay in Zion*, 1943, a volume of poems and the novels *Winter Crook*, 1949, and *The Cobweb*, 1954. In 1951 he received the ANTA playwriting award.

Gide, André (1869–1951), French novelist and playwright. In his dramatic work he specialized in new versions of biblical stories and Greek myths in which his main theme is the conflict between individualism and religious submission: *Saül*, 1896, fp 1922, Théâtre du Vieux-Colombier, dir COPEAU; *Philoctète*, 1898, fp 1937; *Le Prométhée mal enchaîné*, written 1899; *Le Roi Candaule*, 1899, fp 1901; *Bethsabée*, written 1902; *Le Retour de l'enfant prodigue*, 1907, fp 1928; *Oedipe*, fp 1931, in 1949 prod VILAR at Avignon; *Les Caves du Vatican* (adaptation of his own novel), fp 1933, in 1950 at the COMÉDIE-FRANÇAISE in a new version; *Perséphone* (LIBRETTO for Stravinsky), fp 1934; *Le Treizième Arbre*, fp 1935; *Robert ou L'Intérêt général*, 1939–40, fp Tunis 1946. As a dramatist he was best known for his translations of Shakespeare's *Antony and Cleopatra* and *Hamlet*, with which the Compagnie Renaud-Barrault opened their first season in 1946. In 1948 BARRAULT played the lead when the production visited the Edinburgh Festival. G. also dramatized KAFKA's *The Trial* in

collaboration with Barrault for his company, fp 1947, revived at the Odéon 1962.
Bibl: J. C. MacLaren, THE THEATRE OF ANDRÉ GIDE, 1953

Giehse, Therese (1898–1975), German actress. Made her first successful appearance in 1925 at the Munich Kammerspiele under the direction of FALCKENBERG: Mutter Wölffen in HAUPTMANN's *Der Biberpelz*. After 1933 played in Zurich, first at the cabaret Die Pfeffermühle, later at the ZURICH SCHAUSPIELHAUS, and after 1952 mainly at the Munich Kammerspiele and in Zurich. She was one of the great modern German actresses, combining fine craftsmanship with a talent for realizing her characters in carefully observed detail. Her best roles included: BRECHT's *Mutter Courage*, fp Zurich 1941; the title role in GORKY's *Vassa Zheleznova*, BERLINER ENSEMBLE, 1949; Claire Zachanassinn in DÜRRENMATT's *Der Besuch der alten Dame*, Munich 1956, and Mathilde von Zahnd in Dürrenmatt's *Die Physiker*, fp Zurich 1962.
Bibl: W. Drews, 1965

Gielen, Josef (1890–1968), German actor and director. 1924–26 director both at the Dresden Theatre and later also at the Dresden Opera, where he worked in collaboration with Richard Strauss on his operas, *Ariadne auf Naxos*, *Arabella*, *Die schweigsame Frau*. After directing several productions at the Berlin Opera and the BURGTHEATER in Vienna, 1936–39, he emigrated to Brazil (Teatro Cólon, Buenos Aires). He returned to Vienna after the war and was director 1948–56 of the Burgtheater, where he attempted to preserve its tradition by producing classical and contemporary works of world literature. In 1956 appointed director of the Vienna Opera. He also directed opera in Milan, Paris and Buenos Aires.

Gielgud, Sir John (1904–), English actor and director. Knighted in 1953; grand-nephew of ELLEN TERRY. He made his stage début in 1921 as the Herald in *Henry V* at the OLD VIC and first gained popular success in the title role of *Richard of Bordeaux* by DAVIOT, 1932; in 1931 played Malvolio at the opening of the Sadler's Wells Theatre. As an actor, his outstanding characteristic is his fine speaking voice; generally acknowledged as one of the foremost actors of his day. He has excelled in parts such as John Worthing in WILDE's *The Importance of Being Earnest*, 1939; Valentine in CONGREVE's *Love for Love*, 1947. He also directed and acted in: FRY's *The Lady's Not for Burning*, 1948, and ALBEE's *Tiny Alice*, New York 1964; also successful in classic roles, in CHEKHOV's plays, and in SENECA's *Oedipus*, London 1968, dir BROOK. His best parts have been Shakespearean, notably the title role in *Hamlet*, London 1934, New York 1936; in 1935 he alternated as Romeo and Mercutio with OLIVIER; in 1937–38 when manager of the Queen's Theatre, he acted in and directed *Richard II* and *The Merchant of*

George Gershwin's PORGY AND BESS, New York 1935

Michel de Ghelderode's *Pantagleize*, Théâtre National de Belgique, 1970/71

John Gielgud and Pamela Brown in *The Lady's Not for Burning*, by FRY, 1948

Venice (Shylock). Another important Repertory season was in 1944–45 at the Haymarket Theatre, under his management, where he produced SHAKESPEARE, WEBSTER, CONGREVE and MAUGHAM. In the 1950–51 STRATFORD-UPON-AVON season, he played: Angelo in *Measure for Measure*, dir Brook; Benedick in *Much Ado About Nothing*; Prospero in *The Tempest*; *King Lear*; and in 1963 he played Othello. In 1975 he appeared at the NATIONAL THEATRE with Richardson in PINTER's *No Man's Land*, New York 1976. He has also appeared in many films. He is the author of the books *Early Stages*, 1938, and *Stage Directions*, 1963.
Bibl: R. Gilder, JOHN GIELGUD'S HAMLET, 1937

Gignoux, Hubert (1915–), French actor, director and dramatist. Acted with CHANCEREL's company, the Comédiens Routiers, 1931–34. During World War II he was imprisoned in Germany and worked on a PUPPET THEATRE with H. Cordreaux, from which developed the Marionnettes des Champs-Elysées in 1947 with a REPERTORY of plays by MOLIÈRE, COURTELINE, LORCA and COCTEAU. As *instructeur général* for drama he was commissioned by the government in 1945 to deal with the formation of amateur companies; he advocated the decentralization of the French theatre and founded the CENTRE DRAMATIQUE in Rennes, where he helped to establish a reputation with classical and modern productions (GIRAUDOUX, CHEKHOV, SYNGE, PIRANDELLO, etc.); in 1952 he also produced his own play *Les Nouvelles Aventures de Candide*, based on VOLTAIRE. As an actor he gave his best performances as Hamlet and Henry IV (Pirandello). In 1957 took over the management of the Centre dramatique in Strasbourg, where he successfully produced DÜRRENMATT's *The Visit*, 1960, a production which visited Paris; HUGO's *A Mille Francs de récompense*, 1961. His own dramatic works include: *Judas*, *Charles VII*, *Icara* and *L'Ile de la Providence*, Paris 1955.

Gilbert and Sullivan. (1) **Gilbert, Sir William Schwenk** (1836–1911), English dramatist. Knighted in 1907. Began his career as a writer for several humorous papers (e.g. *Fun* magazine) but is best known for his collaboration with the composer (2) **Sir Arthur Sullivan**, which began with the operatic extravaganza *Thespis; or, The Gods Grown Old*, Gaiety Theatre, 1871. Their partnership lasted over 20 years. G.'s LIBRETTI are among the best examples of English humour: ironic, dry, and with a slight tendency to the absurd. After 1882 Gilbert and Sullivan's light operas became known as the Savoy Operas (after the Savoy Theatre): *Trial by Jury*, 1875; *The Sorcerer*, 1877; *HMS Pinafore*, 1878; *The Pirates of Penzance*, 1880; *Patience*, 1881; *Iolanthe*, 1882; *Princess Ida*, 1884; *The Mikado*, 1885; *Ruddigore*, 1887; *The Gondoliers*, 1889; *The Yeoman of the Guard*, 1888; *The Grand Duke*, 1896. Most of these are still in the REPERTORY of the D'Oyly Carte Opera Company and are also produced throughout Britain and the USA by professional and amateur companies. The works G. wrote alone were BURLESQUES, dramatic sketches for entertainers in MUSIC-HALL, romances and more serious plays, e.g. *Sweethearts*, 1874; *Broken Hearts*, 1875; *Dan'l Druce, Blacksmith*, 1876, and *Engaged*, 1877. He financed the building of the Garrick Theatre, which opened in 1889.
Bibl: L. Baily, GILBERT AND SULLIVAN AND THEIR WORLD, 1973

Gilder, Rosamund (1900–), US drama critic and campaigner for the theatre. From 1924 contributor, co-editor and 1945–66 editor of the magazine *Theatre Arts*; leading member of several important public bodies (ANTA, UNESCO, and ITI). She wrote the bibliography *A Theatre Library*, 1931, and (in collaboration with George Freedley) the reference book *Theatre Collections in Libraries and Museums*, 1926. Other works include: *The Letters of Richard Watson Gilder*, 1916, letters of her father Richard Watson, a famous poet and editor of the 1890s; *Enter the Actress*, 1931, and *John Gielgud's Hamlet*, 1937.

Gilles. French theatrical character with a costume similar to that of PIERROT (the famous painting *Gilles* by Watteau is in the Louvre).

Gillette, William (1855–1937), US actor and playwright. The son of a Senator, educated at Harvard and at the Massachusetts Institute of Technology, he made his professional début as an actor in Boston, 1875. Later wrote or adapted from novels and stories a number of plays in which he himself appeared in the lead. These include: *The Professor*, 1881; *Esmeralda* (adapted from a story by Frances H. Burnett), 1881; *Digby's Secretary* (adapted from a German play), 1884; *Held by the Enemy*, 1886, one of the first successful plays dealing with the American Civil War; *She* (after Rider Haggard's novel), 1887; *A Legal Wreck*, 1888; *All the Comforts of Home* (adapted from a German play), 1890; *Too Much Johnson*, 1894; *Secret Service*, 1895, which became one of his greatest successes; *Because She Loved Him So* (adapted from *Jalousie* by Bisson and Leclercq), 1898; *Sherlock Holmes* (based on Sir Arthur Conan Doyle's stories), 1899, in which G. appeared in 1916, successfully revived by the RSC, London, 1974; *Electricity*, 1910. G. was an actor who achieved great effects by understatement, at his best in the roles of cool and superior men of action, such as Captain Thorne in *Secret Service* and as Sherlock Holmes. He wrote *Illusion of the First Time in Acting*, pub in *Publications of the Dramatic Museum of Columbia Univ.*, 1915.

Ginsberg, Ernst (1904–64), German actor. Took an active part in the political life of the 1920s and during his time in BERLIN (VOLKSBÜHNE, Theater am Schiffbauerdamm) was known as an interpreter of young revolutionary heroes. His most important work was at the ZURICH SCHAUSPIELHAUS, 1933–62, where he appeared in many leading roles, his finest probably as Mephistopheles in GOETHE's *Faust* (Parts I and II), but he was also a famous interpreter of MOLIÈRE's characters.
Bibl: E. Brock-Sulzer, 1963

Ginzburg, Natalia (*née* Levi; 1916–), Italian novelist and playwright. She married Professor Leone Ginzburg, a wartime Resistance hero who was killed by the Nazis in 1944. Has written a number of successful novels and short stories. Began writing plays in 1965. Her first play *Ti ho sposato per allegria* (I married you for fun) was staged in Turin with Adriana Ast in 1966. Her second play *Inserzione* (*The Advertisement*) won the Marzotto Prize for European Drama in 1968 and was first performed in English (translation by Henry Reed) at the NATIONAL THEATRE in London with JOAN PLOWRIGHT in the leading role. Has since written a number of radio plays.

Girardi, Alexander (1850–1918), Austrian actor and singer. One of the most famous comedians of Viennese operetta. He was a masterly interpreter of popular songs, in the tradition of the great Viennese folk comedians, and greatly loved by the audience of his time. He appeared 1874–96 at the Theater an der Wien, created Frosch in Johann Strauss's operetta *Die Fledermaus* and Jonathan in Millöcker's *Der arme Jonathan* (Poor Jonathan). After 1896 he appeared at several other theatres including the Raimundtheater, the Deutsches Volkstheater as Argan in MOLIÈRE's *Le Malade imaginaire*, and the BURGTHEATER in RAIMUND's *Der Bauer als Millionär* (The Peasant Millionaire).
Bibl: R. Holzer, DIE WIENER VORSTADTBÜHNEN, 1951; H. Jhering, VON JOSEF KAINZ BIS PAULA WESSELY, 1942

Giraudoux, Jean (1882–1944), French novelist, essayist and playwright. He was a professional diplomat in the Ministry of Foreign Affairs in Paris from 1910; though he had been writing successful stories and novels, it was not until 1928 that he turned to plays and adapted his own novel *Siegfried et le Limousin* into the play *Siegfried*, which was produced by JOUVET, 1928, Comédie des Champs-Elysées. Jouvet directed all but one of G.'s subsequent plays and also supported him in his defence of literary theatre, emphasizing the importance of the text rather than the visual aspects in a production: *Amphitryon 38*, 1929; *Judith*, 1931; *Intermezzo*, 1933; *Tessa*, 1934; *Supplément au voyage de Cook*, 1935; *La Guerre de Troie n'aura pas lieu*, 1935 (adapted by FRY as *Tiger at the Gates*); *Electre*, 1937; *L'Impromptu de Paris* and *Cantique des cantiques*, 1938; *Ondine*, 1939; *L'Apollon de Marsac* (later *L'Apollon de Bellac*), fp Rio de Janeiro 1942; *Sodome et Gomorrhe*, 1943; *La Folle de Chaillot*, fp 1945; *Pour Lucrèce* (*Duel of Angels*), fp 1953. His heroes are often mythological or biblical figures; he takes the myth out of its historical context, giving the characters contemporary preoccupations and, creating a form which is half myth, half allegory, revitalizes it with aesthetic finesse. He uses his archetypal characters as vehicles to explore contemporary and public preoccupations. His

plays, with their precise DIALOGUE which tends to reflective lyricism, extended the world of the French bourgeoisie by introducing elements of irrationality, dream, poetry and myth. He also uses the full gamut of the techniques and illusions of the theatre, but in spite of his delicacy, charm and wit his plays are basically sceptical and bitter. He achieved his greatest impact in France in the 1930s, though his influence there has since waned.
Bibl: G. Mander, 1969; D. Inskip, THE MAKING OF A DRAMATIST, 1958; L. Le Sage; L'ŒUVRE DE JEAN GIRAUDOUX, ESSAI DE BIBLIOGRAPHIE CHRONOLOGIQUE, 1957

Gischia, Léon (1903–), French stage designer. He was a pupil of O. Friesz and LÉGER. 1927–30 he travelled through the USA; in 1937 he collaborated with Léger and Le Corbusier on a pavilion for the Paris World Exhibition. Turned to stage design in 1945 with ELIOT's *Murder in the Cathedral*, dir VILAR, with whom he created the style of the THÉATRE NATIONAL POPULAIRE: simple architectural structures set in open spaces to stimulate the imagination of the audience; to contrast with the simplicity of the stage he designed elaborate COSTUMES; his work became best known with KLEIST's *The Prince of Homburg*, 1952, and CORNEILLE's *Le Cid*, 1961. He has also edited several books on art.
Bibl: H. Parmelin, CINQ PEINTRES ET LE THÉÂTRE, 1956

Gitana, Gertie (Gertrude Mary Astbury; 1889–1957), one of the most popular stars of English MUSIC HALL. She first appeared in London at the Lyceum in 1904 and later at the Holborn Empire. She was famous for her rendering of the song 'Nellie Dean'. She was married to Don Ross, in whose music-hall show *Thanks for the Memory* she played in 1947.

Glasgow Citizens' Theatre. Theatre founded by Scottish enthusiasts under the leadership of BRIDIE in 1943 and housed in the former Princess's Theatre in the working-class Gorbals district. Supported by Glasgow Corporation and the Scottish Arts Council. One of the leading REPERTORY companies in Scotland with an ambitious repertoire of classics and new plays.

Glenville, Peter (1913–), English director. Began his career as an actor in 1934, appeared in 1939 at the OLD VIC as Lucentio in *The Taming of the Shrew*, and directed his first production there in 1944. Best known for his production of *Hamlet*, in which he also played the lead, 1945. Since 1947 he has concentrated on directing plays mainly by SHAW, RATTIGAN, T. WILLIAMS (*Summer and Smoke*), GREENE (*The Living Room*), and was particularly successful with FEYDEAU's *Hotel Paradiso* in 1956. Noted for remarkable productions on BROADWAY: *Rashomon* by F. and M. Kanin after R. Akutagawa, 1959; *Take Me Along*, musical by J. Stein and R. Russell, based on O'NEILL's *Ah Wilderness!*, 1959; *Tchin-Tchin* by S. Michaels based on BILLETDOUX's

Gilbert and Sullivan's *Thespis* at the Gaiety Theatre, 1871, drawing by Alfred Bryan

Gilbert and Sullivan's *The Mikado*, costume designs by Charles Ricketts, 1926

Giraudoux's *Ondine*, 1939, with JOUVET and MADELEINE OZERAY

play, 1962. He also acted in and directed films, e.g. *Becket* in 1964, based on ANOUILH's play.

Gliese, Rochus (1891–1976), German stage designer. His most important work was in collaboration with the director FEHLING, for whom he designed several plays by the Expressionist BARLACH. Later he worked as a guest designer of opera and drama at many German theatres including the BURGTHEATER in Vienna, and the Munich Opera.

Globe Theatre. Famous Elizabethan theatre in Southwark (London) usually associated with SHAKESPEARE. Built in 1599 by C. BURBAGE and five members of the CHAMBERLAIN'S MEN, one of whom was probably Shakespeare. The theatre was open to the sky, with a thatched roof over the stage, its symbol Hercules carrying the Globe. The assumption that originally it had an octagonal layout is unproved. The building was probably similar to the Swan Theatre, built by Francis Langley, *c.* 1594, on Bankside, but larger, more lavish and better equipped technically. It was considered one of the best theatres of the time for fine actors and had a REPERTOIRE which included first productions of contemporary dramatists, in particular SHAKESPEARE. Burnt down in 1612, during a production of the latter's *Henry VIII*, it was rebuilt in 1613, this time with a tiled roof, but was finally pulled down in 1644.
Bibl: J. C. Adams, THE GLOBE PLAYHOUSE, 1943

Gobert, Boy (1925–), German actor and director. Made his début as Oswald in IBSEN's *Ghosts*, Hamburg 1947; subsequently worked at several German theatres (Karlsruhe, Frankfurt) until 1960 when he joined the BURGTHEATER in Vienna. His best performances include: Malvolio in *Twelfth Night*, 1960; Thomas à Becket in FRY's *Curtmantle*, 1961; Sosias in KLEIST's *Amphitryon*, 1963. In 1964 he gave his famous performance in the leading part in STERNHEIM's *Der Snob* at the Renaissance Theatre in BERLIN, dir NOELTE. In 1969 appointed director of the Thalia Theatre in Hamburg.

Godfrey, Thomas (1736–63), the first American dramatist. His tragedy *The Prince of Parthia*, 1759, strongly influenced by SHAKESPEARE, was first performed in New York 1767 by the American Company, and not performed again till it was revived in 1915 by the University of Pennsylvania. ▷HALLAM.

Goering, Reinhard (1887–1936), German dramatist. His play *Die Seeschlacht* (The Sea Battle), is one of the key works of German EXPRESSIONISM (written 1917; fp Berlin 1918, Deutsches-Theater, dir REINHARDT). Other works include (with dates of publication): *Der Erste* (The First), 1918; *Der Zweite* (The Second), 1919; *Die Retter* (The Saviours), 1919; *Scapa Flow*, 1919; *Die Südpolexpedition des Kapitäns Scott* (Captain Scott's Expedition to the South Pole), fp Berlin 1930, State Theatre, dir JESSNER; LIBRETTO for an opera by Zillig, *Das Opfer* (The Sacrifice), published posthumously 1937; *Der Vagabund und das Mädchen* (The Tramp and the Girl), 1931.
Bibl: D. Hoffman (ed), PROSA, DRAMEN UND VERSE, 1962

Goethe, Johann Wolfgang von (1749–1832), German poet, statesman and thinker. One of GERMANY's cultural heroes, he was also outstanding as a dramatic poet and playwright. Studied law and in 1775 became the confidant and friend of Duke Karl August of Saxe-Weimar, and attained high office in the administration of that small but important dukedom which, under his influence, became one of the chief centres of intellectual life in Germany. His first dramatic efforts were of the type of the *Schäferspiel* (shepherd's play ▷ PASTORAL DRAMA) then fashionable in Germany: *Die Laune des Verliebten* (The Lover's Caprice), 1767; *Die Mitschuldigen* (The Accomplices), 1769. Through meeting Herder he became a passionate admirer of SHAKESPEARE and wrote the historical play *Götz von Berlichingen*, an epic chronicle in the STURM UND DRANG style, fp Berlin 1773; started work in the early 1770s on a play about Dr Faustus which occupied him for the rest of his long life. The first version, *Urfaust*, was not discovered and published until 1886. There followed a number of plays in prose dealing with contemporary subjects: *Clavigo*, pub 1774, and *Stella*, fp 1776; *Egmont*, a history play about one of the heroes of the Dutch struggle against Spanish domination, for which Beethoven composed the music, was written *c.* 1775, but first performed as late as 1796, Weimar, with IFFLAND in the title role; the prose version of *Iphigenie auf Tauris*, 1779, was transformed, as the result of impressions gained during a long journey through Italy, 1786–88, into a VERSE DRAMA of classical serenity (final version 1787). From then on G. shed the harsh tones of his earlier style and became a classicist striving for harmony and repose. The tragedy *Torquato Tasso*, 1790, fp 1807, and *Die natürliche Tochter* (The Natural Daughter), 1803, are the other chief expressions of this tendency. In the later stages of the development of the Faust play *Faust, ein Fragment*, 1790; *Faust*, Part I, 1808; *Faust*, Part II, completed 1830, first pub 1833, the classical and the newer, romantic, tendencies are combined in a characteristic mixture. From 1791 he acted as director of the Weimar Court Theatre and remained at its head till 1817. His influence was exerted towards increased artistic and human dignity in performance and in the status of the actors, but he by no means confined himself to a REPERTOIRE which would have shunned the popular successes of the day, notably KOTZEBUE's plays and SINGSPIELE. Having exerted his influence to bring the other leading German poet and dramatist of the epoch, SCHILLER, into the Weimar orbit by securing for him a position as Professor of History at the University of Jena, G. closely collaborated with him from 1794 till Schiller's death in 1805, evolving a theory of drama which deeply influenced the further development of German dramatic writing. The two poets strove to create a world repertoire for the Weimar theatre by staging, and occasionally themselves translating and adapting, plays by VOLTAIRE, GOZZI, RACINE, CALDERÓN and TERENCE. G. resigned from the directorship of the theatre in protest against a visiting troupe with performing dogs.
Bibl: H. Pyritz, GOETHE BIBLIOGRAPHIE 1965; H. Knudsen, GOETHES WELT DES THEATERS, 1946

Goetz, Curt (1888–1960), German dramatist and actor. Began acting in Rostock and Nuremberg; 1911–22 appeared under BARNOWSKY (Lessingtheater, Berlin); particularly successful playing bon-vivants. He made his début as a dramatist with a cycle of one-act FARCES *Nachtbeleuchtung* (Night Illuminations): *Lohengrin, Tobby, Minna Magdalena, Der fliegende Geheimrat* (The Flying Privy Counsellor), and the collection of one-act plays: *Menagerie* (Zoo), *Der Spatz vom Dache* (The Sparrow from the Roof), *Die Taube in der Hand* (A Bird in the Hand), *Der Hund im Hirn* (The Dog on the Brain), *Der Hahn im Korbe* (The Cock in the Basket), Berlin 1920, Künstlertheater. Other works: *Der Lampenschirm* (The Lampshade), 1919; *Ingeborg*, 1922. From 1924 he appeared almost exclusively with his wife, the actress **Valerie von Martens**, in his own and other plays, and founded his own touring company: *Die tote Tante* (The Dead Aunt), 1925, dir REINHARDT; *Hokuspokus* (Magic), 1926–27; *Der Lügner und die Nonne* (The Liar and the Nun), Hamburg 1929, Thalia Theater; *Zirkus Aimée*, Basle 1932; *Mitternachtsdichter* (Midnight Poet), Berlin 1933; *Dr. med. Hiob Prätorius*, Stuttgart 1932; *Dann lieber nach Afrika* (Then Preferably to Africa), with COWARD, Vienna 1949; *Nichts Neues aus Hollywood* (Nothing New from Hollywood), Hamburg 1956, dir/prod GRÜNDGENS. He appeared on stage and in films in the USA, 1939–46, where he also wrote film scripts and co-directed plays. Author of a volume of reminiscences, *Die Memoiren des Peterhans von Binningen*, 1960.

Gogol, Nikolai Vasilyevich (1809–52), Russian novelist, short-story writer and playwright. His reputation is based mainly on his short stories and novel *Myortviye Dushi* (Dead Souls) dramatized by BULGAKOV, dir STANISLAVSKY at the MOSCOW ART THEATRE, 1932. It was produced in Russian during the 1964 WORLD THEATRE SEASON, Aldwych. His early work was praised by PUSHKIN who also inspired him to write his COMEDY *Revizor* (*The Government Inspector* or *The Inspector General*), which was produced in 1836 at the Court Theatre before the Tsar. This masterly play helped to develop the realistic social satirical comedy in Russia – in the tradition of writers like GRIBOYEDOV – to its peak. It was, however, viciously attacked, causing G. to leave Russia for several years. Famous productions of the play include: Stanislavsky, Moscow 1908 and 1921; MEYERHOLD, Moscow 1926. The play was seen in London 1920, and New York 1923. His next most important play was the FARCE *Zhenit'ba*

(*The Marriage*), 1842. He also wrote dramatic sketches, amusing absurd grotesqueries like *Utro delovogo cheloveka* (A Businessman's Morning), 1842; *Tiazhba* (A Lawsuit), 1842; and *Lakeiskaia* (The Servants' Hall), 1842; and *Teatralnyi razyezd posle predstavleniya novoi komedii* (Leaving the Theatre After the Performance of a New Comedy), 1842; and his unfinished farce *Igroki* (The Gamblers), 1842.
Bibl: J. Lavrin, NICOLAI GOGOL 1802–52: A CENTENARY SURVEY, 1951; V. Nabokov, 1944

Gold, Käthe (1907–), Austrian actress, first successful at the Berlin State Theatre, 1934–44, in classic roles by GOETHE, SCHILLER, SHAKESPEARE (Ophelia, Rosalind) and HEBBEL. From 1944 appeared for two years in Zurich; since 1947 one of the leading actresses of the BURGTHEATER ensemble in Vienna.

Goldoni, Carlo (1707–93), Italian playwright. Adapted the COMMEDIA DELL'ARTE to a realistic theatre, which portrayed the life, manners and problems of contemporary Italian society in the tradition of MOLIÈRE's character comedies. Manager, 1737–41, of the Teatro San Giovanni Crisostomo in Venice; 1748–53 resident writer at the Teatro Sant'Angelo; 1753–62 worked for the Teatro San Luca and 1762–65 for the COMÉDIE-ITALIENNE in Paris – during all this time he developed his own style of theatre. His works include five TRAGEDIES, 57 TRAGICOMEDIES, 137 COMEDIES, 57 scenarios for the c. dell'a and numerous LIBRETTI. He portrays women particularly sympathetically, especially in his masterfully written *La Locandiera* (The Mistress of the Inn), 1753, whose heroine Mirandolina provides a superb part (DUSE appeared successfully in it). In *Le Baruffe Chiozzotte* (The Chioggia Affray), 1762, he portrays a social group, the fishermen of Chioggia; it was given a fine production by STREHLER in 1966. Other well-known comedies include: *Il Servitore di due Padroni* (*The Servant of Two Masters*), 1746 (the production by Strehler in 1947 gained international fame); *Il Bugiardo* (*The Liar*), 1750; *La Bottega del caffè* (*The Coffee House*), 1750; *Un Curioso accidente* (A Curious Mishap), 1757; *I Rusteghi* (The Boors), 1760; *L'Impresario delle Smirne* (The Impresario of Smyrna), 1760; *Il Ventaglio* (The Fan), 1764; *Le Bourru bienfaisant* (The Kindly Grouch), 1771, in French. In 1954 Strehler produced three of Goldoni's pieces under the title *La Trilogia della villeggiatura* (Trilogy on Holidays). He also published a volume of reminiscences, which give a lively description of the theatre of his time, *Mémoires*, original edition in French, 1774.
Bibl: N. Mangnini, 1961

Goldsmith, Oliver (1730–74), Irish-born English writer. He established his name first as an essayist, poet and novelist, before turning to drama. He formulated his ideas in his well-known *Essay on the Theatre* attacking the 'modish' sentimental comedy of his day and advocating a 'laughing

Goethe reading to a group of his friends, print by G. M. Kraus

Carlo Goldoni's *The Servant of Two Masters*, design for a 1927 production by REINHARDT

Oliver Goldsmith's *She Stoops to Conquer*

comedy', a mixture of comic, fantastic, ironic and sentimental elements with a strong realistic emphasis, ideas which he successfully realized in two comedies *She Stoops to Conquer*, 1773, and *The Good-Natur'd Man*, 1768.
Bibl: R. Quintano, OLIVER GOLDSMITH: A GEORGIAN STUDY, 1967

Goll, Ivan (1891–1950), Franco-German Expressionist dramatist and poet. He wrote in both French and German: *Der Unsterbliche* (The Immortal One), *Die Chaplinade*, both 1920; *Methusalem oder der ewige Bürger* (Methuselah or the Eternal Bourgeois), fp 1922 Königsberg, also in 1924 at the Dramatisches Theater, BERLIN, a 'satirical drama' with Surrealist dream visions for which he used film sequences; *Lassalles Tod* (Lassalle's Death), 1922; *Der Stall des Augias* (The Augean Stables), 1924, fp Kassel 1926; *Germaine Berton, die rote Jungfrau* (G.B., the Red Maiden), 1925; *Royal Palace*, music WEILL, 1927; *Melusine*, written 1922, fp Wiesbaden 1956.
Bibl: F. J. Carmody, THE POETRY OF IVAN GOLL, 1956

Gombrowicz, Witold (1904–70), distinguished Polish novelist and playwright. Emigrated to Argentina in 1939 and after 1963 settled in Paris; his first play *Iwona, Ksiezniczka Burgunda* (Yvonne, Princess of Burgundy), 1938, fp Cracòw 1957, which the Schillertheater performed at the WORLD THEATRE SEASON, Aldwych, 1971, can be seen as an important precursor of the THEATRE OF THE ABSURD; set in a fairy-tale world, it tells of the intrigues which follow the decision of a prince to marry an ugly, clumsy commoner, Iwona. This was followed by *Ślub* (The Wedding), 1946, fp Paris 1963, and *Operetta*, 1967, successfully produced in Paris by the TNP, in which he portrays the dying Western civilization in the form of a MUSICAL COMEDY. He was strongly influenced by EXISTENTIALISM: the central conflict in his plays (between the individual's self-centredness and society) is always played out in an allegorical, fairy-tale theatre setting: man can never be independent of his environment, even his language is a product of a given situation.

Goncourt. (1) **Edmond de G.** (1822–96) and (2) **Jules de G.** (1830–70), brothers, French writers and art historians. Their novels were naturalistic in approach but captured detail in an almost impressionistic manner. Their 'Diary' is a unique record of French 19th-century literary life. They always had the liveliest interest in the theatre, writing reviews, biographies of actresses, and experimenting in COMEDY, historical drama and milieu studies, e.g. *Henrietta Maréchal*, 1865. Edmond de G. also dramatized his own novels for the stage, e.g. *Germinie Lacerteux*, fp Paris 1888, Odéon, and *La Fille Élisa*, fp by ANTOINE at the Théâtre Libre, 1890.
Bibl: R. Baldick, 1960

Gordon, Ruth (1896–), US actress, playwright and director. Married to KANIN. Accomplished, but not beautiful, she fought hard for recognition which she eventually attained. Her first appearance was as Nibs in *Peter Pan*, 1915 (starring MAUDE ADAMS). She has been seen in many plays, including M. ANDERSON's *Saturday's Children*, 1927; *Serena Blandish*, 1929, a novel by ENID BAGNOLD, dramatized by BEHRMAN; *Hotel Universe* by P. BARRY, 1930; BRIDIE's *A Sleeping Clergyman*, 1934; *Ethan Frome*, 1936, Edith Wharton's novel, dramatized by Owen Davis, with Pauline Lord and Raymond Massey and made her London début at the OLD VIC in 1936, as Mrs Pinchwife in WYCHERLEY's *The Country Wife*, with EDITH EVANS and REDGRAVE. Other appearances include *The Strings, My Lord, are False* by CARROLL, 1942, and Natasha in *Three Sisters* by CHEKHOV in the same year. She wrote *Years Ago*, and *Over 21*, 1944, in which she also acted. One of her best-known later parts was in *The Matchmaker*, 1954, a restaging of WILDER's play, *The Merchant of Yonkers*, 1948. She has also appeared in many films.

Gorelik, Mordecai (1899–), Russian-born US stage designer. He is associated mainly with the GROUP THEATRE, where he worked with directors like CLURMAN, STRASBERG and KAZAN, in a variety of techniques and styles, ranging between realism and EXPRESSIONISM. Author of important theoretical works: *New Theatres for Old*, 1940; 'Stage Design' in *Producing a Play*, ed GASSNER, 1941.

Goring, Marius (1912–), English actor. After appearances as a child actor, toured Germany and France with the English Classical Players in 1931; at the OLD VIC, 1932–34; 1934–35 toured in France, Belgium and Holland with the COMPAGNIE DES QUINZE. By the end of the 1930s he was established as a leading actor in IBSEN and SHAKESPEARE. Played an important part in BBC broadcasts to Germany during the war years. Has since appeared in many classical and modern parts on the stage, in films and on TV in Britain and Germany. G. is a sensitive actor with a fine voice, a brilliant sense of poetry, but also able to give well-observed naturalistic performances. He was married to the actress LUCIE MANNHEIM.

Gorky, Maxim (Alexei Maximovich Pyeshkov; 1868–1936), Russian novelist, essayist, short-story writer, poet and playwright. A superb realistic author in the tradition of CHEKHOV, focusing on the pre-revolutionary stituation in Russian society. He had a working-class origin and was considered an expert on the proletariat and a 'mouthpiece' of the oppressed. He exposed the ills of Tsarism and has been credited with originating the literary theory of SOCIALIST REALISM. His first play was *Meshtchane* (*The Smug Citizens*), 1901, but he achieved great success with his next one, *Na Dne* (*The Lower Depths*), 1902, in STANISLAVSKY's famous naturalistic production at the MOSCOW ART THEATRE, which has remained in the international REPERTORY ever since; the play was also produced by LUGNÉ-POË, Paris 1905, with ELEONORA DUSE and dir REINHARDT, Berlin 1905. Many of G.'s plays were banned from the stage (e.g. *Vragi* (*Enemies*), 1907) until after the Revolution, when he wrote his best dramatic work, a cycle on a changing society: *Somov i drugie* (*S. and the Others*); *Yegor Bulychov i drugie*; and *Dostigaev i drugie*, fp Vakhtangov Theatre in 1932. Other works include *Dachniki* (*Summer Folk*), 1904, *Vassa Zheleznova* (*Mother Z.*), 1910; *Zykovy* (*The Zykovs*), 1913, British première 1976 by the RSC; *Yakov Bogolomov*, 1917 (appeared posthumously in 1941).
Bibl: D. Levin, STORMY PETREL; THE LIFE AND WORK OF MAXIM GORKY, 1965; R. Hare, MAXIM GORKY, ROMANTIC REALIST AND CONSERVATIVE REVOLUTIONARY, 1962

Gorvin, Joana Maria (1922–), German actress. She made her début in 1943 at the Berlin National Theatre under GRÜNDGENS, where she also began her close collaboration with the director FEHLING, at whose theatre she worked, 1945–46, e.g. as Gretchen in GOETHE's *Urfaust*. She later appeared at the Hebbel Theater, BERLIN 1946–48, and at the Munich State Theatre; at the latter in modern classical parts by IBSEN, HEBBEL and LORCA. Later she became one of Gründgen's leading tragic actresses in Hamburg. Her best roles include the name part in STRINDBERG's *Miss Julie*, 1960; Alice in *The Dance of Death*, 1963; and Indra's daughter in *A Dream Play*, 1963. She has also appeared in ALBEE's *Tiny Alice*, 1965.
Bibl: S. Melchinger, SCHAUSPIELER, 1965

Gottsched, Johann Christoph (1700–66), German rationalist critic and teacher. His poetics strongly influenced German drama, and prepared the ground for LESSING. A literary reformer, he attempted to improve the standard of German theatre by adopting the French style of RACINE and CORNEILLE, in theory and in practice, in his best-known play *Der sterbende Cato* (The Dying Cato), 1732, modelled on ADDISON's *Cato*. Together with CAROLINE NEUBER, principal of her own company in Leipzig, with whom he collaborated 1727–41, he formally banned the HANSWURST from the stage. In his theoretical work *Versuch einer kritischen Dichtkunst für die Deutschen* (Attempt at a Critical Poetic for Germany), 1730, he explained his disapproval of SHAKESPEARE (unnatural and apparently without rules), of the opera and of improvisational plays. His trust in the rationalistic attitude, typical of the Enlightment in Germany, made him oppose the irrational, the miraculous and the popular, and led to his being strongly attacked by Bodmer, Breitinger and Lessing. Not until the 20th century was his importance as an innovator in German literature recognized. His wife **Louise G.** (1713–62) wrote model pieces for the new French-style dramas: *Die Hausfranzösin*; *Das Testament*; and *Herr Witzeling*. G. collected translations and original works, mostly of French drama, in his *Deutsche Schaubühne nach den Regeln der alten Griechen und Römer eingerichtet* (The German Stage, Arranged According to the

Rules of the Ancient Greeks and Romans), 6 vols, pub 1740–45.
Bibl: G. Schimansky, 1939

Gozzi, Carlo (1720–1806), Italian writer and playwright. A rival of GOLDONI, whose reputation for truth and naturalness he attacked strongly with lengthy polemics, satires and *fiabe* (fairy-tales), plays which he constructed in the tradition of the COMMEDIA DELL'ARTE, which Goldoni tried to transcend. Contrary to Goldoni's use of everyday language and local dialects, G. wrote his fairy-tale *L'amore delle tre melarance* (The Love of Three Oranges), 1761, in 'pure Tuscan'. This was followed by a fairy-tale about talking animals, magicians and princes, who turn into statues *Il Corvo* (The Raven), 1761; the transformation play *Il Re cervo* (*King Stag*), 1762, and the Chinese fairy-tale *Turandot*, 1764, adapted in 1802 by SCHILLER. He had some impact during his lifetime (the aristocratic conservative G. was opposed to the 'progressive' Goldoni, the dramatist of the bourgeoisie); he later strongly influenced the Romantic movement in Germany (TIECK's fairy-tale dramas; E. Hoffmann's *Prinzessin Brambilla*) and in France (Madame de Staël, MUSSET). Most of his works have been used as LIBRETTI for operas: *The Love of Three Oranges*, Prokofiev, 1921; *König Hirsch*, Henze, 1956; *Turandot*, Busoni, 1918, and Puccini/Alfano, 1926.
Bibl: H. Hoffmann-Rusack, GOZZI IN GERMANY, 1930

Grabbe, Christian Dietrich (1801–36), German playwright. With BÜCHNER one of the most important pioneers of German realistic drama. Rejecting a classical, closed PLOT structure he used a dynamic arrangement of dramatic situations, stressing their epic rather than their theatrical qualities. His structural and stylistic techniques contributed to the genesis of modern EPIC THEATRE. In his essay 'Shakespearo-Manie' (Shakespeare-Mania), 1827, he deals critically with the reception of SHAKESPEARE's plays in Germany. Became a critic at Detmold, until IMMERMANN finally managed to persuade him to join his Düsseldorf theatre for a while as DRAMATURG. His best-known work is the grotesque satirical play *Scherz, Satire, Ironie und tiefere Bedeutung* (*Comedy, Satire, Irony and Deeper Meaning*), written 1822, fp Vienna, 1892; in his historical drama *Napoleon oder die Hundert Tage* (Napoleon or the Hundred Days), 1831, fp Frankfurt 1835, the hero is a victim of historical forces; this was the first German drama in which the populace is the Protagonist of the dramatic action. It was followed by *Die Hermannsschlacht* (The Battle of Hermann), 1836, fp Düsseldorf 1936; and *Hannibal*, 1835, fp Munich 1918. Other works include: *Herzog Theodor von Gothland*, written 1822, fp Vienna 1876; *Nannette und Maria*, 1823; *Marius und Sulla* (fragment), 1827; *Kaiser Friedrich Barbarossa*, 1829; *Aschenbrödel*, 1829; *Kosciusco* (fragment), 1832; *Alexander* (fragment), 1835.
Bibl: H. Bergmann (ed), GRABBE IN BERICHTEN SEINER ZEITGENOSSEN, 1968; W. Steffens, 1966

Gracioso. Comic character of traditional Spanish folk theatre.

Gramatica. (1) **Irma G.** (1870 or 1873–1962), Italian actress. Early in her career in 1887 she worked with the company of C. Rossi and DUSE; in 1892 she became the first leading juvenile actress under Italia Vitaliani; subsequently appeared successfully with several other companies in French 'vogue' plays: MEILHAC and Halévy's *Frou-Frou*; ZOLA's *Nana*; SARDOU's *Odette*. In 1896 she became leading actress of ZACCONI's company (Luise in SCHILLER's *Kabale und Liebe*, Katharina in *The Taming of the Shrew*). At the height of her career, in 1900, she was with the Compagnia Talli-Gramatica-Calabresi, appearing in GIACOSA's *Come le foglie* and VERGA's *Dal tuo al mio*. After 1904 with several troupes, sometimes (after 1928) with her sister Emma. She retired from the theatre in 1938. With her persuasive and natural lively charm, she succeeded in bringing even trivial characters to life. Her sister (2) **Emma G.** (1875–1965) had less natural talent, and was an actress of conscious and hard realism. Among her most famous roles were Nora in *A Doll's House* and the name parts in *Hedda Gabler* (IBSEN); *Rose Bernd* (HAUPTMANN); *Candida* (SHAW). Her wide-ranging REPERTOIRE also included: D'ANNUNZIO, *La Gioconda*, as Sirenetta, 1899; ROSTAND, *La Samaritaine*, 1901; PIRANDELLO; OBEY; and ROSSO DI SAN SECONDO, *Tra vestiti che ballano*, 1928. In the 1930s she toured Europe and in 1945 went to the USA; made many appearances in films and on TV.

Grand Guignol (Théâtre du Grand Guignol), Theatre opened by Max Maurey in Paris (Rue Chaptal) in 1899, now closed. It was devoted to the production of melodramatic horror plays, many by E. A. Poe, which made liberal use of realistic detail; the term *grand guignol* became a generic name for this kind of theatre; one of the earliest writers, probably the true creator of the Grand Guignol was Oscar Méténier, of the Théâtre Libre.
Bibl: C. Antona-Traversi, HISTOIRE DU GRAND GUIGNOL, 1933

Granovsky, Alexander (Abraham Ozark; 1890–1937), Russian actor and director. He was trained by REINHARDT in Germany. In 1919 founded the Jewish Theatre Studio in Leningrad, which later moved to Moscow (Yiddish State Theatre); in 1919 he directed the opening production of MAETERLINCK's *Les Aveugles*, then concentrated on Yiddish plays by, SHOLEM ALEICHEM, Goldfaden and others. After a successful tour in Europe in 1928/29 he did not return to the USSR. In 1930 he produced *Uriel Acosta* for the HABIMAH theatre in BERLIN and under the name of Alexis G., directed films in Germany and France.
Bibl: Toller, Roth, Goldschmidt, etc., DAS MOSKAUER JÜDISCH AKADEMISCHE THEATER, 1928

Granville-Barker, Harley (1877–1946), English playwright, actor, director and

Ruth Gordon with her husband KANIN

Grand Guignol theatre in Paris

Granville-Barker's production of *Androcles and the Lion* by SHAW, 1913

critic of the Edwardian era. As a director he is considered one of the pioneers of modern English theatre. In his early career he acted with GREET's company, and then in POEL's Elizabethan Stage Society, where he became acquainted with SHAW when playing Marchbanks in *Candida* in its first performance in 1900. His management of the ROYAL COURT THEATRE in partnership with VEDRENNE, 1904–07, set a standard for modern English theatre, and raised its quality by encouraging contemporary playwrights and the new drama of ideas; he demanded intelligent and controlled playing by his actors and experimented in stage design and technique. His REPERTOIRE consisted mainly of plays by Shaw and IBSEN, and by MAETERLINCK, HAUPTMANN, SCHNITZLER, YEATS and GALSWORTHY; his SHAKESPEARE revivals, which he mostly directed himself, were particularly important as practical demonstrations of his ideas which were later published in his *Prefaces to Shakespeare*, 1923–47. After World War I he rarely worked in the theatre and concentrated on writing plays and theoretical works; he lectured in many countries including the USA. His main productions: Shaw's *Candida*, 1904, *Fanny's First Play*, 1911, and *Androcles and the Lion*, 1913; EURIPIDES' *Iphigenia in Tauris*, 1912; SHAKESPEARE'S *The Two Gentlemen of Verona*, 1904, *A Winter's Tale*, 1912, *As You Like It*, 1912, *A Midsummer Night's Dream*, 1914. Other theoretical works: *A National Theatre: Scheme and Estimate* (with William Archer, 1907), co-editor of *The Companion to Shakespeare Studies*, 1934. His own plays were naturalistic, using understatement and restraint for dramatic effect; his main purpose was 'to see human emotions in relation to a moral and social order' (Desmond MacCarthy): *The Marrying of Ann Leete*, 1901; *The Voysey Inheritance*, 1905; *Waste*, 1907; *The Madras House*, 1910.
Bibl: C. B. Purdom (ed), THE SHAW-BARKER LETTERS, 1956

Grass, Günter (1927–), German novelist, poet and dramatist. Son of a grocer, he was conscripted into the German army at 17 and later captured by the Americans. After World War II he trained as a stonemason, and then worked as a painter and sculptor in Paris. He now lives in BERLIN. He achieved international fame with his novel *Die Blechtrommel* (*The Tin Drum*), 1959. His early plays are in the tradition of the THEATRE OF THE ABSURD. They include his first full-length play *Die Plebejer proben den Aufstand* (The Plebeians Rehearse the Uprising), fp Berlin 1966, Schillertheater, and London 1970, RSC; and a play about BRECHT and his reaction to the uprising of June 1953 by East Berliners against the Russian occupation. Other works include *Hochwasser* (Flood), Frankfurt 1957; *Onkel, Onkel* (*Uncle, Uncle*), Cologne 1958; *Davor* (Uptight), Berlin 1969, Schillertheater, dir LIETZAU, a drama which takes the form of a debate with five characters, anti-war student activists in conflict with a liberal professor who has renounced his former extremist pacifism; *Die Bösen Köche* (*The Wicked Cooks*), Berlin 1961; and several short plays, among them *Noch zehn Minuten bis Buffalo* (Ten Minutes to Buffalo), 1959.
Bibl: G. Loschutz, GÜNTER GRASS IN DER KRITIK, 1968; Norris Yates, 1967; H. Rischbieter and E. Wendt, DEUTSCHE DRAMATIK IN WEST UND OST, 1965

Grassi, Paolo (1919–), Italian critic, director and manager. In 1941 founded the avant-garde theatre company Palcoscenico, with whom he produced many, mostly contemporary, plays; 1945–47 drama critic and editor of two series of books on the theatre; in 1947 with STREHLER he founded the PICCOLO TEATRO DI MILANO, one of the most important REPERTORY theatres (TEATRO STABILE) in Italy; after Strehler's resignation in 1968, Grassi became its sole director.
Bibl: PICCOLO TEATRO, 1947–58, 1958

Gray, Simon (1936–), English dramatist. Educated at Westminster School and at universities in Canada and France before reading English at Cambridge; now a lecturer in English literature at Queen Mary College, London. Had three novels published before he started writing plays for TV in 1966: *The Caramel Crisis*; *Death of a Teddy Bear*; *A Way with the Ladies*; *Sleeping Dog*, and *Pig in a Poke*. His first stage play was *Wise Child*, 1967, Wyndham's Theatre, with GUINNESS, followed by *Dutch Uncle*, 1969, RSC, and *Spoiled*, 1971; *Butley*, London 1971, dir PINTER, with BATES, and New York 1972; *Otherwise Engaged*, London 1975, with Bates.

Graziano. Name often used for the DOTTORE of the COMMEDIA DELL'ARTE.

Greece. The classical Greek theatre reached its height at the annual festivals in honour of DIONYSOS (origins date back to the DITHYRAMB, the mime and the Dionysiac cult); two of these festivals are important in the development of drama. The LENAEA, occurring in January, was a local festival (while shipping rested) with productions of COMEDIES. From the second half of the fifth century, competitions were held under the auspices of the city states; from *c.* 442 BC TRAGEDIES were also presented. The actual tragedy festival, the main one in Athens, was the City DIONYSIA (or Great Dionysia) which took place from February until the beginning of April. Dramatic performances were given on the south slope of the Acropolis: on each of three consecutive days three tragedies followed by a SATYR PLAY (each TETRALOGY written by one poet) were presented; later, comedies and dithyrambs also formed an important part of the celebrations. The Great Dionysia were directed by the *archon eponymos*, who also chose the three tragic poets. He allocated (probably by lot) a performance each day to a CHOREGOS, a wealthy citizen who had to pay the expenses of dramatic production, providing food for members of the CHORUS and a place for rehearsals, and paying for costumes and special scenery, the musicians and the actors. The poet (e.g. AESCHYLUS, SOPHOCLES, EURIPIDES) wrote the music for his own plays and rehearsed the chorus and, in early times, also took part in the production as an actor. Later these functions became specialized with a CHORODIDASKALOS (chorus teacher) and highly skilled actors. A jury appointed by the State was responsible for choosing the winner, giving an account of the conduct of the festival and fixing the order of the three productions; in the records of early times only the winning poet and the *choregos* are named, later the chief actor or PROTAGONIST is included. Performances were given in an AMPHITHEATRE.
There was no national theatre during Byzantine and Turkish rule; in 1834 Athens had not a single theatre; in 1835 the Théatron Scontzópulos was founded followed by various others, partly with their own ENSEMBLES, but dominated by Italian and French companies; in 1888 founding of a municipal theatre in Athens with a Greek opera company; it was not until 1930 that a NATIONAL THEATRE (Ethnikon) was founded under the direction of Politis, who was succeeded by Rondiris; apart from that, the many commercial theatres are today mainly used as cinemas. After World War II there was a revitalization of classical drama in preserved antique theatres, e.g. festival in EPIDAUROS. Among the revivers of Greek theatre are the directors Christomanos Oeconomou and the younger generation includes Carantinos, Koun, MINOTIS, Mouzenidis, Murat, Solomos and Cacoyannis.
Bibl: A. W. Pickard-Cambridge, THE DRAMATIC FESTIVALS OF ATHENS, 2/1968; G. Else, THE ORIGIN AND EARLY FORM OF GREEK TRAGEDY, 1965; M. Bieber, HISTORY OF THE GREEK AND ROMAN THEATRE, 2/1961, T. B. L. Webster, GREEK THEATRE PRODUCTIONS, 1956; K. Lever, THE ART OF GREEK COMEDY, 1956

Green, Paul Eliot (1894–), US dramatist. Deeply sympathetic to the Black American in his struggle against racial prejudice, e.g. *In Abraham's Bosom*, New York 1926, Provincetown Theatre, awarded the PULITZER PRIZE, which tells the story of a Black American, and the violence and hate he meets when trying to found a school for Black children and his lynching by the mob. He is also concerned with religious fanaticism and superstition, e.g. *The Field God*, 1927, and *Shroud My Body Down*, 1935. In 1937 he created his 'symphonic drama', derived from the American tradition, with dance, chorus and huge parades: *The Lost Colony*, 1937, about the colonization of America; *The Highland Call*, 1939, about the Scots in North Carolina; *The Common Glory*, 1947, portraying Jefferson; *Faith of Our Fathers*, 1950, about Washington; *The Founders*, 1957, about Jamestown Colony, and *Stephen Foster*, 1959. Other works include the one-acters: *The Last of the Lowries*, and *The No 'Count Boy*, 1924; *Fixin's*, 1924; *White Dresses*, 1926; *Hymn to the Rising Sun*, 1930, a dramatic short play about a chain gang; *The House of Connelly*, 1931, about a disintegrating aristocratic family, which play launched the GROUP THEATRE; *Roll,*

Sweet Chariot, 1934, a symbolic play about Black Americans; *Johnny Johnson*, 1936, based on HAŠEK's *The Good Soldier Schweik*, an anti-war play with music by WEILL; *Native Son*, 1941, based on Richard Wright's novel, produced by WELLES.
Bibl: A. Boyd Adams, PAUL GREEN OF CHAPEL HILL, 1951; A. H. Quinn, A HISTORY OF THE AMERICAN DRAMA, 1945

Greene, Graham (1904–), English novelist and playwright. Worked as a film critic for periodicals in the early stages of his career. Author of many outstanding novels, he has written the plays: *The Heart of the Matter*, adapted with DEAN from his own novel, 1950; *The Living Room*, 1953; *The Potting Shed*, 1957; *The Complaisant Lover*, 1959; *Carving a Statue*, 1964. His novel *The Power and the Glory*, was adapted for the stage by CANNAN and Pierre Bost, 1958. Has written a number of screenplays, including *The Fallen Idol* and *The Third Man*, as well as adaptations of some of his novels.

Greene, Robert (1558–92), English dramatist. Travelled widely in England and on the Continent, leading a reckless wandering life. There was no writer in his day who was better able to convey the spirit of the times in England. His autobiographical tract *A Groatsworth of Wit Bought With A Million of Repentance*, pub. 1592, is important in theatre history for its attack on SHAKESPEARE. Among his best plays are the romantic drama *Orlando Furioso*, possibly written in collaboration with the actor Samuel Rowley, 1588–92; *Friar Bacon and Friar Bungay*, *c.* 1589–92 (the themes of love and magic in this play probably influenced Shakespeare); and a historical play, *The Scottish History of James IV*, *c.* 1590–91. Among the other writers with whom he is believed to have collaborated were KYD (*The Spanish Tragedy*) and Shakespeare (*Henry VI*). Though his plays are poorly constructed and careless, they have a high poetic quality.
Bibl: R. Pruvost, 1938

Greet, Sir Ben (Philip Barling; 1857–1936), English ACTOR-MANAGER. Knighted in 1929. Began his career as an actor; first managed open-air productions of SHAKESPEARE's plays in 1886, then founded a company which toured England and the USA, 1902–14; he returned to London in 1914, became one of the founders of the OLD VIC and was responsible for 24 Shakespeare productions, 1915–18; subsequently toured France, produced many plays for schools and open-air theatres. Helped many young actors on stage and in their training.

Gregor, Joseph (1888–1960), Austrian theatre historian. For many years he was head of the theatre collection of the National Library of Austria. His main works include: *Das russische Theater*, 1927; *Das amerikanische Theater und Kino*, 1931; in collaboration with R. Fülöp-Müller he wrote *Weltgeschichte des Theaters*, 1933; and *Geschichte des Österreichischen Theaters*, 1948.

Greece, terracotta statuette of comic actor

Greece, fragment of a crater depicting a costumed actor holding a mask

Gregory, Lady (Isabella Augusta; 1852–1932), Irish dramatist and theatre manager. With YEATS helped to found the Irish National Theatre Society in 1902, the nucleus of the ABBEY THEATRE company, in the formation of which she played an important part; she managed the Abbey Theatre, which opened in Dublin 1904, and wrote many plays for it, mainly one-acters, until her retirement in 1928. Among her best works are the short COMEDIES in the western Irish dialect, such as *Spreading the News*, 1904; *The Rising of the Moon*, 1907, and plays dealing with subjects from the life of the people, based on her interest in Irish literature and history. They included dramatized fairy-tales, e.g. *The Travelling Man*, 1910, and *The Dragon*, 1919; popular historical plays, e.g. the TRAGEDIES *Grania*, 1906, and *Kincora*, 1909; and TRAGICOMEDIES, e.g. *The Canavans*, 1906, and *The White Cockade*, 1905. She also worked with Yeats on many of his plays, e.g. *The Pot of Broth*, 1902, *Cathleen ni Houlihan*, 1902, and *On Baile's Strand*, 1904. She wrote a volume of reminiscences, *Our Irish Theatre*, 1914.
Bibl: E. Coxhead, 1961

Grein, (Jacob) Jack Thomas (1862–1935), English critic and man of the theatre, born in the Netherlands. In 1891 he founded the Independent Theatre Club in London, a non-commercial artistic enterprise, modelled on ANTOINE's Théâtre Libre which opened with IBSEN's *Ghosts*, a spectacular production which gave rise to accusations of obscenity. Until 1898 he produced plays by HAUPTMANN, ZOLA, IBSEN and SHAW, attracting much attention; *Widowers' Houses* produced by G. in 1892 was the first of Shaw's plays to be shown in London. He helped to establish the reputation of Shaw and Ibsen, but did not achieve the continuity of Antoine's theatre. Worked as a critic for *The Sunday Times* until 1918. He also published five volumes of collected *Dramatic Criticism*, 1898–1903; two others appeared in 1921 and 1924.
Bibl: M. Orme, J. T. GREIN; THE STORY OF A PIONEER, 1936

Griboyedov, Alexander Sergeyevich (1795–1829), Russian playwright. Successful diplomat and author of several COMEDIES, the best known of which is *Gore ot uma* (*Woe from Wit*), 1823–24, fp 1831, a brilliant satirical play on topical themes written in verse, which is considered the first great comedy in Russian literature and, according to the poet BLOK, 'unsurpassed in world literature'.
Bibl: S. M. Petrov, 1950

Grieg, Nordahl (1902–43), Norwegian dramatist and poet who was killed in action flying over Berlin. He wrote pacifist, anti-Fascist plays: *Barabbas*, 1927; *En ung manns kjærlighet* (A Young Man's Love), 1927; *Atlanterhavet* (The Atlantic), 1932; *Vår ære og vår makt* (Our Honour and Our Might), 1935, all of which were first performed at the National Theatre in Oslo; followed by *Men imorgen* (But Tomorrow . . .), 1936, and *Nederlaget* (*The Defeat*), 1937, which deals with the Paris Commune in 1871, and inspired BRECHT to write *The Days of the Commune*.
Bibl: H. Beyer, A HISTORY OF NORWEGIAN LITERATURE, 1956

Grillparzer, Franz (1791–1872), Austrian poet and playwright. In his dramatic works he combined elements of popular Viennese theatre and the influence of Spanish BAROQUE DRAMA. Resident playwright at the BURGTHEATER in Vienna 1818–23. His plays combine a surprisingly modern awareness of depth psychology with an ironical attitude to history. Main works: *Die Ahnfrau* (The Ancestress), 1817; the trilogy *Das goldene Vlies* (The Golden Fleece), 1821, consisting of *Der Gastfreund* (The Guest), *Die Argonauten* (The Argonauts), *Medea*; *König Ottokars Glück und Ende* (King Ottokar's Luck and End), 1825; *Ein treuer Diener seines Herrn* (His Master's Faithful Servant), 1828; *Des Meeres und der Liebe Wellen* (The Waves of the Sea and of Love), the story of Hero and Leander, 1831; *Der Traum ein Leben* (The Dream of Life), 1834, *Weh dem, der lügt* (Thou Shalt Not Lie!), 1834. When this last play was condemned by the Viennese aristocracy, G. did not release any more of his plays for production; posthumous works are *Ein Bruderzwist in Habsburg* (Family Strife in Habsburg), 1850, fp 1872; *Libussa* and *Die Jüdin von Toledo* (*The Jewess of Toledo*).
Bibl: H. A. Reger, DAS SPRACHBILD IN GRILLPARZERS DRAMEN, 1968; D. Yates, FRANZ GRILLPARZER, A CRITICAL BIOGRAPHY, 1953

Grimaldi, Joseph (1778–1837). Of English-Italian origin, he was one of the most famous CLOWNS of all time. He began his career as a dancer (his father was ballet master at DRURY LANE) and from 1806 appeared as a clown at COVENT GARDEN, showing exceptional ability as a popular singer, dancer, MIME and actor. He created the typical English clown who has been called 'Joey' ever since.
Bibl: MEMOIRS OF JOSEPH GRIMALDI, 1838

Grock (Adrian Wettach; 1880–1959), one of the best-known CLOWNS of his time. Born in Switzerland, he joined a CIRCUS at the age of 12, performing acrobatic numbers; then went on tour with his family who were Tyrolean singers. In 1903 became partner of the musical clown Brich, with whom he toured Europe and Latin America. In 1907 he joined the famous clown Antonet and after 1911 appeared mainly as soloist in London until 1924 at the Coliseum, and Paris. He was a magnificent performer whose act eventually lasted an hour, consisting mainly of virtuoso musical numbers in which he managed to 'fail' in everything he attempted (though he in fact played 24 instruments expertly). He also wrote autobiographical works: *G. raconté par G.*, 1931; *Sans blague!*, 1948; *Ma vie de clown*, 1957.
Bibl: T. Rémy, LES CLOWNS, 1945

Gropius, Walter (1883–1969), German architect, founder and director of the Bauhaus, 1919–28. In 1927 designed for PISCATOR a 'total theatre', an oval layout in which both a platform stage and part of the auditorium could be moved; this allowed two variations, one in the round (with the audience in a circle), and the other a form similar to the Greek amphitheatre. The whole oval is surrounded by 12 flat screens, which can be used for projections. This plan was, however, never realized.

Grossman, Jan (1925–), Czech director. Studied literature in Prague, and worked as a journalist and editor; became DRAMATURG in Brno, 1949–53, then in Prague under BURIAN, 1955–56; editor, collaborator in the LATERNA MAGICA, 1957–59, and 1961–68 at the Theatre on the Balustrade in Prague where, in 1962, became artistic director of drama (the theatre also has a MIME company run by FIALKA). In 1963 adapted HAŠEK's *The Good Soldier Schweik* for the theatre in Brno and attempted a subtle criticism of the political system in his adaptations and productions – 'critical dramaturgy'; worked closely with HAVEL, whose plays *The Garden Party*, 1963, and *The Memorandum*, 1965, he produced at the Theatre on the Balustrade. Also adapted JARRY's Ubu plays with M. Macourek in 1964 and KAFKA's *The Trial* in 1965.

Grossmith. A family of English actors and entertainers. (1) **George G.** (1847–1912), a singer who appeared in the Savoy operas (▷GILBERT AND SULLIVAN), and his younger brother (2) **Weedon G.** (1852–1919), an actor and playwright, are the joint authors of the famous book *The Diary of a Nobody*, a hilarious picture of Victorian suburban life which has also been adapted for the stage. George's two sons (3) **George G. Jnr** (1874–1935) and (4) **Lawrence G.** (1877–1944) were both distinguished actors.

Grosz, George (1893–1959), German painter, draughtsman and satirist. In the early 1920s he worked at the REINHARDT theatres in Berlin, designed sets for SHAW's *Caesar and Cleopatra*, 1922, and *Androcles and the Lion*, 1923, in a picture-book style. For GOLL's satire on the bourgeoisie, *Methusalem*, he returned to the satirical DADA elements of his early work. PISCATOR allowed him to 'use the stage as a drawing board' for the production of HAŠEK's *The Good Soldier Schweik*, 1928.
Bibl: E. Piscator, DAS POLITISCHE THEATER, 1963

Grotesque ▷THEATRE OF THE GROTESQUE.

Grotowski, Jerzy (1933–), Polish director. Trained in Craców, Moscow and China. In 1967 produced his first play, IONESCO's *The Chairs*. In 1959 with Ludwik Flaszen he took over the management of the Theatre Laboratory *13 Rzedów* (*13 Rows*) in Opole, which in 1965 he moved to Wroclaw, where he established an experimental laboratory theatre. He first based his work on the autonomy of the director; today the actor is the centre of his work, and has to undergo extensive physical and psychological training. G. sees theatre as a ritual act of self-revelation in which the actor violates the last 'sacred' area of life in a secularized society – the sphere of personal privacy. By transgressing such taboos the actor creates the feeling of awe which re-establishes the awareness of the sacred. Famous productions include *Apocalypsis cum figuris*, based on a collection of biblical texts and liturgical chants interspersed with quotations from DOSTOYEVSKY, T. S. ELIOT and Simone Weil: BYRON's *Cain*, 1960; SLOWACKI's *Kordian*, WYSPIAŃSKI's *Akropolis* and MARLOWE's *The Tragical History of Dr Faustus*, all in 1962, and *The Constant Prince* (CALDERÓN/Slowacki, 1965). He outlined his ideas in the book *Towards a Poor Theatre*, 1968. His company has toured Europe and the USA and has had an immense influence on many leading directors, e.g. BROOK.

Group Theatre. A serious and dedicated US movement with high aims which endeavoured to break away from BROADWAY commercialism. It succeeded in deepening the art and content of American theatre but failed after ten years as it proved impossible to combine art theatre with show business. Founded in 1931 by CHERYL CRAWFORD, STRASBERG and CLURMAN, the first production was GREEN's *The House of Connelly*. Other plays include KINGSLEY's *Men in White*, 1933; ODETS's *Waiting for Lefty*, and *Awake and Sing*, 1935, and *Golden Boy*, 1937; R. Ardrey's *Thunder Rock*, 1939. Among actors and directors who had their first training with the Group were KAZAN, STELLA ADLER, John Garfield, Lee J. Cobb and Franchot Tone.

Gründgens, Gustav (1899–1963), German actor, director and manager. One of the leading figures in modern German theatre; he trained under LOUISE DUMONT (Düsseldorf) and in 1923 joined ZIEGEL's company at the Hamburg Kammerspiele, where his first noted appearances included Touchstone in *As You Like It*, 1924; Bluntschli in SHAW's *Arms and the Man*, 1925; Angelo in *Measure for Measure*, 1925, and the title role in BÜCHNER's *Dantons Tod*, 1928. With ERIKA MANN, to whom he was briefly married, K. MANN and Pamela Wedekind, he toured in *Revue zu Vieren*. From 1928 he appeared in BERLIN and established himself mainly in the parts of bon-vivants and genteel gangsters; during this period he made his début as a director of opera. In 1932 he joined the Berlin National Theatre and was appointed INTENDANT in 1934, directing and acting in a great number of plays by SHAKESPEARE, GOETHE, SCHILLER, HEBBEL, GRABBE, etc. Generalintendant of the Düsseldorf Municipal Theatres, 1947–51, and Intendant of the Düsseldorf Schauspielhaus, 1951–55. Intendant of the Deutsches Schauspielhaus, Hamburg, 1955–62, where he produced a number of important modern plays, e.g. Lawrence Durrell's *Sappho*, 1959; BRECHT's *Die heilige Johanna der Schlachthöfe*, 1959; OSBORNE's *The Entertainer*, 1957. As an actor he was praised for his authority, his elegance and wit; probably

Joseph Grimaldi as the clown in *Harlequin Padman or the Golden Fish*, a PANTOMIME at COVENT GARDEN, 1811

Lady Gregory (*right*) with Sir Hugh Lane and two other directors of the Irish National Theatre, SYNGE and YEATS. Drawing by Orpen

George Grosz, programme booklet for the *Schall und Rauch* CABARET

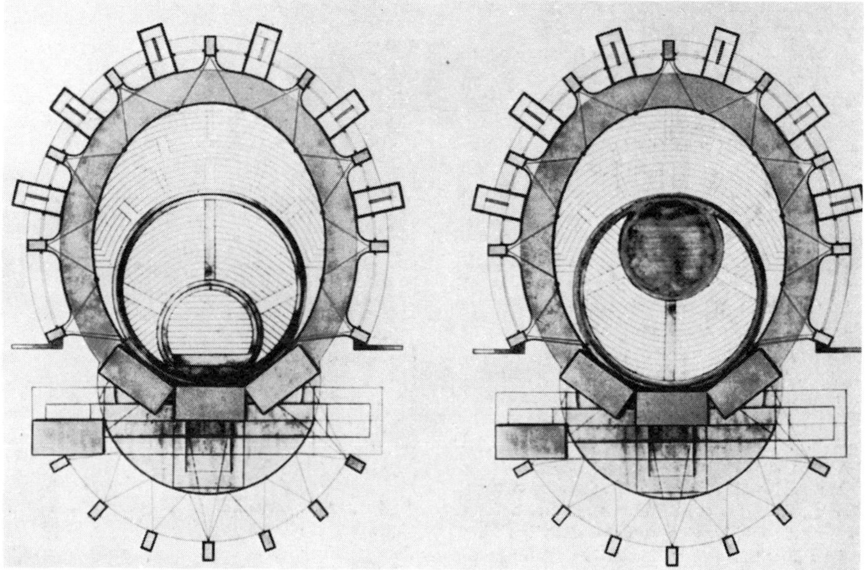

Walter Gropius, design for a theatre

his greatest part was Mephistopheles in GOETHE's *Faust*, which he played from 1932. Bibl: H. Rischbieter (ed), 1963; S. Melchinger, GRÜNDGENS FAUST, 1959

Gryphius, Andreas (1616–64), one of the outstanding poets of the German High Baroque. Since his plays were written without contact with a theatre, they are rarely staged except for occasional revivals of COMEDIES. These include *Horribilicribrifax*, pub 1663, a lively picture of contemporary follies, and *Herr Peter Squentz*, pub 1658. Among his tragedies are *Cardenio und Celinde*, 1647; *Carolus Stuardus*, 1649–63; and *Catharina von Georgien*, 1657.
Bibl: G. Kaiser (ed), DIE DRAMEN DES GRYPHIUS, 1968

Guare, John (1930–), US dramatist. Suddenly gained national attention with his short play *Muzeeka*, New York 1968, Provincetown Playhouse; originally presented at the Eugene O'Neill Memorial Theatre Foundation's Playwrights Conference, Waterford, Conn., and later at the Mark Taper Forum, Los Angeles, it won him a 1969 OBIE AWARD for distinguished playwriting. In 1969 he gained additional prominence with his BROADWAY production of *Cop-Out*, the collective title of two short plays, *Cop-Out* and *Home Fires*. His other works include: *The Loveliest Afternoon of the Year* and *Something I'll Tell You Tuesday*, both presented at the Caffé Cino, New York 1966, and *The House of Blue Leaves*, New York 1970; also produced at the Dublin Festival, 1972. He successfully adapted and wrote the lyrics for a rock-musical version of SHAKESPEARE's *The Two Gentlemen of Verona* at the Public Theatre, New York 1971, and London 1973. Also collaborated on the film script of Milos Forman's *Taking Off*, 1971.

Guarini, Battista (1538–1612), Italian poet, scholar and diplomat. Was Professor of Literature and Philosophy at the University of Ferrara and served the rulers of Ferrara, the Este family, as ambassador in Turin, Venice, Rome and Cracow. His most important dramatic work was *Pastor Fido*, written 1580–83, fp Cremona 1595; inspired by Tasso's *L'Aminta*, it exercised a great influence on PASTORAL DRAMA throughout Europe.

Guignol. French name for the chief character of the traditional popular puppet play, equivalent to the German HANSWURST or English Punch (▷GRAND GUIGNOL).

Guilbert, Yvette (1867–1944), French cabaret singer and actress. One of the most famous DISEUSES of the French theatre, in her early career she achieved little success with the public. Unlike her rivals who attracted attention mainly by their beauty and elegance, she succeeded by her power of expression and simple emotion. At the time when she appeared in the CABARET Divan Japonais her admirers included ZOLA, Daudet, the GONCOURT brothers, Monet and Toulouse-Lautrec. Her first great success came in 1895; in that year she toured the USA, then Europe and North Africa, to return triumphantly to Paris in 1896 at the Moulin Rouge. She established herself from that date as the star of the famous REVUE theatres, e.g. Ambassadeurs, FOLIES-BERGÈRE. She also appeared as a dramatic actress; her best-remembered performance was as Mrs Peachum in BRECHT's *Threepenny Opera*, 1937; in 1926 she played Martha in Murnau's film *Faust*.
Bibl: C. R. Marx, YVETTE GUILBERT VUE PAR TOULOUSE-LAUTREC, 1950

Guild Theatre ▷AMERICAN NATIONAL THEATRE AND ACADEMY.

Guinness, Sir Alec (1914–), English actor. Knighted in 1959. Made his first appearances in minor comic roles, e.g. Osric in GIELGUD's production of *Hamlet*, Touchstone in *As You Like It*. In 1938 achieved great success as Hamlet in the modern dress production by GUTHRIE at the OLD VIC and in the same year played Bob Acres in SHERIDAN's *The Rivals*. His first post-war role was Mitya in his own adaptation of DOSTOYEVSKY's *The Brothers Karamazov*, 1946. In that year he also gave an outstanding performance as the Fool in *King Lear* at the Old Vic, with OLIVIER in the title role, which was followed by two other outstanding performances: Abel Drugger in JONSON's *The Alchemist* and Hlestakov in GOGOL's *The Government Inspector*. He also played Sir Henry Harcourt-Reilly in ELIOT's *The Cocktail Party*, 1949, and in 1961 appeared in his own production of *Hamlet*. He made his later career mainly in films but continued also to appear on stage, e.g. Bridget Boland's *The Prisoner*, 1953, Shakespeare Festival Theatre, Stratford, Ontario; *Hotel Paradiso*, 1956; Bérenger in IONESCO's *Exit the King*, ROYAL COURT, 1963; T. E. Lawrence in RATTIGAN's *Ross*, 1969; the blind barrister in MORTIMER's *Voyage Round My Father*, 1972; *Habeas Corpus* by Alan Bennett, 1973; *Yahoo*, based on J. Swift, 1976.
Bibl: K. Tynan, 2/1955

Guitry. (1) **Lucien G.** (1860–1925), French actor and playwright. After training at the CONSERVATOIRE D'ART DRAMATIQUE he was offered a place with the COMÉDIE-FRANÇAISE, but instead went to the Gymnase Theatre where he made his début as Aimé Tessendier in DUMAS *fils' La Dame aux camélias*, 1878; went on tour to England with SARAH BERNHARDT, playing Don Carlos in *Hernani*; 1882–91 appeared at the Mikhailovsky Theatre in St Petersburg, returned to Paris in 1891 where he worked at the Odéon and the Théâtre Renaissance with RÉJANE and Bernhardt; in 1901 joined the CF as actor and director, a position which he gave up after eight months; 1902–10 took over the management of the Théâtre Renaissance, which soon overshadowed the CF because of the contemporary REPERTOIRE, including plays by France, Brieux, BOURGET and Capus, and outstanding actors. In 1910 he managed the Théâtre de la Porte Saint-Martin; 1912–15 tour; and 1917–18 was particularly successful with his own comedies, *Grand-père* and *L'Archevêque et ses fils*; 1919–24 he appeared in plays by his son Sacha and produced plays by MOLIÈRE, e.g. *Le Misanthrope* and *Tartuffe*. He was a robust actor, admired for his charismatic authority; his voice was mellow with hints of irony. His son (2) **Sacha G.** (1885–1957), a dramatist and actor, wrote more than 100 light plays, brilliant, often frivolous COMEDIES about theatre life and historical personalities in which he acted himself, often with his second wife Yvonne Printemps. He also appeared in and directed films. His plays include: *Le Page*, 1902; *Nono*, 1905; *La Clef*, 1907; *Le Veilleur de nuit*, 1911; *Jean III ou l'Irrésistible vocation du fils Mondoucet*, 1912; *La Prise de Berg-op-Zoom*, 1912; *Deburau*, 1918; *Pasteur*, 1919; *Béranger*, 1920; *Je t'aime*, 1920; *Jacqueline*, 1921; *L'Amour masqué*, 1923; *On ne joue pas pour s'amuser*, 1925; *Mozart*, 1925; *Désiré*, 1927; *Mariette*, 1928; *Charles Lindbergh*, 1928; *Château en Espagne*, 1933; *Le Mot de Cambronne*, 1936; *Louis le bien-aimé*, 1940; *Une Folie*, 1953.
Bibl: A. Madis, SACHA, 1957; S. Guitry, LUCIEN GUITRY, RACONTÉ PAR SON FILS, 1930

Güntekin, Resat Nuri (1889–1956), Turkish novelist and playwright. Began his literary career as a short-story writer and drama critic, 1917–18, before turning to dramatic writing, mainly social satires: *Hülleci* (The Hired Husband), 1935; *Tas Parcast* (A Piece of Stone), 1923; *Eski Sarki* (The Old Song), 1951; and *Yaprak Dökümü* (The Fall of the Leaves), 1943, based on his own novel. Most of his plays are concerned with the people and social problems of Anatolia.

Guthrie, Sir Tyrone (1900–71), English director. Knighted in 1961. Studied at Oxford and first appeared with the Oxford Repertory Company before turning to directing. First worked with the Scottish National Players, 1926–28, in Glasgow and then with the Festival Theatre in Cambridge, 1929–30. His London début as a director came with BRIDIE's *The Anatomist*, 1931. He was twice a director at the OLD VIC, 1933–34 and 1936–37; Administrator of the Old Vic and Sadler's Wells Opera 1939–45, and 1951–52 again at the Old Vic. After the war he founded and ran the Shakespeare Festival Theatre in Stratford, Ontario, 1953–57. In 1962, based on the same ENSEMBLE pattern, he established one of America's first permanent regional theatre companies in Minneapolis where, in 1963, a theatre was named after him. A creative, experimental and highly imaginative artist, his style of production was emphasized by the choreography and quickness of speech. In 1938 he produced a famous modern-dress *Hamlet* with GUINNESS in the lead. Equally outstanding was his production of LINDSAY's *The Three Estates*, a 16th-century Scottish play, for the EDINBURGH FESTIVAL in 1948. But his fame as a director is based primarily on his Shakespearean productions including: (at Stratford, Ontario) *All's Well That Ends Well*; *The Taming of the Shrew*, 1954; (at the Old Vic) *Troilus and Cressida*, 1956; JONSON's *The*

Alchemist, 1963. He also directed opera in Helsinki, Tel Aviv and New York; with WOLFIT he adapted MARLOWE's *Tamburlaine the Great*. G., who had been a radio drama producer for the BBC in Belfast at the start of his career, wrote two important radio plays, which are regarded as a breakthrough in the art of radio drama: *The Squirrel's Cage*, and *The Flowers are not for you to pick*. He adapted the latter for the stage under the title *Top of the Ladder*, 1950. He also wrote several books including: *Theatre Prospect*, 1932; *A Life in the Theatre*, 1960; *Tyrone Guthrie on Acting*, 1971.

Gutzkow, Karl Ferdinand (1811–78), German writer. One of the most prominent members of the literary movement Junges Deutschland, he wrote essays, novels and many plays ranging from historical to family drama and COMEDIES in the tradition of SCRIBE; his only work which is still performed is *Uriel Acosta*, 1846, particularly in Russian (STANISLAVSKY) and Jewish theatres. It deals with conflict of conscience of a Jewish heretic in his struggle for intellectual freedom.
E. W. Dobert, 1968

Gwynn, Nell (Eleanor; 1650–87), one of the first professional actresses in the English theatre. Very popular and admired in her day, her best performances were in COMEDIES, e.g. Florimel in DRYDEN's *Secret Love*. In 1669 she became the mistress of Charles II and in 1670 appeared for the last time on stage in Dryden's *The Conquest of Granada*. The US dramatist Paul Kester (1870–1933) wrote a highly successful play about her, *Sweet Nell of Old Drury*.
Bibl: J. H. Wilson, 1952

Haase, Friedrich (1825–1911), German actor, director and manager. Master of virtuoso detail, whose most famous parts were Marinelli in LESSING's *Emilia Galotti*, and Mephistopheles in GOETHE's *Faust*. He appeared with almost all the major German theatre companies including the Deutsches Landestheater in Prague, Frankfurt, Leipzig, the Royal Theatre in BERLIN, and also on BROADWAY. As a director of the COURT THEATRE in Coburg-Gotha, 1866–68, he attempted to produce model performances in the manner of the MEININGER company. He also played some part in founding the Deutsches-Theater, Berlin, in 1882.
Bibl: P. Schlenther, 1930

Habimah (Hebrew = scene, stage). Jewish theatre company. Formed in Moscow in 1917, visited Palestine in 1928 and settled permanently in Tel Aviv; they have had

Tyrone Guthrie's production of *Peer Gynt*, OLD VIC, 1944

Alec Guinness in *The Government Inspector* by GOGOL, OLD VIC, 1947

Nell Gwynn, portrait from the Lely Studio, 1675

Habimah, dance of the beggars from *The Dybbuk*, New York 1927

their own theatre there since 1945 (▷ ISRAEL). The company, a mixture of amateurs and professionals, gave their first public performance in 1918 with one-act plays by Jewish writers in Hebrew, including ASCH, PERETZ, Katzenelson and Berkowitz, and achieved immediate success; subsequently the Habimah became one of the four studios of the MOSCOW ART THEATRE under STANISLAVSKY. Theatre in Yiddish already existed in Russia and Poland, but the novelty was the use of the ancient Hebrew language. ANSKY's *The Dybbuk* directed by VAKHTANGOV in 1922 became a model production. The company toured Europe, 1925–26, with great success, and, in 1927, the USA, where part of the company broke away and settled, turning from Hebrew to English. The remaining company toured Germany and Italy. After settling in Tel Aviv they formed a kind of NATIONAL THEATRE, touring Europe again 1937–38, the USA 1952, Paris 1954. In Tel Aviv two auditoriums for the Habimah National Theatre were built in a vast cultural complex, opened in 1970. The Habimah has a REPERTORY of world theatre ranging from SOPHOCLES, MOLIÈRE, and SCHILLER to IBSEN, SHAW and A. MILLER; and plays which deal specially with Jewish themes by GUTZKOW, FEUCHTWANGER, Brod, Gronemann, etc. Today the Habimah also has its own drama school; many important European directors have worked there: JESSNER, LINDTBERG, GUTHRIE, etc.
Bibl: G. Hanoch (ed), 1945

Hackett, James Keteltas (1869–1926), US actor. Son of James Henry Hackett, an actor famous for his portrayal of Yankee characters, who was the first American actor to appear in London as a star in 1833, playing Falstaff and several of his Yankee characterizations. J.K.H. was a fine romantic actor who played leading SHAKESPEARE and SHERIDAN roles under DALY in 1892 and in 1895 joined D. FROHMANN's company in New York. He later opened his own theatre, the Wallack, where his production of *Othello*, with sets by URBAN, marked an important step forward in the history of US stagecraft and scenic design.

Hacks, Peter (1928–), German dramatist. Studied in Munich and in 1955 moved to East Berlin, where he worked until 1963 as DRAMATURG at the Deutsches-Theater. Subsequently freelance writer; his works include: *Das Volksbuch vom Herzog Ernst* (The Folk-tale of Duke Ernst), written 1953, fp Mannheim 1967; *Die Eröffnung des indischen Zeitalters* (The Opening of the Indian Age), 1955, Munich Kammerspiele; *Die Schlacht bei Lobositz* (The Battle of Lobositz), East Berlin 1956, Deutsches-Theater; *Moritz Tassow*, East Berlin 1965, Volksbühne, dir BESSON; *Margarete von Aix*, pub 1967; *Amphitryon*, Göttingen 1968, Deutsches-Theater. Adaptations: *Kindermörderin* (The Infanticide), based on H. L. Wagner; *Der Frieden* (Peace), based on ARISTOPHANES, 1962, dir Besson; *Die schöne Helena* (La Belle Hélène), based on MEILHAC and Halévy, 1964, dir Besson; *Polly*, based on GAY, 1966. He started by writing ironic historical dramas, the impact of which was sensational. Combining wit, elegant form, materialism, and erotic frankness, he has developed a style which, though obviously modelled on BRECHT, is very much his own. In *Die Sorgen und die Macht* (Troubles and Authority), East Berlin 1961, he deals with problems among workers in East Germany, and in *Moritz Tassow* with the ideological controversy between utopian and realistic Communism in the post-war era. Both plays were criticized in East Germany by the Party and the State for exhibiting 'decadent' values, and his career received a major setback.
Bibl: H. Rischbieter and E. Wendt, DEUTSCHE DRAMATIK IN WEST UND OST, 1965

Halbe, Max (1865–1944), German dramatist. An exponent of NATURALISM, his best-known works are *Jugend* (Youth), 1893; *Freie Liebe* (Free Love), 1890; *Mutter Erde* (Mother Earth), 1897; *Der Strom* (The Stream), 1903; *Die Friedeninsel* (The Isle of Peace), 1944, etc.

Hall, Peter (1930–), English director and theatre manager. Joined the Arts Theatre in 1954 (artistic director 1955–56) where he staged the first English-language production of BECKETT's *Waiting for Godot*, 1955, and plays by GIRAUDOUX, T. WILLIAMS and LORCA. In 1956 he produced *Gigi* with his first wife Leslie Caron playing the lead and in the same year started work in STRATFORD-UPON-AVON: *Love's Labour's Lost*, 1956; *Cymbeline*, 1957; *Twelfth Night*, 1958; *A Midsummer Night's Dream* and *Coriolanus*, 1959; *The Two Gentlemen of Verona*, 1960. In 1960 he succeeded GLEN BYAM SHAW as director of the Stratford Memorial Theatre, which became the ROYAL SHAKESPEARE COMPANY, and in order to keep a permanent company of actors took over the Aldwych Theatre as a London home, transferring Shakespearean productions from Stratford and also producing new plays by European and English avant-garde writers. He also succeeded in persuading the City of London to build a new theatre in the Barbican redevelopment near St Paul's; in 1968 he retired from active management of the RSC to work on this project. His best-known productions include: *The Wars of the Roses*, a cycle of plays by BARTON based on the three parts of *Henry VI* and *Richard III*, Stratford 1963, London 1964. In 1969 he became director of the Covent Garden Opera but resigned in 1971. He was appointed in 1973 to succeed OLIVIER as director of the NATIONAL THEATRE.

Hall, Willis (1929–), English dramatist. In *The Long and the Short and the Tall*, 1959, he gave a candid and realistic picture of underprivileged soldiers trapped in the Malayan jungle in 1942. He later collaborated with Keith Waterhouse in North-country comedies such as *Billy Liar*, 1960, and *Celebration*, 1961.

Hallam. Family of English actors. They formed the first major company to visit the American colonies and influence the development of theatre there. (1) **Lewis H.** (1714–56) worked at COVENT GARDEN, 1734–41, and at DRURY LANE till he went to America in 1752 with his family and a group of actors; they gave their first performance, *The Merchant of Venice*, at Williamsburg, and in 1753 played JONSON's *The Alchemist* in New York, where they built the Nassau Street Theatre. Their REPERTORY included SHAKESPEARE, LILLO, FARQUHAR, CIBBER, VANBRUGH, GAY and various FARCES. They appeared later in Philadelphia and in Jamaica, 1754–58, where Lewis H. died. His wife took over the management and in 1758 married David Douglass, the manager of a theatrical company. The two companies were amalgamated under Douglass, with (2) **Lewis H. Jr.** (*c.* 1740–1808) as principal actor. Returning to New York, they were renamed The American Company. In 1767 they produced the first original American play in a professional production, GODFREY's *Prince of Parthia*. After the death of his stepfather L.H. took over the management of the American Company in partnership with DUNLAP, John Henry and John Hodgkinson, and, with the latter, built the Park Theatre in New York, 1798.
Bibl: A. H. Quinn, A HISTORY OF AMERICAN DRAMA, 1946

Halliwell, David (1937–), English dramatist. His best-known play is *Little Malcolm and His Struggle Against the Eunuchs*, 1966 (in the USA titled *Hail Scrawdyke*), a satirical fantasy which deals with the origins of Fascism, made into a film, 1975. Since *Little Malcolm*, he has helped to run the Quipu Company, a lunchtime theatre group in London, writing plays and playlets for them, and he has also written for radio. Other works include: *The Experiment*, 1967, a satirical entertainment devised and directed by H. D. Calderisi; *K. D. Dufford Hears K. D. Dufford Ask K. D. Dufford How K. D. Dufford'll Make K. D. Dufford*, 1969; *Muck from Three Angels*, 1970; *A Discussion*, 1970; *A Who's Who of Flapland* (originally a radio play, 1967), fp 1970, ROYAL COURT THEATRE. He is engaged on evolving a new drama technique – 'multi-viewpoint drama' which presents an event from the differing points of view of the characters involved in it.

Hamburgische Dramaturgie. The collected criticism by LESSING of the productions at the Hamburg National Theatre where he was official critic 1767–69 (2 vols, covering 52 performances each; a new edition was published in 1958). The essays were criticisms of individual productions, but developed by Lessing into a general discussion of drama and dramatic technique; he does not depart from ARISTOTLE's theories on drama; in his treatment of catharsis and TRAGEDY he insists that both fear and pity are felt by the spectator who should identify with the hero. The main influence exerted by the Hamburgische Dramaturgie on the development of German drama was L.'s defence of SHAKESPEARE as a model for German playwrights as against the French classical tragedy of RACINE and CORNEILLE – his point of view ultimately prevailed.

Hamilton, Patrick (1904–62), English novelist and playwright. Started as an actor and wrote a number of highly successful plays, among them: the thriller *Rope*, 1929, the story of an actual murder committed solely for thrills by two bored rich young men (distantly based on the Loeb-Leopold case); *Angel Street* (originally *Gaslight*, and later filmed under that title), 1938, about a woman whose husband tries to drive her mad, is a gripping Victorian MELODRAMA; *The Governess*, 1945, another Victorian melodrama, and the romantic historical play *The Duke in Darkness*, 1945. H. also wrote a number of highly effective radio thrillers.

Hamlet. Main character in SHAKESPEARE's play, one of the most multi-faceted in dramatic literature; has provided material for countless theories (between 1870 and 1930 W. Ebisch and L. L. Schücking registered – in a *Shakespeare Bibliography*, Oxford 1931 – *c.* 2,000 studies not including articles in magazines and newspapers). The story of Hamlet is derived from Celtic and Scandinavian legend; first found in written form in the *Historia Danica* (*c.* 1200) by the Danish writer Saxo Grammaticus (1150–1200). The first English Hamlet, so-called *Ur-Hamlet* (which is lost) was probably by KYD, written about 1580, produced in 1594 at the Newington Butts Theatre in London. Shakespeare's version of Hamlet was probably first performed in 1601 at the GLOBE; publication of the first Quarto recorded in the Stationers' Register in 1602; the text used today appeared for the first time in 1604 in the second Quarto edition. In the first production of *Hamlet* Shakespeare himself played the Ghost, R. BURBAGE played Hamlet probably with KEMPE as the first Gravedigger, and Richard Robenson as OPHELIA (first appearance of a woman on the English stage was not until 1656). The part of Hamlet has been a challenge to the greatest actors of all ages: in England BETTERTON, GARRICK, KEAN, OLIVIER; in Germany DEVRIENT, DAWISON, KAINZ, GRÜNDGENS; in France TALMA, MOUNET-SULLY, BARRAULT; others include J. BARRYMORE and GASSMAN.
Bibl: R. Mander & J. Mitchenson, HAMLET THROUGH THE AGES, 1952

Hammerstein. US family of theatre managers and lyric writers. (1) **Oscar H.** (**I** 1847–1919) emigrated from Berlin to the USA at the age of 15. After varied experience in managing REVUES, variety shows and opera, he founded the Manhattan Opera House in 1906 which he sold four years later to the Metropolitan Opera Company. With his sons (2) **William H.** (1874–1914) and (3) **Arthur H.** (1872–1955) he often managed several theatres at one time, the most successful of which was the Victoria, the leading VAUDEVILLE theatre between 1904 and World War I. William's son (4) **Oscar H.** (**II** 1895–1961) was one of the leading MUSICAL COMEDY lyric writers of his time. One of his first shows was *Rose*

Hamlet, etching by Delacroix, 1843

Peter Hall's production of BECKETT's *Waiting for Godot*, Arts Theatre, London 1955

Marie, 1924, music FRIML. He wrote lyrics for *Desert Song*, 1926, music ROMBERG; *Show Boat*, 1927, and *Music in the Air*, 1932, both music KERN. His long and successful collaboration with RODGERS began in 1943 with the THEATRE GUILD production of *Oklahoma!*, based on the stage play *Green Grow the Lilacs* by Lynn Riggs; this was followed by *Carousel*, 1945, based on MOLNÁR's *Liliom*; *South Pacific*, 1949, with MARY MARTIN and Ezio Pinza; *The King and I*, 1941, with GERTRUDE LAWRENCE and Yul Brynner, *The Sound of Music*, 1959, and many others. Together they produced the I. BERLIN musical *Annie Get Your Gun*, 1946, with ETHEL MERMAN, libretto H. and D. FIELDS.

Hammond, Percy (1873–1956), US theatre critic. A Chicago newspaperman, he became drama editor of the *Evening Post* and in 1910 was drama critic of the *Chicago Tribune*. In 1920 he joined the staff of the *New York Herald Tribune* where he worked for 15 years and continued to write reviews when in semi-retirement. His polished, meticulous style, and his wit as well as his attacks on vulgarity and bad taste in the theatre made him one of the outstanding critics of his day.

Hampden, Walter (1879–1955), US actor. Born in New York, he was first seen on the stage in England where he appeared with BENSON's company. After returning to the USA in 1907, he played opposite NAZIMOVA in a series of IBSEN and other contemporary plays. In 1923 he played the lead in ROSTAND's *Cyrano de Bergerac*. He took over the Colonial Theatre in New York, renaming it the Hampden Theatre. Among plays in which he starred while there were BULWER-LYTTON's *Richelieu* and BENAVENTE's *The Bonds of Interest*, both in 1929. In 1947 he was associated with the American Repertory Theatre and played Cardinal Wolsey in SHAKESPEARE's *Henry VIII* with EVA LE GALLIENNE. He was president of the PLAYERS' CLUB for 27 years, till his death.

Hamsun, Knut (1859–1952), Norwegian novelist, poet and playwright. His reputation rests mainly on novels such as *Growth of the Soil*, 1917, *Hunger*, 1890, and *Mysteries*, 1892. He was awarded the Nobel Prize for Literature in 1920. *Hunger* was dramatized by BARRAULT in the 1930s as *Faim*. He wrote six plays somewhat in the tradition of IBSEN and STRINDBERG, including the trilogy *Ved rikets port* (At the Gate of the Kingdom), 1895; *Livets spil* (Game of Life), 1896; *Aftenrode* (Red of Evening), 1898; the VERSE DRAMA *Munken Vendt* (Vendt the Monk), 1902, fp Heidelberg 1926; the historical play *Dronning Tamara* (Tamara the Queen), 1903; and the comedy *Livet i vold* (In the Grip of Life), 1910, fp 1911, MOSCOW ART THEATRE, and in Germany in 1914 by REINHARDT. His novel *Victoria*, 1898, was adapted for the stage by the Austrian dramatist R. Billinger, Vienna 1955.
Bibl: H. Beyer, A HISTORY OF NORWEGIAN LITERATURE, 1956

Handke, Peter (1942–), Austrian playwright. First attracted attention with his word-plays: montages of clichés and contradictory statements which create a linguistic 'field of forces'. Influenced by Wittgenstein's 'language games', he believes that our language, i.e. the vocabulary each individual carries within him, determines his thinking and his being. *Publikumsbeschimpfung* (Offending the Audience), fp Frankfurt 1966, Theater am Turm, consists of an abusive attack on the audience and exposes the shallowness of their existence by listing the linguistic clichés on which it rests. This was followed by *Weissagung* (Prophecy), written 1964; *Selbstbezichtigung* (Self-Accusation), written 1965, fp Oberhausen 1967. His first full-length play *Kaspar* was based on the historical figure of Kaspar Hauser, a boy who appeared on the streets of Nuremberg in the early 19th century, who had obviously been isolated from birth, and who had to be taught the whole of 'civilization'; he was later mysteriously murdered. In the play a character (Kaspar) is created on stage by being taught the language and through it the false consciousness of contemporary man; it was first staged in 1966 at the Theater am Turm and in Oberhausen; in London at the Almost Free Theatre, 1973. *Das Mündel will Vormund sein* (*My Foot My Tutor*), written 1968, is set in a farm-house; two characters act out a master-servant relationship in banal actions without words, fp Theater am Turm, British première Open Space Theatre, 1971. Other works: *Quodlibet* and *Der Ritt über den Bodensee* (*Ride Over Lake Constance*), written 1970, English première, Hampstead Theatre Club, 1974. In 1967 he was awarded the Gerhart Hauptmann Prize.
Bibl: N. Hern, PETER HANDKE, THEATRE AND ANTI-THEATRE, 1971

Hands, Terry (1941–), English director. Studied at Birmingham University and RADA. He started the Everyman Theatre in Liverpool together with two friends, and produced plays by SHAKESPEARE, OSBORNE (*Look Back in Anger*), BECKETT, ARRABAL (*Fando and Lis*) and WESKER's *The Four Seasons*. Left in 1966 to join the ROYAL SHAKESPEARE COMPANY, where he was put in charge of Theatre-go-round, a travelling theatre taking mobile RSC shows to schools, factories, community centres, youth clubs, etc. His formative years, which he spent working on a thrust stage, have conditioned his whole approach towards directing: simple sets, concentration on the actor, his thought and movement. Appointed associate director of the RSC in 1967. Important productions include: TRIANA's *The Criminals*, 1967, Aldwych; *The Merry Wives of Windsor*, 1968, *Richard III*, 1970, *Pericles*, *The Merchant of Venice*, 1971, all at STRATFORD-UPON-AVON; GENET's *The Balcony*, 1971, Aldwych (first public airing of this play since censorship ended); ETHEREGE's *The Man of Mode*, 1971, Aldwych. Produced *Richard III* at the COMÉDIE-FRANÇAISE with HIRSCH in the title role, 1972.

Hansberry, Lorraine (1930–65), Black US dramatist. Wrote in the tradition of Broadway NATURALISM. Her first play *A Raisin in the Sun*, fp New York 1959, with Sidney Poitier, which gained the NYDCC award, was about a Black Chicago family who settled in a White neighbourhood, and the personal and social problems which this created. Another play, *The Sign in Sidney Brustein's Window*, fp New York 1965, dedicated to 'the committed everywhere', shows the gulf between intellectual commitment and a genuine emotional involvement. She captured in her plays the dilemma of Black and White alike, without falling into bitter hatred, combining an understanding of historical causality with a belief in the possibility of change. She sought hope in the capacity of the individual to face reality and retain compassion.

Hanswurst (literally, Johnnie Sausage). Comic figure of the German-speaking theatre, originally derived from Bavarian folk art, who appeared in improvised interludes (*Hanswurstiaden*) between the heroic and sentimental scenes of BAROQUE THEATRE. The name first occurs at the beginning of the 16th century; but the character of Hanswurst was fully developed from the Italian ARLECCHINO and the English CLOWN by the popular Austrian comic actor STRANITZKY at the end of the 17th century.

Happening. A form of avant-garde theatre which arose in the late 1950s and early 1960s: the term became attached to various and very diverse events from Allan Kaprow's *18 Happenings in 6 parts*, staged at the Reuben Gallery, New York, in October 1959. Some Happenings were meticulously planned, others relied on spontaneous actions of the performers and spectators who became participants; what they often had in common was an endeavour to involve the audience to a maximum degree either by presenting them with totally unexpected events which confront them with an uncertainty as to whether they were real or fictitious or by involving them in a series of environments in each of which they may have to play their own role. Happenings can be regarded as an extension of theatre, but also as a development from Dadaist, Surrealist and Pop-Art painting and sculpture. Painters like Kienholz who construct whole 'environments', action painters, sculptors like Tinguely with his self-destroying constructions, can also be regarded as coming close to the Happening. And in fact many of the best-known exponents of the Happening started as painters, Claes Oldenburg, Allan Kaprow, Jim Dine, Ken Dewey, Jean-Jacques Lebel in France, Wolf Vostell in Germany. The composer John Cage is another originator of experiences akin to Happenings. Role-playing and audience participation in poetically structured environments, which is the essence of the Happenings concept, can be found in many age-old popular entertainments: masked balls, 18th-century *fêtes champêtres*, the court masques of INIGO

Happening, arranged by Allan Kaprow, 1962

JONES in England in the 17th century, as well as in many fairground entertainments, presenting the participants with similar situations, surprises and role-playing opportunities. With the potentially enormous resources of modern technology and in the hands of really imaginative artists the Happening seemed capable of developing into a wholly new form of popular entertainment of high artistic quality, in which design, technology, costume and modern methods of manipulation of large crowds might combine to produce memorable experiences for all participants, but it died out after having strongly influenced such people in the theatre as the Becks (LIVING THEATRE), Schechner (PERFORMANCE GROUP), Chaikin (OPEN THEATRE) and others.

Harden, Maximilian (Witkowski; 1861–1927), German critic, essayist and satirist. He wrote in support of the works of IBSEN, TOLSTOY, DOSTOYEVSKY, MAETERLINCK and the Naturalists. In 1889 he became one of the founders of the FREIE BÜHNE, Berlin, with Wolff and BRAHM, and in 1892 founded the weekly political magazine *Zukunft*, which ran till 1922. Published his collected criticism and portraits of theatre personalities in *Literatur und Theater*, 1896, and *Köpfe*, 4 vols, 1905–15; wrote literary criticism, *Kampfgenosse Sudermann*, 1903, and political polemics against Wilhelm II. During World War I he displayed an increasing tendency to Pacifism (polemic against Ludendorff, *Krieg und Friede*, 1917) and Socialism.

Hardwicke, Sir Cedric (1893–1964), English actor. Knighted in 1934. Trained at RADA, started his career in 1912. Joined the BIRMINGHAM REPERTORY THEATRE in 1922 and became one of its most prominent members. Achieved his first major success as Churdles Ash in *The Farmer's Wife* (PHILLPOTTS) which also brought him fame in London when the production was transferred to the ROYAL COURT THEATRE, 1924. At the Malvern Festivals of 1929 and 1930 H. achieved further successes as King Magnus in SHAW's *The Apple Cart*, and Mr Barrett in Rudolf Besier's *The Barretts of Wimpole Street*. After this he frequently appeared in films and increasingly worked in the USA, in both theatre and cinema. An actor of commanding presence and solid characterization.

Hare, David (1947–), English dramatist. Studied at Cambridge. Literary manager and resident dramatist at the ROYAL COURT THEATRE, 1970. Originator and founder of the Portable Theatre. In his first play *How Brophy Made Good*, 1969, he shows the lifestyle of a left-wing intellectual, who is fascinated and corrupted by TV. His next play *Slag*, 1969, set in a girl's school, shows a trio of mistresses trying and failing to achieve their own liberation. He was one of the authors of the group show *Lay-By*, 1971, Royal Court; and also wrote *The Great Exhibition*, 1972, Hampstead Theatre Club, and *Knuckle*, Comedy Theatre, 1974.

Hare, Sir John (J. Fairs; 1844–1921), English ACTOR-MANAGER. Made his first

Hanswurst

appearance in Liverpool in 1864 and in London in 1865 at the Prince of Wales Theatre, where his name is closely linked with that of the playwright ROBERTSON, in whose plays he appeared with great success (e.g. *Society*, 1865). He became manager of the ROYAL COURT THEATRE in 1875 and of the St James's Theatre 1879–88 in partnership with KENDAL (he himself was principal actor and director). He managed the Garrick Theatre, 1889–95, producing several plays by PINERO, and in 1890 achieved resounding success as Benjamin Goldfinch in Sydney Grundy's *A Pair of Spectacles*. After 1895 he toured the USA, appearing mainly in New York. He was knighted in 1907 and retired in 1911.

Harlequin. Columbine's young lover in the English harlequinade; his character was derived from ARLECCHINO of the COMMEDIA DELL'ARTE (▷CLOWN).

Harms, Johann Oswald (1643–1708), theatre painter. The only major one of the 17th century in Germany, he studied in Venice and Vienna and worked in Dresden, Bayreuth and at the Court of Brunswick-Wolfenbüttel and the Opera in Hamburg. Strongly influenced by the Italian style of scenic design which he combined with elements from the Low German and Dutch old masters. He was one of the first designers to use *chinoiserie* (e.g. *Roland*, 1696). His designs included: *Musicalische Opera und Ballett von Wirckung der Sieben Planeten* (Musical opera and Ballet on the Effect of the Seven Planets), by C. Bernhardt, Dresden, 1678; *Die durch Blut und Mord erlangte Liebe oder Nero* (Love Achieved through Blood and Murder or Nero), opera by Handel, Hamburg 1705.
Bibl: F. Richter, 1963

Harrigan, (Ned) Edward (1845–1911), US actor, manager and dramatist. His partnership with the female impersonator Tony Hart (1855–91) brought him fame in New York in 1872. As 'Harrigan and Hart', they produced many successful shows including *The Mulligan Guards* in which Harrigan played Dan Mulligan and Hart his wife Celia. They parted in 1884 after a fire had destroyed the theatre where they were performing. Harrigan continued to act in revivals of his own plays (*Old Lavender*, 1877, and *The Major*, 1881). In 1890 he opened his own theatre, later called the Garrick (it was taken over by MANSFIELD in 1895). He composed a number of songs and over 80 VAUDEVILLE sketches.

Harris, Julie (1925–), US actress. Initially appearing in 11 BROADWAY productions, none of which ran for more than a few days, she nevertheless attracted the attention of the magazines *Variety* and *Theatre World*, finally distinguishing herself in 1950 in CARSON MCCULLERS's *The Member of the Wedding*. Other major parts: Sally Bowles in VAN DRUTEN's *I Am a Camera*, 1951, adapted from ISHERWOOD's novel *Goodbye to Berlin*; in plays by ANOUILH: the title role in *Colombe*, 1954, and Joan in *The Lark* (adapted by LILLIAN HELLMAN), 1955; as Margery Pinchwife in WYCHERLEY's *The Country Wife*, 1957; and as Juliet in SHAKESPEARE's play, 1960. She has also appeared in many films, e.g. KAZAN's *East of Eden*.

Harrison, Rex (1908–), English actor. Began his artistic career with the Liverpool Repertory Theatre. After several years in the provinces and short appearances in London, he achieved a decisive success in 1936 in New York in J. Mallory's *Sweet Aloes*. Since then he has been one of the most popular West End and BROADWAY actors, portraying an updated version of the English gentleman with reserved charm. He has excellent voice technique and is pre-eminent in the art of understatement. He has appeared mainly in comedies by COWARD, RATTIGAN, BEHRMAN, VAN DRUTEN and played Sir Henry Harcourt-Reilly in ELIOT's *The Cocktail Party*, London 1950, and the Duke in FRY's *Venus Observed*, 1952 Broadway production; his greatest success was as Professor Higgins in the musical *My Fair Lady* (LERNER and LOEWE, based on SHAW's *Pygmalion*), 1956. Also well known as a film actor.

Hart, Charles (?–1683), English actor. As a boy played female roles (e.g. Duchess in SHIRLEY's *The Cardinal*, 1641) with the King's Players. After the Restoration in 1660 he became a major actor at the THEATRE ROYAL in KILLIGREW's company, excelling in first performances of DRYDEN's plays, e.g. *The Indian Emperor*, 1665; *Secret Love*, 1667, playing opposite NELL GWYNN; *All for Love*, 1677, and WYCHERLEY's plays, e.g. *The Country Wife*, c. 1673. He was a versatile actor also successful in tragic parts, including Othello and Brutus.

Hart, Lorenz H. (1895/96–1943), US song-writer who worked, from 1918 until his death, with the composer RODGERS; among their greatest successes were *The Boys From Syracuse*, 1938, and *Pal Joey*, 1940.

Hart, Moss (1904–61), US playwright, librettist and director. Began a long and fruitful collaboration with KAUFMAN in 1930 when they wrote the brilliant caricature of Hollywood, *Once in a Lifetime*. Other successful productions on which they worked together include *The Great Waltz*, 1934, music J. Strauss; *You Can't Take It With You*, 1936, a play which won the PULITZER PRIZE; *I'd Rather Be Right*, music RODGERS and lyrics L. HART; *The Man Who Came to Dinner*, 1939, a play about the critic WOOLLCOTT. On his own, M.H. wrote the LIBRETTI for *Face the Music* and *As Thousands Cheer*, 1933, music I. BERLIN; *Jubilee*, 1936, music PORTER; and the BROADWAY hit, *Lady In the Dark*, 1941, music WEILL, lyrics I. GERSHWIN with GERTRUDE LAWRENCE and Danny Kaye; also several plays, including *Winged Victory*, 1943, about the US air force. M.H. directed many of his own plays and also those by others, notably *My Fair Lady*, 1956, based on SHAW's *Pygmalion*, by LERNER, music LOEWE. His autobiography *Act One* was published in 1959.

Bibl: C. Smith, MUSICAL COMEDY IN AMERICA, 1950

Hartog, Jan de (1914–), Dutch writer. Originally a seaman, then an actor, who settled in the USA, where he still lives. He gained world-wide fame with his play *Schipper naast God* (Skipper Next to God), 1942, and with *Het Hemelbed* (fp London 1950, entitled *The Fourposter*). Other works include: *De Ondegang van 'De Vrijheid'* (The Sinking of the SS Freedom), 1937; *De Dood van een Rat* (The Death of a Rat), 1939; *Land in zicht* (Land in Sight), 1935. Also a well-known fiction writer.

Hartung, Gustav (1887–1946), German director and manager. Worked as a director in Bremen, Frankfurt (1914–20) and as INTENDANT of the Darmstadt Municipal Theatre (1920–24; 1931–33). He can claim to have helped establish EXPRESSIONISM in the German theatre; he used anti-illusionistic décor and a style of production reduced to the utmost simplicity: the first productions of UNRUH's *Ein Geschlecht* (A Generation), 1918, *Louis Ferdinand*, 1926; BRUCKNER's *Krankheit der Jugend* (Illness of Youth), 1926; also produced the classics using abstract sets. During World War II H. was a director in Zurich and subsequently in Heidelberg.

Hašek, Jaroslav (1883–1923), Czech essayist, author of CABARET sketches, humorous short stories and COMEDIES. Best known for his great comic novel *The Good Soldier Schweik* which has been dramatized and filmed several times. BRECHT, *Schweik in the Second World War*, written 1943, translated by Ewan McColl, dir JOAN LITTLEWOOD, London 1954, dir KOHOUT, Prague 1963.
Bibl: E. A. Longen, 1947

Hasenclever, Walter (1890–1940), German writer. Major exponent of EXPRESSIONISM, an extreme variety of which was heralded in his heated father-son drama *Der Sohn* (The Son), fp Dresden 1916, Albert Theater. His meeting with REINHARDT at the age of 26 inspired his great anti-war parable *Antigone*, 1917, a proclamation of human rights based on the classical theme, followed by *Der Retter* (The Saviour), 1919; *Die Entscheidung* (The Decision), 1919; *Die Menschen* (The People), 1920; *Jenseits* (Beyond), 1920; *Gobsek*, 1922; *Mord* (Murder), 1926. He then turned to conventional comedy: *Ein besserer Herr* (*A Man of Distinction*), 1927; *Ehen werden in Himmel geschlossen* (Marriages are Made in Heaven), 1928; *Napoleon greift ein* (Napoleon Intervenes), 1930; *Kommt ein Vogel geflogen* (A Bird Came Flying), 1931; *Christoph Columbus*, written with K. Tucholsky, 1932. Produced posthumously; *Münchhausen*, 1947; *Skandal in Assyrien* (Scandal in Assyria), 1957–58.
Bibl: P. J. Cremers & O. Brues, 1922

Hasse, O. E. (1903–), German actor. Trained at REINHARDT's drama school in Berlin; worked with leading German companies including the Munich Kammerspiele,

1930–39; the Hebbel-Theater and Schillertheater in Berlin, 1947–54, and since then has made mainly guest appearances in various German theatres. His reputation is based on modern roles, the best of which include: Mr Antrobus in WILDER's *The Skin of Our Teeth*, 1946; Jupiter in SARTRE's *Les Mouches*, 1948, dir FEHLING; Schwitter in DÜRRENMATT's *Der Meteor*, 1967; Shaw in Jerome Kilty's *Dear Liar*, 1959; Churchill in HOCHHUTH's *Soldaten*, fp Berlin 1967, Freie Volksbühne (▷FREIE BÜHNE).

Hauptmann (1) **Carl H.** (1858–1921), German dramatist. Studied science, and lived in seclusion in the mountains of Silesia. He wrote plays and novels in the spirit of Silesian mysticism: *Waldleute* (Forest People), fp Vienna 1895, Raimundtheater; *Die Bergschmiede* (The Mountain Smith), Munich 1905, Royal Court Theatre; *Die armseligen Besenbinder* (The Poor Broommakers), Dresden 1913, Royal Theatre; *Die lange Jule* (Lanky Julie), Hamburg 1913, Deutsches Schauspielhaus; *Krieg* (War), written 1914; *Tobias Buntschuh*, Berlin 1917, Deutsches-Theater; *Musik*, Leipzig 1920, dir FEHLING; Berlin 1934, State Theatre, etc.

(2) **Gerhart H.** (1862–1946), German dramatist. Brother of Carl H. His early works were influenced by the Naturalist movement in Germany. His first play, *Vor Sonnenaufgang* (Before Dawn), fp Berlin 1889, FREIE BÜHNE, stressed man's oppression through heredity and environment. It was followed by two plays which deal with contemporary bourgeois decadence, *Das Friedensfest* (The Feast of Peace), Berlin 1890, and *Einsame Menschen* (*Lonely Lives*), Berlin 1891; *Kollege Crampton* (*Colleague Crampton*), 1892, a comedy which shows the conflict between the artist and bourgeois society, and a variation on the same theme in tragic form, *Michael Kramer*, 1900; *Gabriel Schillings Flucht* (*G. S.'s Flight*), 1912. In *Die Weber* (*The Weavers*), 1893, the protagonist he created was a collective in revolt against capitalist society, based on the Silesian uprising in 1844. *Der Biberpelz* (*The Beaver Coat*), Berlin 1893, Deutsches-Theater, a witty play, which deals with the private anarchistic class struggle of Mother Wolf, a cunning washerwoman, ranks as one of the best German comedies; its bitter sequel was *Der rote Hahn* (*The Red Cock*), 1901. H. gradually turned from NATURALISM towards a poetic neo-Romanticism.

His legendary neo-romantic dramas in symbolist style include: *Hanneles Himmelfahrt* (The Assumption of Hannele), Berlin 1893; *Die versunkene Glocke* (*The Sunken Bell*), Berlin 1896, Deutsches-Theater; *Der arme Heinrich* (Poor Henry), Vienna 1902, BURGTHEATER; *Elga*, Berlin 1905, Lessingtheater; *Und Pippa tanzt* (And Pippa dances), 1906; *Kaiser Karls Geisel* (Emperor Charles's Hostage), 1908; *Griselda*, Berlin, Lessingtheater, and Vienna, Burgtheater, both 1909. *Florian Geyer*, 1896, is a historical survey of scenes from the German peasant wars. Among his Silesian local dramas with tragic heroes, who succumb to the hardships imposed on them by society, are:

Gerhart Hauptmann's *Der Biberpelz* with THERESE GIEHSE

Julie Harris and ETHEL WATERS in *The Member of the Wedding*, 1950, by CARSON McCULLERS

Rex Harrison in *Monsieur Perrichon's Travels* by LABICHE and Martin, CHICHESTER FESTIVAL, 1976

Fuhrmann Henschel (*Drayman Henschel*), Berlin 1896, Deutsches-Theater; and *Rose Bernd*, 1903. In *Schluck und Jau* (S. and J.), 1900, he shows two proletarian comedians in a feudal setting. *Die Ratten* (*The Rats*), 1911, is a TRAGICOMEDY set in a Berlin tenement house, a realistic play, which at the same time questions the possibility of depicting reality on stage. *Festspiel in deutschen Reimen* (Festival in German Rhymes), 1913, is a patriotic poem celebrating the centenary of the Wars of Liberation. In *Der Bogen des Odysseus* (*The Bow of Odysseus*), 1914, he takes his theme from Greek tragedy, inspired by his personal experiences in Greece. *Die Winterballade* (*Winter Ballad*), 1917, is a dramatic narrative based on a novel by Selma Lagerlöf. 'Dramatic fantasy' and 'dramatic poem' were the sub-titles he gave to his plays on Indian culture and the Spanish conquest: *Indipodhi*, 1922, and *Der weisse Heiland* (*The White Saviour*), 1920. He returned to the psychological realism of his early works in *Dorothea Angermann*, Vienna 1926, and paraphrased the early history of Hamlet in his *Hamlet in Wittenberg*, 1935. He again took a theme from Greek tragedy in his *Die Atriden-Tetralogie* (a TETRALOGY on the story of Agamemnon), written 1940–44, prod 1941–48, including *Iphigenie in Delphi*, 1941; *Iphigenie in Aulis*, 1943; *Agamemnons Tod* (A.'s Death) and *Elektra*, 1947. Other works: *Peter Brauer*, 1921; *Veland*, 1925; *Spuk* (Ghost), 1929; *Vor Sonnenuntergang* (*Before Sunset*), 1932; *Die goldene Harfe* (*The Golden Harp*), 1933; *Die Tochter der Kathedrale* (*The Daughter of the Cathedral*), 1939; *Ulrich von Lichtenstein*, 1939; published posthumously: *Herbert Engelmann*, written 1942, adapted by ZUCKMAYER 1952; *Die Finsternisse* (Darkness), 1952; *Magnus Garbe*, 1956.
H.'s extensive dramatic work is amazingly diverse and varies considerably in style and quality. H. is characterized by compassionate observation of man's sufferings, which establishes him as one of the great German humanitarian writers. His realistic dramas are still an essential part of German REPERTOIRE. He received many honours in his lifetime, and in 1912 was awarded the Nobel Prize for Literature.
Bibl: R. Michaelis, DER SCHWARZE ZEUS, 1962; R. Fiedler, DIE SPÄTEN DRAMEN GERHART HAUPTMANNS, 1954; D. Gerbert, CARL HAUPTMANN, 1952

Havel, Václav (1936–), Czech playwright. One of the most promising writers of his generation in Europe. In 1961 he joined the Theatre on the Balustrade, an avant-garde group in Prague, first as assistant to the artistic director GROSSMAN, later becoming DRAMATURG and resident playwright (all his works were first performed there). He became internationally known with his play *Zahradni slavnost* (*The Garden Party*), 1963, dir KREJČA, a satire on the dehumanizing effects of bureaucracy with a mixture of political comment, Schweikian humour and Kafkaesque intensity which are the characteristics of Havel's work. His other successful plays are *Vyrozumění* (*The Memorandum*), 1965, dir Grossman and *Ztížená možnost soustředeni* (The Increased Difficulty of Concentration), 1968. He has also written concrete poetry.

Hay, Julius (1900–75), Hungarian dramatist who also writes in German. His plays are realistic critical studies concerned with social problems: *Das neue Paradies* (The New Paradise), BERLIN 1932, VOLKSBÜHNE; *Gott, Kaiser und Bauer* (God, Emperor and Peasant), Berlin 1932, Deutsches-Theater. In 1933 he emigrated and went to live in Moscow in 1935 remaining there till 1945. His play *Tisazug*, written in 1936, was first staged in 1945 in Budapest and then in German as *Haben* at the VOLKSTHEATER, Vienna, 1945. Based on a true story, the plot concerns a group of wives who murdered their husbands in a wave of mass-hysteria in Hungary during a period of great land hunger in the 1920s. It has twice been staged in England, in 1955 as *The Midwife* and on the BBC in 1969 as *To Have and to Hold*. Other plays include *Gerichtstag* (Day of Judgment), Berlin 1945, Deutsches-Theater; *Die Brücke des Lebens*, 1950, staged in England at the UNITY THEATRE in 1953 as *The Bridge of Life*; *Der Putenhirt* (The Gooseherd), Berlin 1954, Deutsches-Theater, a savage attack on feudalism. In 1956 he wrote *Gaspar Varros Recht* (Gaspar Varro's Justice), in which he criticized the bureaucracy of the Communist Party; he took part in the uprising in 1956 and was sentenced to six years' imprisonment; released in 1960 he settled in Ascona, Switzerland, in 1965; the works which followed include: *Das Pferd* (The Horse), SALZBURG FESTIVAL, 1964; *Attilas Nächte* (Attila's Nights), Bregenz Festival, 1966.

Hayes, Helen (Helen Brown; 1900–), US actress. First appeared at the age of five at the National Theatre, Washington, D.C., as Prince Charles in *The Royal Family* (R. Marshall); first appearance on BROADWAY in a child's part 1909. Made a triumphant transition to grown-up parts and was particularly noteworthy in: *To the Ladies* by KAUFMAN and CONNELLY, 1922; Cleopatra in SHAW's *Caesar and Cleopatra*, in the THEATRE GUILD's original production, 1925; Victoria in L. Housman's *Victoria Regina*, which involves the whole gamut from girlhood to old age, 1935; Portia in *The Merchant of Venice*, her first Shakespearean role, 1938; Viola in *Twelfth Night*, 1940; London début as Amanda Wingfield in *The Glass Menagerie*, T. WILLIAMS, 1948. Popularly regarded as one of America's greatest actresses. In 1955 the Fulton Theatre in New York was renamed the Helen Hayes Theatre. She was married to the playwright MacARTHUR.

Hazlitt, William (1778–1830), English essayist. The first great London theatre critic. His selected criticism, collected in *A View of the English Stage*, 1818, is one of the most important sources of theatre history in England. He describes in detail the roles played by KEMBLE, KEAN, SARAH SIDDONS and MACREADY. The newspapers and magazines he worked for included the *Morning Chronicle*, *Theatre Champion*, the *Examiner*, the *Edinburgh Review*, *The Times* and the *London Magazine*. His volumes of essays on drama include: *Characters of Shakespeare's Plays*, 1817; *Lectures on the English Comic Writers*, 1819; *Dramatic literature of the Age of Elizabeth*, 1820.

Heartfield, John (originally Herzfelde; 1891–1968), German painter, graphic and stage designer. A member of the DADA circle in Berlin which included his brother Wieland and GROSZ; he was a pioneer of photomontage, designer of political posters and book jackets effective as propaganda. Designer for the Reinhardt-Bühnen in Berlin, 1920–22, e.g. BÜCHNER's *Woyzeck*, 1921, Deutsches-Theater, dir REINHARDT, and at the same time worked with PISCATOR's proletarian theatre and later for the Piscator-Bühne: Franz Jung's *Heimweh*, 1928; WOLF's *Tai Yang erwacht*, fp 1931 – 'a background of inscribed rotating flags which depicted the changes in the political situation' (BRECHT). Emigrated and later participated in the Civil War in Spain, settled in East Berlin after 1945. Designed for the Deutsches-Theater: *Harfe und Gewehr* (from an original play by O'CASEY), 1954; *Sozialaristokraten* by HOLZ, 1955; *Die Illegalen* by G. Weisenborn, 1961.
Bibl: W. Herzfelde, 1962

Hebbel, Friedrich (1813–1863), German dramatist. The son of a bricklayer, he was helped in his youth by generous women, one of whom, the Hamburg writer Amalia Schoppe, bore him two illegitimate children; in 1846 he married the actress CHRISTINE ENGHAUS who became one of the leading ladies of the Vienna BURGTHEATER. H. marks the transition between the VERSE DRAMA of the German classical-romantic tradition (SCHILLER, GOETHE) and the modern psychological play (HAUPTMANN, STRINDBERG); his main subject matter concerns the isolation of the powerful individual of genius, who carries the fate of humanity on his shoulders and has to suffer for it. His first play *Judith*, 1840, opposes a superman, Holofernes, with a woman who is the vessel of God's purpose; determined to kill the oppressor of her people during a night of love, Judith, sexually aroused by her lover, comes into tragic conflict between her duty as a patriot and her sensuality as a woman; *Maria Magdalena*, a play about the life of a simple artisan and his dishonoured daughter, is one of the earliest social tragedies with a lower-class heroine; *Herodes und Mariamne*, 1849, is an exploration of the conflicts of marriage; *Gyges und sein Ring*, pub 1855, fp 1869, is based on the legend of King Cambyses who encounters a young man, Gyges, who has found a ring that can make him invisible. The king invites Gyges to steal into his bedchamber so that the king may display the beauty of his wife to him. This provides the author with another opportunity for psychological exploration of subconscious sexuality much in advance of the times. The trilogy *Die Nibelungen*, 1861, dramatizes the German national epic poem. H. was a

brilliantly intelligent writer whose diaries and theoretical essays are among the finest in German literature.
Bibl: M. Schaub, 1967

Hecht, Ben (1894–1964), US dramatist, novelist and film writer. Inspired by his early career as a journalist, his plays were satirical, witty portrayals of journalism and theatre life, mostly written in collaboration with MACARTHUR: *The Front Page*, 1928, successfully revived London 1972; *Twentieth Century*, 1932, and *Jumbo*, 1935, music RODGERS, lyrics L. HART. Plays he wrote without collaborators include: *The Egotist*, 1922; *To Quito and Back*, 1937; *Winkelberg*, 1958. He also wrote his autobiography, *A Child of the Century*, 1954.

Heckroth, Hein (1901–70), German designer. Worked in major German theatre companies at Frankfurt, 1922; Münster, 1924–26; Essen, 1928–33; designed sets and costumes for the Ballet Jooss 1933–35; emigrated to England and worked at the OLD VIC, Glyndebourne, and the Teatro Colón in Buenos Aires, etc. From 1955 he was resident designer at the Frankfurt Municipal Theatre. He used elements of Impressionism and particularly SURREALISM in his rich, almost baroque décors.

Heijermans, Herman (1864–1924), Dutch dramatist. Began his career as a journalist. His interest in Socialism led him to write plays critical of contemporary society which gave a realistic picture of the middle classes: *Dora Kremer*, 1893; *Ahasuerus*, 1893. His play *Ghetto*, 1898, fp Amsterdam 1898, staged in London and New York 1899, established him in the Dutch theatre; dealing with the fate of the Jewish minority in Amsterdam, he criticized the intolerance and narrow-mindedness of the Jews (he was Jewish himself). He attacked false middle-class morality in *Het zevende Gebod* (*The Seventh Commandment*), 1899; *Schakels* (Links), 1903; *De Opgaande Zon* (*The Rising Sun*), 1908, and *Beschuit met Muisjes* (Blessed Event), 1910. His critical portraits of working-class life: *Ora et Labora* (Pray and Work), 1902; *Het Pantser* (The Suit of Armour), 1901; *Glück auf!* (Good Luck!), 1911, dealt with the exploitation of miners. *Op Hoop van Zegen* (*The Good Hope*), 1900, considered one of his most important plays, shows the lives of Dutch fishermen and their exploitation by the shipowners. His later plays contained symbolic elements and are Socialist allegories: *De Schoone Slapster* (Sleeping Beauty), 1916; *Eva Bonheur*, 1916, fp New York 1924 as *The Devil to Pay*.
Bibl: S. L. Flaxman, HERMAN HEIJERMANS AND HIS DRAMA, 1954

Heinrich Julius, Duke of Brunswick (1564–1613), German playwright. An admirer of the ELIZABETHAN THEATRE in English, he invited a company of actors, under Sackville, the ENGLISH COMEDIANS (*Englische Komödianten*) to perform at his Court in Wolfenbüttel in 1592. In 1593–94 the Duke wrote 11 TRAGEDIES, TRAGI-COMEDIES and COMEDIES in prose for per-

Hein Heckroth, stage design for the opera *Wozzeck* by Alban Berg

Helen Hayes in Laurence Housman's *Victoria Regina*, New York 1935

Ben Hecht and CHARLES MACARTHUR, *The Front Page*, New York 1928

formance at his court. Often crude and relying on superficial effects, they were usually on the subject of matrimonial discord, but in all of them the fool shows great common sense. The influence of this company is evident in these plays which, despite their shortcomings, were important in the development of a national drama in Germany, e.g. *Von der Susanna* (Of Susanna), 1593; *Tragödie von einem ungeratenen Sohn* (Tragedy of a Wicked Son), 1594; *Von einem Buler und Bulerin* (Of a Lover and his Mistress), 1593; *Von einem Weibe* (Of a Woman), 1593; *Von einer Ehebrecherin* (Of an Adulteress), 1594.

Heinz, Wolfgang (1900–), German actor and director. Began his career as an actor at the Berlin National Theatre, 1928–33; at Zurich, 1934–38, and the Scala in Vienna, 1948–56. From 1955 director at the Deutsches-Theater, BERLIN. Appointed INTENDANT of the VOLKSBÜHNE, 1960, and of the Deutsches-Theater, 1963. He is a passionate realistic actor whose best-known parts include: title role in BÜCHNER's *Dantons Tod*, 1939; Mannon in O'NEILL's *Mourning Becomes Electra*, 1943; title roles in SHAKESPEARE's *King Lear* and LESSING's *Nathan der Weise*, 1966. As a director he works in the STANISLAVSKY tradition of psychological realism: CHEKHOV's *The Seagull*; SHAW's *Heartbreak House*; GOETHE's *Faust*, Part II, all at the Deutsches-Theater.

Held, Martin (1908–), German actor. He has worked since 1951 mainly at the Schiller and Schlosspark theatres in BERLIN. His first success came as Wehrhahn in HAUPTMANN's *Der Biberpelz*, 1951, and Leicester in SCHILLER's *Maria Stuart*, 1952. He played in BECKETT's own production of his play *Krapp's Last Tape*, Berlin 1969, Schillertheater. He is at his best in classical modern roles particularly in plays by ANOUILH and BRECHT.

Hellman, Lillian (1905–), US dramatist. Originally a press agent, she later became a play-reader for the Broadway producer Herman Shumlin. Wrote a great number of plays, critical studies of American life, with tight plots and sharp characterization, the best known of which are *The Children's Hour*, 1934, and *The Little Foxes*, 1939, made into a musical in 1949. Her other plays include: *Days to Come*, 1936; *Watch on the Rhine*, 1941; *The Searching Wind*, 1944; *Another Part of the Forest*, 1946; *Montserrat*, 1949 (based on Emmanuel Roblès); *The Autumn Garden*, 1951; *Candide*, 1956, a musical based on VOLTAIRE, music BERNSTEIN; *Toys in the Attic*, 1960; *My Mother, My Father and Me*, 1963 (based on a novel by Burt Blechman). Her autobiography, *An Unfinished Woman*, was published in 1969.
Bibl: J. W. Krutch, AMERICAN DRAMA SINCE 1918, 1957; W. D. Sievers, FREUD ON BROADWAY, 1955

Helmer, Hermann ▷ FELLNER, FERDINAND.

Heminge, John (?1556–1630), English actor. Worked with the CHAMBERLAIN's MEN, of which R. BURBAGE, KEMPE and SHAKESPEARE were partners, which later became the King's Players. Probably the first actor to play Falstaff; his main importance was as an editor with Henry Condell of the First Folio of Shakespeare's plays, printed 1623. He was also a shareholder in the GLOBE and BLACKFRIARS theatres.
Bibl: W. W. Greg, THE SHAKESPEARE FIRST FOLIO, 1955

Henderson, John (1747–85), English actor. Protégé of GARRICK; after playing in the provinces (Bath 1772), he first appeared in London in 1777 as Shylock at the Haymarket Theatre; subsequently he worked at DRURY LANE and went to COVENT GARDEN in 1778. After initial difficulties, due to his small stature and weak voice, he finally achieved success in a variety of roles from Shylock and Hamlet to Falstaff. He was a thoughtful actor, who carefully analyzed his roles and compensated for his vocal weakness with his range of facial expressions.

Henslowe, Philip (?–1616), Elizabethan theatre manager. He played an important part in the development of theatre in SHAKESPEARE's time. Worked as a dyer in the 1580s and was known to be buying property in the City of London. In 1587 he built the Rose Theatre on the Bankside, the Fortune (jointly with ALLEYN) in 1600, and the Hope Theatre, rebuilt from a bear garden in 1613. His step-daughter was married to Alleyn, the principal of the ADMIRAL'S MEN, in 1592. His diaries, discovered in 1790 in the library of Dulwich College (founded by Alleyn), provide one of the most important sources on the ELIZABETHAN THEATRE, its management and relations between the managers and the actors; the latter drew up a document in 1615, accusing H. of mismanagement and even of embezzling their wages. The diaries were edited by W. W. Greg, 1904–08; a new edition was published by R. A. Foakes, 1961.

Hepburn, Katharine (1909–), US actress. Equally celebrated in films and on the stage. She appeared in 1932 as Antiope in J. Thompson's *The Warrior's Husband*; in 1939 as Tracy Lord in *The Philadelphia Story* by P. BARRY; in his *Without Love*, 1942; and in 1950 played her first Shakespearean role, Rosalind in *As You Like It*. First seen in London in 1952 playing the lead in SHAW's *The Millionairess*; in 1955 went on tour to Australia with the OLD VIC company: Portia in *The Merchant of Venice*, Katharina in *The Taming of the Shrew*, Isabella in *Measure for Measure* and in 1957 played Beatrice in *Much Ado About Nothing* (Stratford, Conn.). Her first film was *A Bill of Divorcement* with J. BARRYMORE, 1932, dir George Cukor, with whom she made seven more.
Bibl: T. Cocrofz, GREAT NAMES AND HOW THEY ARE MADE, 1941

Herbert, Jocelyn (1917–), English stage designer. Her name is associated mainly with directors such as RICHARDSON, DEXTER, DEVINE, L. ANDERSON, and GASKILL. She has designed many first productions, including IONESCO's *The Chairs*, 1957, dir Richardson, and *Exit the King*, 1963, dir Devine; WESKER's *Roots*, 1959, *The Kitchen*, 1959, and *Chips with Everything*, 1962, all dir Dexter; BECKETT's *Endgame* and *Krapp's Last Tape*, both 1958, and *Happy Days*, 1963, all three dir Gaskill; BRECHT's *St Joan of the Stockyards*, 1964, dir Richardson. Her designs mainly employ realistic details and empty or highly simplified stage areas. Apart from contemporary plays she has designed several SHAKESPEARE productions: *Richard III*, 1961; *A Midsummer Night's Dream*, 1962; *Othello* and *Julius Caesar*, both 1964.

Hering, Gerhard (1908–), German director and manager. After some experience as a drama critic (1934–41) and DRAMATURG (Konstanz, Stuttgart), he turned to directing and in 1961 was appointed INTENDANT at Darmstadt, where he successfully produced a series of plays by LESSING and GENET. He also wrote essays on drama and the theatre, some of which were collected in the volume *Der Ruf zur Leidenschaft*.

Heroic drama. A shortlived development in English theatre of the Restoration period, which was modelled after French classical TRAGEDY, and written in rhymed couplets. Its chief exponent was DRYDEN whose play *The Conquest of Granada* contained all the elements of the genre. A farcical COMEDY attributed to George Villiers, Duke of Buckingham, called *The Rehearsal*, printed in 1672, was designed to satirize the heroic tragedies of the day, and Dryden's play was a particular target.

Heron, Matilda Agnes (1830–77), US actress. She made her début in Philadelphia in 1851, achieving recognition as Marguerite Gautier in her own version of DUMAS *fils*'s *The Lady of the Camellias*, and made a fortune out of this. She played Medea in EURIPIDES' tragedy and appeared as Nancy in a dramatization of Dickens' *Oliver Twist*. She also acted in a number of her own plays and trained actresses, including her daughter Bijou Heron (1862–1937) who married Henry Miller, a US ACTOR-MANAGER. Their son Gilbert (1884–1967) became a well-known theatre manager in the USA and in England.

Herrand, Marcel (1897–1953), French director and actor. Appeared in 1917 in APOLLINAIRE's *Les Mamelles de Tirésias* at the Vieux-Colombier; subsequently collaborated with COPEAU and PITOËFF, and produced and acted in contemporary poetic plays, e.g. Tzara's *Les Mouchoirs de nuages*, 1924; COCTEAU's *Orphée*. In 1929 he founded the company Le Rideau de Paris which appeared in several theatres until 1939, and at the Théâtre des Mathurins 1939–53: he achieved a literary REPERTOIRE of high standard, supporting new dramatists and discovering major acting talent including MARIA CASARÈS, AUCLAIR, etc. His most famous productions include SYNGE's *The Playboy of the Western World* and *Deirdre*

Lillian Hellman's *The Little Foxes*, New York 1939, with TALLULAH BANKHEAD

Katharine Hepburn and Van Heflin in P. BARRY's *The Philadelphia Story*, THEATRE GUILD, 1939

of the Sorrows; CAMUS's *Le Malentendu*; GENET's *Haute Surveillance*; R. and A. Goetz's *The Heiress* (based on JAMES); 1951–53 he was a producer at the Angers Festival, where he directed SHAKESPEARE's *King John*.

Heywood, John (*c.* 1497–*c.* 1580), English dramatist. Six of his plays are extant and mark the transition from the MORALITY PLAY of the Middle Ages to the Elizabethan COMEDY. His best-known plays are *The Pardoner and the Friar, the Curate, and Neighbour Pratte*, 1513–21; *The Four Ps.*, *c.* 1520–22; *The Play of the Weather*, 1525–33, and *A Play of Love* ?1528–29, pub 1533–34.
Bibl: E. K. Chambers, THE ELIZABETHAN STAGE, 1923, 4 vols.

Heywood, Thomas (*c.* 1573–1641), English dramatist and poet. Originally an actor with HENSLOWE's ADMIRAL's MEN and Worcester's Men, he was a prolific writer who, according to his own records, wrote or collaborated on about 220 plays, of which some 24 are extant; he also wrote PAGEANTS and MASQUES for the Court. Though he wrote history plays (possibly the two parts of *Edward IV*, perhaps written in collaboration with Henry Chettle and others, 1592–99, and *The Rape of Lucrece*, 1606–08), it is for the sympathy and naturalistic style with which he portrayed early 17th-century English bourgeois society that he stands out from his contemporaries. He showed these qualities in COMEDY (*The Wise Woman of Hogsdon*, *c.* 1604); domestic drama (*The English Traveller*, pub 1630); in a blending of everyday English life with foreign adventure (the two parts of *The Fair Maid of the West; or, A Girl Worth Gold*, 1597–1610 and *c.* 1630–31), and above all in his masterpiece *A Woman Killed by Kindness*, 1603. A story of adultery and remorse, this is the one outstanding English domestic TRAGEDY of its period and is remarkable, in its best scenes, for its human understanding, psychological penetration and poetic quality.
Bibl: E. K. Chambers, THE MEDIEVAL STAGE, 1903, 2 vols

Hikmet Ran, Nazim (1901–63), Turkish poet and dramatist. Studied in the USSR. He was a member of the banned Communist Party in Turkey, and was imprisoned 1937–50. After being awarded the Moscow Peace Prize in 1951 he escaped to the USSR. He is one of the most frequently performed playwrights in Socialist countries, notably *Byl li Ivan Ivanovich?* (Did Ivan Ivanovich Exist?), fp Moscow 1956, a satire on the personality cult. Other works include *Kafatasi*, 1923; *Unutalan Adam*, 1935; *Legenda o Ljuby* (Legend of Love), Moscow 1948.

Hildesheimer, Wolfgang (1916–), German writer. Emigrated to London in 1934 where he studied painting and stage design; later became a British army officer and in 1946 was an interpreter at the Nuremberg trials; then worked as a painter and graphic designer. He began his literary career in 1950, writing short stories, radio plays and comedies: *Der Drachenthron* (The Dragon's Throne), fp 1955, dir GRÜNDGENS; new version in 1961 as *Die Eroberung der Prinzessin Turandot* (The Conquest of Princess Turandot). He considers himself a dramatist of the THEATRE OF THE ABSURD, e.g. his lecture 'Erlangen Rede über das absurde Theater' (Erlangen Speech on the Absurd Theatre), 1963. His dramatic works include *Pastorale*, 1958, Munich Kammerspiele; *Landschaft mit Figuren* (Landscape with Figures), BERLIN 1958, Tribüne; *Die Uhren* (The Clocks), Celle 1959, Schlosstheater; *Der schiefe Turm von Pisa* (The Leaning Tower of Pisa), Celle 1959; *Die Verspätung* (The Delay), 1961, and *Nachtstück* (Night-piece), 1963, both Düsseldorf Kammerspiele; a radio play, *Herrn Walsers Raben* (Mr Walser's Ravens), 1960, etc. A TV script, *Nocturno im Grand Hotel*, 1953; LIBRETTO, *Das Ende der Welt* (for the composer Hans Werner Henze), 1953.

Hilpert, Heinz (1890–1967), German actor, director and INTENDANT. As a director followed the realistic tradition of BRAHM, combining a typically Berlin dryness with an appreciation of music and humour. He began in BERLIN as an actor and director at the VOLKSBÜHNE, 1919–25, then joined the Deutsches-Theater, as director in 1926, where his first success came with BRUCKNER's *Die Verbrecher*, fp 1928; ZUCKMAYER's *Der Hauptmann von Köpenick*, fp 1931, and HORVÁTH's *Geschichten aus dem Wiener Wald*, fp 1931. Intendant of the Deutsches-Theater, Berlin, 1934–35; 1938–45 also ran the Theater in der Josefstadt, Vienna; 1950–66 Intendant of the Göttingen Municipal Theatre. His best-known productions include plays by SHAKESPEARE (*Richard II*, *King Lear*), KLEIST and RAIMUND, and after 1945 first productions of some of Zuckmayer's plays.
Bibl: K. H. Ruppel, GROSSES BERLINER THEATER, 1962

Hiob, Hanne (1923–), German actress. Daughter of BRECHT and his first wife Marianne Zoff (▷OTTO ZOFF). Her best known parts include the lead in the first production of Brecht's *Die heilige Johanna der Schlachthöfe*, Hamburg 1959, Deutsches Schauspielhaus, dir GRÜNDGENS, which she repeated in 1968 with the BERLINER ENSEMBLE, and Grusche in *Der kaukasische Kreidekreis*, 1964, ZURICH SCHAUSPIELHAUS.

Hirsch, Robert (1926–), French actor. A member of the COMÉDIE-FRANÇAISE, specializing in HARLEQUIN roles. Trained as a dancer, he became an actor later, joining the CF in 1948 and has been a SOCIÉTAIRE since 1951. He has played the apothecary in MOLIÈRE's *Monsieur de Pourceaugnac*, 1948; Arlequin in MARIVAUX's *Le Prince travesti*, 1950; Sosie in Molière's *Amphitryon*, 1951. His most famous role was Scapin in Molière's *Les Fourberies de Scapin*, 1956, which allowed him to display his talents as a comic actor and a dancer. His best-known parts: (classical) Néron in RACINE's *Britannicus*, 1961; (modern) Raskolnikov in DOSTOYEVSKY's *Crime and Punishment*, 1963, adapted by Arout.

Hirschfeld, Kurt (1902–64), German DRAMATURG, director and INTENDANT. He joined the Darmstadt Municipal Theatre as Dramaturg and director 1930–33, emigrated to Switzerland, where he worked at the ZURICH SCHAUSPIELHAUS 1933–34; he was Dramaturg and deputy director 1938–40, and from 1961 until his death he held the position of Intendant. During World War II developed a REPERTORY of contemporary world literature with first German-language productions of plays by WILDER, first productions of plays by BRECHT, DÜRRENMATT and FRISCH.
Bibl: Günther Schoop, DAS ZÜRICHER SCHAUSPIELHAUS IM ZWEITEN WELTKRIEG, 1957

Histrio (Lat). Professional actor. In pre-Augustan times an actor of orthodox drama. Later applied to all actors: tragic and comic actors, MIMES, PANTOMIMES and actors in ATELLAN FARCES.

Hobson, Sir Harold (1904–), English critic. Since 1944 with *The Sunday Times*, first as assistant literary editor and assistant drama critic and 1947–76 chief drama critic; he also writes reviews for the *Christian Science Monitor* (since 1931) and was TV critic for the *Listener* (1947–51). Author of several books including *Theatre*, 2 vols, 1948; *Verdict at Midnight*, 1952; *The Theatre Now*, 1953; *The French Theatre Today*, 1953. Knighted in 1977.

Hochhuth, Rolf (1931–), German dramatist who lives in Switzerland. Author of two controversial documentary plays based on World War II, *Der Stellvertreter* (translated in Britain as *The Representative*, in the USA as *The Deputy*, fp 1963) and *Soldaten* (*Soldiers*), fp 1967; both at the FREIE VOLKSBÜHNE, Berlin, dir SCHWEIKART. Both are based on documentary material; *The Representative*, a 5-act play in blank verse, is an attack on Pope Pius XII for his failure to prevent the genocide of the Jews by the Nazis; *Soldiers* shows Winston Churchill approving of saturation bombing of German civilians and also implies that Churchill was responsible for the air crash that killed the Polish Prime Minister-in-Exile, General Sikorski. Both plays are over-long, wide-ranging, but effective. *The Representative* was an international success, e.g. dir BROOK in Paris and London; *Soldiers* caused great controversy, particularly in England.
Bibl: E. Bentley (ed), THE STORM OVER THE DEPUTY, 1964

Hochwälder, Fritz (1911–), Austrian dramatist. A self-educated working man, he emigrated to Switzerland in 1938 and lives in Zurich. Became internationally famous with *Das heilige Experiment* (The Holy Experiment), fp Biel 1943, later seen in London under the title *The Strong Are Lonely* with WOLFIT, which deals with the persecution of the Jesuits in Paraguay in the 18th century. His work, which was influenced by KAISER and set in a historical background, includes: *Der Flüchtling* (The Fugitive), 1945, based on a scenario by Kaiser; *Meier Helmbrecht*, 1947; *Der Öffentliche Ankläger* (*The Public Prosecutor*), 1948; *Donadieu*, Vienna 1953, BURGTHEATER; *Die Herberge* (The Inn), Vienna 1957, Burgtheater; *Der Unschuldige* (The Innocent), 1958; *Donnerstag* (Thursday), 1959, a MYSTERY PLAY for the SALZBURG FESTIVAL; *Der Himbeerpflücker* (The Raspberry Picker), written for TV in 1964, fp 1965, ZURICH SCHAUSPIELHAUS; *Der Befehl* (The Order), 1967.

Hoffmann, Paul (1902–), German actor and director. Worked in Dresden (1927–46), Stuttgart (1946–58) and joined the BURGTHEATER in Vienna in 1959, of which he was artistic director 1968–71. Major parts include Mephistopheles in *Faust*, Hamlet, Iago, the title roles in CAMUS's *Caligula*, PIRANDELLO's *Henry IV*, *Kean*, (SARTRE/DUMAS), Kreon in GRILLPARZER's *Medea*, 1960, and the Player in *Rosencrantz and Guildenstern are Dead* by STOPPARD, 1967.

Höflich, Lucie (1883–1956), German actress. From 1903 to 1932 she was connected with the Deutsches-Theater, BERLIN, under REINHARDT; excelled in the portrayals of simple and sincere women of the people, notably HAUPTMANN's *Rose Bernd*, and Gretchen in GOETHE's *Faust*; but she was also a splendid Mrs Alving in IBSEN's *Ghosts*, Berlin State Theatre, 1928, and Nora in *A Doll's House*. After the war she became manager of the theatre in Schwerin, 1946–50.

Hofmannsthal, Hugo von (1874–1929), Austrian poet, playwright and essayist. Major exponent of poetic drama in the early part of this century and one of the founders of the SALZBURG FESTIVAL. His early lyrical one-act VERSE DRAMAS were influenced by the Symbolists (▷SYMBOLISM), particularly MAETERLINCK: *Der Tor und der Tod* (Death and the Fool), pub 1894, fp Munich 1898; *Das Kleine Welttheater* (The Little World Theatre), pub 1897, fp Munich 1929, Residenztheater; *Der Tod des Tizian* (The Death of Titian), written 1892; *Der weisse Fächer* (The White Fan), pub 1898. In his attempt to revive classical plays of the past he was supported by REINHARDT, the producer of most of his plays including: *Elektra* (later made into an opera by Richard Strauss, 1909); *Ödipus und die Sphinx* (Oedipus and the Sphinx), fp BERLIN 1905, Deutsches-Theater; *König Ödipus*, 1907; *Alkestis*, pub 1909; *Das gerettete Venedig* (Venice Preserved), based on OTWAY, fp Berlin, Lessingtheater, des CRAIG. In his later period he wrote mainly COMEDIES and symbolic plays: *Christinas Heimreise* (Christina's Journey Home), Berlin 1910, Deutsches-Theater, dir Reinhardt; *Jedermann*, free adaptation of the English MORALITY PLAY *Everyman*, fp Berlin 1911, dir Reinhardt, and since performed every year at the Salzburg Festival; *Dame Kobold* (The Lady Demon), based on CALDERÓN, 1920; *Der Schwierige* (The Difficult Man), Berlin 1921, Deutsches-Theater; *Der Unbestechliche* (The Incorruptible), Vienna 1923, Raimund-Theater, with PALLENBERG; *Das Salzburger Grosse Welttheater* (The

Salzburg Great World Theatre), Salzburg Festival 1922; *Der Turm* (The Tower), based on Calderón's *Life's a Dream*, Munich 1928, State Theatre. He also wrote LIBRETTI for operas by Richard Strauss: *Der Rosenkavalier*, fp Dresden 1911, Royal Opera House; *Ariadne auf Naxos*, fp Stuttgart 1912; *Die Frau ohne Schatten*, fp Vienna 1919; *Die ägyptische Helena*, fp Dresden 1928; *Arabella*, 1933.
Bibl: G. Erken, HOFMANNSTHALS DRAMATISCHER STIL, 1967; W. Wunberg, DER FRÜHE HOFMANNSTHAL, 1965

Holberg, Ludvig (1684–1754), Danish-Norwegian dramatist, satirist and playwright. A schoolmaster by profession, he wrote about 28 COMEDIES 1722–28 for the first Danish theatre; though showing the influence of PLAUTUS, the COMMEDIA DELL' ARTE and MOLIÈRE (whom he got to know during extensive travel as a young man), he created his own form of satirical comedy, which marked the beginning of drama in Scandinavia; he might be described as the Danish GOLDONI. His most famous works include: *Jeppe ga Bjerget* (Jeppe of the Hill), 1722, and *Den politiske Kandestøber* (The Political Tub-Thumper), 1722. Other works: *Erasmus Montanus*, 1723; *Den Vægelsindede* (The Weathercock), 1723; *Diderich Menschenskrek* (Diderich the Terrible), 1724; *Jacob von Thyboe*, 1724; *Hexerie eller blind Allarm* (Witchcraft or False Alarm), 1724; *Den Stundesløse* (The Fussy Man), 1726; *De Usynlige* (The Invisible Ones), 1726; *Den Danske Comoedies Ligbegængelse* (Last Rites for Danish Comedy), 1727, etc.
Bibl: O. J. Campbell, THE COMEDIES OF HOLBERG, 1914

Holcroft, Thomas (1744–1809), English dramatist. He is credited with the introduction of MELODRAMA to the London stage with his *A Tale of Mystery*, 1802, an adaptation of *Coelina ou l'Enfant de Mystère*, 1800, by the French playwright Guilbert de Pixérécourt (1773–1844) who is remembered chiefly for a long succession of melodramas. H.'s play was frequently revived, the last time in 1937. Among other plays he wrote was a COMEDY *Love's Frailties*, 1794, based on a German original *Das Deutsche Hausvater* by Gemminger. His *Memoirs*, edited by HAZLITT, were published in 1816.

Hölderlin, Friedrich (1770–1843), one of Germany's greatest poets. He wrote only one dramatic work *Der Tod des Empedokles* (The Death of Empedocles), final version 1802; fp Stuttgart 1916, Court Theatre, adapted and directed E. v. Scholz. He also translated SOPHOCLES' *Oedipus Rex*, and *Antigone*, pub 1804, fp 1948, Chur Municipal Theatre, adapted and directed by BRECHT.
Bibl: M. Kohler & E. Kelletat, 1953

Holloway, Stanley (1890–), English actor. Started in REVUE and MUSICAL COMEDY, achieved many of his early successes in PANTOMIME; but also made his mark in SHAKESPEARE: in 1951 he played the First Gravedigger in *Hamlet* at the Old

Hugo von Hofmannsthal, *Jedermann*, Salzburg production

Stanley Holloway in *The Co-Optimists*, London 1921

Rolf Hochhuth, *Soldiers*, London 1958

Vic and Bottom in *A Midsummer Night's Dream* at the EDINBURGH FESTIVAL of 1954. Played Doolittle in the world success *My Fair Lady* (▷LERNER), in New York and London from 1956 onwards, as well as in the film version of the musical in 1964. H. is a fruity comedian who exudes a rich humanity.

Holtei, Karl von (1798–1880), German dramatist. Best known as editor of *Deutsche Blätter für Poesie Literatur, Kunst und Theater*, 1823; *Jahrbuch deutscher Nachspiele*, 1822–24; *Jahrbuch deutscher Bühnenspiele*, 1825–32. In 1825–26 he was secretary to the director, resident playwright and director at the Königstädter Theater, Berlin; 1837–39 director of the Riga theatre; then he travelled, reciting SHAKESPEARE, as he had done earlier. He was a prolific dramatist, in the tradition of French VAUDEVILLE; his best-known works include: *Der alte Feldherr* (The Old Warrior), 1826; *Lenore*, 1828. His autobiography *Vierzig Jahre*, 8 vols, 1832–50, is an important source of theatre history.
Bibl: I. Weithase, HOLTEI ALS VORLESER, 1940

Holz, Arno (1863–1929), German writer, the first major exponent of German dramatic NATURALISM. Collaborated with BAHR and BRAHM, 1884–87, on the paper *Die Freie Bühne*. He exercised considerable influence on G. HAUPTMANN; with the play *Die Familie Selicke* (The Selicke Family), written with J. Schlaf, fp BERLIN 1890, FREIE BÜHNE, he created a prototype of naturalistic drama. Other works include: *Sozialaristokraten* (Social Aristocrats), 1896; *Traumulus*, written with O. Jerschke, 1904.
Bibl: H. Motekat, 1953

Holzmeister, Clemens (1886–), Austrian architect and stage designer. He designed the Neues Festspielhaus in Salzburg, the Landestheater in Linz, and the open-air theatre in Istanbul; his most notable stage designs include: GOETHE's *Faust*, Part I, fp SALZBURG FESTIVAL, 1933, for which he built a complete 'Faust-city' in the rocks of the FELSENREITSCHULE; Mozart's *Don Giovanni*, Salzburg Festival, 1950; Beethoven's *Fidelio*, opening performance at the New Opera House in Vienna, 1955. His daughter **Judith H.** has been with the BURGTHEATER company in Vienna since 1947.

Home, William Douglas (1912–), English dramatist. Son of the 13th Earl of Home and brother of the 14th Earl who became Prime Minister, he started as an actor but took to playwriting and established himself as an accomplished author of highly polished COMEDIES about life in high society; but he has also written the compassionate and serious prison play *Now Barabbas*, 1947. Among his plays are two political comedies: *The Chiltern Hundreds*, 1947, and *The Manor of Northstead*, 1954, and several DRAWING-ROOM COMEDIES *The Reluctant Debutante*, 1955; *Aunt Edwina*, 1959; *The Reluctant Peer*, 1964; *The Secretary Bird*, 1968; *The Jockey Club Stakes*, 1970; *Lloyd George Knew My Father*, 1971; *At the End of the Day*, 1973.

Homolka, Oscar (1901–76), Austrian actor. With his powerful Slavic, high-cheekboned features, he was destined for a career of character acting. He was the first Mortimer in BRECHT's *Edward II*, Munich 1924, and created the title role in his *Baal*, Berlin 1926, with Brecht directing. After emigrating in the early 1930s, he appeared mainly in films, but also, in New York productions, played Edgar, in STRINDBERG's *The Dance of Death*, 1948, and Solness in IBSEN's *The Master Builder*, 1955.

Hopkins, Arthur (1879–1950), US producer and director. Originally a reporter and VAUDEVILLE producer, he made his reputation with high quality plays and strong casts, e.g. O'NEILL's *Anna Christie* and *The Hairy Ape*; M. ANDERSON and Laurence Stalling's *What Price Glory?*, 1924.

Hopkins, John (1931–), English dramatist. Read English at Cambridge and worked for several years as a studio manager in TV. In 1962 he joined the BBC team writing the police series *Z-Cars*, continuing until 1964; subsequently he wrote full-length TV plays including *The Pretty English Girls*, 1964, and *Horror of Darkness*, 1965. In 1966 he consolidated his position as one of the most important dramatists on TV with the TETRALOGY *Talking to a Stranger*; it has been described as 'the first authentic masterpiece written directly for television', and comprises *Any Time You're Ready I'll Sparkle*; *No Skill or Special Knowledge is Required*; *Gladly, My Cross-Eyed Bear*; and *The Innocent Must Suffer*. Other TV plays of this period are *A Game – Like – Only a Game*, 1966; *Some Place of Darkness*, 1967; *Beyond the Sunrise*, 1966. In 1968 his first stage play, *This Story of Yours*, was performed at the ROYAL COURT THEATRE; it was followed in 1970 by *Find Your Way Home*, and in 1974 by *Next of Kin*, NATIONAL THEATRE.

Hörbiger, Paul (1894–) and **Attila** (1896–), Austrian actors. Paul, the elder of the brothers, is above all a character comedian who has appeared in innumerable films and is one of the finest interpreters of the Viennese folk comedies of RAIMUND and NESTROY. Attila, who married the great Austrian actress PAULA WESSELY, started as a leading man, specializing in powerful peasant or lower-class roles, later became a considerable heavy character hero (James Tyrone in O'NEILL's *Long Day's Journey into Night*). For many years he was the Everyman of the SALZBURG FESTIVAL famous outdoor production, originally directed by REINHARDT.

Horniman, Annie Elizabeth Fredericka (1860–1937), English theatre manager and patron. Travels abroad, particularly in Germany, made her aware of the important part played by subsidized theatre in cultural life. She was one of the founders of English REPERTORY theatre and a staunch supporter of the Irish theatre movement. She went to Ireland in 1903 and built the ABBEY THEATRE, which opened in Dublin 1904, and which she financed until 1910. In Manchester she bought and rebuilt the Gaiety Theatre, where she ran a repertory company 1907–17, producing mainly plays of the MANCHESTER SCHOOL (H. Brighouse, HOUGHTON, Monkhouse; these dealt with the life of people in the provinces), and plays by SHAW and the classics. Financially it was unsuccessful; the company was disbanded in 1917 and Miss H. sold the building in 1921.
Bibl: R. Pogson, MISS HORNIMAN AND THE GAIETY THEATRE, 1952

Horovitz, Israel (1939–), US dramatist. He was the first American to be chosen Playwright-in-Residence with the RSC, 1965, and a teaching fellow at RADA, 1961–63. He is a member/playwright of the Eugene O'Neill Memorial Theatre Foundation and has been writing plays for 16 years. His first play *Comeback* was produced in Boston when he was 16 years old. Best noted for his one-act play *The Indian Wants the Bronx*, fp New York 1968, for which he received many awards. Other plays include: *It's Called the Sugar Plum*; *The Honest to God Schnozzola*; *Morning*; *Line*; *Leader*.

Horváth, Ödön von (1901–38), Hungarian-born German playwright. One of the most remarkable writers of his day. His work was gradually rediscovered in Germany in the late 1960s. All his plays reveal strong concern with the German tradition, social change and political movement: *Revolte auf Côté 3018* (Revolt on Peak 3018), 1927, Hamburg Kammerspiele, retitled *Die Bergbahn* (The Mountain Railway), at the VOLKSBÜHNE, Berlin 1929; *Sladek, der schwarze Reichswehrmann* (Sladek, the Black Reichswehr Soldier), Berlin 1929, Lessingtheater; *Italienische Nacht* (Italian Night), Berlin 1931, Theater am Schiffbauerdamm; *Geschichten aus dem Wiener Wald* (*Tales from the Vienna Woods*), Berlin 1931, Deutsches-Theater, dir HILPERT; *Kasimir und Karoline*, 1932, Leipzig Schauspielhaus; *Glaube, Liebe, Hoffnung* (Faith, Love and Hope), fp Vienna 1936; *Hin und Her* (Hither and Thither), 1934, ZURICH SCHAUSPIELHAUS; *Mit dem Kopf durch die Wand* (With One's Head through the Wall), Vienna 1935, Scala; *Figaro lässt sich scheiden* (Figaro is Getting Divorced), Prague 1937, Deutsches-Theater; *Ein Dorf ohne Männer* (A Village without Men), 1937; *Himmelwärts* (Towards the Heavens), 1937; *Der jüngste Tag* (Judgment Day), 1937. Produced posthumously: *Die Unbekannte aus der Seine* (The Stranger from the Seine), 1933, fp Vienna 1949; *Pompeji*, Vienna 1959; *Zur schönen Aussicht* (A Nice View), written 1929; *Rund um den Kongress* (Around the Congress), written 1929. His realistic plays, set among the petty bourgeoisie and the social outcasts of the years before 1933, have gained fresh significance in the productions of the 1960s, mainly *Geschichten aus dem Wiener Wald*, *Kasimir und Karoline* and *Italienische Nacht*. They picture the decadence of society (economic depression,

William Douglas Home, *The Reluctant Debutante*, London 1955

disintegration of values) before Hitler came to power. H.'s apparent ingenuousness allows the audience to apprehend the sadness and banality of life and the sentimentality of most human emotion.
Bibl: K. Kahl, 1966

Horwitz, Kurt (1897–1974), German actor, director and manager. Worked in Munich and Zurich before his appointment as director of the Basle theatre, 1946–50. He was INTENDANT of the Munich National Theatre 1953–58. His best roles include the name parts in: SHAKESPEARE's *King John* and *Julius Caesar* (both 1941); SCHILLER's *Wallenstein*, 1943; Torvald in IBSEN's *A Doll's House*, 1944; and Jupiter in SARTRE's *Les Mouches*, 1944. He produced plays by CLAUDEL, FRISCH, T. WILLIAMS, DÜRRENMATT and CAMUS, and notably a series of MOLIÈRE's plays, most of which starred his friend, the actor GINSBERG: *Tartuffe*, 1951; *L'Avare*, 1952; *L'École des femmes*, 1954, etc.

Hôtel de Bourgogne, Théâtre de l'. The first major theatre in Paris, where many important 17th-century plays were first staged; built in 1548 by the Confrérie de la Passion, who had held the monopoly of acting since the Middle Ages. Soon after the building was finished, religious plays, which formed the most important part of their REPERTORY, were prohibited, and the house was let to visiting companies. With BELLEROSE's Comédiens du Roi the Hôtel de Bourgogne was unrivalled till the establishment in 1634 of the Théâtre du Marais under MONTDORY and the forming of MOLIÈRE's company in 1658; with the merging of these three groups the COMÉDIE-FRANÇAISE was established in 1680. The Hôtel de Bourgogne was used until 1783 by Italian companies.

Houghton, Stanley (1881–1913), English playwright. A leading member of the Manchester school of English regional NATURALISM, the first movement to use non-standard vernacular English as a vehicle for serious drama. His most famous play is *Hindle Wakes*, 1912, in which a young woman, made pregnant by the son of the local mill-owner, refuses to marry him – an Ibsenite new-woman theme transferred to a north of England industrial small-town milieu. H., who also wrote drama criticism for the *Manchester Guardian*, is the author of the following plays: *The Dear Departed*, 1908; *Independent Means*, 1909; *The Master of the House*, 1910; *The Younger Generation*, 1910; *Trust the People*, 1913; *The Perfect Cure*, 1913.

Howard, Bronson (1842–1908), US playwright. Started as a drama critic in his native Detroit, and later in New York where he worked for the *Tribune* and the *Post*. One of the first US playwrights to draw on American characters and social conditions for his subject matter. His first success, in a series of some 20 plays, was *Saratoga*, 1870, which was also produced in England, suitably modified under the title of *Brighton*, 1874; *Lillian's Last Love*, 1873, retitled *The Banker's Daughter*, 1878, and, for production in London with revisions by Albery, again retitled *The Old Love and the New*, 1879; *Young Mrs Winthrop*, 1882; *The Henrietta*, 1887; *Shenandoah*, 1888, a highly successful Civil War play. He was the first US dramatist to rely solely on playwriting for a living; founded the American Dramatists' Club, 1891, and fought for an improvement in the copyright laws to raise the status of playwrights.

Howard, Leslie (1893–1943), English actor. After several London successes he went to the USA in 1920 and made his reputation playing in DRAWING-ROOM COMEDY. He typified the matinée idol – goodlooking, suave in manner and accomplished as an actor. Returning to London he gave a brilliant performance opposite TALLULAH BANKHEAD in *Her Cardboard Lover* (Valerie Wingate/WODEHOUSE, adapted from DEVAL's *Dans sa Candeur naive*, 1926). He was outstanding in SHERWOOD's *The Petrified Forest*, 1935 and as *Hamlet*, 1936, both in New York. He also had a successful film career, one of his best parts being in the famous production *Gone with the Wind*, opposite VIVIEN LEIGH and Clark Gable.

Howard, Sidney (1891–1939), US dramatist. After graduating from the University of California in 1915, he studied playwriting with BAKER (47 Workshop). One of the most important American naturalist writers of plays, he was a founder member of the PLAYWRIGHTS' COMPANY. Among his original plays the best known was *They Knew What They Wanted*, 1924, a modern version of the Tristan and Isolde theme, about a sinning woman, but set in a Californian vineyard, exploring the local idiom. It starred Pauline Lord and R. BENNETT. Awarded the PULITZER PRIZE, it was filmed several times and made into the musical *The Most Happy Fella*. Other works include: *Swords*, 1921, a drama in blank verse; *Lucky Sam McCarver*, 1925; *Ned McCobb's Daughter*, 1926; *The Silver Chord*, 1926; *Salvation*, 1928, written with MacARTHUR; *The Ghost of Yankee Doodle*, 1937, starring ETHEL BARRYMORE, and *Madam, Will You Walk?* (produced posthumously). He often adapted the works of others to provide effective acting vehicles, one of the most successful being *The Late Christopher Bean*, 1932, based on René Fauchois's *Prenez-garde à la peinture*, of which E. WILLIAMS also did an adaptation, and *Yellow Jack*, 1934, taken from Paul Kruif's *Microbe Hunters*.
Bibl: J. W. Krutch, THE AMERICAN DRAMA SINCE 1918, 1957; B. Mantle, CONTEMPORARY AMERICAN PLAYWRIGHTS, 1940

Hroswitha (or **Roswitha**) **von Gandersheim** (*c.*935–*c.*975), Benedictine abbess of Gandersheim in Saxony. She wrote a number of poems as well as plays in medieval Latin. The plays, probably conceived as an answer to or replacement of the COMEDIES of TERENCE in the teaching of Latin are in rhymed Latin prose; they are essentially DIALOGUES, mainly concerned with the triumph of chastity over sensuality. Among these are: *Gallicanus*; *Dulcitus*; *Callimachus*; *Abraham*; *Pafnutius*; *Sapientia*.
Bibl: A. L. Haight, 1965

Hubris (Gk = excessive pride, insolence, arrogance). In Greek TRAGEDY the hero's *hubris* brought him into conflict with the gods and caused his downfall.

Hughes, Langston (1902–67), Black US poet and playwright. Used the language of the American Negro, the speech rhythms of the Harlem district, to express the aspirations and resentments of Black Americans. His earliest plays were openly propagandist and political: *Scottsboro Limited*, 1932, and *Don't You Want to Be Free*, 1936; they were followed by *Little Ham*, 1935, a folk comedy; *Soul Gone Home*, 1937; *Tambourines to*

Glory, 1949, music Jobe Huntley; *The Barrier*, 1950, music Jan Meyerowitz; *Simply Heavenly*, 1957, a musical adapted from some of his own stories, score by David Martin.
Bibl: J. A. Emanuel, 1968

Hugo, Victor-Marie (1802–85), French man of letters, generally regarded as France's greatest Romantic poet. Author of famous novels (*Notre Dame de Paris*; *Les Misérables*, etc.), he also has an important place in the history of drama, although his plays are rarely performed today. Inspired by SHAKESPEARE and the German Romantic poets, he demanded free rein for the poetic imagination in the theatre and the abolition of the restricting rules of French classical drama. The preface to his VERSE DRAMA *Cromwell*, 1827, became the manifesto of the French Romantic school of drama. *Marion Delorme* was forbidden by the censor on political grounds and first performed in 1831, a year after H. had achieved his breakthrough with a performance of his play *Hernani*. On 23 February this play was performed for the first time at the COMÉDIE-FRANÇAISE and was received with hostility as well as enthusiasm by the opposing factions of the audience. But the *bataille d'Hernani*, as the event became known, ended with H.'s triumph and established the Romantics in the French theatre for a long time to come. Other important verse dramas followed: *Le Roi s'amuse*, 1832, which still holds the stage, adapted for opera as *Rigoletto*, and *Ruy Blas*, 1838. In prose he wrote the successful historical dramas *Lucrèce Borgia*, 1833; *Marie Tudor*, 1833; *Angelo, tyran de Padoue*, 1835; but the failure of another verse play *Les Burgraves*, 1843, cooled his enthusiasm for the theatre. Another great verse drama, *Torquemada*, from the third part of his great three-part poem *La Légende des siècles*, 1859–83, which he wrote mainly while in exile in the Channel Isles, 1852–70, was not performed in his lifetime. A play in a completely different vein, the prose MELODRAMA *A Mille Francs de récompense*, written 1866, reached the stage only in 1961, and achieved considerable success as a typical piece of 19th-century sentimental theatre.

Humanist (Scholastic) Drama. Latin drama which was produced in humanist schools (16th and 17th centuries) in Central Europe with themes from the Bible and from Greek and Roman antiquity; mainly written with educational aims to give the pupils practice in the Latin language; in form they were modelled on the concise DIALOGUE of PLAUTUS and TERENCE; e.g. Reuchlin's *Henno*, 1497; Gnapheus' *Acolastus*, 1529, etc. In the Reformation era themes were also taken from the religious struggle. Gradually German texts, at first PROLOGUES, interludes etc., were assimilated and included; later texts were written entirely in German, e.g. Sixt Birk's *Susanna*, 1532. ▷JESUIT DRAMA.
Bibl: R. Newald, DIE DEUTSCHE LITERATUR VON SPÄTHUMANISMUS ZUR EMPFINDSAMKEIT, 2/1957

Huneker, James Gibbons (1860–1921), US music and drama critic. Began his career on the *Morning Advertiser* and *New York Recorder* in 1890; in 1902 moved to the *New York Sun*, and 1912–19 worked for the *New York Times*, subsequently with the *Sun* again for two years. He was an important supporter of European drama on the American stage, e.g. MAETERLINCK, SUDERMANN, WEDEKIND, and particularly IBSEN and STRINDBERG; he also fiercely attacked the superficiality and sentimentality of American plays. His studies of BECQUE, HAUPTMANN and D'ANNUNZIO are remarkable literary works. His books include: *Iconoclasts*; *A Book of Dramatists*; *Egoists*; *Mezzotints in Modern Music*, a novel, *Painted Veils*; a volume of short stories, *Melomaniacs*; and the witty autobiography *Steeplejack*.
Bibl: H. L. Mencken, PREJUDICES, THIRD SERIES, 1922

Hungary. In the 18th century, productions in Catholic monastic schools and Protestant schools as well as German and French companies at Court. In 1790 a National Acting Company emerged under the management of Laszlo Kelemen (1762–1814) who had to compete with the powerful and well-established German theatre. In 1837 the West Hungarian Theatre was opened, becoming in 1840 the National Theatre. It was managed 1878–94 by Ede Paulay, whose work was strongly based on the ideas of LAUBE; in 1883 he first produced *The Tragedy of Man*, written 1861, by Imre Madách (1823–64), a great figure in the history of Hungarian drama. In 1875 the People's Theatre was founded. In the late 19th century a number of private theatrical enterprises came into existence, the first and most important being the Vigszinház (Comedy Theatre) founded in 1896. The playwrights to emerge in this period included Mór Jókai (1825–1904) and Gergely Csiky (1842–91). The first playwright to become internationally acknowledged was MOLNÁR (1878–1952). Operettas also played an important part in the Hungarian theatre, especially at the Kiraly Szinház (since 1903) and Municipal Operetta Theatres (since 1930s) where the works of famous composers like Lehár, Kálmán and Abrahám were performed. In 1904 Sándor Hevesi formed the Thália Society to revitalize Hungarian drama in the manner of other European theatres; he managed the National Theatre, 1922–32, where his REPERTOIRE was based mainly on classical world literature. Outstanding actors were: Árpád Ódry (1876–1937), GIZI BAJOR (1893–1951), Lujza Blaha (1850–1926). In 1949 all Hungarian theatres were taken over by the State and forced into SOCIALIST REALISM. Since 1956 again influenced by all the most important Western and American trends in the theatre; great interest in the works of SHAKESPEARE and rediscovery of MOLNÁR's plays.
Bibl: T. Klaniczay, HISTORY OF HUNGARIAN LITERATURE, 1964

Hunter, Norman C. (1908–71), English dramatist. With a feeling for atmosphere, he portrays disappointed people, ruefully accepting their limited environment. His West End successes were *Waters of the Moon*, 1951; *A Day by the Sea*, 1953; *A Touch of the Sun*, 1958; and *The Tulip Tree*, 1962 – all splendid vehicles for star actors, e.g. SYBIL THORNDIKE, GIELGUD, REDGRAVE.

Hurwicz, Angelika (1922–), German actress. Made her early appearances with touring companies in Germany, in 1945 joined the Deutsches-Theater, Berlin, and left it in 1949 to work with BRECHT and his BERLINER ENSEMBLE with whom she remained till 1957. Since then she has produced and acted at several German theatres; main parts include: Katrin in Brecht's *Mutter Courage*, 1949; Anna in GORKY's *Mother*, 1949; Grusche in Brecht's *Der kaukasische Kreidekreis*, 1954; her main productions: L. N. TOLSTOY's *The Light Shines in Darkness*, 1967; SPERR's *Landshuter Erzählungen*, Wuppertal 1969. Her Grusche is a characteristic example of what Brecht expected of an actress: freshness and naïveté based on analysis and observation. She is the author of *Brecht inszeniert. Der kaukasische Kreidekreis*, 1964.

Huston, Walter (1884–1950), US actor, born in Canada. First BROADWAY appearance was 1905, and he became a star in the 1920s; his greatest successes were in O'NEILL's *Desire Under the Elms*, 1924; *Dodsworth*, 1934, adapted by S. HOWARD from a Sinclair Lewis novel; *Othello*, 1936; *Knickerbocker Holiday*, musical play by M. ANDERSON and WEILL, 1938. He was also well known in films.

Hypokrites (Gk = the one who answers). Principal actor of Greek drama (introduced by THESPIS) who stood opposite the CHORUS; later a general name for actors in the Greek theatre.

Hypothesis (Gk = assumption, assignment). Preface to a Greek drama usually written by a later scholar, containing a synopsis of the PLOT, the setting and dates of performance, titles of other plays on the same subject or by the same author, the names of the CHOREGOS and actors, DIDASCALAE, etc.

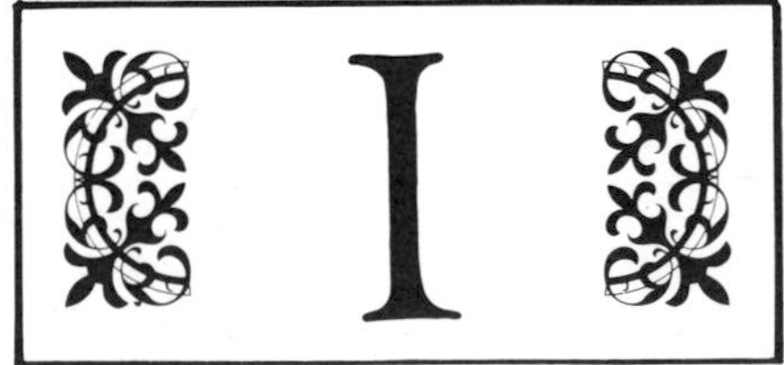

Ibsen, Henrik (1828–1906), Norwegian playwright. Apprenticed to an apothecary, 1844–50; his first play *Catilina* was published under a pseudonym in 1850. His next play *Kjaempehøjen* (*The Warrior's Barrow*) was performed and this led to his appointment in 1851 as stage manager and resident playwright with the newly formed Norwegian National Theatre at Bergen, under the direction of Ole Bull; he worked 1857–62 with the Norske Teatret in Christiania (now Oslo). The plays he wrote under his contract at Bergen were: *Norma*, 1851, a parody of Bellini's opera *Norma*; *Sankthansnatten* (St John's Night), 1853; *Gildet på Solhaug* (*The Feast at Solhaug*), 1855; *Fru Inger til Østråt* (*Lady Inger of Ostrat*), 1855; *Olaf Liljekrans*, 1857. At Christiania, where, owing to the lack of success of the theatre, he was intensely unhappy, he wrote: *Hœrmœnene på Helgeland* (*The Vikings at Helgeland*), 1858; *Kjaerlighedens komedie* (*Love's Comedy*), 1862; *Kongsemnerne* (*The Pretenders*), 1864. Having been awarded a scholarship, he travelled to Rome and spent some years in Italy where he wrote two of his masterpieces, the VERSE DRAMAS *Brand*, pub 1866, the TRAGEDY of an uncompromising idealist, and *Peer Gynt*, 1867, produced in Christiania 1876, an epic TRAGICOMEDY of a man's life and its illusions and false aspirations. These two plays earned him a wide reputation; he then lived mainly abroad, in Italy and Germany, till 1891. Having written two further plays in his earlier vein – *De unges Forbund* (*The League of Youth*), 1869, and *Keiser og Galilœer* (*Emperor and Galilean*), 1873 – he turned to writing a series of realistic plays about contemporary social problems, which caused a stir throughout Europe and made him one of the foremost and most controversial spokesmen of moral and social reform in the latter half of the 19th century. The first of these plays was *Samfundets Støtter* (*The Pillars of Society*), 1877; it was followed by *Et Dukkehjem* (*A Doll's House*), 1879, which started a violent debate on the status of women in marriage; *Gengangere* (*Ghosts*), 1881, shocked the establishment by bringing the topics of venereal disease and sex in marriage on to the stage; *En Folkefiende* (*An Enemy of the People*), 1882, deals with the problem of the dangers of democracy seen as the rule of the majority of mediocre and self-seeking people who try to defeat the outstanding individual who exposes their shortcomings – clearly the outcome of I.'s own feelings about violent and stupid opposition to his social pioneering; in *Vildanden* (*The Wild Duck*), 1884, the other side of the question is aired – here it is the idealistic truth-seeker who brings disaster to ordinary people who might have lived in happy mediocrity with their illusions; *Rosmersholm*, 1886, explores the problems of conventional morality. With *Fruen fra Havet* (*The Lady from the Sea*), 1888, lyrical and symbolical elements tend to come to the fore, while the role of the individual in society and his responsibility towards his fellow men continues to provide the basic theme; the same is true of *Lille Eyolf* (*Little Eyolf*), 1894. *Hedda Gabler*, 1890, one of his most enduring successes, delves into the psychology of a woman whom social convention has denied a creative outlet. In the plays which follow, his technique becomes increasingly symbolical and poetic: *Bygmester Solness* (*The Master Builder*), 1892, is based on his own experience of an old man's infatuation with a young woman and portrays the conflict of the older and younger generations;

Henrik Ibsen, *Little Eyolf*, with MRS PATRICK CAMPBELL, right, as the Rat Wife and ELISABETH ROBINS, left, London 1896

Henrik Ibsen

John Gabriel Borkman, 1896, scrutinizes an old man's guilt after a wasted life; and *Naar vi døde vaagner* (*When We Dead Awaken*), 1899, questions the artist's achievement at the end of his career when he looks back on all his wasted opportunities. The controversies aroused by the social plays of his middle period were so intense at the time, the novelty of his subject matter so shocking, that their brilliance as artistic achievements tended to be overlooked. At one time the opinion prevailed that, as these topics lost their actuality, his plays would be forgotten. The opposite has happened: now that many of his themes are no longer so topical – although some, like those dealing with the status of women, have retained even that impact – it becomes clear that they are profound explorations of the human situation and full of psychological interest and poetic impact. His impact on the European theatre of his time was immense, as was his influence on the evolution of manners and morals. His chief advocate in England was SHAW. ▷ARCHER.
Bibl: M. Meyer, 1967–71, 3 vols

Identification. The term is used in dramatic criticism: (1) to denote the merging of the actor's personality with that of the character he is portraying, the 'becoming identical' with the character; and (2) the tendency on the part of the spectator to identify himself with the feelings and actions of the protagonist on the stage, the spectator's 'being taken out of himself' into the inner world of the character whose fate he is watching with the most intense empathy. Identification in the sense of (1) was postulated and systematically evoked by STANISLAVSKY's methods of actor training, while his pupil VAKHTANGOV and also MEYERHOLD and BRECHT advocated a far more detached attitude of the actor towards the character he plays. This implies that the actor should also approach the character from the outside. Identification in the sense of (2) is a basic psychological condition of all dramatic experience. But Brecht warned against the dangers of total identification between the spectator and the character. He wanted the audience to be critically detached so as to be able to judge the character's actions coolly and intelligently rather than through mere participation in his emotions.

Iffland, August Wilhelm (1759–1814), German actor, dramatist and manager. Early in his career he worked at the COURT THEATRE in Gotha under EKHOF (1777) and met the actors David Beil and Heinrich Beck. All three were engaged by DALBERG at the Court Theatre in Mannheim in 1779, where I. became principal actor of the ensemble, and director; he also wrote essays and his first play *Wilhelm von Schenck*, 1781. His best role was Karl Moor in the original production of SCHILLER's *Die Räuber*. He established his fame as a dramatist with *Verbrechen aus Ehrsucht* (Crimes of Ambition), 1784; other works include: *Die Jäger* (The Foresters), 1785; *Die Hagestolzen* (The Bachelors), 1791. His dramatic works are well constructed, effective plays, amongst the most successful of his time. As an actor he emphasized realistic detail, in the manner of Ekhof, but was also influenced by GOETHE's Weimar style. Having previously toured with great success throughout Germany, he reached the peak of his career with his appointment in 1796 as INTENDANT of the Royal National Theatre, Berlin, which he soon established as one of the leading German theatres; he rebuilt the Theater am Gendarmenmarkt, opening in 1802 with KOTZEBUE's *Die Kreuzfahrer* (The Crusaders). As a director he supervised the editing and rewriting of plays, conducting rehearsals and controlling the making of sets and costumes. His REPERTOIRE was restricted mainly to lavishly produced, 'commercial' plays, for which he was later criticized, but his productions of Schiller's plays had unqualified success. In 1811 he became Generalintendant of all royal theatres of Prussia including the opera house.
Bibl: W. Drews, DIE GROSSEN DER DEUTSCHEN SCHAUSPIELKUNST, 1941

Iffland-ring. A ring which in the late 19th and then in the 20th century was regarded as due to the greatest German actor of his generation, to be bequeathed at his death to the one he considered his worthy successor. Legend has it that IFFLAND wore the ring and passed it on in this manner. In reality the ring, an antique with an Iffland portrait, was probably bought by Theodor Doering in the late 19th century and left to HAASE, who left it to BASSERMANN, from whom it passed in turn to KRAUSS and its present holder, MEINRAD.

Illusionism. A term used in dramatic criticism to describe the theatre of the bourgeois period, *c.* 1750–1910, which aimed at creating maximum illusion of reality on the stage. The contrary tendency is termed an 'anti-illusionistic theatre' which underlines the unreality of the stage, does not want to deceive the public about the fact that they are watching a fictitious event, and delights in the artificiality of the performance.

Ilyinsky, Igor Vladimirovich (1901–), Soviet actor. Joined the MEYERHOLD theatre in 1920 and remained with it till its closure in 1938 when he went to the Maly. He was most successful in satirical comedy, e.g. Khlestakov in GOGOL's *Revizor*. In recent years he has also become well known as a producer.

Immermann, Karl Leberecht (1796–1840), German writer and theatre manager. In 1832 he founded a theatre company and gave 'model productions' at the Düsseldorf theatre, where he was director 1835–37. Influenced by GOETHE's Weimar period, he attempted to provide the German theatre with an international REPERTOIRE and staged works by SHAKESPEARE, CALDERÓN, Goethe, SCHILLER, KLEIST and LESSING. He raised the standard of acting by insisting on controlled, coherent playing and demanded sets to suit a particular type of work, e.g. for Shakespeare's plays he used *Raumbühne* with a large podium (=Theatre-in-the-round). The painters Schirmer and Hildebrand collaborated in designing the sets. For a short time he engaged GRABBE as a literary adviser. In his writing he saw himself as following in the tradition of the German classical and romantic authors: *Das Thal von Ronceval* (The Valley of R.), 1820; *Cardenio und Celinde*, 1826; *Andreas Hofer, der Sandwirt von Passeyer* (A.H., the Innkeeper of Passeyer), 1827; his best-known play *Merlin*, 1832, fp 1918, was inspired by Goethe's *Faust*.
Bibl: M. Windfuhr, IMMERMANS ERZÄHLERISCHES WERK, 1957

Impresario (Ital), A producer or agent involved in promoting productions and visits of theatrical companies, particularly in the field of musical entertainment.

Impromptu (Fr=unprepared, extempore, improvised, an improvised poem). The impromptu has a special tradition in French theatre, where it usually denotes a play in which the dramatist lightly reflects on his own position as a playwright: MOLIÈRE's *L'Impromptu de Versailles* is a critical portrayal of Molière's company and at the same time a reflection on the situation of the theatre in his day. GIRAUDOUX's *L' Impromptu de Paris*, 1937, and IONESCO's *L'Impromptu de l'Alma*, 1956, follow the same pattern.

Improvisation (Lat *improvisus*=unforeseen). Play without precisely predetermined action, text or DIALOGUE (▷EXTEMPORE). The actors of the COMMEDIA DELL'ARTE improvised on a fixed scheme of action, the *canevas*, using variations on a basic stock character and traditional dialogue, passed on by word of mouth, which they adapted to their own personality and to the contemporary situation. They did not 'invent' either the text or the acting style, but varied a pattern that already existed. The comic character ARLECCHINO (the active intriguer) had to address the audience directly and react to local and topical events. Elements of this kind of improvisation existed in the medieval plough and wooing plays, and were later found in the European folk theatre (local FARCES, dialect plays, farcical comedies etc.). Improvisation is also part of the training of actors and has a twofold function: training in observation and the search for individual personal expression. STANISLAVSKY's method, for example, consists of the acting out of unscripted scenes which stimulate the actor's imaginative insight into a character. America's exponents of the METHOD have made innumerable attempts to build whole plays and shows on improvisation. Group improvisation is important in theatre workshops, mainly in OFF-OFF BROADWAY theatres where playwrights work with the actors in avant-garde companies, e.g. LIVING THEATRE, LA MAMA, etc.

India. From the earliest time dance, MIME and drama have formed a unity in India, based on the humanization of the gods (*Shiva*=king of dance, *Brahma*=creator of drama). No exact records of the historical development exist. The basic mythological-theoretical work which examines most thoroughly the principles of Indian drama is *Nātyashāstra* by Bharata (dated between 200 BC and AD 200), who was regarded as the supreme authority according to whose rules dramas were written and performed. He lays down a theory of aesthetics which demands that art should give pleasure, as a step towards the ultimate peace of the mystic's meditation. He writes on the conventions of the stage, defining gesture (24 finger gestures = *Mudra*; 36 eye movements, 16 positions of the feet on the earth and in the air, etc.), dance, décor, rules on playwriting, theatre architecture, poetic composition, etc. He also gives directions for the various socially conditioned rules of walking. The languages employed in classical Indian drama are both Sanskrit, for the persons of high education, and Prakrit used by persons of lower rank. The types of role, costume and mask, intonation of speech and the accompanying instruments were all fixed. Theatre buildings: rectangular in shape, open on all four sides, covered with a roof, divided into areas for actors and the audience. The changing rooms and musicians were located behind a curtain. The classical drama of India incorporates elements of the religious temple dances as well as the earthy jokes of the travelling CLOWN (*Vidushaka*): a fat-bellied bold man, lazy and greedy, shrewd; later a servant's part. The classical Indian drama, also known as Sanskrit drama, starts with a prelude, a DIALOGUE between three characters (*trigata*): the director (actor and producer known as *Sutradhāra*, which means 'thread-holder', derived from the puppet play), the chief actor and the clown. Earliest plays and fragments are dated *c* AD 100 such as the works by Ashvaghosha and Bhasa. From the 2nd and 3rd centuries AD extant: *Cāradatta of Bhāsa*, the story of a rich merchant who became poor through his generosity and who was saved by the virtuous courtesan Vasantasenā. The second version of the same theme written in the 3rd or 4th century, *The Little Clay Cart*, is attributed to King Shudraka. Many versions and adaptations of the play exist. The most highly praised author was KĀLIDĀSA, the Court poet of the Gupta dynasty in the 5th century, whose best-known work *Śakuntalā*, a courtly love story, refined and poetic, is the epitome of classical Indian drama. The Indian drama survived in a moralistic form in Tibet: *Zugiuima*, 11th century; productions in Lhasa until the 20th century. In *c.* 1700 Bhavabhuti wrote his dramas (but without the clown). At the same time FARCES and popular COMEDIES, e.g. the satires on the sexy way of life of monks who were supposed to be ascetic: *Matta vilāsaprahasana* ascribed to King Mahendra-Vikramavarman. Decline of the classical Indian (Hindu and Buddhist) theatre through the invasion of Islam (12th century) and the Moghul empire (16th century), but various features of it survived in folk drama, regional forms of dance drama (complex language of symbolism, a parallel to the rules for Sanskrit rhetoric): Kathakali, Bhārata Nātyam, Khatak and Manipurî. Attempts at a renaissance of classical Indian theatre in the 20th century by TAGORE.

Bibl: J. C. Mathur, DRAMA IN RURAL INDIA, 1964; H. W. Wells, THE CLASSICAL DRAMA OF INDIA, 1963; I. Shekhar, SANSKRIT DRAMA: ITS ORIGINS AND DECLINE, 1960; M. M. Ghose, HISTORY OF HINDU DRAMA, 1951

Indonesia. With Hinduism the Vedantan mythology *Ramayana* and *Mahabharata* (Hindu epics) came to Java. They lent themes and characters to the unique Javanese SHADOW PLAY *wajang kulit* (*Wajang* means 'puppet'; *kulit* means 'leather'), the first records of which go back to the 15th century. The face of the puppet is seen always in profile, the body half-frontal, feet always directed where the puppet looks. Each line, each ornament has its symbolic meaning. The performances last a whole night, about eight to nine hours. They are performed by a single *dalang* ('puppeteer') who speaks the dialogue of all characters, narrates between scenes, sings and conducts the musical ensemble, the *gamelan*. The cast of each play consists often of about 60 puppets, sometimes up to 144, out of the set of many hundreds. During the long history of the *wajang kulit* a great number of cycles of shadow plays came into being; according to the different periods of Javanese history, which they dramatized, each play required new puppet characters. With the infiltration of Islam into Java, the form of *wajang golek* developed ('doll-puppet wajang') which today dominates middle and western Java. It follows basically the structure of the *wajang kulit*, but uses no screen, the figures of the doll-puppets (painted with splendid colours) being seen three-dimensionally. The plays are dramatized stories centring around Prince Menak, a forerunner of Mohammed. The *wajang kulit* in Bali developed concurrently with the Javanese form and includes the standard Pandawa plays, Rama plays and Balinese legends. Here the puppets are more realistic and the performances conducted more as a religious rite. Another important dramatic form, specific for Bali, is the *barong* dance drama, in which central themes of Balinese religion are dramatized.

Bibl: J. R. Brandon, THEATRE IN SOUTH-EAST ASIA, 1967; R. L. Mellema, WAYANG PUPPETS: CARVING, COLOURING AND SYMBOLISM, 1954; B. de Zoete & W. Spies, DANCE AND DRAMA IN BALI, 1938

Inge, William (1913–73), US dramatist. His plays are sentimental, romantic pictures of life in the small towns of the Mid-West. He was a member of the drama faculty of Stephens College, Columbia, Mo., and then worked on the *St Louis Star Times* as theatre critic and taught English at Washington University, St Louis, Mo. Encouraged by T. WILLIAMS, he wrote his first play *Farther Off From Heaven*, fp 1947, Dallas, Texas, and his reputation as a major dramatist became established with *Come Back Little Sheba*, 1950, THEATRE GUILD,

August Iffland as Karl Moor in SCHILLER's *Die Raüber*

India, a Kathakali dance drama

Indonesia, shadow PUPPET

with Shirley Booth; *Picnic*, 1953, which gained the NYDCC award and the PULITZER PRIZE; *Bus Stop*, 1955, dir CLURMAN; and *The Dark at the Top of the Stairs*, 1958, a variation on his first play. Other works: *A Loss of Roses*, 1959; *Natural Affection*, 1963; *Where's Daddy?*, 1966, and a one-acter, *The Disposal*. He won the Academy Award for his screenplay, *Splendour in the Grass*, 1961.

Innamorati (Ital = lovers). Stock characters of the COMMEDIA DELL'ARTE, a young couple who are lovers (▷ANDREINI, FLORINDO).

Intendant. Title given to the artistic director (manager) of a Municipal or State Theatre in Germany; in theatres with separate auditoriums for drama, opera and ballet he is known as Generalintendant; originally an honorary appointment for a member of the Court to supervise the artistic directors.

Interlude. A short dramatic sketch, often taken as the starting point of English drama. The first writer to make the English interlude a complete and independent dramatic form was HEYWOOD. The Players of the King's Interludes were first recorded under Henry VII in 1493 and disappeared under Elizabeth I. ▷INTERMEZZO and ENTREMES.

Intermezzo (Ital=interlude). An insertion of dance or MIME in a play and hence, at a later stage of development, for a short dramatic or musical performance in the intervals of serious plays. The secular drama of the Middle Ages often included insertions of song, dance or mime. With the rediscovery of Greek and Roman drama in the Renaissance and the insistence of the Humanist critics on ARISTOTLE's unities, these illogical insertions of extrinsic elements had to disappear. As a result the Intermezzo became a separate art form, at first a musical interlude, later enlarged by the addition of ballet, choral singing, and ultimately in the spectacular performances of the Baroque period, fireworks and processions. Some Italian theoreticians (Cinthio, Ingegneri) regarded these Intermezzi as a substitute for the choral passages in Greek TRAGEDY. By the 17th century it had developed into so many different varieties of dance and music that the distinctions between the Intermezzo and ballet, MELODRAMA, etc., became very vague. Its development was particularly vigorous in the field of opera. While serious opera, with its stress on mythological and historical subjects gave little opportunity for lighter elements, the Intermezzo had room for COMEDY, extravagant and fashionable COSTUME and realistic acting. From these elements (with the addition of features of the COMMEDIA DELL'ARTE) the Intermezzo grew, at the beginning of the 18th century, into a new genre, the *opera buffa* (comic opera). The French form of the Intermezzo, the *intermède* (*intermédie, entremets*) developed on lines similar to the Italian form at the end of the 16th century. But in France ballet (▷BALLET DE COURT) developed with particular vigour, ultimately into the COMÉDIE-BALLET. In England the INTERLUDE and in Spain the ENTREMES followed different lines of development. ▷MASQUE.

International Theatre Institute (ITI). Central organization for the exchange of ideas, experience and techniques of theatre, founded in 1947 under the auspices of UNESCO with headquarters in Paris. Each country has its own national ITI centre. The ITI publishes a bilingual magazine: *Le Théâtre dans le Monde* (World Theatre), and has annual meetings held in different capital cities.

Ionesco, Eugène (1912–), French playwright of Rumanian origin. Came to France with his parents as a small child, returned to Rumania in his early 'teens, and came back to France shortly before the outbreak of World War II with a scholarship to write his doctoral thesis on Baudelaire. Began to write plays in 1948. His first, *La Cantatrice Chauve* (*The Bald Prima Donna*, in US *The Bald Soprano*), arose from his attempt to learn English. The sentences from his English phrase book turned, for him, into a grotesque play parodying the deadness of the clichés of bourgeois conversation. The play was first performed in 1950 and launched him on a career as a dramatist. It was followed by *La Leçon*, 1951; *Les Chaises*, 1952; *Victimes du devoir*, 1953; *Jacques, ou la Soumission*, 1953; *Amédée ou Comment s'en débarrasser*, 1954; *L'Impromptu de l'Alma, ou le Caméléon du berger* (*The Shepherd's Chameleon*), 1956; *Le Nouveau locataire*, 1957; *Tueur sans gages* (*The Killer*), 1958; *Rhinocéros*, 1959; *Délire à deux* (*Frenzy for Two, or More*), 1963; *Le Roi se meurt* (*Exit the King*), 1962; *Le Piéton de l'air* (*The Stroller in the Air*), 1963; *La Soif et la Faim*, 1966; *Jeux de Massacre*, 1970; *Macbett*, 1972. Ionesco's plays depict a grotesque dream world which expresses the fears, anxieties and obsessions of a sensitive human being in a world which seems to have lost its 'metaphysical dimension' and threatens to degenerate into lifeless and mechanical routine. In the person of Bérenger, who appears in *The Killer*, *Rhinoceros*, *The Stroller in the Air* and *Exit the King*, I. has developed a character (who in some ways represents the author) of a sensitive and ineffectual human being threatened by the insensitivity of other men (who turn into ferocious rhinos) and, above all, by Death. The grotesque humour of his plays conceals the despair of a playwright who is, above all, a poet. He has been involved in a number of polemics against the champions of a political, committed theatre, which he regards as inartistic, because ideologies are better expressed by theoretical writing than by fiction, and totalitarian, because desirous of imposing its views on an unwilling audience. He has expressed these views in numerous essays (collected in the volume *Notes and Counternotes*) and in his diaries, some of which have also been published. ▷THEATRE OF THE ABSURD.
Bibl: P. Vernois, LA DYNAMIQUE THÉÂTRALE D'EUGÈNE IONESCO, 1972; M. Esslin, THE THEATRE OF THE ABSURD, 2/1968

Iran. Puppet theatre since the Middle Ages. Travelling companies up to the 20th century. Professional theatre on European models only since 1950, mainly presenting the work of A. Nishin. Today there are several private theatres in Teheran with a REPERTOIRE of world literature.
Bibl: M. Rezvan, LE THÉÂTRE ET LA DANSE EN IRAN, 1961

Ireland. In the Middle Ages MYSTERY PLAYS were performed in churches in Latin. The first professional theatre seems to have been opened by John Ogilvy in Dublin in 1634. During the Commonwealth, as in ENGLAND, the theatre was prohibited. After the Restoration Ogilvy opened a new theatre in 1662, which became known as the Smock Alley Theatre. By the end of the 18th century there were theatres at Belfast, Cork, Wexford, Waterford, Kilkenny and Limerick. Many Irish actors, singers and playwrights contributed to the English theatre from that time: Thomas Sheridan, 1721–88, became a star actor in London, his son (▷SHERIDAN) was a celebrated playwright and manager of DRURY LANE. Other Irish playwrights of note were GOLDSMITH, FARQUHAR, Kane O'Hara (1713–82), James O'Keefe (1748–1833), James Sheridan Nowles (1783–1862), whose *Brian Borihme*, 1811, was the first play to draw its theme from Irish history; BOUCICAULT became a highly successful writer of melodramas, many of which have Irish subjects; SHAW and WILDE did not use many Irish themes in their work but showed the sharp wit and fantastic sense of humour characteristic of the Irish. While these and many other dramatists of great talent merged into the English theatrical scene, a specifically Irish school of theatre came into being as part of the revival of Irish national feeling and aspirations at the end of the 19th century. Under Douglas Hyde the Gaelic League advocated a revival of the Irish language; an offshoot of the League was the Irish Literary Theatre, founded in 1899 by YEATS, LADY GREGORY and Edward Martyn (1859–1924). The first performance of the Irish Literary Theatre was of Yeats's *The Countess Cathleen*, 1899, Dublin. This was followed by plays by Edward Martyn and George Moore, and a play in Erse, *Casadh an T-Sugain*, by Douglas Hyde. The efforts of the Irish Literary Theatre were continued by the brothers F. and W. FAY and their National Irish Theatre Society which, after having performed in various halls in Dublin, and having also appeared in London, gradually developed into the ABBEY THEATRE, built with the help of ANNIE HORNIMAN and opened on 27 December 1904. The Abbey Theatre became the NATIONAL THEATRE of Ireland and around it arose a group of remarkable playwrights which includes SYNGE, ROBINSON, ERVINE, O'CASEY, CARROLL, BOYLE, George Shiels, etc. Many great actors also came out of the Abbey Theatre, among them SARA ALLGOOD, Maire O'Neill, Barry Fitzgerald, J. McCormack, Cyril Cusack. Another important

theatre which widened the range to include an international REPERTOIRE, the Gate Theatre, Dublin, was opened in 1928 under the direction of MacLIAMMÓIR and Hilton Edwards. After World War II BEHAN and BECKETT were among the Irish playwrights who achieved world-wide acclaim. An annual Theatre Festival in Dublin regularly displays the vitality and talent of Irish actors and playwrights.
Bibl: U. M. Ellis-Fermor, THE IRISH DRAMATIC MOVEMENT, 2/1954; L. Robinson, IRELAND'S ABBEY THEATRE, A HISTORY, 1899–1951, 1951

Irony (Gk = dissimulation). A figure of speech where the speaker says one thing but intends the opposite to be understood. The use of irony can clearly be seen in SHAKESPEARE's *Julius Caesar* in Antony's well-known speech to the citizens. Dramatic irony means the use of words which have inner significance not realized by the person who utters them, e.g. 'I think I shall sleep long tonight' from a character unaware that he is about to be murdered.

Irving. English family of actors. (1) **Henry I.** (John H. Brodribb; 1838–1905), ACTOR-MANAGER, who dominated the theatre in England before the turn of the century. After his first professional appearances he played for about ten years in the provinces, and made his name in 1871 in the MELODRAMA *The Bells* by Leopold Lewis at the Lyceum Theatre; after which he appeared successfully for 12 years in London. In 1873 he took over the management of the Lyceum which was the main attraction of London's theatre life for 23 years with its famous productions of SHAKESPEARE, historically correct sets and costumes, and first-class actors. His principal actress was ELLEN TERRY, who appeared as Ophelia and Portia opposite his Hamlet and Shylock. Apart from Shakespeare his REPERTORY contained only minor melodramas and he avoided modern playwrights. He was frequently criticized as an actor, particularly for his mannerisms, but he had a dynamic personality, supreme grace, a melodic voice, great craftsmanship combined with an intensity of performance which lent his characterizations a touch of mystery and the unusual. Outstanding roles included leads in Tennyson's *The Cup*, 1881, and *Becket*, 1893. Knighted in 1895. His two sons (2) **Henry Brodribb I.** (1870–1919) and (3) **Laurence Sidney I.** (1871–1914) were both actors; the son of the first is the stage designer (4) **Henry Forster I.** (1897–).
Bibl: L. Irving, 1951

Isherwood, Christopher (1904–), English novelist and dramatist. He has lived in the USA since 1940. He wrote several plays in collaboration with AUDEN including: *The Dog Beneath the Skin*, fp London 1936; *The Ascent of F 6*, fp London 1937; *On the Frontier*, fp London 1939. I.'s novel *Goodbye to Berlin* was adapted for the stage by VAN DRUTEN under the title *I Am a Camera*, 1951; in 1967 it was produced as a musical *Cabaret*, and later made into a film.

Eugène Ionesco, *The Chairs*, Paris 1952

Ireland, a scene from SYNGE's *The Playboy of the Western World*, ABBEY THEATRE, with SARA ALLGOOD, Barry Fitzgerald and Arthur Shields

Henry Irving as Shylock, 1879

Henry Irving as Mathias in a scene from *The Bells*, 1871

Israel. The beginnings of the Jewish national theatre date back to the times of the Mandate. In 1928 the HABIMAH, founded in Moscow for performances in Hebrew, settled in Palestine; at that time the only theatre in the country was the Ohel Theatre, which had been founded in 1925 under the patronage of the trade unions. In opposition to the Habimah, the style of which they considered old fashioned, young Jewish people founded the Tel Aviv Theatre in 1942, presenting contemporary plays and musicals which deal with topical problems of modern Israel: Moshe Sha'mir's *Hoo Halach Basadot* (He Walked in the Fields), 1949, a Kibbutz drama; Mossenson's *Kazablan*, 1954, on immigration problems (as a musical). The manager, leading director and actor MILLO took over the management of the newly built Municipal Theatre in Haifa in 1960, which today has the largest subscriptions and the highest subsidy in Israel; Millo runs it as a theatre with an international REPERTOIRE.

Itallie, Jean-Claude van (1936–), Belgian-born US dramatist. One of the most representative writers of the new Underground theatre. His family went to the USA in 1940, when the Germans invaded Belgium. He graduated from Harvard in 1958, having spent most of his senior years directing plays. He then moved to Greenwich Village, doing various jobs, but mostly freelance writing for TV. In 1963 he joined the OPEN THEATRE. His works include the plays: *Pavane*, initially produced by LA MAMA, the experimental theatre club, and later incorporated into the triple bill with the overall title *America Hurrah!*, produced in New York 1966, at the Pocket Theatre, dir Joseph Chaikin; *The Serpent*, 1968, written in collaboration with the Open Theatre group; *War*, initially produced at the Village South Theatre, New York, and then at the Caffé Cino; *Dreams*, initially produced by La Mama and later presented as a part of *6 from La Mama* at the Martinique Theatre; *It's Almost Like Being* and *Hobbies: or Things Are All Right with the Forbushers* (TV play). In his plays he uses a free unconventional technique, based on improvised acting, which produces powerful metaphors for the nightmares and afflictions of contemporary USA.

Italy. In the 15th, 16th and 17th centuries Italy initiated many important developments of the post-medieval European theatre: RENAISSANCE THEATRE; COURT THEATRE; HUMANIST DRAMA; particularly the COMMEDIA DELL'ARTE and RUZANTE. The 18th century is overshadowed by the rivalry between the playwrights GOZZI and GOLDONI. In the 19th century, the virtuoso actor and his travelling company developed from the strolling players of earlier ages: an actor aiming at effect and pathos would at the same time show, in the details of his acting, the beginning of realism. The high point of this intense emotional style was reached by DUSE. Several attempts to establish theatre with a literary programme: PIRANDELLO. After World War II, beginning of a new era with the founding of the PICCOLO TEATRO by STREHLER and GRASSI in 1947; on it were modelled the Teatri Stabili (with ENSEMBLE, REPERTOIRE, subscription and official subsidy) in Rome (1948–54), Trieste, Turin, Naples, Bari, Palermo, Bologna, etc.
Bibl: J. S. Kennard, THE ITALIAN THEATRE, 1964, 2 vols; V. Pandolfi, TEATRO ITALIANO CONTEMPORANEO 1945–59, 1959; S. d'Amico (ed), STORIA DEL TEATRO ITALIANO, 1936

Ivanov, Vsevolod Vycheslavovich (1895–1963), Soviet novelist and dramatist. At the age of 15 he worked with a CIRCUS, then joined a travelling company as an actor and began his literary career in 1920, when he settled in Leningrad. In 1921 he made his reputation with the novel *Bronepoezd 14–69* (*Armoured Train 14–69*) which was adapted for the stage in 1927 and was the first Soviet play to be produced successfully at the MOSCOW ART THEATRE with KACHALOV playing the lead. His other works include: *Blokada* (The Blockade), 1928; *Kompromis Naib-Khana* (Compromise in Naib-chana), 1931; *Kantsler*, 1944; *Lomonosov*, 1953, fp MAT.

Ivernel, Daniel (1920–), French actor. Pupil of the CONSERVATOIRE, he joined the COMÉDIE-FRANÇAISE for a short period and subsequently worked with DULLIN's company; famous for his performances at the THÉÂTRE NATIONAL POPULAIRE, e.g. the title role in IBSEN's *Peer Gynt*, 1958; the Count in *Lorenzaccio* by MUSSET, 1959; Danton in *Danton's Death* by BÜCHNER, 1959, dir VILAR. His greatest successes include: Henry in *Becket* by ANOUILH, Théâtre Montparnasse, dir Anouilh/Roland Piétri; the title role in *Uncle Vanya* by CHEKHOV, CF, 1961, and *Richard III* (SHAKESPEARE/Anouilh), Théâtre Montparnasse, 1964, dir Anouilh/Piétri. Also known as a film actor.

Izumo, Takeda (1691–1756), Japanese dramatist. A major writer, strongly influenced by CHIKAMATSU, he is best known for his puppet plays for the *Kabuki* theatre, e.g. *Sugawara Denju Tenari Kogami* and *Chusingura*.

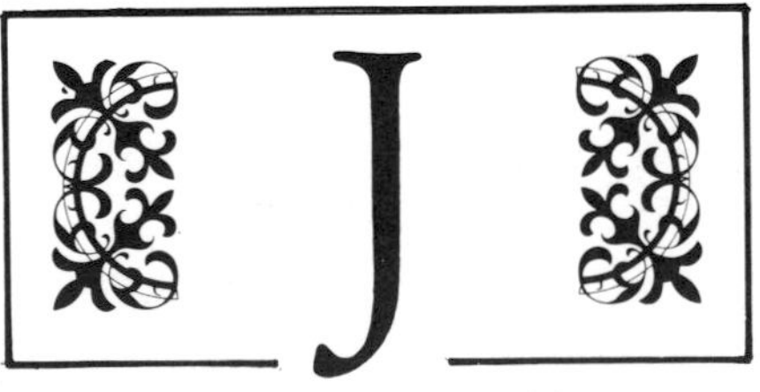

Jackson, Sir Barry Vincent (1879–1961), English theatre manager and director. The son of a rich businessman, he studied architecture. After having worked as a designer and director in amateur theatre, he founded the Pilgrim Players in 1907, which, under the direction of J. A. Pinchard and DRINKWATER, produced classical and modern plays in a style much in advance of its time. Founded the BIRMINGHAM REPERTORY THEATRE in 1913, having built its premises at his own expense. Here under his direction much experimental work was carried out – best known and most discussed probably the production of *Hamlet* in modern dress, 1925. In 1929 he founded the Malvern Festival, where many of SHAW's plays received their first performance. Director of the Shakespeare Memorial Theatre at STRATFORD-UPON-AVON 1945–48. Knighted in 1925.
Bibl: T. C. Kemp, THE BIRMINGHAM REPERTORY THEATRE, 1948

Jacobsohn, Siegfried (1881–1926), German drama critic. In 1905 founded the weekly paper *Die Schaubühne* (since 1918 *Die Weltbühne*), his contributors including POLGAR, BAB, JHERING, K. Tucholsky. His critical writings were collected in book form under the title *Das Jahr der Bühne* (10 vols, Berlin 1912–21), etc. The contemporary writers he praised most highly were STRINDBERG and STERNHEIM; he also viewed with favour REINHARDT's productions of SHAKESPEARE, but objected to the introduction of spectacular diversions. His criticism is impressionistic, full of local Berlin wit and candidly subjective.

Jahnn, Hans Henny (1894–1959), German novelist and dramatist. His visionary dramas of 'black' EXPRESSIONISM deal with the fear of death, nothingness and decay; he shows physical excesses, incest and sodomy as expressions of the search for the meaning of life. Plays: *Pastor Ephraim Magnus*, Berlin 1923, dir BRONNEN; *Die Krönung Richard III* (The Coronation of Richard III), Leipzig 1922; *Der Arzt, sein Weib und sein Sohn* (The Doctor, his Wife and his Son), Hamburg 1928, dir GRÜNDGENS; *Medea*, Berlin 1926, dir FEHLING; *Neuer Lübecker Totentanz* (New Lübeck Dance of Death), an oratorio with COSTUME and dance, music by Y. J. Trede, Hamburg 1964; *Armut, Reichtum, Mensch und Tier* (Poverty, Wealth, Man and Beast). Hamburg and Wuppertal 1948; *Thomas Chatterton*, Hamburg 1956, Deutsches-Schauspielhaus, dir Gründgens; *Der staubige Regenbogen* (The Dusty Rainbow), Frankfurt 1961, dir PISCATOR. His plays were published in *Dramen*, 2 vols, 1963 and 1966.
Bibl: W. Muschg, GESPRÄCHE MIT HANS HENNY JAHNN, 1967

James, Henry (1843–1916), US writer. Spent most of his time in England and became a British subject in 1915. Primarily a novelist, he wrote several plays, some adaptations of his own novels and stories, e.g. *Tenants* and *Disengaged* (based on the story, 'The Solution'). Some were unsuccessfully produced; they were published in 1948. The failure of *Guy Domville*, 1895, deterred him from writing for the theatre apart from *The High Bid*, 1908, and *The Outcry*, 1917. Successful dramatizations of his novels by other writers include: *Berkeley Square*, 1926 (J. L. Balderston/J. C. Squire, based on *The Sense of the Past*); *The Heiress*, 1947 (R. & A. Goetz, based on *Washington Square*); *The Innocents*, 1954 (W. Archibald, based on *The Turn of the Screw*; opera by

Britten in 1959); *The Aspern Papers*, 1959 (MICHAEL REDGRAVE); *The Wings of the Dove*, 1963 (Christopher Taylor). Many of his stories and novels have been successfully adapted for TV.

Jannings, Emil (1884–1950), German actor. After some years with amateur companies in provincial theatres, he made his name in Berlin in 1915 as the schoolmaster in GRABBE's *Scherz, Satire, Ironie und tiefere Bedeutung* and afterwards worked mainly with the Deutsches-Theater in Berlin, acting in Expressionist plays (SORGE, HASENCLEVER, KLEIST) but his best performances were in plays by HAUPTMANN, e.g. Sir Douglas in *Winterballade*, fp 1917, dir REINHARDT; Huhn in *Und Pippa tanzt*, 1919, and the leading role in *Fuhrmann Henschel*, 1932; also noteworthy was his Mephistopheles in GOETHE's *Faust*, 1926. After 1920 he made a reputation as a film actor, notably in *Der blaue Engel* (*The Blue Angel*) with MARLENE DIETRICH.

Japan. The country has produced a remarkable variety of theatre forms, which developed independently, are sharply differentiated from each other and have largely survived until the present day: *Kagura*, the oldest known dance, probably brought from China about 540; *Gigaku* and *Bugaku* mask plays, based on the religious beliefs which originated in China in the 7th and 8th centuries; *Noh* plays from the Samurai culture of the 14th and 15th centuries; *Kyogen*, traditional brief FARCE of Japanese drama, occurring as a comic interlude in the *Noh* plays, which initiated working class social criticism; *Kabuki* theatre, which emerged in the early 17th century with the growing power of the merchant class. The end of the 19th century saw the beginnings of a threatre influenced by the West.

Kagura: two mythological themes (farewell and return of the goddess of the sun; fight of two brothers, in which the sea-god intervenes in favour of the younger brother); the painted faces of the dancing mimes anticipated the paint-mask.

Bugaku (literal meaning, dance and music): on the left of a square podium sat the players of wind instruments, on the right the drummers, and there were two dance groups, one dressed mainly in red, the other in green. Became *c.* AD 820 a ceremonial Court dance.

Noh (original form: *Sarugaku*): popular entertainment by MIMES and CIRCUS artists. In the 14th century the professional *Sarugaku* actors Kanami Kiyotsugu (1333–84) and his son Zeami Motokiyo (1363–1443) developed and established the *Noh* based on the ritualistic code of honour of the Samurai and the contemplation of Zen Buddhism. In 1374 the Shogun Yoshimitsu summoned Kanami and his 11-year-old son to appear at his court. Kanami's play *Komachi at the Grave* is the model for about 100 *Noh* plays by Zeami and the theoretical essays written for his family, who guarded the *Noh* tradition: *Hanaka-gami*, *Kadensho*, *Kyui*. The *Noh* play is acted by the protagonist (*Shite*), the supporting character

Italy, an open-air performance of a comedy in Verona, painting by Marcola Marco

Ivanov, *Armoured Train 14–69*, MOSCOW ART THEATRE, 1927

(*Waki*), the followers (*Tsure*) and the chorus. The female roles are played by men. There exist five categories of plays (one of each category makes up the programme of a production up to the present day): (1) plays of gods, (2) plays of war (Samurai plays), (3) women's plays (wig-plays), (4) dramatic fate of a desperate woman, (5) legend-recounting. The chorus comments in falsetto pitch, but does not intervene in the action. The *Shite* wears a precious mask and a traditional formal brocade costume. Gestures and movements are stylized and in ceremonial slow motion. Stage: a square podium open on three sides, made of polished cedar wood (*Butai*), a temple roof, back wall (*Atoza*) with a painted pine-tree. An open passageway links the changing rooms with the podium. The tradition of *Noh* today is preserved only by a few families of actors.
Kyogen: interludes; clever servants outwit their avaricious masters; hypocritical monks are revealed. Ambiguity (risqué jokes) and vulgarity are taboo. No masks. The protagonist and principal is known as Omo, the second actor as Ado.
Kabuki: the invention of *Kabuki* is attributed to the dancer and amateur priestess Okuni from Izumo (*c.* 1600). She appeared with a group of dancers first in Kyoto, later in Tokyo (1607). Early example: Okuni, mourning for her dead lover, meets his ghost. He appears, disguised as a young woman, on a wooden gangway running through the auditorium called the *Hanamichi* (flower path). It consisted of a raised platform in the *Kabuki* theatre extending through the left side of the auditorium. Used as an additional facility for entries and exits, also as a stage area for special effects. Popular actors used it for their exits and were then applauded by the audience, who would strew flowers on the ground or throw them over their favourite actors. In 1629 performance by women was prohibited in *Kabuki* and since 1652 young boys have also been banned; the female parts were acted by men. One of the most important dramatists was CHIKAMATSU MONZAEMON (1653–1725) whose plays (originally written for the puppet theatre), which deal mostly with the conflicts between love and feudalistic values and manners, were adapted by the *Kabuki* theatre. The *Kabuki* stage, originally similar to that of the *Noh*, by the 18th century was equipped with a curtain, movable décor, trapdoors and revolves. Songs, dance, mime and recitation are combined to achieve a total effect similar to a REVUE. The actors wear masks painted in symbolic colours. Today there are still 350 *Kabuki* actors in Japan.
Joruri: the Japanese puppet theatre founded in the 17th century.
Bunraku (*Ningyo shibai*): popular modern Japanese PUPPET THEATRE using large, almost life-size puppets, manipulated by several handlers; named after Bunrakuen (or Bunrakuken), a puppet-player and manager, who opened the first puppet theatre (Bunraken za) in 1871 in Osaka.
Western tendencies: Tsubuchi Shoyo (1859–1935) translated and produced almost all the works of SHAKESPEARE at the Kabuki-zu of Tokyo, followed by plays of IBSEN, STRINDBERG and HAUPTMANN. In recent decades all literary and theatrical tendencies of the Western theatre have parallels in Japan. Development of the Western-inspired theatre (*Shingeki*) since 1909: opening of the Free Theatre in Tokyo producing plays by Ibsen and GORKY. In 1924 with the founding of the Little Tsukiji-Theatre by Osani Kaoru, the styles of Western theatre were tried, resulting in a director's theatre. In 1928 a revolutionary 'Theatre of the Left' emerged and in 1940 the New Tsukiji-Theatre was established as the new NATIONAL THEATRE under the auspices of the military state. The end of the war in 1945 saw the re-establishment of the Shingeki Theatre and the theatres of the left, *Bungaku-zu* (literary theatre), *Haiyu-zu* (theatre of the actors) and *Mingei* (folk theatre). The most representative dramatists: Kinoshita Junji and YUKIO MISHIMA.
Bibl: S. Miyake, KABUKI, 1965; E. Pound & E. F. Fenellosa, THE CLASSICAL NOH THEATRE OF JAPAN, 1959; A. C. Scott, THE KABUKI THEATRE OF JAPAN, 1955; F. Bowers, JAPANESE THEATRE, 1959

Jarno, Josef (1866–1932), Hungarian-born Austrian actor, director and manager. Began his career as an actor in 1887 at the Deutsches-Theater in Budapest, then worked with the Residenztheater and Deutsches-Theater in BERLIN, 1899–1923 he managed the Theater in der Josefstadt in Vienna, which he made an important theatrical centre with a REPERTORY of French COMEDIES by SARDOU, BERNARD, FEYDEAU, FLERS/CAILLAVET, and introduced writers like IBSEN, CHEKHOV, WEDEKIND, MAETERLINCK, STRINDBERG, SHAW, WILDE, GOGOL, MOLNÁR, etc. During his career as a manager (at one time of three theatres) he also appeared as an actor, and wrote and directed plays.
Bibl: J. Gregor, DAS THEATER IN DER JOSEFSTADT, 1924

Jarry, Alfred (1873–1907), French dramatist. His play *Ubu Roi* caused a scandal when it was staged by LUGNÉ-POË at the Théâtre de l'Œuvre in 1896. Originally a puppet play which he wrote as a LAMPOON on a teacher when a pupil of the lycée at Rennes: it presents a grotesque bourgeois of insatiable rapacity and lack of moral scruple as a monster symbol for the eternal philistine. Ubu makes himself king of Poland, killing and robbing his people. This tale is told in the style of a parody on a Shakespearean history play. The very first word of the text caused a scandal: 'Merde!' J., who increasingly adopted the diction of his character of Ubu in his daily life, wrote a number of sequels to the play: *Ubu Cocu*, pub 1896; *Ubu Enchaîné*, pub 1900. *Ubu sur la Butte*, pub 1906, is an adaptation of *Ubu Roi* for a puppet performance in 1901. *Ubu Roi* is often regarded as the first example of Surrealist theatre which developed into the style of the THEATRE OF THE ABSURD. J. developed his own half-serious, half-parodistic philosophy of pataphysics, the science of imaginary solutions, which ultimately comes down to the ultra-subjectivist position that everything is what you think it ought to be. The Collège de Pataphysique, which has IONESCO, René Clair, Raymond Queneau, Jean Dubuffet and many other prominent writers and artists among its members, carries on a half-serious, half-earnest cult of Jarry. *Ubu Roi* (usually as an adaptation or amalgamation of several of the original plays) has been performed with great success since World War II, notably at the Théâtre National Populaire, Paris, dir VILAR, 1958; at the ROYAL COURT THEATRE, London, 1966; at the Theatre on the Balustrade, Prague, dir GROSSMAN, 1965. His other dramatic works include: *César Antéchrist*, pub 1895; *L'autre Alceste*, pub 1896; *Le Gentilhomme de 1847*, fp 1898; *Par la taille*, one-act play, pub 1906; *L'objet aimé*, pub 1909; *Pantagruel*, opera LIBRETTO, with E. Demolder, music Claude Terrasse, 1911.
Bibl: R. Shattuck, THE BANQUET YEARS, 1959

Jean Potage. Name of a French comic character. ▷HANSWURST.

Jeffers, Robinson (1887–1962), US poet and author of plays in verse. His adaptation of EURIPIDES' *Medea*, 1947, with JUDITH ANDERSON, had a popular success but his next adaptation, *The Cretan Women*, 1954, based on *Hippolytus*, was less well received. His long dramatic poem *Dear Judas*, a retelling of the Gospel story, written 1929, was adapted by M. Myerberg and produced in 1947; *The Tower Beyond Tragedy*, written 1924, an adaptation of the first two parts of AESCHYLUS' *Oresteia*, was performed in 1950.
Bibl: R. Squires, 1956

Jefferson. Family of US actors of English origin: (1) **Thomas J.** (1732–97) appeared at DRURY LANE with GARRICK; his son (2) **Joseph J.** (I; 1774–1832) went to the USA in 1795, was in New York 1796–1803, and then in Philadelphia till 1830 and afterwards on tour. He was a capable comedian, above all in the roles of humorous old men. Of his eight children seven went on the stage. Best known among them was (3) **Joseph J.** (II; 1829–1905), usually called Joe J., who started his stage career at the age of four. The peak of his career was his own adaptation of the Rip van Winkle legend in which he appeared between 1865 and 1880. His performance in the title role displayed a subtle humour with tragic undertones. He wrote his autobiography, an important work in its own right.
Bibl: G. Malvern, GOOD TROUPERS ALL, 1945

Jellicoe, Ann (1927–), English dramatist and director. Trained at the Central School of Speech and Drama in London, she later taught production there; after several productions in the provinces, in 1952 she founded the Cockpit Theatre in London. Her first play *The Sport of My Mad Mother* was awarded third prize in a drama competition sponsored by the *Observer* in 1956 and was subsequently produced at the ROYAL COURT THEATRE; she made her reputation as a dramatist with *The Knack*, Cambridge

1961, Royal Court 1962, later filmed by Richard Lester; her third play was *Shelley*, 1965. She has also translated works by IBSEN (*Rosmersholm*, *The Lady from the Sea*), CHEKHOV (*The Seagull*) and the LIBRETTO for Weber's opera *Der Freischütz*. In 1973 she was appointed literary manager of the Royal Court Theatre.

Jerome, Jerome Klapka (1859–1927), English writer. Worked as a clerk, journalist, schoolmaster, and as a super (walking-on part) with theatrical touring companies, and described his experiences with the latter in *On the Stage and Off*, 1885. Became known as a humorist through his best-selling book *Three Men in a Boat*. As a playwright he had great success with *The Passing of the Third Floor Back*, 1908, in which FORBES-ROBERTSON played the lead; it describes the impact of a Christ-figure on the inmates of a boarding house.
Bibl: A. Moss, 1929

Jessner, Leopold (1878–1945), German director. One of the major innovators of the theatre in GERMANY in the 1920s and influential in the development of EXPRESSIONISM; director of the Berlin State Theatre 1919–30; in his early work in BERLIN he developed an anti-realistic theatre set in almost bare, strictly constructed stage levels often connected by a staircase (known as a 'Spieltreppe' or 'Jessner-Treppe') combined with a concentrated, heightened and coarse language, e.g. SCHILLER's *Wilhelm Tell*, 1919, which was produced as an 'expressionist cry' for freedom, 'revolutionary and anti-nationalistic' (KORTNER); WEDEKIND's *Marquis von Keith*, 1920; SHAKESPEARE's *Richard III*. In all three productions Kortner was the protagonist dominating and advancing the action. His later work tended more to realism, e.g. SCHILLER's *Wallenstein*, 1924; HEBBEL's *Herodes und Mariamne*, 1926; Shakespeare's *Hamlet*, 1926; HAUPTMANN's *Die Weber*, 1928; SOPHOCLES' *Oedipus Rex*, 1929, because of its 'epic' style, much admired by BRECHT.
Bibl: G. Rühle, THEATER FÜR DIE REPUBLIK, 1967

Jesuit drama. Strongest, most individual expression of SCHOOL DRAMA of the 16th and 17th centuries. The plays in Jesuit schools were intended as educational and theological exercises for the pupils; written and performed in Latin with much declamation and gesture. Major productions were performed with great splendour at the end of each school year. The plays were mostly written by the professor of rhetoric and based on classical models; later there developed an individual dramatic form (Pedro de Acevedo in Spain, Stefano Tuccio in Italy, BIDERMANN in Germany, Nicolas Caussin in France, AVANCINI in Austria). The audience consisted first of pupils and their teachers, later guests were also invited, mainly the aristocracy, whose children were educated in Jesuit colleges. In order to enable them to understand the play spectators needed programmes, later a commentator appeared and finally the plays were given, partly or wholly, in the vernacular. Themes were mainly from

Japan, the *Noh* theatre in London with *The Lady Aoi*, 1967

Japan, *Kabuki* theatre, showing the flower path on the left

Joseph Jefferson as Rip van Winkle

the Old and New Testaments, and also from the lives and legends of saints and martyrs and myths of classical antiquity. At first women were prohibited from attending performances, nor were female characters or costumes permitted. But gradually for thematic reasons, this prohibition was modified and eventually discarded (in France there were separate performances for men and women). Varying with different countries and regions, Jesuit theatre was influenced by the national drama; the earliest mention of a Jesuit production appears to date from 1551 in Italy at the Collegio Mamertino at Messina. In 1569 the play *Christus Judex* by Tuccio was performed in the local dialect at Bari; gradually elements of opera also appeared. Apart from the high degree of technical skill and elaborate décor, Jesuit drama was distinguished by the large number of characters who appeared in a play: in Vienna (where the first production took place in 1555), in 1659 *Pietas Victrix* was performed with 36 main characters, 10 allegorical figures, and crowds of members of the senate, and the army, choruses of soldiers, Roman citizens, angels and masks, etc. In Bavaria (Ingolstadt 1558, Munich 1560) and Austria Jesuit drama ranked at times with the professional theatre; in 1608, when Jesuit pupils appeared in Graz before Archduke Ferdinand, they were followed in the second part of the entertainment by the highly professional ENGLISH COMEDIANS. In some European countries profane elements soon entered, particularly in the INTERLUDES; in Spain popular forms of verse were used, e.g. 1556 in a production in Cordoba. Jesuit drama was particularly influential in France through the participation of aristocratic pupils and Court productions.

The great influence of the Jesuits on theatre history is based not so much on the texts of the plays, which were mostly rooted in traditional themes and forms, but on their theatrical technique. Miracles, divine appearances and heroic processions, stimulated the use of mechanical techniques and firework displays. The productions of the Collège Louis-le-Grand in Paris competed with the Académie de danse, the Viennese Jesuit productions with those of the opera. The opulence of the productions – partly financed by aristocratic supporters – met with increasing criticism in the 17th century. With the establishment of the professional theatre, Jesuit drama lost its importance. Among dramatists who were Jesuit pupils and who wrote their first plays for production at colleges were CERVANTES, LOPE DE VEGA (probably), GOLDONI, MOLIÈRE and VOLTAIRE.

Bibl: W. H. McCabe, AN INTRODUCTION TO EARLY JESUIT THEATRE, 1929

Jewish drama ▷YIDDISH THEATRE.

Jhering, Herbert (1888–1977), German critic. Collaborator in the literary magazine *Die Schaubühne*, then drama critic of the *Berliner Börsen-Courier*; supported directors like JESSNER, FEHLING, ENGEL, PISCATOR. An attentive observer of the provincial theatre in GERMANY, interested in the problems of the German theatre system and policy, and one of the first to recognize the importance of BRECHT.

Jig (derived from Ital *giga*=quick dance). Short Elizabethan rhymed FARCE performed by comedians (including a CLOWN) with songs, dance and crude jokes, at the end of a theatrical performance; best known exponents: TARLETON and KEMPE. At the time of the Restoration it was reduced to a short song or dance number at the end of COMEDIES, before the EPILOGUE.

Jodelet (Julien Bedeau; *c.* 1600–60), French actor. Appeared from 1640 at the Théâtre du Marais in CORNEILLE's *Le Menteur* and in a series of FARCES specially written for him in which he played the character of the cunning servant: *Jodelet et le Maître valet*; *Jodelet duelliste*; *Jodelet astrologue*. In 1659 he played the part of the valet in MOLIÈRE's *Les Précieuses ridicules* at the Palais Royal. His brother François Bedeau (1603–63), known as L'ESPY, appeared at the Théâtre du Marais, at the HÔTEL DE BOURGOGNE and, shortly before his death, with Molière at the Palais Royal.

Bibl: S. W. Deierkauf-Holsboer, LE THÉÂTRE DU MARAIS, 1954

Jodelle, Etienne, Sieur du Limodin (1532–73), French writer. Innovator of French classicism, at the same time a member of the Pléiade with Ronsard. His TRAGEDY *Cléopâtre captive*, 1552, performed at the Court of Henri II, was a model for RACINE and CORNEILLE: an antique theme, written in ALEXANDRINES, structured according to ARISTOTLE's theories of drama. Other works include: *Eugène*, 1552, a COMEDY, and the TRAGEDY *Didon se sacrifiant*, written *c.* 1555.

Bibl: H. Chamard, HISTOIRE DE LA PLÉIADE, 1939

Johnston, Denis (1901–), Irish playwright. Trained as a lawyer, he has written scripts for radio and the cinema as well as for the stage; worked as a BBC correspondent during World War II. His plays include: *The Old Lady Says 'No!'*, 1929; *The Moon in the Yellow River*, 1931; *A Bride for the Unicorn*, 1933; *The Golden Cuckoo*, 1939; *The Dreaming Dust* (original title *Weep for the Cyclops*, 1940; revised version with new title, 1954); *Strange Occurrence on Ireland's Eye*, 1956; *The Scythe and the Sunset*, 1958.

Johst, Hanns (1890–), German dramatist; former Nazi party member. From 1935 to 1945 president of the Reichsschrifttumskammer (National Writers Organization) and SS-Brigadeführer. Author of Expressionist plays: *Der junge Mensch* (The Young Man), Munich Kammerspiele, 1919; *Der Einsame* (The Lonely One), 1920, dir Otto Flackenberg; *Der König* (The King), 1920; *Thomas Paine*, 1929; *Schlageter*, Berlin 1933, State Theatre, etc.

Jolson, Al (Asa Joelson; 1883/85–1950), US actor and singer of Russian origin. With his brother Harry J. (1882–1953) and Joe Palmer, he founded the famous trio of comedians Jolson, Palmer and Jolson. From 1913 they worked in collaboration with the SHUBERT brothers in REVUE and shows including: *La Belle Paree*, 1911; *Honeymoon Express*, 1913; *Robinson Crusoe, Jr*, 1916; and *Sinbad*, 1918, which ran for two years. Introduced into it was GERSHWIN's song 'Swanee', written especially for J., which launched the composer on the road to fame. J. made film history with his appearance in the first 'talkie' *The Jazz Singer*, 1927, and made many other films. His last appearance on stage was with the USO in Korea.

Bibl: C. Smith, MUSICAL COMEDY IN AMERICA, 1950

Jones, David (1934–), English director associated with the ROYAL SHAKESPEARE COMPANY. Worked in television as a director and editor of the BBC arts programme 'Monitor'. His notable productions for the RSC include: VIAN's *The Empire Builders*, 1962; MERCER's *Belcher's Luck*, 1966 and *After Haggerty*, 1970; O'CASEY's *The Silver Tassie*, 1969; GRASS's *The Plebeians Rehearse the Uprising*, 1970; GORKY's *Enemies*, 1971, and *The Lower Depths*, 1972.

Jones, Henry Arthur (1851–1929), English dramatist. A commercial traveller by profession, he began his literary career in 1878 with the play *It's Only Round the Corner* and, from that time, concentrated on writing for the stage, using the theatre as a platform for the discussion of social problems. He attracted the attention of SHAW, who preferred him to PINERO and aided his acceptance as one of the new school of dramatists. Though J. was very skilful in his use of naturalistic dialogue and the creation of dramatic tension, the impact of his plays was diluted by melodramatic elements and the lack of a strong theoretical basis. His works include: *A Clerical Error*, 1878; *The Silver King*, 1882, with H. Herman; *Saints and Sinners*, 1884; *Michael and His Lost Angel*, 1896; *The Liars*, 1897; *Mrs Dane's Defence*, 1900.

Bibl: G. B. Shaw, OUR THEATRES IN THE NINETIES, 1932

Jones, Inigo (1573–1652), English architect, artist and stage designer. One of the major exponents of BAROQUE THEATRE, he studied in Italy where he was influenced in architecture by PALLADIO and in theatre design by PARIGI in particular. Attached to Prince Henry's household in 1604 as architect, he took over the production of Court MASQUES (till then controlled by the MASTER OF THE REVELS), and gradually introduced the style and technique of Italian décor into English theatre: three-sided revolving prisms, TELARI, modelled on the ancient Greek PERIAKTOI, with different scenes on each side, SERLIO's two-sided houses with back shutters which opened to show cut-out scenes, flat wings in grooves which brought PERSPECTIVE into play and the proscenium arch in front of flat scenes. He also designed COSTUMES. With the production of *The Masque of Blackness* in 1605, there began J.'s long association with JON-

SON, of whose masques twelve more are known to have been produced with designs by J. Eventually, however, the two men were in conflict over the relative importance of the poet and the scenic artist. After the production of *Chloridia* (1631), the last masque on which they collaborated, the quarrel came to a head. Aided, possibly, by the artistic bias of Charles I's Court, J. succeeded in engineering Jonson's dismissal from his post as author of the masques for the Court in the winter of 1631–32. In retaliation, Jonson satirized J. in his comedy *A Tale of a Tub* (1633). J. also executed designs for masques by the dramatists CHAPMAN and SHIRLEY, and the poets Samuel Daniel, Thomas Campion and Thomas Carew.
Bibl: J. A. Gotch, 1968; A. Nicoll, STUART MASQUES AND THE RENAISSANCE STAGE CRAFT, 1937; R. Southern, CHANGEABLE SCENERY, 1952

Inigo Jones, stage design

Jones, Leroi (1934–), Black US playwright and poet. Has changed his name to the Moslem form **Imamu Amiri Baraka**. Studied English at Howard University, Washington, D.C., where he gained a BA. After a time in Greenwich Village, he moved to Harlem where he founded the Black Arts Repertory Theatre, 1965; later back to his native Newark, N.J., where he directs Spirit House, a Black theatre group and community centre. Won an OBIE AWARD in 1964 for his play *Dutchman*, a violent confrontation on a subway train between a Black man and a White woman. Other plays: *The Slave*, 1964; *The Toilet*, 1964; *Experimental Death Unit 1*, 1965; *A Black Mass*, 1966; *Great Goodness of Life*, 1967; *Madheart*, 1967; *Slave-ship*, 1969; *The Death of Malcom X*, 1969. J. is one of the most talented and also one of the most radical Black revolutionary playwrights and the leader of the extreme and vital Black theatre movement in the USA.

Jones, Margo (1913–53), US producer. She created the influential Theatre-in-the-Round in Dallas which gave opportunities to young playwrights such as T. WILLIAMS and also produced several plays on Broadway.

Robert Edmond Jones, stage set for O'NEILL's *Mourning Becomes Electra*, 1931

Jones, Robert Edmond (1887–1954), US stage designer and director. Studied in Germany at the Deutsches-Theater, Berlin, under REINHARDT. His first design for GRANVILLE-BARKER's production in 1915 of *The Man Who Married a Dumb Wife*, adapted by DUKES from Anatole France, marked the beginning of the modern art of stage design in the USA. He subsequently worked in collaboration with Arthur Hopkins, the Washington Square Players (later THEATRE GUILD) and the PROVINCETOWN PLAYERS (O'NEILL, MACGOWAN). He designed almost all of O'Neill's plays, e.g. *Anna Christie*, 1921, which he also directed; *The Hairy Ape*, 1922; *Desire under the Elms*, 1924; *The Great God Brown*, 1926, also directed; *Mourning Becomes Electra*, 1931; and plays by SHAKESPEARE (*Richard III*, 1920, and *Hamlet*, 1922, both with J. BARRYMORE, the latter production coming

to London; *Macbeth*, 1921, with L. BARRYMORE); CONNELLY, *The Green Pastures*, 1930; PIRANDELLO, CHEKHOV, O'CASEY, etc.
Bibl: R. E. Jones & K. Macgowan, CONTINENTAL STAGECRAFT, 1922

Jonson, Ben (1572/73–1637), English playwright and poet. Contemporary of SHAKESPEARE, whose sharp and witty critical comments on the manners and vices of his day made him one of the most controversial personalities of his time and several times led to his imprisonment. His first spell in prison was brought about by his presumed co-authorship, with Thomas Nashe and the actors Robert Shaw and Gabriel Spencer, of the lost play *The Isle of Dogs*, 1597, a topical satire, the production of which led to the temporary closure of London theatres. J.'s name is especially associated with the Comedy of Humours, which shows individuals controlled by one dominating passion or 'humour'. After the appearance of the first play which is certainly by him, the COMEDY *The Case is Altered*, 1597–98, he developed this genre in *Every Man in His Humour*, 1598, which was presented by the CHAMBERLAIN'S MEN, with Shakespeare playing the part of Kno'well, and in *Every Man out of His Humour*, 1599. In the latter play J., by parodying the style of MARSTON, sparked off the dispute generally known as the WAR OF THE THEATRES, in which several dramatists attacked and counterattacked each other in successive plays. J. took part in the quarrel with two further plays: *Cynthia's Revels; or The Fountain of Self-Love*, 1600–01, and *Poetaster; or The Arraignment*, 1601. J's Roman tragedy *Sejanus his Fall*, 1603, about the favourite of the Emperor Tiberius, was criticized because of its dangerous political implications. The comedy *Eastward Hoe!*, 1605, written with Marston and CHAPMAN, a satire which attacked the politics of James I, led to Jonson being imprisoned again. His major works are the comedies: *Volpone; or The Fox*, 1605–06, the story of an old miser who pretends to be dying in order to unmask the people who desire to inherit his fortune; *Epicoene; or The Silent Woman*, 1609 (▷ARETINO), which ZWEIG used for the LIBRETTO of Richard Strauss's opera *Die Schweigsame Frau*; and *The Alchemist*, 1610, revived many times, by GARRICK and by the OLD VIC. Then followed J.'s second Roman TRAGEDY, *Catiline*, 1611, and the comedy *Bartholomew Fair*, 1614, which vividly evokes a 17th-century London street fair. The failure of his comedy *The Devil is an Ass*, 1616, may have caused his subsequent abstention from the stage until the production of the comedy *The Staple of News* in 1626.
In 1616 J. had been appointed Poet Laureate, and as such wrote MASQUES for Court entertainments, many of them in collaboration with the famous architect and scenic designer I. JONES. He developed the masque into a literary genre of its own and also introduced the anti-masque, a comic parody of the main masque, of which it forms part. Rivalry between J. and Jones, however, eventually erupted in a quarrel which led during the winter of 1631/32 to J.'s dismissal, at Jones's instigation, from his position as author of masques for the Court. J.'s last plays were the comedies, *The New Inn; or the Lightheart*, 1629; *The Magnetic Lady; or Humours Reconciled*, 1632; and *A Tale of A Tub*, 1633. Two plays were left unfinished at his death: the history piece *Mortimer his Fall* (only a short fragment), and the comic pastoral *The Sad Shepherd; or A Tale of Robin Hood*.
Bibl: J. Barish (ed), BEN JONSON, 1963; C. H. Herford & P. Simpson (ed), THE WORKS OF BEN JONSON, 1925–52; G. E. Bentley, SHAKESPEARE AND JONSON, 1945

Jouvet, Louis (1887–1951), French ACTOR-MANAGER and director. An experienced actor, he joined COPEAU at the Théâtre du Vieux Colombier in 1913. Despite his belief that his hard features and slow, heavy diction handicapped him as an actor, he enjoyed considerable success, especially his Aguecheek in *Twelfth Night*, 1914. He was with Copeau in the USA 1917–19, directing and acting, e.g. Géronte in MOLIÈRE's *Les Fourberies de Scapin* and Brendel in IBSEN's *Rosmersholm*, but in 1922 he split with Copeau and formed his own company at the Comédie des Champs-Elysées. Most important in his artistic development was his collaboration with GIRAUDOUX, almost all of whose plays he produced, e.g. *Siegfried* in 1928 as an experimental production, which ran for 303 performances. The collaboration with Giraudoux enabled J. to perfect the neo-classical style he had aimed at – productions reduced to the simplest and most essential stage action, elimination of extraneous effects, controlled movement combined with striking stylized décor, usually designed by BÉRARD. In 1934 J. took over the management of the Théâtre de l'Athénée, where he remained until the end of his life, interrupted only 1941–45 by the war (during which he toured Switzerland and Latin America). After the war he specialized mainly in classical comedies, mainly by his favourite writer Molière: *Dom Juan*, 1947; *L'Ecole des femmes*, 1948; *Tartuffe*, 1950. He was the author of theoretical works: *Réflexions du comédien* (2/1951), *Témoignes*, 1951; *Ecoute, mon ami!*, 1951. He also appeared in films, notably *La Kermesse Heroïque*, 1935.
Bibl: LOUIS JOUVET ET LE THÉÂTRE D'AUJOURD'HUI, 1948

Joyce, (Augustine Aloysius) James (1882–1941), Irish writer. His only preserved drama, *Exiles*, was written during his most fruitful year, 1914, just before he undertook his greatest work *Ulysses*. His early dramatic attempts at the age of 19 were translations of HAUPTMANN's *Michael Kramer* and IBSEN's *When We Dead Awaken*, on which he also wrote an essay. *Exiles* was published in 1918 and had been acted without much success until PINTER directed it in 1970 at the MERMAID THEATRE, London; revived at the Aldwych Theatre, 1971. Some of his prose works were dramatized for the stage: *Ulysses in Nighttown* by Marjorie Barkentin, 1958 (also filmed); *Stephen D.*, 1962, by Hugh Leonard.

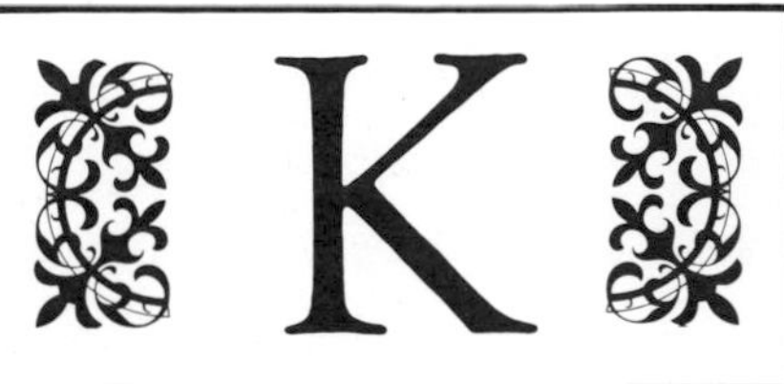

Kabuki ▷JAPAN.

Kachalov, Vassili Ivanovich (1875–1948), Russian actor. After several years in the provinces, he joined the MOSCOW ART THEATRE in 1900 and became one of its leading members. His best-known parts included: Ivan Karamazov in *The Brothers Karamazov* (based on DOSTOYEVSKY, 1910/11); Hamlet in CRAIG's famous production, 1911/12; the Narrator in the adaptation of L. TOLSTOY's *Resurrection*, 1929/30. Also: the Baron in GORKY's *The Lower Depths*, 1902/03; Chatsky in *Gore ot uma* (Woe from Wit), 1906/07, by GRIBOYEDOV, and Vershinin in *Armoured Train 14-69*, 1927/28, by IVANOV, etc.

Kadelburg, Gustav (1851–1925), Hungarian-born German actor and dramatist. Began his career as an actor playing the part of the bon-vivant; later also directed mainly at the Deutsches-Theater, BERLIN, 1883–93. Best known for his COMEDIES written with SCHÖNTHAN and BLUMENTHAL: between 1890 and 1910 he was one of the most frequently performed German playwrights. His first success was *Goldfische* (Goldfish), fp Berlin 1886, Deutsches-Theater. He gained an international reputation as co-author with BLUMENTHAL of the LIBRETTO for the operetta *Im weissen Rössl* (*The White Horse Inn*), fp Berlin 1897, Lessingtheater.

Kafka, Franz (1883–1924), Czech author who wrote in German. His novels and short stories have had a widespread and profound influence on modern drama in Europe. His only play, published posthumously, is *Der Gruftwächter* (The Guardian of the Crypt). Several of his novels have been successfully dramatized: *Der Prozess* (*The Trial*), 1947, by GIDE and BARRAULT, and 1968 by GROSSMAN; *Das Schloss* (*The Castle*), 1953, and *Amerika*, 1957, by Max Brod.
Bibl: R. Gray, 1973; R. Hemmerle, 1958

Kainz, Josef (1858–1910), Austrian actor. First stage successes with the MEININGER company, 1877–80; then at the Munich Court Theatre under the management of POSSART. He became a personal friend of Ludwig II, appearing in his private performances. But the summit of his career was at the Deutsches-Schauspielhaus, Berlin, 1883–89. In 1889 he went to the Berliner Theater, under L. BARNAY, a rival company, but broke his contract and was subsequently banned by the Actors' Union from appearing on any German stage. He then toured Europe and the USA, and in 1892 returned to the Deutsches-Theater, engaged by L'ARRONGE, who broke with the union to engage K. as an actor. In 1895

BRAHM took over the Deutsches-Theater as a champion of NATURALISM; K. left in 1899 to join the Burgtheater Ensemble where he remained until his death. He was considered one of the greatest actors of his time, being specially praised for the melodious beauty and range of his voice, combined with authority and graceful movement; full of poetry and sensitivity, his style has been described as Art Nouveau acting. His important parts included Romeo, Hamlet, Richard II, the heroes of GOETHE, SCHILLER, GRILLPARZER and G. HAUPTMANN.
Bibl: H. Jhering, VON JOSEF KAINZ BIS PAULA WESSELY, 1942; P. Wiegler, 1941; H. Bahr, BRIEFE VON JOSEF KAINZ, 1921; F. Philippi, LUDWIG II UND JOSEF KAINZ, 1913

Kaiser, Georg (1878–1945), German Expressionist playwright. His works were influenced by Nietzsche's philosophy of the superman and by contemporary artists as divergent as HAUPTMANN and Stefan George, with whose literary circle he was connected for some time. In his theoretical essays K. claimed that art should proclaim the synthesis of moral and natural qualities in the new man. His dramas were, therefore, plays of ideas, brilliantly clever in their plotting, but lacking in human substance and characterization; they suffer from a highly stylized clipped language. Later he turned to realistic diction and verse. His works include: *Der Fall des Schülers Vehgesack* (The Case of Student V.), Vienna 1915; *Die Bürger von Calais* (*The Burghers of Calais*), Frankfurt 1917; *Gas I*, Düsseldorf and Frankfurt 1918; *Der gerettete Alkibiades* (Alcibiades Saved), Munich 1920; *Gas II*, Frankfurt 1920; *Die jüdische Witwe* (*The Jewish Widow*), Meiningen and Nordhausen 1921; *Die Flucht nach Venedig* (The Flight to Venice), Nuremberg 1923; *Kolportage*, Berlin and Frankfurt 1924; *Gats*, a play about birth control, Vienna 1925; *Die Papiermühle* (The Paper Mill), Aachen, 1927; *Der Zar lässt sich photographieren* (The Tsar is being photographed), LIBRETTO, music WEILL, Leipzig 1928; *Oktobertag* (October Day), Hamburg 1928; *Zwei Krawatten* (Two Neckties) Berlin 1929; *Mississippi*, Oldenburg and Darmstadt 1930; *Der Silbersee* (The Silver Lake), Leipzig and Magdeburg 1933; *Der Soldat Tanaka*, Zurich 1940; *Zweimal Amphitryon* (A. × 2), Zurich 1944; *Der Gärtner von Toulouse* (The Gardener of T.), Mannheim 1945; *Napoleon in New Orleans*, Karlsruhe 1950, etc.
Bibl: Kaiser, R. Kauf, FAITH AND DESPAIR IN GEORG KAISER'S WORKS, 1955

Kālidasā (?375–?415), a celebrated Indian poet who wrote three well-constructed Sanskrit plays in stanzas of great tenderness and containing fine descriptive passages: the two well-known mytho-pastoral dramas, *Śakuntalā* in seven acts and *Vikramorvasī* in five, and a piece of Court intrigue, inferior to the other two, called *Mālavikagnimitra*, also in five acts. *Śakuntalā* is a classic of Indian literature; it deals with the secret love of King Dusyanta for Śakuntalā, the daughter of a hermit; because of a

Ben Jonson, *Bartholomew Fair*, OLD VIC production, 1950, by DEVINE, set by MOTLEY

Louis Jouvet as Tartuffe in MOLIÈRE's play

James Joyce, portrait by Sean O'Sullivan, National Gallery of Ireland

Franz Kafka, *The Trial*, French adaptation by GIDE and BARRAULT, Paris 1947

curse the king forgets her, but finally finds his way back to her. A translation by Sir William Jones, published in Calcutta, 1790, under the title *The Recovered Ring*, drew the attention of writers in the West to the beauties of Sanskrit literature. It was seen for the first time in English at an open-air performance in Regent's Park by the ELIZABETHAN STAGE SOCIETY in 1899.
Bibl: P. V. Kane, HISTORY OF SANSKRIT POETICS, 1951

Kaminska, Ida (1899–), Jewish actress, director and theatre manager. Made her stage début in 1916, and from 1921 managed the Jewish Art Theatre in Warsaw, which was founded by her mother Esther Rachel K.; 1939–47 she worked in the Soviet Union, 1949–53 in Lódz, 1953–55 in Wroclaw and from 1955 in Warsaw, until finally the theatre was closed in 1968 and she emigrated to the USA. Her most noted parts include: Nora in *A Doll's House* (IBSEN); title role in *Mother Courage* (BRECHT). She has produced plays and dramatizations by PERETZ, SHOLEM ALEICHEM, ASCH.
Bibl: LE THÉÂTRE JUIF DANS LE MONDE, 1931

Kandinsky, Vassily (1866–1944), Russian painter and art theoretician. In 1910 he painted the first non-objective pictures. In 1912 he wrote 'Das Geistige in der Kunst' and in the German Expressionist magazine *Der Blaue Reiter* published the LIBRETTO 'Der gelbe Klang', an early example of the theory he later called 'stage-synthesis' (combining poetry, visual images, colours, light, sound, movement in space etc.). He postulated that the artist should be an engineer; the polytechnic art training and research programmes which K. worked out first in Moscow, later provided the theoretical inspiration behind the Bauhaus in Germany (▷SCHLEMMER). Only once was K. able to put his theories into practice, in a production arranged for the stage of Mussorgsky's piece *Pictures at an Exhibition* (Dessau, 1928).
Bibl: H. Rischbieter (ed), BÜHNE UND BILDENDE KUNST IM 20. JAHRHUNDERT, 1968

Kanin, Garson (1912–), US playwright and director. Started as a musician; then appeared in VAUDEVILLE and made his first appearance in the professional theatre in New York in 1933; became a film director. Wrote the successful play *Born Yesterday* which he directed and produced at the Lyceum Theatre, New York, 1946. Subsequently directed many hits on BROADWAY, among them his own plays: *The Smile of the World*, 1949; *The Rat Race*, 1949; *The Live Wire*, 1950; *Do-Re-Mi*, 1960; *Come on Strong*, 1962. Has also written a number of screenplays in collaboration with his wife, the actress RUTH GORDON, including *Adam's Rib*, *Pat and Mike* and *The Marrying Kind*.

Kantor, Tadeusz (1915–), Polish painter and man of the theatre. Has worked since 1945 as stage designer at the Teatr Stary in Cracow, e.g. CORNEILLE's *Le Cid*, 1945; *Hamlet*, 1958; and since 1955 at the EXPERIMENTAL THEATRE Cricot 2 in Cracow. For his informal productions he used mainly plays by the Surrealist writer WITKIEWICZ: *On a Small Estate*, 1958; *The Madman and the Nun*, 1963; *Cupboard*, 1966; *The Water Hen*, 1968. He adopts the techniques of the HAPPENING for the theatre, using piles of materials, rapid transitions from ecstasy to tranquillity, and audience-involvement. In his theoretical notes he talks of 'autonomous theatre', a 'point O-theatre', of violence and destruction. He has also organized HAPPENINGS in Warsaw, 1965 and 1967, Cracow, 1965, Basle, 1966, Gdynia, 1967.
Bibl: H. Rischbieter (ed), BÜHNE UND BILDENDE KUNST IM 20. JAHRHUNDERT, 1968

Karagöz ▷TURKEY.

Kasperl. Stock character of the old Viennese folk comedy, derived from HANSWURST; created by the actor LAROCHE in 1789 at the Theater in der Leopoldstadt in Vienna. The character has survived in the PUPPET THEATRE.

Kästner, Erich (1899–1974), German satirical writer of poetry, short stories and cabaret sketches. Many of his children's books were successfully dramatized for the stage, foremost among them: *Emil und die Detektive* (Emil and the Detectives), which was also filmed.

Katayev, Valentin Petrovich (1897–), Soviet dramatist. Wrote several COMEDIES, the best known of which is *Kvadratura kruga* (*Squaring the Circle*), fp 1928, MOSCOW ART THEATRE, dir NEMIROVICH-DANCHENKO, New York, 1935, London, 1938, a satire on love, life and the housing problem in the Soviet Union. Other works include: *Doroga tsvetov* (*The Primrose Path*), 1933, produced in New York, 1939; *Rastratchiki* (*The Embezzlers*), 1928; *Avangard* (The Vanguard), 1929; *Million terzanii* (A Million Torments), 1931; *Vremya, vperyod!* (Time, Forward!), 1932; *Domik* (The Little House), 1940; *Sinii platochek* (The Blue Kerchief), 1943; *Otchi dom* (Father's House), 1945; *Den otdikha* (Day Off), 1945.

Kaufman, George S. (1889–1961), US playwright, drama critic, producer and director. Known as the 'Great Collaborator' because almost all his writing was with other authors, including CONNELLY, M. HART, EDNA FERBER, Morrie Ryskind, etc. He also wrote various film scripts, was co-librettist of MUSICALS, directed and produced his own plays and those of other writers. He wrote only two full-length works by himself, *The Cocoanuts*, 1925 (with the Marx Brothers), and *The Butter and Egg Man*, 1925. Most successful works in collaboration include: *Dulcy*, 1921 (starring LYNN FONTANNE), and *Beggar on Horseback*, 1924, based on a German play by Paul Apel, both with Connelly; *The Royal Family*, 1927, with Edna Ferber; the brilliant Hollywood caricature *Once in a Lifetime*, 1930; *You Can't Take It with You*, 1936 (PULITZER PRIZE), and *The Man Who Came to Dinner*, 1939, all with M. Hart; *The Solid Gold Cadillac*, 1953, with H. Teichman. Musicals include: *Of Thee I Sing*, 1930 (Pulitzer Prize) with Ryskind, music GERSHWIN, and *I'd Rather be Right*, 1937 (starring G. M. COHAN), with M. Hart, music and lyrics RODGERS and L. HART, both of which he directed. He also directed, among others, the plays *The Front Page*, 1928, by MACARTHUR and HECHT; *Of Mice and Men*, 1938, by STEINBECK; and the musical *Guys and Dolls*, 1950, by LOESSER.
Bibl: J. W. Krutch, AMERICAN DRAMA SINCE 1918, 1957

Kayssler, Friedrich (1874–1945), German actor, director and manager. In the first half of this century a major figure in the German theatre, who also wrote several plays, *Simplicius*, 1905; *Jan der Wunderbare* (Jan the Wonderful), 1917; *Der Brief* (The Letter), 1927. He began his career in small parts under the direction of BRAHM, 1895; then in the provinces; in 1900 he came to BERLIN and began working in association with REINHARDT; under his direction K. achieved his first major success in *Prinz Friedrich von Homburg* by KLEIST, Deutsches-Theater, Berlin 1907, followed by *Faust I*, 1909, and *Faust II*, 1911; he was also the first Peer Gynt in GERMANY, Lessingtheater, 1913. He was manager of the VOLKSBÜHNE, 1913–33, and engaged directors still unknown at that time, e.g. Ludwig Berger and FEHLING; from 1933 he worked with GRÜNDGENS at the State Theatre, where his greatest successes were as Odoardo in LESSING's *Emilia Galotti*, 1937, and Meister Anton in HEBBEL's *Maria Magdalena*, 1938. Also film actor, and author of *Schauspielernotizen*, 3 vols, 1910–29; a theoretical work, *Von Menschentum zu Menschentum*, 1933; and *Wandlung und Sinn*, 1940.

Kazan, Elia (E. E. Kazanjoglous; 1909–), Greek-born US director and actor. Pupil of BAKER, he began his career as an actor with the GROUP THEATRE in 1932, and made his début there as a director in 1938 with *Casey Jones* by R. Ardrey, whose play *Thunder Rock*, 1939, he also directed. Since 1942 he has concentrated on directing plays and occasionally films. With CHERYL CRAWFORD, STRASBERG and Robert Lewis he founded in 1947 the ACTORS' STUDIO, a workshop for professional actors, and remained there until 1962, when he became associate director of the Lincoln Center Repertory Theatre, from which he resigned in 1965. His major productions include: WILDER's *The Skin of Our Teeth*, 1942, NYDCC AWARD; BEHRMAN's *Jacobowsky and the Colonel*, 1944, based on WERFEL; A. MILLER's *All My Sons*, 1947, NYDCC Award, and *Death of a Salesman*, 1949; plays by T. WILLIAMS: *A Streetcar Named Desire*, 1947; *Camino Real*, 1953; *Cat on a Hot Tin Roof*, 1955, and *Sweet Bird of Youth*, 1959; *J.B.*, 1958, by MacLEISH; etc. K.'s psychological approach to working with actors is orientated towards STANISLAVSKY, and he maintains that 'Directing consists finally in the transformation of psychology into behaviour'.

Kean, Edmund (1787–1833), English actor. Prototype of the English romantic actor, and one of the greatest of all time, he was the illegitimate son of Ann Carey and possibly one Edmund Kean, an architect's clerk (no record of his birth has been found). Abandoned by his mother, he was found and casually cared for by stage people, and eventually joined a group of strolling players until 1814 when he played Shylock at DRURY LANE and his genius was instantly recognized. He created a new style of acting with greater emphasis on facial expression than on voice. K. was a master of tragic parts in which he could portray nobility and virtue and also a touch of malignancy; but he never succeeded in comic parts. He excelled in restrained by-play with occasional sudden outbursts. COLERIDGE said 'To see him act, is like reading Shakespeare by flashes of lightning'. His favourite and most memorable parts included Richard III, Othello, Lear, and Rolla in SHERIDAN's *Pizarro*, though his Hamlet and Coriolanus caused some disappointment. Two of his greatest parts were Sir Giles Overreach in MASSINGER's *A New Way to Pay Old Debts* and Barabbas in MARLOWE's *The Jew of Malta*. His son, **Charles John K.** (1811–68) was a very popular actor, though without the genius of his father; he was an important manager of the Princess Theatre 1850–59; his productions with historically accurate sets and COSTUMES had a great influence on Georg II, Duke of Saxe-Meiningen, who frequently visited London.
Bibl: G. W. Playfair, 2/1950; J. Macqueen Pope, 1960

Keene, Laura (*c.* 1826–73), English-born US actress, one of the first women to manage a theatre. After touring Australia with E. BOOTH in 1854, she settled in the USA and opened a theatre in New York, 1856, under her own name (it was later called the Olympic) with a production of *As You Like It*: she had a good regular company (avoiding the fashion of her time for visiting star-performers) with J. JEFFERSON II and SOTHERN as the leading actors; the latter appeared in one of her most famous productions, *Our American Cousin*, 1858, which established her reputation in the US theatre.

Kelly, George (1887–1974), US actor, playwright and director who learned the craft as a vaudeville actor and sketch writer. He made his stage début in 1908 and his first success with a full-length play was *The Torch Bearers*, 1922. He made his name with *The Show Off*, 1924, and *Craig's Wife*, 1925 (PULITZER PRIZE). Later plays were less successful and his last was *The Fatal Weakness*, 1946. His niece is the former film actress Grace Kelly, now Princess Grace of Monaco.

Kemble. English acting family of the 18th and 19th centuries. The provincial actor (1) **Roger K.** (1721–1802) had twelve children of whom nine worked in the theatre. His eldest daughter, (2) SARAH SIDDONS, is considered one of England's greatest tragediennes. His eldest son, (3)

Edmund Kean as Sir Giles Overreach in *A New Way to Pay Old Debts* by MASSINGER

Kaufman and M. HART, *You Can't Take It with You*, New York 1936

Kasperl, engraving for the *Wiener-Theater Almanach*, 1804

John Philip K. (1757–1823), managed DRURY LANE THEATRE and later COVENT GARDEN. He was also a fine tragic actor (e.g. Brutus, Cato and Coriolanus), and had great dignity with a fine voice technique. J.P.K.'s brother, (4) **Stephen K.** (1758–1822) was a very popular comic actor, excelling particularly as Falstaff (he was himself of vast size). R.K.'s youngest son (5) **Charles K.** (1775–1854) made his début in London as Malcolm in J.P.K.'s production of *Macbeth* and became an accomplished player of such parts as Mercutio, Orlando, Benedick and Romeo. His daughter Frances Anne, known as (6) **Fanny K.** (1809–93), was at first not particularly interested in the theatre but, in order to save her father from bankruptcy, appeared as Juliet with enormous success in 1829 at Covent Garden. Other parts followed: Lady Teazle, Beatrice in *Much Ado About Nothing*, and Bianca in *Othello*. In 1832 she went with her father on a two-year tour to the USA which marked the beginning of many guest star appearances there.

Kempe, William (?–*c*. 1603), English Elizabethan CLOWN. The original Dogberry in *Much Ado About Nothing*, he was one of the CHAMBERLAIN'S MEN from 1594 until 1600. Also popular as a dancer and singer of JIGS.

Kendal, William Hunter (W. H. Grimston; 1843–1917), English ACTOR-MANAGER. From 1866 appeared at the Haymarket Theatre where he met Madge Robertson (1848–1935) whom he married in 1874. They were among the most famous acting couples of the late 19th century. **Madge K.** excelled in contemporary plays by SARDOU (*Dora*, 1878) and PINERO (*The Squire*, 1881); K. was soon overshadowed by the success of his wife and later concentrated on management (St James's Theatre in partnership with HARE, 1879). K. retired in 1908. Madge K. was appointed DBE in 1926.
Bibl: T. E. Pemberton, THE KENDALS, 1900

Kennedy, Adrienne (1931–), Black US dramatist. Grew up in Cleveland, Ohio, and attended Ohio State University, starting to write at 20. Her play *Cities in Bezique*, New York 1969, Public Theatre, has been described as 'two journeys of the mind in the form of theatre pieces'; the director of the production, Gerald Freedman, said about her: 'A.K. is a poet of the theatre. She does not deal in story, character and event as a playwright. She deals in image, metaphor, essence and layers of consciousness.' In *Funnyhouse of a Negro*, fp 1964, OBIE AWARD, as with much of her other work, she is concerned with the problems of identity and self-knowledge. *In His Own Write*, A.K.'s stage adaptation of John Lennon's book, written in collaboration with the author and Victor Spinetti, was produced by the NATIONAL THEATRE at the OLD VIC in 1968. Other plays include: *The Owl Answers*; *A Beast's Story*; *A Rat's Mass*, 1970, LA MAMA; *Lesson and Dead Language*, 1970, Theatre Genesis; *Sun*, London 1971, ROYAL COURT.

Kenny, Sean (1932–73), Irish stage designer. Studied architecture in Dublin and the USA (under Frank Lloyd Wright); worked as a designer in London from 1957. His work was based on elaborate use of modern electronic methods to produce sets which could be moved and transformed in full view of the audience. He advised on the design of the CHICHESTER FESTIVAL theatre. His works include: BEHAN's *The Hostage*, 1959, dir JOAN LITTLEWOOD; *Oliver!*, musical by BART based on Dickens, 1960; *Stop the World – I Want to Get Off*, L. Bricusse/A. Newley, 1961; *Romeo and Juliet*, STRATFORD-UPON-AVON, 1962, dir HALL; *Blitz*, musical by Bart and J. Maitland, 1962; GAY's *The Beggar's Opera*, 1963, dir P. Wood; *Hamlet*, 1963, OLIVIER. K. was able to indulge his ideas most extravagantly in the revue *Casino de Paris*, Las Vegas: he constructed a system of 13 hydraulic movable platforms which could be controlled by only two technicians.

Kern, Jerome (1885–1945), US composer of musicals. Unlike other leading popular composers of his time, e.g. GERSHWIN and BERLIN, who succeeded without any formal musical training, he studied at the New York College of Music and in Europe. His most important musical was *Show Boat*, 1927, lyrics by HAMMERSTEIN II, which influenced the development of this genre: the subject was based on a novel by EDNA FERBER, with songs and dances closely woven into the action. In 1915, at the Princess Theatre, he began a collaboration with Guy Bolton, later joined by WODEHOUSE, evolving a new style of artistically integrated musical including *Very Good Eddie*, 1915; in 1917 there were *Oh Boy!*; *Leave It to Jane*; *Miss 1917*; *Have a Heart*; in 1918 *Oh Lady, Lady* and *Rock-a-Bye Baby*. Other works: *Sally*, 1920; *Sunny*, 1925; *Sweet Adeline*, 1929; *Music in the Air*, 1932; *Roberta*, 1933 and *Very Warm for May*, 1939.
Bibl: D. Ewen, THE STORY OF JEROME KERN, 1955

Kerr, Alfred (1867–1948), German critic. The most prominent and controversial drama critic of his time, he championed IBSEN and G. HAUPTMANN in the German theatre, supporting BRAHM and his company while attacking SUDERMANN and treating REINHARDT's work with much scepticism. He was also the main opponent of BRECHT in BERLIN in the 1920s and 1930s. He emigrated in 1933. K. viewed criticism as an art; his style was pointed, aggressive, sharp, often using fragmented sentences full of irony and sarcasm. His collected critical works were published under the title *Die Welt im Drama*, 5 vols, 1917; revised edition 1954. He also contributed essays to the literary magazine *Neue Rundschau* and acted as drama critic for *Der Tag*, 1909–19, and for the *Berliner Tageblatt*, 1919–33.

Killigrew, Thomas (1612–83), English theatre manager. Author of several plays including *Claricilla*, *The Prisoners* and *The Parson's Wedding*. He founded the present DRURY LANE theatre as the Theatre Royal, 1662, under Charter from Charles II. With DAVENANT he was the holder of a Charter for the Duke's House, later transferred to COVENT GARDEN. After the death of Sir Henry Herbert in 1673, he became MASTER OF THE REVELS, a position in which he was later succeeded by his son **Charles K.** (1665–1725), who, with his half-brother Henry, took over the management of the Theatre Royal in 1671.
Bibl: M. Summer, PLAYHOUSE OF PEPYS, 1935

Kingsley, Sidney (1906–), US playwright and director. Studied at Cornell University, then became an actor. His first play *Men in White*, 1933, the archetype of later hospital plays and TV serials, became a world-wide success; his second play *Dead End*, 1935, which depicted the life of juvenile delinquents and which he himself directed on Broadway, also achieved universal renown. *Ten Million Ghosts*, 1936; *The World We Make*, 1939; *The Patriots*, 1943, and *Darkness at Noon* (adapted from A. Koestler's novel), 1951, NYDCC AWARDS; *Detective Story*, 1949; *Lunatics and Lovers*, 1954; *Night Life*, 1962. K. is a master of the well-constructed play which presents a cross-section of a whole milieu, e.g. a hospital, a police precinct, or a juvenile gang.

Kipphardt, Heinar (1922–), German playwright and essayist. Studied medicine and became a doctor at the Charity Hospital, 1950–59 in East Berlin; at the same time he was chief DRAMATURG at the Deutsches-Theater 1950–53; in 1959 he moved to Düsseldorf, later to Munich. His works include: *Shakespeare dringend gesucht* (Shakespeare Urgently Sought), a satire, fp 1952, Deutsches-Theater; *Der Aufstieg des Alois Riontek* (The Rise of Alois Riontek), a tragi-comic FARCE; *Die Stühle des Herrn Szmil* (The Chairs of Mr Szmil), fp Wuppertal 1961; *Der Hund des Generals* (The General's Dog), fp Munich Kammerspiele, 1962; *In der Sache J. Robert Oppenheimer* (In the Matter of J. Robert Oppenheimer), a documentary play (▷ DOCUMENTARY THEATRE) based on the Oppenheimer case, fp Munich Kammerspiele and FREIE VOLKSBÜHNE, Berlin 1964, dir PISCATOR, which became a world-wide success (VILAR adapted the material relating to the trial for his own Paris production); *Joel Brand* (about Eichmann and the deportation of Hungarian Jews), fp Munich Kammerspiele, 1965; *Die Nacht, in der der Chef geschlachtet wurde* (The Night the Boss was Slaughtered), fp Stuttgart 1967, dir PALITZSCH.
Bibl: H. Rischbieter & E. Wendt, DEUTSCHE DRAMATIK IN WEST UND OST, 1965

Kirkland, Jack (1902–69), US playwright and producer. He wrote a dozen plays, most of them adaptations of novels. His greatest success was *Tobacco Road*, a story of a degenerate sharecropper family, produced in 1933. Taken from a novel by Erskine Caldwell, it ran for 3,182 performances, the second longest-running drama on

BROADWAY, the first having been LINDSAY and CROUSE's *Life with Father*. It was filmed and has been frequently revived.

Kitchen sink drama. Term applied by the press to characterize the plays using lower middle-class speech and locations which changed the accepted mode for English plays – particularly London West End drama after the success of OSBORNE's *Look Back in Anger* at the ROYAL COURT THEATRE in 1956. Up till then, successful commercial plays tended to be located in the main living-room (DRAWING-ROOM COMEDY) rather than in the less elegant locations of the plays of WESKER, PINTER, KOPS, OWEN, ARDEN and others. But the term 'kitchen sink drama' was no more than a very superficial definition of the new school (if it could be called that) of British playwriting, as each of the writers concerned had very different objectives and artistic methods.

Klabund (pseud. of Alfred Henschke; 1890–1928), German poet. He became famous with his play *Der Kreidekreis* (The Chalk Circle) based on a Chinese theme, written for the actress ELISABETH BERGNER, who played the lead in REINHARDT's famous production at the Deutsches-Theater, Berlin, in 1925; the play is still in the REPERTOIRE of many German theatres.

Kleist, Heinrich von (1777–1811), German poet and playwright. Now ranks among the classic German dramatists, although he was never appreciated during his lifetime. This lack of recognition together with the feeling of alienation, despair and financial insecurity drove him to suicide. His dramatic work, influenced by SHAKESPEARE and Greek TRAGEDY, is written in highly stylized verse. He was concerned with the problems of self-knowledge and self-mastery; in the eternal confrontation between the inner and outer world (self and others, emotions and responsibility, desire and reality, the individual and society) only the supreme effort of the protagonist could, he maintained, avert tragedy. In his important essay *Über das Marionettentheater*, 1811, he emphasizes that only self-awareness can lead to knowledge of the outside world. Springing from a deeply emotional personality, K.'s plays anticipated the later discoveries of depth-psychology; his heroes, always precariously poised between crucial choices, have affinities with EXISTENTIALISM. These facts explain the prominent position he came to occupy in France after the war. His plays are: *Die Familie Schroffenstein* (*The Feud of the Schroffensteins*), 1803; *Robert Guiskard*, fragment written 1802/3, fp 1901, Berliner Theater; *Der Zerbrochene Krug* (*The Broken Jug*). Weimar 1808; *Amphitryon*, 1807, fp Berlin 1899, Neues Theater; *Penthesilea*, 1808, fp Berlin 1876, Royal Theatre; *Käthchen von Heilbronn*, Vienna 1810, Theater an der Wien; *Hermannsschlacht*, pub posthumously, 1821, fp Breslau 1860; *Prinz Friedrich von Homburg*, pub posthumously and fp Vienna 1821, BURGTHEATER.

Bibl: J. Geary, HEINRICH KLEIST: A STUDY IN TRAGEDY AND ANXIETY, 1968

Fanny Kemble, portrait by Thomas Sully, 1833

Heinrich von Kleist, *The Prince of Homburg*, *c.* 1875, stage design by Georg II, Duke of Saxe-Meiningen

Thomas Killigrew

Klingemann, Ernst August (1777–1831), German theatre manager. Pupil of the famous Shakespearean translator Eschenburg, who studied philosophy with Fichte, Schelling and A. W. SCHLEGEL at the University of Jena; then turned to the theatre, working with the Walterschen Schauspieltruppe, from which he later formed the Brunswick National Theatre, 1818. He attempted to establish a literary and sophisticated REPERTOIRE, mainly of classical plays, and engaged leading German actors for his theatre including DEVRIENT and F. Esslair. The enterprise went bankrupt in 1826, but reopened in 1828 under the management of a royal INTENDANT with K. as general director, a post he held until his death. His achievement included the first staging of GOETHE's *Faust* in 1829. His other works include: *Über das Braunschweiger Theater*, 1817; *Vorlesungen für Schauspieler*, 1818; *Gesetzliche Ordnungen für das Nationaltheater in Braunschweig*, 1818.
Bibl: H. Buchrath, AUGUST KLINGEMANN UND DIE DEUTSCHE ROMANTIK, 1948

Klinger, Friedrich Maximilian (1752–1831), German dramatist. His early works are representative of the STURM UND DRANG movement in GERMANY: *Otto*, pub 1775, a drama modelled after GOETHE's *Götz von Berlichingen*; *Das leidende Weib* (The Suffering Woman), pub 1775, a social drama on the lines of LENZ; with *Die Zwillinge* (The Twins), fp Hamburg 1776, he won first prize in a drama competition organized by F. L. SCHRÖDER. In his subsequent plays *Die neue Arria* (The new Arria), pub 1776, and *Simsone Grisaldo*, pub 1776, he attempted to combine heroic themes with elements of wild exuberance; *Sturm und Drang* (Storm and Stress), fp Leipzig 1776, gave the new movement its name. His next play *Stilpo und seine Kinder* (S. and his Children), 1880, is representative of his later work, classicist and historical dramas: *Der verbannte Göttersohn* (The Banished Son of God), *Der Derwisch* (The Dervish), *Die falschen Spieler* (The Cardsharpers), etc.
Bibl: W. Kliess, STURM UND DRANG, 1966; C. Hering, 1966

Klucht. In the Dutch late Middle Ages a form of short farcical play, an AFTERPIECE to the main play, the ABELE SPELEN.

Knipper, Olga Chekhova (1870–1959), Russian actress. Made her first appearance at the MOSCOW ART THEATRE under NEMIROVICH-DANCHENKO; most successful in the plays of CHEKHOV, whom she married in 1901: Arkadina in *The Seagull*, 1898; Helena Andreyevna in *Uncle Vanya*, 1899; Anna Petrovna in *Ivanov*, 1904; and Masha in *Three Sisters*, 1901. She was a 'poetic' actress, praised for her psychological subtlety; later she appeared in comic parts, e.g. Shlestova in GRIBOYEDOV's *Gore ot uma* (*Woe from Wit*), 1925.
Bibl: M. Turovskaja, 1959

Knittelvers. German rhyming couplets having four beats. They are found as far back as the 16th century, e.g. as declaimed by SACHS. Later, because of their simplicity, used for 'colloquial' effect, e.g. by GOETHE in his *Urfaust*, and WEDEKIND in the prologue to *Lulu*.

Knoblock, Edward (1874–1945), US playwright who later settled in England. Studied at Harvard where he attended BAKER's playwriting course. Achieved success with *Kismet*, 1911, a romantic Oriental MELODRAMA, in which SKINNER had a triumph as Haji the Beggar. Later filmed and turned into a musical, 1953. He also wrote *Marie-Odile*, 1915, and collaborated with other authors on a number of successful plays, notably *Milestones*, 1911, and *Mr Prohack*, 1927, both with A. BENNETT; *The Good Companions* (with PRIESTLEY, based on the latter's novel), 1931; *Evensong* (with Beverley Nichols, from the latter's novel), 1932. Much sought after as a play-doctor, also worked as a translator and adaptor.

Koch, Gottfried Heinrich (1703–75), German actor and theatre manager. Famous for his innovations in COSTUME design, he dispensed with the stylized French attire which had been worn up to that time and designed costumes to suit the play. In 1771 worked in Berlin, a forerunner of IFFLAND.

Kohout, Pavel (1928–), Czech playwright and director. His best-known plays include: *September Nights*, 1955; *Such a Love*, 1957; *The Third Sister*, 1960. He also adapted novels for the stage: *Around the World in 80 Days* (based on Jules Verne), 1962; *The War of the Molochs* (based on ČAPEK), 1962; *Josef Schweyk* (based on HAŠEK), 1963.

Kokoschka, Oskar (1886–), Austrian graphic artist and painter, whose dramatic works were early examples of an extreme EXPRESSIONISM. In his plays the struggle for freedom is seen in terms of sexual conflict, the language characterized by short, hysterical phrases leading to violent action: *Mörder, Hoffnung der Frauen* (Murderer, Hope of Women), first performed in a temporary open-air theatre set up in conjunction with the Kunstschau in Vienna 1909, staged by K., caused a riot. It was next performed together with *Hiob* (Job) at the Albert Theater in Dresden June 1917 with H. GEORGE and Käthe Richter dir and des by K. *Hiob* and *Der brennende Dornbusch* (The Burning Bush) were presented in 1919, dir K. in Berlin at REINHARDT's Kammerspiele, Job being played by Paul Graetz. They were among the first Expressionist productions in the German theatre. Later K. returned to the theatre as a designer, painting colourful flowing décor for Mozart's *Die Zauberflöte*, Salzburg 1955, and for the RAIMUND cycles at the BURGTHEATER in Vienna; *Moisassurs Zauberfluch* (M.'s Magic Oath), 1960; *Die unheilbringende Krone* (The Fatal Crown), 1961; *Die gefesselte Phantasie* (The Shackled Fantasy), 1962. His autobiography was published in 1974.
Bibl: H. Rischbieter (ed), BÜHNE UND BILDENDE KUNST IM 20. JAHRHUNDERT, 1968

Komisarjevskaya, Vera Fedorovna (1864–1910), Russian actress and producer. Made her stage début in 1891 as Betsy in STANISLAVSKY's production of *The Fruits of Enlightenment* (TOLSTOY), then toured the provinces and in 1896 made her first St Petersburg appearance in SUDERMANN's *Der Schmetterlingsschlacht* at the Alexandrinsky Theatre. In 1904 she founded her own company producing and acting leading roles in IBSEN's *A Doll's House* and *Hedda Gabler* and MAETERLINCK's *Pelléas et Mélisande*. In 1906 she invited MEYERHOLD to produce at her theatre. His tendency to a mechanical style of production and to treat actors like puppets contrasted with her developing interest in SYMBOLISM, which led to a break between them in 1907. From that time the direction was shared by her brother Theodore in partnership with YEVREINOV; in 1908 she toured the USA (Daly's Theatre, New York), retiring from the theatre in 1909.

Komisarjevsky, Theodore (1882–1954), Russian director. Was active at the theatre of his sister, VERA KOMISARJEVSKAYA from 1907, where he took over after MEYERHOLD's departure as manager, at first by himself, later with YEVREINOV producing ANDREYEV's *Black Masks* and IBSEN's *The Master Builder* (both 1907–09); in 1909, after the closure of the theatre, he formed a youth theatre; 1910–18 managed a studio theatre in Moscow, producing plays mainly by Symbolist writers including Andreyev, Kuzmin, Sologub (▷SYMBOLISM); in 1919 he emigrated to England where he produced plays by many authors including SHAKESPEARE at STRATFORD-UPON-AVON (*Macbeth*, 1933; *The Merry Wives of Windsor*, 1935; *Much Ado About Nothing*, 1936, with his wife, PEGGY ASHCROFT, as Beatrice; *King Lear*, 1938) and CHEKHOV; then went to Italy, Paris, New York, Vienna and in 1939 settled permanently in the USA. His best productions and designs were of 19th-century Russian plays (particularly Chekhov, GOGOL and TURGENEV), Russian and other Symbolists (PIRANDELLO, CROMMELYNCK), attempting to synthesize visual and musical elements with dance. Also director of operas and later films (in England). He wrote numerous books on theatre: *Myself and the Theatre*, 1930; *Costume of the Theatre*, 1932; *The Theatre and a Changing Civilization*, 1935.

Koonen, Alice (1899–1974), Soviet actress. Trained under STANISLAVSKY at the MOSCOW ART THEATRE. Wife of the director TAIROV, in whose productions she often played the lead, e.g. Flaubert's *Madame Bovary*, 1939.

Kopit, Arthur (1937–), US playwright. Studied at Harvard, where he had several of his plays produced by the students and won a play-writing contest. Achieved wide acclaim for his play *Oh Dad, Poor Dad, Mamma's Hung You in the Closet and I'm Feelin' So Sad*, 1960, a grotesque FARCE on the theme of the all-devouring mother, written in an Absurdist vein. *The Day the Whores Came Out to Play Tennis*, 1965, is also in this style. But with *Indians*, fp RSC,

London 1968, Aldwych Theatre, his second great success, K. changed his manner by adopting an imaginative documentary technique: the history of the extermination of the American Indian is told in the framework of Buffalo Bill's Wild West Show.

Koppenhöfer, Marie (1901–48), German actress. One of the most important tragediennes of her day, she worked with major companies: Munich Kammerspiele, 1922–25; Deutsches-Theater, BERLIN, 1925–26; State Theatre, Berlin, 1926–44; State Theatre, Munich, 1945–48; and with directors including BRECHT, FALCKENBERG, JESSNER, FEHLING and GRÜNDGENS. Among her major parts were Marie in Brecht's *Im Dickicht der Städte*, 1923, Queen Anne in his *Leben Eduards des Zweiten*, 1924; Amalia in SCHILLER's *Die Räuber*, 1926; KLEIST's *Penthesilea*, 1928, and Kunigunde in *Käthchen von Heilbronn*, 1937; Marion in BÜCHNER's *Dantons Tod*, 1939; title roles in GOETHE's *Iphigenie*, 1943, and GIRAUDOUX's *La Folle de Chaillot*, 1948.

Kops, Bernard (1926–), English dramatist. Member of a Jewish working-class family, he left school at the age of 13. His plays include: *The Hamlet of Stepney Green*, 1958; *Good-bye, World*, 1959; *Change for the Angel*, 1960; *The Dream of Peter Mann*, 1960; his one-act plays *Stray Cats and Empty Bottles* and *Enter Solly Gold*, 1962, were chosen for performance in the provinces by Centre 42. ▷WESKER.

Korneichuk, Alexander Yevdokimovich (1905–72), Soviet dramatist. Communist party official, whose work is committed to orthodox Communism: *Gibeles Kadry* (The Wreck of the Squadron), 1933, fp Red Army Theatre, deals with the scuttling of their own fleet by the Red sailors in 1918; *Platon Krechet*, 1934; *Pravda* (*Truth*), 1937; *Bogdan Khmelnitsky*, 1939, concerned with the Ukrainian peasant uprising against the Poles; *V stepyakh Ukrainy* (The Steppes of the Ukraine), 1942; *Front* (The Front), 1943. His later plays were mainly satirical comedies: *Misya Mistera Perkinsa v stranu Bolshevikov* (Mr Perkins's Mission to the Land of the Bolsheviks), fp 1944, Moscow Theatre of Satire; *Pochemu ulybaks svyozdy* (Why the Stars Smiled), 1956; *Nad Dneprom* (On the Dnieper), 1961, etc.

Körner, Hermine (1878–1960), German actress, director and manager. Made her début at the BURGTHEATER, Vienna in 1898; worked from 1905 to 1909 at the Düsseldorf theatre with LINDEMANN and DUMONT's company (experiences which greatly influenced her work), appeared in major theatres in Germany including BERLIN, Hamburg, Dresden, etc. and worked also as a director and manager (Munich and Dresden). She played many leading parts including the title role in WILDE's *Salomé* and LESSING's *Minna von Barnhelm*; Elizabeth in SCHILLER's *Maria Stuart*; Rebecca West in IBSEN's *Rosmersholm*; Lady Macbeth, Phaedra (RACINE), Iphigenie (GOETHE). Later she became famous for her playing of

Komisarjevsky's production of *King Lear* at Stratford-upon-Avon, 1938

Olga Knipper as Masha in CHEKHOV's *Three Sisters*, 1901

INHALT: OSKAR KOKOSCHKA: Mörder, Hoffnung der Frauen / PAUL LEPPIN: Daniel Jesus / Roman / ALFRED DÖBLIN: Gespräche mit Kalypso über die Musik / SIEGFRIED PFANKUCH: Liegt der Friede in der Luft / PAUL SCHEERBART: Gegenerklärung / KARL VOGT: Nissen als Theaterdirektor / MINIMAX: Kriegsbericht / Karikaturen

Mörder, Hoffnung der Frauen

Von Oskar Kokoschka

Personen:

Mann
Frau
Chor: Männer und Weiber.

Nachthimmel, Turm mit großer roter eiserner Käfigtür, Fackeln das einzige Licht, schwarzer Boden, so zum Turm aufsteigend, daß alle Figuren reliefartig zu sehen sind.

Der Mann

Weißes Gesicht, blaugepanzert, Stirntuch, das eine Wunde bedeckt, mit der Schar der Männer (wilde Köpfe, graue und rote Kopftücher, weiße, schwarze und braune Kleider, Zeichen auf den Kleidern, nackte Beine, hohe Fackelstangen, Schellen, Getöse), kriechen herauf mit vorgestreckten Stangen und Lichtern, versuchen müde und unwillig den Abenteurer zurückzuhalten, reißen sein Pferd nieder, er geht vor, sie lösen den Kreis um ihn, während sie mit langsamer Steigerung aufschreien.

Männer

Wir waren das flammende Rad um ihn,
Wir waren das flammende Rad um dich, Bestürmer verschlossener Festungen!

gehen zögernd wieder als Kette nach, er mit dem Fackelträger vor sich, geht voran.

Männer

Führ' uns Blasser!

Während sie das Pferd niederreißen wollen, steigen Weiber mit der Führerin die linke Stiege herauf.

Frau rote Kleider, offene gelbe Haare, groß,

Frau laut

Mit meinem Atem erflackert die blonde Scheibe der Sonne, mein Auge sammelt der Männer Frohlocken, ihre stammelnde Lust kriecht wie eine Bestie um mich.

Weiber

lösen sich von ihr los, sehen jetzt erst den Fremden.

Erstes Weib lüstern

Sein Atem saugt sich grüßend der Jungfrau an!

Kokoschka's *Mörder, Hoffnung der Frauen*, published in *Der Sturm* (▷WALDEN)

mature parts, such as the title role in GIRAUDOUX's *La Folle de Chaillot*, 1950 and 1959; Hecuba in EURIPIDES' *The Trojan Women*, 1958, and Atossa in AESCHYLUS' *The Persians*, 1960, both adapted by M. Braun.
Bibl: M. Braun, DIE SCHAUSPIELERIN HERMINE KÖRNER, 1964

Kornfeld, Paul (1889–1942), German dramatist. He wrote two early Expressionist plays: *Die Verführung* (The Seduction), 1917, and *Himmel und Hölle* (Heaven and Hell), 1920; later mainly COMEDIES: *Der ewige Traum* (The Eternal Dream), 1923; *Palme oder der Gekränkte* (P. or the Injured), Berlin 1924, Kammerspiele; *Kilian oder die gelbe Rose* (K. or the Yellow Rose), Frankfurt 1926, Schauspielhaus; and the historical drama *Jud Süss*, BERLIN 1930, Theater am Schiffbauerdamm. His German version of KĀLIDĀSA's *Śakuntalā*, Cologne 1925, Schauspielhaus, became well known.

Kortner, Fritz (1892–1970), Austrian actor and director. Trained at the BURGTHEATER, Vienna. Began his career in Mannheim, 1910; from 1911 in BERLIN and Vienna. A powerful personality with ugly but fascinating features, he specialized in heavy character parts. In the 1920s he was regarded as the embodiment of the Expressionist actor. He was a splendid Richard III and Shylock. After 1933 he went to England, where he appeared in some of Korda's films, and later to the USA, where he failed to get recognition as a leading actor but appeared in smaller parts in films. In 1949 he returned to Germany and worked above all as a director, mainly in Munich and Berlin. Irascible and demanding, he insisted on long rehearsals and the total dedication of his actors; he was undoubtedly the most important director in post-war Germany, almost the sole bearer of the great tradition of the 1920s. He concentrated on productions of SHAKESPEARE, MOLIÈRE and the German classics. Among the modern plays he produced was his own marital drama *Zweisprache*, 1964. Autobiography: *Aller Tage Abend*, 1959.

Kott, Jan (1914–), Polish poet, critic and professor of literature at the University of Warsaw. After starting as a Marxist, he turned, in the Stalin era, to criticism of power systems. Inspired by BROOK's production of *Titus Andronicus*, 1955, he explored in his brilliantly original study *Shakespeare, Our Contemporary* (German edition, 1964, under the title *Shakespeare Heute*), the relevance of SHAKESPEARE to our time, mainly using the historical plays to demonstrate the unchanging mechanisms of the power structure. With this book he gained a European reputation and in turn influenced many modern Shakespeare productions, e.g. Brook's *King Lear*, 1963. In all his dramatic criticism he views theatre as a commentary on life in its various aspects – social, political and aesthetic. His most recent work, *Theatre Notebook 1947–67*, was published in 1968. In 1951 and 1955 he was awarded the State Prize in Literature and Literary Studies and in 1964 he received the Herder Award in Vienna. He went to the USA in 1966 to take up a visiting professorship at Yale, and is at present Professor of Comparative Literature at the State University of New York, Stone Brook, N.Y.
Bibl: S. Melchinger, SHAKESPEARE AUF DEM MODERNEN WELTTHEATER, 1964

Kotzebue, August (1761–1819), German playwright. The most popular dramatist of his time, worked in Vienna 1797–99, but spent most of his life in Russia, finally as a personal envoy of Tsar Alexander I. He also edited a weekly literary magazine which violently attacked the nationalist German youth movement and led to his being stabbed to death by a fanatical German student. He wrote about 200 plays, sentimental MELODRAMAS with fine parts for actors which excited audiences but later became unfashionable. Most successful was *Menschenhass und Reue* (Misanthropy and Remorse), 1789; seen in London as *The Stranger* at DRURY LANE, 1798; *Der Opfertod* (The Sacrificial Death) and *Das Kind der Liebe* (The Child of Love). The only play which has remained in REPERTORY till the present day is *Die deutschen Kleinstädter* (The German Small-town People), 1803, a provincial COMEDY.

Krahl, Hilde (1917–), Austrian actress. She began her career in CABARET in Vienna and, from 1936, appeared mainly at the Theater in der Josefstadt. She joined the ENSEMBLE of the BURGTHEATER in 1966. Among her best performances can be counted: the title role in HEBBEL's *Maria Magdalena*, 1942; Louise in SCHILLER's *Kabale und Liebe*, 1942; Schiller's Maria Stuart and SHAKESPEARE's Lady Macbeth, 1960. Her mature performance as the old woman in BRECHT's *Mutter Courage*, Hersfeld Festival 1967, places her in the ranks of the outstanding interpreters of this role, i.e. THERESE GIEHSE, LOTTE LENYA and HELENE WEIGEL.

Krasiński, Zygmunt (1812–59), Polish poet and dramatist. With MICKIEWICZ and SLOWACKI, one of the great Polish romantic writers. His dramatic works – *Nieboska Komedia* (*The Undivine Comedy*), first published 1835, inspired by GOETHE's *Faust* II, a portrait of the 1832 revolution written in poetic prose, and *Irydon* (Iridion), pub 1836 – are considered classic works of Polish literature. They were not performed until 1902 and 1908 respectively. The best known production of *Nieboska Komedia* was by L. SCHILLER in Warsaw in 1926.
Bibl: M. Gardner, 1919

Krasna, Norman (1909–), US producer and dramatist. A journalist by profession until the early 1930s, he became a successful film scriptwriter, later film producer. Made an international reputation as a dramatist with *Sunday in New York*, 1961. Other works include: *Louder, Please*, 1931; *Dear Ruth*, 1944; *Time for Elizabeth* (with Groucho Marx, 1948); *Kind Sir*, 1953; *Who Was That Lady I Saw You With*, 1958, etc.

Kraus, Karl (1874–1936), Viennese satirical writer. In 1889 he formed, edited and wrote (eventually as sole contributor) the critical and satirical magazine *Die Fackel*. K. opposed the theatre of REINHARDT and PISCATOR and attempted by giving recitations to provide new insight into the works of SHAKESPEARE and NESTROY. He favoured BRECHT and WEDEKIND as playwrights, giving a private performance of the latter's *Die Büchse der Pandora* in Vienna in 1905. His dramatic works include *Literatur*, 1921; *Wolkenkuckucksheim* based on ARISTOPHANES, 1923; *Traumstück*, 1923; *Die Unüberwindlichen*, 1928. His best-known work is the immense epic *Die Letzten Tage der Menschheit*, pub 1922, fp 1964 at the Theater an der Wien, in a very abbreviated version; it is a vast canvas of World War I, composed of short satirical and fantastic scenes portraying the horrors of warfare.
Bibl: P. Schick, 1965

Krauss, Werner (1884–1959), German actor. Made his first appearance in provincial theatres with German touring companies. In 1913 REINHARDT engaged him for the Deutsches-Theater, BERLIN, where K. made his name with a series of WEDEKIND plays, 1914, including *Der Kammersänger*, *Der Marquis von Keith* and *Lulu*. Subsequently he appeared in Berlin (State Theatre and Deutsches-Theater) and Vienna (BURGTHEATER) in many leading classical parts including Macbeth, Richard III, Julius Caesar, Lear, Shylock and the heroes of SCHILLER's plays. Among his best-known modern parts were the crippled piper in Reinhardt's production of *Das Mirakel* by Vollmöller, Berlin and New York 1914, King Magnus in SHAW's *The Apple Cart*, Napoleon in *Campo di Maggio*, Giovacchino Forzano's play about the Hundred Days on which his collaborator was Mussolini, and the title role in ZUCKMAYER's *Der Hauptmann von Köpenick*, 1931. He also appeared in many of G. HAUPTMANN's plays, giving one of his most famous performances as Clausen in *Vor Sonnenuntergang*, 1932, seen in London 1933. In his character studies he combined genius and virtuosity, seeming to transform himself completely into the character he was playing.
Bibl: H. Weigel, 1959; J. Bab, KRÄNZE DEM MIMEN, 1954

Krejča, Otomar (1921–), Czech director. Began his career as an actor in Prague in 1945 and from 1950 was at the National Theatre there; in 1956 he turned to directing and soon became the theatre's artistic director, working in collaboration with the DRAMATURG Karel Kraus and the designer SVOBODA: CHEKHOV's *The Seagull*, 1960; *Romeo and Juliet*, 1963; TOPOL's *Carnival's End*, fp 1964. In 1965 he left the Czech National Theatre; in his opinion there was too much bureaucracy and too many non-artistic influences. He founded his own theatre with a small company, the Theatre Before the Gate, which opened in November 1965 with Topol's *The Cat on the Rails*; from 1966 successfully toured foreign countries with productions including Chekhov's *Three Sisters* and SCHNITZLER's *The Green Cockatoo*. In 1971 he was deprived of his position as head of the Theatre Before the Gate by order of the government. His theatre is an actors' theatre extended into psychological realism which is often highly strung, anti-ideological and devoted to the ruthless pursuit of truth advocated by STANISLAVSKY as a young man. He must be considered one of the leading directors of contemporary European theatre.

Krleža, Miroslav (1893–), Croatian writer of short stories, novels and plays. His Symbolist plays (▷SYMBOLISM) are collected under the title *Legende*, 1933; his anti-militaristic work has Expressionist elements, e.g. the TRILOGY *Galicija* or *U logoru*, *Golgota* (Golgotha), 1922, and *Vučjak* (Wolf Village), 1923. Later he turned to realism with another trilogy dealing with the death and self-destruction of the bourgeoisie, written with deep psychological insight and force: *U agoniji* (Agony), 1928; *Gospoda Glembajevi* (The Glembays), 1929; *Leda*, 1930.

Werner Krauss in *The Captain of Köpenick* by ZUCKMAYER and in G. HAUPTMANN's *Before Sunset*

Krones, Therese (1801–30), Austrian actress. One of the greatest players in the Viennese popular theatre, she first appeared on stage at the age of five with her father's travelling company. In 1821 K. F. Hensler offered her a contract at the Leopoldstädter Theater in Vienna, where she created many roles in plays by Gleich, Meisl, Bäuerle and RAIMUND; she also appeared in plays with which she was credited as author, but which were in fact written by her brother Josef (?–1832). Her contemporaries admired her innocence, charm and vitality on stage; she became a legend in her lifetime; GRILLPARZER called her the 'inimitable Krones'. Bibl: O. Rommel, DIE ALT-WIENER VOLKSKOMÖDIE, 1952

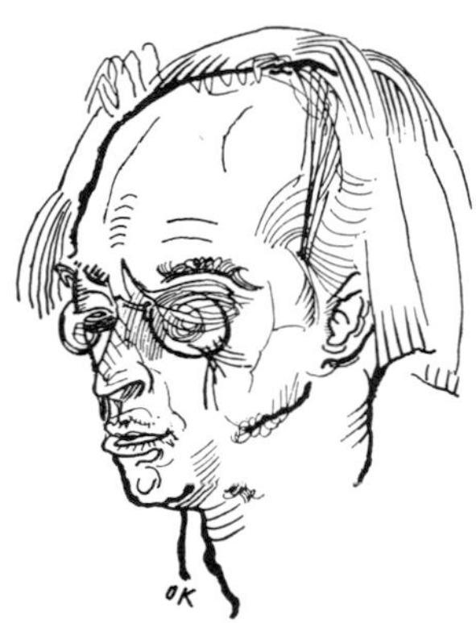

Karl Kraus, sketch by KOKOSCHKA

Kruczkowski, Leon (1900–62), Polish novelist and dramatist. His first novel, *Kordian i cham* (Rebel and Peasant), was adapted for the stage by L. SCHILLER in Warsaw in 1935. After World War II he was appointed chairman of the Polish Writers' Organization (1949–56); he later became a Member of Parliament and of the Polish State Council; he was DRAMATURG of the Polski Theatre in Warsaw 1951–55. His works include: *Odwety* (The Requital), 1948; *Neimcy* (The Germans), fp Craców 1949 (there was a famous production by AXER in 1955), which deals with a scientist during the dictatorship of Hitler; *Juliusz i Ethel*, Warsaw 1954, the case of the Rosenbergs; *Odwiedziny* (The Visit), Warsaw 1955; *Pierwcy dzień wolności* (The First Day of Freedom), 1959; *Smierć gubernatora* (The Death of the Governor), based on ANDREYEV, 1961.

Krutch, Joseph Wood (1893–1970), US theatre critic and writer. Drama critic of the *Nation*, 1924–52, and professor at Columbia University, New York, he has written influential books on drama and theatre, the best known of which is *The American Drama Since 1918*, 2nd ed, 1957.

Therese Krones in RAIMUND's *Der Bauer als Millionär*, 1826

Kummerfeld, Karoline (1745–1814), Austrian actress. Appeared with K. E. ACKERMANN's company, 1758–67, and KOCH's company, 1767–68, in Leipzig where she was greatly admired by GOETHE. Her style of acting was severely criticized by SCHRÖDER. Her volume of reminiscences *Lebenserinnerungen*, 2/1915, is an important source of theatre history.

Kurz, Johann Felix von (known as Bernardon; 1717–84), Austrian actor. Author and actor of original Viennese *Hanswurstiaden* in which he appeared as Bernardon, a character he had created, who was a variation of the traditional HANSWURST: *Der lebendig verbrannte Zauberer* (The Magician burned alive); *Die von Minerva beschützte Unschuld oder Die Vereinigung der Liebesgötter* (Innocence protected by Minerva or the Defence of the Gods of Love). He knew how to combine baroque magical elements with the agility of the COMMEDIA DELL'ARTE. In his later years he had to fight against rationalistic theatre reformers (primarily SONNENFELS, who had the equivalent position in AUSTRIA to GOTTSCHED in GERMANY). His admirers included F. L. SCHRÖDER.
Bibl: O. Rommel, DIE ALT-WIENER VOLKSKOMÖDIE, 1952

Kutscher, Artur (1878–1960), German theatre historian. From 1916 professor at Munich University, where his pupils included many who later became well-known critics, directors and managers; BRECHT also attended his lectures *c.* 1920; he searched for the roots of all acting in ancient MIME theatre and attempted to build up a science of theatre history on this basis. His works include: *Grundriss der Theaterwissenschaft*, 2 vols, 2nd ed 1949; *Wedekind*, rev ed 1964, and his memoirs *Der Theaterprofessor*, 1960.

Kyd, Thomas (1558–94), English dramatist. He was a close friend of MARLOWE. Several plays have been attributed to him, e.g. *Soliman and Perseda*, *c.* 1589–92, and an early version of *Hamlet*, *c.* 1580, but only two are definitely known to be his – *The Spanish Tragedy*, pub *c.* 1592, and later revised by JONSON, on which his reputation is based; and *Cornelia*, pub 1594. The former was the most popular and influential play of its time; an exciting melodramatic TRAGEDY in blank verse in which K. depicts the characters skilfully. Its dramatic craftsmanship and theatrical success inspired the tragedies of revenge of the Elizabethan period.
Bibl: F. Bowers, ELIZABETHAN REVENGE TRAGEDY, 1940

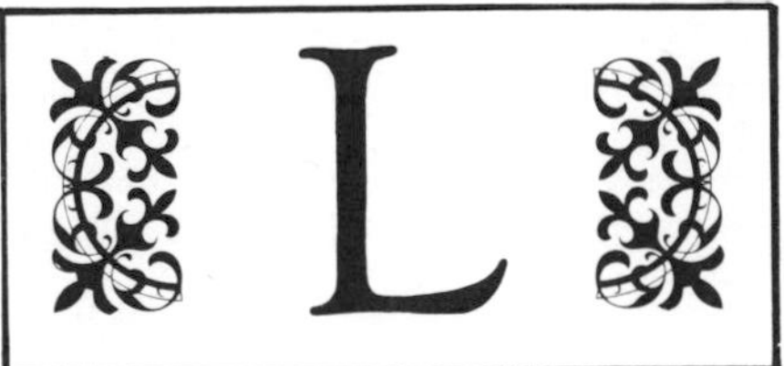

Labiche, Eugène (E. Martin L.; 1815–88), French dramatist. Helped to raise the standard of French FARCE and revived the VAUDEVILLE in the tradition of SARDOU. He wrote more than 150 light comedies attacking human weaknesses with gentle humour. His best-known works include: *Un Chapeau de paille d'Italie* (*The Italian Straw Hat*), 1851, produced as *Horse Eats Hat* in New York, 1936; *Le Voyage de M. Perrichon*, 1860; *La Cagnotte*, 1864.
Bibl; P. Soupoult, 1945

La Chaussée, Pierre Claude Nivelle de (1692–1754), French dramatist. Founder and principal exponent of the *comédie larmoyante*, sentimental plays full of moral pathos which signalled the transition to the DRAME BOURGEOIS. His best-known works include: *Le Préjugé à la mode*, 1735; *Mélanide*, 1741.
Bibl: G. Lanson, *N. de L. C.*, 2/1903

Laffan, Kevin (1922–), English dramatist. Best known as the author of *Zoo, Zoo, Widdershins Zoo*, 1968, which won first prize at the National Union of Students' Drama Festival in 1969; *It's a Two-Foot-Six-Inches-Above-the-Ground World*, 1970, and *The Superannuated Man*, 1971, Dublin Festival.

Lagerkvist, Pär (1891–1974), Swedish dramatist and poet. A major exponent of modern Swedish theatre, his dramatic work falls into two phases: the early plays are characterized by a mood of despair (influenced by STRINDBERG and MAETERLINCK), whereas in his second phase he moves towards realism. His works include: *Sista människan* (*The Last Man*), 1917; a series of one-act plays: *Den svåra stunden* (*The Difficult Hour*), 1918; *Himlens hemlighet* (*The Secret of Heaven*), 1919; *Den osynlige* (*The Invisible One*), 1923; *Han som fick leva om sitt liv* (*He Who Lived His Life over Again*), 1928; *Konungen* (*The King*), 1932; *Bödeln* (*The Hangman*), 1934; *Mannen utan själ* (*The Man Without a Soul*), 1936; *Seger i mörker* (*Victory in the Dark*), 1939; *Midsommardröm i fattighuset* (*Midsummer Dream in the Poor House*), 1941; *Den vises sten* (*The Philosopher's Stone*), 1948; he dramatized his novel *Barabbas*, 1953, which he later made into a film script. He also wrote several essays on the theatre, the most important being 'Modern Theatre', 1918, in which he advocated a symbiosis of realism and SYMBOLISM in the theatre. He was awarded the Nobel Prize for Literature in 1951.
Bibl: A. Gustafson, A HISTORY OF SWEDISH LITERATURE, 1961

La Grange (Charles Varlet; 1639–92), French actor. He joined MOLIÈRE's company in 1659 and played young lovers, e.g. the title role in *Dom Juan*, 1665; Mercure in *Amphitryon*, 1668; Clitandre in *George Dandin*, 1668; Valère in *Tartuffe*, 1669; the hero in RACINE's *Alexandre et Porus* and in other contemporary plays. He kept a register of plays produced at the Palais Royal, which has proved an important historical document of the period.
Bibl: B. E. and G. Ph. Young, LE REGISTRE DE LA GRANGE, 1947

La Mama. Originally 'Café La Mama', an avant-garde theatre founded in New York, 1962, by Ellen Stewart, a fashion designer and theatre enthusiast. Its main function was to enable young playwrights to see their plays for a few performances in inexpensive productions. Became the La Mama Experimental Theatre Club and is now housed in its own premises, built with the aid of foundation money, on 4th Street in the East Village, New York. Many important avant-garde playwrights achieved their first performances and recognition owing to the courage and intuitive feeling for talent which is Ellen Stewart's outstanding gift. Among them are ITALLIE, SHEPARD, MELFI, ROCHELLE OWENS, MEGAN TERRY. The director O'HORGAN is also a product of the La Mama theatre. The troupe has toured widely in Europe.

Lampoon. A coarse, usually short, satire attacking an individual. The word is derived from the French *lampons*=let us drink.

Lang, Alexander Matheson (1879–1948), English ACTOR-MANAGER and dramatist. After touring the USA with LILLIE LANGTRY, the English provinces with ELLEN TERRY and the West Indies with BENSON, he appeared with the latter in London and subsequently under Vedrenne-Barker at the ROYAL COURT THEATRE. Later he took his own company to South Africa, Australia and India with SHAKESPEARE and modern romantic drama. After his return in 1913 he scored his greatest success in the title role in *Mr Wu* by Harry Vernon and Harold Owen at the Strand Theatre, which also resulted in his autobiography *Mr Wu Looks Back*, 1940. He produced several Shakespeare plays for the OLD VIC THEATRE, 1914: *The Taming of the Shrew*, *Hamlet* and *The Merchant of Venice*. Later productions in which he also appeared as an actor: *The Wandering Jew*, by E. Temple Thurston, 1920; *Jew Süss*, adapted by DUKES, based on FEUCHTWANGER, 1929; and *The Chinese Bungalow*, based on a novel by Marion Osmond, in his own adaptation, 1925. He took over the management of the Lyric Theatre in 1918, opening with *The Purple Mask*, his own adaptation. After 1916 he also appeared in films. He was married to the actress Hutin Britton.

Lange, Hartmut (1937–), German dramatist. Chief DRAMATURG at the Deutsches-Theater, East Berlin, 1961–64; moved to West Berlin in 1965. Main works:

Senftenberger Erzählungen (S. Tales), written 1960; *Marski*, a COMEDY about a lone wolf who learns that it is much more pleasant and productive to work in a collective, written 1962/63, fp Frankfurt 1966; *Der Hundprozess/Herakles*, two plays which belong together dealing with Stalin, one showing the negative, the other the positive side of the dictator, fp BERLIN 1968, dir H. Heyme; *Die Gräfin von Rathenow*, 1969, based on KLEIST's novel *Die Marquise von O.*
Bibl: H. Rischbieter & E. Wendt, DEUTSCHE DRAMATIK IN WEST UND OST, 1965

Langer, František (1888–1965), Czech playwright. One of the best modern writers in Czechoslovakia, his social COMEDIES are reminiscent of SHAW and his serious plays are influenced by German EXPRESSIONISM. The first category includes: *Velbloud uchem jehly* (*The Camel Through the Needle's Eye*), 1923, seen on BROADWAY in a THEATRE GUILD production. The second category contains his best-known work *Periférie* (The Outskirts), 1925, a TRAGEDY of existential guilt set in the outskirts of Prague. Other works: *Grand Hotel Nevada*, 1927; *Orbráceni Ferdyše Pištory* (The Conversion of Ferdys Pistora), 1929; *Dvaasedmdesátka* (Prisoners 91), 1937.
Bibl: E. Konrad, 1949

Langhoff, Wolfgang (1901–66), German actor, director and manager. Began his career as an actor in Wiesbaden and Düsseldorf. In the early 1920s his interest in Marxism led him into political activity and he directed plays in amateur working-class theatres; in 1933 he was sent to a concentration camp, where he wrote his autobiography *Die Moorsoldaten*, 1935; then emigrated to Switzerland, appearing in leading parts at the ZURICH SCHAUSPIELHAUS (Faust, Egmont; Brant in O'NEILL's *Mourning Becomes Electra*). As director of the Deutsches-Theater, East Berlin, 1946–62, he emphasized new interpretations of classics, e.g. *Faust*, 1949, *King Lear*, 1957, and supported young dramatists of East Germany, e.g. HACKS.
Bibl: E. Krull, 1962

Langner, Lawrence (1890–1962), British-born US manager and playwright. An important figure in US theatre, he helped to organize the Washington Square Players in 1914 and later the THEATRE GUILD, of which he was first a director and later manager with his wife Armina Marshall and Theresa Helburn. He founded and was first president of the American Shakespeare Festival at Stratford, Conn., and was the author of several plays including *Another Way Out*, 1916; *The Family Exit*, 1917; *Matinata*, 1920; *Henry Behave*, 1926; *These Modern Women*, 1928; *The Pursuit of Happiness*, 1932; *Suzanna and the Elders*, 1939, with Armina Marshall. He also wrote an autobiography, *The Magic Curtain*, 1951, and a book on the history of the Theatre Guild, *The Play's the Thing*.

Langtry, Lillie (Emilie Charlotte le Breton; 1853–1929), English actress.

Karoline Kummerfeld

Thomas Kyd's *The Spanish Tragedy*, title-page dated 1615

Lillie Langtry, 1880

Daughter of the Dean of Jersey, she married the diplomat Edward Langtry and was prominent in London society: close friend of Edward VII. In 1881 she became the first English society lady to appear on the stage; she had a sensational success, more for her beauty and her position in society than her talent. Later she successfully organized her own company touring the English provinces, and the USA with LANG, but she was never considered a serious actress. In 1897 her husband died and ten years later she married Sir Hugo de Bath.

Lardner, Ring (1885–1933), US journalist and humorist. Originally a sports reporter, he became one of America's most acute satirists with a brilliant gift for language. He wrote a number of nonsense playlets which anticipate some of the Surrealist and Absurdist dramas of the 1950s and 1960s: *Clemo-Uti* (The Water Lilies); *The Tridget of Griva*; *I Gaspiri* (The Upholsterers); *Cora or Fun at a Spa*. A more conventional COMEDY *June Moon*, written in collaboration with KAUFMAN, ran for 273 performances on BROADWAY, 1929.

Larionov, Michael (1881–1964), Russian painter and stage designer. With Natalia Goncharova influential in the rapid development of the graphic and plastic arts in RUSSIA before 1914; he evolved a style of non-objective painting, Rayonism. In his designs for the Ballets Russes, after 1915, when he moved to Western Europe, he returned to traditional Russian folklore forms: *Soleil de Nuit* (Rimsky-Korsakov, 1915), *Histoires Naturelles* (Ravel, 1916), *Les Contes Russes*, 1917; *Chout* (Prokofiev, 1921); *Renard* (Stravinsky, 1929). He also worked occasionally as a choreographer and as a librettist; he owned an extensive collection of historical theatre material and incorporated Asian and Turkish forms of theatre in his work.
Bibl: H. Rischbieter (ed), BÜHNE UND BILDENDE KUNST IM 20. JAHRHUNDERT, 1968

Laroche, Johann (known as **Kasperl**; 1745–1806), Austrian comedian. From the middle of the 18th century appeared at the Theater in der Leopoldstadt in Vienna, where in numerous works by MARINELLI and K. F. Hensler he created the character of KASPERL, the most important Viennese variation of HANSWURST.
Bibl: O. Rommel, DIE ALT-WIENER VOLKSKOMÖDIE, 1952

La Roche, Karl von (1794–1884), German actor. Began as a singer in opera and SINGSPIEL. When in Weimar, 1823–33, he was much praised by GOETHE and appeared in the first staging of *Faust*, 1829. After 1833 he joined the BURGTHEATER in Vienna where he was equally successful in tragic and comic parts. His most noteworthy performance was as Malvolio in *Twelfth Night*.

Lasker-Schüler, Else (1869–1945), German Expressionist poet. In her two dramatic works she returns to the milieu of her childhood: factory workers, proletarians, outcasts in Wuppertal around the turn of the century. *Die Wupper*, pub 1909, fp BERLIN 1919, Deutsches-Theater, is still occasionally performed. Her second play deals with a large Jewish family and their exposure to anti-Semitic attacks by the petty-bourgeoisie: *Arthur Aronymus und seine Väter* (A.A. and his fathers) fp 1936, ZURICH SCHAUSPIELHAUS, dir GINSBERG, revived 1968 in Wuppertal.
Bibl: J. P. Wallmann, 1966

Laterna magica. Czechoslovakian revue-style entertainment (▷REVUE) using live action and projected images to produce surprising illusions. Devised by SVOBODA and RADOK in 1957 and originally designed for the Czech pavilion at the World's Fair in Brussels, it is a mixture of drama and film-clips, which has been regularly presented at Prague.

Latin America. Theatre life here has been concentrated from the first in a few cities, mainly Buenos Aires, Santiago, Rio de Janeiro and Mexico City. Soon after the Spanish conquest, still in the 16th century, the COMEDIES of Spanish folk theatre were presented by travelling companies and amateur theatres. The Catholic Church made use of religious plays for its missionary activities. AUTOS SACRAMENTALES in the tradition of CALDERÓN were written by the nun Juana Inés de la Cruz (1651–95), who lived in Mexico. Not until the 19th century did the Latin American theatre develop its own original themes: in 1886 the former CLOWN José J. Podestá produced in Buenos Aires the play *Juan Moreira* based on a Gaucho legend, which initiated the popular genre of Gaucho drama. Most important theatrical activity after 1945 in Buenos Aires, where there are 40 theatres with a world REPERTOIRE. In Chile MARGARITA XIRGU, who emigrated from Spain after the Civil War, ran the Academy of Dramatic Art attached to the NATIONAL THEATRE. In Mexico City, in the last few decades, besides the two big theatres, Palacio de Bellas Artes and Teatro de los Insurgentes, more than 20 medium-sized and smaller theatres have emerged. There are signs of theatrical activity also in all the other Latin American countries; in Cuba, in the service of the government.

Laube, Heinrich (1806–84), Austrian writer and theatre manager. With GUTZKOW the main exponent of the Junges Deutschland movement; important journalist, who for some time edited *Die Zeitung für die elegante Welt*; in 1848 he became a member of the Frankfurt National Assembly. During his time as director of the BURGTHEATER in Vienna, 1849–67, he established a literary REPERTOIRE of a high standard; his style of production emphasized DIALOGUE, strict adherence to the author's text and simplification of décor. In 1869-70 he managed the Leipzig Municipal Theatre, and 1871–79 the Vienna State Theatre which he had founded. His best-known dramatic works are: *Graf Essex* (Lord Essex), Vienna 1856; *Die Karlsschüler* (The Students of the Charles School), Dresden 1846; and *Rokoko*, Dresden 1842. Other works on dramatic theory: *Briefe über das deutsche Theater*; *Das Burgtheater*; *Das norddeutsche Theater*.
Bibl: G. Zobel, HEINRICH LAUBES DRAMATURGIE, 1967; E. Ziemann, HEINRICH LAUBE ALS THEATERKRITIKER, 1934

Laughton, Charles (1899–1962), English actor. Made his stage début at the age of 26 as Ossip in GOGOL's *The Government Inspector*, 1926, followed by the title role in *Mr Prohack*, by A. BENNETT and KNOBLOCK in 1927 at the ROYAL COURT THEATRE. He immediately established himself as one of the best character actors in England with excellent voice control, combining a sense of comic inventiveness with intellectual discipline. From 1933 he appeared at the OLD VIC THEATRE under GUTHRIE in parts such as Lopakhin in *The Cherry Orchard* – considered one of the most brilliant English CHEKHOV interpretations – and Shakespearean roles including Henry VIII, Macbeth, Prospero in *The Tempest*, and Angelo in *Measure for Measure*. He was the first English actor to perform at the COMÉDIE-FRANÇAISE, in 1937, as Sganarelle in MOLIÈRE's *Le Médecin malgré lui*. In 1947 he made his famous appearance in BRECHT's *Galileo* in Los Angeles, which he had adapted in collaboration with the author. Probably his greatest success came as the Devil in an adaptation of the second act of SHAW's *Man and Superman*, under the title *Don Juan in Hell*. In New York he directed plays such as WOUK's *The Caine Mutiny Court Martial*, 1954; Shaw's *Major Barbara*, 1956, and had an outstanding film career.
Bibl: B. Brecht, AUFBAU EINER ROLLE, LAUGHTONS GALILEI, 1956; E. Lanchester, CHARLES LAUGHTON AND I, 1938.

Laurents, Arthur (1920–), US playwright. Graduated from Cornell University and achieved success with his war play *Home of the Brave*, 1945, which was followed by *Bird Cage*, 1950, and *The Time of the Cuckoo*, 1952, which was filmed as *Summertime*, 1955, and became the basis of a musical (with RODGERS), 1965, under the title *Do I Hear a Waltz?*. *A Clearing in the Woods*, 1956, is a psychological drama about race prejudice. L.'s greatest successes have been the LIBRETTI for the musicals *West Side Story*, 1957, music BERNSTEIN, a version of SHAKESPEARE's *Romeo and Juliet* set in New York, and *Gypsy*, 1959, music Jules Styne, a backstage musical about the strip-tease artist Gypsy Rose Lee, and her dominating mother. *Invitation to a March*, 1960, is an entertaining play with a psychological background which ends in fantasy.

Lawler, Ray (1921–), Australian actor and dramatist. Best known for his realistic play *Summer of the Seventeenth Doll*, dir John Sumner, Melbourne 1956 and London 1957, with himself in the leading part. Other works include *Piccadilly Bushman*, Liverpool 1965.

Lawrence, David Herbert (1885–1931), English novelist, whose dramatic work did not achieve recognition on the stage until long after his death. In 1965, at the ROYAL COURT THEATRE, his first play, *A Collier's Friday Night*, written 1906, was directed by Peter Gill who followed it in 1967 with *The Daughter-in-Law*. In 1968 Gill restaged these two plays, together with *The Widowing of Mrs Holroyd*, in a special Lawrence season. Written before World War I they depicted realistically the Nottinghamshire mining community in which L. grew up.

Lawrence, Gertrude (G. Klasen; 1898–1952). English actress who studied under ITALIA CONTI and first appeared in PANTOMIME at the age of 12. She had great vitality and charm. Her career was mainly in MUSICAL COMEDY and REVUE but she had a big success in COWARD's *Private Lives*, 1930. She also appeared in his nine one-act plays, *Tonight at 8.30*, 1934–36. In New York she appeared in a number of productions, including *Pygmalion*, the musicals *The King and I* and *Lady in the Dark*. She married the US theatre manager Richard Aldrich. Her reminiscences were published under the title *A Star Danced*.

Lawson, John Howard (1895–), US dramatist. Made his reputation as a playwright in the 1920s with a series of politically committed plays which incorporated techniques of CABARET and the 'living newspaper'. During the McCarthy era his film scenarios were blacklisted. His works include: *Standards*, 1914; *Servant-Master-Lover*, 1917; *Roger Bloomer*, 1923; *Processional*, 1925; *Nirvana*, 1926; *Loud Speaker*, 1927; *The International*, 1928; *Success Story*, 1932; *The Pure in Heart*, 1934; *Gentlewoman*, 1934; *Marching Song*, 1937; *Parlor Magic*, 1940. He wrote *Theory and Techniques of Playwriting*, 1936.
Bibl: G. Rabkin, DRAMA AND COMMITMENT, 1964

Lazzo. Comic byplay consisting mostly of mimicry in the COMMEDIA DELL'ARTE. There was a standard repertory of *lazzi*, e.g. clowning, tricks, surprise actions, jokes, etc.

Lebedev, Yevgeni Alexeyevich (1917–), Soviet actor. Made his début in 1940 in Tiflis. He was with the Theatre of the Leningrad Komsomol, 1949–56, and from 1949 worked mainly with the director TOVSTONOGOV, playing roles like Rogozhin in DOSTOYEVSKY's *The Idiot*, 1957; Monakhov in GORKY's *The Barbarians*, 1959; the title role in BRECHT's *Arturo Ui*, 1962, dir AXER. He is an outstanding character actor combining finely observed gestures with psychological undertones.

Lecouvreur, Adrienne (1692–1730), French actress. In her 13 years at the COMÉDIE-FRANÇAISE her natural style of acting based on pure emotion prevailed against the academic diction of her rivals Mlle Duclos and Mlle Desmares; she advocated historically accurate COSTUME. She made her début at the CF in 1717 in

Charles Laughton as Tony Pepelli in WALLACE's *On the Spot*, 1930

Adrienne Lecouvreur as Cornélie in *La Mort de Pompée* by Corneille, *c.* 1725

Laterna magica

Ray Lawler's *Summer of the Seventeenth Doll*, 1956

the title role of CRÉBILLON's *Electre*, followed by Monime in RACINE's *Mithridate*, 1717. She excelled in tragic roles including first productions of plays by Crébillon, La Motte and VOLTAIRE: *Artémire*, 1720; *Hérode et Mariamne*, 1724; and in Racine's *Phèdre*, and CORNEILLE's *Bérénice*. Her fame and her hectic love life inspired plays like *Adrienne Lecouvreur*, 1849, by SCRIBE and Legouvé.
Bibl: W. de Spens, 1961; R. L. Voyer de Paulmy, ADRIENNE LECOUVREUR ET MAURICE DE SAXE; LEUR LETTRES D'AMOUR, 1926

Ledoux, Fernand (1897–), French actor. Joined the COMÉDIE-FRANÇAISE in 1921, playing minor roles until the early 1930s and then as a leading actor and director. Major parts include: title roles in MOLIÈRE's *Tartuffe*, 1951, and HOFMANNSTHAL's *Everyman*, Lyons Festival, 1951; he played the lead and directed PIRANDELLO's *Six Characters in Search of an Author*, CF, 1952. He has also appeared in films.

Lee, Nathaniel (1649?–92). English dramatist (▷RESTORATION DRAMA). Author of bombastic and extravagant TRAGEDIES on subjects taken from antiquity, such as Nero, Mithridates, Caesar and Constantine. His first three plays were written in heroic couplets; then he turned to blank verse. His best and most successful plays, both in this style, were *The Rival Queens* (about Alexander the Great), 1677, which remained in the REPERTOIRE for over a hundred years, and *Lucius Junius Brutus*, 1680. In his day his plays were very popular and frequently performed.
Bibl: B. Dobree, RESTORATION TRAGEDY, 1929

Legal, Ernst (1881–1955), German actor, director and manager. Started his career as actor and producer at the State Theatre, BERLIN, 1920–24, and later turned to management; from 1945 to 1952 he was GENERALINTENDANT there. He combined extensive literary knowledge with talent as an organizer and a feeling for COMEDY. He was the first to play Galy Gay in BRECHT's *Mann ist Mann* in 1926. Among his most famous productions were: ZUCKMAYER's *Der Hauptmann von Köpenick*, 1947, and SHAKESPEARE's *The Comedy of Errors*, 1949.
Bibl: H. Barkhoff, 1965

Le Gallienne, Eva (1899–), US actress and producer. Studied at RADA and made her stage début in London in 1914. She went to New York in 1915 and established her career playing Julie in MOLNÁR's *Liliom*, 1921; and developing into a character actress in plays by IBSEN, including Hilda Wangel in *The Master Builder*, 1925, Ella Rentheim in *John Gabriel Borkman*, 1926 and 1946, which she also produced, and *Hedda Gabler*, 1928; and Masha in CHEKHOV's *Three Sisters*, 1926. In 1926 she founded the Civic Repertory Theatre producing a REPERTOIRE of plays from world literature. In 1946 she was associated with the short-lived American Repertory Theatre, which opened with SHAKESPEARE's *Henry VIII* in which she played Katharine of Aragon. Her best known later parts include the title role in SCHILLER's *Mary Stuart*, 1957. Author of two autobiographies: *At 33*, 1934, and *With a Quiet Heart*, 1953.

Léger, Fernand (1881–1955), French designer and painter. Creator of skilful, positive productions of modern civilization and the world of the workers. He saw the circus, the variety theatre and the roller-skating rink as vital centres of life. In his lecture *Le spectacle*, 1924, he argued in favour of a synthesis of forms, rhythms, materials and mass action on a new stage and he realized his ideas in his designs for *Skating Rink*, 1922, and *La Création du Monde*, Paris 1923, Ballets Suédois. The severe style of his hieratic costumes for the ballet *David triomphant*, Paris 1937, greatly influenced the development of costume design.
Bibl: H. Rischbieter (ed), BÜHNE UND BILDENDE KUNST IM 20. JAHRHUNDERT, 1968

Legitimate drama. Phrase used in England and the US to denote traditional drama with spoken DIALOGUE in contrast to MUSICAL COMEDY, REVUE, MUSIC HALL, opera, etc. It arose in the 18th century when only two London theatres, COVENT GARDEN and DRURY LANE, were licensed to perform plays in the true sense of the word; and when, in order to circumvent this law, theatres devoted to musical forms and MIME sprang up. These were the unlicensed theatres whose fare was 'illegitimate' drama. Legitimate drama is sometimes abbreviated to 'legit' drama. ▷LORD CHAMBERLAIN.

Legrand, Marc-Antoine (1673–1728), French actor and dramatist. In 1702 (after a rejection in 1694) he joined the COMÉDIE-FRANÇAISE and became a popular actor of comic parts. He also wrote numerous successful plays for the CF and the COMÉDIE-ITALIENNE dealing with topical themes: the most famous was *Cartouche*, 1721, which portrayed the life of a famous bandit. He was ADRIENNE LECOUVREUR's teacher.

Lehmann, Else (1866–1940), German actress. One of the finest actresses in the tradition of German NATURALISM. She established her reputation in 1889 playing Helene Krause in the première of HAUPTMANN's *Vor Sonnenaufgang*; L'ARRONGE gave her a contract in 1891 at the Deutsches-Theater, BERLIN, where she was to become the leading character actress under the management of BRAHM, appearing mainly in plays by Hauptmann and IBSEN. Her charm and freshness were always controlled and she succeeded in combining the closest approximation to naturalness with skilled craftsmanship.
Bibl: J. Bab, KRÄNZE DEM MIMEN, 1954

Leigh, Vivien (1913–67), English actress. An artist of exquisite beauty and delicate sensibility, she started with Shakespearean roles. In 1937 she played Ophelia, in a performance of *Hamlet* staged by the OLD VIC at Elsinore castle in Denmark, with OLIVIER (to whom she was married 1940–60) in the title role. She achieved world fame as Scarlett O'Hara in the film *Gone with the Wind*, 1939. Another memorable performance was as Blanche du Bois in the London production of T. WILLIAMS's *A Streetcar Named Desire*, 1949. She also starred in the film version 1951.

Leighton, Margaret (1922–76), English actress. She made her first appearance at the BIRMINGHAM REPERTORY THEATRE in 1938 and joined the OLD VIC company in 1944; became established as a leading London actress as Celia Coplestone in ELIOT's *The Cocktail Party*, 1950. Among other successful parts: Masha in CHEKHOV's *Three Sisters*, 1951; Mrs Shanklin and Miss Railton-Bell in RATTIGAN's *Separate Tables*, 1954. In 1946 she made her New York début as Lady Percy in *Henry IV* (Part I) and appeared there with GIELGUD in *Much Ado About Nothing*, 1959; Elaine in MORTIMER's *The Wrong Side of the Park*, 1960, and the lead in IBSEN's *The Lady From the Sea*, 1961, adapted by ANN JELLICOE. She was also well known as a film actress.

Leisewitz, Johann Anton (1752–1806), German writer. His dramatic works belong to the STURM UND DRANG movement in Germany; his *Julius von Tarent* won second prize (after KLINGER's *Die Zwillinge*) in the drama competition organized by F. L. SCHRÖDER in 1775. Schröder produced the play in 1776 in Hamburg. Other works include the short pieces *Die Pfändung* (The Sequestration) and *Der Besuch um Mitternacht* (Midnight Visit).
Bibl: W. Kliess, STURM UND DRANG, 1966

Lekain (Henri-Louis Cain; 1729–78), French actor. Protégé of VOLTAIRE, who saw him in an amateur production and invited him to appear in private productions at his house. In 1750, he made his début at the COMÉDIE-FRANÇAISE as Titus in Voltaire's *Brutus* and rapidly made his name as the leading actor of his time in such parts as the title role in *Œdipe* and Orosmane in *Zaïre* by Voltaire, both in 1751; in CRÉBILLON's *Rhadamiste et Zénobie* and Néron in RACINE's *Britannicus*, both in 1754. A small, plump man with a harsh voice, he overcame these defects through his emotional power, his expressive style of acting and intelligent use of diction. He was also responsible for a number of theatrical reforms; with MLLE CLAIRON he was concerned with introducing historically accurate costumes and sets, and fought for the social recognition of actors. He appeared in the first productions of Voltaire's *Rome sauvée*, *L'Orphelin de la Chine*, *Tancrède*, *Le Triumvirat*, *Les Scythes*, *Sophonisbe*, and in numerous REPERTORY plays and contemporary TRAGEDIES, e.g. Oreste in La Touche's *Iphigénie en Tauride*, 1757; Warwick in La Harpe's *Comte de Warwick*, 1763. In 1775 he was invited to appear in BERLIN before the Court of Frederick the Great.

Lemaître, Antoine-Louis-Prosper; known as **Frédérick** (1800–76). Celebrated French romantic actor, but one who never

worked at the COMÉDIE-FRANÇAISE. Made his début on the Boulevard du Temple at the Variétés-Amusantes, later worked at the Funambules and in 1829 joined the Odéon for a short time, leaving to appear successfully in 1823 as Robert Macaire in *L'Auberge des Adrets*, playing this serious melodramatic part in BURLESQUE style, and gradually added to the part of this great anti-bourgeois robber. He revived this play in 1834, and several times afterwards, under the title *Robert Macaire*, with great success. In his later career he returned to the Odéon to appear as Hamlet and Othello and in romantic plays like VIGNY's *La Maréchale d'Ancre*; DUMAS *père's Richard Darlington* and *Kean*; HUGO's *Lucrèce Borgia*. L., who had appeared under DEBURAU as a MIME at the Funambules, acted with a powerful pose and voice; his admirers praised his passion and power while his enemies attacked him for being loud and vulgar.
Bibl: R. Baldech, LA VIE DE LEMAÎTRE, 1961

Lenaea (Gk *Lenaia*). Annual Athenian festival in honour of DIONYSOS in January/February, celebrated since 450 BC; marked by processions and dramatic competitions (TRAGEDY, COMEDY). ▷DIONYSIA.

Leno, Dan (George Galvin; 1860–1904), English MUSIC HALL star, whose talents comprised acting, singing, dancing and MIME. At the age of four he performed as a dancer in music halls all over England; in 1886 joined DRURY LANE under Augustus Harris, appearing in PANTOMIME, later in other theatres, mainly the London Pavilion. He was a versatile comedian, parodist of the petty-bourgeoisie and provincial types, particularly successful in comic women's parts (Sister Ann, Widow Twankey, the Baroness, Cinderella's Stepmother). He is often compared with Chaplin and GRIMALDI. In 1901 he wrote his autobiography *Dan Leno His Book*.

Lenormand, Henri-René (1882–1951), French dramatist. Influenced by the playwrights STRINDBERG and PIRANDELLO, and also by Freud, he attempted to render visible the effects of the subconscious in his dramatic works. In 1919 he met PITOËFF, who furthered his career by producing most of his plays: *La Folie blanche*, 1905; *Les Possédés*, 1909; *Poussière*, 1914; *Le Temps est un songe*, 1919; *Les Ratés*, 1920; *Le Simoun*, 1920; *Le Mangeur des rêves*, 1922; *L'Homme et ses fantômes*, 1924; *A l'Ombre du mal*, 1924; *Le Lâche*, 1925; *L'Amour magicien*, 1926; *Mixture*, 1927; *Sortilèges*, 1932; *La Folle du ciel*, 1937.
Bibl: M. Descotes, LE DRAME ROMANTIQUE ET SES GRANDS CRÉATEURS, 1955

Lenya, Lotte (1900–), Austrian singer and actress, who married the composer WEILL. One of the best interpreters of BRECHT's plays, she has done much to popularize him internationally. Her reputation rests on roles like the tart Jenny Smith in *Mahagonny*, 1927, and Jenny in *Die Dreigroschenoper*, 1928, both Brecht/Weill. Other parts include: Ismene in SOPHOCLES'

Eva Le Gallienne in IBSEN's *The Master Builder*, 1925

Dan Leno

Vivien Leigh in T. WILLIAMS's *A Streetcar Named Desire*, dir OLIVIER, London 1949

Margaret Leighton as Lady Macbeth, 1952

Lekain as Gengis Khan in VOLTAIRE's *L'Orphelin de la Chine*, COMÉDIE-FRANÇAISE, Paris 1755

Oedipus Rex, 1929; Marion in BÜCHNER's *Dantons Tod*, 1930; Anna I in *Die sieben Todsünden der Kleinbürger*, Brecht/Weill, fp Paris 1933, Théâtre des Champs-Elysées, New York 1958, Frankfurt 1960; Miriam in WERFEL's *The Eternal Road*, New York 1937; Xantippe in M. ANDERSON's *Barefoot in Athens*, New York 1951; in *Brecht on Brecht*, an anthology of his works compiled by George Tabori, New York and London 1962; Brecht's *Mutter Courage*, Ruhr Festival 1965; the leading role in the musical *Cabaret*, based on VAN DRUTEN's play *I am a Camera*, adapted from ISHERWOOD's novel *Goodbye to Berlin*. She has also acted in films and made numerous recordings.

Lenz, Jakob Michael Reinhold (1751–92), German dramatist. Like the young GOETHE, he was one of the major exponents of the STURM UND DRANG movement in Germany, who had great influence on BÜCHNER, GRABBE and BRECHT. His most famous work, *Der Hofmeister* (The Tutor), pub 1774, fp by F. L. SCHRÖDER in Hamburg, adapted by Brecht for the BERLINER ENSEMBLE, 1950, deals with the servitude of badly-off German middle-class intellectuals in the 18th century (based on personal experience). The shameful life of a private tutor, *Der neue Menoza*, pub 1774, is a grotesque comedy (▷GROTESQUE) in which the 'noble savage' assumes the role of critic of contemporary society. *Die Soldaten* (The Soldiers) is a calculated analysis, through language and precise characterization, of the position of Germany at the beginning of the 18th century. Other works include: *Die Freunde machen den Philosophen*, 1776; *Lustspiele nach Plautus* (five free translations of Plautus); dramatic sketches and satires. In his book *Anmerkungen übers Theater*, 1774, he also attempted to define an aesthetic theory of drama.
Bibl: K. Kliess, STURM UND DRANG, 1966

Leonardo da Vinci (1452–1519), Italian painter, sculptor, architect and theatre designer. The wedding festivities at the Court of Lodovico il Moro in the Castello Sforza, Milan (1490), which he was commissioned to arrange, gave him the occasion to construct a large revolving stage for the production of Bellincioni's dramatic poem *Il Paradiso*. Until that time only small revolving turn-tables were known, such as those used by Brunelleschi for religious spectacles in churches in Florence.

Leonidov, Leonid Mironovich (1873–1941), Russian actor and producer. Joined the MOSCOW ART THEATRE in 1903 and became one of its leading members. His brilliant performances included Dmitri Karamazov in an adaptation of DOSTOYEVSKY's novel *The Brothers Karamazov*, the title role in *Peer Gynt*, Lopakhin in *The Cherry Orchard*, and Solyony in *Three Sisters*.

Lermontov, Mikhail Yurievich (1814–41), Russian poet and short-story writer. He also wrote plays in verse, much influenced by SHAKESPEARE and SCHILLER. His first play was *Ispantsy* (The Spaniards), written 1830, pub 1857; the German title of his play *Menschen und Leidenschaften* (Men and Passions), written 1830, pub 1880, was in honour of his literary ideal; he rewrote it in 1831 under the title *Strannyj Chelovyek* (The Strange Man), pub 1857. His finest play was *Maskarad* (*Masquerade*), written 1835, which deals with a husband who poisons his wife under the psychological stress of a corrupt society; it was not performed until 1852 at the Alexandrinsky Theatre and did not make an impression till MEYERHOLD's production at the same theatre in 1917. It was later revived several times and is still in the REPERTOIRE in the Soviet Union.
Bibl: L. Lavrin, 1959

Lerner, Alan Jay (1918–), US dramatist. Gained an international reputation with his LIBRETTI for the musicals *Brigadoon*, 1947; *My Fair Lady*, 1956; and *Camelot*, 1960 – all written in collaboration with LOEWE.

Lernet-Holenia, Alexander (1897–1976), Austrian dramatist, poet and short-story writer. His first play, *Demetrius*, 1926, was a historical drama set in the period following the death of Boris Godunov. His cynical FARCES describing the break-down of moral standards after World War I include the prize-winning *Österreichische Komödie* (Austrian Comedy), 1927; *Ollapotrida* (Hotch-Potch), 1926; *Glastüren* (Glass Doors), 1937. Other works in the Austrian tradition, noted for their theatricality: *Die Frau des Potiphar* (Potiphar's Wife), 1934; *Spanische Komödie* (Spanish Comedy), 1947; *Finanzamt* (Revenue Office), 1957.

Lesage, Alain-René (1668–1747), French dramatist and novelist. His novels *Le Diable boiteux* and *Gil Blas* were satirical portraits of Parisian society. He adapted Spanish playwrights including LOPE DE VEGA and ROJAS and scored his first success in the theatre with the play *Crispin rival de son maître*, 1707, COMÉDIE-FRANÇAISE; his next play *Turcaret*, 1709, a satire on a gross, mean and unscrupulous parvenu, is considered one of the best French COMEDIES. From 1722, after a quarrel with the shareholders of the CF, he wrote only for the Paris fairground theatres, about 100 sketches, mostly in collaboration with other writers like Piron, Fuzelier, Dorneval. His son **René-André L.** (1695–1743), under the name of **Montménil**, became a very popular and successful actor, one of his best parts being the title role in *Turcaret*.

Lessing, Doris (1919–), English writer. She spent much of her youth in Rhodesia. Mainly known as a novelist, she has written the plays *Each His Own Wilderness*, 1958, and *Play With A Tiger*, 1962, which deal with the problems of women in today's rootless society.

Lessing, Gotthold Ephraim (1729–81), one of the most important figures of the literary enlightenment in GERMANY. The first major German drama critic and DRAMATURG and playwright whose work has continued to form an important part of Germany's classical REPERTOIRE. While studying theology (later philosophy and medicine) in Leipzig, he was deeply impressed by CAROLINE NEUBER and her company. His early COMEDIES were written in the traditional French style: *Damon*, *Der Misogyn* (The Misogynist), and *Der junge Gelehrte* (The Young Scholar), fp 1748 by C. Neuber. While working as a journalist in BERLIN, 1748–51, he wrote the philosophical dialogues *Die Juden* (The Jews) and *Der Freigeist* (The Freethinker), and a comedy based on PLAUTUS: *Der Schatz* (The Treasure). In Wittenberg for a year in 1751, to take his final exam as a 'Magister' (Master of Arts). Again in Berlin, 1755–60, he became acquainted with Nikolai, Ewald von Kleist and Moses Mendelssohn. From 1755 onwards he published his *Schriften*, composed of epigrams, literary essays, early plays and *Miss Sara Sampson*, the first German 'bourgeois drama' to be written in the tradition of LILLO, CONGREVE and Richardson. Produced by ACKERMANN's company in Frankfurt in 1755, it was on this play rather than any of his later works that his reputation was based in his lifetime. In 1758 he wrote his *Briefe, die neueste Literatur betreffend*, a standard work of literary criticism (which also includes a *Faust* fragment), and the short TRAGEDY *Philotas*. His treatise on aesthetics, *Laokoön, oder die Grenzen der Malerei und Dichtkunst*, was published in 1766. In 1767 he became Dramaturg at the Hamburg National Theatre, where he wrote his HAMBURGISCHE DRAMATURGIE, 1767–69, which consisted originally of critical assessments of current productions but, after controversy with the actors, was restricted solely to comments on the plays themselves; these reviews add up to a basic critical analysis and polemic against ARISTOTLE and the French classics with SHAKESPEARE held up as an example of true tragedy. Hamburg also saw the production of his first great play *Minna von Barnhelm, oder das Soldatenglück* (M. v. B. or Soldier's Luck), 1767, a comedy in which the action takes place after the Seven Years War in Germany; 'the essential question of the play is, how to achieve peace and freedom' (E. Brock-Sulzer). After the failure of the Hamburg National Theatre, he opened a bookshop with J. C. Bode, which led him into financial difficulties. In 1770 he became librarian to the Duke of Brunswick in Wolfenbüttel, where he wrote his bourgeois drama *Emilia Galotti*, 1772; his bitter struggle against religious orthodoxy, in which his main opponent was Pastor Götze, found expression in his final work *Nathan der Weise* (*Nathan the Wise*), a dramatic poem on religious tolerance, which was published posthumously in Berlin in 1783.
Bibl: H. B. Garland, LESSING, THE FOUNDER OF MODERN GERMAN LITERATURE, 2/1962; E. Brock-Sulzer, 1967; W. Drews, 1965

Levi, Paolo (1919–), Italian dramatist. His reputation rests on well-constructed plays including *Anna e il telefono* (Anna and the Telephone), 1951; *Legittima difesa* (Legitimate Defence), 1952; *Il caso Pinedus* (The P. Case), 1954; *Come per scherzo* (As in jest), 1955; *I Nemici* (The Enemies), 1955; *La Fiera* (The Fair), 1956; *Il Gioco è fatto* (Le Jeu est fait), 1957; *Gli Dei di pietra* (The Stone Gods), 1958; *Fra un mese, fra un anno* (In a month, in a year) based on Françoise Sagan, 1960.

Lewes, George Henry (1817–78), English man of letters. His varied apprenticeship included a short spell as an actor in London. Worked as a journalist, writer of philosophical works, biographer of GOETHE, 1855, and dramatic critic for the *Pall Mall Gazette.* Lived with the novelist George Eliot. Under the pen-name Slingsby Lawrence he wrote a TRAGEDY, *The Noble Heart*, 1849, and a number of COMEDIES and FARCES: *The Game of Speculation*, 1851; *The Lawyers*, 1853; *Wanted a She-Wolf*, 1854; *A Cozy Couple*, 1854; *Give a Dog a Bad Name*, 1854; *Buckstone's Adventure with a Polish Princess*, 1855; *Stay At Home*, 1856; etc. He wrote a book on classical Spanish drama, 1846, and published his collected criticism under the title *On Actors and the Art of Acting*, 1875.

Libretto (Ital=little book). Text of an opera or musical play or outline of the PLOT in ballet. Famous early librettists in Italy were Rinuccini, Apostolo Zeno, Metastasio and later Boito (Verdi's operas); in France the dramatists Quinault, Sedaine, Favart and SCRIBE. In England there are no particularly outstanding librettists apart from GAY (ballad operas), Nahum Tate, Alfred Bunn and W. S. Gilbert who collaborated with Sir Arthur Sullivan (▷ GILBERT AND SULLIVAN). There are many dramatists whose works have served as texts of operas, e.g. HOFMANNSTHAL (*Der Rosenkavalier* and *Ariadne auf Naxos* by R. Strauss); WILDE (*Salome* by R. Strauss); MAETERLINCK (*Pelléas et Mélisande* by Debussy).

Lietzau, Hans (1913–), German director. Started as an actor before making his début as a director in 1943; from 1945 worked almost exclusively as guest director, artistic director and INTENDANT in theatres all over Germany. He produced many first German performances of contemporary playwrights including: ADAMOV's *Ping-Pong*, 1955; GENET's *The Screens*, fp 1961; FRISCH's *Graf Öderland*, 1961; WHITING's *The Devils*, 1961; IONESCO's *Exit the King*, 1963; MÜLLER's *Philoktet*, 1968; GRASS's *Davor*, fp BERLIN 1969, Schillertheater. A strong supporter of the works of the Expressionist writer BARLACH: *Der arme Vetter*, 1956; *Der Graf von Ratzeburg*, 1957; *Die echten Sedemunds*, 1958; *Der blaue Boll*, 1960.

Lillie, Beatrice (1898–), Canadian actress and solo comedienne in REVUE and CABARET. She made her début in 1914 in London with *Not Likely*, achieved great success with *Charlot's Revue* in 1925, which she repeated a year later in New York, and reached the height of her career with the one-woman show *An Evening With Beatrice Lillie*, 1952.

Lerner and LOEWE's *My Fair Lady*, London 1958, costumes by BEATON

Gotthold Lessing, portrait by Anton Graff

Lotte Lenya (right) in *The Seven Deadly Sins* by BRECHT and WEILL, New York 1958

Bibl: E. Short, SIXTY YEARS OF THEATRE, 1951; J. Agate, EGO 3, 1938

Lillo, George (1693–1739), English dramatist. Best known for two plays: *The London Merchant; or The History of George Barnwell*, 1731, DRURY LANE; and *Fatal Curiosity; A True Tragedy of Three Acts*, 1736, Haymarket Theatre. These domestic tragedies had considerable vogue on the continent and influenced playwrights like DIDEROT, LESSING and Z. WERNER.

Lincoln Center for the Performing Arts. Theatre centre in New York City, consisting of a concert hall, opened 1962, the new Metropolitan Opera House (with 3,800 seats) opened 1967, a ballet theatre, the Julliard School of Music, a REPERTORY theatre (the Vivian-Beaumont) opened 1966, a Children's Theatre, and the New York Public Library's Library and Museum of the Performing Arts.

Lindau, Paul (1839–1919), German dramatist, journalist and critic. DRAMATURG and INTENDANT at Meiningen; in BERLIN, Berliner Theater, Deutsches-Theater, then Dramaturg at the Schauspielhaus, 1910–18; wrote several well-made plays in the tradition of SCRIBE and SARDOU: *Maria und Magdalena*, Vienna 1872; *Ein Erfolg* (A Success), Vienna 1874, BURGTHEATER; *Gräfin Lea*, Hamburg 1879.

Lindberg. (1) **August L.** (1846–1916), Swedish actor. After 1872 he made his name as a Shakespearean actor by touring Sweden and in 1882 founded his own travelling company with a literary REPERTOIRE including plays by IBSEN; some were Swedish first productions, e.g. *Ghosts*, 1883. He also staged the first Norwegian production of *Brand*, 1895. After managing various theatres, e.g. in Göteborg, and the Swedish theatre in Helsinki, and directing at the Royal Opera, 1906–15, he became a director and actor at the Royal Dramatic Theatre, Stockholm. After 1900 he gave solo performances, e.g. SHAKESPEARE's *The Tempest*; GOETHE's *Faust*; Ibsen's *Peer Gynt*; SOPHOCLES' *Oedipus Rex*. He visited England and the USA, 1911–12. (2) **Per L.** (1890–1944), son of August, after studying in Berlin under REINHARDT, worked as a director in Göteborg, 1918–23, following the latter's style of mass spectacle in staging plays by Shakespeare and also contemporaries, e.g. STRINDBERG, *The Road to Damascus*, and H. BERGMAN. In Stockholm he made his début with student productions of two Swedish Renaissance plays which he rediscovered 1923–25: Olaus Petri's *Tobie Comedia* and Asteropherus' *Tisbe*. This was followed by a series of experimental productions in the Concert Hall, Stockholm, e.g. AESCHYLUS' *Agamemnon* (designed by the sculptor Carl Milles) using an Expressionist and monumental style. In 1927–29 Per L. founded a club for avant-garde theatre within the Royal Dramatic Theatre, producing plays by H. Bergman, LAGERKVIST, YEATS and SYNGE. Outstanding productions included O'NEILL's *Strange Interlude* and TOLLER's *Hoppla, wir leben!* (*Hoppla, Such is Life!*), strongly influenced by MEYERHOLD and PISCATOR. He reached the peak of his career in 1931–32 and 1934–35 working on productions of *Peer Gynt* and *Hamlet*, with EKMAN as the leading actor, and *The Merchant of Venice*, with Ekman as Shylock. Also published numerous works on dramatic theory, e.g. *Production Problems*, 1927; *G. Ekman*, 1942.
Bibl: S. Lindberg, EN BOK OM PER LINDBERG, 1944; P. Lindberg, AUGUST LINDBERG, 1943

Lindsay, Sir David (1490?–1555), Scottish poet and diplomat, chief herald of Scotland, 1542. His outstanding dramatic work is the MORALITY PLAY *Ane Plaesant Satyre on the Thrie Estaitis*, 1540, which presents a wide-ranging satirical panorama of Man, Society and the Church. GUTHRIE directed a highly successful revival of the play at the EDINBURGH FESTIVAL in 1948 under the title *The Three Estates*, where it was performed several times in subsequent years.

Lindsay, Howard (1889–1968), US playwright, librettist and director. Started as an actor and achieved his first writing successes with *Young Uncle Dudley*, 1929, and *A Slight Case of Murder* (with Damon Runyon), 1935. But his greatest hits originated from his collaboration with CROUSE (1893–1966). They worked together on some 15 plays and musicals, including: *Life with Father*, 1939, in which L. and his wife Dorothy Stickney played the star parts in a five-year run; *State of the Union*, 1945; *Call Me Madam* (LIBRETTO for the I. BERLIN musical), 1950; *The Great Sebastians*, 1955, which starred the LUNTS; *The Sound of Music*, on which L. and Crouse collaborated with RODGERS and HAMMERSTEIN II, 1959, which not only achieved a long run on the stage but became one of the most successful musical films of all time.

Lindtberg, Leopold (1902–), Austrian director. Worked as an actor before directing in BERLIN at the Piscator-Bühne and State Theatre; at the ZURICH SCHAUSPIELHAUS, 1933–45, of which he was director 1965–68; and at the BURGTHEATER in Vienna. A versatile director, he staged plays ranging from BRECHT, WILDER and SARTRE to the classics of world literature. Best known is his SHAKESPEARE cycle of the histories in 1964 at the Burgtheater. He has also directed operas and films.
Bibl: H. R. Hilty (ed), REGIEARBEIT LEOPOLD LINDTBERGS, 1962

Lingen, Theo (1903–), German comic actor. Appeared mainly at the State Theatre in BERLIN, 1930–44; in 1948 joined the BURGTHEATER in Vienna. Also appeared as a guest actor at various German theatres. Among his notable roles are: Malvolio in *Twelfth Night*; Riccot in LESSING's *Minna von Barnhelm*; Krull in STERNHEIM's *Die Kassette*. He has also written a COMEDY, *Theophanes*, Burgtheater 1948, and an autobiography, *Ich über mich*, 1963. He has appeared in many films.

Linklater, Eric (1899–1974), Scottish novelist and poet. Author of witty ironic novels, he has also written the plays: *Crisis in Heaven*, 1944; *The Atom Doctor*, 1950; *Breakspear*, 1958.

Little Tich (Harry Relph; 1868–1928), English MUSIC HALL comic. Began his career in a MINSTREL troupe with whom he later toured the USA; subsequently appeared in PANTOMIMES at DRURY LANE. In his sketches he parodied many well-known personalities including famous actors. He usually performed in enormous boots.

Littlewood, Joan (1914–), English director. She founded and managed the Theatre Workshop until 1973. Coming from a working-class family, she studied at RADA. While working in radio in Manchester she founded, with her husband Ewan McColl, the Theatre Union, an amateur company, which quickly became well known for their experimental productions in halls and out of doors. The group broke up in 1939, reforming in 1945 as Theatre Workshop. In 1953 she moved with the company to their first permanent home, the Theatre Royal in Stratford East, London. Her main aim was to create a theatre for the people. Politically left-wing, she developed an individual style of production, to some degree influenced by BRECHT, with extremely long rehearsals and a collective approach. The company gained world-wide fame with a series of productions that included: B. BEHAN's *The Quare Fellow*, 1956, and *The Hostage*, 1958; SHELAGH DELANEY's *A Taste of Honey*, 1958; the BART/NORMAN musical *Fings Ain't What They Used T'Be*, 1959; and the anti-war revue *Oh What a Lovely War!*, 1963. The company was disbanded in 1973 owing to the continuous threat to the collective effort posed by commercial West End success and the star attraction it had become. L. returned to the Theatre Royal, Stratford East, in 1972.
Bibl: THEATRE WORKSHOP, A BRITISH PEOPLE'S THEATRE, 1957

Littman, Max (1862–1931), German architect. In 1900–02 he built the Prinzregententheater in Munich, virtually a replica of the Bayreuth Festspielhaus (▷BAYREUTH), with a raked auditorium and a sunken orchestra pit, and in 1912 the COURT THEATRE in Stuttgart. After building several other theatres with raked seats, e.g. Schillertheater, BERLIN, 1906–08 and the Munich Künstlertheater, 1908–12, as a 'Relief-Reformbühne' (technical term = reform stage in relief), he returned to the traditional theatre with tiers of galleries.
Bibl: G. J. Wolf, 1931

Liturgical drama (from Liturgy, the service of the Holy Eucharist). Name given to a mass of biblical plays which were performed by the church all over Europe from the beginning of the 12th till the end of the 13th centuries when they had completed their evolution, later development no longer being liturgical. A short play was evolved from the text chanted for the Easter celebration which closely followed the Gospel account of the meeting between the angel at the tomb and the three Marys, further scenes being added later. The Christmas services gave rise to a play on the Nativity. This type of play was found in many countries, being most common in Germany and France, and developing somewhat differently in Italy and Spain. They were the forerunners of the English MYSTERY PLAY, the French *Mystère*, the German PASSION PLAY, the Spanish AUTO SACRAMENTAL and the Italian SACRA RAPPRESENTAZIONE. The 12th-century drama *The Play of Daniel* was revived in 1960 by E. MARTIN BROWNE, and presented in New York, later in England and on the Continent, with music performed on period instruments.

Living Theatre. Theatre group founded *c.* 1950 by Julian Beck and his wife Judith Malina. Both were pupils at PISCATOR's Theatre Workshop in New York, where in 1946 Judith M. made her début as Cassandra in AESCHYLUS' *Agamemnon*. Their first productions were presented in their own apartment and included plays by BRECHT, LORCA, GERTRUDE STEIN and Paul Goodman. In 1951 they moved into the Cherry Lane Theatre, New York. There they produced Gertrude Stein's *Doctor Faustus Lights the Lights*; Kenneth Rexroth's *Beyond the Mountains*; Goodman's *Faustina*; JARRY's *Ubu Roi*. Between 1954 and 1963 productions at various studios included: STRINDBERG's *The Ghost Sonata*, 1954; PIRANDELLO's *Tonight We Improvise*, 1955, and *The Giants of the Mountains*, 1961; RACINE's *Phèdre* – title role Judith M., 1955; and works by Goodman, William Carlos Williams, POUND (*The Women of Trachis*, 1960); BRECHT (*In the Jungle of the Cities*, 1960, and *Man is Man*, 1962). Influenced by the theories of ARTAUD, their work is a testament to absolute non-violence, their aim to form a group of people sharing both their lives and work in the theatre, using meditative exercises. Their presentation of this anti-bourgeois style of life was shown best in the work of one of the group's playwrights, Jack Gelber, *The Connection*, 1959, about drug addiction, and *The Apple*, 1961, and in *The Brig*, by K. H. BROWN, 1963, an anti-military play. They first toured Europe in 1961, appearing at the THÉÂTRE DES NATIONS in Paris. In 1963 the Living Theatre studios were closed down by the US Government because of unpaid taxes. In 1964 they went to Paris, where they first produced *Mysteries and Smaller Pieces* – a programme of scenic exercises, attacks on the audience and demonstrative rituals against violence and war. In 1965 they returned to New York and were again imprisoned; they went back to Europe where they worked in different countries: in Germany, GENET's *The Maids*, Forum Theater, BERLIN; in Italy *Frankenstein*, based on Mary Shelley's novel, a show worked out by the whole company consisting of scenes of terror, mythological PANTOMIMES and horrific effects, fp Venice 1965; this was followed by *Antigone*, 1967, based on Brecht's version of SOPHOCLES' play, translated and adapted by Judith M., who played

Lincoln Center for the Performing Arts: left, New York State Theatre; centre, Metropolitan Opera; right, Philharmonic Hall

Liturgical drama, the stage at Valenciennes, painting by Hubert Caillot, 1547

Joan Littlewood's Theatre Workshop production of *Uranium 235*, 1952

Antigone to Beck's Creon; in France, *Paradise Now*, fp AVIGNON FESTIVAL, 1968, where it caused conflict with local officials, because it encouraged the audience to reject any State decrees against nudity and to establish a new, unrepressive society; in the winter of 1968–69 they toured the USA. The Living Theatre was the most influential group in the 1960s both in America and Europe. Their ideological and aesthetic radicalism, the abolition of barriers between private and artistic existence and also their techniques of presentation (violently expressive movement and speech, developed from long collective exercises and contacts) have been imitated many times or seen as a model for similar experiments, though the rigorous demands of the group almost excluded any long-term followers. It still continues today developing new performance techniques. Others who have been members of the group include: Joseph Chaikin, Steven Ben Israel, Jimmy Anderson, Henry Howard, Luke Theodore and William H. Shari.
Bibl: E. Billeter, THE LIVING THEATRE – PARADISE NOW, 1969

Livings, Henry (1929–), English actor and dramatist. The central character of his realistic COMEDIES of working life in Liverpool is normally the little man, whose unforeseen reactions culminate in a hilarious disaster; FARCE and fantasy are used to show his concern for the forgotten little people, who support the social edifice. In *Stop It, Whoever You Are*, 1961, it is the insignificant Perkin Warbeck, a lavatory attendant in a factory, who is involved in a series of mishaps. The farcical comedy *Big Soft Nellie*, 1961, has as protagonist a 'mother's boy' who is the laughing-stock of his mates. *Nil Carborundum*, 1962, is set in the kitchen of an RAF station; *Kelly's Eye*, fp London 1963, ROYAL COURT THEATRE; *Eh?*, fp 1964, RSC, Aldwych Theatre; *The Finest Family in the Land*, 1972.
Bibl: J. R. Taylor, ANGER AND AFTER, 2/1963

Livy (Lucius Livius Andronicus; *c.* 284–204 BC), Roman poet. Founder of Latin drama in 240 BC, he produced Latin translations of Greek drama at Rome's Ludi Romani.

Lloyd, Marie (Matilda Alice Victoria Wood; 1870–1922), English star of MUSIC HALL. Made her début under the name Bella Delmere in 1885 at the Royal Eagle Music Hall (later known as the Grecian). Had her first major success at the Star Music Hall in Bermondsey with the song 'The Boy I Love Sits Up In The Gallery' in the same year. After having adopted the name under which she later became famous, she conquered the MUSIC HALL of England and Ireland. In 1891 Augustus Hare made her principal girl of the PANTOMIMES at DRURY LANE. In 1898 she fulfilled her life-long ambition to appear as principal boy at the Crown in Peckham in *Dick Whittington*. After an attempt to appear in a musical play *The ABC Girl or Flossie the Frivolous*, by Chance Newton, music G. le Brunn, had failed at the Grand Theatre, Wolverhampton, she returned to music hall, where she remained to the end of her life with the sole exception of one appearance in REVUE (The Revue at the Tivoli, London, 1902). Also visited Paris, BERLIN, and toured the USA. She was small but most attractive, with a peculiar luminosity in her features. She had a delicious cockney humour and her songs gave her opportunity to display her spirit and subtle power of characterization.
Bibl: N. Jacob, OUR MARIE, 1936

Loa. A curtain raiser or PROLOGUE in early Spanish theatre.

Loesser, Frank (1910–69), US composer, lyricist, playwright and producer. He wrote a number of songs for army shows in World War II, including the celebrated 'Praise the Lord and Pass the Ammunition'. Composed lyrics and music for *Where's Charley?*, 1948, and *Guys and Dolls*, 1950, based on the stories of Damon Runyon, which was immensely successful, winning the NYDCC AWARD in 1950, which he won again, together with the PULITZER PRIZE in 1962 for the musical *How to Succeed in Business without Really Trying*.

Loewe, Frederick (1904–), US composer of Austrian origin. Began his career as a pianist in Berlin in the 1920s and, in collaboration with the lyric writer LERNER, is the most successful contemporary composer of musicals in the USA, e.g. *Brigadoon*, 1947; *My Fair Lady*, 1956; *Camelot*, 1960.

Logan, Joshua (1908–), US director and dramatist. Studied acting under STANISLAVSKY in Moscow, later worked at American university theatres in 1928. He made his début as an actor in Boston in 1933 and in the same year was seen in London. Subsequently he worked mainly in the USA as a director of musicals and films. In 1950 he wrote the play *The Wisteria Trees*, an adaptation of *The Cherry Orchard* by CHEKHOV. He wrote LIBRETTI for many musicals in collaboration or alone: *South Pacific*, 1949; *Wish You Were Here*, 1952; *Fanny*, 1954, and *The Flower Drum Song*, 1958. Among his works as a director were: *Knickerbocker Holiday*, 1938; *By Jupiter*, 1942; *Annie Get Your Gun*, 1946; *Picnic*, 1953; *Middle of the Night*, 1956; *The World of Suzie Wong*, 1958; *Mr President*, 1962.

Lonsdale, Frederick (pseudonym of F. Leonard; 1881–1954), English playwright. Obtained his first success with LIBRETTI for MUSICAL COMEDIES: *Betty* (with Gladys Unger, music P. Rubens), 1915; *High Jinks* (music P. Rubens, H. Talbot, J. W. Tate and KERN), 1916; *The Maid of the Mountains* (after R. Evett, music H. Fraser-Simpson), 1917, which ran for 1,352 performances. He then turned to sophisticated DRAWING-ROOM COMEDY: *Aren't We All?* 1923; *Spring Cleaning*, New York 1923; *The Last of Mrs Cheyney*, London 1925, St James's Theatre; *On Approval*, New York 1926; *Canaries Sometimes Sing*, 1929; *Never Come Back*, 1932; *Once Is Enough*, 1938; *But for the Grace of God*, 1946; *Let Them Eat Cake*, produced posthumously, 1959.
Bibl: F. Donaldson, 1957

Lope de Rueda (*c.* 1510–65), Spanish actor and dramatist. A goldsmith by trade, he became a travelling comedian performing in town squares, market places, etc., and in 1554 formed his own company for which he wrote *pasos*, short plays with strong satirical elements with two or three characters: a comic situation with natural DIALOGUE written in dialect – which anticipated the ENTREMESES. Two collected volumes of his work have survived: *El deleitoso* (The Delectable), 1567; and *Registro de representantes* (Register of Representatives), 1570, including his best-known *paso*, *Las aceitunas* (The Olives). His COMEDIES modelled on Italian sources are less significant; some are in prose, e.g. *Eufemia*, *Armelina*, *Medora*, *Los Engañados* (The Deceived), and some in verse, e.g. *Discordia y cuestión de amor* (Discord and Question of Love).
Bibl: J. P. Wickersham, SPANISH DRAMA BEFORE LOPE DE VEGA, 2/1937

Lope de Vega (Lope Felix de Vega Carpio; 1562–1635), Spanish poet and playwright. The son of a craftsman embroiderer, he showed precocious talents; originally destined for the priesthood, he became a soldier, took part in the expedition to the Azores 1583 and with the Armada to England 1588. His passionate nature involved him in numerous love affairs, and led to a period of banishment from Madrid, part of which he spent in Valencia writing plays. After serving as secretary to the Duke of Alba he returned to Madrid in 1600; he entered the priesthood in 1614, but this did not prevent him from continuing to be involved in further passionate love affairs. His later years were overshadowed by the blindness of his mistress, Marta de Nevares, the death of his son at sea and the seduction and abandonment of his daughter by her nobleman lover. Lope was undoubtedly one of the most prodigious literary geniuses of all time, with a vast output of verse and prose, as well as plays. He was said, by an early biographer, to have written some 1,800 plays as well as 400 *autos* (▷AUTO SACRAMENTAL). The titles of 723 plays and 44 *autos* are known; the texts of 426 plays and 42 *autos* are preserved. L. created the form of the classical Spanish drama. His plays are usually in three acts; his strength lies above all in the exposition, while the unravelling of the action follows a fairly rigid and predictable pattern. His handling of metre in drama is free and all his plays show his closeness to the people and popular taste. Yet he was immensely well read and learned.
His dramatic writing comprises numerous COMEDIES of amorous intrigue and honour (COMEDIAS EN CAPA Y ESPADA – cloak-and-sword plays): among which are *La dama boba* (The Goblin Lady); *La discreta enamorada* (The discreet mistress); *El acero de Madrid* (The Sword of Madrid); *La noche*

toledana (The Night of Toledo); *El perro del hortelano* (The Gardener's Dog); *El villano in su rincón* (The Countryman in his Homestead). Among his historical plays, based on Spanish chronicles are: *Peribañez; El mejor alcalde el rey* (The Best Mayor is the King); *Fuente Ovejuna*; *El caballero de Olmedo* (The Knight of Olmedo); *La estrella de Sevilla* (The Star of Seville). Those dealing with events in other countries range from Russia, *El gran duque de Moscovia* (The Grand Duke of Moscovy), to Bohemia, *El Imperial de Otòn* (Otokar's Empire). He also wrote numerous plays on biblical subjects: *La hermosa Ester* (Beautiful Esther) and the lives of Saints, PASTORAL PLAYS and plays on Greek and Roman mythological subjects. *La Dorotea* (1632) is a long novel in dialogue form modelled on *La Celestina*. L. gave an account of his views on the theory of drama in the poem *Arte nuevo de hacer comedias* (The new art of making plays – 1609). L.'s plays were published in his lifetime in various collected editions. The dates of composition and first performance of the extant plays are difficult to establish.
Bibl: H. A. Rennert & A. Castro, VIDA DE LOPE DE VEGA, 1919; S. G. Morley & C. Bruerton, THE CHRONOLOGY OF LOPE DE VEGA'S COMEDIES, 1940

Loraine, Robert (1876–1935), English ACTOR-MANAGER. Son of the actor Herbert Loraine, he first achieved success playing romantic heroes such as D'Artagnan in *The Three Musketeers*, 1899. He developed into a realistic actor in plays by STRINDBERG and particularly SHAW, playing Don Juan in the first production of *Don Juan in Hell*, 1907. He took over the management of the Criterion in 1911, opening with a revival of *Man and Superman*. Other outstanding parts included the title role in *Cyrano de Bergerac*, 1919; Adolf in Strindberg's *The Father*; and many Shakespearean parts (Petruchio, Mercutio).

Lorca, Federico García (1898–1936), Spanish poet and playwright. Major literary personality of the 20th century, he succeeded in integrating the opposing elements of poetry and drama in the theatre. His dramatic work, written in sensual metaphoric language, full of poetic images, depicts man in hopeless conflict between elemental passion and the outdated constraints imposed by society, achieving the pitilessness of classical TRAGEDY. In 1928 L. was already a well-known poet and dramatist in Spain, celebrated particularly for his play *Mariana Pineda*, fp Barcelona 1927, but his most productive years followed an inspiring visit to the USA in 1929; in 1933 he was appointed director of the travelling theatre La Barraca, for which he wrote his most powerful folk plays: *Bodas de sangre*, 1933, translated by Roy Campbell as *Blood Wedding*, London 1947, New York 1949; *Yerma*, 1934; *La Casa de Bernarda Alba* (*The House of B.A.*), 1936, New York 1951, on English TV 1960 and then London 1973, Greenwich Theatre. Other dramatic works include *Amor de Don Perlimplin con Belisa en su jardin* (The Love of D.P. and B. in the Garden), prod 1928, pub 1938; *La zapatera prodigiosa* (The Shoemaker's Prodigious Wife), 1930; *En el retablillo de Don Cristobal* (In the Frame of D.C.), 1935; *Doña Rosita la soltera, or el lenguaje de las flores* (Dona R. the Spinster, or the Language of Flowers), 1935; *Así que pasen cinco años* (When Five Years Pass), pub posthumously 1937. When preparing for a trip to Mexico in 1936, he was arrested and executed by the Falangists in Granada.
Bibl: R. Lema, THE THEATRE OF GARCÍA LORCA, 1963; A. Barea, LORCA, THE POET AND HIS PEOPLE, 1949

Lord Chamberlain. Court official who acted as censor for the theatre in Britain until 1968 when censorship came to an end. The powers of stage control and supervision which became vested in the Lord Chamberlain derived from the functions of the MASTER OF THE REVELS first appointed in the reign of Henry VII. In 1737 this position received statutory recognition. A century later, by the Theatres Act of 1843, the Lord Chamberlain became the licensing authority for stage plays in London, Windsor and other places of royal residence. All plays had to be submitted to him. Outside his area of jurisdiction, local authorities became the licensing authority for plays, but they hardly ever went against his verdict. In the late 19th and 20th centuries it was assumed that private or club performances were outside the jurisdiction of the Lord Chamberlain. This made it possible for experimental and avant-garde drama to deal with hitherto taboo subjects. When a court decision, arising from a club performance of BOND's *Saved*, 1965, held that all public performances, even by a club, should have been licensed by the Lord Chamberlain, the clamour for the abolition of censorship in the interest of experimentation in drama became overwhelming and led to the abolition of his licensing function. The valuable collection of play texts which had accumulated in the Lord Chamberlain's office is now in the British Museum.

Lorre, Peter (1904–64), Hungarian-born German actor and director. He made his début in BERLIN as Fabian in MARIELUISE FLEISSER's *Pioniere in Ingolstadt*, produced by BRECHT, for whom L. became the prototype of the 'epic' actor, following his outstanding performance as Galy Gay in Brecht's *Mann ist Mann*, 1931, directed by the author. Other classic parts included Moritz in WEDEKIND's *Frühlings Erwachen*, 1929; St Just in BÜCHNER's *Dantons Tod*, 1930, both VOLKSBÜHNE; Alfred in HORVÁTH's *Geschichten aus dem Wiener Wald*, Berlin 1931, Deutsches-Theater. A brilliant film actor, notably as the child-murderer in *'M'*, he continued his screen career after emigrating to the USA, e.g. *The Maltese Falcon*.

Lowell, Robert (Traill Spence, Jr; 1917–), US poet. His verse translation of RACINE's *Phèdre* was published in 1961, but he did not emerge as a professionally produced dramatist until 1964, when the

Marie Lloyd

Lope de Vega

Federico García Lorca

American Place Theatre presented the first part of his dramatic TRILOGY *The Old Glory*, dir J. MILLER, which won five OBIE AWARDS for the 1964–65 season and the NYVRDD AWARD; a chronicle of the American character, the three individual plays, which are written in free verse, are held tightly together by the unifying symbol of the national flag. *Benito Cereno, Endecott and the Red Cross* and *My Kinsman, Major Molineux*: the second two owe their sources to Nathaniel Hawthorne and Thomas Marton, while the first and finest play of the trilogy, *Benito Cereno*, was inspired by Herman Melville's novella. It is distinguished by theatrical power, strong narrative full of suspense and richly evocative DIALOGUE. In this short drama L. carries one back to the early 19th century and exposes the roots of present day conflicts and tensions as he probes the ambivalent American attitude towards slavery, servitude and the contemporary Negro.

Löwen, Johann Friedrich (1729–71), German writer and theatre historian. Inspired the founding of the National Theatre in Hamburg of which he was appointed director in 1767. He published the first history of German theatre, 1766, reprinted in 1905 with an introduction and notes by H. Stümke.

Ludi Florales (or *Floralia*). Roman festival in honour of Flora, goddess of Spring. Instituted 238 BC, and at first held at irregular intervals, annually from 173 BC, enlivened by performances of Roman MIMES and other popular entertainers. The mimes performed FARCES which often ended (by popular demand) with veritable strip-tease acts by the actresses.

Ludwig, Otto (1813–65), German dramatist. A 'poetic realist' who disapproved of the German literary tradition of SCHILLER, KLEIST and HEBBEL, and took SHAKESPEARE as his model. His works include: *Hanns Frei*, written 1843, fp 1901; *Die Pfarr-Rose*, Meiningen, 1900; *Das Fräulein von Scuderi*, written 1848, adapted by WILDENBRUCH, fp Vienna 1891, BURGTHEATER; a drama concerned with fate, *Der Erbförster* (The hereditary Forester), Dresden 1850; the tragedy *Die Makkabäer* (The Maccabaeans), Vienna 1852, Burgtheater; *Der Engel von Augsburg, Agnes Bernauerin* (The Angel of Augsburg, A.B.), written 1859, fp Dresden 1897.
Bibl: A. Meyer, 1957

Lugné-Poë (Aurélien-François-Marie Lugné; 1869–1940), French actor and director. One of the leading innovators in the European theatre from the beginning of this century till after World War I. He studied at the CONSERVATOIRE D'ART DRAMATIQUE in Paris, appeared under ANTOINE at the Théâtre Libre, in 1893 took over the famous Théâtre de l'Œuvre, formerly Théâtre d'Art under FORT, and worked there as director and chief actor till 1929, introducing in French modern plays selected from world literature, including nine by IBSEN between 1893 and 1898; MAETERLINCK's *Pelléas et Mélisande*, 1893; STRINDBERG's *The Father*, 1894; JARRY's *Ubu Roi*, 1896, GORKY's *The Lower Depths*, 1905, with ELEONORA DUSE; SCHNITZLER and KAISER. He also revived Elizabethan plays like FORD's *'Tis Pity She's a Whore* and encouraged young playwrights including: ROLLAND, CLAUDEL (*L'Annonce faite à Marie*, 1912, and *L'Otage*, 1914), ACHARD, SALACROU and ROSSO DI SAN SECONDO. Combining the qualities of an excellent actor and director with those of a DRAMATURG, the outstanding features of his work were openness to new ideas and emphasis on the dramatic work throughout the production which was recognized in the name of his theatre. Author of several books on the theatre: *Le Sot du tremplin* and *Acrobaties*, 1931; *Sous les étoiles*, 1933; *Ibsen*, 1937; *Dernière pirouette*, 1946.
Bibl: J. Robichez, ROMAIN ROLLAND ET LUGNÉ-POË: CORRESPONDANCE, 1894–1901, 1957

Lunacharsky, Anatoli Vasilyevich (1875–1933), Russian politician and dramatist. First People's Commissar for Education in Soviet Russia, 1917–29, responsible for the survival of several theatrical institutions after the October Revolution, including the MOSCOW ART THEATRE, and for establishing new Soviet theatres. He also strongly supported proletarian literature and the movement towards SOCIALIST REALISM and protected the leaders of the theatrical avant-garde, including MEYERHOLD, TAIROV and VAKHTANGOV. L. was the author of several historical plays including *Foma Kampanella* (Thomas Campanella), 1920; *Oliver Krompel* (O. Cromwell), 1920; *Faust i gorod* (*Faust and the City*), 1920; *Kanstler i slesar* (Chancellor and Locksmith), 1921; *Osvobozhdonny Don-Kikhot* (The Liberated Don Quixote), 1923.
Bibl: L. Altmann, 1957

Lunt, Alfred (1893–   ), US actor and director. Made his first stage appearance in 1912 and toured with various REPERTORY companies. New York début 1917; first appearance with LYNN FONTANNE (whom he married in 1922) was in 1919, the same year of his first BROADWAY success, *Clarence* by Booth Tarkington. Lunt and Fontanne became one of the most notable husband-wife teams in recent theatrical history, appearing together almost constantly for forty years. In 1923 they appeared with LAURETTE TAYLOR in *Sweet Nell of Old Drury*; in 1924 L. was featured in Sutton Vane's *Outward Bound*, and in that same year they joined the THEATRE GUILD, under whose auspices they had their first spectacular joint success in MOLNÁR's *The Guardsman*. Notable mainly for sophisticated comedy, such as COWARD's *Design for Living*, 1933; SHERWOOD's *Reunion in Vienna*, New York 1931, London 1934, and *Idiot's Delight*, 1935; GIRAUDOUX's *Amphitryon 38*, 1937, adapted by BEHRMAN, they also appeared in more classical works like SHAW's *Arms and the Man*, 1925, and *The Doctor's Dilemma*, 1927; SHAKESPEARE's *The Taming of the Shrew*, 1935; and CHEKHOV's *The Seagull*, 1938. Their last stage performance was in DÜRRENMATT's *The Visit*, New York 1959, London 1960.

Lyly, John (*c.* 1554–1606), English dramatist. The first writer of sophisticated English prose COMEDY. Several times Member of Parliament, he wrote plays almost exclusively for a Court audience, performed by the CHILDREN OF ST PAUL's (of whom he was Vice-Master in 1590) and the CHILDREN OF THE CHAPEL. He was considered a brilliant writer in his day, elegant and full of witty allusions to contemporary situations. His work strongly influenced the ELIZABETHAN THEATRE: *Campaspe*, prod 1580–84, pub 1584; *Sappho and Phao*, prod 1582–84, pub 1584; *Gallathea*, prod 1584–88, pub 1592; *Endimion, the Man in the Moon*, prod 1588; *Midas*, prod 1589–90, pub 1592, and *Mother Bombie*, prod 1587–90, pub 1594, both comedies with themes from TERENCE; and *The Woman in the Moon*, prod 1590–95, pub 1597. He is perhaps best known today for some of the lyrics from these plays, and as the author of the romances *Euphues: The Anatomy of Wit*, 1579, and *Euphues and his England*, 1580, which have a significant place in the early history of the English novel. His elaborate style, full of conceits, gave rise to the adjective 'euphuistic'.
Bibl: J. D. Wilson, 1905

MacArthur, Charles (1895–1956), US playwright and producer. Wrote most of his plays in collaboration with other writers, notably HECHT: among these are *The Front Page*, 1928, the classic comedy-drama about journalists and their world, successfully revived at the NATIONAL THEATRE, 1972, and filmed 1975, and *Twentieth Century*, 1932. His other dramatic work includes *Salvation* (with S. HOWARD), 1925, and *Lulu Belle* (with SHELDON), 1926. M. was married to the actress HELEN HAYES.
Bibl: B. Hecht, CHARLIE, THE IMPOSSIBLE LIFE AND TIMES OF CHARLES MACARTHUR, 1957

MacCarthy, Sir Desmond (1877–1952), English man of letters and drama critic. For many years literary editor of the weekly *New Statesman*, he wrote many play reviews for that paper. A subtle and sensitive judge of plays and actors, he exercised considerable influence. Knighted in 1951.

McClintic, Guthrie (1893–1961), US actor, producer and director. Best known for his productions of SHAKESPEARE and SHAW, his style was characterized by poetic and decorative qualities resulting from his collaboration with the stage designer MIEL-

ZINER. His wife KATHARINE CORNELL starred in many of his productions; e.g. Shaw's *Candida*, 1924, and *Saint Joan*, 1936, Shakespeare's *Romeo and Juliet*, 1933, and *Antony and Cleopatra*, 1947; Rudolf Besier's *The Barretts of Wimpole Street*, 1931; and BEHRMAN's *No Time for Comedy*, 1939, with OLIVIER. Among M.'s outstanding productions in which his wife did not appear: M. ANDERSON's *Winterset*, 1935, and *Hamlet*, 1936 (with GIELGUD).

McCullers, Carson (1917–67), US novelist. Adapted her successful novel *The Member of the Wedding*, 1946, for the stage in 1950. The play achieved world-wide fame and was filmed in 1953. She also wrote the play *The Square Root of Wonderful*, 1958. ALBEE dramatized her novella *The Ballad of the Sad Café*, 1963.

Maccus (Roman). Fool, duffer, a traditional character of the *atellana* (▷ATELLAN FARCE) represented as inn-keeper, soldier, foreigner: a glutton, big-bellied, clumsy, but nevertheless quickwitted and sly.

Macgowan, Kenneth (1888–1963), US theatre critic and producer. Drama critic for the *New York Globe*, 1919–23, and *Vogue*, 1920–24; editor of the *Theatre Arts Magazine*, 1919–25. Associate Director of the PROVINCETOWN PLAYERS, 1924–25; of the Greenwich Village Theatre, 1925–27, and the Actor's Theatre, 1927. He was one of the main supporters of O'NEILL, most of whose plays he was the first to stage; later in the 1930s became best known as a film director. He was head of the department of Theatre Arts at the University of California, 1947–57. His theoretical works include: *The Theatre of Tomorrow*, 1921; *Continental Stagecraft*, with E. JONES, 1922; *Footlights Across America*, 1929; *A Primer of Playwriting*, 1951; co-author of *Theatre Pictorial*, 1953, and *The Living Stage*, 1955.

McGrath, John (1935–), English dramatist. His first play *A Man Has Two Fathers* was staged by the OUDS. Subsequent plays have included *The Tent*, 1958; *Why the Chicken*, 1959; *Events While Guarding the Bofors Gun*, 1966, and *Bakke's Night of Fame*, 1968 (based on the novel *A Danish Gambit* by William Butler), both Hampstead Theatre Club; *Comrade Jacob*, 1969; *Random Happenings in the Hebrides*, 1970; *Unruly Elements*, 1971.

Machiavelli, Niccolò di Bernardo dei (1469–1527), Italian historian and political philosopher. Best known for his treatise on statecraft, *Il Principe* (The Prince), he also wrote a number of COMEDIES including one of the most important of the 16th century: *La Mandragola*, written 1513–20, fp probably 1520. A highly original play, it is an elegant and sharp portrayal of the manners and particularly the vices of the period. Translated by DUKES, it was produced at the Mercury Theatre, 1940, and in 1965 was successfully revived in Milan. Bibl: R. Ridolfi, 1954

MacKaye. (1) **Steele M.** (1842–94), US

Lugné-Poë's production of GORKY's *The Lower Depths*, Théâtre de l'Œuvre, Paris 1905, with ELEONORA DUSE

Alfred Lunt and LYNN FONTANNE in GIRAUDOUX's *Amphitryon 38*, adapted by BEHRMAN, 1937

dramatist, inventor, innovator and theatre producer. Pioneer of the American theatre, who introduced overhead lighting, created a double movable stage and numerous scenic and technical improvements, e.g. folding seats. His best play, *Hazel Kirke*, with which he opened the Madison Square Theatre in 1879, had a run of two years – sensational at that time. Also established the first school of acting in New York, which later became the American Academy of Dramatic Art. He strongly influenced the next two generations with his ingenious plans and ideas. (2) **Percy M.** (1875–1956), his son, also a theatre manager for a short time, was best known as an author of poetic drama, modern MASQUES and spectacles. His works include the VERSE DRAMAS: *The Canterbury Pilgrims*, a COMEDY, 1903; *Jeanne d'Arc*, a TRAGEDY, 1906; *A Thousand Years Ago*, a romantic fantasy, 1913; and a satire, *Anti-Matrimony*, 1910. Later he wrote non-commercial poetic dramas, e.g. the TETRALOGY *The Mystery of Hamlet*, 1949. Percy also wrote several volumes of criticism and a biography of his father entitled *Epoch*, 1927.
Bibl: T. H. Dickinson, PLAYWRIGHTS OF THE NEW AMERICAN THEATRE, 1924

McKenna, Siobhan (1922–), Irish actress. Began her career at the Gaelic Repertory Theatre in Galway, 1940–42; 1942–46 at the ABBEY THEATRE, Dublin, making her London début in 1947. In 1954 she played SHAW's *Saint Joan* for the first time in Dublin, a role she repeated successfully in New York 1956, and London 1964, where she was also seen in BRECHT's *St Joan of the Stockyards*. Other roles include: Madrigal in ENID BAGNOLD's *The Chalk Garden*, New York 1955; Avril in O'CASEY's *Purple Dust*, Glasgow 1953; Viola in *Twelfth Night*, Stratford, Ontario, 1957; Lady Macbeth, Cambridge, Mass., 1959; Pegeen Mike in SYNGE's *The Playboy of the Western World*, Edinburgh 1951, Dublin 1961, and the title role in his *Juno and the Paycock*, London 1973. She has also appeared in a number of films.

Macklin, Charles (M'Laughlin; ?1690–1797), Irish actor. He claimed to have reached the age of 107; this is, however, open to some doubt. A vital active man of the theatre with unbounded energy, of whom it was said that he had 'a rough mind and a rougher manner'. After several years in the provinces and playing small parts at the Lincoln's Inn Fields Theatre, he had his greatest success in 1741 at Drury Lane with a performance as Shylock that made theatre history. The part had until then been conceived as comic; M. achieved a tragic and dignified interpretation ('This is the Jew, That Shakespeare Drew' – Pope). At the Haymarket Theatre he played Iago to FOOTE's Othello, and at COVENT GARDEN Mercutio to S. BARRY's Romeo. He founded a drama school, and tried out many theatrical reforms, anticipating GARRICK, but his erratic personality prevented him from successfully realizing his ideas. He wrote several plays, in which he gave some of his finest performances; two of these works have survived, *Love à la Mode*, and *The Man of the World*, both 1759.

MacLeish, Archibald (1892–), US poet, dramatist and public official. His first volume of poetry, *Tower of Ivory*, appeared in 1917. He won the PULITZER PRIZE twice, and various other awards, for work such as the epic poem, *Conquistador*, 1932, *Collected Poems, 1917–52*, 1953, and for his social drama in modern verse, *J.B.*, 1958, dir KAZAN, a PARABLE play based on the story of Job, affirming modern man's nobler qualities, which ran on BROADWAY for 364 performances. Other stage plays include *Nobodaddy*, pub 1926; *Panic*, 1935, lead played by WELLES, a sophisticated AGITPROP drama about the Wall Street crash; among his radio VERSE DRAMAS are: *The Fall of the City*, 1937; *Air Raid*, 1938; *The American Story*, 1944; *The Trojan Horse*, 1952; *This Music Crept by Me Upon the Waters*, 1953. He was Librarian of Congress, 1939–44, and as Assistant Secretary of State headed the American Delegation which drew up the UNESCO constitution.
Bibl: S. L. Falk, ARCHIBALD MacLEISH, 1965; J. G. Southworth, SOME MODERN AMERICAN POETS, 1951

MacLiammóir, Michéal (1899–), Irish actor, dramatist, stage designer and manager. After varied acting experience in London, he studied painting. Returning to Ireland in 1925, he designed sets for small theatres in Dublin and in 1928 opened the Galway Gaelic Theatre, where he directed many plays, translated MOLIÈRE, CHEKHOV and SHAW into Gaelic and then, with Hilton Edwards, opened the Gate Theatre, Dublin, where he acted and designed sets. His notable performances were in GOETHE's *Faust*; SHAKESPEARE's *Henry IV* and *Hamlet*, and in IBSEN's *Hedda Gabler* as Brack. His plays, most of which he also produced, include *Diarmuid and Grainne*, 1928; *Ill Met by Moon Light*, 1946; *The Mountains Look Different*, 1948; *Home for Christmas*, 1950. He played Iago in WELLES' film of *Othello* and described his experiences in a witty book, *Put Money in Thy Purse*. He also compiled *The Importance of Being Oscar*, 1960, based on the writings of WILDE, in which he gave a brilliant virtuoso solo performance.

McMaster, Anew (1894–1962), Irish actor and actor-manager. Started as an actor in London with Fred Terry. From 1925 he led a Shakespeare company which toured the world, but mainly Ireland. He played all the great Shakespearean roles, Hamlet, Macbeth, Coriolanus, Richard III, Shylock, Othello. For many years his company provided entertainment for the remoter parts of Ireland, where even cinemas were scarce. His powerful performances evoked an immediate response from the simplest rural audiences. Although he was occasionally seen elsewhere (he took over from MARCH in an American touring company's production of O'NEILL's *Long Day's Journey into Night*, and appeared at STRATFORD-UPON-AVON), he preferred the life of a strolling player in Ireland. PINTER acted in his company at the beginning of his acting career, 1951, and has written a moving account of him in the short book *Mac*, 1968.

Macready, William Charles (1793–1873), English actor. Son of the ACTOR-MANAGER William Macready. Made his début as Romeo in Birmingham in 1810, first appearing in London at COVENT GARDEN in 1816 as Orestes in *The Distressed Mother*, an adaptation of RACINE's *Andromaque*. By 1819 he had established himself as a fine tragic actor and a rival to KEAN, whose uncontrolled genius he countered with a restrained acting style governed by intellect. He acted successfully in a variety of parts including Lear, Hamlet and Macbeth. He was seen in the USA in 1826, and again in 1849 as *Macbeth* (▷FORREST); in France in 1828; 1827–39 he managed Covent Garden and 1841–43 the DRURY LANE THEATRE. His memoirs and diaries provide an important source for 19th-century English theatre history.
Bibl: A. C. Sprague, SHAKESPEAREAN PLAYERS AND PERFORMANCES, 1953

Madrigal comedy. The singing of madrigals illustrated by mimed action by masked actors; mainly in Italy between *c.* 1680 and 1720; superseded by the rise of opera.

Maeterlinck, Maurice (1862–1949), Belgian poet and dramatist. A major exponent of SYMBOLISM and aestheticism at the turn of the century, and the forerunner of PIRANDELLO and O'NEILL. His idea about drama lying in silences that reveal the mysteries of man's soul and the universe, as discussed in his book, *Le Trésor des Humbles*, 1896, influenced dramatists like OBEY and J.-J. BERNARD who initiated a 'theatre of silence'. His plays are based on static, mystical inner visions depicting spiritual loneliness and fear of the unseen forces of destiny. The publication of his five-act play *La Princesse Maleine*, 1889, immediately brought him international fame. Most of his works had their première under FORT at the Théâtre d'Art which later became the Théâtre de l'Œuvre under LUGNÉ-POË, M.'s close friend: *L'Intruse*, Paris 1891, Théâtre d'Art; *Les Aveugles*, 1891; *Pelléas et Mélisande*, Bouffes-Parisiens, 1893, dir Lugné-Poë; famous production by REINHARDT, BERLIN 1903; opera by Debussy, Paris 1902, Opéra Comique. Also *Annabelle*, 1894; *Interieur*, 1895; *Aglavaine et Sélysette*, 1896, Odéon; *Monna Vanna* 1902, Nouveau Théâtre, dir Lugné-Poë. Other works include: *Ariane et Barbe-bleue*, 1901; *Joyzelle*, 1903; *L'Oiseau bleu*, fp Moscow 1908, dir STANISLAVSKY; *Marie Madeleine*, 1913; *Les Fiançailles*, 1918; *Le Bourgmestre de Stilmonde*, 1919; *Le Miracle de saint Antoine*, 1921. His most famous non-dramatic work is *La Vie des abeilles*, 1901. He was awarded the Nobel Prize for Literature in 1911.
Bibl: C. Hertrich, 1946; W. D. Halls, MAURICE MAETERLINCK: A STUDY OF HIS LIFE AND THOUGHT, 1960

Maffei, Scipione (1675–1755), Italian poet. His best-known dramatic work is the TRAGEDY *Merope*, 1713, performed in ITALY and at the COMÉDIE-ITALIENNE in Paris, which turned away from the French classicist tradition; it was much admired by VOLTAIRE, whose *Mérope* was dedicated to Maffei.
Bibl: G. Gasperoni, 1955

Magnani, Anna (1908–73), Italian actress. In the 1930s and 1940s she appeared in theatre and REVUE, and also made films. Her finest stage performances were in O'NEILL's *Anna Christie*, and in S. Gantillon's *Maya*, between 1945 and 1946. In this period she also made her most important films: *Ossessione*, dir VISCONTI, 1943, and *Roma città aperta*, R. Rossellini, 1945. Among her best-known later roles was VERGA's *La Lupa*, dir ZEFFIRELLI.

Maistre Pierre Pathelin. Late 15th-century French FARCE of unknown authorship and origins; a comic piece about a fraudulent lawyer, it is considered one of the major French comedies prior to MOLIÈRE.

Make-up. Actor's aid to enhance the appearance of the face and heighten its expressive power: grease-paint, powder, rouge, wigs etc. The intensity of STAGE-LIGHTING makes some make-up indispensable as without it the actors' faces would appear unnaturally pale, but the art ranges from a mere heightening of the natural appearance of the face to highly stylized designs which approximate to wholly artificial masks. This technique forms an important part of an actor's professional skills and involves close study of the shades and highlights that can alter the shape and expressiveness of the face.
Bibl: R. Carson, STAGE MAKE-UP, 1961

Malina, Judith ▷LIVING THEATRE.

Malraux, André (1901–76), French novelist, art critic, orientalist and politician. Politically on the far left in his youth, he travelled in East Asia as an archaeologist, became a supporter of Communist ideology, and fought on the Republican side in the Spanish civil war. Supported De Gaulle as a member of the Free French Forces in World War II. Was Minister of Culture in various Gaullist governments 1958–69. Greatly developed the policy of regionalization in the French theatre and the foundation of numerous Maisons de Culture.

Mamoulian, Rouben (1897–), US director of Georgian origin. Noted particularly for a number of successful musical productions on BROADWAY, the most famous of which were *Oklahoma*, 1943, and *Carousel*, based on MOLNÁR's *Liliom*, 1945. He had a frequent association with the THEATRE GUILD, directing their productions of *Porgy*, 1927; O'NEILL's *Marco Millions*, 1928; TURGENEV's *A Month in the Country*, 1930; GERSHWIN's opera *Porgy and Bess*, 1935.

Manchester School. A regional group of dramatists who developed under the influence of ANNIE HORNIMAN when she was

Steele MacKaye in his own play, *Anarchy*

Michéal MacLiammóir

William C. Macready in BYRON's *Werner* with HELEN FAUCIT

Charles Macklin as Shylock

managing the Gaiety Theatre, Manchester, 1907–17. They produced a strongly realistic style of writing, in a vigorous vernacular, concerned with the social problems of the time. The two outstanding playwrights of this movement were HOUGHTON and Harold Brighouse.

Mann. German family of writers and actors. (1) **Heinrich M.** (1871–1950). Best known for his short stories. He also wrote a number of plays including *Drei Akte* (Three Acts), *Der Tyrann* (The Tyrant), *Die Unschuldige* (The Innocent), *Variété*, 1900; *Schauspielerin* (Actress), 1911; *Die Grosse Liebe* (Great Love), 1913; *Madame Legros*, 1917; *Brabach*, 1919; *Der Weg zur Macht* (The Way to Power), 1920; *Das Strumpfband* (The Garter), written 1902, fp Celle 1965. (2) **Thomas M.** (1875–1955), brother of Heinrich. Author of one dramatic work, *Fiorenza*, a dialogue in three acts based on the life of Lorenzo de' Medici, pub 1905, fp Frankfurt 1907. The most famous production was by REINHARDT in Berlin, 1913. M. also wrote numerous essays on the theatre and about dramatists (LESSING, SCHILLER, CHEKHOV, HAUPTMANN, WEDEKIND, SHAW, etc.). Particularly well known are two essays on Wagner and one on the theatre, *Versuch übers Theater*, 1908. His short story *Die vertauschten Köpfe* (Exchanged Heads) was made into an opera by Peggy Glanville Hicks, fp Louisville 1954, Kentucky Opera. His novella *Death in Venice* was made into a film, dir VISCONTI, 1971, and also into an opera by Benjamin Britten, fp Aldeburgh Festival, 1973. He was awarded the Nobel Prize for Literature in 1929. His daughter (3) **Erika M.** (1905–69) was an actress best known for her appearances in the plays of her brother (4) **Klaus M.** (1906–49), including *Anja und Esther*, 1925, and *Revue zu Vieren* in which he also appeared together with GRÜNDGENS, husband of Erika, and Pamela Wedekind, and which successfully toured Germany. Brother and sister were active 1933–36 in the CABARET Die Pfeffermühle in Zurich, and in 1937 The Pepper Mill in New York, for which K.M. was the main writer. E.M. also prepared a posthumous edition of her father's works. K.M.'s plays include *Gegenüber China* (China Face to Face), Bochum 1929; *Geschwister* (Brothers and Sisters), after COCTEAU, 1932, Munich Kammerspiele; *Athen*, pub 1932; *Der siebente Engel* (The Seventh Angel), written 1946. He wrote the film script for Rossellini's *Paisà*, 1947, and a novel *Mephisto*, 1936, based on the character of Gründgens, his former brother-in-law.
Bibl: A. Kantorowicz, HEINRICH UND THOMAS MANN, 1956; J. Bab, KLAUS MANN ZUM GEDÄCHTNIS (ed E. Mann), 1950; A. Kerr, DIE WELT IN DRAMA III, 1917

Mannheim, Lucie (1899–1976), German actress. Made her early career in BERLIN, appearing at the VOLKSBÜHNE and the State Theatre, 1922–33, where she played in local FARCES as well as classical roles like KLEIST's *Käthchen von Heilbronn*, 1923; Franziska in LESSING's *Minna von Barnhelm*, 1923; Alma in WEDEKIND's *König Nicolò*, 1924; Marie in BÜCHNER's *Woyzeck* and Nora in IBSEN's *A Doll's House*. In 1933 she emigrated to England, and appeared as Nora in London in 1935. Returning to Berlin in 1949 she played leading roles at several theatres, including Rosa in T. WILLIAMS's *The Rose Tattoo*, 1949, Theater am Kurfürstendamm. She was married to the English actor GORING.

Mansfield, Richard (1854–1907), British-born US actor. Made his name in romantic parts such as the title roles in *Cyrano de Bergerac*, and *Beau Brummell*, 1890, a play specially written for him by FITCH. He appeared as Peer Gynt in the first English production of IBSEN's play and introduced the works of SHAW to the USA, appearing in *Arms and the Man*, 1894, and *The Devil's Disciple*, 1897.

Mantle, Robert Burns (1873–1948), US theatre critic. Worked on papers in Denver and Chicago, became drama critic of the New York *Daily News* in 1922 and remained in that capacity on the paper till his retirement in 1943. From 1919 till his death edited the annual series *The Best Plays*, an invaluable reference book.

Manzoni, Alessandro (1785–1873), Italian romantic writer of poetry and prose. He wrote two remarkable TRAGEDIES which have received little attention outside Italy: *Il Conte di Carmagnola*, pub 1820, and *Adelchi*, pub 1822, acted by GASSMAN, 1963.
Bibl: I. Sanesi, 1958

Marais, Jean (1913–), French actor. Studied under DULLIN and in 1937 met COCTEAU, who wrote *Les Parents terribles*, 1938, for him. In 1941 he achieved a major success directing and playing the lead in RACINE's *Britannicus* and in the same year appeared in Cocteau's *La Machine à écrire*. In 1942 he played Cléante in MOLIÈRE's *L'Avare* under Dullin's direction, and in 1946 appeared in two more plays by Cocteau, *Renaud et Armide* and *L'Aigle à deux têtes*. In 1949 he toured the Orient with works by SARTRE, ANOUILH and Cocteau, also in SHAW's plays and classical parts. Has appeared in a number of films.

Marceau, Félicien (1913–), Belgian dramatist, who writes in French. Originally a radio journalist in Belgium, he now lives in Paris. His first stage success was the anti-conformist satire *L'Œuf*, Théâtre de l' Atelier, 1956. Other works: *L'Ecole des moroses*, 1948, one-act play; *Caterina*, 1954, a drama; *La Bonne soupe*, 1958; *L'Etouffe chrétien*, 1960; *Les Cailloux*, 1962; all except *L'Ecole* were produced by BARSACQ. M. himself directed *La Preuve par quatre*, 1964, and *Madame Princesse*, 1965.

Marceau, Marcel (1923–), French mime. After studying under DECROUX, he joined the COMPAGNIE RENAUD-BARRAULT in 1945 (Arlequin in *Baptiste*); left in 1946 to concentrate on MIME, evolving his famous character Bip, based on the 19th-century French PIERROT, a melancholy vagabond with a white clown mask, engaged in a constant struggle with the basic problems of everyday life. His most famous sketches centred around Bip are: *14 juillet*, 1956; *Paris qui rit, Paris qui dort*, 1958; *Le Petit Cirque*, 1958. Apart from this characterization he also developed mime-dramas like: *Mort avant l'aube*, 1947; *Le Manteau*, based on GOGOL, 1951. In *Jardin public*, 1949, he appeared as ten different characters.
Bibl: H. Jhering, MARCEL MARCEAU UND DIE WELTKUNST DER PANTOMIME, 1955

Marcel, Gabriel (1889–1973), French dramatist, critic and Christian existentialist philosopher (▷EXISTENTIALISM). His dramatic works, in style almost like Socratic dialogues, reveal his philosophy and deal with the problems of consciousness: in 1921 *La Grâce* and *Le Cœur des autres*; *Le Regard neuf*, 1922; *La Chapelle ardente*, 1925; *Le Dard*, 1937; *Le Fanal*, 1938, COMÉDIE-FRANÇAISE; *L'Emissaire*, pub 1949; *Les Cœurs avides*, Marseilles 1949; *Le Signe de la croix*, 1951; *Rome n'est plus dans Rome*, 1951; *Le Monde cassé*, pub 1952; *Le Chemin de Crête*, 1953; *La Dimension Florestan*, pub 1953; *Mon temps n'est pas le vôtre*, 1953; *Croissez et multipliez*, 1958.
Bibl: S. Cain, 1961; J. Chenu, LE THÉÂTRE DE GABRIEL MARCEL, 1948

March, Frederic (F. McIntyre Bickel; 1897–1975), US actor. Made his début in 1920 under his own name of Fred Bickel in S. GUITRY's *Deburau* under BELASCO's management, then successfully toured with his wife Florence Eldridge (whom he married in 1927) in plays by SHAW, MOLNÁR and S. HOWARD; in the 1930s appeared mainly in films playing romantic lovers, e.g. in *Anna Karenina* with Greta Garbo, and also character parts. His later stage successes include: Mr Antrobus in WILDER's *The Skin of Our Teeth*, 1942; Dr Stockmann in A. MILLER's *An Enemy of the People*, based on IBSEN, 1950; James Tyrone in O'NEILL's *Long Day's Journey Into Night*, 1956.

Marcus, Frank (1928–), English dramatist. Born in Breslau, Germany, and emigrated to England just before the outbreak of World War II. Studied at St Martin's School of Art, London. His first West End play was *The Formation Dancers*, 1964, Globe Theatre, followed by his COMEDY *The Killing of Sister George*, 1965, which won him the *Evening Standard* award for the 'Best Play of the Year', and which was also a hit on BROADWAY, and a successful film. Among his other works are *Studies of the Nude*, 1967; *Mrs Mouse Are You Within?*, 1968; *Notes on a Love Affair*, 1972. He is drama critic of the *Sunday Telegraph*.

Marinelli, Karl von (1745–1803), Austrian actor and IMPRESARIO. Author of a number of COMEDIES, e.g. *Der Ungar in Wien* (The Hungarian in Vienna), 1773; appeared in leading parts with Mathias Menninger's company and inspired him to found the Theater in der Leopoldstadt in Vienna in

1781, succeeding him later as director. A learned and talented organizer, he engaged actors such as Anton and Friedrich Baumann, the young actor-playwright Anton Hasenhut (who achieved success as the popular comic character 'Thaddädl') and the composer Wenzel Müller. M. raised the standards of the SINGSPIEL and of FARCES and thus the reputation of the traditional Viennese folk theatre, providing a REPERTOIRE of his own plays and adaptations, e.g. *Die Liebesgeschichte von Hirschau oder Kasperl in sechserlei Gestalten* (The Love Story of H. or K. in six shapes), 1782; *Dom Juan, der steinerne Gast* (Don Juan, the Stone Guest), 1783.
Bibl: O. Rommel, DIE ALT-WIENER VOLKSKOMÖDIE, 1952

Marinetti, Filippo Tommaso (1876–1944), Italian writer. The founder of FUTURISM and author of several dramatic works written in French and Italian, e.g. *La Donna è mobile* (Woman is fickle), 1909; *Le Roi Bombance*, 1909; *Poupées électriques*, 1909; *Simultaneità* (Simultaneousness), 1915; *Prigionieri* (Prisoners), 1925. None of these achieved lasting success. Nevertheless the influence of his theoretical writings in which he called for the use of MUSIC HALL techniques and strong physical effects, had a great influence, notably on MAYAKOVSKY and the Surrealists (▷SURREALISM).
Bibl: W. Vaccari, 1959

Marivaux, Pierre Carlet de Chamblain de (1688–1763), French playwright. The son of a banker, he was forced, after bankruptcy, to write for his living. His first play, the COMEDY *Le Père prudent et équitable*, was performed at Limoges in 1706. For the COMÉDIE-ITALIENNE he wrote a number of plays, among them *La Surprise de l'amour*, 1722; *La Double Inconstance*, 1723; *Les Fausses Confidences*, 1737, and *L'Epreuve*, 1740. For the Théâtre Français, M. wrote a TRAGEDY, *Annibal*, 1720, and the comedies: *Les Petits Hommes*, 1727; *La (Seconde) Surprise de l'amour*, 1727; *Le Jeu de l'amour et du hasard*, 1730; *La Réunion des amours*, 1731; *Les Serments indiscrets*, 1732; *Le Petit-Maître corrigé*, 1734; *Le Legs*, 1736; *La Dispute*, 1744; *Le Préjugé vaincu*, 1746. In 1742 he was elected a member of the Académie française. He is a master of French artificial comedy. His PLOTS, though complex, are fairly easily seen through; what distinguishes him is the subtlety and culture of the emotional attitudes he portrays and the deep insights into human nature they reveal. His plays were only rarely successful with his contemporaries; yet they have never disappeared from the REPERTOIRE of the COMÉDIE-FRANÇAISE. The most frequently performed are *Le Jeu de l'amour et du hasard*, *Le Legs*, *L'Epreuve*, *Les Fausses Confidences*, *La (Seconde) Surprise de l'amour*, *Le Préjugé vaincu*, *Arlequin poli par l'amour* and, more recently, *La Double Inconstance*.
Bibl: K. N. McKee, THE THEATRE OF MARIVAUX, 1958

Marlowe, Christopher (1564–93), English poet and playwright. The son of a prosperous shoemaker at Canterbury, he studied at Cambridge, and took his MA in 1587. Had probably, previously, been abroad on some secret government mission. Suspected of holding atheistic views. Was stabbed and killed in a tavern brawl at Deptford at the age of 29, but the motives for the quarrel may well have been political or associated with his secret activities. He was the first of the great Elizabethan dramatists. His earliest play *Tamburlaine the Great*, Part I, 1587, established blank verse as the dominant metre of TRAGEDY and made him famous for 'his mighty line'. His career was associated with the ADMIRAL'S MEN led by ALLEYN, one of the great actors of the period. Part II of *Tamburlaine* followed immediately, 1588; *The Tragical History of Dr Faustus*, probably 1590; *The Jew of Malta*, c. 1590; *Edward II*, 1592. The dates of composition and performance of two other plays, probably written in collaboration with Nashe, are uncertain: *Dido Queen of Carthage*, which may have been written before *Tamburlaine*, and *The Massacre at Paris*. His boldness of construction, characterization and the power and beauty of his verse and imagery would, undoubtedly, had he lived, have made him a very serious rival to his exact contemporary SHAKESPEARE. Indeed, according to some, it was M. who aroused Shakespeare's professional and personal jealousy as the 'rival poet' of the sonnets.
Bibl: D. Cole, SUFFERING AND EVIL IN THE WORKS OF CHRISTOPHER MARLOWE, 1962; H. Levin, THE OVERREACHER, A STUDY OF CHRISTOPHER MARLOWE, 1954; P. Henderson, 1952

Mars, Mlle (Anne-Françoise Hippolyte Boutet; 1779–1847), French actress. Made her début at the COMÉDIE-FRANÇAISE in 1795, at the start of a long, successful career as the leading actress of her time, and the most influential personality of the CF. She was Napoleon's favourite actress, versatile in the classical style, equally successful in COMEDY and romantic drama, including Desdemona in VIGNY's *Le More de Venise* (based on SHAKESPEARE) and Doña Sol in HUGO's *Hernani*. Her last appearances on stage were in her brilliant roles as Elmire in MOLIÈRE's *Tartuffe* and Silvie in MARIVAUX's *Le Jeu de l'amour au hasard*. She retired from the theatre in 1841.
Bibl: M. Descotes, LE DRAME ROMANTIQUE ET SES GRANDS CRÉATEURS, 1955

Marston, John (1576–1634), English playwright. He started writing plays in 1599 for the CHILDREN OF ST PAUL'S. In his first play, the COMEDY *Histriomastix*, he may have irritated JONSON by his portrait of him as Chrisogamus, which was, however, intended to be flattering. The elder poet, in any event, then parodied M.'s extravagant, ranting style in *Every Man out of his Humour*, 1599, thus starting the quarrel known as the WAR OF THE THEATRES. M. participated in the dispute with two other comedies: *Jack Drum's Entertainment*, 1600, and *What You Will*, 1601. By 1603, the quarrel was finally settled, and the rival dramatists collaborated with CHAPMAN on the comedy *Eastward hoe!*, 1605. A passage

Richard Mansfield as Dick Dudgeon in SHAW's *The Devil's Disciple*, 1897

Marcel Marceau

Christopher Marlowe's *Tragical History of Dr Faustus*, title page, 1620

derogatory to the Scots gave offence at Court. Jonson and Chapman were imprisoned, though quickly released. M. appeared to have narrowly escaped. He dedicated to Jonson his best play *The Malcontent*, 1600–04, which was written for the Children of the Queen's Revels; it is a biting satire on the deception and hypocrisy of Renaissance Court life. Other works include a TRAGEDY in two parts, *Antonio and Mellida*, produced 1599–1600, and *Antonio's Revenge*, prod 1599–1601, and the comedies, *The Dutch Courtesan*, prod 1603–04 and *Parasitaster; or The Fawn*, prod 1604–06. M. left the theatre for the Church in 1607.
Bibl: A. Caputi, 1961

Martin, Karl Heinz (1888–1948), German director. Achieved his first outstanding success in 1919 with TOLLER's *Die Wandlung* (with KORTNER playing the lead) at the Tribüne theatre in BERLIN, which he founded with R. Leonhard. This was the first of a series of Expressionist productions by HAUPTMANN, HASENCLEVER, REHFISCH and TOLLER. He also produced modern versions of the classics. He managed the VOLKSBÜHNE, Berlin, 1928–33, producing BÜCHNER's *Dantons Tod*.

Martin, Mary (1913–), US singer and actress. Made her BROADWAY début in 1938 in a musical *Leave it to me* when she sang 'My Heart Belongs to Daddy'. In 1943 she appeared in *One Touch of Venus*, and made her London début in *Pacific 1860*, in 1946. She then starred in the sensationally successful RODGERS and HAMMERSTEIN musicals *South Pacific*, 1949, and *The Sound of Music*, 1959, and between those in a musical version of *Peter Pan*, 1954. In 1964 she appeared in the London production of *Hello, Dolly!*, the musical version of *The Matchmaker*.

Martinelli. Italian family of actors. (1) **Drusiano M.** (mid-16th century–1606/08), a COMMEDIA DELL'ARTE actor who played ARLECCHINO; his reputation is based on his talents as a manager, probably the first to visit England with a regular company, 1577–78; in 1588 he went with the CONFIDENTI company to Spain. As an actor he was overshadowed by his brother (2) **Tristano M.** (*c.* 1556–1630), the most famous Arlecchino prior to G. D. BIANCOLELLI, who changed companies several times (probably a result of his quarrelsome temperament), e.g. in 1601 with the ACCESI; and 1611–13 with ANDREINI in Paris. A witty comedian, T.M. was also famous for his acrobatic prowess.
Bibl: ▷COMMEDIA DELL'ARTE

Masque. A form of entertainment originally featuring the arrival of guests in disguise, bearing gifts; in its early form it was known as 'Disguising' and proved a useful dramatic formula to entertain Queen Elizabeth and generally flourished at the English Court. It combined poetry, music, dance, elaborate COSTUME and spectacular STAGE MACHINERY, allegorical and mythological themes and characters. It reached the height of its development at the Court of James I with the collaboration of JONSON and the stage designer and architect I. JONES. The rivalry between author and stage designer caused a quarrel which led to Jonson's dismissal in the winter of 1631–32, at Jones's prompting, from his post as author of masques for the Court, whereupon Jonson abandoned the form. Notable masques by his successors were SHIRLEY's *The Triumph of Peace* and Thomas Carew's *Coelum Britannicum*, both produced before the Court in 1634, MILTON's *Comus*, though called a masque was strictly speaking a pastoral drama. Produced also in 1634 at Ludlow Castle.
A comic interlude before or during the main masque, which it was intended to parody, was known as the **anti-masque**. Introduced in ENGLAND, early 17th century; Jonson's preface to his play *Masque of Queens*, 1602, contains the earliest recorded use of the term. While the masque praises virtue and beauty, the anti-masque presents a world of vice and darkness. The masque largely disappeared with the outbreak of civil war in 1642 but it has influenced the development of opera, ballet and modern theatre.

Massinger, Philip (1583–1640), English dramatist. Many of his early works (from *c.* 1616) were written in collaboration, chiefly with FLETCHER. When Fletcher died in 1625, M. succeeded him as resident playwright of the King's Players. Of the plays which M. wrote alone the finest are his Comedies of Manners: *A New Way to Pay Old Debts*, 1621–25, one of the most popular English COMEDIES, of which the main character Sir Giles Overreach was, 200 years later, one of the favourite parts of KEAN at DRURY LANE, 1816; and *The City Madam*, 1632. Other works include the tragedies *The Duke of Milan*, 1621–23, and *The Roman Actor*, 1626; and the TRAGICOMEDIES *The Maid of Honour*, *c.* 1621–32; and *The Bondman*, 1623.
Bibl: T. A. Dunn, 1957

Masson, André (1896–), French Surrealist painter. As a stage designer he emphasized simplified sets with decorative elements or dark baroque interiors. Close friend and collaborator of BARRAULT in: CERVANTES' *Numance*, 1937; *Faim*, based on HAMSUN, 1939; SHAKESPEARE's *Hamlet*, 1946; CLAUDEL's *Tête d'or*, 1959; *Wozzeck*, opera by Berg, 1963; also worked with DULLIN on SALACROU's *La Terre est ronde*, 1938; *Médée*, opera by Milhaud, 1940.
Bibl: H. Rischbieter (ed), BÜHNE UND BILDENDE KUNST IM 20. JAHRHUNDERT, 1968

Master of the Revels. English official, first appointed in 1494, active in the time of Elizabeth I and James I, who supervised dramatic entertainments at Court as organizer (master of ceremonies) and later dramatic censor (late 16th to 18th century), a function which became the direct responsibility of the LORD CHAMBERLAIN under the Stage Licensing Act of 1737 (abolished 1968).

Bibl: E. K. Chambers, THE ELIZABETHAN STAGE, 1923, 4 vols

MAT ▷MOSCOW ART THEATRE.

Mathews. (1) **Charles M.** (1776–1835), English comedian, famous for his roles as Falstaff; in SHERIDAN's plays, *The Critic*, as Sir Fretful Plagiary, and *The School for Scandal*, as Sir Peter Teazle. Known above all as an 'entertainer': his one-man shows, originally a programme of comic songs which he linked with imitations and impersonations of different characters, evolved into short plays which were scripted for him by COLMAN the Younger, including *The Actor of All Work*, 1817; *The Trip to Paris*; *Mr Mathews and His Youthful Days*; *The Trip to America*. His son (2) **Charles James M.** (1803–78) did not appear on stage until he was 32 and achieved his first success in his own play *The Humpbacked Lover* and in Rede's FARCE *The Old and the Young Stranger*. He was married to MADAME VESTRIS, appeared at COVENT GARDEN and the Lyceum Theatre and was considered one of the best actors of light comedy. In memory of his father he appeared with his second wife Lizzie Davenport, an American actress, in the 'entertainment' *Mr and Mrs Mathews at Home*.
Bibl: C. F. Armstrong, A CENTURY OF GREAT ACTORS, 1750–1850, 1912

Matthews, James Brander (1852–1929), US theatre historian and playwright. First Professor of Dramatic Literature at Columbia University, New York, 1900–24. Originator of the American tradition of giving lectures and holding seminars specifically for playwrights. He also founded several clubs for writers, actors, historians, copyright specialists. As the *New York Times* drama critic he had great influence on the American theatre and its public. His works include: *Actors and Actresses of Great Britain and the United States* (five volumes, 1886; with Laurence Hutton); *The Development of the Drama*, 1903; *Molière*, 1910; *Shakespeare as a Playwright*, 1913; *Principles of Playmaking*, 1919; autobiography *These Many Years*, 1917.

Mauclair, Jacques (1919–), French actor and director. Studied under JOUVET and appeared 1945–47 at his Théâtre de l' Athénée. Directed his first play in 1947: MOLIÈRE's *Le Mariage forcé*, in which he starred as Sganarelle; with his production of *Cecé* in 1950 he started a series of plays by PIRANDELLO; directed and acted in his own adaptations of DOSTOYEVSKY's *L'Eternel mari*, 1952; plays by ADAMOV, e.g. *La Grande et la Petite Manœuvre*, and *Professeur Taranne*, both 1954; *Ping-Pong*, 1955. He also directed and starred in CHEKHOV's *Ivanov*, 1956, directed IONESCO's *Les Chaises*, 1956, and produced *Uncle Vanya*, COMÉDIE-FRANÇAISE, 1961; directed and acted in *Le Roi se meurt*, 1963. In 1957 he acted in and directed his own play *L'Oncle Otto*. He favours writers whose work reveals reality at different levels. He has been awarded several prizes for his productions, adaptations and writings.

Maugham, William Somerset (1874–1965), English writer of novels, short stories, travel books and memoirs. His COMEDIES in the tradition of WILDE achieved great popularity both in London and New York in the 1920s. The first play to be produced was *A Man of Honour*, with GRANVILLE-BARKER, in 1903; his first big hit was *Lady Frederick*, 1907, which, in the following year, was running in London concurrently with three other of his plays, *Jack Straw*, *Mrs Dot* and *The Explorer*. A prolific author, by the time he gave up writing plays in 1933 he had completed 29, many of them popular DRAWING-ROOM COMEDY successes including *Our Betters*, fp New York 1917, London 1923; *The Circle*, 1921; *The Letter* and *The Constant Wife*, 1927; *The Sacred Flame*, 1928; *The Breadwinner*, 1930; *For Services Rendered*, 1932; *Sheppey*, 1933. He was made a Companion of Honour in 1954.
Bibl: S. Maugham, THE SUMMING-UP, 1938; R. E. Barnes, THE DRAMATIC COMEDY OF W. SOMERSET MAUGHAM, 1968

Maupassant, Guy de (1850–93), French short-story writer and novelist. Among his attempts at drama are: an unperformed verse tragedy, *La Trahison de la Comtesse de Rhune*; a short dialogue in verse, *Histoire du vieux temps*, 1879; a 'pornographic' COMEDY, not contained in his published works, *A la feuille de rose maison turque*, first privately produced 1875; his most successful play which ran for several performances at the COMÉDIE-FRANÇAISE in 1893 was the two-act comedy *La Paix du ménage*. Many of M.'s stories have been adapted for stage, film and TV.

Mauriac, François (1885–1971), French Catholic novelist and dramatist. Author of several plays which deal with human problems from a Christian viewpoint in a style which derives from IBSEN, e.g.: *Asmodée*, 1937, COMÉDIE-FRANÇAISE; *Les Mal aimés*, 1945, CF; *Le Passage du malin*, Rio de Janeiro 1947, Paris 1948; *Le Feu sur la terre*, Lyons 1950. Awarded the Nobel Prize for Literature, 1952.
Bibl: C. Jenkins, 1965

Maximovna, Ita (1914–), German stage designer of Russian origin. Studied in Paris and Berlin, and did her first important work with the director MARTIN (ANOUILH's *Eurydice*, Berlin 1947). Today she is one of the major designers of sets and COSTUMES at leading German theatres and opera houses including the Hamburg State Opera, Deutsche Opera, Berlin, the Vienna State Opera and at La Scala, Milan.

May, Gisela (1924–), German actress. Early successful appearances were at the Deutsches-Theater, BERLIN, 1951–61, where she excelled as Mrs Linde in IBSEN's *A Doll's House*, 1956, and Marie in BÜCHNER's *Woyzeck*, 1958. In 1961 she joined the BERLINER ENSEMBLE, playing leading parts in most of BRECHT's plays. One of her best performances was as Anna I in Brecht's *Die sieben Todsünden der Kleinbürger* (music

Masquers on a floating island, 1621

Masque. Charles I as Philogenes in 'Salmacida Spolia' by DAVENANT and Queen Henrietta Maria in 'Chloridia' by JONSON, 1621

Somerset Maugham's *Penelope* with MARIE TEMPEST, 1909

WEILL) at the Berlin Opera, 1963. She was famous above all for her 'Song Evenings' devoted to the works of Brecht and Tucholsky with which she toured extensively throughout Europe. She has also appeared in many films.
Bibl: W. Carlé, 1960

Mayakovsky, Vladimir Vladimirovich (1894–1930), Soviet poet. Originally encouraged to turn to dramatic writing by GORKY, he took part in the theatrical experiments of the Cubo-Futurists and Constructivists before the October Revolution; worked in close collaboration with MEYERHOLD. His plays support the Revolution and are mostly biting satires on remnants of bourgeois society in utopian terms: *Mysteriya-buff* (*Mystery-Bouffe*), Moscow 1918; *Klop* (*The Bedbug*), Moscow 1929, both dir Meyerhold; *Banya* (*The Bathhouse*), Moscow 1930. *The Bedbug* was first produced in English by a London University group and had its first professional production at the MERMAID THEATRE, 1962. For the CIRCUS he wrote the mass spectacle *Muskva gorit* (Moscow is Burning), celebrating the 25th anniversary of the 1905 Revolution. Shortly afterwards he committed suicide.
Bibl: H. Marshall, 1965; ▷MEYERHOLD

Mehring, Walter (1896–), German writer. Began his career writing CABARET sketches for REINHARDT's Schall und Rauch in BERLIN. One of the founders of DADA; a journalist and political cabarettist. His early Expressionist play: *Die Frühe der Städte* (The Morning of the Cities), was followed by a play written for PISCATOR, *Der Kaufmann von Berlin* (*The Merchant of Berlin*), 1929, which deals with the rise and fall of an Eastern Jew, who comes to Berlin during the inflation.

Mei Lan-fang (1894–1961), leading actor, director and scholar of modern Chinese theatre. First appeared at the Peking theatre, mainly playing female parts, e.g. Tan. His aim was to preserve the Chinese style of acting, especially the *K'in-chu*. He became internationally famous following his wide travels in the USA, where his dramatic MONOLOGUE *A Nun Craves Worldly Vanities* was enthusiastically received, and in the USSR (Moscow, Leningrad) where he was highly praised for his sword dancing and acting in *The Fisherman's Revenge*. His influence on European theatre was great and widespread, e.g. MEYERHOLD, EISENSTEIN, the puppet-player OBRAZTSOV. BRECHT was impressed with his acting style.
Bibl: S. Obraztsov, CHINESE THEATRE, 1965

Meilhac, Henri (1831–97), French dramatist. Author of many COMEDIES and VAUDEVILLES for the Palais Royal and for the Gymnase; with Halévy he wrote LIBRETTI for light operas by Offenbach, Bizet and Massenet and was one of the most important figures in the theatre of his time. He was nicknamed 'Marivaux of the Boulevards'.

Meininger. Troupe of actors of the COURT THEATRE in Meiningen, formed in 1874 by the Duke of Saxe-Meiningen (1826–1914), which had great influence on the theatre throughout Europe. The duke, who directed the plays himself (he is considered to be the first modern director to have emphasized ENSEMBLE playing), was greatly assisted in his work by his morganatic wife, the actress Ellen Franz, and by the actor Ludwig Chronegk. His most important innovations were ensemble training, with special attention to minor parts and crowd scenes, getting away from conventional grouping, the use of gesture and a style of acting in keeping with the period of the play with historically accurate settings and COSTUMES. The troupe toured extensively between 1874 and 1891, and was seen by both ANTOINE and STANISLAVSKY.
Bibl: A. Kruchen, DAS REGIEPRINZIP BEI DEN MEININGERN, 1933

Meinrad, Josef (1913–), Austrian actor. A member of the BURGTHEATER ensemble in Vienna since 1947, he excels mainly in comic Shakespearean parts and particularly in the Viennese folk comedies and FARCES of RAIMUND and NESTROY.

Meistersinger (Ger = master singers). Performers in the late Middle Ages who were members of artisans' guilds in Germany and formed associations dedicated to music and drama. They held singing contests, in which unaccompanied songs were judged according to rigid rules. The centre of the movement *c.* 1500 was the city of Nuremberg. Wagner based his opera *Die Meistersinger von Nürnberg*, 1868, on this fact and the central character on SACHS, the greatest of the poets and playwrights produced by the movement. Their dramatic performances were probably held on open stages.

Melfi, Leonard (1935–), US playwright. Prominent OFF-BROADWAY writer. He attended St Bonaventure University, N.Y., and after spending two years with the US Army in Europe, went to New York City to study acting at the Herbert Berghof-Uta Hagen Studio. He soon began to write, first poetry, then plays that were seen at such EXPERIMENTAL THEATRES as Theatre Genesis, Circle-in-the-Square, the ACTORS' STUDIO and LA MAMA. In 1966 La Mama presented his one-act *Birdbath* as part of *Six from La Mama* at the Martinique Theatre, dir O'HORGAN; his first full-length play *The Jones Man* was seen on BROADWAY, 1968. In 1967 he was awarded a Rockefeller Foundation grant for writing plays.

Melodrama (Gk *melos* = tune and *drama* = action). The use of music to separate incidents in a play and later to emphasize them gave its name to this popular type of play which emerged in the 18th century. The most prolific authors in this genre on the Continent were KOTZEBUE who wrote over 200 melodramas (*Menschenhass und Reue*, 1789, being the most successful), and Guilbert de Pixérécourt (1773–1844), who wrote a long succession of melodramas, the best known of which is *Coelina, ou l'Enfant de mystère* (1800). In America Kotzebue's plays in adaptations by DUNLAP led to a general vogue for melodrama at the expense of more serious works. Pixérécourt's play, adapted by HOLCROFT and put on at COVENT GARDEN in 1802 as *A Tale of Mystery*, was the first English stage production to bear the term melodrama.
The meaning of melodrama came to be synonymous with plays of excessively dramatic content with exaggerated episodes of horror, violence and double-dealing but with virtue ultimately triumphant, while music gradually became less important. The last of the original type of melodrama was PLANCHÉ's *The Brigand* (1829). The setting of Douglas Jerrold's *Fifteen Years of a Drunkard's Life* (1828) heralded a new era of domestic melodrama running concurrently with a fashion for plays with plots based on actual crimes, e.g. *Maria Marten: or the Murder in the Red Barn.* The emergence of a large audience drawn from the middle class made popular a new type of melodrama, notably at the Adelphi. There were the domestic tragedies of the elder DUMAS (*Pauline*, 1840), and *The Corsican Brothers*, 1852, adapted by BOUCICAULT. There were numerous dramatizations of popular novels, Harriet Beecher Stowe's *Uncle Tom's Cabin*, 1852, Mrs Henry Wood's *East Lynne*, 1861, and Miss Braddon's *Lady Audley's Secret*, 1862. Few dramatists of the time invented their own plots and all the melodramas staged by IRVING at the Lyceum had their origins on the Continent. Other ACTOR-MANAGERS had successes with dramatizations of novels, TREE with George du Maurier's *Trilby* (1895), ALEXANDER with Anthony Hope's *The Prisoner of Zenda* (1896), and Fred Terry with Baroness Orczy's *The Scarlet Pimpernel* (1903). By the turn of the century spectacular melodramas were being staged at DRURY LANE with shipwrecks, railway accidents and even earthquakes. In present day parlance 'melodramatic' is usually employed in a pejorative sense to indicate a sentimental play relying on cheaply sensational effects.
Bibl: M. Booth, ENGLISH MELODRAMA, 1965

Melpomene (Gk = the singing one). Greek Muse of TRAGEDY portrayed with a tragic mask in her hand or on her head, with a club and a garland of ivy or vine-leaves.

Menander (*c.* 342–*c.* 291 BC), Greek comic dramatist. Most prominent representative of the New Comedy [▷COMEDY (GREEK)], he wrote over 100 comedies of which 98 titles have survived, but only one complete text – *Dyskolos* (Misanthropist), found in 1958 – and several fragments: two-thirds of *Epitrepontes* (The Arbitration) and sections of *Perikeiromene* (The Girl With her Hair Cut Short), *Samia* (The Girls from Samos), and *Heros* (Hero). His works, in contrast to those of ARISTOPHANES, are non-political, domestic comedies dealing in very subtle ways with everyday situations of romantic love and family life; a common theme is the discovery and recognition of lost children. Social conflicts are presented in

general terms: poor versus rich, country versus city etc. Greatly influenced the Roman comedy of PLAUTUS, TERENCE, and AFRANIUS.
Bibl: T. B. L. Webster, STUDIES IN MENANDER, 2/1960

Mendoza ▷ALARCÓN.

Mercer, David (1928–), English dramatist. Son of an engine driver, he did various odd jobs before going to Durham University. For some time he had ambitions as a painter and also tried novel writing. He wrote his first play *Where the Difference Begins*, 1961, while working as a teacher, and has been a professional writer since its production. His plays are deeply concerned with politics and often examine the disillusionment felt by a committed Marxist as the result of actions by Communist states. Another of his main themes is the alienation of a working-class boy, who has been adopted by the middle class owing to his success as an artist, and who now despises his family. The tensions arising from this situation often lead to mental breakdown in his plays: *The Governor's Lady*, a one-act play, originally written for radio 1960, fp ROYAL SHAKESPEARE COMPANY, 1965, for which, with *Ride A Cock Horse*, 1965, he won the London *Evening Standard* award for the most promising dramatist of the year; a TRILOGY *The Generations* consisting of *Where the Difference Begins*, 1961, *The Climate of Fear*, 1962, and *The Birth of a Private Man*, 1963. TV plays: *A Suitable Case for Treatment*, 1962, filmed as *Morgan*; *For Tea on Sunday*, 1963; *A Way for Living*, 1963; *And Did Those Feet*, 1965; *In Two Minds*, 1967; *The Parachute*, 1968; *The Cellar and the Almond Tree*, 1970; *Let's Murder Vivaldi*, 1968; *On the Eve of Publication*, 1968; *Emma's Time*, 1970. Stage plays: *Belcher's Luck*, 1966, and *After Haggerty*, 1970, all RSC; *Duck Song*, 1974; and *Flint*, 1970.

Meredith, Burgess (1907–), US actor. Made his first appearance with EVA LE GALLIENNE's repertory company and soon established himself as one of the principal young actors in parts such as Mio in M. ANDERSON's *Winterset*, 1935; Marchbanks in SHAW's *Candida*, 1942; the title role in MOLNÁR's *Liliom*, 1940; Christy Mahon in SYNGE's *The Playboy of the Western World*, 1946; Sakini in PATRICK's *The Teahouse of the August Moon*, 1953; Adolphus Cusins in Shaw's *Major Barbara*, 1956; the title role in PIRANDELLO's *Henry IV*, Philadelphia 1958. He also wrote the play *The Durable Maloy*, in collaboration with St Clair McKelway, directed a number of successful productions and has appeared in several films.

Mérimée, Prosper (1803–70), French novelist. In 1925 he published five COMEDIES under the collective title *Le Théâtre de Clara Gazul comédienne espagnole*, which achieved little success during his lifetime; for example, it was not until 1940 that *Le Ciel et l'enfer* was successfully produced by DULLIN. His later comedies are important, e.g. *L'Occasion*, pub 1830, and *La Carosse du Saint Sacrement*, unsuccessfully produced at the COMÉDIE-FRANÇAISE in 1850 (revived 1920 by Dullin at the THÉATRE DU VIEUX-COLOMBIER, produced again in 1926 and 1946). Other works include: *La Famille de Carvajal, Don Quichotte*, and a translation of GOGOL's *The Government Inspector*. But he is best known in the theatre for the adaptation of his novels, e.g. *Carmen* by MEILHAC and Halévy for Bizet's opera, 1875.

Mermaid Theatre. It was largely due to the efforts of MILES that in 1959 the City of London's first new theatre since SHAKESPEARE's time was opened at Puddle Dock, on the bank of the Thames near Blackfriars. The surviving walls of a warehouse, blitzed in 1941, were used for this theatre with 499 seats. Subsidy came from commerce, industry, the general public and the City Corporation. Designed with an open stage and a raked auditorium all on one tier, the most modern STAGE LIGHTING, revolving stage, sound and film equipment were installed. The Mermaid Theatre is now a valuable part of the artistic life of the City, with foyer exhibitions, films, concerts and lectures. It has a fine and varied record of productions including British premières of works by BRECHT, CAMUS, O'CASEY and NAUGHTON. There have also been revivals of such major British dramatists as Shakespeare, FORD, BEAUMONT and FLETCHER, SHAW, plays by the Greek tragedians, and IBSEN, PIRANDELLO and JAMES.

Merman, Ethel (1909–), US star of MUSICAL COMEDY. She is famous for her strong voice and ability to make complicated lines audible. Began her career in CABARET and VAUDEVILLE, and made her theatre début in *Girl Crazy*, 1930. Her first starring role was in PORTER's *Anything Goes*, 1934. Later shows include: *Red Hot and Blue*, 1936; *Du Barry Was a Lady*, 1939; *Panama Hattie*, 1940; *Something for the Boys*, 1943; *Annie Get Your Gun*, 1946; *Call Me Madam*, 1950; *Gypsy*, 1959. She has also appeared in a number of films.

Mertz, Franz (1897–1966), German stage designer. Constructed sets which – dispensing with realistic details – consisted of huge three-dimensional components, such as circular or rock-like shapes, with organic forms floating above the stage. With the director Koch he evolved a disc-shaped stage (known as the Koch-Platte) for the production of ZUCKMAYER's *Gesang im Feuerofen*. After 1948 he worked in collaboration with the director SELLNER in Kiel, Essen, Darmstadt and later in Frankfurt.
Bibl: G. Hensel, 10 JAHRE SELLNER-THEATER, 1962

Messel, Oliver (1904–), English stage designer. Began his career designing for COCHRAN's revues, 1921–31. His elegant and romantic style of sets and COSTUMES made him one of the busiest designers in England and the USA. His designs include: the ballet *Sleeping Beauty*, London, 1946;

Vladimir Mayakovsky, 1925

Burgess Meredith and Ingrid Bergman in MOLNÁR's *Liliom*, 1940

Ethel Merman in BERLIN's *Annie Get Your Gun*, 1946

operas by Strauss: *Ariadne auf Naxos*, 1950, and *Der Rosenkavalier*, 1959, both Glyndebourne; plays by FRY: *The Lady's Not for Burning*, London 1949, and *The Dark is Light Enough*, London 1954, New York 1955. Also SHAKESPEARE's *Romeo and Juliet*, 1951, and Fay and Michael Kanin's adaptation of the Japanese story *Rashomon*, 1959, both New York.

Messemer, Hannes (1924–), German actor. Appeared with the Hanover theatre ENSEMBLE, 1948–50, excelling in parts such as Hamlet, Orin in O'NEILL's *Mourning Becomes Electra*, and Matti in BRECHT's *Herr Puntila und sein Knecht Matti*. Acted at the Bochum theatre 1950–60; his guest performance as Götz in SARTRE's *Le Diable et le Bon Dieu* at the THÉÂTRE DES NATIONS in Paris won him the award of best actor of the year. Other parts include the title role in WEDEKIND's *Der Marquis von Keith*, MacHeath in Brecht's *Die Dreigroschenoper*, and Macbeth. Also well known as actor in German films and on TV.

Method. Name given to an acting system with an introspective approach evolved by STANISLAVSKY for actors at the MAT, later adapted by the GROUP THEATRE in the US in the 1930s, and which came into prominence when it was taken on by the ACTORS' STUDIO.

Meyerhold, Vsevolod Emilyevich (1874–1942), Russian director. One of the great seminal influences of 20th-century theatre, he started as an actor; after training under NEMIROVICH-DANCHENKO he joined the MOSCOW ART THEATRE in 1898 and played the part of Treplyev in CHEKHOV's *The Seagull* in the opening production of the theatre. In 1902 he left STANISLAVSKY and founded his own company to tour throughout Russia. Although he performed many plays from the naturalistic repertoire of the MAT he also produced the neo-romantic and symbolist plays of authors like MAETERLINCK, SCHNITZLER and HAUPTMANN, and gradually developed his own concept of production in opposition to NATURALISM: he regarded the total composition of a production as more important than the Naturalists' concentration on isolated details. In 1905 he took over one of the studios of the MAT to produce Maeterlinck's *La Mort de Tintagiles*; during rehearsals it became clear that M.'s concept was diametrically opposed to the principles and practice of the MAT. The production never opened and M. broke away for the second time from Stanislavsky, of whom however he remained a personal friend throughout his life. After productions in St Petersburg and Tiflis, M. was invited by VERA KOMISARJEVSKAYA to direct IBSEN's *Hedda Gabler* in her theatre, 1906. He realized his concepts with an impressionist décor and COSTUMES in colours symbolizing the characters' attitudes and qualities. Other productions for Komisarjevskaya were: Maeterlinck's *Sœur Béatrice* and *Pelléas et Mélisande*, and WEDEKIND's *Spring's Awakening*. The actors of the company disliked these productions as they felt themselves degraded to mere marionettes. The critics also opposed M.'s ideas and in 1907 he broke with Komisarjevskaya. In 1908 he became a director for plays and opera at the Alexandrinsky and Marinsky Theatres. Apart from many operas he directed plays by HAMSUN, CALDERÓN, SCHNITZLER and MOLIÈRE (*Dom Juan*). In 1913 he directed D'ANNUNZIO's *La Pisanella* in Paris and in 1915 he directed a Russian film version of WILDE's novel *The Picture of Dorian Gray*. After the October Revolution he became a fervent supporter of the Bolshevik cause and proclaimed the 'Theatre October' (i.e. the October Revolution in the theatre): he demanded a political and artistic revolution in the theatre and a fusion of left-wing art and left-wing politics. He became head of the department of theatre in the People's Commissariat for Education and organized mass manifestations, AGITPROP brigades, etc. In collaboration with MAYAKOVSKY he directed the latter's play *Mystery-Bouffe*, 1919. In 1923 he opened his own theatre, the Meyerhold, in Moscow. Towards the end of the 1920s he dissociated himself from agitprop theatre and developed his own style of production which was largely based on elements of music and MIME, CIRCUS, silent film comedies (Chaplin, Keaton) and, after the visit of the great Chinese actor MEI LAN-FANG, 1935, the Chinese style of acting. Principal productions in his own theatre: in 1926, Tretyakov's *Roar China!*; GOGOL's *The Government Inspector*; Mayakovsky's *The Bedbug*, 1929, and *The Bath-house*, 1930. In the early 1930s he was increasingly attacked for 'formalism'. In 1937 his theatre was closed because it did not conform to the rules of the Stalinist doctrine of SOCIALIST REALISM. When, in 1939, M. refused to submit and made an impassioned speech about artistic freedom, he was arrested and died in mysterious circumstances. His mature style treated the play like a symphony: each scene had its function in the overall concept of theme, style and rhythm of the whole. From his actors he demanded complete body control and acrobatic skills (BIO-MECHANICS). In opposition to Stanislavsky's approach (from the inside), M. believed in approaching a part from the outside, through mastery of physical skills and voice control. Like BRECHT he advocated the neat separation of each scene from the next and as such had a great influence on EPIC THEATRE. His writings on the theory of drama and production are collected in *Meyerhold on Theatre*, ed E. Braun, 1969.
Bibl: Ripellino, MAJAKOVSKI ET LE THÉÂTRE RUSSE D'AVANTGARDE, 1965

Mezzetino. A character of the COMMEDIA DELL'ARTE; a variation of BRIGHELLA, made famous by A. COSTANTINI (*c.* 1654–1729) in 1681 with the COMÉDIE-ITALIENNE at the HÔTEL DE BOURGOGNE in Paris, who combined characteristics of both Brighella and SCAPIN. An intriguer who hatched sinister plots, he wore a white-and-red striped costume without a mask.

Mickiewicz, Adam (1798–1855), Polish playwright, poet and patriot. Educated at Vilna University, he was imprisoned for a time by the Russian Government for activities in a secret patriotic student society. He was later, in 1824, ordered to live in exile in Russia where he was admitted to Russian literary circles, meeting PUSHKIN and the Decembrists. He left Russia in 1829 and wandered through Europe, and in 1832 went to Paris. From 1840–44 he was professor of Slavonic studies at the newly formed Collège de France. He died in Turkey while trying to organize a regiment of Poles against the Russians at the outbreak of the Crimean War. His poetry and dramatic work mark the beginning of Polish romanticism. In his most important work, the poetical drama *Dziady*, of which Parts II and IV were published in 1823, Part III in 1832, and Part I posthumously, he expanded his personal experience into the chronicle of a generation, showing the historical stages which led to the conspiracy and uprising on a November night in 1830. It is one of the great plays of Polish literature, known in English by the title of Part III, *Forefathers' Eve*.

Middleton, Thomas (1570–1627), English dramatist. Began writing for HENSLOWE and then for the CHILDREN OF ST PAUL'S; he is believed to have worked with other dramatists such as DEKKER (on the COMEDIES *The Honest Whore*, Part I, 1604, and *The Roaring Girl; or, Moll Cutpurse*, 1604–10) and ROWLEY (on the tragedy *The Changeling*, 1622). Though it is difficult to establish what exactly he did write, a number of plays are attributed to him alone, including comedies in which he satirizes the manners of his time: *A Trick to Catch the Old One*; *A Mad World, My Masters*; *Your Five Gallants* (all 1604–07); *A Chaste Maid in Cheapside*, 1611–13; and the satirical ALLEGORY *A Game at Chess*, 1624, which caused him difficulties with the authorities. As a writer of TRAGEDY he is remarkable for the psychological realism of his characters and his skill in revealing the dark and pessimistic side of human nature, above all in his masterpiece, *The Changeling*, and in *Women Beware Women*, *c.* 1620–27, written by him alone.
Bibl: S. Schoenbaum, MIDDLETON'S TRAGEDIES, 1955

Mielziner, Jo (1901–76), US stage designer. Studied in Philadelphia and Vienna (under STRNAD). After a period as an actor, he started his career at the THEATRE GUILD and became one of the most prominent stage designers in America, winning the PULITZER PRIZE eight times and the NYDCC AWARD seven times. Designed sets for the first performances of many plays by O'NEILL, e.g. *Strange Interlude*, 1928; T. WILLIAMS's *The Glass Menagerie*, 1945, and *A Streetcar Named Desire*, 1947; and A. MILLER's *Death of a Salesman*, 1949. He attempted to reduce his designs to bare essentials, not in an abstract sense but in his selection of details; his designs for musicals are models of scenic technique and visual effect.
Bibl: L. Moussinac, LE THÉÂTRE DES

ORIGINES À NOS JOURS, 1957; M. Gorelik, NEW THEATRE FOR OLD, 1940

Miles, Sir Bernard (1907–), English ACTOR-MANAGER and director. Knighted in 1969. He made his début in a small part in *Richard III*, London 1930, then spent a period with travelling companies and became a successful comedian with sketches and parodies in music hall, e.g. he appeared for three years in a series of REVUES by Herbert Farjeon, while in the same period playing Iago in *Othello*, 1942, and Baudricourt in SHAW's *Saint Joan*, 1947, both at the OLD VIC. Established and ran his own private theatre in St John's Wood, London 1951, until the MERMAID THEATRE opened in 1959 with his own musical play *Lock Up Your Daughters*, music BART, adapted from Fielding. Also a film actor.

Miles gloriosus (Lat). (1) The braggart soldier, a stock character in Roman comedy (▷ROME), who reappeared in Renaissance comedy. (2) Title of an extant comedy by PLAUTUS (*c.* 211 BC). Adaptations and works influenced by *Miles Gloriosus*: UDALL's *Ralph Roister Doister*, 1553; Lodovico Dolce's *Il Capitano*, 1560; Jean Antoine de Baïf's *Le Brave*, 1567; JONSON's *Every Man in His Humour*, 1598; CORNEILLE's *L'Illusion comique*, 1636; HOLBERG's *Jacob von Thyboe*, 1724; and *A Funny Thing Happened on the Way to the Forum*, 1962, by Shevelove, Gelbert and SONDHEIM.

Miller, Arthur (1915–), US dramatist. One of the major exponents of psychological realism; his first BROADWAY play, *The Man Who Had All the Luck*, 1944, was unfavourably received; popular success first came with *All My Sons*, 1947, a family drama in the style of IBSEN, for which he was given the NYDCC AWARD. His next play *Death of a Salesman*, 1949, dir KAZAN, also received this award and the PULITZER PRIZE; it is a modern TRAGEDY, in which the main character is preoccupied with maintaining an illusion of success in business and society. *The Crucible*, 1953, based on the witch trials of the 17th century, was at the same time an attack on McCarthy's 'witch-hunt' against Communism. *A View from the Bridge*, 1955, is a social drama derived from Greek tragedy, set among longshoremen and illegal Sicilian immigrants. Also 1955, *A Memory of Two Mondays*. In *After the Fall*, 1964, dir Kazan, the characters of the lawyer Quentin and Maggie have been assumed to portray M. himself and his former wife, the film actress Marilyn Monroe. *Incident at Vichy*, 1964, a one-act play, deals with a group of people held prisoner by the Germans on suspicion of being Jews. In *The Price* which opened on Broadway in 1968, dir Ulu Grosbard, virtually a sequel to *After the Fall*, two brothers relive their childhood upbringing, M. presents the issues of guilt and responsibility as an example of the recent social history of the USA.

Bibl: R. W. Corrigan, 1969; L. Moss, 1967; S. Hutel, ARTHUR MILLER: THE BURNING GLASS, 1965

Bernard Miles's Mermaid Theatre, London

Meyerhold, costume designs by Nikolai Sapanov for his production of *Columbine's Best Man*, 1910
(1) Columbine's best man (2) a guest

Arthur Miller, *Death of a Salesman*, stage set by MIELZINER

Miller, Jonathan (1934–), English actor, author and director. Qualified as a doctor in 1959. While studying at Cambridge he made his first London appearances in two Footlights revues; then came the satirical four-man REVUE, *Beyond the Fringe*, which was produced first as a Fringe event at the EDINBURGH FESTIVAL, then in London in 1961. It later ran on BROADWAY for 18 months. He directed in New York, e.g. TV revue *What's Going on Now?*; edited Monitor for BBC TV for a year, directed TV films including *Alice in Wonderland*, *Socrates*, with Leo Mckern, and a biography of CHEKHOV, with GIELGUD and PEGGY ASHCROFT. His first London production was *Under Plain Cover*, ROYAL COURT THEATRE, 1962. At the Nottingham Playhouse he has directed *The School for Scandal*, *The Seagull* and *King Lear*. Other productions include: *The Tempest*, 1970, MERMAID THEATRE; *The Merchant of Venice*, 1970, NATIONAL THEATRE; *Twelfth Night*, 1970, Cambridge University Theatre; BÜCHNER's *Danton's Death*, 1971, *The School for Scandal*, 1972; BEAUMARCHAIS's *The Marriage of Figaro*, 1971, all National Theatre; *Three Sisters*, London 1976. He combines his work as a director in theatre with medical research and has, since 1971, been teaching history of medicine at London University. He has written books on Marshall McLuhan and the origins of Victorian spiritualism. He does not think of himself primarily as a director; for him theatre, TV, films are simply media to be used to put ideas across. His sources are in politics, philosophy, anthropology and religion.

Miller, Marilyn (1898–1936), US singer, dancer and actress. Began in VAUDEVILLE, and eventually appeared in the *Ziegfeld Follies*. Successful in musicals such as KERN's *Sally*, 1920 and *Sunny*, 1925; and YOUMANS's *Smiles*, 1930, with FRED and ADELE ASTAIRE. In 1933 she starred in the M. HART-BERLIN revue *As Thousands Cheer*, with ETHEL WATERS and Clifton Webb.

Milligan, Spike (1918–), English comic actor, director and author. Made his first appearance on stage at the age of eight in a Nativity play at the Convent of Jesus and Mary, Poona, India. The radio series *The Goon Show* with Peter Sellers and Harry Secombe brought him to fame in the 1950s. He first came into prominence as a stage actor when he played Ben Gunn in *Treasure Island* at the MERMAID THEATRE in 1961; at the same theatre he gained his next great success in 1963 as co-author, with ANTROBUS, and director of *The Bedsitting Room*, in which he also acted, transferring with the production to the Duke of York's in the same year. In 1964 he played the title role in *Oblomov* by R. Arango, adapted from the novel by Goncharov, at the Lyric, Hammersmith. The play was at first treated seriously, but during its run he gradually sent it up until it became a FARCE, was renamed *Son of Oblomov*, and staged at the Comedy Theatre. M.'s books, comic descendants of Edward Lear, include: *Puckoon*; *Adolf Hitler, My Part in His Downfall*, 1971, vol 1 of his autobiography, filmed with the author playing the part of his own father.

Millo, Josef (1916–), Czech-born Israeli actor, director and manager. Studied in Vienna and Prague with BURIAN. He was director of the Intimate Theatre in Tel Aviv until 1960 when he left to manage the Municipal Theatre in Haifa. His productions include: BRECHT's *The Good Woman of Setzuan*, 1961, and *The Caucasian Chalk Circle*, 1963, des OTTO; GENET's *Le Balcon*; WEISS's *Marat-Sade*; SHAKESPEARE's *Hamlet* and *Richard III* in which he also starred; the production was strongly influenced by KOTT's comment, 'morality of power, which is always immoral'.

Milne, A. A. (Alan Alexander M.; 1882–1956), English writer. Mainly known for his children's classic *Winnie-the-Pooh*, he was also a successful playwright. Among his many plays are: *Wurzel-Flummery*, 1917; *Belinda*, 1918; *Mr Pim Passes By*, 1919; *The Dover Road*, 1921; *To Have the Honour*, 1925 (US title, *Meet the Prince*); *Ariadne or Business First*, 1925; *Success*, 1923 (US title, *Give Me Yesterday*); *The Man in the Bowler Hat*, 1924; *The Ivory Door*, 1928; *The Wind in the Willows*, 1929, a dramatization of Kenneth Grahame's famous children's book, often revived also under the title *Toad of Toad Hall*; *Other People's Lives*, 1935 (US title, *They Don't Mean Any Harm*); *Miss Marlow at Play*, 1937; *Sarah Simple*, 1937; *The Ugly Duckling*, 1940.

Milton, John (1608–74), English poet. The author of the great epic poems *Paradise Lost* and *Paradise Regained*, he also wrote three dramatic works. *Arcades* (written *c.* 1630) is a short MASQUE in honour of the Countess of Derby; a second masque, *Comus*, which is a minor masterpiece, was written on the suggestion of the musician Henry Lawes (1596–1662) and performed at Ludlow Castle on 29 September 1634 – it shows a young virtuous girl attacked by Comus, Circe's son, Lord of Misrule, but successfully defending her chastity against temptation. In his old age M. composed a drama patterned on Greek TRAGEDY, *Samson Agonistes*, pub 1671, a mature work of great originality and sublime poetic expressiveness.

Mime (Gk *mimos*; Lat *mimus*=popular performer, actor). In Antiquity the term mime stood both for the performers themselves and for a literary genre, the popular, vulgar and often obscene performances of itinerant mountebanks, acrobats, jugglers and actors. Originally the mimes confined themselves to acrobatics, juggling, feats of physical dexterity of all kinds, imitation of animals etc. Short farcical and knockabout humorous scenes were also introduced. The first mime plays to be written down were those of Sophron and Epicharmos, both Syracusans active in the 5th century BC; only small fragments of these texts have survived. Classical COMEDY seems to have been influenced by these mime plays, which flourished parallel with it, but on the fringes of respectable theatre. In the later Roman Empire mime reached an extremely wide distribution and popularity. In contrast to classical comedy the performers included women and the performances were often extremely obscene and violent, including realistic execution scenes, for which condemned criminals were made available. At the demand of the audience female mimes had to strip. After the fall of the Roman Empire the tradition of mime seems to have survived among strolling players, jugglers and mountebanks. Whether the Italian COMMEDIA DELL'ARTE is a direct descendant of that tradition is debatable; yet it certainly springs from common origins, like the Roman mime play which relied on fixed character types, it developed fixed types (masks) which formed the basis of improvised plots.

In English usage the term mime is also applied to an art form which in French and German is called PANTOMIME (the word having acquired a different, very specialized meaning in England): this is the depiction of action without the intervention of spoken DIALOGUE, often with musical accompaniment. In Rome this was one of the skills displayed by the mimes. In the 3rd century BC it is said that there were some 6,000 artists of this type, among them many women of outstanding beauty, who even gave silent renderings of scenes from classical literature. On the Paris boulevards in the early 19th century restrictions on legitimate performance led to a revival of the art of mime, notably under the great artist DEBURAU. This art form was revived and brought to a high degree of perfection by DECROUX who elaborated a complete vocabulary of wordless expression. Among his pupils are BARRAULT (who excelled as a mime performing the part of Deburau in Carné's film *Les Enfants du Paradis*) and MARCEAU. The influence of these artists has led to a spread of mime as an autonomous art form to many parts of the world. Among noteworthy mime troups are those of Henryk Tomaszewski in Poland (Wroclaw) and FIALKA's troupe based on the Theatre on the Balustrade in Prague. Another important group led by Lecoq rejects mime as an autonomous art form, but stresses its essential role in the training of all actors. Mime has thus become an important ingredient in all modern actors' training.

Bibl: E. Decroux, PAROLES SUR LE MIME, 1963; A. Nicoll, MASKS, MIMES AND MIRACLES, 1931

Minetti, Bernhard (1905–), German actor. Studied drama in BERLIN and became one of Germany's most prominent performers, appearing in roles such as Mephistopheles in GOETHE's *Faust*, 1936; Marinelli in LESSING's *Emilia Galotti*, 1937; Angelo in SHAKESPEARE's *Measure for Measure*, 1940. One of his finest performances was in BECKETT's *Krapp's Last Tape*. He has also played the title role in *Julius Caesar*, 1963, and Max in PINTER's *The Homecoming*, 1966.

Minks, Wilfried (1931–), Czech-born German stage designer. Studied under

SCHMIDT in Berlin, 1955–57, later worked in theatres in Ulm, Cologne, Stuttgart and with the Bremen Municipal Theatre from 1962. His sets are built as an extension of the auditorium defining the acting areas by large formal structures and employing the techniques of graphic and plastic arts to emphasize details. Most of his work has been carried out in close collaboration with the directors ZADEK, HÜBNER and PALITZSCH.

Minotis, Alexis (1900–), Greek actor and director. A powerful actor in Greek TRAGEDY and SHAKESPEARE, as well as modern roles. Has directed many performances at the ancient theatre of Epidauros. With his wife KATINA PAXINOU, he directed for many years the Greek National Theatre.

Minstrel show. US type of variety show or concert party. Originated in the Southern States between 1820 and 1830. The performers were Whites with black faces (also sometimes referred to as 'burnt-cork minstrels') and there were also Black troupes. In the first part of the performance the CHORUS is arranged in a semi-circle with two comics on either extremity, Mr Tambo and Mr Bones. The master of ceremonies, the only one who appears as a White man, is the 'interlocutor' who acts as straight man to the comics, and introduces the songs. In the second part a series of variety acts or solo performances precede the finale. The most famous black-face comedian was Thomas Dartmouth Rice, who appeared in the character of 'Jim Crow'. The minstrel show, which became a staple of US popular culture, declined with the rise of VAUDEVILLE. Today Black Americans regard the manner in which the Negro was presented as thoroughly degrading.

Miracle Plays ▷MYSTERY PLAYS.

Mise-en-scène (Fr = production). The realization on stage of a dramatic work involving every aspect, dramatic interpretation, direction, design, music and all technical requirements.

Mishima, Yukio (1925–71), Japanese novelist and dramatist. He combined classical Japanese themes with European psychology; best known in Europe for his modern *Noh* dramas (▷JAPAN), published as *Five Modern Noh-Plays*, trans D. Keene, 1957.

Mistinguett (Jeanne-Marie Bourgeois; 1873–1956), French actress, dancer and MUSIC-HALL singer. One of the great stars of the French entertainment world, renowned for her beautiful legs, reputedly insured for 1,000,000 francs, and extravagant costumes. She began her career in 1890 at the Casino de Paris as a singer (under the name Miss Tinguett) and for some time appeared also in straight COMEDY, but her great popularity was achieved after 1910, first at the Moulin-Rouge and at the FOLIES-BERGÈRE where she was partnered by CHEVALIER: *Grande Revue des Folies-Bergère*, 1917, and in the same year her own *Revue Mistinguett*, followed by numerous appearances at the Casino de Paris. At the same time she was successful in SARDOU's *Madame Sans-Gêne*, 1921, in the theatre. She retired from the stage in 1951 and wrote a volume of reminiscences entitled *Toute ma vie*, 1954.
Bibl: J. Charles, CENT ANS DE MUSIC HALL, 1956

Mitterwurzer, Friedrich (1844–97), German actor. Master of psychologically accurate characterization, who originally became famous as a small-part player. His first appearance at the BURGTHEATER in Vienna under LAUBE in 1867 was a failure; his acting was judged eccentric; nevertheless Laube engaged him at the Leipzig Theatre in 1869. In 1871 DINGELSTEDT called him to the Burgtheater, but he soon left, being dissatisfied with the parts he was given. He went on tour and in 1875 became director of the Theater an der Wien in Vienna, leaving in the same year to appear again at the Burgtheater, this time in leading classical roles including Shylock, Macbeth, Iago, Richard III. After 1880 he appeared at various theatres in Vienna and from 1892 at the VOLKSTHEATER, also playing contemporary roles such as Hjalmar in IBSEN's *The Wild Duck*, 1894.
Bibl: J. Bab, KRÄNZE DEM MIMEN, 1954

Mnouchkine, Ariane (1939–), French director. Started with student performances at the Sorbonne in 1964 (*Gengis Khan*) and established a co-operative company of actors, Le Théâtre du Soleil, in 1967, which achieved its first success with a production of WESKER's *The Kitchen* at the Cirque Medrano in Paris. A brilliantly original production of *A Midsummer Night's Dream* followed and ran till June 1968 when the company lost its home in the course of the revolutionary events of the period. But the greatest success of the company and Ariane M. was *1789*, a spectacle about the French Revolution which was first performed at the Milan Sports Palace in 1970, later in Paris and London. In this, as in previous productions, M. creates a spectacle which takes place around and among the audience and involves them by subtle techniques. In *1789* the spectators, who are presented with a number of side shows so that they can wander freely from one to the other, gradually becoming the people of Paris during the storming of the Bastille. In 1972 M. followed her first spectacle (the collective creation of the whole company) with another devoted to the Revolution, *1793*.

Mochalov, Pavel Stepanovich (1800–48), Russian actor. Leading player at the Maly Theatre in Moscow, which he joined in 1830 (first appeared at the BOLSHOI THEATRE from 1825). Usually a romantic hero on stage, he was also a talented comic actor in parts such as Almaviva in BEAUMARCHAIS's *Le Barbier de Séville*. He excelled in tragic parts including the heroes of SCHILLER's and particularly SHAKESPEARE's plays, e.g. *Othello*, *Richard III*, *King Lear*

Marilyn Miller in *Sally*, 1920

Alexis Minotis and KATINA PAXINOU in *Oedipus Rex* by SOPHOCLES

and *Coriolanus*. His greatest role was Hamlet, which the famous critic BELINSKII praised in two essays 'Shakespeare's Hamlet' and 'Mochalov as Hamlet'. Notable appearances in contemporary plays included the leading role in KOTZEBUE's *Menschenhass und Reue* and Chatsky in GRIBOYEDOV's *Gore ot uma*.
Bibl: J. A. Dimitriyev, 1948

Modena, Gustavo (1803–61), Italian actor. Appeared with a travelling company and achieved his first major success as David in ALFIERI's *Saul*, 1824; subsequently gave fine performances in the latter's *Polinice* and *Oreste*, as Leicester in SCHILLER's *Maria Stuart* and Orosmane in VOLTAIRE's *Zaïre*, In 1831 he left the theatre to take an active part in politics and became a propagandist of the Giovane Italia political movement. He travelled to Switzerland, France, Belgium and England; in London he gave successful recitals of Dante's *Divina Commedia*, 1839. On his return to Italy he appeared at different theatres and in 1843 he founded his own company with SALVINI, G. and A. Vestri, and BELLOTTI-BON. During this period his noted parts included the leads in: *Saul*; C. Delavigne's *Louis XI*; VOLTAIRE's *Mahomet*; DUMAS *père's Kean*. In 1847, at the first signs of the uprising of 1848, he was again involved in political activities and published satirical political essays. It was not until 1859 that he returned to the theatre, first in Milan and then in other cities. To the Italian school of acting, stultified with empty rhetoric, M. brought naturalness, realistic expression and a perceptive interpretation of the inner psychology of a role; he anticipated the end of century theatre reforms of STANISLAVSKY, ANTOINE and BRAHM.
Bibl: T. Grandi (ed), GUSTAVO MODENA, SCRITTI E DISCORSI, 1957

Modjeska (Modrzejewska), Helena (1840–1909), Polish-born US actress. She first started appearing in 1860 with amateur companies and later with travelling ensembles and provincial theatres. In 1868 she made her Warsaw début in *Adrienne Lecouvreur* by SCRIBE and Legouvé, and for seven years was Poland's leading actress both in tragic and comic parts. She pioneered SHAKESPEARE in Poland and also supported SLOWACKI's work, and was successful in plays by contemporary writers, including MEILHAC and Halévy (*Frou-Frou*). In 1876 she emigrated to the USA appearing with great success as Adrienne Lecouvreur in San Fancisco, 1877, and on tour. With her own company she toured Poland, 1878–79 and in 1881 came to London, where she appeared in the name parts of *Maria Stuart* (SCHILLER), *Adrienne Lecouvreur, La Dame aux camélias* (DUMAS *fils*), and as Juliet (with FORBES-ROBERTSON as Romeo). She toured extensively 1889–1900 in England, Ireland and the USA, and succeeded in playing Shakespeare in English, her greatest English role being Ophelia. After a short visit to Poland, she retired from the theatre in 1903, apart from a farewell performance in 1905 at the Metropolitan Opera House in New York. With DUSE and BERNHARDT, she was considered one of the leading actresses of her time, at her finest in tragic classical parts, e.g. Lady Macbeth, and in strong emotional parts: Nora in IBSEN's *A Doll's House*. She wrote a volume of reminiscences entitled *Memoirs and Impressions*, 1910.
Bibl: J. Szczublewski, 1959

Moeller, Philip (1880–1958), US playwright and director. Pioneer of poetic theatre (▷VERSE DRAMA) in the USA, and one of the founder members of the Washington Square Players, later THEATRE GUILD, which promoted O'NEILL and SHAW. His noted productions include: Shaw's *The Devil's Disciple* and *Saint Joan*, 1923; *Caesar and Cleopatra*, 1925; *Major Barbara*, 1928; O'Neill's *Strange Interlude*, 1928; *Dynamo*, 1929; *Mourning Becomes Electra*, 1931; *Ah, Wilderness!*, 1933; *Days Without End*, 1934. Other productions: RICE's *The Adding Machine*, 1923; PIRANDELLO's *Right You Are If You Think You Are*, 1927; Stefan Zweig's adaptation of JONSON's *Volpone*, 1928, and Leonhard Frank's *Karl and Anna*, 1929. A collection of his plays written early in his career is published in *Five Somewhat Historical Plays*, 1918.

Moholy-Nagy, László (1895–1946), Hungarian painter and sculptor. Lectured on photography, film and drama at the Bauhaus and with SCHLEMMER wrote *Die Bühne am Bauhaus*. As a stage designer he was at first an Expressionist and later, in the late 1920s, a Constructivist: Offenbach's *Hoffmann's Erzählungen*, BERLIN 1929, Krolloper; MEHRING's *Der Kaufmann von Berlin*, Berlin 1929, Piscator-Bühne, dir PISCATOR; Puccini's *Madame Butterfly*, Berlin 1930, Krolloper.
Bibl: H. Rischbieter (ed), BÜHNE UND BILDENDE KUNST IM 20. JAHRHUNDERT, 1968

Moiseiwitch, Tanya (1914–), English designer. Worked at the ABBEY THEATRE, Dublin, 1935–39; at the Oxford Playhouse, 1941–44; did many designs for the OLD VIC at Liverpool, Bristol and at the New Theatre, London, 1944–46. Designed the Festival Tent at Stratford, Ontario, for GUTHRIE, 1953, and has created many designs there and at the Guthrie Theatre in Minneapolis.

Moissi, Alexander (1880–1935), Austrian actor of Italian/Albanian origin. Discovered by KAINZ and SCHLENTHER, he achieved his first success in Prague, after which he was engaged at the BURGTHEATER in Vienna; in 1906 he went to Berlin to join REINHARDT's company at the Deutsches-Theater. His charismatic personality and the mellow singing quality of his voice (which was also the object of criticism) brought him rapidly into prominence. Under Reinhardt he played Hamlet, Romeo, Oberon, Touchstone; the name part in GOETHE's *Torquato Tasso*; Oswald in IBSEN's *Ghosts*; and Marchbanks in SHAW's *Candida*. One of his most famous parts was Fedya in TOLSTOY's *Redemption, or The Live Corpse* in 1913; and he played in *Jedermann* at the Salzburg Festival from 1922.
Bibl: H. Böhm, 1927

Molander, Olof (1892–1966), Swedish director. Started as an actor. Mainly remarkable as the initiator of a STRINDBERG revival in Sweden. His production of *A Dream Play*, 1935, introduced a new era in the appreciation of that author. Other equally influential productions followed: *The Road to Damascus*, 1937; *The Ghost Sonata*, 1942. He was artistic director of the Royal Dramatic Theatre in Stockholm 1934–38.

Molière (Jean-Baptiste Poquelin; 1622–73), French dramatist, actor and director. Born in Paris, the son of a wealthy upholsterer (*valet-tapissier du roi*), he had an excellent education at the Jesuit Collège de Clermont (later Louis-le-Grand), then studied law, but gave it up *c.* 1642, when he met MADELEINE BÉJART, with whom he founded the Illustre-Théâtre in 1643 and in the following year made his début in Paris. The enterprise was a failure and in 1645 Molière (who was known by this name from 1644) was imprisoned for debt. With the support of friends, he succeeded in forming a new company and toured the provinces 1645–58. The REPERTOIRE comprised TRAGEDY and COMEDY in the tradition of the COMMEDIA DELL'ARTE, some written by M. himself (of which we have only a few of the titles). Despite the vicissitudes of the travelling life, the troupe was fairly stable and had acquired great renown when they finally arrived in Paris in 1658. M. performed the tragedy *Nicomède* for the 20-year-old Louis XIV; this made little impression on the king, but he was amused by the FARCE *Le Docteur amoureux*, which followed it. Louis instantly gave M. permission to alternate with the Italian company directed by Scaramouche (▷FIORILLI) in the Théâtre du Petit-Bourbon. M. who was an excellent character actor in his own comedies, was unconvincing in tragedy. Despite this he attempted several times to build up a repertoire of tragedies, but, added to his weakness, his company could not match the tragic style of the actors of the HÔTEL DE BOURGOGNE and the Théâtre du Marais. Success came only when M. appeared in his comedies: *L'Etourdi*; *Le Dépit amoureux*; *Les Précieuses ridicules*; *Sganarelle ou Le Cocu imaginaire*, 1660. When M. took over the Théâtre du Palais Royal, he opened again with a serious heroic drama *Dom Garcie de Navarre, ou le Prince jaloux*, the first and only failure, which was wiped out by a series of triumphant successes: *L'Ecole des maris*, 1661; *L'Ecole des femmes*, 1663; *La Critique de L'Ecole des femmes*, 1663; *L'Amour médecin*, 1665; *Le Misanthrope*, 1666; *Le Médecin malgré lui*, 1666; *Amphitryon*, 1668; *L'Avare*, 1668; *Les Fourberies de Scapin*, 1671; *Les Femmes savantes*, 1672; and *Le Malade imaginaire*, 1673.
M.'s dramatic works combine criticism of general human failings (greed, hypocrisy) with attacks on contemporary faults (sanctimony; intellectual and social pretentiousness) and support the moderate and reason-

able. Although *Tartuffe* attacks only a false piety, it aroused strong protest and was not performed in public until 1669 (written 1664 and several times performed in private before the Court). *Dom Juan, ou Le Festin de Pierre*, 1665, interpreted as a profession of atheism, had to be removed from the stage and was not published during M.'s lifetime. He was protected by Louis XIV personally from attacks on his private life, among them the accusation that his wife ARMANDE BÉJART (whom he married 1662), a sister or daughter of Madeleine B., was his own daughter. From 1661 he also wrote several plays, LIBRETTI, comedies, BALLETS DE COUR, and FARCES specially for festivities and entertainments at Court: *Les Fâcheux*, 1661; *L'Impromptu de Versailles*, 1663; *Le Mariage forcé*, 1664; *La Princesse d'Elide*, 1664; *George Dandin ou le Mari confondu*, 1668; *Monsieur de Pourceaugnac*, 1669; *Les Amants magnifiques*, 1670; *Le Bourgeois gentilhomme*, 1670; *Psyché*, 1671; *La Comtesse d'Escarbagnas*, 1671.
Bibl: W. G. Moore, MOLIÈRE, A NEW CRITICISM, 1962; R. Fernandez, LA VIE DE MOLIÈRE, 1958; D. B. W. Lewis, MOLIÈRE, THE COMIC MASK, 1959; J. Audiberti, MOLIÈRE DRAMATIQUE, 1954

Molina ▷TIRSO DE MOLINA.

Molnár, Ferenc (1878–1952), Hungarian dramatist, who became a US citizen in 1940. He wrote internationally popular COMEDIES, which mix realism and fantasy with ironic and frivolous elements; brilliant in technique and DIALOGUE. His best-known play is *Liliom*, 1909, New York 1921, THEATRE GUILD, which was adapted as the musical *Carousel* by RODGERS and HAMMERSTEIN II, 1945, and had a Broadway run of more than two years (London production 1950). His other major play *The Guardsman*, 1910, Theatre Guild, 1924, provided an excellent vehicle for the LUNTS. Other successful plays which have been performed in English include *The Devil*, 1907, a modern version of the FAUST legend, which opened in New York, 1908, in two simultaneous productions, at the Belasco Theatre and the Garden Theatre; *The Swan*, 1920; *The Glass Slipper*, 1924; *The Play's the Thing*, 1924 (adapted by WODEHOUSE); *Olympia*, 1927; *The Wolf*, 1974.

Monk, Egon (1927–), German director. Joined the BERLINER ENSEMBLE under BRECHT in 1949, collaborating with him on *Herr Puntila und sein Knecht Matti*, 1949; *Der Hofmeister* (Lenz/Brecht), 1950; on his own directing HAUPTMANN's *Der Biberpelz* and *Der roter Hahn*, Berliner Ensemble 1951. Left East Germany after incurring the disapproval of the authorities with an 'irreverent' production of GOETHE's *Urfaust* in 1953; worked on radio and TV in Hamburg, and was head of TV drama for Norddeutscher Rundfunk, Hamburg, 1960–68. His stage productions include: Křenek's *Der goldene Bock* (The Golden Ram), Hamburg 1964, Staatsoper; S. Lenz's *Das Gesicht* (The Face), Hamburg 1964, Schauspielhaus.

Molière, portrait by P. Mignard

Tanya Moiseiwitch, stage set for *Cyrano de Bergerac* with RICHARDSON, OLD VIC, 1946

Ferenc Molnár's *The Wolf*, Oxford and London 1974, with Edward Woodward, Judi Dench, Leo McKern

Monodrama (Gk *monos*=single). Short solo piece, sometimes supported by silent characters, popularized in GERMANY in the 18th century, mostly written as an actor's virtuoso piece: J. J. Rousseau's *Pygmalion*, 1762, and COCTEAU's *La voix humaine*, 1930.

Monologue (Gk *monos*=single, *logos*= speech). A SOLILOQUY by one person alone on the stage. Important dramatic technique (SHAKESPEARE, GOETHE) for presentation and interpretation of thoughts and feelings. As a device it was taboo in the naturalistic theatre.

Montdory (Guillaume des Gilberts; 1594–1651), one of the first important French actors. A friend and supporter of CORNEILLE, after appearing for several years in the provinces he toured with the latter's first play *Mélite* before appearing in the Paris production in 1630; in 1634 he joined the Théâtre du Marais, at that time second only to the HÔTEL DE BOURGOGNE. An actor of the traditional declamatory style, he appeared in all the important plays of his time, excelling in tragic parts, and created the role of Rodrigue in Corneille's *Le Cid*, 1637. He retired from the stage in 1637.
Bibl: S. W. Deierkauf-Holsboer, LE THÉÂTRE DU MARAIS, 1954

Montherlant, Henry de (1896–1972), French novelist and dramatist. Although his plays have a religious context, he is not a Catholic writer, but is concerned with the conflicts of the human soul – love, religion, sexual obsession – characterized by his noble pessimism and a heroic contempt for the outside world: *L'Exil*, pub 1929, fp 1934, dir DUX; *Pasiphaé*, a dramatic poem, 1938; *Le Reine morte*, 1942, COMÉDIE-FRANÇAISE; *Fils de Personne*, 1943; *Un Incompris*, 1943; *Le Maître de Santiago*, 1948; *Demain il fera jour*, 1949; *Celles qu'on prend dans ses bras*, 1950, a contemporary play dealing with five people and their sufferings caused by love; *Malatesta*, Renaissance tragedy, 1950, Théâtre Marigny, dir BARRAULT; *La Ville dont le prince est un enfant*, Geneva 1953, Paris 1967; *Port-Royal*, 1954, CF; *Brocéliande*, 1956, CF; *Don Juan*, 1958; *Le Cardinal d'Espagne*, fp Vienna 1960.
Bibl: S. Chevally, 1960; L. de Paprade, LE THÉÂTRE DE MONTHERLANT, 1950

Moody, William Vaughn (1869–1910), US dramatist. His work was important in the development of American drama and he was one of the original serious native playwrights. The first of his plays to be staged by Henry Miller (▷HERON) was *The Great Divide*, 1906, produced London 1909, in which year his *The Faith Healer* was seen in New York. He also wrote a religious verse trilogy, *The Masque of Judgement*, 1900, *The Fireraisers*, 1904, and *The Death of Eve*, uncompleted. He edited the works of many English writers including Bunyan, Milton and Scott, and taught at the University of Chicago.
Bibl: David D. Henry, WILLIAM VAUGHN MOODY: A STUDY, 1934; Martin Halpern, WILLIAM VAUGHN MOODY, 1964

Morality plays. Medieval form of drama. The moralities were allegorical plays in which abstract concepts, such as Virtues and Vices, Love, Friendship, Virtue or the Devil were shown battling for the soul of Man. The play of EVERYMAN which originated in the Netherlands is the best-known example and one of the very few English moralities to have remained in the world's repertoire. But the Spanish AUTOS SACRAMENTALES also spring from the same tradition, and some of these are recognized masterpieces, e.g. CALDERÓN's *El gran teatro del mundo*. In the development of English drama the moralities helped to develop the concept of character, particularly in the treatment of different vices which lent themselves to fruity and individualized portraiture of human types. The Comedy of Humours, as developed by JONSON and others, was clearly in some respects a continuation of this technique, the 'irascible' or 'choleric man', for example, being a direct continuation of the vice of Rage or Anger, etc. Even the character of Falstaff might be seen to derive from the vice of Greed or Gluttony. The earliest extant English morality play is *The Castle of Perseverance*, *c.* 1450; one of the finest is Skelton's *Magnyfycence*, 1515. Other notable examples: *Mankind*, *c.* 1466; John Redford's *Wit and Science*, *c.* 1539; Henry Medwall's *Fulgens and Lucrece*, *c.* 1515.
Bibl: E. K. Chambers, THE MEDIEVAL STAGE, 1903, 2 vols

Morelli, Rina (Elvira M.; 1908–76), Italian actress. Member of a long-established Italian acting family. Her uncle **Alamanno M.** (1812–93) had excelled in parts such as the title role in *Kean* (DUMAS *père*), 1845, and in *Hamlet*, 1850, and was also a noted actor in French plays by AUGIER, VIGNY and DUMAS. She was the daughter of the actor Amilcare M. and appeared in the 1930s with many leading Italian companies. Her most significant work was with the director VISCONTI in his production of COCTEAU's *Les Parents terribles* in 1945; with her partner STOPPA she founded the Morelli/Stoppa company, with Visconti as director. Her best-known parts include: Rosalind in *As You Like It*; Cressida in *Troilus and Cressida*; Sonya in CHEKHOV's *Uncle Vanya* and Irina in *Three Sisters*; Laura in T. WILLIAMS's *The Glass Menagerie*, and Blanche in *A Streetcar Named Desire*; Linda in A. MILLER's *Death of a Salesman*; Mathilde in FABBRI's *Figlia d'arte*, for which she was awarded the prize of the THÉÂTRE DES NATIONS festival for the best performance in 1959.

Moreto y Cabaña, Don Augustín (1618–69), Spanish dramatist. Contemporary and close friend of CALDERÓN, he wrote over 100 dramatic works including ENTREMESES, LOAS, religious and Christian dramas, sometimes reworking older themes by TIRSO DE MOLINA and LOPE DE VEGA, whose level of originality and dramatic force he never attained. Nevertheless, he excelled in his use of dramatic technique, particularly in setting the plot, and in his depth of thought and clarity of ideas. Only two of his COMEDIES have remained in the REPERTOIRE: *El lindo don Diego* (The Handsome Don D.), pub 1662; *El desdén con el desdén* (Disdain for Disdain), pub 1654, a plot used later by MOLIÈRE in *La Princesse d'Elide*.
Bibl: E. Caldera, IL TREATRO DI MORETO Y CABAÑA, 1960

Moretti, Marcello (1910–61), Italian actor. From 1940 appeared with several companies playing comic parts, e.g. Mezzetino in GOZZI's *Il Re cervo*, 1940; Puck in *A Midsummer Night's Dream*; best known for his performance in the title role in GOLDONI's *Il Servitore di due Padroni*, dir STREHLER, one of the first productions in 1947 of the newly founded PICCOLO TEATRO DI MILANO, which later toured until 1960 with great success in some 20 countries of Europe, North America and Latin America. He possessed not only the versatility of an ARLECCHINO, but could also contribute acrobatic solo numbers to his performance, e.g. Caliban in *The Tempest*. He also excelled in parts like his famous Chlestakov in GOGOL's *The Government Inspector*, 1953. He left the Piccolo Teatro in 1953, but often made guest appearances, e.g. Wang in BRECHT's *Der Gute Mensch von Setzuan*, 1958.

Morgan, Charles (1894–1958), English novelist, playwright and drama critic. President of the OUDS. Became drama critic of *The Times* in 1926 and retained that position till 1939. Apart from many successful novels he wrote the plays: *The Flashing Stream*, 1938; *The River Line*, 1952 (adapted from the novel); *The Burning Glass*, 1954.

Moriconi, Valeria (1931–), Italian actress. In films from 1953, she made her début in the theatre in 1957 with DE FILIPPO's company, playing the leading role in *De Pretore Vicenzo*; she subsequently appeared in various theatres, mainly under the direction of L. Lucignani. In 1961 at the Piccolo Teatro in Naples she played Daisy in IONESCO's *Rhinocéros*; from this successful production evolved the Compagnia dei Quattro (Enriquez, Moriconi, Mauri, and Scaccis, who was later succeeded by the stage designer Luzzati) which toured in Italy and abroad 1961–64, until the whole group merged with the TEATRO STABILE in Turin in 1965. Her most noted parts include: Katharina in *The Taming of the Shrew*; Puck in *A Midsummer Night's Dream*; Barblin in FRISCH's *Andorra*; title role in GOLDONI's *Mirandolina*. She is also a popular TV actress.

Morley, Robert (1908–), English actor and playwright. Made his stage début in Margate in 1928; toured with BENSON's Shakespearean company in the early 1930s. Had major successes as Oscar Wilde in a play on the writer, London 1936, New York 1938, and as Sheridan Whiteside in *The Man Who Came to Dinner*, London 1941; played the Prince Regent in *The First Gentleman*, 1945; the leading part in his own highly successful play (written with Noel Langley) *Edward, My Son*, 1947. His large bulk, orotund delivery and delicious sense of humour have led him through a long list of subsequent triumphs. Among the other plays which he has written are: *Short Story*, 1935; *Goodness How Sad*, 1937; *Staff Dance*, 1944. He has also adapted and translated a number of foreign plays.

Morris, Clara (1846–1925), US actress. She appeared on the stage as a child, making a great impression in 1872 as Cora the Creole in DALY's play *Article 47*. Though not brilliant as an actress she exercised extraordinary power on her audience and could always be relied on to fill any theatre in which she appeared. Among her best roles were the lead in DUMAS *fils*'s *La Dame aux camélias* (under the title *Camille*), Lady Macbeth, and Julia in Sheridan Knowles' *The Hunchback*.

Mortimer, John (1923–), English dramatist. Son of a barrister, he began his career as a novelist. He made his theatrical début in 1958 with the one-act COMEDY *The Dock Brief*, originally written for radio (won the Italia Prize), part of a double bill with *What Shall We Tell Caroline?*. His full-length plays were all presented in the West End: *The Wrong Side of the Park*, 1960, with MARGARET LEIGHTON and Robert Stephens; *Two Stars for Comfort*, 1962, with Trevor Howard; *The Judge*, 1967. Other works include: *Lunch Hour*; *I Spy*, 1956; *Take Your Hand Baggage*; *Come As You Are*, 1970; *A Voyage Round My Father*, 1971. Has written many radio and TV plays and film scripts and has also adapted two works by FEYDEAU: *A Flea in Her Ear*, 1965, NATIONAL THEATRE, and *Cat Among the Pigeons!*, 1970; and ZUCKMAYER's *The Captain of Köpenick*, 1971, National Theatre.

Moscow Art Theatre. Founded in 1898 by STANISLAVSKY and NEMIROVICH-DANCHENKO with the avowed aim of opposing the grandiloquent and empty theatrical style then prevailing with a new artistic approach based on truth and true ensemble playing. The theatre opened with A. K. TOLSTOY's *Tsar Fyodor Ivanovich*, which was followed by productions of SHAKESPEARE, SOPHOCLES and G. HAUPTMANN. But its first breakthrough came with the success of CHEKHOV's *The Seagull* (in the 1898 season; the play had previously failed in St Petersburg). The seagull motif became the emblem of the MAT. Chekhov's other major plays followed and established the company's reputation. In 1911 Stanislavsky invited CRAIG to direct *Hamlet* and thus made the MAT the focal point of the avant-garde of the day. MEYERHOLD and VAKHTANGOV started as Stanislavsky's followers and pupils at the MAT but broke away when they developed into radical innovators. After the October Revolution the MAT gradually developed into the officially approved model for SOCIALIST REALISM in the theatre throughout the Soviet Union. Although its actors are still among the most skilful in the world, the somewhat dated NATURALISM of its performances makes it an upholder of a great tradition rather than the standard-bearer of modernism that its founders hoped for.

Moscow Art Theatre, the present-day building

Moser, Hans (1880–1964), Austrian actor. After an unremarkable early career with amateur travelling companies, CIRCUSES and variety shows, CABARETS and as a singer of Viennese popular songs, he went on to become a major comic actor of the popular Viennese theatre. In 1920 he was discovered by REINHARDT, who presented him in comic parts first in Vienna and later in BERLIN, where he excelled as Bottom in *A Midsummer Night's Dream* and in the leading role in RAIMUND's *Der Bauer als Millionär*, 1938. From 1931 he had a successful career as a comedian in films and only in his later years returned to the stage, appearing mainly in plays by Raimund, MOLNÁR, and SCHNITZLER.
Bibl: O. M. Fontana, 1965

Mosheim, Grete (1905–), German actress. Trained at the drama school of the Deutsches-Theater, BERLIN, where she appeared 1922–31 and later at several other Berlin theatres. She made her reputation as one of the major German actresses in plays by SHAW: *You Never Can Tell*, 1925, and *Pygmalion*, 1932, as Eliza. After World War II her appearances were mainly as guest artist at the principal German theatres in parts which included Winnie in BECKETT's *Happy Days*, 1961; Mrs Levi in WILDER's *The Matchmaker*, 1955; Hannah Jelkes in T. WILLIAMS's *The Night of the Iguana*, 1963; she played in ALBEE's *Box/Quotations from Chairman Mao Tse-tung/Box*, 1969.

Moskvin, Ivan Mikhailovich (1874–1946), Russian actor. In 1893 he joined the MOSCOW ART THEATRE under STANISLAVSKY and NEMIROVICH-DANCHENKO, whom he succeeded as a director after the latter's death in 1943. Excelled in playing typical traditional Russian characters, the small man fighting against bureaucracy and rapacious businessmen. To his comic parts he brought sharp satirical touches: Epikhodor in CHEKHOV's *The Cherry Orchard*, 1904; Zagoretski in GRIBOYEDOV's *Gore ot Uma* (*Woe from Wit*), 1906; Snegirejev in *The Brothers Karamazov*, 1910; Golutvin in OSTROVSKY's *Even a Wise Man Stumbles*, 1910; Fedya in TOLSTOY's *Redemption or The Live Corpse*, 1911; Opiskin in DOSTOYEVSKY's *The Village Stepanchikovo*, 1917. Among his later roles was the lead in a play about Lenin by POGODIN, *Kremlin Chimes*, 1942. He also acted in films.

Mostel, Zero (Samuel Joel M.; 1915–), US actor. Studied history and graphic arts before appearing first in sketches at a Greenwich Village night club in 1942 and shortly afterwards on BROADWAY in the REVUE *Keep 'Em Laughing*, 1942; the musical *Beggar's Holiday* by Duke Ellington in 1946; the title role in MOLIÈRE's *Le Malade imaginaire* (in his own adaptation), Cambridge, Mass., 1952; Shu Fu in BRECHT's *The Good Woman of Setzuan*, dir BENTLEY, 1956. Probably his greatest stage successes were as Leopold Bloom in Marjorie Barkentin's adaptation of JOYCE's *Ulysses in Nighttown*, 1958, dir MEREDITH, for which he was awarded the first prize for acting at the THÉÂTRE DES NATIONS in Paris; Jean in IONESCO's *Rhinoceros*, 1961; and Pseudolus in a MUSICAL COMEDY adaptation of *Miles Gloriosus* by PLAUTUS, called *A Funny Thing Happened on the Way to the Forum*, 1962. Since 1952 he has been working with the ACTORS' STUDIO and has also appeared in film and TV parts. He is the author of a volume of memoirs *Zero by Mostel*, 1965.

Motley. The name of a team of designers, Audrey Sophia Harris (1902–66), her sister Margaret F. Harris (1904–) and Elizabeth Montgomery (1902–), who produced their first joint stage and COSTUME designs in 1932 (for *Romeo and Juliet* at the OUDS) and became the leading designers of the 1930s in England, where they worked with the OLD VIC and other leading companies and directors. After 1941 they extended their activities to the USA. The team of

Motley was among the first designers in the English-speaking world to aim at collaboration with the director, working closely with him on the text of the play and using costume and sets, not only to achieve pleasing pictorial effects and harmonious colour schemes, but as a means of interpretation of the author's deeper intentions. Their influence can be felt in all subsequent theatre design.

Motokiyo, Zeami (known as **Zeami**; 1363–1443), Japanese dramatist. Most famous writer of *Noh* plays, a master of poetic drama. He was the son of Kanami Kiyotsugu (1333–84). Both directed their own companies, which performed before emperors, and the aristocracy, in Buddhist temples and villages. He was simultaneously playwright, composer, director, actor and dancer, but was also familiar with philosophy and religion. From his huge output of work *c.* 100 plays have survived, also essays and memoirs, which are an important source for the study of the early period of Japanese drama.
Bibl: P. G. O'Neill, A GUIDE TO NOH, 1954

Mounet-Sully (Jean Sully Mounet; 1841–1916), French actor. Leading tragedian of his day. Appeared at the COMÉDIE-FRANÇAISE from 1872 in many major parts including: début as Oreste in RACINE's *Andromaque*; Rodrigue in CORNEILLE's *Le Cid*; Néron in Racine's *Britannicus*, all in 1872; Didier in HUGO's *Marion Delorme*, 1873; Orosmane in VOLTAIRE's *Zaïre*, 1874; title role in J. Lacroix's *Oedipe-roi*, 1881.

Mrożek, Slawomir (1930–), Polish dramatist. Member of the Polish school of the THEATRE OF THE ABSURD, which emerged after the October riots and the Hungarian uprising of 1956 and is therefore much more 'political' than the theatre of IONESCO, BECKETT and PINTER. He describes his world in cataclysmic terms, though always remaining ambiguous and ironical. A Kafkaesque atmosphere and sinister metaphors dominate his works: *Policjanci* (*The Police*), Warsaw 1958; *Meczenstwo Piotra Oheya* (The Martyrdom of Peter O'Heya), Cracόw 1959; *Indyk* (The Turkey Cock), Cracόw 1961; *Na pelnym morzu* (Out at Sea), 1961; *Kąrol* and *Striptease*, Zoppot 1961; *Kynolog w rozterce* (Kynologist in a Dilemma), Wroclaw 1963; *Zabawa* (Party) and *Czarowna noc* (The Enchanted Night), Wroclaw 1963. His play *Tango*, Belgrade 1965, is the first contemporary Polish drama to enter the REPERTOIRE of theatre companies in Western Europe and the USA (▷NUNN). In this frightening symbolic FARCE he deals with the conflict of generations in a situation where the parents have taken part in a revolution and the son's own rebellion must be a return to the old order. He broke with the Polish authorities in 1968 and now lives in the West. His play *Vatzlav*, 1970, is an ALLEGORY portraying the adventures of a shipwrecked slave in a weird modern capitalist society.
Bibl: M. Esslin, THE THEATRE OF THE ABSURD, 2/1968; J. Kott, THEATRE NOTEBOOK 1947–67, 1968

Müller, Heiner (1929–), German dramatist, who lives in East Berlin. His earlier works are models of polemical drama: *Der Lohndrücker* (The Scab, i.e. a worker who accepts work at low wages), Leipzig 1950; *Die Korrektur* (The Correction), Berlin 1958; *Die Umsiedlerin oder das Leben auf dem Lande* (The Re-settler or Life in the Country), which he withdrew after a student production in Berlin in 1961; *Der Bau* (The Building), pub 1965, which used a giant building site suggesting ways in which the construction of East Germany might be carried out; *Philoktet*, based on SOPHOCLES, Munich 1968, Residenztheater, dir LIETZAU. Translated several classical writers, e.g. Sophocles, *Oedipus Rex*, Berlin 1967, Deutsches-Theater, dir BESSON; MOLIÈRE's *Dom Juan*, 1968; SHAKESPEARE's *As You Like It*, 1968.
Bibl: H. Rischbieter & E. Wendt, DEUTSCHE DRAMATIK IN WEST UND OST, 1965

Müller, Traugott (1895–1944), German designer. One of the leading scenic architects in BERLIN in the 1920s and 1930s, e.g. O'NEILL's *Desire Under the Elms*, 1925, Lessingtheater. Became PISCATOR's close collaborator, constructing stages that emphasized the technical possibilities of the theatre: SCHILLER's *Die Räuber*, Berlin 1926, State Theatre; TOLLER's *Hoppla, wir leben!*, Piscator-Bühne, 1927; *Rasputin* by A. N. TOLSTOY/P. Schegolov, Piscator-Bühne, 1927. In 1932 he joined the State Theatre and, with the director FEHLING, evolved a bare stage sloping towards the auditorium: SHAKESPEARE's *Richard III*, 1937, and *Richard II*, 1939; LESSING's *Emilia Galotti*, 1937, dir GRÜNDGENS, for which he covered the stage with stone flooring. Other designs include: Schiller's *Die Jungfrau von Orleans*, 1939; BÜCHNER's *Dantons Tod*, 1939; GOZZI/Schiller's *Turandot*, 1941, dir STROUX.

Munch, Edvard (1863–1944), Norwegian painter. Expressionist innovator whose scenic décor for IBSEN productions transcended NATURALISM in the extreme use of SYMBOLISM: *Peer Gynt*, Paris 1896 and *John Gabriel Borkman*, Paris 1897, both Théâtre de l'Œuvre; *Ghosts*, opening of the Kammerspiele of the Deutsches-Theater, Berlin 1906, dir REINHARDT; *Hedda Gabler*, Berlin 1907, Kammerspiele, dir BAHR.
Bibl: H. Rischbieter (ed), BÜHNE UND BILDENDE KUNST IM 20. JAHRHUNDERT, 1968

Muni, Paul (Meshulom Meyer Weisenfreund; 1895–1967), Polish-born US actor. Son of a Jewish actor, he emigrated with his parents to the USA at the age of eight. He acted until 1926 in both English and Yiddish; his first major part was in RICE's *Counsellor-at-Law*, 1931. Perhaps his most famous role was Loman in A. MILLER's *Death of a Salesman*, 1949. Outstanding films in the 1930s, e.g. Hawk's *Scarface*, Le Roy's *I Am a Fugitive from a Chain Gang*; and screen biographies (ZOLA, Pasteur).

Munk, Kaj (1898–1944), Danish dramatist. A parish priest who was shot resisting the Nazis, his plays of ideas were influenced by Kierkegaard. They dealt with historical characters or themes: *En Idealist* (*Herod the King*), 1928; *Cant*, 1931, about Anne Boleyn; *Ordet* (*The Word*), 1932; *De Udvalgte* (The Elect), 1933, about David; *Sejren* (The Victory), 1937, about Mussolini in Egypt; *Han sidder ved Smeltediglen* (*He sits at the Melting Pot*), 1938, about Hitler's persecution of the Jews; *Egelykke*, 1940; *Niels Ebbesen*, 1942.
Bibl: N. Nojgaard, 1958

Music hall. A form of popular entertainment in England, which developed from musical diversions in public houses; it can be traced back as far as the early 18th century. Special annexes to public houses developed, until by the mid-19th century large and sumptuously decorated theatres were built to accommodate this form of entertainment. The sale of drinks at large bars during performances remained to remind the audience of the growth of the music hall out of the public house. The mainstay of music-hall entertainment was the comic, sentimental or character song, performed by highly popular entertainers, usually with rapturous and raucous participation by the audience. But dramatic sketches (even complete short plays performed by famous stage stars) and comic and variety turns of various kinds also formed part of the programme, as did even ballet and, when the cinematograph was the latest invention, short cinema performances. The music hall produced its own kind of itinerant performers who travelled the country, and often the continents, from hall to hall: LENO, MARIE LLOYD, Albert Chevalier, Vesta Tilley, the great male impersonator, Fred Karno's troupe of knockabout comedians in which Chaplin earned his first laurels. Also LITTLE TICH, Harry Champion, and, in more recent times, Gracie Fields, are some of the names the music hall made world-famous. The great London music halls, Collins's, the Empire, the Metropole, the Alhambra, the Canterbury, and numerous great halls in the outer districts of London and in the provinces, were centres of a genuine people's theatre tradition. After World War I it was the rise of the cinema – a child of the music hall – and after World War II that of TV which led to the decline and virtual demise of this vital form of folk art. The influence of the English music hall on the theatre has been great: the English PANTOMIME is rooted in the music-hall tradition, as was the great era of the silent film comedians like Chaplin, while other great comedians (Buster Keaton, W. C. Fields, the Marx Brothers) came from its American cousin, VAUDEVILLE.
Bibl: C. MacInnes, SWEET SATURDAY NIGHT, 1967; A. Haddon, THE STORY OF THE MUSIC HALL, 1935

Musical comedy (often abbreviated to 'the musical'). A popular form of light entertainment which originated in England and the USA at the end of the 19th century

and fuses elements from BURLESQUE, operetta, REVUE and MUSIC HALL; usually in two acts, with dance numbers and full-scale finales. In England EDWARDES's production of *In Town* (LIBRETTO by A. Rossi and J. T. Tanner, music by F. O. Carr) in 1892 is usually regarded as the opening of the era of the musical comedy. In the USA the first true musicals were productions like *The Belle of New York*, libretto by H. Morton, music by G. A. Kerker, 1898. In the first decades of the 20th century it was largely in the USA that the best composers and most intelligent libretti appeared, notably the musicals of Victor Herbert, FRIML, KERN, I. BERLIN, and RODGERS and HAMMERSTEIN II. In the 1940s the US musical increasingly drew on material of a higher literary quality and more serious artistic intent. The great success of *Oklahoma!* (Rodgers and Hammerstein II, 1943) marked a turning point, giving the musical a claim to be something like genuine folk art, an expression of the national spirit. Works like *West Side Story* (music BERNSTEIN, 1957), which transferred the plot of *Romeo and Juliet* into modern New York with its racial tensions, and *My Fair Lady* (LERNER and LOEWE, 1956), which used SHAW's *Pygmalion*, proclaimed the ability of the musical to deal with literary themes and content. In the era of the mass media, when the theatre has to rely on all the colour and spectacle it can muster, the commercial theatre of BROADWAY and the London West End tends to be dominated by the musical, which is, however, immensely costly to produce and involves great risks for the backers. The history of the musical is one of either fabulous successes or ruinous failures.
Bibl: L. Engel, THE AMERICAN MUSICAL THEATRE, 1967

Musset, Alfred de (1810–57), French poet and dramatist. First influenced by the literary coterie of romantics around HUGO, with whom he broke in 1831. His love affair with George Sand in 1833/34 inspired him to his finest poems and plays. After the failure of his first play *La Nuit vénitienne*, 1830, he continued to write plays solely for publication: *La Coupe et les lèvres*; *A quoi rêvent les jeunes filles*, pub 1832, fp 1851; *Fantasia*, pub 1834, fp 1866; *On ne badine pas avec l'amour*, 1834, fp 1861; *Lorenzaccio*, 1834, fp 1848. He achieved his breakthrough in the theatre in 1847 at the COMÉDIE-FRANÇAISE with *Un Caprice*, written 1837, followed by earlier plays such as *Il faut qu'une porte soit ouverte ou fermée* and *Il ne faut jurer de rien*. He drew female characters with great sensitivity; his central theme was the inspirational and redemptive power of love; he combines the climate of the 19th century with a delicate fantasy reminiscent of SHAKESPEARE. His plays are still in the French REPERTOIRE; many were produced by COPEAU and his followers.
Bibl: H. Lefebvre, ALFRED DE MUSSET, DRAMATURGE, 1955

Müthel, Lothar (1898–1965), German actor and director. Made his early appearances as an actor at the Deutsches-Theater,

Music Hall, The Old Bedford, London. Lithograph by Walter Sickert

Motley, set and costumes for DAVIOT's *Richard of Bordeaux* with GIELGUD and Gwen Ffrangcon-Davies.

BERLIN, 1913–17, e.g. in SCHILLER's *Don Carlos*. After 1917 appeared with leading German companies in Darmstadt, Munich, and toured widely through Germany. With the Berlin National Theatre 1928–29, where his best productions included GOETHE's *Faust* (Part I, 1932); SHAKESPEARE's *Hamlet*, 1937; and G. HAUPTMANN's *Und Pippa tanzt*, 1937. Director of the BURGTHEATER in Vienna 1939–46; 1947–50 actor and director in Weimar, subsequently at the Schlossparktheater and the Schiffbauerdammtheater, Berlin, and 1951–56 artistic director of the Frankfurt Municipal Theatre.
Bibl: R. Biedrzynski, SCHAUSPIELER, REGISSEURE, INTENDANTEN, 1944

Mystery plays (Fr *mystères*; Ger *Mysterienspiele*; Span *Auto sacramental*; Ital *sacra rappresentazione*; also, in English, referred to as miracle plays). Medieval religious plays which derived directly from the Easter liturgy and were performed at Easter, Christmas and later at the feast of Corpus Christi. They grew from the enactment of the Resurrection story to the whole cycle of Old and New Testaments, from Creation to Last Judgment. The biblical story was often intermingled with realistic, dramatic and even humorous interludes which gave insight into the life of the common people and treated the villains (Herod, the Devil) as comic figures. The important development was in the 13th century when they moved from inside the chamber into the open air, and switched from Latin to the vernacular. Performed by trade guilds (archaic meaning of *mystery* =trade) or specially formed *confréries* in France. In England they were acted on movable PAGEANT wagons, and in other countries in open arenas, with the pageants arranged in a circle. In France these Christmas and Easter plays reached their peak in the 14th and 15th centuries, e.g. *La Passion de Semur*; *La Passion d'Arras*; *Le Mystère de la Passion* by Arnoul Gréban. In England four main cycles of mystery plays survive, the Chester, York, Wakefield and Coventry (or Lincoln) cycles. In Germany the mystery play which had originated with Easter plays as far back as the 10th century, flourished longer. The OBERAMMERGAU Passion play, still performed decennially, derives from a 15th-century text. Spain, Italy, Poland and other European countries have a similar tradition of medieval religious drama.
Bibl: A. Grünberg, DAS RELIGIÖSE DRAMA DES MITTELALTERS, 1965; G. Wickham, EARLY ENGLISH STAGES, 1959; G. Cohen, LE THÉÂTRE EN FRANCE AU MOYEN AGE, 2/1948; E. K. Chambers, THE MEDIEVAL STAGE, 1903, 2 vols

Nabis, Les. Group of French painters in the 1890s, who were influenced by Paul Gauguin. They included Pierre Bonnard, Maurice Denis, F. X. Roussel, Paul Serusier and Edouard Vuillard. The group was associated with the director LUGNÉ-POË, for whose Théâtre de l'Œuvre they worked, transferring their colourful textures and shadowy interiors to theatre décor, mostly painted by the artists themselves. The programme notes often contained lithographs by the Nabis. Their anti-bourgeois aims were best illustrated in their collaboration on the first production of JARRY's *Ubu Roi* in 1896.
Bibl: H. Rischbieter (ed), BÜHNE UND BILDENDE KUNST IM 20. JAHRHUNDERT, 1968

Nante (Berlin dialect, abbreviation of 'Ferdinand'). An early 19th-century BERLIN folk character, who first appeared in HOLTEI's play *Ein Trauerspiel in Berlin* (A Berlin Tragedy), 1845. N. is an 'Eckensteher' (a street-corner loafer) and was developed by the actor Friedrich Beckmann into a popular type which was used in a number of other sketches and plays.

Nash, N. Richard (Nathaniel R. Nusbaum; 1913–), US dramatist. He gained worldwide fame with the fantasy play *The Rainmaker*, 1954; later filmed and turned into the musical *110 in the Shade*, 1963. Other works include: *The Second Best Bed*, 1946, a farce about SHAKESPEARE; *Girls of Summer*, 1956; *Keep it in the Family*, 1967. He has also written film and TV scripts.

Nathan, George Jean (1882–1958), US critic. Doyen of New York drama critics; in his 50-year career allegedly saw every single New York première, and exercised considerable influence on the development of American theatre. He supported the drama of ideas, championing modern European playwrights including IBSEN, STRINDBERG, G. HAUPTMANN, SCHNITZLER and SHAW. His most important discovery was O'NEILL, whose earliest works he published in the magazine *The Smart Set* which he edited with H. L. Mencken. His career began in 1905 with the *New York Herald*; he later worked for numerous other papers and magazines such as *Harper's Weekly*, the *Saturday Review of Literature*, *Esquire*, *Newsweek*, *Life*. In 1932 with O'Neill, Theodore Dreiser and others he founded the *American Spectator*. He wrote about 30 books on the theatre, the best of which include: *The Critic and the Drama*, 1922; *The Entertainment of a Nation*, 1942; *The Theatre of the Fifties*, 1953; he edited *Theatre Book of the Year*, 1942/43.
Bibl: I. Goldberg, THE THEATRE OF GEORGE JEAN NATHAN, 1926

National Theatre. From the 17th-century Court, State and National Theatres developed in most European nations, first under the influence of the COMÉDIE-FRANÇAISE, the famous COURT THEATRE of Louis XIV and Louis XV, which later organically developed into a French National Theatre. In the 19th and early 20th centuries the newly emerging nation states needed a National Theatre as an assertion of their national identity and cultural autonomy. In the English-speaking countries the deep influence of puritanism made the idea of a state-subsidized theatre, which might be subservient to the king and a source of frivolous expenditure, or – later – an instrument of political interference in the free play of ideas, almost impossible to envisage. Nevertheless the idea of a British National Theatre was mooted repeatedly from the 18th century onwards. At the beginning of the 20th century SHAW, ARCHER and GRANVILLE-BARKER were the chief advocates; in 1903 Archer and Granville-Barker drew up a concrete plan under the title *A Scheme and Estimates for a National Theatre* which was privately printed and circulated among influential personalities. It was endorsed by prominent theatre people like IRVING, PINERO and BARRIE. In 1910 the movement they had initiated merged with another group advocating a Shakespeare Memorial Theatre. In 1938 a site was acquired in South Kensington but the outbreak of war postponed any possibility of a realization of the sceheme. It was during the war that the role of the OLD VIC as the unofficial National Theatre became clear and so after the end of World War II the idea that the Old Vic should become the nucleus of a British National Theatre gained ground. In 1949 a National Theatre Bill was passed by Parliament, but the implementation of its provisions remained vague. It was only in the early 1960s, on the initiative of the LCC, that the Government finally agreed to create a National Theatre; OLIVIER was appointed director and the new company which was housed in the Old Vic building opened with a production of *Hamlet* (with O'TOOLE in the title role) on 22 October 1963. Shortly afterwards Denys Lasdun was appointed architect to design a new building (opened on the South Bank of the Thames in 1976). Under Olivier the National Theatre achieved a solid reputation and drew large audiences. In the autumn of 1973 HALL took over the direction of the enterprise in preparation for the new building which opened in 1976. It contains an auditorium with a large open stage, another with a proscenium arch stage, and an experimental studio theatre. Among the associate directors appointed by Hall to assist him in the running of the National Theatre are PINTER, J. MILLER, John Schlesinger, the designer BURY, the critic John Russell Brown as literary manager, BLAKEMORE and Olivier. The National Theatre in its new building receives an ARTS COUNCIL subsidy of about £2,000,000 and from the Greater London

Council £300,000.
Bibl: R. Cushman, THE NATIONAL THEATRE, 1963–71. A PICTORIAL RECORD, 1972

National Youth Theatre ▷CROFT.

Naturalism. A movement in the arts which arose in the second half of the 19th century under the influence of the new trends of positivism and scientific thought, insisting on a mercilessly truthful depiction of nature and reality, even if this meant a contravention of age-old ideas of beauty and harmony. The most important theoretician of Naturalism was ZOLA whose books *Le Roman expérimental*, 1880, and *Le Naturalisme au théâtre*, 1882, had a wide impact throughout Europe. Zola based his ideas on the importance of environment and heredity on the character and fate of individuals and advocated the replacement of the old concepts of tragic guilt and destiny by these scientific facts. The need to depict reality as it is, and above all the minutiae of everyday life, made naturalistic drama loose in construction, atmospheric and episodic. Plays like G. HAUPTMANN's *The Weavers*, 1893, in which a whole social class, the weavers, constitute the hero, or GORKY's *The Lower Depths*, Paris 1905, which depicts the fragmented events in the lives of characters assembled by chance in a doss-house, illustrate this tendency as well as the hitherto unheard of concentration on proletarian characters as heroes of TRAGEDY. Whether the later plays of IBSEN, CHEKHOV's major plays, or the more realistic dramas of STRINDBERG belong to Naturalism in the proper sense is a subject of debate. That they reflect many of its ideas is beyond doubt. Many of the theatrical innovators of the turn of the century, ANTOINE and his Théâtre Libre, BRAHM, and STANISLAVSKY were champions of Naturalism.

Naughton, Bill (1910–), Irish-born English dramatist. An important exponent of the regional domestic comedy of the early 1960s. Began by writing radio plays, on which most of his later COMEDIES are based. Main works include: *All in Good Time*, 1963; *Alfie*, 1963; *Spring and Port Wine*, 1965; *June Evening*, 1965, and *Annie and Fanny*, 1967.

Naumachia (Gk = sea battle). Mimed theatrical sea fight; a popular entertainment in ancient Rome, which took place either in a flooded ARENA or on the banks of the river Tiber. Introduced in 46 BC by Julius Caesar. Later revived in the Renaissance in the modified form of water pageants and in the 20th century as water pantomimes in the CIRCUS.

Nazimova, Alla (1879–1945), Russian actress. In 1904 became principal actress of the St Petersburg theatre; subsequently toured Europe and America and in 1906 played IBSEN's *Hedda Gabler* – her first English-speaking part – in New York. She stayed in New York, becoming famous as

Mystery play, the martyrdom of St Apollonia, *c.* 1460, miniature by Jean Fouquet

National Youth Theatre's production by CROFT of TERSON's *Zigger-Zagger*, 1967

Richard Nash, *The Rainmaker*, with Geraldine Page and Darren McGrath, 1954

Alla Nazimova and Eliot Cabot in TURGENEV's *A Month in the Country*, THEATRE GUILD, 1930

an interpreter of Ibsen, and in 1910 appeared at the newly opened Nazimova Theatre in *Little Eyolf.* After some successful years in films, e.g. *Salome*, 1923, she returned to the New York stage at the Civic Repertory Theatre and the THEATRE GUILD in plays by Ibsen, CHEKHOV, TURGENEV, and O'NEILL.

Neagle, Dame Anna (1904–), English actress. Appointed DBE in 1969. Started as a dancer and became a world star with her performance as Queen Victoria in the films *Victoria the Great*, 1937, and *Sixty Glorious Years*, 1938. Has appeared in many highly successful MUSICAL COMEDIES. Married to the film producer Herbert Wilcox.

Neher, Caspar (1897–1962), German stage designer. He was a lifelong friend of BRECHT with whom he collaborated closely. Early in his career he designed many first productions of the latter's plays, directed by the author, as well as productions by other directors such as ENGEL, JESSNER and FEHLING. In the 1930s he studied art history, particularly the Baroque and Renaissance periods; in his opera scenery he recreated historical stage designs, making use of pictorial screens. Worked in Frankfurt 1931–41 and 1934–44 at the Deutsches-Theater, BERLIN, under HILPERT. In 1940 he began a collaboration with SCHUH, mainly on operas: they became known for their productions of Mozart in the Redoutensaal of the Vienna Hofburg and later at the SALZBURG FESTIVAL. From 1948 he worked with Brecht and his BERLINER ENSEMBLE on: *Herr Puntila*, 1949; *Der Hofmeister*, 1950; *Leben des Galilei*, 1957. In his later collaboration with Schuh he developed a new kind of symbolic stylization. His designs for Mozart's opera *Don Giovanni*, 1960, were typical of this style.
Bibl: G. v. Einem and S. Melchinger (ed), 1965

Nemirovich-Danchenko, Vladimir Ivanovich (1858–1943), Russian director and theatre manager. Was co-founder and director of the MOSCOW ART THEATRE, and one of the outstanding personalities of the Russian stage. Studied at Moscow University; began his career by writing novels and a number of conventional plays which were successfully produced at the Maly Theatre. In 1891 he became lecturer in drama at the Moscow Philharmonic Society, among his students being MOSKVIN and MEYERHOLD. In 1897 an important meeting with STANISLAVSKY took place which led to the foundation of the MAT. While Stanislavsky took charge of the productions, N.-D. was responsible for the organization and the literary aspects; it was he who persuaded CHEKHOV to give the performing rights of *The Seagull* to the MAT after its failure at the Alexandrinsky Theatre, and the play subsequently became a triumphant success in 1898. Also worked on several plays as co-director. In 1919 he founded a Music Studio where he made use of his experience at the MAT and developed a new style of production for opera and operetta. In 1926 this theatre was renamed after him. After Stanislavsky's death in 1938, N.-D. became the sole director of the MAT. He wrote a book on its history, *My Life in the Russian Theatre*, 1937, in which he also explored his theories of drama.

Nestroy, Johann Nepomuk (1801–62), Austrian actor and playwright. Began his career in 1822 as a singer at the Vienna Opera. Worked at the German theatre in Amsterdam 1823–25, where he also appeared in plays, then went to Brno. From 1826 played mainly comic parts in Graz and Bratislava and achieved fame as Sansquartier in ANGELY's *Sieben Mädchen in Uniform*, 1827; in 1829 appeared as a guest at the Theater in der Josefstadt in Vienna and in 1831 took up an appointment at the Theater an der Wien (under Karl Carl) where he gained his first success as a playwright with *Der böse Geist Lumpazivagabundus* (The Evil Spirit L.), 1833; in 1838 Carl took over the management of the Leopoldstädter-Theater, which he rebuilt and renamed the Carl-Theater in 1847. After Carl's death in 1854, N. succeeded him as director; in 1860 he retired from the theatre except for guest appearances. He and his famous predecessor RAIMUND were consummate exponents of Viennese folk comedy. Writing mainly for his own troupe, N. produced a great variety of pieces, sure-fire theatrical successes, combining elements of baroque opera, the HANSWURST plays, the SINGSPIEL, themes from the ZAUBERSTÜCK or *Zauberposse* and parody, usually centring on conventional intrigues which derived their special, untranslatable charm from a masterly use of allusive Viennese dialect, the chief source of his humour. An educated member of the middle class rather than a peasant poet, he wrote a kind of satirical, disillusioned theatre. Karl Kraus said of him that 'He wrapped his dynamite in cottonwool. Not until he had established that everything was for the best in the best of all possible worlds, did his world burst wide open.' Of his 80 works the best known are *Das Mädel aus der Vorstadt* (The Girl from the Suburbs), 1841; *Judith und Holofernes*, 1849, and *Einen Jux will er sich machen* (He Wants to Have a Fling), 1842, on which WILDER based his play *The Matchmaker*.
Bibl: R. Preissner, NESTROY, DER SCHÖPFER DER TRAGISCHEN POSSE, 1968; S. Brill, DIE KOMÖDIE DER SPRACHE, 1967; O. Rommel, DIE ALT-WIENER VOLKSKOMÖDIE, 1952

Netherlands. The country's most important contributions to the European theatre of the Middle Ages were: the ABELE SPELEN; the *sotternie* (▷SOTIE); the first version of EVERYMAN; the REDERIJKERS. In the transitional period between the 16th century and the BAROQUE THEATRE the most important dramatist was VONDEL. In 1638 the Schouwburg opened in Amsterdam, a highly developed theatre with a REPERTOIRE including CALDERÓN, CORNEILLE and GRYPHIUS; from 1655 with professional actors and in 1644 equipped with a wing-stage. It burnt down in 1772 and was rebuilt in 1774. The repertoire in the 18th century consisted of French TRAGEDIES and contemporary Dutch COMEDIES (by Pieter Langendijk, Thomas Asselijn, Pieter Bernagie) with a high standard of acting. The company made many guest appearances in foreign countries. In about 1800, the actor Marten Corver and his pupils established a more natural and simple style of acting. In the 19th century the Schouwburg was rented to travelling companies and guest groups, since then it has had no resident company. Towards the end of the 19th century literary tendencies were dominant: De Koninklijke Vereeniging Het Nederlands Tooneel (Royal Society of Netherlands Theatre; 1876–1932) produced French comedies and SHAKESPEARE and brought together the best actors including Louis Bouwmeester, a celebrated Shylock. Under the management of Louis Henri Crispin the Nederlands Tooneel organization was oriented towards the French Théâtre Libre (▷ANTOINE), producing IBSEN, HAUPTMANN and MAETERLINCK. From 1910 to 1925 the most outstanding and influential directors and personalities of Dutch theatre were: Willem Royaards (*As You Like It* and *A Midsummer Night's Dream*), in the festive style of REINHARDT, and Eduard Verkade, influenced by CRAIG's *Hamlet*. In 1935 Albert von Dalsum (1889–1971) and August Dufresne (1893–1962) produced LAGERKVIST's sensational play *The Hangman*, which had an anti-Fascist protest as its underlying theme; it was taken off the stage for political reasons. From 1945 there have been permanent companies in Amsterdam, The Hague, Rotterdam, Arnhem and Tilburg as well as touring companies. Their REPERTORY is international, including the classics of world literature; among the best new dramatists is the Flemish writer CLAUS, born 1929.
Bibl: DE AMSTERDAMSE SCHOUWBURG VAN 1637, 1959; B. Hunningher, EEN NEUW NEDERLANDS TOONEEL, 1950

Neuber, Friedrike Caroline (*née* Weissenborn; 1697–1760). Also known as 'die Neuberin', she was the first and most important German professional actress and manager. With the support of the famous critic GOTTSCHED she crusaded for 'good taste' on the German stage and introduced many reforms, helping to raise the standard of German acting and purify the REPERTOIRE. In 1727 she appeared as 'Court comedienne' with her company in Leipzig, producing French classical TRAGEDIES and COMEDIES adapted by Gottsched. She was dedicated to abolishing the old vulgar style of German folk theatre, improvised clowning comedies and popular FARCES; her efforts led later to the disappearance of the HARLEQUIN from the German stage. Under Gottsched's direction she had HANSWURST banished from the theatre; he was symbolically burned in a famous ceremony at Leipzig in 1737. As C.N. was a fine actress herself, she appeared in many leading parts, helped to train many talented young actors, with an emphasis on regularity and order; she also wrote several INTERLUDES and PASTORAL PLAYS. Between 1739 and 1741 she and Gottsched gradually drifted apart, and this led to her ridiculing him in the play *Der Sterbende Cato* (The Dying Cato). She subsequently toured Germany and Russia (1740) unsuccessfully till her company finally broke up. Her association with Gottsched prior to their break is considered a turning-point in German theatre and marked the beginnings of modern acting. Bibl: K. Reinholz, EDUARD DEVRIENTS GESCHICHTE DER DEUTSCHEN SCHAUSPIELKUNST, 1846–74, 2/1967; W. Drews, DIE GROSSEN DES DEUTSCHEN SCHAUSPIELS, 1941

Neue Sachlichkeit (Ger=new objectivity). German literary and artistic movement in the 1920s, a reaction against EXPRESSIONISM. In contrast to the latter's emotionalism and high-flown language, the new movement strove for factual, documentary treatment of the real world, stressing technology, sport, jazz. As the USA was regarded as the home of the 'modern' technological civilization, the writers and painters of the Neue Sachlichkeit often used American themes and backgrounds; BRECHT passed through such a period. Other writers either used the documentary approach for social criticism, e.g. BRUCKNER in *Die Verbrecher* (The Criminals), 1928, which showed a cross-section through a block of flats and traced the different ways the inhabitants broke the moral law. Other plays in this vein were Peter Martin Lampel's *Revolte im Erziehungshaus* (Revolt in the House of Correction), 1928, and the reconstruction of the Dreyfus affair by REHFISCH and Herzog, *Die Affäre Dreyfus*, 1929. One of its chief exponents among directors was PISCATOR who constructed a number of performances from newspaper reports, using documentary film, diagrams of statistics, etc.

Nichols, Mike (1931–), US actor, writer and director. Started in CABARET, partnering Elaine May. Achieved immense success as a director with SIMON's *Barefoot in the Park*, New York 1963. Has since directed many of the same author's hits (*The Odd Couple*, 1965; *Plaza Suite*, 1968). Also an excellent film director.

Nichols, Peter (1927–), English dramatist. Wrote TV plays for about ten years before he finally achieved recognition on the stage with *A Day in the Death of Joe Egg* in 1967, GLASGOW CITIZENS' THEATRE. His best known TV plays are: *Ben Spray*, 1961, and its sequel *Ben Again*, 1962; *The Big Boys*, 1961; *The Reception*, 1961; *Promenade*, 1961; *The Hooded Terror*, 1963; *The Continuity Man*, 1963, originally a stage play; *When the Wind Blows*, 1965. One of his main themes is the violence beneath the surface of ordinary, apparently conventional family life. Since *Joe Egg* he has had four further TV plays produced (*The Gore, Daddy Kiss It Better, Hearts and Flowers, The Common*) and has scripted the screen version of *Joe Egg*, filmed by P. Madek 1972, and written the stage plays: *The National Health*, NATIONAL THEATRE, 1969, a black comedy, set in a hospital, which portrays the life and sufferings of

Netherlands, Schouwburg stage setting of a general's camp and tent, after W. Writs from 'Atlas van de Stad Amsterdam'

Caroline Neuber as Elizabeth I of England in Thomas Corneille's *Le comte d'Essex*

Johann Nestroy, scene from *Lumpazivagabundus*

six patients in a ward and contrasts it with a romanticized TV version of hospital life; *Forget-Me-Not Lane*, Greenwich Theatre, 1971, transferred to the West End, an ironical comedy that takes up most of his earlier themes, and is mainly concerned with the 'genetic gap' that eventually turns us into our parents; *Chez Nous*, Globe Theatre, 1974, a domestic comedy with bitter undertones, set in a converted French farmhouse. This play covers a variety of themes, middle-class hypocrisy, the equivocal nature of friendship, deep-rooted male competitiveness, which emerge through the interaction of the four chief characters, the central one being a nervy paediatrician who has written a best-seller called *The Nubile Generation*. Another play is *The Freeway*, National Theatre, 1974.

Nicolet, Jean-Baptiste (1728–96), French acrobat and actor. The son of a puppet-player, he had in 1760 a booth on the Boulevard du Temple, which he soon transformed into a permanent theatre, where he was allowed to perform plays for which the COMÉDIE-FRANÇAISE and COMÉDIE-ITALIENNE had licences; in 1772 Louis XV granted it the title 'Spectacle des grands danseurs du roi'; after the Revolution in 1792 it became the Théâtre de la Gaîté, where he successfully produced CORNEILLE, RACINE and MOLIÈRE.

Nicoll, Allardyce (1894–1976), Scottish-born theatre historian. Professor of English Literature at London and Birmingham, later head of the Drama Department of Yale University, where he started to accumulate a vast wealth of theatrical material. He has written a number of books on the theatre including: *World Drama from Aeschylus to Anouilh*, 1949; *History of English Drama 1660–1900*, 6 vols, 1952–59; *The Development of the Theatre*, 4/1956; *The Theatre and Dramatic Theory*, 1962; *The Elizabethans*, 1957; *The World of Harlequin*, 1963; *English Drama; a modern viewpoint*, 1968.

Niessen, Carl (1890–1969) German theatre historian. Head of the Drama Department of the University of Cologne, 1929–55, and responsible for founding the extensive collection of historical material on theatre. Author of many essays and books including his unfinished *Das Handbuch der Theaterwissenschaft*, publication of which began in 1949.

Noah, Mordecai Manuel (1785–1851), US dramatist. Author of a number of well-written plays dealing with American historical subjects employing lavish décor and lighting. His plays remained in REPERTORY for many years: *The White Pilgrim*, 1812, translation of *Le Pélerin Blanc* by Pixérécourt; *The Siege of Tripoli*, 1820 (now lost); *The Grecian Captive*, 1822.

Noelte, Rudolf (1921–), German director. Leading exponent of a radical realistic style of production based on the tradition of FEHLING, with whom he worked early in his career. Made his début as a director in 1948 with BORCHERT's *Draussen vor der Tür*, but achieved his first success with M. Brod's adaptation of KAFKA's *Das Schloss*, 1953. For a brief period in 1959 he managed the Kurfürstendamm Theater in BERLIN and with his production of STERNHEIM's *Die Kassette*, 1960, heralded a new series of productions of the latter's satirical COMEDIES as realistic portrayals of German society. Other productions by N. include CHEKHOV's *Three Sisters*, 1965, and KLEIST's *Der Zerbrochene Krug*, 1966.

Noh play ▷JAPAN.

Norman, Frank (1931–), English writer. Writing from personal experience of the London underworld and of prison life, he wrote the scripts of two of JOAN LITTLEWOOD's musical successes: *Fings Ain't Wot They Used T'Be*, 1959, music BART, and *A Kayf Up West*, 1964, music Stanley Myers.

Norway. Visiting performances by Danish companies in the 18th century. The first theatre in the Norwegian language was the 'Dramatic Society', 1794–1828, in Bergen with a comedy REPERTOIRE. In 1849 founding of the Norwegian theatre in Bergen by the musician Ole Bull, where from 1851 to 1857 IBSEN worked as DRAMATURG and director and where in 1855 his play *Lady Inger of Ostrat* was first performed. BJØRNSTJERNE BJØRNSON was director there from 1857 till 1863 when it was closed down. From 1857 until bankruptcy put an end to it, the Norwegian theatre in Christiania (Oslo) was under the artistic direction of Ibsen, and from 1865 to 1867 was managed by Bjørnson. At the instigation of BJØRN BJØRNSON (Bjørnstjerne's son) a NATIONAL THEATRE was founded in Christiania in 1899, which reached its artistic peak in 1907, and was under the direction of Halfdan Christensen 1911–23. A Norwegian-language theatre was founded in 1913; its outstanding manager and director was Knut Hergel, who was director of the National Theatre 1946–60. Biggest theatre in Oslo: Folk Theatre, which opened in 1933, after 1945 managed by Hans Jacob Nilsen. Other permanent theatres are in Bergen and Trondheim; there also exist a number of state-subsidized travelling companies.
Bibl: H. Beyer, A HISTORY OF NORWEGIAN LITERATURE, 1956

Novelli, Ermete (1851–1919), Italian actor. One of the greatest performers of his time, he first appeared in COMEDY, but it was in TRAGEDY that he made his reputation, combining technical virtuosity with great sensitivity for modernity. After several years with travelling companies, he became the leading comic character under BELLOTTI-BON, 1877–83, appearing in plays by GOLDONI, GIACOSA, DUMAS, SCRIBE, etc. From 1883 until his death he had his own company which at first produced 'fashionable' plays ranging from Najac to MOSER/SCHÖNTHAN and touring successfully, e.g. in Spain, 1886–87, and Latin America, 1890; it was not until 1890 that he appeared in tragic parts such as Othello, Shylock, and Hamlet where his scene with his father's Ghost became famous; it was said that he made the audience see the apparition. Another of his great parts was the title role in Aicard's *Le Père Lebonnard*, which he also translated and adapted. However, his attempt in 1900 to found a permanent theatre in Rome – Casa di Goldoni – with a classical REPERTOIRE and new plays was a failure.
Bibl: A. Camilleri, I TEATRI STABILI IN ITALIA, 1898–1918, 1959

Novello, Ivor (David Ivor Davies; 1893–1951), British composer, dramatist and actor. Son of musical parents, he showed talent for composing light music from his earliest years. During World War I he contributed to the score of a number of MUSICAL COMEDIES and made a great hit with his patriotic song 'Keep the Home Fires Burning'. He made his début as an actor in 1921 in S. GUITRY's *Deburau*, adapted by GRANVILLE-BARKER, at the Ambassadors' Theatre, and began writing plays and musical comedies in 1924. His first play, *The Rat*, 1924, was written in collaboration with CONSTANCE COLLIER. Among others, in many of which he appeared himself, were *Symphony in Two Flats*, 1929; *I Lived with You*, 1932; and *We Proudly Present*, 1947. From 1935 to 1945 he worked as author, composer and leading actor (SHAKESPEARE's *Henry V*, 1938) at DRURY LANE. He wrote, composed and played the lead in four successive musicals at Drury Lane: *Glamorous Night*, 1935; *Careless Rapture*, 1936; *Crest of the Wave*, 1937; and *The Dancing Years*, 1939, revived in 1942, running for the rest of World War II. At the time of his death he was appearing in his own *King's Rhapsody*.

Nunn, Trevor (1940–), English director. Studied at Cambridge where he acted, and directed many plays for the Marlowe Society, the Amateur Dramatic Club and a Footlights Revue. In 1962 he went to the Belgrade Theatre, Coventry, as a trainee-director and remained there as a resident director (putting on plays by ARDEN, BRECHT, A. MILLER, IBSEN and SHAKESPEARE) till 1965 when he joined the ROYAL SHAKESPEARE COMPANY as an associate director. His productions included, as co-director, Bolt's *The Thwarting of Baron Bolligrew*, London, Aldwych 1965; *Henry IV*, Parts I and II, *Henry V*, and the first revival for 300 years of TOURNEUR's *The Revenger's Tragedy*, at STRATFORD-UPON-AVON 1966. In 1966 he acted in and produced MROŻEK's *Tango* at the Aldwych and revived VANBRUGH's *The Relapse* there in 1967. In 1968, at the age of 28, he was appointed Artistic Director of the RSC in succession to HALL. Other notable productions include *King Lear*, Stratford 1968; *The Taming of the Shrew*, Stratford 1967, Aldwych and then Los Angeles 1968; *Much Ado About Nothing*, Stratford 1968, Aldwych and Los Angeles 1969; ALBEE's *A Delicate Balance*, Aldwych 1969; *The Winter's Tale*, Stratford 1969, which then toured Japan and Australia; *Henry VIII*, 1969, and *Hamlet*, 1970, at Stratford. He then spent a year preparing a season of Shakespeare plays under the general title *The Romans*, which included *Coriolanus*, *Julius Caesar*, *Antony and Cleopatra* and *Titus Andronicus*, first produced 1972. Married to the actress Janet Suzman.

Nušić, Branislav (1864–1938), Serbian diplomat, journalist, DRAMATURG, theatre manager (Skopje, Sarajevo). A writer of great versatility, he became very popular with his COMEDIES which in later years were vehicles for sharp social criticism.

NYDCC (New York Drama Critics Circle) Award. Established in 1935 by a group of New York critics, in protest against the awarding of the PULITZER PRIZE for a sentimental adaptation by Zoë Akins of Edith Wharton's *The Old Maid*. The first play to receive the award was M. ANDERSON's *Winterset*, 1936, in which year the Pulitzer Prize went to SHERWOOD's *Idiot's Delight*. In 1938 the Critics' Award went to STEINBECK's *Of Mice and Men*, and the Pulitzer Prize to *Our Town* by WILDER. NYDCC Award winners have been T. WILLIAMS, SAROYAN, A. MILLER, LILLIAN HELLMAN, VAN DRUTEN and O'NEILL. It is also awarded to foreign plays and musicals.

NYVRDD/New York Vernon Rice Drama Desk Award. Annual award, named after late New York drama critic, for promising playwrights.

Obaldia, René de (1918–), French dramatist. Well known for his poetry and the novel *Fugue à Waterloo*, 1956, for which he was awarded the Surrealists' Prix de l'Humour noir. His dramatic works are mostly COMEDIES with strong surrealist elements; he began by writing one-act plays: *Le Grand Vizir*, 1956; *Le Défunt* and *Le Sacrifice du bourreau*, 1957. His first full-length play *Génousie* was first performed in 1960 by the TNP. Other works include: *Le Satyre de la Villette*, 1963, Théâtre de l'Atelier, dir BARSACQ; *Du Vent dans les branches de Sassafras*, 1965, dir R. Dupuy; one-act plays: *L'Azote*, 1960; *Les Jumeaux étincelants*, 1960; *Poivre de Cayenne*, 1961; *Le Général inconnu*, 1964; *Le Cosmonaute agricole*, 1965; *L'Air du large*, pub 1966.

Oberammergau. Village in Upper Bavaria, famous for its traditional religious drama. During the plague epidemic of 1633 the villagers made a vow to perform a PASSION PLAY; it was first staged in 1634 and every ten years thereafter was enacted by the village people as a mass spectacle. The original version was a combination of two texts (a passion play of the 15th century in the Swabian dialect of Augsburg and a

NYDCC Award winner, *The Glass Menagerie* by T. WILLIAMS, with LAURETTE TAYLOR and Eddie Dowling, 1945

Ivor Novello in *Perchance to Dream*, London 1945

Oberammergau, PASSION PLAY

play by the Augsburg MEISTERSINGER Sebastian Wild). The script has been revised and rewritten several times, the text used today being based on an 1810 version by P. Ottmar Weiss. It became internationally known after the appearance of the actor E. DEVRIENT and today has its own festival theatre. The most recent performance was in 1970.

Obey, André (1892–1975), French dramatist. Best known for his early work written for the COMPAGNIE DES QUINZE where he worked as resident dramatist 1929–32: *Le Viol de Lucrèce*, *La Bataille de la Marne*, and *Noé* (all 1931) were staged in accordance with COPEAU's ideas. Together with J.-J. BERNARD and other dramatists, he created a 'theatre of silence', inspired by the ideas of MAETERLINCK who believed that drama lies in silences that reveal the mysteries of man's soul and the universe. After leaving the C. des Q. in 1932 he wrote French adaptations of SHAKESPEARE, SOPHOCLES and AESCHYLUS and a *Don Juan* (a later version was entitled *L'Homme de cendres*, 1949). In 1946/47 he was briefly director of the COMÉDIE-FRANÇAISE. His later works include: *Lazare*, 1951; *Plus de miracles pour Noël* (*Frost at Midnight*), 1957.

Obie (Distinguished Play) Award. An annual prize initiated by *The Village Voice*, a Greenwich Village paper published in New York, at the end of the 1955–56 theatre season, in order to give recognition to theatrical achievement in the OFF-BROADWAY theatre.

Obraztsov, Sergei Vladimirovich (1901–), Russian puppet master. Studied painting 1918–26 and was then an actor in STANISLAVSKY's theatre until 1936. In 1920 he started to use puppets and created the Soviet Puppet Theatre. Today there are over 100 professional PUPPET THEATRES, all indebted to him. Since 1931 he has been in charge of the State Central Puppet Theatre which he founded in Moscow. Actor, producer, theoretician and organizer, he also makes his own puppets which are of various sizes to give the illusion of perspective. Through his puppets he portrays real-life situations, involving suffering, passions and dreams, even politics, creating a theatre of dazzling wit and invention, full of moral and political jokes. Particularly well known are: *An Unusual Concert* and *Aladdin and His Wonderful Lamp*, 1940; *Mowgli* (by N. Gernet, based on Kipling, 1945); *King Stag* (by E. Speranski, based on GOZZI). He has also written several books including *The Puppet-Master*, 1938; *My Profession*, 1950; *Chinese Theatre*, 1965.

O'Casey, Sean (John Casey; 1880–1964), Irish dramatist. His realistic plays combine great artistic quality with social and political awareness. The plots are based on the lives and characters of people from the Dublin slums, and on events like the Irish struggle for freedom which O'C. knew intimately. His work belongs to the genre of tragic satire in which COMEDY and satire have tragic implications, a form of literature rarely treated so masterfully. His first plays were all produced at the ABBEY THEATRE, Dublin; *The Shadow of a Gunman*, 1923, with which he made his reputation; *Juno and the Paycock*, 1924, and *The Plough and the Stars*, 1926, but a riot by Irish patriots on the first night of this play caused O'C. to leave Ireland and he settled in England. He refused to allow his plays to be performed in Ireland for some years after YEATS had rejected *The Silver Tassie*, pub 1928, which marked a change in style tending towards the stylization of EXPRESSIONISM and SYMBOLISM, developed in his next play, with a London setting, *Within the Gates*, fp London 1934, Everyman Theatre. Two one-act FARCES, *The End of the Beginning* and *A Pound on Demand*, were written during this period. Other full-length plays include *Purple Dust*, written 1938/39, fp 1944; a farcical comedy, *The Star Turns Red*, fp 1940, and *Oak Leaves and Lavender*, written 1942, pub 1946, both invoking the use of Symbolism to reinforce the Marxist ideas of his heroes; and in the final phase of his work, *Red Roses for Me*, a redramatization of *The Star Turns Red*, fp Dublin 1943, Olympia, his first Irish première for 17 years; *Cock-A-Doodle Dandy*, pub 1949, a rewrite of *Oak Leaves and Lavender*, fp New York 1958, London 1959; *The Bishop's Bonfire*, fp 1955; *The Drums of Father Ned*, fp 1959. In 1961 he wrote a further three one-act plays, the best of which is *Behind the Green Curtains*. He also wrote two volumes of drama criticism: *The Flying Wasp*, 1937, and *The Green Crow*, 1957.
Bibl: G. Fallon, SEAN O'CASEY, THE MAN I KNEW, 1965; S. Cowasje, SEAN O'CASEY, THE MAN BEHIND THE PLAYS, 1965; R. Hogan, THE EXPERIMENTS OF SEAN O'CASEY, 1960

Odeon (Lat *odeum* from Gk *oideion*). In ancient GREECE a covered, circular building used for the *proagon*, a parade preceding dramatic festivals, musical events, and legal trials. One of the earliest examples was built by Pericles in Athens in 444 BC. The other Odeon in Athens (still well preserved) was given by Herodes Atticus to the city in 170 BC. Today a popular name given to cinemas and theatres, e.g. Odéon in Paris.

Odets, Clifford (1906–63), US dramatist, actor and director. Began acting professionally after graduating from high school. In 1928 he joined the acting company of the THEATRE GUILD. When CLURMAN, STRASBERG, and CHERYL CRAWFORD founded the GROUP THEATRE in 1931 he was among the actors and, from 1935 to 1940, he was their major playwright; his first seven plays were written for and produced at the Group Theatre. They dealt with social topics, mainly in Marxist terms, dividing humanity into two classes (characteristic of all his plays) – exploiter and exploited – and for the latter, the victims of ignorance, he showed genuine sympathy. His works include: *Waiting for Lefty*, 1935, about the cab-strike in New York; *Till the Day I Die*, 1935, anti-Nazi play; *Paradise Lost*, 1935; *Golden Boy*, 1937, about a professional boxer; *Rocket to the Moon*, 1938; *Night Music*, 1940; *Clash by Night*, 1941; *The Big Knife*, 1949; *The Country Girl*, 1949, prod as *Winter Journey*, London 1952; *The Flowering Peach*, 1954. Wrote several film scripts and was also a film director.

Oedipus. King of Thebes who, in fulfilment of a pronouncement of the oracle at Delphi, unwittingly murdered his father Laius and married his mother Jocasta. Became king after solving the riddle of the sphinx but, when his sin was discovered, blinded himself and went into exile. He appears in SOPHOCLES' *Oedipus Rex*, after 429 BC, and *Oedipus at Colonus*, 407/6 BC; in EURIPIDES' *Oedipus* (lost) and *Phoenician Women*, and in SENECA's *Oedipus* and *Phoenician Women*. AESCHYLUS' lost *Oedipus* formed part of the Theban TETRALOGY. Adaptations and works influenced by *Oedipus Rex*: SACHS, *Die unglückhaftige Königin Jokasta*, 1550; CORNEILLE, *Oedipe*, 1659; VOLTAIRE, *Oedipe*, 1718; DRYDEN and LEE, *Oedipus*, 1679; HOFMANNSTHAL, *Ödipus und die Sphinx*, 1905; GIDE, *Oedipe*, 1931; COCTEAU, *La Machine infernale*, 1934. ELIOT's *The Elder Statesman*, 1958, is based on *Oedipus at Colonus*.

Oehlenschlaeger, Adam Gottlob (1779–1850), Danish poet and playwright. His work signalled the beginning of Danish romanticism. Also wrote a number of lyrical plays based on Scandinavian mythology with symbolic and allegorical elements which owed much to German HEROIC DRAMA (e.g. SCHILLER); *Sanct Hans Aften-Spil* (A Play of Midsummer Night), 1803; *Aladdin etter den forunderlige lampe* (Aladdin and the Wonderful Lamp), 1805; *Hakon Jarl*, 1807; *Baldur hin Gode* (Baldur the Good), 1807; *Axel og Valborg* (Axel and Valborg), 1810; *Correggio*, 1811; *Helge*, 1814.

Oenslager, Donald (1902–76), US stage designer. Pupil of BAKER, he started working in collaboration with O'NEILL and MACGOWAN for the PROVINCETOWN PLAYERS and at the Greenwich Village Theatre, New York, later with McCLINTIC, HAMMERSTEIN II, KAUFMAN and LAUGHTON. From 1925 he was considered one of the leading designers on BROADWAY. Extremely versatile, he worked in drama, opera, musicals and ballet.

Off-Broadway. A term used to denote that part of the New York theatre which does not fall under the concept of BROADWAY (i.e. the fully commercialized sector). The distinction has its artistic aspect, as the Off-Broadway theatre is more adventurous in producing plays of literary merit or social relevance, and more experimental with staging techniques, but also – and closely connected with it – an economic aspect: union rates for actors and technicians are not as high, the restrictions imposed by the unions on operating conditions not as stringent as on Broadway. In the late 1960s the Off-Broadway scene was further enriched by the rise of a publicly supported sector, notably PAPP's New York Public Theatre, in 1973 extended to include the two non-musical theatres in the LINCOLN CENTER. ▷OBIE.

Off-Off-Broadway. The sector of the New York theatre which is outside the ambit even of OFF-BROADWAY theatre. The concept spread in the early 1960s when avant-garde groups sprang up in cafés and cellars in Greenwich Village. Similar style productions are to be found in London's Soho. Here the performers are even less well paid (or not at all), than in the Off-Broadway theatre and both artistically and politically they tend to be more extreme. Off-Off-Broadway has produced many outstanding talents, notably from groups like the LA MAMA, Joseph Chaikin's OPEN THEATRE, Richard Schechner's PERFORMANCE GROUP, Charles Lullam's The Theater of the Ridiculous, the BREAD AND PUPPET THEATRE, the LIVING THEATRE, Richard Foreman's Ontological Hysteric Theatre and Robert Wilson's Byrd Hoffman School of Birds.

O'Horgan, Tom (1927–), US composer, musician, singer, actor and director. Came to prominence as a director at LA MAMA. The originality of his approach lies in his unconventional treatment of stage illusion (with the actors narrating the play, changing parts etc.) and his bold combination of visual and musical effects with the text. In directing ROCHELLE OWENS's *Futz*, 1967, and Foster's *Tom Paine*, 1968, he tried to realize his aim of recreating the Greek and Renaissance concept of the actor/musician/dancer. These ideas also dominated his approach in his internationally successful production of *Hair* and his controversial film version of *Futz*, which he directed and for which he wrote the score. Also wrote the score for the film *Alex in Wonderland*, and achieved considerable success with *Lenny*, 1971, a play by Julian Berry and music by O'H. based on the life and words of Lenny Bruce. Directed *Jesus Christ Superstar*, 1971.

Okhlopkov, Nikolai Pavlovich (1900–67), Soviet director. Began as an actor in Irkutsk, where in 1921 he produced the mass spectacle *The Struggle of the Toilers against Capital* on the market place with workers, students and soldiers. In his next production, MAYAKOVSKY's *Mystery-Bouffe*, he set parts of the action in the auditorium. He appeared 1924–30 under the direction of MEYERHOLD and also in films; 1934–38 he was artistic director of the Realistic Theatre in Moscow, where, with the stage designer Yakov Stoffer, he experimented with various stage forms (derived from the Greek and Elizabethan theatre, the stylized forms of Japanese and Chinese theatre and the theatre of the Middle Ages). He was aiming at a theatre based on emotion with full communication between actor and spectator, in which the audience is 'involved' in the true sense of the word: he built gangways leading into the auditorium with platforms spread throughout, employing mass action based on his experience with open-air productions and the use of music. Characteristic productions of this

Clifford Odets, *Waiting for Lefty*, GROUP THEATRE, 1935

Oedipus Rex, REINHARDT's production at COVENT GARDEN, 1912

Sean O'Casey, *Shadow of a Gunman*, THEATRE WORKSHOP, 1957

time included: *Othello*; *Mother* by GORKY; and *Razbeg* by V. Stavski. Also worked at the Intimate Theatre and Vakhtangov Theatre, and in 1943 became director of the Theatre of the Revolution, renamed the Mayakovsky Theatre 1954. In 1957 he revived his 1934 production of POGODIN's *Aristocrats* which had led to the closing of the Realistic Theatre: the play is set in a labour camp and O. directed it in the style of a grotesque carnival. Other noted productions include: *Hamlet*, 1954, in which the seats were on a two-storey steel scaffold; *Medea*, set in a concert-hall with seats built as an amphitheatre; and ARBUZOV's *It happened in Irkutsk*.
Bibl: A. Bejlin, 1953

Old Vic Theatre. Opened in London, 1818, as the Coburg Theatre, it was renamed the Victoria Theatre in 1833 and eventually became known as the Old Vic. Originally a theatre for sensational MELODRAMAS, variety and MUSIC HALL, it acquired a bad reputation as a brothel and was closed early in 1880. In the same year Emma Cons, a social reformer and the first woman member of the London County Council, bought it and reopened it as a temperance amusement place called the Royal Victoria Hall and Coffee Tavern. Her attempt to educate the audience included concerts, lectures and Shakespearean productions. Emma Cons's niece LILIAN BAYLIS (1874–1937) took over the management in 1912 and produced classical drama and opera only, the first season being devoted to SHAKESPEARE. In 1931 when the opera found a new home at the Sadler's Wells Theatre the Old Vic became the first permanent London home for productions of classic plays, mainly Shakespeare. After the death of Lilian Baylis in 1937, GUTHRIE became manager. In 1941 the theatre was badly damaged and subsequently closed: the New Theatre in the West End provided a temporary home where OLIVIER, RICHARDSON and John Burrell staged their famous seasons. In 1950 the Old Vic was restored and reopened, managed by SAINT-DENIS, DEVINE and GLEN BYAM SHAW and 1953–58 by Michael Benthall. In 1963 the Old Vic became the temporary home of the NATIONAL THEATRE company under the direction of Olivier.
Bibl: A. Dent (ed), A THEATRE FOR EVERYBODY; THE STORY OF THE OLD VIC AND SADLER'S WELLS, 1945

Oldfield, Anne (1683–1730), English actress. One of England's most famous performers, she was discovered by CIBBER in whose play *The Careless Husband* in 1794 she played Lady Betty Modish and achieved the first major success of a triumphant career. Among the parts for which she achieved the highest praise by the writers of her time (e.g. Cibber, FIELDING and VOLTAIRE) were: Sylvia in FARQUHAR's *The Recruiting Officer*, 1706, and Mrs Sullen in his *The Beaux' Strategem*, 1707; Marcia in ADDISON's *Cato*, 1713; Cleopatra in Cibber's *Caesar in Egypt*, 1724 (all these were the original productions); Lady Brute in VANBRUGH's *The Provok'd Wife*, 1730.
Bibl: E. Robins, TWELVE GREAT ACTRESSES, 1900

Olesha, Yuri Karlovich (1899–1960), Russian novelist and playwright. A supporter of the October Revolution, he openly criticized Stalinist repression in the arts in 1934 and fell into disgrace with the regime, but survived the purges. His plays reflect the ideological conflicts of the revolution: *Tri tolstyaka* (Three Fat Men), 1928; *Zagovor Chuvstv* (The Conspiracy of Feelings), 1929; *Spisok Blagodeyanii* (*A List of Assets*), 1931; *Chorny Chelovyek* (The Black Man), 1932.

Olivette. A stock character of the COMÉDIE-ITALIENNE, partner of PIERROT.

Olivier, Laurence Kerr, Lord (1907–), English actor and director; knighted 1947, created a life peer 1970. Married to the actress JOAN PLOWRIGHT since 1961. He made his début in 1922 as Katharina in a school production of SHAKESPEARE's *The Taming of the Shrew*; 1926–28 worked at the BIRMINGHAM REPERTORY THEATRE and in 1935 appeared at the New Theatre, London, where with GIELGUD he alternated the parts of Romeo and Mercutio; PEGGY ASHCROFT played Juliet. In 1937 he joined the OLD VIC company where he made his reputation, being particularly outstanding in the title role in a production of *Hamlet* in its entirety. In 1944 he became co-director with R. Richardson; in 1963 he was appointed director of Britain's first NATIONAL THEATRE (at the Old Vic). The opening production was *Hamlet* with O'TOOLE. In 1961 he became director of the CHICHESTER FESTIVAL THEATRE, directing all plays of the first season in 1962 (*Uncle Vanya, The Broken Heart* and *The Chances*), continuing working there until 1965 when he was succeeded by CLEMENTS. He ranks with BURBAGE, GARRICK and IRVING as one of the finest English actors of all time. His qualities include versatility, intelligence, disciplined acting with a range extending from lyricism to deep passion and supreme comic character acting. Some of his most famous performances include the title roles in Shakespeare's *Henry IV*, 1937; *Coriolanus*, 1938; *Richard III*, 1944; *Richard II*; *Macbeth*; *King Lear*; alternating the roles of Caesar and Antony in SHAW's *Caesar and Cleopatra* and Shakespeare's *Antony and Cleopatra*, 1951, with VIVIEN LEIGH (his second wife) as Cleopatra. Other notable parts: *Oedipus Rex* (trans by YEATS) followed, on the same evening, by Mr Puff in SHERIDAN's *The Critic*, 1945; the Duke in FRY's *Venus Observed*, a part written specially for him, 1950, and *Othello*, which production was filmed. He has been equally successful in modern drama such as OSBORNE's *The Entertainer*, 1957; Berenger in IONESCO's *Rhinoceros*, 1960; O'NEILL's *Long Day's Journey into Night*, 1972; E. DE FILIPPO's *Saturday, Sunday, Monday*, National Theatre, 1973. He has acted in a number of films, including Hitchcock's *Rebecca* and in his own film versions of *Henry V*, *Hamlet* and *Richard III*.
Bibl: F. Barker, THE OLIVIERS, 1953

Olympia. City in Elis, principal site of the cult of Zeus in ancient Greece. The Olympic Games were held there in his honour.

O'Neill, Eugene (1888–1953), US dramatist. The first major playwright born in the USA. He was strongly influenced by IBSEN and STRINDBERG and, in some plays, by German EXPRESSIONISM. He was the son of the actor **James O'Neill** (1848–1920), best known for his magnificent acting in the title role of G. H. Andrew's adaptation of DUMAS *père*'s *The Count of Monte Cristo*, in which he appeared from 1883 for about eight years in some 6,000 performances and again repeatedly in later years: 1912 also in film. E.O'N. decided to become a writer after an unsettled childhood and serious illness, 1912–13. He went to study at Harvard under BAKER at the 47 Workshop, 1914–15, and then worked with the PROVINCETOWN PLAYERS, who produced his early one-act plays first in Provincetown, Mass., and later in New York, at their Greenwich Village Theatre. Some of O'N.'s one-act plays were published in the magazine *Smart Set*, the editor of which, NATHAN, was instrumental in getting *Beyond the Horizon* produced on BROADWAY, 1920. It was an outstanding success and O'N. was then established as America's leading dramatist. He received the PULITZER PRIZE for this play, an award he received on three other occasions. Productions of *Desire Under the Elms*, 1925, *Marco Millions*, 1927, and *Strange Interlude*, 1928, took Broadway by storm. However, after the productions of *Ah, Wilderness!*, 1933, and *Days without End*, 1934, he retired from the theatre and for the next twelve years refused to allow any of his new plays to be produced. In 1936 he was awarded the Nobel Prize for Literature, the first American dramatist to be so honoured. Sometime after this he began to write a number of his most important works: *The Iceman Cometh*, 1939, fp New York 1946; *Long Day's Journey Into Night*, written 1940–41, fp Stockholm 1956, New York 1956; *A Moon for the Misbegotten*, written 1943, fp Stockholm 1954, revived New York 1974; *A Touch of the Poet*, written 1940, fp Stockholm 1957; and *Hughie*, fp Stockholm 1956. Shortly before his death he destroyed the manuscripts of several unfinished works. Other plays are *Bound East for Cardiff*, 1916, *The Long Voyage Home*, 1917 and *Ile*, 1917, produced Provincetown; *The Moon of the Caribbees*, New York 1919; *The Emperor Jones*, New York 1920; *Anna Christie*, 1921, awarded the Purlitzer Prize (film with Greta Garbo, 1930), musical *New Girl in Town*, 1957; *The Hairy Ape*, New York 1922; *All God's Chillun Got Wings*, New York 1924; *The Great God Brown*, New York 1926; *Mourning Becomes Electra*, New York 1931; *More Stately Mansions*, written 1938, fp Stockholm 1962. The Coronet Theatre in New York has been renamed the Eugene O'Neill Theatre.

Bibl: H. M. Bream, 1965; J. Gassner (ed), O'NEILL: A COLLECTION OF CRITICAL ESSAYS, 1964; A. & B. Gelb, O'NEILL, 1962

Open Theatre. US OFF-OFF-BROADWAY theatre company, founded in 1963 by Peter Feldmann and Joseph Chaikin, both former members of the LIVING THEATRE. Their work was based on concentration and improvisation exercises aiming to explore new styles of acting and production. Chaikin's actors evoke sympathy which lures the audience deeper into the game of discovery, because the audience relationship is to him 'caused neither by the actor nor the audience but the silence between them'. His best and most characteristic work was *The Serpent*, 1968, produced in collaboration with the playwright ITALLIE, a brilliant exploration of the Book of Genesis with a special kind of theatrical magic. Sounds and gestures were used as a language in themselves within the specific improvisational situation. The Open Theatre was political in the most basic sense – it dealt with individuals and their relationship to life. Another writer-collaborator was MEGAN TERRY (*Viet Rock*).

Ophüls, Max (1902–57), German theatre and film director. Worked with many leading German companies, directing plays by JONSON (*Volpone*), BÜCHNER, SHAKESPEARE, KLEIST, SHAW and PAGNOL. He was in the USA 1941–49, and in 1950 went to France to continue directing films, in which field he had started in Berlin in the 1930s (*Liebelei*, 1933): *La Ronde*, 1950, and *Lola Montez*, 1955. His last and probably most famous production in the theatre was BEAUMARCHAIS's *The Marriage of Figaro*, Hamburg 1957. His work was atmospheric, full of subtle nuances, inspired on the one hand by the COMMEDIA DELL'ARTE and on the other by the music of Mozart. Wrote a volume of reminiscences *Spiel im Dasein*, pub posthumously, 1959.

Orchestra (Gk = dancing place). Area in the Greek theatre where the CHORUS performed; a circular space between the spectators and the raised stage.

Oresteia. TETRALOGY by AESCHYLUS (fp 458 BC) of which the TRILOGY *Agamemnon*, *Choephori* and *Eumenides* has survived; the SATYR PLAY *Proteus* is lost. Some adaptations of and works inspired by the *Oresteia*: SOPHOCLES' *Electra*; EURIPIDES' *Electra*; SENECA's *Agamemnon*; VOLTAIRE's *Oreste*, 1750; ALFIERI's *Oreste*, 1786; O'NEILL's *Mourning Becomes Electra*, 1931; SARTRE's *Les Mouches*, 1943; G. HAUPTMANN's *Die Atriden-Tetralogie*, 1940–44.

Orpheus. Greek mythological character (or perhaps a real personage, the Thracian founder of Orphism), son of a Thracian river god Oeagrus (or Apollo) and the Muse Calliope. According to legend his skill with the lyre and as a singer was such that he attracted wild beasts, trees, even stone. When his wife Eurydice, pursued by

Laurence Olivier as Othello, NATIONAL THEATRE, 1964

Eugene O'Neill's *The Iceman Cometh*, New York 1946

Aristaeus, was fatally bitten by a snake, Orpheus descended into Hades and so charmed the infernal powers with his music that he was permitted to bring her back to the Upper World provided that he did not turn round to look at her on the way. Breaking this condition, he lost her forever. The Orpheus theme has been dramatized several times: LOPE DE VEGA, 1630; CALDERÓN, 1663; KOKOSCHKA, 1919; COCTEAU, 1926; ANOUILH, 1941; T. WILLIAMS, 1957; used for opera by Gluck 1762, and Haydn (rediscovered in 1950), Offenbach, 1858.

Orton, Joe (1933–67), English playwright. His first play was written for radio: *The Ruffian on the Stair*, 1964. It was followed by his first great stage success *Entertaining Mr Sloane*, a black comedy in which a young man is the object of desire and jealousy on the part of a middle-aged lady and her brother. *Loot*, 1966, and *What the Butler Saw* (produced posthumously, 1968) were also highly successful. His comic effects spring from his combination of sordid and outrageous situations with a stylized high-comedy DIALOGUE derived from WILDE and COWARD. He was murdered by the man with whom he lived.

Osborn, Paul (1901–), US dramatist. Studied at Yale under BAKER and made his name as a playwright mainly with two works, *On Borrowed Time*, 1938, based on L. E. Watkin's novel, and *The World of Suzie Wong*, 1958, based on the novel by Richard Mason. Other dramatizations of novels include *A Bell for Adano*, 1944 (John Hersey) and *Point of No Return*, 1951 (J. P. Marquand). He has also written a number of original plays, among which were *Hotbed*, 1928; *A Ledge*, 1929; *The Vinegar Tree*, 1930; *Oliver Oliver*, 1934, and *Morning's at Seven*, 1939.

Osborne, John James (1929–), English dramatist. Wrote for trade journals at the age of 17. Joined a touring theatrical company and began acting in 1948. With Antony Creighton, a fellow actor, he wrote *Personal Enemy*, 1955, and *Epitaph for George Dillon*, 1958, not produced until after he had finished his play, *Look Back in Anger*, 1956, ROYAL COURT THEATRE, dir T. RICHARDSON, which established him as the original 'angry young man' of post-war English drama. Other plays: *The Entertainer*, 1957, Royal Court, dir Richardson, with OLIVIER; the musical *The World of Paul Slickey*, 1959; *A Subject of Scandal and Concern*, TV play, 1960, dir Richardson, with BURTON; *Luther*, Nottingham 1961, Theatre Royal, with FINNEY, dir Richardson; *Plays for England* (one-acters, *The Blood of the Bambergs*, dir DEXTER, and *Under Plain Cover*, dir J. MILLER), 1962; *Inadmissible Evidence*, 1964, dir A. Page; *A Patriot for Me*, 1965, all Royal Court; *A Bond Honoured*, 1966, NATIONAL THEATRE, dir Dexter, with Robert Stephens, an adaptation of LOPE DE VEGA's play *La Fianza satisfecha*; *Time Present*, 1968; *The Hotel in Amsterdam*, 1968; *West of Suez*, 1971; *A Sense of Detachment*, 1972. In association with Richardson, Osborne founded Woodfall Films, for which he wrote the screenplay of *Tom Jones*, 1964, and other films.
Bibl: R. Hayman, 1968; J. R. Taylor, ANGER AND AFTER, 2/1963

Ostrovsky, Alexander Nikolayevich (1823–86), Russian playwright. Author of about 80 plays. In 1843 worked as a clerk at the Arbitration Court and later at the Commercial Tribunal, where he got to know the merchant class which he pitilessly portrayed in his COMEDIES, giving a realistic, irreverent presentation of this group of society and their amoral behaviour. His strength lies in the characteristic episodes, the emotional atmosphere and the richness of the minor roles. His first comedy *Bankrot* (The Bankrupt), written 1849, was banned, but eventually performed in 1861 in a toned-down version entitled *Svoi Lyudi – sochtiomsya* (*It's a Family Affair – We'll Settle It Ourselves*); the original version was not seen until 1881. Among his other early plays were: *Ne v svoi sani ne sadis* (Don't Ride a Sledge That Isn't Yours), 1853; *Byednost' ne porok* (*Poverty Is No Crime*), 1854; *Ne tak zhivi kak khochetsya* (Don't Live as You Like It), 1855; *Staryi drug luchshe novykh dvukh* (One Old Friend Is Better Than Two New Ones), 1854; and *Groza* (*The Thunderstorm*), 1860, which attacks traditional attitudes and values and is considered his best play. In his comedies he attacks social conventions and hypocrisies: *Na vsyakogo mudretsa dovolno prostoty* (*Even A Wise Man Stumbles*), 1868; *Bechenye dengi* (Easy Money), 1870; *Les* (*The Forest*), 1871; *Volki i ovtsy* (*Wolves and Sheep*), 1875. A year before his death he took up the post of director of the Moscow Imperial Theatre and the drama school.
Bibl: A. Dubinskaya, 1951

O'Toole, Peter (1932–), Irish-born actor. Began his career in 1955 at the Bristol Old Vic, where he became the leading actor, attracting the attention of London critics. He made his first London appearances in 1957 and 1959, and joined the ROYAL SHAKESPEARE COMPANY in Stratford-upon-Avon in 1960, where he excelled as Shylock. Other notable parts include: Petruchio in *The Taming of the Shrew*; the title role in BRECHT's *Baal*, 1963; and Hamlet in the opening production of the NATIONAL THEATRE in 1963. In 1973 he returned to the Bristol Old Vic and appeared with great success in CHEKHOV's *Uncle Vanya*. Has also appeared in a number of films.

Otto, Theo (1904–68), German stage designer. Studied at the Academy of Art in Kassel and, at the State Theatre there, designed FEUCHTWANGER's *Vasantasena*, 1924–25. Then worked in BERLIN, first as assistant director at the State Opera, and 1928–33 as designer at the State Theatre. In 1933 he emigrated to Switzerland, working at the ZURICH SCHAUSPIELHAUS, and after World War II with the BERLINER ENSEMBLE, at the Vienna BURGTHEATER, and in Milan, London and New York. He also designed GRÜNDGENS' famous *Faust* productions in Hamburg, 1957–58. First productions of BRECHT's plays in Zurich during World War II: *Mutter Courage, Der gute Mensch von Setzuan*; after the war premières of plays by FRISCH and DÜRRENMATT. He designed the sets for opera productions by RENNERT and SELLNER; with GASSMAN he worked in Syracuse on AESCHYLUS' *Oresteia*, 1959. Among his outstanding qualities are his visual sense, dramatic technique, ability to create magical effects and efficiency in carrying out his objectives. His sets were either aesthetic and abstract or baroque and extravagant, depending on the play. His works on dramatic theory include: *Nie wieder*, a diary in pictures, introduction by Brecht, 1949; and *Meine Szene*, introduction by Dürrenmatt, 1965.
Bibl: G. Schoop, DAS ZÜRICHER SCHAUSPIELHAUS IM 2. WELTKRIEG, 1957

Otway, Thomas (1652–85), English dramatist. With DRYDEN the most prominent tragic writer of his time. After an unsuccessful attempt at acting, he turned to writing and achieved his first success with *Alcibiades*, 1675, in which ELIZABETH BARRY, for whom he cherished a hopeless passion to the end of his life, made her name as an actress. *Alcibiades* is a rhymed HEROIC DRAMA, as is its successor, *Don Carlos; Prince of Spain*, 1676, one of the best examples of the genre. In his later TRAGEDIES, Otway abandoned the heroic form and brought his own interpretation, and psychological understanding, to the style and spirit of SHAKESPEARE and his contemporaries. *The Orphan; or, the Unhappy Marriage*, 1680, is a fine study in pathos. *Venice Preserved; or a Plot Discovered*, 1682, a genuinely tragic treatment of a human dilemma in a political setting, is his masterpiece and the greatest tragedy of the late 17th-century English theatre. It has probably been more often revived and translated than any other English classic apart from Shakespeare. He also wrote three strongly satirical comedies, *Friendship in Fashion*, 1678, *The Soldier's Fortune*, 1680, and its sequel, *The Atheist*, 1683. The best interpreters of parts in his plays were Elizabeth Barry and BETTERTON.
Bibl: A. M. Taylor, NEXT TO SHAKESPEARE: OTWAY'S 'VENICE PRESERVED' AND 'THE ORPHANS', 1950

OUDS ▷ OXFORD UNIVERSITY DRAMATIC SOCIETY.

Owen, Alun (1926–), Welsh-born author and dramatist. Began his career as assistant stage manager in repertory 1942; appeared at the BIRMINGHAM REPERTORY THEATRE, the OLD VIC and with the ENGLISH STAGE COMPANY. His most characteristic style is the new NATURALISM used in a romantic nostalgic way to evoke the local colour of Liverpool, where he spent his youth. He seizes on the idiomatic language of the city and the dramatic conflict implicit in the clash of race and religion between the local people, the Welsh, and Irish from both north and south of the Border in *Progress to the Park*, 1959. *The Rough and* *the Ready Lot*, 1959, is a carefully constructed historical play dealing with mercenary officers in a revolutionary army in South America just after the American Civil War. Other plays include: *Two Sons*, 1957; *A Little Winter Love*, 1963; *Maggie May*, 1964; *The Game*, 1965. Most of his writing has been for TV: *No Trams to Lime Street*, 1959; *After the Funeral, The Ruffians*, both 1960; *The Ways of Love, The Rose Affair*, 1961; *You Can't Win 'Em All, Dare to be a Daniel, The Hard Knock*, all 1962; *The Stag, The Strain, A Local Boy, Lena O My Lena*, all 1963. He also scripted several films including *The Criminal*, 1960; *A Hard Day's Night*, 1964, for the Beatles.

Owens, Rochelle (1936–), US dramatist. Studied at the New School for Social Research in New York and at the Uta Hagen-Herbert Berghof Studio. She worked at numerous jobs, wrote poetry, which from 1959 began to appear in several magazines; she has since had three books of poems published, and contributed to many literary journals and anthologies. International theatrical prominence came with her first play *Futz*, written 1962, presented at LA MAMA, 1967, dir O'HORGAN, subsequently touring England and Europe; 1968 returned OFF-BROADWAY, Theatre De Lys, where it ran for 233 performances and won an OBIE AWARD. It was also filmed in 1969 by O'Horgan. Since then she has written a number of full-length and short plays including: *The Queen of Greece*; *Istanboul*; *He Wants Shih!*; *Belch, Homo*; *Kontraption*; and *The Karl Marx Play*; her first play to be produced was *The Strip Game* at the Judson Poets' Theatre; subsequently her plays have been produced OFF-OFF-BROADWAY, in regional and college theatre, on TV and abroad. She is a member of the Playwrights' Union, of the ACTORS' STUDIO, and the New Dramatists' Committee.

Oxford University Dramatic Society. The principal amateur drama society among the undergraduates of Oxford; there are also numerous college drama societies as well as the Experimental Theatre Club (ETC), founded in 1885. The OUDS stages its productions in the University Theatre (the Oxford Playhouse), often under well-known professional directors. Its performances attract wide attention in the press and a successful appearance by a student actor or a notable production by a student director is frequently a stepping stone to a professional career in the theatre. Many of the best English actors and directors have come to the fore through the OUDS, arguably because the democratic structure of the society, which compels competition for election to the leading positions within it, brings out the qualities which are needed in the highly competitive professional theatre world.

Ozeray, Madeleine (1910–), French actress. Her name is associated with JOUVET with whom she worked as leading actress at the Théâtre de l'Athénée: Hélène in GIRAUDOUX's *La Guerre de Troie n'aura pas*

John Osborne, *Look Back in Anger*, ROYAL COURT THEATRE, 1956, with MARY URE, BATES and Kenneth Haigh

Paul Osborn's dramatization of *A Bell for Adano*, New York 1940, with MARCH

Thomas Otway, *Venice Preserved*, with GARRICK, painting by Zoffany, 1762–63

lieu, 1935; *Ondine*, 1939; with Jouvet she went on tour through the USA, appearing in the title role of CLAUDEL's *L'Annonce faite à Marie*, 1941. Other leading parts in: C. Péguy's *Jeanne d'Arc*, 1947; LORCA's *La zapatera prodigiosa*, 1948, etc.

Pageant. The term originally designated one scene in a MYSTERY PLAY; hence applied to the platforms or carts on which single tableaux were represented. Later applied to spectacular shows, in particular elaborately staged processions to the *trionfi* of the Italian Renaissance. In more recent times in England and the US an even more specialized meaning developed: a pageant, or 'historical pageant' is a series of historical scenes or tableaux presented in the course of local celebrations or festivals usually concerned with depicting the history of the place or institution (e.g. school) concerned. People associated with this form of entertainment included Louis Napoleon Parker (1852–1944), English dramatist and pageant master, who depicted several patriotic pageants during World War I, and the American P. MacKAYE (1875–1956), a son of S. MacKAYE, and P. GREEN whose pageant drama *The Lost Colony* is immensely popular and produced annually.

Pagliaccio (Ital = buffoon). Comic character of Italian folk comedy. The costume was white and consisted of long, wide trousers, a wide loose frock with long sleeves covering the hands, large buttons, ruff and a pointed felt hat. ▷PIERROT.

Pagnol, Marcel (1895–1974), French dramatist and film-maker. He is best known for his play *Topaze*, 1928, and the TRILOGY *Marius*, 1929, *Fanny*, 1931 (both later made into films), and *César*, film version 1933, adapted and performed on stage in 1946. They are essentially sentimental popular folk plays set in Marseilles, where he was born, and the south of France. From 1933 to 1955 he worked almost entirely in films as writer, producer and director, notably *La Femme du boulanger*, 1938. Other plays, none very successful, include: *La Belle Meunière*, 1948; *Le Rosier de Madame Husson*, 1949; *Manon des sources*, 1953; *Judas*, 1955. He also translated and adapted SHAKESPEARE's *Hamlet* and *A Midsummer Night's Dream*.
Bibl: L. Combaluzier, LE JARDIN DE PAGNOL, 1937

Palitzsch, Peter (1918–), German director. First worked at the VOLKSBÜHNE, Dresden, till he joined the BERLINER ENSEMBLE in the 1950s and, with BESSON and WEKWERTH, became one of BRECHT's most important younger co-workers; he also collaborated on important publications about Brecht's productions, e.g. *Theaterarbeit*, 1952. A pupil of Brecht, he developed the analytical intelligence and clarity which are his characteristics as a director. In his productions he always attempts to combine analysis of the play's structure with practical staging as defined by Brecht. He left the Berliner Ensemble after the erection of the Berlin Wall in 1962. Since 1957 he has directed at several theatres in Germany, mainly plays by Brecht: *Leben Eduards des Zweiten* (after MARLOWE), Stuttgart 1957; *Mann ist Mann* and *Herr Puntila und sein Knecht Matti*, Wuppertal and Cologne 1966; *Der gute Mensch von Setzuan* and *Der Prozess der Jeanne d'Arc*, Ulm 1960 and 1961; *Der kaukasische Kreidekreis*, Bremen 1964; *Mutter Courage*, Cologne 1964. Also: SHAKESPEARE's *The Taming of the Shrew*, Ulm 1960; BÜCHNER's *Dantons Tod*, Stuttgart 1962; Shakespeare's *The Merchant of Venice*, Hanover 1963; WALSER's *Überlebensgross Herr Krott*, Stuttgart 1963; and *Der schwarze Schwan*, 1964; WEISS's *Die Ermittlung*, 1966; BARTON/HALL Shakespeare cycle *The Wars of the Roses*, 1967. P. was artistic director of the Stuttgart Municipal Theatre, 1966–72, when he was appointed artistic director of the Municipal Theatre at Frankfurt.

Palladio, Andrea (Andrea di Pietro Monaro; 1508–80), Italian architect. He resurrected many of the architectural principles and methods of antiquity and had a decisive influence on the revival of the classical style in European architecture. As regards theatre architecture, his most important work is the TEATRO OLIMPICO, Vicenza, built, after his plans, by his pupil Scamozzi between 1580 and 1584: it transfers the basic shape of an outdoor amphitheatre indoors with a semi-circular auditorium and a stage with a permanent street-scene set with three-dimensional houses receding in perspective. Perfectly preserved, the Teatro Olimpico is still in use today.

Pallenberg, Max (1877–1934), Austrian actor. Started as a comedian in operetta and was discovered as a potentially great serious actor by REINHARDT, who brought him to his Deutsches-Theater in BERLIN in 1914. A small man with a broad face, he was a creative actor who could make the most insignificant part stand out through the sheer inventiveness of his imagination, also often by improvising and extemporizing (P. was feared by actors appearing with him as he tended not to give them their cues). Among his finest creations was the Good Soldier Schweik in PISCATOR's production of an adaptation of HAŠEK's novel in Berlin, 1928. In the SALZBURG FESTIVAL 1933 he played Mephistopheles in Reinhardt's production of GOETHE's *Faust*. He died in an aircrash, aged 57. He was married to the great MUSICAL COMEDY actress Fritzi Massary.

Palliata (Lat *pallium* = Greek cloak – 'drama in Greek robes') or *fabula palliata*. Roman COMEDY adapted from Greek sources with Greek names, costumes and settings, which borrows themes from Greek life and literature, e.g. all extant comedy of this type including plays by PLAUTUS, CAECILIUS STATIUS, TERENCE, etc., in contrast to the *fabula togata* which was set in a Roman background. ▷FABULA.

Pandolfi, Vito (1917–), Italian critic and director. His first success was with *L'Opera dello straccione*, based on GAY's *The Beggar's Opera*, which he produced while still a student at the Accademia dell'arte drammatica in Rome, 1943; later he made his reputation as a fine director of contemporary plays, e.g. CAMUS's *Le Malentendu*, Bologna 1949, and with his revival of the COMMEDIA DELL'ARTE, e.g. *La Fiera delle maschere* – adaptation of c. dell'a. scenarios, which he wrote with SQUARZINA and L. Salce, performed at the BIENNALE 1947; and *Scenario*, Brussels 1951. He also contributed to numerous magazines. His books on the theatre include: *Antologia del grande attore*, 1955; *Teatro del dopoguerra italiano*, anthology, 1956; *Teatro tedesco espressionista*, anthology, 1956; and particularly *Il Teatro drammatico dalle origini ai nostri giorni*, 1959, and *Teatro italiano contemporaneo, 1945–59*, 1959.

Pantalone (derived from San Pantalene, patron saint of Venice). A COMMEDIA DELL'ARTE character; an avaricious Venetian merchant, suspicious, amorous, and always betrayed by his wife. He wore red trousers, a red doublet and a light black cloak with sleeves (*zimarra*). Physical characteristics are: a half mask with a long hooked nose and a thin pointed beard. Variations are Pandolfo and Bartolo. Later Pantalone was COLOMBINA's father, guardian or old husband in the Harlequinade.

Pantomime. In most European languages the term denotes what in England is usually referred to as MIME. This is due to the fact that in England the term has become attached to a specific form of folk entertainment which developed from the Harlequinade (▷HARLEQUIN) in the 19th century. English pantomime, usually performed during the Christmas season, with runs extending well into the New Year, is a highly formalized, indeed ritualized, genre which merges elements from drama, MUSIC HALL, the CIRCUS and today even pop-music. The basic story line comes from the traditional fairy-tale or other children's literature (Cinderella, Dick Whittington, Robinson Crusoe, Aladdin), but the thread of the plot is continually interrupted by variety turns (jugglers, acrobats), popular songs, children's ballet and extended comic routines. Traditionally the male hero is played by a long-legged actress (principal boy), while the chief comedian appears in 'drag' as a 'dame' (e.g. Widow Twankey). A Demon King and a Good Fairy also figure in most traditional pantomime. The origins of pantomime in COMMEDIA DELL'ARTE and BAROQUE THEATRE are also revealed in the tradition of spectacular scene-changes (transformation scene) and the large proportion of topical and often improvised material included. English pantomime is ideal family entertainment because it combines a children's story with a great deal of sexual innuendo which the parents can enjoy while it remains unnoticed by the children.

Papp, Joseph (1921–), US producer and director. Managing director of the Actors' Laboratory Theatre, Hollywood, 1948–50, he founded the New York Shakespeare Festival in 1954, at the Emmanuel Presbyterian Church, which then moved to open-air premises in Central Park. His determination to provide free theatre for the multitude attracted the attention of philanthropists which enabled the Delacorte Theatre to be built in Central Park in 1962. He has won many awards including the Shakespeare Club of New York City Award for Unusual Service in Bringing Shakespeare to the People, 1957. Another civic enterprise instigated by him was the New York Public Theatre. Housed in the former Astor Library which contains five auditoriums and is sponsored by the City of New York, it opened in 1967. The sensational hippy musical *Hair* had its inception there, and many of the most promising developments and experiments in US theatre have been under its aegis.

Parabasis. Principal song of the CHORUS in the Greek Old Comedy (ARISTOPHANES), which was addressed directly to the audience, and originally came at the end of the play; later also came in the middle. One part was the poet's self-defence, a response to his critics and an appeal to the judges, the other part was a ritual hymn to the gods.

Parable (from Gk=placing side by side, hence comparison). An allegorical or moral tale, designed to illustrate an abstract principle by a concrete instance. BRECHT wrote a number of dramatic parables, or parable plays, to illustrate, for example, the Marxist concept of alienation in *The Good Woman of Setzuan*, or the socialist attitude to property in *The Caucasian Chalk Circle*.

Parigi, Giulio (before 1580–1635/36), Italian architect. One of the first scenic designers to work in opera, whose work influenced FÜRTTENBACH and I. JONES. He was a pupil of BUONTALENTI whom he succeeded in 1608 as architect at the Court of the Medici, at which he was responsible for the décor for festivities. He was succeeded in 1628 by his son **Alfonso P.** (?–1656).
Bibl: H. Tintelnot, BAROCKTHEATER UND BAROCKE KUNST, 1939

Parodos (Gk='side passage'). (1) Formal component of Greek drama: the song of the CHORUS as they enter the orchestra. (2) *parodoi* (pl.): part of the Greek semicircular AMPHITHEATRE, the passageways on both sides of the *skene*.

Paryla, Karl (1905–), Austrian actor and director. Began his career in Vienna and then worked with several companies in Germany and in 1938 went to Zurich,

Pantomime, *Sleeping Beauty*

Parigi, engraving of scene from the LIBRETTO for *Il Solimano*, 1620

Joseph Papp's musical *Hair*, 1968

achieving fame in comic character parts, mainly in NESTROY farces. After World War II he joined HEINZ at the short-lived Theater in der Scala in Vienna and in 1956 went with him to BERLIN to work at the Deutsches-Theater, where he appeared in parts such as St Just in BÜCHNER's *Dantons Tod*, and Truffaldino in GOLDONI's *Il Servitore di due Padroni*; he also began directing plays, e.g. SCHILLER's *Wallenstein*, 1958. In more recent years his successful productions include: WEISS's *Marat/Sade*, Hamburg 1965; and *Gesang vom Lusitanischen Popanz*, Berlin 1967; ROJAS' *Celestina*, Cologne 1966; ARISTOPHANES' *Peace*, Dortmund 1968; and Schiller's *Don Carlos*, Wiesbaden 1968.

Passion play. Pageant productions of the Passion of Christ, developed from the medieval *Osterspiele* (Easter play) which were first performed in churches and later as open-air spectacles in the market place. The most important early example was the Old Frankfurt Passion Play founded in 1350, of which some scenic notes in Latin are preserved – it lasted two days – and from which developed the Frankfurt Play of 1493. The Alsfeld Passion Play dating from 1501 lasted three days and had parts for not less than 172 actors. The most famous Passion Play to survive (dating from 1634) is performed decennially in OBERAMMERGAU, Bavaria; the most recent performance was in 1970.
Bibl: W. Werner, STUDIEN ZU DEN PASSION UND OSTERSPIELEN DES DEUTSCHEN MITTELALTERS, 1963

Pastoral drama. A dramatic genre, based on pastoral poetry about the simple life of shepherds, which originated in ancient GREECE and continued into the 17th century. Pastoral poetry expressed the romantic involvement of city dwellers with the simple rustic life. The best examples were written in Italy, e.g. TASSO's *L'Aminta*, 1573, and GUARINI's *Pastor Fido*, fp Cremona 1595, and in Spain, the dramatic *églogas* of ENCINA, which served as sources for later English romances and drama, e.g. SHAKESPEARE. Native pastoral elements in England can also be found in LYLY's *Euphues*, MILTON's *Comus* and in PEELE's work. Pastoral romance and drama flourished in England in the 17th century (FLETCHER, *The Faithful Shepherdess*, 1608) and survived in the 18th century with GAY's work. Notable examples in France: Théophile de Viau's *Pyrame et Thisbe*, Hôtel de Bourgogne, 1621, and Racan, *Bergeries*, 1625. The first German opera *Daphne*, music Schütz, based on Rinuccini, 1627, was a pastoral.

Pataphysics ▷JARRY.

Patrick, John (J. Patrick Goggan; 1907–), US dramatist. Became internationally known with *The Teahouse of the August Moon*, 1953 (based on a novel by Vern Sneider), which won both the PULITZER PRIZE and the NYDCC AWARD. A delightful service COMEDY, it shows how the American colonel in charge of an occupied Okinawan village is won over to the Japanese way of life. Other works include *The Hasty Heart*, 1945; *The Story of Mary Surratt*, 1947 and *Lo! and Behold*, 1951.

Patrick Campbell, Mrs ▷CAMPBELL.

Paxinou, Katina (1900–74), Greek actress. The leading performer of her generation in Greece, she appeared after 1927 mainly under the direction of MINOTIS, whom she married in 1940, in Athens and New York (1930–31). In 1932 she joined the Athens National Theatre, playing major parts: Clytemnestra in AESCHYLUS' *Agamemnon*, 1932; the name part in O'NEILL's *Anna Christie*, 1932, which she also translated; Mrs Alving in IBSEN's *Ghosts*, 1934; the leading roles in SOPHOCLES' *Electra*, 1936, and WILDE's *Lady Windermere's Fan*, 1937; she toured Europe in 1939 and was seen in English versions of *Ghosts*, London 1940, and of *Hedda Gabler*, New York 1942. She acted in films in Hollywood (notably Hemingway's *For Whom the Bell Tolls*) and returned to Greece in 1950, where she appeared in classical and contemporary plays, e.g. as Jocasta in Sophocles' *Oedipus Rex*, 1952; and the title role in LORCA's *The House of Bernarda* Alba, 1954. She also appeared in a number of TV plays, e.g. Lorca's *Blood Wedding* as the mother, England 1959.

Peele, George (?1558–?1597), English dramatist. A friend and contemporary of Thomas Nashe, GREENE, and MARLOWE. He wrote verse, PAGEANTS and several plays, the best of which is *The Arraignment of Paris*, a romantic PASTORAL DRAMA first performed *c.* 1581–84 by the CHILDREN OF THE CHAPEL at the Court of Elizabeth I, pub 1584. *The Old Wives' Tale*, produced *c.* 1588–94, pub 1595, is considered an important landmark in the development of English COMEDY for P.'s use of parody. Other works include: *The Battle of Alcazar*, prod 1588–89, pub 1594; *Edward I*, prod 1590–93, pub 1595, and *The Love of King David and Fair Bethsabe*, prod *c.* 1581–94, pub 1599.
Bibl: I. Ribner, THE ENGLISH HISTORY PLAY IN THE AGE OF SHAKESPEARE, 1959

Peking Opera ▷CHINA.

Percy, Esmé (1887–1957), English actor. Studied with SARAH BERNHARDT in Paris, joined the BENSON company in 1904; appeared as Romeo with the Elizabethan Stage Society in 1905; 1909–11 with ANNIE HORNIMAN's company in Manchester. In 1924 became producer of the Macdona Players, a company dedicated to the work of SHAW. In his later years a character actor of impish charm and demonic power, and an excellent director.

Peretz, Yitschok Leybush (1852–1915), Polish-born Yiddish short-story writer, poet, playwright and essayist. He is regarded as the father of Yiddish literature. For about ten years a highly successful lawyer, he was forced to abandon this career in 1888 for political reasons. In 1889 he became book-keeper of Gmine, the Jewish community organization in Warsaw. From his early youth he was completely involved in Yiddish literature, and in all kinds of literary and educational activities: editing magazines, writing short stories. He soon played a leading role in Jewish literary life encouraging Yiddish cultural activities. In an attempt to raise the quality of Yiddish theatre, he wrote several dramas, mainly in verse, which were theatrical poems to justify his belief that theatre should 'only portray what man sees in his dreams': *Di Goldene Keyt* (The Golden Chain); *Klezmer* (Musicians), also known as *Vos in Fidele Shtekt* (That Which is in a Violin); *Banakht Oyfn Altn Mark* (In the Old Market Place at Night) – all published 1907; *In Polish oyf der Keyt* (Chained in the Synagogue Vestibule), pub 1908.
Bibl: M. Samuel, PRINCE OF THE GHETTO, 1948; A. A. Ruback, PERETZ, PSYCHOLOGIST OF LITERATURE, 1935

Performance Group. US avant-garde company based in New York. Conceived and founded by Richard Schechner, former editor of the *Drama Review*. Like the other US avant-garde theatres it rejects conventional contexts and interpretations of the theatre. It emphasizes the physical aspects of theatre and has introduced the environmental concept. The Group's most characteristic and famous production was *Dionysus 69*, an adaptation of EURIPIDES' *The Bacchae*. The actors are trained in a heightened acrobatic technique. They make the theatrical experience a physical adventure, attempting to expand the audience's understanding of liberty, drawing them into the action. The actors move from primitive rites to group therapy, each actor talking about his fears as honestly as he can. They employ myth and ritual in an attempt to go beyond appearances, and approach the rhythms of contemporary life.

Periaktos. Movable scenic device used on the Roman stage from about 79 BC, perhaps even earlier in the Hellenistic theatre. According to Vitruvius, they were triangular prisms, one on either side of the stage. Painted on all three sides with different scenes, each could be revolved on its axis. The turning of both signified the transition from one play to the next, and the moving of only the right *periaktos* a change of scene. ▷AMPHITHEATRE

Périer, François (F. Gabriel Pilu; 1919–), French actor. Made his début in 1938 in C. A. Puget's *Les Jours heureux*, followed by numerous roles in BOULEVARD THEATRE such as in ACHARD's *Colinette*, 1942, and Puget's *Le Saint-Bernard*, 1946; but was also successful in parts like Hugo in SARTRE's *Les Mains sales*, 1948; probably his best-known part was the title role in A. Roussin's *Bobosse*, 1950, a part written for him. In 1952 with FRESNAY he took over the management of the Théâtre de la Michodière, producing J.-P. Aumont's *Un Beau dimanche*, 1952; MacDougall/T.

Allan's *Gog and Magog*, 1959. In 1969 he gave a noted performance as Götz in Sartre's *Le Diable et le Bon Dieu* at the TNP. Has also appeared in numerous films.

Perioche (Gk = circumference). In the performances of the JESUIT DRAMA of the Baroque era, which were in Latin, an outline of the PLOT in the vernacular, which was provided to enable the audience to follow the play. First used at Munich in 1597.

Peripety (Gk *peripeteia* = sudden change). A reversal of fortune; sudden unexpected change for the better (COMEDY) or for the worse (TRAGEDY). It was described by ARISTOTLE in his *Poetics* as one of the three elements of PLOT, the other two being recognition and suffering.
Bibl: R. Petsch, WESEN UND FORMEN DES DRAMAS, 1945

Perspective (Lat *perspicere* = to see through). In graphic art the technique of representing three-dimensional space on one plane – depicting proportions and relationship between objects so that the viewer will receive an impression of distance. Discovered by the Italian painters of the Renaissance and first employed in the theatre by Giovanni da Udine (Ferrara 1508) and PERUZZI. It reached its zenith in the space fantasies of GALLI-BIBIENA.
Bibl: G. Schöne, DIE ENTWICKLUNG DER PERSPEKTIVBÜHNE, 1933

Peruzzi, Baldassare (1481–1536), Italian architect and theatre painter. One of the first scenic designers to employ PERSPECTIVE for theatrical scenery; in 1518 he was responsible for the scenery for BIBBIENA's comedy *Calandria* in Rome.
Bibl: H. Tintelnot, BAROCKTHEATER UND BAROCKE KUNST, 1939

Petit-maître. In 18th-century French theatre name of a particular character type: a servant or villain, who wore the COSTUME of a cavalier.

Petrolini, Ettore (1886–1936), Italian actor and variety performer. He appeared mainly in parodies and sketches, generally writing his own material: *Napoleone*, *Nerone*, *Romani a Roma*. In his later career he also gave fine performances in straight plays like MOLIÈRE's *Le Médecin malgré lui*, 1925.

Phallus (Gk *phallos* = male organ). Artificial over-sized cod-piece made of leather, which was a feature of the COSTUME worn by the actors of antiquity (CHORUS and buffoons) in MIME, COMEDY, PHLYAKES and SATYR PLAYS.

Phelps, Samuel (1804–78), English ACTOR-MANAGER. Originally a journalist, he started his theatrical career with amateur companies, then travelled in the provinces before being called by MACREADY to appear in heroic parts at COVENT GARDEN. In 1843 he went into management, taking over Sadler's Wells and turning it into the leading Shakespearean theatre of his day. By the time of his resignation in 1862 he had performed all except four of SHAKESPEARE's plays, mostly appearing himself in the lead, excelling as Lear and Othello. His *Antony and Cleopatra*, 1849, was the first revival since 1661.
Bibl: J. Coleman, MEMOIRS OF SAMUEL PHELPS, 1886

Philipe, Gérard (1922–59), French actor. Studied at the CONSERVATOIRE D'ART DRAMATIQUE in Paris. First success in 1945 in the title role in CAMUS's *Caligula*. In subsequent years he made his career in films, returning to the stage in 1951 to work with VILAR at the TNP, playing the lead in CORNEILLE's *Le Cid*; later excelled in plays such as KLEIST's *The Prince of Homburg*, 1951; HUGO's *Ruy Blas*, 1954; SHAKESPEARE's *Richard II*, 1955; MUSSET's *Lorenzaccio*, 1953, *Les Caprices de Marianne*, 1958, and *On ne badine pas avec l'amour*, 1959, dir René Clair.
Bibl: A. Philipe, SOUVENIRS, 1960

Phillips, Stephen (1864–1915), English actor and playwright. The son of a clergyman, he joined BENSON's company in 1885 and worked as an actor for seven years, after which he took up clerical employment to be able to devote himself to writing. His best-known play which achieved great success at the time and was regarded as the augury of a great career for its author as a major dramatic poet was *Paolo and Francesca*, pub 1900, fp 1902, a romantic VERSE DRAMA in a Shakespearean vein. Great acclaim also greeted *Herod*, 1900, his first play to be performed. In his later plays he did not live up to his early promise: *The Sin of David*, 1904; *Nero*, 1906; *Faust*, 1908; *Pietro of Siena*, 1910; *Armageddon*, 1915; *Harold*, pub 1927.

Phillpotts, Eden (1862–1960), English novelist and playwright. An exceptionally prolific writer whose work mainly deals with the landscape and rural life in the west of England. His most successful play is *The Farmer's Wife*, a delightful rural COMEDY, fp 1916, BIRMINGHAM REPERTORY THEATRE; in London at the ROYAL COURT THEATRE in 1924, where it ran for more than 1,300 performances. Other plays include: *Devonshire Cream*, 1924; *Jane's Legacy*, 1925; *Yellow Sands* (written in collaboration with his daughter **Adelaide P.**, 1926); *The Purple Bedroom*, 1926; *The Blue Comet*, 1927; *The Runaways*, 1928; *A Cup of Happiness*, 1932.

Phlyakes (named after Phlyax, a demon of the woods in the service of Dionysos). Form of Doric FARCE in the Greek cities of southern Italy (Paestum, Tarentum) in the 4th–3rd centuries BC: the actors of the genre wore COSTUMES with grotesquely padded stomach and buttocks, a PHALLUS and mask, in amusing sketches taken from everyday life. Little of this material has survived; in Tarentum it was the writer Rhinton (300 BC) who gave the genre its literary form, on which the later ATELLAN FARCE was modelled.

Samuel Phelps as Cardinal Wolsey in *Henry VIII*, painting by FORBES-ROBERTSON, at the GARRICK CLUB, London

Perspective, title page engraving from *Deutsche Schaubühne*, 1655

Gérard Philipe in *The Prince of Homburg*, by KLEIST, at the AVIGNON FESTIVAL, 1954

Picasso, Pablo (1881–1973), Spanish painter and sculptor, who lived in France. The enormous variety of his work also included stage designs, which were often modified versions of old stage forms or had the character of collage: *Parade* – ballet devised by COCTEAU with décor by P. and music by Satie, performed by Diaghilev's Ballets Russes, 1917; other works for the Ballets Russes included: *Le Tricorne*, music de Falla, 1919; *Pulcinella*, music Stravinsky, 1920; *Cuadro Flamenco*, 1921. Further works: *Antigone*, by Cocteau, music Honegger, Théâtre de l'Atelier, Paris 1922; *Mercure*, ballet, music Satie, Paris 1924; *Oedipus Rex*, by SOPHOCLES, Paris 1947; *Icare*, ballet, Paris 1962, Opéra. He also wrote two avant-garde plays: *Le Désir attrapé par la queue*, 1941, a playful *atelier* joke and a late example of DADA, which in 1944 was given a reading under the direction of CAMUS with Simone de Beauvoir, SARTRE, Michel Leiris and Raymond Queneau, and *Les Quatre petites filles*, 1952.
Bibl: G. Cooper, PICASSO ET LE THÉÂTRE, 1967

Piccolo Teatro (della Città) di Milano. The first permanent theatre to be established in ITALY after World War II, founded in 1947 by STREHLER and GRASSI. It opened with GORKY's *The Lower Depths* dir Strehler, who remained the leading director till 1968. His most famous productions were revivals of classics, e.g. SHAKESPEARE, GOLDONI, and first performances of BRECHT's plays in Italy.
Bibl: PICCOLO TEATRO 1947–58, 1958

Pickelherring. Name of the CLOWN in early English COMEDY; mainly associated with the actor Robert Reynolds (fl 1610–40) of Queen Anne's Men, who travelled to Germany in 1616 with the ENGLISH COMEDIANS and successfully appeared on the Continent up to *c.* 1640.

Pierrot (Fr=little Peter). Originally a character of the COMMEDIA DELL'ARTE: the simple, awkward, shy, melancholy servant, dressed in a white costume with a mask. Pierrot developed as the CLOWN counterpart of HARLEQUIN; originally derived from Pedrolino (first played by Giovanni Pellerini) of the c. dell'a. The earliest French version was created in 1682 in Paris by the Italian actor Giovanni Battista Giaratoni. Later the mime DEBURAU developed his own variation at the Funambules: the naïve, clumsy, childish figure, at once comic and pathetic, who became legendary. The new lease of life that Deburau gave to Pierrot survives in many clowns today.
Bibl: K. Dick, 1960

Pinero, Sir Arthur Wing (Pinheiro; 1855–1934), English dramatist, knighted in 1909. A leading figure in the years between 1885 and World War I, he started as an actor in Edinburgh, later appeared in London under IRVING. In 1877 his first play *£200 a Year* was produced at the Globe Theatre and in 1881 *The Money Spinner* at St James's Theatre. Subsequently he achieved great popularity with his FARCES at the ROYAL COURT THEATRE: *The Magistrate*, 1885; *The Schoolmistress*, 1886; *Dandy Dick*, 1886; *The Cabinet Minister*, 1890. *The Profligate*, 1889, was the first of his more serious plays, studies of the social climate of the day. The most famous of these were: *The Second Mrs Tanqueray*, 1893, with MRS PATRICK CAMPBELL; *The Notorious Mrs Ebbsmith*, 1895; *Trelawny of the 'Wells'*, 1898; *Iris*, 1901; *Letty*, 1903; *His House in Order*, 1906; *Mid-Channel*, 1909.
Bibl: H. H. Fyfe, SIR ARTHUR PINERO'S PLAYS AND PLAYERS, 1930

Pinget, Robert (1919–), Swiss-born French writer, lawyer, journalist and painter, who also taught languages in England. After settling in Paris in 1946, he started writing prose in 1951 and became one of the leading exponents of the *nouveau roman*. Several of his dramatic works were staged: *Lettre morte*, 1959, an old man's letter to his son, who has left him; *La Manivelle* (*The Old Tune*), a radio play, which was first produced by the BBC in an English translation by BECKETT – French première in Paris, 1962; other works include: *L' Hypothèse*, one-act play, pub 1961, fp 1965; *Ici ou ailleurs*, pub 1961.
Bibl: M. Esslin, THE THEATRE OF THE ABSURD, 2/1968

Pinter, Harold (da Pinta; 1930–), English playwright and director. Started as an actor in provincial REPERTORY under stage name of David Baron. Published poetry from the age of 19. First short play, *The Room*, written 1957 for Bristol University Drama Department, together with another short play *The Dumb Waiter* (fp in German, Frankfurt 1959) was produced at the Hampstead Theatre Club, London 1960, and transferred to the ROYAL COURT. His first full-length play, *The Birthday Party*, fp London 1958, was a commercial failure, but his breakthrough came with *The Caretaker*, with BATES fp Arts Theatre Club, London 1960, transferred to Duchess Theatre. First radio and TV successes: *A Slight Ache*, radio play, 1959; *A Night Out*, on radio, then TV, 1960. Other plays: *The Dwarfs*, for radio, fp 1960; *The Collection*, 1962, and *The Lover*, 1963, TV plays, both later successfully staged; *The Homecoming*, full-length stage play, 1965; *Tea Party*, TV play, 1965; *The Basement*, TV play, 1967; *Landscape* and *Silence*, TV plays, 1969; *Old Times*, stage play, Aldwych, 1971; *A Slight Ache* and *Landscape* were produced as a double bill at the Aldwych, 1973; *No Man's Land*, stage play, 1975, with GIELGUD and RICHARDSON. Pinter has written a number of screenplays, adaptations of novels by other writers: *The Servant*, 1963; *The Pumpkin Eater*, 1963; *The Quiller Memorandum*, 1966; *Accident*, 1966; *The Go-Between*, 1969. His successful stage productions in London include: *The Man in the Glass Booth*, by R. SHAW, 1967; *Exiles*, by JOYCE; *Butley*, by GRAY, 1971. Pinter's originality as a dramatist lies in his impeccable ear for spoken language; he reproduces all the repetitions, tautologies and logical nonsense of actual speech. By renouncing a too closely defined exposition of the characters – because he feels that no man can really know what motivates another and that any pretension to such knowledge would be impertinent – and often leaving the end of his plays as open as situations in real life, he produces a highly poetic combination of extreme NATURALISM with mystery and the ambiguity of a dream. He is a fine craftsman and makes superb use of rhythms and silences.
Bibl: M. Esslin, 2/1973; R. Hayman, 1968

Pirandello, Luigi (1867–1936), Italian playwright. He ranks in importance with GOLDONI in the Italian theatre and also had a major influence on the development of modern European drama. Though his work was influenced by the THEATRE OF THE GROTESQUE (▷CHIARELLI) his dramatic antecedents were the Greeks, SHAKESPEARE and IBSEN. He confronts his audience with the problems of personality and identity, man's inability to communicate – his processes of self-discovery, self-construction and self-destruction and the shifting boundary between illusion and reality, truth and make-believe, on the stage as well as in daily life. In 1925 he founded his own theatre group, which he managed until 1928 as a REPERTORY and touring company. Awarded the Nobel Prize for Literature 1934. Main works: *Lumiè di Sicilia* (Sicilian Limes), 1910; *Pensaci, Giacomino!* (*Just think, Giacomino!*), *Professor Toti*, 1916; *Liolà*, 1916; *Così è (se vi pare)* (*Right You Are – If You think You Are*), 1917; *Il giuoco delle parti* (*The Rules of the Game*), 1918; *Tutto per bene* (*All for the Best*), 1920; *Sei personaggi in cerca d'autore* (*Six Characters in Search of an Author*), 1921; *Enrico IV*, 1922; *Vestire gli ignudi* (*To Clothe the Naked*), 1922; *La vita che ti diedi* (*The Life I Gave You*), 1923; *Ciascuno a suo modo* (*Each in his Own Way*), 1924; *Diana e la Tuda* (*Diana and Tuda*), 1926; *L'amica delle mogli* (*The Wives' Friend*), 1927; *La Nuova Colonia* (*The New Colony*), 1929; *O di uno o di nessuno* (*Of One or of No one*), 1929; *Questa sera si recita a soggetto* (*Tonight We Improvise*), 1930; *Come tu mi vuoi* (*As You Desire Me*), 1930; *Quando si è qualcuno* (*When One is Somebody*), 1933; *Non si sa come* (*One does not Know How*), 1934; *I giganti della Montagna* (*The Giants of the Mountains*), unfinished, 1937. His plays are often revived, especially *Six Characters. Henry IV* was performed at Her Majesty's Theatre, London, 1974, with HARRISON in the leading part.
Bibl: L. Ferrante, 1958

Pirchan, Emil (1884–1957), German stage designer. Established his reputation in the 1920s with designs for JESSNER's Expressionist productions at the Berlin National Theatre, including: WEDEKIND's *Der Marquis von Keith*, 1920; SHAKESPEARE's *Richard III*, 1920, and *Othello*, 1921; SCHILLER's *Wilhelm Tell*, 1923. Also responsible for many productions in foreign countries. He worked with the BURGTHEATER in Vienna 1936–48. Professor at the Academy of Art in Vienna until his death, and at the State Academy in Berlin. He also wrote several books on actors and dancers: *Fanny Elssler*,

1940; *Harald Kreutzberg*, 1941; *Marie Geistinger*, 1947; and on scenic design: *Bühnenmalerei*, 1946; *2000 Jahre Bühnenbild*, 1949; *Kostümkunde*, 1952.

Piscator, Erwin (1893–1966), German director and manager. A follower of REINHARDT, he was the son of a Protestant clergyman. In 1914 he started his career as an actor at the COURT THEATRE in Munich; during war service he became a pacifist and socialist. After a year as director of the Tribunal Theatre in Königsberg, he went to Berlin in 1920, as director first of the Proletarian Theatre, then of the Central Theatre, and 1924–29 as artistic director of the VOLKSBÜHNE, where his productions included Paquet's *Fahnen*, 1924, with slide projections; and *Sturmflut*, 1926, with documentary film inserts; GORKY's *The Lower Depths*, 1926, set against the background of revolution, inflation and unemployment; SCHILLER's *Die Räuber*, Prussian State Theatre, 1926, with an emphasis on a political documentary interpretation, with the character of Spiegelberg in a Lenin-mask representing the true revolutionary; WELK's *Gewitter über Gottland*, 1927 – medieval pirates as revolutionaries – film projections of the Russian October Revolution ending with a still of Lenin. Politically he was too close to the Communists for the Social Democrat Volksbühne, so he left and formed the Piscator-Bühne in the Theater am Nollendorfplatz, where he produced: TOLLER's *Hoppla, wir leben!*, 1927, with a multiple set, film inserts and slides; A. N. TOLSTOY's *Rasputin*, with a stage built like a globe to symbolize the earth; an adaptation (by a group of writers which included BRECHT) of Hašek's novel *The Good Soldier Schweik*, 1928, with GROSZ's drawings, presenting Schweik's march, as a back projection. 1928 saw the collapse of the Piscator-Bühne, following which P. directed plays at several other Berlin theatres including M. ANDERSON's anti-war play *What Price Glory?*, 1929, showing the march of ragged, dishevelled soldiers, again using a moving back-projection; and F. Wolf's *Tai Yang erwacht*, 1931, a parable-play. P.'s work in the theatre of the late 1920s was the most important attempt to create a political revolutionary theatre. Using Expressionist techniques, he was the first director to use documentary material (▷DOCUMENTARY THEATRE), to employ vast STAGE MACHINERY, film inserts, slides, animated cartoons to strengthen the argument of the play, to speed up the action and to heighten the emotional impact. His collaborators included the playwrights Brecht, Gasbarra, MEHRING, Toller, etc., the designer MÜLLER, who worked on stage construction and made symbolic machines. P.'s ultimate aim was to create a team of playwrights, designers, DRAMATURGS, and musicians, thereby dispensing with the need to work from completed scripts. Brecht described the differences between their work: for P. the content was in the foreground, while for Brecht form took precedence. P.'s excited, missionary-style theatre was

Pinero's *Trelawny of the 'Wells'*, with G. DU MAURIER, 3rd from left, IRENE VANBRUGH, 3rd from right, BOUCICAULT far right

Erwin Piscator's production of SCHILLER's *Die Räuber*, 1926, with EBERT 3rd from left

Harold Pinter, *Old Times*, with Colin Blakeley, DOROTHY TUTIN and Vivien Merchant, RSC 1970

utopian and demanded emotional audience involvement: 'I want a play without décor, without costumes, yes, even without clothes, naked, not in body, not in soul, to discover finally where the truth lies . . . to find laws, by which we can live and be happy.' He was in the USSR 1931–36, in Paris 1936–39, in New York 1939–51, where he became director of the Dramatic Workshop of the New School of Social Research. He directed numerous productions and had many pupils. From 1951 onwards he returned occasionally to Germany to direct plays including Schiller's *Die Räuber*, Mannheim 1957; his own adaptation of L. TOLSTOY's *War and Peace*, Berlin; STRINDBERG's *The Dance of Death* (I and II), Hamburg 1957; SARTRE's *Les Séquestrés d'Altona*, Essen 1958; KAISER's *Gas* (I and II), Bochum 1958; STERNHEIM's *1913*, Munich 1960; GENET's *Le Balcon*, Frankfurt 1962. In 1962 he took over the management of the FREIE VOLKSBÜHNE, Berlin, where he remained until his death: here he produced HAUPTMANN's *Die Atriden Tetralogie*, 1962; HOCHHUTH's *Der Stellvertreter*, fp 1963; KIPPHARDT's *In der Sache J. Robert Oppenheimer*, fp 1964; WEISS's *Die Ermittlung*, fp 1965. P's works on dramatic theory include: *Das politische Theater*, 1929, rev ed 1964; *Schriften zum Theater*, 2 vols, 1968.

Bibl: G. Rühle, THEATER FÜR DIE REPUBLIK, 1967; Marie Ley-Piscator, THE PISCATOR EXPERIMENT, 1967

Pit. The term pit, derived from the Elizabethan cockpit, originally designated the sunken area between stage and lower boxes, used for standing spectators. In the 19th century these boxes became a raised circle and the pit extended underneath. Later only the rows of cheap unreserved seats at the back of the auditorium were known as the pit, with more expensive stalls in front and an orchestral pit between these and the stage. Rarely used in theatrical terminology today.

Pitoëff, Georges (Georgy Pitoyev; 1884–1939), French actor and director of Russian origin. He directed his own amateur company in Petrograd before settling with his wife **Ludmilla P.** (1895–1951) in Paris after World War I where he exerted a great influence on the French theatre. In 1915–16 they appeared in Geneva in productions in Russian, then started a company which consisted of amateur and professional actors and attempted to build up a REPERTOIRE of world literature. After touring from 1919, they appeared in various Paris theatres including that of COPEAU; P. took his company to the Théâtre des Arts in 1924 and from there to the Mathurins. P. himself was a fine actor, but was also good at adapting, translating and producing. He supported dramatists including CLAUDEL, ANOUILH and COCTEAU, and introduced Paris to the works of CHEKHOV, as well as SHAKESPEARE, SHAW and PIRANDELLO in productions based on scenic simplicity. As an actor he was at his best playing sensitive characters like Pirandello's *Henry IV*, 1925, and Shakespeare's *Hamlet*, 1922–29, several times; his wife was best as Nora in IBSEN's *A Doll's House*, Marthe in Claudel's *L'Echange*, and particularly as Saint Joan (Shaw), 1925, and the same role in *Le Vray Procès de Jeanne d'Arc*, Arnaud/Pitoëff, 1929. He was ably assisted in his work by his wife, who continued to direct the company after his death, touring the USA and Canada. Many of his productions were later revived by his son **Sacha P.**, who is best known as a film actor.

Pizzi, Pier Luigi (1930–), Italian stage designer. His first designs, seen at the Piccolo Teatro in Genoa in 1951, were for ANOUILH's *Léocadia*, directed by G. C. Castello, with whom he collaborated in the following years. Characteristic of his style is the elegance and taste of productions like FEYDEAU's *La Puce à l'oreille*, 1951; SHAW's *Mrs Warren's Profession*, 1956. He has since collaborated mainly with the director DE LULLO, turning more to realism: Patroni Griffi's *Anima nera*, Comp. De Lullo-Falk-Guarnieri-Valli-Albani, 1960. Also responsible for many opera designs.

Planché, James Robinson (1796–1880), English writer, playwright, librettist, designer, musician and COSTUME historian. The descendant of a French Huguenot family who settled in England in the 17th century, he was one of the most versatile and fascinating men of the Victorian theatre. At the end of his life he could claim to have written or collaborated in the writing of some 175 works of the theatre, plays, BURLESQUES, EXTRAVAGANZAS, PANTOMIMES and LIBRETTI. He is the author of the libretto of Weber's *Oberon* and translated the libretti of Mozart's *The Magic Flute*, Rossini's *William Tell* and many other well-known operas into English. He wrote numerous comic burlesques and pantomimes, excelling above all in rhymed couplets with the most outrageous rhymes. His adaptation of a French MELODRAMA *The Vampyre; or The Bride of the Isles*, 1820, was the first vampire play in English MELODRAMA. For MADAME VESTRIS and MATHEWS at the Olympic Theatre, he wrote a long series of burlesque extravaganzas, perhaps best known among them *The Riquet with the Tuft*, 1836. There can be no doubt that these exercised a formative influence on later authors, notably W. S. GILBERT. He published a notable *History of British Costume*, 1834, and he designed, among others, KEMBLE's production of *King John*, 1824. An expert on heraldry, he was Rouge Croix Pursuivant of Arms at the College of Heralds. He wrote an amusing autobiography *Recollections and Reflections*, 1872.

Planchon, Roger (1931–), French director, actor and dramatist. Since 1951 he has run his own company, opening the Théâtre de la Comédie de Lyon in 1952, where he directed and appeared in leading parts in plays including: MARLOWE's *Dr Faustus*; JONSON's *Volpone*, 1950–51; ADAMOV's *Professor Taranne*, 1952–53; MOLNÁR's *Liliom*, 1953–54; BRECHT's *The Good Woman of Setzuan*, 1954–55; IONESCO's *La Leçon* and *Les Victimes du devoir*, 1956–57; ADAMOV's *Paolo Paoli*, 1956–57. In 1957 he moved with his company to the Théâtre de la Cité de Villeurbanne (in a suburb of Lyons), opening with SHAKESPEARE's *Henry IV* (Parts I and II) and playing Prince Hal. In 1959 he also gave a successful season in Paris at the invitation of BARRAULT; from that date the company created the first CENTRE DRAMATIQUE in the provinces. Influenced by Brecht, VILAR, and also by Elizabethan drama, P. attempted to evolve a theatre for factory workers. He became internationally known with his adaptation of DUMAS's *The Three Musketeers*, 1957–58, shown at the EDINBURGH FESTIVAL and the Piccadilly Theatre, London 1960, playing D'Artagnan; Brecht's *The Good Woman of Setzuan*, 1958–59, and *Schweik in the Second World War*, 1961–62; and his productions of classics, with emphasis on historical and social aspects, including MOLIÈRE's *George Dandin*, 1957–58; Marlowe's *Edward II*, 1960–61, which he also adapted; Molière's *Tartuffe*, 1962–63; Shakespeare's *Troilus and Cressida*, 1963–64. Other productions included his own plays: *La Remise*, 1961–62; *Patte blanche*, 1964–65; *Bleu, blanc, rouge, ou les Libertins*, Avignon Festival 1967; *L'Infame*, 1971. Also produced first play by GATTI, *La Vie imaginaire de l'éboueur Auguste Geai*, 1962, dir J. Rosner, sets by ALLIO, who designed most of P.'s productions. In 1972 he was appointed co-director of the TNP.

Bibl: E. Copfermann, LE THÉÂTRE POPULAIRE POURQUOI?, 1965; M. Corvin, LE THÉÂTRE NOUVEAU EN FRANCE, 1963

Plater, Alan (1935–), English dramatist. Trained as an architect in Newcastle, but turned to full-time writing when his radio play *Smoke Zone* was broadcast in 1961. He worked for the BBC's TV series *Z-Cars* and also for *Softly, Softly*. All his subsequent plays were adapted from TV to the stage or vice versa: *A Smashing Day*, on TV 1962, became a full-length stage play in 1966. *So Long, Charlie*, 1963; *See the Pretty Lights*, 1963, staged in 1970; *Ted's Cathedral*, 1964, later produced in Stoke-on-Trent; *The Incident*, 1965; *To See How Far It Is*. Another stage play was a reworking of the TV play *The Nutter* as *Charlie Came to Town*, 1966, which led to his most successful show, the musical documentary about coal-mining *Close the Coalhouse Door*, 1968; it was followed by *Don't Build a Bridge, Drain the River*, 1970, and *Simon Says . . .*, 1970, the last three in collaboration with the composer Alex Glasgow.

Plautus, Titus Maccius (*c.* 251–184 BC), Roman comic playwright. He was born into a poor family (probably slaves) in Sarsina, Umbria, and at an early age went to Rome, where he worked in the theatre in a minor position. It has also been said that while writing his first COMEDIES he worked as a merchant or a labourer in a flour mill (which is doubted by modern scholars), and later became famous and wealthy by writing. Some scholars think that he received the name Maccius from having played the role of Maccus (▷ATELLAN FARCE). About 130 plays are ascribed to him, of which 21 have survived. These extant comedies are all free adaptations and versions (condensations of two or more plays into one) of plays of the New Comedy (▷COMEDY (GREEK)). He used Greek PLOTS, settings and main characters, but adapted them to local Roman conditions. His language is rich in alliteration, jokes (obscene and effective), puns, topical allusions, plays on words, humorous invective, exaggerations, etc. The plots are usually simple and theatrical, the effectiveness of each twist in the action being more important than the composition as a whole; they usually deal with love affairs confused through trickery and misunderstanding. The stock characters are: fathers, sons, wives, innocent young girls, scheming slaves, braggart warriors, lovers, parasites, old men in love, courtesans, etc.; P. specialized in improbable situations, brawls, disputes, humorous MONOLOGUES by slaves, interspersed with songs, which almost give the plays the character of MUSICAL COMEDY. Only four dates of performances are recorded: *Miles Gloriosus* (The Braggart Soldier), *c.*211 BC, based on the Greek comedy *Alazon*; *Cistellaria* (The Casket Comedy), 201 BC, based on MENANDER's *Synaristosae*; *Stichus*, 200 BC, based on Menander's *Adelphoi*; *Pseudolus*, 191 BC. *Amphitruo*, 186 BC, one of his most successful comedies, has been translated and adapted by many dramatists such as ROTROU, MOLIÈRE, KLEIST, DRYDEN, GIRAUDOUX, KAISER; unlike AESCHYLUS, SOPHOCLES and EURIPIDES, P. treated the Amphitryon theme as a comedy. Other plays are: *Asinaria* (The Comedy of Asses), based on Demophilus' *Onagos*; *Aulularia* (about the character of a greedy man), based on Menander; *Bacchides*, based on the latter's *Dis Exapaton*; *Captivi* (The Captives), which LESSING, the 18th-century German critic, considered the finest play ever written; *Casina*, based on Diphilus' *Clerumenoe*; *Curculio*; *Epidicus*; *Menaechmi* (The Twin Menaechmi) – several times adapted (most famous version is SHAKESPEARE's *The Comedy of Errors*); *Mercator* (The Merchant), based on Philemon's *Emporos*; *Mostellaria*, based on *Phasma*, possibly by Theognetus; *Persa* (The Girl from Persa); *Poenulus* (The Carthaginian), based on *Carchedonois*, possibly by Menander; *Rudens* (original by Diphilus); *Trinummus* (The Three Penny Day), based on Philemon's *Thesauros*; *Truculentus*; *Vidularia* (a fragment). Since the Renaissance P. has had a decisive influence on modern comedy, and has been translated, adapted and imitated by many great dramatists including ARIOSTO, JONSON and MOLIÈRE. ▷MILES GLORIOSUS.

Bibl: E. Segal, ROMAN LAUGHTER: THE COMEDY OF PLAUTUS, 1968; G. E. Duckworth, THE NATURE OF ROMAN COMEDY, 1952; W. Beare, THE ROMAN STAGE, 3/1965

Playbill ▷PROGRAMME.

Players' Club. New York theatre club founded in 1888 which is run on the lines of the GARRICK CLUB in London. E. BOOTH, who was its first president, followed by J. JEFFERSON and J. DREW, donated a house for it. It contains a large collection of theatrical relics and has a library which was opened in 1957 as the Walter Hampden Memorial Library. ▷HAMPDEN.

Playfair, Sir Nigel (1874–1934), English ACTOR-MANAGER and director. Knighted in 1928. Ran the Lyric Theatre, Hammersmith, in London 1918–34. His most notable achievement was the revival of GAY's *The Beggar's Opera* with sets and costumes by FRASER which ran for some 1,500 performances and had, through its use of stylization and colour, a lasting influence on the development of the concept of the unity between design and direction in English theatre. In exemplary productions of English high comedy (CONGREVE, WILDE) he developed artists like EDITH EVANS and GIELGUD.

Playwrights' Company. Formed in New York in 1937 by the authors, RICE, SHERWOOD, M. ANDERSON, S. HOWARD, and BEHRMAN, the purpose being to organize a producing company to put on their own plays. In their first season in 1938–39 they scored successes with Sherwood's *Abe Lincoln in Illinois*, Anderson's *Knickerbocker Holiday*, Behrman's *No Time for Comedy*. After World War II it gradually lost its importance, with only Anderson and Rice active.

Plot. The sequence of external events, action or intrigue of a play, usually divided into exposition – the introduction of the basic situation and the characters; developments; climax and solution.

Plowright, Joan Anne (1929–), English actress. Married since 1961 to OLIVIER; after appearing in small parts at the OLD VIC and in the provinces, she attracted notice in the role of the cabin boy in WELLES's adaptation of Melville's *Moby Dick*, 1955, and had an outstanding success as Margery Pinchwife in WYCHERLEY's *The Country Wife*, 1956, with the ENGLISH STAGE COMPANY. Her best roles have been mainly in plays by contemporary playwrights: IONESCO's *The Chairs* and *The Lesson*, 1957–58; Jean Rice in OSBORNE's *The Entertainer*, 1958; Beatie Bryant in WESKER's *Roots*, Coventry and London 1959; Daisy in Ionesco's *Rhinoceros*, 1960; Josephine in SHELAGH DELANEY's *A Taste of Honey*, New York 1961. Other roles: SHAW's *Saint Joan*, CHICHESTER FESTIVAL, 1963 and OLD VIC, where she also played: Hilde Wangel in IBSEN's *The Master Builder*, 1964; Masha in CHEKHOV's *Three Sisters*, 1967; Rosaline in *Love's Labour's Lost*, 1968; Portia in *The Merchant of Venice*, 1970; the leading female role in E. DE FILIPPO's *Saturday, Sunday, Monday*, 1973, with Olivier.

Plummer, Christopher (1929–), Canadian actor. Started in REPERTORY in Canada, came to New York in 1954 and rose to prominence as a Shakespearean

Christopher Plummer as Richard III, Stratford-upon-Avon 1961, set designed by JOCELYN HERBERT

Joan Plowright as Sonya in CHEKHOV's *Uncle Vanya*, dir OLIVIER; CHICHESTER FESTIVAL 1962

actor at the Stratford, Conn., Festival Theatre, in 1955 (Mark Antony), and at Stratford, Ontario, 1956 (Henry V, Hamlet). At STRATFORD-UPON-AVON in 1961 (Benedick in *Much Ado*, and Richard III). Played King Henry in ANOUILH's *Becket* in London 1961/62. On the basis of these performances became one of the acknowledged international STARS of stage and screen, seen by millions as the male lead in *The Sound of Music*, one of the most successful films of all time.

Poel, William (1852–1934), English actor and director. Passionately interested in SHAKESPEARE, he devoted his life to a reform of Shakespearean production. Founded the Elizabethan Stage Society in 1894 to mount productions of Shakespeare on a reconstructed Elizabethan stage. His main achievement was to show that what the 18th and 19th centuries had regarded as flaws in the construction of Shakespeare's and other Elizabethan plays – the sequence of short, seemingly disconnected scenes – was in fact their strength and that it was not necessary to 'improve' these plays by forcing them into the mould of 'classical' five-act drama. The present approach to Shakespeare production in England, with its emphasis on the flow of the action with the minimum of elaborate scene-changes, is largely due to his efforts and influence.

Poelzig, Hans (1869–1936), German architect and teacher of architecture. Designed functional buildings and was responsible for transforming the Zircus Schumann in BERLIN into the Grosses Schauspielhaus, with 5,000 seats, which opened in 1919 with REINHARDT's production of AESCHYLUS' *Oresteia*. His other work as a designer included: JOHST's *Der König*, Dresden 1920, with G. Linnebach; SOPHOCLES' *Oedipus Rex*, Berlin 1929, National Theatre, dir JESSNER.

Poetic drama ▷VERSE DRAMA.

Pogodin (Stukalov), Nikolai Fyodorovich (1900–62), Soviet dramatist. A journalist by profession, he was first successful with his 'documentary' plays of the first years after the Revolution: *Temp* (Tempo), 1930; *Poema o topore* (*Poem About an Axe*), 1931. Plays dealing with the building and development of Soviet society after the Revolution: *Snyeg* (The Snow), 1932; *Moy drug* (*My Friend*), 1932; *Posle balla* (After the Ball), 1932; *Aristokraty* (*Aristocrats*), fp by OKHLOPKOV at the Vakhtangov Theatre, 1934, a COMEDY which deals with the formation of a gang of criminals engaged in digging a canal from the Baltic to the White Sea; followed by the Lenin TRILOGY *Tchelovek s ruchem* (The Man With the Gun), 1937; *Kremlyovskie kuranti* (*Kremlin Chimes*), 1942, new versions 1954 and 1956 – the latter seen in London in 1964 in a production by the MOSCOW ART THEATRE; *Tretya patetichevskaya* (The Third Pathétique), 1959. Also successful were his war plays *Moskovskie nochi* (Moscow Nights), 1942; *Lodochnitsa* (The Ferryboat Girl), 1943. Other works include: *Missuriisky-valts* (Missouri Waltz), 1950, an anti-American play ridiculing Truman; *Sonet Petrarki* (Petrarch's Sonnet), 1956.
Bibl: N. Zayzev, 1958

Poland. From the 13th to the 17th centuries MYSTERY PLAYS and passion PAGEANTS with comic and realistic elements (Mikolaj Wilkowiecka's *The Story of the Glorious Resurrection of our Lord* is still revived, notably the adaptation by L. SCHILLER, 1923, and by DEJMEK, 1961); 16th to 18th centuries, JESUIT DRAMA; in the 17th century performances by English strolling players and Italian opera and COMMEDIA DELL'ARTE companies. In 1724 Augustus II established the first public theatre building near Warsaw Castle, which became in 1765 the first Polish NATIONAL THEATRE; managed 1783–94 and 1799–1814 by BOGUSLAWSKI (1757–1829), the 'father of the Polish theatre'. The suppression of the movement for national independence by Tsarist Russia, also strongly affected the theatre. The National Theatre was rebuilt and when it opened in 1833 the name 'National Theatre' being forbidden, it became the Teatr Wielki (Big Theatre), mainly used for opera; attached to it was a small house for drama (Teatr Rozmaitosci), since 1924 Teatr Narodowy (National Theatre).
The greatest achievements in Polish Romantic literature consisted of the work of authors who were persecuted and suppressed; among the most outstanding were MICKIEWICZ (*Forefathers' Eve*), SLOWACKI and KRASIŃSKI (*The Undivine Comedy*). The greatest Polish comic writer was Aleksander Fredro (1827–93) whose sentimental COMEDIES enjoyed great success during his lifetime. The 19th century saw such brilliant actors as DAWISON and Helena Modrzejewska (MODJESKA); both won international fame appearing in Europe and the USA. The Garden Theatre in Warsaw tended towards NATURALISM and its most representative dramatist was the former actress GABRIELA ZAPOLSKA (1860–1921); in her satirical comedies she was concerned with moral, psychological and social problems of her time, e.g. *Zabusia*, 1896; *Panna Maliczewska* (A Miss What's Her Name), 1912. One of the most creative periods in Poland was *c.* 1890–1914: ENSEMBLE theatre in Cracow under naturalistic and symbolist influences; SYMBOLISM and EXPERIMENTAL THEATRE dominated the work of the great theatre reformer and dramatist of the time, WYSPIANSKI (1869–1907), also director and painter. Distinctive theatres were founded in Lódz, 1908, by Aleksander Zelwerowicz; in Warsaw, Teatr Polski, 1913, by SZYFMAN, and Teatr Reduta, 1919, by Juliusz Osterwa. Major director of the period between the wars: L. Schiller (1887–1954), who worked in Warsaw and Lódz. One of the most respected writers of this time was Jerzy Szaniawski (1886–). During the German occupation 1939–44 theatrical performances were prohibited, and buildings destroyed. After 1945 revivals of the national drama of the great Romantics. The line of development in 20th-century Polish drama, extending from WITKIEWICZ whose grotesque drama plays were the first examples of the THEATRE OF THE ABSURD, to GOMBROWICZ has been continued in the works of RÓZIEWICZ and MROŻEK, both influenced by IONESCO and DÜRRENMATT who wrote anti-totalitarian political parables in absurdist style; Mrożek is probably Poland's best-known playwright abroad. Another respected dramatist greatly concerned with social and political issues is KRUCZKOWSKI (1900–62). Many theatrical experiments were made by KANTOR and GROTOWSKI. Today in Warsaw there are three leading theatres with a REPERTOIRE of world literature: National Theatre – until 1968 under the management of K. Dejmek; Dramatic Theatre under Marian Meller; Contemporary Theatre under AXER. KRYSTYNA SKUSZANKA's theatre in Nova Huta near Cracow, which she managed until 1963, also gained an international reputation. Altogether Poland has today about 100 professional theatres.
Bibl: J. Kott, THEATRE NOTEBOOK 1947–67, 1968; W. Csato, THE POLISH THEATRE, 1963

Polgar, Alfred (1875–1955), Austrian writer and critic. Wrote law, parliamentary reports and drama reviews in Vienna; in 1925 became drama critic in BERLIN of *Die Weltbühne* and *Das Tagebuch*; 1933–38 was back in Vienna and in 1940 emigrated to the USA; after the war he made several trips to Europe. An outstanding critic and essayist of the 1920s and 1930s with a brilliant literary style, he also wrote satires and comedy sketches.

Political theatre. Drama has always had political implications. One of the oldest-known plays, *The Persians* by AESCHYLUS, even has openly propagandist aims (the raising of the morale of the Athenians and a strengthening of their self-confidence). That SHAKESPEARE's and MARLOWE's plays abounded in topical political allusions is a commonplace, but the use of drama as a consciously employed tool of political action is a relatively recent development, the first instances of which are probably provided by the theatre for political agitation of the Russian Revolution. Here groups of actors were sent to focal points (factories) to convert audiences to the party's point of view. In Germany PISCATOR and BRECHT worked on similar lines and so did, partially under direct influence from the German example, the Living Newspaper of the New Deal era in the USA in the 1930s. In the totalitarian states of the 20th century (Nazi Germany, Soviet Russia and the East European Communist states after World War II) the theatre became a direct instrument of political indoctrination and propaganda. But it is debatable whether these efforts were not self-defeating: predictability is the annihilation of the excitement and suspense which are the life-blood of drama; politically tendentious theatre in a country where only one opinion can prevail is totally predictable. On the other hand the audience in such countries develops a special sensibility for implied subversive meanings. In Nazi Germany humanist sentiments in plays by SCHILLER and GOETHE were wildly applauded; in

Poland and Czechoslovakia during the Stalinist era the national classics became politically explosive. The rise of writers of political allegory and satire, MROZEK in Poland, HAVEL in Czechoslovakia, prepared the ground for periods of struggle for greater freedom of thought in these countries. In areas where free expression of political opinions is allowed the weakness of political theatre (such as the underground theatre in the USA during the Vietnam War) is that it tends to preach to the converted. Its main problem, therefore, is that of finding the right audience: street theatre and theatre for political agitation in factories, etc., seems to be the answer.

Popov, Alexei Dmitrevich (1892–1961), Soviet producer and actor. Joined the MOSCOW ART THEATRE in 1912, then worked with VAKHTANGOV at the First Studio and 1923–30 as actor and director at the Third Studio (after 1926 the Vakhtangov Theatre) and was important in the development of the company. First directed GROTESQUE productions following the style of Vakhtangov, e.g. MÉRIMÉE's *Théâtre de Clara Gazul*, and later turned to modern Soviet plays and Stanislavskian realism. From 1930 he directed at the Theatre of the Revolution; outstanding productions included POGODIN's *Poem About an Axe* and *My Friend*, and *Romeo and Juliet*; after 1936 he directed at the Red Army Theatre, e.g. his famous *The Taming of the Shrew*, 1937. Later productions which won acclaim were: a revival of GOGOL's *The Government Inspector*, 1951; a new version of Pogodin's *Kremlin Chimes*, 1956; and the dramatization of Sholokhov's *Virgin Soil Upturned*, 1957.

Popov, Oleg Konstantinovich (1930–), Russian CLOWN. Trained at the State School of Circus Art in Moscow and began his career as a tightrope artiste. In 1955 he joined the Moscow State Circus as a clown. His character is derived from the 'Auguste de soirée', whose main function was to amuse and entertain the audience between acts. P. developed this role and gave it new meaning and importance; he became the boyish, comic character with the charm of a naughty child, who gets entangled in various problems with stage props and even the mechanics of scene-changing, and always wins in the end, with his talents as a juggler, MIME, musical clown and tightrope artiste. He imitates and parodies the 'straight' numbers and so links the various elements in the whole performance. His many tours in Western Europe and in the USA have won him international fame; he is today considered the greatest living clown. Bibl: V. Angarski & E. Viktorov, 1964

Porter, Cole (1892–1964), US composer. Wrote popular songs, stage and film musicals, almost all of them with his own lyrics. He studied music at Harvard, but did little writing professionally till 1928, when he composed the music for the REVUE *Paris*, which brought him international fame. His greatest hits were: *Gay Divorce*, 1932, with ASTAIRE and Claire Luce; and *Kiss Me, Kate*, 1948, musical

Hans Poelzig's design for the auditorium of the Grosses Schauspielhaus in BERLIN, 1919

Cole Porter's musical *Kiss Me, Kate*, 1948, with Patricia Morison and Alfred Drake

based on SHAKESPEARE's *The Taming of the Shrew*. He also wrote the lyrics and music for *See America First*, 1916; *Hitchy-Koo*, 1919; *Greenwich Village Follies of 1924*; *Wake Up and Dream*, and *Fifty Million Frenchmen*, 1929; *The New Yorkers*, 1930; *Nymph Errant*, 1933; *Anything Goes*, 1934; *Jubilee*, 1935; *Red Hot and Blue*, 1936; *The Sun Never Sets*, 1938; *Leave It to Me*, 1938; *You Never Know*, 1938; *Du Barry Was A Lady*, 1939; *Panama Hattie*, 1940; *Let's Face It*, 1941; *Seven Lively Arts*, 1944; *Around the World*, 1946; *Can-Can*, 1953; *Silk Stockings*, 1955.
Bibl: C. S. Smith, MUSICAL COMEDY IN AMERICA, 1950; A. Green & J. L. Laurie, SHOW BIZ, 1951

Portugal. The earliest important Portuguese playwright was VICENTE (*c.* 1465–*c.* 1536), the Court poet of Manuel I and the founder of a popular folk theatre, which declined under the oppression of the Inquisition and Spanish rule. In the 17th century the Court opera dominated, with only one theatre performing drama in Portuguese: the Teatro do Bairro-Alto, where 1733–38 the works of Antonio José da Silva were first staged and between 1767 and 1770 the first Portuguese productions of MOLIÈRE took place. In 1838 in the Teatro dos Condos the drama *Auto de Gil Vicente* by Almeida Garrett (1799–1854) had its first performance. He was a dramatist who initiated the Teatro National D. Maria II, which opened in 1834 and has remained a permanent theatre for the most important companies and actors. Since 1929 the group of the acting couple Amélia Rey-Colaco and Robles Monteiro have worked there with a world REPERTOIRE; they have also toured the most important cities in Portugal.

Possart, Ernst von (1841–1921), German actor, director and INTENDANT. As an actor he embodied the stately classical 19th-century style. Became artistic director of the Munich Court Theatre in 1878; in 1895 succeeded K. v. Perfall as Intendant of the COURT THEATRE. He also founded the Prinzregententheater in Munich as a home for the operas of Richard Wagner. Also author of several books: *Der Lehrgang des Schauspielers*, 1901; *Die Kunst des Sprechen*, 1907.
Bibl: R. Crodel, DER SCHAUSPIELER ERNST VON POSSART, 1927

Posse (farce). German name for a form of slapstick COMEDY centred around a comic character. Difficult to distinguish from FARCE and *Schwank*, the *Posse* nevertheless had its own tradition, as local farce (or dialect farce); there exist other variations like the *Bauern Posse* (peasant farce) in Bavaria and the Tyrol. In Vienna writers of the genre included STRANITZKY, KURZ, A. Bäuerle, forerunners of the literary *posse* of NESTROY (satirical farce) and RAIMUND (magical farce). In Berlin in the 19th century the most representative writers in the genre were Voss, ANGELY, HOLTEI, Glassbrenner, Kalisch; of minor importance were local writers of other cities, e.g. Baermann in Hamburg and Niebergall in Darmstadt.

Pound, Ezra (1885–1972), US poet, an important literary innovator. With E. Fenellosa he translated *Noh* plays (▷JAPAN) 1916, and wrote a free version of SOPHOCLES' *Trachiniae* (*The Women of Trachis*), fp Darmstadt, 1956, dir SELLNER.

Power, Tyrone (1795–1841), Irish actor. He first appeared on stage in 1815 but made little impression until 1826 when he began to specialize in Irish roles such as Sir Lucius O'Trigger in SHERIDAN's *The Rivals*. He also acted in his own plays, among them *St Patrick's Eve*, 1832; *Paddy Cary, the Boy of Clogheen*, 1833, and *Flannigan and the Fairies*, 1836. In 1840 he left for America, but was drowned on the return journey. A son, Harold, was father of (2) **Tyrone Edmond P.** (1869–1931), a prominent member of DALY's Company, 1890–98. The latter's son, (3) **Tyrone P.** (1914–58), had a distinguished film career though he had also been on stage, with KATHARINE CORNELL in *Romeo and Juliet*, 1930, and *Saint Joan*, 1936. He appeared in London in 1950 in *Mister Roberts* by Thomas Heggan and LOGAN.

Prampolini, Enrico (1894–1956), Italian director and designer. Painter of the Futurist movement (▷FUTURISM), who edited theoretical art magazines and with MARINETTI wrote a manifesto, in which they advocated a 'synthetic' theatre. P. partially realized his ideas with the Teatro del Colore, Rome 1920, and subsequently with the Teatro Sintetico, 1921–22, the Teatro degli Indipendenti and the Teatro delle Arti, 1923, with BRAGAGLIA, and a Futurist MIME theatre, 1927–28, Paris-Milan.
Bibl: G. Frette, SCENOGRAFIA TEATRALE 1909–54, 1955

Preetorius, Emil (1883–1973), German stage designer and illustrator. A contributor to the magazines *Jugend* and *Simplizissimus*. In 1909 he founded a school for illustration and book design; 1926–35 he was a teacher at the Academy of Art in Munich (illustration and stage design). He designed several productions for the Munich Künstlertheater and from 1923 at the Munich Kammerspiele (under the direction of FALCKENBERG), but he is best known for his décor for the BAYREUTH Wagner Festival (1933–41 for productions of H. Tietjen). Subsequently designed opera and plays for several important theatres in Germany and abroad.
Bibl: R. Adolph, 1960

Prehauser, Gottfried (1699–1769), Austrian actor. Was chosen by STRANITZKY to succeed him as HANSWURST at the Theater am Kärntnertor in Vienna. P. was a master of quick-fire cynical comedy – sometimes he played up to eight parts with different COSTUMES in one evening. He became particularly well known for his satirical songs.
Bibl: O. Rommel, DIE ALT-WIENER VOLKSKOMÖDIE, 1952

Price, Stephen (1783–1840), US theatrical entrepreneur. He was probably the first modern IMPRESARIO in America as distinct from an ACTOR-MANAGER; a theatrical speculator. Associated with the management of the Park Theatre, New York, from 1808, he arranged guest appearances of famous European actors. He briefly also managed DRURY LANE, London 1826.

Priestley, John Boynton (1894–), English dramatist, novelist and critic to whom recognition first came with a volume of verse, *The Chapman of Rhymes*, 1918. In 1931 he achieved a triumph with his novel *The Good Companions* (which he dramatized with KNOBLOCK; it was later filmed, and in 1974 made into a musical); he subsequently established himself as one of the most entertaining dramatic writers of his day. He was a master of characterization, mainly writing about Yorkshire people, their hopes and aspirations. One of his best plays is *Time and the Conways*, 1937, in which he experiments with the concept of time: the first and third acts are set in the present, but the second act takes place 20 years in the future. One character retains memories of the future in the third act. Other works include *Dangerous Corner*, 1932; *I Have Been Here Before*, 1937; *Laburnum Grove*, 1933; *Eden End*, 1934; *When We Are Married*, 1938; *Music at Night*, 1938; *Johnson over Jordan*, 1939; *The Long Mirror*, 1940; *They Came to a City*, 1943; *An Inspector Calls*, 1946; *Ever Since Paradise*, 1946; *The Linden Tree*, 1947; *Summer Day's Dream*, 1949; *Dragon's Mouth*, 1952; *Take the Fool Away*, 1954; *Doomsday*, 1958; *The Rack*, 1959.
Bibl: D. Hughes, 1958

Proclemer, Anna (1923–), Italian actress. First appeared in UNIVERSITY THEATRE, then in 1942–43 joined the Compagnia Teatro delle Arti, under the direction of BRAGAGLIA; her greatest success came in 1948 as Nina in CHEKHOV's *The Seagull* at the PICCOLO TEATRO DI MILANO directed by STREHLER; in 1952 she played Viola in *As You Like It* at the Piccolo Teatro in Rome and 1952–53 Ophelia in *Hamlet* at the Teatro delle Arti, dir GASSMAN and L. SQUARZINA. Since 1955 she has co-managed several touring companies, appearing since 1956 particularly with ALBERTAZZI's company in plays like D'ANNUNZIO's *La Figlia di Jorio* (awarded S. Genesio Prize, 1958); IBSEN's *Ghosts*, etc.

Programme. Printed information for the audience containing the title of the play, author and cast, used in European theatres since the middle of the 18th century (COVENT GARDEN and DRURY LANE, London 1737). Originally published for notice and distribution in coffee houses – a function later superseded by posters, newspaper advertisements, etc. In the 18th century the programme also gave information about ticket prices, times of performances and future productions. Nowadays, performance details are often supplemented with biographies of actors and historical articles; sometimes very elaborately designed – especially for FESTIVALS and NATIONAL THEATRES.

Prologue (Gk *prologos*=foreword). An introductory speech before the opening of the action of the play, by one or several of the actors; sometimes even takes the form of a short introductory playlet performed by the actors in the play. Also the speaker of the prologue.

Prompter. Person in theatres and opera-houses who cues actors and reminds forgetful ones of their lines. **Prompt Side** and **Opposite Prompt** are technical terms for stage left and stage right.

Proscenium. In the modern theatre the opening through which the spectator sees the stage; also the proscenium arch which frames the opening and the walls of which this arch is a part. Proscenium doors (doors of entrance) were a special feature of the English Restoration theatre; three doors were built on each side of the fore-stage running into the lower box tier.

Protagonist (Gk *protagonistes*=first fighter). In the ancient Greek theatre the chief actor, today the central character in a dramatic work. ▷ANTAGONIST.

Provincetown Players. An experimental group of US actors and dramatists, whose aim was to revitalize the American drama and who first staged many of O'NEILL's early plays. Founded in 1915 by Susan Glaspell (1882–1948) and her husband George Cram Cook, its purpose was to give 'the American playwrights a chance to work out their ideas in freedom'. They opened in spring 1916 with Boyce's *Constancy* and S.G.'s *Suppressed Desires* at the Wharf Theatre, Provincetown, Mass., later moving to New York, Greenwich Village (Playwright's Theatre), and in 1918 in the same street opened the Provincetown Playhouse. Productions included O'Neill's 'sea-plays', *Bound East for Cardiff*, 1916; *The Long Voyage Home*, 1917; *Ile*, 1917; *The Moon of the Caribbees*, 1919, and other early works such as *The Emperor Jones*, 1920; *The Hairy Ape*, 1922; *All God's Chillun Got Wings*, 1924; *Desire Under the Elms*, 1925 (a later BROADWAY production set O'Neill on the road to fame); works by other American dramatists including: Edna St Vincent Millay's *Aria Da Capo*, 1919; Dreiser's *The Hand of the Potter*, 1921; P. GREEN's *In Abraham's Bosom*, 1926; plays by European writers like HASENCLEVER's *Jenseits*, 1925; STRINDBERG's *The Ghost Sonata*, 1924, and *A Dream Play*, 1926. The leading directors were James Light and R. E. JONES. For a while they operated in conjunction with the Greenwich Village Theatre, including operatic productions like GILBERT AND SULLIVAN's *Patience*, 1924, dir R. E. Jones; *Orpheus*, 1926, a short version of Gluck's *Orpheus and Eurydice*, dir Light. In 1929 they moved to the Garrick Theatre but lack of success and the economic crisis of the time forced the company to disband and several members joined the THEATRE GUILD.
Bibl: H. Deutsch & S. Hahau, THE PROVINCETOWN PLAYHOUSE: STORY OF A THEATRE, 1931

Puecher, Virginio (1927–), Italian director. Started his career as assistant to STREHLER at the PICCOLO TEATRO DI MILANO, then in 1948–49 worked for some time as a journalist, before rejoining the Piccolo Teatro in 1955. Since 1957 directed his own productions, notably: BALZAC's *Mercadet*, Piccolo Teatro, 1959; ZAVATTINI's *Come nasce un soggetto cinematagrafico*, Venice Festival 1959; and plays by O'NEILL, e.g. *Long Day's Journey Into Night*, Compagnia Ricci, 1958, and *A Moon for the Misbegotten*, TEATRO STABILE, Genoa 1959. Other productions: T. WILLIAMS's *Summer and Smoke*, Compagnia Brignone-Santuccio, Rome 1959; SHAKESPEARE's *Henry V*, Teatro Stabile, Bologna, and Piccolo Teatro, 1967; WEISS's *The Investigation*, Piccolo Teatro, 1966. He also directed operas: MANZONI's *La Sentenza*, Bergamo, Festival della novità 1960; Paisiello's *Nina*, Piccola Scala, Milan 1961.

Pulcinella (Neapolitan, *pollecenella* = young turkey). One of the comic servants of the COMMEDIA DELL'ARTE: a coarse, boorish, selfish servant, also known as Policinella (Fr Polichinelle); originally a popular CLOWN figure, who was adopted by the Neapolitan c. dell'a. in 1570. His costume was white and voluminous, later the patchwork costume of the HARLEQUIN, a pointed hat, black half-mask, beard, fat belly, sometimes a humped back. He was the central character of numerous improvised FARCES in the south of Italy and later also gained popularity in several variations, also in the north. The character was probably definitively established by FIORILLO.

Pulitzer Prize (Pulitzer Play Award). One of several literary prizes established by the US publisher Joseph Pulitzer (1847–1911), awarded annually since 1917 by Columbia University, New York, for the best 'original American play performed in New York'. Among playwrights who have received this award are O'NEILL, four times, the first one being for *Beyond the Horizon*, 1920, the last one posthumously for *Long Day's Journey Into Night*, 1956. S. HOWARD won it in 1924 for *They Knew What They Wanted*; SHERWOOD won it three times, for *Idiot's Delight*, 1936; *Abe Lincoln in Illinois*, 1939 and *There shall be no Night*, 1940. T. WILLIAMS won it in 1947 for *A Streetcar named Desire*, and in 1955 for *Cat on a Hot Tin Roof*. WILDER won it three times, for *The Bridge of San Luis Rey*, 1927; *Our Town*, 1938 and *The Skin of Our Teeth*, 1942. LINDSAY and CROUSE won it in 1945 for *State of the Union* and ALBEE in 1966 for *A Delicate Balance* and in 1975 for *Seascape*. ▷NYDCC for the setting up of a critics' award when they became dissatisfied with the Pulitzer choices.

Punch and Judy ▷PUPPET THEATRE.

Puppet Theatre. In a wider sense the term comprises a number of forms of theatre without the use of live actors, i.e. SHADOW PLAYS, mechanical theatre which uses automata, TOY THEATRES, etc. In the narrower sense there are three main types,

Puppet, or marionette, from the COMMEDIA DELL'ARTE

Punch and Judy show

J. B. Priestley's *An Inspector Calls*, London 1946, with GUINNESS and MARGARET LEIGHTON

according to the nature of the puppets employed: glove puppets, marionettes which are moved by strings attached to the limbs from above, and puppets moved by sticks from below or as in China by slides from the back. Movable puppets are known to have existed in ancient Egypt. There are reports of puppet theatre in ancient Greece and it was widespread throughout the Roman Empire. The attacks of many of the Christian fathers and Islamic theologians on the wickedness of theatre often make an exception for puppet theatre. It was an important part of popular entertainment and folk culture throughout Europe into the 19th century. The comic PROTAGONIST is always at the centre: Polichinelle or Punch, derived from the PULCINELLA of the COMMEDIA DELL'ARTE; in Germany HANSWURST or KASPERL. In the Near East and Asia puppet theatre is also a widespread form of popular entertainment, best known being the Javanese shadow play *Wajang Kulit* (*wajang*=puppet; *kulit*=leather) and the Turkish *Karagöz*. Since the beginning of the 20th century there have been efforts towards the revival of puppet theatre as a serious art form. The most remarkable modern puppeteer is OBRAZTSOV, head of the Moscow State Puppet Theatre. Many important artists of this century have occupied themselves with puppet theatre, among them Natalia Goncharova, Paul Klee, Sophie Tauber-Arp, A. Calder and Bil Baird in the USA. After World War II there have been efforts towards a merging of live and puppet theatre and towards an abstract puppet theatre.
Bibl: G. Speaight, PUNCH AND JUDY: A HISTORY, 2/1970; R. Baird, THE ART OF THE PUPPET, 1965

Pushkin, Alexandr Sergeyevich (1799–1837), Russian writer. First of the great Russian poets, short-story writers and dramatists to be well versed in Western European literature, his favourite writers being MOLIÈRE, SHAKESPEARE and BYRON. From this background he started to search for a truly national drama, based on Russian themes and folklore. With his dramatic and particularly his poetic works he exercised great influence on the Russian theatre and the development of Russian as a literary language. Many of his poetic works were adapted for ballet, e.g. *Ruslan and Ludmilla*, 1821, ballet by Glushkovsky (1825 dramatized by Shakovsky, 1858, opera by Glinka); others were made into operas: *Eugene Onegin* (novel in verse, 1825–32; opera by Tchaikovsky, 1879), etc. His main dramatic work was the TRAGEDY, *Boris Godunov* (opera by Mussorgsky, 1870), based on a political theme, completed in 1825, but published only in 1830 because of censorship problems. It was first produced in 1870 in St Petersburg and in 1880 in Moscow; but only in 1907, after the MOSCOW ART THEATRE production, did it find a permanent place on the Russian stage. His work for the theatre also includes four 'little tragedies', completed in 1830: *Skupoi rytsar* (The Avaricious Knight), fp St Petersburg 1852, prod STANISLAVSKY 1889–90; *Motsart i Salieri* (Mozart and Salieri), St Petersburg 1932, and MAT 1915 (made into an opera by Rimsky-Korsakov 1898); *Kamyenni gost* (The Stone Guest), fp St Petersburg 1847, MAT 1915; *Pir vo vremya chumy* (The Feast During the Plague), fp 1899, MAT 1919.
Bibl: D. S. Mirsky, 1963; H. Troyat, 1959, 2 vols

Quadflieg, Will (Friedrich Wilhelm Q.; 1914–), German actor. After many appearances with different German provincial companies, came to BERLIN in 1937; 1940–45 at the Schillertheater. After World War II he was engaged at the Hamburg Schauspielhaus and in Zurich (from 1949) and founded his own touring company, Die Schauspieltruppe, with MARIA BECKER and Robert Freytag. He excelled at playing classical heroes, e.g. in SCHILLER's *Don Carlos*; GOETHE's *Faust*, dir GRÜNDGENS; *Macbeth*, BURGTHEATER 1964; *Othello*, Berlin 1966, which he also directed; Prospero in *The Tempest*, Salzburg 1968. He has also appeared in modern plays, e.g. as Julian in ALBEE's *Tiny Alice*, Hamburg 1966, and in DYER's *Staircase*, Berlin 1968.
Bibl: S. Melchinger, SCHAUSPIELER, 1965

Quaglio (also Quaglia, Qualio, Qualia). Italian family of painters from Lenno (between Como and Lugano), who from the late 18th century till the beginning of this century worked mainly in Germany. Among the many Italian families of artists, they stand out by reason of their continuity; in six generations there were about 15 members of the family who worked as stage designers, decorators and architects in Kassel, Dresden, Vienna and Munich. The best known were (1) **Lorenzo I** (1730–1804), a Late Baroque scenic designer; in 1758 appointed Court architect of the Mannheim theatre, designed works by Salieri, Galuppi, Hasse, Paisiello, etc., extended the Schlosstheater and built the National Theatre in Mannheim, at the time considered the most modern theatre in Germany. After working in Dresden and studying in Italy he worked in Zweibrücken, and in 1778 was appointed Court architect in Munich and designed the first production of Mozart's *Idomeneo*, 1781. (2) **Domenico** (Dominik) **II** (1787–1837) was more important as a painter, decorator and lithographer. (3) **Simon** (1795–1837) was appointed in 1828 director of scenic art at the Munich Court Theatre. (4) **Angelo II** (1828–90) collaborated with Richard Wagner, designed many of his works and became an important theatre figure in Munich under the direction of POSSART. (5) **Eugen** (1857–1942) worked as a stage designer in Munich, Berlin, Stuttgart and Prague.

Qualtinger, Helmut (1928–), Austrian actor, CABARET artist and author. With Carl Merz and Gerhard Bronner he wrote the scripts for many cabarets in Vienna and also acted in them. From 1953 appeared also in straight plays: Prince of Wales in *Kean*, SARTRE/DUMAS, Vienna 1955; Wondrak in HOCHWÄLDER's *Donnerstag*, SALZBURG FESTIVAL 1959, and in a great number of NESTROY roles such as Knieriem in *Lumpazivagabundus*, Vienna 1965. In 1962, in Vienna, he created his popular character Herr Karl, text written with Carl Merz, a typical Austrian who survives all political upheavals through his opportunism and adaptability. From 1963 he gave solo-recitations of works by KRAUS, e.g. *Die letzten Tage der Menschheit*, and in 1965 appeared in his own play *Die Hinrichtung*, VOLKSTHEATER, Vienna. He is at once a comedian and moralist, able to adopt any Viennese and Austrian dialect and to use the speech and ideas of different social classes with great versatility, conveying surprising insights with simple comic lines.

Quayle, Antony (1913–), English actor and director. Made his stage début in 1931. He made his breakthrough after 1945, his most famous role being Iago in 1947 in Stratford and London. He was director of the Shakespeare Memorial Theatre, STRATFORD-UPON-AVON, 1948–56, where he acted and directed: Petruchio in *The Taming of the Shrew*, 1948; Falstaff in *Henry IV*, 1950, *Othello*, 1954; and in *The Merry Wives of Windsor*, 1955. Among other noted parts are Eddie in A. MILLER's *A View from the Bridge*, 1956; James Tyrone in O'NEILL's *Long Day's Journey Into Night*, 1958; Marcel Blanchard in FEYDEAU's *Look After Lulu*, adapted by COWARD, 1959; ARBUZOV's *Old World*, RSC 1976, with PEGGY ASHCROFT. Also many film and TV parts.

Queen's Men (more accurately: Queen Elizabeth's Men). One of the major Elizabethan acting companies that flourished between 1583 and 1590. Formed by the MASTER OF THE REVELS after the queen, who had preferred boys' companies in the first two decades of her reign, expressed a renewed interest in adult actors. The company, which included the famous CLOWNS TARLETON and Singer, and actors like R. WILSON and William Johnson (the latter two from the Earl of Leicester's company), appeared at the Bull and Bell Theatres, and was frequently asked to act at Court. After 1590 they declined and in 1594 combined with Sussex's company under HENSLOWE. In the same year the Lord Chamberlain's Company which included BURBAGE, KEMPE and SHAKESPEARE was formed and finally eclipsed the Queen's Men.

Quintero ▷ALVAREZ QUINTERO.

Quintero, José (1924–), US director. With Theodore Mann founded the Theatre Circle in the Square in 1950, an OFF-

BROADWAY arena theatre, which first made its name in 1952 with the production of T. WILLIAMS's *Summer and Smoke*. He directed SCHNITZLER's *Der Reigen* as *Merry-go-Round*, 1954; he became best known for his productions of O'NEILL plays including *The Iceman Cometh*, 1956; and *Long Day's Journey Into Night*, Helen Hayes Theatre, 1956. Other productions: O'Neill's *A Moon for the Misbegotten*, Spoleto Festival, 1958; (at the Circle) BEHAN's *The Quare Fellow*, 1958, WILDER's *Our Town*, 1959, GENET's *The Balcony*, 1960, D. THOMAS's *Under Milk Wood*, 1961, and O'Neill's *Desire Under the Elms*, 1963; *Strange Interlude*, Hudson Theatre, 1963; *Marco Millions*, ANTA, Washington Square Theatre, 1964. Also active as a film and TV director.

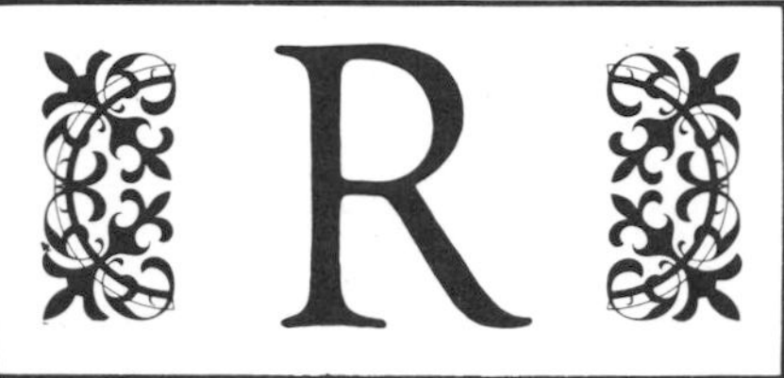

Angelo Quaglio, design for *Tristan and Isolde*, 1865

Rabe, David (1940–), US dramatist. Taught playwriting and film criticism at Villanova University, Pennsylvania. First came into prominence as a playwright with his Vietnam study *The Basic Training of Pavlo Hummel*, first presented by PAPP at the New York Public Theatre, 1971, where in the same year his second play *Sticks and Bones* was successfully produced.

Rachel (Elisabeth Rachel Félix; 1821–58), French tragedienne. Daughter of a poor Jewish merchant, she sang as a child on the streets, studied at Saint-Auclaire's drama school and for some time at the CONSERVATOIRE D'ART DRAMATIQUE, but had to discontinue her studies in order to earn a living. She was engaged by the director of the Gymnase Théâtre, where she appeared in 1837 in *La Vendéenne* by Dupont, a performance which was enthusiastically received by the French critic Jules Janin (*Journal des Débats*), who assisted her career. In 1838 she made her début at the COMÉDIE-FRANÇAISE, first with little response from the audience, but when she played in revivals of great French TRAGEDIES by, e.g. CORNEILLE and RACINE, she was recognized as the greatest actress of her day; the title role in *Phèdre* (Racine) was considered her finest part. She also appeared in a number of modern plays including the first production of *Adrienne Lecouvreur*, 1849, written for her by SCRIBE and Legouvé. She toured Europe with her best classical roles, and was particularly successful in London 1841, and the USA 1855, also in Russia. After returning to France, she contracted tuberculosis and died at the age of 38. She was thin and not particularly beautiful, but her emotional range encompassed a restrained fiery passion.
Bibl: J.-P. Stephan, 1958; S. Chavalley, RACHEL EN AMÉRIQUE, 1957

Rachel in *Horace* by CORNEILLE, COVENT GARDEN 1841

Racine, Jean Baptiste (1639–99), French playwright and poet. Educated mainly in Jansenist schools; a member of literary groups while still a student. Among his friends were such writers as La Fontaine, Boileau and MOLIÈRE, who greatly influenced and encouraged his dramatic writing and in 1664 performed his tragedy *La Thébaïde, ou les frères ennemis*, Palais Royal, which, however, was a failure. For this reason, after his *Alexandre et Porus*, 1665, had run for a fortnight at Molière's Palais Royal, R. handed it over to the HÔTEL DE BOURGOGNE, which had among other advantages a higher reputation in TRAGEDY. But his action created a scandal in Paris and made him a lifelong enemy of Molière. After the death of MLLE DU PARC, his mistress, who was the first *Andromaque*, Hôtel de Bourgogne, 1667, R. fell in love with the actress LA CHAMPMESLÉ, for whom he wrote *Bérénice*, 1670; *Iphigénie*, 1674, and *Phèdre*, 1677. In 1668 his only comedy *Les Plaideurs* was a failure when first produced, but it is today still in the classical REPERTOIRE of French COMEDY. R. then reverted to tragedy, with *Britannicus*, 1669; *Bajazet*, 1672; *Mithridate*, 1673; establishing himself as a master in this field, ranking with CORNEILLE. After *Phèdre* he retired from the theatre, probably because his enemies had persuaded the playwright Nicolas Pardon to write a play on the same theme and to perform it within two days; Pardon's work, written in less difficult verse than R.'s *Phèdre*, was much more successful. In 1677 R. was appointed Royal Historiographer. This ended his career as a playwright, except for two biblical tragedies which he wrote 12 years later, at the request of Mme de Maintenon, for her girls' school at Saint-Cyr: *Esther*, Saint-Cyr 1689, CF, 1721; *Athalie*, Saint-Cyr 1690/91, CF, 1716.

R.'s heroes are the victims of an inevitable fate, which becomes manifest in their destructive passions. The conflict in his plays is simply stated, the PLOT economically developed, concentrating on the fortunes and ultimate destiny of the hero. In his biblical tragedies destiny is replaced by divine power. His language is extremely simple, economic and precise, and achieves its effect by musicality and rhythmic virtuosity. Except for the lyrical choruses in the biblical tragedies, his plays are written in ALEXANDRINES.

Bibl: R. Barthes, SUR RACINE, 1964; B. Weinberg, THE ART OF JEAN RACINE, 1963; J. C. Lapp, ASPECTS OF RACINIAN TRAGEDY, 1956; E. Vinaver, 1951; F. Mauriac, 1928

RADA ▷ ROYAL ACADEMY OF DRAMATIC ART.

Radok, Alfred (1914–76), Czech director. In 1945 he was appointed opera director at the Prague Theatre of the 5th of May (Smetana Theatre) and in 1957 at the National Theatre (drama). In that year, together with the stage designer SVOBODA, he founded the famous LATERNA MAGICA, a mixture of drama and film clips. He remained artistic manager of the Laterna Magica until 1960, after which he directed at the National Little Theatre and abroad, e.g. IBSEN's *Hedda Gabler*, 1964; ROLLAND's *Le Jeu de l'amour et de la mort*, 1964; *The Swedish Match*, based on Hans Andersen, Prague 1964, Vienna 1965, Dortmund 1966; GORKY's *The Last Ones*, Munich 1965; LORCA's *The House of Bernarda Alba*, Berlin 1967. Left Czechoslovakia after the Russian occupation, 1968, and thereafter worked in Western Europe.

Raffaëlli, Michel (1929–), French painter, guitarist and stage designer. Best work in the theatre has been in collaboration with the director SELLNER: Schönberg's opera *Moses und Aron*, Berlin 1959; in Darmstadt: CALDERÓN's *The Mayor of Zalamea*, 1959; AUDIBERTI's *La Fête noire*, 1960; LORCA's *The House of Bernarda Alba*, 1961; and for the Théâtre de la Cité de Villeurbanne: GOLDONI's *La Trilogia della villeggiatura*, 1963; dir J. Rosner.

Raimu (Jules-Auguste-César Muraire; 1883–1946), French actor. Began his career in MUSIC HALL and was discovered by S. GUITRY, who chose him for his play *Faisons un rêve*, 1916. His greatest success was probably the title role in PAGNOL's *Marius*, 1929, in the sequels *Fanny* and *César*, and in the screen versions. After 40 years in the theatre R. became a member of the COMÉDIE-FRANÇAISE, where his finest performances included: Monsieur Jourdain in MOLIÈRE's *Le Bourgeois gentilhomme*, 1944 and Aragon in *Le Malade imaginaire*.

Raimund, Ferdinand (1790–1836), Austrian playwright and actor. With NESTROY the greatest folk dramatist writing in German. After appearing with several travelling companies between 1808 and 1813, he was engaged by the poet Gleich at the Theater in der Josefstadt in 1814 and in the following year appeared in Gleich's FARCE *Die Musikanten am Hohen Markt* (The Musicians in the High Market), which established him as the most popular actor of his time. From 1817 he appeared in folk comedies at the Leopoldstädter Theater, the leading Viennese company at that time. He wrote adaptations and interludes for plays in the REPERTOIRE; inspired by his successful adaptation of Meisl's *Die Prinzessin mit der langen Nase* (The long-nosed Princess), he started his first play *Der Barometermacher auf der Zauberinsel* (The Barometer Maker on the Magic Island), a farce with songs. With R. in the title role, the play was a resounding success and in the following years his reputation both as actor and dramatist grew. In 1828 he was appointed manager of the Leopoldstädter Theater, but emotional disturbances led him to take his own life eight years later. His theatre has its roots in the Baroque ZAUBERSTÜCK and the old Viennese farce; in some of his plays he also inclined towards German idealism and aspired to standards set by SHAKESPEARE and GRILLPARZER. His work combines naïve and realistic scenes with fairy-tale elements: *Der Diamant des Geisterkönigs* (The Fairy King's Diamond), 1824; *Moissasurs Zauberfluch* (M.'s Magic Curse), 1827; *Die Gefesselte Phantasie* (Fantasy in Chains), 1828; *Die Unheilbringende Krone* (The Fatal Crown), 1829. His masterpieces are generally considered to be: *Das Mädchen aus der Feenwelt, oder der Bauer als Millionär* (The Girl from Fairyland, or The Peasant Millionaire), 1826; *Der Alpenkönig und der Menschenfeind* (The King of the Alps and the Misanthropist), 1828; *Der Verschwender* (The Prodigal), 1834.

Bibl: K. Kahl, 1967; H. Weigel, FLUCHT VOR DER GRÖSSE, 1960

Randone, Salvo (Salvatore R.; 1906–), Italian actor. Made his first stage appearance in 1926 and in 1941 successfully appeared with the Compagnia del Teatro delle Arti (dir BRAGAGLIA) as Daniel in SCHILLER's *Die Räuber*, and as Luka in GORKY's *The Lower Depths*, in the opening production of the PICCOLO TEATRO DI MILANO dir STREHLER. Since World War II he has worked with many leading Italian companies and theatres, under the direction of COSTA (Malvolio in *As You Like It*, 1950), Strehler (Raimondo Navarra in VERGA's *Dal tuo al mio*, 1956), GASSMAN (alternating as Othello and Iago, 1956). He is at his best in old and modern classics, e.g. PIRANDELLO, ELIOT (Becket in *Murder in the Cathedral*, 1957–58), and in the plays of 19th- and 20th-century Italian writers including Verga, GIACOSA, BETTI and FABBRI.

Raphael (1483–1520), Italian painter. His sole important contribution to the theatre was the décor for *I Suppositi* by ARIOSTO in honour of Pope Leo X, performed during the Roman carnival in 1519.

Rattigan, Terence (1911–), English dramatist, author of several successful light COMEDIES, followed by serious plays on topical themes, clearly constructed and theatrically effective. Though they may not plumb great depths, they always provide excellent acting vehicles; STARS who have appeared in his plays include the LUNTS, HARRISON and GUINNESS. Major works: *French Without Tears*, 1936 and the musical version *Joie de vivre*, music R. Stolz, 1960; *After the Dance*, 1939; *While the Sun Shines*, 1943; *Love in Idleness* (later entitled *Oh Mistress Mine*), 1944; *The Winslow Boy*, 1946; *Playbill* with *The Browning Version* and *Harlequinade*, 1948; *Adventure Story*, 1949; *Who Is Sylvia?*, 1950; *The Deep Blue Sea*, 1952; *The Sleeping Prince*, 1953; *Separate Tables*, 1954 (double bill); *Variations on a Theme*, 1958; *Ross*, 1960; *Like Father, Like Son*, 1961; *Heart to Heart*, 1962 (for TV); *Man and Boy*, 1963; *In Praise of Love*, 1973 (double bill). Many of his plays have been filmed.

Raupach, Ernst (1784–1852), German dramatist. Author of more than 100 successful plays, aimed at crude theatrical effects, which imitated the works of SCHILLER, GOETHE and particularly KOTZEBUE; his outstanding work is *Der Müller und sein Kind* (The Miller and His Child), 1835. Other works: *Der Traum, ein Märchen* (The Dream, a Fairytale), 1822; *Isidor und*

Ferdinand Raimund

Racine, *Les Plaideurs*, 1668

Olga oder Die Leibeigenen (I. and O. or the Serfs), 1826; *Der versiegelte Bürgermeister* (The Sealed-up Burgomaster), 1829; *Der Zeitgeist* (The Spirit of the Times), 1835.

Raynal, Paul (1885–1971), French dramatist. Best known for his World War I play *Le Tombeau sous l'Arc de Triomphe*, 1924, COMÉDIE-FRANÇAISE. Other works include: *Le Maître de son cœur*, 1920; *La Francerie*, 1933; *Le Matériel humain*, written 1936, fp 1948; *Napoléon unique*, 1936, dir COPEAU; *A souffert sous Ponce Pilate*, 1939; *Au Soleil de l'instinct*, 1932.

Reade, Charles (1814–84), English novelist. Best known as the author of *The Cloister and the Hearth*, he also wrote a number of plays: *Gold*, 1853; *Masks and Faces* (in collaboration with Tom Taylor), 1852; *The Courier of Lyons*, 1854; revived in 1877 as *The Lyons Mail*, it was one of IRVING's greatest successes in MELODRAMA. R. dramatized ZOLA's *L'Assommoir* (with C. Warner) under the title *Drink*, 1879.

Rederijkers. Rhetoricians. A society in the Netherlands devoted to poetry, drama and theatre; founded at the end of the 14th century, it reached its peak in the 16th century. Membership was primarily middle class; the patron was an aristocrat or patrician. Annual competitions (*landjuwel*) were held with allegorical spectacles and FARCES, which were preceded by a magnificent procession.

Michael Redgrave in STRINDBERG's *The Father*, 1947

Redgrave, Sir Michael (1908–), English actor. Knighted in 1959. Studied at Cambridge and turned to the theatre at the age of 26, joining the Liverpool Repertory Company in 1934. Versatile and intelligent, he has appeared since the late 1930s with many leading English companies, beginning with the OLD VIC in 1936–37, then under GIELGUD at the Queen's Theatre, 1937–38, and later with SAINT-DENIS at the Old Vic, 1950–52. He now ranks with Gielgud and OLIVIER as one of the major old-guard actors in the English theatre. His best parts include Rakitin in TURGENEV's *A Month in the Country*, 1943; Hamlet and Richard II, 1950–51, Old Vic, and Prospero at STRATFORD-UPON-AVON where, in the 1952–53 season, he also played Shylock, Lear and Antony with PEGGY ASHCROFT as Cleopatra. In 1955 he played Hector in GIRAUDOUX's *Tiger at the Gates*, in London and New York, and in 1958 he went to the USSR with his earlier *Hamlet* production. He has also appeared successfully in films, and has written two books on the art of acting: *The Actor's Ways and Means*, 1953, and *Mask or Face*, 1959. His daughter **Vanessa R.** (1937–) first appeared with her father in 1958 in *A Touch of the Sun* by HUNTER, and soon established herself as an outstanding stage and screen actress. She achieved her first great success as Stella Dean in BOLT's *The Tiger and the Horse*, 1960. Her other well-known parts include: Rosalind in *As You Like It*, Stratford-upon-Avon 1962; title role in IBSEN's *The Lady from the Sea* and Nina in CHEKHOV's *The Seagull*, 1964; the title role in a dramatiza-

Terence Rattigan's *Flare Path*, 1942

tion of Muriel Spark's novel *The Prime of Miss Jean Brodie*, 1966, and Gilda in a revival of COWARD's *Design for Living*, 1973. M.R.'s wife **Rachel Kempson** (1910–), his son **Corin R.** (1939–) and his other daughter **Lynn R.** (1944–) are also successful on stage and in films.

Regnard, Jean-François (1655–1710), French dramatist. Wrote crude FARCES and COMEDIES, first for the COMÉDIE-ITALIENNE, 1688–96, and 1694–1708 for the COMÉDIE-FRANÇAISE. He had great talent for witty DIALOGUE and comic situations, and was often compared with MOLIÈRE, but his work suffered from weakness in character development. His best plays include: *Le Joueur*, 1696; *Le Distrait*, 1697; and especially *Le Légataire universel*, 1708, which remained on stage until the 20th century.

Rehan, Ada (A. Crehan; 1860–1916), US actress. One of the leading comic performers of her day, she appeared 1879–99 with DALY's company. She overcame her tendency to stylization with her charm and sparkling technique. Her roles were mainly in Shakespearean and classical COMEDY; her most famous was probably Katharina in *The Taming of the Shrew*; other greatly admired roles included Lady Teazle (*The School for Scandal*), Rosalind (*As You Like It*), Sylvia (FARQUHAR's *The Recruiting Officer*).
Bibl: M. Felheim, THE THEATRE OF AUGUSTIN DALY, 1956

Rehberg, Hans (1901–63), German dramatist. Author of historical plays, whose heroic nihilism was particularly acceptable under the Third Reich: *Cecil Rhodes*, 1932; Prussian dramas: *Der grosse Kurfürst* (The Great Elector), 1934, *Friedrich I*, 1935, *Friedrich Wilhelm I*, 1935, and *Der Siebenjährige Krieg* (The Seven Years War), fp Berlin 1938, State theatre, dir GRÜNDGENS who also played in it; Renaissance dramas: *Die Königin Isabella*, Berlin 1939, dir Gründgens; *Heinrich und Anna*, 1942; *Heinrich VII*, Munich 1947, and *Elisabeth und Essex*, 1949, etc.; the Agamemnon dramas: *Der Gattenmord* (The Murder of the Husband), fp 1953, Düsseldorf Theater, dir Gründgens, and *Der Muttermord* (The Matricide), Stuttgart 1953; *Rembrandt*, Duisburg 1956.
Bibl: U.-K. Ketelsen, HEROISCHES DRAMA, 1968

Rehfisch, Hans José (1891–1960), German novelist and dramatist. Wrote documentary plays and satirical COMEDIES on topical themes: *Wer weint um Juckenack?* (Who Weeps for J.?), fp 1924; 1925 VOLKSBÜHNE, Berlin, dir PISCATOR; *Nickel und die 36 Gerechten* (N. and the 36 Just Men), fp 1925, performed simultaneously at 13 theatres; *Die Affäre Dreyfus* (The Dreyfus Affair), written with W. Herzog, fp 1929, Volksbühne; *Wasser für Canitoga* (Water for C.), written with O. E. Eis, under the pseudonym G. Turner, Bochum and Vienna, 1936, made into a film with ALBERS; *Oberst Chabert* (Colonel Chabert), based on a short story by BALZAC, fp Hamburg 1955. R.'s plays were published in two volumes in 1966.

Reichel, Käthe (1926–), German actress. Made her début with the BERLINER ENSEMBLE in 1951 as the maid servant in *Die Mutter* (BRECHT based on GORKY, 1951), and subsequently appeared in many leading roles including Margarethe in GOETHE's *Urfaust*, 1952; Shen Te in Brecht's *Der gute Mensch von Setzuan*, Rostock 1955, Berliner Ensemble 1957; Sophie von Beeskow in STERNHEIM's *1913*, Berlin 1964, Deutsches-Theater. Her reputation rests on politically committed acting, particularly as Saint Joan in: *Der Prozess der Jeanne d'Arc zu Rouen 1431* (Brecht/Seghers), Berliner Ensemble 1952, dir BESSON; *Saint Joan* (SHAW), 1956, 1965; *Die heilige Johanna der Schlachthöfe* (Brecht), Stuttgart and Rostock 1961, dir Besson. She was a close friend of Brecht.

Reicher, Emanuel (1849–1924), German actor. After several years in the provinces, went to BERLIN in 1887, made his début in 1888 as Othello at the Royal Theatre and appeared in the same year as Iago. He was one of the founders of the FREIE BÜHNE in 1889; from 1894 worked at the Deutsches-Theater and in 1899 founded an academy of dramatic art, later a dramatic society. He was a pioneer of the naturalistic school of acting, who excelled in plays by HAUPTMANN, IBSEN and WEDEKIND.

Reigbert, Otto (1890–1957), German stage designer. Best known for his collaboration with the director FALCKENBERG, most of whose productions he designed: BRECHT's *Trommeln in der Nacht*, 1922; BRONNEN's *Vatermord*, 1922; BARLACH's *Der tote Tag*, 1924; STRINDBERG's *Carl XII*, 1924; SHAKESPEARE's *Troilus and Cressida*, 1925; WEDEKIND's *Lulu*, 1928.

Reinhardt, Max (1873–1943), German director and manager. Made his début as an actor in 1893 in Salzburg and in 1894 joined the Deutsches-Theater, BERLIN, under the direction of BRAHM, appearing mainly in the roles of old men: Pastor in G. HAUPTMANN's *Die versunkene Glocke*, 1896; Foldal in *John Gabriel Borkman*, 1897, and Engstrand in *Ghosts*, 1900, by IBSEN. Gradually he turned away from Brahm's NATURALISM and in 1898 founded the Sezessionsbühne with other members of the Brahm Ensemble and toured with MAETERLINCK's *The Intruder* in 1899. In 1901 he appeared in the CABARET 'Schall und Rauch' as well as at the Deutsches-Theater; and the next year he formed his own Kleines-Theater; in 1903 the Neues-Theater where he successfully produced GORKY's *The Lower Depths*, in which he played Luka, 1903; WILDE's *Salomé*, 1903; SCHILLER's *Kabale und Liebe*, 1904. His final breakthrough came with his production – the first of many – of SHAKESPEARE's *A Midsummer Night's Dream* in 1905. The same year he took over the management of the Deutsches-Theater, Berlin; his brother Edmund was appointed administrative director, a post he held in all of R.'s theatrical enterprises. In his poetic, brilliantly acted and lavishly decorated productions of Shakespeare the most prominent German actors of his time appeared (BASSERMANN, SCHILDKRAUT, WEGENER, KAYSSLER, MOISSI, Camilla Eibenschütz, Else Heims, TILLA DURIEUX, LUCIE HÖFLICH, GERTRUD EYSOLDT), as well as some very fine character actors and comedians (Hans Wassmann, Alfred Abel, ARNOLD, Wilhelm Diegelmann). In 1906 R. opened – adjacent to the Deutsches-Theater – the Kammerspiele (chamber theatre) with a production of *Ghosts*; here also his famous productions of WEDEKIND's *Spring's Awakening*, 1906, and STRINDBERG's chamber plays.
His most characteristic productions made use of the widest possible range of dramatic effects: SOPHOCLES' *Oedipus Rex*, 1910 in the Concert Hall in Munich, then in the Zircus Schumann in Berlin, 1911 in Zircus Busch in Vienna; AESCHYLUS' *Oresteia*, 1911; Vollmöller's *The Miracle* (from 1911 in Berlin, Vienna, Budapest, London, New York). R. was director of the VOLKSBÜHNE, Berlin, 1915–18. In 1917 he founded an avant-garde theatre, Das junge Deutschland, where he produced two Expressionist plays: SORGE's *Der Bettler*, 1917, and GOERING's *Die Seeschlacht*, 1918; but the Expressionists' striving towards stylization, ecstasy, political involvement was essentially alien to him. His diverse, far-reaching, in some ways often eclectic, sensual and beguiling theatrical productions were heavily attacked by critics even before World War I, mainly by KERR. He was considered the theatrical exponent of the Wilhelminian era. In 1919 he opened the Grosses Schauspielhaus in Berlin, rebuilt by the architect POELZIG to replace the original Zircus Schumann, with Shakespeare's *Hamlet* and ROLLAND's *Danton*. In 1917 he founded with Richard Strauss and HOFMANNSTHAL the SALZBURG FESTIVAL where he staged a new production of the latter's adaptation of *Jedermann*, performed since 1920 in front of the cathedral, and his *Das Salzburger Grosse Welttheater*, Kollegienkirche 1922; GOETHE's *Faust* I, FELSENREITSCHULE 1933–37. He had previously produced operas including Strauss's *Der Rosenkavalier*, fp Dresden 1911, and *Ariadne auf Naxos*, fp Stuttgart, 1912.
It was the success of JESSNER and EXPRESSIONISM that drove R. from Berlin; in October 1920 he appointed Felix Holländer to run his theatres there and moved to Vienna. In the Redoutensaal of the Vienna Hofburg he produced: CALDERÓN/Hofmannsthal's *Dame Kobold*, 1922, and Goethe's *Clavigo*, 1922; and in 1924 opened the newly renovated Theater in der Josefstadt with GOLDONI's *The Servant of Two Masters*, followed by Schiller's *Kabale und Liebe* and Hofmannsthal's *Der Schwierige*. He proclaimed the actor to be the centre of the theatre and referred to his newly founded theatre as 'the actors of the Theater in der Josefstadt under the direction of Max Reinhardt'. In the same year he returned to Berlin and opened a new theatre, the Komödie am Kurfürstendamm, with PIRANDELLO's *Six Characters in Search of an Author*, 1924, and at the Deutsches-Theater successfully directed SHAW's *Saint Joan*, 1924, and

The Apple Cart, 1929. The world economic crisis also affected R.'s theatres. He kept away from Berlin 1929–32, and in 1933 moved to Austria, having formally handed over the Deutsches-Theater to the German people in a letter to Goebbels; in 1938 he went to the USA and settled in Hollywood where he married the actress HELENE THIMIG. His main achievement was that he finally established the director's theatre in Central Europe. He carefully planned his productions and came to the rehearsals with a detailed *Regiebuch* (production script) but was nevertheless open to suggestions from actors. His intuitive understanding of actors, his feeling for ENSEMBLE playing, for DIALOGUE and the dramatic function of the set formed the basis of his genius.
Bibl: H. Braulich, 1966

Réjane (Gabrielle-Charlotte Réju; 1856–1920), French actress. Made her début in 1875 at the Vaudeville and later appeared alternately there and at the Odéon in many plays which are forgotten today. She was an extremely attractive woman, possessed of great sensibility and charm, and in her heyday was considered one of the most 'modern' and finest comic actresses of her generation. Her prominent admirers included Marcel Proust. Among her finest parts were: E. DE GONCOURT's *Germinie Lacerteux*, 1888; MEILHAC's *Ma Cousine*, 1890; SARDOU's *Madame Sans-Gêne*, 1893; Berton/Simon's *Zaza*, 1898. In 1906 she opened her own theatre in Paris, Théâtre Réjane (former Théâtre Nouveau), where she acted and produced COMEDIES, mainly by Niccodemi.
Bibl: C. Antona-Traversi, 1931

Renaissance theatre. Initially the rediscovery of classical texts, mainly the COMEDIES of PLAUTUS and TRAGEDIES of SENECA. First produced by the Humanists: *Hippolytus*, 1486, by Pomponius Laetus, and Plautus' *Menaechmi*, 1486, at the Court of the d'Este family in Ferrara. Theatre architecture and stage design was based on VITRUVIUS' treatise *De Architectura*: a *skene* (▷AMPHITHEATRE) with five entrance doors, and an open front stage was used for the production of TERENCE's *Poenulus*, 1513, Rome, on the Capitol. First German Humanist production based on the Roman model: Reuchlin directed his own play *Henno* in 1497 at Pforzheim. Rapid development of various forms: SCHOOL DRAMA, COURT THEATRE, PASTORAL PLAYS, tragedies and comedies.
Humanist tragedies: horror-dramas including Giraldi's *Orbecche*, performed 1541, in one basic décor, in Ferrara; JODELLE's *Cléopâtre captive*, 1552, by the Hôtel de Reims in Paris before a set representing the façade of a palace.
Humanist comedies: productions of Plautus in Ferrara before a backdrop depicting a street; 1509 ARIOSTO's *I Suppositi*, also performed 1519 in Rome with a set by RAPHAEL depicting the city of Ferrara (an English translation by George Gascoigne was performed at Gray's Inn in 1566). In 1513 *La Calandria* by BIBBIENA was performed in Urbino, in a set with some three-

Max Reinhardt's production of *The Miracle* by Vollmöller at Olympia, London, 1912

Ada Rehan and DREW in *The Railroad of Love*

Réjane as the Prince de Sagan, a photograph which was inscribed to Proust

Renaissance theatre, production of TERENCE's *Giudonis Juvenalis*, 1493

dimensional elements; when it was revived in 1518 in Rome, PERUZZI designed a set with a fully three-dimensional perspective. Renaissance theatre architecture reached its height in the building of the Teatro Olimpico, designed by PALLADIO, in Vicenza, which opened in 1584 with a production of SOPHOCLES' *Oedipus Rex*. In 1520 MACHIAVELLI's *La Mandragola* was presented in Florence and Rome.
Pastoral plays: TASSO rehearsed and produced his *L'Aminta* in 1573 on the Island of Belvedere in the Po at the country villa of the d'Este family. GUARINI's *Pastor Fido* (The Faithful Shepherd) was presented in Cremona in 1595. It was performed in English in 1601, and in Latin by the King's College Men, 1605.
Court festivities: displays of power as well as claim to political power were the motivation for the *trionfi* (triumphal processions with elaborately designed floats), e.g. Milan 1490, a festival was presented by order of Lodovico Sforza to win the favour of the young Isabella of Aragon. Lodovico himself developed the idea, B. Bellincioni wrote the oration, LEONARDO designed the décor and costumes (a movable system of planets, costumes for gods and goddesses, masks for wild men and legendary animals). From the *trionfi* later developed opera and ballet; in England interludes and MASQUES. The *trionfi* marked the transition to the BAROQUE THEATRE.

Renaud, Madeleine (1903–), French actress. She trained at the CONSERVATOIRE D'ART DRAMATIQUE and made her début in 1921 as Cécile in MUSSET's *Il ne faut jurer de rien* at the COMÉDIE-FRANÇAISE, where she remained for 25 years. In the same year she made a historic appearance as Agnès in MOLIÈRE's *L'Ecole des femmes*, a part in which she appeared for about 10 years. Her wide range included Angélique in Molière's *George Dandin*, parts in plays by MUSSET, MARIVAUX, FLERS and CAILLAVET, H. BERNSTEIN, etc. In 1940 she married BARRAULT (her third husband) and appeared under his direction in 1943 in CLAUDEL's *Le Soulier de satin*, She left the CF with him in 1946 and together they founded the Compagnie Renaud-Barrault, which has greatly enriched theatrical life in France, and has also toured extensively abroad. She has appeared in leading roles in almost all their productions: Molière's *Amphitryon*, 1947; CAMUS's *L'État de siège*, 1948; MONTHERLANT's *Malatesta*, 1950; SARDOU's *Madame Sans-Gêne*, 1957; Winnie in BECKETT's *Oh les Beaux Jours*, 1963; Madame Verdúret-Balades in BILLETDOUX's *Il faut passer par les nuages*, 1964; M. DURAS's *Des Journées entières dans les arbres*, 1966. She has also acted in many films.

Rennert, Günther (1911–), German director. He was INTENDANT of the Hamburg State Opera, 1946–56, and then guest director in Hamburg, Stuttgart, Milan, London, Glyndebourne and New York till his appointment in 1967 as Intendant of the Munich State Opera. One of the leading contemporary directors of opera, he has rediscovered many rarely performed works and staged first productions of many modern operas. His productions are well thought out, highly imaginative and often in a playful vein. Apart from opera he has also directed straight plays: GOGOL's *The Government Inspector*, 1958; BRECHT's *Leben des Galileï*, 1955; GIRAUDOUX's *La Folle de Chaillot*, 1960; MOLIÈRE's *Tartuffe*, 1964, etc.
Bibl: W. E. Schäfer, 1962

Renoir, Pierre (1885–1952), French actor. Son of the painter Auguste R., he made his stage début in 1908 at the Odéon and reached the peak of his career during the 24 years he worked with the director JOUVET, in several GIRAUDOUX plays: first in the title role of *Siegfried*, fp 1928, then as Jupiter in *Amphitryon 38*, 1929; and as Ulysse in *La Guerre de Troie n'aura pas lieu*, 1935; then as MOLIÈRE's Dom Juan, 1949, and as Orgon in *Tartuffe*, 1950. After Jouvet's death he succeeded him as a director of the Théâtre de l'Athénée. He also appeared in many films.

Repertoire (Fr=stock list). The stock of parts (of an actor) or of plays (of a company of actors) which are ready to be performed, or which can form the programme of a given season.

Repertory (Anglicized form of repertoire). When a company of actors has several plays ready for production and performs them alternately rather than *en suite* (the same play every evening until the run definitely ends) they are said to be appearing 'in repertory'. Where permanent companies exist, particularly if they are subsidized National Theatres like the COMÉDIE-FRANÇAISE or the BURGTHEATER, they have a large REPERTOIRE of plays which can be performed in a varied repertory. In Britain the movement for the establishment of permanent companies, particularly outside London where the habit of touring West End successes had spread towards the end of the 19th century, became known as the 'repertory movement' and led to the establishment of repertory theatres in many of the larger provincial centres. The impulse came from ANNIE HORNIMAN who, after participating in the foundation of the ABBEY THEATRE in Dublin, started repertory theatres in Manchester and Liverpool in the first decade of the 20th century. But most of the so-called repertory theatres which have since been established in Britain do not present plays in genuine repertory, but usually for runs of three weeks. In Britain the NATIONAL THEATRE and the ROYAL SHAKESPEARE COMPANY, both at Stratford-upon-Avon and at their London headquarters, are the only companies which regularly present plays in genuine repertory.

Restoration drama. Term applied to plays written during the period following the restoration of the monarchy in England with the installation of Charles II as king in 1660. The ban on theatrical entertainment, imposed by the Puritans in 1642 was finally raised, and DAVENANT and KILLIGREW were given patents to re-open public theatres (e.g. THEATRE ROYAL, DRURY LANE, 1662). As part of the reaction to the long era of Puritanism, a wealth of dramatic writing ensued, the chief figures in this field being DRYDEN, ETHEREGE, WYCHERLEY, CONGREVE, J. VANBRUGH and FARQUHAR. The plays were generally witty comedies of manners, noted for their uninhibited style and sometimes licentious content.

Revolving stage. A circular movable platform which enables fast scene changes to be made. Used by LEONARDO in Milan 1490, and by the Japanese *Kabuki* theatre from 1658. In modern European theatre introduced in Munich in 1896, to enable quick scene changes of three-dimensional sets in naturalistic theatre.

Revue (Fr=survey, march-past). A form of theatrical performance consisting of a loosely connected sequence of sketches, songs, dance-numbers etc. Developed in England (by Albert de Courville, André Charlot, Alfred Butt, COCHRAN) and in Germany, notably BERLIN, in the 1920s. In the USA it took the form of spectacular musical shows (ZIEGFELD, George White). In England 'intimate revue', introduced by Cochran, concentrated on wit and grace rather than large-scale spectacle, by employing fine high-comedy actors like GERTRUDE LAWRENCE, BEATRICE LILLIE and COWARD. The genre declined after World War II.

Rhetoric. The ancient art of oratory, in antiquity regarded as one of the foremost branches of human skill. Elaborate rules of exposition, style and techniques of persuasion were worked out by Roman authors like CICERO (*De Inventione*) and notably Quintilian (*Institutio Oratoria, c.* AD 95). These rules exercised an important influence on literature throughout the Middle Ages and the Renaissance, and therefore, indirectly on the art of composition of speeches in plays. A link between rhetoric itself and the public theatrical performances was formed by such French groups of poets and orators as the Rhétoriqueurs, or the Dutch REDERIJKERS. With the coming of more realistic modes of playwriting, based on the observation of actual habits of speech rather than the copying of ideal models of elaborate speechmaking, the influence of rhetoric on drama declined.

Ricci, Renzo (1899–), Italian actor. First appeared with the company of ZACCONI and IRMA GRAMATICA. In 1930 he formed his own company, 1935–39 worked with Laura Adani and after 1946 with Eva Magni. He was one of the first Italian ACTOR-MANAGERS; within the artistic framework of the TEATRO STABILE, he developed a director's theatre. Among directors who worked for his company were STREHLER (CAMUS's *Caligula*), SQUARZINA (IBSEN's *An Enemy of the People*) and Ferrero (ELIOT's *The Cocktail Party*). His roles ranged from BOULEVARD plays (HARTOG's *The Fourposter*, 1952) to classical parts (Tiresias in AESCHYLUS' *The Persians*, 1950); he excelled in SHAKESPEARE, e.g. as Bassanio in *The Merchant of Venice* (Venice 1934, dir REIN-

HARDT), title roles in *Hamlet, Othello, Macbeth, King Lear, Richard III* (PICCOLO TEATRO DI MILANO, 1952, dir Strehler).

Riccoboni. (1) **Luigi Andrea R.** (known as Lelio; 1676–1753), Italian actor. From 1699 tried to start a theatre in Northern Italy after the French model in antithesis to the COMMEDIA DELL'ARTE. From 1716 he managed the COMÉDIE-ITALIENNE in Paris under the protection of the Duke of Orléans, and 1729–31 he was Comptroller of the Royal Household in Parma, returning to Paris in 1733. LESSING included some of R.'s *canevas* (scenario of the c. dell'a.) in his *Theatralische Bibliothek.* He also wrote several books on the theatre including a history of the Italian Theatre in 2 vols, published in Paris 1728 and 1731, and *Riflessioni sulla rappresentazione*, 1738. His son (2) **Antonio Francesco R.** (known as Lelio *fils*; 1707–72), appeared 1726–50 with the Comédie-Italienne in Paris, wrote several COMEDIES and in 1750 published *L'Art du théâtre* (in the same year Lessing published the German version; rev. edition 1954) in which he discusses the extent to which feeling should dominate acting. His wife, (3) **Marie-Jeanne de la Boras** (known as Madame R.; 1713–92), was the author of several comedies in the style of MARIVAUX and was a friend of DIDEROT.
Bibl: E. A. Crosby, MADAME RICCOBONI, 1924

Rice, Elmer (E. L. Reizenstein; 1892–1967), US dramatist, director and producer. He was successful with his first play *On Trial*, New York, 1914, and also with *The Adding Machine*, 1923, a grim satirical fantasy on the world of automation. After his next play *Street Scene*, 1929, awarded the PULITZER PRIZE (new version with music by WEILL, 1947), he turned to directing as well, and from 1931 produced most of his own plays. In 1937, with S. HOWARD, BEHRMAN, SHERWOOD and M. ANDERSON, he formed the PLAYWRIGHTS' COMPANY, which produced the plays of the dramatists involved. Other works include: *Counsellor-at-Law*, 1931; *We, the People*, 1933; *Judgment Day*, 1934; *Not for Children*, pub 1935, fp 1951; *American Landscape*, 1938; *Dream Girl*, 1945; *The Winner*, 1954. His productions of other playwrights' work: Sherwood's *Abe Lincoln in Illinois*, 1938; M. Anderson's *Journey to Jerusalem*, 1940; Behrman's *The Talley Method*, 1941.
Bibl: J. W. Krutch, THE AMERICAN DRAMA SINCE 1918, 1957

Rich, Claude (1929–), French actor. Successful in Paris BOULEVARD THEATRE, but since 1955 has made his career mainly in films. His best stage appearances include: Sébastien in Françoise Sagan's *Un Château en Suède*, 1960, dir BARSAQ; title role in VITRAC's *Victor, ou les enfants au pouvoir*, 1962, dir ANOUILH and R. Piétri; Lenny in PINTER's *The Homecoming*, 1966.

Richardson, Sir Ralph (1902–), English actor. Knighted in 1947. First professional appearance in 1921. With the BIRMINGHAM REPERTORY THEATRE, 1926. First London

Elmer Rice's *The Adding Machine*, New York 1923

Ralph Richardson as Falstaff at the OLD VIC, 1945

Madeleine Renaud in GENET's *Les Paravents*, at the Théâtre de France, 1967

appearance in the same year; joined the OLD VIC THEATRE company in 1930 and soon became one of the leading actors in Britain, and played many parts in SHAKESPEARE, SHAW and a number of other classical and modern authors. Toured the USA for the first time in 1935. Co-director 1944–47, with OLIVIER and John Burrell, of the Old Vic company in its famous seasons at the New Theatre, London. During this period he gave outstanding performances as Falstaff, Uncle Vanya, Peer Gynt, and created the part of Inspector Goole in PRIESTLEY's *An Inspector Calls*. His range is prodigious. He excels in the parts of ordinary people who suddenly reveal demonic qualities or profound emotion, e.g. a modern EVERYMAN in Priestley's *Johnson over Jordan*, 1939, or a mysteriously ordinary inmate of a mental asylum in STOREY's *Home*, 1970.

Richardson, Tony (1928–), English director. Appointed associate director of the ENGLISH STAGE COMPANY in 1956, his first success came with OSBORNE's early plays including *Look Back in Anger*, 1956; *The Entertainer*, 1957 (title role, OLIVIER); *Luther*, 1961 (title role FINNEY), both of which he also directed on BROADWAY, 1963, as well as BRECHT's *Arturo Ui*, 1963, and T. WILLIAMS's *The Milk Train Doesn't Stop Here Anymore*, 1964. In London, he was responsible for notable productions of IONESCO's *The Chairs*, 1957, and CHEKHOV's *The Seagull*, 1964, with his wife VANESSA REDGRAVE in the lead. In 1959 he directed *Othello*, with ROBESON, at STRATFORD-UPON-AVON. In London he staged the first English production of Brecht's *St Joan of the Stockyards*, 1969. His work with Prospect Productions for which he directed SHAKESPEARE's *Richard II* and MARLOWE's *Edward II*, 1964, with Ian McKellen in both title roles, was also outstanding. He is one of the leading directors in England; his style is realistic, always conscious of the social context. He is also one of the exponents of Free Cinema London and has directed several films, e.g. *Look Back in Anger*, *Tom Jones* and *The Charge of the Light Brigade*. In 1969 he founded the Free Theatre in London which opened with a production of *Hamlet*.

Richelieu (Armand Jean du Plessis, Cardinal de; 1585–1642), French statesman and patron of the theatre. Helped to establish professional theatre in France and inspired a group of playwrights – CORNEILLE, ROTROU, BOISROBERT, Colletet and Claude de l'Etoile – who wrote several plays based on his ideas, e.g. *La Comédie des Tuileries*, 1635. He also patronized the actor MONTDORY, whom he often invited to his palace to play before him, and was a friend of Corneille, whom he championed in the famous literary quarrel over *Le Cid* in 1637.
Bibl: L. Battifol, RICHELIEU ET CORNEILLE, 1936

Ristori, Adelaide (1822–1906), Italian actress. Member of an acting family, she was already appearing on stage at the age of 14 in a successful production of *Francesca da Rimini* (S. Pellico). From 1838 she was leading lady of several companies, excelling in parts such as Juliet in *Romeo and Juliet*; GOLDONI's *La Locandiera*; SCHILLER's *Maria Stuart*, and in ALFIERI's *Antigone*, *Ottavia* and *Rosamunda*. After her marriage in 1847 she retired for some time from the theatre. From 1853 till her retirement in 1885 she mostly toured in Europe and the USA (first appearance 1866). In her Paris début in 1855 she won instant acclaim from the audience and the critics (DUMAS PÈRE, Janin, GAUTIER, etc.). She was praised for the dignity and strength of her acting, and soon became a serious rival to RACHEL.
Bibl: G. Di Martino, 1908

Rittner, Rudolf (1869–1943), Austrian actor. Working in the field of German NATURALISM, he was discovered by BRAHM during his period as a drama critic and engaged by him in 1894 at the Deutsches-Theater, BERLIN. He became an outstanding interpreter of IBSEN and HAUPTMANN, excelling as Oswald in Ibsen's *Ghosts* and creating the title role in Hauptmann's *Fuhrmann Henschel*, 1898. He mainly played opposite the actress ELSE LEHMANN; both represented Brahm's style of acting, emphasizing 'naturalness' as against any kind of virtuosity. In 1907 he retired at the peak of his career, and devoted the rest of his life to farming.
Bibl: J. Bab, KRÄNZE DEM MIMEN, 1954

Robbins, Jerome (1918–), US choreographer and director. In 1949 appointed associate director (with Balanchine) of the New York City Ballet, and in 1958 formed his own company – Ballets: USA. As a choreographer he prefers abstract ballet without PLOT; as a director of musicals his charm and spontaneity are overwhelming. His productions include one of the greatest successes in American post-war theatre: *West Side Story*, 1957, of which he did both the choreography and direction, music L. BERNSTEIN, LIBRETTO by LAURENTS. Other works: *On the Town* (music L. BERNSTEIN), 1944, and *Billion Dollar Baby*, 1945, both by Betty Comden and Adolph Green; *The King and I*, 1951, musical by RODGERS and HAMMERSTEIN II, dir VAN DRUTEN, des MIELZINER. His best-known production of a straight play is KOPIT's *Oh, Dad, Poor Dad, Mamma's Hung You in the Closet and I'm Feeling So Sad*, 1962. He also produced BRECHT's *Mother Courage*, 1963, and directed the musical *Fiddler on the Roof*, 1964, which gained international renown.
Bibl: A. H. Franks, TWENTIETH-CENTURY BALLET, 1954

Robertson, Thomas William (1829–71), English playwright. From a theatrical family, he became an actor, but later gradually drifted towards journalism. His main contribution to English theatrical history is the introduction of serious social comment and a realistic style into what was then the highly melodramatic mode of English playwriting. He wrote: *Society*, 1865; *Ours*, 1866; *Caste*, 1867; *Play*, 1868; *School*, 1869, and *The M.P.*, 1870. As portraits of society, their realism earned them the sobriquet 'cup and saucer comedies' because so much emphasis was laid on accurately reproducing actual modes of human behaviour. He influenced the way they were produced and in some ways was also a precursor of the modern notion of the director. *Caste* is regarded as one of the precursors of NATURALISM on the British stage; it is still in the REPERTOIRE.

Robeson, Paul (1898–1976), Black US actor and singer. Son of a Methodist preacher, he obtained his LLB from Columbia University Law School in 1922. Made stage début in New York 1921 in *Simon the Cyrenian*. First outstanding parts were the lead in revivals of *All God's Chillun Got Wings*, 1924, and *The Emperor Jones*, 1925, both by O'NEILL. He sang in the London production of EDNA FERBER's *Show Boat*, 1928. He played *Othello* in London 1930 and in New York 1943. He undertook concert tours throughout Europe and the USA. Politically left-wing, he anticipated the Civil Rights movement. His autobiography, *Here I stand*, was published 1958.

Robey, Sir George (1869–1954), English MUSIC HALL artist and actor. Knighted shortly before he died in 1954. Nicknamed 'the Prime Minister of Mirth', he made his début in the halls in 1891 and became one of the most popular performers, a figure of portentous dignity. Also acted in 'legitimate' theatre, notably as Falstaff in *Henry IV*, Part I, London 1935, His Majesty's Theatre, and appeared in films, his most noteworthy performance being his Sancho Panza opposite Chaliapin's Don Quixote in G. W. Pabst's film (1933). Wrote two autobiographical volumes *My Life up to now* and *Looking Back on Life*.

Robins, Elisabeth (1862–1952), US actress. She passed the greater part of her life in London where she first appeared in 1889. She became identified with the introduction of IBSEN and played many leading roles in the first productions of *The Pillars of Society*, 1889; *A Doll's House* and *Hedda Gabler*, 1891. She also acted in *The Master Builder*, *Rosmersholm*, *Brand*, *Little Eyolf* and *John Gabriel Borkman*, and played the title role in *Mariana* by ECHEGARAY in 1897. She then retired and devoted herself to writing novels and two volumes of theatrical reminiscences.

Robinson, Lennox (1886–1958), Irish man of the theatre. Playwright, critic manager, actor, and director, he was intimately connected with the development of the ABBEY THEATRE, Dublin, where for many years he was manager and artistic director, and where his first play, *The Clancy Name*, 1908, was produced. Other plays: *Harvest*, 1910; *Patriots*, 1912; *The Dreamers*, 1913; *The White-Headed Boy*, 1916; *The Lost Leader*, 1918; *Crabbed Youth and Age*, 1922; *The Big House*, 1926; *The Far-Off Hills*, 1928; *Give a Dog*, 1928; *Ever the Twain*, 1929; *All's Over Then?*, 1932; *Is Life Worth Living?*

(alternative title: *Drama at Inish*), 1933; *Church Street*, 1934; *When Lovely Woman*, 1936; *Killycreggs in Twilight*, 1937; *Forget-Me-not*, 1941; *The Lucky Finger*, 1948. A realist both in his political and social TRAGEDIES as in his COMEDIES, he gave a vivid picture of Irish life, displaying consummate skill in construction and characterization. Also noteworthy are his two volumes of autobiography *Three Houses*, 1938, and *Curtain Up*, 1942. He edited *Lady Gregory's Journals*, 1946, and wrote *Ireland's Abbey Theatre, a History, 1899–1951*, 1951. He published several volumes of critical essays.

Robinson, Madeleine (M. Svoboda; 1916–), French actress. A leading figure of the BOULEVARD THEATRE, she trained under DULLIN. She made her breakthrough in the theatre with the leading part in Ducreux's *Musique légère*, 1942. She toured widely in Latin America with CLAUDEL's *L'Otage* and BOURDET's *Hyménée*. In *Le Soif*, 1949, written for her by H. BERNSTEIN, she played the lead with Claude Dauphin and Jean Gabin.

Robson, Dame Flora (1902–), English actress. She was appointed a DBE in 1960. Trained at RADA and made her début in 1921 with GREET and Fagan's company at the Oxford Playhouse. After leaving the stage for four years, she returned in 1928 and soon became one of England's most popular character actresses, e.g. in the lead in O'NEILL's *Desire Under the Elms*, 1931; Olwen Peel in PRIESTLEY's *Dangerous Corner*, 1932; Ella Downey in O'Neill's *All God's Chillun Got Wings*, 1933. With the OLD VIC THEATRE company 1933–34: Katharine in *Henry VIII*, Isabella in *Measure for Measure*. In 1938 she went to Hollywood to make films and also appeared in plays in New York (*Ladies in Retirement*, 1940; *Damask Cheek*, 1942). Back in London, she appeared as Thérèse Raquin in *Guilty*, based on ZOLA, 1944; Lady Cicely in SHAW's *Captain Brassbound's Conversion*, 1949; in Lesley Storm's *Black Chiffon*, 1949; the governess in *The Innocents*, based on JAMES's *The Turn of the Screw*; Mrs Alving in IBSEN's *Ghosts*, Old Vic, 1958; the title role in BRECHT's *Mother Courage*, TV 1959; in an adaptation by REDGRAVE of James's *The Aspern Papers*, 1959; Mrs Borkman in Ibsen's *John Gabriel Borkman*, 1963.

Rodgers, Richard (1902–), US composer. Early in his career worked with L. HART, for whose lyrics he composed music for student productions, 1918. Their first great success came with *The Garrick Gaieties*, 1925, which led to a continuous collaboration resulting in the famous musicals: *The Connecticut Yankee*, 1927; *I Married an Angel*, 1937; *The Boys From Syracuse*, 1938; *Pal Joey*, 1940, *By Jupiter*, 1942, and many others. Hart wrote intelligent verse with punchy lines; after his death in 1943, R. found a new partner in HAMMERSTEIN II. With him, less sophisticated than Hart and also more sentimental, R. surpassed even his former successes, particularly with *Oklahoma!*, 1943; *Carousel*, 1945, based on

Jerome Robbins' production of *West Side Story*, New York 1957

George Robey as Dame Hubbard in *Goody-Two-Shoes*

Flora Robson in O'NEILL's *Desire Under the Elms*, London 1931

Rodgers and HAMMERSTEIN musical *Oklahoma!*, THEATRE GUILD, 1943

MOLNÁR's *Liliom*; *South Pacific*, 1949; *The King and I*, 1951; *The Sound of Music*, 1959. When Hammerstein died in 1961, R. wrote his own lyrics as well as music for *No Strings*, 1962, and has since collaborated with SONDHEIM among others.
Bibl: D. Ewen, PANORAMA OF AMERICAN POPULAR MUSIC, 1957; C. Smith, MUSICAL COMEDY IN AMERICA, 1950

Rojas, Fernando de (1465–1541), Spanish writer. Either wrote or completed *La Celestina*, a piece in DIALOGUE divided into acts, also known as *Tragicomedia de Calisto y Melibea*. The first part was written in 1499 and, because of its extraordinary length and its uninhibited depiction of low life, was probably never meant for stage performance, but the beauty of the language and vivid realism of the characterization made it a popular work of world literature. The matchmaker Celestina in particular became a classical character of Spanish literature. The play also influenced drama in Spain and England, and modern adaptations are still being staged; English versions by John Rastell, *c.* 1530; James Mabbe, 1631; Phyllis Hartnoll, 1959.
Bibl: N. Bataillon, LA CELESTINA, 1961

Rolland, Romain (1866–1944), French novelist and dramatist. He is today remembered most for his ten-volume novel *Jean Christophe*, 1903–12. He attempted to supplant the commercial theatre with one for the people, and also wrote two monumental play cycles, *Tragédies de la foi* and *Tragédies de la révolution* which expressed his idealism, often in symbolic terms. The cycle plays included: *Les Loups*, 1898, inspired by the Dreyfus case; *Le Triomphe de la raison*, 1899; *Danton*, 1900 (famous production by REINHARDT, Berlin 1919); *Le Quatorze Juillet*, 1903; *Le Temps viendra*, 1903; *Le Jeu de l'amour et de la mort*, 1928; *Pâques fleuris*, pub 1926, and *Les Léonides*, pub 1928, fp 1948. Other historical plays include *Robespierre*, 1938, fp Leipzig 1952. He was awarded the Nobel Prize for Literature, 1915.
Bibl: W. T. Starr, 1950; M. Descotes, 1948.

Roller, Alfred (1864–1935), Austrian stage designer. His first sets were for the Viennese Hofoper in 1903, under the direction of Mahler, including Wagner's *Tristan und Isolde*, in which colour was used to reinforce the music. With his movable sets for Mozart's *Don Giovanni*, 1905, he made a decisive contribution towards freeing the stage from romantic illusionism. He gained international renown with his designs for Richard Strauss's *Der Rosenkavalier*, Dresden 1911, dir REINHARDT. In 1935 he designed sets for *Parsifal* at the BAYREUTH Festival. His collaboration with Reinhardt resulted in two other famous productions: AESCHYLUS' *Oresteia*, Munich 1911, and SOPHOCLES' *Oedipus Rex*, Berlin 1911, Zircus Schumann.

Romains, Jules (Louis Farigoule; 1885–1972), French poet, novelist and playwright. His early dramatic work, like his novels, proclaims the philosophy of life of *Unanimisme* (superiority of the group as against the individual). He was, for a time, a collaborator at COPEAU's Théâtre du Vieux-Colombier, where his second play *Cromedeyre-le-Vieil* was first staged in 1920; and Copeau's pupils, JOUVET, DULLIN and PITOËFF successfully produced R.'s later plays. His best known ones are probably his satires on the medical profession, *Knock ou le Triomphe de la médecine*, successfully directed and acted by Jouvet in 1923, and *Donogoo-Tonka*, 1930. Several of his plays are still in the REPERTOIRE of the COMÉDIE-FRANÇAISE.

Romberg, Sigmund (1887–1951), Hungarian-born US composer of operettas and MUSICAL COMEDIES. Came to New York at the age of 21, worked as a café pianist, then started his own orchestra. Having composed a number of highly successful popular songs, he entered into a connection with the Shubert management for whom he wrote a number of hit operettas: *Maytime* (LIBRETTO by Rida Johnson Young, based on a German original), 1917; *Sinbad* (in collaboration with JOLSON, libretto by H. Atteridge), 1918; *Blossom Time* (adapted from Berté's Viennese original with music taken from the melodies of Franz Schubert; American libretto by D. Donnelly), 1921; *The Student Prince* (based on the German play *Alt Heidelberg*, libretto by Donnelly), 1924, one of R.'s greatest triumphs; *The Desert Song*, another major hit (libretto by O. Harbach, HAMMERSTEIN II and F. Mandel), 1926; *New Moon*, which contained some of R.'s most popular tunes (libretto by Hammerstein II, F. Mandel and L. Schwab), 1928. In 1930 he went to Hollywood to work for the cinema. After the war he turned from old-fashioned operetta to the new genre of the American musical: *Up in Central Park* (libretto by H. and D. FIELDS), 1947; *The Girl in Pink Tights* (libretto by J. Chodorov and J. FIELDS), 1954. His fertility of invention and the size of his output – in addition to his most successful works quoted above, he wrote many others, alone or in collaboration with other composers, as well as adapting numerous European originals – made R. one of the most popular composers of light music of all time.

Rome. The theatre of ancient Rome is strongly dependent on Greek models. Its history starts with the translation of Greek COMEDIES by LIVY (*c.* 284–204 BC) and reaches its peak in the comedies of PLAUTUS and TERENCE, which, however, are all based on Greek originals from which they are freely adapted. In the plays of Plautus the main emphasis is on theatrical effectiveness and vulgar popular humour, whereas Terence has more literary ambitions, writes much more carefully constructed, well-made PLOTS and avoids the more coarse-grained effects. In spite of its reliance on Greek plots, the Roman comedy – through its use of Roman RHETORIC, Roman modes of thought and speech – must be regarded as an original contribution to the development of European theatre: it has had a considerable influence on the SCHOOL DRAMA of the Renaissance, on MOLIÈRE, GOLDONI, HOLBERG, KLEIST and many other European playwrights. Side by side with this genre, performed in Greek costume and labelled *fabula palliata* (after the Greek garment, the *pallium*, ▷PALLIATA) there existed the original Roman popular comedy, the *fabula atellana* (▷ATELLAN FARCE) which relied on a large number of stock-types (the slaves MACCUS and Buccus, the fool Pappus, the hunchback DOSSENUS), rather like the later Italian COMMEDIA DELL'ARTE. A direct continuity from the *fabula atellana* to the c. dell'a. has been suggested, but remains unproven. A third genre, the *fabula togata* (after the *toga*, the characteristic Roman garment), relies on purely Roman subject matter but is more refined and regular (▷FABULA). Its main representatives are Titinius, Atta, of whose works only a few lines are extant, and AFRANIUS (44 titles of his plays are known and about 400 lines preserved). While the Greek theatre building developed from the orchestra, the area where the CHORUS danced, in the Roman theatre the stage itself is of major importance from the very beginning. The buildings which have been preserved are all of relatively late date; but one basic feature is important from the outset: the stage shows the façade of a house with three doors, which can also stand for the doors of three different houses. The action thus is deemed to take place in the street. Entrance to the performances of Roman comedy was free; they were financed – as were the gladiatorial contests – by gifts of patrons, mostly public officials, i.e. state funds. The popular comedy was eventually overtaken in popularity by the Roman *pantomimus*. Performances of TRAGEDY in public were not customary in Rome. Instead there were recitations in private, usually by a single actor, who concentrated on the highlights of the plays. The only completely preserved Roman tragedies, those of SENECA, were not written for full-scale performance but for recitation. ▷COMEDY, TRAGEDY.
Bibl: G. E. Duckworth, THE NATURE OF ROMAN COMEDY, 1967; W. Beare, THE ROMAN STAGE, 3/1965; M. Bieber, THE HISTORY OF THE GREEK AND ROMAN THEATRE, 2/1961

Ronconi, Luca (1913–), Italian director. Trained at the Accademia Nazionale d'Arte Drammatica in Rome; for several years appeared with GASSMAN's company, later turned to directing and in 1966 gained his first notable success with a production of his own adaptation of MIDDLETON's *The Changeling*. Other well-known productions include: SHAKESPEARE's *Measure for Measure*, 1967, *Richard III*, and Giordano Bruno's *Candelaio*, both 1968, all with the ensemble of the TEATRO STABILE in Turin. With the Teatro Libero di Roma, R. produced a highly original adaptation of ARIOSTO's *Orlando Furioso*, 1969, in which he revived the tradition of Italian folk spectacle in a freely-structured space.

Roscius (Quintus Roscius Gallus; *c.* 125–62 BC), Roman actor. Best in comic roles

(parasite, procurer), but also appeared in TRAGEDY; a friend of Cicero, who defended him in a trial in 76 BC with a famous speech. According to Diomedes it was R. who first introduced the mask to hide his squint. Born a slave, he won his freedom through acting and also became so rich (Cicero tells us that his yearly income amounted to 6 million *sestertii*) that in his later years he dispensed with any sort of salary.
Bibl: F. W. Wright, CICERO AND THE THEATRE, 1931

Rose Theatre. Opened by HENSLOWE on the south bank of the Thames in 1587 with a capacity of 2,500 spectators. It is not known which company first played there, but 1594–1600 the ADMIRAL'S MEN (with whom SHAKESPEARE was associated) settled there. The theatre was pulled down *c.* 1606.
Bibl: E. K. Chambers, THE ELIZABETHAN STAGE, 1923, 4 vols

Rossi, Ernesto (1827–96), Italian actor, one of the greatest of his time. He performed from 1846 with MODENA's company, whose psychological approach served him as a model. In 1855 he appeared successfully in Paris with the famous Italian actress ADELAIDE RISTORI. He reached the zenith of his career as manager of his own company, founded in 1864, with a REPERTOIRE of classical Italian TRAGEDIES, e.g. ALFIERI, romantic dramas (HUGO, DUMAS), and adaptations (*Enrico Faust* by Montazio, after GOETHE), in many of which he starred. He became widely known for his interpretations of SHAKESPEARE, particularly *Hamlet* and *Othello*, Paris 1866; he also appeared in *Le Cid*. From 1870 he was on tour almost continuously in Latin America, Russia, Egypt, the USA and Germany in Shakespearean roles including Hamlet, Othello, Lear, Macbeth, Coriolanus, Richard III, Shylock etc.; he gained enormous success particularly in Latin countries, where Shakespeare was still largely unknown. He represented the confident virtuoso actor, his interpretation of characters relying on precisely observed details.
Bibl: C. Guetta, 1906

Rosso di San Secondo, Pier Maria (1887–1956), Italian dramatist and novelist. His grotesque and lyrical dramas were influenced by CHIARELLI and PIRANDELLO. Their recurring themes, such as the conflict between reality and illusion, freedom and social convention, are treated with great dramatic power, particularly in his best-known play *Marionette, che passione!* (Puppets, what a Passion!), Milan 1918, which shows man as a puppet of fate. Other major works include: *La bella addormentata* (The Sleeping Beauty), Milan 1919; *Primavera* (Spring), Milan 1919; *L'ospite desiderata* (The Longed-for Guest), Milan 1921; *Amara*, Modena 1923; *I peccati di gioventú* (The Sins of Youth), Milan 1923; *L'avventura terrestre* (The Earthly Adventure), Milan 1924; *Par fare l'alba* (It seems dawn), Rome 1919; *L'illusione dei giorni e delle notti* (The Illusion of Days and Nights), Milan 1925; *La Signora Falkenstein*, Milan 1929; *Lo*

Roman actor, statuette in Vatican Museum

Roman stage, copy of wall-painting at Pompeii showing the basic façade of a house with three doors

Ernesto Rossi as Hamlet, 1876

spirito della morte (The Spirit of Death), Rome 1941; *Finestre* (Windows), Palermo 1954. He also translated Goethe's *Die Geschwister* and wrote several books on the theatre, including *Luigi Pirandello*, 1916.
Bibl: L. Pirandello, SAGGI, 1960; G. Calendoli, IL TEATRO DI ROSSO DI SAN SECONDO, 1956

Rostand, Edmond (1868–1918), French poet and dramatist. Best known for his VERSE DRAMA *Cyrano de Bergerac*, 1897, written for the elder COQUELIN, which became a favourite with many theatre audiences in Europe and the USA. Though sentimental and over-romantic, it is saved by a sense of humour. His other well-known play, which also reveals great theatrical craftsmanship, is *L'Aiglon*, 1900, dealing with the fate of Napoleon's son, a part which SARAH BERNHARDT played with resounding success at the age of 56. Other works include: *Les Romanesques*, 1894; *La Princesse lontaine*, 1895; *La Samaritaine*, 1897; *Chantecler*, 1910, with L. GUITRY; *La Dernière nuit de Don Juan*, 1922 posthumously. His son **Maurice R.** (1891–) is also a dramatist, best known for his play *L'Homme que j'ai tué*, 1930.

Rothe, Hans (1894–), German dramatist and translator. Worked as a DRAMATURG, first in Leipzig, 1920–25, then in BERLIN, Deutsches-Theater, 1926–30. In 1934 he emigrated to the USA, where he lectured on drama, 1947–53; now lives in Florence. He wrote several plays, *Keiner für alle* (No one for all), 1928; *Saint Eugénie*, 1941, but is best known for his SHAKESPEARE translations in colloquial German, which are virtually free adaptations and have been severely criticized. He published a treatise under the title *Shakespeare als Provokation*, 1961.

Rotrou, Jean de (1609–50), French dramatist. With CORNEILLE the leading playwright in the first half of the 17th century. At the age of 19 he became resident dramatist at the HÔTEL DE BOURGOGNE, writing TRAGI-COMEDIES and COMEDIES. The first French writer to take a Spanish dramatist as a model for his works, e.g. he translated LOPE DE VEGA. His *Venceslas*, 1647, was based on a comedy by ROJAS, the main character of Ladislas providing an excellent part for Montfleury and later for actors such as BARON, LEKAIN and TALMA. He also wrote a number of versions of the Amphitryon theme, of which *Les Sosies*, 1638, based on PLAUTUS, is considered his best play.
Bibl: R. Rigal, LE THÉÂTRE FRANÇAIS AVANT LA PÉRIODE CLASSIQUE, 1901; H. C. Lancaster, A HISTORY OF FRENCH DRAMATIC LITERATURE IN THE 17TH CENTURY, 1929–42, 9 vols

Rowe, Nicholas (1674–1718), English playwright. Studied law and was admitted to the Middle Temple in 1691, but later devoted himself wholly to literature. He wrote some successful TRAGEDIES: *The Fair Penitent*, 1703; *The Tragedy of Jane Shore*, 1714; *The Tragedy of Lady Jane Grey*, 1715. Other tragedies, *Ulysses*, 1705, and *The Royal Convert*, 1707, and a COMEDY *The Biter*, 1704, were less well received. But his greatest importance lies probably in his being the first critical editor of SHAKESPEARE. His edition, in six volumes, 1709, enlarged by the Poems to nine volumes, 1714, also contained the first biography of Shakespeare and remains one of the bases of all works on the same subject. He became Poet Laureate in 1715.

Rowley, William (*c.* 1585–1626), English actor and playwright. Of unknown origin, he was popular as an actor of fat clownish parts. He wrote some plays by himself – *All's Lost by Lust*, 1619; *A Shoemaker a Gentleman*, *c.* 1608; *A New Wonder, A Woman Never Vexed*, *c.* 1610; *A Match at Midnight*, *c.* 1607 – but mainly collaborated with other authors, having a particular talent for low comedy and MELODRAMA. Among the more notable of these collaborations are: *The Witch of Edmonton* (with DEKKER and FORD), 1621; *The Maid in the Mill* (with FLETCHER), 1623; *The Changeling* (with MIDDLETON), 1622; *The Spanish Gipsy* (with Middleton), 1623. In 1662 an edition of the play *The Birth of Merlin or The Child has found its Father* appeared with a title page claiming that it was written by R. in collaboration with SHAKESPEARE. While R. may have been connected with this play, Shakespeare almost certainly was not. It has also been suggested that some portions of the latter's *Pericles* were written by R.

Royal Academy of Dramatic Art (London). One of Britain's leading drama schools, it was founded in 1904 by TREE.

Royal Court Theatre. Opened in Sloane Square, London, in 1870. It first gained its place in the history of theatre under the joint management of GRANVILLE-BARKER (1877–1946) and VEDRENNE (1867–1930) in the period from 1904 to 1907 when it became the focal point of endeavours to introduce the modern, post-Naturalist theatre to ENGLAND – with performances of SCHNITZLER, HAUPTMANN, MAETERLINCK, YEATS, Granville-Barker's own plays and, above all, SHAW. Half a century after the close of that exciting period in its history the Royal Court again became the source of a revolution in English drama, when DEVINE established his ENGLISH STAGE COMPANY in the old house: OSBORNE, PINTER, WESKER, BOND, STOREY and many other important authors were launched here or at the Theatre Upstairs in the same building.

Royal Shakespeare Company. One of Britain's leading dramatic companies. It is subsidized by the ARTS COUNCIL. It received its present name in 1961, having emerged from the Stratford-upon-Avon Shakespeare Memorial Theatre Company. Ever since GARRICK had staged a SHAKESPEARE Jubilee at Stratford, Shakespeare's birthplace, in 1769, there had been efforts to establish a Shakespeare festival there. This was started on a modest scale in 1879. In 1926 the Victorian theatre building burned down. A new modern theatre was opened in 1932. Gradually the festival season was extended so that the festival lasted from April to the late autumn. When HALL was appointed director of the company in 1960 he decided that to establish a permanent ENSEMBLE and develop its own style he would have to keep the company together for the whole year and so he established a London home for the company at the Aldwych Theatre, where, apart from Shakespeare, the company could also tackle modern avant-garde drama. With BROOK and SAINT-DENIS as co-directors, Hall developed a distinctive modern Shakespeare style, staging BRECHT, PINTER and other contemporary authors. In 1968 one of the young directors who had emerged under Hall, NUNN (1940–) took over the artistic direction of the company from Hall. A new London home for the RSC is being built at the Barbican in the City of London.

Róziewicz, Tadeusz (1921–), Polish poet, dramatist and stage designer. Member of the Resistance movement during World War II; his poems expressed in agonizing style his disillusionment with post-war Poland, which is also the theme of his first Surrealist drama, *Kartoteka* (The Card Index), fp Warsaw 1960. His other dramatic works include *Grupa Laokoona* (The Laokoön Group), fp Warsaw 1962; *Swiadkowie, albo nasza mala stabilizacja* (The Witnesses, or Things Are Almost Back to Normal), fp Warsaw 1963; *Akt przery wany* (The Interrupted Act), fp Ulm, Germany, 1965.

Rozov, Victor Sergeyevich (1913–), Soviet dramatist. He began by writing about the problems of young people and his plays have been very popular in the USSR. In 1957 the Contemporary Theatre in Moscow opened with his play *Vechno zhivye* (Alive for Ever), directed by YEFREMOV, on which the internationally successful film *Letyat zhuravli* (The Cranes are Flying), 1957, was based. Among his best known plays are *Neravny boi* (Unequal Combat), 1960, whose hero is a 16-year-old boy; *V dobry chas* (The Lucky Hour), about a boy who questions the world of grown-ups but eventually love and his work enable him to find the true path; *V den Svadby* (On the Day of the Wedding), 1963, a Chekhov-like presentation of a family. *V poiskach radosti* (*In Search of Happiness*), written 1955, was performed in England on TV in 1960.

RSC ▷ROYAL SHAKESPEARE COMPANY.

Rubinstein, Ida (1885–1960), dancer and actress of Russian-Jewish origin. An admirer and disciple of Isadora Duncan, she made her first successful appearance with the Ballets Russes in Paris, acting and dancing the title role in *Cléopâtre*, 1909, and in *Martyre de Saint Sébastien* by D'ANNUNZIO, music Debussy, 1911. Later a series of mime dramas with music were written specially for her: *La Pisanella* by D'Annunzio, music Pizzetti, Paris 1913, dir MEYERHOLD; *Perséphone*, by GIDE, music Stravinsky,

1934, choreography Kurt Jooss; *Jeanne d'Arc au Bûcher* by Claudel, music Honegger, Basle 1938. She managed her own company 1928–34, whose earliest appearances were at the Paris Opéra. Diaghilev said of her: 'I introduced to the dance a mysterious, extravagant, biblical Rubinstein.'

Rudkin, (James) David (1936–), English dramatist. He established himself with his first play *Afore Night Come*, presented by the RSC, 1962, revived by them at The Other Place, STRATFORD-UPON-AVON, 1974. The play, set 'in an orchard in a rural pocket on the crust of the Black Country' and written in dialect, shows a group of casual labourers, suddenly confronted with the arrival of an Irishman, whom they mark as a 'scapegoat' and victim, and whom they finally murder ritualistically. He has since written TV plays, e.g. *Children Playing*, 1967; a libretto for the Western Theatre Ballet, *The Stone Dance*, 1963; plays: *Cries from Casement as His Bones Are Brought to Dublin* and *Ashes*, 1973.

Rudolf, Leopold (1911–), Austrian actor. Made his début in 1937; after several appearances in the German provinces joined the company in the Theater in der Josefstadt in Vienna, where he rapidly established himself as one of the leading actors. At his best with the complex neurotic characters of IBSEN, STRINDBERG and PIRANDELLO he also became very popular in comic roles in NESTROY FARCES and in plays by HOFMANNSTHAL and SCHNITZLER.

Ruggeri, Ruggero (1871–1953), Italian actor. Worked 1891–98 with NOVELLI's company; in 1900 achieved an outstanding success as Aligi in D'ANNUNZIO's *La Figlia di Jorio*, which he repeated in 1934. He was a modern actor with a great sense of spontaneity, notably in plays by D'Annunzio, PIRANDELLO, *Enrico IV*, *Sei personaggi in cerca d'autore*, 1925; GIRAUDOUX, *Siegfried*, 1930, and also in high comedy and in classical roles, ALFIERI's *Oreste*, 1949.

Rühmann, Heinz (1902–), German actor. Appeared for several years with leading German companies, but his formative period came at the Munich Kammerspiele, which he joined in 1925, under the direction of FALCKENBERG. After initially playing young leading men he was soon recognized as an outstanding comic actor; his first great success was as Puck in *A Midsummer Night's Dream*. In the late 1920s he appeared successfully in English and French light comedies in Munich and the State Theatre, BERLIN, 1938–44. After World War II made guest appearances at various theatres, e.g. as Loman in A. MILLER's *Death of a Salesman*; Estragon in BECKETT's *Waiting for Godot*, Munich Kammerspiele 1953–54, dir KORTNER, etc. One of Germany's most popular film stars, he played the lead in the film version of ZUCKMAYER's *Der Hauptmann von Köpenick*.

Rumania. Early Oriental influence in the popular PUPPET THEATRE; simple dramatic forms in religious PAGEANTS and festivals which form an important part of Rumanian folk culture. Not until the 19th century with the struggle for independence did a unified national culture develop, leading finally to the formation of national drama, strongly influenced by touring companies from foreign countries. From 1829 to 1835 the dramatic society in Bucharest was responsible for the development and support of a national theatre and a training school for actors, which produced the famous brothers Costache (1815–87) and Iorgu Caragiale, leading figures in the Rumanian theatre, as directors and actors. In 1852 the newly built Teatrul des Mar (Big Theatre) was opened, known since 1854 as the National Theatre, managed by Costache Caragiale. His nephew ION LUCA CARAGIALE was one of the first important playwrights of social COMEDIES whose plays have since formed the most important part of the REPERTOIRE. The director Paul Eusty (d. 1944) supported and conveyed the ideas of ANTOINE and STANISLAVSKY and directed plays by MAETERLINCK and WEDEKIND. Among the best known 20th-century playwrights are: Ion Slavici (1848–1925), Nicholas Iorga (1871–1940), and Victor Eftima (1889–). Since 1963 there have been 82 theatrical companies in Rumania, 42 of them specifically for plays.
Bibl: P. Hanes, HISTOIRE DE LA LITTÉRATURE ROUMANE, 1934

Russia ▷USSR.

Rutherford, Dame Margaret (1892–1972), English actress. Appointed DBE in 1967. Turned to the stage in her early 30s and her performance in 1938 as Aunt Bijou Furze in GIELGUD's production of *Spring Meeting* (M. J. Farell/J. Perry) established her overnight as an outstanding comedienne. Her subsequent successes include Madame Arcati in COWARD's *Blithe Spirit*, 1941; Lady Bracknell in WILDE's *The Importance of Being Earnest*, 1947; Lady Wishfort in CONGREVE's *The Way of the World*, 1953, and Minerva Goody in *Farewell, Farewell Eugene* (R. Ackland), based on J. Vari), London 1959, New York 1960. She also acted in films. Particularly good in COMEDY, she also portrayed certain types of sinister, unpredictable old ladies.

Ruzante (or Ruzzante; real name Angelo Beolco; 1502?–43), Italian actor and dramatist. The invention of the COMMEDIA DELL' ARTE has been attributed to him. He was the director of a strolling company for which he wrote plays in the dialect of Padua and in which he played the chief character: a shrewd, rebellious peasant boy, a critic of princes and the bourgeoisie. Other members of his company also appeared as stock characters, e.g. M. A. Alvarotto as Menato, G. Zanetti as Vezzo. His plays were rediscovered and revived in the 20th century: *Anconitana*, fp 1522?, COPEAU 1927; *La Moschetta*, fp 1528, DE BOSIO, Turin 1960, TEATRO STABILE.

Ida Rubinstein as Cleopatra, 1909

Margaret Rutherford as Miss Prism in WILDE's *The Importance of Being Earnest* (film version 1958)

Sabbatini, Niccoló (1574–1654), Italian architect. He designed the Teatro del Sole in Pesaro and was the author of a treatise on stage design and technique *Pratica di fabricar scene e macchine ne' Teatri*, 1638.

Sachs, Hans (1494–1576), Nuremberg cobbler, MEISTERSINGER and the most important exponent of the FASTNACHTSPIEL (carnival play). He turned out 4,000 songs, epigrammatic poems, and more than 200 dramatic works including 63 TRAGEDIES, 65 COMEDIES and numerous Fastnachtspiele. The sources of his serious plays were mainly biblical or taken from classical antiquity, chronicles and popular books; they were written in KNITTELVERS and used basic dramatic technique to convey themes with clearly defined moral purpose. The performances took place on a simple podium with stairs leading up, right and left. The actors usually appeared in contemporary costumes except for pagans, Turks, Angels and Devils, who wore fantasy costumes. The acting was according to established conventions: sleeping was indicated by a sitting posture, lying on the floor meant death; in the same way gestures were prescribed according to fixed rules. Highly praised by his contemporaries, S. fell into oblivion during the Renaissance and Baroque period; he was rediscovered in the STURM UND DRANG era (GOETHE, *Ein Fastnachtsspiel vom Pater Brey*) and appreciated by the Romantics. Wagner portrayed him in his opera *Die Meistersinger*. S. expressed great admiration for Luther in his poems *Die Wittenbergische Nachtigall* (The Wittenberg Nightingale), 1523, and *Ein Epitaphium oder Klagred ob der Leych M. Luthers* (Epitaph or Funeral Oration on the Corpse of Luther), 1546. His major works include: (tragedies) *Der Wüterich Herodes* (The Tyrant Herod), 1552; *Tragedia König Sauls* (The Tragedy of King Saul), 1557; (dramas) *Der Hörnen Sewfried* (Siegfried with the Horny Skin), 1537; *Die ungleichen Kinder Evä* (The Unequal Children of Eve), 1553; (farces) *Schlauraffenland* (Land of Milk and Honey), 1530; *Das Narrenschneiden* (The Cutting Down of Fools), 1543; *Der Schwanger Bauer* (The Pregnant Peasant), 1544; *Der Teufel mit dem alten Weib* (The Devil and the Old Woman), 1545; *Der fahrend Schüler im Paradeiss* (The Wandering Scholar in Paradise), 1550, *Das Kelberbrüten*, 1551; *S. Peter mit der Geiss* (St Peter with the Goat), 1555.
Bibl: H. Kindermann, MEISTER DER KOMÖDIE, 1952

Sacra Rappresentazione. 15th-century Italian religious drama, comparable with the AUTO SACRAMENTAL in the Spanish theatre and the MYSTERY PLAY in England and France.

Sadovsky. Russian family of actors. (1) **Prov Mikhailovich S.** (1818–72) in 1838 joined the Imperial Maly Theatre in Moscow, first playing minor parts but rapidly achieving prominence in comic roles in OSTROVSKY's plays and parts such as Osip in GOGOL's *The Government Inspector*. With the actor SHCHEPKIN he is regarded as the founder of the realistic school of Russian acting. His son, (2) **Mikhail Provich S.** (1847–1910), and daughter-in-law, (3) **Olga Osipovna Sadovskaya** (1850–1919), were also leading members of the Maly Theatre as were their children, (4) **Elisaveta Mikhailovna** (1870–1934) and (5) **Prov Mikhailovich S.** (1874–1947), who was director as well of the theatre from 1944. Among his best parts were Chatsky in GRIBOYEDOV's *Gore ot Uma* (*Woe from Wit*), and Brutus in SHAKESPEARE's *Julius Caesar*.

Sagert, Horst (1934–), German designer. A leading stage designer in East Germany, his best-known work has been carried out in collaboration with the director BESSON at the Deutsches-Theater, Berlin: O'CASEY's *Red Roses for Me*, 1963; MOLIÈRE's *Tartuffe*, 1963; SHVARTS's *Drakon*, 1965; SOPHOCLES/MÜLLER's *Ödipus Tyrann*, 1967. Other works: BRECHT/WEILL's *Mahagonny*, Berlin 1964, Deutsche Staatsoper; Brecht's *Turandot oder der Kongress der Weisswäscher*, fp Zurich 1969.

Sainete. The term used for a short comic interlude in the Spanish theatre of the 17th–19th centuries, usually between the acts or at the end of a long play. The most important writer of this form was Ramón de la Cruz. A revival of the genre can be found in the 20th century, e.g. in the works of the brothers ALVAREZ QUINTERO.

Saint-Denis, Michel (1897–1971), French actor and director. Worked extensively in England and the USA. Began his career in Paris as stage manager and assistant director at the Théâtre du Vieux-Colombier under his uncle COPEAU, and in 1931 reorganized the latter's Les Copiaux as the COMPAGNIE DES QUINZE, where he produced *Noé*, *Le Viol de Lucrèce* and *Bataille de la Marne*, all by OBEY. Despite widespread recognition, the company finally disbanded and S.-D. went to London, where he founded a school, the London Theatre Studio, in 1936 and directed several productions, mainly at the OLD VIC: ROWLEY's *The Witch of Edmonton*, 1936; SOPHOCLES/YEATS's *Oedipus Rex*, 1945; TURGENEV's *A Month in the Country*, 1949. He was head of the Old Vic theatre school 1946–52 and 1950–52 also associate director of the Old Vic. He returned to France to become director of the CENTRE DRAMATIQUE in Strasbourg. Appointed artistic adviser to the Lincoln Center Project in New York in 1962, and of the Julliard School attached to LINCOLN CENTER. In 1962 he also became one of the artistic directors of the RSC (CHEKHOV's *The Cherry Orchard*, 1962). He was undoubtedly one of the decisive influences in post-war British theatre. Many of the best actors and directors of the younger generation were trained by him at the Old Vic school. Author of *Theatre: The Rediscovery of Style*, pub 1960.

Sainte-Beuve, Charles-Augustin de (1804–69), French critic. One of France's greatest critical authors, he wrote essays for several journals from 1848, later published in a series of volumes *Causeries du lundi*, *Nouveaux lundis*, *Premiers lundis*. His main literary work was: *Histoire de Port-Royal*, 6 vols, 1840–59; *Châteaubriand et son groupe littéraire sous l'Empire*, 1861. His articles on the dramatic works of CORNEILLE, RACINE, VOLTAIRE, BEAUMARCHAIS, MARIVAUX and the early French classicist writers were published under the title: *Tableau historique et critique de la poésie française et du théâtre français au XVIe siècle*, 1828. He also wrote plays and novels and many other books of theatrical and literary criticism.

Sainthill, Loudon (1919–69), stage designer of Australian origin. He came into prominence in the London theatre in the 1950s. His colourful and painterly style was particularly effective in his ballet designs. He also designed a number of Shakespearean productions.

Salacrou, Armand (1899–), French dramatist. Began his career as a Communist journalist (contributor to *L'Humanité* and *L'Internationale*) and in 1923 became a member of the Surrealist group that has to some extent influenced his dramatic work. Several of his plays were produced by DULLIN, a close friend: *Patchouli*, 1930; *Atlas-Hôtel*, 1931; *Une Femme libre*, 1934, milieu-comedy; *La Terre est ronde*, a drama about Savonarola, in which he depicts the parallels between religious fanaticism and Fascism, Théâtre de l'Atelier, 1938. *Les Nuits de la colère*, Resistance-drama, was given by the Compagnie Renaud-Barrault, dir BARRAULT, 1946. Other works: *La Vie en rose*, 1931; *L'Inconnue d'Arras*, 1935; *Histoire de rire*, 1939; *L'Archipel Lenoir*, 1947; *Dieu le savait*, 1950; *Sens interdit*, 1953; *Boulevard Durand*, 1960, etc.
Bibl: P. L. Mignon, 1960

Saltikov-Schedrin, Mikhail Yevgrafovich (1826–89), Russian novelist and satirist. Wrote two plays which were not performed during his lifetime: *Smert Pazukhina* (The Death of Pazukhin), written in 1857, was published in 1893 and fp 1901, revived by the MOSCOW ART THEATRE and performed in New York 1914. It portrays a family waiting for the death of a rich merchant. *Shadows* was found after his death and fp Moscow 1914. Some of his other work was also later dramatized.

Salvini. Family of Italian actors. (1) **Tommaso S.** (1829–1915), son of the actor Giuseppe S., he was with MODENA's company from 1843, whom he greatly admired and took as his model. He was first successful in TRAGEDY with ADELAIDE

Loudon Sainthill, design for a scene in *Romeo and Juliet*

Tommaso Salvini as Othello

Michel Saint-Denis teaching a group of students at the OLD VIC school

RISTORI's company, particularly as Mortimer in F. V. SCHILLER's *Maria Stuart*, and in ALFIERI's *Oreste*, 1848. After a year away from the theatre studying Shakespearean roles, he achieved resounding successes as Othello and Hamlet, 1854. His reputation extended all over Europe, his travels took him to Spain, England, Germany, Latin America, USA and Russia, where STANISLAVSKY saw his Othello and was greatly impressed by his charm and naturalness, the thoroughness of his interpretation and his complete identification with the part. His REPERTOIRE also included *King Lear, Saul* (Alfieri), *Zaïre* (VOLTAIRE), and plays by SCRIBE, IFFLAND and GOLDONI. His son, (2) **Gustavo S.** (1859–1930), was also a successful actor, while his grandson, (3) **Guido S.** (1893–), was a stage designer and assistant director at the Teatro d'Arte under PIRANDELLO in Rome; he has done much to popularize the latter's plays with productions in Prague, Vienna and Budapest. He formed and managed a young company of actors 1930–31; in 1934 worked with REINHARDT on his production of *The Merchant of Venice* at the Biennale, then turned to opera direction with Verdi's *Falstaff* at the SALZBURG FESTIVAL in 1935. He taught stage production at the Accademia Nazionale dell'Arte Drammatica in Rome 1938–44 (SQUARZINA was among his pupils), directed numerous first productions of plays by contemporary Italian playwrights and also worked as a guest director abroad (e.g. London, Helsinki).
Bibl: G. Salvini, 1955

Salzburg Festival. Founded in 1917 by REINHARDT, the composer R. Strauss and HOFMANNSTHAL, whose adaptation of *Jedermann* was first performed in 1920 in front of Salzburg Cathedral, and has been given annually ever since. In 1922 the *Salzburger Grosse Welttheater* (Hofmannsthal, based on CALDERÓN) was first produced in the Kollegienkirche and in 1933 GOETHE's *Faust* in the FELSENREITSCHULE, all three under the direction of Reinhardt. In 1926 the Festspielhaus opened with its programme of operas, at first mainly by Mozart and later by other composers – which became the focal point of the Festival. In 1961 the new Festspielhaus opened with Goethe's *Faust* (Parts I and II), directed by LINDTBERG.
Bibl: J. Kaut, FESTSPIELE IN SALZBURG, 1965

Sandrock, Adele (1863–1937), German actress of Dutch origin. Made her début in 1879 in BERLIN and after several appearances in Vienna, Berlin and Budapest, went on tour with a *Hamlet* parody in 1898. She worked with the ENSEMBLE of the Deutsches-Theater, Berlin, 1905–10, and subsequently at several other Berlin theatres, mainly in BOULEVARD plays. She began her career playing young heroines in works by KLEIST and LESSING, later became one of the greatest tragediennes of her time, excelling as SHAKESPEARE's Lady Macbeth and SCHILLER's Maria Stuart. She was also good in COMEDY parts and starred in many German films. In her later career she played formidable comic ladies. She published a volume

of reminiscences under the title *Mein Leben*, 1940.
Bibl: H. Jhering, VON JOSEF KAINZ BIS PAULA WESSELY, 1942

Sands, Diana (1934–73), US actress. The first Black actress to appear on the New York stage in leading roles, e.g. SHAW's *Saint Joan* and Cassandra in GIRAUDOUX's *Tiger at the Gates* (translation by FRY from the original play entitled *La Guerre de Troie n'aura pas lieu*), both Lincoln Center, 1967. After several OFF-BROADWAY appearances, she made her breakthrough in 1959 in LORRAINE HANSBERRY's *A Raisin in the Sun*; then appeared in the REVUE *Brecht on Brecht* (G. Tabori, 1962), in the CABARET 'The Living Premise', 1964, and in BALDWIN's *Blues for Mister Charlie*, 1964 – a performance W. Kerr described as: 'A complex beat on the drums, a rhythmical outcry . . . Miss Sands speaks, no, sings those lines in Sophocleic cadences – wild pulsing beats, which can only be controlled by the great strength of this actress.' She was also the first Black actress to appear in a part written for a White woman, in B. Manhoff's *The Owl and the Pussycat*, 1964.

San Francisco Mime Troupe. Founded 1959, to counter the stifling clichés of contemporary theatre. The troupe plays in parks and streets, and maintains its own indoor theatre in San Francisco. The SFMT is much influenced by all forms of popular entertainment and also uses a modern form of COMMEDIA DELL'ARTE, taking themes and plays from 17th-century Italy and Spain, e.g. adaptations of GOLDONI's *L'Amante militare* and LOPE DE RUEDA's *Los Olivos*.

Sanjust, Filippo (1925–), Italian stage designer. Best known for his décor for VISCONTI's productions, including Verdi's *Don Carlos*, 1958, COVENT GARDEN. Later worked with other leading European directors such as DE FILIPPO, SELLNER, PUECHER, mainly in opera, e.g. H. W. Henze's *The Young Lord*, Berlin 1965. Other works include: MOLIÈRE's *Le Bourgeois gentilhomme*, Berlin 1968.

Sarcey, Francisque (François Sarcey de Sutières; 1827–99), French critic. The most influential drama critic of his day, who wrote for *L'Opinion Nationale*, 1859–67, and for *Le Temps*, 1867–99.
Bibl: L. Straus-Horkheimer, 1937

Sardou, Victorien (1831–1908), French dramatist. With SCRIBE, the most prolific writer of the WELL-MADE PLAY; he treated historical and social matters without detailed characterization, but with ingenious PLOTS and stage effects. His output was enormous, *c.* 80 plays including social satires, PAGEANTS, historical spectacles, MELODRAMAS, LIBRETTI, FARCES – most of them successful, because of their topicality and the great players who appeared in them, e.g. SARAH BERNHARDT (*Fédora*, 1882; *Théodora*, 1884, *La Tosca*, 1887, later an opera by Puccini). His best-known works include: *Les Pattes de mouche*, 1860, produced in London as *A Scrap of Paper*; *Dora*, 1877, adapted for the English stage in 1878 as *Diplomacy* and which became the model for WILDE's *An Ideal Husband*; *Divorçons*, 1880, with Emile de Majac and *Madame Sans-Gêne*, 1893, with RÉJANE.
Bibl: E. Bentley (ed), LET'S GET A DIVORCE AND OTHER PLAYS, 1958

Saroyan, William (1908–), US novelist and dramatist. Most distinctive play *The Time of Your Life*, 1939. His essential theme is the victory of good over corruptive materialism. His best works are characterized by their vigorous spontaneous quality, e.g. *My Heart's in the Highlands*, 1939; *The Beautiful People*, 1941; *Across the Board on Tomorrow Morning*, 1942; *Hello Out There*, 1943; *The Cave Dwellers*, 1957.
Bibl: H. R. Floan, 1966

Sarrazin, Maurice (1925–), French actor and director. Formed the Grenier de Toulouse in 1945 with friends, a company which was recognized in 1949 as the Centre Dramatique du Sud-Ouest. He first attracted attention with *Carthaginois*, 1946, a free adaptation of PLAUTUS' *Poenulus*, with which he won a drama competition for young companies. Apart from productions of MOLIÈRE's *Les Fourberies de Scapin*, 1950, and SHAKESPEARE's *The Taming of the Shrew*, 1951, he also staged contemporary plays including BRECHT's *Mother Courage*, 1959, 1965; GATTI's *Chronique d'une planète provisoire*, 1963, and *Le Poisson noir*, 1964. His company appeared several times successfully in Paris. He has also directed operas.

Sartre, Jean-Paul (1905–), French philosopher, novelist, essayist and playwright. One of the chief exponents of EXISTENTIALISM which places its main emphasis on man's existential experience as against abstract ideals, he was naturally prone to embody his ideas in the form of concrete experiences of individual characters, at first in novels and stories, but later, after the outbreak of World War II, also in plays. His first dramatic effort was a PASSION PLAY, *Bariona*, which he wrote for performance in a prisoner-of-war camp to show his solidarity with some Catholic priests who shared his captivity in 1940. After his release he dealt with the problems of the German occupation in the guise of a retelling of the story of Orestes in *Les Mouches*, 1943. The idea that an individual's personality is determined by the view others have of him is embodied in *Huis Clos* (English titles used: *In Camera*, *No Exit*, 1944); *La Putain respectueuse* (*The Respectful Prostitute*), 1947, deals with racial tension in the American South. *Les Mains sales*, in England *Crime Passionel*, 1949, earned him the hostility of the extreme Left, with whom he had sympathized, by concentrating on the mixed motives behind the liquidation of a high Communist functionary in Eastern Europe. Other plays: *Morts sans sépulture*, 1946 (prod London 1947 as *Men without Shadows*, New York 1948 as *The Victors*), a philosophic naturalistic four-act play in which captured Resistance fighters question the meaning of their suffering even as they undergo tortures vividly depicted on stage; an ambitious but less successful play which sets out to demonstrate the uselessness of God, *Le Diable et le Bon Dieu*, 1951; *Kean, ou désorde et génie*, after DUMAS *père*, written for BRASSEUR; *Nekrassov*, 1955, a political farce; *Les Séquestrés d'Altona*, 1959, a large-scale drama about a family which embodies in its various members the anguish of Germany in the post-Nazi era, and is an adaptation of EURIPIDES' *The Trojan Women*, 1965. His plays are conventional in form and language but rich in original ideas and brilliantly posed problems. Awarded the Nobel Prize for Literature in 1964, he refused it.
Bibl: F. Anderson, 1971

Sastre, Alfonso (1926–), Spanish dramatist. First came into prominence with his play *La mordaza* (The Bite), 1954. Other works include: *Uranio 235* (Uranium 235), 1946; *Cargamento de sueños* (Cargo of Dreams), 1949; *Escuadra hacia la muerte* (*Condemned Squad*), 1953; *La cornada* (*Death Thrust*), 1960. His dramas deal critically with social topics and are frequently performed in Spain.

Satyr play. The fourth play of a TETRALOGY, it followed the tragic TRILOGY as performed in ancient GREECE. It had a comic plot with elements of BURLESQUE and simple action (▷AFTERPIECE). It was named after the CHORUS, who were dressed as satyrs (originally woodland demons in the service of DIONYSOS with horses' tails, hooves and other animal characteristics). All the Greek dramatists wrote satyr plays but AESCHYLUS, Achaeus and Aristias were considered masters of the form. The only complete extant example is EURIPIDES' *The Cyclops*, though fragments of SOPHOCLES' *Ichneutae* and Aeschylus' *Dictyulci* and *The Isthmiasts* also survive.

Sauer, Oscar (1856–1918), German actor. One of the leading naturalistic actors of BRAHM'S ENSEMBLE, whose portrayals of petty bourgeois and proletarian characters were held to be the most true to life of any actor of his time and he was highly praised by his fellow actors and critics for his profound and unobtrusive realism. After 16 years in the provinces, first as a *bon-vivant* in drama and operetta, he joined the Lessingtheater in 1890 under BLUMENTHAL and from 1897 worked with Brahm at the Deutsches-Theater, excelling as Gregers Werle in IBSEN's *The Wild Duck*, and Judge Brack in *Hedda Gabler*. Among his later parts were: Pastor Manders in Ibsen's *Ghosts* and the title role in HAUPTMANN's *Michael Kramer*.
Bibl: H. Jhering, VON JOSEF KAINZ BIS PAUL WESSELY, 1942

Saunders, James (1925–), English playwright. Started his career as a schoolmaster. Attracted attention with the witty Absurdist one-act plays *Alas, Poor Fred*, 1959; *Barnstable*, 1960; *A Slight Accident*, 1961; broke through to the West End of London with *Next Time I'll Sing to You*, 1962, a brilliant Pirandellian theatricalization of the life of a man who has completely withdrawn from the world. Another full-length play, *A Scent of Flowers*, 1964, which examined the reasons for a girl's suicide, achieved international success. Other plays: an adaptation of the novel *The Italian Girl*, 1968, in collaboration with the author, Iris Murdoch; *The Borage Pigeon Affair*, 1969; *The Travails of Sancho Panza*, 1969, a play for children, based on Don Quixote. Has also written plays for TV and radio.

Savits, Jocza (1847–1915), German director of Hungarian origin. Worked at the Munich COURT THEATRE from 1885 to 1906. Notable for being one of the first 19th-century directors to insist on performing SHAKESPEARE with a minimum of scenery to allow the rhythm of the fluid construction to achieve its effect. For this he devised his Shakespeare stage, a simple platform divided into forestage and backstage by a curtain which allowed a rapid succession of SCENES.

Scamozzi, Vicenzo (1552–1616), Italian architect. He completed the TEATRO OLIMPICO, Vicenza, after the death of his master Palladio, and designed on his own the Teatro Olimpico, Sabbioneta.
Bibl: F. Barbieri, 1952

Scaramuccia. A character of the COMMEDIA DELL'ARTE; a variation of the CAPITANO from Naples, created and perfected by the Italian actor T. FIORILLI (1608–94). Known in France as Scaramouche.

Scarron, Paul (1610–60), French dramatist. His FARCES were mostly adaptations of Spanish models, in which the actor JODELET excelled as the knowing servant, a forerunner of Scapin and Figaro: *Jodelet ou Le Maître valet*, 1643, Théâtre du Marais; *Le Jodelet souffleté*, 1645. Other works: *Don Japhet d'Arménie*, 1647; *L'Ecolier de Salamanque*, 1654. The plays were performed by three leading Paris theatres of the time: Théâtre du Marais, HÔTEL DE BOURGOGNE, and by MOLIÈRE's company, and were later taken into the repertoire of the COMÉDIE-FRANÇAISE. In his *Roman comique* (2 vols, 1651–57) S. gives an excellent portrayal of the life of travelling companies in the provinces.
Bibl: N. F. Phelps, THE QUEEN'S INVALID, 1951

Scene (Gr *skene*=tent, booth, stage). The term is used for 'stage', but also, in the subdivision of plays into acts and scenes, for a section of a play, usually between the entrances and exits of characters, so that each scene comprises the action between a given number of characters until one of them leaves, or new ones enter, thus constituting a different constellation of persons on the stage. In plays with frequent changes of setting, the term 'scene' can also stand for each section of an act with a different décor or scenery. An outline of the action of a play scene by scene is a scenario.

Schall, Ekkehard (1930–), German actor. After appearing in Frankfurt and BERLIN, he joined the BERLINER ENSEMBLE

Victorien Sardou with SARAH BERNHARDT at a fête in her honour

Jean-Paul Sartre's *Le Diable et le Bon Dieu*, Paris 1951

in 1952, where he soon became one of that company's leading actors. He has played José in BRECHT's *Die Gewehre der Frau Carrar*, 1952; Wu Tsan in *Der Tag des grossen Gelehrten Wu* (Brecht/PALITZSCH/Weber, 1955); Shawn Koegh in SYNGE's *The Playboy of the Western World*, 1956; in Brecht's *Arturo Ui*, 1959; *Die Tage der Kommune*, 1962, and *Coriolan*; Oppenheimer in KIPPHARDT's *In der Sache J. Robert Oppenheimer*, 1964.

Schalla, Hans (1904–), German director and manager. Began his career as an actor and director with several German companies and in 1949 was appointed INTENDANT of the Bochum theatre, where he continued the SHAKESPEARE cycles started by his forerunner SCHMITT (more than 30 productions since 1949). His effective and concise style of production, highly simplified sets and bold COSTUMES were applied to an outstanding REPERTOIRE, which included weeks devoted to the theatre of specific countries, e.g. the USA and France, and made the Bochum theatre into one of the leading German companies. His productions of SARTRE's *Le Diable et le Bon Dieu*, 1956, and WEDEKIND's *Der Marquis von Keith*, 1957, were presented at the THÉATRE DES NATIONS in Paris.

Schéhadé, Georges (1910–), Syrian-born French poet and dramatist. Educated in Paris, has lived mainly in Beirut. His dramas are full of powerful surrealistic images and lyrical qualities in an attempt to revive poetic drama on the French stage (like H. Pichette, AUDIBERTI, J. Supervielle): *La Soirée des proverbes*, Paris 1954, dir BARRAULT; *Histoire de Vasco*, fp Zurich 1956, Paris 1957, dir Barrault; *Les Violettes*, fp Bochum, Germany, 1960, dir SCHALLA; *Le Voyage*, Paris 1961, dir Barrault.
Bibl: L. C. Pronko, AVANT-GARDE, THE EXPERIMENTAL THEATER IN FRANCE, 1962

Schellow, Erich (1915–), German actor. Made his début as Mortimer in SCHILLER's *Maria Stuart* and immediately established himself as an outstanding actor of heroic parts, mainly in plays by Schiller, KLEIST, SHAKESPEARE (*Hamlet*) and GIRAUDOUX (mostly under the direction of KORTNER). After 1960 he took on a new role as character actor in leading parts in classical and modern plays including: Möbius in DÜRRENMATT's *Die Physiker*, 1962; George in ALBEE's *Who's Afraid of Virginia Woolf?*, 1963; title roles in SOPHOCLES' *Oedipus Rex* and *Oedipus at Colonus*, SALZBURG FESTIVAL 1965, dir SELLNER; GOETHE's *Faust* II, 1966; the Boss in GRASS's *Die Plebejer proben den Aufstand*, Munich 1967.

Schenk, Otto (1930–), Austrian director and actor. After some experience of acting at the Vienna BURGTHEATER and directing in EXPERIMENTAL THEATRES, he joined the Theater in der Josefstadt in 1955 as actor and director. Later he established himself as director of opera and in TV. Notable productions include: plays, O'NEILL's *Ah, Wilderness!*, Vienna 1960; HORVÁTH's *Kasi mir und Karoline*, Vienna 1963, Munich 1969, and *Geschichten aus dem Wiener Wald*, Munich 1966; BÜCHNER's *Dantons Tod*, Vienna, 1967; operas, G. von Einem's *Dantons Tod*, Vienna Festival, 1963; Mozart's *Die Zauberflöte*, SALZBURG FESTIVAL, 1963.

Schikaneder, Emanuel (1751–1812), Austrian actor, director, singer, dramatist and manager. Formed his own travelling company in 1777. He was a supporter of the German opera of Gluck, Haydn and Mozart, whom he first met in Salzburg in 1780. The culmination of his career was his management of the Theater an der Wien, which opened in 1801. His collaboration with Mozart resulted in his best remembered work, the LIBRETTO for *Die Zauberflöte*, 1791. He also wrote a great number of FARCES, COMEDIES, SINGSPIELE and ZAUBERSTÜCKE.
Bibl: E. v. Kormorzynski, 1951

Schildkraut, Rudolf (1862–1930), German actor. Son of a Jewish family, he was raised in Rumania and trained for the stage in Vienna under MITTERWURZER. He worked 1900–05 at the Hamburg theatre and from 1905 under REINHARDT at the Deutsches-Theater, BERLIN, excelling as Shylock, Lear and Mephistopheles (GOETHE's *Faust*). In 1920 emigrated to the USA, where he appeared first at the Yiddish People's Theatre but from 1922 acting also in English. In 1925 he founded his own Yiddish theatre. His son, **Joseph S.** (1895–), was trained in Germany and the USA; he made his stage début in New York in 1910 and appeared under Reinhardt in Germany (with his father in Schmidtbonn's *Der verlorene Sohn*, 1913); in 1920 Joseph S. followed his father to the USA, where he achieved his greatest success in the title role in IBSEN's *Peer Gynt*, 1923. He became a very popular actor on stage and in films. One of his later successes was the father in *The Diary of Anne Frank* by Frances Goodrich and Albert Hackett, New York, 1955.

Schiller, Friedrich von (1759–1805), German poet and dramatist. He ranks as one of the most important in his country. As a protégé of Duke Karl Eugen of Württemberg, he was educated from 1773 at the Hohe Karlsschule and from 1775 studied medicine to become an army doctor in Stuttgart in 1780. His early poetic work shows strong influence of Swabian pietism and also of the Enlightenment. In his thesis, 1780, *Zusammenhang der tierischen Natur des Menschen mit seiner geistigen* (The connection between man's animal and spiritual nature), he posed the question of man's physical and metaphysical freedom. He wrote his first play, *Die Räuber* (The Robbers) in 1781, at the age of 22. A subtly effective drama, it was staged with great success in 1782 at the Mannheim National Theatre, dir IFFLAND. He then managed to avoid further service under Duke Karl Eugen and fled to Mannheim where he was appointed resident dramatist in 1783. His next two plays were produced there in 1784: *Kabale und Liebe* (Intrigue and Love), a most effective denunciation of feudalism, which had a *succès fou*, and *Fiesko*, an attempt to portray the character of an ambitious politician, entangled in his own emotions and problems. Two years later he paid his first visit to Weimar where he published the VERSE DRAMA *Don Carlos*, fp Hamburg 1787, by SCHRÖDER. In this play he constructed a complicated web of intrigue and misunderstanding, centred on characters who are in a state of emotional confusion; the weak Carlos, completely lacking in self-control, his father Philip II of Spain, isolated by his ambition, and the idealist Posa whose humanitarianism is tinged with fanaticism. In the same year he wrote his famous historical essay *Geschichte des Abfalls der Vereinigten Niederlände* (History of the Secession of the Netherlands) pub 1788, followed by *Geschichte des Dreissigjährigen Krieges* (History of the Thirty Years War), 1791–93. In 1789 he was appointed professor of history at Jena. He made intensive studies of Kantian philosophy which resulted in the essay *Über die ästhetische Erziehung des Menschen in einer Reihe von Briefen* (Letters on the Aesthetic Education of Mankind), 1775, and, in the same year, founded the magazine *Die Horen*, with the publisher Cotta.
Among his friends were W. von Humboldt and GOETHE, who produced his *Wallenstein* TRILOGY at Weimar in 1798 (*Wallensteins Lager*, *Die Piccolomini* and *Wallensteins Tod* – W.'s Camp, the P.s, W.'s Death). After going to Weimar in 1799, S. wrote his most dramatically telling play, *Maria Stuart*, in which the carefully balanced contrast between the two queens makes for highly effective theatre. In 1801 *Die Jungfrau von Orleans* (The Maid of Orleans) was first produced in Leipzig. S. is one of the most powerful writers in the history of drama. With their high-flown idealism and poetic language, his plays became the most popular and frequently quoted, and, after SHAKESPEARE, the most often produced classic dramas in the 19th century in Germany and Eastern Europe where the emergent national schools of drama were strongly influenced by the formal structure of his work. His impact was less in France and the Anglo-Saxon countries.
In order to widen the REPERTOIRE of the Weimar theatre, S. translated and adapted Shakespeare's *Macbeth*, 1800; GOZZI's *Turandot*, 1802; RACINE's *Phèdre*, 1805. Posthumous publications include the translation of *Der Parasit* and *Der Neffe als Onkel* (both after Picard); stage versions of LESSING's *Nathan der Weise* and Goethe's *Egmont* and *Iphigenie*. In 1803 *Die Braut von Messina* and in 1804 *Wilhelm Tell* were first staged in Weimar. A fragment of a play, *Demetrius*, was also published posthumously.
The turn of the century saw a renewal of interest in his dramatic work. BRAHM directed *Kabale und Liebe*, 1894, as the opening production of his Deutsches-Theater; REINHARDT revived this in 1904 and later *Don Carlos*. In 1919 JESSNER made his début as a director in the State Theatre, Berlin with *Wilhelm Tell*, produced in

Expressionist style; PISCATOR gave a production of *Die Räuber* at the State Theatre in 1926 with a social revolutionary interpretation.
Bibl: F. Burschell, 1968; R. Albrecht, SCHILLERS DRAMATISCHER JAMBUS, 1967; T. Mann, VERSUCH ÜBER SCHILLER, 1955

Schiller, Leon (1887–1954), Polish director. He studied theatre history and drama in Paris (1907–09) and had his first essays published in CRAIG's magazine *The Mask*. He returned to Warsaw to work in CABARET and also as a journalist. After studying music in Vienna (1916–17) he became DRAMATURG in Warsaw and took over the management of the Boguslawski Theatre in 1924, where he produced SHAKESPEARE and the Polish Romantics. His best-known production was KRASIŃSKI's *The Undivine Comedy*, 1926. He aimed at a 'monumental' and 'total' theatre, which has to be understood as a counterbalance to the 'limited' bourgeois theatre of his time restricted to petty realism; he sought autonomy for the theatre from literature, involving equal emphasis on acting, music, scenery, lighting, according to the theories of Craig. Over the years, under the influence of the revolutionary Russian theatre, he also developed his use of the theatre as a platform to reveal social mechanisms. After the closing of the Boguslawski Theatre because of political opposition (his last production of BRECHT's *The Threepenny Opera* caused a furore) he went to Lvov, where he directed his most remarkable productions of the pre-war period: MICKIEWICZ's *Forefathers' Eve* and TRETYAKOV's *Roar China!*, which led to his imprisonment. Back in Warsaw in 1932 he took over the management of the New Atheneum Theatre and also became director of the National Theatre Institute; during this period he also worked as a guest director in Poland and abroad, and directed films. In 1941 he was interned for several months in Auschwitz; during the war years, after his release, he worked with amateur companies and in the front line. He was manager of the Lódz theatre 1946–49, where he produced ROJAS's *La Celestina*, 1947, and GORKY's *The Lower Depths*, 1949. In 1950 he moved to the Polski Theatre and later lectured, mainly on drama, and worked as a guest director abroad, e.g. *Halka* by S. Moniuszko, Berlin Opera 1953. He also wrote numerous essays, articles, notes to plays and on political theatre; a collection of his writings was published in 1961 under the title *Teatr Ogromny*.

Schinkel, Karl Friedrich (1781–1841), German architect and painter. He designed the Schauspielhaus auf dem Gendarmenplatz in BERLIN (1818–24) and was also the most important stage designer of German classicism: Mozart's *Die Zauberflöte*, 1816; SCHILLER's *Die Jungfrau von Orleans*, 1817; KLEIST's *Käthchen von Heilbronn*, 1818; Schiller's *Don Carlos*, 1819; GOETHE's *Iphigenie*, 1821, and *Faust*, 1832; he also designed many operas for the Royal Theatre in Berlin and was the author of several books on stage design including *Dekorationen an*

Friedrich von Schiller, a scene from *Wallensteins Lager*

Joseph Schildkraut in *The Diary of Anne Frank*, New York 1955

Karl Friedrich Schinkel, design for a stage set

den beiden Königlichen Theatern in Berlin, 1819–24; *Sammlung von Theaterdekorationen*, 1862; *Lebenswerk*, 11 vols, 1938ff.
Bibl: P. O. Rave, 1953

Schisgal, Murray (1926–), US dramatist. His early one-act plays, including *The Typists, The Postman, A Simple Kind of Love*, were first staged by the BRITISH DRAMA LEAGUE in London in 1960. After his next play *Ducks and Lovers*, 1961, also first staged in London, came the BROADWAY première of *The Typists* and *The Tiger* (a new version of *The Postman*) in 1963 under the direction of Arthur Storch, which established him as a dramatist in the tradition of the THEATRE OF THE ABSURD. This was surpassed by the success of his next play *Luv*, London 1963, and New York 1964, dir NICHOLS. Other work: *Knit One, Purl Two*, 1963.

Schlegel, August Wilhelm von (1767–1845), German writer. Best remembered as a literary critic and translator of SHAKESPEARE; the edition of 1797–1810, for which he translated 17 plays, is named after him and his collaborator TIECK; the Schlegel-Tieck translations are still, in spite of their romanticism, the versions most often performed in Germany. He also translated Dante, CERVANTES and CALDERÓN. His series of lectures *Über die dramatische Kunst und Literatur* given at Vienna, pub 1809–11, was the first attempt to trace the development of world drama.
Bibl: M. E. Atkinson, AUGUST VON SCHLEGEL AS A TRANSLATOR OF SHAKESPEARE, 1958

Schlegel, Johann Elias (1719–49), German dramatist of the Enlightenment. An uncle of A. SCHLEGEL, his early work was strongly influenced by GOTTSCHED. When he had freed himself of this influence, he discovered and championed SHAKESPEARE in GERMANY and was the forerunner of LESSING and the STURM UND DRANG movement. He wrote classical dramas: *Die Geschwister in Taurien* (Brother and Sister in Tauris), 1737, later entitled *Orest und Pylades*; *Hekuba*; *Dido*; *Die Troerinnen*; *Lukretia*; historical dramas: *Hermann*, 1743; *Canut*, 1746; COMEDIES: *Der geschäftige Müssiggänger* (The Busy Idler), 1741; *Der Gärtnerkönig* (The Gardener King), 1746; *Der Triumph der guten Frauen* (The Triumph of Good Women), 1748. From 1743 he lived in Copenhagen and wrote a number of essays on the Danish theatre; and in 1741 *Vergleichung Shakespeares und Andreas Gryphius* (Comparison between Shakespeare and GRYPHIUS).
Bibl: H. Schonder, 1941

Schlemmer, Oskar (1888–1943), German painter and dancer. An important figure in the German theatre in the 1920s; before World War I he was already preoccupied with the idea of combining dance and graphic art. His attempts to create a choreography of abstract figures in space led to his *Triadisches Ballet* and his work in Berlin at the Bauhaus (with MOHOLY-NAGY he wrote *Die Bühne am Bauhaus*). In addition he designed sets for the conventional stage using the graphic techniques of his paintings, e.g. in KOKOSCHKA's play *Mörder, Hoffnung der Frauen*, Stuttgart 1921: *Tsar Golod* by ANDREYEV, Berlin 1924, VOLKSBÜHNE; *Wer weint um Juckenack?* by REHFISCH, dir PISCATOR, Berlin 1925, Volksbühne; *Don Juan und Faust* by GRABBE, Weimar 1925; *Hamlet*, Berlin 1925, Volksbühne; *Die glückliche Hand*, opera by Arnold Schönberg, Berlin 1930, Krolloper.
Bibl: H. Rischbieter (ed), BÜHNE UND BILDENDE KUNST IM 20. JAHRHUNDERT, 1968

Schlenther, Paul (1854–1916), German critic and manager. From 1883 editor of the *Deutsche Literatur-Zeitung*; in 1886 he became a critic on the *Vossische Zeitung*, BERLIN, supporting in particular the works of IBSEN and HAUPTMANN. He was also one of the founders of the FREIE BÜHNE; 1898–1910 director of the Vienna BURGTHEATER, afterwards returning to Berlin, where he worked again as a critic for the *Berliner Tageblatt*. Author of a number of books on the theatre including *Frau Gottsched und die bürgerliche Komödie*, 1886; *Gerhart Hauptmann*, 1897; *Adolf von Sonnenthal*, 1906; editor of a volume of collected criticism by BRAHM, 1913.
Bibl: K. Böhla, PAUL SCHLENTHER ALS THEATER KRITIKER, 1935

Schmidt, Willi (1910–), German designer and director. Began his career as a stage designer in BERLIN (VOLKSBÜHNE, Deutsches-Theater, State Theatre) and after 1945 gained rapid success as a director, with a style characterized by lucidity and formal balance: STERNHEIM's *Die Hose*, 1947, Deutsches-Theater; ANOUILH's *L'Invitation au château*, 1959, Renaissancetheater; GIRAUDOUX's *Amphitryon 38*, 1961, Schlossparktheater; GOETHE's *Clavigo*, 1963, and A. MILLER's *The Price*, 1968, both Schillertheater.

Schmitt, Saladin (1883–1951), German director and manager. As manager of the Bochum theatre, 1918–48, he helped establish this provincial theatre as one of the leading companies in Germany. His most successful period was when he produced a series of major classical works, tending towards a cerebral and educational theatre: SHAKESPEARE's historical plays, 1927; GOETHE, 1928; HAUPTMANN, 1932; SCHILLER, 1933; a second Shakespeare cycle, 1937; HEBBEL, 1939; GRABBE, 1940; GRILLPARZER, 1942.
Bibl: K. Dornemann (ed); BLÄTTER DER ERINNERUNG, 1964

Schneider, Alan (1917–), US director. Born in the USSR, he has lived in the USA since 1922; professor of drama at Washington University, St Louis, Mo., 1944–48. In 1944 made his first appearance as an actor in the professional theatre: M. ANDERSON's *Storm Operation*, PLAYWRIGHTS' COMPANY, New York; in 1948 trained as an actor under STRASBERG at the ACTORS' STUDIO; made his BROADWAY début as a director with *A Long Way from Home*, based on GORKY, 1948. Other successes: Liam O'Brien's *The Remarkable Mr Pennypacker*, 1954; and *Anastasia*, by Guy Bolton, adapted from Marcelle Maurette's play, 1954. His Broadway successes gave him the prestige and chance to support and encourage the work of new young playwrights, and he became known as the 'ABB' (ALBEE, BRECHT, BECKETT) director; he directed Beckett's *Waiting for Godot*, 1956; *Endgame*, 1958; *Krapp's Last Tape*, 1960, and *Happy Days*, 1961; Brecht's *The Caucasian Chalk Circle*, 1961; *Man is Man*, 1962, and *The Threepenny Opera*, 1963; Albee's *Who's Afraid of Virginia Woolf?*, 1962; *The Ballad of the Sad Café*, 1963 (from MCCULLERS); and *Tiny Alice*, 1964. He also directed for the screen, *Film*, in 1964, based on a script by Beckett, with Buster Keaton in the leading role.

Schneider-Siemssen, Günther (1926–), German stage designer. Since 1962 he has worked mainly in Vienna for the BURGTHEATER and the State Opera, where his best-known work includes: Debussy's opera *Pelléas et Mélisande*, 1962; SCHILLER's *Die Räuber*, Burgtheater, 1965, dir LINDTBERG. Other works: Offenbach's opera *Hoffmanns Erzählungen*, Stuttgart 1965; HORVÁTH's *Kasimir und Karoline*, Theater in der Josefstadt, 1965, dir SCHENK, etc.

Schnitzler, Arthur (1862–1931), Austrian dramatist. A doctor by profession; in his best plays he achieved a Chekhovian balance between psychological insight and objective toughness. He portrayed with great skill Viennese characters and atmosphere at the turn of the century; *Anatol*, a series of one-act episodes, was written 1888–91 and the first complete performance was given in Czech in 1893, in German in 1910, Vienna and BERLIN; *Liebelei*, Vienna 1895, BURGTHEATER; *Freiwild* (Easy Prey), fp Berlin 1896, Deutsches-Theater. Subsequently he collaborated closely with the director BRAHM until the latter's death. Productions of his plays include: (in Berlin) *Das Vermächtnis* (The Bequest), 1898; *Lebendige Stunden* (Living Hours), 1902; *Der Puppenspieler* (The Puppeteer), 1903; *Der einsame Weg* (The Lonely Path), 1904; *Der tapfere Kassian* (Brave Cassian), 1904; *Der Ruf des Lebens* (*The Call of Life*), 1906; *Das weite Land* (The Distant Land), 1911; and *Professor Bernhardi*, 1912; (in Vienna) *Der grüne Kakadu* (*The Green Cockatoo*), 1899, together with *Paracelsus* and *Die Gefährtin* (The Companion); *Zwischenspiel* (Interlude), 1905; *Der junge Medardus* (Young M.), 1910; (in Breslau) *Der Schleier der Beatrice* (*The Veil of Beatrice*), 1900. *Der Reigen* (The Round Dance), pub 1900, fp in Hungarian, Budapest 1912, had its first German production in Berlin 1920; it consisted of a series of DIALOGUES, each of them centred on the sex act, and was originally banned as obscene, but later achieved fame in much attenuated form as the film *La Ronde*. Other plays: *Komödie der Worte* (Comedy of Words), Vienna 1915; *Fink und Fliederbusch* (Finch and Lilac-bush), Vienna 1917. His son, **Heinrich S.** (1902–), actor, DRAMATURG, professor in the USA 1942–55, became director at

the Theater in der Josefstadt, Vienna, in 1958, directing mainly his father's works.
Bibl: C. Melchinger, 1969; H. Reichert and H. Salinger (ed), STUDIES IN ARTHUR SCHNITZLER, 1963

Scholz, Wenzel (1787–1857), Austrian actor. Began his career at the BURGTHEATER 1814–15; after a period in Graz, 1819–26, he returned to Vienna, where he appeared at the Theater in der Josefstadt, Theater an der Wien and the Carltheater and rapidly established himself as one of the most popular figures of his time. From 1832 until his death he was a close friend of NESTROY, who wrote a part for him in almost all his plays.

Schönemann, Johann Friedrich (1704–82), German actor. Appeared 1730–40 with CAROLINE NEUBER's company and formed his own in 1740, opening with RACINE's *Mithridate* in Lüneburg (with EKHOF, ACKERMANN and SOPHIE SCHRÖDER). He travelled in north and east Germany, concerned with raising the cultural level in the audience and, in accordance with GOTTSCHED's demands, dispensed with the HANSWURST interludes; in competition with Gottsched's *Deutsche Schaubühne* he published several volumes of his REPERTOIRE under the title *Schönemannsche Schaubühne*, 1748. In 1753–54, with Ekhof, he made the first attempt to establish a German school of acting.
Bibl: H. Kindermann, THEATERGESCHICHTE DER GOETHEZEIT, 1948; H. Devrient, JOHANN F. SCHÖNEMANN UND SEINE SCHAUSPIELERGESELLSCHAFT, 1895

Schönherr, Karl (1867–1943), Austrian dramatist. His powerful and realistic plays of Tyrolean peasant life, in the tradition of ANZENGRUBER, made him one of the most popular writers of his day in AUSTRIA: *Der Judas von Tirol* (The Judas of Tyrol), 1897 and 1927; *Der Bildschnitzer* (The Woodcarver), 1900; *Sonnwendtag* (Day of the Solstice), 1902; *Kärrnerleut'* (Draymen), 1904; *Erde* (Earth), 1907; *Das Königreich* (The Kingdom), 1908. His greatest successes were: *Glaube und Heimat* (Faith and Fatherland), 1910; *Der Weibsteufel* (The Female Devil), 1915.
Bibl: K. Paulin, 1950

Schönthan, Franz von (1849–1913), Austrian dramatist and actor. Famous for his innumerable farcical comedies (▷POSSE), mostly written in collaboration with MOSER and KADELBURG. His best-known piece is *Der Raub der Sabinerinnen* (The Rape of the Sabine Women), 1885, written with his brother Paul, which still remains in the REPERTOIRE.

School drama. Latin and, later, German plays during the Renaissance and Restoration era, developed under the influence of Humanism. They were original plays and adaptations, written by scholars for productions at schools and universities. In the 16th century themes were taken mostly from the Bible and classical antiquity. At

Oskar Schlemmer's *Grosse Brücken Revue*

School drama, an illustration from *Brockman Laurentis Bühne*, Cologne 1581

the time of the Reformation in GERMANY, preludes and interludes, eventually the whole play, were written in German. A separate form developed in JESUIT DRAMA. School drama reached its literary peak in the 16th century, but with the emergence of professional theatre in Germany during the 17th century, it declined in importance.

Schreyvogel, Joseph (1768–1832), Austrian critic and theatre manager. He was a friend of GOETHE, SCHILLER, Herder, Fichte and WIELAND. He collaborated on several literary magazines and 1807–08 edited, under a pseudonym, the Vienna *Sonntagsblatt*. His period as manager (officially 'artistic secretary') of the BURGTHEATER in Vienna, 1814–32, heralded its most successful era. He raised the level of the REPERTOIRE with productions of classical world literature (SHAKESPEARE, Goethe, Schiller, CALDERÓN), encouraged and produced GRILLPARZER, and built up an excellent ENSEMBLE, including, e.g. ANSCHÜTZ, despite constant opposition and censorship.
Bibl: E. Haeussermann, DIE BURG, 1964; J. Gregor, GESCHICHTE DES ÖSTERREICHISCHEN THEATERS, 1948

Schröder, Ernst (1915–), German actor and director. Studied under SCHMITT in Bochum; after varied experiences as an actor and drama teacher, his career really began in 1951 as an actor and director with major German theatre companies, including the Schillertheater, Schlossparktheater in BERLIN, the Munich Kammerspiele and the Zurich theatre. Characteristic parts included Mark Antony in *Julius Caesar*, 1952; the title role in MOLIÈRE's *Tartuffe*, Crofts in SHAW's *Mrs Warren's Profession*, 1955. Later he excelled in contemporary plays in parts such as de Sade in WEISS's *Marat/Sade*, 1964, and Hamm in BECKETT's *Endgame*, 1967, dir Beckett. His most remarkable productions include: GOETHE's *Faust*, Part II, 1966, in which he also played Mephistopheles; GOMBROWICZ's *The Wedding*, 1968; both at the Schillertheater. Author of the book *Die Arbeit des Schauspielers*, 1966.
Bibl: S. Melchinger, SCHAUSPIELER, 1965

Schröder, Friedrich Ludwig (1744–1816), German actor and theatre manager. He was the son of the actress Sophie Schröder and stepson of the theatre manager ACKERMANN who married her in 1749. He first appeared on stage at the age of three, and trained as an acrobat and dancer; but under the influence of EKHOF, who appeared in his stepfather's company, he devoted himself entirely to acting. In 1771 he took over from Ackermann the management of the Hamburg National Theatre, which he ran with his mother for the next ten years; here he produced e.g. LESSING's *Emilia Galotti*, 1772, and LILLO's *The London Merchant*, 1773. He supported the playwrights of the STURM UND DRANG movement and was the first to perform GOETHE's *Götz von Berlichingen* and *Clavigo* in 1774; he organized a drama competition which was won by KLINGER with his play *Die Zwillinge*, 1776; produced H. L. Wagner's *Die Reue nach der Tat*, 1776, and LENZ's *Hofmeister*, 1778. He appeared in these plays, mostly in comic parts and supporting roles such as Marinelli in *Emilia Galotti*, Carlos in *Clavigo*, Lerse in *Götz von Berlichingen*. The most important elements of his first management were his productions of SHAKESPEARE, which helped enormously to establish his plays in the German REPERTOIRE – though at the beginning they were somewhat modified versions of the originals which he adapted himself, often cutting whole acts and adding happy endings. He started in 1776 with a successful production of *Hamlet* (title role first played by Johann Brockmann with S. as the Ghost, in 1778 Hamlet played by S. himself); this was followed in the same year by an unsuccessful *Othello*; subsequently well received productions included *The Merchant of Venice*, 1778, with S. as Shylock; *Measure for Measure*, 1778; *King Lear*, 1778, with S. in the title role. Personal and financial difficulties led him to give up management and he then made a triumphant tour throughout Germany as a guest artist; in 1781 he joined the ENSEMBLE of the Vienna BURGTHEATER, in 1785 appeared in Altona, and 1786–98 managed the Hamburg National Theatre for the second time; he produced contemporary works by KOTZEBUE, IFFLAND and by himself (*Portrait der Mutter*, *Die unglückliche Heirat*, *Der Vetter von Lissabon*) of lesser quality but bringing more financial reward. S. also founded an organization for retired actors, retiring himself in 1798, though he took over the management of the Hamburg National Theatre once more (1811–12) during a crisis. He ranks with Ackermann and Ekhof as one of the founders of the great school of realistic acting in Germany; his discerning manner of acting strongly influenced the Burgtheater style; his carefully prepared Shakespeare productions did much to help build up a literary REPERTOIRE in the German theatre.
Bibl: D. Hadamoczik, F. L. SCHRÖDER IN DER GESCHICHTE DES BURGTHEATERS, 1961; K. Bowe, EKHOF, SCHRÖDER, IFFLAND, 1956

Schröter, Corona (1751–1802), German actress and singer. In 1776 she joined the Weimar theatre as a singer, also appearing in the parts of young comic heroines and in tragic roles, including GOETHE's *Iphigenie* in the first production of the play in 1779. She subsequently performed as the heroine in many of Goethe's plays.
Bibl: G. Sichardt, DAS WEIMARER LIEBHABERTHEATER UNTER GOETHES LEITUNG, 1957

Schuch, Franz (?–1764), Austrian actor and manager. Viennese HARLEQUIN, who in 1741 formed the Schuch travelling company, which appeared mainly in Germany (Gotha, Frankfurt, Leipzig). It developed into one of the leading German companies of the day with an ENSEMBLE of the finest actors including EKHOF, Brückner, Mecour, Brandes and later Sophie Hensel, one of the greatest players of heroic roles of her time. After S.'s death his son Franz took over the management.

Schuh, Oscar Fritz (1904–), German director and manager. Director at the Hamburg Opera, 1932–40, and 1940–50 at opera houses in Vienna, Milan, Rome and Venice. His best-known productions were of Mozart operas for the SALZBURG FESTIVAL (*Figaro*, *Don Giovanni*, *Die Zauberflöte*). With the stage designer NEHER, responsible for first productions of operas including *Dantons Tod* (G. v. Einem, 1947); *Antigone* (C. Orff, 1949). From 1951 he directed straight plays in BERLIN, where he was appointed director of the Theater am Kurfürstendamm in 1953; INTENDANT of the Hamburg theatre 1963–68. Characteristic of his interest in psychological drama are his productions of STRINDBERG, O'NEILL and FRISCH.
Bibl: O. F. Schuh & R. W. Willnauer, BÜHNE ALS GEISTIGER RAUM, 1963

Schuster, Ignaz (1779–1835), Austrian actor. One of the most popular players of the Viennese folk theatre, he joined the Leopoldstädter Theater company in 1801, where he remained for the rest of his life. He appeared in many of the local SINGSPIELE, in plays by Adolf Bäuerle and in the *Staberliaden* by Karl Carl.

Schwartz, Arthur (1900–), US composer and producer. Originally trained as a lawyer and teacher. He wrote the music for *Grand Street Follies*, 1926, and *The Little Show*, 1929. With Howard Dietz as lyricist, he collaborated on a number of other musicals including *The Second Little Show*, 1930; *Three's a Crowd*, 1930; *The Band Wagon*, 1932. Among his later shows are *Inside USA*, 1948; *A Tree Grows in Brooklyn*, 1951, and *Jennie* (starring MARY MARTIN), 1963.

Schweikart, Hans (1895–1975), German director and manager. Began his career as an actor and director at several German theatres, including BERLIN (Deutsches-Theater), Munich (Kammerspiele) and Vienna; he was artistic director of the Residenztheater in Munich 1934–38, and INTENDANT of the Munich Kammerspiele 1947–62. Subsequently worked as a guest director, mainly in Munich and Berlin. He ran the Munich Kammerspiele in the tradition of FALCKENBERG as an actor's theatre with emphasis on psychological nuances. Apart from his famous Shakespearean productions at the Residenztheater, he was best known for staging the premières of contemporary plays by DÜRRENMATT, HACKS and HOCHHUTH. He also worked as film director and script writer, 1938–42, and was the author of several books on the theatre and one successful COMEDY *Ich brauche dich* (I need you), 1942.

Scofield, Paul (1922–), English actor. After appearing with a student repertory company and on tour during World War II, he joined the BIRMINGHAM REPERTORY THEATRE, where he achieved his first success as the Bastard in SHAKESPEARE's *King John* in 1945. A year later he moved with JACKSON, who was appointed director of the Memorial Theatre, to STRATFORD-UPON-

AVON where he remained until 1948, appearing in leading Shakespearean roles including Hamlet, Henry IV and Don Armado in *Love's Labour's Lost*, dir BROOK. In the following years he played a great variety of parts, notably the twin brothers Hugo and Frederic in *Ring Round the Moon*, 1950 (FRY's adaptation of ANOUILH's play *L'Invitation au château*); the title role in Shakespeare's *Richard II*, dir GIELGUD, 1952; Pierre in OTWAY's *Venice Preserved*, 1953. In 1955–56 he appeared for a season with Brook at the Phoenix Theatre: in GREENE's *The Power and the Glory*, as the priest; in ELIOT's *The Family Reunion*; and as Hamlet. Another outstanding role was Sir Thomas More in BOLT's *A Man for All Seasons*, 1960. In 1962 came his famous performance as Lear in Brook's production with the ROYAL SHAKESPEARE COMPANY, which was seen in Paris in 1963, and made a world tour in 1964. He appeared in Shakespeare's *Timon of Athens*, 1965–66; *Macbeth*, also RSC, dir HALL, 1967; at the ROYAL COURT in the first production of OSBORNE's *Hotel in Amsterdam*, 1968, and in CHEKHOV's *Uncle Vanya*, 1970, at the OLD VIC in PIRANDELLO's *The Rules of the Game*, 1972, as West in Christopher Hampton's *Savages*, 1973, Royal Court, and most recently in FUGARD's *Dimetos*, 1976.

Paul Scofield in BROOK's production of *King Lear*, 1962

Friedrich Schröder as Falstaff in 1780

Scotland. In the 15th and 16th centuries MORALITY PLAYS and festival PAGEANTS. The drama of the Middle Ages reached its peak with one great play, the poetic satire *Ane Plaesant Satyre on the Thrie Estaitis*, 1540, by SIR DAVID LINDSAY (?1490–1555). From the 17th to the 18th century religious prohibitions and strong licensing laws rendered the theatre almost non-existent. Theatres were either closed or burnt down, e.g. the first Scottish Playhouse, which had been opened in 1736; however, in 1756 the Rev. John Home's *Douglas* was successfully produced there, despite opposition from the Church. In the 19th century stock companies in Edinburgh and Glasgow, where mostly English plays were performed. The first prominent dramatist was BARRIE, whose *The Little Minister*, 1897, was enormously successful in both Scotland and England, but John Brand (1869–1947) is considered the father of modern Scottish drama. He is best known for his comedy *The Glen is Mine*, 1923. Due to his influence and the founding of the first professional theatre, the Scottish Players Limited, many others were encouraged to become playwrights: John Ferguson (1873–1928), Dr Gordon Bottomly (1874–1948), BRIDIE (1888–1951). After World War I the Scottish National Players emerged, a group of actors who mainly produced works by Scottish native dramatists, including Bridie, Brandane, Joe Corrie, Ferguson, Neil Gunn and Robin Millar. The Scottish National Theatre Society, formed in 1922, failed in its attempt to found a NATIONAL THEATRE, but worked with great effectiveness until the 1930s. Today there are a number of REPERTORY companies, notably at the GLASGOW CITIZENS' THEATRE and Lyceum in Edinburgh; the annual EDINBURGH FESTIVAL, founded 1947, is an international event.

Scotland, settings by Alexander Nasmyth for Sir Walter Scott's *Heart of Midlothian*, 1819–20

Scribe, Eugène (1791–1861), French dramatist and librettist. A master of the WELL-MADE PLAY, he wrote about 400 dramatic works, sometimes with collaborators, including VAUDEVILLE scripts, COMEDIES, LIBRETTI (for *opéra comique*), and full-length plays. The success of his plays is based on his enormous talent for fusing a simple but precise PLOT with themes based on social topical situations and manners, full of suspense and ingenious COUPS DE THÉÂTRE, as in *Bertrand et Raton*, one of his best known and most brilliant comedies, or *Le Verre d'eau*, 1840, translated as *The Ladies' Battle* and *The Queen's Gambit*, 1883. As resident dramatist of the Théâtre du Gymnase, he was required to write 12 plays a year, though he sometimes managed to write 18; half a dozen of his works were later included in the REPERTOIRE of the COMÉDIE-FRANÇAISE. Major works include: *Une Nuit de la Garde Nationale*, 1815; *Le Solliciteur ou l'Art d'obtenir des places*, 1817; *Le Charlatanisme*, 1825; *Le Mariage de raison*, 1826; *Malvina, ou le Mariage d'inclination*, 1828; *La Frontière de Savoie*, 1834; *Le Mariage d'argent*, 1827; *L'Ambitieux*, 1834; *La Camaraderie, ou la Courte échelle*, 1837; *La Calomnie*, 1840; *Une Chaîne*, 1841; *Le Puff, ou Mensonge et vérité*, 1848, etc. His only tragedy *Adrienne Lecouvreur*, 1849, with E. Legouvé, in which RACHEL first excelled, later provided a famous leading part for SARAH BERNHARDT and other great actresses.
Bibl: N. C. Arvin, EUGÈNE SCRIBE AND THE FRENCH THEATRE 1815–60, 1924

Segal, Alex (1915–), US director. Best known for his work in TV, since 1951 ABC-TV New York. Has also successfully produced several stage plays including M. Levin's *Compulsion*, 1957; KRASNA's *Who Was That Lady I Saw You With?*, 1958; L. Coleman's *Jolly's Progress*, 1959; F. Bauer/M. Dubey *We Take the Town*, 1962; D. Wassermann's *One Flew Over the Cuckoo's Nest*, 1963. He has been awarded a number of prizes for his TV productions and in 1949 the Peabody Award for his work at the ACTORS' STUDIO.

Sellner, Gustav Rudolf (1905–), Austrian director and manager. Appointed INTENDANT of the Darmstadt theatre in 1951, in 1962 he took over the management of the Berlin Opera. In Darmstadt with his DRAMATURG Egon Vietta (and later Claus Bremer) and the stage designers MERTZ and RAFFAELLI, he developed a style of production that emphasized simplicity and choreographic elements, and was widely influential in Germany in the 1950s; his REPERTORY was mainly Shakespearean, but he also successfully produced new adaptations of Greek TRAGEDIES, as well as many examples of the THEATRE OF THE ABSURD, e.g. IONESCO's *The Killer*, first staged in Darmstadt, 1958. He also directed GOETHE's *Iphigenie* at the Ruhrfestspiele, 1956, a series of plays by SOPHOCLES at the BURGTHEATER in Vienna, 1960–63, and SHAKESPEARE's *The Tempest* at the Hamburg Schauspielhaus. Author of *Theatralische Landschaft*, 1962.
Bibl: G. Hensel, KRITIKEN. EIN JAHRZEHNT SELLNERTHEATER IN DARMSTADT, 1962

Semper, Gottfried (1803–79), German architect. After Schinkel the most important architect of the 19th century in Germany. Designed and built the COURT THEATRE in Dresden (1838–42), the Neues Hoftheater (Opera House, 1870–78) and the BURGTHEATER in Vienna (1870–88). He also wrote several treatises on architecture including *Kleine Schriften*, 1884, and *Der Stil*, 2 vols, 1878–79.
Bibl: E. Stockmeyer, 1939

Seneca, Lucius Annaeus (the Younger; *c.*4 BC–AD 65), Roman philosopher and writer of TRAGEDY. His are the only completely preserved Roman tragedies; they were not designed to be produced but to be declaimed (a single actor recited all the parts or the most important scenes of the play, or they were acted by MIMES accompanied by DIALOGUE or music), therefore they have no development of PLOT and character, but are composed as eulogies of passion and greatness in superb RHETORIC, showing man in the crucial battle between the Stoic absolutes of passion and reason. His works greatly influenced classical French tragedy, and the earliest English tragedy, e.g. *Gorboduc*, fp 1561, London, Inner Temple Hall, as well as SHAKESPEARE's *Richard III*, *c.*1593, and RENAISSANCE and BAROQUE THEATRE generally. The titles of S.'s nine extant tragedies are: *Hercules Furens, Troades, Phoenissae, Medea, Phaedra, Oedipus, Thyestes, Agamemnon, Hercules Oetaeus*; most critics do not consider *Octavia*, the only surviving Roman *fabula praetexta* (▷FABULA), to be his work.
Bibl: E. F. Watling, INTRODUCTION TO SENECA'S FOUR TRAGEDIES

Serlio, Sebastiano (1475–1554), Italian painter and architect. After years of practical work as a painter and theatre architect, he published a work, *Regole generali di Architettura*, in Venice 1551. Part II, which contained six chapters on how to build stages and scenery, appeared first in Paris in 1545 under the title *Le Second Livre de la perspective*, and was translated into English in 1611 as *The Second Book of Architecture*. Much of it was based on drawings and notes made by PERUZZI who was studying the works of VITRUVIUS during the time that S. was his pupil. S.'s book had great influence on the development of the Renaissance stage and architecture in general, in particular that part which dealt with PERSPECTIVE.
Bibl: G. Schöne, DIE ENTWICKLUNG DER PERSPEKTIVBÜHNE, 1933

Servetta. Servant maid in Italian comedy, the female counterpart of the ZANNI. Also known as Fantesca, Serva, Zagna; the most frequently used names are Franceschina, Pasquella, Smeraldina, COLOMBINA, Spinetta, Olivetta, for variations of the same basic character.

Seyler, Abel (1730–1800), German ACTOR-MANAGER. Originally a merchant, he married the actress Sophie Hensel, and took his own company all over Germany from 1769. He gave guest performances of *Hamlet* and *Macbeth* at the Mannheim National Theatre, the management of which he took over in 1781, and was director of the COURT THEATRE in Schleswig, 1783–92. He was one of the pioneers of the German National Theatre, supporting the dramatists of the STURM UND DRANG era and contributing to the popularity of SHAKESPEARE on the German stage.

Seyler, Athene (1899–), English actress. Made her début in 1909 in London and has since then appeared in the London theatre almost without interruption, mainly in DRAWING-ROOM COMEDY and modern plays, but also in RESTORATION DRAMA and SHAKESPEARE. One of the wittiest comediennes of her time. Elected President of the Council of the ROYAL ACADEMY OF DRAMATIC ART in 1950.

Seyrig, Delphine (1932–), French actress. Appeared from 1952 at various theatres in Paris and the provinces, before going to the USA, where she worked 1956–60 (ACTORS' STUDIO, OFF-BROADWAY roles, TV). Made her breakthrough in France with a film role in Resnais's *Last Year in Marienbad*, and on stage as Nina in CHEKHOV's *The Seagull*, Théâtre Moderne, dir PITOËFF. She gave an outstanding performance as Natalia in TURGENEV's *A Month in the Country*, 1962, Théâtre de l'Atelier, dir BARSACQ. She also appeared successfully in PINTER's *The Collection* and *The Lover*, 1965. Has appeared in a number of films, notably Buñuel's *The Discreet Charm of the Bourgeoisie*, 1973.

Shadow play. A form of PUPPET PLAY in which the moving silhouettes of the characters appear on a screen of paper lit from behind. The figures are articulated so that their limbs can be moved by sticks from below or by concealed strings. Originating in the Far East, it is particularly highly developed in INDONESIA (Bali, Java). From there the shadow play reached the Middle and Near East, especially TURKEY where the *Karagöz* shadow play became a popular folk entertainment. In the 18th century Les Ombres Chinoises became the fashion in France. In ENGLAND this developed into the Galanty Show, performed at country fairs. The animated silhouettes of Lotte Reininger's fairy-tale films must be regarded as a revival of the shadow play, which, in its techniques, can be considered a precursor of the animated film cartoon.

Shadwell, Thomas (*c.*1642–92), English dramatist. Followed the Comedy of Humours in the tradition of JONSON, whose disciple he claimed to be, rather than the fashionable Comedy of Manners (▷COMEDY). He satirized early RESTORATION DRAMA and the HEROIC DRAMA of DRYDEN, which led to intense literary quarrels with the latter, whom he succeeded as Poet Laureate. He also adapted SHAKESPEARE; his version of *The Tempest*, called

The Enchanted Island, 1674, was an operatic spectacle with emphasis on the STAGE MACHINERY and scenery of the time. His best plays include: *The Sullen Lovers, or The Impertinents*, 1668, based on MOLIÈRE's *Les Fâcheux*; *Epsom-Wells*, 1672; *The Squire of Alsatia*, 1688; *Bury-Fair*, 1689.
Bibl: A. S. Borgman, THOMAS SHADWELL, HIS LIFE AND COMEDIES, 1928

Shaffer. (1) **Anthony S.** (1926–), English dramatist. After a number of TV scripts and the play *The Savage Paradise*, 1963, he wrote the thriller *Sleuth*, 1970, which became a commercial hit in the West End, on BROADWAY and as a film. (2) **Peter S.**, twin brother of A.S., is also a dramatist. Began as a writer of TV plays, e.g. *Balance of Terror*, *The Salt-land*, and achieved his first success in the theatre with *Five Finger Exercise*, 1958. This was followed by two one-act plays, *The Private Ear* and *The Public Eye*, 1962, and the text of a revue for JOAN LITTLEWOOD, *Merry Roosters Panto*, 1963. His best-known works are *The Royal Hunt of the Sun*, a historical drama about the Spanish conquest of Peru, successfully performed by the NATIONAL THEATRE company at the CHICHESTER FESTIVAL, and in London 1964; and *Equus*, 1973, National Theatre, and in New York 1974.

Shakespeare, William (1564–1616), English dramatist. Undoubtedly the greatest and most influential playwright of modern times. Relatively little is known about his life: the entry in the Stratford-upon-Avon parish church register of baptisms is dated 26 April 1564, hence his presumed birth-date is 23 April. His father, John Shakespeare, is referred to as a glover, but is also known to have traded in barley, timber and wool. Little is known about his early life, except that he married Anne Hathaway at Stratford in 1582 and had a daughter Susanna in May 1583, and two further children, the twins Hamnet and Judith, in February 1585. First mention of one of his plays, *Henry VI, Part I*, by HENSLOWE, March 1592. In 1594 he appears as one of the partners of the company of the CHAMBERLAIN'S MEN, together with KEMPE and R. BURBAGE. There are also references to his having appeared as an actor in various plays. The fact that he acquired a house in Stratford in 1597 shows that he achieved prosperity. In 1599 he became one of the 'householders' of the new GLOBE THEATRE, with a one-tenth share. In 1610 he sold his share and retired to Stratford.
Of his 37 plays only sixteen were printed in his lifetime, mainly in corrupt quarto editions. Seven years after his death on 23 April 1616, his former colleagues with the King's Men (as the CHAMBERLAIN'S MEN later became known), Heminge and Condell, published a collected edition containing 36 plays, the First Folio (1623). S. had written his plays for his acting company, who performed them at the Swan and the Globe as well as on special occasions at Court. It is certain that he did not prepare them for publication. The Folio texts are based on prompt copies, often imperfect and misread by the printer. His plays are

Shakespeare's *Titus Andronicus*, sketch illustrating first scene, *c.* 1594

Shakespeare Memorial Theatre, Stratford-upon-Avon

Shakespeare, *Romeo and Juliet*, production by NUNN, RSC 1976

usually grouped in five periods (but the exact dating of composition and performances must often remain a matter for conjecture). (1) The early period: *Henry VI*, Part I (1589/90); *Henry VI*, Part II and Part III (1590/91); *Richard III* and *Titus Andronicus* (1592/3); *The Comedy of Errors* and *The Taming of the Shrew* (1593/94). (2) A period of (mainly) lyrical plays: *The Two Gentlemen of Verona* and *Love's Labour's Lost* (1594/95); *Romeo and Juliet*, *Richard II* and *A Midsummer Night's Dream* (1595/96); *King John* and *The Merchant of Venice* (1596/97). (3) The period of the mature histories and COMEDIES: *Henry IV*, Parts I and II (1597/98); *Much Ado about Nothing*, *Henry V*, *The Merry Wives of Windsor* (1598/99); *Julius Caesar*, *As You Like It* and *Twelfth Night* (1599–1600). (4) The period of the problem plays (or the TRAGICOMEDIES): *Troilus and Cressida* (1601/02); *All's Well That Ends Well* and *Measure for Measure* (1603/04); and the great TRAGEDIES: *Hamlet* (1600/01); *Othello* (1602/03); *Timon of Athens* (1604/05); *King Lear* and *Macbeth* (1605/06); *Antony and Cleopatra* (1606/07); *Coriolanus* (1607/08). (5) The period of the romances: *Pericles, Prince of Tyre* (1608/09); *Cymbeline* (1609/10); *The Winter's Tale* (1610/11); *The Tempest* (1611/12); *Henry VIII* (1612/13). A number of other plays have been ascribed to S., notably *Edward III* (*c.* 1590–95) and *The Two Noble Kinsmen* (1613–16); the latter may have been written in conjunction with FLETCHER, who may also have collaborated on *Henry VIII*. His plays, written for a truly popular theatre, were undervalued in the 18th century because they lacked elegance. Nevertheless, they retained their popularity in the REPERTOIRE, although they were often performed in adaptations which provided alternative endings and took other liberties with the text. It was only in the early 19th century, under the influence of critics like COLERIDGE and HAZLITT, that his true greatness as a poet and dramatist began to be appreciated. But even in the 19th century the staging of his plays tried to press them into the mould of the five-act well-made play. Towards the end of the 19th century directors like POEL and GRANVILLE-BARKER insisted on restoring the flow of the action written for a stage which had a minimum of scenery by using simple all-purpose sets. Outside Britain his influence on the rise of German classical drama was decisive. LESSING was the chief advocate of S. as a model of true tragedy as against the artificiality of the French model, tied down by its rigid rules of three unities. In France itself S. became the watchword of the Romantic movement in drama, of which HUGO was the protagonist. In many of the emergent national cultures of central and southern Europe translations of S. constituted the first step towards a national revival of drama. S.'s greatness lies in his profound insight into human nature, the richness of his characterization and the beauty and strength of his language, in verse or prose. Throughout the world to play the big Shakespearean roles is the ambition of every actor aspiring to greatness. ▷HAMLET.

Bibl: the literature of Shakespeare is too immense to be listed even in a brief selection. A useful encyclopaedia on the work of Shakespeare is F. E. Halliday, A SHAKESPEARE COMPANION, 1964, which also contains an extensive bibliography.

Shaw, George Bernard (1856–1950), Irish playwright, critic, socialist and moralist. Started as music critic and was drama critic of the *Saturday Review* 1895–98, conducting a vigorous campaign in favour of the socially conscious drama of IBSEN. After an abortive collaboration on a play with Ibsen's translator ARCHER, he wrote a spirited attack on slum landlordism in his play *Widowers' Houses*, 1892. Aware of the difficulty of getting plays so different from the usual fare of the London theatre performed, Shaw tried to make his plays readable by adding extensive stage-direction, and prefaced them with essays, often lengthy, on social, political or philosophical themes. Yet, however strong the didactic and propagandist objectives of S.'s plays have been in his own mind, their effect arises largely from his exuberant interest in people, his wit, love of paradox and his brilliant handling of dramatic DIALOGUE. One of the founders of the Fabian Society, he was a lifelong socialist and later developed his own vitalist philosophy, a belief in a life force which inspires the forward movement of evolution. His main plays are: *The Philanderer*, 1893, fp 1907; *Mrs Warren's Profession*, 1893, fp 1902; *Arms and the Man*, 1894; *Candida*, 1895; *The Man of Destiny*, 1895, fp 1897; *You Never Can Tell*, 1895, fp 1899; *The Devil's Disciple*, 1896/97, fp 1897; *Caesar and Cleopatra*, 1899, fp 1907; *Captain Brassbound's Conversion*, 1900; *Man and Superman*, 1901–03, fp 1905; *John Bull's Other Island*, 1904; *How He Lied to Her Husband*, 1905; *Major Barbara*, 1905; *The Doctor's Dilemma*, 1906; *Getting Married*, 1908; *Misalliance*, 1910; *The Dark Lady of the Sonnets*, 1910; *Fanny's First Play*, 1911; *Androcles and the Lion*, 1912; *Pygmalion*, 1913; *Heartbreak House*, 1920; *Back to Methuselah*, 1922, a cycle of five full-length plays; *Saint Joan*, 1923; *The Apple Cart*, 1929; *Too True to Be Good*, 1932; *Village Wooing*, 1933, fp 1934; *The Millionairess*, 1936; *In Good King Charles's Golden Days*, 1939. He received the Nobel Prize for Literature in 1925. His influence as political pamphleteer and pioneer of socially committed drama has been immense but it is also significant that the plot of one of his plays, *Pygmalion*, should have formed the basis of one of the most successful musicals of all time, *My Fair Lady*.
Bibl: Dan H. Laurence (ed), COLLECTED LETTERS, 1965; R. Mander & J. Mitchenson, THEATRICAL COMPANION TO SHAW, 1955; L. Kronenberger, GEORGE BERNARD SHAW, A CRITICAL SURVEY; E. Bentley, 1950; F. Harris, 1938

Shaw, Glen Byam (1904–), English actor and director. A sensitive and elegant performer, he appeared in a number of notable productions of the classics but gradually turned to directing. After World War II he became one of the three artistic heads of the OLD VIC, with SAINT-DENIS and DEVINE, and in 1952 was appointed co-director of the Shakespeare Memorial Theatre at STRATFORD-UPON-AVON with QUAYLE, and, after the latter's resignation in 1956, sole director of the company until 1959. Has since directed plays and opera.

Shaw, Irwin (1913–), US novelist, critic and playwright. A member of the GROUP THEATRE, he wrote a number of plays dealing critically with social topics, notably the anti-war one-acter *Bury the Dead*, 1936, and *The Gentle People*, 1939, about simple people dealing forcefully with a racketeer. Other plays are *Siege*, 1937; *Quiet City*, 1939; *Sons and Soldiers*, 1944; *The Assassin*, 1945, about the murder of Admiral Darlan in Algiers. His novel *The Young Lions*, 1948, about Hitler's Germany, was adapted successfully as a film.

Shaw, Robert (1927–), English actor, novelist and dramatist. His early work includes the plays *Off the Mainland*, 1956, and *The Pets*, 1960, a TV play adapted from his own novel *The Hiding Place*. *The Man in the Glass Booth*, 1967, based on his own novel, was directed in London and on BROADWAY by PINTER and starred Donald Pleasance.

Shchepkin, Mikhail Semyonovich (1788–1863), Russian actor. Son of a serf, he was an important figure in the development of a realistic style of acting in his country. He combined passion with technical perfection, his characters always being clinically observed and truthfully presented. His style of acting was later exemplified in the plays of OSTROVSKY, CHEKHOV and GORKY; STANISLAVSKY considered him to be the founder of the Russian art of acting. Among his best work were performances in GOGOL's *The Government Inspector*, and GRIBOYEDOV's *Gore ot Uma* (*Woe from Wit*); in SHAKESPEARE's COMEDIES, e.g. *The Merchant of Venice* (Shylock), and in *Hamlet* (Polonius); in the comedies of SHERIDAN and MOLIÈRE, and also in some of SCHILLER's plays. TURGENEV wrote a number of comedies for him.
Bibl: J. Sobolev, 1933.

Shchukin, Boris Vasilievich (1894–1939), Soviet actor. In 1920 joined VAKHTANGOV at what became the Third Studio of the MOSCOW ART THEATRE, playing leading roles. One of his finest parts was Tartaglia in Vakhtangov's last and most famous production, GOZZI's *Turandot*, in 1922. In the following years he gave fine performances in plays by OSTROVSKY and GOGOL, and after 1925 specialized in plays by contemporary playwrights including KATAYEV, POGODIN, AFINOGENOV, etc.
Bibl: P. Nobicki, 1945

Sheldon, Edward Brewster (1886–1946), US dramatist. Studied playwriting at Harvard with BAKER at the 47 Workshop and achieved his first success with *Salvation Nell*, 1908. His next play *The Nigger*, 1909, raised hopes that he might become a serious dramatist who would not shy away from pressing social problems: the play deals with the governor of a southern State who discovers that he has Negro blood in his veins. *The Boss*, 1911, also deals realistically with American politics. But his subsequent work belied these hopes and was on the lines of romantic MELODRAMA: *The Princess Zim-Zim*, 1911; *Egypt*, 1912; *The High Road*, 1912, and *Romance*, 1913, his greatest popular success. *The Garden of Paradise*, 1914, is an adaptation of Hans Andersen's fairy-tale *The Little Mermaid*. Other plays: *Bewitched*, with S. HOWARD, 1924; *Lulu Belle*, with MacARTHUR, 1926; *Dishonored Lady*, with Margaret Ayer Barnes, 1930.

Shelley, Percy Bysshe (1792–1822), English romantic poet and dramatist. He wrote several dramatic works in verse: *Prometheus Unbound*, a lyrical drama, pub 1820; *Oedipus Tyrannus, or Swellfoot the Tyrant*, a burlesque, pub 1820; *Hellas*, a lyrical drama, pub 1822. These were unsuccessful on the stage. His best-known work for the stage is *The Cenci*, pub 1819, which has been revived several times; important in theatre history for ARTAUD's adaptation. His other dramatic work includes translations of EURIPIDES' SATYR PLAY *The Cyclops*, scenes from GOETHE's *Faust* and scenes from CALDERÓN's *El magico prodigioso*.
Bibl: E. S. Bates, A STUDY OF SHELLEY'S 'THE CENCI', 1908

Shepard, Sam (1943–), US underground playwright. Raised near Los Angeles, he acted his way to New York with Bishop's Company Repertory Players and spent many years writing plays for OFF-BROADWAY, among them *Chicago*, *Red Cross*, *Cowboys*, *Rock Garden*, *4-H Club*, *Dog* and *Icarus's Mother* (ROYAL COURT, Theatre Upstairs, London 1971); *Melodrama Play*, fp LA MAMA (repertory) in Europe; *Fourteen Hundred Thousand*, National Educational TV network; *La Turista*, American Place Theatre, and Royal Court, Theatre Upstairs. His first full-length play *Operation Sidewinder*, was given at the Lincoln Center, New York 1970; another, *The Tooth of Crime*, London 1972, at the Open Space Theatre. One of his sketches is included in the review *Oh! Calcutta!* He has received numerous OBIE AWARDS, has written films in Hollywood, contributed to Antonioni's *Zabriskie Point*, and is a passionate drummer.

Sheridan, Richard Brinsley (1751–1816), Irish-born dramatist, manager and politician. His most famous play *The School for Scandal*, 1777, remains one of the finest examples of the English Comedy of Manners (▷COMEDY). He was the son of the actor Thomas S. and the novelist Frances S. Nearly all his work ridicules the sentimentality of his time with agile wit and presents excellent character portrayals: *The Rivals*, comedy, 1775; *The Duenna*, comic opera, 1775; *A Trip to Scarborough*, comedy, 1777 (an adaptation of VANBRUGH's *The Relapse*, 1696); *The Critic, or a Tragedy Rehearsed*, burlesque, 1779. *Pizarro*, 1799, is a TRAGEDY based on KOTZEBUE. In 1776 S. bought GARRICK's share in the THEATRE

George Bernard Shaw, portrait by Augustus John

Shaw's *Saint Joan*, with SYBIL THORNDIKE, London 1924

Sheridan, *The School for Scandal*, 1778

ROYAL, DRURY LANE, rebuilding it in 1794, where despite persistent financial difficulties, he remained until its destruction by fire in 1809. He became a Member of Parliament in 1780.
Bibl: O. Sherwin, 1960; W. A. Darlington, 1951

Sherriff, Robert Cedric (1896–1975), English dramatist. Educated at New College, Oxford. For several years, as a young insurance official, he wrote plays for an amateur society. His first London production, *Journey's End*, was presented by the Stage Society at the Apollo Theatre, 1928, with OLIVIER as Stanhope; after its outstandingly successful production at the Savoy, 1929, it was translated and performed throughout the world. The most recent revival was in London 1973. It is a profoundly moving war play with an all male cast in a dug-out before St Quentin on the eve of the March offensive of 1918. Other plays: *Badger's Green*, 1930; *Windfall*, 1933; *St Helena*, 1935, with Jeanne de Casalis; *Miss Mabel*, 1948; *Home at Seven*, 1950; *The White Carnation*, 1953; *The Long Sunset*, 1955; *The Telescope*, 1957. He has also written novels and screenplays for many famous films, e.g. *The Invisible Man*, *Lady Hamilton*, *Goodbye Mr Chips*, *Mrs Miniver*. His autobiography *No Leading Lady* was published in 1968.
Bibl: J. C. Trewin, DRAMATISTS OF TODAY, 1953

Sherwood, Robert Emmet (1896–1955), US dramatist. Made his reputation with urbane comedies as well as more serious plays with social and political content. His earliest success was *The Road to Rome*, 1926, with JANE COWL. This was followed by *Reunion in Vienna*, THEATRE GUILD 1931, with the LUNTS; *The Petrified Forest*, New York 1935, dir HOPKINS, with L. HOWARD; *Idiot's Delight*, Theatre Guild 1935, with the Lunts; *Abe Lincoln in Illinois*, 1938, dir RICE, the first play put on by the PLAYWRIGHTS' COMPANY; *There Shall Be No Night*, 1940, again with the Lunts. He won three PULITZER PRIZES. President of ANTA in 1949 he had several wartime appointments and wrote many of President Roosevelt's speeches.
Bibl: R. B. Schumann, ROBERT E. SHERWOOD, 1964; J. W. Krutch, THEATRE IN OUR TIME, 1954

Shirley, James (1596–1666), English dramatist. Wrote some 40 dramas among the best of which are the COMEDIES, which provide a link between those of JONSON and the writers of RESTORATION DRAMA, such as *The Witty Fair One*, 1628; *The Gamester*, 1633; and *The Lady of Pleasure*, 1635; and the TRAGEDIES such as *The Maid's Revenge*, 1626; *The Traitor*, 1631; *Love's Cruelty*, 1631; *The Cardinal*, 1641. He also wrote a number of MASQUES including *The Triumph of Peace*, 1634; *The Triumph of Beauty*, pub 1646. After MASSINGER's death in 1640, he became resident playwright of the King's Men (GLOBE and BLACKFRIARS THEATRES) and was London's leading dramatist when the theatres were closed by the Puritans in 1642. He enjoyed considerable popularity during the early days of the Restoration but died as the result of terror and exposure during the Great Fire of London.

Sholem Aleichem (Schalom Rabinowitz; 1859–1916), Jewish novelist. A journalist in Kiev till he emigrated to the USA in 1905, he wrote several novels and short stories about the life of East European Jews and of American immigrants. His best-known character is the milkman, Tevye, in the novel of the same title, which in 1964 became the successful Broadway musical *Fiddler on the Roof*, and was subsequently filmed. Many of his stories were dramatized for the stage by Jewish companies (M. Schwartz in New York; GRANOVSKY in Moscow) and were also translated into Hebrew to become part of the REPERTOIRE of the HABIMAH THEATRE: e.g. *Der Oysvurf* (The Treasure), written 1908; *Shver tsu zayn a Yid* (It's Hard to Be a Jew), written 1914, produced in New York with MUNI; *Dos Groyse Gevins* (Grand Prize; also known as '200,000'), written 1914; *Tevye der Milkhiker* (Tevye the Milkman), written 1915. A one-act play, *The World of Sholem Aleichem*, New York 1953, London 1955, based on short stories by S. A. and PERETZ, was written by A. Perl. S.A. wrote the memoirs of his childhood in *The Great Fair*, pub 1955.
Bibl: M. Waife-Goldberg, MY FATHER, SHOLEM ALEICHEM, 1968

Showboat. Name given to the floating theatre of the great rivers of the west in America, particularly the Mississippi and the Ohio, which represented an early and successful attempt to bring drama to the pioneer settlements. The first record of one dates from 1817 under Noah Ludlow (▷S. SMITH); William Chapman, formerly an actor in London and New York, became the first manager of a showboat, a large flat boat with a structure on it labelled 'Theatre'. The interior was long and narrow with a shallow stage at one end and benches in front, the whole being lit by candles. Here Mr and Mrs Chapman and their five children played one-night stands along the rivers. The chief productions were MELODRAMAS like KOTZEBUE's *The Stranger* or fairy-tales such as *Cinderella*. The Chapmans eventually sold their boat to Smith who lost it in a collision. A more elaborate showboat was the floating Circus Palace of Spaulding and Rogers, built in 1851. The great showboat era ended with the outbreak of Civil War in 1861 and it was never so popular again though it still continued. The subject was vividly described in EDNA FERBER's popular novel *Show Boat*, 1935, dramatized for stage and screen.

Shtraukh, Maxim Maximovich (1900–74), Soviet actor. Worked 1921–25 at the Prolet-cult theatre, and 1921–24 appeared in many of EISENSTEIN's films, e.g. *Battleship Potemkin*. From 1929 he worked at the Meyerhold Theatre and in films. His most memorable performances were as Lenin in KORNEICHUK's *Truth* and Eisenstein's *Three Songs on Lenin*, and, on stage, in VISHNEVSKY's *The Unforgettable Year 1919*, 1949.

Shubert. US family of theatre managers and directors. (1) **Sam S.** (1876–1905), after varied experiences in the theatre business, formed his own touring company in 1894. Later, with his brothers, (2) **Lee S.** (1875–1935) and (3) **Jacob J. S.** (1880–1963), he moved to New York, where they fought against the powerful THEATRICAL SYNDICATE by forming the Shubert Theatre Corporation which soon controlled a major part of the theatre in New York and all over the USA. They owned 15 of 32 active commercial theatres in New York, also seven out of nine in Chicago, two of the three in Detroit and all theatres of Boston, Baltimore, Cincinnati, Los Angeles, Philadelphia, Pittsburgh and other cities. In 1949 the government invoked the anti-trust laws against them, and six years later Jacob J. S. sold 12 of the Corporation's playhouses.
Bibl: J. Stagg, THE BROTHERS SHUBERT, 1968

Shvarts, Yevgeni Lvovich (1896–1958), Soviet writer and dramatist. Only moderately popular during his lifetime, he was a brilliant wit, one of a few whose works are free of Marxist cant and criticize the essence of the authoritarian state. Best known for his satirical fairy-tale dramas, some written originally for children but which entered the REPERTOIRE of professional adult theatre: *Ten* (The Shadow), 1933, about the Stalinist era; *Drakon* (*The Dragon*), 1943, which debunks political tyranny. Other plays include adaptations of Hans Andersen's stories: *Goly Korol* (The Naked King), 1934, from *The Emperor's New Clothes*; *Snezhnaya koroleva* (The Snow Queen), 1938, and other well-known fairy-tales like *Little Red Riding-Hood* as *Krasnaya shapochka*, 1937. Many of his plays, banned under Stalin, were restaged in the 1960s by AKIMOV, who produced his last play, *An Ordinary Miracle* at the Leningrad Comic Theatre in 1958. A famous production of *Drakon* by BESSON was staged in Berlin 1960, Deutsches-Theater.

Siddons, Sarah (*née* Kemble: 1755–1831), English actress. One of the greatest tragediennes of the English stage. The eldest daughter of R. KEMBLE, she married the actor William Siddons at the age of 18. On the strength of her appearances in the provinces, GARRICK engaged her for DRURY LANE, but her Portia in 1775 was a failure and she returned to the provinces; however, back in London in 1782, she won acclaim as a tragic actress: as Isabella in SOUTHERNE's *The Fatal Marriage*, Belvidera in OTWAY's *Venice Preserved*, 1782; and in a series of Shakespearean roles including Isabella in *Measure for Measure*, 1783, Constance in *King John*, 1783, Ophelia, 1785, Katharine in *Henry VIII*, 1788, and Gertrude in *Hamlet*, 1795. She also gave fine performances in contemporary plays, e.g. KOTZEBUE's *The Stranger* and *Pizarro*, 1799, but her best part was Lady Macbeth, in which she made her farewell appearance in 1812. She was praised for her beauty, intelligence and nobility. HAZLITT said of her: 'Power was seated on her brow; passion emanated from her breast as from a shrine. She was tragedy personified . . .' Bibl: Y. French, 1954

Sievert, Ludwig (1887–1968) German stage designer. He made his début in 1912 in Freiburg with designs for Wagner's opera-cycle *Der Ring des Nibelungen*, strongly influenced by APPIA. During his period at the Mannheim National Theatre, 1914–19, under the direction of C. Hagemann, with the director WEICHERT and the conductor Furtwängler, he turned from his early *fin de siècle* style towards EXPRESSIONISM. Especially important was his collaboration with Weichert in Frankfurt, from 1919, on several Expressionist plays by HASENCLEVER, WEDEKIND and KOKOSCHKA.
Bibl: K. MacGowan & R. E. Jones, CONTINENTAL STAGECRAFT, 1923

Simon, Neil (1927–), US dramatist. In his early career collaborated with his brother Danny on summer REVUES, shows for TV and sketches for the BROADWAY revue *Catch A Star*. When his brother went to Hollywood, N.S. did TV work for *Caesar's Hour, Sergeant Bilko* and the Garry Moore show. Made his great start on Broadway with the hit *Come Blow Your Horn*, 1961, also a big success later in London. This was followed by the LIBRETTO for the musical *Little Me*, 1962, and further Broadway triumphs, some also with later London productions: *Barefoot in the Park*, 1963; *The Odd Couple*, 1965; *Plaza Suite*, 1968; *Promises, Promises*, another musical, 1968; *The Last of the Red Hot Lovers*, 1969, and *The Gingerbread Lady*, 1970.

Simoni, Renato (1875–1952), Italian dramatist, director and critic. His plays are important examples of psychological drama, but he is best known for his LIBRETTI including: *Turandot* for Puccini; *Madame Sans-Gêne* for Giordano; *Dibruck* for L. Rocca. His work as a director consisted mainly of productions of plays by GOLDONI. He was also the author of several books: *La Vedova*, 1902; *Carlo Gozzi*, 1903; *Tramonto*, 1906; *Il Matrimonio di Casanova*, 1910; *Congedo*, 1910, and of collected critical and historical essays: *Nomi e cose d'ieri*, 1952, and *Trent'anni di cronaca drammatica*, 1959.
Bibl: A. Cibotto, DRAMMA, 1952

Simonov, Konstantin Mikhailovich (1915–), Soviet novelist and poet. Author of several plays on topical themes (awarded several Stalin prizes), most of which are still frequently revived in the USSR: *Istoriya odnoi lyubi* (The Story of a Love), 1940, prod Leningrad 1954, dir AKIMOV; *Russkie lyudi* (The Russian People), 1942, prod London 1943 as *The Russians* by the OLD VIC; *Zhdi menya* (Wait for Me), 1943; *Tak i budet* (And So It Will Be), 1944; *Shuzhaya ten* (A Foreign Shadow), 1950; *Dobroe imya* (A Good Name), 1953.

Sarah Siddons, as The Tragic Muse, 1789, portrait by Reynolds

The World of Sholem Aleichem, produced by Sam Wanamaker, London 1955

Simonov, Reuben Nikolaievich (1899–1969), Soviet actor and director. In 1920 he joined the Third Studio of the MOSCOW ART THEATRE (which in 1926 became the Vakhtangov Theatre), playing TRUFFALDINO and PANTALONE in GOZZI's *Turandot.* In his own productions he followed the tradition of VAKHTANGOV: HUGO's *Marion Delorme*, 1926 and HECHT/MacARTHUR's *The Front Page*, 1930. In 1928 he formed his own studio theatre with students, which in 1937 amalgamated with the Leningrad Domsomol Theatre and was forced in the direction of SOCIALIST REALISM. During his post-war period as director of the Vakhtangov Theatre his most successful productions included: POGODIN's *Missuriisky-valts*, 1950; GORKY's *Foma Gordeyev*, 1956; ARBUZOV's *Irkutskaya istoriya*, 1960. During a guest visit to the THÉÂTRE DES NATIONS, Paris 1963 he successfully revived Vakhtangov's 1922 production of *Turandot.*

Simonson, Lee (1888–1967), US stage designer. Began his career with the Washington Square Players, who in 1919 formed themselves into the THEATRE GUILD, of which he was associate director for several years. S.'s style tended to simplification, reduction to a graphic outline and monumental architecture: TOLLER's *Masse Mensch* as *Man and the Masses*, 1924, which he also directed; SHAW's *Back to Methuselah*, 1922; O'NEILL's *Marco Millions*, 1927. Author of two books on stage design: *The Stage is Set*, 1932, and *The Art of Scenic Design*, 1950.

Simpson, Norman Frederick (1919–), English dramatist. His work is extravagant fantasy, but based on social realities. Nonsense and satire are mingled with parody, always with an evident philosophical view, and forceful social comment. He came into prominence with *A Resounding Tinkle*, which won first prize in the *Observer* 1957 Playwrights' Competition, fp ROYAL COURT THEATRE, 1957. Later works: *The Hole*, 1958; *One Way Pendulum*, 1959; *The Form*, 1961; *The Cresta Run*, 1965.
Bibl: M. Esslin, THE THEATRE OF THE ABSURD, 2/1968; J. R. Taylor, ANGER AND AFTER, 2/1963

Singspiel. Name given to a form of light German drama with inserted songs and instrumental music, analogous to the English BALLAD OPERA. While the Italian opera buffa was acted and sung by singers, the *Singspiele* were performed by actors. They became widely popular in the 18th century in Vienna, BERLIN and particularly Leipzig (Weisse, 1726–1804; J. A. Hiller, 1728–1804). Texts for *Singspiele* were written by GOETHE (*Erwin und Elmire*, 1775; *Jery und Bätely*, 1779; and *Claudine von Villa Bella*, 1776) and WIELAND (*Alceste*, 1773). From the tradition of the *Singspiel* came Mozart's *Die Entführung aus dem Serail*, 1782.

Siparium (Lat = curtain). Front curtain and backdrop, which was portable and used originally by mime actors. It was drawn aside or pulled up. Occasionally a combination of AULEUM and *siparium* was used: the *auleum* was raised and the *siparium* drawn to the sides.

Sjöberg, Alf (1903–), Swedish director. Began his career as an actor and made his début as a director in 1931 at the Royal Dramatic Theatre in Stockholm, where his best-known productions include: GOGOL's *The Government Inspector*, 1932; SHERIDAN's *The Rivals*, 1934; BATY's *Crime and Punishment* (after DOSTOYEVSKY), 1936; SHAKESPEARE's *As You Like It*, with sets reminiscent of Watteau, *The Merchant of Venice*, 1944, in Venetian style, *Twelfth Night*, 1946, in Renaissance costumes, and *Hamlet*, 1960. Other productions: MILLER's *Death of a Salesman*, 1949; IBSEN's *Rosmersholm*, 1959; BRECHT's *Mother Courage*, 1968.

Skagestad, Tormod (1920–), Norwegian director and manager. Joined the Norske Teater, Oslo, in 1953 as a director and took over its management in 1960. His greatest success was in creating a Norwegian theatre language, amalgamating the dialects of the country. He dramatized Sigrid Undset's novel *Kristin Lavransdatter* and successfully produced plays by O'NEILL, LORCA and RACINE; his production of IBSEN's *Peer Gynt* became internationally famous and toured in many countries.

Skinner, Otis (1858–1942), US actor. Discovered as a Shakespearean actor by E. BOOTH, later worked with DALY's company 1884–89, and with Booth, 1889, and in the same year played Claudius, Bassanio, Laertes and Macduff with HELENA MODJESKA's company. Best remembered for his performances as Haji in KNOBLOCK's *Kismet*, 1911. His other famous roles include: Falstaff in *Henry IV*, Part I, 1926, and in *The Merry Wives of Windsor*, 1928. He was also the author of several volumes of reminiscences including *Footlights and Spotlights*, 1924, and *The Last Tragedian*, 1939. His daughter **Cornelia Otis S.** (1901–) was a celebrated actress and DISEUSE, who toured successfully throughout the USA with her solo programme of sketches: *The Wives of Henry VIII*, *Empress Eugénie*, *The Loves of Charles II*, *The Mansion on the Hudson*. She also appeared successfully on stage as Angelica in CONGREVE's *Love for Love*, 1940; Mrs Erlynne in WILDE's *Lady Windermere's Fan*, 1946; and as Katherine Dougherty in *The Pleasure of His Company*, 1958, which she wrote together with S. Taylor. She is also the author of a book on SARAH BERNHARDT entitled *Madame Sarah*, 1968.

Skuszanka, Krystyna (1924–), Polish director. Following several productions at Opole 1953–55, she managed the theatre in the new industrial town of Nova Huta 1955–63 (SHAKESPEARE's *Measure for Measure*); with her production of GOZZI's *Turandot* (in collaboration with Jerzy Krasowski) she gained international reputation at the THÉÂTRE DES NATIONS, Paris 1956. Among her other famous productions is Shakespeare's *The Tempest*, 1959. In 1963 appointed artistic director of the Polski Theatre in Warsaw and since 1964 (with Krasowski) director of the Polski Theatre and the theatre in Wroclaw. Her style of production always conveys contemporary relevance – even with classical texts: for example, in *Measure for Measure* the décor consisted of concentration camp watchtowers, and the play was directed as a polemic against Fascism.

Slevogt, Max (1868–1932), German painter. The theatre plays an important part in his impressionistic paintings. His interest in music and décor led him to design sets: (for REINHARDT) SHAKESPEARE's *The Merry Wives of Windsor*, 1904, and HEBBEL's *Gyges und sein Ring*, 1907, and (for BRAHM) HAUPTMANN's *Florian Geyer*, 1904. He later expressed his enthusiasm for Mozart in stage designs for *Don Giovanni*, Dresden 1924, and *Die Zauberflöte*, BERLIN 1929.
Bibl: H.-J. Imiela, 1968

Slowacki, Juliusz (1809–49), Polish poet and dramatist. With MICKIEWICZ and KRASIŃKI one of the great exponents of Romantic drama in POLAND. From 1831 he lived in exile, mostly in Paris. He is best known for the patriotic play *Kordian*, written 1834. His other works include (dates of publication given): *Mondowe*, 1832; *Maria Stuart*, 1832; *Balladyna*, 1839; *Horsztynski*, fp 1879; *Beatrix Cenci*, written in French, 1840; *Lilla Weneda*, 1840; *Mazeppa*, 1841; *Fantasy*, fp 1867; *Skiadz Marek*, 1843; *Sen srebne Salomei*, 1844; *Samuel Zborowski*, 1845, etc. S. was, after occasional productions at the end of the 19th century, rediscovered in the 20th century. Today his plays are part of the national classical REPERTOIRE in Poland.
Bibl: P. Hertz, 1961

Smith, Maggie (1934–), English actress. Made her first appearance in 1952 in a student performance at the Oxford Playhouse and was originally successful in revue (*New Faces*, New York 1956; Bamber Gascoigne's *Share My Lettuce*, London 1957). In 1959 she joined the OLD VIC for a year, appearing in many leading roles including Maggie Wylie in BARRIE's *What Every Woman Knows*; she appeared in the West End as the lead in the one-act plays by P. SHAFFER, *The Private Ear* and *The Public Eye*, 1962; also in Jean Kerr's *Mary, Mary*, 1963. At the NATIONAL THEATRE 1964–71: Desdemona in *Othello*, 1964, with OLIVIER; Hilda Wangel in IBSEN's *The Master Builder*, 1964; Beatrice in SHAKESPEARE's *Much Ado About Nothing*, 1965, dir ZEFFIRELLI. At the CHICHESTER FESTIVAL, 1965, she appeared in the title role in STRINDBERG's *Miss Julie*. Has also starred in films.

Smith, Oliver (1918–), US stage designer. First worked for a PUPPET THEATRE, and in 1941 joined the Ballets Russes in Monte Carlo where he was very successful with his sets for *Rodeo*, choreography by Agnes de Mille, 1942. In 1944 started his close collaboration with ROBBINS in New York including: *Fancy Free*, 1944; *Interplay*, 1945; *Facsimile*, 1946; *The Age of Anxiety*, 1950. Established himself as one of the most successful stage designers on BROADWAY, mainly in ballet and musicals: *Billion Dollar Baby*, 1945; *Carousel*, 1945; *My Fair Lady*, 1956; *West Side Story*, 1957; *The Sound of Music*, 1961. His style of décor is atmospheric and supremely stylish.

Smith, Sol (1801–69). Pioneer of US theatre on the frontier. He ran away from home as a child and joined a series of itinerant companies. He formed a partnership with Noah Ludlow (▷SHOWBOAT), dominating the St Louis stage till 1851, building there the first permanent theatre west of the Mississippi. He published three books on the theatre, the third, *Theatrical Management in the West and South*, 1818, combining the first two.

Socialist Realism. A catch-phrase used in the USSR in the jargon of Stalinism: it denotes an approach to literature in general, and drama in particular, in which the emphasis is on the depiction of conditions in society not as they actually are, but as they *ought* to be. The demand for realism arose from the reaction of the masses to the avant-garde works of the artists who had supported the Bolshevik revolution (MAYAKOVSKY, BLOK, MEYERHOLD, etc.), as they were difficult to understand and seemed a waste of resources, apart from being useless as political propaganda. This led to a demand by Stalin, who, unlike Trotsky, was far from being an intellectual himself, that art should shun abstraction, fantasy and obscurity, that it should, in fact, be realistic. Yet the real social situation was far from being attractive. Hence works which dwelt on the inefficiency, the shortages, and the muddles of the Soviet regime, were labelled naturalistic, and the term Socialist Realism was coined to distinguish politically acceptable descriptions of social reality from those which could be harmful by revealing too much of reality. It is one of the ironies of this development that the most devotedly Communist theatre men, like Meyerhold and BRECHT, whose works were too abstract, conflicted with the official line and suffered in consequence, while the late 19th century realism of the MOSCOW ART THEATRE was found acceptable and was elevated to the status of a model of an orthodox Soviet theatrical style. Even in the period of de-Stalinization, the Russian authorities persisted in their opposition to a more open approach to the theatre.

Sociétaire (Fr=shareholder, co-operative member). Member of the COMÉDIE-FRANÇAISE, which is run as a co-operative. The *sociétaires* are shareholders of the theatre and decide upon the admission of new members, on casting and choice of plays, etc.

Soliloquy. In a soliloquy a person speaks alone, or utters thoughts aloud regardless of the presence of others. The word is usually applied to such speeches by a character in a play; the device used by playwrights (e.g. SHAKESPEARE) to express the chief characters' private thoughts. The Naturalists rejected soliloquy as something which does not occur in real life. Modern playwrights (e.g. BRECHT), reacting against NATURALISM, have returned to its use.

Son et lumière. A mixed media entertainment involving lighting, music and dramatized commentary, usually given at places famed in history – from the Parthenon to the Tower of London. First staged at the châteaux of the Loire in the 1950s.

Sondheim, Stephen (1930–), US composer and lyricist. Wrote the lyrics for *West Side Story* (music by BERNSTEIN, choreography and direction by ROBBINS), 1957; *Gypsy*, 1959. Music and lyrics for *A Funny Thing Happened on the Way to the Forum*, 1962; *Company*, 1970; *Follies*, 1971, and *A Little Night Music*, 1975.

Sonnenfels, Josef von (1733–1817), Austrian lawyer and progressive statesman. Like GOTTSCHED in Germany, he fought the vulgarity of the Viennese theatre and opposed the HANSWURST. In his *Briefe über die wienerische Schaubühne* he imitated and parodied LESSING's *Hamburgische Dramaturgie*; he also inspired the emperor, Joseph II, to raise the BURGTHEATER to the status of COURT and NATIONAL THEATRE.

Sonnenthal, Adolf von (1834–1909), Austrian actor. Following several appearances in the provinces, he made his début at the Vienna BURGTHEATER in 1856 as Mortimer in SCHILLER's *Maria Stuart* and rapidly established himself as one of the leading actors of the Burgtheater ensemble. In 1870 also director at, and for a short time (1887–90) manager of, the Burgtheater. Strongly influenced by the Italian virtuoso style of ROSSI and SALVINI, he was convincing more through his impressive appearance and the formality of his acting than by versatility or spontaneity; his Hamlet was too 'healthy', his Othello more lover than soldier, despite which he was one of the most popular actors of his time. His outstanding parts included: Leicester in Schiller's *Maria Stuart*, the title role in GOETHE's *Clavigo*; Alfonso in GRILLPARZER's *Die Jüdin von Toledo*; the title role in SHAKESPEARE's *Richard II*; but he also excelled in contemporary bon-vivant roles in plays by BAUERNFELD, FREYTAG, LINDAU, SCRIBE and SARDOU.
Bibl: J. Bab & W. Handl, DEUTSCHE SCHAUSPIELER, 1908

Sophocles (497/6–406 BC), Greek tragic playwright. He is said to have written 123 plays, of which seven tragedies and a fragment of a SATYR PLAY have survived: *Ajax*, after 450; *Antigone*, 442?; *Trachiniae*, after 438; *Oedipus Rex*, after 429; *Electra*, after 413; *Philoctetes*, 409; *Oedipus at Colonus*, produced posthumously 401 BC. He stands between the monumental simplicity of AESCHYLUS and the psychological variety of EURIPIDES. In the following centuries Euripides was more appreciated, but ARISTOTLE (in his *Poetics*) considered S.'s work as a model for TRAGEDY. He turned away

Lee Simonson, stage set for O'NEILL's *Dynamo*, New York 1929

Stephen Sondheim, *A Little Night Music*, London 1975, with Hermione Gingold

Maggie Smith as Mrs Sullen in FARQUHAR's *The Beaux' Stratagem*, NATIONAL THEATRE, 1970

from Aeschylean trilogic composition with a continuous story, presenting instead three self-contained plays in each TRILOGY; accordingly he focuses more on the solitary individual rather than on the divine law, as Aeschylus did. S.'s innovations changed the form of tragic performance; he introduced a third speaking actor, a practice which Aeschylus also adopted; he probably also introduced a fourth actor. He raised the number of chorus performers from 12 to 15; his CHORUS intervenes little in the action, its function being mainly to comment on the action. He was also the first dramatist to use painted scenery.
Bibl: T. Woodward (ed), SOPHOCLES, A COLLECTION OF CRITICAL ESSAYS, 1966; F. J. H. Letters, THE LIFE AND WORK OF SOPHOCLES; C. M. Bowra, SOPHOCLEAN TRAGEDY, 1944

Sorano, Daniel (1920–62), French actor. Joined SARRAZIN's company Le Grenier de Toulouse in 1945, excelling in roles like the slave Milfion in *Le Carthaginois* (an adaptation of PLAUTUS), Creon in ANOUILH's *Antigone*, and particularly as Scapin in MOLIÈRE's *Les Fourberies de Scapin*, 'He played with his hands, fingers and feet, with his ears and forehead . . . that is Scapin' (F.-J. Gauthier). In 1952 he appeared as the Gravedigger in a production of *Hamlet* by the COMPAGNIE RENAUD-BARRAULT at the Zurich Festival and soon afterwards was contracted by VILAR for the AVIGNON FESTIVAL and the TNP, Paris (until 1959), where his finest parts included Sganarelle in Molière's *Dom Juan*, 1953, and Figaro in BEAUMARCHAIS' *Le Mariage de Figaro*, 1956. With his rough features and toothy face, he seemed destined to play only comic parts, but shortly before his death, he gave a powerful performance as Shylock in *The Merchant of Venice* (Odéon, Théâtre de France, 1961; dir M. Jamois).

Sorge, Reinhard Johannes (1892–1916), German poet and dramatist. His early works were strongly influenced by Nietzsche. In 1912 he wrote *Der Bettler*, one of the earliest German Expressionist plays; it was directed by REINHARDT at the Deutsches-Theater, BERLIN, in 1917, with GERTRUDE EYSOLDT, HELENE THIMIG, WEGENER and JANNINGS. He was converted to Catholicism and his later plays dealt with Christian themes, e.g. *Metanoeite*, three MYSTERY PLAYS, 1915, fp Berlin 1922. Other works (dates denote publication) include: *König David*, 1916; *Gericht über Zarathustra*, 1921; *Mystische Zwiegespräche*, 1922; *Der Sieg des Christos*, 1924.
Bibl: C. Hill and R. Ley, THE DRAMA OF GERMAN EXPRESSIONISM, 1960

Sorma, Agnes (Martha Karoline Zaremba; 1865–1927), German actress. In 1883, after several years in the provinces, she joined the Deutsches-Theater, BERLIN, under L'ARRONGE. Worked under BARNAY at the Berliner Theater 1891–94 and under BRAHM at the Deutsches-Theater 1894–98. She then toured widely in Holland, Italy, Russia, and Sweden. Among her many admirers were T. MANN and G. HAUPTMANN who were fascinated by her charm and the intensity of emotion she displayed in her major parts, including SHAKESPEARE's Ophelia, Portia, and SHAW's Candida. For many years she had an international reputation, especially between 1904 and 1908, when she worked under REINHARDT in Berlin.
Bibl: J. Bab, 1927

Sothern, Edward Askew (1826–81), English actor and playwright who went to the USA and achieved a sensational success in the part of the bewhiskered, silly English Lord Dundreary at the opening performance of Tom Taylor's play *Our American Cousin* in New York, 1858. The part, originally a small one, was built up by him with a wealth of comic embellishment until it became one of the leading roles and the main attraction of the play. A number of BURLESQUE sketches were specially written for the type S. had created, e.g. *Dundreary Married and Done For*, 1864, and *Dundreary a Father*, 1886. The long sidewhiskers in which S. had appeared became known as 'dundrearies'. He wrote a number of romantic MELODRAMAS: *David Garrick*, 1864; *A Crushed Tragedian*, 1874. His son **Edwin Hugh S.** (1859–1933) became a leading romantic actor, but also continued the Dundreary tradition. He was married to the US actress Julia Marlowe (1866–1950) and acted in many plays with her.

Sotie. In 15th- and 16th-century France the name given to a popular theatrical form of topical satire, presented as a prelude to the main performance and named after the main character, the fool (*sot*). The best-known authors of the genre are Pierre Gringoire and Jean Bouchet (their surviving plays are attacks on the Pope). The Dutch form derived from it, the *Sotternie* (also known as *Klucht*), was presented at the end of the performance.
Bibl: B. Groth, UNTERSUCHUNG ZUR GATTUNGSGESCHICHTE DER SOTIE, 1969

Soubrette. Comic female role, the lady's maid or chamber maid, who first appeared in French COMEDY. Several French historians and critics distinguish between the *servantes* (servants) in MOLIÈRE (e.g. Dorine in *Tartuffe*; Nicole in *Le Bourgeois gentilhomme*) and the subtle and clever soubrettes in MARIVAUX's plays (Lisette in *Le Jeu de l'amour et du hasard)*. An early example of the soubrette is Susanna in BEAUMARCHAIS's *Le Mariage de Figaro*. In comic opera, and also in operetta, the soubrette developed into a character type, full of naïve charm; in the best examples she possessed some of the qualities of Molière's characters: rebelliousness, dry common sense and native wit, e.g. Franziska in LESSING's *Minna von Barnhelm*.

South Africa. The African Theatre, opened in Cape Town in 1801, presented amateur productions in English, Dutch, French and German and occasionally invited foreign companies. Two other small theatres were founded in 1843, and in 1855 the first semi-professional company, the Drawing Room Theatre. The first big theatre, the Standard Theatre in Johannesburg, was built in 1891. Subsequently three others were built there, and also in other cities – Cape Town, Pretoria, Durban, etc. Leading figure during this time was Leonard Rayne (1869–1925), actor, director and manager, who also invited many foreign guests to appear in his company. Drama in Afrikaans emerged at the beginning of the 19th century and was produced by many companies travelling through the country. The two leading groups were the Cape Town Repertory Theatre Society (founded in 1921) and the Johannesburg Repertory Theatre (founded in 1927). In 1947 the South African National Theatre Organization was founded to co-ordinate diverse theatrical activities in the country and helped to raise the standard of the touring companies, which perform in both official languages. Several South African theatres are state-subsidized.

Southerne, Thomas (1659–1746), Irish-born dramatist. His first play, *The Loyal Brother, or The Persian Prince*, 1682, a TRAGEDY with a contemporary political theme, was followed by the domestic drama *The Disappointment, or The Mother in Fashion*, 1684. S.'s understanding of the world and of human motives were most effectively expressed in his next two tragedies: *The Fatal Marriage, or The Innocent Adultery*, 1694; and *Oroonoko, or The Royal Slave*, 1695, his masterpiece, a story (based on a novel by APHRA BEHN) of a noble Indian slave betrayed by his European masters. S. wrote three more tragedies (the last produced in 1726) and also three COMEDIES: *Sir Anthony Love, or The Rambling Lady*, 1690; *The Wives' Excuse, or Cuckolds Make Themselves*, 1691, and *The Maid's Last Prayer, or Any rather than Fair*, 1693.

Soyinka, Wole (1934–), Nigerian dramatist. Educated in the universities of Ibadan and Leeds; spent some time at the ROYAL COURT THEATRE, London, as a play-reader. Returned to Nigeria in 1960, where he started his own theatre group, The 1960 Masks, and later The Orisun Theatre. Director of the Drama school at Ibadan University, 1967, where he had taught English. Imprisoned in Nigeria during the civil war and has now left the country permanently. Plays: *A Dance of the Forests*, pub 1963; *Five Plays*, pub 1964; *The Lion and the Jewel*, fp Royal Court Theatre, 1966; *The Road*, pub 1965; *Kongi's Harvest*, pub 1967; *The Swamp Dwellers, The Strong Breed*, pub 1969; *Madmen and Specialists*, fp at the Eugene O'Neill Theater Center, Waterford, Conn., August 1970, pub 1971. S. writes in English with a strong mixture of African flavour and idiom. His plays reflect the struggle between the old world of African ritual and belief in spirits and the corruptions of modern life. He was awarded the John Whiting Award of the ARTS COUNCIL OF GREAT BRITAIN in 1966/67. His adaptation of EURIPIDES' *The Bacchae* was presented at the OLD VIC in 1973, and *The Trials of Brother Jero*, fp Hampstead Theatre Club 1966, was revived in a double bill with

Jero's Metamorphosis, Bristol 1974.

Spaić, Kosta (1923–), Yugoslav director. Since 1962 director of the State Theatre Academy in Zagreb and since 1964 manager and organizer of the annual Theatre Festival at Dubrovnik. Besides works by native contemporary playwrights (B. Kreft, M. Bozic, J. Kastelan) he has directed mainly modern classical works, including LORCA's *La Casa de Bernarda Alba*, *Bodas de Sangre*, *Doña Rosita*; GIRAUDOUX's *Pour Lucrèce*, *Apollon de Bellac*; O'NEILL's *The Iceman Cometh*; IONESCO's *Les Chaises*; also classics, e.g. SHAKESPEARE's *Measure for Measure* and MOLIÈRE's *Dom Juan*. He has also worked as a guest director abroad and is known for several operatic productions.

Spain. Greek theatre probably existed at Saguntum, also Roman theatre, PANTOMIME and gladiators up to the time of the Visigoths (5th to 7th centuries). The Arab invasion in the 8th century killed the beginnings of Christian theatre in Spain. From the 13th century onward there was religious drama. Secular, literary drama starts with the works of ENCINA (*c.* 1469–1529?), who took his themes from medieval LITURGICAL DRAMA, but his characters were full-blooded and vigorous Renaissance types. His great accomplishment was to secularize church drama. The most advanced dramatic text of the post-medieval period was published in 1499 in Burgos, titled *La comedia de Calisto y Melibea* (The Comedy of Calisto and Melibea) which was discovered and later finished by ROJAS, called *La tragicomedia de Calisto y Melibea*. Under the title *La Celestina* it became widely known in Europe.
As well as appearances of touring Italian companies various forms of drama emerged in the second half of the 16th century: PASTORAL DRAMA in the form of *églogas* (eclogue = a dialogue between shepherds), ENTREMESES and AUTOS SACRAMENTALES. Presented first at the Court, later in market-places and finally in the CORRALES, open yards of private houses or inns, on a simple stage and using galleries for scenes in a tower or behind a window. One of the first managers was LOPE DE RUEDA, who formed his own company modelled after the strolling COMMEDIA DELL'ARTE companies and toured the country performing his own plays. These were *entremeses* and dramas in prose, Spanish plays of the pastoral type and adaptations of Italian COMEDIES. The first playwright to adapt subjects taken from Spanish history and to make use of traditional ballads was Juan de la Cueva (1550–1610); *entremeses* were cultivated by CERVANTES.
In 1580 in Madrid monks rebuilt the theatres Corral de la Pacheca and Corral de la Cruz; they charged a fixed entrance fee; performances took place in the afternoon; décor was stripped to bare essentials, but the costumes were splendid. They had a large and lively audience. A great number of large, well-equipped companies emerged. In 1598 theatres were closed by decree of Philip II following pressure to preserve public morals, but they were reopened in 1600, though only eight (after 1615 twelve) companies were licensed; women were not allowed to appear on stage until 1608, and then not in men's clothes, and there was severe censorship. The *Sigle de Oro* (golden era) of the Spanish theatre occurred 1621–65 under Philip IV, who himself wrote plays and even appeared as an actor. In this great period, which coincided with Spanish political supremacy in Europe, the main representative writers were LOPE DE VEGA, TIRSO DE MOLINA and CALDERÓN. The latter, whose books were written partly for popular theatre, partly for the Court, was appointed director in 1635 of BUEN RETIRO, the COURT THEATRE where BAROQUE THEATRE reached its peak. By this time there were 40 companies with more than 2,000 actors in Madrid, and about 300 companies in the whole country.
Continual clerical criticism and attack, particularly in the first half of the 18th century, led to the closing down of many Spanish theatres; in the period of neo-classicism the folk theatre and the *autos sacramentales* were criticized. In Barcelona and Madrid the Italian opera flourished. From *c.* 1830 romantic drama, influenced by HUGO, reached its zenith with *Don Juan Tenorio* by José Zorrilla, 1844. From the folk theatre the ZARZUELA survives. Towards the end of the 19th century new romantic (ECHEGARAY), realistic (BENAVENTE) and satirical-grotesque (VALLE-INCLÁN) dramatic literature. At that time the system of travelling companies and STAR appearances prevailed. With the Spanish Civil War in 1936 the rising development of the realistic and poetic folk theatre of LORCA and the actress MARGARITA XIRGU was abruptly terminated. After 1945 strong censorship made it difficult for the Spanish theatre to develop a REPERTORY of world literature and the idea of a director's theatre arrived very late in comparison with other European countries. Today there are three state-subsidized theatres in Madrid, but, Barcelona excepted, very little theatrical activity in other cities. Most popular author is SASTRE.
Bibl: J. P. Wickersham Crawford, SPANISH DRAMA BEFORE LOPE DE VEGA, 3/1967; N. D. Shergold, A HISTORY OF THE SPANISH STAGE FROM MEDIEVAL TIMES UNTIL THE END OF THE 17TH CENTURY, 1967; A. Valbuena Prat, HISTORIA DEL TEATRO ESPAÑOL, 1956

Spencer, Colin (1933–), English novelist and dramatist. Studied at Brighton Art College. Had four novels published before he wrote his first play, *The Ballad of the False Barman*, fp Hampstead Theatre Club, 1966, a musical fantasy. His next play *Spitting Image*, fp Hampstead Theatre Club, 1968, transferred to the West End, is a light-hearted social satire about two homosexuals who find out that one of them is expecting a baby. His subsequent plays include: *Matrix or the Sphinx Mother*, 1971, and *Trial of Saint George*, fp Soho Poly Theatre, 1972.

Sperr, Martin (1944–), German dramatist. One of the most interesting young

Spain, *Tragicomedia de Calisto y Melibea*, title page, Toledo 1526

Spain, corral theatre in the 17th century, performance at Corral del Principe, Madrid, reconstruction drawing by Juan Comba y Garcia

E. H. Sothern portrayed in *If I were King* by Justin Huntly McCarthy, poster designed by JOHN BARRYMORE

playwrights to emerge in Germany in the 1960s; a writer of realistic plays, set in villages and small towns, which are microcosms of social behaviour; best known are *Jagdszenen aus Niederbayern* (Hunting Scenes from Lower Bavaria), Bremen 1966; *Landshuter Erzählungen* (Tales from Landshut), a fight between two peasant entrepreneurs over a local monopoly, Munich Kammerspiele, 1967.

Squarzina, Luigi (1922–), Italian director. Made his name mainly with contemporary playwrights like A. MILLER (*All My Sons*, 1947) and MacLEISH (*J. B.*, 1958) and supported the works of young Italian dramatists including BETTI, FABBRI, d'Errico, Prosperi. He took over the management of the TEATRO STABILE, Genoa 1963–69. One of the leading figures in contemporary Italian theatre, he is primarily a DRAMATURG and director; he has also written several plays and adaptations. He emphasized interpretation rather than charismatic acting. Also the author of several essays on the theatre, published in magazines like *Sipario*.

Stadttheater (Ger = Municipal Theatre). Theatres which, in contrast to the STATE THEATRES, subsidized by the State and under the Ministries of Culture, are financed and run by municipal authorities. Most German cities with more than 50,000 inhabitants pride themselves in financing a *Stadttheater*, which often presents opera, operetta and straight plays, mostly in two different auditoriums. Originally these theatres were leased to entrepreneurs who were able to make a profit. It was only after the rise of the cinema that municipal subsidies had to be used to keep the theatres open so that they passed into direct municipal administration.

Stage lighting. Artificial stage light came into use in the 16th century when theatre, which had been an almost exclusively outdoor activity, moved inside. Until the end of the 19th century the usual sources of light were: chandeliers, concealed ceiling and side-lighting from candles in candleholders or oil lamps, concealed or open footlights, lighting for backdrops and concealed lights in the wings. To reinforce the light of candles and oil-lamps mirrors were used; additionally, for special effects, torches with metal reflectors. The intensity of the light could be controlled by the use of silk ribbons or movable cylinders. In spite of the abundance of light sources this technique was not very effective as each change had to be effected in hundreds of places. The first decisive improvement came with the introduction of gaslight, first used in entrance halls and auditoriums of London theatres. From 1817 gaslight was also used on the stage, first at the Lyceum; its advantages were much greater intensity and ease of control, its disadvantage the great fire hazard it represented. In the period of stage lighting by gas, from 1820 to 1880, more theatres burned down than ever before or since. Soon after the appearance of Edison's electric lightbulb the first theatre was fitted out with electric stage lighting (Brno, 1883). At the end of the 1880s most of the larger theatres were equipped with electric light. Today the director and lighting designer have at their disposal the whole gamut of infinitely variable light sources which are increasingly capable of being automatically controlled and pre-set electronically.

Stage machinery. The use of mechanical devices to create spectacular effects in the theatre goes back to antiquity. Little is known about the stage machinery of the Greek theatre (▷AIOREMA, AMPHITHEATRE), but the Romans are known to have employed various devices. Modern stage machinery goes back to Italy and the Renaissance when the first permanent indoor theatre buildings were erected (hence the PROSCENIUM stage is still, in French, called *théâtre à l'Italienne*). Bramante and PERUZZI introduced painted backdrops in perspective and, to facilitate quick changes, TELARI (derived from the Greek PERIAKTOS): prisms with portions of a different design painted on each of their three sides which could be quickly turned to produce instant scene changes. As early as the mid-15th century there were machines which could make angels fly through the sky or appear suddenly as cotton-wool clouds opened. In the 17th century Giacomo Torelli (1608–78) who worked in Venice and later in France was a most fertile inventor of stage machinery, particularly for quick scene changes by a system of movable wings. In the 19th century the stage became increasingly mechanized: an elaborate grid above the stage allows scenery to be lifted and lowered (*flown*) by ropes and pulleys. In many theatres the whole stage can be moved sideways or lowered hydraulically so that whole sets can be moved into view in an instant. The REVOLVING STAGE (first used in Munich, 1896) also allows quick scene changes. But modern trends towards theatre in the round and away from the proscenium arch, which is an essential element in the creation of illusion by separating the spectator from the magic world of the stage behind its picture frame, may well result in a reduction in the importance of stage machinery.

Stanislavsky, Konstantin Sergeyevich (1863–1938), Russian director, actor, theoretician and one of the greatest teachers of acting. He came from an upper middle-class family, studied drama and singing under F. P. Komisarjevsky, father of VERA K. and THEODORE K., himself a playwright and director, and played for a short time in VAUDEVILLE, operetta, drama and COMEDY. In 1888 together with the elder Komisarjevsky and Fedotov, he founded the Society of Literature and Art, aimed at the systematic presentation of good plays, in mostly amateur productions. At first S. worked as an actor in this amateur group playing, e.g. Ferdinand in SCHILLER's *Kabale und Liebe*; later he became its director. In 1891 he produced for the first time L. TOLSTOY's comedy *The Fruits of Enlightenment* and a dramatization of DOSTOYEVSKY's *The Village Stepanchikovo*; he became well known through his productions of, e.g., G. HAUPTMANN's *Hanneles Himmelfahrt* and *Die versunkene Glocke*, and SHAKESPEARE's *Othello*. In 1897 he met NEMIROVICH-DANCHENKO, with whom he founded the MOSCOW ART THEATRE in 1898. He concentrated on the development of direction and dramatic acting, while Nemirovich-Danchenko mainly worked on the selection of plays and organization. The first production of the MAT was A. K. TOLSTOY's *Tsar Fyodor Ivanovich*, but his breakthrough came with CHEKHOV's *The Seagull* on 17 December 1898, followed by other famous productions of Chekhov's plays – *Uncle Vanya*, 1899; *Three Sisters*, 1901; *The Cherry Orchard*, 1904. Regardless of the theatre's traditions and the expectations of the audience, he demanded inner truth instead of the traditional style of acting which relied upon external dramatic effect. To achieve this, he aimed in his productions for accuracy in décor and COSTUMES and developed for the actor a series of techniques to reach the essence of the personality he was to portray, beginning with information about the historical situation, and through improvisation and concentration exercises; this 'system' was propagated and used (specially by his pupil SULERZHITSKY) and has had widespread influence up to the present day, notably in the 'Method', a style of acting originating in the ACTORS' STUDIO. He realized the limits of his detailed realism and he supported other non-naturalistic concepts, particularly those of MEYERHOLD, whose symbolic production of MAETERLINCK's *La Mort de Tintagiles* reached the stage of the dress rehearsal, but was never publicly performed. With Meyerhold, as well as his other pupils, he was linked by lifelong friendship, even during the years of Stalinism. Several studio theatres were attached to the MAT, the First Studio founded in 1913, directed by Sulerzhitsky, the Second Studio in 1916, the Third Studio in 1920, directed by VAKHTANGOV (from which the HABIMAH THEATRE developed). Several tours abroad made the MAT internationally famous. Among his other principal productions during his early years were: IBSEN's *Hedda Gabler*, 1899; Chekhov's *Uncle Vanya*, 1899; Ibsen's *An Enemy of the People*, 1900; GORKY's *Children of the Sun* and *The Lower Depths*, both 1902. After 1905 S., influenced by SYMBOLISM, directed Maeterlinck's *The Blue Bird*, 1908; Shakespeare's *Hamlet*, 1911, together with CRAIG; Tolstoy's *Resurrection*, 1911; MOLIÈRE's *Le Malade imaginaire*, 1913. After the Revolution his work also included the production of political plays, e.g. IVANOV's *Armoured Train 14–69*, 1927, but concentrated increasingly on operatic works at the Opera Studio of the BOLSHOI THEATRE. Among his last productions were: *Othello*, 1932; *Dead Souls*, 1932, dramatization of GOGOL's novel by BULGAKOV; Molière's *Tartuffe*, 1939, finished by Kedrov and Toporkov. Almost all of his productions were directed in collaboration with other directors including NEMIROVICH-DANCHENKO, Luchski, Sanin, Sulerzhitsky, MOSKVIN, Sudakov, Gorchakov, etc. S.'s ideas and methods are recorded in his many books, among them *My Life in Art*, 1924; *An Actor Prepares*, 1926; *Stanislavsky Rehearses Othello*, London and New York 1948; *Building a Character*, 1950; *The Seagull, produced by K.S.S.* (edited by S. D. Balukhaty, London 1952).

Star. An actor of exceptional popularity and drawing power. The star system is a creation of the BROADWAY stage and the Hollywood film industry. With its emphasis on the personality of the star actor, which is elaborately built up by mass publicity, the system tends to force an actor into a very circumscribed range of roles which correspond exactly to his 'image' and thus reduce his skill as an actor. The public comes to see the actor rather than the play or the character he portrays. In the commercial theatre the fact that the willingness of a star actor to appear may secure financial backing for a play also distorts the priorities of genuine theatrical art: for example, a play which is outstanding but does not contain a part capable of attracting a big star may have less chance of being produced than a mediocre play with an effective star part, and once a star has decided to appear in a play he may well override the wishes of the director. These weaknesses of the star system have been powerful arguments in the debate about the creation of publicly subsidized theatres in the English-speaking countries.

State theatre. Theatres owned and subsidized by the state. In GERMANY many of the COURT THEATRES of the kingdoms and principalities which made up the Wilhelmine Empire became State Theatres when the country adopted a republican form of government in 1918. Hence theatres in the capitals of some of the German regions still carry the label *Staatstheater*. There are State Theatres in many other West European countries, notably in Scandinavia. In Eastern Europe all theatres are State-owned and run.

Steckel, Leonard (1901–71), Hungarian-born German actor and director. Began his career in BERLIN in the 1920s (Piscator-Bühne, VOLKSBÜHNE, Deutsches-Theater), emigrating to Zurich in 1933, where he acted and directed until his death, apart from guest appearances in Bochum, Munich, Basle, Berlin and Vienna. For a short period 1958–59 he was also Intendant at the Kurfürstendamm Theater, Berlin. During his time in Zurich he concentrated on direction, at first mainly in classical and later in modern plays. His best acting roles included villainous and malevolent characters, e.g. the name part in *Richard III*; Caliban in *The Tempest*; in Brecht's plays, he was the first Galileo, 1943, and the first Puntila in *Herr Puntila und sein Knecht Matti*, 1947, revived in 1949 by the BERLINER ENSEMBLE; but he gained his greatest successes as Loman in A. MILLER's *Death of a Salesman*, and as Schwitter in DÜRRENMATT's *Der Meteor*, fp 1966.

Steele, Sir Richard (1672–1729), Irish-born politician, essayist, pamphleteer and

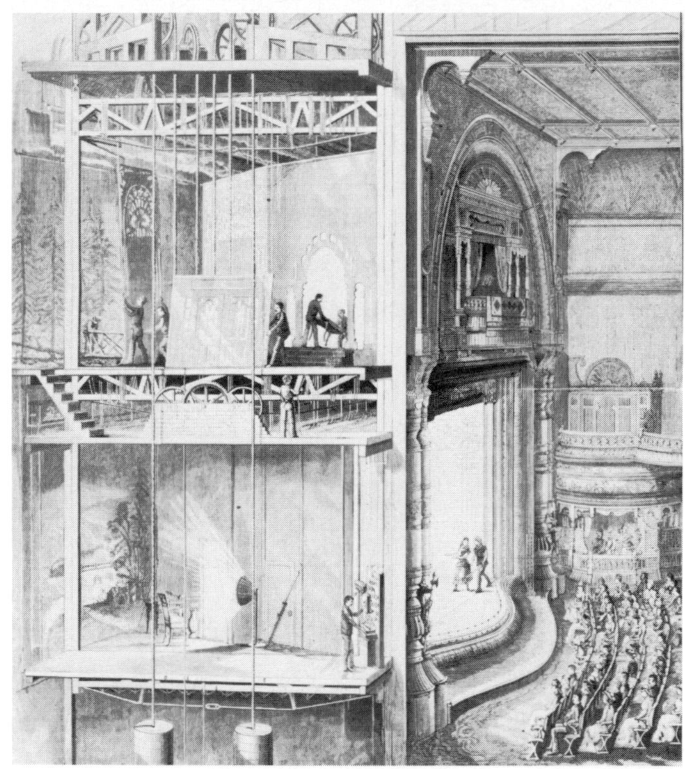

Stage machinery, the movable stage at Madison Square Garden, New York, 1884

Stage lighting, theatre lit by Edison lamps, 1883

Konstantin Stanislavsky in GORKY's *The Lower Depths*

dramatist. He was editor of the weekly magazines *The Tatler*, *The Spectator* (with ADDISON) and *The Guardian* to which Addison and Pope contributed. He wrote moralistic, sentimental COMEDIES, which are in contrast with the cynicism of much RESTORATION DRAMA. His most important play, *The Conscious Lovers*, was successfully produced by CIBBER at DRURY LANE in 1722, with a cast including BOOTH, Wilkes and ANNE OLDFIELD; it exercised great influence on the French COMÉDIE LARMOYANTE. His other comedies are *The Funeral, or Grief A-la-Mode*, 1701; *The Lying Lover, or The Ladies' Friendship*, 1703; *The Tender Husband, or The Accomplished Fools*, 1705. He founded and edited the first English theatre magazine *The Theatre*, which appeared twice weekly 1719–20.
Bibl: J. Loftis, 1952

Stein, Gertrude (1874–1946), US novelist and poet. Her unique, simplistic prose style influenced the works of ELIOT, POUND, Hemingway, John Dos Passos and others. She was the author of some dramatic works including: *Four Saints in Three Acts* (music by Virgil Thomson), pub 1929, fp Hartford, Conn., 1934; *Yes Is for a Very Young Man*, Pasadena, Calif., 1946; *The Mother of Us All* (music Thomson), Columbia University, N.Y., 1947; *It Happened a Play*, written 1913, revised as *What Happened*, 1964, and won an OBIE AWARD.
Bibl: J. M. Brinnin, THE THIRD ROSE: GERTRUDE STEIN AND HER WORLD, 1959

Steinbeck, John (1902–68), US novelist. As a playwright he is best known for dramatizations of his own novels including: *Of Mice and Men*, 1937; *The Moon is Down*, 1942; *Burning Bright*, 1950. His novel *Sweet Thursday* was used by RODGERS and HAMMERSTEIN II for their musical *Pipe Dream*, 1955. He was awarded the Nobel Prize for Literature in 1962.

Steinrück, Albert (1872–1929), German actor and director. He achieved his greatest success at the Munich Hoftheater, 1908–20. Made his name in leading classical parts; played the title role in BÜCHNER's *Woyzeck* in the first professional production of the play in 1915, and was the first German actor to play Higgins in SHAW's *Pygmalion*, 1913. He was highly praised in the title role of SHAKESPEARE's *King Lear*, 1913, and as Iago in *Othello*, 1921; one of his finest parts was Dr Schön in WEDEKIND's *Erdgeist*, and Mephistopheles in GOETHE's *Faust*.

Stern, Ernst (1876–1954), Bucharest-born German stage designer. Studied painting in Munich, later became contributor to the magazines *Jugend* and *Simplizissimus* and worked for the cabaret 'Die elf Scharfrichter' in Munich (as Tobias Loch, the café artist). In 1904 he made his début as a designer for Bodmann's *Die Krone*; the following year he went to BERLIN where in 1907 he began his close collaboration with REINHARDT and other directors including WINTERSTEIN and MARTIN. When Reinhardt left Berlin in 1921, S. worked almost exclusively on operas and operettas; in 1929, and again from 1934 onwards, in England, with COWARD and E. Charell, mainly designing musicals. In his 16 years' collaboration with Reinhardt his best works included: (at the Deutsches-Theater, Berlin) SHAKESPEARE's *A Midsummer Night's Dream*, 1905; *As You Like It*, 1907; *Hamlet*, 1909; *Henry IV*, 1912, and *Macbeth*, 1916, and GOETHE's *Faust II*, 1911; also Vollmöller's *The Miracle*, London 1911, Olympia; BÜCHNER's *Dantons Tod*, 1916; IBSEN's *John Gabriel Borkman*, 1917; G. HAUPTMANN's *Die Winterballade*, 1917. He worked with WOLFIT on a series of Shakespeare productions 1943–45.
Bibl: C. Niessen, MAX REINHARDT UND SEINE BÜHNENBILDER, 1968; K. MacGowan and R. E. Jones, CONTINENTAL STAGECRAFT, 1923

Sternheim, Carl (1878–1942), German dramatist. Son of a banker, he published the literary magazine *Hyperion* with F. Blei, 1908–10. In 1911, REINHARDT presented his bourgeois COMEDY *Die Hose* (Bloomers) at the Deutsches-Theater, Berlin. *Die Hose*, the first of his great cycle of satirical middle-class comedies, *Aus dem bürgerlichen Heldenleben* (Scenes from the Heroic Life of the Middle Classes), was a brilliant *exposé* of the hypocritical prudery of the Wilhelmine era. It became *succès de scandale* and was immediately banned because of the indelicacy of its subject, which concerned a lady losing her knickers in embarrassing circumstances. It led to S.'s taking up residence abroad and from 1930 he lived permanently in Brussels. Other plays in this cycle include *Die Kassette* (The Money Box), 1911; *Bürger Schippel* (*Schippel*), 1913, concerning the hero's rise to middle-class status; *Der Snob*, 1914, which deals with the second generation of the Schippel family, the further climbing of a petty-bourgeois and his successful adaptation to high society; the next play in the series, *1913*, deals with the third generation and portrays the decadence of capitalist society. Then followed *Der Kandidat* (The Candidate), after FLAUBERT, 1915; *Das leidende Weib* (The Suffering Woman), after KLINGER, 1916; *Der Scharmante* (The Charmer), based on MOLIÈRE, 1917; *Tabula rasa*, 1919. His dramas were first classed as Expressionist because of the clipped style of DIALOGUE but successful revivals in the 1960s showed his realism. His twelve comedies are perhaps the best to have been written in Germany in the 20th century, but he gradually lost his sure touch and his plays became less coherent as he strained them to cover increasingly implausible situations. Other works: *Perleberg*, also called *Mihlow* or *Der Stänker*, 1917; *Die Marquise von Arcis*, 1919, translated by DUKES as *The Mask of Virtue*, fp London, 1935, with VIVIEN LEIGH making her West End début; *Der entfesselte Zeitgenosse*, 1921; *Manon Lescaut*, after Prévost, 1921; *Der Nebbich*, 1922; *Das Fossil*, 1923; *Die Schule von Uznach oder Neue Sachlichkeit*, 1926; *Die Königin*, 1929. *Bürger Schippel* and *Der Snob* were most recently revived (as *Schippel* and *The Snob*), London 1974/75.
Bibl: W. Wendler, 1965; H. Sokel, THE WRITER IN EXTREMIS, 1959

Stichomythia (Gr *stichos* = a line of verse; *mythos* = speech). In Greek drama a passage of DIALOGUE in which each character has one line of verse to speak, in passages of heated argument. When each character has two alternate lines we have *distichomythia*; when each character speaks half a line of verse: *hemistichomythia*.

Stock company. A theatrical company attached to one theatre, as against a strolling or touring company. The term was used in the 19th century; today in ENGLAND one would speak of the resident companies of REPERTORY theatres in the provinces, of the ENSEMBLES of the subsidized national companies like the NATIONAL THEATRE or the ROYAL SHAKESPEARE COMPANY. The stock companies of the 19th century had a large REPERTOIRE (their stock in trade) and the parts were allocated according to the type each actor represented (leading man, leading lady, ingénue, juvenile lead, low comedian, etc.). In the USA companies which provide a repertoire of plays in holiday resorts are called 'summer stock'.

Stoppa, Paolo (1902–), Italian actor. Worked with several companies 1927–37, joined the Teatro Eliseo in Rome 1938–41, where, among other parts, he played the title role in Sharoff's *The Gambler*, 1939–40, based on DOSTOYEVSKY. In 1945 he met VISCONTI and with him as director and the actress RINA MORELLI as his partner developed one of the most prominent Italian post-war companies. Among his best parts were Raskolnikov in BATY's adaptation of Dostoyevsky's *Crime and Punishment*, 1946; Ali in GOLDONI's *L'Impresario delle Smirne*, 1947; Trappola in *Il cervo*, based on GOZZI's *Il re cervo* adapted and directed by STREHLER, 1948; Loman in MILLER's *Death of a Salesman*, 1951; probably his finest performances were in CHEKHOV's plays (Andrey in *Three Sisters*, 1952; *Uncle Vanya*, 1955) and also in Jerome Kilty's *Dear Liar*, dir author.

Stoppard, Tom (originally Straussler; 1937–), Czech-born English dramatist. Began his career as a journalist in Bristol, subsequently in London as a freelance. He started writing for the stage in 1960. His first play *A Walk on the Water* was produced on TV in 1963, and on stage in Hamburg and Vienna in 1964. His TV plays include *A Separate Peace* and *Teeth*, and radio plays *The Dissolution of Dominic Boot*; *M Is for Moon Among Other Things*; *If You're Glad I'll Be Frank*; and *Albert's Bridge*, which won the Prix Italia in 1968. In 1964 he went to BERLIN for five months on a Ford Foundation grant and on his return he started work on *Rosencrantz and Guildenstern are Dead*, fp Oxford Theatre Group at the EDINBURGH FESTIVAL, 1966, NATIONAL THEATRE, 1968, dir Derek Goldby; it has been translated and produced in numerous European countries and in the USA. This play marked his breakthrough as a writer and is still the basis of his reputation. His subsequent work has included: *Enter a Free Man*, a stage version of *A Walk on the Water*, 1968; *The Real Inspector Hound*, 1968; *After Magritte*, 1970, one-act play; *Jumpers*, 1972, National Theatre; *Travesties*, 1974, Aldwych; *Dirty Linen*, 1976, Arts Theatre. He is the author of the novel *Lord Malquist and Mr Moon*.

Storey, David (1933–), English dramatist. A teacher who wrote successful novels (*This Sporting Life*, 1960; *Flight Into Camden*, 1960, and *Radcliffe*, 1963) before he turned to drama in 1963, inspired by L. ANDERSON, who filmed *This Sporting Life*, which the author scripted. Revised and rewrote his first play, *The Restoration of Arnold Middleton*, written 1959, it appeared on stage in 1967. This production was quickly followed by *In Celebration*, 1969, ROYAL COURT THEATRE, dir Anderson, a family drama and, like *Arnold Middleton*, a study of a man at the end of his tether. *The Contractor*, 1969, dir Anderson, is about a marquee for a wedding reception in a garden and the people who set it up – the physical action of raising the tent and taking it down encompasses the entire action. In *Home*, 1970, dir Anderson, with GIELGUD and RICHARDSON, there is little external action: two old gentlemen meet two less genteel ladies in what turns out to be a mental home. *The Changing Room*, 1971, shows a Rugby League team before, during and after the match. Here too, as in *The Contractor*, the outwardly strictly naturalistic action becomes symbolic of life itself. In 1973 he wrote *The Farm* and *Cromwell*.

Stranitzky, Anton Joseph (1676–1726), Austrian actor. Originator of the Viennese version of the HANSWURST and creator of the Viennese folk theatre. From 1699 he travelled with touring companies in southern Germany; in 1705 went to Vienna and a year later formed his own company with whom he moved into the Kärntnertor Theater in 1712. In the plays he produced there (which took their themes mostly from contemporary Italian operas) he starred as Hanswurst, the comic figure, in peasant costume. As an actor-playwright he was the founder of a tradition which lasted until NESTROY.
Bibl: M. Enzinger, DIE ENTWICKLUNG DES WIENER THEATERS VOM 16. ZUM 19. JAHRHUNDERT, 1918–19, 2 vols

Strasberg, Lee (1901–), Polish-born US director. Began his career as assistant director in 1924 at the THEATRE GUILD, and in 1931 founded the GROUP THEATRE with CLURMAN and CHERYL CRAWFORD. He was the most prominent director of the company, until his disagreement with Clurman led to a final split in 1937; he was responsible for the opening production in 1931 of *The House of Connelly* by P. E. GREEN, and several other plays. Artistic director of the ACTORS' STUDIO, founded in 1947. His style of production involves solid and consistent ensemble acting; he adapted STANISLAVSKY's ideas to American theatre (the 'Method');

Ernst Stern, costume design for MOLIÈRE's *Le Bourgeois gentilhomme*

John Steinbeck, *Burning Bright* with Howard da Silva and Kent Smith, New York 1950

Tom Stoppard, *Rosencrantz and Guildenstern are Dead*, Nottingham Playhouse production with John and Peter McEnery

Lee Strasberg and CLURMAN, two of the founders of the GROUP THEATRE

in 1934 he went on an educational trip to the USSR and made use of the inspiration derived from MEYERHOLD's productions in his direction of M. Levy's *Eagle Guy*, 1934. His major productions include: *Johnny Johnson*, musical by Green and WEILL, 1936; ODETS's *Clash by Night*, 1941, and *The Big Knife*, 1949; HARTOG's *Skipper Next to God*, 1948; IBSEN's *Peer Gynt*, 1951.
Bibl: R. E. Hethmon (ed), STRASBERG AT THE ACTORS' STUDIO, 1965; H. Clurman, THE FERVENT YEARS, 1945

Stratford-upon-Avon. SHAKESPEARE's birthplace, and site of the Shakespeare Memorial Theatre (▷ROYAL SHAKESPEARE COMPANY).

Straub, Agnes (1890–1941), German tragedienne. After 1915 appeared mainly in BERLIN and made her reputation in plays by HEBBEL such as *Herodes und Mariamne*, 1921, dir Falckenberg, and *Judith*, 1922, both Deutsches-Theater, and as Kriemhild in *Die Nibelungen*, 1924, Berlin State Theatre. She also gave fine performances in Expressionist plays by JAHNN and BRONNEN; probably her most famous role was as Cecile in GOETHE's *Stella*, Berlin 1920.
Bibl: H. Jhering, VON JOSEF KAINZ BIS PAULA WESSELY, 1942

Strehler, Giorgio (1921–), Italian director. After working as an actor and drama critic of the newspaper *Milano Sera*, he undertook a number of productions which eventually led to the foundation of the PICCOLO TEATRO DI MILANO (1947), which under the administrative guidance of GRASSI – and between 1955 and 1968 the joint directorship of Grassi and S. – became Italy's leading permanent theatre. It opened with GORKY's *The Lower Depths*; in the same season Strehler directed GOLDONI's *Il Servitore di due Padroni* which became a classic and toured the world for many years with the brilliantly acrobatic MORETTI in the title role – after the latter's death Ferruccio Soleri took over. In the first years the Piccolo Teatro and S. concentrated mainly on plays by Goldoni and SHAKESPEARE, supplemented by CHEKHOV and BRECHT. S.'s direction is characterized by brilliantly intelligent basic concepts which are carried through with immense precision, logic and plasticity. Brecht deeply appreciated S.'s work on *The Threepenny Opera* and wrote to him in 1956, shortly before he died: 'You have created my work anew'. Another great Brecht production by S. was *Galileo*, 1963. Among other authors whose work S. directed are PIRANDELLO, BÜCHNER, DÜRRENMATT and WEISS. He has also directed many operas at La Scala and the SALZBURG FESTIVAL.

Strindberg, August (1849–1912), Swedish playwright and novelist. S.'s childhood was overshadowed by the bankruptcy of his father, a shipping merchant, his mother's death when he was 13 and his father's remarriage to his housekeeper. He read medicine at Uppsala University, became an actor, failed, returned to university to study modern languages; worked as a journalist, 1872–74, and was an assistant at the Royal Library in Stockholm from 1874 to 1882. After this he spent various periods abroad in France, Austria and Germany. He returned to Sweden in the last years of his life. He was married three times: in 1877 to the actress Siri von Essen (the divorced wife of Baron Wrangel) from whom he was divorced in 1891; the Austrian journalist Frida Uhl, from 1893 to 1897; and the Norwegian actress Harriet Bosse from 1901 to 1904. The failure of his first marriage and his suspicions about the paternity of his children were at the roots of his misogyny. During the crisis of his second marriage, from 1894 to 1896, he suffered a series of mental breakdowns in Austria and Paris which he described in his moving autobiographical book *Inferno*. The Inferno-crisis was a watershed in his artistic development. In the plays he wrote in the aftermath of this crisis he broke away from the romantic VERSE DRAMAS of his youth and the naturalism of his middle period and created, in plays like *Spöksonaten* (*The Ghost Sonata*), 1907, *Ett drömpsel* (*A Dream Play*), 1901, and the three parts of *Til Damaskus* (*The Road to Damascus*), 1900, a new form of subjective drama presenting the fantasies of a deeply disturbed mind which blazed the trail for the subsequent development of Expressionist, Surrealist and Absurdist drama (▷EXPRESSIONISM, SURREALISM). But all of his plays are driven by the intensity of his vision and the manic drive of his passion. He wrote more than 60 plays among which the most important are: historical dramas, *Mäster Olof*, 1872–77; *Hemsöborna* (The People of Hemsö), 1889; *Himmelrikets mycklar* (The Keys of Heaven), 1892; *Folkungasagan* (The Folkung Saga), 1899; *Gustav Vasa*, 1899; *Erik XIV*, 1899; *Gustav Adolf*, 1900; *Kristina*, 1901; *Carl XII*, 1901, and *Gustav III*, 1902; naturalistic plays about the relationships of men and women: *Kamraterna* (Comrades), 1886/87; *Fadren* (*The Father*), 1887; *Fröken Julie* (*Miss Julie*), 1888; *Fordringsägare* (*Creditors*), 1888; *Leka med elden* (Playing with Fire), 1892; *Brott och Brott* (Crimes and Crimes), 1899; *Dödsdansen* (*The Dance of Death*), Parts I and II, 1900; folk and fairy-tale plays: *Lycko-Pers resa* (Lucky Peter's Journey), 1882; *Kronbruden* (*The Crown-Bride*), 1901; *Svanevit* (*Swanwhite*), 1901, and *Abu Casem's tofflor* (*Abu Casem's Slippers*), 1908; religious plays: *Advent, ett mysterium* (Advent), 1898; *Påsk* (*Easter*), 1900; *Lammet och vilddjuret* (The Lamb and the Beast), 1903, and *Stora landsvägen* (*The Great Highway*), 1901. He is also the author of a number of novels and stories and series of moving autobiographical books.
Bibl: J. Lamm, 1971; E. Sprigge, THE STRANGE LIFE OF AUGUST STRINDBERG, 1949; C. E. W. L. Dahlstrom, STRINDBERG'S DRAMATIC EXPRESSIONISM, 1965

Strittmatter, Erwin (1912–), German novelist and dramatist. Works as an editor and freelance writer in East Germany. His novels and dramatic works mainly deal with peasant life, e.g. the COMEDY *Katzgraben* (Cat's Grave), 1953, BERLINER ENSEMBLE, dir BRECHT; *Die Holländerbraut* (The Dutch Bride), 1960, Deutsches-Theater, dir BESSON.

Strnad, Oskar (1879–1935), Austrian stage designer. In 1909 Professor of Architecture at the Vienna Polytechnic. It was not until 1919 that he turned to stage design with HASENCLEVER's *Antigone*; from 1924 he collaborated closely with REINHARDT in Vienna and Salzburg, e.g. Strauss's opera *Ariadne auf Naxos*, 1927; SHAKESPEARE's *A Midsummer Night's Dream*, 1926, both in Salzburg; SHAW's *Saint Joan*, 1926. During the same period he also worked for theatres in Cologne, Amsterdam and the Maggio Musicale in Florence (Mozart's *Die Entführung aus dem Serail*, 1935). S. distinguished between atmospheric and rhythmical works. For 'atmospheric' plays (e.g. Shakespeare's *The Merchant of Venice*, 1924, and HOFMANNSTHAL's *Der Schwierige*, 1924) he designed historically accurate sets, and for 'rhythmical' plays (SCHILLER, IBSEN) he preferred simple architectural solutions (realistic portals, staircases, walls).
Bibl: O. Niedermoser, 1965

Stroux, Karl Heinz (1908–), German director and manager. Began his career as an actor and director at the VOLKSBÜHNE, BERLIN, 1928–31; worked in Darmstadt and Wiesbaden, 1945–48, and in Berlin, Düsseldorf and Wuppertal, 1949–55. In 1955 he was appointed director of the Düsseldorf Schauspielhaus which was rebuilt in 1970, where he gained his reputation mainly with first productions of IONESCO's plays, and also produced classical world drama including EURIPIDES, ARISTOPHANES, SHAKESPEARE, SCHILLER, GOETHE and KLEIST.

Sturm-Bühne. A short-lived theatre in Berlin, founded in 1918 by WALDEN and Lothar Schreyer. It attempted to develop an Expressionist style of theatre, parallel to the development in Hamburg of the *Kampfbühne*.

Sturm und Drang (Ger = storm and stress). An 18th-century movement in German literature and drama, which took its name from KLINGER's play of that title (originally titled *Der Wirrwarr*, 1776). Representative dramatists included Klinger, LENZ, LEISEWITZ, Maler Müller, GOETHE in his early works (*Götz von Berlichingen*) and SCHILLER (*Die Räuber*). Theoreticians and critics of the movement included G. Gerstenberg, Herder and Merck. It was during this period that SHAKESPEARE received widespread acceptance on the German stage, and became the idol and model of all the *Sturm und Drang* dramatists.
Bibl: G. Mattenklott, MELANCHOLIE IN DER DRAMATIK DER STURM UND DRANG, 1968; W. Kleiss, STURM UND DRANG, 1966

Suassuna, Arina (1920–), Brazilian dramatist. Left-wing Catholic writer, who first became known with his *Auto da Compadecida* (Testament of Compassion), a modern MYSTERY PLAY, first performed by amateur company. Other works include: *O Santo e a porca* (The Saint and the Pig),

Josef Svoboda, stage design for GOGOL, *The Government Inspector*, Prague 1948

O Casamento suspeitoso (The Suspicious Marriage), both 1958; *Auto de João da Cruz* (Testament of St John of the Cross).

Sudermann, Hermann (1857–1928), German dramatist. His work was compared at the turn of the century with that of G. HAUPTMANN. His plays, theatrically effective, well-made, sentimental dramas which provide great acting roles, were frequently produced during his lifetime, but have rarely been revived since, though some have been adapted for TV, 1974. He scored his first success with *Die Ehre* (Honour), Berlin 1889, Lessingtheater, but is best remembered for his drama *Heimat* (known in England and the USA as *Magda*), 1893, Lessingtheater, in which DUSE and BERNHARDT both played the lead in German in London 1895, at the same time. The following year MRS PATRICK CAMPBELL played it in English in London, and later New York. Other works include: *Sodoms Ende* (Sodom's End), 1890; *Die Schmetterlingsschlacht* (The Battle of the Butterflies), 1894; *Das Glück im Winkel* (Happiness in a Quiet Corner), 1895; *Morituri*, 1896; *Johannes*, 1898; *Johannisfeuer* (Midsummer Fire), 1900; *Der Sturmgeselle Sokrates* (The Stormy Socrates), 1903; *Der Bettler von Syrakus* (The Beggar of Syracuse), 1911; *Die Lobgesänge des Claudian* (The Paeans of Claudian), 1914; *Die Raschoffs*, 1919, etc.
Bibl: I. Leux, 1931

Sukhovo-Kobylin, Alexander Vasilievich (1817–1903), Russian dramatist. Under suspicion of having murdered his mistress, he was gaoled 1850–57. After his release he used his personal experience of the law to write his TRILOGY *Kartiny proshedshevo* (Pictures of the Past), including the plays *Svadba Krechinskovo* (The Wedding of Krechinsky), *Delo* (The Law Case), and *Smert Tarelkina* (The Death of Tarelkin). His works were regarded as dangerous and banned by the censor, which finally led him to give up the theatre; today his plays are in the Soviet REPERTORY. He was a great friend and admirer of GOGOL.
Bibl: I. Klejner, DRAMATURGIA SUKHOVO-KOBYLIN, 1961

Sulerzhitsky, Leopold Antonovich (1872–1916), Russian director. Painter, singer, dancer and novelist, in the last 10 years of his life he turned to the theatre, where he was a versatile reformer and innovator, more influential with his personality than his artistic works. In 1905 he joined the MOSCOW ART THEATRE and became an ardent admirer of STANISLAVSKY and propagandist of his 'system', making attempts to plan a theatre as an artists' commune. He assisted Stanislavsky in the direction of MAETERLINCK's *L'Oiseau bleu* and of *Hamlet*. Later, he took over the First Studio of the MAT, where his most successful productions included G. HAUPTMANN's *Das Friedensfest* and plays by Volkenstein, HEIJERMANS, Berger, etc.

Sullivan, Sir Arthur ▷GILBERT AND SULLIVAN.

Surrealism. An extremist movement in literature and the arts which evolved in Paris from DADA, *c.* 1924. In its early stages it represented an attempt to reach back to a pre-conscious dream state from which the freakish images that crowd the subconscious could be captured and expressed by a kind of pure psychic automatism unimpeded by critical or moral principles. It was strongly influenced by psychoanalytic theories and appeared at one time to have affinities with Oriental mysticism. The term was invented by APOLLINAIRE in the preface to his play *Les Mamelles de Tirésias*. The movement was led by André Breton whose manifestos of 1924, 1930 and 1934, calling for an imaginative evocation of the dream world and the refusal of the individual to be limited by reality, kept pace with his changing theories. Surrealism was more common in painting than in drama, where it was foreshadowed by JARRY's *Ubu Roi* and also by STRINDBERG's plays *The Road to Damascus* and *A Dream Play*; both ARTAUD and VITRAC produced Surrealist drama in the Théâtre Alfred-Jarry, founded 1927. The movement spread overseas and gradually became absorbed in the mainstream of Western drama; traces can be seen in the THEATRE OF THE ABSURD and THEATRE OF CRUELTY.

Svoboda, Josef (1920–), Czech stage designer. Studied architecture in Prague; became a leading designer first at the Prague Opera and in 1948 of the Prague National Theatre while also Professor of Architecture at the Prague Polytechnic. Best known as the creator of the Polyvision and Diapolycran systems used for the Czech pavilion at the Brussels World Fair, from which he developed the LATERNA MAGICA. He has designed 400 sets in theatres all over the world, including East and West BERLIN, Moscow, Vienna, Milan, Venice, Munich, Brussels, London and Boston, Mass. He also designed the Czech pavilion at the World Fair in Montreal. His stage designs include: (in Prague) HÖLDERLIN's *Empedokles*, Verdi's *Tosca*, 1947; Hrubin's *A Sunday in August*, 1958, dir KREJČA; *Hamlet*, 1959, dir J. Pleskot; CHEKHOV's *The Seagull*, 1960, dir Krejča; SOPHOCLES' *Oedipus Rex*, 1963, dir M. Machacek; (in Munich) Orff's *Prometheus*, dir EVERDING; (in London) Strauss's opera, *Die Frau ohne Schatten*. In the operatic field he collaborated mainly with the director Václav Kašlik. His role is principally that of a technician; he makes more use of machinery, lighting and electronic devices than any other contemporary stage designer; 'He creates dreamlike images on stage by his use of realistic, abstract spaces, structures and curtains of light. His theatre is the embodiment of illusionism on stage – with the technology of the present and of the future.' (H. Rischbieter).

Sweden. Religious plays since the 12th century. Since the Reformation, SCHOOL DRAMA; its biblical themes were soon secularized into COMEDY and realism (*Thisbe* by Magnus Olai Asteropherus, 1609). Appearances of the ENGLISH COMEDIANS. In 1667 the first permanent theatre was built in Stockholm: the Comedy House in the Lions' Den. Student performances at Uppsala University and Stockholm between 1682 and 1691. In 1700 the Grand Ballroom in Stockholm was converted into a theatre, where in the 18th century mainly French companies appeared. In 1766 a COURT THEATRE was founded in DROTTNINGHOLM. During the reign of Gustav III (1771–92), who was infatuated with the theatre, activities increased greatly: the Royal Opera was founded in 1782, and in 1788 the Royal

Dramatic Theatre, which has remained the leading Swedish theatre with the status of a NATIONAL THEATRE (with I. BERGMAN as director 1963–66, succeeded by Erland Josephson). Tendencies towards a director's theatre in Sweden since the MEININGER company appeared there in 1889. Among leading players of this century are: Anders de Wahl (1869–1956), Pauline Brunius (1881–1954), EKMAN (1890–1938), Marta Ekström (1899–1952). Little drama of importance until STRINDBERG, Sweden's most prominent and influential playwright; he was DRAMATURG at the Intimate Theatre in Stockholm 1907–09, under the management of August Flack; for it he wrote a number of so-called 'chamber plays'. The other noted dramatist LAGERKVIST saw theatre somewhere between Strindberg's expressive drama and IBSEN's psychological realism. The works of Strindberg and Lagerkvist are fixed points in the development of Swedish drama, which most later dramatists followed: BERGMAN, DAGERMAN, Lars Forssell. Today there is considerable theatrical activity, with over ten permanent theatres in Stockholm and important municipal theatres in Göteborg, Malmö, Uppsala. The Riksteater, founded in 1933, is a State-subsidized touring company which comprises several ensembles and gives about 2,000 performances annually in 600 different places.
Bibl: N. Brunius, SWEDISH THEATRE, 1968; A. Gustafson (ed), A HISTORY OF SWEDISH LITERATURE, 1961

Swinarski, Konrad (1929–75), Polish director. Disciple of BRECHT and AXER; he established an international reputation with the first production of WEISS's *Marat/Sade* at the Schillertheater, BERLIN, in 1963. Other well-known productions include: Brecht's *Die Dreigroschenoper*, 1958; DÜRRENMATT's *Ein Engel kommt nach Babylon*, 1961, and *Frank V*, 1962; MAYAKOVSKY's *The Bedbug*, 1964, etc.

Switzerland. Earliest forms of drama were religious plays at Muri and St Gallen and, most famous, the medieval MYSTERY PLAYS performed at Lucerne on a multiple stage. Great theatrical activity in the 16th and 17th centuries; the struggle between Protestants and Catholics developed the theatre of both factions as a means of self-presentation and propaganda. JESUIT DRAMA; plays by CALDERÓN at Einsiedeln (still performed by villagers today). Ban on theatres due to puritan influence in Zurich and Geneva; only peasant theatre in remote Alpine valleys. During the 18th century an increasing number of foreign companies appeared in Switzerland. In the 19th century municipal theatres were founded, first in Lucerne and Zurich. The most important professional theatre is the Zurich Schauspielhaus, which reached its zenith during the management of the director A. Reucker 1901–21, and between 1938 and 1945 was the most important independent German-speaking theatre, particularly under the direction of WÄLTERLIN and HIRSCHFELD, the DRAMATURG. It was at this time also that Switzerland began to be a major contributor to world drama, chiefly through the works of HOCHWÄLDER, FRISCH and DÜRRENMATT. Today there are a number of subsidized theatres, in Basle, Berne, Lucerne, St Gallen, Biel-Solothurn. Slower development of theatre in the French-speaking part of the country.
Bibl: E. Müller, SCHWEIZERISCHE THEATERGESCHICHTE, 1944

Sydow, Max von (1929–), Swedish actor. Worked at the Malmö Municipal Theatre under I. BERGMAN, 1955–60, later joined the Royal Dramatic Theatre at Stockholm. A tall man with a thoughtful face, he was an impressive Peer Gynt, 1957, Alceste in MOLIÈRE's *Le Misanthrope*, 1957; Faust in GOETHE's play, 1958, and Victor in LORCA's *Yerma*, 1961. Frequently cast by Bergman in his films, he achieved worldwide recognition and has appeared in many Hollywood films as well as Swedish ones.

Symbolism. An important movement in French literature which began about 1880 with the poems of Mallarmé and Verlaine, and whose precursor was Baudelaire. It signified a departure from the traditional conventions governing both theme and technique in French poetry. The Symbolists wished to liberate the technique of versification in every way that would make for fluidity, holding that the function of poetry was to evoke, that its matter should be impressionistic and intuitive, and poetic images should be symbols of the state of the poet's soul. Symbolism in the theatre was encouraged by FORT who founded the Théâtre d'Art in 1890 for the production of Symbolist plays by authors such as MAETERLINCK. This later became the Théâtre de l'Œuvre under LUGNÉ-POË who succeeded Fort in 1893. Other dramatists to come under the influence of Symbolism were ANDREYEV and YEVREINOV in Russia, HOFMANNSTHAL and G. HAUPTMANN in his later plays (*Die versunkene Glocke*) in Germany, SYNGE (*The Well of the Saints*), O'CASEY (*Within the Gates*), YEATS (his early plays) in Ireland, and O'NEILL in the USA.

Synge, John Millington (1871–1909), Irish dramatist. With YEATS the leading figure in the Irish Dramatic Movement. As a young man he wandered through Europe; in Paris he met Yeats, who inspired him to write and return to Ireland, where he lived a life of rural simplicity, deriving the material for most of his plays from the life and characters of country people. His plays have dramatic and poetic force, firm scenic structure, subtle characterization and rich lively humour as well as deep seriousness. Main works: *In the Shadow of the Glen*, 1903; *Riders to the Sea*, 1904; *The Tinker's Wedding* (his only play not performed at the ABBEY THEATRE, Dublin), written 1904, fp London 1909; *The Playboy of the Western World*, first full-length play, 1907; *Deirdre of the Sorrows*, 1910 posthumous (unfinished).
Bibl: A. Price, SYNGE AND THE ANGLO-IRISH DRAMA, 1961; U. Ellis-Fermor, THE IRISH DRAMATIC MOVEMENT, 2/1954

Szyfman, Arnold (Arnold Stanislav Zygmunt Schiffman; 1882–1967), Polish director and manager. Founded the first literary CABARET in Warsaw in 1908; in 1913 formed the Teatr Polski, which he managed with interruptions (1915–18, 1939–45, 1949–55) until 1957, when he became honorary director. Apart from the Teatr Polski he also managed several other theatres in Warsaw and Lódz, and was generally looked upon as one of the best organizers of the Polish NATIONAL THEATRE in the 20th century. His outstanding productions include: *Hamlet*, 1922, 1947; KRASIŃSKI's *The Undivine Comedy*, 1920; *Pygmalion*, 1925; *Romeo and Juliet*, 1931; AESCHYLUS' *Oresteia*, 1947.

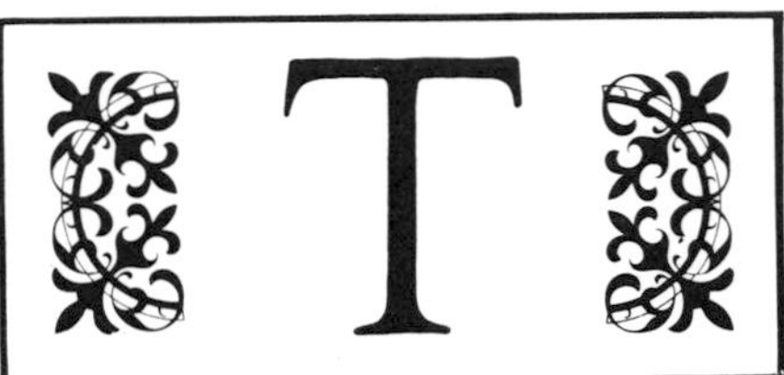

Tagore, Sir Rabindranath (1861–1941), Indian poet, playwright, novelist and philosopher. The first modern playwright in India to achieve world renown. He received the Nobel Prize for Literature in 1913 and was knighted in 1915. He studied law in England and later established in Bolpur the Santiniketan ('abode of peace'), which became a famous international institute, where he lectured on Oriental philosophy. His dramatic works (he wrote about 50) are varied in form, containing song, MIME and dance, combining lyrical and symbolic elements. Inspired by Sanskrit drama and Bengali folk drama, he wrote mainly in Bengali, often translating his own plays into English. Among his earlier ones, usually in verse, are *Vis Barjan* (Sacrifice), 1890; *Chitrangada* (translated as *Chitra*), 1892, based on the Hindu *Mahabharata*. Later plays are generally in prose, heavily weighted with SYMBOLISM, e.g. *Raja* (King of the Dark Chamber), 1910; *Dakghar* (The Post Office), 1912, one of his most popular plays in Europe; *Rakta Karavi* (Red Oleanders), 1924. His dance dramas include *Chitrangada*, 1936, based on the earlier play, and *Shyama*, 1933, taken from a Buddhist legend.
Bibl: K. Chandrasekharan, TAGORE, A MASTER SPIRIT, 1963; Sir S. Radhakrishnan, THE PHILOSOPHY OF RABINDRANATH TAGORE, 1961; E. Thompson, TAGORE, POET AND DRAMATIST, 1948

Tairov, Alexander Yakovlevich (1885–1950), Soviet director. One of the greatest innovators of the early 1920s, his work made an important contribution to the theory of stage technique. He began his career as an actor under MEYERHOLD in St Petersburg, where he directed his first plays (1910–11), leaving in 1913 to work in Moscow. Here in 1914 he formed the Kamerny Theatre with which he was associated until his death. His opening production was KĀLIDĀSA's *Śakuntalā*. With his designer ALEXANDRA EXTER, he developed a scenic décor strongly inspired by Cubism: a stage area divided into platforms with scaffolding, poles and squares of coloured fabric. The actors employed elements of MIME, clowning and REVUE; he used COMMEDIA DELL'ARTE themes (R. Lothar's *King Arlecchino*, 1917) preferring the fantastic (E. T. A. Hoffmann's *Prinzessin Brambilla*, 1920) while maintaining the supremacy of purely theatrical effects, of the artistry and virtuosity of actor, designer and director as against the written text. His ideas were most successfully realized in the adaptation of the operetta *Giroflé-Girofla* (Lecocq, 1922; the lead was played, as in many other of his productions, by his wife ALICE KOONEN), in which these theatrical elements were dominant; these ideas were less applicable in his productions of serious drama which included CLAUDEL's *L'Echange* and *L'Annonce faite à Marie*, 1918; SHAW's *Saint Joan*, 1924; O'NEILL's *The Hairy Ape* and *Desire Under the Elms*, both 1926, and *All God's Chillun Got Wings*, 1929. His productions caused a sensation when he toured Europe 1925–30. His *Notes of a Director*, written 1921, were published in 1923 as *The Theatre Unchained*. Under the pressure of Stalinism T. was forced to work under supervision, to return to a more traditional style and eventually his theatre was taken over by a committee, but, unlike Meyerhold, he was able to continue his work until one year before his death. His essays are collected in *Theatre October*, 1967.

Bibl: L. Schreyer, ERINNERUNGEN AN STURM UND BAUHAUS, 1956

Talli, Virgilio (1858–1928), Italian theatre manager. Began his career as an actor with various companies and in 1900 took over the management of the famous Compagnia Talli-Gramatica-Calabresi, of which RUGGERI and later LYDA BORELLI were also members. He managed the Teatro Argentina in Rome as a *semistabile* (semi-permanent) theatre from 1918 to 1921; 1921–23 with the State-subsidized Compagnia Nazionale, organized the tours of ELEONORA DUSE, and in 1926 was appointed director of the Teatro Arcimboldi in Milan. He foreshadowed the modern director's theatre in his skilful selection of actors and his daring REPERTOIRE; apart from commercial plays, he produced works by VERGA, D'ANNUNZIO, PIRANDELLO, ROSSO DI SAN SECONDO. He discovered and supported a number of famous actors.

Talma, François-Joseph (1763–1826), French actor. One of the greatest French tragic actors, who also reformed stage costume. He made his début at the COMÉDIE-FRANÇAISE in 1787, where he received immediate acclaim in the title role of CHÉNIER's *Charles IX*, 1789. He was a strong supporter of the Revolution and a friend of Marat and Danton. In 1791 he left the CF with a group of actors to form the Théâtre de la République. After the reconstitution of the CF in 1799, he played

August Strindberg, self-caricature. Inscription reads 'Nyklerhelens folger' (Consequence of sobriety), 1882

Sweden, poster for the Royal Dramatic Society, designed by Skawarius *c.* 1938

J. M. Synge at a rehearsal of *The Playboy of The Western World*, sketch by Jack Yeats

Rabindranath Tagore, 1912

François-Joseph Talma as Néron in RACINE's *Britannicus*, portrait by Delacroix

the title role in CORNEILLE's *Le Cid*, the opening production there. Napoleon, a great admirer, chose him in 1808 to appear in Erfurt before an audience of five kings in *La Mort de César* by VOLTAIRE. T.'s acting style was based on sensitivity and naturalness, opposed to the exaggerated declamatory style of his time. He admired SHAKESPEARE and appeared in several of his plays (*Macbeth*, *Othello*, *Hamlet*) but despite his popular success he was unable to gain acceptance for Shakespeare from critics. Despite his friendship with many important politicians and artists of his time, his extravagant life-style eventually forced him to work in the provinces and abroad. Apart from leading roles in contemporary tragedies, he also appeared in other plays by Corneille (*Cinna*, Sévère in *Polyeucte*, *Nicomède*), RACINE (Oreste in *Andromaque*, Néron in *Britannicus*, *Bajazet*, Achille in *Iphigénie*) and Voltaire (*Oedipe*, Brutus in *La Mort de César*, Séide in *Mahomet*), etc.
Bibl: A. Augustine-Tierry, 1942

Tarasova, Alla Konstantinovna (1898–1973), Russian actress. Appeared from 1916 at the MOSCOW ART THEATRE (touring in Europe and US 1922–24) in leading roles including: Anya in CHEKHOV's *The Cherry Orchard*; Irina in *Three Sisters*; Sonya in *Uncle Vanya*; Gruschenka in *The Brothers Karamazov* (based on Dostoyevsky). Among her mature roles were: Masha in *Three Sisters*, 1937, and the title role in SCHILLER's *Maria Stuart*. She was considered the major exponent of STANISLAVSKY's acting method in her depiction of the subtlest emotional feelings, particularly in Chekhov's plays. In 1947 she was appointed director of the MAT, a post she held until 1954.

Tardieu, Jean (1903–), French poet and dramatist. Began writing poetry and prose in 1927 in the style associated with Prévert and Queneau. His dramatic works, 16 sketches published in two volumes (*Théâtre de chambre*, 1955, and *Théâtre II: poèmes à jouer*, 1960), include FARCES, parodies and poems, and are exercises in style reminiscent of SURREALISM. They were produced in the 1950s, mostly by Michel de Ré and Jacques Poliéri in Paris avant-garde theatres. His works include (with dates of first performances): *Qui est là?*, 1949; *Un Mot pour un autre*, 1950; *La Politesse inutile*, 1950; *Oswald et Zénaïde, ou Les Apartés*, 1951; *Ce que parler veut dire*, 1951; *Il y avait foule au manoir, ou Les Monologues*, 1951; *Faust et Yorick*, 1951; *Un Geste pour un autre*, 1951; *Conversation-Sinfonietta*, 1951; *Les Amants du Métro*, a ballet comedy 'without dance and music', 1952; *Eux seuls le savent*, 1952; *Le Meuble*, 1954; *La Serrure*, 1954; *Le Guichet*, 1955; *La Sonate et les messieurs, ou Comment parler musique*, 1955; *La Société Apollon, ou Comment parler des arts*, 1955; *Une Voix sans personne*, 1956; *Les Temps du verbe, ou Le Pouvoir de la parole*, 1956; *L'ABC de notre vie*, 1959; *Rythme à trois temps*, 1959; and his early verse drama: *Tonnerre sans orage, ou Les Dieux inutiles*, written 1944. He also translated GOETHE's *Iphigénie* and *Pandora*, poems by HÖLDERLIN and plays by P. Pörtner etc.
Bibl: M. Esslin, THE THEATRE OF THE ABSURD, 2/1968

Tarleton, Richard (?–1588), English CLOWN, the most famous of the ELIZABETHAN THEATRE who worked with the QUEEN'S MEN from 1583 until his death. His performances were largely EXTEMPORE and he was also a famous exponent of the JIG. He wrote several scripts, of which the second part only of *The Seven Deadly Sins* is preserved. He is said to have been the model for Yorick in *Hamlet*.
Bibl: E. K. Chambers, THE ELIZABETHAN STAGE, 1923, 4 vols

Tartaglia. A character of the COMMEDIA DELL'ARTE, especially popular in Naples; related to the DOTTORE.

Tasso, Torquato (1544–95), Italian poet. His PASTORAL DRAMA *L'Aminta*, staged in 1573 on the Belvedere island in the river Po, is, with GUARINI's *Pastor Fido*, fp Cremona 1595, the most outstanding 16th-century example of this form. The drama *Torrismondo*, pub 1587, a mixture of TRAGEDY and romance, dealing with the incestuous love of two sisters, is reminiscent of SOPHOCLES' *Oedipus Rex*. He also wrote an unfinished COMEDY, *Intrighi d'amore*. He is the hero of a play by GOETHE.
Bibl: A. Tortoreto, 1957

Tate, Harry (1872–1940), English MUSIC HALL comedian. He is best remembered for his golfing, motoring and fishing sketches. He also appeared in the earliest REVUES at the London Hippodrome and in 1935 played the King in the PANTOMIME *The Sleeping Beauty*.

Taylor, Cecil P. (1929–), Scottish-born dramatist. Member of a Glasgow Jewish family, he is mainly interested in left-wing types, especially their inconsistencies and misconceptions. Most successful in a brief comedy *Allergy*, 1966, about a Glasgow journalist torn between Marxist principles and the need for personal security. *Bread and Butter*, 1966, is his outline biography of two Jewish couples in the Gorbals between 1931 and 1965. *Happy Days are Here Again*, 1965, is a political fantasy. The musical *Who's Pinkus Where's Chelus?*, 1967, is a piece of Jewish folklore with songs by Monty Norman.

Taylor, Laurette (1884–1946), US actress. She was married to the dramatist J. Hartley Manners, in whose play *Peg o'My Heart* she had a triumphant success (600 performances in New York, 500 in London). Her last memorable appearance was as Amanda Blake in T. WILLIAMS's *The Glass Menagerie*, 1945.

Teatro Campesino, El. One of the most prominent and successful US theatre troupes concerned with developing revolutionary propaganda; it represents the Union of Farm Workers from southern California. Productions consist of sketches and songs based on topical problems of migrant Mexican farm labourers in California, using primitive theatrical devices to gain effects of great immediacy.

Teatro Olimpico (Vicenza, Italy). One of the most important theatre buildings of the Renaissance, a variation on the antique Roman stage form; a semicircular, high-tiered auditorium, geometrically constructed stage (*scenae frons*) with three doors and a perspective view on the wing-alleys. The theatre, with 950 seats, was built of wood. The design was based on the plans of PALLADIO (1509–80) and built by his son Scilla and his pupil SCAMOZZI (1552–1616). It became a model for theatre architecture of the Renaissance.
Bibl: L. Magagnato, TEATRI ITALIANI DEL CINQUECENTO, 1954

Teatro stabile. Italian for permanent ENSEMBLE theatre.

Telari (Ital, *telaio* = frame). A form of stage décor in the early Renaissance (used by the Italian architect BUONTALENTI), derived from the Greek PERIAKTOS, which foreshadowed WINGS; three-sided revolving prisms right and left on stage which were differently painted on each side. In combination with a movable back-drop, the *telari* system made a quick change of scenery possible. The principle of the system was employed by the German architect FURTTENBACH in 1641 and was described by him in 1663 in his treatise *Mannhaffter Kunstspiegel*.

Tempest, Dame Marie (Mary Susan Etherington; 1864–1942), English actress. She was appointed DBE in 1937. Trained as a singer, she first appeared in operetta and MUSICAL COMEDY. Later she was successful as a straight actress, notably as Kitty in *The Marriage of Kitty* (an adaptation of a French play by Cosmo Gordon-Lennox, her second husband). Later she appeared in leading roles, mainly in modern COMEDIES, e.g. Judith Bliss in COWARD's *Hay Fever*, 1925, a part written for her.

Ter-Arutunian, Rouben (1920–), Russian-born US stage designer. Emigrated with his family first to France and Germany (trained in BERLIN and designed his first sets for the Dresden Opera in 1943 and in Vienna 1944), then studied in Paris 1947–50; settled in the USA in 1951. In his designs he often employs synthetic fabrics, metal and plastic. After working for TV, he became well known through his rebuilding of the stage for the American Shakespeare Festival in Stratford, Conn., a construction modelled on the Elizabethan theatre. He worked on numerous Shakespearean productions at the same theatre including: *King John*, 1956; *Measure for Measure*, 1956; *Much Ado About Nothing*, 1957; *The Merchant of Venice*, 1957. Other works include: BRECHT's *Arturo Ui*, New York 1963, dir T. RICHARDSON; HOCHHUTH's *The Deputy*, New York 1964; WHITING's *The Devils*, New York 1965, dir M. Cacoyannis; also worked on ballets, e.g. Brecht's *The Seven Deadly Sins*, New York City Ballet, 1958, choreography Balanchine, and on operas, e.g. Gluck's *Orpheus and Eurydice*, Hamburg Opera, 1963.

Teatro Olimpico at Vicenza by Palladio, 1580–84

Ellen Terry, photograph by Julia Cameron

Terence, sketch from a 12th-century copy of his comedies illustrating *Woman of Andros*

Terence (Publius Terentius Afer; *c.* 190–159 BC), Roman comic dramatist. Translated and adapted Greek comedies by MENANDER and other playwrights of the New Comedy (▷COMEDY (GREEK)), in many cases improving on the original. He introduced new characters but was more respectful of dramatic structure and logic of action than PLAUTUS. While the latter introduced Roman manners and habits, T. adhered closely to the original, often announcing his changes in the PROLOGUE. Though his language was more refined than that of Plautus and his plays imbued throughout with culture and refinement, they were theatrically less effective; Julius Caesar criticized his work for lacking the necessary *vis comica*. In the Middle Ages his works were read and acted in schools, particularly because of his perfect use of the Latin language and the absence of crude jokes, buffoonery, etc. In the 10th century the German nun HROSWITHA tried to imitate his style. Of his works only six are extant; *Andria* (The Woman of Andros), 166 BC; *Hecyra* (The Mother-in-Law), 165 BC; *Heauton-timorumenos* (The Self-tormentor), 163 BC; *Eunuchus*, 161 BC; *Phormio*, 161 BC; *Adelphi* (The Brothers), 160 BC.
Bibl: W. Beare, THE ROMAN STAGE, 3/1965; G. F. Duckworth, THE NATURE OF ROMAN COMEDY, 1952

Terry, Dame Ellen Alice (1847–1928), English actress. Daughter of the actor Benjamin Terry (1818–96) and Sarah Ballard (1819–92); made her first appearance on stage at the age of eight. She left the stage twice, the first time (1864) to marry the painter G. F. Watts, and shortly afterwards for six years during her relationship with Edward Godwin, an architect and stage designer, when she had two children: Edith Craig (1869–1947) and E. G. CRAIG. She returned to the stage in 1867 as Katharina in *The Taming of the Shrew*, with IRVING as Petruchio. In 1878 she started a collaboration with Irving which lasted for 24 years. She was highly successful playing Shakespearean heroines including Ophelia, Portia, Olivia and Beatrice. She was the embodiment of charm and wit; it was SHAW who said that the whole age was in love with her. After leaving Irving in 1902, she managed the Imperial Theatre for some time, where Craig designed his first sets. Shaw, with whom she corresponded (their letters have been published), wrote for her the part of Lady Cecily in *Captain Brassbound's Conversion*, Court Theatre, 1906. Her second marriage in 1878 was to an actor, Charles Kelly (1839–85). Her third husband was an American actor James Carew (1876–1938); this marriage (1907) lasted only two years but thereafter she appeared only rarely on stage. She toured the USA and Australia giving readings and lectures on Shakespeare. She was made a DBE in 1925. GIELGUD is her grand-nephew.
Bibl: E. G. Craig, ELLEN TERRY AND HER SECRET SELF, 1931

Terry, Megan (1932–), US playwright. Regarded as one of the most compelling and successful of OFF-OFF-BROADWAY dramatists. Took a Bachelor of Education degree at the University of Washington and worked as a teacher before devoting herself wholly to dramatic writing. She came first to national prominence with her explosive play *Viet Rock*, in which she recreated 'the ambience of the Vietnam war and our feelings about it'. Originally presented by LA MAMA in New York, the play was chosen by Robert Brustein for production at the Yale Drama School. In 1966 it reappeared under her direction at the Martinique Theatre in New York. An active and principal proponent of the Off-Off-Broadway movement, she was a member of Joseph Chaikin's OPEN THEATRE and a director of its playmaking workshop. A number of her own plays originated at the Open Theatre including: *Keep Tightly Closed in a Cool Dry Place*; *Calm Down Mother*; *Coming and Goings*; *The Magic Realists* (Open Theatre at La Mama). Other stage works: *Miss Copper Queen on a Set of Pills*, Cherry Lane Theatre, New York; *The People versus Ranchman*, Firehouse Theatre, Minneapolis; *The Key Is on the Bottom*, Mark Taper Forum, Los Angeles; *Home*, 1968, televised by National Educational TV.

Terson, Peter (1932–), English dramatist. Born in Newcastle-on-Tyne, the son of a carpenter, he began his career in the theatre as a resident dramatist at the VICTORIA THEATRE, STOKE-ON-TRENT, which is strongly committed to the local community. Here a series of his plays were produced: *A Night to Make the Angels Weep*, 1964; *All Honour Mr Todd*, 1965; *The Mighty Reservoy*, 1966; *I'm in Charge of These Ruins*, 1967; *The Ballad of the Artificial Mash*, 1967. He collaborated with the company on the documentary musical, *The Knotty*, 1966, which deals with the history of the North Staffordshire Railway. Has also written plays specifically for the NATIONAL YOUTH THEATRE: *Fuzz*, *Zigger-Zagger*, 1967; *The Apprentices* and *Spring-Heeled Jack*, 1970, and TV plays: *The Last Train through the Harecastle Tunnel*, 1969, and *The 1861 Whitby Lifeboat Disaster*, which he later rewrote as a full-length stage play. Most recent works include: *Prisoners of War*, 1970, and *The Samaritan*, Stoke 1971. His plays, which show the conflict between rural traditions and the forces of change, combine great talent for humour with the power of poetry in the racy DIALOGUE.

Terzieff, Laurent (1935–), French actor. Made his début in 1953 in a small part in ADAMOV's *Tous contre tous*. Subsequently he appeared at several avant-garde theatres in BRECHT's *The Exception and The Rule*, 1955, dir Jean-Marie Serreau; as Louis Lane in CLAUDEL's *L'Echange*, 1957, and Cébès in his *Tête d'or*, Odéon 1959, dir BARRAULT; he played his first great classical part in 1964, the title role in CORNEILLE's *Nicomède*, TNP at the Avignon Festival; he also appeared in ALBEE's *The American Dream* and *The Zoo Story*, 1965; SCHISGAL's *Luv*, 1965; MROŻEK's *Tango*, 1967, which he also directed. He is also a well-known director and film actor.

Tetralogy. (1) In ancient drama a group of four plays: three tragedies (TRILOGY) and a SATYR PLAY, which were performed together at a dramatic contest. (2) A series of four plays with a unified theme, e.g. HAUPTMANN's tetralogy on the House of Atreus (*Iphigenie in Delphi*, 1941; *Iphigenie in Aulis*, 1944; *Agamemnons Tod*, 1945; *Elektra*, 1945).

Thalia (Gr *thaleia* = blossoming). The Muse of Comedy, shown with a comic mask and shepherd's staff; today the symbol for the art of acting in general.

Theatre, The. The earliest of the London playhouses. Erected by J. BURBAGE in the parish of St Leonard's, Shoreditch, on a plot he had leased in April 1576. Burbage, having originally been a carpenter by trade, designed and built the playhouse himself, a circular building with three galleries. It was opened in the summer of 1577. Used for displays of fencing and other physical spectacles, it was also occupied by a number of acting companies, among them Leicester's Men (1576–78); the QUEEN'S MEN, between 1583 and 1589 intermittently; the ADMIRAL'S MEN, 1590–91; and the CHAMBERLAIN'S MEN, to which Burbage himself belonged, 1594–99. After Burbage's death his son CUTHBERT B. pulled The Theatre down, 1598, and used the timbers to build the GLOBE THEATRE.

Théâtre de France. The second French State theatre in Paris, after the COMÉDIE-FRANÇAISE; housed in the beautiful Théâtre de l'Odéon, originally known as the Salle de Luxembourg, the second house of the Comédie; it was managed 1959–68 by BARRAULT.

Théâtre des Nations. International festival founded in 1954, held annually in spring in Paris, which presents outstanding productions of every theatrical form, by companies from many countries; 1957–64 held at the Théâtre Sarah Bernhardt, managed by A. M. Julien; 1965–68 at the Théâtre de l'Odéon, managed by BARRAULT. High points include the great acting ENSEMBLES: the OLD VIC in SHAKESPEARE, the MOSCOW ART THEATRE in CHEKHOV, the BERLINER ENSEMBLE in BRECHT. Since 1960 an increasing number of companies from East Asia and Africa, since 1965 also many experimental groups have been invited. There is also a festival magazine, which appears eleven times a year, *Théâtre: drame, musique, dance*.

Théâtre du Vieux-Colombier ▷COPEAU.

Théâtre Français. ▷COMÉDIE-FRANÇAISE.

Theatre Guild, The. A subscription theatre society, founded in New York in 1919, many of whose founders (MOELLER, LANGNER, SIMONSON, Helen Westley, Theresa Helburn) were former members of the Washington Square Players. In its heyday (1930s and '40s) the leading force in high-quality productions of generally ambitious European and US plays; also instituted successful subscription series in cities outside New York, 'Theatre Guild Production' becoming a national hall mark. After the failure of the inaugural production (BENAVENTE's *Bonds of Interest*) the Guild achieved immediate success with *John Ferguson*, a naturalist play by ERVINE; by 1920 there were about 30,000 seasonal subscribers. Apart from first US productions of SHAW (*Heartbreak House*, 1920; *Back to Methusaleh*, 1922); O'NEILL (*Strange Interlude*, starring LYNN FONTANNE, 1928; *Mourning Becomes Electra*, 1931), P. BARRY (*The Philadelphia Story*, starring KATHARINE HEPBURN, 1939), BEHRMAN, M. ANDERSON and SHERWOOD, the Guild also presented foreign plays including MOLNÁR's *Liliom*, 1921; KAISER's *From Morn to Midnight*, 1922; ČAPEK's *R.U.R.*, 1922; WERFEL's *Goat Song*, 1926. In 1931 the Guild produced *Of Thee I Sing*, book by KAUFMAN and Morrie Ryskind, sing G. and I. GERSHWIN, (PULITZER PRIZE), and in 1935 première of *Porgy and Bess*; from 1943 the enormously successful musicals of RODGERS and HAMMERSTEIN, *Oklahoma!* and *Carousel*, 1945 (based on *Liliom*). Among the actors of the Guild were: Lunt and Fontanne, Dudley Digges, Helen Westley, Edward G. Robinson. The most important director and stage designer were MOELLER and SIMONSON respectively. Guests from Europe included REICHER and COPEAU. Bibl: W. P. Eaton, *The Theatre Guild: the First Ten Years*, 1929.

Theatre-in-the-round. A theatre building in which the acting area is surrounded by the auditorium on all sides. Also called arena theatre. Notable examples: Théâtre en Rond de Paris, 1954, designed by André Villiers; VICTORIA THEATRE, STOKE-ON-TRENT, 1962, designed by Stephen Joseph.

Théâtre Italien. ▷COMÉDIE-ITALIENNE.

Théâtre Libre. ▷ANTOINE.

Théâtre National Populaire. ▷VILAR; G. WILSON.

Theatre of Cruelty. The term, coined by ARTAUD, has often been misunderstood. It does not denote a theatre in which violence and physical cruelty play an important part, but was meant to embody Artaud's demand for a theatre which so completely involves the spectator and changes him through the depth of his experience that he suffers with the characters on the stage, rather than being able to leave the theatre as the same person who entered it.

Theatre of the Absurd. A term often applied to the plays of such writers as BECKETT, IONESCO, ADAMOV, GENET, which, deriving from the Surrealist movement of the 1930s, achieved considerable success in the 1950s and 1960s. At first sight these plays dispense with the traditional techniques of dramatic construction and characterization. The exposition is often vague, little or nothing is said about the previous history of the characters; the characters

themselves are fluid, changing their personalities during the action abruptly and often illogically; the action often remains obscure or involves fantastic and grotesque incidents. But if one sees these plays as daydreams, fantasies of their authors, which depict their inner life of anxieties, obsessions and wish-fulfilment dreams, it becomes clear that they depict a reality of their own – the inner reality of their authors and perhaps the realities of the fantasy and dream life of humanity at large. Being an expression of one human being's inner life, these plays are akin to lyrical poetry which is also concerned with metaphors for states of mind rather than narrative about the external world. Hence the action of the plays of the Theatre of the Absurd can also be regarded as presenting images or metaphors, three-dimensionally materialized on stage. Plays like Beckett's *Waiting for Godot* or Ionesco's *The Chairs* are poetic images of basic human predicaments. The Theatre of the Absurd has provided the dramatists of the generation which followed its flowering with the technical means to express a whole range of subjects hitherto denied to the stage; at the same time audiences, which at first received the seemingly nonsensical and obscure action of this type of drama with bewilderment have become accustomed to a new convention that they now find easily acceptable to them.
Bibl: M. Esslin, THEATRE OF THE ABSURD, 2/1968

Theatre of the Grotesque. A form of the comic in which dark, exaggerated and outrageous features predominate. The term may derive from the Italian *grotta*=cave: in the Renaissance, strange and distorted frescoes found in ancient ruins aroused an interest in the grotesque. In dramatic literature grotesque comedy, scurrility and strangeness lead to a form of TRAGICOMEDY where the ridiculous and the sad combine; Romanticism contains a strong trend towards the grotesque. It draws attention to the disharmony, the inner contradictions of reality and often relies on the combination of incompatible elements. Grotesque features appear in 19th-century farce (NESTROY, GOGOL, COURTELINE, FEYDEAU) and in Expressionist drama (late STRINDBERG, WEDEKIND, STERNHEIM). In Italy CHIARELLI initiated a grotesque theatre (*teatro grottesco*) which influenced PIRANDELLO. Features are also found in the great silent screen comedies of Chaplin and Buster Keaton. BRECHT used grotesque elements in many of his plays. They predominate in the plays of BECKETT, IONESCO and the other dramatists of the THEATRE OF THE ABSURD and in DÜRRENMATT's comedies of paradox.
Bibl: J. L. Styan, THE DARK COMEDY, 1962

Theatre Royal ▷DRURY LANE.

Theatre Union. Co-operative theatre organization, founded in New York City in 1932, to present and support contemporary plays on social themes and political radicalism, with low admission prices and

Theatre-in-the-round, VICTORIA THEATRE, STOKE-ON-TRENT, set by Alex Bunn for *Frankenstein* by CAMPTON

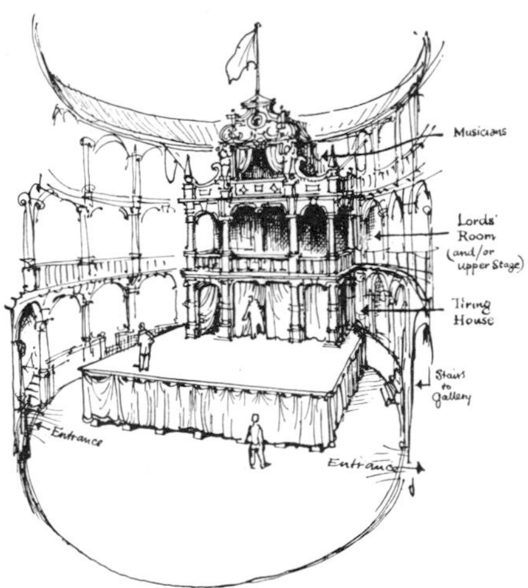

The Theatre, reconstruction of JAMES BURBAGE's playhouse, built 1576

Theatre Guild production of SHAW's *Heartbreak House*, New York 1920

free entry for the unemployed. The founders included S. HOWARD, SHERWOOD, M. ANDERSON, MUNI and RICE. Before it broke up in 1937, it had become a model for similar organizations in other cities in the USA.

Theatre Upstairs ▷ROYAL COURT.

Theatre Workshop ▷LITTLEWOOD.

Theatrical Syndicate. Association of US businessmen formed in 1896 including the firm of Klaw and Erlanger, C. FROHMAN, A. Hayman, S. Nixon and J. Fred Zimmerman. For sixteen years they controlled most of New York's theatres and many in other cities. They were sufficiently powerful to harm those who opposed them, e.g. forcing MRS FISKE to play in second-rate theatres on tour and SARAH BERNHARDT to appear in a tent. Both these players, together with BELASCO, helped eventually to break the syndicate. ▷SHUBERT.

Theologeion (Gk = stage of the gods). Scaffold, flat roof of the *skene*, where, from *c.* 500 BC, gods made their appearance in Greek drama.

Theorikon (Gk). 'View money', tokens of bronze or lead given by the *polis* to citizens in Athens to enable them to visit the theatre free; introduced by Pericles; repealed for a period between 411 and 409 BC.

Thespis (6th century BC), Greek poet and dramatist of Icaria in Attica. The legendary 'ancestor' of drama, he was probably the first writer to introduce a leader of the CHORUS, since he was the first to employ a solo actor. It is also said that he was the first producer of a drama at the Dionysian Festival in Athens. The belief that he travelled with his actors round the country on his 'Thespis cart' is not substantiated.

Thimig. Family of Austrian actors. (1) **Hugo T.** (1854–1944), comic character actor at the BURGTHEATER in Vienna, which he joined in 1874, excelling in plays by GOLDONI (e.g. TRUFFALDINO in *Il Servitore di due Padroni*) and SHAKESPEARE; after World War I considered representative of the Burgtheater-style. His children Helene, Hermann and Hans also became actors. (2) **Helene T.** (1889–1974) began her career in 1919 with REINHARDT at the Deutsches-Theater, BERLIN, where she remained until 1933 playing many leading comic and poetic roles, including Ophelia, Rosalind in *As You Like It*, and Gretchen in GOETHE's *Urfaust*. She married Reinhardt and they lived in Hollywood from 1938 until his death in 1943; she returned to Vienna in 1946, and joined the Burgtheater. In 1948 she was appointed director of the famous Max Reinhardt drama school in Vienna. Her mature roles included: Christine in O'NEILL's *Mourning Becomes Electra*, 1946; the mother in LORCA's *Blood Wedding*, 1951; Mrs Alving in IBSEN's *Ghosts*, 1955. (3) **Hermann T.** (1890–1976) made his career playing leading parts at the Deutsches-Theater, Berlin 1914–24, and the Theater in der Josefstadt, Vienna 1924–32, then worked for two years in films. Returned to the stage in the popular Viennese farces of RAIMUND and in the classical comic roles of Shakespeare and MOLIÈRE. (4) **Hans T.** (1900–) from 1918 acted both at the Burgtheater and the Theater in der Josefstadt, also often in COMEDIES by Shakespeare (e.g. Tranio in *The Taming of the Shrew*) and in the satirical FARCES of NESTROY.
Bibl: J. Handl, SCHAUSPIELER DES BURGTHEATERS, 1955

Thoma, Ludwig (1867–1921), German short-story writer and humorist. His dramatic works include: *Moral* (Moral) fp Berlin 1908; *Die Medaille*, Munich 1901; *Die Lokalbahn* (The Local Train), Munich 1902; *Lottchen's Geburtstag* (Lottie's Birthday), Stuttgart 1911; *Magdalena*, Berlin 1912.
Bibl: F. Brehm, ZEHN HABEN NEUN MEINUNGEN, KRITIK UND KRITIKER BEI LUDWIG THOMA, 1958

Thomas, Dylan (1914–53), Welsh poet and dramatist. His finest dramatic work is *Under Milk Wood*, 'A Play for Voices', written for radio, first broadcast by the BBC 1954; it also became a successful stage play, first presented at the EDINBURGH FESTIVAL 1956. One of the most ingenious pieces of poetic drama ever written, it shows T.'s great humour and sense of characterization as well as his genius for poetry. Posthumously his play *The Doctor and the Devils*, pub 1953, was performed at Wuppertal, Germany, 1959, in a translation by Erich Fried, and at the Edinburgh Festival, 1961.
Bibl: E. Olson, 1961; J. M. Brinnin, DYLAN THOMAS IN AMERICA, 1955; C. Thomas, LEFTOVER TO KILL, 1953

Thomas, Gwyn (1913–), Welsh writer, wit and dramatist. Best known as a playwright for *The Keep*, 1962, a realistic COMEDY of character in a South Wales home, strengthened by the sardonic twist of a surprise ending, and *Jackie the Jumper*, 1963, a period play with music set in the Chartist era.

Thomas, Walter Brandon (1856–1914), English actor, dramatist and songwriter. Best known for his FARCE *Charley's Aunt*, 1892, centring around a transvestite joke; it was first staged with great success and had a four-year run at the Royalty Theatre (in which T. starred); it became one of the greatest theatrical triumphs of all time and has since been played all over the world. It has been filmed and made into the musical *Where's Charley?* by ABBOTT and LOESSER, fp New York 1948.

Thorndike, Dame Sybil (1882–1976), English actress. Appointed a DBE in 1931. She began her career touring with GREET for four years in England and the USA. After her London début in 1908, she was the leading lady at ANNIE HORNIMAN's Repertory Theatre in Manchester. She married the actor CASSON in 1908. She was at the OLD VIC 1914–18, playing Shakespearean heroines and characters like Puck in *A Midsummer Night's Dream*, Launcelot Gobbo in *The Merchant of Venice*, and the Fool in *King Lear*. Her most distinguished performances after World War I include: Saint Joan in SHAW's play, 1923, and classical roles, e.g. Hecuba in EURIPIDES' *The Trojan Women*, 1919; Lady Macbeth at the Odéon, Paris 1921. During World War II she toured the provinces as Lady Macbeth, Medea and Candida (Shaw). After the war she appeared in many contemporary plays displaying great versatility: Isabel Linden in PRIESTLEY's *The Linden Tree*, 1947, Lady Monchensey in T. S. ELIOT's *Family Reunion*, 1957.
Bibl: J. Casson, LEWIS AND SYBIL, 1972

Thulin, Ingrid (1929–), Swedish actress and director. After training 1948–50 she worked at several Swedish theatres including the Royal Dramatic Theatre, Stockholm 1950–52, New Theatre, Stockholm 1952–53, and Municipal Theatre, Malmö 1955–60, where she excelled as Anitra in IBSEN's *Peer Gynt*, 1957, dir I. BERGMAN. Another noted performance was the title role in STRINDBERG's *Fröken Julie*, Municipal Theatre, Stockholm 1960. Since 1948 she has mainly worked in films (with Bergman, e.g. *Silence*, 1964) and in TV since 1955, also in the USA.

Tidblad, Inga (1901–75), Swedish actress. Her first success was as Ariel in *The Tempest*; she later established herself as one of the leading interpreters of SHAKESPEARE and STRINDBERG in Sweden. She played Ophelia in HAMLET at the Swedish Theatre, Stockholm 1922, and in 1932 became principal actress at the Royal Dramatic Theatre, Stockholm: Juliet in *Romeo and Juliet*, 1936; Rosalind in *As You Like It*, 1938; Portia in *The Merchant of Venice*, 1944; Viola in *Twelfth Night*, 1946; the Queen in *Hamlet*, 1960; leading roles in Strindberg's *Swanwhite*, 1926, *A Dream Play*, 1947, *Miss Julie*, 1949, and *Queen Christina*, 1961.
Bibl: S. Melchinger, SCHAUSPIELER, 1965

Tieck, Ludwig (1773–1853), German dramatist, novelist, poet, translator and director. One of the most important writers of the Romantic period, his main contribution to the development of German drama was the famous Schlegel-Tieck translation of the complete works of SHAKESPEARE, 1828–33, which was undertaken by A. W. SCHLEGEL, BAUDISSIN and Dorothea Tieck (T.'s daughter), and edited and revised by T. himself. His dramatic work is today largely of historical interest, many of the themes being taken from fairy-tales which are treated satirically: *Ritter Blaubart* (Bluebeard the Knight), 1796; *Die verkehrte Welt* (The Upside-down World), 1798, and *Der gestiefelte Kater* (Puss in Boots), 1797. In 1825 he became DRAMATURG at the Hoftheater in Dresden, where he was responsible for its emphasis on a literary REPERTORY including works by Shakespeare, CALDERÓN and KLEIST. He was a director at the Royal Theatre in BERLIN, 1840–48.
Bibl: P. C. Matenko, LUDWIG TIECK

AND AMERICA, 1954; E. Zeydel, LUDWIG TIECK, THE GERMAN ROMANTICIST, 1933

Tirso de Molina (Gabriel Téllez; 1571/84–1648), Spanish dramatist. He ranks as a master of COMEDY with CALDERÓN and LOPE DE VEGA. He wrote about 400 plays, of which 86 are preserved. He led the contemplative life of a monk, and his plays reveal a strong concern with the individual, displayed with wit and irony; he had great psychological insight and was particularly adept at characterization. His high moral tone was always to the forefront, and even more evident than in the comedies of Lope de Vega, whom he greatly admired. But he was so heavily criticized by the Church that after 1626 he virtually stopped writing plays. His only comedy still in the REPERTOIRE is *Don Gil de las calzas verdes* (Don Gil of the Green Trousers). He was also the author of *El burlador de Sevilla y Convidado de piedra* (The Joker of Seville and the Stone Guest), the first of many plays based on the Don Juan theme.
Bibl: I. L. McClelland, TIRSO DE MOLINA, STUDIES IN DRAMATIC REALISM, 1948

TNP=Théâtre National Populaire. ▷ VILAR.

Tofano, Sergio (1886–), Italian actor. Appeared in 1913 under TALLI, and became his protégé. He later established his name with leading companies of his day, excelling mainly in light COMEDY; since 1931 also as manager or associate manager. After World War II he worked exclusively in REPERTORY companies: T. dei Satiri di Roma (BRECHT's *Mother Courage*, 1952–53); at the PICCOLO TEATRO DI MILANO (Filippo in GOLDONI's *La Trilogia della villeggiatura*, 1954), and also at the TEATRO STABILE, Turin, 1961. His acting was thoughtful and restrained. He also worked as a director, stage designer and dramatist (under the pseudonym 'Sto').

Toller, Ernst (1893–1939), German playwright. Played an active part in political life; was one of the leaders of the short-lived Bavarian revolutionary government in 1919, and was later sent to prison. Emigrated in 1933 first to England, thence to the USA: committed suicide in New York in 1939. His themes reflect his strong political and social interest in basic religious and ethical questions. His major works include: *Die Wandlung* (*Transfiguration*), fp 1919, Tribüne, Berlin, with KORTNER, dir MARTIN, on the conversion of a poet from love of his country to universal love of mankind; *Masse-Mensch* (*Man and the Masses*), Berlin 1922, dir PISCATOR; *Der deutsche Hinkemann*, 1923; *Hoppla, wir leben!*, 1927, produced at the Gate Theatre, London 1929, as *Hoppla!*, which reveals his pessimistic view of man's plight and the impossibility of achieving universal human understanding. Other works: *Die Maschinenstürmer*, which deals with the Luddites, 1922, prod London 1923 as *The Wreckers*; *Der entfesselte Wotan* (Wotan unchained), 1923; *Die Rache des verhöhnten Liebhabers*

Dylan Thomas, *Under Milk Wood*, 1956

Sybil Thorndike and RICHARDSON in IBSEN's *Peer Gynt*, GUTHRIE production, OLD VIC, 1940

Ernst Toller, *Man and the Masses*, designed and directed by SIMONSON, New York 1924

(The Vengeance of a Mocked Lover), 1928; *Bourgeois bleibt Bourgeois* (Bourgeois remains Bourgeois), 1929, written with HASENCLEVER; *Feuer aus den Kesseln* (Fire from the Furnace), 1930; *Wunder in Amerika* (Miracle in America), written with Hermann Kesten; *Blind Man's Buff*, 1935, written with JOHNSTON; *No More Peace!*, 1937, lyrics adapted by AUDEN, music EISLER; *Pastor Hall*, written 1939, pub 1946. Bibl: H. F. Garten, MODERN GERMAN DRAMA, 1959; A. Kerr, DIE WELT IM DRAMA, 1954

Tolstoy, Alexei Konstantinovich (1817–75), Russian diplomat, friend of Alexander II. Author of a number of poems, short stories and a historical TRILOGY which idolized feudal Russia: *Smert Ivana Groznogo* (The Death of Ivan the Terrible), 1866; *Tsar Fyodor Ivanovich*, 1868; and *Tsar Boris*, 1870. The second play was banned until 1898 when it was produced by STANISLAVSKY at the MOSCOW ART THEATRE.

Tolstoy, Alexei Nikolayevich (1882–1945), Soviet novelist and dramatist. Author of several historical dramas which dealt with the themes of the Revolution and reinterpreted traditional values. His two-part drama *Ivan Grozny* (Ivan the Terrible), 1943, praised the tsar as the man who had united Russia. His other works include *Rasputin*, 1928; *Pyotr Pervy*, a three-part epic novel, pub 1929–34, in English, 1936, as *Peter the Great*, dramatized by the author, and *Put k pobede* (The Road to Victory), 1939.

Tolstoy, Leo Nikolayevich (1828–1910), Russian writer. Began writing for the theatre under the influence of M. V. Lentovsky (Moscow People's Theatre). His dramatic works consist of several plays in a strong naturalistic style with highly moral themes. *Vlast tmy* (*The Power of Darkness*), written 1886, was banned for ten years in Russia, having its first production by ANTOINE at the Théâtre Libre, Paris 1888; in 1903 it was directed with great success by STANISLAVSKY and NEMIROVICH-DANCHENKO at the MOSCOW ART THEATRE. It was followed by *Plody prosveshcheniya* (*The Fruits of Enlightenment*), 1889, a popular COMEDY. *Zhivoi trup* (*Redemption*, also known as *The Live Corpse*), written 1900, fp MAT 1911, dir Stanislavsky and Nemirovich-Danchenko, lead played by MOSKVIN. His last play *I svet vo tmye svetit* (*The Light Shines in Darkness*) remained unfinished and was published posthumously 1911–12. Several of his novels have been successfully dramatized and performed all over the world, including *Voskresenie* (*Resurrection*), *Anna Karenina* and *Voina i mir* (*War and Peace*). The best-known dramatization of the latter has been that by PISCATOR, Berlin 1957. The last mentioned has been successfully filmed recently, both in the USSR and USA, and was the subject of a BBC TV serial in 1973. Bibl: H. Troyat, 1967; K. L. Stanislavsky, 3/1933

Topol, Josef (1935–), Czech dramatist. Since 1965 he has worked in close collaboration with the director KREJČA at the Divadlo za Branou (Theatre Before the Gate), Prague. His plays reveal deep concern with the revolutionary changes which took place when socialism became entrenched in CZECHOSLOVAKIA, and deal also with eternal questions of life and death. His works include: *Púlnočni vítr* (The Midnight Wind), 1955; *Jejich den* (Their Day), 1959; *Konec masopustu* (The End of Shrovetide), 1963; *Kočka na kolejích* (*The Cat on the Rails*), 1965; *Slavík k večeři* (Nightingale's Dinner Invitation), 1967. He translated and adapted CHEKHOV's *The Seagull*, 1960, and SHAKESPEARE's *Romeo and Juliet*, 1963.

Torres Naharro, Bartolomé de (mid-15th century–*c.* 1531), Spanish writer. One of the great forerunners of Spanish drama, particularly of LOPE DE VEGA, with his main work *Propaladia*, 1517. This was a collection of love-songs, satires, romances, epistles, songs and six COMEDIES (*Serafina*, *Trofea*, *Soldatesca*, *Tinellaria*, *Himenea*, *Jacinta*), with a PROLOGUE which is the first important theoretical essay on dramatic technique (he distinguishes between two types of play: *comedia a noticia* and *comedia a fantasia*). Bibl: A. R. Rodriguez Monina, 1936

Totò (1898–1967), Italian actor (real name Antonio de Curtis Gagliardi Duca Comneno di Bisanzio). Member of an ancient artistocratic family, he made his career mainly in REVUE, VARIETY, operettas and, especially after 1950, in films. He was one of the greatest Italian comedians of his time, characterized by his feeling for mimic expression, and also a fine tragedian. One of his most memorable performances was in an adaptation of DUMAS's *The Three Musketeers*, 1928, in which he set out to satirize militarism.

Toulouse-Lautrec, Henri de (1864–1901), French painter and graphic artist. His paintings and lithographs captured the atmosphere of MUSIC HALLS, CIRCUSES, dance halls, CABARETS and characters of the Parisian *belle-époque*; together with the NABIS, he exercised a strong influence on the productions of LUGNÉ-POË; he designed the programme and several sets, e.g. for JARRY's *Ubu roi*, 1896; Jourdain's *Le Gage*, 1898, etc. Bibl: H. Rischbieter (ed), BÜHNE UND BILDENDE KUNST IM 20. JAHRHUNDERT, 1968

Tourneur, Cyril (1575–1626), English dramatist. Two extant TRAGEDIES, *The Revenger's Tragedy*, 1606–07, and *The Atheist's Tragedy; or The Honest Man's Revenge*, 1607–11, are ascribed to him, his authorship of the former (by which his name chiefly lives) being uncertain. Endowed with a great sense of the theatre, and intermittent poetic force, he presents a world of horror and extravagant evil which links his work with that of WEBSTER. Bibl: U. Ellis-Fermor, THE JACOBEAN DRAMA, 2/1955

Tovstonogov, Georgii Alexandrovich (1915–), Soviet director. Began his career as an actor and assistant director in Tbilisi in 1935, directing his first production in 1938. He worked in Moscow 1946–49 and 1950–56 in Leningrad (Theatre of the Leningrad Komsomol); he took over the management of the Gorky Theatre in Leningrad in 1956 and made it into one of Russia's leading theatres by the individual style of his productions, which include: VISHNEVSKY's *An Optimistic Tragedy*, 1956; GORKY's *The Barbarians*, 1959; Stein's *The Ocean*, 1961; CHEKHOV's *Three Sisters*, 1965.

Toy theatre. Miniature theatres (including scenery) made of cardboard, which enjoyed great popularity in England 1810–60. Today they provide a unique record of the theatre history of the 19th century. Major collections: British Museum (Print Room); Victoria and Albert Museum; and Museum of London. Among famous private collections was that of Benjamin Pollock. Bibl: G. Speaight, THE HISTORY OF THE ENGLISH TOY THEATRE, 2/1969

Tragedy (from Gk *tragos*=goat, *ode*=song; i.e. the songs which accompanied the sacrifice of a goat during the feast of DIONYSOS). One of the two basic genres of drama, originally applied to the serious plays which formed the Greek dramatic festivals, as distinct from the comic ones (▷COMEDY), originating about the middle of the 6th century BC. Much has been written about the exact definition of tragedy, which ARISTOTLE considered the noblest form of poetry and for which he prescribed a number of rules. As yet no agreement has ever been reached on such a definition: the loftiness of theme and treatment, the nobility with which the hero suffers his misfortune and recognizes the justice of his suffering (in atonement for his tragic guilt), and which purges the spectator's mind and heart through terror and pity, leading to catharsis (the elevated feeling that results from a deep, moral experience combined with the aesthetic pleasure caused by such feelings even in the face of the hero's most dire misfortunes) – all these aspects of tragedy have been endlessly discussed. Yet in the 19th century writers like BÜCHNER (who in *Woyzeck* made a lowly and disturbed individual, without any loftiness of mind or elevation of feeling, a passive victim of circumstance) and the Naturalists who followed him, created tragedy from material and by methods which totally contradicted the traditional views and definitions of the genre. Not even the definition of tragedy as a play with a sad ending entirely covers the discussion: some tragedies – e.g. KLEIST's *The Prince of Homburg*, but also many of EURIPIDES' plays which are resolved by the appearance of a *deus ex machina* – have a happy ending. There are thus not one, but many definitions and different kinds of tragedy: the classical Greek tragedy described, if not wholly defined, by Aristotle; French classical tragedy which follows rules which the French critics of the time had deduced (though not quite correctly) from Aristotle; English Elizabethan tragedy (which mixes lofty and low, poetic and coarsely prosaic elements with immense theatrical effect in defiance of all rules); Spanish classical tragedy; German classical tragedy (GOETHE and SCHILLER) which emulated Greek models while worshipping at the shrine of SHAKESPEARE as well; and the modern tragedies of great dramatists like IBSEN, STRINDBERG, HAUPTMANN or BRECHT. The one element which all these different types of drama have in common is that of compassion (Aristotle's pity and terror) with suffering humanity.

Tragicomedy. From PLAUTUS (who invented the word) to LESSING ('an important action among distinguished persons which has a pleasant ending'), a term denoting a play which does not correspond to the usual definition of COMEDY or TRAGEDY; in Plautus' terminology, a play in which gods and tragic heroes (characters of tragedy) are of equal importance with slaves, who until then had existed solely as comic characters, e.g. gods disguised as slaves, etc. The term was later also applied to plays which did not end with the death of the hero (CORNEILLE first called his *Le Cid* a tragicomedy). More recently attempts have been made by modern analysts to contrast this purely 'external' definition with an organic conception of plays in which the tragic and comic elements are mutually interdependent, as in the works of SHAKESPEARE, LENZ, BÜCHNER, WEDEKIND, DÜRRENMATT, BECKETT or IONESCO.
Bibl: J. L. Styan, THE DARK COMEDY, 1962; M. T. Herrick, TRAGICOMEDY IN ITALY, FRANCE AND ENGLAND, 1962

Travers, Ben (1886–), English dramatist. Wrote some of the best examples of early 20th-century FARCE, which from 1925 were performed for almost a decade at the Aldwych Theatre, London, and became known as 'Aldwych farces'. Situation comedy at its best, the farces are the closest equivalent in English drama to FEYDEAU. The plays follow a carefully worked-out formula – familiar characters from everyday life in a succession of outrageously embarrassing situations, which, though as stereotyped as those of TERENCE and PLAUTUS, T. could always fit into some new and unexpected tangle. His name is closely linked with that of Tom Walls, who presented, directed and acted in his plays: *The Dippers*, 1922; *A Cuckoo in the Nest*, 1925; *Rookery Nook*, 1926; *Thark*, 1927; *Plunder*, 1928; *Mischief*, 1928; *A Cup of Kindness*, 1929; *A Night Like This*, 1930; *Turkey Time*, 1931; *Dirty Work*, 1932; *A Bit of a Test*, 1933; *Oh Mistress Mine*, 1936; *Banana Ridge*, 1938; *Spotted Dick*, 1939; *She Follows Me About*, 1943; *Outrageous Fortune*, 1947; *Wild Horses*, 1952; *Nun's Veiling*, 1953 (revised version of *Oh Mistress Mine*). His play, *The Bed Before Yesterday*, written in 1976, at the age of 90, had an amazing success. He wrote his autobiography, *Vale of Laughter*, 1957.
Bibl: J. C. Trewin, DRAMATISTS OF TODAY, 1953

Leo Tolstoy, *The Fruits of Enlightenment*, MOSCOW ART THEATRE, 1911

Toy Theatre, by Benjamin Pollock

Travesty (Ital *travestire* = to disguise, dress up). Ridiculing of an established dramatic work. In contrast to parody, which exposes the formal devices of an author by exaggerating them, travesty transposes characters and situations of a work to banal surroundings and language, e.g. the Greek god and heroes in Offenbach's *Orpheus in the Underworld* act and speak like people in a frivolous Paris salon; Holofernes, in NESTROY's Hebbel-parody *Judith and Holofernes*, speaks like the boastful soldiers of the Viennese folk theatre. Parody and travesty merge in BRECHT's *Arturo Ui*: the Nazi uprising is travestied as a power struggle by greengrocers, while the character Ui parodies Hitler in exaggerated larger-than-life detail.

Tree, Sir Herbert Draper Beerbohm (1852–1917), English ACTOR-MANAGER, half brother of Max Beerbohm. His chief acting successes were in roles which required his gift for impersonation. In 1887 he took over the management of the Comedy Theatre and later in the same year the Haymarket Theatre where he produced *Hamlet*, with himself in the title role, and GEORGE DU MAURIER's *Trilby*, 1895, in which he scored a major success as Svengali. He built Her Majesty's Theatre, which opened in 1897, and founded RADA in 1904. He was knighted in 1909. His REPERTOIRE, apart from topical contemporary plays, included works by SHAKESPEARE (*Richard II*), GOETHE (*Faust*, 1908) and SHAW (*Pygmalion*, 1914). His productions were visual interpretations aiming at magnificent effects; as an actor too he relied on effects, excelling in bizarre and eccentric parts. In 1883 he married the actress **Helen Maud Holt** (known as Lady T., 1863–1937) with whom he appeared in many leading parts; she established herself mainly in COMEDIES by Shakespeare, SHERIDAN and Shaw. Their daughter **Viola T.** (1884–1938) made her début in Edinburgh as Viola in *Twelfth Night*, subsequently appearing mainly at the Haymarket Theatre. Her son **David T.** also became an actor.
Bibl: H. Pearson, 1956

Tretyakov, Sergei Mikhailovich (1892–1939), Russian dramatist and journalist. His plays *Slushai Moskva!* (Moscow! Feel!) and *Protivogazy* (Gas-Masks) were produced in 1923–24 by EISENSTEIN; his best known play, written after a journey to China, was *Rychi Kifai!* (*Roar, China!*), directed in 1926 by MEYERHOLD's pupil, V. Fedorov; it dealt with the exploitation of Chinese coolies by white imperialists. His play *Khochu rebyonka* (I Want a Child), 1926, was adapted for the German stage by BRECHT, who was a close friend. He subsequently became a victim of the Stalinist purges.

Triana, José (1931–), Cuban dramatist. Spent four years in Madrid, but returned to Cuba after Castro's revolution and has written several plays since then. *La Noche de los asesinos* (*The Criminals*), the first Cuban play to be staged in London, at the Aldwych 1967 (dir HANDS), was written in the THEATRE OF CRUELTY genre and was influenced by ARRABAL.

Trilogy. A group of three plays with a unified theme, originally the three TRAGEDIES performed at the festival of DIONYSOS (which were followed by a SATYR PLAY to form a TETRALOGY), e.g. AESCHYLUS' *Oresteia*.

Trionfi (Ital = triumphs, processions). Allegorical presentations of 15th- and 16th-century Italy, mainly performed on carts during processions on festive occasions, e.g. in Florence, 1477, at the marriage of Ferrante I and Joanna of Aragon; in Rome, 1499, the Trionfi di Vespasiano e Tito, in the presence of Alexander VI and Lucrezia Borgia.

Truffaldino. A character of the Italian COMMEDIA DELL'ARTE; a variation on the second ZANNI.

Try-out. A performance, usually in the provinces, of a new play or production before it is presented to the critics of the metropolis (London or New York). Essentially the try-out represents rehearsals in front of an audience, whose reaction can be studied so that last-minute alterations or improvements can be made. It is an unwritten law that try-out performances must not be reviewed by metropolitan critics, although they can be reviewed in local papers.

Turgenev, Ivan Sergeyevich (1818–83), Russian novelist, short-story writer and poet. Wrote several plays between 1843 and 1852 which, in their concentration on the inner self, anticipate CHEKHOV, particularly in the play *Mesyats v derevne* (*A Month in the Country*), written 1849–51, produced by the Maly Theatre in Moscow 1881 and 1892, and triumphantly revived at the MOSCOW ART THEATRE in 1909, dir STANISLAVSKY; it has become popular in the European REPERTOIRE, particularly in England, e.g. Royalty Theatre, 1926; OLD VIC company at the New Theatre, 1949, and Yvonne Arnaud Theatre, Guildford, 1965, both with REDGRAVE as Rakitin; Chichester 1974, with DOROTHY TUTIN. Other plays were written for the actor SHCHEPKIN: *Where It's Thin, It Breaks*, 1848, one-act COMEDY; *The Bachelor*, 1849; *Penniless; or, Scenes from the Life of a Young Nobleman*, 1846; *The Parasite*, 1848.
Bibl: D. Magarshack, TURGENEV, A LIFE, 1954

Turkey. Although Islam was hostile to theatre, two forms have existed in Turkey for centuries: village theatre, folklore-style or ritualistic plays to celebrate the cycle of the seasons, fertility and animal rituals, etc., which derived from pre-Islamic ritual cult plays, still popular today, performed by peasants; and folk theatre, performed by professional actors at festivities of the sultans and folk festivals during Ramadan, the time of fasting, still performed today.
Besides the diversity of village regional theatre, there are three main forms of folk theatre. (1) *Meddah* (= singer of praise), a solo performer with great talent for imitation, derived from the storyteller, a traditional figure throughout the Orient. (2) *Karagöz*, the SHADOW PLAY, which came to Turkey from the Far East via India and Egypt in the 16th century, and soon became one of the most popular forms of theatrical entertainment; the plays use puppets, and there are two main characters, Karagöz ('black eye', originally referring to a Turkish gipsy), a popular and crude CLOWN, from whom the theatre derives its name, and Hacivat, a half-educated petty-bourgeois; also the female character Zenne as well as popular types from the Ottoman multi-nation state. (3) *Orta Oyunu* (= play in the middle; term used since *c.* 1830, although its origins can be found in the 17th century) with an acting area surrounded by the audience and without décor, indicating a very archaic form of theatre. PLOTS, themes, main and supporting characters closely related to those of the shadow play, e.g. Kavuklu (= man who wears a turban), rogue and buffoon; Pisekar, leading actors who devise the play, cunning rather than crudely comic; Zenne (female part acted by men); and other popular characters. The actors remained in fixed positions on the acting area throughout the performance. It was not until the early 19th century that the Turkish theatre turned towards Western forms; visits from many touring companies from Europe. In 1868 the first permanent theatre was founded in Istanbul, in the European manner, under the management of the Armenian Güllü Agop, whose ensemble also included a number of Turkish actors, but no actresses; in 1882 this theatre was closed down and destroyed by the order of an anti-European Sultan. Ahmed Vefik Pasha, governor of Bursa, built his own theatre there, giving the young Turkish artistic theatre a home between 1882 and 1885, and the possibility for development. In 1914 ANTOINE was appointed to found a drama school within the conservatoire known as Dar-ül-Bedayi (place of art) but because of the outbreak of World War I he managed to complete only the preparations. In 1921, from this drama school, by then separated from the conservatoire, the first modern Turkish theatre with the same name developed; in 1930 it became a municipal theatre, in Turkish *Sehir Tiyatrosu*, so called since 1934. This is the oldest national theatre to be subsidized by the State. Its first leading director was Ertugral Muhsin, who acquired his practical knowledge in BERLIN and Moscow. It was managed 1952–58 by the director and stage designer Max Meinecke, since 1962 a drama professor in Ankara. In 1936 foundation of a State conservatoire in Ankara, now capital of the Turkish Republic; director of the department for opera and drama (later including a studio theatre) from 1936 to 1948 was the German actor and director EBERT. A new State theatre, designed by the architect Paul Bonatz, was opened in 1948. Between 1948 and 1958 important artists worked there including Renato Mordo and Arnulf Schröder. Today there are six theatres in Ankara and one each in

Izmir, Bursa and Adana, at all of which the State theatre performs. Since 1958 the director has been EBERT's pupil Cüneyt Aydin Gün. In 1969 opening of the 'house of culture' in Istanbul, where the State theatre, both drama and opera, appears. The number of private theatres in Istanbul and Ankara has increased in recent years. Most of the plays produced are on social topics. One of the most prominent Turkish dramatists was HIKMET.

Bibl: M. And, A HISTORY OF THEATRE AND POPULAR ENTERTAINMENT IN TURKEY, 1963

Tutin, Dorothy (1930–), English actress. She made her début in 1949, and appeared at the OLD VIC, 1950–51. She achieved real recognition with her performance of Rose Pemberton in the first production of G. GREENE's *The Living Room*, 1953; this was followed by Sally Bowles in VAN DRUTEN's *I Am a Camera*, 1954; ANOUILH's *The Lark*, 1955; Hedwig in IBSEN's *The Wild Duck*, 1955; and numerous Shakespearean roles at STRATFORD-UPON-AVON, including Juliet, Viola, Ophelia (all in 1958); and Cressida (1960, 1962); Joanne in WHITING's *The Devils*, 1961; Queen Victoria in W. Francis' *Portrait of a Queen*, 1965; the lead in Turgenev's *A Month in the Country*, CHICHESTER FESTIVAL, 1974; Maggie in BARRIE's *What Every Woman Knows*, 1974.

Tyler, Royall (1757–1826), US playwright. Author of the first American COMEDY *The Contrast*, produced by Thomas Wignell in 1787. It was revived several times. Published in 1790, George Washington headed the list of subscribers.

Tynan, Kenneth (1927–), English drama critic. An early champion of ANOUILH on the English stage and an advocate of BRECHT. He was on the staff of the *Observer*, 1954–58 and 1960–63, and wrote for the *New Yorker*, 1958–60. He was Literary Manager of the NATIONAL THEATRE 1963–73. In 1969 devised the much discussed erotic revue *Oh! Calcutta!*, and in 1976 *Carte Blanche*. Author of several works on the theatre including: *He That Plays the King*, 1950; *Alec Guinness*, 1953; *Curtains*, 1961, and *Tynan Right and Left*, 1967.

Udall, Nicholas (1505–56), English scholar, headmaster of Eton College, then of Westminster School. Author of the earliest known English comedy *Ralph Roister Doister*. Date of first performance uncertain; it may have been between 1534 and 1541 while he was at Eton or about 1553 after he had moved to Westminster. It was not printed till *c.* 1566. It was strongly influenced by PLAUTUS and TERENCE. Most of his other dramatic works (plays,

Turkey, *karagöz* puppets

Herbert Beerbohm Tree as Mark Antony in *Julius Caesar*, 1898

Kenneth Tynan's *Oh! Calcutta!*, London 1969

PAGEANTS, DIALOGUES) are lost or exist in fragmentary form.

Unamuno, Miguel de (1864–1936), Spanish philosopher, essayist, novelist and playwright. Author of 11 plays, the best known of which is his treatment of the Don Juan theme *El Hermano Juan, o el mundo es teatro* (Brother John, or The World of the Theatre), 1929. His short dialogue-novel *Nada menos que todo un hombre* (Nothing Less than a Whole Man), 1920, was dramatized by Julio de Hoyos in 1925. Other dramatic works include: *Fedra* (Phaedra), 1918; *Sombras de sueño* (Dream Visions), 1920; *El otro* (Cain and Abel), 1932.
Bibl: G. Torrente Ballester, TEATRO ESPAÑOL CONTEMPORANEO, 1957

United States of America. ▷USA

Unity Theatre. A British left-wing theatre group of amateur actors (often, however, with a strong admixture of professionals) formed in 1936 as part of the struggle against Nazism and Fascism. Its small theatre in the King's Cross area of London saw the first performances of many important left-wing plays of the period (e.g. BRECHT's *Señora Carrar's Rifles*, ODETS's *Waiting for Lefty*) and many hard-hitting satirical REVUES. This tradition is vigorously continued to the present day.

University theatre. Theatrical activity within the framework of universities can be grouped under three headings: (1) performances designed to facilitate theatrical research, e.g. reconstructions of performances of historically interesting plays which have no chance of being produced in the professional theatre. Some of the German universities which provide courses in *Theaterwissenschaft* (theatre and drama studies) have facilities for such performances. (2) The teaching of the skills of acting, directing, stage design and stagecraft with a view to training professional practitioners in the theatre or teachers at elementary or secondary level who will be able to stage performances in schools. This type of university theatre is above all prevalent in the USA, where most universities are equipped with splendid facilities, which also enable them to provide something akin to a regular REPERTORY theatre for the students and teaching staff of large campuses and the populations of university towns which may not have a professional theatre. (3) Amateur performances by student societies: in Britain this form of university theatre (notably the OUDS in Oxford and the ADC in Cambridge, which have the use of well-equipped theatre buildings) is a breeding ground of successful professional actors and directors, even in universities without a drama department. In Britain the NUS annual festival of student drama has produced a wealth of talent. International student drama festivals, such as those at Nancy and Wroclaw, provide evidence that the universities are a fertile ground for experimentation in new forms of theatre.

Unruh, Fritz von (1885–1971), German Expressionist dramatist. He is best known for his play *Ein Geschlecht* (A Generation), Frankfurt 1918, an impassioned avowal of his belief in humanity and pacificism. Other works: *Jürgen Wullenweber*, 1910; *Offiziere* (Officers), BERLIN 1911, Deutsche-Theater, dir REINHARDT; *Louis Ferdinand, Prinz von Preussen*, pub 1913, fp Darmstadt 1920; *Vor der Entscheidung* (Before the Crisis), 1914; *Platz* (Space), 1920, sequel to *Ein Geschlecht* (the third part of the TRILOGY, *Dietrich*, was published as a fragment in 1960); *Stürme* (Storms), 1922; *Rosengarten* (Rose Garden), 1923; *Heinrich aus Andernach*, 1925; *Bonaparte*, 1927; *Phäa*, 1930: *Zero, Berlin in Monte Carlo*, 1932. He emigrated in 1932 and spent the years of World War II in the USA, returning to Germany in 1952, but his later plays: *Duell an der Havel* (Duel on the Havel), 1953; *Wilhelm von Oranien*, 1953, and *17 Juni*, 1954, found little response, and a number of others have remained unperformed.
Bibl: F. Rasche (ed), 1965

Unruh, Walther (1898–), German engineer, professor, theatre technician. Studied drama in Leipzig, electronics and technical engineering in Dresden. He was technical director of the Badisches Staatstheater, Karlsruhe, 1924–25; Mannheim National Theatre, 1925–34; and Hamburg State Opera, 1934–35. Since 1945 world-renowned consultant in theatre architecture and technique. Author of *Hilfsbuch für Bühnentechnik* and *ABC der Theatertechnik*, 1950, and editor of the *Bühnentechnische Rundschau*.

Unzelmann. Family of German actors. (1) **Karl Wilhelm Ferdinand U.** (1753–1832), actor and singer, worked 1774–81 as leading man, singer and dancer with DÖBBELIN's company and 1788–1823 appeared at the Royal National Theatre in BERLIN as Hamlet, Franz Moor in SCHILLER's *Die Räuber*, Posa in his *Don Carlos* and Leporello in Mozart's opera *Don Giovanni*, 1790. He married the actress and singer Friederike Bethmann (*née* Flittner; 1768–1815), who became famous as (2) **Friederike Bethmann-Unzelmann**. She was a friend of GOETHE, Schiller, KOTZEBUE and IFFLAND and appeared at various German theatres, notably as Luise in Schiller's *Kabale und Liebe*, 1785, Ophelia in SHAKESPEARE's *Hamlet*, 1785, and many other roles in plays by Schiller, LESSING and Kotzebue. She also sang magnificently as Constanze in Mozart's opera *Die Entführung aus dem Serail*, 1788. Their son, (3) **Karl Wolfgang U.** (1786–1843), was a successful comedian; best known is his TRUFFALDINO in GOLDONI's *Il Servitore di due Padroni*, 1812.
Bibl: I. Laskus, 1927

Urban, Joseph (1872–1933), Viennese-born US stage designer and architect. After his early work in Austria and Germany (SCHNITZLER's *Zwischenspiel*, Vienna 1905; GOETHE's *Faust* I, 1906; *Faust* II, 1907, BURGTHEATER) he emigrated in 1912 to the USA, where with R. E. JONES, SIMONSON and BEL GEDDES, he became one of the leading stage designers of the 'New Stagecraft' generation, following the theories of APPIA and CRAIG in productions of opera, drama and musicals. Apart from his work for the Metropolitan Opera (e.g. Wagner's *Parsifal*, 1920; Verdi's *Falstaff*, 1925) he designed REVUES for ZIEGFELD, musicals (*Show Boat*, KERN and HAMMERSTEIN II, 1927), and for HACKETT's Shakespearean productions. He also built the Ziegfeld Theatre, which opened in New York 1927 (now demolished).

Ure, Mary (1933–75), English actress. Made her début as Amanda in ANOUILH's *Time Remembered*, 1954; her first great success came as Alison Porter in OSBORNE's *Look Back in Anger*, ROYAL COURT, 1956; a year later she made her New York début in the same part. She also gave fine performances as Desdemona in *Othello*, STRATFORD-UPON-AVON 1959, and Lucille in GIRAUDOUX's *Duel of Angels*, 1960. Married to Osborne, 1957–62, subsequently to the actor and playwright R. SHAW.

USA. European travelling companies in the 17th and 18th centuries met with strong opposition from the Puritan element in the American colonies. In 1763 a company of English actors, under HALLAM, billed itself as 'The American Company'. In the 19th century the theatrical scene was still largely dominated by European touring companies, but towards the end of the century the commercial theatre of New York developed as the centre of a vigorous traffic of road companies which covered the country. The beginnings of an American school of playwriting emerged from MELODRAMAS and COMEDIES at first modelled on European successes. At the beginning of the 20th century first efforts to establish ENSEMBLE playing and REPERTORY theatre: the PROVINCETOWN PLAYERS with plays by O'NEILL from 1916, and in the 1930s the GROUP THEATRE and the THEATRE GUILD. At the same time the consolidation of the highly skilful commercial theatre of BROADWAY, notably the growth of the American musical, spectacular REVUE, but also from the 1930s the work of serious dramatists (O'NEILL, WILDER, T. WILLIAMS). During the depression the Roosevelt administration encouraged the growth of a socially conscious theatre (FEDERAL THEATRE PROJECT) and left-wing troupes flourished for a time. After World War II the OFF-BROADWAY theatre grew as a counterweight to the over-commercialized BROADWAY scene; at the same time regional theatres were established throughout the country (e.g. the Guthrie Theatre at Minneapolis, Minn., the Arena Theatre in Washington, D.C., the Mark Taper at Los Angeles, Calif.). Political dissent in the period of the Vietnam War led to a further development of underground theatre (▷OFF-OFF-BROADWAY) which was highly adventurous in experimental forms (IMPROVISATION, audience participation, HAPPENINGS). Another important development of the 1960s was the establishment of the LINCOLN CENTER in New York. There are signs that public subsidy may at last become a significant factor in the development of theatre in a society whose Puritan roots tended to lead to drama being regarded with suspicion. The New York Public Theatre, under PAPP, also points in the direction of publicly supported serious drama. Another important new element in the US theatre is the vigorous growth of Black theatre in the 1960s and 1970s.

Bibl: D. C. Blum, A PICTORIAL HISTORY OF AMERICAN THEATRE, 1960; B. Hewitt, USA 1665–1957, 1959; J. W. Krutch, THE AMERICAN DRAMA SINCE 1918, 1957; A. S. Downer, FIFTY YEARS OF AMERICAN DRAMA, 1900–50, 1955; A. H. Quinn, A HISTORY OF THE AMERICAN DRAMA FROM THE BEGINNING TO THE CIVIL WAR, 1946.

USSR. No religious drama emerged from the rich liturgy of the Russian Orthodox church. In the 17th century there was some influence from Polish JESUIT DRAMA. From 1672 Baroque productions at the Court of the Tsars, directed by the Protestant pastor Johann Gottfried Gregory (1631–75), who was of German origin: *Artaxerxes*, 1672; *The Comedy of Young Tobias*, 1673; *The Comedy of Holofernes*, 1674; *Pagliaccio and Tamerlan*, 1675. After 1703 there was in Moscow the Comedy House (on what is now Red Square) and the beginning of a Russian REPERTOIRE, e.g. Feofan Prokopovich (1681–1736), with guest appearances of the COMMEDIA DELL'ARTE, of the German NEUBER company (1740), and the Theatre of the Cadet College (1749, *Khorev* by Alexei Petrovich Sumarkov). From 1757 professional theatre with subsidies from the Court; the Bolshoi (large) Theatre, used mainly for opera and ballet, and the Maly (little) Theatre used for drama and MUSICAL COMEDY, in St Petersburg and Moscow. Censorship hindered or postponed performances of Russian plays, e.g. LERMONTOV's *Masquerade*, written 1835, produced 1852 in a cut version, 1864 in full version, and GRIBOYEDOV's *Gore ot Uma* (*Woe from Wit*), pub 1833. Attempts at reform by GOGOL and the actor SHCHEPKIN (1836 performance of Gogol's *The Government Inspector* in the presence of Tsar Nicholas I, with Shchepkin in the title role). From 1853 OSTROVSKY (1823–86) dealt in his comedies with the transition of a feudal to a capitalist society. His attempts at reform (directed against sentimentality and cheap effects in the fashionable VAUDEVILLES and among the actors) succeeded only in 1885, one year before he died, when he became director of the Moscow Maly Theatre. After 1882 the establishment of private theatres was permitted; guest appearances of the German MEININGER company; in 1898 foundation of the MOSCOW ART THEATRE by NEMIROVICH-DANCHENKO and STANISLAVSKY. Greatest flowering of the realistic theatre with the authors: CHEKHOV, TOLSTOY and GORKY. The Russian theatre has since, through the influence of Stanislavsky, been imbued with the strict ENSEMBLE principle, long rehearsal periods and a repertoire retained over many years, a director's theatre. In the

Fritz von Unruh, *Ein Geschlecht*, 1918, with EBERT on the left

Joseph Urban, design for Act II of Wagner's *Parsifal*, New York 1918

Unity Theatre production of *Plant in the Sun* with ROBESON, 1938

first decade of the 19th century symbolist tendencies in the works of ANDREYEV, MEYERHOLD, and the influence of FUTURISM. In the first years after the Revolution from 1917, Theatre-October, the fusion of theatre and propaganda, mass-meeting and play: YEVREINOV and Meyerhold. Simultaneous development of many forms of stylized theatre, the use of acrobatics, COMMEDIA DELL'ARTE, the breaking away from use of the proscenium arch, Constructivist designs: TAIROV, VAKHTANGOV, EXTER, Stenberg, YAKULOV, MAYAKOVSKY, GRANOVSKY, the HABIMAH, OKHLOPKOV. In the 1930s State interference and bans, and the imposition of SOCIALIST REALISM. Liquidation of Meyerhold, BABEL and TRETYAKOV. The Stanislavsky system became dogma and was declared compulsory. After 1967 gradual attempts at a revival of the tradition of Meyerhold; Okhlopkov became director of the Mayakovsky Theatre in Moscow. Mayakovsky's plays were revived in the Theatre of Satire. In the 1960s important foundations of new theatres: the Contemporary Theatre in Moscow, directed by YEFREMOV with plays criticizing Stalinism; the Taganka Theatre in Moscow directed by Yuri Lyubimov, which revived some of the tendencies of the Theatre-October. The most important legitimate theatre is the Gorky Theatre in Leningrad, directed by TOVSTONOGOV.

Since the 1930s theatre has also been spreading in the Soviet Republics: 1931 Vladivostok, 1932 Novosibirsk, 1933 Alma-Ata, 1934 Tashkent. In 1930 the first Art Olympiad was held in Moscow with 17 theatres representing different Republics. Development of *kolkhoz* (collective) theatres, CHILDREN'S THEATRE, army theatre, and a widely based amateur theatre movement. In 1965: about 470 professional theatres, of which 50 for opera and ballet; 36 youth and children's theatres, 73 PUPPET THEATRES. Subsidies amounting to about 36 million roubles per year.

Bibl: V. Alexandrovna, A HISTORY OF SOVIET LITERATURE 1917–64, 1964; M. Slonim, RUSSIAN THEATRE FROM THE EMPIRE TO THE SOVIETS, 1961; N. A. Gortchakov, THE THEATRE IN SOVIET RUSSIA, 1957

Ustinov, Peter Alexander (1921–), English actor, dramatist and director. Author of witty COMEDIES with serious themes, which he extends into the realms of extravagant, but always tongue-in-cheek fantasy. He has also acted in many films and written film scripts. He trained in London under SAINT-DENIS, making his stage début in 1939 in the Players' Theatre, a London club which is run in the style of a Victorian cabaret, with his own sketches, and in the REVUES *Diversion*, 1940, and *Diversion No. 2*. His best-known plays, in many of which he also acted, include: *The House of Regrets*, 1942; *The Banbury Nose*, 1944; *The Indifferent Shepherd*, 1948; *The Love of Four Colonels*, 1951; *Romanoff and Juliet*, 1956; *The Empty Chair*, 1956; *Photo Finish*, 1961; *The Life in My Hands*, 1966; *Halfway Up the Tree*, 1967; *The Unknown Soldier and his Wife*, 1973.

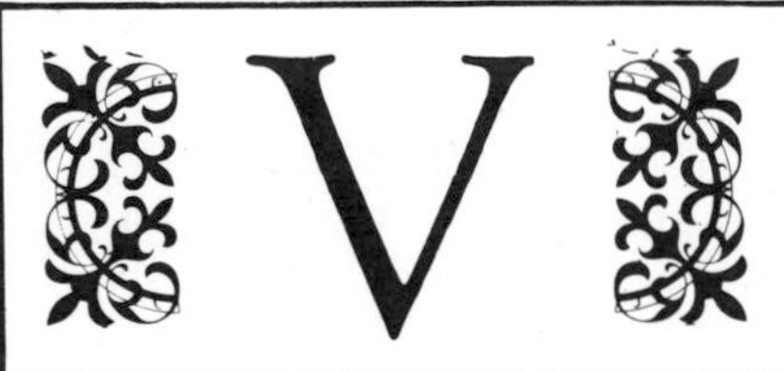

Vakhtangov, Eugene V. (1883–1922), Russian actor-director. Founder of a theatre in Moscow which is named after him. He trained at the drama school of the MOSCOW ART THEATRE which he joined in 1911 as assistant and actor and in 1914 he directed, at the First Studio attached to it, HAUPTMANN's *The Feast of Reconciliation* in an Expressionist rendering so overheated that it dismayed even STANISLAVSKY and NEMIROVICH-DANCHENKO, whose devoted pupil and follower he was. Apart from his work as director of the First Studio, he also appeared in small parts at the MAT and worked with student groups (Mansurov-Studio), from which in 1917 emerged the Moscow Dramatic Studio under V.'s management (incorporated in 1920 as Third Studio of the MAT). At the First Studio he produced IBSEN's *Rosmersholm* in 1918 and in the same year MAETERLINCK's *The Miracle of Saint Anthony*; for the opening of the Hebrew Theatre in 1918 he directed an evening of one-act plays by ASCH, PERETZ, Katznelson and Berkovich. But his most famous productions came in 1921: (at the First Studio) STRINDBERG's *Eric XIV*; (Third Studio) GOGOL's *The Marriage*, and (Habimah Studio) ANSKY's *The Dybbuk*, with which production he laid the foundation for the REPERTOIRE of the Jewish Studio of the Art Theatre which later became the HABIMAH and toured many European countries until it found a new home in Palestine. His career ended with his most important production, GOZZI's *Turandot*, which he did not live to see. After his death the Third Studio remained under the management of his widow and was renamed Vakhtangov Theatre in 1926.

Bibl: N. A. Gortchakov, VAKHTANGOV, METTEUR EN SCÈNE, 1959

Valentin, Karl (1882–1948), Bavarian dialect comedian. From 1899 appeared as a club comedian, at first with little success; in 1907 after an improvised solo performance at the Baderwirt-Restaurant in Munich he was engaged at the Frankfurter Hof. In 1911 he met Liesl Karlstadt, his pupil who became his partner and collaborator; before the outbreak of World War I they wrote some 400 sketches and FARCES, some of which were filmed. He excelled in the role of a simple, awkward workman battling with objects and the pitfalls of language. Among his greatest admirers was BRECHT, on whom he exercised a strong influence. Published works: *Lachkabinett*, 1952; *Gesammelte Werke*, 1961; *Die Jugendstreiche des Knaben Karl*, 1968.

Bibl: M. Ophüls, SPIEL IM DASEIN, 1959

Valère, Simone (S. Gondoff; 1923–), French actress. Has been with the COMPAGNIE RENAUD-BARRAULT since 1946, mainly playing the role of SOUBRETTE in plays by MARIVAUX (Lisette in *La (Seconde) Surprise de l'amour*) and MOLIÈRE (Zerbinette in *Les Fourberies de Scapin*), but also giving fine performances in corresponding roles by contemporary dramatists (Daisy in IONESCO's *Rhinocéros*). Also well known as a film actress.

Valéry, Paul (1871–1945), French poet and essayist. Wrote a novel in dialogue form *Mon Faust* (1945, read in a matinée performance at the COMÉDIE-FRANÇAISE, fp Théâtre de l'Œuvre 1962 with FRESNAY). Author of ballet libretti including *Amphion*, music Honegger, written for IDA RUBINSTEIN, who appeared in it in 1931; *Semiramis*, 1934; *Cantate du Narcisse*, 1944; and theoretical works on the theatre, *Mes théâtres*, 1942, and *L'Ame et la dance*, 1921.

Bibl: C. Whiting, 1960; A. Gide, 1947

Valle-Inclán, Ramón Maria del (1866–1936), Spanish novelist, poet and dramatist. Author of a number of satirical plays, most important of which are the *esperpentos*, farcical plays in which he ridicules the pretences and evasions of contemporary society, conveyed in the jargon of the Madrid underworld: *Luces de Bohemia* (Bohemian Lights), 1929; *Farsa y licencia de la reina castiza* (Farce and Licence of the Well-bred Queen), 1920; *Los cuernos de don Friolera* (The Horns of Don Friolera), 1921; *Las galas del difunto* (The Funeral of the Departed), 1927; *La hija del capitán* (The Captain's Daughter), 1927; *Ligazón* (The Connection), 1927.

Bibl: Anthony N. Zahareus, RAMON DEL VALLE-INCLÁN: AN APPRAISAL OF HIS LIFE AND WORKS, 1968; A. del Saz, EL TEATRO DE VALLE-INCLÁN

Valli, Romolo (1925–), Italian actor. Joined the ensemble of the PICCOLO TEATRO DI MILANO in 1952, appearing in a number of leading roles under the direction of STREHLER: Northumberland in BRUCKNER's *Elizabeth of England*, 1952; the First Actor in PIRANDELLO's *Sei personaggi in cerca d'autore*, 1953. In 1954 he founded the COMPAGNIA DEI GIOVANI with DE LULLO, ROSSELLA FALK, BUAZZELLI, and A. M. Guarnieri, where he excelled in parts such as Gaston in COLETTE's *Gigi*, 1955, and Frank in *The Diary of Anne Frank*, Frances Goodrich and Albert Hackett, 1957.

Van Druten, John (1901–57), US playwright of British origin. A highly accomplished craftsman who achieved a sensational success with *Young Woodley*, 1925. There followed: *Diversion*, 1928; *London Wall*, 1931; *There's always Juliet*, 1931; *Behold We live*, 1932; *The Distaff Side*, 1933; *Old Acquaintance*, 1940; *The Voice of the Turtle*, 1943; *I Remember Mama*, 1944; *Bell, Book and Candle*, 1950; *I Am a Camera* (based on ISHERWOOD), 1951.

Vanbrugh. Stage name of the English actresses (1) Violet Augusta Mary Barnes (1867–1942) and (2) her sister Irene (1872–1949). **Violet V.** appeared in BURLESQUE and later joined the KENDALS, accompanying them to the USA. She subsequently played Anne Boleyn in *Henry VIII* under IRVING's direction. In 1894 she married the ACTOR-MANAGER Arthur Bourchier, in whose productions (Royalty Theatre, Garrick Theatre) she achieved resounding success in many leading parts. With TREE at His Majesty's she appeared as Katharine (*Henry VIII*) and Lady Macbeth. She had a mellow melodious voice and was particularly praised for her use of gesture. **Dame Irene V.** was considered one of the best actresses of her generation and an outstanding interpreter of contemporary plays, mainly PINERO: Rose in *Trelawny of the 'Wells'*, 1898, Sophie Fullgarney in *The Gay Lord Quex*, 1899, and Letty in the same play, 1903. She also gave notable performances in plays by WILDE, H. A. JONES, BARRIE, MAUGHAM, and COWARD. She was made a DBE in 1941. The Vanbrugh Theatre at RADA was named in honour of Violet and Irene by their brother, Sir Kenneth Ralph Barnes (1878–1957), for many years its director.

Vanbrugh, Sir John (1664–1726), English playwright and architect (▷RESTORATION DRAMA). As architect he was responsible for the Queen's Theatre in the Haymarket which he built for BETTERTON's company. He proved himself an important dramatist in his plays *The Relapse, or Virtue in Danger*, 1696 (a parody of CIBBER's *Love's Last Shift*, later adapted by SHERIDAN as *A Trip to Scarborough*, 1777), *The Provok'd Wife*, 1697, and *The Confederacy*, 1705, adapted from Dancourt. He was a master of character portrayal, of naturalistic, witty DIALOGUE, and in depicting the manners of his time. His unfinished play *A Journey to London* was completed and produced by Cibber in 1728 as *The Provok'd Husband*.
Bibl: L. Whistler, SIR JOHN VANBRUGH, ARCHITECT AND DRAMATIST 1664–1726, 1939; B. Dobree (ed), THE COMPLETE WORKS OF SIR JOHN VANBRUGH, 1927–28

Vaneck, Pierre (P. Van Hecke; 1931–), French actor of Belgian origin. Achieved his first success as Jimmy Porter in OSBORNE's *Look Back in Anger*, 1958, followed in 1959 by an excellent performance as Stavrogin in CAMUS's *Les Possédés*, Avignon 1963 (later at the TNP); as Hector in GIRAUDOUX's *La Guerre de Troie n'aura pas lieu*; in 1965 as Hamlet at the TNP.

Variety. A mixed performance, consisting of a variety of turns or numbers: songs, acrobats, short sketches etc. In England most variety used to be performed in MUSIC HALLS; in America in VAUDEVILLE or BURLESQUE houses. Also the name of a US theatrical newspaper.

Vasari, Giorgio (1511–74), Italian painter, architect and scenic designer. Master of the 16th-century Tuscan school, he worked mainly for the Medici. In 1536 he was responsible with Tribolo and Gherardi for the design of the triumphal entry of Charles V into Florence and in 1541 with Battista del Tasso and Tribolo for the christening of Prince Francesco. In 1542 he built a theatre in Venice, in 1555 again served the Medici and in 1565 designed the wedding festivities for Prince Francesco and Anne of Austria. His reputation today rests mainly on his work as an art historian, with his *Le Vite de' più eccellenti Architetti, Pittori, e Scultori Italiani* which contains his autobiography as well as biographies of many of his contemporaries.
Bibl: H. Tintelnot, BAROCKTHEATER UND BAROCKE KUNST, 1939

Vaudeville. The term originally denoted popular satirical songs; it is believed to derive from Val-(Vau-)de-Vire, a region of Normandy where such songs originated. It gradually developed into a term denoting light musical plays, as staged by strolling players who wanted to circumvent the monopoly of legitimate (i.e. spoken) drama held by the COMÉDIE-FRANÇAISE. By the 18th century vaudeville was popular in France, Austria and elsewhere as light COMEDY interspersed with ballads. It was this association with popular song which led to the use of the term by the mid-19th century in USA for a variety theatre corresponding to the English MUSIC HALL, in which popular character songs, interspersed with sketches and other variety numbers formed the staple ingredient of the programme. American vaudeville reached vast popularity and became big business in the USA in the second half of the 19th century, where a number of chains or circuits of variety theatres were established by managers like Percy C. Williams, Benjamin Franklin Keith, who later teamed up with Edward Franklin, Albee, and Martin Beck, who controlled the powerful Orpheum circuit. With the invention of motion pictures these at first became part of the programme of vaudeville variety; gradually they killed vaudeville, to which the advent of radio and TV eventually gave the *coup de grâce*.

Vauthier, Jean (1910–), French writer of Belgian origin. First became known for *Le Personnage combattant*, the monologue of a writer confronting his destiny, staged and acted by BARRAULT at the Petit Marigny in 1956. The same theme appeared in his first play *Capitaine Bada*, 1952, where the hero is trapped in the struggle between his own life and literature. Characteristic for V.'s texts are his detailed stage directions. Other works include: *L'Impromptu d'Arras*, 1951; *La Nouvelle Mandragore*, based on MACHIAVELLI's *La Mandragola*, 1952; *Les Prodiges*, fp Berlin 1959; *Le Rêveur*, 1961; *Chemise de nuit*, 1962; *Badadesque*, 1965.

Vedrenne, John E. (1867–1930), English theatre manager. Started in business and as a concert promoter. Together with GRANVILLE-BARKER he managed the famous Vedrenne-Barker seasons at the ROYAL COURT THEATRE, 1904–07, one of the most important pioneer efforts to establish serious drama in London with productions of SHAW, IBSEN, Masefield and Granville-Barker's own plays. He managed the

Peter Ustinov in his own play, *The Unknown Soldier and his Wife*, London 1973

Violet Vanbrugh as Katharine in *Henry VIII*

Karl Valentin, scene from a sketch with BRECHT (at left)

Queen's Theatre, 1907; the Lyric Theatre (1910 – with Lewis Waller) and the Royalty (1911 – with Dennis Eade).

Velthen, Johannes (1640–93), German ACTOR-MANAGER. One of the first outstanding German theatre managers, whose importance in theatre history was, however, originally greatly overestimated, e.g. in J. F. Löwen's *Geschichte des deutschen Theaters*, 1776. He studied at the universities of Wittenberg and Leipzig, and in 1665 joined the company of Karl Andreas Paulsen, whose daughter Catharine Elisabeth (?–*c.* 1712) he married some years later. In 1678 he finally founded his own company, the Kursächsische Komödianten which had a repertory of 87 plays including 14 by MOLIÈRE, and plays from the REPERTOIRE of the ENGLISH COMEDIANS, e.g. *The Rich Jew of Venice*. In 1685 he entered the service of Elector Johann Georg III of Saxony at Dresden, with whom he remained until 1692. After V.'s death the management of the company was taken over by his widow.

Venice Festival ▷BIENNALE.

Verga, Giovanni (1840–1922), Italian novelist and playwright. His distinguished literary output includes historical novels, and, later in his career, powerful realistic portrayals of his native Sicily. Almost all his plays were adaptations of his novels, like his most famous *Cavalleria Rusticana* (Rustic Chivalry), 1884, in which DUSE gained a triumphant success; later it formed the LIBRETTO for Mascagni's opera. His play *La lupa* (The She-Wolf), 1896, has remained in REPERTORY to the present day (revived 1966, dir ZEFFIRELLI, with ANNA MAGNANI). Other works include: *La caccia al lupo* (The Wolf-hunt), 1901; *La caccia alla volpe* (The Fox-hunt), 1901, both one-act plays; *Dal tuo al mio* (From Yours to Mine), 1903; *Rose caduche*, pub posthumously, 1928, never performed.
Bibl: G. Raya, 1961

Verismo (Ital *verità*=truth). Name given to a school of art which developed in Italy in the last two decades of the 19th century; the Italian equivalent of NATURALISM. Notable examples are the works of VERGA, BERTOLAZZI, *El nost' Milan*, and the operas of Mascagni, Leoncavallo, Puccini, etc.

Verneuil, Louis (Louis Collin-Barbie du Bocage; 1893–1952), French dramatist. Member of a wealthy family who made his early career in REVUE and later wrote a number of successful BOULEVARD comedies, some of which became BROADWAY hits, including: *Mademoiselle ma mère* (*Oh Mama!*), 1920; *Régine Armand*, 1922 (one of SARAH BERNHARDT's last roles); *Le Fauteuil 47*, 1923, triumphant success with 700 performances in Paris, 4,000 in the provinces, toured the country and was translated into many languages; *Le Mariage de maman* (*First Love*), 1924. In 1940 he moved to the USA and there wrote film scripts as well as plays. In 1950 he directed his first play to be written in English, *Affairs of State*.

Verse drama. From earliest times verse was used in drama to remove the action from the trivia of everyday life and elevate it to the plane of the mythical, royal or sublime. Gods, heroes and kings, who were not supposed to be concerned with the minutiae of existence, had to speak an elevated language. It was only in COMEDY and in DIALOGUE ascribed to comic characters that prose gradually gained a foothold in drama. In Elizabethan TRAGEDY, for example, most of the elevated passages remained in blank verse while comic episodes, but also more down-to-earth passages of the chief tragic character, could be in prose (like Hamlet's instructions to the actors). With the rise of NATURALISM verse was increasingly banished from the stage, simply because it does not occur in real life. In the 20th century, neo-romantic movements in literature have attempted to bring verse back into modern drama (HOFMANNSTHAL, MAETERLINCK, ROSTAND *c.* 1910; DUNCAN and ELIOT in England and M. ANDERSON in the USA in the 1930s; FRY in the 1940s and 1950s) while didactic dramatists (BRECHT, AUDEN, ISHERWOOD) used verse to compress their social or moral message in easily memorable form. The use of verse represents a definite ALIENATION EFFECT by removing the action from realism. But it must be emphasized that verse drama is not synonymous with poetic drama: the poetry *of* the stage is produced by the conjunction of movement, light, situation and speech – which may be in prose. Verse drama is poetry *on* the stage.
Bibl: D. Donoghue, THE THIRD VOICE, 1959

Vestris, Françoise-Rose (*née* Courgaud; 1743–1804), French actress who made her début at the COMÉDIE-FRANÇAISE in 1768 as Aménaide in VOLTAIRE's *Tancrède*. She distinguished herself mainly in tragic parts, her best-known performance being in Voltaire's *Irène* in 1778, which was highly praised by the author. Other noted parts included: Gabrielle in Belloy's *Gabrielle de Vergy*, 1777; Catherine de Medici in CHÉNIER's *Charles IX*, 1789, etc.

Vestris, Madame (*née* Lucia Elisabetta Bartolozzi; 1797–1856), English actress, wife of the French ballet dancer Armand Vestris (1788–1825) who abandoned her in 1820. A singer, who preferred to appear in light entertainment, she was at her best in BURLESQUE or high COMEDY. After a successful performance in a burlesque of Mozart's *Don Giovanni* called *Giovanni in London* (1817, by William Moncrieff), she played in Paris and then returned to London playing alternately at COVENT GARDEN and DRURY LANE. In 1830 she took over the Olympic Theatre, opening with *Olympic Revels* by PLANCHÉ. While there she took into her company the younger CHARLES MATHEWS whom she married in 1838. She was an excellent manageress and made many improvements, being one of the first to use historically correct details and real, as opposed to fake, properties; in 1832 she introduced the box-set complete with ceiling on to the London stage.
Bibl: C. J. Williams, MADAME VESTRIS, A THEATRICAL BIOGRAPHY, 1973

Vian, Boris (1920–59), French poet, novelist and dramatist. Also jazz-trumpeter, engineer, *chansonnier*, film actor, jazz critic and translator (Raymond Chandler, Peter Cheyney, James Cain, Nelson Algren, STRINDBERG, etc.). He was one of the most remarkable figures of post-war Paris and with IONESCO the most important exponent of the Collège de Pataphysique (▷JARRY). His best-known play was *Les Bâtisseurs d'Empire, ou Le Schmürz*, fp by VILAR at the Théâtre Récamier 1959, which shows a family trying to escape from a mysterious, unidentified, terrifying noise, with all the characters dying in the course of the play. They are accompanied by a silent passive character called Schmürz whom they constantly kick for no obvious reason. The play is a poetic image of mortality and the fear of death. Other plays include: *L'Equarissage pour tous*, fp 1950; *Le Goûter des généraux*, 1964.
Bibl: M. Esslin, THE THEATRE OF THE ABSURD, 2/1968

Vicente, Gil (*c.* 1465–*c.* 1536), Portuguese dramatist. Known as the 'founder of the Portuguese theatre', he wrote over 40 plays, 17 in Portuguese, 11 in Spanish and 16 in both languages. After 1502 he held the post of deviser of Court entertainments. The dramatic structure of his plays remained in the medieval tradition of MORALITY PLAYS, MYSTERY PLAYS and FARCES; in content they are close to Humanism (inspired by the ideas of Erasmus) fighting religious oppression, particularly anti-semitism, and glorifying the joys of life. They had great influence on the Spanish AUTO SACRAMENTAL. Main works: *Farsa da India*, a play about adultery, 1509; *Moralidade dos quatro tiempos* (Morality of the Four Seasons), 1513; the trilogy of the ships – *Barca do Inferno* (Ship of Hell), 1517, *Barca do Purgatório* (Ship of Purgatory), 1518, and *Barca de Glória* (Ship of Glory), 1519; *Moralidade de Alma*, 1518; *Farsa de Inês Pereira*, 1523; *Clérigo da Beira*, 1530; *Juiz da Beira*, 1526.
Bibl: A. Braamkamp Freire, 2/1944

Victoria Theatre, Stoke-on-Trent. One of England's leading professional REPERTORY theatres and the main permanent THEATRE-IN-THE-ROUND in Britain. Founded in 1962 by the pioneer of this type of theatre, Stephen Joseph, as a permanent home for his touring Studio Theatre Company. From the first Peter Cheeseman has been the director, responsible to Joseph's company, and since 1967 to a local body of trustees. Cheeseman's aim is the creation of a theatre with roots in the local community, its history and needs: hence his policy of creating locally devised documentary plays. A result of this policy is the employment of resident playwrights, notably TERSON. The theatre's achievements are widely recognized and the productions have toured abroad.
Bibl: J. Elsom, THEATRE OUTSIDE LONDON, 1971

Vidal, Gore (1925–), US novelist and playwright. Author of a number of light satires, principally *Visit to a Small Planet*, 1957, a FARCE about a man from outer space. In more serious vein *The Best Man*, 1960, and *Weekend*, 1968, deal with the manœuvres of presidential aspirants in an election year. He adapted DÜRRENMATT's *Romulus der Grosse* as *Romulus*, 1962, and has written several screenplays (including that of T. WILLIAMS's *Suddenly Last Summer*), TV drama and many novels.
Bibl: R. L. White, 1968

Viertel, Berthold (1885–1955), German director, poet and actor. Writer of Expressionist poems; author and actor in the Viennese cabaret 'Simplizissimus', 1912–14, DRAMATURG and director of the Vienna VOLKSBÜHNE, editor and drama critic of the *Prager Tageblatt*; director at the Dresden State Theatre, 1918–22. In BERLIN 1922 he directed HEBBEL's *Judith* at REINHARDT's Deutsches-Theater, and BRONNEN's *Vatermord* (Patricide), with which he had great success. In 1923 he founded his own company (Die Truppe), opening with SHAKESPEARE's *The Merchant of Venice*, followed by Robert Musil's *Vinzenz oder die Freundin bedeutender Männer* (Vincent or the Girlfriend of Important Men); however, he soon left the company to work as a freelance director. He went to the USA in 1927 and directed films and plays (BRECHT's *Fear and Misery of the Third Reich*, New York 1945). Returning to Europe in 1949, he produced GORKY's *Vassa Zheleznova* for the BERLINER ENSEMBLE, and from 1951 directed in Vienna at the BURGTHEATER plays by T. WILLIAMS, e.g. *A Streetcar Named Desire*, 1951, CHEKHOV and Shakespeare. He also wrote a COMEDY, essays and other literary works including dramatic adaptations. A collection of his works edited by E. GINSBERG was published in 1956 under the title *Dichtungen und Dokumente*.
Bibl: H. Jhering, VON REINHARDT BIS BRECHT, 1958–61, 3 vols

Vietnam had a theatre as long ago as the Middle Ages. Its classic *hat cheo* (satirical folk plays) and *hat boi* (a type of opera) genres were in the early 20th century modified into the *chai luong* – serious spectacles with DIALOGUE, singing, music and dance derived from Chinese opera and fiction, the socio-historical themes of which were adapted to modern Vietnamese settings. *Chai luong* has remained the most popular entertainment to the present day. The other modern Vietnamese theatre genre, *kich*, derived from the French; it is a one-act representational drama on contemporary subjects produced without music or song. Professional *chai luong* and *kich* troupes have performed throughout Vietnam and on radio. During the fighting of 1960s and 1970s classic *hat cheo* was widely produced as propaganda.
Bibl: F. Bowers, THEATRE IN THE EAST, 1956; Song Ban, THE VIETNAMESE THEATRE, 1960

Vigny, Alfred-Victor, Comte de (1797–1863), French poet, dramatist and novelist. An outsider among the Romantics, he was a master of form and a forerunner of the Parnassiens. His early dramatic works were adaptations of SHAKESPEARE: *Roméo et Juliette*, 1828; *Shylock* (adapted from *The Merchant of Venice*), 1830; *Othello, ou le More de Venise*, 1829. For the actress MARIE DORVAL, with whom he had an affair, he wrote the charming one-act comedy about marital infidelity, *Quitte pour la peur*, 1833. His second original play *La Maréchale d'Ancre*, 1831, Odéon, was an unsuccessful historical melodrama. His best work was the romantic tragedy *Chatterton*, successfully premièred at the COMÉDIE-FRANÇAISE in 1835 with Marie Dorval in the lead.
Bibl: P. G. Castex, 1952; G. Bonnefoy, LA PENSÉE RELIGIEUSE ET MORALE D'ALFRED DE VIGNY, 1944

Vilar, Jean (1912–70), French actor, director and manager. Appointed director of the Théâtre National Populaire in 1951. A pupil of DULLIN, he worked at the Théâtre de l'Atelier as stage manager and acted in minor roles. In 1941 he toured with a company of young actors and in 1943 took over the Théâtre de Poche, where he produced MOLIÈRE's *Dom Juan*; Sigurd Christiansen's *En reise i natten* (The Journey in the Night); STRINDBERG's *The Dance of Death*; ELIOT's *Murder in the Cathedral*. In 1947 he founded and organized the AVIGNON FESTIVAL which, with its REPERTOIRE of classical world literature, became an international event: SHAKESPEARE's *Richard II*; CORNEILLE's *Le Cid*; BÜCHNER's *Danton's Death*; GIDE's *Oedipe*; KLEIST's *The Prince of Homburg*. This led to his appointment as director of the TNP in which he endeavoured to create a theatre for the masses in the huge Palais de Chaillot (2,700 seats at low prices). He produced Shakespeare, PIRANDELLO, CHEKHOV, Kleist and BRECHT (*Mother Courage*) in addition to French classics, for an audience that had seldom been to a theatre. In this huge auditorium with a simple podium stage he developed a style of production which relied on bare scenic essentials and emphasized COSTUME, free movement, grand gesture and striking grouping of the actors. He was the author of the book *De la tradition théâtrale*, 1955.

Visconti, Luchino (Conte L. V. di Modrone; 1906–76), Italian director and stage designer. He is mainly known for his work as a representative of neo-realism in the cinema. In the theatre he favoured psychological drama, which he directed with great regard for historical accuracy (sometimes designing the productions himself) mainly in collaboration with the Morelli-Stoppa company which he joined in 1946: ANOUILH's *Antigone*, 1945; A. MILLER's *Death of a Salesman*, 1951, with DE LULLO, M. Mastroianni, and *A View from the Bridge*, 1958; CHEKHOV's *Uncle Vanya*, 1955; FABBRI's *Figlia d'arte*, 1959; and (in Paris) FORD's *'Tis Pity She's a Whore*, 1961. His productions of opera include: Verdi's *La Traviata*, Milan 1955, La Scala, with Maria Callas; *Don Carlos*, Covent Garden, 1958; and *Der Rosenkavalier*.

Madame Vestris

Jean Vilar in PIRANDELLO's *Henry IV*, Théâtre de l'Atelier

Vishnevsky, Vsevolod Vitalievich (1900–51), Soviet dramatist. His plays demonstrated the contradictions of the Revolution and were successfully produced mainly in Socialist countries. His greatest success was *Optimisticheskaya tragediya* (*An Optimistic Tragedy*), 1932, fp by TAIROV at the Kamerny Theatre 1934, which dealt with the defeat of anarchy in the Revolution; his reputation rests on this and his last play *Nezabyvayemy 1919-y* (*The Unforgettable Year 1919*), 1949, of which Stalin is the hero; both plays are still in the REPERTOIRE of Soviet theatre. Other works: *Pervaya konnaya* (The First Cavalry Army), 1929; the musical play *Wide Spreads the Sea*, 1943, with Alexander Kron and Alexander Azarov; *U Sten Leningrada* (At the Walls of Leningrad), 1944.

Vitaly, Georges (1917–), Russian-born French director. Best known for his productions of AUDIBERTI's plays: *Le Mal court*, 1947, Théâtre de Poche; *La Fête noire*, 1948; *Les Naturels de Bordelais*, 1953; *Le Quallou*, 1958; *L'Effet Glapion*, 1959; *Pomme, pomme, pomme*, 1962. In 1953 he took over the management of the Théâtre La Bruyère, with the aim of reviving VAUDEVILLE theatre with works by FEYDEAU, LABICHE, Guiton and Bréal.

Vitrac, Roger (1899–1952), French playwright. One of the best dramatists to emerge from the Surrealist movement which followed DADA, a development in art in which he was involved with Tristan Tzara and André Breton in Paris. With his friend ARTAUD he founded the Théâtre Alfred Jarry in 1927, for which he wrote *Les Mystères de l'amour*, 1927; and *Victor, ou les Enfants au pouvoir*, 1928. In the latter he parodies the themes of the typical bourgeois play and the values of bourgeois mentality, through the eyes of a nine-year-old child seven feet tall, who combines cynicism and naïveté as he observes the stupidity and narrowness of the family. Both plays were directed by Artaud, but were unsuccessful at the time; *Victor* shocked the audience. It was not until 1946 that Michel de Ré revived it for the stage. In 1962 it was put on again successfully at the Théâtre Ambigu under the direction of ANOUILH, who also directed the play in 1963 in Germany at the Munich Kammerspiele. Other works include: *Le Peintre*, pub 1930; *Le Coup de Trafalgar*, 1934; *Camelot*, 1936; *Les Demoiselles du large*, 1938; *Le Loup-garou*, 1940, dir R. Rouleau; *Le Sabre de mon père*, 1951, dir DUX.
Bibl: M. Esslin, THE THEATRE OF THE ABSURD, 2/1968

Vitruvius (Marcus V. Pollio; 88–26 BC), Roman architect and author of the ten-volume treatise *De Architectura*. In the fifth of these he deals with Roman theatre construction. The discovery of this manuscript in St Gall in 1414, printed in 1484, and published with illustrations in 1511, greatly influenced the building and style of RENAISSANCE and BAROQUE THEATRES in the recreation of Roman models, e.g. TEATRO OLIMPICO in Vicenza. An Italian translation appeared in 1531.

Volksbühne. German working-class organization for the encouragement of theatre-going. Originated in BERLIN in 1890 under the name Freie Volksbühne (Free People's Theatre). The inspiration for the enterprise came from the example of the FREIE BÜHNE and the Socialist movement's desire to raise the cultural level of the masses. At first the Volksbühne organized Sunday matinées for workers in theatres hired for the purpose with actors engaged for specific plays. Later, tickets at reduced prices were made available to members at existing theatres. In 1967 the Volksbühne had about 400,000 members in the German Federal Republic. The Volksbühne movement was much afflicted by internal quarrels; it split in 1892 and one of its factions, the Neue Freie Volksbühne, flourished and opened its own theatre in 1914. After it was reunited in 1919, PISCATOR was its artistic director 1924–27. His radical and revolutionary productions led to further internal dissensions which eventually induced him to leave and found his own theatre. The main – social democratic – body of the Volksbühne pursued a policy of educating the working class without emphasis on a particular political line. Gradually the movement spread from Berlin to the rest of Germany. Closed down by the Nazis, the Volksbühne was re-founded after 1945. In 1962, Piscator, returned from exile, became director of a new theatre, the Freie Volksbühne in Berlin. Since 1919 there have been rival Christian and nationalist organizations, collectively known as the Bühnenvolksbund. Since their amalgamation in 1945 the Christian groups have been known as the Bund der Theatergemeinden (Association of theatre groups).
Bibl: W. G. Oschilewski, FREIE VOLKSBÜHNE, 1965

Volkstheater ▷WIENER VOLKSTHEATER.

Voltaire (François Marie Arouet; 1694–1778), French philosopher and poet. The son of a notary, he studied at the Jesuit Collège de Clermont and became one of the major influences in 18th-century philosophy, science and literature. He was not a major poet and dramatist in the manner of CORNEILLE and RACINE; his plays tend to lose themselves in RHETORIC and abstraction, but this does not diminish his importance in the history of the theatre. His first TRAGEDY *Œdipe*, fp 1718, established him as a dramatist and was followed by *Artémire*, 1720, and *Mariamne*, pub 1725. After a disagreement with the aristocracy, which led to his imprisonment, he went into exile in England 1726–29, where he was deeply impressed by productions of SHAKESPEARE's plays – 'a most powerful and barbaric genius'; V.'s later works owed much to him: *Brutus*, 1730, was inspired by *Julius Caesar*, as was *La Mort de César*, written 1731, which after a private performance, was staged by the COMÉDIE-FRANÇAISE, 1743. *Zaïre*, 1732, inspired by *Othello*, was highly successful and ranks with *Mérope*, 1743 as V.'s best play. His *Lettres Anglaises* which praise the English originals, brought him disgrace at Court; he escaped in 1734 to the castle of Mme du Châtelet; in 1744 he became historian to the King and in 1746 was appointed a member of the Académie française. Later he was harassed again for his 'free thinking' and went to the Court of Frederick the Great where he remained until 1753, then again fell into disfavour. He travelled to Alsace and Switzerland, where he settled in 1755. In 1778 he returned to Paris to see the first production of his last play *Irène*, and died there at the moment of achieving his most triumphant success. Other principal dramatic works: *Adélaïde du Guesclin*, 1734; *Alzire*, 1736; *L'Enfant prodigue*, 1736; *Mahomet*, 1741; *Sémiramis*, 1748; *Nanine*, 1749; *Oreste*, 1750; *Rome sauvée, L'Orphelin de la Chine*, 1755; *Tancrède*, 1760. He also wrote several COMEDIES (mainly for the entertainment of his patrons, e.g. Mme du Châtelet), carelessly written tragedies (e.g. *Olimpie* which he wrote in six days), LIBRETTI (most of which were never set to music) and numerous philosophical essays on the theatre. Some plays achieved great popularity after his death, including *La Mort de César* during the French Revolution; and even in the early 19th century he was more frequently produced at the CF than either Racine or Corneille.
Bibl: H. C. Lancaster, FRENCH TRAGEDY IN THE TIME OF LOUIS XIV AND VOLTAIRE 1715–92, 1950, 2 vols; G. Bengesco, LES COMÉDIENNES DE VOLTAIRE, 1912

Vondel, Joost van den (1587–1679), Dutch dramatist, poet and man of letters. His reputation rests mainly on his plays which are representative of the Baroque Humanist movement. He also made a number of translations and adaptations of the classics (SENECA, SOPHOCLES, Virgil) which strongly influenced his work. His themes were mainly taken from the Bible and classical antiquity, e.g. *Josef*, 1635; *Elektra*, 1639; *Koning Edipus*, 1660; *Koning David in Ballingschap*, 1660, etc. For the opening of the new Municipal Theatre in Amsterdam, in 1637, he wrote *Gysbreght van Aemstel*, a drama on the decline of earthly grandeur which emphasizes the importance of eternal values like humility and obedience to the commands of God. It is still performed annually in Holland on New Year's day.
Bibl: J. G. Bomhoff, 1950

Voskovec, Jiří (George J. Wachsmann; 1905–), Czech actor and dramatist. He was associated with his collaborator WERICH under the collective name, Voskovec and Werich. From their *Vest pocket revue*, 1927, developed one of the liveliest theatres (*Osvobozené divadlo*, Prague) in Czechoslovakia between the two wars. With the director J. Honzl and the composer J. Jezek they produced at first plays by other writers, but later appeared exclusively in their own works: *Smoking Revue*, 1928; *The Gorilla from the Machine*, 1928; *The Dynamite-Island*, 1930; *Robin, the Robber*, 1932. As actors, they modelled themselves on US silent movie comedians; Voskovec was the rational thinker, Werich the tough instinctive character. They combined parodies of famous film and theatre clichés with political allusions, which eventually necessitated their emigration to the USA in 1938. Their attempt to reopen their theatre after the war failed and they have appeared in REPERTORY companies. Since 1948 Voskovec has been in the USA, appearing as a straight actor, notably as the male lead in *Romanoff and Juliet*, 1957, by USTINOV, and as Dr Neuross in K. Wittlinger's *Do You Know the Milky Way?*, 1961, translated from the German *Kennen Sie die Milchstrasse?*, 1955.

Voltaire's apotheosis in his play *Irène*, COMÉDIE-FRANÇAISE, 1778

Wagner, Wieland (1917–66), German opera director. Grandson of Richard Wagner. From 1951 he took over the management of the BAYREUTH FESTIVAL jointly with his brother Wolfgang W. (1919–). With a series of boldly imaginative productions without the conventional romantically pictorial sets, and relying largely on lighting effects to create a sense of space and design, he revolutionized the staging of Wagner at Bayreuth and throughout the world.

Herwarth Walden, drawing by KOKOSCHKA

Walbrook, Anton (Adolf Wohlbrück; 1900–67), German actor, who acquired British nationality in 1947. He made his early appearances in Berlin, 1920–26 worked in Munich (with HERMINE KÖRNER at the Schauspielhaus and under FALCKENBERG at the Kammerspiele); 1927–30 in Dresden and 1930–35 at the Barnowsky-Bühnen in Berlin. He went to London in 1937 where he made his début as Otto in COWARD's *Design for Living* at the Haymarket Theatre, later as Kurt Müller in LILLIAN HELLMAN's *Watch on the Rhine*, and Hjalmar Ekdal in IBSEN's *The Wild Duck*, both 1942. After two guest appearances in Düsseldorf 1951, he played again in London as Cosmo Constantine in the musical *Call Me Madam* (LINDSAY/CROUSE/BERLIN), 1952, and Hans van Maasdijk in *Masterpiece* (Ward/Russell), 1961. Also well known as a film actor.
Bibl: W. Holl, DAS BUCH VON ANTON WALBROOK, 1935

Wieland Wagner, set for *Parsifal* at Bayreuth, 1951

Walden, Herwarth (Georg Lewin; b. 1878, missing, presumed dead, in the Soviet Union, 1941), German novelist and critic. Founded the weekly magazine *Der Sturm* in 1910 and also wrote several Expressionist plays, including (dates indicate year of publication): *Weib* (Wife), 1917; *Kind* (Child), 1918; *Trieb* (Desire), 1918; *Menschen* (Mankind), 1918; *Glaube* (Belief), 1920; *Sünde* (Sin), 1920; *Die Beiden* (Both), 1920; *Letzte Liebe* (Last Love), 1920.

Walkley, A. B. (Alfred Bingham; 1855–

1926), English drama critic. Reviewed plays in *The Times* from 1900 to 1926. His reviews have been collected in a number of volumes: *Drama and Life*, 1907; *Pastiche and Prejudice*, 1921; *More Prejudice*, 1923; *Still More Prejudice*, 1925.

Wallace, Edgar Horatio (1875–1932), English journalist, novelist and dramatist. He began as a crime reporter, and was the first successful writer of detective plays in the theatre. Most of his works – he wrote *c.* 170 – are based on his early thrillers; among the most famous are: *The Ringer*, 1926; *On the Spot*, 1930; *The Case of the Frightened Lady*, 1931, etc. He also wrote two volumes of reminiscences: *People: A Short Autobiography*, 1926, and *My Hollywood Diary*, 1932.
Bibl: M. Lane, 1938

Wallace, Nellie (1870–1948), English MUSIC-HALL performer. She was particularly brilliant in grotesque character comedy songs. Also appeared in PANTOMIME, one of the few successful female 'Dames' of the genre.

Wallack. Family of actors of English origin, important in the development of the US theatre. (1) **Henry John W.** (1790–1870) was invited to the USA in 1819 and in 1824 became leading actor of the Chatham Garden Theatre in New York. His brother, (2) **James William W.** (1795–1864), made his first appearance in New York in 1818, and successfully played young leading men. The Wallacks took over several theatres in New York and in the 1860s became one of the leading companies in the USA until the rise of E. BOOTH and DALY. John Johnstone, known as (3) **Lester W.** (1820–88), a son of J. W. W. and Susan Johnstone, and his cousin James William W. Jr, known as (4) **Jim W.** (1818–73), son of H. J. W., continued the family tradition.
Bibl: M. J. Moses, FAMOUS ACTOR-FAMILIES IN AMERICA, 1906

Walser, Martin (1927–), German novelist and dramatist. His books include *Ehen in Philippsburg* and *Halbzeit*, and he established himself as one of the most important contemporary German dramatists with: *Der Abstecher* (The Detour), fp Munich Kammerspiele, 1961, originally written as a radio play; *Eiche und Angora* (*The Rabbit Race*), fp Berlin 1962, Schiller Theater, a 'German chronicle'; *Überlebensgrosser Herr Krott* (Over-lifesize Herr K.), Stuttgart 1963, the character of Krott being a personification of Capitalism; *Der schwarze Schwan* (The Black Swan), Stuttgart 1964, drama of conscience and guilt of a young man, whose father was guilty of Nazi war crimes; *Zimmerschlacht* (Indoor Battle), Munich Kammerspiele, 1967.

Wälterlin, Oskar (1895–1961), German director and manager. Began as an actor and director in Basle 1919–25, and managed the same theatre from 1925 to 1932. Director of the Opera in Frankfurt 1933–38, and from 1938 until his death director of the Zurich Schauspielhaus. In 1933 many notable German theatrical personalities who were unwilling or unable to work in Hitler's Germany came to Zurich after the occupation of Austria and Czechoslovakia. The Zurich Schauspielhaus under W.'s direction became the centre of anti-Hitler German theatre. Here some of BRECHT's plays (*Mutter Courage, Der Gute Mensch von Setzuan, Leben des Galilei*) were first produced. He also supported native Swiss dramatists, notably FRISCH and DÜRRENMATT.
Bibl: G. Schoop, DAS ZÜRICHER SCHAUSPIELHAUS IM 2. WELTKRIEG, 1957

War of the Theatres. A quarrel which caused a stir in the Elizabethan theatrical world from 1599 until 1601, and in which JONSON, MARSTON, DEKKER and possibly SHAKESPEARE took part. In *Every Man out of His Humour*, 1599, Jonson put into the mouth of one of his characters, Clove, speeches which parodied Marston's extravagant style. Jonson may have been provoked by Marston's portrait of him (inept, though intended to be flattering) as Chrisoganus, in his first play, *Histriomastix*, produced early in the year. Marston duly retaliated by caricaturing Jonson in his next play, *Jack Drum's Entertainment*, 1600. Jonson retorted by satirizing both Marston and Dekker in *Cynthia's Revels*, 1600–01, and within a few weeks started work on *Poetaster*, intended to crush both these dramatists decisively. Jonson was probably forestalled by Marston's *What You Will*, in which he is caricatured, before the production of *Poetaster*, 1601, set in the time of Augustus, in which he ridicules Marston's person and style in the character of Crispinus, as well as Dekker in the character of Demetrius. In this play Jonson represents himself as Horace. In *Satiromastix*, produced later that year, Dekker takes all three of these characters from *Poetaster*, giving Horace an interpretation which caricatures Jonson, as well as introducing another of Jonson's characters in *Poetaster*, Tucca, to castigate him. Jonson, who had offended not only dramatists but actors, soldiers and lawyers with certain allusions in *Poetaster*, narrowly avoided prosecution and ceased writing comedies for some years. The 'war' had now ended, having increased attendance at the theatres and apparently without causing any lasting rift between the contestants. An allusion in the anonymous play, *The Return from Parnassus*, Part Two, *c.* 1602, suggests that Shakespeare took part in the quarrel. It has been suggested that he may have satirized Jonson in the character of Jaques (*As You Like It*, 1599) or of Ajax (*Troilus and Cressida*, 1602). Alternatively he may have acted Horace in *Satiromastix* (which was produced by BURBAGE's company) and, in doing so, have parodied Jonson's mannerisms.
Bibl: R. S. Small, THE STAGE QUARREL BETWEEN BEN JONSON AND THE SO-CALLED POETASTERS, 1899

Warde, Frederick Barkham (1851–1935), US actor. After an apprenticeship in touring companies, appeared successfully in SHAKESPEARE at Booth's Theatre, New York. Formed his own company in 1881 and starred in many Shakespeare plays as well as in romantic historical dramas. Retired from the stage in 1919. Also lectured on drama and wrote a book on *The Fools of Shakespeare*, 1913, plus his autobiography *Fifty Years of Make-Believe*, 1920.

Warfield, David (1866–1951), US actor. Started in California, came to New York in 1891, then appeared in VAUDEVILLE, MUSICAL COMEDY and BURLESQUE, where he developed a successful line of German and Jewish characters. BELASCO saw him in one of these impersonations and cast him in a comic-sentimental part as a Jew in *The Auctioneer* by Lee Arthur and Charles Klein, 1901, in which he achieved a sensational success; he followed this with an even greater triumph, as a German musician who emigrates to America and finds his long-lost daughter, in *The Music Master* (also by Arthur and Klein), 1904. His third great success was achieved in Belasco's play *The Return of Peter Grimm*, 1911. He appeared repeatedly in these three roles. In 1922 Belasco starred him as Shylock in *The Merchant of Venice*.

Warren, William (1767–1832), US actor of English origin. Went to Philadelphia in 1796 and became manager of the Chestnut Street Theatre. He was an excellent character actor, particularly in parts as old men. His son **William W.** (1812–88) also became an actor who spent most of his career in Boston.

Washington Square Players. A US company which evolved into the THEATRE GUILD.

Waters, Ethel (1900–), US actress and singer. She made her début in VAUDEVILLE, 1917, and played the circuits for the next ten years, making her BROADWAY début in *Africana*, 1927. She appeared in the *Blackbirds of 1930*, the M. HART-BERLIN *As Thousands Cheer*, with MARILYN MILLER, 1933, and *Cabin in the Sky*, 1940. Plays include *Mamba's Daughters*, 1938, by Dorothy and Dubose Heyward which brought her recognition as an actress of the first rank, and CARSON McCULLERS' *The Member of the Wedding*, 1950, with JULIE HARRIS. She has devoted much time to sacred music and has appeared in Billy Graham's Youth for Christ rallies. Famous popular songs of the 1930s such as 'Dinah' and 'Stormy Weather' were introduced by her. She has also appeared in films.

Webster, John (?1580–?1634), English dramatist. His best-known original plays are *The White Devil*, 1609–12, and *The Duchess of Malfi*, 1612–14, passionate TRAGEDIES of love and political intrigue in Renaissance Italy, full of horror and exceptional cruelty, but validated by the macabre power of imagination, the dramatic force of their greatest scenes and the beauty of their poetry. They also provide great acting parts (notably Vittoria Corombona in the former play and the title role

in the latter) and have remained in the REPERTOIRE up to the present day. Another extant play is the TRAGICOMEDY, *The Devil's Law Case*, 1610–19. W. may have written the tragedy *Appius and Virginia* in collaboration with T. HEYWOOD; he also collaborated on plays with DEKKER, FORD, MARSTON and ROWLEY.
Bibl: T. Board, THE TRAGIC SATIRE OF JOHN WEBSTER, 1955; U. M. Ellis-Fermor, THE JACOBEAN DRAMA, 1955

Wedekind, Frank (1864–1918), German dramatist. His extremely radical style of presentation made him a forerunner of the Expressionists and one of the main influences on BRECHT. He attempted to penetrate to a fundamental sphere of reality; he heightened his action by bizarre and grotesque effects to reveal the hypocrisy of the bourgeois mentality, and by dispensing with nuances portrayed the seamier side of human behaviour, particularly with regard to sex. He depicted a world of adventurers, prostitutes, with elements of the CIRCUS, BURLESQUE and particularly CABARET (for some time he wrote for the satirical magazine *Simplizissimus*, and in 1901 joined the cabaret 'Die elf Scharfrichter', singing ballads to his own lite accompaniment). After 1905 he also appeared in his own plays. In 1906 he worked with his wife Tilly Newes, at the Deutsches-Theater, BERLIN, both appearing in the première of his *Frühlings Erwachen* (*Spring's Awakening*), written in 1891, under the direction of REINHARDT. In 1908 he went to live in Munich, acting and touring in his own plays until 1917. Main works: *Der Liebestrank* (The Love Potion), FARCE, 1891–92, Nuremberg 1905, Intimes Theater; *Erdgeist* (Earth Spirit), Part I of *Lulu*, 1893–94, Berlin 1902, Kleines Theater; *Die Büchse der Pandora* (Pandora's Box), Part II of *Lulu*, 1893–94, fp Nuremberg 1905, Intimes Theater, with *Erdgeist* under the general title *Lulu*; *Der Kammersänger*, 1897, Berlin 1899, Neues Theater, dir Reinhardt; *Der Marquis von Keith*, Munich 1902, revived 1920 by JESSNER in a famous Expressionist production, and London 1974, RSC; *König Nicolò oder So ist das Leben* (King Nicolo or Such is Life), Munich 1902; *Hidalla*, also called *Karl Hetmann, der Zwergriese* (Karl Hetman, the Giant Midget), Munich 1905; *Tod und Teufel* (Death and the Devil), also called *Totentanz*, Nuremberg 1906; *Musik*, Nuremberg 1908; *Die Zensur*, 1907, Munich 1909; *Oaha, die Satire der Satire*, later called *Till Eulenspiegel*, Munich 1911; *Schloss Wetterstein*, Zurich 1917; *Franziska*, Munich, Kammerspiele 1911; *Simson, oder Scham und Eifersucht* (Simson, or Shame and Jealousy), Berlin 1914, Lessing Theater; *Herakles*, Munich 1919, Prinzregententheater; *Bismarck*, written 1916, Weimar 1926.
Bibl: T. Wedekind, ICH WAR WEDEKINDS LULU, 1969; F. Rothe, FRANK WEDEKINDS DRAMEN, 1968; H. F. Garten, MODERN GERMAN DRAMA, 1959

Wegener, Paul (1874–1948), German actor. Studied law in Leipzig before making his début as an actor in Rostock. In 1906 he joined the Deutsches-Theater, Berlin, under REINHARDT, with whom he worked closely during his acting career. He scored his first major success as Oberst Kottwitz in KLEIST's *Prinz Friedrich von Homburg* and very soon made a reputation as a player of mature classical heroes, notably Holofernes in HEBBEL's *Judith*, 1909 dir Reinhardt; Kandaules in *Gyges und sein Ring*, 1907; Shakespearean roles (Lear, Henry IV, Macbeth, Richard III, Othello); SOPHOCLES' *Oedipus Rex*; and IBSEN's *John Gabriel Borkman*. One of his last and finest parts was the title role in LESSING's *Nathan der Weise*, 1945, opening production of the Deutsches-Theater after the war. He set off opposing moods against one another: elementary strength against barbaric ferocity, wise composure against sly humour.
Bibl: H. Jhering, VON JOSEF KAINZ BIS PAUL WESSELY, 1942

Weichert, Richard (1880–1961), German director. Began his career as an actor and gained his first stage experience in Düsseldorf under Louise Dumont-Lindemann, where he also made his début as a director. He then went to Mannheim where he directed 1914–18. During that time his production of HASENCLEVER's *Der Sohn* set the style for Expressionist productions: stylized set, emphasis on lighting, and use of following lights; W. was first a director and later INTENDANT at the Frankfurt Städtische Bühnen (1918–32) where he supported the works of Hasenclever (*Antigone, Ein besserer Herr*), the early BRECHT (*Trommeln in der Nacht*, 1922) and BRONNEN. Director at the State Theatre, Munich, 1932–33, subsequently at the VOLKSBÜHNE, Berlin (KLEIST's *Amphitryon*, 1939). He was also guest director of several productions in Vienna and worked as artistic director in Frankfurt 1947–65.
Bibl: H. Heym (ed), FRANKFURT UND SEIN THEATER, 1963

Weigel, Helene (1900–71), German actress and manager. Married BRECHT in 1928. After a brief training in Vienna, she appeared in several German theatres in Frankfurt and BERLIN. In 1932 she played the title role in Brecht's *Die Mutter* (after GORKY). In 1933 she had to leave Germany, and appeared only occasionally while in exile: in Brecht's *Die Gewehre der Frau Carrar*, Paris 1937, Copenhagen 1938; *Furcht und Elend des Dritten Reiches*, Paris 1938. Returning from the USA in 1948, she appeared in Switzerland (Chur) in the title role of SOPHOCLES' *Antigone*. She became the head of the BERLINER ENSEMBLE (of which Brecht was officially 'artistic director') in 1949. Principal parts: *Mutter Courage*, 1949, dir Brecht/ENGEL; *Die Mutter*, 1951; *Gewehre der Frau Carrar*, 1952; title role in BAIERL's *Frau Flinz*, 1961; Volumnia in Brecht's *Coriolan* (after SHAKESPEARE), 1964; Mrs Luckerniddle in *Die heilige Johanna der Schlachthöfe*, 1968.
Bibl: DIE SCHAUSPIELERIN HELENE WEIGEL, 1959

Weill, Kurt (1900–50), German composer. A pupil of Busoni, he started by writing

Frank Wedekind's *Lulu* with Julia Foster, an English adaptation by BARNES, fp Nottingham Playhouse 1970

Helene Weigel in BRECHT's *Mother Courage*

chamber music, while working as coffee-house pianist. His first one-act operas were *Der Protagonist* (LIBRETTO by KAISER), Dresden 1926; *Royal Palace* (libretto by GOLL), Berlin 1927, Krolloper. In 1927 he entered upon his collaboration with BRECHT, first on the song play *Mahagonny*, Baden-Baden 1927, from which later came the opera *Aufstieg und Fall der Stadt Mahagonny*; after a work based on Kaiser's *Der Zar lässt sich fotographieren*, Leipzig 1928, he achieved his greatest success with *Die Dreigroschenoper* by Brecht after GAY, Theater am Schiffbauerdamm, 1928, which won international fame (in New York, 1952, adapted by Elisabeth Hauptmann in collaboration with Brecht, it had a run of 2,611 performances). *Happy End*, 1929, was an unsuccessful attempt in the genre of *Die Dreigoschenoper*; he also wrote music for Brecht's *Lehrstücke* including: *Der Flug der Lindberghs*, 1921; *Der Jasager*, 1930; *Die sieben Todsünden der Kleinbürger*, Paris 1933. In 1933 he emigrated to the USA where he established himself as a composer for musicals, e.g. *A Kingdom for a Cow*, 1935; *Knickerbocker Holiday*, 1938; *Lady in the Dark*, 1941; *Love Life*, 1948; *Street Scene*, 1947; *Lost in the Stars*, 1949. He was married to the actress and *chansonnière* LOTTE LENYA.
Bibl: S. Schmidt-Joos, DAS MUSICAL, 1965

Weise, Christian (1642–1708), German dramatist. Teacher at a grammar school in Weissfels, 1670, headmaster in Zwittau, 1678, where he wrote and produced about 70 plays (61 have survived) for performances by his pupils; in a moralizing vein and involving as many actors as possible in supporting roles, the plays were written in prose and incorporated elements from the plays of strolling comedians (PICKELHERRING). The highly moral themes were taken from the Old Testament (*David, Absalom*) and history (*Regnerus in Schweden*); at the end of the play festivals, which lasted three days (at first presented during carnival, later in autumn) a COMEDY was presented. His version of SHAKESPEARE's *The Taming of the Shrew*, the *Comödie von der bösen Catharina*, was also performed by travelling companies.
Bibl: W. Eggert, CHRISTIAN WEISE UND SEINE BÜHNE, 1935

Weiss, Peter (1916–), German playwright, painter, film director and journalist. Exiled by the Nazis in 1934, he studied painting in Prague, emigrating to Sweden in 1939, where he had his first exhibition in 1940. In 1946 he wrote his first poems in Swedish, followed by several attempts at drama: *Der Turm* (*The Tower*), influenced by Kafka, Stockholm 1948; *Die Versicherung* (The Insurance), a surrealistic series of scenes on the fall of bourgeois society, written 1952. He also wrote autobiographical novels, *Abschied von den Eltern* (Leavetaking), 1961 and *Fluchtpunkt* (Vanishing Point), 1962, and a PUPPET PLAY, *Nacht mit Gästen* (Night with Guests), fp Berlin 1963, Schiller-Theater. He distinguished himself as a dramatist with *Die Verfolgung und Ermordung Jean Paul Marats dargestellt durch die Schauspielgruppe des Hospizes zu Charenton unter Anleitung des Herrn de Sade*, known generally as *Marat/Sade*, fp Berlin 1963, Schiller Theater, dir SWINARSKI; in English, dir BROOK with the ROYAL SHAKESPEARE COMPANY 1963, later New York. It is essentially a DIALOGUE on revolution and violence, between the socialist Marat and the extreme individualist de Sade, set in a lunatic asylum. His next play *Die Ermittlung* (*The Investigation*), 1965, is a concise documentary presentation of the Frankfurt trials of some of the Auschwitz guards. In *Gesang vom lusitanischen Popanz* (*Song of the Lusitanian Bogey*), 1967, he attacks Portuguese colonialism in Africa, fp Stockholm 1967, then Rome 1969, dir STREHLER. *Diskurs über die Vorgeschichte und den Verlauf des lang andauernden Befreiungskrieges in Viet Nam als Beispiel für die Notwendigkeit des bewaffneten Kampfes der Unterdrückten gegen die Unterdrücker sowie die Versuche der Vereinigten Staaten von Amerika die Grundlagen der Revolution zu vernichten* (Discourse on the Historical Background and the Course of the Continuing Struggle for Liberation in Vietnam as an Example of the Necessity of Armed Warfare by the Oppressed against their Oppressors and Furthermore on the Attempts of the United States of America to Annihilate the Basic Principle of the Revolution), fp Frankfurt 1968, BUCKWITZ. This documentary drama is a narrative of over 2,000 years of Vietnamese history and an attack on American imperialism. Other works: *Wie dem Herrn Mockimpott das Leiden ausgetrieben wird* (How Mr M. cast out grief), a MORALITY PLAY, fp Hanover 1968; *Hölderlin*, 1971.
Bibl: G. Braun (ed), MATERIALEN ZU MARAT/SADE, 1967

Wekwerth, Manfred (1929–), German director. Pupil and follower of BRECHT, started by directing amateur companies till 1951 when he joined the BERLINER ENSEMBLE; he made his début as a director with Brecht's *Die Mutter*, Vienna 1953 featuring HELENE WEIGEL. His productions at the Berliner Ensemble include: Brecht's *Der kaukasische Kreidekreis*, 1954, and BECHER's *Winterschlacht*, 1955, both dir together with Brecht; SYNGE's *The Playboy of the Western World*, 1956, VISHNEVSKY's *An Optimistic Tragedy*, 1958, and Brecht's *Der aufhaltsame Aufstieg des Arturo Ui*, 1959, all dir with PALITZSCH; Brecht's *Die Tage der Kommune*, 1962, KIPPHARDT's *In der Sache J. R. Oppenheimer*, 1965, and Brecht's *Die heilige Johanna der Schlachthöfe*, 1968, all dir with J. Tenschert. He is also the author of two books on the theatre: *Theater in Veränderung*, 1960, and *Notate*, 1967.

Welk, Ehm (1884–1966), German writer. Mainly known as the author of short stories and novels, e.g. *Die Heiden von Kumnerow*, 1937; he also wrote several plays for the theatre including *Gewitter über Gottland* (Storm over God's Land), 1926, dir PISCATOR; *Kreuzabnahme* (Descent from the Cross), 1929; *Michael Kobbe*, 1931; *Schwarzbrot* (Black Bread), 1932. Awarded the National Prize of East Germany.

Well-made play. A term frequently used of plays modelled on French 19th-century bourgeois drama, notably those of SCRIBE and SARDOU, ridiculed by SHAW as 'Sardoodledom'. In modern times often used in a derogatory sense. BENTLEY has pointed out that although the 'well-made' play is a form of classical TRAGEDY, degenerate in so far as the PLOT is ingeniously contrived, with arresting situation, intrigue and suspense, it is mechanical and devoid of feeling.
Bibl: J. R. Taylor, THE RISE AND FALL OF THE 'WELL-MADE PLAY', 1967

Welles, (George) Orson (1915–), US actor and director. While travelling in Europe he made his first appearance aged 16 in Dublin 1931 in FEUCHTWANGER's *Jew Süss* and worked at the ABBEY THEATRE and Gate Theatre before returning to the USA to tour with KATHARINE CORNELL, in *Romeo and Juliet*, as Mercutio, and in *Candida* as Marchbanks, etc. He made his New York début as Tybalt and soon established himself as an outstanding actor/director. In 1936 he directed for the FEDERAL THEATRE PROJECT a Negro version of *Macbeth*, and other plays, including MARLOWE's *Dr Faustus* in which he played the title role. With John Houseman (1902–) who had also been at the Federal Theatre, he founded the Mercury Theatre where he directed and played Brutus in a sensational modern-dress *Julius Caesar*. He was also responsible for the famous broadcast *The War of the Worlds*, 1938, which gave such a realistic impression of a Martian invasion that it caused a panic in the USA. After the failure of his adaptation of Jules Verne's *Around the World in 80 Days*, 1946, he did not appear on the New York stage for ten years. He first appeared in London in 1951 as Othello and in 1955 played Lear on TV (and in 1956 on BROADWAY) and acted in his own adaptation of *Moby Dick*. He also produced IONESCO's *Rhinoceros* with OLIVIER in the lead at the ROYAL COURT THEATRE, London 1960. His productions challenge convention; he was a controversial figure in the film industry. His film *Citizen Kane*, 1941, is one of the great classics of the cinema.
Bibl: P. Nolde, THE FABULOUS ORSON WELLES, 1956

Werfel, Franz (1898–1945), Czech-born Austrian writer. Famous for his novels, especially *Die Vierzig Tage des Musa Dagh* (The Forty Days of Musa Dagh), 1933, he began his career as a poet and then wrote a free adaptation of EURIPIDES' *The Trojan Women*: *Die Troerinnen*, Berlin 1916. Other plays followed, based on the German tradition of Romanticism and EXPRESSIONISM; *Der Besuch aus dem Elysium* (The Visit from Elysium), Berlin 1918; *Spiegelmensch* (Mirror Man), Leipzig 1921, a verse trilogy based on the Faust legend; and *Schweiger* (The Silent One), Prague 1923, portraying a schizoid personality. His next play *Bockgesang* (*Goat Song*), 1921, produced by the THEATRE GUILD in New York 1926, a horrific symbolic work on the brutality of man in rebellion, caused a sensation.

Kurt Weill and BRECHT's *The Threepenny Opera*, Berlin 1928

After this he turned to historical drama with an increasingly Catholic bias; *Juarez und Maximilian*, 1925; *Paulus unter den Juden* (St Paul among the Jews), 1926; *Das Reich Gottes in Böhmen*, about 15th-century Austrian Hussites whose bestiality destroys the ideals of their leader, 1930; *Der Weg der Verheissung* (The Eternal Road), 1935, produced by REINHARDT in New York 1937, with music by WEILL, a dramatization of biblical accounts of the sufferings of the Jews; *In einer Nacht* (In One Night), 1937. He was married to Alma Mahler, widow of the composer Gustav Mahler. He emigrated to the USA in 1938, where his popular novel, *The Song of Bernadette*, was filmed. His last play was a COMEDY, *Jacobowsky and the Colonel*, adapted by BEHRMAN, New York 1944, fp in German, Basle 1944.
Bibl: L. B. Foltin (ed), 1961

Werich, Jan (1905–), Czech actor. Worked until 1948 in collaboration with VOSKOVEC, then took over the management of the ABC-Theatre in Prague where with Miroslav Hornicek he produced part of the REPERTORY of Voskovec and Werich presented in a new form. Also a well-known film actor and script writer.

Orson Welles in Othello, London 1951

Werner, Oskar (1922–), Austrian actor. As a young man he worked with the Vienna BURGTHEATER, 1941–49, subsequently appearing in Vienna at the VOLKSTHEATER and the Theater in der Josefstadt; 1952–54 he played at the ZURICH SCHAUSPIELHAUS and after 1955 starred in several parts again at the Burgtheater. For some time he had his own company. Recently he has acted mainly in films in France (*Jules et Jim*). On stage he excelled in playing young lovers and sensitive characters, e.g. Clitandre in MOLIÈRE's *Le Misanthrope*, 1946; and title role in *Hamlet*, 1952, 1956; GOETHE's *Torquato Tasso*, 1960; ANOUILH's *Becket*, 1961.

Werner, Zacharias (1768–1823), German dramatist. An exponent of the Romantic movement, his play *Der 24 Februar*, Weimar 1810, introduced *Schicksalstragödie* (tragedy of fate) to Germany. This genre concerns a blind fate wreaking its fury on an insignificant character in contrast to classical TRAGEDY where great individuals pit themselves against anonymous supernatural forces. Other works include: *Martin Luther oder die Weihe der Kraft*, 1807; *Attila, König der Hunnen*, 1808; *Wanda, Königin der Sarmanten*, 1810; *Die Weihe der Urkraft*, 1814.

Arnold Wesker directing his play *Their Very Own and Golden City*, Aarhus, Denmark 1974

Wesker, Arnold (1932–), English playwright, a major exponent of post-war English social drama. Born in the East End of London of Eastern European Jewish parentage, his dramatic works are largely autobiographical. His first play, *The Kitchen*, written 1957, fp 1959, is based on his experience as a confectionery apprentice in a London hotel. *Chips with Everything* was derived from his conscript service in the Royal Air Force, fp ROYAL COURT THEATRE 1962, it was later transferred to the West

End and voted best play of the year. In 1963 it had a successful run on BROADWAY. Several of his other plays first opened at the Belgrade Theatre in Coventry, i.e. *Chicken Soup with Barley*, 1958; *Roots*, 1959; *I'm Talking about Jerusalem*, 1960, and were later transferred to the Royal Court, London, where they were staged as a TRILOGY in 1960. Other works: *Their Very Own and Golden City*, written 1964, which won the Italian Premio Marzotto Drama Award, had its première at the Belgian National Theatre in Brussels and was first performed in London, 1966, at the Royal Court, dir GASKILL; *Four Seasons*, fp Coventry 1965, Belgrade Theatre, transferred to West End; *The Friends*, fp Stockholm 1970, dir author; *The Old Ones*, fp Royal Court, 1972, dir DEXTER; *The Wedding Feast*, fp Stockholm 1974.
In 1962 he founded Centre 42, with headquarters in a converted engine shed in London (Roundhouse), a cultural movement for popularizing the arts, primarily with trade union support and participation, which gained the active co-operation of well-known personalities from all walks of life. It failed, eventually, largely through the indifference of the trade unions and was dissolved in 1970. W.'s *The Nottingham Captain*, fp Centre 42, 1962, was a documentary for which he wrote the LIBRETTO, Wilfred Josephs the classical score and Dave Lee the jazz score.
W. has also written articles and several books including *Love Letters on Blue Paper*, 1974, a collection of short stories and *Say Goodbye, You May Never See Them Again*, 1974, in collaboration with John Allin, a painter.

Wessely, Paula (1908–), Austrian actress. Went on the stage at 16 and immediately attracted attention with her freshness and natural charm. From 1929 she appeared mainly at the Theater in der Josefstadt in Vienna, until 1938 under the management of REINHARDT. Under his direction she played Gretchen in GOETHE's *Faust* at the SALZBURG FESTIVAL and a succession of great classical parts. In the 1930s she also achieved international fame as a film actress. Since 1953 she has been a member of the ensemble of the Vienna BURGTHEATER.
Bibl: H. Jhering, VON JOSEF KAINZ BIS PAULA WESSELY, 1942

West, Mae (1893–), US actress. In 1897 she started appearing in children's parts in a small theatre company in Brooklyn, N.Y.; later she established herself in VAUDEVILLE and made her BROADWAY début in *Folies Bergère*, 1911, subsequently starring in her own successful shows including *Sex*, 1926; *The Drag*, 1926; *Diamond Lil*, 1928; *The Constant Sinner*, 1931, all celebrating the sexually emancipated woman. She became the sex symbol of the American cinema in the 1930s. In the 1940s she returned to the stage in drama and vaudeville. She also wrote her own film scripts in the tradition of stars like Charlie Chaplin and Buster Keaton.

Whitehead, E. A. (1933–), English dramatist. Born in Liverpool, educated in Cambridge; his occupations have included that of milkman, postman, bus-driver, teacher and finally advertising. Winner of the George Devine Award for 1970. Became known in the theatre with his first play *The Foursome*, first performed at the ROYAL COURT, Theatre Upstairs, 1971, in the same year transferred to the Fortune Theatre. Appointed resident dramatist at the Royal Court 1971. His most recent play is *Alpha Beta*, Royal Court, 1972, with FINNEY.

Whiting, John (1917–63), English dramatist. Started his career as an actor; began to write plays in the 1950s (*Saints Day*, 1951) but his first play to be successfully staged was the satirical drama *A Penny for a Song*, 1951, Haymarket Theatre, later revived in a new version by the RSC, followed by *Marching Song*, 1954, and *The Gates of Summer*, 1956. After writing film scripts for some years (e.g. *Talk of the Devil*, 1956; *The Reason Why*, 1958; *Young Cassidy*, 1960), he scored his greatest success with *The Devils*, fp 1961, RSC, dir HALL, an adaptation of Aldous Huxley's *The Devils of Loudun* about a case of mass hysteria in 17th-century France. Other works include: *Conditions of Agreement*, 1946, and *No Why*, one-act play, fp 1964.

Whitworth, Geoffrey (1883–1951), British man of the theatre. Founded the BRITISH DRAMA LEAGUE in 1919 and became its first secretary and later its director and chairman. He retired from active work with the League in 1948. W. was also one of the most active champions of the cause of a British NATIONAL THEATRE and wrote a book *The Theatre of My Heart*, 1930, advocating its cause.

Wieland, Christoph Martin (1733–1813), German critic, essayist, librettist and dramatist. Like LESSING, he was a major author of the German Enlightenment and one of the most controversial personalities of his time. Editor, 1773–1810, of *Die Deutsche Merkur*, the first important literary magazine in Germany. His dramatic works, *Lady Johanna Gray oder der Triumph der Religion* (Lady J.G. or the Triumph of Religion), after ROWE, 1758; *Alceste*, a SINGSPIEL after EURIPIDES, 1773; and translations (ARISTOPHANES' *The Clouds*, 1798, and *The Birds*, 1806; and SHAKESPEARE), 1762–66, were unsuccessful on stage. His reputation rests mainly on his early recognition of Shakespeare and of the young GOETHE and LENZ.
Bibl: J. Hecker, 3/1960

Wieman, Mathias (1902–71), German actor. His career is closely associated with the directors REINHARDT, at the Deutsches-Theater, BERLIN, from 1924, and HILPERT. He played many leading parts both in classical and particularly in modern plays (IONESCO's *Le Roi se meurt*, 1964; Gregory Salomon in A. MILLER's *The Price*, 1968). Also well known as a film actor.

Wiener Volkstheater. Theatres in Viennese suburbs (Kärntnertortheater, Leopoldstädter Theater, Theater in der Josefstadt, Theater an der Wien), which were established at the beginning of the 18th century. Their REPERTORY first consisted of HANSWURST plays starring the folk comedian STRANITZKY (1712 at the Kärntnertortheater) and his successor PREHAUSER. In 1781 MARINELLI took over the management of the Leopoldstädter Theater where great folk comedians like LAROCHE (as 'KASPERL'), Anton Hasenhut and Ignaz Schuster appeared. Marinelli was succeeded by C. F. Hensler as manager for whom the playwrights Gleich, A. Bäuerle and Meisl worked. Marinelli also presented SINGSPIELE by the composer Wenzel Müller. Mozart's *Die Zauberflöte*, 1791, was produced under the direction of SCHIKANEDER at the Theater an der Wien; this great opera is clearly derived from the Viennese SINGSPIEL and *Zauberposse* (▷ZAUBERSTÜCK) of the Viennese folk theatre, and Mozart's *Die Entführung aus dem Serail* also bears the marks of these influences. The fully developed literary form of folk comedy was achieved in the *Zauberpossen* of RAIMUND (under the ACTOR-MANAGER Karl Carl), and in the FARCES of NESTROY (with the comedian SCHOLZ).
Bibl: M. Dietrich, JUPITER IN WIEN, 1967; A. Bauer, 150 JAHRE THEATER AN DER WIEN, 1952; O. Rommel, DIE ALT-WIENER VOLKSKOMÖDIE, 1952; J. Gregor, DAS THEATER IN DER WIENER JOSEFSTADT, 1942; F. Hadamowsky, DAS THEATER IN DER WIENER LEOPOLDSTADT, 1934

Wilbrandt, Adolf von (1837–1911), German dramatist and manager. A journalist by profession, he wrote a number of derivative dramatic works, his TRAGEDIES modelled on SCHILLER and his COMEDIES on FREYTAG. Among his best-known plays are: *Jugendliebe* (Young Love), Vienna 1871, BURGTHEATER; *Gracchus der Volkstribun* (Gracchus, People's Tribune), Munich 1872; *Die Eidgenossen* (The Sworn Comrades), Vienna 1896. As artistic director of the Burgtheater, 1881–88, he concentrated on a classical REPERTOIRE. He was married to the Burgtheater actress, Auguste Baudius.
Bibl: R. Wilbrandt, 1937

Wilde, Oscar (1854–1900), Irish-born English poet, playwright, novelist, critic and aesthete. For his children he wrote *The Happy Prince and Other Tales*, 1888. Two years later appeared his famous novel, *The Picture of Dorian Gray*, later dramatized, and eventually made into a film. His reputation as a dramatist was made with his self-described 'trivial comedies for serious people', with flashing epigrams, farcical PLOTS and sparkling DIALOGUE: *Lady Windermere's Fan*, 1892; *A Woman of No Importance*, 1893; *An Ideal Husband*, 1895, and his masterpiece, *The Importance of Being Earnest*, 1895, one of the most brilliant, and most frequently revived, COMEDIES in the English language. Using the conventional dramatic structure of his time, he transcended it by his sense of style and the brilliant paradox of his wit. His lyric prose drama, *Salomé*, written in French, which epitomizes his attitude to aesthetic decadence, received its

first performance in France with SARAH BERNHARDT in the title role. It was banned in England till 1905 in which year Richard Strauss used the play for the LIBRETTO of his sensuous and melodramatic opera. An unfinished one-act VERSE DRAMA, *A Florentine Tragedy*, written 1893/94, was completed by Sturge Moore and produced 1906. W.'s relationship with the young poet Lord Alfred Douglas brought about his trial for homosexual offences, for which he was convicted and sent to prison for two years. During that time he wrote a philosophical essay, *De Profundis*, and a moving poem, *The Ballad of Reading Gaol*, 1898. He died in self-imposed exile in France.
Bibl: R. Hart-Davies (ed), THE LETTERS OF OSCAR WILDE, 1962; J. E. Agate, OSCAR WILDE AND THE THEATRE, 1962; St. John Ervine, 1961

Oscar Wilde, portrait by A. S. Boyd

Wildenbruch, Ernst von (1845–1909), German dramatist. The son of a Prussian diplomat, his derivative historical dramas supported the new Germany united under the Hohenzollerns, which earned him the praise of Kaiser Wilhelm II; *Die Quitzows*, 1888; *Der neue Herr* (The New Master), 1891, on Wilhelm II and Bismarck; *Heinrich und Heinrichs Geschlecht* (Henry and Henry's Dynasty), 2 parts, 1896; *Die Rabensteiner*, 1907, etc.
Bibl: F. Sengle, DAS DEUTSCHE GESCHICHTSDRAMA, GESCHICHTE EINES LITERARISCHEN MYTHOS, 1952

Wilder, Thornton Niven (1897–1975), US novelist and dramatist. First became famous with his novel *The Bridge of San Luis Rey*, 1927. In his plays he uses anti-naturalistic devices and presents situations which involve humanist cultural and educational ideas in the context of everyday life in America. In 1926, when his first novel *Cabbala* was published, the American Laboratory Theatre in New York produced his play *The Trumpet Shall Sound*. Most of his early works, written between 1915 and 1927, are short dramatic pieces written for UNIVERSITY THEATRES (Oberlin and Yale), published under the title *The Angel That Troubled the Waters and Other Plays*, 1928. In 1931 he published some one-act plays, the most important being *The Long Christmas Dinner*; *The Happy Journey to Trenton and Camden*; *Pullman Car Hiawatha*. In all of them the emphasis was on improvisation: a stage manager appears, addresses the audience directly; the scenery is stripped to bare essentials. His masterpiece, *Our Town*, 1938, uses this style to present a panoramic view of American life. It was followed in 1942 by the controversial *The Skin of Our Teeth*, starring TALLULAH BANKHEAD, produced in London 1945 with VIVIEN LEIGH. He received the PULITZER PRIZE for both these plays. He had great success with *The Matchmaker*, London 1954, dir GUTHRIE, New York 1955, a revised version of his *The Merchant of Yonkers*, 1938, which was an adaptation of NESTROY's Viennese FARCE *Einen Jux will er sich machen*. In 1963 it was adapted as a musical *Hello, Dolly!*. In 1955 his *A Life in the Sun* was presented at the EDINBURGH

Thornton Wilder's *The Skin of Our Teeth*, 1945, with MARCH, Florence Eldridge, and Frances Heflin

Mae West in *Diamond Lil*, 1928

FESTIVAL: an adaptation of EURIPIDES' *Alcestis*, it was technically modelled on Greek TRAGEDY and the SATYR PLAY. In 1961 he began a series of 14 plays, seven on the deadly sins and seven on the ages of man; three of them were staged in New York in 1962 under the title *Plays for Bleecker Street* (*Someone from Assisi, Infancy, Childhood*).
Bibl: M. Goldstein, THE ART OF THORNTON WILDER, 1965

Wildgans, Anton (1881–1932), Austrian dramatist. After studying law, he worked from 1912 as a freelance writer. He was director 1921–23 and 1930–31 of the BURGTHEATER in Vienna. Author of sentimental dramas employing the literary styles and devices of his time (ranging from NATURALISM to EXPRESSIONISM): *In Ewigkeit, Amen!*, FREIE VOLKSBÜHNE, Vienna 1913; *Armut*, Deutsches Volkstheater, Vienna 1915; *Liebe*, 1915; *Dies Irae*, Burgtheater 1919; *Kain*, Rostock 1921.
Bibl: L. Wildgans, 1955

Williams, Clifford (1926–), English director. Came into prominence with his productions of LORCA's *Yerma*, 1957; DÜRRENMATT's *The Marriage of Mr Mississippi*, 1959; O'NEILL's *A Moon for the Misbegotten*, 1960. For the RSC he directed SHAKESPEARE's *The Comedy of Errors*, Stratford and London 1962, and *The Merchant of Venice*, 1965, and MARLOWE's *The Jew of Malta*, London 1965. For the NATIONAL THEATRE he directed the much discussed all-male production of *As You Like It*, 1969.

Williams, (George) Emlyn (1905–), Welsh-born actor, dramatist and director. Made his first appearances as an actor in 1927 in *And So to Bed*, J. B. Fagan, and in O'CASEY's *The Silver Tassie* in 1929. His breakthrough as an actor and author came with *Night Must Fall*, London and New York 1935. His other outstanding roles include: Angelo in *Measure for Measure*, OLD VIC, 1937; Sir Robert Morton in RATTIGAN's *The Winslow Boy*, 1946; The Man in MORTIMER's *Lunch Hour*, 1961; Sir Thomas Moore in the American production of BOLT's *A Man for All Seasons*, 1962. Some of his best performances have been in his own plays: *Spring 1600*, 1934; *He Was Born Gay*, 1937; *The Corn is Green*, 1938; *The Light of Heart*, 1940; *The Morning Star*, 1941; *The Druid's Rest*, 1943; *The Wind of Heaven*, 1945; *Someone Waiting*, 1953; *Beth*, 1958. He had great success as Charles Dickens in a series of readings from the novels in 1951. He has also appeared in many films. In 1961 he published *George*, and in 1973, *Emlyn*.
Bibl: R. Findlater, 1956

Williams, Heathcote (1941–), English playwright. Started his writing career with a book on the orators of Hyde Park *The Speakers*, 1964. His first play *The Local Stigmatic*, 1967, caused a stir through the rawness of its language and the harshness of its treatment of an incident of teenage violence. His most notable play hitherto *AC/DC* – an exploration of the world and language of the media and the drug culture – achieved considerable success when it was produced at the ROYAL COURT THEATRE, London 1970.

Williams, Tennessee (1911–), US playwright. One of the most important playwrights to emerge in the USA since World War II, and with A. MILLER the principal representative of psychological realism in the US theatre; in his plays he attempts to present dramatic parables on stage both to amuse and shock the audience. With his mastery of the subtleties of speech and gesture, he has created some of the most powerful and entertaining characters in American drama. He began by writing one-act plays, some of which were produced by university and summer-theatre groups. The first was a FARCE, *Cairo! Shanghai! Bombay!*, 1935. The most successful were *Candles to the Sun*, 1936, dealing with suffering coal-miners, and *The Fugitive Kind*, 1937, about St Louis's Skid Row. In 1939 he received a citation from the GROUP THEATRE for a set of three one-act plays, under the title *American Blues*, and then was awarded a scholarship for a playwriting seminar given by GASSNER who persuaded the THEATRE GUILD to produce W.'s first full-length play *Battle of Angels*, 1940 (it did not, however, reach BROADWAY); later it was rewritten as *Orpheus Descending*, 1956, which was made into a film with Marlon Brando (the film was given the title of his earlier play, *The Fugitive Kind*). W. made his name with *The Glass Menagerie*, 1945, a semi-autobiographical play, and his reputation was firmly established with *A Streetcar Named Desire*, 1947, for which he was awarded a PULITZER PRIZE; he received another for *Cat on a Hot Tin Roof*, 1955. Other important plays are *Summer and Smoke*, 1947; *The Rose Tattoo*, 1950; *Camino Real*, 1953; *Suddenly Last Summer*, 1958; *Sweet Bird of Youth*, 1959, and *The Night of the Iguana*, 1961. *The Milk Train Doesn't Stop Here Anymore*, first presented as a one-acter at the Spoleto Festival, 1963, and later on BROADWAY.
Bibl: E. M. Jackson, THE BROKEN WORLD OF TENNESSEE WILLIAMS, 1966

Wilson, Georges (1921–), French actor, director and manager. After several years in the provinces as an actor, from 1951 he worked in Paris, engaged in 1952 by VILAR at the Théâtre National Populaire, where he appeared in almost all productions, and at the AVIGNON FESTIVAL which was linked with the TNP: Père Timothée in VAUTHIER's *La Nouvelle Mandragore*, Sganarelle in MOLIÈRE's *Le Médecin malgré lui*; Polyclète in CORNEILLE's *Cinna*; Macduff in *Macbeth*; title roles in BÜCHNER's *Danton's Death*, and in JARRY's *Ubu Roi*; Arnolphe in Molière's *Les Femmes savantes*, 1958; title role in BRECHT's *Galileo*, 1963, which he also directed. In 1963 he succeeded Vilar as director of the TNP, producing and acting in DÜRRENMATT's *Romulus the Great*, 1964; title role, OSBORNE's *Luther*, 1964; Puntila in Brecht's *Mr Puntila and His Servant, Matti*, 1964; Claudius in *Hamlet*, 1965.

Wilson, Robert (*c.* 1550–*c.* 1605), Elizabethan actor and playwright. With Leicester's company in 1572, joined the QUEEN'S MEN in 1583. He was praised for his wit and learning and is probably the author of the play *Three Ladies of London*, published in 1584 by 'R.W.'. It deals with a generous Jewish money-lender, and may have been intended as a reply to a lost play *The Jew* which is believed by some to have been the source of *The Merchant of Venice*.

Wilson, Sandy (1924–), English composer, librettist of musical plays and lyricist. First achieved success with *The Boy Friend*, 1953, a satirical pastiche of a 1920s MUSICAL, for which he wrote LIBRETTO and music. Originally written for the Players' Theatre (▷USTINOV), it ran for five years in London's West End and was filmed in 1973 by Ken Russell. Another successful musical play he wrote and composed was *Valmouth* (based on Ronald Firbank's novel), 1958.

Wimmer, Maria (1910–), German actress. Trained in Leipzig and first appeared on stage in Stettin, 1930–33. Subsequently she played a wide range of parts in leading German repertory companies including those at Frankfurt, Hamburg (Deutsches Schauspielhaus), Munich (Residenztheater and Kammerspiele, with the director KORTNER), and at Düsseldorf. She established herself as one of Germany's leading actresses specializing in classical tragic roles including the heroines of SCHILLER, GOETHE, HEBBEL, KLEIST and STRINDBERG, and in modern classics by O'NEILL, T. WILLIAMS and CLAUDEL, among others.

Wing. Before the coming of three-dimensional wholly enclosed sets, the sides of the stage were masked by a series of flats (painted canvas-covered wooden frames) which, while allowing actors to pass through them, gave the illusion of a continuous side wall in perspective. For interior sets wings have largely been superseded today, but they still appear in exterior sets (as trees etc.) or in PANTOMIME (to allow quick transformation scenes). To watch a performance 'from the wings' still means to watch from behind the scene on the stage. ▷ALEOTTI.

Winterstein, Eduard von (1871–1961), Austrian actor. From 1898 worked with BRAHM at the Deutsches-Theater, BERLIN, and subsequently was at the Lessingtheater for two years; from 1903 he was with REINHARDT's ensemble. He appeared at the Berlin Schillertheater 1938–44 and in 1945 left to work again at the Deutsches-Theater, East Berlin. He played many classical roles, particularly young leading men; e.g. Ferdinand in SCHILLER's *Kabale und Liebe*, 1904, and Tellheim in LESSING's *Minna von Barnhelm*, 1904; later heavy character parts, e.g. Kent in *King Lear*, 1908, and the title role in HAUPTMANN's *Fuhrmann Henschel*, 1916, and Lessing's *Nathan der Weise*, 1945, 1955. He also wrote a volume of reminiscences entitled *Mein Leben und meine Zeit*, 2 vols, 1942 and 1947.
Bibl: H. Jhering & F. Wisten, 1961

Peg Woffington as Mrs Ford in *The Merry Wives of Windsor*, 1751

Witkiewicz, Stanislaw Ignacy (1885–1939), Polish philosopher, painter, novelist and playwright. He created his own theory of aesthetics based on 'pure form' which he published in a series of articles from 1918–22 in the magazine *Teatr*. The most original man of letters in Poland between the wars and one of the forerunners of contemporary European literature and drama. His plays have since been produced in France, Germany, and Scandinavia, and translated into French, German and English. He participated in the Russian Revolution as a 'white' officer and 'red' political commissar; he shot himself the day after the Red Army entered Poland's Eastern territories. He wrote about 30 grotesque dramas (▷ THEATRE OF THE GROTESQUE), anti-realistic in style, with an overwhelming emphasis on cruelty and the absurd, revealing the agony and decay of the first quarter of the 20th century. (He was a catastrophist – forerunner of EXISTENTIALISM). His main works: *Tumor Mózgowicz*, 1921; *Kurka Wodna* (*The Water Hen*), 1922; *Pragmatisci* (The Pragmatics), Warsaw 1921; *Nadobnisie i Koczkodany* (*The Madman and the Nun*), written 1922, fp Vienna 1962; *Sonata Metafizyka Dwoglowego cielecia* (The Metaphysics of a Calf with Two heads), Posen 1928; *Matwa* (The Cuttle-fish), Craców 1933; *Szewcy* (The Shoemakers), written 1934, etc.
Bibl: J. Kott, THEATRE NOTEBOOK 1947–67, 1968

Emlyn Williams in his own play, *The Wind of Heaven*, 1945, with DIANA WYNYARD

Wodehouse, P. G. (Sir Pelham Grenville W.; 1881–1975), English writer who lived for many years in the USA. He was the creator of the famous comic character Jeeves. Apart from his vast output of comic stories and novels, W. was a prolific practitioner of the theatre. He collaborated on many COMEDIES and musicals, and adapted a number of foreign plays, notably some of the comedies of the Hungarian playwright MOLNÁR. Among his most notable successes are: (with Ian Hay) *A Damsel in Distress*, 1928, *Baa Baa Black Sheep*, 1929 and *Leave it to Psmith*, 1930; (with Guy Bolton) *Who's Who*, 1934 and *Anything Goes*, 1934, music and lyrics by PORTER, 1934, which was later revised by LINDSAY and CROUSE. Knighted shortly before his death.

Tennessee Williams's *A Streetcar Named Desire*, New York 1947, with Marlon Brando and Jessica Tandy

Woffington, Peg (*c.* 1714–60), Irish-born English actress. At the age of ten acted in children's companies in Dublin and then worked at the Smock Alley theatre, where she appeared as Mrs Peachum, Ophelia and the boy's part Sir Harry Wildair in FARQUHAR's *The Constant Couple*, 1740, in which she was seen by John Rich who engaged her for COVENT GARDEN. She made her début as Sylvia in Farquhar's *The Recruiting Officer* in 1740 and in the same year revived her performance as Sir Harry Wildair. She toured in Ireland 1742–47 with GARRICK, whose mistress she was for some time, and appeared at DRURY LANE Theatre in such Shakespearean parts as Cordelia, Rosalind and Portia, and Belvidera in OTWAY's *Venice Preserved*. After 1748, with short interruptions, she was again at

Covent Garden. One of the most celebrated actresses of her day, she was a woman of great beauty and wit, spirit and elegance, excelling as great ladies, e.g. Millamant, Lady Townly, Lady Betty Modish.
Bibl: J. C. Lucey, 1952

Wolf, Friedrich (1888–1953), German dramatist. A Communist, he was the author of a number of plays on historical and contemporary subjects in the style of SOCIALIST REALISM: *Das bist du* (That You Are), Dresden 1919; *Tamar*, Frankfurt 1922; *Kolonne Hund*, Hamburg 1927; *Cyankali*, Berlin 1929, against the abortion law; *Die Matrosen von Cattaro* (The Sailors of C.), Berlin 1930; *Professor Mamlock*, Zurich 1934, against the anti-semitism of the Nazis, achieved international success; *Beaumarchais*, 1946; *Thomas Münzer*, Berlin 1953; *Das Schiff auf der Donau* (The Ship on the Danube), Berlin 1955, etc. He spent the years of the Hitler regime in the USSR and played an important part in East Germany after the war.

Wolfe, Thomas (1900–38), US novelist and author of several plays, including *The Return of Buck Gavin*, 1924; *Welcome to Our City*, pub 1923; *Mannerhouse*, 1948, published posthumously; *Look Homeward Angel*, adapted from his novel of that title by Ketti Frings, won the PULITZER PRIZE in 1957.

Wolfit, Sir Donald (1902–68), English man of the theatre, knighted in 1957. The last of the great ACTOR-MANAGERS, he made his first appearance in York and in London in 1924 as Phirous in *The Wandering Jew*. He was at the OLD VIC 1929–30 and at STRATFORD-UPON-AVON 1936–37, appearing in many Shakespearean roles – Cassio in *Othello*, Claudius in *Hamlet* (he played the lead in 1933), and King Lear in 1936, probably his major achievement. In 1937 he formed his own company with a largely Shakespearean REPERTORY; he appeared in the main role himself in most productions: *Hamlet*; *Macbeth*; *Othello*; *Oedipus Rex*; *Volpone*; ROSTAND's *Cyrano de Bergerac*; *King Lear*, 1943, 1947; in 1951 at the Old Vic the title role in MARLOWE's *Tamburlaine the Great*. His performances in IBSEN's plays were also much praised: Manders in *Ghosts*, 1959; *John Gabriel Borkman*, 1963. He published an autobiography *First Interval* in 1955.
Bibl: R. Harwood, 1971

Wolter, Charlotte (1834–97), German actress. Began her career in ballet, then trained as an actress in Vienna. After several appearances in Brünn, BERLIN and Hamburg, she joined the Vienna BURGTHEATER in 1861, where she established herself as an outstanding tragedienne, appearing in the lead in classical plays (GOETHE's *Iphigenie*, SHAKESPEARE's *Macbeth*), and in French vaudeville plays (SCRIBE's *Adrienne Lecouvreur*). She scored a triumphant success as Messalina in WILBRANDT's *Arria und Messalina*, which was written for her. The Viennese critics at first disapproved of her 'naturalistic' acting, but her uninhibited style was soon recognized as a necessary break from the inflexible tradition of the Burgtheater, particularly her sensuality and her famous stage screams, known as '*Woltersschrei*'. Her COSTUMES, which were often designed by her husband, the Irish Count O'Sullivan, added to her stage presence.
Bibl: J. Bab, KRÄNZE DEM MIMEN, 1954

Women's parts (in European theatre). Greek TRAGEDY and COMEDY excluded women from the stage. Only in Roman MIME did women appear on stage, at first mainly as strip dancers (the actresses were prostitutes). With the end of classical antiquity, the growing influence of the church and the emergence of religious plays, women were again prohibited from appearing on stage (occasional exceptions: in 1333 it is recorded that in Toulon a young girl appeared as the Virgin Mary in a religious play at Christmas; the same happened in Metz in 1468). Women as professional actresses first appeared in medieval secular plays in Spain and in the Italian COMMEDIA DELL'ARTE. In the JESUIT THEATRE, in MORALITY PLAYS and the ELIZABETHAN THEATRE, women's parts were played by men or boys. From about the middle of the 17th century professional actresses were finally accepted. Among the earliest outstanding figures were: in the BAROQUE THEATRE in the Netherlands after 1655, Adriana Noozeman; in England after 1666, NELL GWYNN, in Germany, beginning 18th century, CAROLINE NEUBER; in France Marie Ferée.

Wood, Charles (1932–), English dramatist. The army recurs as a central theme in almost everything he has written. His first two plays were *Traitor in a Tin Helmet* and *Prisoner and Escort* (both written for TV, the first broadcast 1961); the second was presented on stage as a part of a triple bill *Cockade* in 1963, with *Spare* and *St Thomas*. In contrast to the straight NATURALISM of his earlier works stand his two major plays *Dingo* and *H*, vast spectacles which employ many theatrical devices. In these two plays he gives a comprehensive picture of war. *Dingo*, Bristol 1967, and ROYAL COURT THEATRE the same year, dir Reeves, is a savage anti-militarist cartoon which sets out to deflate heroic myth and to expose the devices by which war-time Britain insulated itself from the facts of death. *H*, 1968, NATIONAL THEATRE, is a historical PAGEANT. A non-military play *Fill the Stage With Happy Hours*, 1966, Nottingham Playhouse, is based on his experiences in the theatre. He has also written a triple bill *Welfare*, Liverpool 1970, comprising *Tie Up the Ballcock*, *Meals on Wheels*, and the one-acter *Labour*; and *Veterans*, 1972, Royal Court, with GIELGUD. He has written many film scripts, e.g. the Beatles' film, *Help*; English dialogue for Fellini's *Satyricon*; Skolimovski's *Adventures of Gerard*; and John Schlesinger's *Hadrian VII*; Richard Lester's *How I Won the War* and RICHARDSON's *Charge of the Light Brigade*. For TV: *The Drill Pig*, 1964; *A Bit of a Holiday*, 1969, and its sequel *A Bit of Family Feeling*, 1971.

Woollcott, Alexander (1887–1943). US journalist and drama critic. Best remembered for his witty essays (*Shouts and Murmurs*, 1922; *While Rome Burns*, 1934, etc.), he was the prototype of Sheridan Whiteside in *The Man Who Came to Dinner*, 1939, by KAUFMAN and M. HART. He was more interested in players than plays, often misjudging important plays of his time, including those of O'NEILL. He collaborated with Kaufman on two plays, *The Channel Road*, 1929, and *The Dark Tower*, 1932, and appeared on stage in three plays, including acting with the touring company in *The Man Who Came to Dinner*.
Bibl: Edwin P. Hoyt, ALEXANDER WOOLLCOTT: THE MAN WHO CAME TO DINNER, 1968

World Theatre Season. ▷DAUBENY.

Worth, Irene (1916–), US actress. Made her first noteworthy appearance in London as Ilona in Molnár's *The Play's the Thing*, 1947, and in 1949 in Edinburgh as Celia in ELIOT's *The Cocktail Party*. She worked with the OLD VIC company, giving two memorable performances as Desdemona in *Othello*, 1951–52, and Portia in *The Merchant of Venice*, 1953. She is one of the leading actresses in England and the USA, mainly in parts characterized by strong personality and passion. Important successes include the title role in SCHILLER's *Maria Stuart*, 1958, Mathilde von Zahnd in DÜRRENMATT's *The Physicists*, London 1963, and the lead in *Tiny Alice*, New York 1963, by ALBEE with GIELGUD; Jocasta in BROOK's production of SENECA's *Oedipus*, RSC 1965. She has also appeared in many films and TV plays.

Wotruba, Fritz (1907–), Austrian sculptor. From his piled-up landscape-like sculptures he derived his décors for SELLNER's large-scale classical productions, e.g. a series of SOPHOCLES' plays at the Vienna BURGTHEATER: *Oedipus Rex*, 1960; *Antigone*, 1961; *Electra*, 1963, and Wagner's cycle *Der Ring des Nibelungen*, Deutsche Oper, Berlin 1967.
Bibl: H. Rischbieter (ed), BÜHNE AND BILDENDE KUNST IM 20. JAHRHUNDERT

Wouk, Herman (1915–), US novelist. Gained international fame with his novel *The Caine Mutiny*, 1929, which he adapted for the stage under the title *The Caine Mutiny Court Martial*, 1954; later filmed. Other dramatic works include: *The Traitor*, 1949; *Nature's Way*, 1957.

Wuolijoki, Hella (1886–1954), Finnish playwright. Wrote several successful dramas in which she recorded the life of Finnish farmers; her work *Iso-Heikkilän isäntä ja hänen renkinsa Kallel* was used by BRECHT, who stayed with her in 1940, as the basis for his play *Herr Puntila und sein Knecht Matti*, 1940–41.

Wycherley, William (1640–1716), English playwright (▷RESTORATION DRAMA). One of the major exponents of the Comedy of Manners (▷COMEDY). Though CONGREVE

far surpasses him in beauty of style and technical smoothness, W. is unrivalled by any other Restoration dramatist in the satirical power, savage wit and sheer theatrical effectiveness with which he mirrors the social conditions and especially the sexual morality of his age. Of his four comedies the best are *The Country Wife*, 1675, adapted in 1766 by GARRICK as *The Country Girl*, and *The Plain Dealer*, 1676; both have been frequently revived and are still in the REPERTOIRE. His other plays, written earlier, are *Love in a Wood; or, St James's Park*, 1671; *The Gentleman Dancing-Master*, 1672.
Bibl: R. A. Zimbardo, WYCHERLEY'S DRAMA: A LINK IN THE DEVELOPMENT OF ENGLISH DRAMA, 1965

Wynyard, Diana (1906–64), English actress. Made her London début in 1925. Her great beauty and sensitive portrayal of passion made her of one of the most popular leading ladies of her day. She appeared in many West End COMEDIES, but also in plays by SHAW (*Candida*, 1937) and SHAKESPEARE (Stratford-upon-Avon 1948–49; as Beatrice opposite GIELGUD in *Much Ado About Nothing*, London 1952).

Wyspiański, Stanislaw (1869–1907), Polish dramatist, designer and painter. Continued the great Polish romantic tradition of MICKIEWICZ and SLOWACKI. His plays were based on national themes, representative of the symbolic and neo-romantic trend based on the ideas of Wagner and Nietzsche. The themes were taken from classical antiquity, the Bible and contemporary life. His work inspired L. SCHILLER (founder of the modern style of direction in Poland) in his monumental productions, in which he realized the greatest variety of spiritual meaning and expression in a synthesis of verbal and visual images. He often designed the sets for his plays. *Wesele* (*The Wedding*), 1900, a drama of waiting, disillusionment, immaturity and total inertia, is regarded as his finest work; in it the characters are waiting for the morning of the Polish uprising. It is probably the single most original Polish play. Other works: *Warszawianka* (The Warsovienne), written 1898, and *Protesilas i Laodamia*, written 1899, both fp 1903 with MODJESKA; *Meleager*, fp 1908; *Klatwa* (The Curse), fp 1909, *Sedziowie* (The Judge), fp 1911; *Legion*, fp 1911; *Noc listopadowa* (November Night), fp 1908, *Akropolis*, fp 1916, adaptation by GROTOWSKI 1962. W. also translated and adapted SHAKESPEARE's *Hamlet*, 1905, and CORNEILLE's *Le Cid*, 1907, both of which he directed and designed.
Bibl: T. Backvis, 1952

Xirgu, Margarita (1888–1969), Spanish actress. Began her career with amateur companies. In 1910 she joined the Teatro Principal, Barcelona; after 1914 worked in Madrid. In 1936 toured Cuba and Mexico, and for political reasons remained in Latin America after the outbreak of the Civil War. Thereafter she was working as an actress, director and teacher. Her outstanding roles have been particularly in plays by Spanish writers, including LOPE DE VEGA, UNAMUNO, VALLE-INCLÁN, and LORCA, but she also appeared in a wide range of plays, such as SHAW's *Saint Joan*, Seneca's *Medea*, and works by PIRANDELLO.

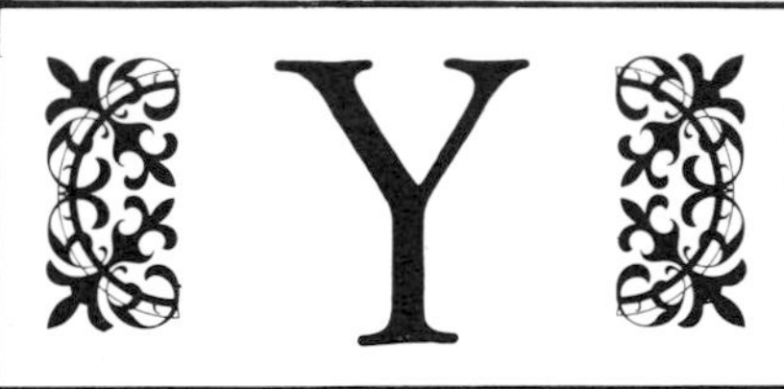

Yablochinka, Alexandra Alexandrovna (1868–1964), Russian actress. Made her début in 1888 at the Maly Theatre in Moscow, where she remained until her death, playing a great range of roles including Ophelia, Cordelia, Desdemona; leading parts in plays by WILDE and GALSWORTHY, and in Russian plays by, e.g. GRIBOYEDOV, GORKY, Romashov, and KORNEICHUK.

Yakulov, Georgi Bogdanovich (1884–1928), Russian painter and stage designer. Combined fantastic and grotesque elements in his work, most of which was done in collaboration with TAIROV at the Moscow Kamerny Theatre: CLAUDEL's *L'Echange*, 1918; *Princess Brambilla*, based on E. T. A. Hoffmann's story; *Giroflé-Girofla*, MIME drama by Lecoq. He also designed for the Ballets Russes in Monte Carlo and for the HABIMAH theatre, e.g. SOPHOCLES' *Oedipus Rex*.

Yeats, William Butler (1865–1939), Irish poet and playwright. Innovator and leading figure of the Irish Dramatic Movement, who with LADY GREGORY founded the ABBEY THEATRE, which opened in Dublin in 1904. His dramatic work consists mainly of poetic plays of great beauty, unexcelled in his time. He greatly influenced other Irish dramatists like SYNGE and O'CASEY. In his later *Plays for Dancers* he made use of the style of the Japanese *Noh* play (▷ JAPAN), but took his basic themes from Irish myth and legend. For the Abbey Theatre he also translated the two OEDIPUS

Donald Wolfit in MARLOWE's *Tamburlaine the Great*, 1951

W. B. Yeats, portrait by Augustus John

Irene Worth as Jocasta in SENECA's *Oedipus*, RSC 1965

tragedies of SOPHOCLES. Principal plays: *The Countess Cathleen*, 1892; *The Land of Heart's Desire*, 1894; *Cathleen ni Houlihan*, 1902; *The Pot of Broth*, 1902; *The Hour-Glass*, 1903; *The King's Threshold*, 1904; *The Shadowy Waters*, 1900; *On Baile's Strand*, 1904; *Deirdre*, 1907; *The Unicorn from the Stars*, 1908; *Four Plays for Dancers*, 1921; *The Player Queen*, 1922; *The Cat and the Moon*, 1924; *Fighting the Waves*, 1929; *Purgatory*, 1929; *The Words upon the Window-pane*, 1934; *The Death of Cuchulain*, 1939. All years are those of publication, except *Purgatory* which is fp and *Death of Cuchulain*, which is probably fp also as Yeats died on 28 January 1939. He received the Nobel Prize for Literature in 1923.
Bibl: H. Vendler, Y.'S VISION AND THE LATER PLAYS, 1963; P. Ure, Y. THE PLAYWRIGHT, 1963; R. Ellman, Y., THE MAN AND THE MASKS, 1949; Joseph Hone, W.B.Y. 1865–1939, 2/1963; U. M. Ellis-Fermor, THE IRISH DRAMATIC MOVEMENT, 1939; Lady Gregory, OUR IRISH THEATRE, 1931

Yefremov, Oleg Nikolayevich (1927–), Russian director. Trained under NEMIROVICH-DANCHENKO; worked as an actor at the Moscow Children's Theatre; début as director 1955. Founded the Studio of Young Actors in 1957, which he renamed the Contemporary Theatre in 1958. He is endeavouring, in his productions of anti-dogmatic Soviet plays about contemporary subjects, to develop a style, realistic yet imaginative, in the tradition of VAKHTANGOV.

Yefros, Anatoly Vassilyevich (1925–), Russian director. Trained at the Moscow Theatre Academy; since 1951 has worked as a director with a number of the leading theatres in the Soviet Union and directed plays by ROZOV, KATAYEV, GOGOL, and others. At the Film Actors' Studio he directed a notable production of IBSEN's *Hedda Gabler*, 1957; at the Yermolov Theatre BRECHT's *Visions of Simone Machard*, 1959; and at the Contemporary Theatre DE FILIPPO's *Nobody*, 1962. In 1964 he became a staff director at the Moscow Komsomol Theatre, and he is a professor at the Theatre Academy. He prefers plays which deal with the everyday life of contemporary people. Has also worked with CHILDREN'S THEATRES and as a film director.

Yegorov, Vladimir Yevgenevich (1878– ?), Russian stage designer. At the MOSCOW ART THEATRE 1905–13, where, in collaboration with STANISLAVSKY and NEMIROVICH-DANCHENKO, he designed specifically functional sets adapting symbolist elements to the psychological realism of the productions. His Art Nouveau décor for MAETERLINCK's *Bluebird*, 1908, dir Stanislavsky, became famous when the MAT toured Europe. His other works include: ANDREYEV's *The Life of Man*, 1907, dir Stanislavsky; IBSEN's *Rosmersholm*, 1907, dir Nemirovich-Danchenko. After 1916 he worked mainly as a designer in films.

Yermolova, Maria Nikolayevna (1853–1928), Russian actress. A great tragedienne who excelled in accurate observation and realistic acting; anticipated STANISLAVSKY's 'Method' style of acting in many of its features and was greatly admired by him. Made her first impact in the title role of LESSING's *Emilia Galotti*, 1870; was also a great Judith in GUTZKOW's *Uriel Acosta*, 1879; Mary Stuart in SCHILLER's TRAGEDY, 1886; Klärchen in GOETHE's *Egmont*, 1888; Phèdre in RACINE's play, 1890. Her greatest role, however, was the lead in Schiller's *Maid of Orleans*, 1884. In 1930 one of the studios of the Moscow Maly Theatre was renamed after her.

Yevreinov, Nikolai Nikolayevich (1879–1953), Russian dramatist and director. Managed the Old Theatre in St Petersburg 1907–08 and 1911–12. Between 1908 and 1909 at the Dramatic Theatre he produced among others D'ANNUNZIO's *Francesca da Rimini* and WILDE's *Salomé*; until 1917 he worked at several small theatres as a producer, also performing his own MONODRAMAS. After the Revolution he started to direct large mass spectacles, e.g. *The Storming of the Winter Palace* with about 8,000 extras. In 1925 he emigrated to France. He was one of the great Russian theatre reformers at the beginning of the century; his wide range as a producer included plays from the Middle Ages, e.g. Rutebeuf's *Le Miracle de Théophile*. His dramatic work was Symbolist in style, exemplified in *The Theatre of the Soul*, 1912, and his best work *The Chief Thing*, 1921. He expounded his theories in a controversial book *The Theatre For Oneself*; his theoretical works align him with the view of MEYERHOLD and TAIROV.

Yiddish theatre. Plays in Yiddish or Hebrew have existed since the Middle Ages. In the 19th century in Eastern Europe travelling popular singers combined their songs with DIALOGUE in Yiddish and thus created one-act plays. In 1876 the first Jewish Theatre was founded in Jassy by the actor, director, and playwright, Abraham Goldfaden (1840–1908), who wrote and acted in *The Witch*, 1879; *Shulamith*, 1880. The anti-Jewish feeling after the murder of Alexander II led to the prohibition in 1883 of all productions in Yiddish in Russia and the existence of the Yiddish theatre was threatened until the Revolution in 1917. Many artists emigrated to New York, including Goldfaden in 1887. Israel Gradner, an actor under the latter, founded a Jewish Theatre in New York. The Yiddish theatre there was at first concerned with the European situation until Jacob Gordin (1853–1909) revitalized the theatre with his own plays, e.g. *The Jewish Lear*, 1892; *God, Man and Devil*, 1900. The playwrights Salomon Libin (*Broken Hearts*, 1903) and Leo Kobrin followed Gordin in his attempt to deal with the social problems of Jewish families in New York. The Jewish artistic theatre in Odessa, founded by the playwright Perez Hirschbein, was active 1908–10, influenced by STANISLAVSKY and by SYMBOLISM. Later the Vilna Company continued this tradition from 1916. Some members of this company went to New York, where they joined the director Maurice Schwartz and produced mainly works by SHOLEM ALEICHEM and Ossip Levich (Golem). The most important Yiddish theatre which took part in the Soviet AGIT-PROP was the Moscow Jewish State Theatre, managed until 1927 by GRANOVSKY, whose REPERTOIRE was also based on the works of S. Aleichem. Like all the other Yiddish theatres in Soviet Russia, it was closed in 1948. The HABIMAH THEATRE, founded in 1917 in Moscow, from its inception performed plays in Hebrew rather than Yiddish, in accordance with Zionist aims, and moved to Palestine in 1928. For the Jewish Art Theatre in Warsaw ▷IDA KAMINSKA, PERETZ.
Bibl: A. Madison, YIDDISH LITERATURE: ITS SCOPE AND MAJOR WRITERS, 1968

Youmans, Vincent (1898–1946), US composer and songwriter. He wrote songs typical of the 1920s for such musicals as *Two Little Girls*, 1921; *Wildflower*, 1924; *No, No, Nanette*, 1925; *Hit The Deck*, 1927, and *Smiles* (with FRED and ADELE ASTAIRE), 1930.

Young, Stark (1881–1963), US drama critic. On the staff of the *New Republic*, 1921–47, and 1924–25 also critic of the *New York Times*. He supported many of the 'imaginatively theatrical' Latin writers including MOLIÈRE, LORCA and D'ANNUNZIO against the 'teutonic' realists like IBSEN, STRINDBERG and their followers. He was a well-educated and well-read man, whose collected critical writings were published in six volumes. He translated works by CHEKHOV and several from Spanish and Italian. He also wrote many plays. Criticism: *Immortal Shadows*, 1948; *The Flower in Drama and Glamour*, 1955. Dramatic works (with dates of publication): *Guenevere*, 1906; *The Saint*, 1925; a collection of plays and theoretical essays was published under the title *The Pavilion*, 1951.

Yugoslavia. Before the formation of the South Slav state in 1918 the country was split into a multitude of political and cultural units. In the 16th century the Serbo-Croat language was used in Dalmatia (which was under Venetian rule) by the Renaissance dramatists of Dubrovnik (Ragusa), who modelled themselves on Italian comedy writers of the period. Most notable among these was Marin Držić. In the 17th and 18th centuries Slovenia and Croatia (under Austrian rule) were largely dependent on the visits of German-speaking strolling players. Into the first half of the 19th century German-speaking actors dominated in the parts under Austrian rule. 1839–41 there was a Serbian strolling company in Zagreb, the capital of Croatia. In 1860 the German actors left Zagreb and a Croat National Theatre was founded. In Serbia the first permanent theatre was established at Belgrade in 1842. In 1869 a Serbian National Theatre was established there which performed plays by Serbian authors (K. Trivković, J. Subotić, M. Ban) as well as European classics, and soon afterwards IBSEN. After 1890 the Serbian theatre took its guidelines from Russia and France. 1911 the Russian director A. V. Andreyev came to Belgrade. The leading playwright of the period was NUŠIĆ (1864–1938). After 1945 vigorous state support for drama in all the national republics of Yugoslavia. Festivals were established in Dubrovnik, Split, Novi Sad.

Yurski, Sergey Yurevich (1935–), Russian actor. Since 1961 with the Gorky Theatre at Leningrad. A tranquil character actor, he has also appeared in MIME and in films.

Peter Zadek's *Little Man, What Now?*, Bochum 1972

Zacconi, Ermete (1857–1948), Italian actor. Son of strolling players, in 1884 he became the leading man in the Giovanni Emanuel company and was soon considered Italy's outstanding actor. In 1894 he founded his own company and successfully produced young contemporary dramatists, e.g. he introduced IBSEN's *Ghosts* to Italy (playing Oswald himself) and plays by HAUPTMANN, GIACOSA, MAETERLINCK. In 1899 he went on tour with DUSE with D'ANNUNZIO's *La Gioconda* and *La Gloria* to Russia, Austria and Germany. He reached the peak of his career in 1900 with memorable performances as Hamlet and Othello; and in the title role of Hauptmann's *Fuhrmann Henschel* and MUSSET's *Lorenzaccio*. His style was naturalistic, and he created a character through precise psychological detail.
Bibl: G. Pardieri, 1960

Zadek, Peter (1926–), German director. In 1933 he emigrated to England. Directed in London 1949–59: WILDE's *Salomé*; ELIOT's *Sweeney Agonistes*; GENET's *The Maids* and *The Balcony*; also TV films and radio plays. Back in Germany he directed as a guest VAUTHIER's *Capitaine Bada*, Cologne 1960, and DORST's *Grosse Schmährede an der Stadtmauer*, Berlin 1962, Schiller Theater. Later started a fruitful collaboration with the designer MINKS and the INTENDANT Kurt Hübner, first in Ulm and later in Bremen, where his productions included: *Held Henry* (adaptation of SHAKESPEARE's *Henry V*); BEHAN's *The Hostage*, 1962, and *The Quare Fellow*, 1964; ANN JELLICOE's *The Knack*, 1964; WEDEKIND's *Frühlings Erwachen*, 1965; T. Valentin's *Die Unberatenen*, 1965; SCHILLER's *Die Räuber*, 1967, in comic-strip costumes; Shakespeare's *Measure for Measure*, 1967; O'CASEY's *The Silver Tassie*, 1967; *Kleiner Mann, Was Nun?* (*Little Man, What Now?*), based on Hans Fallada's novel, Bochum 1972, and WORLD THEATRE SEASON, London 1973, Aldwych. His extravagant imagination, abetted by the stage designs of Minks, leads sometimes to a mere accumulation of clever ideas; at his best his solutions are convincing in their aesthetic radicalism, e.g. Shakespeare's *Measure for Measure*.

Zanni from the COMMEDIA DELL'ARTE, with PANTALONE on the left

Zanni. The two male servants of the COMMEDIA DELL'ARTE; the name is used as both singular and plural (▷SERVETTA). The origins of the characters are obscure but are possibly to be found in the *sanniones* of the ATELLAN FARCE or simply in the Christian names Gian, Zuan or Zan. The Z. are servants from Bergamo speaking mainly in dialect. From early times the character of Z. was divided into two roles: the first Z.'s task was to instigate the action of the COMEDY with intrigues and ideas, while the second Z. interrupted the action with comic gags, e.g. LAZZI. The first Z. was the wily, superior villain, the second an incompetent clown, though sometimes shrewd. The first Z. was usually a city servant, who wore a light jacket from which developed a stylized livery; the second was mostly a farm labourer with a patched ragged outfit, which later became a coloured patchwork costume. The first Z. was usually known as BRIGHELLA (also

Buffeto, Flautino, Coviello). The second soon became more important than the first Z. and was the prototype for other characters who have since changed greatly in function and appearance: ARLECCHINO, TRUFFALDINO, MEZZETTINO, FRITELLINO, Pasquino, Tabarino, Tortellino, Trappolino (▷FIORILLO), Trivellino, Bagolino.
Bibl: ▷COMMEDIA DELL'ARTE

Zapolska, Gabriela (G. Piotrowska; 1860–1921), Polish dramatist and actress. She began her career in 1881, appeared in Paris in 1889 and 1892–95 at the THÉÂTRE LIBRE, subsequently in Warsaw, Lemberg and Craców. Author of about 40 plays, still in the Polish theatre REPERTOIRE, which are critical portrayals of social realities according to the naturalist definition (illness, prostitution, discrimination against women). She became known in Europe with her drama *Moralnošč pani Dulskiej* (The Moral of Mrs Dulska), 1906. The MELODRAMA *Zarewitsch*, 1917, served as LIBRETTO for the operetta *The Tsarevitch* by Franz Lehár.

Zarzuela. Portuguese and Spanish musical play or operetta, which derived its name from the Palacio de la Zarzuela of Philip IV, where they were first performed. It had its origin in the Spanish folk theatre. It is an attractive form of theatrical entertainment (plays with frequent musical interpolations) which still enjoys great popularity.
Bibl: R. Mindlin, 1965

Zauberstück (magic fantasy play). A theatrical form, particularly popular in Austria, which mixed realistic and fantastic elements either in FARCE (*Zauberposse*) or opera (best-known example, Mozart's *The Magic Flute*). The style reached its peak in the magical plays of RAIMUND and the satires of NESTROY.

Zavadski, Yuri Alexeyevich (1894–), Soviet actor and director. Began his career as an actor under VAKHTANGOV in 1916, in whose famous production of GOZZI's *Turandot* he appeared as Kalaf. In 1924 he opened his own studio where he attempted to combine STANISLAVSKY's method with the innovations of Vakhtangov; compelling adaptations with an emphasis on circus elements. His best-known productions include his own adaptation of JONSON's *Volpone*, 1932; SHAW's *The Devil's Disciple*, 1933; OSTROVSKY's *Volki i ovsty* (Wolves and Sheep), 1934. His studio was closed down in 1934; he then worked at various theatres following the ideas of SOCIALIST REALISM, and in 1940 was appointed director of the Mossoviet Theatre, where he has produced plays by SHAKESPEARE, GOLDONI and contemporary dramatists. He was twice awarded the Lenin Prize: 1947 for *The Merry Wives of Windsor* and 1965 for a revival of LERMONTOV's *Masquerade*.

Zavattini, Cesare (1902–), Italian film-script writer. His best-known work includes the scripts for *Open City*, dir Roberto Rossellini, and for de Sica's *Bicycle Thieves*, 1948, and *The Miracle of Milan*, 1951. He also wrote the stage play *Come nasce un soggetto cinematografico* (How a Screenplay is Born), PICCOLO TEATRO DI MILANO at the VENICE FESTIVAL, 1959, dir PUECHER.

Zeffirelli, Franco (1923–), Italian director and stage designer. Began his career as assistant to VISCONTI, for whose productions he also designed the sets. He established his name with his designs for T. WILLIAMS's *A Streetcar Named Desire*, 1948; SHAKESPEARE's *Troilus and Cressida*, 1949, and CHEKHOV's *Three Sisters*, 1951. In 1953 he turned to directing, at first operas, e.g. *Cenerentola* (Rossini) and *La Traviata* (Verdi) with Maria Callas, then also drama, including his internationally famous Shakespeare productions of *Romeo and Juliet*, OLD VIC, 1960; *Othello*, STRATFORD-UPON-AVON, 1961; *Hamlet*, 1963; *Much Ado About Nothing*, 1965; also ALBEE's *Who's Afraid of Virginia Woolf?*, 1963, and E. DE FILIPPO's *Saturday, Sunday, Monday*, London 1973, NATIONAL THEATRE, with OLIVIER and JOAN PLOWRIGHT. He has worked in opera houses throughout the world, including COVENT GARDEN and the Metropolitan. His productions are characterized by their distinctive atmospheric quality evolved from the rich, historically exact, scenic details and the charming naïveté and spontaneity of the acting. Also a well-known film director.

Ziegel, Erich (1876–1950), German actor, director and manager. Began his career as an actor at the Hoftheater, Munich, and in 1913 took over the management of the Munich Kammerspiele, which he ran until 1916. In 1918 he founded the Hamburg Kammerspiele, which became one of the leading provincial theatres, with an emphasis on modern REPERTORY (it opened with a week of WEDEKIND's plays, followed by plays by SORGE, BARLACH and GOERING) and support for young talented theatre people including ENGEL, KORTNER and GRÜNDGENS. He managed the Deutsche Schauspielhaus, Hamburg, 1926–28, but returned to the Kammerspiele; in 1934 he worked in BERLIN and in 1935 became director of the Vienna Kammerspiele.
Bibl: P. Mohring, THEATERSTADT HAMBURG, 1948

Ziegfeld, Florenz (1868–1932), US theatre manager, whose name became a by-word for three decades for REVUES and musicals. His famous theatrical revue *The Ziegfeld Follies* ran for 24 editions, between 1906 and 1943, under the slogan 'An American Institution' and 'Glorifying the American Girl'. A star-maker, he discovered artists like FANNY BRICE, W. C. Fields, and Eddie Cantor, and among the wide range of performers who appeared under his aegis were Anna Held (his first wife, later a very popular comedienne), CHEVALIER, ASTAIRE, Lupino Lane, Billie Burke, etc. Others who worked in association with him included the stage designer URBAN, the composers I. BERLIN, GERSHWIN and RODGERS, and the librettists LARDNER and HAMMERSTEIN II. The great attractions of his revues were the variety turns, the stylish sets and his perfectly trained troupe, the Ziegfeld Girls, typifying American beauty. Many became motion picture STARS, including, in the early days, Olive Thomas, Mae Murray and Marion Davies; later Irene Dunne and Paulette Goddard. Apart from his revues and musicals, he produced numerous plays.
Bibl: M. Farnsworth, THE ZIEGFELD FOLLIES, 1956

Ziegler, Klara (1844–1909), German actress. Made her stage début in Bamberg in 1862; in 1865 she was engaged at the Gärtnerplatz Theater, Munich, under the direction of Adolf Christensen, whom she married in 1876. She appeared very successfully at Leipzig, 1867–68, in GOETHE's *Iphigenie*, the opening production of the new Municipal theatre. She was the last important representative of the Hoftheater style, relying on recitation rather than on acting, and interpreting classical roles as aesthetic monologues with the emphasis on beauty of diction and gesture rather than on inner truth and emotion; she excelled, e.g. as Orsina in LESSING's *Emilia Galotti*, and in KLEIST's *Penthesilea*. She also made guest appearances in Berlin under the direction of BARNAY and toured throughout Europe.

Zoff, Otto (1890–1963), Czech-born German novelist, editor and DRAMATURG. He emigrated in 1941 to France and later to the USA. Best known for his adaptations of classics. Other works: *Kerker und Erlösung* (Prison and Deliverance), 1917; *Der Schneesturm* (The Snowstorm), 1919; *Die zwei Abenteurer* (The Two Adventurers), 1926; *Rosen und Vergissmeinnicht* (Roses and Forget-Me-Nots), 1933; *The Huguenots*, 1942; *Die Glocken von London* (after Dickens's *The Chimes*), 1958. His sister, **Marianne Z.**, was BRECHT's first wife and later married the comedian LINGEN.

Zola, Emile (1840–1902), French novelist, dramatist, critic and pamphleteer, famous for his intervention in the Dreyfus affair in 1898. The publication of his letter *J'accuse* resulted in a year of exile in England. He is best known for his novels, some of which he dramatized, e.g. *Thérèse Raquin*, written 1868, and also wrote directly for the theatre, though without great success: *Madeleine Férat*, 1868, *Les Héritiers Rabourdin*, 1874; *Le Bouton de rose*, 1878; *Renée*, 1880, written for SARAH BERNHARDT. He was an opponent of Romanticism and developed the theoretical basis of NATURALISM in his novels, and also in the theatre, his theories being elaborated in his well-known essay, *Le Naturalisme au théâtre*, 1878.
Bibl: L. A. Carter, ZOLA AND THE THEATRE, 1963

Zolkowski. Family of Polish actors. (1) **Alojzy Fortunat Z.** (1777–1822) appeared in Warsaw after 1798 as Karl Moor in SCHILLER's *Die Räuber*, and the servant in an adaptation of GOLDONI's *Il Servitore di due Padroni*; he adapted French VAUDEVILLE and wrote satires, which he also published. His wife and three children were also actors,

the best-known of whom was his son (2) **Alojzy Z.** (1814–89), a brilliant comedian in contemporary vaudeville, but also remembered for his fine performance as Polonius in *Hamlet*.
Bibl: E. Szwankowski, 1956

Zuckmayer, Carl (1896–1977), German novelist and dramatist. For a time DRAMATURG in Kiel, where his adaptation of TERENCE's *Eunuchus* in 1923 provoked a scandal. Later he worked at the Deutsches-Theater, BERLIN. His early plays were strongly influenced by the Expressionist movement: *Kreuzweg* (Crossroads), Berlin 1920, State Theatre, dir JESSNER; *Pankraz erwacht oder die Hinterwälder* (Pankraz awakes or the Backwoodsman), Berlin 1925, Deutsches-Theater, dir HILPERT. This period also includes an unfinished play *Die Wiedertäufer* (The Anabaptist). After the enthusiastic reception of his COMEDY *Der fröhliche Weinberg* (The Gay Vineyard), 1925, he turned to the new drama of REALISM with *Schinderhannes*, Berlin 1927, Lessingtheater; *Katharina Knie*, 1928; *Kakadu Kakada*, a children's play, Berlin 1929, Deutsches-Theater; *Der Hauptmann von Köpenick* (*The Captain of Köpenick*), Berlin 1931, Deutsches-Theater, dir Hilpert, a satirical comedy based on a real event in which an unemployed ex-convict hoodwinks the Prussian military by wearing a borrowed uniform (title role played by KRAUSS). Following Hitler's rise to power he emigrated to Switzerland in 1933, where he wrote *Der Schelm von Bergen* (The Rogue of Bergen), 1934, and *Bellmann*, 1938. In 1939 he went to the USA and after World War II divided his time between the two countries. His third period started with the first post-war play to pose the question of guilt and responsibility for the crimes of Nazi Germany, *Des Teufels General* (*The Devil's General*), which proved a success in Zurich 1946, New York and London 1953; there followed *Barbara Blomberg*, 1949; *Der Gesang im Feuerofen* (The Song in the Fiery Furnace), 1950, on the Resistance; *Das kalte Licht* (The Cold Light), 1955, dir GRÜNDGENS; *Die Uhr schlägt eins* (The Clock strikes One), 1961, dir Hilpert; *Das Leben der Horace W. Tabor* (The Life of Horace W. Tabor), 1964; *Der Kranichtanz* (Crane's Dance), 1966; *Der Rattenfänger* (Pied Piper), Zurich 1974. He also wrote the autobiography *Als wär's ein Stück von mir*, 1965 (English translation *A Part of Myself*).
Bibl: FÜLLER DER ZEIT CARL ZUCKMAYER UND SEIN WERK. ZUM 50. GEBURTSTAG DES DICHTERS, 1956

Zurich Schauspielhaus ▷WÄLTERLIN.

Zefferelli's production of DE FILIPPO's *Saturday, Sunday, Monday*, London 1973, with JOAN PLOWRIGHT and Frank Finlay

Ziegfeld Follies, 1910, with FANNY BRICE

INDEX OF PLAY TITLES

Authors' names appear in brackets. CAPITALS denote a separate entry.

ILLUSTRATION CREDITS

t = top of page · m = middle of page · b = bottom of page

Joseph Abeles Studio, New York 13m
Agence de Presse Bernand, Paris 149t, 157b, 229b
Antikensammlungen, Munich 125t
Courtesy of the Art Institute of Chicago. Gift of Emily Crane Chadbourne 151t
Chris J. Arthur, London 273b
Ashmolean Museum, Oxford 113b
Australian Information Service, London 169b
Bauhaus Archives 127b
Bertorelli Collection, Milan 13t, 73t, 211m
Biblioteca Nacional, Madrid 25m, 55b
Bibliothèque de l'Arsenal, Paris 81b
Bibliothèque de l'Opera, Paris 81t
Bibliothèque Nationale, Paris 23m (courtesy M. Loeb), 75t, 131t
Bildarchiv Foto Marburg 219t
Bochum Theater 293t
Bodleian Library, Oxford 107t, 265b
From the Drawings Collection of the British Architectural Library, London 113t
Courtesy of the Trustees of the British Museum, London 69b, 121b, 133b, 153m, 289t
Bulloz, Paris 31bl, 59m, 109m, 171br, 263br
Central Press, London 153t
By permission of Circle in the Square, New York 207b
Nobby Clark, London 199m
Gerhard Cohn, Johannesburg 181m
Donald Cooper, London 51t, 111m, 141b, 253m
Culver Pictures, New York 17b, 57t, 129b, 135m, 139b, 159m, 187b, 219b, 259tr, 287m, 287b
From the collection of Sir Peter Daubeny 11b (photo Barry Comber), 81m (photo Ugo Mulas)
Devonshire Collection Chatsworth. Reproduced by Permission of the Trustees of the Chatsworth Settlement 79b, 155t (photos Courtauld Institute of Art, University of London)
By courtesy of the Trustees of the Dickens House 53t
Zoë Dominic, London 45m, 51b, 135b, 217b, 277t, 291b, 295t
Drottningholms Theatermuseum 87t (photo Beata Bergstrom)
By permission of the Governors of Dulwich College Picture Gallery 15m, 53bl, 251t
Ellinger, Salzburg 141t
Fitzwilliam Museum, Cambridge 249t
Copyright The Frick Collection, New York 21tr
By kind permission of the Garrick Club 213t
Giraudon, Paris 65tr, 193t, 199t
Harlingue-Viollet, Paris 37b
Harvard Theatre Collection 85m, 85b, 103br, 137b, 139t, 153b, 201t, 227ml, 237t (Angus McBean Photograph), 269b
John Haynes, London 27t
Louis Held 167t
Hessisches Landesmuseum, Darmstadt 121t
Hirmer Fotoarchiv, Munich 15b
The Hoblitzelle Theatre Arts Library The Humanities Research Center, The University of Texas at Austin 67bl, 171tl, 203m
John Holte, Stratford-upon-Avon 105m
Houston Rogers, London 17m, 131b, 209t
Indian Embassy, Paris 263bl
Douglas H. Jeffrey, London 253b
Peter H. Juley & Son, New York 189b
Keystone Press, London 53br, 173b, 221m
Alfred Kröner Verlag, Stuttgart 255m
Raymond Laniepce, Paris 67t
Collection Lázaro, Madrid 177m (photo Mas)
Library of Congress, Washington D.C. 33tr, 65b
© 1966, Lincoln Center for the Performing Arts – photographed by Bob Serating 175t
Lipnitzki-Viollet, Paris 45b, 59t, 79tl, 103bl, 157ml, 213b, 239b, 279b
From the Mander & Mitchenson Theatre Collection, London 23br, 29bl, 61t, 61mr, 71t, 75b, 91m, 93t, 103t, 121m, 137m, 141m, 143, 169tl, 185b, 197b
Mansell Collection, London 145b
By kind permission of the Marquess of Bath, Longleat House 247t
Angus McBean 23t, 83t, 97t, 117b, 173t, 207t
Metropolitan Museum of Art, New York. Alfred Stieglitz Collection through Miss Georgia O'Keeffe, 1949 265m
Municipal Gallery of Modern Art, Dublin 101b
Museo La Scala, Milan 43b
Museum of the City of New York 79m, 105b, 155b, 255b, 289b
Museum of London 9b, 63b
Collection, The Museum of Modern Art, New York. Purchase Fund. 243t
National Gallery of Ireland, Dublin 157mr, 287t
National Gallery of Scotland, Edinburgh 245b
National Library of Ireland, Dublin 149bl
National Portrait Gallery of Ireland, Dublin 291m
National Portrait Gallery, London 129mr
National Theatre, Prague 261
Morris Newcombe, London 11m
Herb Nott, Toronto 57b
The Nottingham Playhouse 21b, 259m (photos Allan Hurst), 111t
Österreichische Nationalbibliothek, Vienna titlepage, 25t, 25b, 31t, 109t, 115b, 159b, 165b, 201m, 201b, 225tl, 245tr
P.A. Interpress, Warsaw 99m
Pathik Art Studio, Ahmedabad 147m
Pennsylvania Academy of Fine Arts, Philadelphia. Gift of Mrs John Ford, 1843 61t
Pic, Paris 91b
The Pierpont Morgan Library, New York 119t
Private Collection 27b
Radio Times Hulton Picture Library, London 39b, 89b, 167b, 203t, 215t, 235b
Rheinisches Bildarchiv, Cologne 243b
Ken Rimmell 61b
Roger-Viollet, Paris 71m, 87m, 123m
Schiller National Museum, Marbach am Neckar 241t
Helga Schmidt-Glassner, Stuttgart 77t
Science Museum, London 257m
Scottish Tourist Board 91m
By permission of the Governors of the Shakespeare Theatre, Stratford-upon-Avon 245tl, 247b
Georges Sirot Collection 227mr
Edwin Smith 221t, 247m, 271b, 273t
S.C.R., London 151b, 163m, 195, 271t
Collection George Speaight 273t
Staatliche Museen zu Berlin 41t
Staatliche Schlösser, Garten und Seen Museumabteilung, Munich 223t
Stadt Galerie, Munich 49t
Tate Gallery, London 115t
Theatre Collection, The New York Public Library at Lincoln Center, Astor, Lenox and Tilden Foundations 9t, 11t, 17t, 31br, 33m, 65tl, 73m, 117t, 179b, 183t, 205t, 229t, 231t, 253t
Theatermuseum, Munich 83m, 89t, 135t, 137t, 147t, 213m, 275t, 283b, 285t
Théâtre National de Belgique 117m (photo Jiři Jiru)
Theatersammlung der Universität, Hamburg 161m
Tropenmuseum, Amsterdam 147b
C. Vajenti 265t
Vatican Museums, Rome 233t
©John Vickers – London 35m, 49b, 115m, 129ml, 129t, 149br, 157t, 175b, 193m, 205b, 221b, 225m, 225b, 229m, 237b, 251b, 269t, 269m, 275b, 289m, 291t
Victoria and Albert Museum, London 19m, 35t, 39t, 39m, 47b, 53m, 55t, 87b, 91b, 99t, 107b, 113b, 119m, 159t, 197t, 209b, 231mr, 239t, 249b, 259tl
Enthoven Collection 13b, 19t, 29br, 43t, 43m, 47m, 47t, 57m, 65m, 67br, 73b, 91t, 97m, 105t, 123b, 145t, 161b, 171tr, 177t, 181bl, 181br, 203b, 205m, 211t, 223b, 227t, 231ml, 233b, 237m, 279t
Victoria Theatre, Stoke 267t (photo Richard Smiles)
Martin von Wagner Museen, University of Würzburg 125b
Clifford Wallace Inc., New York 211b